Annotated Commercial Crime Insurance Policy

THIRD EDITION

TONI SCOTT REED AND
CARLETON R. BURCH, EDITORS

AMERICAN BAR ASSOCIATION
Defending Liberty
Pursuing Justice

TABLE OF CONTENTS

Exhibit F
Crime Protection Policy For Public Entities
Standard Form No. SP 00 02 04 12

Introduction

It has been thirty years since the Fidelity and Surety Law Committee of the American Bar Association published the *Annotated Commercial Blanket Bond* as an important reference material and compilation of case law discussing the interpretation of standard form provisions in what was then referred to as a blanket bond. In the years since, the work has been updated and expanded with a supplement to the *Annotated Commercial Blanket Bond*, published in 1991, and with the *Annotated Commercial Crime Policy (Second Edition)*, published in 2006. As time has marched on, so too has the development of various standard forms of what are now more generally referred to as commercial crime policies or mercantile policies. What these forms have in common over their years of development is that they were designed to provide coverage for various defined hazards to commercial businesses. They began in formats that tended to follow the forms of a financial institution bond, but over time they have become distinct in many different ways. There have been a substantial number of changes and updates to the insuring agreements and coverage terms for these policies over time, particularly those available in various standard forms and in manuscripted versions over the last decade. For that reason, the Fidelity and Surety Law Committee felt that it was timely and important to publish the current edition of this book, now titled the *Annotated Commercial Crime Insurance Policy (Third Edition)*.

The three prior publications that have described the scope of the development of the case law over the decades have served as invaluable tools and references for the publication of this book. The purpose of the Third Edition is to provide annotations of all major cases decided based upon the language of any number of forms of commercial crime or mercantile policies, focusing on the standard forms that have been issued, but also addressing any particular manuscripted language that has become widely used or has been reviewed by courts.

In certain instances, the historical roots of these various insurance forms and the development of the general coverage of mercantile insurance over time can be very important to the explanation of coverage that exists in a particular policy. The history of these products, provided in Chapter 1 of this Third Edition, can serve as an important explanation of that background, as well as for the substantial changes that have occurred over time, particularly over the last two decades.

To summarize, there has been a colorful history of the development of these coverages. As Chapter 1 details, there are deep roots in history for these particular types of policies. In the mid-1980s, the Insurance Services Office, Inc. ("ISO") and the Surety Association of America (now the Surety and Fidelity Association of America, or "SFAA") jointly issued commercial crime forms that were designed to be part of package policies and combined with other commercial lines. Those products focused on fidelity and certain other traditional coverage agreements in separate forms that could be combined as needed or desired. In later periods, the SFAA and ISO began to issue separate policies and coverage forms of their own drafting.

Since 2000, there have been a series of stand-alone policies and provisions that could be combined with other packages issued as forms by the SFAA and ISO. During that time period, the SFAA language covering employee dishonesty and the ISO language covering employee dishonesty diverged, with the SFAA form continuing to include coverage for employee dishonesty, utilizing the manifest intent standard, and with the ISO form referencing coverage for employee theft. At the same time, various insurance companies began to draft their own proprietary and manuscripted forms that address both traditional insurance agreements and terms, and that also address more modern coverage language and risks. Some of the most notable of the insurance agreements and definitions that are appearing in company-specific forms include coverage for technology, computer, and electronic risks or causes of loss. As technology continues to develop, so too do the various forms of coverage made available for losses arising out of the use of technology.

The proliferation of the various forms of commercial crime or mercantile insurance available on the market has certainly made the reporting of the case law in this area a more challenging task. For that reason, the authors have organized their chapters in ways to assist the reader in locating helpful authority. In each chapter, standard form language is quoted and cited. Where there are multiple forms of standard language, the alternatives are quoted. Following the standard form language, each chapter identifies major categories of decisions reached by courts, and also provides annotations of the specific decisions that interpret the form language. Where non-standard language has been addressed by a court, there are additional subdivisions within the annotations describing those cases or notes that the decision addresses non-standard language. Where the language or provision has been addressed by a court in the context of another type of insurance product, including the financial institution bond, certain cases are discussed as well. Finally, there is a list of secondary sources on each subject included in each chapter, broken down by subdivision, which may be helpful.

As a reference tool, the most recently issued forms of commercial crime and mercantile policies promulgated by ISO and the SFAA are included in the Appendix of the book. In most instances, the authors have focused on the most recent form language, but where needed, they have made reference to other standard language as well.

Like its predecessor editions, this Third Edition has sought to include all of the major cases that have construed the relevant insuring agreements, definitions, exclusions, conditions, and general terms. Cases decided over the last decade are new additions to this book, but all of the older case law that remains relevant or informative is reported as well.

This Third Edition contains what we hope are very helpful comments from the authors, all highly experienced professionals who focus on this area of law, on the individual elements that are covered in each chapter. The annotations that are included begin with any applicable decisions by the United States Supreme Court, and then include decisions by the Unites States Circuit Courts of Appeals, organized numerically by circuit, decisions by the United States District Courts, organized alphabetically, and finally decisions by the state courts, organized alphabetically and by highest to lowest court. The annotations appear in reverse chronological order, beginning with the most recent case law first.

All of the authors of the chapters have commented how important the earlier editions of the book have been to the development of this Third Edition. On behalf of ourselves and the current authors, we extend our deepest gratitude to the contributors who were involved in the production of the earlier three editions. Their names are listed in the acknowledgements to this Third Edition. William F. Haug, Carolyn Pratt Perry, Lana M. Glovach, and Cole S. Kain, all of whom were editors of earlier editions, deserve our sincere thanks and recognition as well.

As the editors of this Third Edition, we thank our friend and colleague Gary Valeriano, Chair of the Fidelity and Surety Law Committee, for entrusting this project, and the accompanying program where it will be presented, to us. For the real expertise and work that it took to translate all the authoritative writing into an actual book, we thank the individuals at Strasburger & Price, LLP, who made the formatting and the publication details of the book possible, in particular,

Marianna Green and Christine Grey. This book is not the first rodeo for either Marianna or Christine, so certainly we are indebted to them for providing their professional expertise and dedication to detail.

Finally, we thank all the authors for the careful research and preparation of the materials included in the book. Their depth of experience and thorough preparation made the editing process a streamlined and enjoyable endeavor. We hope that this reference material is a very helpful tool to its readers and to all students of the law in this subject area.

TONI SCOTT REED
Strasburger & Price, LLP
Dallas, Texas
Editor and Program Chair
November 2015

CARLETON R. BURCH
Anderson, McPharlin & Conners LLP
Los Angeles, California
Editor and Program Chair
November 2015

EDITORS

TONI SCOTT REED • Partner in the Dallas, Texas office of Strasburger & Price, LLP. Ms. Reed is a graduate of Southern Methodist University, B.B.A. and B.A. *summa cum laude* 1990, and J.D. *cum laude* 1993. Ms. Reed is Chair Elect Presumptive and Vice Chair of the Fidelity & Surety Law Committee.

CARLETON R. BURCH • Partner in the Los Angeles, California and Las Vegas, Nevada offices of Anderson McPharlin & Conners, LLP. Mr. Burch is a graduate of Colorado College B.A., *cum laude*, 1984, and the University of California, Hastings College of Law, J.D. 1987.

AUTHORS

SAMUEL J. ARENA, JR. • Partner with the Philadelphia, Pennsylvania office of Stradley Ronon Stevens & Young, LLP. Mr. Arena is a graduate of Ursinus College, B.A. *magna cum laude* 1979, and Villanova University School of Law, J.D. *cum laude* 1983. Mr. Arena is a past Chair of the Fidelity & Surety Law Committee.

DENNIS J. BARTLETT • Member with Brosseau Bartlett Seserman, LLC, in Greenwood Village, Colorado. Mr. Bartlett is a graduate of the University of Notre Dame, B.A.A. *cum laude* 1980, and J.D. *cum laude* 1985.

RICHARD E. BAUDOUIN • Associate in the New Orleans, Louisiana office of Krebs Farley, PLLC. Mr. Baudouin is a graduate of the University of Texas, B.A. 2001, and Loyola University New Orleans College of Law, J.D. *cum laude* 2007.

WILLIAM T. BOGAERT • Partner with the Boston, Massachusetts law firm of Wilson Elser Moskowitz Edelman & Dicker, LLP. Mr. Bogaert is a graduate of Clark University, B.A. *with honors* 1976, and Boston College Law School, J.D. *cum laude* 1985.

CARLETON R. BURCH • Partner in the Los Angeles, California and Las Vegas, Nevada offices of Anderson McPharlin & Conners, LLP. Mr. Burch is a graduate of Colorado College B.A., *cum laude*, 1984, and the University of California, Hastings College of Law, J.D. 1987.

GRACE WINKLER CRANLEY • Shareholder with Leo & Weber in Chicago, Illinois. Ms. Cranley is a graduate of the University of Illinois, B.A. 1986, and the Illinois Institute of Technology Chicago-Kent College of Law, J.D. 1993.

CARLA C. CRAPSTER • Associate in the Dallas, Texas office of Strasburger & Price, LLP. Ms. Crapster is a graduate of Texas A&M University, B.A. *summa cum laude* 2005, and the University of Texas School of Law, J.D. *with high honors* 2008.

CHARCRETIA V. DIBARTOLO • Partner in the Boston, Massachusetts office of Hinshaw & Culbertson, LLP. Ms. DiBartolo is a graduate of Washington University, B.A. 1988, and Washington University School of Law, J.D. 1991.

BRETT D. DIVERS • Founding shareholder of the law firm of Mills Paskert Divers. Mr. Divers is a graduate of Dartmouth College, B.A. 1989, and University of Florida College of Law, J.D. *with honors* 1992.

ROBERT J. DUKE • Corporate Counsel with The Surety & Fidelity Association of America in Washington, D.C. Mr. Duke is a graduate of Loyola University Maryland, B.B.A. *summa cum laude* 1988 and M.B.A. 1992, and the Columbus School of Law, Catholic University of America, J.D. *summa cum laude* 2005.

BRIAN M. FALCON • Member in the Indianapolis, Indiana office of Frost Brown Todd, LLC. Mr. Falcon is a graduate of Ball State University, B.S. 1998, and the Indiana University Robert H. McKinney School of Law, J.D. 2003.

MATT J. FARLEY • Partner in the New Orleans office of Krebs Farley, PLLC, in New Orleans, Louisiana. Mr. Farley is a graduate of Tulane University, B.A. *summa cum laude* 1974, and Tulane University Law School, J.D. *cum laude* 1977.

ROBERT M. FLOWERS • Second Vice President, Crime, FI Bond, Cyber and Kidnap & Ransom Claim with Travelers in Hartford, Connecticut. Mr. Flowers is a graduate of the University of Nevada, B.A. 1996. Mr. Flowers is a Vice Chair of the Fidelity & Surety Law Committee.

ANN I. GARDINER • Bond Claims Manager with ABA Insurance Services Inc., in Mayfield Heights, Ohio. Ms. Gardiner is a graduate of Indiana University of Pennsylvania, B.S. *with honors* 1987, and Case Western Reserve University School of Law, J.D. *with honors* 1990.

BRANDON J. HELD • Associate with the Tampa, Florida office of Mills Paskert Divers. Mr. Held is a graduate of the University of Florida, B.S. *cum laude* 2002 and M.S. 2003. He also is a graduate of Stetson University, M.B.A. 2007, and Stetson University College of Law, J.D. *cum laude* 2007.

GINGER JOHNSON • Specialty Claim Analyst with The Hanover Insurance Group in Itasca, Illinois. Ms. Johnson is a graduate of Northern Illinois University, B.A. 1984.

MICHAEL KEELEY • Partner in the Dallas, Texas office of Strasburger & Price, LLP. Mr. Keeley is a graduate of the University of Arizona, B.S. *summa cum laude with honors* 1977, and the University of Arizona School of Law, J.D. *cum laude* 1981. Mr. Keeley is a past Chair of the Fidelity & Surety Law Committee, Editor-in-Chief of the Fidelity Law Journal, Advisor Emeritus to the Fidelity Law Association, Advisor to the Surety & Fidelity Association of America and past Editor-in-Chief of the Tort & Insurance Law Journal.

ANDREW S. KENT • Counsel in the West Orange, New Jersey and New York City offices of Chiesa Shahinian & Giantomasi PC. Mr. Kent is a graduate of Rutgers College, B.A. 1989, and Rutgers School of Law, Newark, J.D. 1992.

JAMIE L. KESSLER • Associate in the Boston, Massachusetts office of Hinshaw & Culbertson, LLP. Ms. Kessler is a graduate of Gettysburg College, B.A. 2008, and Suffolk University Law School, J.D. *cum laude* 2011.

JAMES A. KNOX • Counsel with Christensen & Ehret, LLP, in Chicago, Illinois. Mr. Knox is a graduate of Southern Methodist University, B.A. 1980, and the University of Texas School of Law, J.D. 1984. Mr. Knox is a former Editor-in-Chief of the Fidelity & Surety Digest and Chair of the Defense Research Institute's Fidelity & Surety Committee.

MARK J. KRONE • Senior Associate in the Los Angeles, California office of Anderson McPharlin & Conners, LLP. Mr. Krone is a graduate of the University of Colorado, B.S. 1989, and Fordham University School of Law, J.D. 1995. Mr. Krone is a Vice Chair of the Fidelity & Surety Law Committee.

MEGAN M. MANOGUE • Assistant Vice President and Chief Claims Officer with Berkley FinSecure in Towson, Maryland. Ms. Manogue is a graduate of Loyola College, B.A. 1986, and the University of Baltimore School of Law, J.D. 1989.

SA'ADIYAH K. MASOUD • Associate with the Boston, Massachusetts law firm Wilson Elser Moskowitz Edelman & Dicker, LLP. Ms. Masoud is a graduate of Duke University, B.A. 1998, and Boston University School of Law, J.D. 2003.

RICHARD S. MILLS • Partner in the New York City office of McElroy Deutsch Mulvaney & Carpenter, LLP. Mr. Mills is a graduate of Pennsylvania State University, B.S. 1982, and New York Law School, J.D. 1986.

JOHN W. MORRIS • Partner in the Morristown, New Jersey office of McElroy Deutsch Mulvaney & Carpenter, LLP. Mr. Morris is a graduate of Montclair State University, B.A. 1988, and the University of Dayton School of Law, J.D. 1991.

THOMAS R. OROFINO • Associate in the New York City office of Sedgwick, LLP. Mr. Orofino is a graduate of Villanova University, B.S. 2004, and Seton Hall University School of Law, J.D. 2009.

CAROL A. PISANO • Partner in the New York City office of McElroy Deutsch Mulvaney & Carpenter, LLP. Ms. Pisano is a graduate of the State University of New York, B.A. *summa cum laude* 1976, and Hofstra University, Maurice A. Deane School of Law, J.D. *with honors* 1979.

SCOTT L. SCHMOOKLER • Partner in the Chicago, Illinois office of Gordon & Rees, LLP. Mr. Schmookler is a graduate of Bradley University, B.A. 1993, and IIT-Chicago Kent College of Law, J.D. 1996.

ARMEN SHAHINIAN • Member of the West Orange, New Jersey and New York City offices of Chiesa Shahinian & Giantomasi PC. Mr. Shahinian is a graduate of Brown University, A.B. 1971, and New York University, J.D. 1974. Mr. Shahinian is a past Chair of the Fidelity & Surety Law Committee, Advisor Emeritus to the Fidelity Law Association, Advisor to the Surety & Fidelity Association of America, and is a member of the Board of Directors of the Surety Claims Institute, and Editor-in-Chief of its Newsletter.

CAROL Z. SMITH • Member with the Overland Park, Kansas law firm of Gilliland & Hayes, P.C. Ms. Smith is a graduate of the University of Kansas, B.A. 1984, and the University of Kansas School of Law, J.D. 1987.

A. NICOLE STOVER • Associate in the Cherry Hill, New Jersey office of Stradley Ronon Stevens & Young, LLP. Ms. Stover is a graduate of Washington and Lee University, B.A. *magna cum laude* 2001, and Pennsylvania State University Dickinson School of Law, J.D. 2004.

D.M. STUDLER, M.ACC., CPA • Managing Member with Studler Doyle & Company, LLC, Chicago, Illinois. Ms. Studler is a graduate of Indiana University, B.S. 1987, and The University of Texas, Masters in Accounting, *summa cum laude* 1990. Ms. Studler is a Vice Chair of the Fidelity & Surety Law Committee.

SUSAN K. SULLIVAN • Partner in the Los Angeles, California office of Sedgwick, LLP. Ms. Sullivan is a graduate of the University of Washington, B.A. *with honors* 1987, and the University of California, Los Angeles School of Law, J.D. 1991.

GARY J. VALERIANO • Partner in the Los Angeles, California office of Anderson McPharlin & Conners, LLP. Mr. Valeriano is a graduate of California State University, Northbridge, B.A. 1974, and Loyola University School of Law, J.D. 1979. Mr. Valeriano is Chair of the Fidelity & Surety Law Committee.

KENNETH D. WATNICK • Senior Counsel in the Los Angeles, California office of Anderson McPharlin & Conners, LLP. Mr. Watnick is a graduate of Cornell University, B.S. 1987, and Duke University School of Law, J.D. 1990.

JUSTIN D. WEAR • Partner with Manier & Herod in Nashville, Tennessee. Mr. Wear is a graduate of the University of the South, *magna cum laude* B.A. 2001, and the University of Tennessee College of Law *summa cum laude* J.D. 2004. Mr. Wear is a Vice Chair of the Fidelity & Surety Law Committee.

MICHAEL J. WEBER • Shareholder with Leo & Weber in Chicago, Illinois. Mr. Weber is a graduate of Indiana University, B.S. 1980, and Indiana University at Bloomington School of Law, J.D. 1983.

KEITH WITTEN • Member with the Overland Park, Kansas law firm of Gilliland & Hayes, PC. Mr. Witten is a graduate of Auburn University, B.A. *with honors* 1968, and the University of Kansas School of Law, 1971.

CONTRIBUTORS TO SECOND EDITION

Julie Alleyne
Samuel J. Arena, Jr.
Julia E. Bell
Lisa A. Block
William T. Bogaert
Jonathan M. Bryan
Carleton R. Burch
David M. Burkholder
CharCretia V. DiBartolo
David T. DiBiase
Karen K. Fitzgerald
Edward G. Gallagher
Melissa L. Gardner
Lana M. Glovach
Eric M. Hurwitz
Cole S. Kain
Michael Keeley

James A. Knox, Jr.
Thomas H. McNeill
Richard S. Mills
Dolores A. Parr
Richard L. Pemberton
Martha L. Perkins
Carol A. Pisano
Scott L. Schmookler
Armen Shahinian
Sandra M. Stone
D.M. Studler, M.ACC., CPA
John J. Tomaine
Thomas J. Trautner, Jr.
Gregory R. Veal
Christopher R. Ward
Keith Witten
William H. Woods

CONTRIBUTORS TO FIRST EDITION
and SUPPLEMENT

Mark E. Aronson
Robert A. Babcock
William T. Bogaert
James F. Crowder, Jr.
James L. Csontos
David T. DiBiase
Karen K. Fitzgerald
Jeanne M. Forneris
William J. Hacker
William F. Haug
John B. Hayes
John W. Hinchey
James D. Huegli
Frank Mays Hull

G. Kevin Kiely
James A. Knox
James F. Moran
Edgar L. Neel
Hugh M. Palmer
Carolyn Pratt Perry
Douglas M. Reimer
Bernard A. Reinert
Hugh B. Reynolds, Jr.
Charles F. Seeman
Deanna L. Seward
H. Bruce Shreves
James Smirz
C. Cullen Sylvester

Chapter 1

History and Development of Mercantile Crime Policies*[1]

This chapter will address the history of the standard forms currently available in the market, the Crime Protection Policy issued by The Surety & Fidelity Association of America[2] and the Commercial Crime Policy issued by the Insurance Services Office.[3]

The roots of the mercantile crime policy forms used in today's market can be traced to financial institution bond forms. Financial institution bond forms began their evolution in the early 1900s in response to the expansion of the banking industry. As the number of banks and bank employees grew, and the magnitude and volume of bank employees increased, so did the necessity for protection against different types of improper conduct, including employee dishonesty.[4]

The growth of other commercial (non-financial) enterprises spawned the need for protection of these industries as well against losses stemming from employee dishonesty and wrongful acts by others. In 1940, the first stand-alone mercantile crime policy, the Comprehensive Dishonesty, Disappearance and Destruction Policy, was introduced. This was followed by the appearance of the Blanket Crime Policy in 1957. Both of these mercantile forms were modeled after financial institution

---

* By Robert J. Duke, The Surety & Fidelity Association of America, Washington, D.C.
1 This article draws from and builds on prior articles regarding the history of mercantile crime policies: Robert Duke et al., *History and Development of Mercantile Crime Policies—Their Interpretation and Construction,* in COMMERCIAL CRIME INSURANCE COVERAGE Ch. 1 at 1 (Randall I. Marmor & Susan Koehler Sullivan eds. 2015) and Carol A. Pisano and Robert Duke, *Interpretation and Construction of the Commercial Crime Policy,* in COMMERCIAL CRIME POLICY Ch. 1 at 1 (Randall I. Marmor & John J. Tomaine eds. 2d ed. 2005).
2 Hereinafter SFAA.
3 Hereinafter ISO.
4 *See* discussion *infra* at Section B.2.

1

bonds, such as the Bankers Blanket Bond, and were predecessors to the mercantile crime forms that are used in the market today.

A. Historical Perspective—Bonds Generally: The Past

1. The Foundation—Surety Bonds

Any examination of the development of mercantile crime policies must begin with a brief review of surety bonds. Financial Institution Bonds, which insure the honesty of the institution's employees, and provide coverage for other crime risks, were first developed in the beginning of the twentieth century. However, the history of Financial Institution Bonds begins with the history of surety bonds, which is centuries old.

A surety bond is a three-party agreement by which one party (the surety) guarantees the obligation owed by a second party (the principal) to a third party (the obligee).[5] Suretyship, the guaranteeing of one's debt to another, is an ancient concept that has existed for thousands of years. Principles of suretyship were referenced in the eleventh century in the Magna Carta.[6] In the Merchant of Venice, Shakespeare created a surety bond that most assuredly would not be available in the market today, a pound of flesh that secured Antonio's repayment of a loan from Shylock.[7]

Surety bonds provide the benefit of financial security in the event that a certain obligation is not performed. One such obligation that has been secured by bonds over the years is an employee's obligation to remain faithful and honest to her employer, the guarantee of fidelity. Thus, fidelity protection originally was provided by way of a surety bond. The employee would be the principal, and his or her obligation of honesty owed to the employer, the obligee, would be secured by a surety. In the late 1800s and early 1900s, as a means to enhance their employment prospects, household servants in England would offer to

---

5   John B. Fitzgerald et al., PRINCIPLES OF SURETYSHIP 1.3 (2d ed. 2003).

6   Magna Carta of 1215, Ch. 9 ("Neither we nor our bailiffs will seize for any debt any land or rent, so long as the chattels of the debtor are sufficient to repay the debt; nor will those who have gone surety for the debtor be distrained so long as the principal debtor is himself able to pay the debt.").

7   WILLIAM SHAKESPEARE, THE MERCHANT OF VENICE, act 1, sc.3.

provide a fidelity bond to their employers.[8] Professional individual sureties would conduct a background check of the individual and would pay the employer for his losses caused by the employee's dishonesty.[9] During the industrial revolution, corporate sureties moved onto the scene and soon replaced individual sureties in securing the honesty of employees in various commercial enterprises.[10] As commercial activity expanded, obtaining a separate bond for each employee became cumbersome.[11] Corporate sureties developed fidelity bonds that covered the dishonest acts of multiple employees: name schedule bonds and position schedule bonds. Thus began the progression of fidelity bonds from a three-party surety product to the form it takes today, a two-party insurance agreement.

2. The History of Financial Institution Bond Forms

The development of policies covering employee dishonesty and other risks for financial institutions, particularly commercial banks, influenced much of the development of mercantile crime policies. Therefore, a brief discussion of the development of coverage for commercial banks provides insight into the development of mercantile crime policies.

The rapid growth of the banking industry in the early 1900s, which required the hiring of many but mostly inexperienced employees, exposed banks' need for employee dishonesty and other coverages.[12] Insurers responded to the demand by providing various types of "honesty insurance." Unfortunately, the banking community had more crime exposures than just unfaithful employees, including robbery and theft. Because insurance regulation at the time prohibited United States companies from offering a form that provided multiple coverages, a bank

---

8   David A. Lewis, *History of Fidelity Coverage: Types of Commercial Crime Policies, in* COMMERCIAL CRIME POLICY, Ch. 1 at 1-7 (Gilbert J. Schroeder ed., 1st ed. 1997).

9   *Id.*

10 *Id.*

11 Robert A. Babcock, *History of Fidelity Coverage, in* COMMERCIAL BLANKET BOND ANNOTATED, Ch. 1 at 1-3 (William F. Haug ed. 1985).

12 Edward G. Gallagher et al., *A Brief History of the Financial Institution Bond in* FINANCIAL INSTITUTION BONDS, SECOND EDITION, Ch. 1, at 6 (Duncan L. Clore ed., 1998).

had to purchase a number of separate bonds and policies to be fully covered (or obtain such product from Lloyd's of London).[13] In 1912, the New York State Commissioner of Insurance permitted insurers to combine various types of unrelated coverages for financial institutions into a single bond.[14] Four years later, the Surety Association of America—now called The Surety & Fidelity Association of America ("SFAA")—with the guidance of the American Bankers Association, developed the "Bankers Blanket Bond," the first standard form, multiple-line insurance against certain commercial risks, and the forerunner of the modern "Financial Institution Bond."[15]

The first Bankers Blanket Bond, Form 1, was a two-party agreement that provided banks protection against employee dishonesty, loss of property on the premises and in transit through robbery or theft, loss by false pretenses and other risks.[16] Coverage forms for commercial banks have gone through several iterations throughout the years, all the way up to the current Financial Institution Bond, Standard Form No. 24 (2011 Edition) (Form 24). Nevertheless, the form retains its basic structure of a two-party insuring agreement offering multiple coverages under a single policy.

The form for commercial banks has served as a template for mercantile crime polices. The drafting history of the Form 24 can provide insight into the meaning and intent of certain terms in mercantile crime policies.[17] For example, a new definition of "dishonesty" was established in the Form 24 in response to bad case law,[18] first by rider SR

13   Robin V. *Weldy, History of the Bankers Blanket Bond and the Financial Institution Bond Standard Form No. 24 with Comments on the Drafting Process, in* SECOND SUPPLEMENT: ANNOTATED BANKERS BLANKET BOND, Ch. 1, at 3 (Harvey C. Koch ed., 1988) [hereinafter Weldy-Supplement].
14   *Id.*
15   Weldy-Supplement, *supra* note 11, at 4.
16   Gallagher, *supra* note 10, at 7.
17   *See,* Robert J. Duke, *A Concise History of the Financial Institution Bond, Standard Form No. 24, in* ANNOTATED FINANCIAL INSTITUTION BOND, THIRD EDITION, Ch.4, § 1 at 533 (Michael Keeley, ed. 2013).
18   For example, in *Mortgage Corp. of N.J. v. Aetna Casualty and Surety Co.,* 115 A.2d 43 (NJ 1955), the insured mortgage company's employee was responsible for preparing progress reports upon which the insured relied when disbursing construction loan funds. The employee's responsibilities included visiting the job sites to determine the extent of work in progress. Inclement weather intervened, and the employee only relied on the

6019 and then by incorporation into the 1980 form. As revised, coverage under the fidelity insuring agreement was limited to dishonest acts committed by an employee with the "manifest intent" to cause the insured to sustain a loss and to obtain a financial benefit. Prior to the revision, the fidelity insuring agreement covered loss "through any dishonest act." Case law had developed over the years such that a dishonest act amounted to mere negligence.[19]

In addition, Rider SR 6019 added four exclusions:

(i) Potential income . . . including but not limited to interest and dividends, not realized by the Insured because of a loss covered under this bond.

(ii) All damages of any type for which the Insured is legally liable, except compensatory damages arising from a loss covered under this bond.

(iii) All costs, fees and other expenses incurred by the Insured in establishing the existence of or amount of loss covered under this bond.

(iv) Loss resulting from payments made or withdrawals from a depositor's account involving funds erroneously credited to such account . . . .[20]

These revisions were incorporated into the 1980 Form 24.[21] At the same time, similar new language was incorporated into SFAA's mercantile crime policies (Comprehensive Dishonesty, Disappearance and Destruction Policy and Blanket Crime Policy).

Similarly, case law pertaining to a provision in a Financial Institution Bond may be relevant to and affect a mercantile crime policy provision,

---

borrower's representations. These proved false and the borrower defaulted on its loans. The insured sought to recover under its Brokers Blanket Bond, which provided coverage for "[a]ny loss through any dishonest, fraudulent or criminal act" of the insured's employees. The court held that the intent of the employee was not a factor to consider but only that his conduct was wrongful.

19 Frank L. Skillern, *The Insuring Agreements, Section 1—Insuring Agreement (A)—Fidelity, in* ANNOTATED BANKER BOND (Frank L. Skillern ed., 1980).

20 The Surety & Fidelity Association of America, Rider SR 6019.

21 The Surety & Fidelity Association of America, Statement of Change, Bankers Blanket Bond, Standard Form No. 24, Revised July 1980.

even if the language in the Financial Institution Bond and the mercantile crime policy are different. For example, in *Home Savings Bank, SSB v. Colonial American Casualty and Surety Company*,[22] the North Carolina Court of Appeals did not give effect to the condition in the Financial Institution Bond, whereby the bond automatically terminates as to an employee upon the discovery of that employee's prior dishonesty. In 1985, the insured learned that one of its employees had embezzled from a prior employer (another bank). When it applied for the bond in 2001, the bank did not mention that it was aware of the employee's prior embezzlement. The same employee embezzled again, this time from the insured, and the insured sought coverage under the 2001 bond. The insurer argued that there never was coverage for the employee because at the commencement date of the bond the insured knew of prior dishonest acts. The court incorrectly held that the automatic termination provision was ambiguous because it could mean that coverage terminates only if the insured initially discovers prior dishonesty after the coverage commences.

To address this misinterpretation, changes were made to the Financial Institution Bond, first to the 2008 edition of the Standard Form No. 25, and then in all other Financial Institution Bonds (Form Nos. 14, 15 and 24) in 2011. In particular, clarifying language was added to the termination condition:

> Termination of this bond as to any Employee terminates liability for any loss caused by a dishonest or fraudulent act committed by such Employee after the date of such termination.

An exclusion also was added:

> Loss resulting directly or indirectly from the dishonest or fraudulent acts of an Employee if any Insured . . . knows, or knew at any time, of any dishonest or fraudulent act committed by such Employee at any time . . . without regard to whether knowledge was obtained before or after commencement of this bond.

---

22   598 S.E.2d 265 (N.C. App. 2004), *Pet. for Rev. dismissed as moot* 609 S.E.2d 770 (N.C. 2005).

The 2012 edition of the Crime Protection Policy added the following language to the Cancellation as to Any Employee Condition:

Whether such discovery occurs prior to or after commencement of this Policy, there is no coverage under Insuring Agreement 1 for loss or losses resulting from acts committed by that employee after the date of such discovery.

A driving factor of form revision is the importance of assuring that the coverage of the risk is capable of being underwritten and priced reasonably. Whether the insured is a financial institution or a commercial business, this interest is the same. Therefore, many of the revisions of financial institution bond forms also are appropriate for mercantile crime policies.

3.   The Evolution and Development of Mercantile Crime Policies

Almost thirty years after SFAA first introduced a uniform policy for commercial banks that offered multiple coverages, SFAA and the National Bureau of Casualty & Surety Underwriters ("National Bureau") offered the Comprehensive Dishonesty, Disappearance and Destruction Policy of July 1, 1940.[23] A memorandum from SFAA to its member companies[24] describes the new so-called "3-D Policy," as follows:

As a result of a growing demand for so-called comprehensive coverage for commercial concerns, the Surety Association of America and the National Bureau of Casualty and Surety Underwriters appointed a Joint Committee to explore the situation and to draft an appropriate form for consideration.

This Joint Committee has about completed its work and has submitted to the Surety Association and the National Bureau a Comprehensive Dishonesty, Disappearance, and Destruction Policy designed to grant in the one instrument the type of

---

23   Edward G. Gallagher, *The Crime Protection Policy*, V FID L.J. 185,186 (1999).
24   Memorandum dated May 3, 1940, from E. Vernon Roth, Assistant Secretary to Chief Executives of member companies.

fidelity, burglary, robbery and forgery protection necessary to
meet the requirements of the average commercial organization.

The 3-D Policy offered five coverages in the basic contract:

- Employee Dishonesty Coverage;
- Loss Inside the Premises Coverage;
- Loss Outside the Premises Coverage;
- Money Orders and Counterfeit Currency Coverage;
- Depositors' Forgery Coverage.[25]

Under the 3-D Policy, the insured could select a separate limit for
each coverage. Coverage was provided for losses that were sustained
during the policy period. The limit of liability for employee dishonesty
coverage is extended over the whole loss, regardless of the number of
employees (Form A), or on a per-employee basis (Form B). Covered acts
were "fraudulent or dishonest acts." As previously noted, this
subsequently was amended to "employee dishonesty."
      In 1957, SFAA and the National Bureau developed a Blanket Crime
Policy as an alternative to the 3-D Policy.[26] The content of the coverages
under the Blanket Crime Policy was the same as that offered under the 3-
D Policy, except that the Blanket Crime Policy offered a single limit for
all coverages, and the insured was required to obtain all coverages.[27]
      The 3-D Policy and Blanket Crime Policy were available for use in
the market until 1986, when as part of the movement in the insurance
industry to simplify policy forms, SFAA and ISO introduced simplified
Commercial Crime forms. These forms were structured so that they
could be written either as the Commercial Crime Coverage Part of the
Commercial Package Policy (along with other commercial lines of
insurance), or as a separate monoline Commercial Crime Policy.[28] On

---

25   Lewis, *supra* note 6, at 1-8 - 1-9.
26   Gallagher, *supra* note 21, at 187.
27   Other crime coverage forms available at the time included Commercial
      Blanket Bond, Money & Securities Broad Form, Money Orders and
      Counterfeit Paper Currency Coverage, and Depositors Forgery Bond. SFAA
      and National Bureau, Press Release, March 13, 1957.
28   Not all would agree that the Commercial Crime Policy represented a
      simplification. In response to the filing of the policy with the Virginia
      Department of Insurance, the Department's Deputy Commissioner

July 1, 1986, SFAA and ISO announced they would cease supporting stand-alone, "non-simplified" polices such as the 3-D Policy and Blanket Crime Policy.[29] The Commercial Crime Policy provided coverage similar to the 3-D Policy and Blanket Crime Policy. The modular format of the policy allowed for the attachment of a variety of SFAA and ISO crime coverage forms, and was designed to fit ISO's package of policies in other commercial lines by sharing Common Policy Conditions.[30] The policy also could be written as a stand-alone policy. The policy had Crime General Provisions that governed various crime coverage forms, including:

- Coverage Form A: Employee Dishonesty
- Coverage Form B: Forgery or Alteration
- Coverage Form C: Theft, Disappearance and Destruction— Money and Securities (Inside and Outside the Premises);
- Coverage Form D: Robbery and Safe Burglary—Other Property (Inside and Outside the Premises); and
- Coverage Form F: Computer Fraud

SFAA and ISO had joint responsibility for the Crime General Provisions. SFAA had sole responsibility for the forms and rating rules for Coverage Forms A and B. ISO had responsibility for the remaining coverage forms. Coverage was provided initially on a loss sustained basis only and then in 1997, SFAA and ISO issued a separate Crime General Provisions form on a discovery basis.

Notably, the transition from the stand-alone crime policies to the new package policies generally did not involve any material change in substance, but rather, a change in structure and organization.[31] For

---

commented, "I have no intention of subjecting the citizens of the State of Virginia to this mess." Memorandum to file from Robin V. Weldy (quoting Deputy Commissioner Peter Synott at a March 6, 1986, meeting involving the Department of Insurance, SFAA and ISO) (March 7, 1986) (on file with SFAA).

29   Gallagher, *supra* note 21, at 188.

30   *Id.*

31   Carol A. Pisano & Richard S. Mills, *The Development of the Commercial Crime Policy: 66 Years of Evolution—The Policy's History, Construction, and Interpretation, in* ANNOTATED COMMERCIAL CRIME POLICY, SECOND EDITION Ch 1 at 6 (Cole S. Kain & Lana M. Glovack *eds.* 2006).

example, in the filing letter to state insurance regulators in connection with the Commercial Crime Policy, SFAA staff noted that the policy's employee dishonesty coverage "is the equivalent of the presently existing Employee Dishonesty Insuring Agreement [that] is found in the Comprehensive 3-D Policy, Blanket Crime Policy and Commercial Blanket Bond. There is no intent to either increase or decrease coverage. Only format and language is changed."

B. Mercantile Crime Coverage Forms: The Present

In 1997, SFAA and ISO filed the Crime General Provisions (Discovery Form) to convert the Commercial Crime Policy from loss sustained to discovery.[32] Thereafter, SFAA members expressed a desire to develop a stand-alone policy similar to the 3-D Policy, and SFAA set out on its own to develop a stand-alone crime policy containing employee dishonesty, burglary and theft coverages. Effective March 1, 2000, SFAA introduced the Crime Protection Policy ("CPP").[33] The CPP was written on a discovery basis. Later that same year, ISO introduced two versions of the Commercial Crime Policy that combined employee theft, forgery and other crime coverages on both a discovery and loss sustained basis.[34] ISO also introduced coverage form equivalents for use with package polices.

1. Crime Protection Policy

The CPP is an all-inclusive policy that contains six basic insuring agreements. Two additional insuring agreements may be added by endorsement. The eight insuring agreements are:

1. Employee Dishonesty
2. Forgery or Alteration
3. Inside the Premises
4. Outside the Premises
5. Computer Fraud

---

32   Gallagher, *supra* note 21 at 189.
33   Hereinafter CPP.
34   ARTHUR L. FILTNER ET AL., COMMERCIAL CRIME INSURANCE AND FINANCIAL INSTITUTION BONDS 1.3 (2d ed. 2002). ISO retained the name Commercial Crime Policy on its new coverage forms.

6. Money Orders and Counterfeit Paper Currency
7. Loss of Client's Property
8. Funds Transfer Fraud

Insuring Agreement 1 uses the manifest intent definition of "dishonesty" that was used in SFAA's prior mercantile crime forms. A modified "theft" coverage was considered, but the manifest intent language was continued because it was thought to be more precise and, in some circumstances, more beneficial to the insured.

Insuring Agreement 2 covers loss resulting directly from forgery or alteration of checks, drafts, or similar written promises.

Insuring Agreement 3 provides coverage for loss inside the insured's premises. Money and securities are covered for theft, disappearance, and destruction. Other property is covered for robbery and safe burglary. The premises and the insured's safe, cash register, or strong box are covered for damage from actual or attempted theft, robbery, or safe burglary.

Insuring Agreement 4 covers loss of money, securities and other property while outside the insured's premises in the custody of an armored motor vehicle company or a messenger. The covered causes of loss for money and securities are theft, disappearance, and destruction. Other property is covered for actual or attempted robbery.

Insuring Agreement 5 covers loss directly caused by the fraudulent use of a computer causing a transfer of property from inside the insured's premises or a bank to someone outside the premises.

Insuring Agreement 6 covers loss from the insured's acceptance of money orders that are not paid or are counterfeit U.S. or Canadian currency.

Insuring Agreement 7 covers loss of a client's money, securities, or other property resulting from a dishonest act committed by the insured's employee. In the context of this insuring agreement, dishonesty is defined in terms of manifest intent to cause the client to sustain a loss.

Insuring Agreement 8 covers loss resulting from a fraudulent instruction to a financial institution to transfer funds from the insured's account.

The substance of coverages provided by the CPP compared to the old Commercial Crime Policy (developed by SFAA and ISO) were largely the same. There were a few minor differences:

- The CPP integrated the provisions regarding coverage for employee benefit plans directly into the policy form.
- The CPP included a Consideration Clause that establishes the relationship between premium payment and the payment of losses. It is similar to the clause in the financial institution bonds.
- The CPP added a condition that only the highest deductible may be applied in cases where multiple deductibles apply to a loss.
- Section E.14 stated that, if two or more coverages of the policy apply to a loss, the policy will pay the lesser of: (a) the amount of the actual loss or (b) the highest limit applicable to the coverages. The old Commercial Crime Policy paid the lesser of the amount of the loss of the sum of the limits of the applicable coverages.

2. Crime Protection Policy, 2012 Revisions

In 2012, SFAA made revisions to the CPP. Most of the changes previously were made to the Financial Institution Bonds in recent years, starting with the changes in the 2004 edition of the Financial Institution Bond Standard Form No. 24. As a general matter, the revisions provided clarification rather than expanded or reduced coverage compared to the 2000 edition of the CPP. The more significant revisions are noted below.

Insuring Agreement 1

SFAA changed the term "financial benefit" to "improper financial benefit," which is in the revised edition of the Financial Institution Bonds. Also, the phrase regarding benefits "earned in the normal course of employment" is replaced by benefits "received" by the Employee. The purpose of the change is to strengthen the effect of the language, to preclude an argument that wages, salaries, or commissions generated through a dishonest scheme were not in the normal course of employment and therefore not excluded from the meaning of an "improper financial benefit."

In addition, in the 2012 edition, Insuring Agreement 1 covers "loss" generally (rather than loss of money, securities, and other property). This formulation has worked well in the Financial Institution Bonds and reflects more fully the intent of the fidelity insuring agreement—to protect the insured against loss directly caused by employee dishonesty. From a practical perspective, the revision likely will not alter coverage because the insured's loss will involve "money, securities and other property."

Insuring Agreement 3

Insuring Agreement 3 was revised to include a requirement that a perpetrator of a theft must be physically present on the premises at the time of the loss. This requirement is included in the recent editions of the Financial Institution Bonds.

Insuring Agreements 3 and 4

The scope of coverage was amended from loss of "money" to loss of "cash," which is a newly defined term in the 2012 edition. The risks under Insuring Agreement 3 and Insuring Agreement 4 contemplate in-person events, rather than electronic transactions. Thus "cash" (defined as paper money and coins) would be the item lost under these insuring agreements, rather than "money" (as more broadly defined).

Insuring Agreement 5

Insuring Agreement 5 (Computer Fraud) was revised to reflect the intent of coverage, which is coverage for "computer to computer" transaction. The coverage is not intended to extend to every loss that involves a computer, even tangentially. The revision also was in response to bad case law that suggested that the mere use of an e-mail in a dishonest scheme could bring a loss within computer crime coverage.[35] In addition, a few new exclusions hone the coverage: a confidential information exclusion, a data breach costs exclusion, a debit/credit card exclusion, and an exclusion for failure to follow security procedures.

Among the other revisions in the 2012 edition were the following:

The definition of "money" was revised to make explicit that the meaning does not refer exclusively to paper bills and coins. "Money" is defined to consist of "cash" (a newly defined term—paper currency and

---

35 *See, e.g.*, Owens, Schine & Nicola, P.C. v. Travelers Cas. and Sur. Co. of America, 2010 WL 4226958 (Conn. Super. September 20, 2010), vacated at 2012 WL 12246940 (Conn. Super. Ct. Apr. 18, 2012).

coins), deposits on account and travelers checks, register checks, and money orders.

The definition of "employee" was revised to better reconcile the definition with the exclusion involving temporary employees. The definition includes persons furnished to the insured on a short-term or seasonal basis. However, the definition also excludes persons leased to the insured by a labor leasing firm. As originally drafted, the definition might suggest that the exclusion "swallows" the temporary employee part of the definition. The exclusion was meant to refer to persons providing services to the insured on a long-term basis that usually are provided by an employee (such as bookkeeping services). Persons intended to be covered are those furnished temporarily or on a short-term basis under certain conditions. Therefore, the definition has been revised to add an exception to the exclusion.

As part of the revisions of Insuring Agreement 5, certain exclusions were added to further define the scope of coverage, including an exclusion for failure to follow "Security Procedures." "Security Procedure" is a newly defined term, which includes procedures to verify a "payment order." "Payment order" is also a defined term and is based on the definition set forth in the Uniform Commercial Code (§ 4A-103).

Losses related to the theft, disappearance and destruction of confidential information are excluded in the 2012 edition. This is an exclusion that is common on company forms.

An exclusion for data breach costs was added. As electronic commerce expands and electronic transactions become more prevalent, an increasing exposure for companies is the costs incurred when the company's computer system (or the computer system of the bank) is breached. When a system is breached, federal and state privacy laws require the company to take certain measures, such as notifying customers that their personal information has been stolen. Although a breach may cause a loss that is covered under the CPP's Insuring Agreements, the CPP is not intended to cover the compliance costs incurred as a result of the breach. Coverage for these costs can be obtained by other insurance that is available commercially.

A number of Conditions were revised to track revisions previously made to Financial Institution Bonds.

The inclusion of property "for which the Insured is legally liable" in the Ownership of Property Condition has led to claims that the legal liability of the Insured is covered. This Condition was amended to "codify" cases, such as in *Lynch Properties Inc. v. Potomac Ins. Co.*, 140

F3d 622 (5th Cir. 1998), which correctly held that the Insured must be responsible for the property prior to the events giving rise to the loss.

Similar to the language in the Financial Institution Bond, the Cancellation As to Any Employee Condition (applicable to Insuring Agreement 1) states that the policy is cancelled as to an employee upon discovery of a dishonest act, whether the discovery occurred prior to or after the commencement of the policy.

As part of the rollout of the 2012 edition of the CPP, SFAA also released a CPP for Public Entities. The CPP for Public Entities includes the provisions that are necessary to accommodate coverage for public entities and tracks the provisions in Form O and Form P of the earlier Commercial Crime Policy. Similar to Form O, the limit of insurance for the CPP for Public Entities is on a per loss basis. By endorsement, the limit of insurance can apply on a per employee basis (similar to Form P).

3.   Crime Protection Policy, 2014 Revisions

The CPP had offered employee dishonesty coverage on a blanket basis. That is, the insuring agreement covered the acts of all employees, as defined in the policy. In 2014, SFAA released an endorsement (SE 01 62) that converted the coverage to a schedule basis (i.e., coverage extends to the acts of employees named in the schedule).

4.   New Insuring Agreement 9

In 2015, SFAA introduced the new Insuring Agreement 9, Fraudulently Induced Transfers. Coverage for Funds Transfer Fraud, Insuring Agreement 8, covers loss of funds caused by a fraudulent instruction to a financial institution to transfer funds from the insured's account. Thus, the coverage contemplates that the instruction purportedly sent from the insured to the insured's bank was fraudulent or phony, and then the bank acted on those phony instructions and wired funds to the fraudsters account.

In recent months, businesses have experienced a fraudulent scheme that was not contemplated under Insuring Agreement 8. In particular, the fraudster impersonates a vendor, customer, or employee of the insured and contacts the insured, requesting a wire transfer of funds. Then, based on this phony information, a legitimate employee of the insured contacts the bank to place the order for a wire transfer. Thus, the instruction sent from the insured to the bank is legitimate, as it is sent by a legitimate employee intending to do so. However, the employee was fraudulently induced into contacting the bank and making the order for the wire transfer. The exposure for such scams can be significant. According to the Federal Bureau of Investigation Internet Crime Complaint Center, between October 2013 and December 2014 such scams resulted in losses totaling $214,972,503.30.[36] However, as noted, the scam was not contemplated under the coverage provided under Insuring Agreement 8.

Insuring Agreement 9 covers loss caused by a "fraudulently induced transfer" in which funds are transferred out of the insured's premises or banking premises. A "fraudulently induced transfer" is defined as a transfer resulting from a payment order (to make a wire transfer) or check, made or written on the good faith reliance of the instruction provided by a person impersonating an employee, customer, vendor or owner of the insured. The form establishes internal controls as a condition precedent. Specifically, before sending the payment order or issuing the check, the insured is required to verify the instruction by calling back the purported employee, customer, vendor, or owner at a predetermined telephone number or through some other verification methodology approved by the insurer.

Also in 2015, Insuring Agreement 8 was revised to ensure there is no unintended overlap of coverage between "traditional" funds transfer fraud coverage and the new coverage for fraudulently induced transfers. In addition, the coverage now uses the term "payment order" to refer to a specific instruction to the bank to transfer a specific amount. SFAA observed that "instruction" in the prior version could refer to either an instruction received from some party to the insured or an instruction sent by the insured to the bank to wire funds. The definition of "payment order," which already is included in the Crime Protection Policy, is based on the definition of "payment order" from the Uniform Commercial Code.

---

36 Brian Donohue, *FBI: Business Email Compromise Scams Steal $214M in 2014*, Threatpost, January 28, 2015, https://threatpost.com/fbi-business-email-compromise-scams-steal-214m-in-2014/110715.

5. *ISO's Commercial Crime Policy*[37]

A significant difference between the ISO Commercial Crime Policy and the SFAA Crime Protection Policy is ISO's use of "employee theft language" in the fidelity coverage rather than "employee dishonesty" with the manifest intent standard. Under the ISO Commercial Crime Policy, the insured must prove that it was deprived of its covered property as a direct result of the unlawful taking.

The 2013 edition of the ISO Commercial Crime Policy contains the following insuring agreements:

1. Employee Theft—this insuring agreement provides coverage for loss of, or damage to, "money," "securities," and "other property" resulting directly from "theft" committed by an "employee," whether identified or not, acting alone or in collusion with other persons. "Theft" means the unlawful taking of property to the deprivation of the Insured.

   For the purposes of this Insuring Agreement, "theft" shall also include the undefined term "forgery" to emphasize that the Insuring Agreement includes all employee acts that result in a covered loss, including forgery losses caused by employees.

2. Forgery Or Alteration—This insuring agreement provides coverage for loss resulting directly from "forgery" or alteration of checks, drafts, promissory notes or similar written promises, orders or directions to pay "money" made or drawn by the insured or its agent. Substitute checks as defined in the Check Clearing for the 21st Century Act (Check 21) are treated the same as the original it replaced.

   If the insured is sued for refusing to pay any instrument covered under this insuring agreement, reasonable legal expenses incurred by the insured with the consent of the insurer are also covered.

3. Inside The Premises—Theft Of Money And Securities—this insuring agreement provides coverage for loss of "money" and "securities" inside the insured's "premises" or a "financial institution" premises:

---

37 Special thanks to Robert Olausen, Principal, Crime/Fidelity & Financial Institutions of ISO Insurance Programs and Analytic Services, for furnishing the information regarding the ISO Commercial Crime Policy.

- Resulting directly from theft committed by a person present inside such "premises" or "financial institution premises"; or
- Resulting directly from disappearance or destruction.

Also covered is damage to the "premises" or its exterior resulting directly from actual or attempted "theft" and damage to locked containers inside the "premises" such as safes, vaults, and cash registers, from actual or attempted "theft" of or unlawful entry into those containers.

4. Inside The Premises—Robbery Or Safe Burglary Of Other Property—this insuring agreement provides coverage for loss of or damage to property other than "money" and "securities" inside the insured's "premises" resulting directly from an actual or attempted "robbery" of a custodian or "safe burglary."

5. Outside The Premises—This insuring agreement provides coverage for loss of "money" and "securities" in the care and custody of a "messenger" or armored motor vehicle company resulting directly from theft, disappearance, or destruction.
Also covered is loss or damage to "other property" in the care and custody of a "messenger" or an armored vehicle company resulting directly from an actual or attempted "robbery."

6. Computer And Funds Transfer Fraud—this insuring agreement was rewritten with the 2013 edition of the policy, in response to recent court decisions construing Computer Fraud coverage. The Insuring Agreement provides coverage for loss resulting directly from a fraudulent entry of "electronic data" or "computer program" into, or change of "electronic data" or "computer program" within, a "computer system" owned, leased or operated by the insured that causes "money," "securities," or "other property" to be transferred, paid or delivered; or that causes the insured's account at a "financial institution" to be debited or deleted.
Also covered, is loss resulting directly from a "fraudulent instruction" directing a "financial institution" to transfer, pay or deliver "money" or "securities" from the insured's "transfer account."
The Insuring Agreement requires that there has to be an actual fraudulent entry or change of electronic data or computer program by an outside person (hacker) for coverage to apply, not just the incidental use of a computer to cause loss.

Two new exclusions also apply to the revised Insuring Agreement:

- The Authorized Access exclusion explicitly denies coverage for losses involving fraudulent entry or change of electronic data or computer programs by persons with authorized access to the insured's computer.

- The Fraudulent Instructions exclusion explicitly denies coverage for loss from an employee acting on fraudulent instructions (e.g., e-mail instructions) to transfer money, securities or other property or to debit or delete the insured's account.

7. Money Orders and Counterfeit Money—this insuring agreement provides coverage for loss resulting directly from the insured having accepted, in good faith, in exchange for merchandise, "money" or services, money orders that are not paid upon presentation and "counterfeit money" acquired during the regular course of business.

In response to recent court decisions involving data breaches, ISO also introduced a Confidential Or Personal Information Exclusion and a Data Security Breach Exclusion (the latter stating that data breach expenses are an indirect consequence of loss, and are not covered).

In 2015, the ISO Commercial Crime Policy was further revised, mainly to include an exclusion for virtual currency and to change the definition of "fraudulent instructions," which applies to the Computer And Funds Transfer Fraud Insuring Agreement.

Addressing new exposures in the Crime marketplace, ISO recently introduced new coverage endorsements to:

- Provide coverage for insured's transacting business using virtual currency; and
- Provide coverage for fraudulent impersonation scams where the insured is tricked into transferring money, securities, or other property by someone impersonating an employee, customer, or vendor of the insured.

C. Conclusion

The standard industry mercantile forms are rooted in over 100 years of development. A practitioner interpreting the forms today can draw from an extensive pool of drafting history and case law. Terms and provisions found in current forms must be viewed in the context of their development. They have evolved over the years in response to case law and the market demand for relevant coverage. It is safe to say that the standard form will continue to evolve in response to court decisions and fraudsters and dishonesty employees finding new ways to steal with a 21st-century gloss.

Chapter 2

Loss and Causation*

Coverage under Commercial Crime Policies ("CCP") and other fidelity policies requires a direct and immediate link between the covered peril and the insured's loss of property. The importance of this requirement is underscored by the repeated use of "directly" and its variants throughout the policy. Although loss "resulting directly" from a covered event mandates something more exacting than proximate cause, a minority of courts eschew a contractual-causation standard in favor of a tort-causation standard. Accordingly, this chapter explores cases that have applied the various causation standards, ranging from a contractually based "direct means direct" approach to proximate cause and "but for" causation analyses.

Inasmuch as the body of case law frequently simultaneously calls upon bankers' bonds, fidelity bonds, policy riders and the CCP to interpret "direct," this chapter examines CCP, financial institution bonds and their brethren in an effort to isolate and explore causation and loss as components of a fidelity/crime claim.

Additionally, this chapter collects cases that examine causation from the perspective of the types of loss that can be fairly considered to be "resulting directly." For example, it is not uncommon for an insured to seek coverage under the CCP for its liability to third parties arising from employee dishonesty. For the most part, courts do not consider such losses to result directly from the peril, and those cases are collected herein. Similarly, insureds often seek indemnification for loss in market value or the movement of funds between accounts. As such, it is necessary to identify whether the loss is an actual, as opposed to the theoretical or bookkeeping, loss.

---

*   Carleton R. Burch, Anderson McPharlin & Conners, LLP, Los Angeles, California and Las Vegas, Nevada, and Kenneth D. Watnick and Mark J. Krone, Anderson McPharlin & Conners, LLP, Los Angeles, California.

OUTLINE OF ANNOTATIONS

ANNOTATIONS

A. Cases Decided Under Commercial Crime Policies

1. "Loss" Generally

(a) SFAA Form

E.D. Mich. 2008. Employee's embezzlement of funds from escrow accounts held by the insured title company was direct loss within the scope of the Crime Protection Policy. *Phillip R. Seaver Title Co. v. Great Am. Ins. Co.*, 2008 WL 4427582 *amended on reh'g in part* 2008 WL 4966890.

(b) Other Forms

D. Minn. 2005. The district court found that questions of fact precluded either party's cross motion for summary judgment. The insured's customer had pledged assets in several accounts as security to a third-party lender. The customer induced the insured to release a freeze in consideration of the payment of those funds to Baltic Bank for the purchase of certain certificates of deposit. These CDs were in turn accepted as collateral under the prior pledge arrangement. The loan went into default and upon liquidation, the certificates were shown to have no value. It was thereafter discovered that Baltic Bank was a "shell" bank controlled by insured's customer and that the CDs were worthless. The lender sued the insured and a settlement ultimately was reached. The court held that the loss occurred when the money was wire transferred initially, not when the settlement was entered into, but that it could not grant summary judgment to either party due to the factual questions it believed existed on the remaining coverage issues. *RBC Dain Rauscher Inc. v. Fed. Ins. Co.,* 370 F. Supp. 2d 886.

S.D.N.Y. 2005. The district court affirmed an arbitration award in favor of the insurer under its CrimeGuard policy. The insured had invested funds in a foreign subsidiary and asserted that it had done so based on false information provided to it by an employee of the subsidiary. No evidence appeared in the record that the employee embezzled any property of the insured or gained any improper financial benefits from the transaction. An investigation, accounting, and report were performed and issued pursuant to the terms of the policy. The dispute was then submitted to arbitration. The arbitrator concluded that there was not in fact a loss resulting directly from the theft under the policy and thus found in favor of the insurer. Because of the posture of the matter before the district court—a petition to confirm the arbitration results—the legal analysis of the coverage issues is fairly brief. *Nat'l Union Fire Ins. Co. of Pittsburgh, Pa. v. Dana Corp.,* 2005 WL 857352.

E.D. Pa. 1971. Insured has suffered loss recoverable under the commercial crime coverage form where employee used company funds to cover previous embezzlements in a lapping scheme. *John B. White, Inc. v. Providence Wash. Ins. Co.,* 329 F. Supp. 300.

Ala. 1982. Verdict recovered by computer services "software" company against ex-employees who had copied computer data and programs, but subsequently returned original tapes to employer before starting competitor firm, held compensable under employer's bond. Under the circumstances, employer had property interest in computer programs and their copying by ex-employees constituted conversion of tangible personal property, and jury's award of damages as to resulting financial loss to employer was supported by ample evidence. *Nat'l Sur. Corp. v. Applied Sys., Inc.,* 418 So. 2d 847.

Ariz. App. 1975. The Arizona Court of Appeals reviewed a garnishment claim on a motor vehicle dealer's license bond, which applied to loss suffered by any person "by reason of any unlawful act" of the insured. Injured plaintiffs/judgment creditors, who were unable to collect punitive damages from defendant insured, could not collect punitive damages from the insured's surety under its bond. *Harper v. Home Ins. Co.,* 533 P.2d 559.

Cal. App. 1985. Insurer was held liable under its commercial blanket bond where the insured's employee made numerous fraudulent misrepresentations regarding a potential loan, inducing the insured to enter into the loan transaction. The insured sustained the loss upon the date the fraudulent loan defaulted, and not the date upon which the insured discovered the fraud. *Pac.-S. Mortgage Trust v. Ins. Co. of N. Am.,* 212 Cal. Rptr. 754.

Cal. App. 1948. An insured hotel in Los Angeles stored the day's receipts, together with guest property, in the hotel safe. It suffered a loss of the day's receipts and guest property as a result of the wrongful abstraction of such by an employee. The insurer honored the claim for the stolen receipts, but disputed coverage for the insured's liability for the guests' property. The court of appeal affirmed the judgment of the trial court that the bond in question was obligated to indemnify the insured for its liability to its guest, citing language in the policy that obligated the insurer to indemnify the insured for loss "through . . . wrongful abstraction, willful misapplication, or other . . . dishonest act or acts committed by any one or more of the employees of the plaintiffs . . . ." *Alberts v. Am. Cas. Co. of Reading, Pa.,* 200 P.2d 37.

Fla. App. 1980. The insured's employees submitted a false financial statement to induce a bank to purchase an installment contract for the sale of a truck, and the insured repurchased the contract. The court held that the fidelity bond, containing a "loss resulting from" insuring clause, covers an insured's monetary losses incurred in settlement with third parties of a suit for damages caused by dishonest or fraudulent acts of insured's employees. *Southside Motor Co. v. Transamerica Ins. Co.,* 380 So. 2d 470.

La. App. 1968. Where an employee reported a prior shortage and made restitution to the insured, the insured employer thereafter was entitled to recover under its blanket crime policy for subsequent embezzlement by same employee due to a lack of evidence that the employee's prior reimbursement notified the insured of his prior "fraudulent or dishonest" conduct. *Salley Grocer Co. v. Hartford Acc. & Indem. Co.*, 223 So. 2d 5, *writ refused*, 222 So. 2d 883 (1969).

Me. 1953. Where comprehensive Dishonesty, Disappearance and Destruction policy insured against loss through employee dishonesty, insured's inability to trace dishonest acts of employees to entirety of claimed loss of 5,449 chickens prevented recovery for entire amount of the claimed loss. Rather, insured could only recover the portion of loss that evidence demonstrated was stolen by employees. *Lipman Bros., Inc. v. Hartford Acc. & Indem. Co.*, 100 A.2d 246.

Mass. App. 2005. An employee of the insured stole a relatively small amount from the insured, but a significantly large amount from another entity controlled by the same persons who controlled the insured. That second entity was not a named insured under the Employee Dishonesty Policy before the court. The court held that the funds from the second entity were not the insured's property and thus the loss was not a direct loss of the insured's covered property. It went on to conclude that the policy did not provide liability coverage for the insured and thus the insurer was not held to indemnify payments made by the insured to satisfy its liability to the other entity. *Atlas Metals Prods. Co. v. Lumberman's Mut. Cas. Co.*, 829 N.E.2d 257.

Miss. App. 2005. The insured automobile dealer was sued by its borrower. The borrower alleged that he had suffered damage to his credit rating as a result of various acts of the insured's employees and that a power of attorney used to help effectuate the lease that was at issue was forged, although the customer did not disavow the lease itself. The court held that under Mississippi law, it did not appear that the insured would suffer a loss as a direct result of employee dishonesty. It also rejected contention that the claims fell within the forgery or alteration coverage form of the specific policy as it did not apply where an employee of the insured had not been implicated. It also denied recovery of defense costs and expenses incurred in defending the suit brought by the customer as the policy expressly excluded such amounts. *Watson Quality Ford, Inc. v. Great River Ins. Co.*, 909 So. 2d 1196.

Miss. 1968. Loss occurs when a misappropriation of funds is made by the insured's employee; insured is not required to reimburse the missing funds before the surety becomes liable on the bond. *Am. Nat. Ins. Co. v. U. S. Fid. & Guar. Co.*, 215 So. 2d 245.

2.   Insured's Legal Liability as "Loss"

La. App. 1994. The Court of Appeals, applying Louisiana law, affirmed the decision of the trial court that the Louisiana direct action statute did not give a third-party claimant a right of direct action against the commercial crime policy issued to the insured, as such actions could only be brought against liability insurers. The court held that the commercial crime policy covered only the loss of money, securities, and other property directly resulting from employee dishonesty. It thus concluded that the policy was not a liability policy and affirmed the dismissal of the direct action. *State Through Dep't of Transp. & Dev. v. Acadia Parish Police Jury*, 631 So. 2d 611.

Wis. App. 2008. Theft of money from third party by insured's employee was not a direct loss of property under insured's commercial crime policy. The policy did not cover the insured's vicarious liability for damages to a third party. *Meriter Health Servs., Inc. v. Travelers Cas. & Sur. Co. of Am.*, 758 N.W.2d 112.

3.   Causation: Loss "Resulting Directly From" Dishonesty

2d Cir. 1989 (N.Y.). Brokers Blanket Bond did not provide coverage for loss to corporation through the sole owner's reckless trading because there was no evidence that the owner manifestly intended to cause the corporation a loss, or to obtain an improper financial benefit for himself. A manifest intent provision and trading loss exclusion of the standard form Brokers Blanket Bond limit protection under the bond to losses due to embezzlement or embezzlement-like acts. *Glusband v. Fittin, Cunningham & Lauzon, Inc.*, 892 F.2d 208.

2d Cir. 1988 (N.Y.). Fidelity bond providing indemnity for losses "sustained" during the bond period had prospective operation only, and thus covered only those acts committed during the bond period. Under New York law, in order to recover under fidelity bond covering losses resulting from either "dishonest or fraudulent acts," fraud must be proven by clear and convincing evidence, and dishonesty is proven merely by a preponderance of the evidence. When two or more causes of loss are disjunctively stated in the context of a fidelity bond, it is sufficient that the loss be caused by any one of them. *Leucadia, Inc. v. Reliance Ins. Co.*, 864 F.2d 964, *cert. denied*, 490 U.S. 1107.

6th Cir. 2012 (Ohio). Insured sought coverage under Blanket Crime Policy's computer fraud endorsement after hackers downloaded credit card and checking account information pertaining to the insured's customers. The court held that the loss of customer credit card and bank account information, resulting in the insured incurring costs for charge backs, card reissuance, account monitoring, and fines imposed by VISA/MasterCard, was a loss to the insured. *Retail Ventures, Inc. v. Nat'l Union Fire Ins. Co. of Pittsburgh, Pa.*, 691 F.3d 821.

6th Cir. 1987 (Tenn.). Fidelity bond covering losses resulting directly from dishonest or fraudulent acts of employees did not cover loss to insured broker-dealer by employee's violation of trading limit, because employee's intent was to make money, not to cause her employer to lose money, and "dishonest or fraudulent acts" under bond were limited to those committed with manifest intent to cause the insured to sustain loss. *Mun. Sec., Inc. v. Ins. Co. of N. Am.*, 829 F.2d 7.

9th Cir. 1988 (Cal.). Employee's fraudulent bond-trading activities were not excluded from coverage by trading loss exclusion of Brokers Blanket Bond, because broker's losses were not caused by employee's trades, but by his dishonesty. The trading loss exclusion was held not to exclude coverage merely if it is shown that a trade occurs anywhere in the chain of events resulting in a loss to the insured. Actual loss occurred not when employee traded bonds, but later when employee wrongfully retained sales proceeds or when rightful owners claimed bonds that employee stole. *Ins. Co. of N. Am. v. Gibralco, Inc.*, 847 F.2d 530.

D.C. Cir. 1988. Fidelity bond issued to air traffic controllers union did not cover actions of union officials in appropriating funds for a strike that resulted in a discharge of most of the union membership and the bankruptcy of the union. Fund appropriation did not reflect a corrupt intent to deceive or defraud union membership and did not reveal a breach of financial integrity. *Skirlick v. Fid. & Dep. Co. of Md.*, 852 F.2d 1376, *cert. denied,* 488 U.S. 1007.

D.C. Cir. 1970. Covered losses are not limited to the physical loss of "money, securities and other property," but can include consequential pecuniary loss through payments made from the insured's funds due to employee "misconduct." *Imperial Ins., Inc. v. Employers' Liab. Assur. Corp.,* 442 F.2d 1197.

N.D. Ill. 1986. Commissions paid to employees, but not earned by them in normal course of employment, are excluded from fidelity bond coverage. Losses resulting directly from a transfer of funds to third parties will be indemnified, even if underlying motive for providing third-party benefits was to enable employees to acquire more unearned commissions. Intention to benefit third party with a tax deduction did not result in a "direct" loss to the insured, because tax deductions did not cause funds to be taken from insured. Funds that originated as commissions to employees and which were then transferred to third parties were excluded from coverage to same extent as the unearned commissions were excluded. *Hartford Acc. & Indem. Co. v. Wash. Nat'l Ins. Co.,* 638 F. Supp. 78.

D. Md. 1985. Insured has the burden of proving how missing money was spent in order to prove a loss under a Commercial Blanket Bond. *Towne Mgmt. Corp. v. Hartford Acc. & Indem. Co.,* 627 F. Supp. 170.

Ill. App. 1989. The insured bank sought indemnity under a Bankers Blanket Bond for court costs and attorneys' fees incurred by obligee in defense of an underlying action by a customer alleging that the insured had intentionally and negligently interfered with his business relationships. The insured bank was not entitled to indemnity for attorneys' fees and court costs under the "Fidelity" provisions of the bond because the course of action at issue in the underlying action was "determined at a high level to be in the best interests of the Bank. . . ." In short, there was no employee dishonesty involved, so the loss was not covered. *State St. Bank & Trust Co. of Quincy v. U.S. Fid. & Guar. Co.,* 539 N.E.2d 779.

Ill. App. 1971. In action under blanket position bond, without conclusive evidence as to who actually stole funds, the jury must determine whether the acts of a store manager who was not implicated in the theft itself but had fraudulently falsified weekly reports and concealed monetary shortages were the proximate cause of plaintiff's eventual loss and could find coverage under insuring clause covering "loss through" dishonesty. *Daniel Grocer Co. v. New Amsterdam Cas. Co.*, 266 N.E.2d 365.

E.D. La. 2011. Insured who lost money after investing in a hedge fund that invested with Bernard Madoff sought coverage under computer fraud insuring agreement of commercial crime policy. Though the court stated that "direct" means immediate or proximate, as distinguished from remote, the insured's loss was too many steps removed from Madoff's fraud to be direct. *Methodist Health Sys. Found., Inc. v. Hartford Fire Ins. Co.*, 834 F. Supp. 2d 493.

La. App. 1968. To be compensable under a Blanket Crime Policy, loss must be actually suffered as a result of the dishonesty or fraud of an insured's employees. The policy in question provided coverage for losses that the insured "sustain[ed] through any fraudulent or dishonest conduct" of its employees. *Salley Grocer Co. v. Hartford Acc. & Indem. Co.*, 223 So. 2d 5 *writ refused sub nom. Salley Grocer Co. v. Hartford Acc. & Indem. Co.*, 222 So. 2d 883 (1969).

Md. 1989. Under Comprehensive Dishonesty, Disappearance and Destruction policy insuring against loss resulting directly from employee dishonesty, the court concluded that a third party that has suffered a loss as a result of the dishonesty of an employee of the insured may not predicate a claim against the fidelity insurer solely on the fact that the dishonesty rendered the insured legally liable to the third party. *Three Garden Village Ltd. P'ship v. U.S. Fid. & Guar. Co.*, 567 A.2d 85.

N.D. Ohio 2014. An employee of the insured stole from a related company and insured sued to obtain employee theft coverage under commercial crime policy. In denying insurer's motion to dismiss, the court held that "resulting directly" should be analyzed under a proximate cause standard. *Transtar Elec., Inc. v. Charter Oak Fire Ins. Co.*, 2014 WL 252023.

B. Cased Decided Under Other Fidelity Coverages

1. "Loss" by "The Insured," Generally

3d Cir. 2002 (Pa.). The Third Circuit, applying Pennsylvania law, reviewed a claim under insured's Blanket Employee Dishonesty policy that covered "direct loss caused by any fraudulent or dishonest acts" committed by its employees. The insured conducted clinical trials for experimental drugs. Nurses employed by the insured falsified observations of the patients, thus rendering the studies useless. As a result, the insured performed each study again without charge to its clients. The Third Circuit held that the insured was entitled to indemnity because the insured's loss resulting from rerunning the studies was proximately caused by the nurses' misconduct. *Scirex Corp. v. Fed. Ins. Co.,* 313 F.3d 841.

4th Cir. 1989 (N.C.). Bankers Blanket Bond covered certain losses resulting directly from false pretenses committed by person on the premises of the insured or in which the property is deposited. However, under North Carolina law it did not cover loss to the bank through securities fraud orchestrated by a person telephoning from another state when he made the misrepresentations to obtain bank's money. The "on premises" requirement precludes coverage for losses from fraud perpetrated by telephone or computer, except in rare cases where the perpetrator phones or uses a computer hookup from the bank's property or from property of a custodian entrusted by the bank to safeguard funds. *S. Nat'l Bank of N.C. v. United Pac. Ins. Co.,* 864 F.2d 329.

4th Cir. 1984 (Va.). Diversion of labor from a construction site could not be considered "property" under a Dishonesty, Disappearance and Destruction policy, covering loss of money or property by general contractor, absent a definition of "property" that specifically includes manpower. Policy language indicates that coverage for loss of only tangible property such as money and securities was contemplated. *G&C Constr. Corp. v. St. Paul Fire & Marine Ins. Co.,* 731 F.2d 183.

4th Cir. 1982 (S.C.). The bond that covered direct loss to credit union through employee's failure "to well and faithfully perform his duties" insures against employee negligence. *M.B.A.F.B. Fed. Credit Union v. Cumis Ins. Soc'y, Inc.,* 681 F.2d 930.

5th Cir. 2006 (Miss.). A natural gas seller tapped into the pipe downstream of the meter and recirculated the gas back into the line upstream of the meter, causing insured to pay for the same gas again. The insured claimed coverage for "direct physical loss of or damage to Covered Property," which property did not include money. The court held there was no coverage because the insured's overpayment for the recirculated gas was a loss of money, rather than covered property. *Hartford Ins. Co. of Midwest v. Mississippi Valley Gas Co.*, 181 F. App'x 465.

5th Cir. 1987 (La.). Insured's employees submitted bids for projects through their wholly owned companies, which were lower than the bids that they submitted on behalf of the insured. The potential income exclusion in comprehensive Dishonesty, Disappearance and Destruction policy excluded from coverage a claim for contract profits lost by employees' subversion of the bids. The court found a question of fact as to whether the insured's payment of travel expenses in furtherance of bid scheme, and salaries paid to them, was a loss of property caused "directly from one or more fraudulent or dishonest acts" of employees. *Diversified Grp., Inc. v. Van Tassel,* 806 F.2d 1275.

5th Cir. 1981 (Tex.). Attorney fees and court costs expended in defense of lawsuits alleging conspiracy to defraud through forgery and check kiting scheme perpetrated by director of bank and facilitated by bank president were recoverable under Bankers Blanket Bond because a judgment against the bank in suit would constitute a valid and collectible loss under bond. The bond provided indemnity for "loss through" any dishonest or fraudulent act of an employee. *First Nat'l Bank of Bowie v. Fid. & Cas. Co. of NY,* 634 F.2d 1000.

5th Cir. 1969 (Fla.). Shareholder-customers of corporate insurance clearinghouse or broker (which managed USAFORM Hail Pool for shareholder-customers) could not bring suit as third-party beneficiaries under the reinsurance pool's fidelity bond. A bonding company is not liable under a fidelity bond until the insured itself has suffered a proven loss. *Am. Empire Ins. Co. of S.D. v. Fid. & Dep. Co. of Md.,* 408 F.2d 72, *cert. denied,* 396 U.S. 818.

5th Cir. 1950 (Tex.). Insured is allowed indemnity under a fidelity bond providing indemnity for "loss through" employee dishonesty for secret profits or commissions earned by its dishonest employee who failed to account for such earned profits. *Eagle Indem. Co. v. Cherry*, 182 F.2d 298.

6th Cir. 2012 (Mich.). Insured's employee diverted funds from a company that was controlled by insured and from which the insured received income, but which was not insured under the CrimeShield policy. Judgment was affirmed in the insurer's favor because the theft from controlled company was not a direct loss to the insured in that it was not a loss "without anything intervening." *Tooling, Mfg. & Technologies Ass'n v. Hartford Fire Ins. Co.*, 693 F.3d 665.

6th Cir. 2012 (Ohio). Insured sought coverage under computer fraud endorsement after hackers downloaded credit card and checking account information pertaining to the insured's customers. The phrase "resulting directly from" in the insuring agreement imposed a proximate cause standard. *Retail Ventures, Inc. v. Nat'l Union Fire Ins. Co. of Pittsburgh, Pa.*, 691 F.3d 821.

6th Cir. 1990 (Ohio). "Missing" securities underlying repurchase agreements qualified under blanket bond as "property" because insured had an interest in securities even though it did not own them. The insured bank must show that loss was an unexplainable, mysterious loss within terms of bond, rather than a mere failure to deliver the securities promised (and thus a breach of contract), to be entitled to summary judgment. Blanket bond is excess to any coverage available from Securities Investors Protection Corporation. *First Fed. Sav. & Loan Ass'n of Toledo v. Fid. & Dep. Co. of Md.*, 895 F.2d 254.

7th Cir. 1989 (Wis.). Former employees' issuance of deceptive title insurance commitments and policies were excluded from coverage under blanket fidelity bond by provision excluding losses resulting from contracts of insurance. *Cont'l Corp. v. Aetna Cas. & Sur. Co.*, 892 F.2d 540.

7th Cir. 1980 (Ill.). A question of fact was found so as to require reversal of a grant of summary judgment. An insurer is not liable under the terms of fidelity bond covering loss through dishonest or fraudulent acts of the insured's employee for losses occasioned by negligence, carelessness, inattention to business, mistakes, errors in judgment, incompetency or other acts or omissions not amounting to conscious wrongdoing or involving moral turpitude. However, employee's actions need not reach the point of personal profit before coming within the terms of the bond. *Cent. Nat'l Life Ins. Co. v. Fid. & Dep. Co. of Md.,* 626 F.2d 537.

7th Cir. 1970 (Ill.). Insured bank's losses incurred through check kiting scheme were covered by Bankers Blanket Bond as a loss through false pretenses. *First Nat'l Bank of Decatur v. Ins. Co. of N. Am.,* 424 F.2d 312, *cert. denied,* 398 U.S. 939.

8th Cir. 1983 (Ark.). An insured bank did not suffer loss recoverable under its Bankers Blanket Bond when the bank president fraudulently induced a customer to purchase "participation interest" in a loan, and subsequently redeemed such interest from the aggrieved customer, and thereby transferred the interest to another willing customer who purchased the participation interest from the bank without recourse. *Bank of Mulberry v. Fireman's Fund Ins. Co.,* 720 F.2d 501.

8th Cir. 1979 (Ark.). Insured sustained loss recoverable under its bond when an inexperienced agent negligently released documents in reliance upon a purchaser's fraudulent misrepresentations. The language of the employee fidelity bond evidenced its intent to cover loss sustained by the bank "through" false pretenses. *Perkins v. Clinton State Bank,* 593 F.2d 327.

8th Cir. 1971 (Mo.). In suit to recover on a fidelity bond, an insured was awarded judgment for loan losses caused by its employee's falsification and forgery of credit applications. It also was entitled to recover kickbacks received by same employee when the employee referred potential and rejected customers of the corporation to other lending institutions for personal profit, and the corporation consequently suffered pecuniary loss. *Boston Sec., Inc. v. United Bonding Ins. Co.,* 441 F.2d 1302.

8th Cir. 1934 (Neb.). Insurer is not liable under bond unless competent evidence demonstrates that insured actually suffered a pecuniary loss through employee dishonesty. An insured's attempt to demonstrate loss through its bookkeeping ledgers was inadmissible hearsay. *Am. Employers' Ins. Co. v. Roundup Coal Mining Co.*, 73 F.2d 592.

9th Cir. 2002 (Cal.). An employee of the insured allegedly stole trade secrets from the insured and sold them to a competitor. As a part of this scheme, he allegedly stole copies of the various formula for the insured's products. The court rejected the contention of the insured that such acts were the direct cause of the loss, and also rejected its contention that the value of the intellectual property copied onto such papers was the value of its loss, holding that such loss should be measured by the value of the sheets of paper on which the formula had been copied. *Avery Dennison Corp. v. Allendale Mut. Ins.*, 47 F. App'x 41.

9th Cir. 1990 (Or.). Under Oregon law, losses sustained by a credit union because of officer's disbursement of improper loan did not qualify as loss of "money" under fidelity bond, but did qualify as a loss of "property," where bond defined "property" to include "securities," which included both checks and mortgages. *Portland Fed. Employees Credit Union v. Cumis Ins. Soc'y, Inc.*, 894 F.2d 1101.

9th Cir. 1986 (Cal.). For purposes of recovery under its Comprehensive Dishonesty, Disappearance and Destruction policy, proper measure of insured's equipment loss through employee's fraudulent sales was the stipulated fair market value or wholesale list price, and not insured's cost of remanufacture. Insured was not entitled to recover freight payments because those were costs that insured would ordinarily have absorbed. "Other property" within the meaning of the policy did not include employee commission on fraudulent sales, because the policy clearly excluded fraudulent or dishonest commissions. *James B. Lansing Sound, Inc. v. Nat'l Union Fire Ins. Co. of Pittsburgh, Pa.*, 801 F.2d 1560 *amended*, 981 F.2d 1549.

9th Cir. 1979 (Cal.). When an employee knowingly pays more for an item than it is worth, with the intention of enriching the person from whom purchase is made, such act is an act of dishonesty, and loss through such act potentially would have been recoverable under the fidelity bond before the court, except for applicable exclusions. *Research Equity Fund, Inc. v. Ins. Co. of N Am.*, 602 F.2d 200, *cert. denied*, 445 U.S. 945.

9th Cir. 1975 (Cal.). An insured savings and loan association merged with another association, against which there were pending lawsuits pertaining to allegedly dishonest acts committed by its employees. The insured brought action against its bonding company under a Form 22 Savings and Loan Blanket Bond to recover legal fees incurred following the merger in defending the lawsuits, which had continued against the merged associations. The insurer was not liable for the legal fees and expenses because the insured's acquisition of the liabilities of the merged association did not amount to a "loss" under its bond. *Fid. Sav. & Loan Ass'n v. Republic Ins. Co.*, 513 F.2d 954.

9th Cir. 1974 (Cal.). The Ninth Circuit affirmed the grant of summary judgment, holding that insurer is not liable under a Bankers Blanket Bond containing a "loss through" insuring clause when the subject funds were used by officers of the insured to meet general corporate expenses. *Bass v. Am. Ins. Co.*, 493 F.2d 590.

11th Cir. 1986 (Fla.). Under a fidelity bond excluding coverage for any loss that a "reasonable person" should have discovered prior to the bond period, negligence or inattention by bank's employees precluded recovery, notwithstanding the general principle of Florida law that nothing short of actual discovery by insured employer will defeat recovery. The opinion includes a detailed discussion of instruction given to jury on this point. *Royal Trust Bank, NA., v. Nat'l Union Fire Ins. Co. of Pittsburgh, Pa.*, 788 F.2d 719.

D.C. Cir. 1970. Insurer held liable for loss under fidelity policy covering loss "through any fraudulent or dishonest act or acts committed by any of the Employees" when insured's employee fraudulently issued excessively high-risk fire and casualty insurance policies, on which the insured had to pay large claims to its policyholders. *Imperial Ins., Inc. v. Employers' Liab. Assur. Corp.*, 442 F.2d 1197.

D.D.C. 2004. The district court granted the motions to dismiss filed by the insurer and insurance agent. The insured's client asserted that it was a loss payee on a fidelity bond provided by Federal. The court held that the complaint failed to state a cause of action for breach of contract, as it was the plaintiff and not the insured that suffered the loss. The bond provided that "[o]nly the first named Insured shall have any right to claim, adjust, receive or enforce payment of any loss." *Cambridge Holdings Grp., Inc. v. Fed. Ins. Co.,* 357 F. Supp. 2d 89.

E.D. Cal. 2011. Insured sought employee coverage under its commercial property insurance policy after its employee diverted funds intended for tax payments to another of the insured's accounts, with the eventual goal of diverting the funds to herself. The court dismissed the action because the insured's tax penalties and interest were not a direct physical loss of, or damage to, covered property. *J & J Pumps, Inc. v. Star Ins. Co.,* 795 F. Supp. 2d 1023.

N.D. Cal. 1986. Insured's Bankers Blanket Bond, which excluded from coverage losses resulting from the extension of credit on uncollected items of deposit, did not cover bank's loss from credit card fraud scheme utilizing credit card sales, notwithstanding the doctrine of concurrent causation. *Bay Area Bank v. Fid. & Dep. Co. of Md.,* 629 F. Supp. 693.

D.D.C. 1980. Where a third party suffers a loss for which the insured is legally obligated to pay restitution, loss to the insured accrues when the third party demands compensation from insured for purpose of determining whether a proof of loss was submitted in a timely fashion. *Fid. & Dep. Co. of Md. v. President & Dir. of Georgetown Coll.,* 483 F. Supp. 1142.

E.D. Mich. 2010. Loss of brokerage fees that the insured would have collected from a subsidiary, but for an employee of the subsidiary dishonestly diverting the brokerage income, was an indirect loss excluded by the CrimeShield policy. *Tooling, Mfg. & Technologies Ass'n. v. Hartford Fire Ins. Co.,* 2010 WL 3464329 *aff'd* 693 F.3d 665.

W.D. Mo. 1980. The Bankers Blanket Bond covering the bank against loss to bank of property through false pretenses did not include loss through action of officer of two companies in depositing checks made payable to one company in the account of another company. No false pretense was practiced on the bank because the bank knew of the overt use of the accounts even though it did not know of the underlying fraudulent transfers in anticipation of bankruptcy. A loss of property by false pretenses under bond is loss due to a false or misleading statement made to the bank to its detriment. *Columbia Union Nat'l Bank v. Hartford Acc. & Indem. Co.,* 496 F. Supp. 1263, *aff'd,* 669 F.2d 1210.

D.N.J. 2011. Auto manufacturer's recalculation of a performance bonus due to the insured auto dealership after discovery that insured's employees had manipulated customer satisfaction surveys was not a loss of covered property. *Jack Daniels Motors, Inc. v. Universal Underwriters Ins. Co.*, 2011 WL 346500 aff'd, 446 F. App'x 504.

D.N.J. 1983. This opinion, arising under a Bankers Blanket Bond, rejected a claim for loss suffered by the bank when fictitious certificates of deposit were given as partial security for a loan. The court rejected the contention that the loss might be covered under Insuring Agreement (D) of the subject bond because the instruments, in their signature, were wholly fictitious and thus any forgery was not a direct cause of the loss. *Liberty Nat'l Bank v. Aetna Life & Cas.*, 568 F. Supp. 860.

S.D.N.Y. 1986. Share of profits from stock loan department taken by employees of securities broker-dealer qualified as an "emolument" within meaning of fidelity bond exclusion for "salary, commissions, fees, or other emoluments" received by the insured, even if that share of profits was dishonestly earned. *Morgan, Olmstead, Kennedy & Gardner, Inc. v. Fed. Ins. Co.*, 637 F. Supp. 973, *aff'd*, 833 F.2d 1003 (2d Cir.).

W.D. Va. 1989. Bank officer's actions in depositing money received by a loan participation agreement into borrower's account instead of using money to reduce bank's liability on loan, and in falsifying debit slip used to wire bank's money to participating bank when it called its loan, qualified as dishonest acts committed with an intent to harm bank under Bankers Blanket Bond. *U.S. Fid. & Guar. v. Cit. Bk. of Tazewell*, 718 F. Supp. 471.

E.D. Va. 1975. "False pretenses" within the meaning of the Bankers Blanket Bond included the action of the partner of a used car partnership in signing and depositing checks of its corporate floor planner after its authority to utilize the checks had been withdrawn because the deposit of these checks was intended to deceive. The definition of "property" under the bond was broader than tangible items and included rights and evidences of debts lost through partnership's scheme. *Clarendon Bank & Trust v. Fid. & Dep. Co. of Md.*, 406 F. Supp. 1161.

Cal. App. 2007. The insured advertising agency's customer base and business collapsed after discovery that its employee manipulated prize payouts for promotional games. The court of appeal rejected the insured's contention that its loss of business and litigation costs was a loss of covered property resulting directly from employee dishonesty. *Simon Mktg. v. Gulf Ins. Co.*, 57 Cal. Rptr. 3d 49.

Haw. Sup. 2006. Insured could not recover attorney fees and costs incurred in litigation arising from conduct of its dishonest employee, as those payments were not "direct financial loss" within the meaning of its employee dishonesty policy. *House of Fin., Inc. v. Fin. Solutions Ins. Servs., Inc.*, 138 P.3d 754.

Ill. App. 1990. Insurer was obligated under "Employee Dishonesty Commercial Blanket Coverage" to indemnify insured advertising services corporation for losses through employee's falsification of documents to create the appearance of having mailed documents that were actually discarded. *Northbrook Nat'l Ins. Co. v. Nehoc Adver. Servs., Inc.*, 554 N.E.2d 251.

Kan. 1970. A blanket bond unambiguously covers only the insured against employee defalcation. A plaintiff who has recovered judgment against insured, therefore, cannot maintain garnishment proceedings against the insurer. *Ronnau v. Caravan Int'l Ins. Corp.*, 468 P.2d 118.

La. App. 1999. The insured sought recovery under a commercial crime policy for the loss attributed to its employee. The employee had confessed to such embezzlements. However, the evidence at trial was found to be insufficient to corroborate the amount of theft or when the alleged dishonesty occurred. The court held that the insured must prove the dishonesty actually took place during the policy term of the form at issue, and that it directly caused the loss. *Provincial Hotels Inc. v. Mascair*, 734 So. 2d 136.

La. App. 1974. Employees cannot recover under their employer's Brokers Blanket Bond for commissions that they alleged were fraudulently withheld from them when they left the employment of the insured brokerage company. *Herbert v. Mayeur & Co.*, 296 So. 2d 446.

Md. 1950. Where a fidelity policy insured against loss of property due to employee fraud or dishonesty, such policy did not cover the loss of profits resulting from employee's contracts to himself. *Levy v. Am. Mut. Liab. Ins. Co.,* 73 A.2d 892.

Mass. App. 1992. The Court of Appeals, applying Massachusetts law, held that the trial judge properly instructed a jury that a finding that the alleged principal had committed one of the alleged acts of theft should not in and of itself be sufficient to prove that she had committed others. The court thus held that coverage under a financial institution bond required the insured to prove that all transactions were the direct result of dishonesty and that all losses result directly from such before indemnity will be owed. *Cambridge Trust Co. v. Commercial Union Ins. Co.,* 591 N.E.2d 1117.

Mich. App. 1992. The Court of Appeals of the State of Michigan examined the efforts of a judgment creditor of the insured to recover its judgment from the insured's "broker's blanket bond." The court held that the bond was not a liability policy and thus not subject to garnishment. It went on to conclude that because the only potential loss to the insured was the return of the allegedly unearned commissions, such would not give rise to a "loss" compensable under the broker's blanket bond, but rather a return of money to which the insured was not otherwise entitled. *Bralko Holdings, Ltd. v. Ins. Co. of N. Am.,* 483 N.W.2d 929.

Minn. 1989. Bank that unknowingly accepted fake stock certificates as collateral for loan was not entitled to recover on Bankers Blanket Bond for financial loss stemming from loan's default, because bank did not have actual physical possession of the securities before making the loan. The court stated that the failure to follow sound business practices and verify authenticity is a business risk taken by banks, not an insured risk covered by the Bankers Blanket Bond. Moreover, fake stock certificates did not fall within bond's definition of "counterfeited." *Nat'l City Bank of Minn. v. St. Paul Fire & Marine Ins. Co.,* 447 N.W.2d 171.

R.I. 1970. Insured's employee's admitted theft of thirty bars of precious metal would only support loss through dishonest acts of employees for the value of the thirty bars and not the amount that the insured claimed was lost during the period of employee's employment. *Danal Jewelry Co. v. Fireman's Fund Ins. Co.,* 264 A.2d 320.

Vt. 2014. Insured town's treasurer embezzled over $300,000, which its insurer reimbursed. The insurer, however, declined to reimburse interest on the embezzled funds. The court held that the policy covered the interest that could have been earned on the embezzled funds. *Town of Ira v. Vermont League of Cities & Towns–Prop. & Cas. Intermunicipal Fund, Inc.,* 109 A.3d 893.

Va. 1986. When a note was made out incompletely and later completed in an unauthorized manner, the bank did not suffer an insurable loss within the terms of its Bankers Blanket Bond at the time it made payment in reliance on the altered note because bank was a holder in due course of the note and had the right to enforce the note against the maker as a matter of law. No "loss" is incurred by paying value for a valid and enforceable instrument. *Virginia Capital Bank v. Aetna Cas. & Sur. Co.,* 343 S.E.2d 81.

Wash. App. 1982. The Court of Appeals of the State of Washington, applying Washington law, held that the bond covered only actual as opposed to theoretical losses. However, the court appears to have concluded that accrued but unpaid interest that was charged off could be included in the value of the bank's actual loss. This decision, like the *Estate of Jordan* decision, is outside the mainstream of precedent on this issue. *Puget Sound Nat'l Bank v. St. Paul Fire & Marine Ins. Co.,* 645 P.2d 1122.

   2.   When Does "Loss" Occur

1st Cir. 1966 (Mass.). Where an employee dishonestly cashed his employer's checks and caused the insured bank to pay out its own funds, the bank sustained loss under a Bankers Blanket Bond at the time the employee cashed the checks. *Aetna Cas. & Sur. Co. v. Guar. Bank & Trust Co.,* 370 F.2d 276.

5th Cir. 1970 (Tex.). Discovery of "loss" occurs under a Bankers Blanket Bond on the date fraud was discovered, not on the date the obligee was called upon to indemnify the loss. *FDIC v. Aetna Cas. & Sur. Co.,* 426 F.2d 729.

10th Cir. 1994 (Utah). The Tenth Circuit affirmed a jury verdict for the FDIC arising from the alleged acts of dishonesty of a bank employee in making a loan. The court held that in this case the loss occurred at the time the insured transacted the loan, not when the loan proved to be partially uncollectible. The court reasoned that the disbursement of funds was an act that resulted directly from the alleged dishonest or fraudulent acts. The District Court's opinion also contains an extensive discussion, and quotes jury instructions. *FDIC v. United Pac. Ins. Co.,* 20 F.3d 1070.

Ill. App. 1979. The date of "loss" is the date the dishonest acts occurred, and not when the insured was required to pay settlement costs based on the fraudulent acts. *Reserve Ins. Co. v. Gen. Ins. Co. of Am.,* 395 N.E.2d 933.

Mass. 1931. "Loss" means deprivation or dispossession of money or property of the bank due to the dishonest, criminal, or fraudulent acts of its officers. *Fitchburg Sav. Bank v. Mass. Bonding & Ins. Co.,* 174 N.E. 324.

N.D. 1979. Insurer was held liable for loss resulting from the acts of its insured's employee when the employee embezzled funds prior to the expiration of the fidelity policy, and later transferred new funds to insured's accounts to conceal the original loss after the policy had expired. The opinion also contains an analysis of the different elements required to prove "bad faith" and to support an award of punitive damages. *Corwin Chrysler-Plymouth, Inc. v. Westchester Fire Ins. Co.,* 279 N.W.2d 638.

3. Bookkeeping Entries as "Loss"

5th Cir. 1980 (Fla.). Insurer, under a Fidelity Blanket Bond, is not liable for insured's alleged loss when employees took permanent investment funds and deposited them to a general account of the insured, because the insured merely experienced a "shifting of liabilities." *Everhart v. Drake Mgmt., Inc.,* 627 F.2d 686.

5th Cir. 1975 (Fla.). A loss under a fidelity bond is not established by showing that funds were wrongfully diverted from one account within a corporation and applied to another account within that same corporation. No loss is established if wrongfully appropriated monies were used to pay legitimate corporate obligations. Burden is on the insurer to prove that money was used for valid corporate expenditures. *Fid. & Dep. Co. of Md. v. USAFORM Hail Pool, Inc.,* 523 F.2d 744 *cert. denied,* 425 U.S. 950.

5th Cir. 1972 (Fla.). Where employees misused funds in a special "premium account" of the insured corporation, in that such trust fund was used to pay corporate obligations rather than used for trust purposes, the insured suffered no loss, and coverage did not attach. *Fid. & Dep. Co. of Md. v. USAFORM Hail Pool, Inc.,* 463 F.2d 4.

5th Cir. 1941 (Tex.). A surety's obligation to indemnify its insured bank against "direct loss sustained" refers to actual present loss, rather than theoretical, bookkeeping loss. *Cont'l Cas. Co. v. First Nat'l Bank of Temple,* 116 F.2d 885.

7th Cir. 1994 (Ind.). The Seventh Circuit, applying Indiana law, held that a question of fact existed as to whether the proceeds of a bank money order that was used to disburse loan proceeds, and which allegedly bore a forged endorsement, actually reached the borrower. It thus held that summary judgment could not be granted either to the insured bank or to its insurer. The court could not conclude on the record before it whether the insured bank had suffered an actual loss as a direct result of the forgery, or whether it was a bookkeeping loss. *Cincinnati Ins. Co. v. Star Fin. Bank,* 35 F.3d 1186.

C.D. Cal. 1987. Federal book entry securities are "property" for purposes of Savings and Loan Blanket Bond. The provision of the bond covering loss of property while the property is "lodged or deposited within any offices or premises located anywhere . . ." is not limited to property in any of the insured's premises, but provides coverage for loss occurring while property is lodged or deposited within any person's offices or premises. *Fed. Sav. & Loan Ins. Corp. v. Transamerica Ins. Co.,* 661 F. Supp. 246.

S.D. Ga. 2007. Direct loss requires an actual present loss, not a theoretical or bookkeeping loss. Where the dishonest bank employee fraudulently issued loans to repay prior loans, the financial institution bond applied only to the actual depletion of the insured bank's funds.

Citizens Bank & Trust Co. v. St. Paul Mercury Ins. Co., 2007 WL 4973847.

N.D. Ill. 2011. Holding that a "modest causal horizon is appropriate in a non-fidelity policy, the court rejected insurer's contention that "loss resulting directly from dishonest acts" was limited to an actual depletion of the insured's bank account. Accordingly, the court found that the allegedly dishonest acts were not direct theft, yet the acts directly caused the insured to incur the cost of litigation and settlement. *Alliant Credit Union v. CUMIS Ins. Soc., Inc.*, 2011 WL 941257.

S.D. Miss. 2012. Fictitious loan entered on the insured bank's books to pay off prior legitimate loan was only a bookkeeping or theoretical loss, which is not a loss covered under the terms of the financial institution bond. *BancInsure, Inc. v. Peoples Bank of the S.*, 866 F. Supp. 2d 577.

W.D. Mo. 2010. Transfers of funds from trust accounts to insured's operating accounts amounted to a bookkeeping or theoretical loss that was not sufficient for a fidelity bond to provide coverage. Coverage requires that there be a direct loss or the actual depletion of the insured's funds caused by the employee's dishonest acts. *Tactical Stop-Loss LLC v. Travelers Cas. & Sur. Co. of Am.*, 2010 WL 2802203 *aff'd*, 657 F.3d 757.

D.P.R. 2004. The insured's employees caused it to lose track of transactions, eventually causing the insured to write off millions to balance its accounting records. The district court denied the insurer's motion for summary judgment, holding that under Puerto Rico law, questions of fact remained as to whether the claimed loss was a an actual depletion of funds or a non-covered "bookkeeping or theoretical" loss. *Oriental Fin. Grp. v. Fed. Ins. Co.*, 309 F. Supp. 2d 216.

N.D. Ill. 2006. The insured auto dealer's employee dishonestly overpaid for purchases and accepted underpayments for sales. Although the court held that direct loss requires an actual depletion of funds, it denied summary judgment on the basis that the insured had not provided competent evidence of the intrinsic values of the cars as basis of comparison against the purchase and sales prices. *Patrick Schaumburg Automobiles, Inc. v. Hanover Ins. Co.*, 452 F. Supp. 2d 857.

D. Utah 2010. Direct loss under a credit union bond is limited to the actual depletion of bank funds caused by the employee's dishonest acts and does not include the impact of the real estate market on value of the improper loans between the time they were issued and the time they failed. *Transwest Credit Union v. Cumis Ins. Soc., Inc.*, 2010 WL 3791310.

Colo. 1935. A bookkeeping entry that reveals an account deficiency is not a "loss" recoverable under a Savings and Loan Blanket Bond with "loss through" acts of dishonest employees where there is no direct evidence of employee dishonesty. *Am. Sur. Co. v. Capitol Bldg. & Loan Ass'n*, 50 P.2d 792.

Ga. App. 2008. An insured law firm's employee stole funds over several years in a complex check kiting scheme. Payments between the law firm's accounts were not a loss to the insured, and thus not covered. *Lee, Black, Hart & Rouse, P.C. v. Travelers Indem. Co.*, 662 S.E.2d 889.

Iowa 1979. Dishonest and fraudulent acts covered by fidelity bond include acts in disregard of an employer's interest that are likely to subject the employer to loss. The opinion does not describe or quote the bond in detail. Bank president's acts—in transferring funds from one account to another without authorization, making false records, making false reconciliation of accounts with other banks, crediting checks to improper accounts, making false reconstruction of checking accounts and holding overdrafts as cash items—qualified as dishonest and fraudulent under terms of bond. *FDIC v. Nat'l Sur. Corp.*, 281 N.W.2d 816.

Minn. 1992. The Minnesota Supreme Court held that the insured bank did not sustain any loss within the meaning of its bond for that portion of the loss whereby the insured's employee misapplied bank funds to pay off outstanding loans from the insured to himself, his sons, his insurance agency, and his former business partner from other bank funds without evidence that the insured was precluded from otherwise recovering on the loans. It thus held that loss does not include bookkeeping or theoretical losses, but only actual depletion of the insured's assets. *Transamerica Ins. Co. v. FDIC*, 489 N.W.2d 224.

Minn. 1957. A preponderance of the evidence established that the managing officer of an insured bank had fraudulently caused the insured to suffer loss by deducting certain income from clients' accounts. The surety was therefore held liable under its fidelity bond for the amount of loss. *Prior Lake State Bank v. Nat'l Sur. Corp.,* 80 N.W.2d 612.

N.Y. App. 2012. Insured investment management company sought to recover under its fidelity bond losses that its various investing entities sustained after selecting Bernard Madoff as an outside investment advisor. The court held that no reasonable interpretation of the term "loss" in the context of the bond allowed for coverage of the fictitious gains that Madoff reported to his investors. *Jacobson Family Investments, Inc. v. Nat'l Union Fire Ins. Co. of Pittsburgh, PA,* 955 N.Y.S.2d 338.

N.Y. App. 1988. A bank employee who intentionally failed to debit customer's account for dishonored checks and instead took funds from unrelated frozen account intended loss to be sustained by the insured bank, and thus his actions were "dishonest" for purposes of fidelity policy and Bankers Blanket Bond. *Nat'l Bank of Pakistan v. Basham,* 531 N.Y.S.2d 250, *aff'd,* 541 N.Y.S.2d 345 (1989).

N.Y. Sup. 1967. Surety held not liable for loss where a ledger card representing an account in insured's savings and loan association disappeared and the insured had to pay funds to the assignee of the account. Since the ledger card had no intrinsic value, it did not constitute evidence of debt. *Metro. Sav. & Loan Ass'n v. Hanover Ins. Co.,* 286 N.Y.S.2d 129.

Vt. 2014. Insured town's treasurer embezzled over $300,000, which its insurer reimbursed. The insurer, however, declined to reimburse interest on the embezzled funds. The court held that the policy covered the interest that could have been earned on the embezzled funds. This decision is contrary to mainstream precedent with respect to interest. *Town of Ira v. Vermont League of Cities & Towns–Prop. & Cas. Intermunicipal Fund, Inc.,* 109 A.3d 893.

Wash. 1993. In this decision, the Washington State Supreme Court held that the shifting of internal liabilities without a corresponding reduction in the insured's net assets can constitute a covered loss under a commercial crime policy. This decision construed the policy as a statutory bond. *Estate of Jordan v. Hartford Acc. & Indem. Co.*, 844 P.2d 403.

Wash. App. 1982. The Court of Appeals for the State of Washington, applying Washington law, held that the bond covered only actual as opposed to theoretical losses. However, the court appears to have concluded that accrued but unpaid interest which was charged off could be included in the amount of the bank's actual loss. This decision, like the *Estate of Jordan* decision, is outside the mainstream of precedent on this issue. *Puget Sound Nat'l Bank v. St. Paul Fire & Marine Ins. Co.*, 645 P.2d 1122.

4. Insured's Legal Liability as "Loss"

5th Cir. 1985. Attorney fees and court costs incurred in defending fraud action were recoverable under fidelity bond when any liability in the fraud action would have been a collectible loss under the bond. According to the court, neither the terms of the bond "nor Texas law required that insured suffer an actual collectible loss, only that it be threatened with a potential collectible loss." *Cont'l Sav. Ass'n v. U.S. Fid. & Guar. Co.*, 762 F.2d 1239, *modified in part on other grounds*, 768 F.2d 89 (5th Cir.).

5th Cir. 1976 (La.). A surety on a Bankers Blanket Bond was not liable for its insured's loss where the insured bank attempted to pay its own debts with the proceeds of a check deposited in a customer's account, and the check was later returned for insufficient funds. *Calcasieu Marine Nat'l Bank of Lake Charles v. Am. Emp. Ins. Co.*, 533 F.2d 290.

6th Cir. 1997 (Ky.). The Sixth Circuit, applying Kentucky law to a Form 24 Bankers Blanket Bond, held that amounts paid by the bank to resolve claims by third parties against the bank for the employee's alleged dishonest conduct directed against those third parties were not covered under the bond. While the bulk of the discussion is directed towards the question of the manifest intent of the employees, the opinion also analyzes the question of whether the loss incurred by the bank in resolving third-party claims was a loss "resulting directly from" the acts in question. *Peoples Bank & Trust of Madison Cnty. v. Aetna Cas. & Sur. Co.,* 113 F.3d 629.

7th Cir. 1989 (Wis.). The Seventh Circuit, applying Wisconsin law, reviewed a claim under a Form 25 Insurance Companies Blanket Bond made by Continental on its bond with Aetna. Continental claimed it suffered losses when its employee engaged in a series of fraudulent real estate scams involving in part the issuance of fraudulently procured title insurance policies. It held that Continental's losses on its title insurance policies were excluded by an exclusion for such payments and that its payments for settlement of claims brought against it by third parties also duped by its employee were not covered as such were not resulting directly from the employee's alleged dishonesty. *Cont'l Corp. v. Aetna Cas. & Sur. Co.,* 892 F.2d 540.

8th Cir. 2015 (Minn.). The insured bank's employee convinced two non-customers to put money into an advance payment scam relating to an estate in Africa. Both men made the checks payable to the bank, and the employee wired the funds to an account in Hong Kong. The Eighth Circuit held that the insured bank sustained loss resulting directly from dishonest or fraudulent acts of the employee. Although the insured's loss resulted from its liability to the two investors, it briefly held the non-customers' money in its accounts, and was thus legally liable for the money. Also under Minnesota law, a loss of third-party funds entrusted to the insured through employee theft or fraud may be considered a loss "resulting directly from" the fraudulent acts of an employee. *Avon State Bank v. BancInsure, Inc.,* 2015 WL 3465985.

8th Cir. 1990 (Ark.). The Eighth Circuit, applying Arkansas law to a dispute arising under an unnamed fidelity bond issued by National Union to a securities brokerage firm in Arkansas, held that the bond was given to comply with an Arkansas statute requiring the bonding of brokerages, and under such statute such bonds were to provide indemnity for recoveries by third parties against the insured where the third party had lost property held by the insured. In reaching its decision, it appears that the court construed the bond as a statutory bond. It expressly noted that, generally speaking, fidelity bonds are not to be considered liability insurance. *Foster v. Nat'l Union Fire Ins. Co. of Pittsburgh, Pa.,* 902 F.2d 1316.

8th Cir. 1990 (Iowa). The Eighth Circuit, applying Iowa law, held that a covered loss occurred when the insured was legally liable for the conduct of its officer and thus was not able to enforce fraudulently executed notes against the customers. It thus had to "settle" those claims by advancing funds to its customers to pay off the notes. It reached this conclusion by finding that Bankers Blanket Bonds, before they were required to comply with Iowa Code § 524.705 (1970), also under that statute, were required to provide such indemnity. The bond in question was a Bankers Blanket Bond Standard Form No. 24. *First Am. State Bank v. Cont'l Ins. Co.,* 897 F.2d 319.

8th Cir. 1987 (Iowa). The district court, applying the law of the State of Iowa, held that the Bankers Blanket Bond at issue was not a liability policy under Iowa law. It thus concluded that judgment creditors of the insured bank could not pursue a claim under the bond under an Iowa statute that would allow such claims against a liability insurer. *Anderson v. Employers Ins. of Wausau,* 826 F.2d 777.

9th Cir. 2006 (Cal.). Assignee of insured bank could not recover under bank's financial institution bond ("FIB") for losses caused it by the dishonesty of the bank's employees. The insured bank's assignment of rights under its FIB did not confer standing to bring a claim for losses suffered by parties other than the insured bank. *BNY Midwest Trust Co. v. Nat'l Union Fire Ins. Co. of Pittsburgh, PA,* 213 F. App'x 563.

9th Cir. 1981 (Cal.). Loss sustained by a savings and loan association on certificates of deposit that association had had on deposit with bank that failed, due in part to dishonest acts of bank's officers, was not entirely recoverable under its blanket bond. In determining the cause for an association's loss, the fact finder must consider the failure of borrowers to repay their valid debts as well as evidence of dishonest loans. *Fid. Sav. & Loan Ass'n v. Aetna Life & Cas. Co.,* 647 F.2d 933.

10th Cir. 1994 (Okla.). The Tenth Circuit, applying Oklahoma law, found that the fidelity policy at issue did not obligate St. Paul to indemnify its insured for the insured's liability for the theft of its clients' funds by an employee. *In Re Ben Kennedy & Assoc.,* 40 F.3d 318.

D. Colo. 2011. Insured claimed coverage for employee dishonesty for its settlement with a third party after its employees fraudulently induced the party to enter into a contract with the insured and a business in which the employees had an interest. The court held there was no coverage because the underlying lawsuit did not involve property for which the insured had legal liability. The phrase "property for which [the insured] is legally liable" referred to an interest that existed apart from a third party's claim of employee dishonesty. *Qwest Commc'ns Int'l, Inc. v. QBE Corporate Ltd.*, 829 F. Supp. 2d 1037.

D. Conn. 2002. The court held that the insured's "employee dishonesty protection rider" limited its coverage to losses to the insured directly resulting from employee dishonesty and thus did not obligate the insurer to indemnify the insured's bankruptcy trustee for claims against the estate by the insured's customer for tax liabilities of those customers. *Finkel v. State Farm Fire Marine Ins. Co.*, 2002 WL 1359672.

N.D. Ill. 2012. An insured law firm reimbursed one of its partners after one of the firm's secretaries embezzled from the personal account of the partner, which account she administered. The court held that the insured could not recover under its employee dishonesty coverage because losses suffered by a third party that the insured subsequently reimburses are not direct losses. *Sperling & Slater, P.C. v. Hartford Cas. Ins. Co.*, 2012 WL 6720611.

D. Kan. 1993. This opinion involved the direct action by the credit union against the securities dealer blanket bond issued in favor of a brokerage house. The credit union asserted that the direct action was authorized by Arkansas Code Annotated § 23-42-305. The court held that the bond was not a liability policy and thus did not define the existence of such a direct action right under the Arkansas statute. It went on to find that any obligation that the insurer might have had to indemnify the brokerage under the bond did not arise until the insured made the payment that it was legally obligated to make to a third party. *Sch. Employees Credit Union v. Nat'l Union Fire Ins. Co. of Pittsburgh, Pa.*, 839 F. Supp. 1477, *aff'd*, 52 F.3d 338.

E.D. Ky. 2011. The insured provided payroll services, which included issuing payroll directly from the client's account to the client's employees. Using the control over the client's account given to her, the insured's employee embezzled from the client. The court held that there was no direct loss under the employee dishonesty coverage because the funds were never in the insured's "care, custody or control." *Monroe Guar. Ins. Co. v. Radwan Brown & Co.*, 2011 WL 1102694.

E.D. Ky. 1990. Applying Kentucky law, the district court held that the fidelity bond in question was a common law bond and thus would not allow a direct action against it by the alleged victim. *Thornsberry v. Western Ins. Co.*, 738 F. Supp. 209.

E.D. Mich. 1992. Applying Michigan law, the district court held that a Brokerage Blanket Bond obligated the carrier to indemnify the insured for amounts paid by it to resolve claims against the partnership arising from alleged dishonesty of certain of its partners. *Manley, Bennett, McDonald & Co. v. St. Paul Fire & Marine Ins. Co.*, 807 F. Supp. 1287.

W.D. Mo. 1984. A bank that did not claim any interest in funds that were deposited in a special account could not claim that it suffered a "loss" when a bank officer later removed such funds for his own use. *Shearson/Am. Express, Inc. v. First Cont'l Bank & Trust Co.*, 579 F. Supp. 1305.

D.N.J. 1994. The court held that the financial institution bond did not give rights to any third parties. Rather, it existed only for the benefit of the named insured. *Resolution Trust Corp. v. Moskowitz*, 845 F. Supp. 247, *opinion vacated in part and on other grounds*, 1994 WL 475811.

Bankr. N.D. Ohio 1988. The bankruptcy court held that the brokers bond at issue obligated the insurer to indemnify the insured's bankruptcy trustee for losses incurred as a result of claims made by investors duped by the employee allegedly operating a Ponzi scheme at the insured. *In Re Baker & Getty Fin. Servs., Inc.*, 93 B.R. 559.

D. Or. 1968. An insured bank that authorized a loan to a borrower who gave forged or counterfeited stock certificates as collateral for the loan has sustained a loss "through" this conduct, which loss was covered by its bond, regardless of the insured's possible remedy against the makers of the note. *Citizens Bank of Oregon v. Am. Ins. Co.*, 289 F. Supp. 211.

S.D. Tex. 2014. A Florida lawyer allegedly committed acts of fraud and dishonesty, resulting in claims against the insured title company. With respect to claims by third parties against the insured, the court held that third-party liability was not loss that results directly within the meaning of the financial institution bond. *Stewart Info. Servs. Corp. v. Great Am. Ins. Co.*, 997 F. Supp. 2d 650.

D. Utah 2008. Insured wholesale lending company had to repurchase mortgage loans after discovering that its employee falsified documents to close loans. The court adopted the "direct means direct" approach and held the financial institution bond's exclusion for indirect loss barred coverage for insured's liability to repurchase the defective mortgages. *Direct Mortgage Corp. v. Nat'l Union Fire Ins. Co. of Pittsburgh, PA*, 625 F. Supp. 2d 1171.

S.D. W. Va. 1973. Bank incurred a loss under a Bankers Blanket Bond when its employee fraudulently and dishonestly represented that certain automobiles were accounted for. Notwithstanding the subject automobiles were collateral for a loan and were in possession of banker's debtor, their loss was held to constitute a "loss" under broad terms of the bond. Bank's liability to second bank, which suffered loss on promissory notes due to the fraudulent acts of first bank's employee, also was covered. *First Nat'l Bank of W. Hamlin v. Maryland Cas. Co.*, 354 F. Supp. 189.

E.D. Wis. 2010. Mortgage lender's contractual obligation to repurchase loans that did not comply with the lender's underwriting requirements due to employee dishonesty was not a direct loss under a mortgage Bankers Blanket Bond. In reaching its holding, the court rejected that "direct" is synonymous with "proximately" or "proximate cause" for purposes of coverage under a fidelity bond. *Universal Mortgage Corp. v. Württembergische Versigherung, AG*, 2010 WL 3060655, *aff'd* 651 F.3d 759.

Colo. App. 2012. Assignees of bankrupt lender could not recover their investment losses under lender's employee theft coverage of mortgage bankers bond. "Direct financial loss" sustained by the insured referred only to the immediate loss of the insured's property, not damage to third parties, including investors. *Abady v. Certain Underwriters at Lloyd's London*, 317 P.3d 1248.

Ill. App. 2004. The Illinois Appellate Court held that where the insured bank settled with a third party that had purchased a loan originated at the bank by an allegedly dishonest employee to himself, the amounts paid to resolve that third-party claim would not be deemed to be a loss resulting directly from the employee's dishonesty. In so doing, the court held that the phrase "loss resulting directly from" was unambiguous and that it mandated a stricter causational standard than proximate cause. *RBC Mortgage Co. v. Nat'l Union Fire Ins. Co. of Pittsburgh, Pa.*, 812 N.E.2d 728.

Ill. App. 1989. When senior management approved the conduct of its president, which a suit against bank alleged to be fraudulent, the bank was not entitled to indemnity for court costs and attorney fees in its defense of that suit. *State Street Bank & Trust Co. of Quincy v. U.S. Fid. & Guar. Co.*, 539 N.E.2d 779.

La. App. 1983. The employee dishonesty coverage under a "comprehensive 3-D" policy was intended to insure against the loss of insured's own property. Accordingly, such policy did not cover the legal liability of an insured cleaning service to its customer for damages resulting from a fire in customer's building set by employee of insured in order to cover the employee's theft of the customer's cash box. *Gulf Bldg. Servs., Inc. v. Travelers Indem. Co.*, 435 So. 2d 477.

La. App. 1976. The Louisiana Court of Appeals held that an insured bank could maintain an action against its bonding company even though directors of the insured bank had reimbursed the bank for sums that were fraudulently taken by an employee. The bank's liability to the directors was a "loss" covered by the bond. *Sugarland State Bank v. Aetna Ins. Co.*, 330 So. 2d 336.

Mass. Super. 2005. Insurer was not liable to bank under financial institution bond for amount the bank owed a customer resulting from dishonesty by customer's employee because the FIB does not cover indirect losses associated with third-party liability. *Commerce Bank & Trust v. St. Paul Mercury Ins. Co.*, 2005 WL 4881101.

Mich. App. 2008. Business Owners Property Policy did not obligate insurer to pay for a third party's non-economic losses related to the loss of or damage to property caused by the fraudulent conduct of the insured's employees. *First Mountain Mortgage Corp. v. Citizens Ins. Co.*, 2008 WL 4604689.

Minn. 2004. The Court of Appeals for the State of Minnesota reviewed a claim by an insured under a Crime Loss Indemnity policy issued by St. Paul Fire and Marine Insurance Company. The policy provided indemnity, subject to its other terms and conditions, for "loss sustained by the insured by reason of any claim first made against the insured during the policy period directly caused by theft or forgery by any employee of the insured for which loss the insured is liable . . . ." The employees of Cargill allegedly stole germplasm developed by a rival, Pioneer. Litigation ensued and Cargill resolved the underlying case by settlement. The fidelity insurers declined coverage. The Court of Appeals affirmed the grant of summary judgment. In so doing, it held that "we conclude that the language of clause (A)(2) does not support Cargill's assertion that the clause provides general liability coverage or creates a duty to defend or settle [claims] against Cargill by third parties . . . . We conclude that the provision . . . covers only Cargill's direct losses, not claims arising from a third-party's direct losses, it requires that the insured's loss—and not the third-party's claim be directly caused by employee theft in order for coverage to become available . . . ." *Cargill, Inc. v. Nat'l Union Fire Ins. Co. of Pittsburgh, Pa.*, 2004 WL 51671.

Neb. 1981. A Bankers Blanket Bond did not insure against insured bank's liability to a third party for a judgment obtained against the bank on the grounds of alleged fraud and misrepresentation by a bank employee. *Omaha Bank for Coops. v. Aetna Cas. & Sur. Co.*, 301 N.W.2d 564.

N.H. 1981. A Bankers Blanket Bond, insuring against loss through the insured having purchased, acquired, accepted, sold, or extended credit on the faith of a written instrument that proves to have been raised, altered, lost, or stolen, was held to cover negligent acts by employees of bank, and indirect losses to bank, where no indirect loss exclusion is present. *Exeter Banking Co. v. New Hampshire Ins. Co.* 438 A.2d 310.

N.Y. App. 2013. An employee of an insured commodities futures broker exceeded his margin by making unauthorized trades from his personal trading account, resulting in a large unsecured loss, which the insured was required to pay to the clearing house. Holding that a "direct financial loss" required a proximate cause analysis, the court found that the unauthorized trades were the direct and proximate cause of the insured's loss because the trades caused a near instantaneous shortfall for which the insured was automatically responsible. *New Hampshire Ins. Co. v. MF Global, Inc.*, 970 N.Y.S.2d 16.

N.Y. App. 2003. Insured sought a declaration that the insurer would be obligated to indemnify it for various fees, costs, and lost interest attributable to thefts of funds by employees. The appellate division affirmed the dismissal of the complaint by the trial court. In so doing, it relied upon New York law stating that the policies in question were not liability policies and that such an interpretation as urged by the insured would convert them into such. *Ernst & Young, LLP v. Nat'l Union Fire Ins. Co. of Pittsburgh, Pa.*, 758 N.Y.S.2d 304.

N.Y. App. 1998. The Appellate Division of the New York Supreme Court reviewed a claim by an insured for losses it incurred as a result of the settlement of various insider-trading suits against it. The primary layer of coverage was afforded under Lloyd's standard form No. 14 Blanket Bond. Among other matters, the court held that the bonds in question did not obligate the insurers to indemnify the insured for the amounts paid in settlement as such payments were not a direct result of the alleged dishonest conduct. *Aetna Cas. & Sur. Co. v. Kidder, Peabody & Co.*, 676 N.Y.S.2d 559.

N.Y. Sup. 1993. Drexel Burnham Lambert filed suit under multiple bonds identified as "Bankers and Brokers Blanket Bonds." The court held that the bonds were not liability insurance policies and did not provide indemnity for alleged losses incurred as a result of third-party claims against Drexel Burnham, where the losses were occasioned by settlements of clients brought by third parties. The court stated, "[Employees] frauds were not committed against Drexel, but against members of the investing public, the companies they manipulated, and the federal regulatory agencies. In short, they did not steal *from* the company, they stole *for* the company." *Drexel Burnham Lambert Group, Inc. v. Vigilant Ins. Co.*, 595 N.Y.S.2d 999.

N.Y. 1980. The judgment creditor of an obligee has no cause of action against a fidelity bond issued to the judgment debtor because the fidelity bond insures only against a direct loss of the insured, not against liability asserted by a third person. *175 E. 74th Corp. v. Hartford Acc. & Indem. Co.,* 51 N.Y.2d 585.

5.   Effect of Insured's Collateral or Salvage Rights

2d Cir. 1979 (N.Y.). The court held that a surety that was obligated to reimburse its insured brokerage house for the amount of settlement in customers' actions could not set off profits realized by the insured from transactions that were the subject of the suit. *H.S. Equities, Inc. v. Hartford Acc. & Indem. Co.,* 609 F.2d 669.

5th Cir. 1967 (Tex.). The Fifth Circuit rejected an insurer's argument that, under a Brokers Blanket Bond, its insured should offset losses by the amount of profits earned for the company by its dishonest employee. *Nat'l Sur. Corp. v. Rauscher, Pierce & Co.,* 369 F.2d 572.

8th Cir. 1971 (Mo.). An insurer is obligated to indemnify its insured bank for loss attributable to a depreciation of collateral pledged to the bank in connection with a dishonestly induced loan transaction. *U.S. Fid. & Guar. Co. v. Empire State Bank,* 448 F.2d 360.

E.D. Va. 1969. An insured bank is not barred from collecting net losses from its insurer when the insured had attempted to mitigate its losses by consolidating loans and taking additional security. *Arlington Trust Co. v. Hawkeye-Security Ins. Co.,* 301 F. Supp. 854.

Tex. App. 1969. Neither public policy nor fidelity bond terms required insured employer to file charges against or prosecute an employee who embezzles funds as a prerequisite to recovery under the bond. *Commercial Standard Ins. Co. v. J.D. Hufstedler Truck Co.,* 443 S.W.2d 54.

6.   Causation: Loss "Resulting Directly From" Dishonesty

1st Cir. 1998 (Mass.). In this case, decided under an Employee Theft policy, the First Circuit held that a diversion of funds by a third-party tax and payroll service's chief executive officer fell within the authorized representative exclusion of the employee theft policy and thus did not constitute a direct loss because the policy's exclusion encompassed all acts resulting from the officer's power to divert funds. *Stop & Shop Cos. v. Fed. Ins. Co.*, 136 F.3d 71.

2d Cir. 1988 (N.Y.). The Second Circuit, applying New York law to a mortgage broker's fidelity bond, held that for a given loss to be covered, it must have been the direct result of a dishonest or fraudulent act of an employee or agent and thus required the establishment of a direct causational link between an alleged act of dishonesty and the claimed loss. It rejected the contention that a general pattern of dishonesty would suffice. *Leucadia Inc. v. Reliance Ins. Co.*, 864 F.2d 964.

2d Cir. 1978 (N.Y.). An investment company's employee purchased securities using dishonest methods to manipulate the price. He caused the insured to suffer a loss by the scheme to buy high and sell low. Such losses were held to be covered under a statutory bond. *Index Fund, Inc. v. Ins. Co. of N. Am.*, 580 F.2d 1158, *cert. denied*, 440 U.S. 912.

3d Cir. 2000 (N.J.). The Third Circuit, applying New Jersey law, reviewed a claim under a Savings and Loan Blanket Bond Form 22. It reversed the District Court's grant of summary judgment in favor of the insurer, holding that a genuine issue of material fact as to whether the loss incurred by the bank should be deemed a loss resulting directly from the "alleged dishonesty" of the employees. In so doing, the District Court equated the phrase "resulting directly from" with "proximately caused by." This reasoning was followed by the New Jersey Supreme Court in *Auto Lenders Acceptance Corp. v. Gentilini Ford, Inc.*, discussed below. *Resolution Trust Corp. v. Fid. Dep. & Co. of Md.*, 205 F.3d 615.

3d Cir. 1992 (Pa.). The Third Circuit reviewed the question of whether losses on a mortgage were "resulting directly from" a forgery of a notary's acknowledgment within the meaning of the forgery exception to the loan exclusion and the Bankers Blanket Bond form at issue in that case. The court held that the forged signature was the "proximate cause" of losses sustained by the bank making the loan in question and that as such, it was a loss "resulting directly from" the forgery. *Jefferson Bank v. Progressive Cas. Ins. Co.*, 965 F.2d 1274.

4th Cir. 1962 (Va.). The insured savings and loan association's bond provided for indemnity of loss through forgery. The insured sought recovery for the failed repayment of a loan secured by real property. It claimed that the loss resulted from forged endorsements on six checks it issued pursuant to the loan. However, the court found that the insured's loss was not caused by forged endorsements, but rather was through the failure of the security. *Piedmont Fed. Sav. & Loan Ass'n v. Hartford Acc. & Indem. Co.,* 307 F.2d 310.

5th Cir. 1998 (Tex.). The Fifth Circuit, applying Texas law, addressed the claim of Lynch Properties for the theft by one of its employees of funds of the mother of the owner of the insured from her personal accounts. The court held that any legal liability that Lynch might have to Mrs. Lynch would not give rise to a covered loss, in that the original loss was not a property owned by Lynch Properties or that it held or was legally liable in the terms of the bond. *Lynch Props., Inc. v. Potomac Ins. Co. of Ill.,* 140 F.3d 622.

5th Cir. 1995 (La.). The Fifth Circuit, applying Louisiana law, held that a general pattern of dishonesty in connection with an alleged loan loss scheme was sufficient to establish causation of a loss uncovered under the bond before it. In so doing, it relied on case law construing forms that provided coverage for loss "through" employee dishonesty, as opposed to "resulting directly from" employee dishonesty as set forth in the bond before it. *FDIC v. Fid. & Dep. Co. of Md.,* 45 F.3d 969.

5th Cir. 1992 (Ky.). In this case, applying Kentucky law to a complex loan loss claim under a Bankers Blanket Bond for loan losses caused by the alleged dishonest acts of Kevin DeWitt, the Fifth Circuit appears to adopt a causational standard requiring only that the insured establish that "but for" the employee's act, the injury would not have occurred. It should be noted that the Fifth Circuit, in an unpublished opinion following the insurer's petition for rehearing, held that the insured would still need to establish that the loss was proximately caused by the employee's alleged dishonesty. *First Nat'l Bank of Louisville v. Lustig,* 961 F.2d 1162.

5th Cir. 1978 (Fla.). The court held that a surety that issued Bankers Blanket Bond was liable for its insured's loss if the acts of the insured's former president in issuing two letters of credit without authorization and without following proper bank procedures were done willfully and with the intent to deceive the bank. *Eglin Nat'l Bank v. Home Indem. Co.*, 583 F.2d 1281.

5th Cir. 1966 (Tex.). Brokers Blanket Bond covered loss sustained by the insured when it settled claims against it when an employee made fraudulent misrepresentations that induced the purchase of water bonds, and aggrieved purchasers subsequently brought action against the insured broker. The court allowed the insurer to defend on the theory that the insured settled as a volunteer, but found that it had not done so. *Nat'l Sur. Corp. v. Rauscher, Pierce & Co., Inc.*, 369 F.2d 572, *cert. denied*, 386 U.S. 1018.

5th Cir. 1934 (Tex.). A bank sustained loss recoverable under its Bankers Blanket Bond when the bank president persuaded the insured bank to loan money to companies in which the president had concealed personal interests, and the bank subsequently sustained loss through such loans. *Maryland Cas. Co. v. Am. Trust Co.*, 71 F.2d 137.

6th Cir. 2013 (Ky.). The insured bank issued a loan after the borrower assigned a life insurance policy that he claimed had a cash value of over a million dollars, but in fact the policy had a surrender value of $65,000 and had already been assigned to several banks. Although the assignment documents contained a forgery, the court affirmed summary judgment in the insurer's favor because the loss resulted directly from the fact that the collateral was worthless, and the same loss would have ensured if the signature had been genuine. *Forcht Bank, N.A. v. BancInsure, Inc.*, 514 F. App'x 586.

6th Cir. 2012 (Ohio). An investment advisor employed by the insured siphoned funds from customer accounts that were held by a third party but were accessible only to the insured's investment advisor staff. The court held that the customer assets were "held by someone else under circumstances which make the Insured responsible for the Property prior to the occurrence of the loss," and thus were "covered property." Thus, the theft of those assets by the insured's employee was a direct loss under either a proximate causation standard or something more exacting. *First Defiance Fin. Corp. v. Progressive Cas. Ins. Co.*, 688 F.3d 265.

6th Cir. 2008 (Mich.). A commercial lending bank sought coverage under financial institution bonds for losses allegedly resulting from forged mortgage documents received from mortgage intermediaries. Holding that "resulting directly" requires more than proximate cause, the court affirmed insurer's summary judgment because the insured's loss did not result directly from forged documents, but because the collateral represented in the documents did not exist. *Flagstar Bank, F.S.B. v. Fed. Ins. Co.*, 260 F. App'x 820.

7th Cir. 2011 (Wis.). Insured loan originator was contractually required to repurchase loans after its employee funded substandard mortgages in exchange for kickbacks. The insured's mortgage Bankers Blanket Bond did not cover the insured's losses sustained as a result of the insured's third-party contractual liability. *Universal Mortgage Corp. v. Württembergische Versicherung AG*, 651 F.3d 759.

7th Cir. 1983 (Ill.). Willfulness and the intent to deceive must be present for an employee's actions to be dishonest or fraudulent within the meaning of a blanket fidelity bond. Although the conduct of the employee need not result in personal profit, the mere negligence, incompetence, or error in judgment of the employee is not sufficient for coverage to attach. *Rock Island Bank v. Aetna Cas. & Sur. Co.*, 706 F.2d 219.

7th Cir. 1979 (Ill.). Where a bank president approved unsecured loans to a small circle of friends, relatives and business associates, authorized the refinancing of such loans when they became due, was involved in transactions involving forged documents, and converted bank funds to his own use, the conduct of such employee fell within the terms of a blanket bond protecting against loss through the dishonest or fraudulent acts of employees. *First Nat'l Bank Co. of Clinton v. Ins. Co. of N Am.*, 606 F.2d 760.

7th Cir. 1971 (Ind.). A bank employee who negligently failed to send checks for collection and subsequently tried to conceal the cancelled checks and ledger was both dishonest and negligent from the outset, and the bank suffered loss through the employee's dishonest misconduct. *Citizens State Bank v. Transamerica Ins. Co.,* 452 F.2d 199.

8th Cir. 2015 (Minn.). The insured sought to recover loan losses on the strength of an allegedly forged personal guaranty. Applying a proximate-cause analysis, the court held that insured bank would have suffered the identical loss had the guaranty not been forged because the guaranty was worthless at the time the loan was made. *BancInsure, Inc. v. Highland Bank,* 779 F.3d 565.

8th Cir. 1994 (Mo.). The Eighth Circuit held that an exclusion in the financial institution bond for "loss caused by any employee" excluded losses caused in part by negligence of the employees where coverage was sought under the "forgery or alteration" coverage and the "on premises" coverage of the subject bond. The case was decided under Missouri law. *Empire Bank v. Fid. & Dep. Co. of Md.,* 27 F.3d 333.

8th Cir. 1988 (Neb.). A former employee whose dishonesty resulted directly in a loss by the bank during policy period was covered by Bankers Blanket Bond, unless the insured discovered employee's dishonesty before the bond went into effect. *First Sec. Sav. v. Kansas Bankers Sur. Co.,* 849 F.2d 345.

8th Cir. 1970 (S.D.). Insured sought to recover under its Savings and Loan Blanket Bond, which insured against loss through forgery or alteration of, on, or in any instrument. Act by developer, pursuant to obtaining mortgage loan from insured federal savings and loan association, of forging contractor's signature to lien waiver constituted a covered loss, notwithstanding claim that waiver was without any possible relationship to loss that resulted solely from the house not being located on lot in question, where forged instrument constituted such an element of reliance that without it loan would not have been made. *First Fed. Sav. & Loan Ass'n of Beresford v. Aetna Ins. Co.,* 431 F.2d 267.

9th Cir. 2010 (Mont.). Bank's loss was directly caused by the worthlessness of the underlying collateral, not defects in the security documents. *Bank of Bozeman v. BancInsure, Inc.,* 404 F. App'x 117.

9th Cir. 2002 (Cal.). The Ninth Circuit reviewed a claim under a Financial Institution Bond issued in favor of a title insurer, holding that the fidelity insurer was not obligated to indemnify it for claims made against it by the California Department of Insurance for deficiencies in escrow accounts that the insured was required to cure by way of statute. The court held that title insurer had not suffered a direct loss because the escrow accounts held property of third parties, not the insured. The court placed particular emphasis on the regulatory scheme, holding that "the statutory scheme which imposed liability on United General was put in place to compensate third parties for potential shortfalls . . . ." *United Gen. Title Ins. Co. v. Am. Int'l Group, Inc.* 51 F. App'x 224.

9th Cir. 2000 (Cal.). The Ninth Circuit, applying California law, affirmed the grant of summary judgment in favor of the insurer. Gene Shirley, an alleged employee of the insured, had allegedly engaged in a series of fraudulent representations, causing third-party investors to part with funds that were diverted by Shirley and his cohorts as a part of a large Ponzi scheme. The scheme collapsed and the investors sued the insured, and others. The insured resolved the cases by settlement. The court of appeals rejected the insured's argument that because it was legally liable for the acts of Shirley, its settlement payment was a "direct loss" of property for which it was "legally liable." The court held that the employee theft policy was not a liability policy and that the settlement payment was not such a direct loss. It concluded, "we hold that 'direct' means 'direct' and that in the absence of a third-party claims clause, Vons' policy did not provide indemnity for vicarious liability for tortious acts of its employee." *Vons Cos. v. Fed. Ins. Co.,* 212 F.3d 489.

9th Cir. 1999 (Cal.). In this case, the Ninth Circuit reversed a grant of summary judgment against the insurer on claims brought against it under employee theft policies issued to various insureds that fell victim to a third-party tax and payroll service's chief executive officer's diversion of their tax payments. The Ninth Circuit held that the loss fell within the policy's authorized representative exclusion. The court cited and concurred with the *Stop & Shop* opinion by the First Circuit. *Stanford Univ. Hosp. v. Fed. Ins. Co.,* 174 F.3d 1077.

9th Cir. 1997 (Cal.). In this unpublished decision, the Ninth Circuit, applying California law, held that expenses incurred by the insured bank after its employees violated an IRS levy were not covered under a fidelity bond as they were not losses "resulting directly from" acts covered under the bond. It held that the only direct loss was the loss actually diverted by the employees, which the insurer had paid. It expressly distinguished and declined to follow *Jefferson Bank. United Sec. Bank v. Fid. & Dep. Co. of Md.,* 1997 WL 632606.

9th Cir. 1986 (Cal.). Plaintiff sought recovery under Bankers Blanket Bond for loss resulting from payor bank's refusal to pay checks allegedly bearing forged endorsements. The court found that insured bank's own conduct in crediting the checks to customer's account and permitting subsequent withdrawal of funds set in motion a chain of events that proximately caused loss and brought it within exclusion that excluded from coverage loss resulting from payments made or withdrawals from any depositor's account by reason of uncollected items of deposit. *Mitsui Mfrs. Bank v. Fed. Ins. Co.,* 795 F.2d 827.

9th Cir. 1981 (Cal.). Where loans were made to uncreditworthy borrowers for the purpose of purchasing bank stock, such loans were "dishonest" and surety was liable for loss under provisions of blanket bond. *Fid. Sav. & Loan Ass'n v. Aetna Life & Cas. Corp.,* 647 F.2d 933.

10th Cir. 1972 (N.M.). Applying New Mexico law, the Tenth Circuit held that a savings and loan association could not recover on a Savings and Loan Blanket Bond for losses sustained when evidence established that the officer and the bookkeeper of the insured association made serious mistakes, were generally negligent, but did not act dishonestly, fraudulently or criminally, within the coverage of the bond. *New Mexico Sav. & Loan Ass'n v. U.S. Fid. & Guar. Co.,* 454 F.2d 328.

C.D. Cal. 2015. Accountancy corporation arranged for transfer of funds from its client's bank account to overseas bank accounts after receiving fraudulent e-mail instructions from a third party who had hacked into client's e-mail account. The accountancy corporation reimbursed its client for lost funds and asserted a claim under its crime policy. The court ruled that accountancy corporation had not suffered a direct loss. A direct loss does not occur unless the hacker infiltrates the insured's computer system and causes an immediate depletion of funds from the insured's account. Because there were intervening circumstances between the hacking event and the insured's loss, the loss was not a direct loss. *Taylor & Lieberman v. Fed. Ins. Co.*, 2015 WL 3824130.

S.D. Cal. 2014. Ponzi schemer conspired with employees of an insured title company to steal his clients' money to sell and refinance condominium units, for which the title company was the escrow officer. The fraudster, who was not an employee, routinely forged his investors' signatures on grant deeds and other escrow closing documents. On cross-motions for summary judgment, the court held that the title company sustained a direct loss with respect to victims' property that was misappropriated while in insured's possession. *Fid. Nat. Fin., Inc. v. Nat'l Union Fire Ins. Co. of Pittsburg, PA*, 2014 WL 4909103.

C.D. Cal. 2014. Every pay period the insured transferred funds to the account of its payroll service company for the payment of payroll and payroll taxes. Although the payroll service company made payroll for the insured's employees, it did not remit tax payments, instead diverting the funds for its own use. The insurer obtained summary judgment on several bases, including that the diversion of funds after the insured transferred them to the payroll service company's account is not a direct loss. *Pestmaster Servs., Inc. v. Travelers Cas. & Sur. Co. of Am.*, 2014 WL 3844627.

N.D. Cal. 2012. Forgeries on account control agreements given in security for loans were not the direct cause of the bank's loss under its financial institution bond. The instant cause of the loss was the fact that the borrower did not have any collateral. *Valley Cmty. Bank v. Progressive Cas. Ins. Co.*, 854 F. Supp. 2d 697.

S.D. Fla. 1970. A bank employee who fraudulently made loans to a company without checking the credit of the borrower and exceeded his scope of authority in making the loan caused the insured to suffer loss recoverable under its Bankers Blanket Bond. The court also allowed recovery of the costs in liquidating the loans and collateral as having been incurred through the dishonest acts. *Miami Nat'l Bank v. Pa. Ins. Co.*, 314 F. Supp. 858.

N.D. Ill. 2014. Prior to the FDIC's takeover, the insured bank loaned money to a customer to finance an equipment lease, and received an assignment of the lease as collateral. The lease schedules, however, contained a forgery and the equipment never existed. Employing a "but for" causation standard, the court held that the leases were themselves the collateral rather than merely describing or valuing collateral, thus the bank's losses resulted directly from the forged signatures on those leases. *FDIC v. RLI Ins. Co.*, 2014 WL 2598736.

S.D. Ind. 2014. Insured bank made loans after the borrower pledged stock certificates containing forged signatures. The court held that, if the collateral represented in the stock certificates was worthless, then there would not be loss resulting directly from the forgery under the financial institution bond. *FDIC v. Fid. & Deposit Co. of Maryland*, 2014 WL 6775410.

E.D. Mo. 2007. Direct losses of covered property by forgery include loss that is proximately caused by the employee's forgery. In the absence of exclusionary language in the policy, third-party claims proximately caused by the forgery are covered. *Graybar Elec. Co. v. Fed. Ins. Co.*, 2007 WL 1365327.

W.D. Mo. 1993. In this case arising under Missouri law, the district court held that the allegedly dishonest conduct of the bank's president was so attenuated from the actual loss that the independent superseding cause of the negligence of bank employees were deemed to be the direct cause of the loss and not the alleged dishonesty. It also appeared that the bank knew or should have known of the alleged loss prior to the inception of the bond. *Empire Bank v. Fid. & Dep. Co. of Md.*, 828 F. Supp. 675.

D.N.J. 1977. The acts of insured's directors were dishonest and fraudulent when they knowingly listed renewal loans as new loans, authorized unsecured loans in direct violation of company instructions, and made false oral and written reports. The court held that losses attributable to such acts were recoverable under the insured's fidelity bond. *Midland Bank & Trust Co. v. Fid. & Dep. Co. of Md.*, 442 F. Supp. 960.

N.D. Ohio 2010. The court employed proximate cause analysis to determine that employee's siphoning of funds from customer investment accounts was a direct loss to the insured. *First Defiance Fin. Corp. v. Progressive Cas. Ins. Co.*, 688 F. Supp. 2d 703 *aff'd*, 688 F.3d 265.

D. Or. 2011. Bank sued bond issuer to recover losses allegedly resulting from forged guaranties. On motions for summary judgment, the court held that "resulting directly from" means that the loss suffered must be a direct consequence of extending credit in reliance on a forgery. *Columbia Cmty. Bank v. Progressive Cas. Ins. Co.*, 2011 WL 2457913.

D. Or. 2001. The insured, a national discount securities brokerage firm, sought indemnity from its bond for losses resulting directly from alterations on checks it received from its clients. The district court held that even though the insured's bank had debited the insured's account as a remedy for the insured's breach of transfer warranties, the breach proximately caused the bank's right to set off, thus the insured's loss results directly from the alteration and indemnity was afforded under the bond. *Bidwell & Co. v. Nat'l Union Fire Ins. Co. of Pittsburgh, Pa.*, 2001 WL 204843.

D.P.R. 1972. An insurer was liable on a Bankers Blanket Bond in which the insured established, through a preponderance of the evidence, that its losses were not accidental, but were sustained as a result of the dishonest, fraudulent, and criminal conduct of its employees. *Banco de San German, Inc. v. Maryland Cas. Co.*, 344 F. Supp. 496.

D. Utah 2014. The insured bank, which was in the business of factoring, sued to recover its factoring fraud loss under its financial institution bond after a customer electronically altered electronic account statements to reflect higher receivables than actually existed. On summary judgment, the court held that the bank's loss resulted directly from making over-advances because its customer fraudulently altered its accounts receivable. In the court's view, whether the loss resulted from the fraudulent alteration or the fact that the invoices contained false representations was a distinction without a difference. *Transp. Alliance Bank, Inc. v. BancInsure, Inc.*, 2014 WL 684691.

E.D. Va. 1969. A bank did not accurately report or record past-due accounts, assured officials that business was fine, and gave unauthorized loans and loans in excess of approved credit. The court held that such conduct was dishonest and that the loss suffered through this conduct was covered. *Arlington Trust Co. v. Hawkeye Sec. Ins. Co..* 301 F. Supp. 854.

W.D. Wash. 2011. Insured credit card processor could not recover under policy's computer fraud coverage for deductions from a reserve account by bank to cover chargebacks resulting from a merchant fraudulent chargeback scheme. "Direct" means without any intervening agency or step, without any intruding or diverting factor. Here, the insured's loss resulted directly from its contractual obligation to cover any chargeback losses incurred by the bank, not from computer fraud. *Pinnacle Processing Grp., Inc. v. Hartford Cas. Ins. Co.*, 2011 WL 5299557.

Ariz. App. 1977. A question of fact existed as to whether an employee's dishonest act was causally related to the monetary losses sustained by employer to a degree sufficient to bring it within the coverage of the insured's fidelity bond. Accordingly, the court reversed a directed verdict in favor of the insurer. *J.R. Norton Co. v. Fireman's Fund Ins. Co.*, 569 P.2d 857.

Conn. Super. 2010. Here, the fraudster e-mailed the insured law firm for assistance in a collection matter. Shortly after entering a retainer agreement, the law firm received an "official check" from the so-called debtor. The insured subsequently wired the funds to an account designated by the purported client, only to learn that the check was fraudulent and it was out the wired funds. The court denied the insurer's summary judgment motion with respect to computer crime coverage on the basis that the e-mails were the "proximate cause and 'efficient cause'" of insured's loss, which set the chain of events in motion that led to the entire loss. Pursuant to stipulation, the court's memorandum of decision was later vacated. *Owens, Schine & Nicola, P.C. v. Travelers Cas. & Sur. Co. of Am.*, 2010 WL 4226958 *vacated*, 2012 WL 12246940.

Ill. App. 2004. The Illinois Court of Appeals held that where the insured bank settled with a third party that had purchased a loan originated at the bank by an allegedly dishonest employee to himself, the amounts paid to resolve that third-party claim would not be deemed to be a loss resulting directly from the employee's dishonesty. In so doing, the court held that the phrase "loss resulting directly from" was unambiguous and that it mandated a tighter causational nexus than that of proximate cause be shown to obtain indemnity under the Financial Institution Bond. *RBC Mortgage Co. v. Nat'l Union Fire Ins. Co. of Pittsburgh, Pa.,* 812 N.E.2d 728.

Ill. App. 1983. Loss suffered by a licensed futures commodity merchant as a result of employee dishonesty was covered by the undefined dishonesty clause of a merchant's fidelity bond as existing prior to effective date of "new" definition of "dishonesty," but loss suffered after endorsement to insured's bond was not covered. *Mortell v. Ins. Co. of N. Am.,* 458 N.E.2d 922.

Iowa 1999. The city's fire department lost a master key to all public school buildings in the district. The city replaced the locks on the schools to avoid possible theft or damage. The city made a claim for this expense under its Public Employee's Blanket Bond. The court held that this expense was not a direct loss to the city within the meaning of the bond. *City of Burlington, Iowa v. Western Sur. Co.,* 599 N.W.2d 469.

Kan. App. 2007. Insured bank that was liable for its customer's misuse of trust funds could not recover under its Financial Institution Crime Bond for on-premises loss. The insured's loss did not result directly from theft. The insured's loss was caused by its deviation from the ordinary standards of banking practice. *Citizens Bank, N.A. v. Kansas Bankers Sur. Co.,* 149 P.3d 25.

La. App. 1972. Absent evidence that an employee was influenced by personal interests in making a loan, the employee did not commit fraud or misconduct within the terms of employer fidelity bond when he loaned money to a customer in violation of the instructions of the insured company. *W.H. Hodges & Co. v. Hanford Acc. & Indem. Co.,* 262 So. 2d 542, *cert. denied,* 266 So. 2d 223.

Mich. App. 1982. The words "fraud" and "dishonesty" in fidelity bonds include acts that show a "want of integrity" or "breach of trust"; but acts amounting to mere irregularity, mistake, or error of judgment are excluded. *Gen. Elec. Credit Corp. v. Wolverine Ins. Co.,* 327 N.W.2d 449.

Minn. 1976. A bankers fidelity bond did not cover losses suffered by reason of fraud, dishonesty or breach of fiduciary duty when the bank, through its board of directors, had knowledge of acts complained of, appreciated their fraudulent nature, and condoned, acquiesced or participated in them. The bond at issue provided indemnity for loss by reason of "employee dishonesty." *Farmers & Merch. Bank of Pierz v. St. Paul Fire & Marine Ins. Co.,* 242 N.W.2d 840.

Mont. 2006. The term "direct loss" in the context of employee dishonesty coverage applies to consequential damages incurred by the insured that were proximately caused by the alleged dishonesty. *Frontline Processing Corp. v. Am. Econ. Ins. Co.,* 149 P.3d 906.

Neb. 1976. A surety was held not liable for loss under a Bankers Blanket Bond where an injured plaintiff obtained judgment against the insured bank for losses incurred by its reliance on the fraudulent misrepresentations of the bank's employee. *Foxley Cattle Co. v. Bank of Mead,* 244 N.W.2d 205.

N.J. 2004. New Jersey Supreme Court, construing a "building and personal property coverage form" in a "commercial package" insurance policy, held that the insured suffered a direct loss of coverage property when it established that it had sold automobiles on the strength of fraudulent sales contracts and that "direct loss" would be equated with "proximate cause." *Auto Lenders Acceptance Corp. v. Gentilini Ford, Inc.,* 854 A.2d 378.

Pa. Commw. 1981. Insurance brokers who paid kickbacks to the Director of Bureau of Insurance caused insured Commonwealth of Pennsylvania to sustain loss recoverable under fidelity bond that covered loss sustained through the failure of employees to faithfully perform their duties. *Commonwealth v. Ins. Co. of N Am.,* 436 A.2d 1067.

Tex. App. 1976. An agent who failed to remit premium payments to insurance companies and who made unauthorized personal expenditures out of the account into which the premiums were deposited was guilty of fraud and dishonesty within the meaning of a fidelity bond. *Lawyers Sur. Corp. v. Am. Public Life Ins. Co.,* 540 S.W.2d 842.

Wash. App. 1990. The Washington Intermediate Court of Appeals applied Washington law to a dispute relating to a "comprehensive fidelity insurance policy." The court equated language in the bond requiring that a loss result "directly from" the alleged dishonesty to be equivalent to the tort concept of proximate cause, holding that the language meant that the dishonest or fraudulent acts had to be the proximate cause of the loss in order for coverage to be established. In so doing, the court upheld a jury instruction that defined proximate cause as ". . . a cause which in a direct sequence, unbroken by any independent cause, produces the injury complained of and without which such injury would not have happened." *Hanson PLC v. Nat'l Union Fire Ins. Co. of Pittsburgh, Pa.*, 794 P.2d 66.

Wis. App. 2003. The Wisconsin Court of Appeals applied Wisconsin law to a claim arising under a Financial Institution Bond Standard Form 24. Allegedly dishonest employees of the bank entered into a scheme in which they would fraudulently confirm that a third party was a customer of the bank and had sufficient sums on deposit to cover down payments on a loan to be originated by a mortgage company not connected with the bank. After multiple defaults on such loans, the scheme was uncovered. The mortgage companies made claims against the bank. The court refused to find the bond a contract of adhesion and held that amounts paid to resolve such claims are not losses "resulting directly from" employee dishonesty, but rather claims for vicarious liability and thus indirect in nature. The report contains a useful survey of case law on the topic. *Tri City Nat'l Bank v. Fed. Ins. Co.*, 674 N.W. 2d 617.

SECONDARY SOURCES

Paul R. Devin & Lauren D. Song, *Loss & Causation: The Alpha & Omega of Fidelity Claims Analysis, in* COMMERCIAL CRIME POLICY 15-1 (Gilbert J. Schroeder ed., 1997).

David T. DiBiase & Carleton R. Burch, *Loss & Causation, in* ANNOTATED COMMERCIAL CRIME POLICY, 43-82 (Cole S. Kain & Lana M. Glovach eds., 2d ed. 2006).

David T. DiBiase & Tracey Santor, *Causation of Loss—The Overlooked Ingredient to Covered Loss, in* COMMERCIAL CRIME POLICY, 373 (Randall I. Marmor & John J. Tomaine eds., 2d ed. 2005).

Peter Haley, *Loss & Causation, in* ANNOTATED FINANCIAL INSTITUTION BOND 99 (Michael Keeley ed., 2d ed. 2004).

John W. Hinchey, *Loss & Causation, in* ANNOTATED BANKERS BLANKET BOND (Frank L. Skillern, Jr., ed., 1st ed. 1980 & Supp. 1983).

Michael Keeley et al., *Insuring Agreement (E)—Revisited, in* XVII FIDELITY L.J. 203, 245-260 (2011).

Stephen M. Kranz et al., *Can Direct Mean Direct? Untangling the Web of Causation in Fidelity Coverage, in* XVI FIDELITY L.J. 153 (2010).

James J. Moran, Jr. & William T. Bogaert, *Loss & Causation, in* COMMERCIAL BLANKET BOND ANNOTATED 15 (Carolyn Perry ed., Supp. 1991).

James J. Moran, Jr., *Loss & Causation, in* COMMERCIAL BLANKET BOND ANNOTATED 23 (William F. Haug ed., 1985).

Edgar L. Neel & Timothy Markey, *What is a Loss?, in* COMMERCIAL CRIME POLICY 207 (Randall I. Marmor & John J. Tomaine eds., 2d ed. 2005).

Scott L. Schmookler & Pat Duffy, *The Compensability of Third Party Losses, in* COMMERCIAL CRIME POLICY 229 (Randall I. Marmor & John J. Tomaine eds., 2d ed. 2005).

Gary J. Valeriano & Carleton R. Burch, *The Interpretation of a Direct Loss Under Fidelity Bonds, in* 33 THE BRIEF (Summer 2004).

Gary J. Valeriano, *Direct Loss & Causation, in* COMMERCIAL CRIME INSURANCE COVERAGE, 351-392 (Randall I. Marmor & Susan K. Sullivan eds., 2d ed. 2015).

Karen Wildau, *Evolving Law of Third-Party Claims Under Fidelity Bonds: When is Third Party Recovery Allowed?*, 25 TORT & INS. L.J. 92 (1989).

Chapter 3

The Insuring Agreements—

Employee Dishonesty Coverage*

As discussed more thoroughly in Chapter 1 of this book, the modern stand-alone crime insurance policy for commercial institutions—that is, non-banks and other financial institutions—developed from earlier packaged policies, including the Comprehensive Dishonesty, Disappearance and Destruction Policy, the Blanket Crime Policy, and the Commercial Crime Policy,[1] the latter of which was a joint effort between the Surety & Fidelity Association of America[2] and the Insurance Services Office, Inc.[3] That original Commercial Crime Policy offered ten different coverages, including employee dishonesty as well as a separate coverage form for "Theft, Disappearance and Destruction of Money and Securities."[4] In March 2000, the SFAA and ISO each issued stand-alone crime insurance policies.[5] The Crime Protection Policy,[6] which is the subject of this chapter, was issued by the SFAA. It included six insuring agreements, including coverage for losses caused directly by employee dishonesty, similar to the SFAA's standard form Financial Institution Bond.[7] The current version of the CPP was issued by the SFAA in 2012,

---

* By Michael Keeley and Carla C. Crapster, Strasburger & Price, LLP, Dallas, Texas, and Ann I. Gardiner, ABA Insurance Services Inc., Mayfield Heights, Ohio.

1 *See* Chp. 1 herein, at 8.

2 Hereinafter SFAA.

3 Hereinafter ISO.

4 *See* Edward G. Gallagher and Robert Duke, *A Concise History of Fidelity Insurance, in* HANDLING FIDELITY BOND CLAIMS, 18 (Michael Keeley & Sean Duffy eds., 2d ed. 2005).

5 ISO's Commercial Crime Policy, which provides coverage for employee theft, not employee dishonesty, is the subject of Chapter 4 of this book.

6 Crime Protection Policy, SP 00 01 03 00 (SAA 2000) reprinted in COMMERCIAL CRIME POLICY (Randall R. Marmor & John J. Tomaine eds., 2d ed. 2005) [hereinafter CPP].

7 Financial Institution Bond, Standard Form No. 24 (SFAA 1986), *reprinted in* ANNOTATED FINANCIAL INSTITUTION BOND (Michael Keeley ed., 3d ed. 2013).

and is the result of revisions over time so that it now more closely follows the SFAA's employee dishonesty insuring agreement from its standard form Financial Institution Bond.

This chapter summarizes the long history of cases involving five important issues commonly arising in employee dishonest claims. Because employee coverage in the CPP closely resembles that of the standard form Financial Institution Bond, the overwhelming majority of the cases involve the latter policy, but nevertheless are directly applicable to employee dishonesty coverage under the CPP.

1. **Employee Dishonesty**
    We will pay for loss resulting directly from dishonest acts committed by an employee, whether identified or not, acting alone or in collusion with other persons, with the manifest intent to:
    a. **Cause you to sustain loss; and**
    b. **Obtain an improper financial benefit for:**
        (1) **The employee; or**
        (2) **Any person or organization intended by the employee to receive that benefit.**
    As used in this Insuring Agreement, an improper financial benefit does not include any employee benefits received in the course of employment, including: salaries, commissions, fees, bonuses, promotions, awards, profit sharing or pensions.[8]

COMMENT

The majority of published opinions construing crime insurance involve Insuring Agreement (A), employee dishonesty. Historically, the firestorm of controversy with such claims involved the intent of coverage and the precise meaning and proper application of the manifest intent requirement of Insuring Agreement (A) of the Financial Institution. The manifest intent requirement was added, first by Rider in 1976, and then by amendment to the 1980 standard form Bankers Blanket Bond.[9] And, it is carried over to the SFAA's CPP.

---

8   Crime Protection Policy, SP 00 01 04 12 (SFAA 2012).
9   *Id.* at 993.

While courts readily accepted the fact that the SFAA added the "manifest intent" language to the bond in order to limit coverage for dishonest claims to embezzlement-type acts, there was great divergence of opinion in the courts as to the precise meaning of the term. Early on, some courts concluded that a purely objective standard should be followed in defining the term "manifest intent," such that an employee could be found to have the manifest intent to cause the insured a loss if the natural consequences of the employee's actions were a loss.[10] But few recent cases have adopted this standard. Rather, the debate has largely moved on to whether an insured must establish that its employee acted with the "specific intent," or "purpose," to cause the insured to sustain a loss, or whether it was adequate to show that the employee knew that a loss was "substantially certain" to follow from the employee's actions. While the first standard—the specific intent test—is purely a subjective one, the latter standard—the substantial certainty test—contains an objective element.

To date, the Second, Third, Fourth, and Fifth Circuits have adopted the specific intent standard. The Sixth, Seventh, and Tenth Circuits appear to have adopted the substantial certainty test. Perhaps the most thorough analysis of the differing standards by a court to date is in *Resolution Trust Corp. v. Fidelity & Deposit Co. of Maryland.*[11] In this case, the Third Circuit adopted the specific intent standard after first reviewing the purpose and history behind this provision of the bond. After carefully considering the distinction between the two primary standards, including adoption of the general intent and specific intent standards in older criminal law cases and in tort law, as well as under the Model Penal Code, it concluded that the specific intent standard should be applied. The court held that the term "manifest intent" required the insured "to prove that the employee engaged in dishonest or fraudulent acts with the specific purpose, object or desire both to cause a loss and to obtain a financial benefit."[12]

Unfortunately, while the Third Circuit's actual holding seems to leave no question that it adopted the specific intent test, as all too often is the case, the application of this test to the facts seems inconsistent with

---

10   *See, e.g.,* Transamerica Ins. Co. v. FDIC, 465 N.W.2d 713 (Minn. Ct. App. 1991), *rev'd in part on other grounds,* 489 N.W.2d 224 (Minn. 1992) (a person is deemed to intend the natural consequences of his or her actions).

11   205 F.3d 615 (3d Cir. 2000).

12   *Id.* at 642.

the court's holding. Problematically, the court observed that a jury may consider evidence tending to establish an employee's reckless behavior, as well as circumstantial proof of the substantial likelihood of loss, and infer from those circumstances an intent to cause a loss. This dicta seems contrary to the court's holding that neither an employee's recklessness nor knowledge that a result was substantially certain to occur would satisfy the language of the policy, absent an inference of specific intent.

While there is a significant body of case law construing the other important issues arising in employee dishonesty claims, they generally have not been as controversial. For instance, it seems well settled that in addition to having the manifest intent to cause the insured to sustain a loss, the employee also must have the same intent to obtain a financial benefit. And, while the "employee benefits" carve-out from the financial benefit requirement once engendered significant debate, it is now well settled that there is no coverage under Insuring Agreement (A) for losses that amount to employee benefits, including salaries, commissions, fees, bonuses, promotions, awards, profit sharing, or pensions.

In addition to the SFAA's standard form CPP, there are various proprietary forms on the market. For example, some insurers, presumably due to market pressures, have shied away from the manifest intent language and instead simply require proof of an intent to cause a loss. At first glance, it might seem that the deletion of the word "manifest" results in more liberal coverage. But arguably not. The word "intent," on its own, is easily understood as referring to one's purpose or design.[13] And it is difficult to know a person's intent without looking at the facts that manifest that intent. In short, as always is the case, it is critical to ensure that the language of the policy considered by the court is applicable to the claim that is being analyzed.

OUTLINE OF ANNOTATIONS

A. Meaning of Dishonest or Fraudulent Acts
B. Manifest Intent
C. Collusion
D. Financial Benefit
E. Benefits of Employment

---

13 WEBSTER'S THIRD NEW INTERNATIONAL DICTIONARY 1376 (1976).

ANNOTATIONS

A. Meaning of Dishonest or Fraudulent Acts

2d Cir. 2000 (N.Y.). The bank made several loans to a limited partnership engaged in a construction project. A bank trustee allegedly knew that one of the partners was committing fraud against the bank and stealing from the construction project, but did not disclose his knowledge to the bank. The bank trustee also failed to disclose that he had an existing business relationship with the partner. Trustee continued to remain silent while the bank issued additional loans to the partnership. The court held that the trustee's failure to disclose knowledge of fraudulent conduct pertaining to a loan constituted a dishonest act under the financial institution bond. *FDIC v. Nat'l Union Fire Ins. Co. of Pittsburgh, Pa.*, 205 F.3d 66.

2d Cir. 1988 (N.Y.). The Court of Appeals held that, under New York law, different standards of proof applied to the terms "dishonest acts" and "fraudulent acts" in a fidelity bond issued to an investment firm. Fraud must be proven by "clear and convincing" evidence; dishonesty is proven merely by a "preponderance of the evidence." The trial judge had erroneously instructed the jury by failing to distinguish the two terms and by requiring "clear and convincing" evidence of dishonesty to establish coverage. The error was harmless, however, because the record failed to show that the employee acted with the manifest intent to cause a loss and to obtain a financial benefit for himself or others, even under the lower evidentiary standard. *Leucadia, Inc. v. Reliance Ins. Co.*, 864 F.2d 964.

2d Cir. 1979 (N.Y.). The insured, a stockbroker, filed a claim under its brokers blanket bond for churning and false representations made by one of its employees to third-party customers. Insurer refused to provide a defense and later denied coverage, contending that the bond did not cover dishonesty to third parties. The appellate court affirmed the district court's holding that the misconduct of the insured's employee constituted dishonest and fraudulent acts and that the bond provided coverage for dishonesty directed at third parties since the bond failed to indicate otherwise. *H.S. Equities, Inc. v. Hartford Accident & Indem. Co.*, 464 F. Supp. 83 (S.D.N.Y. 1978), *aff'd*, 609 F.2d 669.

3d Cir. 2002 (Penn.). Nurses employed by a drug-testing firm falsified patient records during clinical trials. The falsifications rendered the drug studies worthless. In an action under a blanket employee dishonesty policy, the court of appeals held that submitting falsified patient records was irrefutably dishonest. *Scirex Corp. v. Fed. Ins. Co.*, 313 F.3d 841.

4th Cir. 1979 (S.C.). In an action on a fidelity bond, an employee of the insured mortgage broker admitted that he advanced construction monies to contractors without the required prior approval of HUD and falsely certified the dates and amounts of the advances to HUD. On the issue of notice, the employee's conduct was held to be dishonest as a matter of law. The court noted that: (1) fraudulent or dishonest conduct need not amount to a crime and need involve only bad faith or a want of integrity or untrustworthiness or a disposition to lie or cheat or a faithlessness to a trust; and (2) there need not be an intent to profit or cause a monetary loss to the employer. *C. Douglas Wilson & Co. v. Ins. Co. of N. Am.*, 590 F.2d 1275.

4th Cir. 1965 (S.C.). Individuals controlled several interrelated companies that were all covered under the same blanket fidelity bond. After all of the companies went into bankruptcy, the trustee made a claim under the bond for "losses" on behalf of third parties making claims against the individuals' estates for fraudulent and dishonest acts by the companies' employees. The trustee alleged that the employees, with the full knowledge and consent of all appropriate officers and directors, deceived and misled the insurance commissioner and various banks in order to make the companies' financial statements appear better than they were. The insurer contended the acts complained of were not covered under the bond because they did not amount to fraud or deception against any of the companies. In agreement with the insurer, the appellate court held that the bond only protected against loss due to fraud perpetrated on the insured corporations and that deception practiced on third parties was not covered under the bond. *Kerr v. Aetna Cas. & Sur. Co.*, 350 F.2d 146.

4th Cir. 1934 (N.C.). The making of an unauthorized loan approved by directors was held not to constitute a dishonest act under a fidelity bond. The court pointed out that directors repeatedly approved renewals of the loan and, though it involved a technical violation of the banking laws, the employee involved did not intend to injure the bank. *Fid. & Deposit Co. of Md. v. People's Bank of Sanford,* 72 F.2d 932.

4th Cir. 1930 (W. Va.). A bank's cashier misappropriated bank funds and used the funds in a business he owned. The Fourth Circuit held that the words "fraud" and "dishonesty" in a bond are to be given a "broad significance" and covered the cashier's conduct. *Brandon v. Holman,* 41 F.2d 586.

4th Cir. 1915 (W. Va.). An agent received money allegedly due the company, which he spent, contending that he had valid offsets. The court held the conduct constituted dishonesty under two surety bonds. The agent had a duty to hold funds for the principal until the dispute over offsets was settled. The court held that the meaning of "fraud and dishonesty" extends beyond criminal acts and that the words are to be given a broad meaning. *Citizens Trust & Guar. Co. v. Globe & Rutgers Fire Ins. Co.,* 229 F. 326.

5th Cir. 1995 (La.). Chief lending officer engaged in a pattern of dishonest conduct, receiving bribes and kickbacks in connection with loans, and failed to disclose his business relationships with borrowers. The bank did not have to prove a dishonest act for each loan; instead, a general pattern of dishonesty, whereby the officer was motivated by separate instances of bribery to make multiple loans, was sufficient under the bank's fidelity bond. *FDIC v. Fid. & Deposit Co. of Md.,* 45 F.3d 969.

5th Cir. 1985 (Tex.). A third party's suit against the bank president and the bank resulted in a judgment against the bank and was a covered loss under the fidelity bond based upon the "loss through" language. Although the third-party suit primarily alleged a claim for breach of contract for failing to make a loan for which the third party had paid a commitment fee, this allegation "potentially" included the bank president's dishonest and fraudulent act of embezzling the commitment fee. *Cont'l Sav. Ass'n v. USF&G,* 762 F.2d 1239.

5th Cir. 1981 (La.). The president of a bank permitted borrowers to collect the proceeds of life insurance policies pledged as collateral for two loans made by the bank. These acts were found to be dishonest, but no coverage existed under the bankers bonds. *Cent. Progressive Bank v. Fireman's Fund Ins. Co.,* 658 F.2d 377.

5th Cir. 1981 (Tex.). To constitute a dishonest or fraudulent act under a bankers blanket bond under Texas law, the employee must have some degree of intent to perform a wrongful action, though the intent need not be to the extent required by criminal law. There must be a physical act plus a mental state. Mere negligence, carelessness, or incompetence is insufficient. *Merch. & Farmers State Bank of Weatherford, Tex. v. Fid. & Cas. Co. of N.Y.,* 791 F.2d 1141.

5th Cir. 1981 (Tex.). Lawsuits were filed against the bank alleging conspiracy to defraud through a forgery and check kiting scheme perpetrated by a bank director and facilitated by the bank's president. The allegations were held to fall within the fidelity clause of the bankers blanket bond. *First Nat'l Bank of Bowie v. Fid. & Cas. Co. of N.Y.,* 634 F.2d 1000.

5th Cir. 1978 (Fla.). A bank claimed loss arising from the alleged dishonesty of a former president in issuing letters of credit without authorization and without following proper bank procedures. The court held that an employee's acts do not need to be criminal nor is it necessary that the employee personally benefit or intend to benefit to give rise to coverage. However, willfulness and an intent to deceive are necessary elements for acts to be dishonest and fraudulent. More than negligence, mistake, carelessness, or incompetence must be present. The court also held that an act that is dishonest and fraudulent under the bankers blanket bond is excluded under the standard exclusion in the directors and officers liability insurance policy as "acts of active and deliberate dishonesty committed with actual dishonest purpose and intent." *Eglin Nat'l Bank v. Home Indem. Co.,* 583 F.2d 1281.

5th Cir. 1977 (La.). The insured suffered trading losses when an employee-broker speculated in the commodities market. The broker used the insured's membership in the Chicago Board of Trade to gain access to the floor of the exchange. In an action on a brokers blanket bond, the court held that the broker's conduct was dishonest. The employee used the insured's credit, knew that the insured would have to pay any loss sustained, and gave the insured bad checks to allow deception to continue. *Howard, Weil, Labouisse, Friedrichs, Inc. v. Ins. Co. of N. Am.*, 557 F.2d 1055.

5th Cir. 1970 (Tex.). Bank director placed the interests of third parties ahead of the interests of the bank in various real estate transactions. In an action on bankers blanket bonds, the court found that the director's actions were dishonest, that the director disregarded his responsibilities to the bank, and that he concealed his conflict of interest. *FDIC v. Aetna Cas. & Sur. Co.*, 426 F.2d 729.

5th Cir. 1966 (Tex.). Insured brokerage company's employee misstated facts to water bond purchasers. The bond purchasers filed suit against the insured. Insured, in turn, notified its insurer of the pending suit and demanded that the insurer fulfill its indemnity bond obligation to defend the suit under a brokers blanket bond. The insurer refused to defend the insured, alleging that the bond did not cover the suit. Once the insured settled with the bond purchasers, it brought an action against the insurer. Affirming the lower court's judgment, the appellate court held that the bond covered the employee's misconduct. The court further noted that even though the insured could have settled the suit without sustaining a loss, the insured was allowed to recover because it acted as a prudent uninsured security dealer, the insured sustained damages as a principal due to the fraudulent acts of its agent, and the bond did not limit the type or amount of losses covered. *Nat'l Sur. Corp. v. Rauscher, Pierce & Co.*, 369 F.2d 572.

5th Cir. 1956 (Fla.). The court adopted the rule that there must be an element of moral turpitude or want of integrity for an act to be dishonest under a fidelity bond. *Glenn Falls Indem. Co. v. Nat'l Floor & Supply Co.*, 239 F.2d 412.

5th Cir. 1950 (Tex.). Action of employee in purchasing steel in insured's name and diverting it to the open market at a secret personal profit was held to constitute fraudulent and dishonest conduct under a fidelity bond. *Eagle Indem. Co. v. Cherry*, 182 F.2d 298.

5th Cir. 1934 (Tex.). The insured claimed that its president had insolvent persons execute notes and secretly used the proceeds to finance his stock market operations. The president's acts were held dishonest under a bankers blanket bond as a matter of law. The court noted that "[i]nsurance against dishonest acts is insurance of fidelity; it is intended to, it does, guarantee openness and fair dealing on the part of the bank's officers. It is intended to, it does, underwrite that the bank's officers shall act with common honesty and an eye single to its interests. It guarantees that the bank shall at all times have the benefit of the unbiased, critical, and disinterested judgment of the president in regard to the loans it makes." *Md. Cas. Co. v. Am. Trust Co.,* 71 F.2d 137.

5th Cir. 1931 (Ala.). Cashier allowed a customer to overdraw his account in violation of a resolution of board of directors and state law. The Fifth Circuit approved the jury instruction that "personal dishonesty" had broader meaning than "criminal" and might include any acts that showed a want of integrity and intentional breach of trust. The Fifth Circuit noted that it was not necessary that the cashier acted with any purpose of personal profit and that any illegal or unauthorized taking of funds of bank intentionally perpetrated by the employee was an act of personal dishonesty under the fidelity provision of a surety bond. The court also held that the issue of dishonesty was one of fact for the jury. *USF&G v. Bank of Thorsby,* 46 F.2d 950.

5th Cir. 1918 (Ala.). The Fifth Circuit held that the issue of whether the acts of a cashier were authorized and directed by president of insured was properly submitted to the jury. The bond specifically provided that the insurer would not be liable for an act done or left undone by a named employee in obedience to or in pursuit of any instructions or authorization received from the employer or any superior officer. *USF&G v. Walker,* 248 F. 42.

5th Cir. 1917 (Ala.). An employee-bookkeeper received immediate credit on his representation that the check was good. The check was later dishonored. Language in the fidelity insuring agreement was held broad enough to cover loss due to fraud or dishonesty of an employee in connection with transactions not connected with the rendition of service for which employee was hired. *Md. Cas. Co. v. First Nat'l Bank,* 246 F. 892.

6th Cir. 1966 (Ohio). Actions by employee in misrepresenting values of vehicles to inflate their loan values was held to constitute dishonest conduct under a commercial blanket bond. To constitute "dishonesty," the court noted that the conduct need not amount to a crime or be an intent to profit or to cause a monetary loss to the employer; the conduct need only involve bad faith or a want of integrity or untrustworthiness or a disposition to lie or cheat or a faithlessness to a trust. *City Loan & Savs. Co. v. Employers' Liab. Assurance Corp.*, 249 F. Supp. 633 (N.D. Ohio 1964), *aff'd without opinion*, 356 F.2d 941.

6th Cir. 1934 (Mich.). President and principal stockholder of the insured bank committed a series of acts that the receiver of the bank contended were dishonest and criminal. The Sixth Circuit held that whether such acts were covered by the schedule fidelity bond was an issue of fact to be decided by the jury. As to whether the teller, who made false entries in connection with certain of the transactions, was also guilty of dishonest and criminal conduct, it was held to be issue of fact for the jury. However, the court stated that making a false entry alone would not be sufficient to impose liability on bonding company; something more was needed; e.g., knowledge that the entries were false or an intent to aid others in fraudulent conduct. The court went on to state that circumstances from which such knowledge and intent may reasonably be inferred were sufficient to raise a fact issue and support the jury verdict. Also, the court held that the jury verdict for the receiver on additional loss on the theory that loans to third parties were actually loans to the president of the insured and, therefore, involved dishonest and criminal conduct, was supported by the evidence. *USF&G v. Barber*, 70 F.2d 220.

7th Cir. 1983 (Ill.). Although the facts of an employee's conduct may have been undisputed, the characterization of that conduct was a separate question of fact. Because the inferences to be drawn from the employee's conduct could reasonably show dishonesty under the blanket bond on the one hand, or error of judgment, incompetence, or negligence on the other hand, summary judgment was reversed. *Rock Island Bank v. Aetna Cas. & Sur. Co.,* 706 F.2d 219.

7th Cir. 1980 (Ill.). In an action on a fidelity bond, the lower court's judgment was reversed and case was remanded for a jury determination of whether the employees' conduct constituted dishonest or fraudulent acts. *Cent. Nat'l Life Ins. Co. v. Fid. & Deposit Co. of Md.,* 626 F.2d 537.

7th Cir. 1979 (Ill.). The words "dishonest" and "fraudulent" used in a fidelity bond are to be given broad meaning. They are broader than their "criminal" meaning and include acts that show a want of integrity or breach of trust. The following conduct of a bank president was held to be dishonest and fraudulent as a matter of law: (1) approving seventy-two loans to eight friends, relatives, and business associates, most without security, and all of whom were out of the territory and were refinancing the loans when they came due; (2) continuing to purchase participations from another bank owned by his brother-in-law, in violation of the instructions of the board of directors; and (3) diverting monies to himself that belonged to the bank from credit life commissions. *First Nat'l Bank Co. v. Ins. Co. of N. Am.*, 606 F.2d 760.

7th Cir. 1971 (Ind.). The court held that whether an employee's conduct constitutes dishonesty under a bankers blanket bond is a question of fact. The words "dishonest" and "fraudulent" are to be given a broad meaning, and it is not necessary to show that an employee benefited personally for the act to be dishonest. Bank vice president fraudulent entries and failure to charge back dishonored checks were sufficient evidence of dishonesty. *Citizens State Bank v. Transamerica Ins. Co.*, 452 F.2d 199.

7th Cir. 1953 (Ill.). Insured claimed that the manager of construction loan department failed to follow instructions and established procedures that constituted dishonesty under the brokers blanket bond. The court held that the words "dishonest" and "fraudulent" are to be given a broad meaning, but that mere negligence, mistake or error in judgment or acts resulting from incompetence are not dishonest. Furthermore, dishonesty is a question of fact for the jury. *Irvin Jacobs & Co. v. Fid. & Deposit Co. of Md.*, 202 F.2d 794.

7th Cir. 1932 (Ind.). The cashier of a bank agreed with another bank to rediscount its notes. The president of the other bank was forging the notes involved and the cashier discovered that some of the notes were not genuine but continued the arrangement. The total amount of notes purchased was far in excess of the bank's capital stock. Finding coverage for the insured under a blanket indemnity bond, the court held that dishonest acts do not have to involve criminal liability of the employee and that if the employee's conduct indicates a "reckless, willful, and wanton disregard for the interest of the employer—if it be an act manifestly unfair to the employer and palpably subjects him to likelihood of loss—a fact question of liability for loss thereby ensuing, as from a dishonest act, is fairly raised." *London & Lancashire Indem. Co. v. Peoples Nat'l Bank & Trust Co.,* 59 F.2d 149.

8th Cir. 1993 (S.D.). In an action on two financial institution bonds, the Court of Appeals held that jury instruction correctly included broad definition of "dishonest" and "fraudulent," which permitted the jury to find dishonesty if an employee acts in disregard of employer's interest, subjecting the employer to a likelihood of loss. *First Dakota Nat'l Bank v. St. Paul Fire & Marine Ins. Co.,* 2 F.3d 801.

8th Cir. 1975 (Mo.). A bank president's acts in creating a "check floating" operation involving his bank and two other banks were held to constitute dishonest and fraudulent conduct under a bankers blanket bond. The court stated that conduct does not have to involve a criminal offense to be dishonest and that it is dishonest and fraudulent conduct if an employee creates a conflict of interest and acts in his own interest or acts in disregard of his employer's interest, subjecting the employer to the likelihood of a loss. *First Nat'l Bank of Sikestown v. Transamerica Ins. Co.,* 514 F.2d 981.

8th Cir. 1971 (Mo.). The office manager of a small loan company falsified credit applications to improve the apparent financial condition of applicants and received a kickback for referring potential customers to other lenders. The court held that the receipt of kickbacks was dishonest within terms of the fidelity bond because such conduct was inimical to best interests of the employer. *Boston Sec., Inc. v. United Bonding Ins. Co.,* 441 F.2d 1302.

8th Cir. 1971 (S.D.). The president of the insured used the insured's funds to make advances to another corporation, of which he was also president, in violation of the insured's bylaws. The president's actions were held to be dishonest under the fidelity bond as a matter of law. The court noted that the words "fraudulent or dishonest" are to be given a broad meaning and may be inferred from the facts, but must be proven by a preponderance of the evidence. It is not necessary that the employee benefit. *Gen. Fin. Corp. v. Fid. & Cas. Co. of N.Y.,* 439 F.2d 981, *rev'g.* 311 F. Supp. 353.

8th Cir. 1935 (Iowa). A bank's cashier permitted overdrafts to be paid for a bank customer with whom he had a business relationship and aided another customer in a check kiting scheme. There was evidence to support the jury's finding of dishonesty. The court held that the word "dishonest" in a fidelity bond is to be given a broad meaning and may be something short of criminality. *Fid. & Deposit Co. of Md. v. Bates,* 76 F.2d 160.

8th Cir. 1906 (Iowa). Employee in charge of insured's operation dealt with a customer in violation of the employer's instructions, concealed his conduct, and falsified reports. The evidence showed that the employee was using some of the insured's monies in his own affairs. The Eighth Circuit held that employee's conduct was dishonest and fraudulent under a fidelity bond as a matter of law. The acts involved "a breach of trust, a want of financial integrity, coupled with deceit and concealment, and resulting in financial loss to the employer." The Eighth Circuit also held that the terms "dishonesty" and "fraud" within the bond are not restricted to criminal acts. *USF&G v. Egg Shippers Strawboard & Filler Co.,* 148 F. 353.

9th Cir. 1991 (Or.). A production credit association made loans to a cattle company whose president and principal stockholder also was a director of the production credit association. The director had falsified the loan documents by inflating the cattle inventory. The director disappeared and the loans were never repaid. The court held that the director's failure to disclose his fraud and dishonesty to the production credit association was conduct covered by the association's fidelity bond. *Interstate Prod. Credit Ass'n v. Fireman's Fund Ins. Co.,* 944 F.2d 536 *rev'g* 735 F. Supp. 225 (D. Or. 1990).

9th Cir. 1981 (Cal.). When determining whether employees of a bank acted dishonestly in accepting deposits with knowledge of the bank's insolvency, under a standard savings and loan blanket bond the court should look to the definition of "dishonesty" rather than its definition under the National Bank Act. *Fid. Sav. & Loan Ass'n v. Aetna Life & Cas. Co.,* 647 F.2d 933.

9th Cir. 1979 (Cal.). An employee who knowingly pays more for an item than it is worth with the intention of enriching the person from whom the purchase is made is guilty of theft and, thus, is dishonest under a fidelity bond. *Research Equity Fund, Inc. v. Ins. Co. of N. Am.,* 602 F.2d 200.

9th Cir. 1963 (Wash.). In an action on a bankers blanket bond, the court noted that the dictionary definitions of "dishonesty" and "fraud" have similar meanings and that implicit in each is the concept of bad faith or an intent to accomplish some wrongdoing. The court approved of a jury instruction that emphasized the wrongful intent and affirmed the trial court judgment for the bonding company. *Sherwood & Roberts-Kennewick, Inc. v. St. Paul Fire & Marine Ins. Co.,* 322 F.2d 70.

10th Cir. 1972 (N.M.). An employee authorized overdisbursement on interim construction loans resulting in loss to the insured and, on instruction from the president of the insured, lied to a member of the board of directors concerning the extent and condition of the insured's construction financing program. In an action on a savings and loan blanket bond, the court held that a jury could have reasonably concluded that the employee and president did not act dishonestly, but had the best interests of the insured in mind. Even though there was ample evidence to conclude that they exercised poor judgment, made serious mistakes, and were generally negligent in handling the affairs of the insured, the jury's verdict was supported by substantial evidence. *N.M. Sav. & Loan Ass'n v. USF&G,* 454 F.2d 328.

10th Cir. 1971 (Okla.). Four employees of the insured made disbursements to another company pursuant to the terms of a contract. The insured argued that interlocking directorates between the companies made the contract invalid and, therefore, that the disbursements were unauthorized and the acts of the employees who disbursed the monies were dishonest and fraudulent within the meaning of the bond. The court found that the contract was valid and made in good faith and, therefore, that the employees' conduct was not dishonest under the blanket honesty bond. *W. Fid. Corp. v. Ins. Co. of N. Am.,* 437 F.2d 752.

10th Cir. 1969 (Okla.). A fidelity bond indemnified against loss "through the fraudulent or dishonest misapplication, misappropriation, or conversion committed by any one or more of the Employees. . . ." The court held that coverage under the quoted language was not limited to employee embezzlement for direct personal benefit, but included loss through obtaining the insured's money through fictitious assignments and conversion of trust fund monies paid upon valid accounts. *Ins. Co. of N. Am. v. Greenberg,* 405 F.2d 330.

D.C. Cir. 1988. The Court of Appeals held that the actions of a labor union's officers in planning and executing an air traffic controller strike did not constitute "fraudulent or dishonest acts" within the meaning of a fidelity bond. In light of a rider specifically deleting faithful performance coverage and the legislative history of the Labor-Management Reporting and Disclosure Act, pursuant to which the bond had been issued, the court would not apply a broad reading of the terms "fraudulent" and "dishonest." *Skirlick v. Fid. & Deposit Co.,* 852 F.2d 1376.

D.C. Cir. 1970. The court approved a jury instruction on the issue of dishonesty that stated, "there must be found to exist a compelling sense of conscious wrong rather than a mere omission or act amounting to negligence or mere lack of judgment." *Imperial Ins., Inc. v. Employers' Liab. Assurance Corp.,* 442 F.2d 1197.

N.D. Cal. 1994. The court held that dishonest acts must be against the insured employer in order to trigger coverage under the "dishonesty" provision of a general liability policy. There was no evidence that any employee committed dishonest acts against the employer, and the court held that dishonest acts against a third-party claimant and assignee of the employer did not trigger employer's dishonesty coverage. *Fireman's Fund Ins. Co. v. Nat'l Bank for Coops.,* 849 F. Supp. 1347, 1362.

D. Colo. 2015. In a motion in limine, the court ruled to keep out all evidence that the insured's employees had engaged in "constructive fraud." The court noted that willfulness and an intent to deceive are necessary elements for an employee's acts to be "dishonest and fraudulent" under a fidelity bond. It held that constructive fraud lacked these elements. *Centrix Fin. LLC v. Nat'l Union Fire Ins. Co.,* No. 09-cv-01542, 2015 U.S. Dist. LEXIS 70497.

D. Del. 1977. A receiver of insolvent securities brokerage firm brought action to recover under excess insurance policies for losses resulting from recoveries against the insured based on securities law violations. The court discussed the meaning of "dishonest acts" as used in the policy. After quoting Webster's ("not honest, lying, cheating, etc.") and

Black's ("disposition to lie, cheat or defraud; untrustworthiness, lack of integrity;"), the court applied these definitions to the several fact situations involved in the cases previously decided against the insured. *Stargatt v. Avenell,* 434 F. Supp. 234.

D.D.C. 1962. Insured brought action on brokers blanket bond. The court found that the allegedly dishonest employee was himself duped by friends who used him in a fraudulent scheme and, therefore, the employee's conduct was not dishonest or fraudulent. The court held that "there must exist a compelling sense of conscious wrong rather than a mere omission or act amounting to negligence." *Sade v. Nat'l Sur. Corp.,* 203 F. Supp. 680.

S.D. Fla. 1970. The insured's vice president allowed a customer to exceed the authorized and statutory loan limits and allowed lessees of customer to be shown as a borrower. The court held that the officer's acts were dishonest and fraudulent under bankers blanket bonds. The court noted: (1) the terms "dishonest" and "fraudulent" are broader and more comprehensive than "criminal" and include acts that show a want of integrity or breach of trust; (2) acts or a course of conduct demonstrating an intentional breach of trust or a reckless disregard for the interests of employer are dishonest or fraudulent within bond; and (3) knowingly making unauthorized loans is a breach of trust that constitutes fraud or dishonesty within bond. *Miami Nat'l Bank v. Penn. Ins. Co.,* 314 F. Supp. 858.

D. Idaho 2010. The insured sought coverage for embezzlement by its employee. The insurer's investigation revealed that the same employee had engaged in a prior act that was arguably dishonest or fraudulent, which the insurer argued should terminate the bond as to that employee. The employee's previous misdeed consisted of changing the due date on her own loan account. The employee had a loan with the bank, which was also her employer (the insured). The bank actually had a program that would allow its employees to push back the due date of a loan, but only if certain requirements were satisfied. The dishonest employee who unilaterally pushed back her own date did not meet these requirements. The court concluded that a jury should decide whether the employee's prior acts were dishonest or fraudulent. *Pioneer Fed. Credit Union v.*

Cumis Ins. Soc'y, Inc., No. 1:08-CV-496, 2010 U.S. Dist. LEXIS 145761.

N.D. Ill. 1988. Credit union sought reimbursement under a "Credit Union Discovery Bond" for losses resulting from investments made by credit union's treasurer. The court held that the terms "fraud" and "dishonesty" in a fidelity bond are given a broad meaning. Dishonesty includes a reckless, willful, and wanton disregard for the interests of the employer. A fact question precluding summary judgment is raised if an act is manifestly unfair to the employer or subjects the employer to a likelihood of loss. *N. Side "L" Fed. Credit Union v. Cumis Ins. Soc'y, Inc.*, No. 87 C 7150, 1988 U.S. Dist. LEXIS 12010.

E.D. Ill. 1926. Cashier requested stockholders and directors to sign accommodation notes upon agreement that the notes would be limited in amount and used only as collateral for bank's loans from correspondent banks. After the bank closed and the cashier disappeared, these notes were found in the records of the bank as part of its assets. The court held that the cashier was guilty of fraud and dishonesty under a surety bond. The court stated that the word "dishonesty" is to be given a broad significance and taken most strongly against the bonding company. *Aetna Cas. & Sur. Co. v. Commercial State Bank*, 13 F.2d 474.

S.D. Iowa 2005. Financial institution crime bond held to be a statutory bond under Iowa law and, thus, liberally construed. The court further held that "dishonest" and "fraudulent" included acts that showed a "want of integrity," "breach of trust," as well as "acts in disregard of employer's interest, which are likely to subject the employer to loss." This could be shown by a failure to disclose true financial condition of borrowers, serving the borrowers' interests rather than the bank's, and by making "straw man" loans. *Kan. Bankers Surety Co. v. Farmers State Bank*, 408 F. Supp. 2d 751.

D. Kan. 1989. Applying Kansas law, the court held that the words "dishonest" and "fraudulent" in a comprehensive dishonesty, disappearance, and destruction policy are to be given a broad meaning. Their connotation is broader than the word "criminal" and includes acts that show a want of integrity or breach of trust. An employee acted dishonestly by arranging to receive kickbacks from customers. *Koch*

Indus., Inc. v. Nat'l Union Fire Ins. Co. of Pittsburgh, Pa., No. 89-1158-K, 1989 U.S. Dist. LEXIS 15703.

W.D. La. 1993. Bank employee issued letter of credit to borrowers without authority and agreed to release collateral on a loan they already owed, knowing that they were in financial trouble. When the bank later refused to release the collateral, the borrowers sued the bank. The bank brought suit against its bonding company on a blanket bond for costs to defend against borrowers' suit, claiming the suit was caused by the employee's dishonest acts. The court disagreed, finding that any connection between the borrowers' suit and the employee's acts was too tenuous to trigger coverage under a "costs of defense" provision and that issuing a letter of credit without authority may not be a dishonest act. *Farm Credit Bank of Tex. v. Fireman's Fund Ins. Co.*, 822 F. Supp. 1251.

D. Mass. 2010. As a result of an error made by an employee of the insured, paychecks intended for the insured's president were deposited in the bank account of an information technology (IT) support worker. The insured attempted to recover the amounts mistakenly paid under an employee dishonesty and theft provisions of a financial institution bond. The insurers agreed to pay for the amounts that were wrongly paid to the IT support worker while he was employed with the insured, but not the amounts that the worker received after he quit working for the insured. The court held that the employee dishonesty and theft provisions required the insurers to indemnify the insured for the full amount that was mistakenly paid to the worker because the worker's dishonest passivity in maintaining his silence after receiving grossly inflated paychecks began while he was working for the insured and the worker did not commit any affirmative act that aggravated the loss after he stopped working for the insured. *FundQuest Inc. v. Travelers Cas. & Sur. Co.*, 715 F. Supp. 2d 202.

D.N.J. 1977. Ship loans were made without the prior approval or authorization of the insured's board of directors or executive committee and in violation of lending limits and collateral requirements set by the board. The loans were regularly renewed without reduction and renewals were disguised as new loans in monthly reports to the board. The president of the insured and its attorney handled the loans and concealed from the board the true facts concerning the handling of these loans. The court held that the acts of the president and attorney were dishonest and fraudulent within the meaning of the bankers blanket employee fidelity bond and the excess bank employee dishonesty bond. The court noted that: (1) fidelity bonds are to be broadly construed; (2) the clear intent of the bond is to protect the insured against wrongful acts of employees, which, though not criminal, display significant lack of probity, integrity or trustworthiness; and (3) coverage does not extend to acts that constitute mere negligence, mistake, error in judgment, or incompetence. *Midland Bank & Trust Co. v. Fid. & Deposit Co. of Md.,* 442 F. Supp. 960.

D.N.J. 1971. The president of a bank made a loan allegedly in violation of the orders of the board of directors. The court held that the president's acts were not dishonest or fraudulent under a bankers blanket bond. The court pointed out that no reason for the alleged violation of the board's orders was shown, the president had nothing to gain, did nothing to conceal the transaction or alter the records, and brought the loan up for board review in a routine way. The definition of "dishonesty" from *Mortgage Co. of New Jersey v. Aetna* was adopted. *Essex County State Bank v. Fireman's Fund Ins. Co.,* 331 F. Supp. 931.

D.N.M. 1979. The president of a bank made loans in excess of the bank's legal lending limit to cover overdrafts, which were not reported to the bank's board of directors. The court held that the president acted with the intent to injure the bank, and his actions were dishonest and fraudulent as defined in the Bankers Blanket Bond and Excess Bank Employee Dishonesty Blanket Bond. *Plaza Del Sol Nat'l Bank v. Firemen's Ins. Co.,* No. 78-073-B, 1979 U.S. Dist. LEXIS 12876.

W.D. Okla. 1973. An employee of the insured made loans to another company and pledged the insured's assets as collateral for the loans. In an action on a "Comprehensive, Dishonesty, Disappearance and Destruction Policy," the court held that the acts of the employee were unwise but not dishonest, where the loans were approved in advance or subsequently ratified by insured's board of trustees. The fact that the board of trustees may not have understood all that it approved at a time when it had all of the facts at its disposal did not make the acts dishonest. Dishonesty does not include good faith business judgment that results in financial disaster. *Alfalfa Elec. Coop., Inc. v. Travelers Indem. Co.,* 376 F. Supp. 901.

D.P.R. 1991. The court held that the words "fraud or dishonesty" in a savings and loan blanket bond are given a broad meaning and are ordinarily held to extend beyond acts that are criminal. The words include any act showing a lack of integrity, breach of trust or abstraction of funds, together with deceit and concealment. However, mere negligence, mistake, or error in judgment does not suffice, and an intent to deceive must be present in order for an employee's actions to be dishonest. *FDIC v. CNA Cas. of P.R.*, 786 F. Supp. 1082.

D.P.R. 1972. In an action on two fidelity bonds, a shortage in a correspondent account was held to have been sustained through the dishonest and fraudulent conduct of employees, despite a lack of sufficient evidence to convict the principal employee in a criminal proceeding and the lack of records due to their destruction. Evidence of fraud and dishonesty was found to be "clear and convincing no matter what standard of proof is applied." *Banco de San German, Inc. v. Md. Cas. Co.,* 344 F. Supp. 496.

M.D. Tenn. 1990. Bank director who authorized unsound loans to third parties to enable the third parties to purchase shares in his company acted dishonestly within the meaning of a bankers blanket bond. The director failed to adequately check the borrowers' financial statements, failed to reveal his conflict of interest to the board, and violated bank policy by failing to recuse himself from voting on the loans. The court noted that the phrase "dishonest or fraudulent acts" has received varying interpretations. After a review of the many opinions interpreting the phrase, the court determined that the paradigmatic case of dishonesty exists where an employee has cheated and deceived his employer by furthering his own interests at the employer's expense, and covered up his misdeeds. *FDIC v. St. Paul Fire & Marine Ins. Co.,* 738 F. Supp. 1146, *aff'd in part, vacated in part by* 942 F.2d 1032 (6th Cir. 1991).

E.D. Va. 1969. A bank's officer made unauthorized loans, loans in excess of approved lines of credit, renewed overdue loans without authority, and made inaccurate reports in connection with these loans. The court held that the officer's conduct was dishonest and fraudulent under the blanket bankers bond. The court noted that: (1) the terms "dishonest" and "fraudulent" as used in policy are broader than the term "criminal," and include acts that show a want of integrity or breach of trust; (2) knowingly making unauthorized loans is such a breach of trust; (3) intent to deceive is an essential element of fraud or dishonesty, but such intent may be inferred from officer's reckless disregard; and (4) knowingly making false reports to superiors constitutes evidence of intent to deceive. *Arlington Trust Co. v. Hawkeye Sec. Ins. Co.*, 301 F. Supp. 854.

S.D. W. Va. 1973. An assistant cashier filed false reports concerning collateral in connection with floor plan financing for a car dealer, resulting in a judgment against the insured in favor of a bank that purchased some of the loans. The court held that the conduct of the employee was dishonest and fraudulent under a bankers blanket bond as a matter of law. The court adopted a broad definition of "dishonesty" as set out in *Mortgage Company of New Jersey v. Aetna Casualty & Surety Company*. The court noted that the evidence established that the employee made representations of fact purportedly based upon personal knowledge when he did not know if they were true or not. *First Nat'l Bank of W. Hamlin v. Md. Cas. Co.*, 354 F. Supp. 189.

Ariz. Ct. App. 1973. Insured claimed the trial court erred in sustaining the insurer's objection to the admissibility of an underlying lawsuit and numerous letters from dissatisfied customers, and contended that the exhibits should be introduced as business records to prove the fraudulent and dishonest acts of one of its employees to recover under a commercial blanket bond. The appellate court affirmed the lower court's decision and held that the exhibits were not prepared "in the regular course of business at or near the time of the condition or event" as required by the applicable state statute. *Horizon Corp. v. Home Ins. Co.*, 511 P.2d 175.

Ariz. Ct. App. 1971. In an action on fidelity bonds, the court held that though a criminal act is not required, there must be some conduct from which can be implied as an intent to deceive, cheat, or defraud. *Md. Cas. Co. v. Clements*, 487 P.2d 437.

Cal. Ct. App. 1984. Insurer claimed the trial court's instructions to the jury on the meaning of "fraud or dishonesty" under a commercial blanket bond constituted prejudicial error. The appellate court held that the trial court correctly instructed the jury that they needed to find an actual intent to defraud, not a mere negligent misrepresentation. *Pacific-Southern Mortgage Trust Co. v. Ins. Co. of N. Am.*, 156 Cal. App. 3d 37.

Cal. Ct. App. 1940. The bank president secretly borrowed money from the insured through a nominee, knowing that the nominee could not repay and did not intend to do so. The court held that the president's acts were dishonest under the fidelity bond and that fidelity insurance is intended to, and does, guarantee openness and fair dealing on the part of the bank's officials with the bank. *Pac. Indem. Co. v. Hargreaves*, 98 P.2d 217.

Ill. App. Ct. 1998. Bank employee's failure to report suspicious activity that indicated a check kiting scheme in connection with a customer's account was a dishonest act under the bank's fidelity bond. The employee had been charged with the responsibility of monitoring accounts for check kiting. His failure to fulfill his job duties was dishonest. The court held that an employee's act need not be technically criminal nor benefit him personally to qualify as dishonest. *Oxford Bank & Trust v. Hartford Accident & Indem. Co.*, 698 N.E.2d 204.

Ill. App. Ct. 1979. Dishonesty within an "Insurance Companies Blanket Bond" included an act that is manifestly unfair to the employer; palpably subjects employer to a likelihood of loss; indicates a reckless, willful, and wanton disregard for the interest of the employer; and constitutes wrongful acts which, although not criminal, nevertheless display a significant lack of probity, integrity or trustworthiness. *Reserve Ins. Co. v. Gen. Ins. Co.*, 395 N.E.2d 933.

Ill. App. Ct. 1963. The solicited sale of unregistered securities was a criminal misdemeanor under Illinois law without regard to the person's intent. However, the court reasoned that the jury could have found the requisite intent to make the act of the salesmen-employees dishonest as well as criminal, pointing out that the question of dishonesty is one of fact for the jury. The court concluded that the acts could be both criminal and dishonest under a brokers blanket bond. The court cited cases adopting the broad definition of "dishonesty." *Home Indem. Co. v. Reynolds & Co.*, 187 N.E.2d 274.

Ind. Ct. App. 1937. The act of the bank cashier in paying checks of the bank's president, who had insufficient funds to cover the checks, was held not to constitute dishonesty under a cashier's fidelity bond in the absence of a showing of some intent or purpose of the cashier. The term "dishonesty" was held to include an element of deceit or bad faith on the part of the person charged and not to include error of judgment or injudicious exercise of discretion. *State v. Jay,* 10 N.E.2d 737.

Iowa 1979. Evidence that a bank officer transferred funds from one account to another without authorization, made false records and false reconciliation of accounts with other banks, credited checks to improper accounts, falsely reconstructed checking accounts, and held overdrafts as cash items was held to support a finding that the bank officer was guilty of fraudulent and dishonest acts under a fidelity bond. The terms were held to include acts that show a want of integrity or breach of trust and acts in disregard of employer's interest that are likely to subject the employer to loss. Knowingly making unauthorized loans in excess of authority was held to constitute dishonest and fraudulent conduct. *FDIC v. Nat'l Sur. Corp.,* 281 N.W.2d 816.

Iowa 1929. Intentional wrongful entry or omission to make an entry on the books of a bank for the purpose of deception was held to be a dishonest act under an individual fidelity bond. The court noted that the bond does not cover loss through negligence, inadvertent conduct, or error in judgment. *Andrew v. Hartford Accident & Indem. Co.,* 223 N.W. 529.

Kan. 1989. Bank director secured several loans from the bank. The loans were allegedly secured by cattle that the bank later discovered did not exist. The director also deposited several insufficient funds checks with the bank. The court held that the words "dishonest" and "fraudulent" in a bankers blanket bond are to be given a broad meaning and that the director's actions manifestly represented a series of dishonest and fraudulent acts. *First Hays Banshares, Inc. v. Kan. Bankers. Sur. Co.,* 769 P.2d 1184.

Kan. Ct. App. 2005. An employee's surreptitious and unauthorized act of raising her personal credit limit constituted dishonest conduct. The court adopted a broad definition of "dishonest" and concluded that conduct may be dishonest even if the employee does not intend to harm the insured. The terms "dishonest" and "fraudulent" are not ambiguous and therefore are not subject to rules of construction. *Troy State Bank v. BancInsure, Inc.,* No. 92,115, 2005 Kan. App. Unpub. LEXIS 120.

Ky. 1938. Insured grocery store filed a claim under its fidelity bond when its employee improperly extended credit to one of the insured's customers, who subsequently failed to pay his bill. The court, in agreement with the trial court, found no basis for recovery under the terms of the indemnity policy, concluding that while such extension of credit was unauthorized and improper, it did not provide evidence sufficient to show an intent of the manager to commit a fraud or to be dishonest in such a way that an insurance recovery was warranted. *Jellico Grocery Co. v. Sun Indem. Co.*, 114 S.W.2d 83.

La. 1939. Bankers blanket bonds at issue covered loss caused through an act of larceny or embezzlement. The court held that an employee who becomes indebted to his employer through mistake or carelessness, or who uses funds of the employer for his personal use with no intent to defraud, is not guilty of embezzlement nor of a dishonest act within the meaning of a fidelity bond. *Curran & Treadway, Inc. v. Am. Bonding Co.*, 192 So. 335.

La. 1932. In an action on a blanket fidelity policy, the court held that the act of an employee in drawing his salary for one month in advance but not attempting to hide it was wrongful and perhaps unlawful, but not dishonest. *Bank of Commerce & Trust Co. v. Union Indem. Co.*, 142 So. 156.

La. Ct. App. 1972. An employee owed a customer $500 and made a loan to the same customer on behalf of insured. The court held that there was no evidence the personal debt had any influence on the employee in making a loan. The employee was liable to the insured for violating instructions, but the conduct was held not to be dishonest or fraudulent under the fidelity bond. *W. H. Hodges & Co. v. Hartford Accident & Indem. Co.*, 262 So. 2d 542.

Md. 1975. A bank employee allegedly concealed and misrepresented the financial condition of a borrower. The employee was a "financial consultant" to the borrower and attended meetings of its board. The court noted that fraud and dishonesty as used in the bankers blanket bond includes any act showing a want of integrity or breach of trust, but the bonding company is not liable for the consequences of acts done in actual good faith, without intentional fault. This includes constructively or technically fraudulent acts innocently done, even though they constitute a breach of obligation by the person whose fidelity is insured. The court also held that an insurer is not liable for loss occasioned by mere negligence, carelessness, inattention to business, mistake, errors in judgment, incompetency, or other acts or omissions not denoting conscious wrongdoing or involving moral turpitude. *First Nat'l Bank of S. Md. v. USF&G*, 340 A.2d 275.

Md. App. 1928. A bank president discounted notes, which were in names of fictitious companies, and the board approved the notes. The bank president knew he was insolvent at the time he discounted the notes and received the money. The court held that the president acted dishonestly under the surety bond by withholding from the bank vital information concerning his insolvency. *Nat'l Sur. Co. v. State,* 161 N.E. 573.

Mass. 1931. A bank employee paid a debt with checks from an insurance company of which he was a director and then repaid the insurance company with a check drawn on the bank. The check was later covered by a note from a third person and subsequently covered in part by another note. The cashier's conduct was held to be criminal as a matter of law, and the loans involved were held to be fraudulent within the meaning of the indemnity bond. *Fitchburg Sav. Bank v. Mass. Bonding & Ins. Co.,* 174 N.E. 324.

Mich. Ct. App. 2011. The court stated in a footnote that the phrase "any fraudulent or dishonest act" was not defined and could therefore be construed as ambiguous in terms of what falls within its parameters. But the court held that whatever else it may mean, it clearly included acts committed that resulted in pleading guilty to a felony offense involving elements of fraud or dishonesty. *Alcona County v. Mich. Mun. League Liab. & Prop.*, No. 292155, 2011 Mich. App. LEXIS 473.

Minn. 1976. Insured bank filed a claim under its bankers fidelity bond to recover its legal fees after one of its customers filed suit against the bank and its officers for breach of fiduciary duty. Reversing the lower court's judgment, the appellate court concluded that the purpose of the fidelity bond was to cover losses by dishonest or fraudulent acts of employees whereby the employer was rendered liable to third parties. It further held that the fidelity bond did not cover losses suffered by reason of fraud, dishonesty, or breach of fiduciary duty when the bank, through its board of directors, had knowledge of the acts complained of, appreciated their fraudulent nature, and condoned, acquiesced, or participated in them. *Farmers & Merchs. State Bank of Pierz v. St. Paul Fire & Marine Ins. Co.*, 242 N.W.2d 840.

Minn. 1957. In an action on a bankers blanket bond, the court held that coverage for acts of fraud and dishonesty extends beyond acts that are criminal. The court also held that loss due to dishonesty can be established by circumstantial evidence. *Prior Lake State Bank v. Nat'l Sur. Corp.*, 80 N.W.2d 612.

Minn. 1953. The employee whose conduct was in question was the manager of a liquor store. In an action on a blanket fidelity bond, the court held that evidence provided only a conjectural basis for an inference that any dishonest act was attributable to the accused employee. Evidence of dishonesty was held insufficient to submit to jury and directed verdict for bonding company was affirmed. The court noted that dishonesty is not established by proof of employee's mistakes or negligence. *Village of Plummer v. Anchor Cas. Co.*, 61 N.W.2d 225.

Minn. 1926. In an action on a fidelity bond, there was insufficient evidence to establish that the employee had a "culpable" part in the transaction at issue. *Liberty State Bank v. Am. Sur. Co. of N.Y.*, 206 N.W. 706.

Minn. Dist. Ct. 2010. The insureds were banks that serviced or participated in loans to Louis Pearlman. An attorney involved in preparing documents necessary for the loans forged certain documents in connection with the loans. The loans eventually went into default and the insureds sought to recover the loss under a fidelity bond. The court considered whether the attorney's actions constituted dishonesty. The court held that the term "dishonesty" did not refer solely to criminal conduct. It held that "[m]isrepresentation of facts and deliberate deception by pretense and stealth constitute dishonest and fraudulent conduct within the meaning of a fidelity bond," and dishonesty "includes any acts done in breach of [the employee's] duty to the bank: and any wilful [sic] omissions to discharge the duties of his office." Ultimately, the court held that there was a question of fact as to whether the attorney's actions were "dishonest." *Alerus Fin. Nat'l Ass'n v. St. Paul Mercury Ins. Co.*, No. 27-CV-09-3344, 2010 Minn. Dist. LEXIS 290.

Neb. 1981. A dishonesty insuring agreement in the bankers blanket bond issued to a group of farm credit banks does not insure the bank against the consequences of its own torts. *Omaha Bank for Coops. v. Aetna Cas. & Sur. Co.*, 301 N.W.2d 564.

N.H. 1932. Bank employee discovered shortages, but instead of reporting them to the directors, he transferred the shortages to inactive accounts, preventing examiners from discovering the discrepancy. The court held that the words "fraud" and "dishonesty" were to be broadly interpreted to include any acts that show a want of integrity or a breach of trust under the fidelity bond. *Exeter Banking Co. v. Taylor*, 160 A. 733.

N.J. 1978. A branch manager knowingly misrepresented the value of an insured's collateral on a large loan. The court found this conduct to be dishonest and fraudulent under the bankers blanket bond. The court adopted the definition of "dishonesty" found in *Mortgage Corp. of New Jersey v. Aetna Casualty & Surety Co.* The court noted that the subjective intent of the employee may have been blameless, but the nature of his acts indicated that he put the interests of the customer above those of the insured. *Nat'l Newark & Essex Bank v. Am. Ins. Co.*, 385 A.2d 1216.

N.J. 1955. The employee's job was to personally inspect the progress of construction projects on which the insured was making loans and to issue certifications that the insured would use to make loan disbursements. In an action on a brokers blanket bond, the court held: (1) fidelity bonds are to be construed broadly; (2) the clear intent of the bond is to protect employer against employees' wrongful acts, which though not criminal, nevertheless display significant lack of probity, integrity, or trustworthiness; (3) the absence of motive of personal profit or gain does not establish that conduct was not dishonest; and (4) mere neglect or incompetence is not dishonesty. Under the facts, the employee deceived his employer, and it did not matter that his deceptions were not accompanied by intent to cause actual monetary loss to employer and were influenced by motives of personal comfort or convenience rather than by personal profit or gain. *Mortgage Co. of N.J. v. Aetna Cas. & Sur. Co.,* 115 A.2d 43.

N.Y. App. Div. 2012. The phrase "dishonest or fraudulent acts" must be given its ordinary meaning and broadly include acts that demonstrate a want of integrity or a breach of trust or moral turpitude affecting the official fidelity or character of the employee. It was dishonest for an employee to sign the name of another without consent in order to approve transactions that the employee forging the signatures lacked authority to approve. *Capital Bank & Trust Co. v. Gulf Ins. Co.,* 91 A.D.3d 1251, 1253.

N.Y. 1930. A teller allowed a depositor to cash out-of-town checks in spite of the bank's rule that payment against uncollected items of deposit was not to be made without consent of the bank's president or another bank officer. In an action on a bankers bond, the court held that the question of whether an employee's acts were dishonest or criminal was a question of fact for the jury. Writing for the court, Judge Cardozo noted that "[d]ishonesty, unlike embezzlement or larceny, is not a term of art . . . the measure of its meaning is not a standard of perfection, but an infirmity of purpose so opprobrious or furtive as to be fairly characterized as dishonest in the common speech of men." *World Exch. Bank v. Commercial Cas. Ins. Co.,* 173 N.E. 902.

N.Y. 1926. In an action on a surety bond, an employee authorizing overdrafts was "dishonest" only if his actions were done with a dishonest intent and purpose. *First Nat'l Bank of Edgewater v. Nat'l Sur. Corp.,* 152 N.E. 456.

N.C. 1932. The loss sustained by the insured solely by reason of overdrafts allowed by the cashier, without authority of the board of directors, was not covered by the cashier's bond. The court stated that the cashier was civilly but not criminally liable for the loss. *Bank of Peachland v. Fairley,* 162 S.E. 229.

Ohio App. 1930. In an action on a fidelity bond, it was improper to instruct the jury that an employee who loaned money to himself and others, in violation of his authority or when not authorized by the board of directors, was not guilty of dishonesty or fraud. *Massillon Mortgage Co. v. Independence Indem. Co.,* 174 N.E. 167.

Pa. 1939. In an action on an indemnity bond, the court held that fidelity coverage protects the insured against any acts of its employees involving moral turpitude or want of integrity or any act done with the intent to defraud the insured for the personal profit of the employee. *Miners Sav. Bank of Pittston v. Royal Indem. Co.,* 9 A.2d 543.

S.C. 1926. The language in a fidelity bond, which covered loss by any act of fraud, dishonesty, forgery, theft, embezzlement, unlawful abstraction, or willful misapplication, implies positive acts of wrongdoing. Mere negligence or carelessness is not sufficient. *Salley v. Globe Indem. Co.,* 131 S.E. 616.

Tex. 1964. The court held that to constitute fraudulent and dishonest conduct under a fidelity bond, the employee must have some degree of intent to perform the wrongful act. There must be a physical act plus the mental state, though the intent need not be of the degree required for criminal conduct. Mere negligence, carelessness, or incompetence is insufficient. If the employee has knowledge of and aids in concealing another person's wrongful conduct, the employee is guilty of the same wrongful conduct. *Great Am. Ins. Co. v. Langdeau,* 379 S.W.2d 62.

Tex. 1935. The directors of a newly organized bank declared dividends to themselves as stockholders, in violation of the law. The vice president who participated in the declaration was liable for dishonesty despite the fact that the dividend was declared by a vote of the directors. *First State Bank of Temple v. Metro. Cas. Ins. Co. of N.Y.,* 79 S.W.2d 835.

Tex. 1929. The president of a bank embezzled funds through schemes involving the manipulation of books. In an action on a fidelity bond, the court found that the scheme could not have been carried out without false entries made by the bookkeeper, and it was impossible for the bookkeeper not to have discovered the fraud; therefore, the bookkeeper aided and assisted the president in the scheme. *Austin v. Neiman,* 14 S.W.2d 794.

Tex. Civ. App. 1977. In an action on a fidelity bond, the employee's use of union funds for personal expenses was a "misappropriation" as a matter of law despite the intent of the employee to repay. The wrongful intent was established by the employee's intent to use the funds personally. *Downer v. Amalgamated Meatcutters and Butcher Workmen of N. Am.*, 550 S.W.2d 744.

Tex. Civ. App. 1976. An insurance agent failed to remit the rightful share of premium payments that came into his hands and made unauthorized personal expenditures out of a bank account into which premiums were deposited. The court found that the agent's conduct was dishonest and fraudulent within the meaning of the blanket indemnity bond because it involved his intent to perform the wrongful act. *Lawyers Sur. Corp. v. Am. Pub. Life Ins. Co.*, 540 S.W.2d 842.

Tex. App. 1964. The court held that there was no direct evidence of fraud or dishonesty under a fidelity bond, only an inference. The court stated that the insured's records were inept and incomplete. The difficulty of providing proof did not excuse a lack of evidence. *Home Indem. Co. v. Gonzalez*, 383 S.W.2d 857.

Tex. App. 1933. In an action on a fidelity bond, the evidence established that a bank's funds were abstracted by someone, and a bonded employee made false entries that concealed and aided in the perpetration of the fraud. *Shaw v. Cone*, 56 S.W.2d 667.

Tex. App. 1925. An insurance agent's unexplained failure to remit premiums to a company constituted fraud and dishonesty within the meaning of a position fidelity bond. "Fraud" and "dishonesty" were found to be synonymous. *Nat'l Sur. Co. v. McCutcheon*, 270 S.W. 1062.

Wash. 1993. An escrow company obtained a fidelity bond as required by Washington's Escrow Agent Registration Act. The vice president of the escrow company diverted funds from escrow trust accounts to the company's operating account in order to cover general operating expenses. In an effort to avoid detection, he occasionally shifted money back from the general operating account to the trust account, and he filed false operating reports. The court held that the resulting losses were covered by the company's fidelity bond. According to the court, a fraudulent or dishonest act is any act showing a want of integrity, breach of trust, or abstraction of funds, together with deceit and concealment.

Furthermore, the bond language limiting coverage to acts performed with the manifest intent to cause a loss and obtain financial benefit impermissibly narrowed the coverage for dishonest acts required by the Escrow Agent Registration Act, which required coverage for any dishonest act. *Estate of K.O. Jordan v. Hartford Accident & Indem. Co.*, 844 P.2d 403.

Wash. 1935. The president of the insured bank made loans in violation of a statute requiring approval of the board of directors. The court held that the president's acts were dishonest and fraudulent within the meaning of the bankers blanket bond. The court noted that: (1) dishonesty is to be given a broad and comprehensive meaning; and (2) the question of dishonesty is a question of fact. The court also found that the violation of state banking law is the "violation of a public, as well as a private, trust" and, therefore, is not innocent of a dishonest motive or intent. *Hansen v. Am. Bonding Co.,* 48 P.2d 653.

Wis. 1927. A bank president obtained unsecured personal loans from the bank without the authority of the board of directors, and allowed overdrafts in his checking account. He did not conceal the transactions, and they were fully revealed on the books of the bank. The court held that the president's acts did not constitute fraud or dishonesty under the individual fidelity bond, though the acts were irregular and violated banking laws. The court stated that it was not the purpose of the bond to indemnify the bank against losses arising out of transactions of which the bank had knowledge and consented, and that no fraud or deceit was practiced. The transactions were open and plainly revealed by the bank's books and records. *Parker v. Sprague,* 214 N.W. 361.

B. Manifest Intent

1st Cir. 2003 (Mass.). An employee of the insured, a charitable organization, engaged in unauthorized fraudulent fundraising from individual donors, and used the funds for personal expenses. The court held that the "manifest intent" language in the commercial crime policy limited coverage to conduct intended to lead to a dimunition of the insured's assets. The insured had not suffered a covered loss because the employee intended to enrich himself at the expense of the donors rather than by inflicting a loss on his employer. *Fireman's Fund Ins. Co. v. Special Olympics Int'l, Inc.*, 346 F.3d 259.

2d Cir. 2000 (N.Y.). A bank made several loans to a limited partnership engaged in a construction project. A bank trustee allegedly knew that one of the partners was committing fraud against the bank and stealing from the construction project, but did not disclose that fact to the bank. The Second Circuit held that the trustee's failure to inform the bank of the fraud and theft established manifest intent as required under the fidelity bond as a matter of law. The Second Circuit noted that the New York Court of Appeals had not yet addressed the "manifest intent" requirement. Reviewing the various approaches employed by different courts, the Second Circuit concluded that the test was essentially a subjective inquiry into the employee's state of mind, with a necessary objective requirement in that the employee's actions can circumstantially establish that the employee acted with the manifest intent to cause the insured a loss. To establish manifest intent, the insured must show that the employee acted with the specific purpose to harm the insured. Reckless behavior alone does not suffice, and actions that will possibly benefit the employer do not establish manifest intent as a matter of law. Inconsistent with its earlier statement, the court went on to reason that manifest intent does not require that the employee actively wish for or desire a particular result, but can exist when a particular result is substantially certain to follow from the employee's conduct. *FDIC v. Nat'l Union Fire Ins. Co. of Pittsburgh, Pa.*, 205 F.3d 66.

2d Cir. 1989 (N.Y.). In an action on a brokers blanket bond, the court of appeals held that the trial court had erroneously refused to give an instruction on "manifest intent." A new trial was not necessary, however, because the evidence was insufficient to establish either element of the manifest intent requirement. First, investment firm owner's conduct in making risky investments was reckless and imprudent, but there was no evidence that he intended to cause a loss. Second, there was no evidence that he intended to obtain a financial benefit or that he misappropriated funds. *Glusband v. Fittin Cunningham & Lauzon, Inc.*, 892 F.2d 208.

3d Cir. 2004 (Pa.). The insured was a bank that loaned customers money to pay insurance premiums for auto policies. Part of the bank's collateral was the right to cancel the policy and receive the return premium. It was therefore critical that the bank identify a default and cancel the defaulted policy promptly. A third-party operator had responsibility for identifying defaults but failed to do so. The insured bank sought coverage for the nonpayment of loans, but coverage was denied because the operator lacked intent to confer a financial benefit on itself. The operator received only normal payments, such as bonuses and commissions, in exchange for its performance—no additional funds for failing to catch defaults as it had promised. *Hudson United Bank v. Progressive Cas. Ins. Co.*, 112 F. App'x 170.

3d Cir. 2003 (N.J.). The Third Circuit applied a specific intent standard and held that the district court correctly found that the receiver of an insolvent bank was not entitled to recover under a financial institution bond. The undisputed evidence showed that the loan officer who advised bank to make an uncreditworthy loan did not act with the manifest intent to obtain a financial benefit for himself or for a third party. *FDIC v. Nat'l Union Fire Ins. Co. of Pittsburgh, Pa.*, No. 01-2524, 2003 U.S. App. LEXIS 2096.

3d Cir. 2000 (N.J.). The Third Circuit considered two questions with respect to manifest intent: (1) the appropriate construction of the term "manifest intent," and (2) the type of circumstantial evidence relevant to the insured's burden of proof. The case includes a brief discussion of the history of the "manifest intent" requirement, and contrasts two different approaches—general intent versus specific intent—adopted by various jurisdictions. The Third Circuit predicted that the Supreme Court of New Jersey would conclude that the "specific intent" definition more closely comports with the savings and loan blanket fidelity bond drafters' intent. According to the Third Circuit, manifest intent is characterized by the mental state "purposefully" and is analogous to the Model Penal Code definition of "specific intent." *RTC v. Fid. & Deposit Co. of Md.*, 205 F.3d 615.

4th Cir. 1996 (Va.). Insured's employee altered customer purchase orders, resulting in the shipment of useless products to customer. Insured sustained losses when customer refused to accept delivery. The Fourth Circuit held that to satisfy the manifest intent requirement of the employee dishonesty insurance policy, insured must demonstrate that employee had specific intent to accomplish a particular purpose, analogous to the intent required by the criminal law. Summary judgment was inappropriate because fact issues remained as to whether employee possessed manifest intent to benefit employee or a third person. *Gen. Analytics Corp. v. CNA Ins. Cos.*, 86 F.3d 51.

4th Cir. 1993 (N.C.). President of securities firm pleaded guilty to fraud and embezzling from firm's clients. The court held that president's guilty plea and other statements established his manifest intent to defraud as required under the blanket bond. *In re Waddell Jenmar Sec., Inc.*, No. 92-2158, 1993 U.S. App. LEXIS 9535 (unpublished table opinion).

4th Cir. 1934 (N.C.). The making of an unauthorized loan, approved by directors, was not a dishonest act. Directors repeatedly approved renewals of the loan, and, although it involved a technical violation of the banking laws, the employee involved did not intend to injure the bank. *Fid. & Deposit Co. of Md. v. People's Bank of Sanford*, 72 F.2d 932.

5th Cir. 1996 (La.). Insurers defeated bank's bad faith claim that was based upon insurer's denial of coverage under a bankers blanket bond for dishonest acts committed by a loan officer. The Fifth Circuit held that coverage was "fairly debatable" because the definition of "manifest intent" had not yet been determined under Kentucky law. Though the majority of courts have adopted a subjective test, there existed uncertainty under Kentucky law as to whether manifest intent was based on the subjective intent of the loan officer or on the objective result of his conduct. Furthermore, the insurers reasonably contested coverage based on factual questions regarding the loan officer's intent. *First Nat'l Bank of Louisville v. Lustig (Lustig II)*, 96 F.3d 1554.

5th Cir. 1992 (La.). This case presents a thorough discussion of the manifest intent issue and implicitly recognizes the specific intent requirement of manifest intent. A loan officer admitted he had fabricated credit references on several loans, but maintained that he did so to obtain recognition from his employer, not for personal gain from customers. The Fifth Circuit held that a finding that an employee acted dishonestly is not enough to trigger coverage under a bankers blanket bond; there can be no manifest intent when the employee hopes to benefit the employer, regardless of the likelihood or certainty of loss. According to the Fifth Circuit, there is a continuum of dishonest acts: at one end are acts of embezzlement that benefit the employee at the expense of the employer; and at the other end are acts that benefit both the employer and the employee. The court also held that when determining the employee's purpose, all surrounding circumstances must be considered, including the employee's conduct, not just the employee's explanation. Though the court held that manifest intent could be inferred from reckless conduct, the standard is nevertheless a subjective standard that seeks to determine the employee's intent. *First Nat'l Bank of Louisville v. Lustig (Lustig I)*, 961 F.2d 1162.

6th Cir. 2012 (Ohio). The employee of insured bank was an investment advisor who transferred money from his clients' brokerage accounts into his own account. The insured was forced to reimburse the clients for their losses. In deciding whether the employee had the manifest intent to cause the insured a loss, the court held that the phrase "manifest intent" "does not establish a subjective standard; it establishes an objective one, meaning 'apparent or obvious.'" The court followed the substantial certainty test, holding that as long as the dishonest employee realized that his conduct was substantially certain to result in a loss to the insured, manifest intent was present. The court found that the substantial certainty test was "assuredly" met. *First Defiance Fin. Corp. v. Progressive Cas. Ins. Co.*, 688 F.3d 265.

6th Cir. 2012 (Ohio). A bank employee transferred funds from a client's brokerage account into his own account. The employee had the manifest intent to cause the bank a loss because it was "absolutely certain" that a loss would result from his theft. The court noted, "An insured meets the requirement [of proving manifest intent] where 'a particular result is substantially certain to follow from conduct.'" The court also noted that the employee's actions could not have benefited the bank—bank embezzlement is a zero-sum game; the employer must lose for the employee to win. *First Defiance Fin. Corp. v. Progressive Cas. Ins. Co.*, 688 F.3d 265.

6th Cir. 2005 (Ohio). President of insured "borrowed" over $3 million from insured and signed promissory notes for the repayment of the funds. He ultimately was fired, having paid back only $550,000. Insured sought coverage under two insurance contracts that included "employee dishonesty coverage forms." The court upheld district court's denial of summary judgment for the insurer because although it was possible that the employee did not have the manifest intent to cause the insured a loss by virtue of having signed promissory notes for the funds, it was equally plausible that the promissory notes were a "sham" to make it appear that he was only borrowing the money. *Century Bus. Servs., Inc. v. Utica Mut. Ins. Co.*, 122 F. App'x 196.

6th Cir. 1998 (Ky.). The Sixth Circuit held that the bankers blanket bond did not provide coverage for certain fraudulent acts of the insured's employees. However, the court of appeals disavowed any language in the district court's opinion that could be construed as meaning that "manifest intent" requires an employee to actually receive a personal monetary benefit. The law of the circuit requires only that the employee intended to have received such a benefit. *Ins. Co. of N. Am. v. Liberty United Bancorp., Inc.*, No. 96-6502, 1998 U.S. App. LEXIS 3781 (unpublished table opinion).

6th Cir. 1997 (Ky.). Bank employees defrauded bank customers by inducing customers to purchase a business and to procure a loan from the bank for the purpose of purchasing the business. The bankers blanket bond did not cover damages resulting from a lawsuit filed against the bank by customers who had been defrauded by bank employees. The bond covers loss suffered by a third party only if dishonest employees know or expect loss will migrate to the bank. Too many contingencies intervened between fraud and eventual loss to the bank to conclude that dishonest employees held manifest intent to cause the bank's loss. *Peoples Bank & Trust Co. of Madison County v. Aetna Cas. & Sur. Co.*, 113 F.3d 629.

6th Cir. 1991 (Tenn.). The Sixth Circuit held that there was no coverage under a bankers blanket bond for the losses caused by a former bank president who made bad loans to his friends and business associates. In finding that the bank president did not have the manifest intent to cause the bank a loss, the court rejected a purely objective standard, noting that the principle that a person is presumed to intend the natural and probable consequences of his actions had been undermined in recent years. The court instead stated that manifest intent does not necessarily require the employee to actively wish for or desire a particular result, but does require more than a mere probability, and that manifest intent exists when a particular result is substantially certain to follow. Furthermore, the bond covered fraud not bad business judgment. The bank president's conduct fell somewhere between embezzlement, the classic scenario for coverage whereby the employee gains at the employer's expense, and a scenario in which the employee causes a loss while intending to benefit the employer. Thus, a question of fact was presented that was properly decided in favor of the insurer by the district court. Because the former bank president was also a shareholder, it was highly unlikely that he intended to injure the bank, and far more likely that he intended all parties to benefit. *FDIC v. St. Paul Fire & Marine Ins. Co.*, 942 F.2d 1032.

6th Cir. 1987 (Tenn.). Broker dealer's trader violated company policy by making trades in excess of her inventory limit. The court held there was no coverage for the resulting losses under the broker dealer's fidelity bond because the trader did not have the manifest intent to cause her employer a loss. Instead, her evident motive initially was to make money for her employer, and then to cover up and recoup losses that threatened her job security. *Mun. Sec., Inc. v. Ins. Co. of N. Am.*, 829 F.2d 7.

7th Cir. 1992 (Ill.). The Seventh Circuit held that the trial court's failure to give jury instructions on the definition of "manifest intent" was a reversible error because the term has a technical meaning under the law. Finding no Illinois cases directly on the point, the court looked to the law of other jurisdictions. Cases holding that manifest intent exists when a particular result is substantially certain to follow, and that manifest intent does not require that the employee actively wish for or desire a particular result, were consistent with Illinois law. Citing *Lustig I*, the court held that the jury should not inquire solely into the subjective motive or purpose of the employee and that the fidelity bond's manifest intent requirement could be inferred from reckless conduct. *Heller Int'l Corp. v. Sharp*, 974 F.2d 850.

7th Cir. 1983 (Ill.). Although the facts of an employee's conduct were undisputed, the characterization of that conduct was a separate question of fact. Because the employee's conduct could reasonably show dishonesty on the one hand, or error of judgment, incompetence, or negligence on the other, summary judgment was reversed. *Rock Island Bank v. Aetna Cas. & Sur. Co.*, 706 F.2d 219.

8th Cir. 2001 (N.D.). Insurer that paid bank's employee dishonesty claim under financial institution bond sought declaration that it was entitled to a refund of a portion of the proceeds. The court of appeals held that the district court did not err by finding that the employee did not have the requisite manifest intent as to some of the loans and that the insurer was entitled to a refund for those loans that did not meet the financial institution bond criteria. Noting that North Dakota courts had not ruled on the definition of "manifest intent," the court of appeals held that the district court correctly adopted the dictionary definition to conclude that "manifest intent" means "clearly evident intent," and that it was reasonable to draw the inference that a person intends the natural and probable consequences of his acts. *BancInsure, Inc. v. BNC Nat'l Bank, N.A.*, 263 F.3d 766.

8th Cir. 1993 (S.D.). In an action on a bankers bond, the Eighth Circuit held that a jury instruction on manifest intent in connection with a claim on a bankers bond, which stated that a "person is deemed to intend the natural consequences of his actions," was not erroneous because any potential adverse effect of this language was cured by qualifying language contained in the remainder of the instruction. When read as a whole, the instruction indicated that the jury had a choice whether to draw an inference from employee's conduct. *First Dakota Nat'l Bank v. St. Paul Fire & Marine Ins. Co.*, 2 F.3d 801.

8th Cir. 1989 (Minn.). The bankers special bond at issue contained a duty-to-defend clause. The court held that there was no duty to defend and no coverage for customer's claim that bank president forged customer's signature on a mortgage deed and note. The bond's manifest intent provision was written in the conjunctive, requiring the intent to both cause a loss to the bank and to benefit the employee. Bank president's alleged forgery could only have been done with the intent to benefit the bank, and thus there was no coverage. *Red Lake County State Bank v. Employer's Ins. of Wausau*, 874 F.2d 546.

9th Cir. 1991 (Cal.). Employees of insured government contractor falsified test results on products supplied by the contractor. Fines and penalties incurred by the contractor were not covered by insured's employee dishonesty policy. The employees did not have the manifest intent to cause the employer a loss, but apparently intended to benefit their employer by falsifying the test results. *Genisco Tech. Corp. v. Seaboard Sur. Co.*, No. 90-55480, 1991 U.S. App. LEXIS 10165.

10th Cir. 1994 (Utah). In this loan-loss case, the Tenth Circuit noted that Utah had not yet considered the meaning of "manifest intent," and the court turned to other jurisdictions to determine that manifest intent exists when a particular result is substantially certain to follow from an employee's conduct, and that manifest intent may be inferred from recklessness and other circumstantial evidence. Using this standard, the court found that the president's guilty plea alone did not conclusively establish manifest intent as required under the savings and loan blanket bonds, and that his intent would be a question of fact given his subjective proclamations that he intended to benefit his employer. *FDIC v. Oldenburg*, 34 F.3d 1529.

10th Cir. 1994 (Utah). The Tenth Circuit rejected insurer's argument that the jury should have been instructed that "manifest intent" requires that the employee actively wish for or desire a particular result. The court held that the jury was properly instructed that "manifest intent" exists when a particular result is substantially certain to follow from the employee's conduct and that fidelity bond's manifest intent requirement may be inferred from an employee's reckless conduct. *FDIC v. United Pac. Ins. Co.*, 20 F.3d 1070.

10th Cir. 1991 (Utah). A savings and loan association sued its insurer under a fidelity bond for losses incurred as a result of default on loans that were made by a former loan officer without loan committee approval. The Tenth Circuit affirmed summary judgment for insurer, holding that the possibility that the loan officer used poor judgment in making loans did not establish manifest intent to cause a loss. *First Fed. Sav. & Loan Ass'n of Salt Lake City v. Transamerica Ins. Co.*, 935 F.2d 1164.

M.D. Fla. 2011. Three employees of the insured filed workers compensation claims, which the insured paid. The insured later discovered the claims were fraudulent and sought reimbursement under an Employee Dishonesty Policy. In deciding whether the employees had the requisite manifest intent to cause the insured a loss, the court noted that the Eleventh Circuit has never decided whether to apply the substantial certainty test, the objective approach, or the specific intent test. The court did not resolve the question of which test applies. Instead, it held that under any of the tests, the employees had the requisite manifest intent. It rejected the insured's argument that the employees knew the insured had insurance to cover their workers compensation claims, and that the employees therefore intended to deprive the insurer rather than the insured. It held that both the insured and insurer were listed on the compensation checks that were made out to the dishonest employees, which the court held supported the conclusion that the employees had the manifest intent to injure the insured. *Bailey Indus. v. Amerisure Mut. Ins. Co.*, No. 5:10-cv-72-Oc-25, 2011 U.S. Dist. LEXIS 135945.

N.D. Ill. 2012. The insured's employee had embezzled from the account of a third party. The insured ultimately bore responsibility for the loss. In determining whether the insured had the requisite manifest intent, the court followed the substantial certainty test, but held that even that test was not satisfied. Because the dishonest employee had stolen from someone other than the insured, the court held that it was not substantially certain that the insured would actually suffer a loss. *Sperling & Slater, P.C. v. Hartford Cas. Ins. Co.*, No. 12 C 761, 2012 U.S. Dist. LEXIS 125897.

N.D. Ill. 2000. The insured's salesman allegedly bribed a customer's purchasing agent to purchase parts at inflated prices. The customer sued the insured for disgorgement of profits. The loss claimed was the disgorgement of profits resulting from the salesman's actions. The loss was not covered by the insured's CrimeGuard policy, which covered losses resulting from "dishonesty." The court found that the salesman did not have the manifest intent to cause his employer to disgorge profits obtained through his scheme. Such intent would require the absurd assumption that the salesman intended for his conduct to be discovered. *Williams Elecs. Games, Inc. v. Barry*, No. 97 C 3743, 2000 U.S. Dist. LEXIS 11154.

N.D. Ill. 1992. The bank alleged that its loan officer acted dishonestly by attempting to conceal a bank customer's overdrawn and delinquent accounts. The district court rejected a specific intent standard and held that to establish manifest intent, the bank need only show that the loan officer acted with the same degree of intent as required by the law of intentional torts. According to the district court, the purpose of the bankers blanket bond is to insure the bank from losses stemming from intentional torts committed by bank employees. *Affiliated Bank/Morton Grove v. Hartford Accident & Indem. Co.*, No. 91 C 4446, 1992 U.S. Dist. LEXIS 5919.

S.D. Iowa 2005. Bank employee issued "straw man" loans and failed to disclose financial condition of borrowers. The court held the financial institution crime bond to be a statutory bond under an Iowa statute that did not include "manifest intent" language. However, because "intent" was an element of "fraud" and "dishonesty" in the statute, the court did not consider the bond's "manifest intent" language as surplusage. The court further held that Iowa would likely apply a "clearly evident" or "results substantially certain to follow" intent standard and noted that "manifest intent" is ill suited for determination on summary judgment. *Kan. Bankers Sur. Co. v. Farmers State Bank*, 408 F. Supp. 2d 751.

D. Mass. 2010. An employee deposited the paycheck of the bank's CEO into his own account, instead of his own pay. He then complained that he was not receiving his own pay (without mentioning that he was receiving the CEO's pay). The court granted summary judgment for the insured, which necessarily required a conclusion that the employee had the manifest intent to cause the bank a loss. *FundQuest Inc. v. Travelers Cas. & Sur. Co.*, 715 F. Supp. 2d 202.

E.D. Mich. 2008. The insured was an escrow company. One of its escrow agents was taking funds meant for various closings and negotiating the funds for her own personal use. The court held that the agent had the requisite manifest intent to cause the insured a loss. The court noted that there was a dearth of Michigan law on the interpretation of the term "manifest intent," but the court followed Sixth Circuit law holding that the requisite manifest intent is present if the employee's actions are substantially certain to result in a loss to the insured. *Phillip R. Seaver Title Co. v. Great Am. Ins. Co.*, No. 08-CV-11004, 2008 U.S. Dist. LEXIS 78568.

D. Minn. 2001. Insurer paid the bank for sums its employee had embezzled, but denied coverage for sums paid by the bank to settle misrepresentation claims in lawsuit filed by bank customer and customer's creditor. The bank claimed the litigation was a direct consequence of the employee's embezzlement scheme and that the employee had the manifest intent to cause the losses incurred in the litigation. In an action on a financial institution bond, the district court held that an employee manifestly intends to cause loss when such loss is a natural consequence of the employee's actions. Under this standard, the bank failed to show that the employee's actions at issue in the litigation were part of the embezzlement scheme. *First Nat'l Bank of Fulda, Minn. v. BancInsure, Inc.*, No. Civ. 00-2002 DDA/FLN, 2001 U.S. Dist. LEXIS 21967.

D.N.J. 2012. The insured was a credit union. Some of its employees sold loans that the credit union had made without authorization. The court held that the employees had acted with the requisite manifest intent. The court held that the presence of such intent "could not be clearer," given that loans were illegally sold on the secondary market and the proceeds were not given to the insured. *Sperry Assocs. Fed. Credit Union v. Cumis Ins. Soc'y, Inc.*, No. 10-00029 (DRD), 2012 U.S. Dist. LEXIS 26839.

D.N.J. 2001. A loan officer concealed from the bank his knowledge that loans made to a large construction project were uncollectible and that the construction project was in danger of being unprofitable. The court applied a subjective standard to determine that the losses were not covered by the bank's financial institution bond. The court held that even if the loan officer was substantially certain the bank would suffer a loss, there was no evidence that his specific purpose was to cause the loss. *FDIC v. Nat'l Union Fire Ins. Co. of Pittsburgh, Pa.*, 146 F. Supp. 2d 541.

D.N.J. 1991. Predicting how the Supreme Court of New Jersey would rule, the district court rejected the insured's argument that a savings and loan blanket bond covered actions that were reckless or wanton, but taken without the subjective intent to cause a loss. The term "manifest intent" unambiguously required employee to act with "some degree of dishonest intent" to obtain a benefit and to cause a loss to the insured. *Oritani Sav. & Loan Ass'n v. Fid. & Deposit Co. of Md.*, 821 F. Supp. 286.

D.N.J. 1983. Under Insuring Agreement (A) of Bankers Blanket Bond, the question of intent to cause the insured a loss was one of fact, precluding summary judgment, and if an intent to benefit anyone financially was shown, the bank's loss would be covered. *Liberty Nat'l Bank v. Aetna Life & Cas. Co.,* 568 F. Supp. 860.

D.N.M. 1979. The president of a bank made loans in excess of the bank's legal lending limit to cover overdrafts, and the loans were not reported to the bank's board of directors. The court held that the president acted with the intent to injure the bank, and his actions were dishonest and fraudulent as defined in the Bankers Blanket Bond and the Excess Bank Employee Dishonesty Blanket Bond. *Plaza Del Sol Nat'l Bank v. Firemen's Ins. Co.,* No. 78-073-B, 1979 U.S. Dist. LEXIS 12876.

S.D.N.Y. 2009. The court adhered to the "substantial certainty" test and found that actions can circumstantially establish that an employee acted with the manifest intent to cause the insured a loss. *U.S. Alliance Fed. Credit Union v. Cumis Ins. Soc'y, Inc.,* No. 93 Civ. 10317 (PGG), 2009 U.S. Dist. LEXIS 83047.

Bankr. S.D.N.Y. 1992. A stockbroker employee violated a securities firm's established policy by trading from his own account without sufficient liquid assets to cover potential losses. The resulting losses were not covered by the firm's security dealer blanket bond. The court held that fidelity bonds covered losses due to embezzlement or embezzlement-like acts and were not issued to cover reckless or improvident trading losses or violations of the insured's orders. Though the employee intended to make money, he did not have the manifest intent to cause his employer a loss. *In re J.T. Moran Fin. Corp.,* 147 B.R. 335.

N.D. Ohio 2010. Employee of insured bank was an investment advisor who transferred money from his clients' brokerage accounts into his own. The insured was forced to reimburse the clients for their losses. In deciding whether the employee had the manifest intent to cause the insured a loss, the court held that the phrase "manifest intent" "does not establish a subjective standard; it establishes an objective one, meaning 'apparent or obvious.'" The court followed the substantial certainty test, holding that as long as the dishonest employee realized that his conduct was substantially certain to result in a loss to the insured, manifest intent was present. *First Defiance Fin. Corp. v. Progressive Cas. Ins. Co.*, **688** F. Supp. 2d 703, aff'd in part and rev'd in part by **688** F.3d 265.

S.D. Ohio 1998. A bank's CEO made a loan in excess of his lending authority. Evidence that the CEO was angry at the chairman of the board for failure to pay bonuses and that the CEO had made the unauthorized loan to "get back at the bank" was sufficient to raise a genuine issue of material fact that the CEO intended to harm the bank. *First Bank of Marietta v. Hartford Underwriters Mut. Ins. Co.*, 997 F. Supp. 934.

Bankr. N.D. Ohio 1988. The bankruptcy court applied an objective standard to find that an employee of a brokerage firm who falsely represented to customers his authority to sell shares at discounted prices had the manifest intent to cause his employer a loss. The court held that an employee has the manifest intent to cause a loss when he knows to a substantial certainty that his employer will sustain a loss, and an individual is presumed to intend the natural consequences of his acts. Thus, there was coverage under a securities dealer blanket bond because it strained credulity to believe that the employee did not know his employer would be responsible to compensate investors whose funds had been converted. *In re Baker & Getty Fin. Servs., Inc. v. Nat'l Union Fire Ins. Co. of Pittsburgh, Pa.*, 93 B.R. 559.

W.D. Pa. 2001. The former administrator of a guardianship estate pleaded guilty to embezzling funds from the estate. The subsequent administrator sued for benefits under an employee dishonesty policy issued to the former administrator's employer, a county guardianship service. The district court adopted the analysis of the Third Circuit because the Pennsylvania Supreme Court had not ruled on the meaning of "manifest intent." According to the Third Circuit, "manifest intent" means the employee acted with the specific purpose, object, or desire to cause the loss to the insured. Manifest intent may be proven by circumstantial evidence indicating the employee acted with reckless disregard for a substantial risk of loss, but mere recklessness or knowledge that a result was substantially certain to occur would not satisfy the policy language. *Shoemaker v. Lumbermens Mut. Cas. Co.*, 176 F. Supp. 2d 449.

E.D. Pa. 1995. In an action on an insurance contract containing an employee dishonesty coverage form, the court predicted that the Pennsylvania Supreme Court would reject a purely objective test of manifest intent and instead would hold that manifest intent under employee dishonesty coverage is determined by the external indicia of the employee's subjective intent. Deviating from a Pennsylvania Superior Court case, however, the court also predicted that the Pennsylvania Supreme Court would find that manifest intent could be established if the employee either desired the loss to result from her actions or knew that the loss was substantially certain to result. *Good Lad Co. v. Aetna Cas. & Sur. Co.*, No. Civ. A. 92-5678, 1995 U.S. Dist. LEXIS 9456.

E.D. Pa. 1992. The court applied an objective standard to determine that losses caused by a salesman's violation of his employer's policy restricting credit sales were covered by a fidelity policy. The court held that manifest intent requires more than a mere probability of loss, but does not require that an employee wish for or desire the result. *Keystone Floor Prods., Inc. v. Home Ins. Co.*, Civ. A. No. 91-1998, 1992 U.S. Dist. LEXIS 5310.

Bankr. E.D. Pa. 1992. Former employee's guilty plea to mail fraud charge was sufficient to establish coverage under a fidelity bond. Though the court stated it did not appear that specific intent to defraud was sufficient to establish coverage, it nevertheless appeared that the employee engaged in embezzlement or embezzlement-like acts. The employee removed and utilized employer's funds in a manner that permitted the inference that he intended to benefit himself at his employer's expense. It was clear from external manifestations of the employee's behavior that he had the requisite manifest intent to trigger coverage. *In re Lloyd Sec., Inc.*, Nos. 90-0985S, 91-1090S, 1992 Bankr. LEXIS 1452.

D.P.R. 2008. The insured's employees altered and manipulated account reconciliations. The insured prevailed in a trial against its insurer, successfully proving that coverage applied under an employee dishonesty provision. The insurer filed a renewed motion for judgment as a matter of law, contending that there was insufficient evidence to prove intent. The court disagreed. It held that as long as the employees were acting with knowledge that their actions were substantially certain to cause the insured a loss, that was sufficient to prove a loss. The insurer conceded that the evidence showed as much. Thus, the court denied the motion. *Oriental Fin. Grp., Inc. v. Fed. Ins. Co.*, 598 F. Supp. 2d 199.

D.P.R. 2004. A group of employees manipulated the reconciliations of cash accounts and concealed the true cash account balances, causing a loss to the bank. The court refused to grant summary judgment to the insurer, holding that the three crucial questions—whether a "loss" resulted; whether the employee had engaged in dishonest or fraudulent acts; and whether the acts were committed intentionally to obtain a benefit or to cause the financial group a loss—were properly left for trial because they were imbued with questions of intent. *Oriental Fin. Grp. v. Fed. Ins. Co.*, 309 F. Supp. 2d 216.

N.D. Tex. 2004. A retail securities brokerage firm sought coverage under a financial institution bond when two of its employees violated company policy and engaged in unauthorized trades in their employee accounts, resulting in a loss. Although both employees testified that they made the trades with the intent to make money for themselves, the court granted summary judgment in favor of the insurer and held the employees lacked the manifest intent to cause the brokerage firm's losses. The court concluded that knowledge that the employees would bear responsibility for any losses generated by the unauthorized trades merely acted as a "security blanket" to allow them to engage in the trades and did not create a fact issue on whether they had the manifest intent to cause the insured a loss. *Investors Trading Corp. v. Fid. & Deposit Co. of Md.*, Civ. A. No. 3:02-CV-2176-P, 2004 U.S. Dist. LEXIS 25906.

N.D. Tex. 1996. The court held that manifest intent does not require that the employee actively wish for or desire a particular result, but exists when a particular result is substantially certain to follow from the employee's conduct. Citing *Lustig I*, the court stated the employee's intent should be determined from her subjective motive and purpose, as well as by inferences from tangible manifestations of behavior. Under this standard, there was no coverage under the insured's crime policy because the funds embezzled by the employee did not belong to the insured. Thus, the employee did not intend to cause her employer a loss as a matter of law. *Lynch Props., Inc. v. Potomac Ins. Co. of Ill.*, 962 F. Supp. 956.

S.D. Tex. 1993. A bank president employed poor banking practices, failed to follow internal procedures, and misrepresented the condition of borrowers and the value of their collateral. The loss was not covered under a standard bankers bond because there was no evidence that the bank president intended to cause a loss, and no evidence that the loss was the result of anything other than incompetence and bad judgment. *Progressive Cas. Ins. Co. v. First Bank*, 828 F. Supp. 473.

W.D. Va. 1989. The bank's CEO made loans in excess of his lending authority and deposited participation funds into a borrower's account rather than using the funds to reduce the bank's liability. The court applied an objective standard to determine that the CEO had the manifest intent to cause the bank a loss, and that the loss was covered under the bankers blanket bond. Referring to the criminal law, the court noted that it can be inferred that a person intends the natural and probable consequences of his acts. *USF&G v. Citizens Bank of Tazewell*, 718 F. Supp. 471.

W.D. Wash. 2012. The court refused to apply the bond's manifest intent requirement, holding that the requirement was "repugnant to the Escrow Act, which 'requires that the bond cover "any fraudulent or dishonest acts" that result in a loss,' not merely those 'committed with the specific intent listed in the bond.'" *Ritchie v. Capitol Indem. Corp.*, No. C11-1903RAJ, 2012 U.S. Dist. LEXIS 106804.

Ala. 1986. The bank sued the insurer for losses resulting from activities of the bank president and for bad faith in delaying payment. A directed verdict on the bankers blanket bond claims should not have been entered because there was conflicting evidence regarding the "manifest intent" by the president to cause the bank a loss. Furthermore, the character and amounts of the claims constantly changed while the insurer was investigating, and this uncertainty justified the delay in handling those claims. *Ins. Co. of N. Am. v. Citizensbank of Thomasville*, 491 So. 2d 880.

Conn. Super. Ct. 1997. Insurance agency's employee retained payments that were due to customers of the insurance company. The insurance company reimbursed its customers and sought reimbursement from the agency. The agency's employee dishonest policy did not apply because the acts were not intended to cause the agency a loss. Instead, the acts caused a direct loss to the insurance company, and only an indirect loss to the agency. *ITT Hartford Life Ins. Co. v. Pawson Assocs., Inc.*, No. 940361910S, 1997 Conn. Super. LEXIS 1646.

Ill. App. Ct. 2013. The insured was a meat-packing company. One of its employees had been unlawfully implanting veal calves with hormones and steroids, concealing that fact from customers, competitors, and the federal government, and allowing the insured to make fraudulent claims that its veal did not contain steroids. The insured sought to recover the resulting loss, but the court noted that the employee had not acted with the intent to harm the insured, but had instead acted with the hope of benefiting the insured. *Ind. Ins. Co. v. Brown Packing Co.*, No. 1-11-3039, 2013 Ill. App. Unpub. LEXIS 988.

Ill. App. Ct. 1998. Bank employee embezzled funds from the bank and also failed to report suspicious activity that indicated a check kiting scheme in connection with a customer's account, even though the employee had been charged with the responsibility of monitoring accounts for check kiting. In an action on a financial institution bond, the court held that employee had the manifest intent to harm the bank when he desired to cause the consequences of his action or believed that the consequences were substantially certain to result. The employee's willful failure to perform his job, together with other evidence of embezzlement, outweighed any evidence of his attempts to pursue his employer's interests and was sufficient to find he had the manifest intent to cause his employer a loss from the check kiting scheme. *Oxford Bank & Trust v. Hartford Accident & Indem. Co.*, 698 N.E.2d 204.

Ill. App. Ct. 1998. In an action on fidelity insurance policies, the insurers moved to stay the lawsuit filed by the insured pending resolution of the insurers' prior-filed action in England, which was subject to English law. The court held that a stay of the coverage proceedings was appropriate, in part because a potential key issue, the meaning of "manifest intent," was an issue of first impression in England, and an issue of intense debate among American courts. Thus, it would be difficult for an Illinois court to predict how an English court would decide the matter. *Philips Elecs., N.V. v. N.H. Ins. Co.*, 692 N.E.2d 1268.

Ill. App. Ct. 1983. Summary judgment was granted to the insurer under a brokers blanket bond with a 1976 rider adding the manifest intent requirement because no manifest intent to cause the insured a loss was shown and because the employee received no financial benefit from the unauthorized trading except commissions. *Mortell v. Ins. Co. of N. Am.,* 458 N.E.2d 922.

Mass. Ct. App. 2005. An employee of insured company embezzled funds from another company with whom the insured provided administrative services. The court held that the employee did not have the manifest intent to cause the insured a loss where there was no factual dispute that the employee knew she was taking funds from the other company and not from the insured. Therefore, there was no coverage under the blanket employee dishonesty protection policy. Common incidents of ownership between the two companies involved did not alter the analysis because the employer was the only applicant and the only named insured. *Atlas Metals Prods. Co. v. Lumbermans Mut. Cas. Co.,* 829 N.E.2d 257.

Mich. Ct. App. 2006. The insured's employees had committed various wrongful acts in connection with certain real estate transactions. The insured was sued for those acts. The insured sought recovery from its insurer for the amounts it had to pay. As to employee dishonesty, the court held, with very little discussion, that the employees had not manifestly intended to cause the loss, and thus affirmed the holding that coverage could not apply under the employee dishonesty provision. *Five Star Real Estate v. Kemper Cas. Ins. Co.,* No. 258602, 2006 Mich. App. LEXIS 1626.

Minn. Ct. App. 1995. In an action on a financial institution bond, the court held that the following facts supported the conclusion that the employee intended to cause the bank a loss: the bank's employee coerced a customer into signing a promissory note and giving the loan proceeds to the employee; both the employee and customer declared bankruptcy; and the bank did not receive payments on the debt. The evidence in the record also supported the conclusion that the employee acted with the intent to benefit himself. *Citizens State Bank of Big Lake v. Capitol Indem. Corp.,* No. C1-95-321, 1995 Minn. App. LEXIS 929.

Minn. Ct. App. 1991. A bank's president, who was also the majority shareholder, disregarded regulators' instructions to write off problem loans and instead cashed certificates of deposit and used the proceeds to pay off the loans. The president also took the bank's money for his own personal use and falsified the bank's records. The court of appeals held that the resulting losses were covered by the bank's financial institution bond because the bank president's conduct demonstrated an intolerable disregard for established banking rules, regulations, and laws, and because a person is deemed to intend the natural consequences of his actions. The natural consequences of the president's fraud was a loss to the bank, thus, there could be no dispute that the loss was covered by the bond. *Transamerica Ins. Co. v. FDIC*, 465 N.W.2d 713, *rev'd in part on other grounds*, 489 N.W.2d 224 (Minn. 1992).

Minn. Ct. App. 1985. The employer sued under a commercial blanket bond to recover losses incurred when a sales manager submitted false orders, ordered unnecessary merchandise, and misused the company credit card. There was no evidence of manifest intent to harm the employer and to obtain a financial benefit for the employee other than benefits earned in the normal course of employment. *Benchmark Crafters, Inc. v. Nw. Nat'l Ins. Co.*, 363 N.W.2d 89.

Minn. Dist. Ct. 2010. The insureds were banks that serviced or participated in loans to Louis Pearlman. An attorney involved in preparing documents necessary for the loans forged certain documents in connection with the loans. The loans eventually went into default and the insureds sought to recover the loss under a fidelity bond. The court analyzed whether the attorney had the requisite intent to cause the insured a loss. It applied the substantial certainty test, asking whether there was a genuine issue of fact as to whether the lawyer's actions were taken with knowledge that the natural and probable consequences of the conduct was to cause the insured a loss. The court held that there were questions of fact on this issue and denied the insurer's motion for summary judgment. *Alerus Fin. Nat'l Ass'n v. St. Paul Mercury Ins. Co.*, No. 27-CV-09-3344, 2010 Minn. Dist. LEXIS 290.

N.J. 2004. Insured auto dealership sought coverage for its losses under the employee dishonesty provision of a "Commercial Package" insurance policy with a "Master Pak for Property" endorsement after its employee fraudulently provided installment contract approvals for several otherwise unqualified customers. The court adopted the substantial certainty test and concluded that summary judgment was inappropriate for either party because neither side offered sufficient evidence regarding the employee's intent when he falsified credit applications on behalf of the individual borrowers. The court therefore held that the issue of manifest intent was an issue of material fact for jury determination and remanded the case to the Law Division for further proceedings. *Auto Lenders Acceptance Corp. v. Gentilini Ford, Inc.*, 854 A.2d 378.

N.J. Super. Ct. Law Div. 1993. A senior loan officer of a savings and loan took certain actions without board approval, causing his employer to acquire unenforceable mortgage loans. The resulting losses were not covered because the employer's conduct was consistent with an intent to benefit his employer, not to cause it a loss. The court rejected the insured's argument that intent to cause a loss could be inferred from recklessness or from the loss itself. *N.J. Sav. & Loan Ass'n v. Fid. & Deposit Co. of Md.*, 660 A.2d 1287.

N.Y. App. Div. 1998. Insured broker-dealer sought coverage for payments made to settle class actions filed by shareholders of public companies that were the subject of various insider trading schemes perpetrated by insured's employee. The court noted that coverage is triggered by acts of embezzlement, at one end of a continuum of dishonest employee conduct, but not triggered by dishonest acts at the other end of the continuum, which, though they result in loss, were intended by the employee to benefit the employer. There was no coverage under the fidelity blanket bonds in this case because there was no evidence that the employee had the manifest intent to cause his employer a loss. *Aetna Cas. & Sur. Co. v. Kidder, Peabody & Co.*, 676 N.Y.S.2d 559.

N.Y. App. Div. 1988. In an action on a bankers blanket bond, a bank employee allowed a customer to receive immediate credit for five checks from certain drawers, even though the employee knew that checks from these drawers had previously been dishonored. When the five checks again were dishonored, the employee attempted to conceal the loss by debiting an unrelated account. The court of appeals held that the loss was covered. The court found that the employee acted with the requisite manifest intent because he knew the bank would ultimately bear the responsibility for the loss. The dissent, by contrast, stated that the employee may not have acted with manifest intent. According to the dissent, the employee's plea allocution indicated that the employee's initial crediting of the customer's account demonstrated an error in judgment that the employee later attempted to conceal from his superiors. *Nat'l Bank of Pakistan v. Basham*, 531 N.Y.S.2d 250.

N.Y. Sup. Ct. 2006. The insured broker dealer's client was running a Ponzi scheme. The insured's employees helped the client cover up the truth by falsifying documents. The insured itself pleaded guilty to securities fraud. The court agreed with the insurer that the bond did not cover the loss. The dishonest employees were stealing for, rather than from, the insured. *HSBC USA Inc. v. Gulf Ins. Co.*, No. 603413/04 (no published opinion).

N.Y. Sup. Ct. 1995. Stock broker employees made unauthorized trades on customers' accounts, without the customers' knowledge, as part of a scheme to artificially raise a publicly traded company's stock prices. The securities firm sustained losses when the scheme was detected by regulators and the firm was unable to meet margin calls. The court stated that the manifest intent provision limited protection under the bond to losses due to embezzlement or embezzlement-like acts. Thus, coverage was not triggered because the employees did not have the manifest intent to cause a loss, but intended to make money. *Cont'l Bank, N.A. v. Aetna Cas. & Sur. Co.*, 626 N.Y.S.2d 385.

Ohio App. 1993. A bank vice president used his access to bank computers to create fictitious loans. He converted the funds to his personal use and also applied the funds from the fictitious loans to pay off actual delinquent loans. Insurer relied on testimony of the vice president that he did not intend to cause the bank a loss, but merely to create the appearance that he was doing a good job by bringing past-due accounts current. In an action on a financial institution bond, the court of appeals determined that under the natural-and-probable-consequences test, the jury could infer that the vice president intended to cause the bank a loss and to obtain a financial benefit for himself. *First Nat'l Bank of Dillonvale v. Progressive Cas. Ins. Co.*, 640 N.E.2d 1147.

Pa. Super. Ct. 1995. In an action on a financial institution bond, the court recognized two distinct lines of cases construing "manifest intent" language. One line of cases applies an objective or "natural and probable consequences" test by which coverage is triggered if the natural and probable consequences of an employee's acts are financial harm to the bank, and benefit to the employee or others. The second line of cases applies a subjective test by which coverage is triggered only if the employee was substantially certain a particular result would be achieved. The court adopted the subjective test and held that the fact finder could consider the employee's testimony and external indicia or circumstantial evidence of subjective intent. *Susquehanna Bancshares, Inc. v. Nat'l Union Fire Ins. Co. of Pittsburgh*, 659 A.2d 991.

Pa. Ct. of Common Pleas 1988. Bank employee was convicted under a criminal statute under which guilt could be established by proof of reckless disregard of the bank's interests. The court held that the conviction was not sufficient to conclusively establish coverage under the bankers blanket bond. While reckless disregard might have been sufficient to establish coverage under older bonds, the current requirement of manifest intent means that conduct amounting to reckless disregard would not be covered. *Luzerne Nat'l Bank v. Hanover Ins. Co.*, 49 Pa. D. & C.3d 399.

Wash. 1993. The vice president of an escrow company diverted funds from escrow trust accounts to the company's operating account. The apparent purpose of the diversion was to cover general expenses. The court held that the resulting losses were covered by the company's fidelity bond. According to the court, a person acts with manifest intent when the person desires to achieve the particular consequences of the act or knows that the consequences are substantially certain to follow from the act. The court held that the vice president knew that his embezzlement of funds from the trust account was substantially certain to result in a loss in that the company would be unable to meet its obligations as trustee of the escrow funds. *Estate of K.O. Jordan v. Hartford Accident & Indem. Co.*, 844 P.2d 403.

Wash. Ct. App. 1990. An employee of a meat-processing company knowingly overpaid a supplier of raw materials. The supplier had allegedly threatened the employee that the supply of materials would be cut off if the employee failed to pay the inflated prices. The court held that the resulting losses were covered under a comprehensive fidelity insurance policy. According to the court, an employee has the manifest intent to cause his employer a loss when he desires to cause the consequences of his act or believes that they are substantially certain to result. The court determined that the jury could have found that the employee desired or was substantially certain that the supplier would obtain a benefit at his employer's expense. *Hanson PLC v. Nat'l Union Fire Ins. Co. of Pittsburgh, Pa.*, 794 P.2d 66.

Wis. Ct. App. 2003. Bank employees schemed to fraudulently obtain mortgage loans for insufficiently funded borrowers who did not otherwise qualify for the loans. The court noted in a footnote that the employees lacked manifest intent to cause the bank a loss because the losses did not result from the scheme but from the defaults on the loans. *Tri City Nat'l Bank v. Fed. Ins. Co.*, 674 N.W.2d 617.

C. Collusion

4th Cir. 1930 (W. Va.). A cashier worked in the bank, along with his children. Together, they misappropriated bank funds and used the funds in a business the family owned. The Fourth Circuit held that the word "connivance" in the financial institution bond meant "an agreement or consent, indirectly given, that something unlawful be done by another." The evidence was sufficient to establish that the cashier connived with his family and that the loss was covered by the fidelity bond. *Brandon v. Holman*, 41 F.2d 586.

6th Cir. 1992 (Tenn.). Insurer contended that the trial court improperly instructed the jury that mere silence could constitute collusion. The district court had approved the following jury instruction: "In determining whether a director or officer was in collusion with [the employee], you may consider the silence of that person or his or her failure to report the dishonesty to the Board of Directors or regulatory authorities as evidence of collusion." The Sixth Circuit agreed with the district court's finding that the instruction did not "equate silence with collusion: it simply states the logical conclusion that silence may be considered as evidence of such collusion." *FDIC v. Aetna Cas. & Sur. Co.*, 947 F.2d 196.

10th Cir. 1994 (Utah). The president and general counsel of a bank were accused of making fraudulent loans to a company that the president of the bank owned. Some bank employees knew of those loans, but the insurer failed to establish that those employees were not in collusion with the president and general counsel. Because the insurer admitted that the employees who were alleged to have made the discovery worked on the loans with the dishonest employees, the court upheld the finding of collusion made by the trial court. *FDIC v. Oldenburg*, 34 F.3d 1529.

10th Cir. 1991 (Okla.). A vice president's silence after learning of the chairman of board's check kiting scheme, which allowed the chairman to continue the scheme, was sufficient to uphold a finding of collusion. *Adair State Bank v. Am. Cas.*, 949 F.2d 1067.

S.D. Ala. 2006. There was not enough evidence to support an inference of collusion between two employees, where one employee set up a dummy account for the other. *Cont'l Cas. Co. v. Compass Bank*, No. 04-0766-KD-C, 2006 U.S. Dist. LEXIS 13009.

D. Ariz. 1994. The court upheld summary judgment for insurer as to collusion (for purposes of discovery/termination) because the mere fact that bank officers followed the president's orders in funding and documenting an illegal loan was not sufficient to create a fact issue on collusion. *Resolution Trust Corp. v. Aetna Cas. & Sur. Co.*, 873 F. Supp. 1386.

D. Ariz. 1990. The district court held that the bond did not cover a bank officer's conduct in making an under-collateralized loan to illiquid borrowers. Under Insuring Agreement (A) of the Financial Institution Bond, loans would be covered only if the bank could demonstrate that the bank officer was in collusion with borrowers. According to the district court, "collusion" is synonymous with "conspiracy." The fact that loans were allegedly supported by worthless collateral or that loans were made negligently or recklessly did not create an inference of conspiracy. *Standard Chartered Bank v. Milus*, 826 F. Supp. 310.

D. Mont. 1990. Two employees who actively attempted to disclose to the other board members the wrongdoing of one another were not in a collusive relationship but instead were adverse to one another. *Fed. Sav. & Loan Ins. Corp. v. Aetna Cas. & Sur. Co.*, 785 F. Supp. 867.

S.D. Tex. 1993. The bank president made numerous unsound loans. The loss was not covered under the bankers blanket bond because there was no evidence of collusion. The court stated that in order to trigger coverage, there must be more than evidence of a borrower's gain. There must be some evidence of the banker's secret personal gain from which collusion may be inferred. *Progressive Cas. Ins. Co. v. First Bank*, 828 F. Supp. 473.

Ill. App. Ct. 1991. Two employees rented post office boxes and opened checking accounts under the auspices of nonexistent companies and then submitted fraudulent invoices to their employer. They also diverted the insured's funds by fraudulently submitting personal expenses for payment. The scheme was accomplished by mutual approval of each other's expense reports. Finding no Ohio cases construing the collusion requirement of a comprehensive crime policy, the court looked to Tennessee law. The court held that collusion does not require the employees to jointly initiate a common scheme. Collusion is established if each employee begins stealing independently, but later becomes sufficiently concerned and implicated in each other's fraud. The employees were deemed to have acted in collusion when they discovered or became aware of each other's scheme and overtly assisted, not merely in concealing the fraud, but in perpetrating it. *Purdy Co. of Ill. v. Transp. Ins. Co., Inc.*, 568 N.E.2d 318.

Minn. Dist. Ct. 2010. The insureds were banks that serviced or participated in loans to Louis Pearlman. An attorney involved in preparing documents necessary for the loans forged certain documents in connection with the loans. The loans eventually went into default and the insureds sought to recover the loss under a fidelity bond. The court analyzed whether any collusion had occurred. It relied on a dictionary definition of "collusion": "secret agreement or cooperation, especially for an illegal or deceitful purpose." The court also noted that collusion could be proven through circumstantial evidence. Ultimately, the court held that there was a question of fact on whether any collusion had occurred. It noted that there was some evidence suggesting that the dishonest attorney had colluded with bank officials. *Alerus Fin. Nat'l Ass'n v. St. Paul Mercury Ins. Co.*, No. 27-CV-09-3344, 2010 Minn. Dist. LEXIS 290.

D. Financial Benefit

2d Cir. 1989 (N.Y.). In an action on a brokers blanket bond, the court of appeals held that the trial court had erroneously refused to give an instruction on "manifest intent." A new trial was not necessary, however, because there was no evidence to prove that the investment firm owner intended to obtain a financial benefit when he recklessly and imprudently made risky investments. *Glusband v. Fittin Cunningham & Lauzon, Inc.*, 892 F.2d 208.

3d Cir. 2004 (Pa.). In an action on a financial institution bond, the court held that it was not sufficient simply to show that a financial benefit to a third party occurred. Rather, the insured had to show that the employee acted with manifest intent to obtain the benefit for himself or a third party. *Hudson United Bank v. Progressive Cas. Ins. Co.*, 112 F. App'x 170.

5th Cir. 1995 (La.). A chief lending officer engaged in a pattern of dishonest conduct, receiving bribes and kickbacks in connection with loans, and failed to disclose business relationships with borrowers. In an action on a bank's financial institution bond, the court held that the evidence supported an inference that the chief lending officer would not have approved risky loans that probably would have caused the bank a loss had he not had a personal stake in the outcome. *FDIC v. Fid. & Deposit Co. of Md.*, 45 F.3d 969.

6th Cir. 1998 (Ky.). The Sixth Circuit held that the bankers blanket bond did not provide coverage for certain fraudulent acts of the insureds' employees. However, the court of appeals disavowed any language in the district court's opinion that could be construed as meaning that "manifest intent" requires an employee to actually receive a personal monetary benefit. The law of the circuit requires only that the employee intended to have received such a benefit. *Ins. Co. of N. Am. v. Liberty United Bancorp., Inc.*, No. 96-6502, 1998 U.S. App. LEXIS 3781 (unpublished table opinion).

8th Cir. 1993 (S.D.). A bank's successor brought suit against insurer under a financial institution bond for dishonest acts of bank president. The court of appeals held that unrealized gain on stock purchased by the bank president did not constitute a financial benefit for the purposes of the bond. *First Dakota Nat'l Bank v. St. Paul Fire & Marine Ins. Co.*, 2 F.3d 801.

N.D. Ill. 1992. A bank alleged that a loan officer acted dishonestly by attempting to conceal a bank customer's overdrawn and delinquent accounts. The district court held that the overdrafts the loan officer attempted to conceal were "loans" within the meaning of Insuring Agreement (A) of the Bankers Blanket Bond, but that there was an issue of material fact regarding whether the loan officer obtained a financial benefit in excess of $2,500. *Affiliated Bank/Morton Grove v. Hartford Accident & Indem. Co.*, No. 91 C 4446, 1992 U.S. Dist. LEXIS 5919.

S.D. Iowa 2005. Analyzing a financial institution crime bond, held to be a statutory bond under Iowa law, the court gave effect to language in the bond requiring a financial benefit in the case of loan losses, despite potential inconsistency with the statute, which did not have such a requirement. The court then held that where there are dishonest loans forming part of the same course of conduct, it is not necessary to demonstrate a financial benefit as to each individual transaction where language in the bond referred to "transactions" in the aggregate. *Kansas Bankers Surety Co. v. Farmers State Bank*, 408 F. Supp. 2d 751.

E.D. La. 2007. Employees participated in a fraudulent mortgage scheme. Insurer moved for summary judgment and argued that the bank had not shown any financial benefit to the employee. The bank, however, argued that one of the employees received a free property appraisal from one of the appraisers allegedly involved in the scheme. The court found that the alleged free appraisal raised an issue of fact and denied the insurer's motion as to Insuring Agreement (A). *First Guar. Bank v. BancInsure, Inc.*, No. 06-3497, 2007 U.S. Dist. LEXIS 30934.

M.D. La. 2008. An employee was misrepresenting that apartments were being rented so that he would receive commissions that he was not entitled to. Employer sought coverage under its Commercial Crime Policy for what it believed were lost rents it would otherwise receive. The court granted the insurer summary judgment. It concluded that the employee received no financial benefit other than commissions, which were not considered financial benefits under the policy. Thus, the lost rent did not result from covered employee dishonesty. *Palm Hills Props., L.L.C. v. Cont'l Ins. Co.*, No. 07-668-RET-SCR, 2008 U.S. Dist. LEXIS 56095.

S.D. Miss. 2010. A bank customer borrowed money from several banks and gave them each first liens on a single piece of real estate as collateral. An attorney schemed with the customer and certified to each bank that the property was unencumbered. The customer defaulted, causing the insured bank a loss. Insurer denied coverage because there was no showing of an improper financial benefit to the attorney (who was also the insured's employee). The court disagreed and pointed to the many perks that the customer/borrower provided to the attorney in exchange for providing false statements to banks. The court considered whether those perks and payments were "in connection with" the improper statements or whether they were in connection with legitimate services that the attorney provided. The word "connection" had broad meaning, and there clearly was some connection between the improper benefits the customer was paying to the attorney and his provision of fraudulent documents to the banks. *Peoples Bank of the S. v. BancInsure, Inc.*, 753 F. Supp. 2d 649.

D.N.J. 1983. In an action on a bankers blanket bond, the court held that the question of intent to cause the insured a loss is one of fact, precluding summary judgment. If an intent to benefit anyone financially was shown, the bank's loss would be covered. *Liberty Nat'l Bank v. Aetna Life & Cas. Co.,* 568 F. Supp. 860.

S.D. Ohio 1998. Bank's CEO made a loan in excess of his lending authority. In an action on a financial institution bond, the district court rejected the bank's argument that alleged enhancement of CEO's prestige in the community and enhancement of CEO's performance at the bank constituted financial benefits sufficient to trigger coverage. *First Bank of Marietta v. Hartford Underwriters Mut. Ins. Co.*, 997 F. Supp. 934.

Bankr. E.D. Pa. 1987. Debtor's president and other high-level employees borrowed substantial sums through debtor and then fraudulently attempted to liquidate the obligations upon which they were personally liable. Employees invaded debtor's escrow accounts and used the funds to retire debt obligations that were personally guaranteed by the employees. In an action on a fidelity bond, the bankruptcy court held that retirement of personally guaranteed debts constituted a financial benefit to the employees. *In re Leedy Mortgage Co.*, 76 B.R. 440.

S.D. Tex. 1993. A bank president employed poor banking practices, failed to follow internal procedures, and misrepresented the condition of borrowers and the value of their collateral. The court held that the loss was not covered under a standard bankers bond. There was no evidence that the bank president intended to obtain a financial benefit, and no evidence that the loss was the result of anything other than incompetence and bad judgment. *Progressive Cas. Ins. Co. v. First Bank*, 828 F. Supp. 473.

Cal. Ct. App. 2002. In an action on a financial institution bond, the court of appeals affirmed summary judgment for the insurer. The burden was on the insured mortgage lender to demonstrate that employees who allegedly participated in a fraudulent loan scheme acted with intent to receive a financial benefit. The mortgage lender failed to adduce evidence establishing that the value of a benefit received by employees exceeded $2,500. *Mortgage Assocs., Inc. v. Fid. & Deposit Co. of Md.*, 129 Cal. Rptr. 2d 365.

Ga. Ct. App. 2008. The insured was a law firm whose employee was engaged in a check kiting scheme to take money from the firm's escrow account. She would shuffle money among different files, creating an artificial float and siphoning off funds. But the employee had deposited some of the checks at issue back into the escrow account. The court held that under these circumstances, not only was there no loss, but there also was no financial benefit to the employee. *Lee, Black, Hart & Rouse, P. C. v. Travelers Indem. Co.*, 291 Ga. App. 838.

Ill. App. Ct. 1983. Summary judgment was granted to the insurer pursuant to a brokers blanket bond with 1976 rider language adding a manifest intent requirement. No manifest intent to cause the insured a loss was shown and the employee received no financial benefit from the unauthorized trading except commissions. *Mortell v. Ins. Co. of N. Am.*, 458 N.E.2d 922.

Minn. Ct. App. 1995. In an action on a financial institution bond, the court held that the following facts supported the conclusion that the employee intended to cause the bank a loss: the bank's employee coerced a customer into signing a promissory note and giving the loan proceeds to the employee; both the employee and customer declared bankruptcy; and the bank did not receive payments on the debt. The evidence in the record also supported the conclusion that the employee acted with the intent to benefit himself. *Citizens State Bank of Big Lake v. Capitol Indem. Corp.*, No. C1-95-321, 1995 Minn. App. LEXIS 929.

Minn. Ct. App. 1985. The employer sued the insurer on a commercial blanket bond to recover losses incurred when a sales manager submitted false orders, ordered unnecessary merchandise, and misused the company credit card. The court held that there was no coverage for the loss. The court rejected the insured's argument that the employee's four months of employment before the fraud was discovered satisfied the financial benefit requirement of the bond. *Benchmark Crafters, Inc. v. Nw. Nat'l Ins. Co.,* 363 N.W.2d 89.

N.J. 2004. An auto dealership employee fraudulently provided installment contract approvals for several otherwise unqualified customers. The dealership sought coverage for its losses under its "Commercial Package" insurance policy with a "Master Pak for Property" endorsement containing an "Employee Dishonesty" provision. The court denied summary judgment in both parties' motions, and remanded the case for jury determination of whether the employee obtained a financial benefit at the dealership's expense. The court further noted that had the insurer wanted to ensure that coverage under this policy would be limited to circumstances where the employee acted with the specific intent to benefit himself or another, it could have done so by replacing the term "manifest intent" with the phrase "specific intent or desire" in the policy. *Auto Lenders Acceptance Corp. v. Gentilini Ford, Inc.*, 854 A.2d 378.

Ohio Ct. App. 1993. A bank vice president used his access to bank computers to create fictitious loans. He converted the funds for his personal use and also applied the funds from the fictitious loans to pay off actual delinquent loans. Insurer relied on testimony of the vice president that he did not intend to cause the bank a loss, but merely to create the appearance that he was doing a good job by bringing past due accounts current. In an action on a financial institution bond, the court of appeals determined that under a natural-and-probable-consequences test, the jury could infer that the vice president intended to cause the bank a loss and to obtain a financial benefit for himself. *First Nat'l Bank of Dillonvale v. Progressive Cas. Ins. Co.*, 640 N.E.2d 1147.

Pa. Super. Ct. 1999. A bank employee colluded with a bank customer to defraud the bank by manipulating a floor plan financing system in order to obtain financing for nonexistent vehicles. In an action on a financial institution bond, the court of appeals affirmed summary judgment for insurer. The bank failed to show that an employee who colluded with the bank customer in the fraudulent loan scheme obtained a financial benefit in excess of $2,500. Unrealized gain on stock purchase and sale did not constitute a financial benefit. *First Philson Bank, N.A. v. Hartford Fire Ins. Co.*, 727 A.2d 584.

Wash. 1993. The vice president of an escrow company diverted funds from escrow trust accounts to the company's operating account in order to cover general operating expenses, including payments on debts for which vice president was personally liable. The Supreme Court of Washington held that the diversion of funds constituted a financial benefit to the vice president under a comprehensive fidelity insurance policy. Furthermore, to the extent the diversions kept the company afloat, the vice president benefited in his role as a shareholder. *Estate of K.O. Jordan v. Hartford Accident & Indem. Co.*, 844 P.2d 403.

E. Benefits of Employment

3d Cir. 2004 (Pa.). In an action on a fidelity bond, the insured argued that it was fraudulently induced to overpay nonexistent profits to an entity, presumably considered an "employee," with which it had a profit-sharing agreement in exchange for that entity's administration of an insurance premium financing program. The insured argued that fraudulently obtained financial benefits are not benefits of employment because they are not, by definition, earned in the normal course of employment. The court disagreed, holding that "in the normal course of employment" merely defined a type of excluded benefits, namely those the insured provides knowingly to its employees as part of a compensation scheme, and thus the insured had not made a prima facie case for coverage. *Hudson United Bank v. Progressive Cas. Ins. Co.*, 112 F. App'x 170.

3d Cir. 2000 (N.J.). The court of appeals held that "golden handcuff payments" obtained dishonestly were not covered by the Savings and Loan Blanket Bond. The bond does not provide coverage when the employee's purpose is to obtain the type of financial benefit that the insured knowingly provides its employees as part of its compensation scheme and as a result of the employment relationship. Exclusionary language "earned in the course of employment" describes the character of the payment at issue rather than the frequency with which the payment is received by the employee. The opinion includes a collection of cases interpreting the employee benefits language of the bond. *RTC v. Fid. & Deposit Co. of Md.*, 205 F.3d 615.

5th Cir. 2003 (Tex.). Unauthorized pay increases that the controller of a car dealership gave herself and another employee were not covered by car dealership's commercial crime policy. The language of the policy unambiguously exempted from coverage salaries obtained due to employee dishonesty from coverage. *Performance Autoplex II LTD v. Mid-Continent Cas. Co.*, 322 F.3d 847.

6th. Cir. 1987 (Tenn.). A broker-dealer's trader violated company policy by making trades in excess of her inventory limit. The court held that commissions the trader received and was not entitled to were not covered because the language of the fidelity bond explicitly excluded dishonest or fraudulent acts intended to enhance the employee's regular compensation. *Mun. Sec., Inc. v. Ins. Co. of N. Am.*, 829 F.2d 7.

8th Cir. 2010 (Iowa). The insured employed a technician who illegally obtained more than $100,000 by overstating on his time cards the number of hours that he worked. The court held that coverage could not apply because the hourly wages that the technician obtained dishonestly were plainly within the category of benefits of employment for which there was no coverage. *R & J Enterprizes v. General Cas. Co.*, 627 F.3d 723.

9th Cir. 1986 (Cal.). Employee of a stereo equipment manufacturer perpetrated a complex fraud that enabled him to collect commissions on fraudulent sales of stereo equipment. The insured brought suit for the commissions and other losses incurred as a result of the scheme. The insured argued that the commissions were covered because fraudulent sales were not its normal course of business. The court rejected the argument and held that the Comprehensive Dishonesty, Disappearance and Destruction insurance policies unambiguously excluded commissions. The court reasoned that, if the insured were correct, the exclusion of commissions would have no meaning or effect because fraud or dishonest acts are not usually part of the normal course of business. The court also rejected the argument that the commission payments qualified as "other property" covered by the policy. *James B. Lansing Sound, Inc. v. Nat'l Union Fire Ins. Co. of Pittsburgh, Pa.*, 801 F.2d 1560.

M.D. Ala. 1997. A car salesman dishonestly obtained commissions by allegedly manipulating a government price discount program. The insured car dealership suffered losses resulting from chargebacks to the manufacturer because of the improper discounts. The district court rejected the insured's argument that the policy was ambiguous. The unearned commissions were excluded because they were received "in the normal course of business," a term that the court construed as merely defining the type of excluded benefit. The insurer was not liable because the allegedly dishonest employee sought an excluded benefit. *Auburn Ford Lincoln Mercury, Inc. v. Universal Underwriters Ins. Co.*, 967 F. Supp. 475.

N.D. Ill. 1986. Life insurance salesmen perpetrated a fraudulent scheme to sell life insurance policies with the intent to obtain greater commissions. The district court predicted that the Illinois Supreme Court would find that the fidelity bond language was unambiguous and excluded coverage for all types of commissions, whether earned or unearned, if obtained dishonestly. *Hartford Accident & Indem. Ins. Co. v. Wash. Nat'l Ins. Co.*, 638 F. Supp. 78.

M.D. La. 2008. A dishonest employee embezzled money by receiving commissions when he misrepresented that apartments had been rented. The insured claimed lost rent for the apartments. Insurer was entitled to summary judgment because the bond required a financial benefit to the employee or someone else, when employee benefits, including commissions, were not a financial benefit. *Palm Hills Props., L.L.C. v. Cont'l Ins. Co.*, No. 07-668-RET-SCR, 2008 U.S. Dist. LEXIS 56095.

S.D. Miss. 2010. A bank customer borrowed money from several banks and gave each of them first liens on a single piece of real estate as collateral. An attorney schemed with the customer and certified to each bank that the property was unencumbered. The customer defaulted, causing the insured bank a loss. Insurer denied coverage because there was no showing of an improper financial benefit to the attorney (who also was the insured's employee). The court disagreed and pointed to the many perks that the customer/borrower provided to the attorney in exchange for providing false statements to banks. The court considered whether those perks and payments were "in connection with" the improper statements, or whether they were in connection with legitimate services that the attorney provided. The word "connection" was broadly defined, and there was clearly some connection between the improper benefits the customer was paying to the attorney and his provision of fraudulent documents to the banks. *Peoples Bank of the S. v. BancInsure, Inc.*, 753 F. Supp. 2d 649.

S.D.N.Y. 1986. An employee entered into an agreement with a third party involving stock loan transactions, which resulted in an artificial increase in the department's net profits and ultimately increased the employee's income under a profit-sharing formula. The employee's acts did not meet the definition of "fraudulent and dishonest acts" under the employee fidelity bond because the gain he sought was associated with his employment. As long as the financial benefits to him were in the form of salary, commissions, fees, or other emoluments of his employment, it was irrelevant whether they were honestly or dishonestly earned. *Morgan, Olmstead, Kennedy & Gardner, Inc. v. Fed. Ins. Co.*, 637 F. Supp. 973.

Bankr. E.D. Pa. 1987. A debtor's president and other high-level employees borrowed substantial sums through the debtor and then fraudulently attempted to liquidate the obligations, for which they were personally liable. The bankruptcy court held that the actions had no connection to their compensation, and thus, the fidelity bond's exclusionary clause for salary did not apply. *In re Leedy Mortgage Co.*, 76 B.R. 440.

M.D. Tenn. 1990. A bank director caused the bank to issue checks to a company in which the director was a stockholder. A portion of the funds was used to buy a life insurance policy for the director. The director designated the payment as "fees" in the monthly financial statement reviewed by the board. The director also instructed the bank's controller to issue monthly checks payable to the director for "executive committee fees," even though the director performed no services in exchange for the payments, and he admitted that the fee designation was for the purpose of concealing the payments. The district court stated that recovery is barred by the "employee benefits" provision when two conditions are satisfied: (1) the employer knowingly pays the funds to the employee; and (2) the employee defrauds the employer into believing the employee has earned the funds as compensation for his work. Neither condition was satisfied and the payments to the company and "executive committee fees" constituted pure embezzlement, which the FDIC was entitled to recover under a bankers blanket bond. *FDIC v. St. Paul Fire & Marine Ins. Co.*, 738 F. Supp. 1146, *aff'd in part, vacated in part by* 942 F.2d 1032 (6th Cir. 1991).

D. Utah 1984. Loan officers made loans to persons of questionable credit in order to collect the commissions. The district court held that the fidelity bond unambiguously excluded coverage for commissions. *Verex Assurance, Inc. v. Gate City Mortgage Co.*, Civ. No. C 83 0506W, 1984 U.S. Dist. LEXIS 21545.

Ala. 2002. Employees of the transit authority issued payroll checks in excess of their salaries to themselves. The losses were covered by the transit authority's fidelity policy. According to the court, the embezzled funds were not "salaries" because the funds exceeded the fixed compensation the employees were entitled to be paid. *Cincinnati Ins. Co. v. Tuscaloosa County Parking & Transit Auth.*, 827 So. 2d 765.

Ill. App. Ct. 1983. Salesmen employed by a licensed futures commodity merchant allegedly used fraud and deception to induce customers to purchase commodity options. The customers sued the merchant, and the merchant sought coverage under a brokers blanket bond. It was undisputed that the salesmen did not gain anything except a commission from the unauthorized trading alleged in the customer complaints. Thus, the court held that there was no coverage with respect to the customer claims. *Mortell v. Ins. Co. of N. Am.*, 458 N.E.2d 922.

Md. Ct. Spec. App. 2003. An employee was substantially overpaid during several payroll periods due to a data entry error. The employee ran from the building when confronted and never returned the overpaid funds. The court held that the "salary and benefits exclusion" clearly and unambiguously excluded coverage. The court observed that the "salary and benefits" exclusion has been in standard fidelity bonds since 1980 and that its purpose is twofold: (1) to avoid involving insurers in employer-employee disputes over salary, commissions, and benefits when the conduct of the employee is within the internal control of the employer; and (2) to counteract a trend in court decisions expanding coverage beyond the limit intended by the insurers. *ABC Imaging of Wash., Inc. v. Travelers Indem. Co. of Am.*, 820 A.2d 628.

Mich. Ct. App. 2012. The insured's employee in charge of payroll was cutting two paychecks to herself instead of the one that she was entitled to receive. The insurer argued that the loss was not covered because the benefit the employee received was additional salary. The court disagreed. It held that the employee's embezzlement more closely resembled the scenario of an employee making an improper "loan" from the company to herself, than it did a plan by an employee to induce her employer to erroneously issue her a salary check greater than her actual salary. The money taken by the employee was not salary. It was not included in her regular paycheck and she did not pay income tax or other withholding on the money. The court held that the money should not be considered salary simply because she stole it from the payroll account instead of a cash register. *Amerisure Ins. Co. v. DeBruyn Produce Co.*, 825 N.W.2d 666, 667.

Minn. Ct. App. 1985. The employer sued the insurer on a commercial blanket bond to recover losses incurred when a sales manager submitted false orders, ordered unnecessary merchandise, and misused the company credit card. The court held that there was no coverage for the loss. It was uncontroverted that the employee did not gain anything except his regular salary and expenses from the fraudulent acts. *Benchmark Crafters, Inc. v. Nw. Nat'l Ins. Co.*, 363 N.W.2d 89.

Minn. Dist. Ct. 2010. The insureds were banks that serviced or participated in loans to Louis Pearlman. An attorney involved in preparing documents necessary for the loans forged certain documents in connection with the loans. The loans eventually went into default and the insureds sought to recover the loss under a fidelity bond. The court analyzed whether the attorney had received an improper financial benefit. The court noted that the term "financial benefit" did not include employee benefits earned in the normal course of business. The evidence showed that the dishonest attorney had not received anything other than the fees he would normally charge. But, the insured argued that these fees were not earned in the normal course of employment because they were the result of work performed with a divided loyalty, amounting to a conflict of interest. The law required the attorney to return any such fees. The court rejected this argument and stated that the fees were earned in the normal course of business, regardless of whether they were earned through proper professional conduct. *Alerus Fin. Nat'l Ass'n v. St. Paul Mercury Ins. Co.*, No. 27-CV-09-3344, 2010 Minn. Dist. LEXIS 290.

Miss. Ct. App. 2005. Crooks used an altered power of attorney to lease a car from the insured dealership. The person who executed the power of attorney sued the crooks, the insured, and others. Insured sought to compel the insurer to provide a defense. The court affirmed summary judgment for the insurer in part because the only benefit to an employee was a commission, which was not a financial benefit under the policy. *Watson Quality Ford v. Great River Ins. Co.*, 909 So. 2d 1196.

N.J. Super. Ct. Law Div. 1993. A savings and loan association sought to recover under a "Servicing Contractor Rider" the commissions and fees it had paid to a mortgage debt servicing contractor. The contractor, who had also procured the mortgages and sold them to the savings and loan, defaulted on its obligations and later was found to have engaged in criminal conduct in connection with the mortgages. The rider excluded coverage for commissions and fees earned in the normal course of business. The court held that the commissions and fees were excluded from coverage because the contractor would have been entitled to receive them had it properly performed the services it had contracted to provide. The court noted that cases interpreting similar bond language did not require the commissions and fees be earned honestly for the exclusion to apply. *N. Jersey Sav. & Loan Ass'n v. Fid. & Deposit Co. of Md.*, 660 A.2d 1287.

N.Y. App. Div. 2002. An employee of a clothing manufacturer created fake purchase orders. Although the insured did not pay bonuses to its employees, the employee apparently was motivated by the hope of obtaining some form of extra compensation for generating a large sales volume. The insured sustained a loss when it manufactured the garments and then could sell them only below cost. The court held that the loss was not covered by the insured's fidelity insurance policy. The exclusion for employee benefits did not depend on the employee's receipt or entitlement to a bonus or other normal form of financial benefit, but on the employee's intent to obtain such benefit. *Jamie Brooke, Inc. v. Zurich-Am. Ins. Co.*, 748 N.Y.S.2d 5.

N.Y. App. Div. 2000. Insured's comptroller allegedly embezzled funds from a payroll account by secretly and fraudulently paying himself an unauthorized salary, commissions, and bonuses. The court held that, if the allegations were true, the insured's employee dishonesty policy endorsement would provide coverage because the insured did not knowingly make the payments and because the policy provided protection from embezzlement or theft. *Klyn v. Travelers Indem. Co.*, 709 N.Y.S.2d 780.

Pa. Super. Ct. 1999. A bank employee colluded with a bank customer to defraud the bank by manipulating a floor plan financing system in order to obtain financing for nonexistent vehicles. In an action on a fidelity bond, the court of appeals affirmed summary judgment for the insurer. Shares of the bank's stock received by employee through an employee stock option plan (ESOP), salaries, and bonuses were benefits earned in the normal course of business and thus were not covered. *First Philson Bank, N.A. v. Hartford Fire Ins. Co.*, 727 A.2d 584.

Tex. App. 1997. An employee dishonesty policy did not cover losses incurred when two employees manipulated the time card system to obtain compensation for time they did not work. *Dickson v. State Farm Lloyds*, 944 S.W.2d 666.

Wash. 1993. The vice president of an escrow company diverted funds from escrow trust accounts to the company's operating account in order to cover general operating expenses. The Supreme Court of Washington held that, to the extent the diversions kept the company afloat, the diversion of funds constituted a financial benefit to the vice president in his role as a shareholder, and such benefit was not excluded as an employee benefit earned in the normal course of business under the fidelity bond. *Estate of K.O. Jordan v. Hartford Accident & Indem. Co.*, 844 P.2d 403.

SECONDARY SOURCES

Elizabeth K. Ainslie, *The Major Provisions of the Financial Institution Bond*, *in* 2-8 BUSINESS INSURANCE LAW AND PRACTICE GUIDE § 8.03 (2015).

Samuel J. Arena, Jr. et al., THE MANIFEST INTENT HANDBOOK (Samuel J. Arena, Jr., et al. eds., American Bar Association 2002).

Robert A. Babcock, *History of Fidelity Coverage, in* COMMERCIAL BLANKET BOND ANNOTATED 3 (William F. Haug ed., 1985).

Scott D. Baron et al., *Recent Developments in Fidelity and Surety Law*, 41 TORT & INS. L.J. 429 (Winter, 2006).

George Biancardi, *Underwriting and Claim Issues in a Changing Market: A Commercial Crime Perspective* (unpublished paper presented at ABA TIPS FSLC, Toronto, Can., Aug. 1998, on file at the Stradley Library, No. 2870).

Thomas J. Burnside, *When Crime and Fraud Benefit the Employer: "Manifest Intent" or "Business as Usual"* (unpublished paper presented at the Northeast Surety & Fidelity Claims Association Claims Conference, Iselin, N.J., Oct. 1993, on file at the Stradley Library, No. 3064).

Norman R. Carpenter, *The Catch 22 of the Manifest Intent: Inferring the Obvious* (unpublished paper presented at ABA TIPS FSLC, Chicago, Ill., Aug. 1995, on file at the Stradley Library, No. 2467).

Gary M. Case, *"Manifest Intent": The Search for an Evidentiary Standard* (unpublished paper presented at the Northeast Surety & Fidelity Claims Association Claims Conference, Hartford, Conn., Nov. 1992, on file at the Stradley Library, No. 2150).

Jeffrey A. Ford & John S. Torkelson, *The Current Status of Manifest Intent Requirement in Fidelity Bonds* (unpublished paper presented at Surety Claims Institute, Lansdowne, Va., June 1997, on file at the Stradley Library, No. 2686).

Edward G. Gallagher et al., *A Brief History of the Financial Institution Bond, in* FINANCIAL INSTITUTION BONDS 3 (Duncan L. Clore ed., 2d ed. 1998).

Robert M. Horkovich et al., *Insurance Coverage for Employee Theft Losses: A Policyholder Primer on Commonly Litigated Issues*, 29 U. MEM. L. REV. 363 (Winter 1999).

Institution Bonds and Commercial Crime Policies (unpublished paper presented to the ABA Fidelity and Surety Law Committee Mid-Winter Meeting, New York, N.Y., Jan. 22, 1999, on file at the Stradley Library, No. 2932).

Robert H. Jerry & Michele L. Mekel, *Cybercoverage for Cyber-Risks: An Overview of Insurers' Responses to the Perils of E-Commerce*, 8 CONN. INS. L.J. 7 (2001).

Glenn R. Kazlow, *Division Among the Circuits: The Courts Wrestle with the Meaning of "Manifest Intent"* (unpublished paper presented at NBCA, Pinehurst, N.C., Oct. 2000, on file at the Stradley Library, No. 3064).

Michael Keeley & Christopher A. Nelson, *Critical Issues in Determining Employee Dishonesty Coverage*, 44 TORT & INS. L.J. 933 (Spring, 2009).

Michael Keeley & John R. Riddle, *Commercial Crime Policy Insuring Agreement 1: Employee Dishonesty and Employee Theft Coverage*, 1-120 APPLEMAN ON INSURANCE (2015).

Michael Keeley & Justin Melkus, *An Introduction to Fidelity Insurance: Essential Terms, Background, and History*, 10-111 APPLEMAN ON INSURANCE (2015).

Michael Keeley & Lisa Block, *"Manifest Intent"—The Waters Are Clearing; Or Are They?*, Fidelity & Surety Law Committee Newsletter (ABA TIPS Fidelity & Surety Law Comm.), Fall 2000.

Michael Keeley & Sean Duffy, *Investigating the Employee Dishonesty Claim: Interviewing Witnesses, Obtaining Documents, and Other Important Issues, in* HANDLING FIDELITY BOND CLAIMS 151 (Michael Keeley & Timothy M. Sukel eds., 1999).

Michael Keeley, *Critical Loan Loss Issues Under Insuring Agreement (A) of the Financial Institution Bond* (unpublished paper presented at ABA TIPS FSLC Mid-Winter, New York, N.Y., Nov. 1993, on file at the Stradley Library, No. 2120).

Michael Keeley, *Employee Dishonesty Claims: Discerning the Employee's Manifest Intent*, 30 TORT & INS. L.J. 915 (1995).

Michael Keeley, *Employee Dishonesty: The Essential Elements of Coverage Under Insuring Agreement (A); Where Are We Now With "Manifest Intent," in* FINANCIAL INSTITUTION BONDS 41 (Duncan L. Clore ed., 2d ed. 1998).

Christopher Kirwan, *Mischief or "Manifest Intent"?   Looking for Employee Dishonesty in the Uncharted World of Fiduciary Misconduct*, 30 TORT & INS. L.J. 183 (Fall 1994).

David T. Knight & Jeffrey D. Murphy, *Check Kiting Insuring Agreement (A)* (unpublished paper presented at So. S.&F. Claims Conference, Atlanta, Ga., Apr. 1993, on file at the Stradley Library, No. 2171).

Jane Landes et al., *Does a Criminal Conviction Equal Dishonesty? Criminal Intent Versus Manifest Intent*, 24 TORT & INS. L.J. 785 (1989).

Law Journal Press, INSURANCE COVERAGE DISPUTES § 11.03 (2015).

Robert L. Lawrence, *Manifest Intent and Insuring Agreement (A)— Where Are We Now?* (unpublished paper presented at ABA TIPS FSLC, Atlanta, Ga., Sept. 1994, on file at the Stradley Library, No. 1143).

T. Scott Leo, *Combined Fidelity and Liability Policies and the Role of the Litigator in the Next Cycle of Claims* (unpublished paper presented at ABA TIPS FSLC, New York, N.Y., July 2000, on file at the Stradley Library, No. 3069).

Randall I. Marmor, et al., *Recent Developments in Fidelity and Surety Law*, 39 TORT & INS. L.J. 421 (Winter, 2004).

Ronald G. Mund, *"Dishonesty v. Business Judgement v. Negligence: The Bankers Blanket Bond v. The Directors' and Officers' Liability Policy"* (unpublished paper presented at ABA TIPS FSLC, New York, N.Y., Jan. 1986, on file at the Stradley Library, No. 57).

Ronald G. Mund, *New Fidelity and Financial Institution Bond Endorsements and Case Law Interpreting Them* (unpublished paper presented at Surety Claims Institute, Hershey, Pa., June 1999, on file at the Stradley Library, No. 2978).

Dolores A. Parr & Gail K. Donovon, *Back to the Future: Proposed Fidelity Coverage for Financial Institution Bonds and Commercial Crime Policies* (unpublished paper presented to the ABA Fidelity and Surety Law Committee Mid-Winter Meeting, New York, N.Y., Jan. 22, 1999, on file at the Stradley Library, No. 2932).

Sam H. Poteet & H. Rowan Leathers, III, *Financial Institution Bond, Standard form 24)—Common Law or Statutory Bond? and Consequences of Such a Decision on Surety Defenses Such as Manifest Intent and Notice Requirements* (unpublished paper presented at the Third Annual Conference of the Southern Surety & Fidelity Claims Association, Atlanta, Ga., May 1992, on file at the Stradley Library, No. 2093).

Toni Scott Reed & Kevin White, *What is Employee Dishonesty, in* COMMERCIAL CRIME POLICY 31 (Randall I. Marmor & John J. Tomaine, eds., 2005).

Toni Scott Reed, *What is Employee Dishonesty and Employee Theft?*, *in* COMMERCIAL CRIME INSURANCE COVERAGE (Randall I. Marmor & Susan Koehler Sullivan, eds., 2014).

Paul H. Robinson & Jane A. Grail, *Element Analysis in Defining Criminal Liability: The Model Penal Code and Beyond*, 35 STAN. L. REV. 681 (1983).

Roger P. Sauer & Eric B. Levine, *Excluding Expert Testimony in Fidelity Bond Cases: A Practical Guide for Defense Counsel*, THE BRIEF, Summer 2002, at 66 (publication of the American Bar Association).

Frank L. Skillern, Jr., *Fidelity Coverage: What is Dishonesty?*, *in* BANKERS AND OTHER FINANCIAL INSTITUTION BONDS (1979).

Carol Z. Smith et al., *Recent Developments in Fidelity and Surety Law*, 50 TORT & INS. L.J. 367 (Winter, 2015).

Carol Z. Smith et al., *Recent Developments in Fidelity and Surety Law*, 49 TORT & INS. L.J. 205 (Fall, 2013).

Carol Z. Smith et al., *Recent Developments in Fidelity and Surety Law*, 48 TORT & INS. L.J. 237 (Fall, 2012).

Graves L. Stiff, III & Thomas L. Seldon, *Criminal Conduct and Manifest Intent: An Update* (unpublished paper presented at Nat'l Bond Claims Institute, Pinehurst, N.J., September 1992, on file at the Stradley Library, No. 2093).

Christopher R. Ward et al., *Recent Developments in Fidelity and Surety Law*, 47 TORT & INS. L.J. 215 (Fall, 2011).

Christopher R. Ward et al., *Recent Developments in Fidelity and Surety Law*, 44 TORT & INS. L.J. 459 (Winter, 2009).

Christopher R. Ward et al., *Recent Developments in Fidelity and Surety Law*, 42 TORT & INS. L.J. 475 (Winter, 2007).

Ron A. Yarbrough & Gregory L. Kennedy, *"Thou Shall Not Steal"— Manifest Intent and the Eighth Commandment in the New*

Millennium (unpublished paper presented at ABA TIPS FSLC, San Francisco, CA, January 2000, on file at Stradley Library No. 3024).

Chapter 4

The Insuring Agreements—

Employee Theft Coverage*

As discussed in Chapter 1, there are two modern standardized forms of crime insurance for commercial institutions on the market today.[1] One is the Crime Protection Policy[2] issued by the Surety and Fidelity Association of America.[3] It is written on an employee dishonesty basis, similar to the standard form Financial Institution Bond[4] issued by the SFAA. The second is the Commercial Crime Policy,[5] issued by the Insurance Services Office, Inc.[6] The CCP provides coverage not for losses caused by employee dishonesty, but for loss of or damage to money, securities, and other property resulting directly from "theft" committed by an employee.

At the time ISO adopted the employee theft language, several companies had already begun offering it as an alternative to coverage for employee dishonesty. There appears to have been several reasons for this movement. First, some in the industry believed that "theft," as opposed to the manifest intent requirement of the employee dishonesty insuring agreement that was more commonly used, would be more readily understood because "theft" is a more common term than "manifest intent." Second, there was a growing body of case law interpreting the manifest intent requirement, but courts continued to disagree over its

---

* By Michael Keeley and Carla C. Crapster, Strasburger & Price, LLP, Dallas, Texas, and Megan M. Manogue, Berkley FinSecure, Towson, Maryland.
1 See Chp. 1 herein, at 1.
2 Crime Protection Policy, SP 00 01 04 12 (SFAA 2012) [hereinafter CPP]; see App. herein, at 911.
3 Hereinafter SFAA.
4 Financial Institution Bond, Standard Form No. 24 (SFAA 1986) [hereinafter FIB], reprinted in Annotated Financial Institution Bond (Michael Keeley ed., 3d ed. 2013).
5 Commercial Crime Policy, CR 00 22 08 13 (ISO Props., Inc. 2012) [hereinafter CCP]; see App. herein, at 877.
6 Hereinafter ISO.

precise meaning and application. Thus, there was some thought that the theft language would avoid continued court battles. Finally, some thought that commercial entities would prefer a policy providing coverage for employee theft. Importantly, while using different language, it appears that in the vast majority of claims, coverage will not differ. Ultimately, fidelity bond coverage, regardless of form, is intended to be limited in scope, providing coverage for employee embezzlement and embezzlement-type losses.

There is a long history of cases discussing various issues that arise in the context of employee dishonesty claims. Some of those, including who is an "employee," and the meaning of a "direct" loss, also arise in the context of employee theft claims. Those cases are annotated in Chapter 3 of this book. Because the CCP was not issued until 2000, there is a much thinner body of case law discussing the meaning of "employee theft." Those cases are annotated in this chapter.

A.   Insuring Agreements[7]

1.   Employee Theft

We will pay for loss of or damage to "money," "securities" and "other property" resulting directly from "theft" committed by an "employee," whether identified or not, acting alone or in collusion with other persons.

For the purposes of this Insuring Agreement, "theft" shall also include forgery.

F.   Definitions[8]

23.   "Theft" means the unlawful taking of property to the deprivation of the Insured."

CCP, Insuring Agreement 1.
8   CCP, Definitions, 23.

COMMENT

The primary issue involved in analyzing the theft insuring agreement of the CCP is determining precisely what is intended to be covered. While "theft" is defined by the CCP to mean "an unlawful taking," one might ask exactly what constitutes an "unlawful taking." Does the employee have to act intentionally in order for his taking to be unlawful? Or, is it enough if his taking is not purposeful, but his actions are substantially certain to result in a "taking." And what precisely is a taking?

Query whether it is appropriate to look to the meaning of the term "theft" under state criminal law to determine when an act is unlawful. Problematically, there are substantive and procedural differences amongst various states' criminal offenses. Moreover, intent standards applicable to various crimes in the same jurisdiction often vary significantly. For example, under the Model Penal Code, the intent standards applicable to particular crimes include four distinct mental states: purposely, knowingly, recklessly, and negligently.[9] Applying one of these mental states as opposed to another may significantly affect the coverage analysis and lead to inconsistent results. On the other hand, the Model Penal Code and similar state criminal laws may also provide a basis to argue in favor of a standard similar, if not identical to, manifest intent. More specifically, the Model Penal Code provides that a "theft" occurs when a person "unlawfully takes, or exercises unlawful control over, movable property of another *with purpose* to deprive him thereof."[10] Reference to the actor's "purpose" suggests that the actor must have a subjective intent that the victim suffer a loss. Accordingly, this language of the Model Penal Code may support an argument that the manifest intent cases remain, at least to some extent, relevant to a theft coverage analysis.

In cases involving a simple embezzlement by an employee, the absence of "manifest intent" language likely will make little difference to the outcome of a coverage analysis under the theft insuring agreement. In simple embezzlement cases, there is rarely any debate as to whether the employee intended to cause a loss to the insured and to financially benefit. As a result, the outcome under a traditional employee dishonesty

---

9   MODEL PENAL CODE § 2.02(2) (2015).
10   *Id.* at § 223.2(1) (emphasis added).

insuring agreement and a theft insuring agreement should be identical in most, if not all, simple embezzlement cases. But, query whether in a more sophisticated embezzlement scheme, the lack of "manifest intent" language in the theft insuring agreement could influence a court's decision. For instance, if an employee engages in a fraudulent scheme to conceal previously sustained losses, with the intent of benefiting the employer, there clearly would not be coverage under a traditional dishonesty insuring agreement because the employee did not have the manifest intent to cause a loss to the insured or receive a financial benefit. There is a strong argument to be made that such activity by the employee should likewise not constitute "theft" under a theft insuring agreement. But it is possible that a court might rely on the "unlawful" nature of the activity by the employee and the fact that such activity ultimately resulted in the loss of money to the "deprivation of the Insured" to conclude that a covered "theft" occurred, regardless of the employee's ultimate motive. In short, the departure from traditional manifest intent language in the theft insuring agreement potentially opens the door for courts to reach results that vary from the well-rehearsed conclusions under traditional employee dishonesty insuring agreements.

The risk that a court would hold that a "theft" has occurred without any specific intent to cause the employer a loss should be tempered by the requirement for an "unlawful *taking*." Several recent cases have emphasized that not every loss caused by an employee's fraud or dishonesty is the result of a true *taking*. For example, the Western District of Texas has held that an employee did not engage in "theft" when he forged letters of credit on behalf of a customer of the insured.[11] The employee was engaging in this conduct so that the insured would continue selling product to the customer, even though the insured did not have sufficient credit to continue buying the product. The dishonest employee believed that it was in the insured's best interest to continue selling product and that the customer would be able to pay despite its credit problems. The court held that even though the loss had come about as a result of the employee's dishonesty, the dishonest employee had never had control over the property, meaning that he had never engaged in a taking. The loss at issue in this case should not have been covered

---

11   Tesoro Refining & Mktg. Co. LLC v. Nat'l Union Fire Ins. Co. of Pittsburgh, Pa., No. SA:13-CV-931-DAE, 2015 U.S. Dist. LEXIS 45168 (W.D. Tex. Apr. 7, 2015).

under an employee dishonesty insuring agreement because of the lack of manifest intent to cause a loss. But the requirement of a "taking" served a similar purpose in this particular case. Because the employee, though dishonest, had never actually possessed the property himself (because he did not intend to benefit from it or cause his employer a loss), there was no taking. This case illustrates that the taking requirement may sometimes serve the same purpose of ensuring that a commercial crime policy does not cover those instances where the employee has no intent to cause the insured a loss.

It is important to keep in mind that various insurers utilize their own versions of employee theft coverage.[12] And, as courts and commentators further weigh in on the appropriate interpretation and application of theft coverage, it is possible that the language of the theft insuring agreement will evolve. Therefore, when analyzing coverage under a theft insuring agreement, careful attention must be paid to the language of the insuring agreement and its particular definition of "theft."

OUTLINE OF ANNOTATIONS

A. Theft
B. Deprivation to the Insured

ANNOTATIONS

A. Theft/Intent

6th Cir. 2012 (Ohio). Hackers accessed the insured's computer system to obtain financial information of the insured's retail customers. They then used that information to steal from the customers. The insured had to make the customers whole, and sought to recover its loss under a commercial crime policy. The policy covered loss resulting directly from theft by "Computer Fraud." The court applied a proximate cause standard in applying the "resulting directly from" language, and thus held that the hackers' theft had resulted in a covered loss. The Sixth

---

12   *See id.* at 40.

Circuit affirmed the award of summary judgment in favor of the insured. *Retail Ventures, Inc. v. Nat'l Union Fire Ins. Co.*, 691 F.3d 821.

6th Cir. 2012 (Mich.). The insured was a trade association that had created an insurance agency to accept commissions from insurers who used the trade association to broker policies. An employee of the agency, which was distinct from the trade association, diverted those commissions from the agency (his employer). The court held that the insured was not entitled to coverage under an employee theft provision because the insured's loss did not result directly from the employee's theft. Although the employee had breached his fiduciary duty to the trade association, he had not directly caused a loss to it at the moment he diverted the funds from the agency. *Tooling, Mfg. & Techs. Ass'n v. Hartford Fire Ins. Co.*, 693 F.3d 665.

11th Cir. 2015 (Ala.). The insured's CEO made false statements in the application for the insurance policy at issue. It was also the CEO of the insured who was engaged in the wrongdoing that caused the loss the insured sought to recover from its insured. The CEO had stolen funds from the insured both before and after submitting the application. The court held that the CEO lied about whether the insured had the very checks and balances in place that would have presented his theft. The court held that the misrepresentations were material and made with the intent to deceive. The court rejected the argument that coverage had to apply because the CEO was acting adversely to the insured's interest. Instead, the court held that because the CEO was the sole contact for the insurer, the burden of any wrongdoing he engaged in fell on the insured rather than the insurer. The court affirmed the award of summary judgment in favor of the insurer. *Scottsdale Indem. Co. v. Martinez, Inc.*, 2015 U.S. App. LEXIS 10427.

11th Cir. 2011 (Ala.). An employee of the insured real estate company was also a board member who had influence over which properties the company purchased. He recommended that the insured purchase properties in which he had a financial interest without disclosing his interests to the company. When the insured found out, it argued that it could have purchased these properties at a much lower price, and sought to recover its loss from its insurer. The policy at issue covered employee theft, which was defined as the unlawful taking of money to the deprivation of the insured. The court agreed with the insurer (and the district court) that the employee's conduct, though dishonest, was not theft. It held that the employee had not "taken" money from his employer. *Hartford Fire Ins. Co. v. Mitchell Co.*, 440 F. App'x 759.

N.D. Ala. 2015. The insured's CEO made false statements in the application for the insurance policy at issue. It was also the CEO of the insured who was engaged in the wrongdoing that caused the loss the insured sought to recover from its insured. The CEO had stolen funds from the insured both before and after submitting the application. The court held that CEO lied about whether the insured had the very checks and balances in place that would have presented his theft. The court held that the misrepresentations were material and made with the intent to deceive. The court rejected the argument that coverage had to apply because the CEO was acting adversely to the insured's interest. Instead, the court held that because the CEO was the sole contact for the insurer, the burden of any wrongdoing he engaged in fell on the insured rather than the insurer. Following this same reasoning, the court also held that the dishonest employee's knowledge of her own thefts was imputed to the insured, resulting in the thefts being discovered before commencement of the policy, and not during the policy period. The court awarded summary judgment to the insurer. *Scottsdale Indem. Co. v. Martinez, Inc.*, 2014 U.S. Dist. LEXIS 135129.

Bankr. N.D. Ga. 1995. Four loans were alleged by trustee of insured to have constituted "theft." "Theft" was defined as "the unlawful taking of money . . . to the deprivation of the Insured." The insurers argued that no theft had taken place. The court stated that if the employee was unaware that a borrower had submitted false invoices backing the loans, he might not have been involved in an unlawful taking. If, however, the employee knew invoices submitted to obtain the loans were bogus and that the borrower had no intention of repaying, the transfers would have been unlawful takings. The insurer and insured filed cross motions for summary judgment. The court granted summary judgment to the insurers on two of the four loans because although the insured had shown that the employee had duped the insured's own lender into financing the loans, it had not shown that the employee was aware that the borrower in those transactions did not intend to repay its loan, nor that the employee was involved in fabricating invoices submitted with respect to the other. As to the two other transactions, the court refused to grant summary judgment on the "theft" issue. In one of those transactions, the trustee had admitted in pleadings that it was possible that a theft had not occurred (despite a payment made by the borrower to the employee after the loan). In the other, the court held that a theft did not occur as a matter of law merely because the employee had a business dealing with the insured or may have been reckless in issuing the loan. *In re Prime Comm. Corp.*, 187 B.R. 785.

E.D. Ky. 2010. The insurance policy at issue covered loss resulting from theft but it excluded loss resulting from wrongful conversion or embezzlement. The insured had suffered a loss as a result of its employees' taking of cattle that belonged to the insured. The employees had access to the cattle and were entrusted with transporting them. But the employees sold the cattle and kept the proceeds for themselves. The insurer argued that the employees' acts constituted conversion or embezzlement but not theft. The policy did not define "theft," "wrongful conversion" or "embezzlement." The court held that the terms were ambiguous and had to be construed in favor of coverage. It therefore concluded that the employees' conduct constituted theft. The court granted the insured's motion for summary judgment as to whether coverage applied. *Meridian Citizens Mut. Ins. Co. v. Horton*, 2010 U.S. Dist. LEXIS 28797.

E.D. La. 2004. Employee of insured manipulated accounts receivable to cause delinquent accounts to appear current to make herself and her department look better. As a result, the insured employer paid $200,000 in undeserved merit raises and bonuses to the employee and others and ultimately was forced to write off over 5 million in accounts receivable. Analyzing a CrimeShield policy that covered "loss of . . . 'money' . . . and 'other property' which results from theft by an 'employee,' whether or not identifiable, while acting alone or in collusion with other persons," the court held that a "theft" had unquestionably occurred because the account manipulation was an "unlawful taking" that deprived the insured of its property. However, the lost accounts receivable were not recoverable under the policy because they were not "other property" as defined under Louisiana law. Only the $200,000 in undeserved raises and bonuses were recoverable as they were monies paid out of pocket by the insured as a direct result of the employee's scheme. *Morris Kirschman & Co., L.L.C. v. Hartford Fire Ins. Co.*, 2004 U.S. Dist. LEXIS 17427.

N.D. Ill. 2009. The insured was an automobile dealer. One of its employees was helping customers falsify their credit applications to obtain cars they could not afford. A bank that had a lending arrangement in place with the insured would lend funds to these customers in reliance on their credit applications. The dishonest employee would receive a kickback from the customers he was helping to perpetuate this fraud. Eventually, many of the customers defaulted on their loans and the insured suffered a loss. The insured sought coverage under the employee theft provision of a commercial crime policy. The court held that the dishonest employee had engaged in theft because he had aided and abetted the customers in unlawfully taking the vehicles from the dealership, and the loaned funds from the bank that loaned the customers money on the faith of the falsified credit applications. The court was not persuaded by the argument that coverage could not apply because the theft affected the insured only indirectly, because it had directly affected only the lending institution. The court noted that the policy did not require the stolen property to be owned or possessed by the insured. Instead, it required only that the insured was "legally liable for the loss." The court thus granted the insured's motion for summary judgment. *Taylor Chrysler Dodge, Inc. v. Universal Underwriters Ins. Co.*, No. 08 C 4522, 2009 U.S. Dist. LEXIS 91187.

N.D. Ill. 2000. A "Crimeguard" policy defined a covered loss as "the direct deprivation of the Insured by a single act or series of related acts resulting from [the unlawful taking] of [money held by the Insured] to the deprivation of the Insured." The court held that an employee's payment of bribes to the insured's customer in exchange for the customer's purchase of items from the insured at inflated prices, ultimately resulting in the insured having to refund profits from the transactions, did not constitute "theft," which was defined more narrowly than "fraudulent or dishonest acts" found in other policies. Under another applicable policy using "manifest intent" language, the court held that for the loss to be covered, the employee would have had to intend that the insured pay back the profits, which would absurdly assume that the employee intended that his scheme be discovered. Thus, no coverage existed under that policy either. *Williams Elec. Games v. Barry*, 2000 U.S. Dist. LEXIS 425.

N.D. Ind. 2007. The trustee and secretary of a pension fund authorized the fund to purchase land for significantly more than it was worth, in exchange for a kickback. This caused the insured, which was the pension fund, to suffer a loss. It sought to recover under a commercial crime policy, apparently under an "employee theft" provision, but the opinion does not make clear exactly what language the policy included. The sole issue in the opinion is whether the claim for coverage was barred by a contractual two-year limitations provision in the policy. The court held that the provision was unenforceable because the policy was purchased to comply with ERISA. The court also held that there were issues of fact as to whether the insurer waived its right to enforce the limitations provision due to delay in analyzing and investigating the claim. *Ind. Reg'l Council of Carpenters Pension Trust Fund v. Fid. & Deposit Co. of Md.*, No. 2:06-CV-32 PS, 2007 U.S. Dist. LEXIS 15429.

E.D. Ky. 2014. The insured's employee was a salesman responsible for collecting funds for goods sold. He was pocketing some of the money that he should have been remitting to the company. The court held that the employee's actions clearly met the definition of "theft" and, even if they had not, that they would clearly have met the definition of "employee dishonesty." But coverage nonetheless could not apply because the same employee had engaged in the same wrongful scheme before, and the insured had allowed him to stay on despite his misdeeds as long as he repaid the money. The policy included language precluding coverage for a loss caused by an employee whom the insured knew had committed a prior dishonest act. Thus, coverage could not apply. The court awarded summary judgment in favor of the insurer. *Westfield Ins. Co. v. Jackson Wholesale Co.*, 2014 U.S. Dist. LEXIS 2306.

W.D. Mich. 2010. The insured was an automobile dealer who contended that two of its employees had engaged in three separate wrongs. First, it argued that the two employees used funds received on vehicle sales to pay current expenses rather than paying a lender, which the lending agreement required. Second, the two employees used income received after a certain date to pay expenses incurred before that date, which was also improper. Finally, the insured argued that the two employees provided inaccurate and incomplete information about the financial condition of the insured before selling stock in the insured to a third party. The court held that none of these wrongs constituted a "theft," which the policy defined as the unlawful taking of property to the deprivation of the insured. *Coopersville Motors, Inc. v. Federated Mut. Ins. Co.*, 771 F. Supp. 2d 796.

D.N.J. 2008. The insured, an automobile dealer, had an employee who was engaged in two separate dishonest schemes. First, he was embezzling money from his employer by converting to his own use money orders that the employer meant for third parties. Second, he was allowing customers of the insured to purchase cars far beyond what their credit would allow by falsifying their credit applications. Many of these customers defaulted on their loans to the insured, causing it to suffer a loss. The insured had a commercial crime policy in place that covered employee theft. The court held that the employee's conversion of money orders constituted a theft, but also held that the employee had engaged in only one "occurrence" of theft, even though multiple instances of the same misconduct had occurred. As to the employee's practice of falsifying credit applications, the court held that it did not constitute a "theft." The court noted that the policy defined theft as the unlawful "taking" of money, securities or other property to the deprivation of the insured. The court held that although the employee's actions may have been dishonest, they were not a "theft." *Pine Belt Auto. v. Royal Indem. Co.*, No. 06-5995 (JAP), 2008 U.S. Dist. LEXIS 84393.

E.D.N.Y. 2014. The insured was a specialty pharmacy and disease-management company. Its former employee had been responsible for purchasing pharmaceuticals for the insured. But unfortunately, that employee was obtaining pharmaceuticals for his employer from illegal sources. The employee would then dispense those medications to the insured's customers, most of whom were on Medicaid. When the scheme came to light, the New York State Attorney General sued the insured for claiming and obtaining reimbursement from Medicaid for the pharmaceuticals that were not eligible for reimbursement since they were obtained outside "legitimate" streams of commerce. The court denied the insurer's motion to dismiss, noting that dismissals are appropriate only if the terms in the policy are clear and unambiguous. But here, the court held that there were ambiguities in the policy language. With very little analysis, and no explanation of which terms were ambiguous, the court held that whether a "theft" had occurred could not be decided on a motion to dismiss because several of the key terms were open to different interpretations. *Allion Healthcare, Inc. v. Arch Ins. Co.*, No. CV 14-0147, 2014 U.S. Dist. LEXIS 137282.

S.D.N.Y. 1998. Several employees engaged in a scheme to cause losses, including the taking of unauthorized personal advances. The term "theft" was defined as "the unlawful taking of Money, Securities, or other property." The court noted that other courts had looked to state criminal law to define the term "theft." The New York criminal laws equated "theft" with "larceny," which included "wrongful taking, obtaining or withholding of another's property," including by false pretenses. The court ultimately decided that fact issues precluded it from granting summary judgment, but the court arguably implied that coverage could possibly exist based upon a theft by false pretense. *Titan Indus. Corp. v. Fed. Ins. Co.*, No. 94 Civ. 0726, 1998 U.S. Dist. LEXIS 23650.

N.D. Ohio 2013. Guyan International hired the insured to administer its employee benefit plan. But the insured's employees had a practice of delaying payment of employee benefits as long as possible and using the funds that Guyan International had deposited with the insured to pay for the insured's operating expenses. But no employee actually took Guyan International's funds or embezzled them. When the scheme came to light and it became clear that the insured did not have all of Guyan's funds, as it should have, a claim for insurance coverage followed. The policy at issue covered loss resulting directly from employee theft, which was defined as the unlawful taking of property. The court noted that neither "unlawful" nor "taking" was defined in the policy. It looked to Ohio's definition of "theft." The court held that theft was not limited to an embezzlement-like act but instead could encompass any fraudulent or dishonest criminal act. The court held that when the insured exercised control over the Guyan funds without Guyan's consent, it deprived Guyan of the plan funds for immediate payment, which constituted a theft. *Guyan Int'l, Inc. v. Prof'l Benefits Adm'rs, Inc.*, No. 5-10-CV-823, 2013 U.S. Dist. LEXIS 46297.

W.D. Tenn. 2009. An employee of the insured had access to the personal bank account of one of the insured's executives. She abused that access by stealing funds from it for her own personal use. Importantly, however, the funds she stole were not in the *insured's* bank account. The insured sought to recover the stolen money from its insurer, under an employee theft provision. But the policy at issue included an "Ownership" clause, which provided that coverage for employee theft was limited to theft of property owned by the insured or for which the insured was legally liable, or that the insured held. Here, none of those tests were satisfied. Thus, the court awarded summary judgment in favor of the insurer. *Loeb Props. v. Fed. Ins. Co.*, 663 F. Supp. 2d 640.

W.D. Tex. 2015. The insured was in the oil refinery business. After refining the fuel, the insured would sell it to a third party, Enmex, on credit. Unfortunately, Enmex could not afford to buy as much of the fuel from the insured as it was actually purchasing. One of the employees in the insured's credit department was lying and forging letters of credit to make it appear that Enmex had more collateral available to secure its purchase of the fuel than it actually had. When Enmex was ultimately unable to pay for the fuel, the insured suffered a loss and sought to recover it from the insurer. The policy at issue covered direct loss from employee theft, which was defined as unlawful taking to the deprivation of the insured. The Employee Theft insuring agreement added that "For purposes of this Insuring Agreement, 'theft' shall also include forgery." The insured relied on this language to argue that "theft" had occurred here because the dishonest employee had been forging letters of credit. But the court disagreed. It held that an unlawful taking required either possession of the property by the employee or the employee's dominion or control over the property. The fuel sold to Enmex had therefore not been part of a "theft" because the dishonest employee did not exercise control over the fuel at any time, he merely ensured that it was sold to Enmex. The court granted the insurer summary judgment, and denied the insured's motion for partial summary judgment. *Tesoro Refining & Mktg. Co. LLC v. Nat'l Union Fire Ins. Co. of Pittsburgh, Pa.*, No. SA:13-CV-931-DAE, 2015 U.S. Dist. LEXIS 45168.

Cal. App. 2007. The insured was a marketing company responsible for putting together promotional games and contests for McDonalds, one of its clients. One of the insured's employees organized a network of accomplices and coconspirators to funnel high-value winning game pieces to specific individuals. The dishonest employee received kickbacks from the "winners." When the scheme came to light, the insured faced a number of lawsuits, and sought to recover part of its eventual losses from its insurer. The policy at issue covered "direct losses of Money, Securities or other property caused by Theft or forgery by any Employee of any Insured." The insured argued that the dishonest employee had engaged in theft of the winning game pieces that he helped funnel into the hands of his accomplices. The court seemed to agree that there had been a theft, but it held that the resulting loss was borne by McDonalds, not the insured (the marketing company whose employee orchestrated the scheme). The court therefore affirmed the award of summary judgment in the insurer's favor. *Simon Mktg., Inc. v. Gulf Ins. Co.*, 57 Cal. Rptr. 3d 49.

Bankr. N.D. Ga. 1995. An employee made loans, relying on invoices as collateral. Those invoices turned out to be false and the loans went into default. The court concluded that "whether the losses were the results of theft, 'taking' by [the principal] that was 'unlawful'" turns on whether the principal was aware that the invoices were false and that the customer had no intent to repay the loan. The court stated, "If he knew that invoices were bogus and that a customer had no ability or intention of repaying, the transfers would have been an unlawful taking by [the principal]." In other words, the court held that no "theft" or "taking" had occurred unless the principal knew that the advanced funds would not be repaid. *In re Prime Commercial Corp.*, 187 B.R. 785.

Ill. Ct. App. 1993. The insured was a paper distributor. It claimed a loss as a result of "unidentifiable" employee theft. The insurer denied coverage, contending that there was no proof that an employee theft had occurred and that the loss was based solely on an inventory calculation. The court granted summary judgment in favor of the insured, but the jury awarded no damages. On appeal, the court held that the summary judgment was improperly granted and that there were fact issues regarding the claimed theft. The primary issue was whether a theft had occurred at all. Thus, the case does not provide much guidance on the meaning of "theft." *Bradner Central Co. v. Fed. Ins. Co.*, 628 N.E.2d 1129.

Mass. Dist. Ct. 1992. The principal managed the insured's day-trading program that was governed by strict guidelines. By accident, the principal violated these guidelines, and the insured suffered significant losses as a result. To cover up his mistake, the principal continued to violate the guidelines in the hopes that he would win back his losses and avoid having to confess his error. The court found that the principal did not intend to deprive the insured of its money, but was hoping to recoup the losses he negligently caused. The court stated: "The mere fact that Mr. Mourad made misrepresentations in Apollo's corporate records does not trigger coverage unless there was also an intent to defraud Apollo, rather than make money for it." The court held that no "taking" occurred because the principal had merely gambled with the insured's money in the hopes of winning it back. *Apollo Computer, Inc. v. Fed. Ins. Co.*, No. 900-0288-C (no published opinion).

Minn. App. 2004. The improper use of genetic information was held not to constitute a "taking" and, thus, was not a "theft." The court rejected the insured's proposed definition derived from statutory definitions of larceny because the term "theft" was unambiguous. *Cargill, Inc. v. Nat'l Union Fire Ins. Co.*, 2004 Minn. App. LEXIS 33.

N.Y. App. 2010. The insured invested, on behalf of its employees, in a company run by Bernie Madoff. The insured sought to recover under an Employee Theft provision and a Premises, Computer Fraud, and Funds Transfer Fraud provisions. The court held that the insured could not recover under more than one provision, and that there had not been more than one instance of Employee Theft, which prevented the insured from recovering multiple policy limits. *Cumberland Packing Corp. v. Chubb Ins. Corp.*, 958 N.Y.S.2d 306.

Ore. App. 2000. The court reversed a summary judgment rendered in favor of an insurer on an employee theft policy insuring an overseas insured. The insurer accepted, solely for purposes of its motion, that the employee's acts of accepting checks post-dated to an extent beyond the insured's policies, granting excessive discounts to customers, accepting kickbacks in access of local norms, and selling in volumes indicating that the customer was reselling the products in other countries in competition with the insured in violation of company policy, constituted "theft," defined as the "unlawful taking of money . . . to the deprivation of the insured." At issue was when the insured discovered its loss and, thus, whether its claim was timely. The court held that knowledge that the employee violated company policy did not necessarily imply discovery of "theft" because, without more, those acts are not covered losses, as they do not demonstrate intent to harm, rather than help, the employer. The court found that "unlawful taking" meant that the employee had to intend to commit theft, which could not be shown by violation of company policy alone. Thus, issues of fact remained and the case was reversed and remanded. *Nike, Inc. v. Nw. Pac. Indem. Co.*, 999 P.2d 1197.

B. Deprivation to the Insured

N.D. Ohio 2015. One individual owned two companies. Each company had separate employees, separate bank accounts, and separate insurance policies. But there was some overlap between the two. For example, they were run out of the same office, and one bookkeeper worked for both corporations. Unfortunately, that bookkeeper was dishonest. He was stealing—but only from the second company. The insurer for the second company paid the applicable limit of its policy for the loss. The *other* company then also submitted a claim and sued its insurer, seeking to recover the remainder of the loss. In a brief opinion, the court granted summary judgment to the insurer. The court emphasized the language in the policy stating that it covered theft "to the deprivation of the insured."[13] Here, it was not the insured that suffered the loss but the other company, which, although owned by the same person, was distinct. *Transtar Elec., Inc. v. Charter Oak Fire Ins. Co.*, No. 3:13CV1837, 2015 U.S. Dist. LEXIS 44202.

N.D. Ohio 2014. The insured was an electrical contractor. An employee of the insured had access to the financial records and accounts of the insured's customer, which she abused by stealing that customer's money for her own use. The insured sought to recover the loss under the employee theft provision. Theft was defined in the policy as the unlawful taking of property money, securities or other property to the deprivation of the insured. The insurer argued that coverage could not apply because the employee had stolen from the customer, not from the insured. The court disagreed, for purposes of ruling on the insurer's motion to dismiss. It held that the definition of "theft" was not limited to property that belonged to the insured. Instead, the key language was "to the deprivation of the insured." The court found that the employee's taking had ultimately deprived the insured according to the pleadings. The court also rejected the insurer's argument that the loss did not result "directly"

---

13   *Id.* at *7-8.

from the theft. *Transtar Elec., Inc. v. Charter Oak Fire Ins. Co.*, No. 3:13CV1837, 2014 U.S. Dist. LEXIS 8000.

Bankr. N.D. Ga. 1995. Insurers argued that no "theft" had occurred because the funds lost through loans to third-parties were asserted to be those of the insured's financer, obtained illegally by the employee, rather than the insured's own funds, and thus there was no "deprivation" to the insured, as required under the definition of "theft." The court held that this argument had no merit, stating that regardless of whether the funds had been obtained from the financer illegally, the insured was under the same obligation to repay them. Thus, the insured had suffered a deprivation, irrespective of who had legal title to the lost funds. *In re Prime Comm. Corp.*, 187 B.R. 785.

E.D. La. 2004. Employee of insured manipulated accounts receivable to cause delinquent accounts to appear current to make herself and her department look better. As a result, the insured employer ultimately was forced to write off over 5 million in accounts receivable. The loss of the accounts receivable was a "deprivation" to the insured as required by the policy's definition of "theft," but it was not recoverable because accounts receivable were held not to be "other property" as defined under Louisiana law. On the other hand, $200,000 in undeserved raises and bonuses paid as a result of employee's scheme was recoverable, as it was money paid out of pocket by the insured as a direct result of the employee's scheme. *Morris Kirschman & Co., L.L.C. v. Hartford Fire Ins. Co.*, 2004 U.S. Dist. LEXIS 17427.

Minn. App. 2004. A provision in policy covering loss resulting from "theft" was held not to be ambiguous and to cover only direct loss to the insured, not loss to third parties. Furthermore, the third party did not suffer a deprivation by the insured's use of proprietary genetic information because the insured's use of the information did not deprive the third party of its own use of the information. *Cargill, Inc. v. Nat'l Union Fire Ins. Co.*, 2004 Minn. App. LEXIS 33.

Pa. County Ct. 2013. The insured was a grocery store, whose employee was allowing customers to take merchandise without paying. The court held that the insured had suffered a loss due to employee theft. The policy included an exclusion relating to a loss that could be proved only through inventory records. But the court found that this exclusion did not apply because the insured could substantiate its loss with proof beyond its inventory records. *Natrona Heights Supermarket, Inc. v. Firemen's Ins. Co.*, 2013 Pa. Dist. & Cnty. Dec. LEXIS 105, *aff'd*, 2014 Pa. Super. Unpub. LEXIS 2701 (Pa. Super. Ct. 2014).

SECONDARY SOURCES

Michael Keeley & John R. Riddle, *Commercial Crime Policy Insuring Agreement 1: Employee Dishonesty and Employee Theft Coverage*, 1-120 APPLEMAN ON INSURANCE (2015).

Michael Keeley & Justin Melkus, *An Introduction to Fidelity Insurance: Essential Terms, Background, and History*, 10-111 APPLEMAN ON INSURANCE (2015).

Toni Scott Reed, *Employee Theft Versus Manifest Intent: The Changing Landscape of Commercial Crime Coverage*, 36 TORT & INS. L.J. 43 (Fall, 2000).

Toni Scott Reed, *What is Employee Dishonesty and Employee Theft?*, in COMMERCIAL CRIME INSURANCE COVERAGE (Randall I. Marmor & Susan Koehler Sullivan, eds., 2014).

Toni Scott Reed & Kevin White, *What is Employee Dishonesty, in* COMMERCIAL CRIME POLICY 31 (Randall I. Marmor & John J. Tomaine, eds., 2005).

Scott L. Schmookler, *Claims Arising From a Fraud on a Third Party*, 10-130 APPLEMAN ON INSURANCE § 130.02 (2015).

Carol Z. Smith et al., *Recent Developments in Fidelity and Surety Law*, 50 TORT & INS. L.J. 367 (Winter, 2015).

Chapter 5

The Insuring Agreements—
Forgery or Alteration*

Loss caused by forgery and alteration is a frequently occurring loss. The issues of what constitutes forgery, which is a defined term, and alteration, which is not a defined term, are litigated frequently.

A commonly used commercial crime policy form is published by the Insurance Services Office ("ISO"). That form provides the following coverage for Forgery or Alteration:

> 2. **Forgery or Alteration**[1]
>   a. **We will pay for loss resulting directly from "forgery" or alteration of checks, drafts, promissory notes, or similar written promises, orders or directions to pay a sum certain in "money" that are:**
>   **(1) Made or drawn by or drawn upon you; or**
>   **(2) Made or drawn by one acting as your agent;**
>   **or that are purported to have been so made or drawn.**
>   **For the purposes of this Insuring Agreement, a substitute check as defined in the Check Clearing for the 21st Century Act shall be treated the same as the original it replaced.**

---

*   By Dennis J. Bartlett, Brosseau Bartlett Seserman, LLC, Greenwood Village, Colorado.

1   Commercial Crime Policy (Discovery Form), Standard Form No. CR 00 22 08 13 (Insurance Services Office, Inc. 2012). The ISO Commercial Crime Policy Claims Made Form, Standard Form No. CR 00 23 08 13 (Insurance Services Office, Inc. 2012) Forgery and Alterations coverage provision is identical. The policy form sponsored by the SFAA is very similar, the major difference being the SFAA form does not expressly deal with a "substitute check" as defined under the Check Clearing for the 21st Century Act.

b. **If you are sued for refusing to pay any instrument covered in Paragraph 2 a. on the basis that it has been forged or altered, and you have our written consent to defend against the suit, we will pay for any reasonable legal expenses that you incur and pay in that defense. The amount that we will pay is in addition to the Limit of Insurance applicable to this Insuring Agreement.**

COMMENT

The Forgery or Alteration coverage provides indemnity for a direct loss sustained by the Insured as maker or drawer of certain enumerated negotiable instruments (see UCC 3-104) or "similar written promises, orders or directions to pay a sum certain in 'money'" that: 1) are "[m]ade or drawn by" the Insured; or 2) are "drawn upon" the Insured; or 3) are "[m]ade or drawn by" an agent of the Insured; or 4) purport to be "made or drawn by" the Insured; or 5) purport to be "drawn upon" the Insured; or 6) purport to be "[m]ade or drawn by" an agent of the Insured. The particular written documents that are identified in this coverage are often specifically defined in the relevant policies, as well. Therefore, care should be taken to review the particular definitions that govern each item. The term "forgery" is defined in the policy, but the term "alteration" is not. Courts frequently turn to the definition of "alteration" contained in UCC 3-407, "Alteration."

Common claims that involve checks arise out of the Insured's failure to exercise its rights against the drawee bank under UCC 4-406, "Customer's duty to discover and report unauthorized signature or alteration."

To enable the maker or drawer of a forged or altered instrument to assert its defenses to a suit brought "for refusing to pay any instrument covered in Paragraph a.," Section 2.b. provides indemnity "for any reasonable legal expenses" incurred and paid by the Insured in defending such suits. The written consent of the insurer to the defense is an express condition precedent to such coverage. Payments made by the Underwriter under Section 2.b. are in addition to the applicable Limit of Insurance.

OUTLINE OF ANNOTATIONS

A. Forgery
B. Alteration
C. Instruments Not Covered
D. Case on Direct Loss Requirement

ANNOTATIONS

A. Forgery

5th Cir. 2010 (Tex.). An insurance agent's son, Charles McMahon, Jr., who was authorized to endorse and deposit checks, created forged applications for premium financing and submitted those to its insured, AFS/IBEX, which financed insurance premiums. When the premium financing checks were received at the insurance agency the son endorsed the checks "Charles McMahon Insurance Agency" and deposited those checks into the son's personal account. The court rejected Great American's argument, which relied upon the UCC for support as to the meaning of "forgery" because the policy defined the term "forgery." The court also rejected Great American's argument that relied upon the definition of "forgery," which excluded "a signature which consists in whole or in part of one's own name" because that would mean there is no coverage if the forger shares any part of the name being signed. The court rejected Great American's argument because of that "absurd" result and noted: "[f]or example, if a person named Bob Smith stole Bob Jones's check book and endorsed a check "Bob Jones," there would be no coverage because "Bob" was part of the endorsement and also part of the endorser's name." Finally, the court rejected the argument that there was no forgery because the son was authorized to endorse checks. The son's authority was to endorse checks and deposit them in the proper account. He was not authorized to endorse these fraudulently obtained checks and deposit them in his personal account. *Great Am. Ins. Co. v. AFS/IBEX Fin. Ser. Inc.*, 612 F.3d 800.

9th Cir. 2005 (Cal.). Genuine withdrawal receipts were not forgeries even though they were used to fraudulently induce payment. The court defined forgeries as "[a] false or altered document made to look genuine by someone with the intent to deceive." *Bell Gardens Bicycle Casino v. Great Am. Ins. Co.*, 124 F. App'x 551.

C.D. Cal. 2015. The insured CPA firm managed funds for a client and a partner at the CPA firm had a power of attorney that authorized him to make electronic transfers from the client's bank account. A third party hacked the client's e-mail account and sent a series of e-mails to the CPA requesting wire transfers to the Far East. Two of the e-mail requests were followed before the fraud was discovered and the CPA firm was not able to recover all the money sent oversees from the client's bank account. Among other things, the CPA firm asserted there was coverage under its forgery coverage. The court granted Federal Insurance summary judgment, holding the loss was not a direct loss and in so ruling, the court rejected the CPA firm's argument that because of the power of attorney, it held the client's funds as a bailee or trustee. In rejecting that argument, the court relied upon the fact that the funds were held in the client's bank account, not by the CPA firm. *Taylor and Lieberman v. Fed. Ins. Co.,* No. CV-14-3608 RSWL. 2015 U.S. Dist. Lexis 79358.

D. Del. 2013. A law firm which fell victim to a check scam scheme by depositing what appeared to be a bank check and wiring out the money to its "client" asserted coverage for the loss of funds under its forgery coverage. Continental argued: (1) the law firm had not proven the signature on the check was forged; and (2) the check was a counterfeit, not a forgery. The court rejected both arguments holding it was a virtual certainty the scammer would not have signed his or her real name to the check. The court also held a counterfeit check was equivalent to a forged check. *Morris James LLP v. Cont'l Cas. Co.*, 928 F. Supp. 2d 816.

N.D. Ind. 1996. Forged supporting documents used to draw upon a sight draft (that was not forged) were construed as a single document providing coverage. "Drawn upon you" is an ambiguous term that includes both the drawee bank and the insured. Further, under Indiana law, that court held that "[r]esulting directly from" is equivalent to proximate cause in insurance contracts. *Omnisource Corp. v. Transcont'l Ins. Co.*, 949 F. Supp. 681.

Ind. App. 2003. A title company depositing a check in contravention of closing instructions was neither a forgery nor an alteration of the check. *Utica Mut. Ins. Co. v. Precedent Cos., LLC*, 782 N.E.2d 470.

B. Alteration

D. Nev. 2013. The court denied summary judgment for Federal Insurance on whether coverage for an alteration existed. The third-party payroll service provider swept funds from its customer Orgill/Singer's account. The service provider altered the IRS Form 941 sent to the IRS with the deposit to reflect a lower amount and would pay that lower amount only, keeping the difference. Noting that normally alterations occur where a tortfeasor increases the amount of a check, the court went on to state that an alteration theory can lie where: "(1) the alleged alteration did not occur with respect to the transfer between the victim and the tortfeasor but rather between the tortfeasor and a third party whom the tortfeasor has promised to pay on behalf of the victim; and (2) the tortfeasor has not fraudulently increased the amount to be paid the victim but rather has taken from the victim exactly the amount the victim intended to pay." *Orgill/Singer & Assocs., Inc. v. Fed. Ins. Co.*, 943 F. Supp. 2d 1141.

Ky. App. 2013. The dishonest employee prepared unauthorized checks payable to herself or her husband and hid them in batches of checks to be signed. Auto Owners argued the checks were not forgeries but rather, the employee deceived her employer to sign legitimate checks. The court, noting forgery was not defined in the policy, held under the applicable criminal statute a "forged instrument is defined as a written instrument which has been falsely made, completed, or altered." Without explaining how, the court found the employee was "essentially altering checks prior to their completion by the owner." *Piles Chevrolet Pontiac Buick, Inc. v. Auto Owners Ins. Co.*, No. 2011-CA-002317-MR, 2013 Ky. App. Unpub. LEXIS 397.

Wisc. App. 2008. The insured college hired a third party to process the college's workers' compensation claims. The college would send the third party money to process approved claims through the third party's account and would replenish the account with funds to cover claims and the fee owed the third party for its services. The third party sent the college altered or "dummy" check ledgers that showed money being disbursed to third-party health-care providers. The third party never sent the health care providers the checks and instead kept the money that had been paid by the college. The court rejected coverage under the forgery or alteration clause because the unmailed checks were not forgeries. The dummy check ledger arguably may have been altered but it was not a covered instrument. *Milwaukee Area Technical Coll. v. Frontier Adjusters of Milwaukee*, 752 N.W.2d 396.

C. Instruments Not Covered

5th Cir. 2002 (Tex.). Baptist Health's accounting department paid invoices when signed as approved by Baptist Health's financial services department. An employee created invoices with forged financial services approvals, which were then paid by accounting department. The Fifth Circuit concluded the "instruments covered" language was not ambiguous but had a definite legal meaning. Internal, signed invoices were not "[d]rawn upon you," and thus were not covered instruments. *Travelers Cas. & Sur. Co. of Am. v. Baptist Health Sys.*, 313 F.3d 295.

5th Cir. 2002 (Tex.). Forged documents supporting a sight draft drawing upon a letter of credit were not construed as a single document providing coverage. "Drawn upon you" is not ambiguous and has a definite legal meaning. Neither the letter of credit nor the sight draft was a covered instrument because they were drawn upon a bank and not upon Parkans. The court applied the same reasoning to hold there was no coverage under a following form excess policy and ruled for the Zurich and the excess carriers as a matter of law on Parkans' bad faith claim. *Parkans Int'l LLC v. Zurich Ins. Co.*, 299 F.3d 514.

D. Mass. (2012). CustomMade Ventures alleged that Sentinel, under the forgery coverage, owed it a defense against a lawsuit based upon a forged or altered e-mail that purported to promise a certain salary per month and a defined track to partnership. The court, in ruling for Sentinel, stated: "The e-mail here is not similar to a check, draft, or promissory note and it is not a negotiable instrument." The e-mail was not a signed, unconditional written order directing someone to pay a sum certain of money. *CustomMade Ventures Corp. v. Sentinel Ins. Co.*, No. 11-10365-DPW, 2012 U.S. Dist. Lexis 131964.

E.D. Ky. (2011). A dishonest employee of Radwan, which processed payroll for third-party Radwan client, redirected payments for terminated employees of the third party to the dishonest employee's personal account. Radwan had authority to transfer funds from the client's account. When the client's employees would leave, the dishonest Radwan employee would send orders to the client's bank directing the bank to transfer money to the dishonest Radwan employee's account. The court held the order to the client's bank directing it to transfer funds was not a covered instrument. *Monroe Guar. Ins. Co. v. Radwan Brown & Co.*, No. 09-247-JBC, 2011 U.S. Dist. Lexis 30263.

Ky. App. 2009. Forged financing applications and related documents such as odometer statements, title applications, purchase contracts and warranty disclaimers for the purchase and sale of vehicles were not covered instruments. Therefore, the forgery and alteration coverage did not apply. *Frank Shoop, Inc. v. TIG Ins. Co.*, No. 2007-CA-000691-MR, 2009 Ky. App. Unpub. LEXIS 11.

Miss. App. 2005. A forged power of attorney used to sign a car lease was not a covered instrument. The lease was not forged. The power of attorney was not a check, draft, promissory note or order to pay a sum certain of money. *Watson Quality Ford, Inc. v. Great River Ins. Co.*, 909 So. 2d 1196.

D. Case on Direct Loss Requirement

7th Cir. 2011 (Wisc.). This case is not a commercial crime policy case. The case provides an excellent overview of the cases that hold "direct means direct" versus the more liberal "proximate cause" standard. The case dealt with losses suffered by a mortgage originator who sold mortgages to investors. The court, in concluding Wisconsin would follow the direct means direct line of cases, held "a loss resulting from an insured's liability to third parties in not a direct loss under a fidelity bond, even if the liability resulted from a covered act." *Universal Mortgage Corp. v. Würtembergische Versigherung AG*, 651 F.3d 759, 762.

SELECTED SECONDARY SOURCES

Michael R. Davisson, *The Other Insuring Agreements of Commercial Crime Policies*, *in* COMMERCIAL CRIME POLICY 285 (Randall I. Marmor & John J. Tomaine eds., 2d ed. 2005).

Michele L. Fenice & Adam P. Friedman, *Section 4—Insuring Agreement (D)—Forgery or Alteration*, *in* ANNOTATED FINANCIAL INSTITUTION BOND 86 (Michael Keeley ed., 3d ed. 2013).

Adam P. Friedman & Andrew S. Kent, Chapter 121. Commercial Crime Policy Insuring Agreement (2)—Forgery or Alteration, New Appleman on Insurance Law Library Edition (2015).

Scott L Schmookler, *Insuring Agreement D, in* FINANCIAL INSTITUTION BONDS 313 (Duncan L. Clore ed., 3d ed. 2008).

Chapter 6

Insuring Agreements—

Other Coverages*

This chapter surveys cases and authorities involving those insuring agreements of commercial crime insurance policies that provide coverage for loss caused by non-employees resulting directly from the perils of "theft,"[1] disappearance, destruction, "robbery," "safe burglary," unpaid money orders and "counterfeit" currency. Also included in this chapter are cases that examine coverage for loss suffered by an "employee benefit plan" resulting directly from fraudulent or dishonest acts committed by an "employee."

The most recent iterations of the Commercial Crime Policy (collectively referred to as the "CCP") copyrighted by the Insurance Services Office, Inc. ("ISO") in 2012[2] delineate the Insuring Agreements and the "Employee Benefit Plans" Condition that are the subject of this chapter as follows:

- Insuring Agreement A.3.—Inside The Premises—Theft of Money and Securities;
- Insuring Agreement A.4.—Inside The Premises—Robbery Or Safe Burglary Of Other Property;

---

* By Robert M. Flowers, Travelers Bond and Specialty Insurance, Hartford, Connecticut, John Morris, McElroy, Deutsch, Mulvaney & Carpenter, LLP, Morristown, New Jersey, and Richard S. Mills and Carol A. Pisano, McElroy, Deutsch, Mulvaney & Carpenter, LLP, New York, New York.

1 Unless the context suggests otherwise, the inclusion of quotation marks around words or phrases in this chapter generally denotes that the word or phrase is a defined term in most commercial crime policy forms.

2 Commercial Crime Policy, CR 00 22 08 13 (Insurance Services Office, Inc. 2012) (Discovery Form) and Commercial Crime Policy, CR 00 23 08 13 (Insurance Services Office, Inc. 2012) (Loss Sustained Form) (collectively referred to as the "CCP") *reprinted in* COMMERCIAL CRIME INSURANCE POLICY, 785, 799 (Randall I. Marmor & Susan Koehler Sullivan, eds. 2014).

- Insuring Agreement A.5.—Outside The Premises;
- Insuring Agreement A.7.—Money Orders and Counterfeit Currency; and
- Condition E.1.h.—Employee Benefit Plan.

The latest edition of the Crime Protection Policy (the "CPP") published by the Surety & Fidelity Association of America ("SFAA") in 2012 organizes and titles these insuring agreements in a manner almost identical to the CCP. One exception is that the CPP combines Insuring Agreement A.3. and A.4 of the CCP into one insuring agreement (Insuring Agreement B.3.) simply titled: "Inside the Premises."[3] As their titles reveal, Insuring Agreements A.3. and A.4. of the CCP are distinguished based on the perils insured and the types of property covered. While the CPP makes similar distinctions, it does so via subparagraphs contained in a single insuring agreement.[4]

This chapter is divided into five subsections corresponding to the four insuring agreements and one condition listed above. The language of the particular insuring agreement or condition that is the subject of each subsection is quoted at the beginning of that subsection. For a reference point, the quoted language is from the versions of the CCP that were copyrighted in 2012. If there is a significant difference between the quoted versions of the CCP and the version of the CPP that also was released in 2012, it will be noted in this Introduction or in the Comment that appears immediately below the quoted policy provision.

Numerous words and phrases in the insuring agreements and "Employee Benefit Plans" Condition that are reproduced below appear in quotation marks. The quotations marks denote that those words and phrases are specifically defined in the Definitions section of the CCP.[5] For the most part, the same words and phrases are defined in the CPP[6], although, on occasion, the two policy forms use different terminology. For example, the CCP utilizes the defined phrase "financial institution

3   Crime Protection Policy, SP 00 01 04 12 (Surety & Fidelity Association of America 2012) (referred to herein as the "CPP") *reprinted in* COMMERCIAL CRIME INSURANCE COVERAGE, 769 (Randall I. Marmor & Susan Koehler Sullivan, eds. 2014).
4   *Id.*
5   CCP, *supra* note 2, at 785, 795-98, 799, 811-814. Defined words in the CPP appear in bold print, instead of quotation marks. CPP, *supra* note 3, at 772.
6   Compare, CCP, Section F. Definitions, *supra* note 2, at 795-98, 811-814 *with* CPP, Section C. Definitions, *supra* note 3, at 773-75.

premises,"[7] while the CPP continues to use the differently defined term "banking premises."[8] As might be expected, the particular policy provisions that are the subject of this chapter are inextricably dependent upon the application of words and phrases that are expressly defined in the policy forms.

While this chapter will include cases that discuss relevant policy definitions in the context of the insuring agreements and condition that are the subject of this chapter, it will not include cases that address these definitions in the context of other sections of the policy where the same words and phrases are used. The reader is encouraged to review Chapter 9 of this book, which annotates cases that examine particular policy definitions in the broader context of the entire commercial crime policy, rather than in the context of only those policy provisions under discussion here. Court rulings made with regard to a particular defined word or phrase in the context of another insuring agreement or policy provision will be persuasive authority when analyzing coverage under the policy provisions that are the subject of this chapter.

Likewise, with regard to Condition E.1.h. of the CCP, which provides that "employee benefit plans" identified in the policy's Declaration are included as insureds with regard to loss resulting directly from fraudulent or dishonest acts committed by an "employee"[9], this chapter will not delineate cases addressing the definition of an "employee" outside the context of "employee benefit plans," nor will it include cases discussing what constitutes a fraudulent or dishonest act. For cases generally discussing the types of acts that constitute fraud or dishonesty, the reader is directed to Chapter 4 of this book. Cases that discuss the definition of "employee" are annotated in Chapter 8, however, proceed cautiously: Only one subsection of the "employee" definition[10] is relevant to coverage for "employee benefit plans"; it is

---

7   CCP, *supra* note 2, at 797, 813.

8   CPP, *supra* note 3, at 773. Pre-2012 editions of the CCP also utilized the term "banking premises." *See*, Julie Alleyne, William H. Woods & Jonathan M. Bryan, The Insuring Agreements—Other Coverages, *in* ANNOTATED COMMERCIAL CRIME POLICY, SECOND EDITION 157 (Cole S. Kain & Lana M. Glovack eds. 2006); Commercial Crime Policy, CR 00 21 05 06 (Insurance Services Office, Inc. 2005) (Loss Sustained Form).

9   CCP, *supra* note 2, at 790-91, 804-5.

10   CCP, Definition F.7.a.(4), *supra* note 2, at 796, 812; CPP, Definition 5.c., *supra* note 3, at 773.

unlikely that cases dealing with other subsections of the definition will be relevant to the analysis of who is an "employee" for purposes of applying the "Employee Benefit Plans" Condition.

In addition to containing conditions and exclusions that are generally applicable to all insuring agreements, the CCP and CPP contain specific conditions and exclusions applicable only to designated insuring agreements.[11] With regard to the CCP, the following specific exclusions apply to Insuring Agreements A.3. (Inside The Premises—Theft of Money and Securities); A.4. (Inside The Premises—Robbery Or Safe Burglary Of Other Property); and A.5. (Outside The Premises):

- Exclusion D.3.a.—Accounting Or Arithmetical Errors or Omissions;
- Exclusion D.3.b.—Exchanges or Purchases;
- Exclusion D.3.c.—Fire;
- Exclusion D.3.d.—Money Operated Devices;
- Exclusion D.3.e.—Motor Vehicles Or Equipment and Accessories;
- Exclusion D.3.f.—Transfer Or Surrender of Property;
- Exclusion D.3.g.—Vandalism;
- Exclusion D.3.h.—Voluntary Parting Of Title To Or Possession Of Property.[12]

The CPP contains similar exclusions specifically applicable to Insuring Agreement B.3. (Inside the Premises) and B.4. (Outside the Premises) of that policy form, with two exceptions: (1) the Fire Exclusion under the CPP is applicable to all insuring agreements; and (2) the Motor Vehicles Or Equipment and Accessories Exclusion under the CPP is only applicable to the "Outside the Premises" Insuring Agreement (i.e., Insuring Agreement B.4.).[13]

---

11   CCP, *supra* note 2, at 786-95, 800-11; CPP, *supra* note 3, at 775-83.
12   CCP, *supra* note 2, at 788-89, 802-03.
13   CPP, *supra* note 3, at 775-77.

Regarding the existence of specific conditions, Condition E.4.a—titled: "Armored Motor Vehicle Companies"—is specifically applicable to Insuring Agreement A.5. of the CCP (Outside The Premises).[14] Condition E.4.a. states that with regard to loss involving an armored motor vehicle company, Insuring Agreement A.5. will only respond to that portion of a loss that cannot be recovered under the insured's contract with the armored motor vehicle company, or from insurance issued for the benefit of the armored motor vehicle company's customers.[15] The CPP contains a corresponding specific condition applicable to the "Outside the Premises" Insuring Agreement (Insuring Agreement B.4.) that is embodied in subparagraph b. of that policy form's "Other Insurance" Condition.[16]

Both the CCP and the CPP also contain a specific condition—titled: "Special Limit Of Insurance For Specified Property"—that is applicable to Insuring Agreements A.4. (Inside The Premises—Robbery Or Safe Burglary Of Other Property) and A.5. (Outside The Premises) of the CCP, and to Insuring Agreements B.3. (Inside the Premises) and B.4. (Outside the Premises) of the CPP.[17] This condition states that a special $5,000 per occurrence limit of insurance applies to specified categories of property including: (1) precious metals, precious or semiprecious stones, pearls, furs, and certain partially completed articles; and (2) manuscripts, drawings, and records, or the cost of reconstructing them or their contents.[18]

Lastly, the CPP contains a specific condition applicable to Insuring Agreements B.3. (Inside the Premises) and B.4. (Outside the Premises).[19] This Condition—titled: "Duties in the Event of Loss"—requires the insured to notify the police if the insured has reason to believe that a loss involves a violation of law.[20] A similar specific condition applies to Insuring Agreement B.6. of the CPP (Money Order and Counterfeit Paper Currency). This Condition obligates the insured to notify the

---

14 CCP, *supra* note 2, at 795, 811.
15 *Id.*
16 CPP, *supra* note 3, at 780.
17 *Id.* at 782; CCP, *supra* note 2, at 795, 811.
18 *Id.*
19 CPP, *supra* note 3, at 782.
20 *Id.*

police if it has reason to believe that it accepted "counterfeit" paper currency or counterfeit money orders.[21]

A. Insuring Agreement A.3.: Inside The Premises—Theft Of Money And Securities

Insuring Agreement A.3. of the CCP states:

Inside The Premises—Theft Of Money And Securities
We will pay for:
a. **Loss of "money" and "securities" inside the "premises" or "financial institution premises":**
    (1) Resulting directly from "theft" committed by a person present inside such "premises" or "financial institution premises"; or
    (2) Resulting directly from disappearance or destruction.
b. **Loss from damage to the "premises" or its exterior resulting directly from an actual or attempted "theft" of "money" and "securities", if you are the owner of the "premises" or are liable for damage to it.**
c. **Loss of or damage to a locked safe, vault, cash register, cash box or cash drawer located inside the "premises" resulting directly from actual or attempted "theft" of, or unlawful entry into, those containers.[22]**

COMMENT

Subsection A.3.a.

Insuring Agreement A.3.a. of the CCP provides coverage for loss of "money" (or under Insuring Agreement B.3.a. of the CPP, for loss of "cash"[23]) and "securities" resulting directly from the perils of "theft," disappearance and destruction.[24] Under the CPP, "cash" is a separately

---

21   *Id.* at 783.
22   CCP, *supra* note 2, at 785; 799.
23   CPP, *supra* note 3, at 772.
24   CCP, *supra* note 2, at 785, 799.

defined term[25], and is a subcategory of the more broadly defined term "money."[26] "Money" also is defined more broadly in the CCP than "cash" is defined in the CPP.[27]

The CPP defines "cash" as United States or Canadian bills (i.e., paper money) or coins having a face value and accepted as legal tender.[28] Under the CCP, "money" is defined to include, *inter alia*, currency, coins and bank notes (in current use and having a face value), as well as travelers checks and money orders held for sale to the public.[29] By using the more narrowly defined word "cash" in Insuring Agreement B.3.a.— Inside the Premises (and also in Insuring Agreement B.4.—Outside the Premises[30]), instead of the broader term "money," the drafters of the CPP are emphasizing that the "Inside the Premises" and "Outside the Premises" Insuring Agreements envision coverage for *in person* transactions, not electronic ones[31]; logically, because paper money and coins are tangible; they cannot be transferred electronically.

In the case of "theft," Insuring Agreement A.3.a. only affords coverage when the thief is present inside the "premises" or inside the "financial institution premises"[32] ("banking premises" under the CPP").[33] Generally, the issues to be resolved regarding this requirement are: (1) whether actual presence of the perpetrator inside the insured's place of business or financial institution is necessary, or is a constructive or metaphorical presence sufficient (such as, for example, "theft" facilitated over the telephone); and (2) if actual presence is required, must all of the acts constituting the "theft" be committed while the perpetrator is inside the "premises" or "financial institution premises." Insuring Agreement B.3.a. of the CPP seeks to eliminate the first of these issues and to clarify

---

25 CPP, *supra* note 3, at 773.

26 *Id.* at 774.

27 *Compare*, CCP, Definition F.16., *supra* note 2, at 797; 813 *with* CPP, Definition C.2., *supra* note 3, at 773.

28 CPP, *supra* note 3, at 773.

29 CCP, *supra* note 2, at 797; 813.

30 CPP, *supra* note 3, at 773.

31 Robert Duke, Carol A. Pisano & Richard S. Mills, *History and Development of Mercantile Crime Policies—Their Interpretation and Construction, in* COMMERCIAL CRIME INSURANCE COVERAGE, 1 (Randall I. Marmor & Susan Koehler Sullivan, eds. 2014).

32 CCP, *supra* note 2, at 785; 799.

33 CPP, *supra* note 3, at 772.

the genuine intent of this coverage by inserting the modifier *physically* before the word "present"; expressly requiring that the thief be: *physically* present at the time of the loss to trigger coverage.[34]

The language requiring the presence of the perpetrator inside the "premises" or inside the "financial institution premises" was not contained in the 2002 version of the CCP[35], but is contained in the 2012 edition.[36] The requirement of physical presence was newly added in the 2012 version of the CPP.[37] However, such a requirement has long been a necessary element of "on premises" coverage under the Financial Institution Bond and its predecessor, the Bankers Blanket Bond.[38] For that reason, there is substantial case law addressing the physical presence issue in the context of coverage for banks and financial institutions. Since these cases provide guidance and are instructive with regard to the issues under discussion here, they are included in the annotations below.

Another issue encountered when evaluating coverage for claims under this insuring agreement is what constitutes the "premises" for purposes of determining whether coverage is triggered. Although the term "premises" is defined as the "interior portion of any building" that the insured occupies in conducting its business[39], questions may nonetheless arise regarding the breadth of the definition.

For example, in *Brightpoint, Inc. v. Zurich American Insurance Co.*[40], which involved a claim under the computer fraud insuring agreement of a commercial crime policy, the insured argued that the interior of any building where one of its employees is present and acting on its behalf constitutes the insured's premises under the definition. The

---

34 *Id.*

35 Alleyne, Woods & Bryan, *supra* note 8. *The Insuring Agreements—Other Coverages, in* ANNOTATED COMMERCIAL CRIME POLICY, SECOND EDITION 160 (Cole S. Kain & Lana M. Glovack eds. 2006).

36 The requirement that the perpetrator be present inside the "premises" or "financial institution premises" was also contained in the edition of the CCP copyrighted by ISO in 2005. Commercial Crime Policy, CR 00 21 05 06 (Insurance Services Office, Inc. 2005) (Loss Sustained Form).

37 Duke, Pisano & Mills, *supra* note 31, at 11-12; CPP, *supra* note 3, at 772.

38 Christopher C. Novak, Todd D. McCormick & Thomas R. Orofino, *The Other Insuring Agreements of Commercial Crime Policies, in* COMMERCIAL CRIME INSURANCE COVERAGE, 282 (Randall I. Marmor & Susan Koehler Sullivan, eds. 2014).

39 CCP, *supra* note 2, at 798; 799; CPP, *supra* note 3, at 774.

40 No. 1:04-CV-2085-SEB-JPG, 2006 WL 693377 (S.D. Ind. Mar. 10, 2006).

court rejected the insured's construction of the definition, holding that the insured's interpretation was overly broad and could be wrongly deemed to "include literally any building anywhere a Brightpoint employee might find himself during business hours."[41]

Subsections A.3.b. and A.3.c.

Insuring Agreement A.3.b. of the CCP provides coverage for damage to the "premises" or its exterior that occurs during the course of an actual or attempted "theft" of "money" and "securities," but only if the insured is the owner of the "premises" or is liable for damage to it.[42] Certain types of containers—locked safes, vaults, cash registers, cash boxes or cash drawers—that are located inside the "premises" are covered by Insuring Agreement A.3.c. for loss or damage to those containers resulting directly from "theft" (actual or attempted) or unlawful entry into them.[43] Insuring Agreement B.3.c. of the CPP provides coverage substantially similar to that provided by subparagraphs b. and c. of Insuring Agreement A.3. of the CCP.[44]

OUTLINE OF ANNOTATIONS

A. Inside the Premises
B. Disappearance or Destruction
C. Money or Securities
D. Safe
E. Exclusions

---

41 *Id.* at *6.
42 CCP, *supra* note 2, at 785; 799.
43 *Id.*
44 *Compare*, CCP, Insuring Agreement A.3. subparagraphs b. and c., *supra* note 2, at 785; 799 *with* CPP, Insuring Agreement B.3.c., *supra* note 3, at 772.

ANNOTATIONS

A. Inside the premises

3d Cir. 1993 (N.J.). Quoting the American Bankers Association, *Digest of Bank Insurance* (4th ed.), the court held that actual physical presence of the defrauder on the bank's presence is required to invoke "On Premises" coverage under a Savings and Loan Blanket Bond; constructive presence is insufficient: "Generally, false pretenses occur during a face-to-face meeting between a bank employee or other custodian and a party to the fraud. Unless this happens on the premises of the insured bank, the loss is not . . . covered under [the On Premises] Insuring Agreement (B). Losses caused by false pretenses over the telephone are not covered unless it can be proved that the call came from a person who was on the premises of the insured bank." *Oritani Savings & Loan Ass'n v. Fidelity and Deposit Co.*, 989 F.2d 635, 642.

4th Cir. 1989 (N.C.). A bank employee was fraudulently induced to purchase fictitious treasury bonds during telephone calls with a customer. The court held that the "On Premises" insuring clause of a Bankers Blanket Bond afforded no coverage, finding that "[t]he crucial factor in determining whether the 'on premises' requirement has been satisfied is . . . [the defrauder's] location when he engages in misrepresentations." The fact that the defrauder was not in the bank's offices or on the premises where the bank kept its money when he made the misrepresentation that prompted the bank to depart with $2.8 million was fatal to the bank's claim. *S. Nat. Bank of N. Carolina v. United Pac. Ins. Co.*, 864 F.2d 329, 331-33.

7th Cir. 2013 (Wis.). "On Premises" insuring agreement of a standard Financial Institution Bond does not cover a fraud orchestrated from outside a financial institution's premises, even if the defrauder's agent (a courier) enters the bank's offices and picks up the cashier's checks that the defrauder fraudulently caused the bank to issue. To trigger coverage the bank would have to prove that the courier was guilty of fraud or larceny. Because such proof was lacking, the court of appeals affirmed the district court's decision that "On Premises" coverage was not afforded for the bank's loss. *Bankmanagers Corp. v. Fed. Ins.* Co., 712 F.3d 1163, 1165-66 *affirming in relevant part* 11-C-871, 2012 WL

4023328 (E.D. Wis. Sept. 12, 2012) *judgment corrected*, 2013 WL 790760 (E.D. Wis. Mar. 4, 2013).

7th Cir. 2009 (Ill.). Loss from fraudulent scheme perpetrated against the insured bank by repeated exchanges, on the bank's premises, of bad checks for money orders was a loss from false pretenses that occurred on the insured's premises and was covered by the "On Premises" insuring agreement of a Financial Institution Bond despite that the actual loss occurred when the checks tendered in exchange for the money orders were dishonored off premises by the issuing bank. Coverage applied because false pretenses were committed on the insured's premises by the exchange of bad checks for money orders with the intention to defraud. *First State Bank of Monticello v. Ohio Cas. Ins. Co.*, 555 F.3d 564, 569-70.

7th Cir. 2005 (Ill.). Financial institution bond's "On Premises" fraud coverage did not cover loss resulting from off-premises fraudulent withdrawal of funds. *Private Bank & Trust Co. v. Progressive Cas. Ins. Co.*, 409 F.3d 814, 816-18 *affirming Private Bank v. Progressive Casualty Insurance Co.*, 2004 WL 1144048 (N.D. Ill. May 18, 2004).

7th Cir. 1991(Ill.). "On Premises" insuring agreement of a Financial Institution Bond did not provide coverage for loss stemming from the depositing of misappropriated checks because the checks were not stolen on the bank's premises; no loss occurred when the deposit was made; and funds in excess of the bond's deductible were not received by the perpetrator while he was present on the bank's premises. *Alpine State Bank v. Ohio Casualty Ins. Co.,* 941 F.2d 554, 561-62.

N.D Ill. 2004. Construing a Financial Institution Bond, the court rejected the argument that a loss should be deemed to occur "on premises" if some of the acts constituting a theft by false pretenses occurred inside the bank, but the thief was outside the bank when the loss actually occurred. To trigger "On Premises" coverage "requires the physical presence of the person causing the loss at the time that the loss occurs." Although the thief was present on the bank's premises when he used false pretenses to open an account into which he deposited stolen checks, because he was not physically present when he telephoned and effectuated a transfer of the stolen funds to purchase gold coins, the "On Premises" coverage was not triggered. *Private Bank v. Progressive Casualty Insurance Co.*, 2004 WL 1144048, *3-4 (May 18, 2004) *aff'd* 409 F.3d 814, 816-18 (5th Cir. 2005).

E.D. Ky. 2011. The insured provided payroll services to clients. The payroll funds were transferred directly from the client's accounts to the accounts of the clients' employees based on instructions furnished by the insured. One of the insured's employees stole from a client by continuing to direct payment to someone who had left the client's employ. The insured repaid the loss to the client and made a claim under the employee dishonesty coverage of a business owner's property policy. The court held that there was no direct loss as required by the policy. The insured did not have custody of the funds that the employee embezzled, and the policy did not provide liability insurance. The policy also contained a Money and Securities insuring clause, there was no coverage under that section because the insured did not have use and custody of the money involved. The money was transferred directly from the client's account to the account of the embezzler. Finally, there was no forgery or alteration of a covered instrument. *Monroe Guaranty Insurance Co. v. Radwan Brown & Co., PSC*, 2011 WL 1102694.

E.D. Wis. 2012. An employee of the bank's customer telephoned the bank and, using her employer's funds, purchased cashier's checks made payable to her personal creditors. The customer sought recourse from the bank and the bank sought "On Premises" coverage under its Financial Institution Bond. The district court found that the loss occurred when the bank complied with the defrauder's requests and issued the cashier's checks, and not when the defrauder's courier(s) obtained possession of the checks; for that reason, the "On Premises" insuring clause was held inapplicable. The court noted that ample authority existed to support the conclusion that off-premises fraud perpetrated by telephone is not a risk the drafters of the financial institution bond intended to insure against under the "On Premises" insuring agreement. *Bankmanagers Corp. v. Fed. Ins.* Co., No. 11-C-871, 2012 WL 4023328, *6-8 (Sept. 12, 2012) *judgment corrected*, 2013 WL 790760 (E.D. Wis. Mar. 4, 2013) *aff'd in relevant part*, 712 F.3d 1163 (7th Cir. 2013).

Kan. Ct. App. 2007. The insured bank permitted checks fraudulently drawn by a customer acting as a trustee on trust accounts to be deposited into the customer's personal and business accounts at the bank. The Trust sought to recover the amount of the checks wrongly accepted by the bank for deposit, and the bank sought "On Premises" coverage from its insurer under a Financial Institution Bond. The court found that while "[i]t is obvious the bond covers theft of property *from* the bank," the bond does not cover the bank's loss when the bank later becomes liable to a third party (i.e., the Trust) from which the money was stolen. Moreover, even if the loss was deemed to have occurred when the deposits were made and not when the bank was held liable for permitting them, coverage would still be inapplicable because the checks were deposited by the customer's employee, and not by the customer who was the thief. It was error for the trial court to attribute acts by the perpetrator's employees to be "on premises" conduct by the perpetrator. *Citizens Bank, N.A. v. Kansas Bankers Sur. Co.*, 149 P.3d 25 (unpublished decision).

La. Ct. App. 1967. Robbery that took place on a platform adjacent to the insured's pharmaceutical premises did not occur "inside the premises" under a Money and Securities Broad Form Policy. *Singerman v. Nat'l Sur. Corp.*, 196 So. 2d 291-93.

B. Disappearance or Destruction

Ark. 1969. The insured sought to recover deposits that were alleged to have mysteriously disappeared from a night depository. The court found that there was insufficient evidence to prove that the deposits actually were made to establish coverage for "disappearance." *Fireman's Fund Ins. Co. v. Fort Smith Pizza Co.*, 442 S.W. 2d 238, 239.

C. Money or Securities

6th Cir. 2004 (Tenn.). A casino suffered a loss when it extended gambling credit to a patron in exchange for fraudulent bank checks. The court stated that gambling credit is a form of Money or Securities as defined in a Blanket Crime Policy. *Harrah's Entertainment, Inc. v. ACE American Insurance Co.*, 100 F. App'x 387, 390.

D.N.J. 2011. Two employees of a car dealership filled out Audi's customer surveys pretending that they were customers of the dealership. Based on the fraudulently completed surveys the dealership "earned" a bonus from Audi. When Audi discovered the fraud it determined that based on genuine survey responses, the dealership was not entitled to a bonus. The insured sued its insurer claiming that the bonus it did not receive was a covered loss covered under the theft and forgery provisions of the policy. The court granted the insurer's motion to dismiss and held that the lost opportunity to receive the bonus was not Money, Securities or Other Property covered by the policy. *Jack Daniels Motors, Inc. v. Universal Underwriters Insurance Co.*, 2011 WL 346500.

Tex. 1974. The court ruled in favor of the insured, finding that a coin collection came within the definition of "money" and "securities." "Money" was defined as "currency, coins, bank notes and bullion." This result is unlikely today, as "money" and "cash" are defined under modern crime policy forms as currency "in current use." *Nat'l Sur. Corp. v. Seale*, 506 S.W.2d 579.

Tex. App. 1973. Insurer denied coverage on the grounds that a coin collection did not come within the definition of "money" because the coins were no longer in circulation and were collector's items. The court interpreted the term "coin" literally and ruled that the coins came within the definition of "money." Modern crime policy forms have responded to this wrongful expansion of coverage by defining "money" and "cash" as currency "in current use." *Nat'l Sur. Corp. v. Seale*, 499 S.W.2d 753, 754.

D. Safe

Ga. App. 1977. Insured's strongbox was taken when its establishment was broken into. The strongbox was located in a liquor storage room, and the door to the room did not contain a combination lock. The court, in *dicta*, commented on the term "safe" and concluded that the strongbox and liquor storage room did not come within the dictionary definition of "safe." *Zurich Ins. Co. v. Waite*, 240 S.E.2d 914, 916.

S. C. App. 2002. One of the insured's convenience stores was burglarized, and $1,940 in cash was stolen from an ATM. The portion of Plaintiff's claim for the ATM cash was denied by the insurer. The court found that the ATM qualified as a safe under the common definition of "safe." *Mixson, Inc. v. Am. Loyalty Ins. Co.*, 562 S.E.2d 659, 661.

E. Exclusions

6th Cir. 2004 (Tenn.). Court found that loss resulting from the extension of gambling credit in exchange for forged cashier checks was not covered under "On Premises" insuring agreement of a Blanket Crime Policy because the loss was "due to the giving and surrendering of Money and Securities in any exchange or purchase," which was excluded from coverage. *Harrah's Entm't, Inc. v. Ace Am. Ins. Co.*, 100 F. App'x 387, 390-91.

7th Cir. 2009 (Ill.). Loss covered by the "On Premises" insuring agreement of a Financial Institution Bond was not excluded by the bond's "employee" exclusion, which eliminated coverage under that insuring agreement "for loss caused by an Employee" of the insured. The bank's employee violated bank policy when he unknowingly accepted bad checks from a customer in exchange for money orders. The court distinguished between employees that cause a loss and those that fail to prevent one, holding that "because all such transactions are handled—at one level or another—by a bank employee," to apply the "employee" exclusion in the later circumstance would be an overly broad interpretation of the exclusion that would "eviscerate much of the coverage granted under the bond." *First State Bank of Monticello v. Ohio Cas. Ins. Co.*, 555 F.3d 564, 571-72.

N.D. Tex. 2008. Loss stemming from checks tendered to insurance agent in fraudulent premium financing scheme where perpetrator endorsed and deposited checks without authorization, was excluded from coverage under "Inside the Premises/Theft" Insuring Agreement because of the policy's "Theft by Trickery" exclusion, which applied where the insured voluntarily parted with title or possession to money, but coverage was found under Forgery or Alteration Insuring Agreement. *Great Am. Ins. Co. v. AFS/IBEX Fin. Servs., Inc.*, No. CIV. A. 307-CV-924-O, 2008 WL 2795205, *13-14 (July 21, 2008), *aff'd*, 612 F.3d 800, 807-08 (5th Cir. 2010).

SECONDARY SOURCES:

Julie Alleyne, William H. Woods & Jonathan M. Bryan, *The Insuring Agreements—Other Coverages*, *in* ANNOTATED COMMERCIAL

CRIME POLICY, SECOND EDITION 157 (Cole S. Kain & Lana M. Glovack eds. 2006).

John V. Burch & Timothy J. Burson, *Other Insuring Agreements in Commercial Crime and Other Fidelity Policies—An Update, in* COMMERCIAL CRIME POLICY 5-1 (Gilbert J. Schroeder, ed. 1997).

Michael R. Davisson, *The Other Insuring Agreements of Commercial Crime Policies, in* COMMERCIAL CRIME POLICY 285 (Randall I. Marmor & John J. Tomaine, eds., 2d ed. 2005).

Christopher C. Novak, Todd D. McCormick & Thomas R. Orofino, *The Other Insuring Agreements of Commercial Crime Policies, in* COMMERCIAL CRIME INSURANCE COVERAGE, 282 (Randall I. Marmor & Susan Koehler Sullivan, eds. 2014).

B. Insuring Agreement A.4.: Inside The Premises—Robbery Or Safe Burglary Of Other Property

Insuring Agreement A.4. of the CCP states:

Inside The Premises—Robbery Or Safe Burglary Of Other Property
We will pay for:
a.   Loss of or damage to "other property":
  (1)   Inside the "premises" resulting directly from an actual or attempted "robbery" of a "custodian"; or
  (2)   Inside the "premises" in a safe or vault resulting directly from an actual or attempted "safe burglary".
b.   Loss from damage to the "premises" or its exterior resulting directly from an actual or attempted "robbery" or "safe burglary" of "other property", if you are the owner of the "premises" or are liable for damage to it.

c. Loss of or damage to a locked safe or vault located inside the "premises" resulting directly from an actual or attempted "robbery" or "safe burglary".[45]

COMMENT

Insuring Agreement A.4.a. of the CCP (Insuring Agreement B.3.b. of the CPP[46]) provides coverage for loss of "other property" inside the "premises": (1) resulting directly from the peril of "robbery" (actual or attempted) of a "custodian"; or (2) resulting directly from the peril of "safe burglary" (actual or attempted) from a safe or vault.[47]

Insuring Agreement A.4.b. of the CCP provides coverage for damage to the "premises" or its exterior that occurs during the course of an actual or attempted "robbery" or "safe burglary" of "other property," but only if the insured is the owner of the "premises" or is liable for damage to it.[48] Lastly, a locked safe or vault that is located inside the "premises" is covered by Insuring Agreement A.4.c. for loss or damage resulting directly from an actual or attempted "robbery" or "safe burglary."[49] Insuring Agreement B.3.c. of the CPP provides coverage substantially similar to that provided by subparagraphs b. and c. of Insuring Agreement A.4. of the CCP.[50]

OUTLINE OF ANNOTATIONS

A. Inside the premises
B. Money
C. Robbery
D. Visible signs of forced entry

---

45 CCP, *supra* note 2, at 785-86, 799-800.
46 CPP, *supra* note 3, at 772.
47 CCP, *supra* note 2, at 785-86, 799-800.
48 *Id.* at 786; 800.
49 *Id.*
50 *Compare*, CCP, Insuring Agreement A.4., subparagraphs b. and .c., *supra* note 2, at 786; 800 *with* CPP, Insuring Agreement B.3.c., *supra* note 3, at 772.

ANNOTATIONS:

A. Inside the premises

Mich. 1944. Three robbers forced the insured, his wife and employees back into their cafe. The day's receipts were left in the car. One robber went out to the car and brought the money back into the cafe. All three robbers left. The court ruled that the robbery took place "inside the premises" of the cafe at the time the robbers brought the money back there and then departed. *Saks v. St. Paul Mercury Indem. Co.,* 14 N.W.2d 547, 548.

Wash. 1935. Robbers first approached the owner with a gun outside the premises and forced him back inside the premises, where they took cash and other valuables from the owner and from the safe. The court ruled that the robbery was consummated at the time that the money or property was taken; thus, the claim fell within the "inside the premises" portion of the policy's coverage, not outside the premises. *Cartier Drug Co. v. Md. Cas. Co.,* 42 P.2d 37, 38-9.

B. Money

Mo. App. 1965. The court determined that US Collector's coins taken during a safe burglary came within the policy's definition of "money" and not "other property," relying primarily on the fact that the insured was not in the business of dealing in rare coins and that the policy was clear in including coins under the definition of "money." This result is unlikely today, as "money" and "cash" are defined under modern crime policy forms as currency "in current use." *Cornblath v. Firemen's Fund Ins. Co.,* 392 S.W.2d 648, 650.

C. Robbery

2d Cir. 2012 (N.Y.). The court of appeals affirmed summary judgment in favor of the insured agreeing with the district court that the policy's definition of "robbery" was ambiguous and therefore had to be construed in favor of the insured's interpretation, which the court found was reasonable. "Robbery" was defined as "the unlawful taking of insured property . . . from an Employee . . . by violence, threat of violence or other overt felonious act committed in the presence and cognizance of such person . . . ." The court held that the fraudulent act itself, or its criminal nature, did not have to be apparent to, and observed by the insured's employee at the time of its occurrence. For coverage purposes, it was sufficient that the fraud was perpetrated in the employee's presence; the taking was felonious; and the employee was aware that imposters took money. *VAM Check Cashing Corp. v. Fed. Ins. Co.,* 699 F.3d 727, 729-34 *affirming VAM Check Cashing Corp. v. Fed. Ins. Co.,* 787 F. Supp. 2d 264.

S.D.N.Y. 2011 (N.Y.). Loss caused by imposters who tricked the insured's cashier into handing over $120,000 constituted an "overt felonious act committed in [cashier's] presence and cognizance," and thus constituted a covered "robbery" within the definition of the term as used in the Crime Insurance Policy. Finding that the policy's definition of "robbery" was ambiguous, the court construed the definition in favor of coverage despite that there was no violence or threat of violence, and notwithstanding that the cashier was not aware that a felony was being committed when she communicated with and delivered the money to the imposters. *VAM Check Cashing Corp. v. Fed. Ins. Co.,* 787 F. Supp. 2d 264, 268-72 *aff'd* 699 F.3d 727.

Minn. App. 2008. The insured sustained a loss when it lent money to a thief. It sought coverage from its insurer for "robbery," defined to include the taking of property by one who has committed an "obviously unlawful" act witnessed by the person with custody of the property. The appellate court affirmed the trial court's finding of no coverage because the act was not perceived to be unlawful at the time the property was surrendered. "Obviously unlawful" refers to the time the act is committed; not a subsequent realization. When the fraud occurred, the insured believed the loans were legitimate and would be profitable. The act was not perceived to be unlawful until later. Therefore, coverage for "robbery" was not triggered. *Sela v. St. Paul Travelers Companies, Inc.,* 2008 WL 495734, *2-4 (February 26, 2008) (unpublished decision).

Pa. 1951. The court addressed the difference between "robbery," which was covered under the policy, and "burglary," which was not covered, ruling that a majority of the losses suffered did not come within the policy terms because it was due to a burglary. *Hunt Motor Co., Inc. v. Fid. & Cas. Co. of New York,* 78 Pa. D. & C. 49, 50-51.

D. Visible signs of forced entry

Fla. 1956. The court agreed with the insurer's declination of coverage, finding there was no evidence that entry into the safe was done by force and violence. The safe was simply removed from the premises, and the court could not infer, for purposes of coverage, that the felons forcibly gained access into the safe and thereby left marks on the safe. *Moore v. General Cas. Co. of Am.,* 91 So. 2d 341, 341-42.

Fla. App. 1975. The insured's premises were broken into and the safe was opened without any evidence of forced entry on the safe. The court affirmed the insurer's denial of coverage because there were no signs of forced entry on the safe as required by the policy. *Rosie O'Grady's Warehouse, Inc. v. Charter Oak Fire Ins. Co.,* 319 So. 2d 632, 633.

Kan. 1962. Entry into the safe during a burglary was obtained by manipulating the combination lock on the exterior door of the safe, while the interior door's lock was punched out. The court concluded that the phrase "visible signs of force and violence" is an evidentiary requirement in the policy and not a prerequisite to coverage. *Ferguson v. Phoenix Assur. Co.,* 370 P.2d 379, 381-83.

La. App. 1971. Burglars forced the insured to open his safe at gunpoint, and the court found that this did not satisfy the clear requirement in the policy that there be visible marks on all doors of the safe for there to be coverage under the policy. The court ruled that this condition in the policy was not prohibited by statute or void as against public policy. *Lichtentag v. Millers Mut. Fire Ins. Co.,* 250 So. 2d 105, 106-07.

Neb. 1968. The court held that the loss did not come within the scope of coverage under the safe burglary policy in question because the safe had no signs of forced entry or violence on the outside door of the safe. *Hazuka v. Md. Cas. Co.,* 160 N.W.2d 174, 176-77.

N.Y. App. 1992. Insured suffered losses as a result of a safe burglary, but the court confirmed the insurer's denial of coverage because there were no signs of forced entry as required by the policy. *Prince Check Cashing Corp. v. Fed. Ins. Co.,* 582 N.Y.S.2d 751.

Ore. 1957. The safe from which cash and property were taken only contained scratches on the outer surface of the door of the safe, but there is no evidence that those scratches contributed to the opening of the safe. Therefore, the court ruled that the loss did not come within the scope of coverage. *Inglis v. General Cas. Co.,* 316 P.2d 546, 547-48.

SECONDARY SOURCES:

Julie Alleyne, William H. Woods & Jonathan M. Bryan, *The Insuring Agreements—Other Coverages*, in ANNOTATED COMMERCIAL CRIME POLICY, SECOND EDITION 157 (Cole S. Kain & Lana M. Glovack eds. 2006).

John V. Burch & Timothy J. Burson, *Other Insuring Agreements in Commercial Crime and Other Fidelity Policies—An Update*, in COMMERCIAL CRIME POLICY 5-1 (Gilbert J. Schroeder, ed. 1997).

Michael R. Davisson, *The Other Insuring Agreements of Commercial Crime Policies*, in COMMERCIAL CRIME POLICY 285 (Randall I. Marmor & John J. Tomaine, eds., 2d ed. 2005).

Christopher C. Novak, Todd D. McCormick & Thomas R. Orofino, *The Other Insuring Agreements of Commercial Crime Policies*, in COMMERCIAL CRIME INSURANCE COVERAGE, 282 (Randall I. Marmor & Susan Koehler Sullivan, eds. 2014).

C. Insuring Agreement A.5: Outside The Premises

Insuring Agreement A.5. of the CCP states:

Outside The Premises
We will pay for:

a. Loss of "money" and "securities" outside the "premises" in the care and custody of a "messenger" or an armored motor vehicle company resulting directly from "theft", disappearance or destruction.

b. Loss of or damage to "other property" outside the "premises" in the care and custody of a "messenger" or

an armored motor vehicle company resulting directly from an actual or attempted "robbery".[51]

COMMENT

Insuring Agreement A.5.a. of the CCP provides coverage for loss "outside the premises" of "money" and "securities" in the care and custody of a "messenger" or armored motor vehicle company. To trigger coverage, the loss must result directly from the perils of "theft," disappearance or destruction.[52] Insuring Agreement A.5.b. of the CCP provides coverage for loss resulting directly from an actual or attempted "robbery" occurring "outside the premises" of "other property" while that property is in the care and custody of a "messenger" or armored motor vehicle.[53]

As the following annotations demonstrate, the primary issue that has been litigated under this provision is the level of control and supervision that the "messenger" or armored motor vehicle company must maintain over the insured property to meet the undefined "care and custody" component of this Insuring Agreement. The mere fact that the "messenger" or armored motor vehicle company may leave property unattended, or that the property is not physically in their possession does not *ipso facto* negate the existence of "care and custody" over that property. Generally, in evaluating the "care and custody" element of coverage, the courts will consider the steps taken by the "messenger" or armored motor vehicle company to safeguard the property in their absence (e.g., was the property left in a locked vehicle; was it feasible for a guard to keep the property in personal custody); how long was the absence, and what was the reason for the absence.

Pursuant to the Armored Motor Vehicle Companies Condition of the CCP (Condition E.4.a.)[54] and the "Other Insurance" Condition of the CPP[55], loss involving an armored motor vehicle company is only covered to the extent that the loss that cannot be recovered under the insured's

---

51   CCP, *supra* note 2, at 786, 800.
52   *Id.*
53   *Id.*
54   CCP, *supra* note 2, at 795, 811.
55   CPP, *supra* note 3, at 780.

contract with the armored motor vehicle company, or from insurance carried for that company's customers.

Insuring Agreement B.4. of the CPP is structured differently, but provides coverage substantially similar to Insuring Agreement A.5. of the CCP[56]; however, there are distinctions: For example, the causation language used in Insuring Agreement A.5. is loss *resulting directly from*[57]; Insuring Agreement B.4. of the CPP uses the less stringent *resulting from* causation standard.[58] Also, Insuring Agreement B.4.a. of the CPP uses the word "cash" in place of the more broadly defined word "money" that is contained in Insuring Agreement A.5.a. of the CCP.[59]

OUTLINE OF ANNOTATIONS

A. Care and custody
B. Disappearance
C. Outside the premises

ANNOTATIONS

A. Care and custody

Ga. App. 1969. Money was taken from an employee's car while he stopped to purchase a sandwich for lunch. The court found that the money did not have to be carried on the employee's person, and the fact that the money was locked in the glove compartment and the car was locked was sufficient to satisfy the "care and custody" requirement. *Atlanta Tallow Co., Inc. v. Firemen's Fund Ins. Co.,* 167 S.E.2d 361, 362.

---

56   *Compare,* CCP, Insuring Agreement A.5., *supra* note 2, at 786; 800 *with* CPP, Insuring Agreement B.6, *supra* note 3, at 773.
57   CCP, *supra* note 2, at 786, 800.
58   CPP, *supra* note 3, at 773.
59   *Id.* The reader is referred to the COMMENT to Section 1 of this chapter and footnotes 23-31, inclusive, which collectively discuss the significance of this distinction.

Ga. App. 1967. After withdrawing cash from the bank and before returning to the store, employee stopped at home for lunch, leaving the cash in the car, which then was stolen. The court found no coverage because the stolen or lost money was not in the immediate custody or possession of the messenger at the time of the loss. *Cleveland Ave. Liquor Store, Inc. v. Home Ins. Co.*, 156 S.E.2d 202, 203.

Nev. 1970. While the insured's security guard was making a chip exchange at a casino, two bags of chips left in the insured's car were taken. The court interpreted the "in the care and custody" element of coverage to mean protective custody and not personal custody. This requirement is satisfied when the messenger makes reasonable efforts to protect and secure the insured property. *Home Indem. Co. v. Desert Palace, Inc.*, 468 P. 2d 19, 21-2.

N.J. Super. 1977. The insured's payroll was taken from the job superintendent's truck while he was at the job site. Transportation of the payroll was within his job duties. The court ruled that the payroll was within his "care and custody" while it was in the truck because he locked the truck, placed the keys in his pocket and remained near where the truck was parked. *Deleson Steel Co., Inc. v. Hartford Ins. Group*, 372 A.2d 663, 665.

B. Disappearance

Tenn. 1969. The court reasoned that when the money dropped into the depository and the messenger lost sight and access to the money, it qualified as a "disappearance" under the policy. *Swindler v. St. Paul Fire & Marine Ins. Co.*, 444 S.W.2d 147, 148-49.

C. Outside the premises

7th Cir. 1942 (Wis.). Robbers entered the office in which the insured conducted his business and forced him into another office next door, in which he did not conduct any business, at which time they stole diamonds from him. The court ruled that the policy was clear that "premises" for purposes of the policy was the interior of the office in which the insured conducted his business; thus, there was no coverage under the policy because the insured was outside the premises when the robbers took the diamonds from him. *Axt v. London & Lancashire Indem. Co.,* 131 F.2d 370, 371.

SECONDARY SOURCES:

Julie Alleyne, William H. Woods & Jonathan M. Bryan, *The Insuring Agreements—Other Coverages,* in ANNOTATED COMMERCIAL CRIME POLICY, SECOND EDITION 157 (Cole S. Kain & Lana M. Glovack eds. 2006).

John V. Burch & Timothy J. Burson, *Other Insuring Agreements in Commercial Crime and Other Fidelity Policies—An Update,* in COMMERCIAL CRIME POLICY 5-1 (Gilbert J. Schroeder, ed. 1997).

Michael R. Davisson, *The Other Insuring Agreements of Commercial Crime Policies,* in COMMERCIAL CRIME POLICY 285 (Randall I. Marmor & John J. Tomaine, eds., 2d ed. 2005).

Christopher C. Novak, Todd D. McCormick & Thomas R. Orofino, *The Other Insuring Agreements of Commercial Crime Policies,* in COMMERCIAL CRIME INSURANCE COVERAGE, 282 (Randall I. Marmor & Susan Koehler Sullivan, eds. 2014).

D. Insuring Agreement A.7.: Money Orders And Counterfeit Money

Insuring Agreement A.7. of the CCP states:

Money Orders And Counterfeit Money
We will pay for loss resulting directly from your having, in good faith, accepted in exchange for merchandise, "money" or services:
a.   Money orders issued by any post office, express company or "financial institution" that are not paid upon presentation; or

b.   **"Counterfeit money" that is acquired during the regular course of business.**[60]

COMMENT

Insuring Agreement A.7. of the CCP covers loss resulting directly from the good faith acceptance of merchandise, "money," or services: (1) in exchange for certain types of money orders that are dishonored when presented; or (2) in exchange for "counterfeit money" that is received in the usual course of business.[61] Insuring Agreement B.6. of the CPP, is substantially similar to Insuring Agreement A.7. of the CCP, except that instead of the defined term "counterfeit money" that is used in Insuring Agreement A.7. of the CCP, Insuring Agreement B.6. covers loss stemming from "counterfeit" paper currency of the United States or Canada.[62] Under the CPP, if the insured believes that it has accepted "counterfeit" money orders or "counterfeit" paper currency, it is required to notify the police.[63]

OUTLINE OF ANNOTATIONS

A. "Money Orders"
B. "Counterfeit"

ANNOTATIONS:

A. Money Orders

6th Cir. 2004 (Tenn.). Insured drafted its own Blanket Crime Policy covering loss for "any post office or express money order, issued or purporting to have been issued by any post office or express company." Insured accepted $1.5 million in counterfeit cashier's checks. Court determined that cashier's checks were not "express money orders" and

---

60   CCP, *supra* note 2, at 786, 800.
61   *Id.*
62   *Compare*, CCP, Insuring Agreement A.7., *supra* note 2, at 786, 800 *with* CPP, Insuring Agreement B.6., *supra* note 3, at 773.
63   CPP *supra* note 3, at 783.

were not issued by an "express company." *Harrah's Entm't, Inc. v. Ace Am. Ins. Co.*, 100 F. App'x 387, 389-92.

7th Cir. 1996 (Ill.). "Money orders differ from cashier's checks and certified checks in that the latter contain the signature of a bank official, while money orders do not." *Center Video Industrial Co, Inc. v. Roadway Package System, Inc.*, 90 F. 3d 185, 189.

Colo. 1988. Insured sold equipment and was given a counterfeit bank cashier's check. Court held that bank cashier's check was "not a money order issued by the post office or by an express company." *Computer Works, Inc. v. CNA Ins. Cos.*, 757 P.2d 167, 169.

N.J. 1997. Observing the public perception of a money order is at "odds with legal reality": a "money order 'has the characteristic of a check in that it constitutes a draft drawn on a bank and is payable on demand.'" *Trump Plaza Assoc. v. Haas*, 300 N.J. Super 113, 118 (quoting *Newman v. First Nat'l State Bank of Toms Rivers, NJ*, 173 N.J. 598, 601 (App. Div. 1980)).

B. Counterfeit

5th Cir. 1990 (Tex.). Bogus stock certificates were not "counterfeit" for purposes of insuring Agreement E of Bankers Blanket Bond, because there never existed any genuine certificates that the bogus certificates could be said to imitate; *Reliance Insurance Company v. Capital Bancshares, Inc./Capital Bank*, 685 F. Supp. 148 (N.D. 1988), *aff'd* 912 F.2d 756, 757-58 (citing *Bank of the Southwest v. National Surety Company*, 477 F.2d 73 (5th Cir.1973); and, *National City Bank of Minneapolis v. St. Paul Fire & Marine Insurance Company*, 447 N.W.2d 171, 178-80.)

Conn. Super Ct. 2010. Rejecting insurer's contention that fraudulent bank check constituted counterfeit money or money order within meaning of exclusion from crime policy. *Owens, Schine & Nicola, P.C. v. Travelers Cas. & Sur. Co. of Am.*, No. CV095024601, 2010 WL 4226958, *9 (Sept. 20, 2010) *vacated by* No. FBT-CV-09-5024601-S., 2012 WL 12246940.

SECONDARY SOURCES:

Julie Alleyne, William H. Woods & Jonathan M. Bryan, *The Insuring Agreements—Other Coverages*, in ANNOTATED COMMERCIAL CRIME POLICY, SECOND EDITION 157 (Cole S. Kain & Lana M. Glovack eds. 2006).

John V. Burch & Timothy J. Burson, *Other Insuring Agreements in Commercial Crime and Other Fidelity Policies—An Update*, in COMMERCIAL CRIME POLICY 5-1 (Gilbert J. Schroeder, ed. 1997).

Michael R. Davisson, *The Other Insuring Agreements of Commercial Crime Policies*, in COMMERCIAL CRIME POLICY 285 (Randall I. Marmor & John J. Tomaine, eds., 2d ed. 2005).

Christopher C. Novak, Todd D. McCormick & Thomas R. Orofino, *The Other Insuring Agreements of Commercial Crime Policies*, in COMMERCIAL CRIME INSURANCE COVERAGE, 282 (Randall I. Marmor & Susan Koehler Sullivan, eds. 2014).

E. Condition E.1.h.: Employee Benefit Plans

The Employee Benefit Plans Condition of the CPP states:

Employee Benefit Plans
The "employee benefit plans" shown in the Declarations (hereafter referred to as Plan) are included as Insureds under Insuring Agreement A.1., subject to the following:
(1) If any Plan is insured jointly with any other entity under this Policy, you or the Plan Administrator is responsible for selecting a Limit of Insurance for Insuring Agreement A.1. that is sufficient to provide a Limit of Insurance for each Plan that is at least equal to that required under ERISA as if each Plan were separately insured.
(2) With respect to loss sustained or "discovered" by any such Plan, Insuring Agreement A.1. is replaced by the following:

> We will pay for loss of or damage to "money", "securities" and "other property" resulting directly from fraudulent or dishonest acts committed by an "employee", whether identified or not, acting alone or in collusion with other persons.
>
> (3) If the first Named Insured is an entity other than a Plan, any payment we make for loss sustained by any Plan will be made to the Plan sustaining the loss.
>
> (4) If two or more Plans are insured under this Policy, any payment we make for loss:
>
> (a) Sustained by two or more Plans; or
>
> (b) Of commingled "money", "securities" or "other property" of two or more Plans;
>
> resulting directly from an "occurrence", will be made to each Plan sustaining loss in the proportion that the Limit of Insurance required under ERISA for each Plan bears to the total of those limits.
>
> (5) The Deductible Amount applicable to Insuring Agreement A.1. does not apply to loss sustained by any Plan.[64]

COMMENT

Pursuant to Condition E.1.h. of the CCP "employee benefit plans" that are named in the policy's declarations are included as insureds under Insuring Agreement A.1.—Employee Theft.[65] However, in order to satisfy ERISA, subparagraph (2) of Condition E.1.h. replaces the "theft" trigger of Insuring Agreement A.1. with an "employee" dishonesty trigger.[66]

The "Employee Benefit Plan" Condition in the CPP is substantively similar to Condition E.1.h. of the CPP[67]; however, because Insuring Agreement B.1. of the CPP is already subject to an "employee"

---

64 CCP, *supra* note 2, at 790-91, 804-05.

65 *Id.*

66 *Id.* The "theft" vs. "dishonesty" coverage triggers under "employee" fidelity insuring agreements are discussed in Chapters 3 and 4 of this publication.

67 *Compare*, CCP, Condition E.1.h., *supra* note 2, at 790-91, 804-05 *with* CPP, Condition 8., *supra* note 3, at 778-79.

dishonesty trigger,[68] an amendment to that Insuring Agreement to meet the requirements of ERISA was not necessary. Insuring Agreement B.1 of the CPP—Employee Dishonesty—contains a manifest intent requirement.[69] There is no manifest intent requirement included in the Condition E.1.h. amendment to Insuring Agreement A.1. of the CCP.[70]

For purposes of the "Employee Benefit Plans" Condition, the term "employee" is defined in Definition F.7.a.(4) of the CCP and in Definition 5.c. of the CPP to include: (1) trustees, officers, employees, and managers of "employee benefit plans" (but administrators or managers that are independent contractors are excluded); and (2) the insured's directors and trustees while they are engaged in handling "money," "securities," and "other property" belonging to an "employee benefit plan." Although the words "employee" and "manager" are defined in both the CCP and CPP, those definitions do not apply in this context.[71]

The "Employee Benefit Plans" Condition places the burden of purchasing a Limit of Insurance sufficient to comply with the Employee Retirement Income Security Act ("ERISA") on the insured or the Plan Administrator.[72] No deductible apples to a loss sustained by a covered "employee benefit plan."[73]

ANNOTATIONS:

2d Cir. 2011 (N.Y.). Affirming dismissal of complaint bereft of factual allegations from which it could be inferred that Bernard Madoff was a trustee, and thus, an employee, of the insured plan: fact that plan funds passed through third-party intermediary was found to "negate[]"the plausibility that Madoff was affiliated with insured ERISA plan. *Schupak Group, Inc. v. Travelers Casualty and Surety Company of America*, 2011

---

68   CPP, *supra* note 3, at 772.
69   *Id.*
70   CCP, *supra* note 2, at 790-91, 804-05.
71   CCP, Definition F.7.a.(4), *supra* note 2, at 785, 796, 799, 812 (the words under discussion are not in quotation marks); CPP, Definition 5.c., *supra* note 3, at 772-73 (the words under discussion are not in bold type).
72   CCP, *supra* note 2, at 790-91, 804-05; CPP, *supra* note 3, at 778-79.
73   *Id.*

WL 2214756, **2 (June 8, 2011) *affirming Schupak Group, Inc. v. Travelers Casualty and Surety Company of America*, 2010 WL 1487737.

5th Cir. 1988 (La.). The court addressed the terms "fiduciary," "plan official" and "employee" under the ERISA policy, ultimately ruling that the failed institution did not come within the definition of these terms for purposes of coverage because it was merely a party from whom the actual plan administrator had purchased negotiable instruments. The terms "fiduciary" and "plan official" are not utilized in Definition F.7.a.(4) of the Commercial Crime Policy or in Definition 5.c. of the Crime Protection Policy forms copyrighted in 2012. *Carroll L. Wood, III, D.D.S. v. CNA Ins. Cos.*, 837 F.2d 1402, 1403.

7th Cir. 2011 (Ill.). Declining to find that aggrieved beneficiary of ERISA plan lacked standing as asserted under adverse domination theory to sue the Plan's ERISA insurers. *Peabody v. Davis*, 636 F.3d 368, 370.

9th Cir. 1996 (Cal.). The insured suffered losses as a result of investments in second deeds of trust through a company managed by Glickman. The insured sought coverage for Glickman's dishonesty as a trustee under the policy's definition of "employee," arguing that Glickman was a fiduciary that had to be bonded under ERISA and that the term "fiduciary" was synonymous with "trustee" for purposes of the policy. Without deciding whether Glickman was a fiduciary, the court concluded that there was no coverage because even if Glickman were a fiduciary requiring bonding under ERISA, a fiduciary is not also a trustee, as the term "trustee" is more restrictive than "fiduciary." Furthermore, the ERISA bond does not provide coverage for all persons that must be bonded by ERISA, only those categories of persons as stated in the policy. *Joseph Rosenbaum, M.D., Inc. v. Hartford Fire Ins. Co.*, 104 F.3d 258, 261-62.

N.D. Ala. 2004. ERISA class action plaintiffs did not have legally protectable interest that would entitle them to intervene as of right in consolidated action pending before same court in which insurers sought rescission and declaratory judgment regarding policies that could provide coverage for claims asserted in ERISA litigation; proposed intervenors' interest in securing pool of insurance money to draw upon was not only purely economic, but also theoretical, considering no judgments had been obtained against insureds. *In re Healthsouth Corporation*, 219 F.R.D. 688, 691.

N.D. Cal. 1991. Profit-sharing plan beneficiary sought recovery against insurers under an ERISA bond. The court determined that a plan beneficiary has standing to prosecute a claim under the policy as a real party in interest. *Isola v. Hutchinson,* 780 F. Supp. 1299.

N.D. Ind. 2007. Declining to enforce ERISA bond's two-year suit limitation as the same was found to be in derogation of Indiana law governing public bonds, and applying state statute of limitations to find action on the bond to be timely. *Indiana Regional Council of Carpenters Pension Trust Fund v. Fidelity & Deposit Company of Maryland,* 2007 WL 683795, *3-4.

D. Ore. 2008. Limit of liability for "any one loss" arising under ERISA fiduciary coverage was modified and capped by the policy's Total Liability clause; the court declined to incorporate ERISA statute into policy. Since coverage terminates immediately upon discovery of dishonesty, coverage for the defalcator terminated prior to inception of policy. *United Association Union Local No. 290 ex rel. U.A.U. Local No. 290 Plumber, Steamfitter & Shipfitter Indus. 401(k) Plan & Trust v. Fed. Ins. Co.,* No. CIV.07-1521-HA, 2008 WL 3523271, *4.

D. Ore. 2005. District court declined to exercise jurisdiction under Declaratory Judgment Act over coverage disputes arising out of ERISA bond that would necessarily be resolved in parallel state court action. *Hartford Fire Insurance Co. v. Office and Professional Employees International Union Local No. 11,* 2005 WL 1981291, *2-3 (August 15, 2005)

S.D.N.Y 2010. Insured failed to adequately plead affirmative element of breach of contract claim (i.e., performance of insurance contract's cooperation clause by refusing to provide books or records, e.g., DOL Form 5500) so as to raise plausible inference that person to whom ERISA plan's funds were ultimately entrusted, Bernard Madoff, was a plan "employee" within coverage of ERISA Compliance Bond defining "employee" as "[a] trustee, an officer, employee administrator or manager, except an administrator or manager who is an independent contractor"). *Schupak Group, Inc. v. Travelers Casualty and Surety Company of America*, 2010 WL 1487737, *4-6 (April 13, 2010)

S.D.W.Va. 2011. Coverage for that portion of loss consisting of unpaid benefits was clearly precluded, however, the court found that the definition of "fiduciary" requiring a natural person, and excluding independent contractors was ambiguous; and held that insurer's argument that policy's definition evinced insurer's clear intent to restrict coverage to exclude entities (like third-party claim administrators) who would be required by ERISA to maintain their own insurance was inconsistent. *Guyan Int'l, Inc. v. Travelers Cas. & Sur. Co.*, No. CIV.A. 3:10-1244, 2011 WL 6225398, *5.

Ore. App. 2010. Investment firm and its principals were independent contractors beyond the scope of the definition of "employee" contained in identical provisions of ERISA compliance bonds issued by Travelers and Hartford insurance companies. *Employers-Shopmens Local 516 Pension Trust v. Travelers Casualty and Surety Company of America*, 235 P.3d 689, 494-95.

SECONDARY SOURCES

Julie Alleyne, William H. Woods & Jonathan M. Bryan, *The Insuring Agreements—Other Coverages*, in ANNOTATED COMMERCIAL CRIME POLICY, SECOND EDITION 157 (Cole S. Kain & Lana M. Glovack eds. 2006).

Edward G. Gallagher et al., A COMPLETE GUIDE TO THE ERISA BONDING REQUIREMENT (1994).

Chapter 7

The Insuring Agreements—

Electronic Coverages*

Technological advances have revolutionized the manner in which business is now conducted. Today's business environment is driven by information assets and network connectivity. While these advances have added a great deal of value to all participants in the global marketplace, they have also created additional risks for which businesses must be aware. As reliance on technology has increased, so too have the risks associated with information security and computing, referred to here as "cyber" risks. Businesses must accept that cyber risks are now a routine part of doing business in today's technology-driven age.[1]

However, keeping pace with appropriate security measures is both challenging and costly. The types of cyber threats are constantly changing, targeting new users and new platforms at a rapid pace.[2] Add to that the fact that business leaders may lack a clear understanding of the nature and magnitude of today's cyber threats, it should not be surprising that defensive strategies aimed to thwart internal and external cyber attacks commonly fall short of the intended objectives.

Because cyber risks cannot be eliminated completely, it is common for organizations to implement security measures only to the extent feasible, and to seek to shift any remaining risks to a willing third party (commonly, an insurer).[3] In the case of cyber risk, however, traditional

---

*   By Justin D. Wear, Manier & Herod, Nashville, Tennessee.

1   See PRICEWATERHOUSECOOPERS, LLP, KEY FINDINGS FROM THE 2013 US STATE OF CYBERCRIME SURVEY 1 (2013), http://www.pwc.com/en_US/us/increasing-it-effectiveness/publications/assets/us-state-of-cybercrime.pdf.

2   EMC CORPORATION, THE CURRENT STATE OF CYBERCRIME TWENTY THIRTEEN: AN INSIDE LOOK AT THE CHANGING THREAT LANDSCAPE 1 (2013), http://www.emc.com/collateral/fraud-report/current-state-cybercrime-2013.pdf.

3   MICHAEL E. WHITMAN AND HERBERT J. MATTORD, READINGS & CASES IN INFORMATION SECURITY: LAW & ETHICS 76 (Cengage Learning 2010).

forms of insurance coverage were not necessarily drafted with potential cyber liability or loss in mind. In turn, these policies often provide little if any coverage for cyber losses. Given the lack of coverage for information security, computing, and other forms of cyber risk, insurers sought to fill an unmet demand by insureds seeking to mitigate exposure from cyber attacks. From this, the market for cyber insurance was born.

Cyber insurance is still a relatively new phenomenon, commonly offered as a standalone policy or an endorsement to existing coverage. Given its infancy, it should come as no surprise that the scope of cyber insurance coverage varies significantly from policy to policy. There is also relatively little case law interpreting the scope of cyber coverages. What follows is a discussion of case addressing three (3) types of electronic coverages—the Computer Fraud coverage, the Electronic Funds Transfer Fraud coverage, and non-standard electronic coverages. Insureds often pursue computer crime claims under the Computer Fraud or the Electronic Funds Transfer Fraud provisions. Although each insuring agreement imposes different elements of coverage, both are intended to limit coverage to instances in which a fraudster, without the insured's knowledge, accesses the insured's computer system and steals property (either via directly transferring funds or causing the insured's bank to transfer funds) without any intervening action by the insured. The case law regarding computer crime is still evolving and courts have not always reached consistent results.

A. Computer Fraud Insuring Agreement

We will pay for your direct loss of, or your direct loss from damage to, Money, Securities and Other Property directly caused by Computer Fraud.

"Computer Fraud" is defined as:

The use of any computer to fraudulently cause a transfer of Money, Securities or Other Property from inside the Premises or Banking Premises:
1.   to a person (other than a Messenger) outside the Premises or Banking Premises; or
2.   to a place outside the Premises or Banking Premises.

B. Funds Transfer Fraud Insuring Agreement

We will pay you for your direct loss of Money and Securities contained in your Transfer Account on deposit at a Financial Institution directly caused by Funds Transfer Fraud.

"Funds Transfer Fraud" is defined as:

1. **an electronic, telegraphic, cable, teletype or telephone instruction fraudulently transmitted to a Financial Institution directing such institution to debit your Transfer Account and to transfer, pay or deliver Money or Securities from your Transfer Account which instruction purports to have been transmitted by you, but was in fact fraudulently transmitted by someone other than you without your knowledge or consent;**

2. **a fraudulent written instruction, other than one covered under Insuring Agreement B., issued to a Financial Institution directing such Financial Institution to debit a Transfer Account and to transfer, pay or deliver Money or Securities from such Transfer Account by use of an electronic funds transfer system at specified intervals or under specified conditions which written instruction purports to have been issued by you but was in fact fraudulently issued, Forged or altered by someone other than you without your knowledge or consent; or**

3. **an electronic, telegraphic, cable, teletype, telefacsimile, telephone or written instruction initially received by you which purports to have been transmitted by an Employee, but which was in fact fraudulently transmitted by someone else without your or the Employee's consent.**

OUTLINE OF ANNOTATIONS:

A. Computer Fraud
B. Funds Transfer Fraud
C. Non-Standard Electronic Coverages

ANNOTATIONS

A. Computer Fraud

C.D. Cal. 2015. Taylor and Lieberman, the insured accounting firm (the "Firm"), had power of attorney to make transfers from a client's account. In response to fraudulent e-mails purportedly sent by the Firm's client, the Firm's employee made two wire transfers to bank accounts in Asia. When the client disavowed the e-mails, the Firm was able to recover some of the transferred funds and reimbursed the client for the remainder. The insured asserted a claim under the Forgery, Computer Fraud, and Funds Transfer Fraud coverages of the subject policy. Each of these coverages required a direct loss sustained by an insured, and the court found that the loss from reimbursing the client was not a direct loss. The original transfers were of the client's funds from the client's account. The Firm sustained a loss only when it later reimbursed the client. The court held that this was not a direct loss and granted summary judgment to Federal Insurance Company. *Taylor and Lieberman v. Federal Insurance Co.*, 2015 WL 3824130.

C.D. Cal. 2014. Travelers was awarded summary judgment under its Computer Fraud insuring agreement. The insured, Pestmaster Services, Inc. ("Pestmaster"), retained Priority 1 Resource Group ("Priority 1") to handle preparation of Pestmaster's payroll, payment of payroll taxes and delivery of payroll checks. In order to allow Priority 1 to perform the agreed upon payroll and payroll tax services, Pestmaster executed an ACH authorization that authorized Priority 1 to obtain payment of Priority 1's approved invoices by initiating ACH transfers of funds from Pestmaster's bank account to Priority 1's bank account. For each payroll period, Priority 1 would prepare and deliver invoices to Pestmaster reflecting amounts owed for employee salaries and payroll taxes. Once Pestmaster approved payment of the invoices, Priority 1 would initiate an ACH transfer and move sufficient funds from Pestmaster's bank account to Priority 1's account in order to pay the amounts approved by Pestmaster. Although Priority 1 would typically complete Pestmaster's payroll on a Friday, it was not required to pay payroll taxes until the following Wednesday. Thus, the funds transferred to Priority 1's account would remain in Priority 1's account for several days until Priority 1 was required to pay the payroll taxes.

Pestmaster discovered that Priority 1 had failed to remit payroll taxes to the IRS from 2010-2011 in the amount of $373,136, and it sought coverage under the policy. The court held that the Computer Fraud provision was not implicated. The court stated that this insuring agreement is potentially implicated "when someone 'hacks' or obtains unauthorized access or entry to a computer in order to make an unauthorized transfer or otherwise uses a computer to fraudulently cause a transfer of funds." Priority 1 did not hack or obtain unauthorized access to Pestmaster's computer, and the court distinguished between "fraudulently causing a transfer" (which may implicate coverage) and "causing a fraudulent transfer." Because Priority 1 had access to Pestmaster's account, its conduct equated to "causing a fraudulent transfer," and not "fraudulent causing a transfer." Finally, the court held that Priority 1's use of a computer was merely incidental to the scheme, and that the claimed loss did not result directly from the use of a computer. *Pestmaster Services, Inc. v. Travelers Casualty and Surety Co. of America*, 2014 WL 3844627.

E.D. La. 2011. The insured, Methodist Health System Foundation, Inc. ("Methodist"), suffered a loss involving the infamous Bernie Madoff Ponzi scheme. Specifically, Methodist invested in Meridian Diversified Fund, which invested a portion of its holdings in Tremont Hedge Fund, which invested a portion of its holdings in Bernard L. Madoff Investment Securities, Inc. When the Ponzi scheme collapsed, Methodist sought coverage under a commercial crime provision substantially similar to the Computer Fraud insuring agreement. Methodist argued that coverage was implicated because Madoff used computers to create false documents that misled investors and gave the appearance of a legitimate investment operation. The court disagreed, and awarded summary judgment to Hartford Fire Insurance Company. The court held that the use of computers was not the direct cause of loss. *Methodist Health System Foundation, Inc. v. Hartford Fire Ins. Co.*, 2011 WL 2607107.

N.D. Tex. 2008. Great American Insurance Company ("Great American") filed a declaratory judgment action seeking a declaration that crime insurance policies issued to AFS/IBEX Financial Services, Inc. ("AFS") did not provide coverage for a loss involving checks issued by AFS and payable to Charles McMahon Insurance Agency. AFS provided premium financing in the insurance industry. AFS entered into an agreement with Charles Owen McMahon, Sr. ("McMahon Sr."), the owner of the Charlie McMahon Insurance Agency. This agreement contemplated that McMahon Sr. would create and sign premium finance applications on behalf of insureds. AFS would then send a check to the insurance company for the purchase price of the insurance, and the insureds would send regular payments to AFS. McMahon Sr.'s son, Charles Owen McMahon, Jr. ("McMahon Jr."), was an insurance agent and owner of McMahon Insurance Services. McMahon Jr. worked in an office adjoining the offices of McMahon Sr.'s agency. McMahon Jr. was also the office manager at McMahon Sr.'s agency, and had responsibility for submitting applications for premium financing to Defendant under his father's contract with Defendant. McMahon Jr. exploited this business relationship by submitting approximately 122 false applications to dupe AFS into issuing checks for the premium financing made payable to "Charles McMahon Insurance Agency." McMahon Jr. endorsed these checks "Charles McMahon Insurance Agency" and deposited the funds into his own personal bank account. McMahon Sr. was unaware of the fraudulent applications submitted to AFS.

AFS sought coverage under a Forgery insuring agreement, as well as a Computer Fraud insuring agreement and a Funds Transfer Fraud insuring agreement. Great American was awarded summary judgment under the Computer Fraud provision, successfully arguing that no computer actually caused the transfer of any funds from AFS' account. The court noted that "the language of these provisions indicate that they are designed to cover losses directly stemming from fraud perpetrated by use of a computer." *Great American Ins. Co. v. AFS/IBEX Financial Services, Inc.*, 2008 WL 2795205.

Conn. Super. Ct. 2010. The court held that using an e-mail to initiate a fraudulent scheme implicated the Computer Fraud insuring agreement. The insured, a law firm called *Owens, Schine & Nicola, P.C.* (the "Law Firm"), was contacted via an e-mail message from an individual claiming to be a North Carolina attorney. The e-mail message stated that the North

Carolina attorney was seeking the Law Firm's assistance collecting a debt for one of the attorney's China-based clients. Shortly thereafter, the Law Firm received an e-mail purporting to be from the director of the Chinese client. The following week, the purported client notified the Law Firm that the debtor had agreed to pay its debt and the Law Firm should expect a check in the mail. The next day, the Law Firm received what appeared to be an "Official Check" drawn on Wachovia Bank and made payable to the Law Firm in the amount of $198,610. The purported client sent the Law Firm instructions via e-mail to wire the funds from the Law Firm's trust account at Chase Bank to a South Korea account, after deducting $1,500 in fees for the Law Firm's assistance regarding the collection. After the funds were wired, it was determined that the "Official Check" was fraudulent and had not been honored by Wachovia.

The Law Firm submitted a claim to Travelers and litigation ensued. Travelers argued that the Computer Fraud provision required that a loss result from a third party hacking into the Law Firm's computer system, such as using a computer to manipulate numbers or events. The court disagreed and determined that 17 e-mails exchanges between the Law Firm and purported client constituted "computer fraud." According to the court, "the policy [was] ambiguous as to the amount of computer usage necessary to constitute computer fraud. This ambiguity is resolved in favor of the [insured]." A "computer hacking" incident was not required. The court also equated direct cause with proximate cause and held that the e-mails sent from the imposter directly caused the loss because the e-mails "set the chain of events in motion that led to the entire loss." *Owens, Schine & Nicola, P.C. v. Travelers Casualty & Surety Co. of America*, 2010 WL 4226958. The judgment in favor of the Law Firm was vacated at 2012 WL 12246940 (Conn. Super. Ct. Apr. 18, 2012).

N.Y. Super. Ct. 2010. The insured, Cumberland Packing Corp. ("Cumberland") suffered a loss involving the Bernie Madoff Ponzi scheme. Cumberland began investing with Madoff in 2002 on behalf of its employees through the Cumberland Employee's Pension Plan and Trust. Cumberland also made separate investments with Madoff beginning in 2005. When the Ponzi scheme collapsed, Cumberland submitted a claim of approximately $11 million under a variety of insuring clauses. Chubb paid $3.5 million but denied the balance of the claim under, *inter alia*, the Computer Fraud and the Funds Transfer

Fraud insuring clauses. The court held that coverage was precluded by a number of exclusions, including (1) loss caused by an Employee (as Madoff qualified as an Employee as a fiduciary of the pension plan), and (2) loss caused by a fraudulent, dishonest, or criminal act of an "authorized representative." *Cumberland Packing Corp. v. Chubb Ins. Corp.*, 958 N.Y.S. 2d 306.

Wis. Ct. App. 2008. This case involves theft from the insured Milwaukee Area Technical College (the "College") by Frontier Adjusters of Milwaukee and its former owner, Michael D. McNichols. The College hired McNichols and Frontier Adjusters of Milwaukee to process the College's workers' compensation claims. Under the agreements, Frontier Adjusters of Milwaukee evaluated the College's workers' compensation claims, and was supposed to pay those that had been approved. The payments were to be made from a Frontier Adjusters of Milwaukee bank account controlled by McNichols. The College replenished the money in that account by periodically sending checks to McNichols. The College also paid to Frontier Adjusters of Milwaukee an administrative fee. McNichols used his arrangement with the College to steal money that the College gave him to pay the workers' compensation claims. McNichols informed the College that he had sent checks to healthcare providers when, in reality, he had not done so. Instead, he kept the checks made payable to the healthcare providers in a box, unsent. McNichols would also send dummy check ledgers to the College that represented that he had paid the healthcare providers. The College sent the replenishment checks to McNichols based on the dummy check ledgers. McNichols put the replenishment money in the Frontier Adjusters of Milwaukee bank account and then stole that money by issuing checks from that account. The College sought coverage from St. Paul Travelers under, inter alia, the Computer Fraud insuring agreement. According to the College, coverage was implicated because McNichols used a computer to print the fraudulent ledgers and to manage the Frontier Adjusters of Milwaukee bank account into which he put the College's replenishment funds. The court held that it need not determine whether the Computer Fraud provision was implicated because the claim was precluded by the "authorized representative" exclusion. The policy excluded coverage for "any dishonest or criminal acts committed by any of your...authorized representatives whether acting alone or in collusion with other persons or while performing services for you or otherwise." The College asserted that it never "authorized" McNichols to steal from it, but that was insufficient to prevent the exclusion from applying. The trial court's award of summary judgment to St. Paul Travelers was affirmed. *Milwaukee Area Technical College v. Frontier Adjusters of Milwaukee*, 2008 WL 1787682.

B. Funds Transfer Fraud

C.D. Cal. 2015. Taylor and Lieberman, the insured accounting firm (the "Firm"), had power of attorney to make transfers from a client's account. In response to fraudulent e-mails purportedly sent by the Firm's client, the Firm's employee made two wire transfers to bank accounts in Asia. When the client disavowed the e-mails, the Firm was able to recover some of the transferred funds and reimbursed the client for the remainder. The insured asserted a claim under the Forgery, Computer Fraud, and Funds Transfer Fraud coverages of the subject policy. Each of these coverages required a direct loss sustained by an insured, and the court found that the loss from reimbursing the client was not a direct loss. The original transfers were of the client's funds from the client's account. The Firm sustained a loss only when it later reimbursed the client. The court held that this was not a direct loss and granted summary judgment to Federal. *Taylor and Lieberman v. Federal Insurance Co.*, 2015 WL 3824130.

C.D. Cal. 2014. Travelers was awarded summary judgment under its Computer Fraud insuring agreement. The insured, Pestmaster Services, Inc. ("Pestmaster"), retained Priority 1 Resource Group ("Priority 1") to handle preparation of Pestmaster's payroll, payment of payroll taxes, and delivery of payroll checks. In order to allow Priority 1 to perform the agreed upon payroll and payroll tax services, Pestmaster executed an ACH authorization that authorized Priority 1 to obtain payment of Priority 1's approved invoices by initiating ACH transfers of funds from Pestmaster's bank account to Priority 1's bank account. For each payroll period, Priority 1 would prepare and deliver invoices to Pestmaster reflecting amounts owed for employee salaries and payroll taxes. Once Pestmaster approved payment of the invoices, Priority 1 would initiate an ACH transfer and move sufficient funds from Pestmaster's bank account to Priority 1's account in order to pay the amounts approved by Pestmaster. Although Priority 1 would typically complete Pestmaster's payroll on a Friday, it was not required to pay payroll taxes until the following Wednesday. Thus, the funds transferred to Priority 1's account would remain in Priority 1's account for several days until Priority 1 was required to pay the payroll taxes.

Pestmaster discovered that Priority 1 had failed to remit payroll taxes to the IRS from 2010-2011 in the amount of $373,136, and it sought coverage under the policy. The court held that the Funds Transfer Fraud provision was not implicated. According to the court, the Funds Transfer Fraud insuring agreement generally provided coverage for loss involving a fraudulent instruction to Pestmaster's bank instructing a transfer of funds when, in reality, Pestmaster was unaware of the instruction, the instruction was forged or altered, etc. The court held that coverage was not implicated under this provision because it "does not cover authorized or valid electronic transactions, such as the authorized ACH transfers in this case, even though they are, or may be, associated with a fraudulent scheme." All of the instructions from Priority 1 to Pestmaster's bank, while in the furtherance of a fraudulent scheme, were authorized and proper. The fact that Priority 1 simply stole the funds once they were properly transmitted did not trigger coverage. *Pestmaster Services, Inc. v. Travelers Casualty and Surety Co. of America*, 2014 WL 3844627.

C.D. Cal. 2014. A payroll processor defrauded the insured, Southern California Counseling Center ("SCCC"). SCCC authorized the processor to debit SCCC's bank account for funds that were supposed to be used to pay SCCC's payroll tax obligations. Instead, the funds were diverted to the use of the president of the processor. SCCC submitted a claim to Great American Insurance Company ("Great American"). The insuring clause at issue was subject to an exclusion for acts of SCCC's authorized representatives. The district court followed Ninth Circuit precedent and found that an authorized representative was someone authorized by SCCC to have access to the stolen funds; that is, someone whom SCCC empowered to act on its behalf. Applying this meaning, the payroll processor was an authorized representative, and the loss was not covered. The court rejected SCCC's argument that the processor never intended to apply the funds properly and so the agreement authorizing the processor to act on SCCC's behalf was void ab initio and the processor was not an authorized representative. The court found that there was fraud in the inducement to the agreement and it was voidable, as opposed to void ab initio. SCCC knew what it was signing and intended to authorize the processor to act on its behalf. The court also noted that SCCC's argument "would render the authorized representative exclusion a nullity." The court granted summary judgment to Great American and denied SCCC's cross-motion for summary judgment. *Southern California Counseling Center v. Great American Insurance Co.*, Case No. 2:13-cv-5468.

S.D. Ind. 2006. The insured, Brightpoint, Inc. ("Brightpoint") submitted a claim to Zurich American Insurance Company ("Zurich") for loss involving the theft of pre-paid phone cards. The fraudsters utilized fraudulent purchase orders, post-dated checks, and purported bank guaranty of checks to be transmitted via facsimile to Brightpoint. On the day of the alleged theft, Brightpoint received the usual documents by facsimile and Brightpoint's representative met with the fraudster near Brightpoint's office and exchanged the cards for the original documents. Zurich was granted summary judgment because the allegedly fraudulent facsimiles (facsimiles came within the subject coverage) did not directly cause the surrender of the money. The court stated, "Only after Brightpoint received the physical documents would it release the phone cards and, based on established practices of Brightpoint, the cards would not have been turned over simply on the basis of a facsimile. The fraud in this instance occurred through the use of the unauthorized checks and guaranties, not the manipulation of numbers or events through the use of a computer, facsimile machine or other similar device." The court expressly rejected Brightpoint's argument that coverage was implicated if a computer was used and a loss subsequently followed. According to the court, the insured's "expansive interpretation of the term "directly related" represents a distortion of the policy terms." *Brightpoint, Inc. v. Zurich American Ins. Co.*, 2006 WL 693377.

N.D. Tex. 2008. Great American Insurance Company ("Great American") filed a declaratory judgment action seeking a declaration that crime insurance policies issued to AFS/IBEX Financial Services, Inc. ("AFS") did not provide coverage for a loss involving checks issued by AFS and payable to Charles McMahon Insurance Agency. AFS provided premium financing in the insurance industry. AFS entered into an agreement with Charles Owen McMahon, Sr. ("McMahon Sr."), the owner of the Charlie McMahon Insurance Agency. This agreement contemplated that McMahon Sr. would create and sign premium finance applications on behalf of insureds. AFS would then send a check to the insurance company for the purchase price of the insurance, and the insureds would send regular payments to AFS. McMahon Sr.'s son, Charles Owen McMahon, Jr. ("McMahon Jr."), was an insurance agent and owner of McMahon Insurance Services. McMahon Jr. worked in an office adjoining the offices of McMahon Sr.'s agency. McMahon Jr. was also the office manager at McMahon Sr.'s agency, and had responsibility for submitting applications for premium financing to Defendant under his father's contract with Defendant. McMahon Jr. exploited this business relationship by submitting approximately 122 false applications to dupe AFS into issuing checks for the premium financing made payable to "Charles McMahon Insurance Agency." McMahon Jr. endorsed these checks "Charles McMahon Insurance Agency" and deposited the funds into his own personal bank account. McMahon Sr. was unaware of the fraudulent applications submitted to AFS.

AFS sought coverage under a Forgery insuring agreement, as well as a Computer Fraud insuring agreement and a Funds Transfer Fraud insuring agreement. Great American was awarded summary judgment under the Computer Fraud provision, successfully arguing that no computer actually caused the transfer of any funds from AFS's account. The court noted that "the language of these provisions indicate that they are designed to cover losses *directly* stemming from fraud perpetrated by use of a computer." *Great American Ins. Co. v. AFS/IBEX Financial Services, Inc.*, 2008 WL 2795205.

N.Y. Super. Ct. 2010. The insured, Cumberland Packing Corp. ("Cumberland") suffered a loss involving the Bernie Madoff Ponzi scheme. Cumberland began investing with Madoff in 2002 on behalf of its employees through the Cumberland Employee's Pension Plan and Trust. Cumberland also made separate investments with Madoff beginning in 2005. When the Ponzi scheme collapsed, Cumberland submitted a claim of approximately $11 million under a variety of insuring clauses. Chubb paid $3.5 million but denied the balance of the claim under, *inter alia*, the Computer Fraud and the Funds Transfer Fraud insuring clauses. The court held that coverage was precluded by a number of exclusions, including (1) loss caused by an Employee (as Madoff qualified as an Employee as a fiduciary of the pension plan), and (2) loss caused by a fraudulent, dishonest, or criminal act of an "authorized representative." *Cumberland Packing Corp. v. Chubb Ins. Corp.*, 958 N.Y.S. 2d 306.

C. Non-Standard Electronic Coverages

1st Cir. 1999. Stop & Shop Companies, Inc. ("Stop & Shop") sought coverage when an entity retained by Stop & Shop to process and pay taxes stole Stop & Shop's funds. Stop & Shop's On Premises coverage included the "Computer Theft of Money and Securities within or from the Premises." Meanwhile, the subject policy excluded coverage for loss due to the "[t]heft or any other fraudulent, dishonest or criminal act . . . by any [e]mployee, director, trustee or authorized representative of the Insured whether acting alone or in collusion with others." The court held that coverage was excluded pursuant to the "authorized representative" exclusion. The court held that an "authorized representative" encompassed "either a person or company empowered to act on an entity's behalf." *Stop & Shop Companies, Inc. v. Federal Ins. Co.*, 136 F.3d 71.

6th Cir. 2014. The insured, Bank of Ann Arbor (the "Bank"), received a fax purporting to be from a customer requesting that $196,000 from the customer's home equity line of credit (HELOC) be wired to a bank in South Korea. The Bank verified the instruction by (1) comparing the signature on the fax with the signature on file for the customer and (2) calling the customer. The call confirmed the instruction. The Bank was unaware that the telephone number for the customer in its records had been changed a few days earlier via a fax purportedly from the customer. The Bank wired the funds. When the imposter attempted to repeat the fraud a few days later, another employee of the Bank looked up the prior number and called the true customer who denied making the transfer. Everest National Insurance Company ("Everest") had issued a financial institution bond ("FIB") to the Bank, and the Bank sought coverage under Insuring Agreement (D). Everest denied the claim based on the FIB's loan loss exclusion and a rider entitled Electronic/Computer Systems Rider. The Bank sued, was awarded summary judgment, and the Sixth Circuit affirmed. The reported decisions did not address the Electronic/Computer Systems Rider.

With regard to the FIB's loan loss exclusion, the court considered the purpose of the provision and concluded, "Plaintiff did not lose $196,000 as a result of giving out a loan or extension of credit. Plaintiff lost $196,000 because an individual forged the signature of its true customer and thereby managed to get $196,000 transferred from the true customer's HELOC to an account in South Korea, which resulted in the money being stolen. The plain language of the bond covers this type of loss and the exclusion in section 2(e) clearly does not apply."

Finally, after summary judgment was granted by the district court, Everest filed a motion for reconsideration and argued, for the first time, that the faxed transfer instruction was not an "original" document as required by Insuring Agreement (D). The motion for reconsideration was denied, and on appeal, the Sixth Circuit held that Everest had waived this potential defense by not citing it as a basis for denial of coverage. The Sixth Circuit also held that the district court did not abuse its discretion in refusing to grant reconsideration since the argument that the fax was not an "original" could have been made in opposition to the Bank's summary judgment motion. *Bank of Ann Arbor v. Everest Nat'l Ins. Co.*, 2013 WL 665067, *aff'd* 563 F. App'x 473 (6th Cir. 2014). Denial of Everest's motion for reconsideration reported at 2013 WL 1914232 (E.D. Mich. May 8, 2013).

6th Cir. 2012. Computer hackers utilized the local wireless network at a DSW shoe store to access the main computer system or the insured, Retail Ventures, Inc. ("Retail Ventures"). Once in the main computer system, the hackers downloaded credit card and checking account information for more than 1.4 million customers of 108 DSW stores. The hackers then used the stolen customer credit card and checking account information to initiate unauthorized transactions on the customers' accounts. Retail Ventures made a claim under the Computer and Funds Transfer Fraud Endorsement of their Blanket Crime Policy to recover "expenses for customer communications, public relations, customer claims and lawsuits, and attorney fees in connection with investigations by seven state Attorney Generals and the Federal Trade Commission (FTC)." The largest portion of Retail Ventures' alleged loss stemmed from credit card charge backs, credit card reissuance, account monitoring, and fines by VISA/MasterCard.

The Computer and Funds Transfer Fraud Endorsement covered "Loss which the Insured shall sustain resulting directly from . . . [t]he theft of any Insured property by Computer Fraud." National Union Fire Insurance Company of Pittsburgh, Pa. ("National Union") denied the claim, in part, on the grounds that Retail Ventures did not suffer a loss "resulting directly from" the theft of customer credit card and checking account information. National Union argued that the "'resulting directly from" language unambiguously required that the theft of property by computer fraud be the "sole" and "immediate" cause of the insured's loss." The theft of customer information, standing alone, appeared to have caused no loss to Retail Ventures; it was the subsequent use of the information that resulted in an eventual loss to Retail Ventures.

The district court disagreed and the Sixth Circuit affirmed an award of summary judgment in favor of Retail Ventures. The Sixth Circuit equated direct cause with proximate cause and held that Retail Ventures' loss from customer credit card charge backs, card reissuance, account monitoring, and fines were losses "resulting directly from" Computer Fraud. *Retail Ventures, Inc. v. National Union Fire Insurance Co. of Pittsburg, Pa.,* 691 F.3d 821.

9th Cir. 2015. The insured, First National Bank of Northern California (the "Bank") sought coverage regarding wire transfers from its customer's account based on what turned out to be fraudulent instructions. After reimbursing the customer, the Bank sought to recover on its financial institution bond (the "FIB"). The FIB included a Fraudulent Instructions Insuring Clause that provided coverage if the Bank "suffers a loss directly from . . . having in good faith . . . transferred funds on deposit in a Customer's account in reliance upon a fraudulent telephonic voice instruction" transmitted to the Bank "which purports to be from . . . [among others] an individual person who is a Customer of" the Bank. For purposes of the Fraudulent Instructions Insuring Clause, a Customer is defined as "an entity or natural person" that

(i) has a Written agreement with the Insured authorizing the Insured to rely on telephonic voice or Telefacsimile Device instructions to make transfers;

(ii) has provided the Insured with the names of persons authorized to initiate such transfers; and

(iii) with whom the Insured has established an instruction verification procedure other than voice recognition.

The Bank had a standard form agreement authorizing wire transfers based on telephone or facsimile instructions, but had not secured the customer's signature or ascent to it. Travelers therefore was awarded summary judgment, and the Ninth Circuit affirmed. The court rejected the Bank's argument that the signed signature card regarding the account somehow incorporated by reference the non-signed, standard form agreement authorizing wire transfers based on telephone or facsimile instructions. The requisites for incorporation by reference under California law were not met, and the district court properly found that the signature card and other documents did not qualify as a written agreement under the bond. *First National Bank of Northern California v. St. Paul Mercury Insurance Co.*, 2013 WL 61026 (N.D. Cal. Jan. 3, 2013), *aff'd* 2015 WL 2225044 (9th Cir. May 11, 2015).

9th Cir. 1999. The insured, Stanford University Hospital (the "Hospital"), sought coverage when a payroll processor stole the Hospital's funds. The Hospital's On Premises coverage included the "Computer Theft of Money and Securities within or from the Premises." The Ninth Circuit held that coverage was excluded pursuant to the "authorized representative" exclusion. The court commented that "the plain meaning of the 'authorized representative' language in the crime insurance policies is not ambiguous and covers those who by authorization of the insured are given access to and permitted to handle the insured's funds. No other interpretation would make sense in terms of the crime insurance policy. The 'authorized representative' provision excludes coverage for misappropriation of funds by those individual or entities authorized by the insured to have access to the funds—in essence, those whom the insured empowers to act on its behalf." *Stanford Univ. Hospital v. Federal Ins. Co.*, 174 F.3d 1077.

S.D. Fla. 1997. The insured, Peoples Telephone Company ("Peoples"), sought coverage from Hartford under a crime policy for loss involving stolen information. Peoples provided cellular phones for rental car fleets. Lists containing combinations of electronic serial numbers and mobile telephone identification numbers ("ESN/MIN combinations"), which are necessary to activate and use cellular phones, allegedly was stolen by a Peoples employee. The employee allegedly sold the lists to third parties, who, in turn, used the number combinations to program (or "clone") other cellular phones. As a result, Peoples claims to have incurred significant charges for unauthorized telephone usage. Peoples sought coverage for usage charges billed to Peoples by its cellular telephone providers, plus deactivation/reactivation charges incurred by Peoples to disconnect the stolen numbers and install new numbers on its cellular phone inventory. At issue was whether the stolen information constituted "property other than money and securities" under the subject policy, which was defined as "tangible property other than money and securities that has intrinsic value." The court held that the stolen information was not tangible property, and Hartford Fire Insurance Company was awarded summary judgment. *Peoples Telephone Co. v. Hartford Fire Insurance Co.*, 36 F. Supp. 2d 1335.

D. Minn. 2014. The State Bank of Bellingham (the "Bank") suffered a loss of $485,000 when unknown criminals transferred that amount from an account at the Bank to an account at a bank in Poland. The transfer could not be reversed. The Bank used FedLine for wire transfers, and its security procedures included two separate users to authorize transfers, several passwords (including ones generated by tokens), and various firewalls and anti-virus services. The investigation of BancInsure, Inc. ("BancInsure") showed that the Bank's employees used the computer for such things as e-mail and visits to Facebook, that the tokens for two users were left in the computer's USB ports, and that one employee would commonly enter information for herself and the supposed second employee. By clicking on a link in an e-mail, the Zeus virus was introduced into the computer, and for various reasons the anti-virus systems failed to prevent the virus from working. The result was that the criminals obtained the information needed to initiate the fraudulent wire transfer.

BancInsure did not dispute that the loss resulted from a fraudulent transfer within the Computer Systems Fraud insuring agreement, which provides coverage for:

Loss resulting directly from a fraudulent
(1)   entry of Electronic Data or Computer Program into, or
(2)   change of Electronic Data or Computer Program within
any Computer System operated by the Insured, whether owned
or leased, or any Computer System identified in the application
for this Bond, or a Computer System first used by the Insured
during the Bond Period, provided the entry or change causes
(1)   property to be transferred, paid or delivered,
(2)   an account of the Insured or of its customer to be added,
       deleted, debited or credited, or
(3)   an unauthorized account or a fictitious account to be
       debited or credited.
In this Insuring Agreement (H), fraudulent entry or change shall
include such entry or change made by an employee of the
Insured acting in good faith
(1)   on an instruction from a software contractor who has a
       written agreement with the Insured to design, implement or
       service programs for a Computer System covered by this
       Insuring Agreement (H), or
(2)   on an instruction transmitted by Tested telex or similar
       means of Tested communication identified in the
       application for this Bond purportedly sent by a customer,
       financial institution, or automated clearing house.

BancInsure asserted that several exclusions and the Bank's alleged lack
of cooperation barred the claim. The court held that none of the
exclusions asserted by BancInsure—including loss caused by an
Employee and lost resulting directly or indirectly from the theft of
confidential information—rose to the level of an overriding cause of the
loss. The acts of the insured's employees, theft of confidential
information, and failure to keep the anti-virus protections up to date were
not an overriding cause of the loss as required by Minnesota law to
defeat coverage. The court concluded, "Thus, even if those
circumstances 'played an essential role' in the loss, they were not
'independent and efficient causes' of the loss. In other words, without the
fraudster's actions, there would have been no loss even if all of the other
circumstances existed." Finally, the court also rejected BancInsure's
defense based on the Bank's breach of the cooperation provision of the

bond because the lack of cooperation had not prejudiced BancInsure. *State Bank of Bellingham v. BancInsure, Inc.*, 2014 WL 4829184.

E.D. Pa. 2014. An employee of the insured, Sb1 Federal Credit Union (the "Credit Union"), made several wire transfers to accounts in Thailand based on e-mail requests and faxed transfer instructions purportedly transmitted by an accountholder. The Credit Union sought coverage under, *inter alia*, a Funds Transfer insuring agreement in the subject credit union bond. The Funds Transfer insuring agreement provided coverage for:

> Loss resulting directly from fraudulent instruction through E-mail, Telefacsimile or Telephonic means received by the Insured from a person who purports to be the Accountholder, the Accountholder's authorized representative or an Employee but is not the Accountholder, provided:
> (a)   the Insured performed a Callback Verification with respect to such instruction, or
> (b)   the Insured followed a commercially reasonable security procedure set forth in a written funds transfer agreement, signed by the Accountholder or the Accountholder's authorized representative, that governs the transaction and instruction.

The insurer, Berkley Regional Insurance Company ("Berkley"), filed a motion to dismiss, which was granted. The Credit Union's employee did not follow the Credit Union's own requirement for a telephone verification callback. The employee did request that the "accountholder" send a copy of his driver's license or passport to verify his identity, but the imposter explained by e-mail that he was traveling and could not make a copy.

The Credit Union argued that verification of the signature on the faxed transfer instruction was a "commercially reasonable security procedure" under the insuring agreement. The court did not reach the question of whether a signature comparison could be a security procedure, although it noted that the Pennsylvania UCC said it was not. The complaint failed as a matter of law because the accountholder had "membership and account agreements" with the Credit Union, but they were not written, signed by the accountholder or authorized funds transfers as required by the Funds Transfer insuring agreement. *Sb1 Federal Credit Union v. FinSecure LLC*, 2014 WL 1395036.

W.D. Wash. 2011. The insured, Pinnacle Processing Group, Inc., ("Pinnacle"), was a company that processed credit card transactions for merchants. In short, merchants would contract with Pinnacle to lease a credit card terminal so the merchant's customers could pay for goods and services with credit cards. At the end of each day, a third party called Merrick Bank would deposit funds in the merchant's account equal to the sum of all credit card transactions. Merrick Bank was reimbursed by the financial institutions that issued the credit card to the consumers (the "Issuing Banks"). In the event a credit card transaction had to be reversed or refunded (either through error, fraud, or a returned item), funds were returned to the Issuing Banks by Merrick Bank, and Merrick Bank was reimbursed by the merchant. If for some reason Merrick Bank could not be reimbursed (if, for example, the merchant is insolvent or has disappeared), Pinnacle was required to reimburse Merrick Bank. Pinnacle established a $250,000 reserve account that Merrick Bank could draw from to reimburse chargebacks that were not reimbursed by the merchant. When Merrick Bank withdrew from the reserve account, Pinnacle was required to replenish those funds within two days.

From December 8, 2008 through December 17, 2008, Pinnacle processed $228,000 worth of credit card transactions from a jeweler. In January 2009, there were $228,044 of chargebacks that were not paid by the jeweler and therefore paid by Pinnacle. The "purchases" that resulted in the chargebacks were alleged to be fraudulent. Pinnacle sought coverage under an endorsement that provided coverage for loss resulting directly from Computer Fraud. The endorsement defined Computer Fraud as:

> [A]ny act of stealing property following and directly related to the use of any computer to fraudulently cause a transfer of that property from inside your premises or from a banking institution or similar safe depository, to a person (other than a "messenger") outside those premises or to a place outside those premises.

Hartford Casualty Insurance Company argued that coverage was not implicated because there was no "direct loss," and the court agreed. The court held that direct means "without any intervening agency or step:

without any intruding or diverting factor." In this matter, Pinnacle's loss did not occur until (1) Merrick Bank was unable to recover the chargeback funds from the merchant banks; (2) Merrick Bank deducted funds from Pinnacle's reserve account; and (3) Pinnacle fulfilled its contractual obligation to replace those deducted funds. The court held that finding coverage under these facts would render the word "directly" to be superfluous. *Pinnacle Processing Group, Inc. v. Hartford Cas. Ins. Co.*, 2011 WL 5299557.

N.J. App. Div. 2005. Morgan Stanley Dean Witter & Co. ("Morgan Stanley") sued numerous insurance carriers seeking to recover over $21 million Morgan Stanley paid to defend and settle a lawsuit brought by First Tokyo Index Trust Limited ("First Tokyo"). The First Tokyo lawsuit involved fraudulent conduct by First Tokyo's investment advisor, London and Bishopsgate International ("London/Bishopsgate"), a company affiliated with a prominent English businessman named Robert Maxwell. The relationship between Morgan Stanley and London/Bishopsgate began when the companies executed a written custodial services agreement, in which Morgan Stanley agreed to safeguard money and property that was owned and held by London/Bishopsgate. As custodian, Morgan Stanley was to be responsive to London/Bishopsgate's instructions, which could come from several persons specifically authorized to issue instructions on behalf of London/Bishopsgate. London/Bishopsgate also identified which of the authorized persons served as its authorized signatories. In order to facilitate receipt of any instructions, Morgan Stanley provided London/Bishopsgate with computer software allowing access to Morgan Stanley's computer programs.

After London/Bishopsgate and Morgan Stanley entered into the custodial services agreement, London/Bishopsgate entered into an investment management contract with First Tokyo. Under this contract, First Tokyo agreed to allow London/Bishopsgate to manage its investments. To effectuate this agreement, London/Bishopsgate opened an account with Morgan Stanley, where it also held accounts for eight other clients. The account opened by London/Bishopsgate to manage First Tokyo's investments was entitled "Client Account: 00040056 First Tokyo Index Trust." Two years later, an entity called Headington Investments Limited ("Headington"), which owned 75% percent of London/Bishopsgate, announced that it was making a public offer to purchase First Tokyo. After the offer became unconditional, Headington requested that there be no change to First Tokyo's securities portfolio without Headington's consent. Therefore, First Tokyo instructed London/Bishopsgate to cease trading on its behalf. No one informed Morgan Stanley that London/Bishopsgate no longer had authority to trade for First Tokyo. Despite revocation of London/Bishopsgate's authority, London/Bishopsgate subsequently instructed Morgan Stanley to liquidate the bulk of First Tokyo's portfolio in five different transactions. Through each of these transactions, the sale proceeds were delivered to London/Bishopsgate-affiliated accounts. The transactions were accomplished through instructions sent by computer, fax, and voice to Morgan Stanley by persons associated with and specifically authorized by London/Bishopsgate to do its business. After discovering the loss, First Tokyo sued Morgan Stanley.

In its complaint against the carriers, Morgan Stanley asserted coverage under three insuring agreements protecting Morgan Stanley against fraudulent instructions communicated by voice, fax, and computer. The carriers were awarded summary judgment by the trial court, but the appellate court reversed in part—affirming summary judgment with regard to the fax instructions and computer instructions insuring agreements, but reversing with regard to the voice instructions insuring agreement. The court described coverage with regard to fax instructions as "imposter coverage," and the instructions received by Morgan Stanley were unquestionably not sent by an imposter. Coverage also was not implicated under the computer instructions insuring agreement, as an exclusion expressly precluded coverage for "loss by reason of the input of Electronic Data at an authorized electronic terminal . . . or a Customer Communication System by a customer or other person who had authorized access to the customer's authentication mechanism." *Morgan Stanley Dean Witter & Co. v. Chubb*, 2005 WL 3242234.

N.Y. 2015. The insured, Universal American Corp. ("Universal"), suffered a loss when an authorized user of its computer system submitted Medicare claims for services that were never rendered. Universal sought coverage under a Computer System Fraud rider to the subject policy. The rider provided coverage for:

Loss resulting directly from a fraudulent
(1)   entry of Electronic Data or Computer Program into, or
(2)   change of Electronic Data or Computer Program within the
       Insured's proprietary Computer System
...
provided that the entry or change causes
(a)   Property to be transferred, paid or delivered,
(b)   an account of the insured, or of its customer, to be added,
       deleted, debited or credited, or
(c)   an unauthorized account or a fictitious account to be
       debited or credited

National Union Fire Insurance Company of Pittsburgh, Pa. ("National Union") prevailed at the trial court and appellate court levels, and National Union's judgment was affirmed by Court of Appeals of New York (New York's highest court). The court held that the rider applies to loss resulting directly from fraudulent access to the computer system, and not from loss resulting directly from the content submitted by authorized users. Thus, the court distinguished between fraudulent entry of data (which may be covered) and entry of fraudulent data (which is not covered). *Universal American Corp. v. National Union Fire Insurance Company of Pittsburgh, Pa.*, 959 N.Y.S. 2d 849, *aff'd* 972 N.Y.S. 2d 241, *aff'd* 2015 WL 3885816 (N.Y. June 25, 2015).

Pa. Commonw. Pl. 2001. Northside Bank ("the Bank") sought coverage under an insurance policy issued by American Casualty Co. of Reading, Pa. ("American Casualty") for a computer crime loss. The Bank opened an account incident to a merchant services agreement with a company known as Dakco PC Product Division Inc. ("Dakco"). Dakco then proceeded to accept orders for merchandise, and take payment by debit and credit cards. Dakco electronically transmitted the debit and credit card authorizations to the Bank and upon receipt, the Bank transferred money into Dakco's account. Eventually, it was discovered that Dakco never delivered the purchased merchandise to its customers, and they exercised their rights under federal law to rescind their obligation to pay for the unshipped merchandise. When these customers refused to pay, their creditors, in turn, refused to pay, or charged back the amounts paid to the Bank. When the Bank went to charge back Dakco, it found Dakco's accounts depleted. The Bank sustained a loss of about $300,000.

The Bank sought coverage under a Computer Fraud insuring provision, which provided coverage for:

> Loss resulting from the insured having in good faith and in the usual course of business transferred, paid or delivered any funds or property, established any credit, debited any account or given any value or assumed any liability as the direct result of any fraudulent electronic instruction or advice transmitted to or from the insured through
> (1)   the insured's computer system;
> (2)   any shared network or facility for any automated teller machine or point-of-sale terminal in which the insured participates; or
> (3)   a corporate customer cash management system.

The Bank also sought coverage under an Electronic Funds Transfer insuring provision, which provided coverage for:

> Loss resulting directly from the insured having in good faith and in the usual course of business transferred, paid or delivered any funds or property, or established any credit or given any value on the faith of, or assumed any liability or otherwise acted upon, any *fraudulent electronic instruction or advice* transmitted to the insured through an electronic funds transfer system.

For both insuring provisions, the phrase "fraudulent electronic instruction or advice" was defined as:

> (a)   an electronic instruction or advice purporting to have been sent by another financial institution or automated clearing house or by a customer of the insured, and which instruction or advice is intended to deceive and is not in fact sent by said financial institution or automated clearing house or by said customer; or
> (b)   an electronic instruction or advice which is modified or altered with intent to deceive after being sent by another financial institution or automated clearing house or by a customer of the insured.

The Bank argued that the instructions it received were "modified or altered with intent to deceive" under subsection (b) of the definition of "fraudulent electronic instruction or advice." The court disagreed and American Casualty was awarded summary judgment. The court opined that the terms "modified" and "altered" were unambiguous and that the Bank paid the electronic instructions it received in their unmodified and unaltered language. The court also commented "A review of the insurance policy *in toto*, and the electronic fund transfer and computer crimes coverage in particular, establishes that the purpose of the coverage was to protect the Bank from someone breaking into the electronic fund transfer system and pretending to be an authorized representative or altering the electronic instructions to divert monies from the rightful recipient. That is simply not what happened in this case." *Northside Bank v. American Cas. Co. of Reading*, 2001 WL 34090139.

SELECTED SECONDARY SOURCES

ANNOTATED COMMERCIAL CRIME POLICY (Cole S. Cain, et al. ed., 2d ed., 2006).

ANNOTATED FINANCIAL INSTITUTION BONDS (Michael Keeley ed., 3d ed. 2013).

Commercial Crime Policy, ISO CR 00 22 08 13(Revised 2012).

Crime Protection Policy (Revised 2012).

FINANCIAL INSTITUTION BONDS (Duncan L. Clore ed., 3d ed. 2008)

Jeffrey S. Price & Michael J. Sams, *E-Gad . . . Is That Loss Covered?: Claims Made and Coverage Available For Losses Arising out of or Related to Electronic Data* (2011) (presented at the 2011 Midwinter Meeting of the American Bar Association, Tort Trial & Insurance Practice Section, on file with author).

Scott L. Schmookler, *Computer and Funds Transfer Fraud, in* COMMERCIAL CRIME INSURANCE COVERAGE, 299 (Randall Marmor and Susan Sullivan, ed., 2014).

Justin D. Wear, *The Computer Crime Endorsement* (2014) (presented at the 2014 Midwinter Meeting of the American Bar Association, Tort Trial & Insurance Practice Section, on file with author).

Chapter 8

Definition of Employee*

The definition of "employee" is of central importance to understanding and determining coverage under modern forms of commercial crime insurance policies. Fidelity coverage generally protects insureds against direct loss caused by embezzlement or similar acts committed by employees as insiders, but often expressly limits or excludes coverage for loss caused by an "employee" of the insured, other than for embezzlement-type loss. The reason for this is that the employer/employee relationship is unique, and poses very different risks than exist between an insured and a third party not hired and supervised by it. However, there are relationships that are similar to employment in structure, function and risk, as to which insureds may seek, and insurers may be willing to offer, fidelity coverage. Hence, a crime policy's express definition of "employee" assists both the insurer and the insured in defining and understanding the nature and limits of coverage offered.

The 2012 ISO Commercial Crime Policy[1] defines a covered "employee" as follows:

> 7. **"Employee":**
>   a. **Means:**
>   (1) **Any natural person:**
>   (a) **While in your service and for the first 30 days immediately after termination of service, unless such termination is due to "theft" or any other dishonest act committed by the "employee";**
>   (b) **Whom you compensate directly by salary, wages or commissions; and**

---

* By Armen Shahinian and Andrew S. Kent, Chiesa Shahinian & Giantomasi PC, West Orange, New Jersey and New York, New York.

[1] Commercial Crime Policy (Discovery Form), CR 00 22 08 13 (F)(7) (Insurance Services Office, Inc. 2012) (Discovery Form), *reprinted in* COMMERCIAL CRIME INSURANCE COVERAGE 785 (Randall I. Marmor & Susan Koehler Sullivan eds., 2015).

    (c)   Whom you have the right to direct and control while performing services for you;

(2)   Any natural person who is furnished temporarily to you:

    (a)   To substitute for a permanent "employee" as defined in Paragraph 7.a.(1) above, who is on leave; or

    (b)   To meet seasonal or short-term workload conditions;

    while that person is subject to your direction and control and performing services for you;

(3)   Any natural person who is leased to you under a written agreement between you and a labor leasing firm, to perform duties related to the conduct of your business, but does not mean a temporary "employee" as defined in Paragraph 7.a.(2);

(4)   Any natural person who is:

    (a)   A trustee, officer, employee, administrator or manager, except an administrator or manager who is an independent contractor, of any "employee benefit plan", or

    (b)   Your director or trustee while that person is engaged in handling "money," "securities" or "other property" of any "employee benefit plan";

(5)   Any natural person who is a former "employee", partner, "member", "manager", director or trustee retained by you as a consultant while performing services for you;

(6)   Any natural person who is a guest student or intern pursuing studies or duties;

(7)   Any natural person employed by an entity merged or consolidated with you prior to the effective date of this Policy;

(8)   Any natural person who is your "manager", director or trustee while:

      (a)   **Performing acts within the scope of the usual duties of an "employee"; or**

      (b)   **Acting as a member of any committee duly elected or appointed by resolution of your board of directors or board of trustees to perform specific, as distinguished from general, directorial acts on your behalf.**

  b. **Does not mean:**

    Any agent, broker, factor, commission merchant, consignee, independent contractor or representative of the same general character not specified in Paragraph 7.a.

COMMENT

Commercial crime policy forms have evolved over time, but the basic definition of "employee" has remained relatively constant for decades. There consistently has been some requirement in the definition that the employer must directly compensate, and have the right to govern, control, and/or direct, the "employee." The Comprehensive Dishonesty, Disappearance and Destruction Policy (hereinafter referred to as the "3-D Policy"), Blanket Crime Policy, and Commercial Blanket Bonds that preceded the Commercial Crime Policy all included similar language, as does the Surety and Fidelity Association of America's Crime Protection Policy. As such, cases interpreting those forms provide guidance in the analysis of who is an "employee" under a Commercial Crime Policy.

The Commercial Crime Policy (Discovery Form), originally released in 2001 by the Insurance Services Office and most recently revised in 2012, continues to utilize the earlier forms' basic definition of "employee," but also includes in the definition of "employee" other categories of individuals such as temporary or leased employees, former employees or managers brought back by the former employer in a consulting capacity, guest students and interns.

Until 2004, the language setting forth the employer's right to "direct and control" was not contained in the Financial Institution Bond. The absence of that language played a crucial role in some courts' analysis of who was a covered "employee" under a Financial Institution Bond notwithstanding the fact that the right to govern and direct is inherent in the nature of an employer-employee relationship. Therefore, because of the lack of "direct and control" language in the older versions of the Financial Institution Bond, the principles established in cases involving such bonds may not be fully applicable to cases involving the Commercial Crime Policy. Nonetheless, because some courts have relied upon precedents involving Financial Institution Bonds in interpreting the Commercial Crime Policy and vice versa, analysis of such cases is required.

In determining whether an individual is an "employee" for purposes of invoking coverage under a fidelity bond, courts have focused primarily on whether, and to what extent, the employer maintains control over the individual. Some courts, when analyzing the issue, have drawn a distinction between whether the employer has a theoretical right to control the individual and whether the employer has actually exercised that right.

Courts also have looked at factors other than control in determining who is a covered "employee" under a commercial crime policy or fidelity bond, including the manner in which the individual is compensated, how the individual is treated for workers' compensation, health insurance, and other benefits, and whether the individual is treated as an employee for income tax purposes.

Because most commercial crime policies define "employee" as a person whom the employer has "the right to direct and control," some courts have relied upon the absence of that language in the definition of "employee" in some policies as support for finding the issue of control to be irrelevant in the analysis, notwithstanding the fact that the right to direct and control is inherent in the employer-employee relationship (as recognized by other courts).

Sometimes issues arise as to whether an individual was acting in his "employment capacity" at the time he caused the alleged loss. This issue has arisen in situations involving dual employment, where the individual while purporting to act for one employer cheats or steals from his other, insured employer. Questions regarding employment capacity may also arise when a part-time or borrowed employee, or temporary employee, steals from the employer during non-working hours.

The involvement of entities that lease employees may also complicate the analysis of who is a covered "employee." Commercial crime policies issued prior to 1997 did not specifically address leased employees. In 1997, the commercial crime policy form was revised to state that the definition of "employee" does not include any "person leased to you by a labor leasing firm." Since at least 2002, however, commercial crime policies include persons leased under written agreements with labor leasing firms under Subpart (a)(3).

Commercial crime polices generally do not cover outside attorneys retained by the insured. Coverage will generally be available, however, for in-house attorneys who fit the policy's basic definition of "employee." Cases involving Financial Institution Bonds are inapposite because under such Bonds, the term "employee" is specifically defined to include "an attorney retained by the Insured, and an employee of such attorney, while performing legal services for the Insured."

Similarly, third-party data processors are treated as "employees" under the Financial Institution Bond, but not under the Commercial Crime Policy. Under Subpart (b) of the Commercial Crime Policy, such third-party data processors generally must be regarded as agents or independent contractors, and not as "employees."

The analysis of who is a covered "employee" may be affected by either a consolidation or a merger involving an insured. Commercial crime policies and 3-D Policies traditionally included special provisions regarding consolidations and mergers, but the issue was not expressly referenced within the definition of "employee." The most current version of the Commercial Crime Policy, at Subpart (a)(7), now specifies that the term "employee" extends to "[a]ny natural person employed by an entity merged or consolidated with you prior to the effective date of this Policy."

With respect to directors, commercial crime policies and fidelity bonds, including the Commercial Crime Policy and Financial Institution Bond, generally provide that a director will not be considered a covered "employee" except in circumstances in which the director is performing functions ordinarily performed by an employee in connection with the performance of an executive task. Because the language regarding directors in the Commercial Crime Policy, 3-D Policy, and Financial Institution Bond are functionally similar, cases concerning directors generally have been used interchangeably as guiding precedent. Earlier forms of commercial crime policies provided that an employee "does not mean" a director, except when the director was acting as an employee. Subpart (a)(8) in the most current version of the Commercial Crime Policy is structured a little differently. The definition of "employee" now expressly does include a manager, director, or trustee, but only while performing "acts within the scope of the usual duties" of an "employee." Presumably, the purpose of this change in structure was to avoid the misperception that the limitation of coverage for directors was an exclusion, as opposed to merely definitional, and thereby avoid the misapplication of judicial doctrines by which exclusions in insurance policies should be very narrowly applied.

When an insured discovers a loss but is unable to identify the employee causing the loss, courts have generally held that so long as the insured can reasonably prove that its loss was caused by employee dishonesty or employee theft, the insurer may not deny the claim. Some forms of crime policies, including the 3-D Policy, reference "unidentifiable employees." The Commercial Crime Policy contains an exclusion that precludes the insured from proving a fidelity loss that is dependent upon an inventory computation or a profit and loss computation. The Commercial Crime Policy and Financial Institution Bond, however, do not contain a specific reference to "unidentifiable employees."

Other issues that may affect employee coverage in commercial crime policies include special endorsements that modify the definition of "employee," or special circumstances such as the possible application of a statute requiring the insured to obtain fidelity coverage with respect to individuals other than those whom the insurer agreed to cover in its policy's definition of "employee."

Insurers may defend against claims for coverage under commercial fidelity policies and bonds where an owner-wrongdoer who dominates the insured is alleged to be a covered "employee" of the insured. Under the Commercial Crime Policy, the right to direct and control the owner-wrongdoer is essential to the coverage determination. If the dishonest "employee" is not, in fact, subject to the direction and control of any superior officer or independently functioning board of directors, but so dominates the insured by virtue of stock ownership and/or control of the board of directors as to be beyond its control and direction, such an individual likely falls outside of the policy's express definition of "employee."

In cases involving the older forms of the Financial Institution Bond or the predecessor Bankers Blanket Bond where there was no "right to control" language, sometimes variations on the so-called "alter ego defense" have been adopted by the courts. In such circumstances, some courts have focused on whether the insured has forfeited coverage by imputing knowledge by the wrongdoer/alter ego of the wrongdoing to the insured. Thus, if a court finds that the wrongdoer's knowledge of his or her own wrongdoing is imputed to the insured, the fidelity insurer may establish that the insured failed to satisfy the bond's notice requirements or that coverage terminated upon commission of the first instance of activity in furtherance of the alleged fraud or dishonesty by virtue of the insured's immediate discovery of such dishonest conduct terminating coverage as to such dishonest "employee." Additionally, where the wrongdoer so dominates the insured that his or her acts must be regarded as the acts of the insured itself, public policy may prevent the insured from recovering for what are in essence its own intentional and wrongful acts.

The scenario of the dominance of an insured by a wrongdoer is colloquially referred to in the fidelity insurance context as the "alter ego defense." However, that is a misnomer, particularly under policies such as the Commercial Crime Policy. A dominant corporate actor is simply not under the direction or control of the insured, and hence does not meet the policy's basic definition of "employee." Determining the absence of fidelity coverage in this context is not akin to veil-piercing or the "alter ego doctrine" in corporate law, and does not implicate an affirmative defense. Rather, coverage fails because the malefactor is not an "employee" as defined in the policy, and no fidelity coverage exists.

OUTLINE OF ANNOTATIONS

A. Key Factors: Control and Direct Compensation
   1. Commercial Crime Policies
   2. Other Policies or Bond Forms
B. Capacity of Employee
   1. Commercial Crime Policies
   2. Other Policies or Bond Forms
C. Leased Employees and Professional Employer Organizations
   1. Commercial Crime Policies
   2. Other Policies or Bond Forms
D. Merger and Former Employees
   1. Commercial Crime Policies

E. Managers, Directors, or Trustees
    1. Commercial Crime Policies
    2. Other Policies or Bond Forms
F. ERISA Trustees
    1. Commercial Crime Policies
    2. Other Policies or Bond Forms
G. Unidentifiable Employees
    1. Commercial Crime Policies
    2. Other Policies or Bond Forms
H. Endorsements or Other Policies Expanding the Definition of
    Employee
    1. Attorneys
    2. Data Processors
    3. Investment Advisors
    4. Other Endorsements
I. Other Circumstances
    1. Commercial Crime Policies
    2. Other Policies or Bond Forms
J. The Alter Ego Defense
    1. Commercial Crime Policies
    2. Other Policies or Bond Forms

ANNOTATIONS

A. Key Factors: Control and Direct Compensation

1. Commercial Crime Policies

5th Cir. 1969 (Miss.). An insured was permitted to recover under a fidelity insurance policy where the wrongdoer was found to meet the definition of "employee" under the policy. The court noted that the insured had exercised its right to control the sales and collections performed by the wrongdoer, and that the wrongdoer was in the regular service of the insured's business. *New Orleans Furn. Mfg. Co. v. Great Am. Ins. Co.,* 413 F.2d 1278.

D. Kan. 1995. The president of a parent company who oversaw the financial affairs of both the parent company and its subsidiaries did not meet the definition of an "employee" under a commercial crime policy issued to one of the subsidiary companies. The court focused on the policy criteria that an "employee" must be a person "whom you compensate directly by salary, wages or commissions. . ." The court noted that the president was not an employee of the subsidiary company because he was not compensated directly by the subsidiary. *T.S.I. Holdings, Inc. v. Buckingham*, 885 F. Supp. 1457.

N.D.N.Y. 2014. Three affiliated companies with common ownership each obtained fidelity coverage under policies defining "employee" as a natural person in the service of the insured, whom the insured has the right to direct and control, and compensates "directly by salary, wages or commissions." The three companies, however, structured their business in such a way that there was some sharing of employees among the companies, and certain employees were paid through a master payroll account held by one of the companies, but into which all three companies made deposits. The court deemed the direct compensation clause from the policies' definition of "employee" ambiguous as applied to the insureds' corporate payroll structure, reasoning that to hold otherwise would render the fidelity coverage inoperative. The court further held that the alleged dishonest individual was an "employee" of all three insureds for coverage purposes. *Dataflow, Inc. v. Peerless Ins. Co.*, No. 3:11-CV-1127, 2014 WL 4881534.

W.D. Pa. 2014. An employee of a recruiting and placement firm ("MRI") requested that her employment be terminated and she entered into an agreement with MRI under which she would henceforth be regarded as "self-employed" or would continue to provide services to MRI through a different employer. MRI later accused her of dishonesty. MRI sought to recover under its insurance policy, which included coverage for employee dishonesty and which defined "employee" similarly to a Commercial Crime Policy. The court granted summary judgment in favor of the insurer and against MRI. Although the alleged wrongdoer still provided services for MRI and received some direct compensation from MRI, the court found that she was an "independent contractor" and not an "employee" as defined in the policy. *Mgm't Recruiters of Pittsburgh-North, Inc. v. Travelers Indem. Co. of Am.*, No. 2:13-cv-201, 2014 WL 201070.

E.D. Va. 2007. A jewelry store sought to recover under its Commercial Crime Policy for a theft committed by an alleged employee. The policy defined employee as a natural person in the service of the insured, subject to its right to direct and control, and whom the insured compensates directly by salary, wages, or commissions, but not an agent, broker, factor, commission merchant, consignee, independent contractor, or representative of the same general character. The alleged thief was a friend of the store's owner, who was permitted to live in an apartment above the store, and who on the date of the theft had opened the store and worked there all day. However, he was paid no salary or commissions, except for a single commission check for sales made on a consignment-like arrangement through a side-business that on occasion had purchased jewelry from the insured store. On those facts, the court granted the fidelity carrier's motion for summary judgment, concluding that the insured's single consignment-style payment to the thief did not render him a directly compensated employee under the policy. *Carytown Jewelers, Inc. v. St. Paul Travelers Cos., Inc.*, No. 3:06cv312, 2007 WL 174020.

Ga. Ct. App. 1992. An outside salesman did not meet the definition of "employee" under an employee dishonesty policy. The court noted that the insured did not exercise control over the hours worked by the salesman, and did not give specific instructions regarding dealing with customers. The court rejected the insured's arguments that control was maintained because the salesman's contract would be terminated if he did not sell enough merchandise, and because the insured directed the salesman not to sell merchandise in Virginia or New York. *N.S. Co., Inc. v. Cincinnati Ins. Co.*, 416 S.E.2d 859.

N.Y. App. 1983. The court affirmed a denial of summary judgment where factual issues existed as to whether a wrongdoer met the definition of an "employee" under a fidelity insurance policy. The court noted that because there were conflicting affidavits, the court could not determine whether the wrongdoer met the three-prong test of being an employee: (1) being compensated by the insured in the form of wages, salary, commissions, or otherwise; (2) remaining subject to the direction and control of the insured in terms of performance of duties; and (3) not being a broker, agent, factor, commission merchant, cosignee or contractor, or other general agent. *175 Check Cashing Corp. v. Chubb Pac. Indem. Group*, 464 N.Y.S.2d 118.

Ohio Ct. App. 2004. The court affirmed summary judgment dismissing a claim against a commercial crime policy where the wrongdoer was the business partner of the insured, and thus did not meet the definition of an "employee." *Roberts v. Maichl,* No. C-040002, 2004 WL 1948718.

2. *Other Policies or Bond Forms*

4th Cir. 1942 (N.C.). The court denied coverage under a bankers blanket indemnity bond where an insured bank lent money to a company, and requested that the president of the company be responsible for collections on the outstanding notes. The insured argued that the president was therefore acting as an employee of the insured bank. The court found, however, that the president was acting as an agent, independent in the manner and method of his collection, and not subject to the control of the insured bank other than being responsible for the prompt remittance of payments on the notes. *Nat'l Bank of Burlington v. Fid. & Cas. Co. of N.Y.,* 125 F.2d 920.

6th Cir. 1992 (Ky.). A representative of a part owner of an insured bank was determined not to meet the definition of "employee" under a bankers blanket bond and excess bank employee dishonesty bond because the representative was controlled by a separate legal entity, and not by a manager or officer of the insured. *Bank of Cumberland v. Aetna Cas. & Sur. Co.,* 956 F.2d 595.

6th Cir. 1977 (Ohio). A real estate appraiser hired by a savings and loan association did not meet the definition of an "employee" under a bankers blanket bond. The court noted that "the right to control is the hallmark of an employer-employee relationship," and found that the insured did not exert control because no instructions, directions, or exercise of control was asserted over the manner in which the appraiser performed inspections. Additionally, the court noted that that the appraiser was never furnished with a W-2 form, income taxes and social security deductions were not withheld, fringe benefits were not provided, and the appraiser was not listed as an employee for purposes of workers' compensation or unemployment benefits. *Third Fed. Sav. & Loan Ass'n of Cleveland v. Fireman's Fund Ins. Co.,* 548 F.2d 166.

6th Cir. 1969 (Mich.). An individual met the definition of an "employee" under a fidelity bond. The court articulated that the principal test of an employer and employee relationship was control. In reviewing the facts of the case, the court found that the employer maintained very close supervision and control over the individual through daily contact and instruction. *William H. Sill Mortg., Inc. v. Ohio Cas. Ins. Co.,* 412 F.2d 341.

8th Cir. 1935 (Ark.). The court allowed coverage under a fidelity bond where an insured had specifically applied for the bond to cover the wrongdoer as an employee. The court did not consider the control factor. Rather, the court noted that the insurer was aware of the insured's relationship with the wrongdoer from the bond application. As such, the court held that insurer's knowledge of this relationship estopped the insurer from denying that the wrongdoer was an employee. *Emp'rs Liab. Assur. Corp. v. Wasson,* 75 F.2d 749.

9th Cir. 1991 (Cal.). The insured's former president, director and sole shareholder was determined to be covered under a financial institution bond's definition of "employee" because the bond failed to incorporate "the right to control" as an element of the definition of "employee." *FDIC v. New Hampshire Ins. Co.,* 953 F.2d 478.

10th Cir. 1994 (Colo.). An insured bank's former president met the definition of an "employee" under a financial institution bond where the language of the bond defined "employee" to include "an officer or other employee of the insured, while employed in, at, or by any of the insured's offices or premises. . ." In an unpublished decision, the court determined that the absence of "govern and direct" language in the bond made the issue of control irrelevant. *FDIC v. Kan. Banker's Sur. Co.,* 17 F.3d 1436 (table), No. 93-1051, 1994 WL 55595.

M.D. Ala. 2013. A dentist obtained an insurance policy for his practice that included coverage for employee dishonesty. The policy's definition of "employee" was limited in relevant part to persons whom the insured compensated directly by salary, wages, or commissions. The alleged thief was the insured's spouse. The court granted the fidelity carrier's motion for summary judgment because the insured failed to produce any evidence that he had paid his spouse any salary, wages or commissions. *Chancey v. Cincinnati Ins. Cos.,* No. 1:12-CV-679, 2013 WL 1908387.

N.D. Cal. 2001. The court granted summary judgment dismissing a claim for employee dishonesty coverage. The facts established that the alleged malefactor was the sole director, officer, and shareholder of the insured, and that he did not have an immediate supervisor. The court concluded that no reasonable jury could find that the wrongdoer was an "employee" of the insured and subject to its control. *Beck v. State Farm Fire and Cas. Co.*, No. C 00-36362, 2001 WL 492449.

S.D.N.Y. 2001. An officer of the insured met the definition of an "employee" under an excess crime policy because the policy defined employees as "the Assured's officers, clerks, servants and other employees while employed by the Assured," and did not include any language regarding the right to govern or control. The court opined that the absence of such language from the policy rendered the issue of control irrelevant to determining who was an "employee" as defined under the policy. *SEC v. Credit Bancorp, Ltd.*, 147 F. Supp. 2d 238.

S.D.N.Y. 1984. An insured's claim for coverage under a credit union discovery bond for dishonest acts of employees was denied because the insured's money broker and the insured's bank did not meet the commonly accepted and traditional meaning of the word "employee." The court noted that neither the money broker, nor the bank received any wages or salary, and were not under the insured's direction and control. *IBM Poughkeepsie Emp'ees Fed. Credit Union v. Cummis Ins. Soc'y, Inc.*, 590 F. Supp. 769.

S.D. Oh. 2007. A manufacturing company engaged a third-party payroll service, which stole certain tax withholding funds provided by the manufacturer for payment to the Internal Revenue Service. The insured sought to recover under a business policy that included employee dishonesty coverage. The policy defined "employee" as a natural person in a service usual to the insured's business operations, whom the insured pays by salary, wages, or commission, and that the insured has the "exclusive right to direct" in the "performance of their service," but not including "any broker, factor, commission merchant, consignee, contractor, or other agent or representative." The court held that the third-party payroll service was unambiguously not an employee as defined in the policy, and that the employee dishonesty coverage therefore did not cover the insured's claimed loss. *Florists' Mut. Ins. Co. v. Ludy Greenhouse Mfg. Corp.*, 521 F. Supp. 2d 661.

Bankr. N.D. Ohio 2010. The insured had fidelity coverage under a Financial Institution Bond, defining "employee" as a natural person compensated directly by the insured and under its direction and control. In reliance upon certain documents produced by the insured and representations made by the insured in its Proof of Loss that a wrongdoer was its employee, the insurer ("Federal") made a large payment to the insured in partial satisfaction of its claim. Thereafter, the insured provided additional information establishing that the wrongdoer was an independent contractor and not an employee. Federal asserted a counterclaim against its insured to recover the payment, asserting that it was fraudulently obtained or was the result of a mutual mistake. The insured moved to dismiss, arguing that the wrongdoer's status as either an employee or an independent contractor was an issue of law and not of fact, and that a mistake or misrepresentation as to the law will not support a claim for rescission based upon mutual mistake or fraud. The court denied the motion in part, finding that Federal had adequately alleged misrepresentations of fact for purposes of its claim for mutual mistake, but dismissed the fraud claim because Federal had not alleged with specificity that the subject misrepresentations were knowingly false or recklessly made. *In re Cont'l Capital Inv. Servs., Inc.*, 439 B.R. 111.

Bankr. N.D. Ohio 1988. A wrongdoer who operated out of an insured's corporate office, received health benefits from the insured and held himself out to the public as an employee of the insured met the definition of an "employee" under a group fidelity bond. The court noted that the evidence demonstrated the existence of the insured's right to control the wrongdoer, and that the absence of actual control was irrelevant. *In re Baker & Getty Fin. Servs., Inc.*, 93 B.R. 559.

Del. Super. Ct. 1930. The vice president of the insured's holding company met the definition of "employee" under a blanket position bond because the vice president was listed in the insured's schedule of positions and was actively supervised by the insured. The court reasoned that the bond was intended to protect both the holding company and its subsidiary companies, and the vice president was under the control of the holding company as well as of the insured. *Penn. Car Co. v. Hartford Acc. & Indem. Co.*, 151 A. 665.

Ky. Ct. App. 2013. A car dealership ("Piles") suffered a loss as a result of its bookkeeper issuing unauthorized checks. Piles had an insurance policy providing limited coverage for employee dishonesty, and also for forgery and alteration. The forgery coverage, however, excluded recovery for loss caused by an "employee" of the insured. When the bookkeeper first began providing her services for Piles, she was paid by and under the control of a different company. The court therefore held that forgery coverage was available as to checks issued prior to, but not after, the date when the bookkeeper became a direct employee of Piles. *Piles Chevrolet Pontiac Buick, Inc. v. Auto Owners Ins. Co.*, Nos. 2011-CA-002317-MR & 2011-CA-002340-MR, 2013 WL 2120319.

La. 1938. An insured was denied coverage under a primary blanket fidelity bond. The insured had a contract with a branch manager who maintained his own employees. The employees of the branch manager did not meet the definition of "employee" under the insured's bond because the insured's contract with the branch manager did not provide the insured with any control over the branch manager's employees or responsibility for their compensation. *Ark. Fuel Oil Co. v. Nat'l Sur. Corp.*, 184 So. 560.

Mich. 1933. A marketer and transporter did not meet the definition of "employee" under an embezzlement and larceny bond. The court determined that the relationship was that of a vendor-vendee, not employer-employee. Among other things, the court noted that the insured's right to supervise the marketer and transporter was restricted because the insured was not entitled to control the means by which the marketer and transporter conducted sales. *Stone v. Harris*, 251 N.W. 322.

Neb. 1988. A gasoline distributor suffered losses at several stations because of fraudulent acts by the stations' operators. The court found that the station operators were not employees under an employee blanket bond because the insured did not treat the operators as employees. The operators were not recorded in the insured's books and records, and no taxes were withheld from them. Rather, the operators made their profit by selling gasoline at a higher price than the insured charged them. *Jones v. Emp'rs Mut. Cas. Co.*, 432 N.W.2d 535.

N.Y. App. 2013. A commodities broker paid solely on a commission basis, which payments were recorded on 1099 forms, was alleged to have caused an insured a loss due to dishonest conduct. The fidelity carrier moved for summary judgment, arguing that the insured had not suffered a direct financial loss. Although the issue was not addressed by the parties in their motion papers, the lower court entered summary judgment in favor of the insured and opined that the broker was an employee as a matter of law under the policy. The policy defined employee to include "(i) a person under an implied contract of employment or services with the insured; (ii) a person working under the direct control and supervision of the insured; or (iii) a person who is paid by the insured under their payroll system." The policy further provided, however, that the term "employee" does not mean an independent broker. Reversing the trial court, the appellate panel held that there were questions of fact as to whether the wrongdoer fell within the independent broker exclusion, and also as to whether he worked under the direct control and supervision of the insured. The appellate panel also observed that the court below had acted improvidently in granting summary judgment on an issue that was outside of the subject matter of the motion before it. *N.H. Ins. Co. v. MF Global, Inc.*, 970 N.Y.S.2d 16.

Pa. 1950. A purchasing agent retained to buy and sell automobiles on behalf of the insured did meet the definition of an "employee" under a blanket position bond. The bond defined "employees" as persons in the regular service of the insured, in the ordinary course of business, and "whom the insured has the right to govern and direct at all times in the performance of such service." The court noted that the insured had the right to direct the places the purchasing agent worked, and the purchasing agent was responsible to continually keep in touch with and report to the insured. *Feller v. New Amsterdam Cas. Co.*, 70 A.2d 299.

W. Va. App. 2001. The appellate panel reversed the lower court's grant of summary judgment in favor of an insurance carrier, finding that there was an issue of fact regarding whether the insured's construction manager met the definition of an "employee" under a general liability policy with coverage for employee dishonesty. The court noted that the question of whether a person is an employee or independent contractor depends on the facts in any given case, and all elements must be considered together. Among the elements to be considered are the manner of selection of the person who is to do the work, how the person is to be paid for such work, the right to hire and to fire, and most importantly, the right or power of control or supervision in connection with the work to be done. The court found that the lower court overlooked the fact that while an employer's actual exercise of the right to control may prove, or tend to prove, the existence of a right to control, the failure to exercise a duly reserved right does not, by itself, prove the absence of that right. *Mountain Lodge Ass'n v. Crum & Forster Indem. Co.,* 558 S.E.2d 336.

B. Capacity of Employee

1. Commercial Crime Policies

10th Cir. 1948 (Okla.). Two individuals did not meet the definition of "employees" under a blanket honesty insurance policy. The court refused to recognize an alleged oral agreement as creating an employer-employee relationship where the written contract at issue merely contemplated a business venture without establishing the insured's ability to control the actions of the alleged wrongdoers. *Brewer v. Nat'l Sur. Corp.,* 169 F.2d 926.

Mo. Ct. App. 1981. A wrongdoer did not meet the definition of an "employee" under an employee fidelity policy. The insured hired the wrongdoer each morning and terminated the wrongdoer with pay at the close of each working day. Because the theft at issue occurred after the wrongdoer was terminated from employment, the court held that the wrongdoer did not meet the definition of an "employee" under the policy at the time of the loss. *Citizens Ins. Co. of N.J. v. Kan. City Comm. Cartage, Inc.,* 611 S.W.2d 302.

N.J. 1972. Coverage was upheld under a commercial crime policy where employees stole plumbing materials from their workplace after business hours. The court held that the time the loss occurred was irrelevant and that the perpetrators were just as much "employees" in the evening as they were during normal business hours. *C&H Plumbing & Heating, Inc. v. Empr's Mut. Cas. Co.,* 287 A.2d 238.

2. Other Policies or Bond Forms

4th Cir. 1984 (Va.). Where a contract between the insured and a third-party contractor made it clear that the contractor was, in fact, a subcontractor, and the fidelity bond expressly excluded subcontractors from its definition of "employees," coverage under the bond was denied. *G&C Constr. Corp. v. St. Paul Fire & Marine Ins. Co.*, 731 F.2d 183.

5th Cir. 1977 (La.). A commodities dealer was determined to be acting as an "employee" within the meaning of a brokers blanket bond despite using bad checks to cover losses to the insured from orders placed through a personal account. The court noted that the bond covered any loss through any dishonest or fraudulent act of an employee. The court did not see any reason to distinguish the case of a broker who colludes with a customer to meet trading calls with bad checks, from the case where the broker and the customer are one and the same. *Howard, Weil, Labouisse, Friedrichs, Inc. v. Ins. Co. of N. Am.*, 557 F.2d 1055.

8th Cir. 1967 (Iowa). An individual serving as the president of the insured and who worked as a contractor for the insured met the definition of an "employee" under a commercial fidelity bond. The court noted that nothing in the bond prevented an employee from serving in a dual employment capacity, and the court specifically found that while acting as a contractor, the individual was subject to the control, direction, and ultimate discharge of the corporation and its board of directors. *Wooddale, Inc. v. Fid. & Dep. Co. of Md.*, 378 F.2d 627.

10th Cir. 1937 (Okla.). A bank employee, who was also the treasurer of a municipality, embezzled funds from the municipality using accounts he maintained with the insured bank. The insurer attempted to disclaim coverage under a fidelity bond, arguing that the embezzlement was performed by the individual in his capacity as treasurer of the municipality, and that, therefore, the bank was not liable for the same. The court granted coverage, reasoning that the bank was responsible for the loss regardless of the capacity in which its employee was acting when the funds were embezzled. *Md. Cas. Co. v. Queenan,* 89 F.2d 155.

S.D. Ind. 2002. Coverage was upheld under a property policy for losses resulting from a fire set by an individual who was an employee, director, officer and shareholder of the insured. The court accepted the insured's argument that the policy covered acts of destruction committed by employees. Although the court acknowledged the common law principle, which precludes coverage for intentional acts of insureds, the court found that the ambiguity in the policy concerning employees who are also directors, officers, and shareholders of the insured should be resolved in favor of the insured. *Thompson Hardwoods v. Transp. Ins. Co.*, No. NA 00-74-C H/K, 2002 WL 31040703.

D.N.D. 1997. Coverage under a property policy was denied where an employee, who was also an officer, director, and shareholder of the insured, committed arson. The policy excluded coverage for losses resulting from a "dishonest and criminal act" by any employee, director, etc., but the exclusion did not apply to "acts of destruction by employees." The court noted that because the employee who started the fire was also an officer, director, and shareholder, the exception for acts of destruction by employees was inapplicable. *Kabob House, Inc. v. Houston Gen. Ins. Co.*, 17 F. Supp. 2d 1090.

E.D.N.Y. 1977. An insured bank argued that a mortgage-servicing contractor was a covered "employee." The court found that the mortgage service contractor was a covered "employee" under a service contractors rider, but not the main insurance policy. The court noted that if service contractors were intended to be covered as employees under the main insurance policy, there would be no reason for the coverage language in the rider. *Hudson City Sav. v. Hartford Acc. & Indem. Co.*, 440 F. Supp. 41.

E.D. Pa. 1990. The court determined that a wrongdoer who set fire to the insured's property while off duty still met the definition of an "employee" under an "all risk" policy with an exclusion for dishonest acts of employees. The court reasoned that the policy did not limit the time period in which the act must occur, and therefore must be construed against the insurer. *Transp. Ins. Co. v. Didaniele,* Nos. 88-4802 & 88-8322, 1990 WL 149222.

Ga. Ct. App. 1964. Coverage under a fidelity bond issued on behalf of a tax commissioner was declined for acts committed by the tax commissioner in his capacity as Agent of State Revenue Commissioner for the licensing of motor vehicles in the county. *Sanders v. U.S. Fid. & Guar. Co.*, 134 S.E.2d 831.

Kan. 1932. Coverage was denied under a fidelity bond where the treasurer of the insured embezzled funds from checks issued to a bank for the purchase of securities. The fidelity carrier argued that the treasurer, who was also the president of the bank where the checks were made payable, was not acting as treasurer of the insured when he embezzled the funds. The court found this contention to lack merit because the checks were given to the wrongdoer as treasurer of the insured, not as president of the bank. *Ft. Scott Bldg. & Loan Ass'n v. McAfee*, 10 P.2d 851.

Pa. 1933. The wrongdoer, a seller of musical instruments, entered into an agreement with the insured to act as the collector of accounts that he sold to the insured. The wrongdoer received no payment, but was compensated by the possibility of securing as customers those who came to his store to pay on the accounts. Later, the wrongdoer entered into a separate agreement for consignment sales of pianos. The wrongdoer absconded with the money. The insured's claim was denied on the ground that the wrongdoer was not an employee, but rather an independent contractor. The court found that the wrongdoer met the definition of "employee" under the surety bond at issue with respect to his agreement to act as the collector of accounts. The court permitted coverage because the insurer had knowledge of the insured's relationship with the wrongdoer. The court denied coverage, however, with respect to the agreement for consignment sales of pianos because the wrongdoer was defined as an independent contractor under the agreement. *Frederick Invest. Co. v. Am. Sur. Co. of N.Y.*, 169 A. 155.

S.D. 1916. An insured's manager/cashier, who was responsible for misappropriating the insured's funds, met the definition of an "employee" under a fidelity bond. The fidelity carrier argued that because the manager/cashier was compensated on a net profit basis for a period of time, the manager/cashier was a partner in the business instead of an employee. The court disregarded this argument, reasoning that the change in method of compensation was irrelevant. *Adams Co. v. Nesbit*, 159 N.W. 869.

Tex. App. 1937. An insurer argued that coverage should be denied under a fidelity bond where the insured ("CVC") had an agreement with an individual to sell butter, but the CVC shipped the butter to a company in which the individual was a minority shareholder. The court found that coverage existed because the individual met the definition of an "employee" under the bond. The court noted that CVC paid salary to the individual directly and that it was irrelevant that the individual sold the butter through a separate corporation because the individual was not in the exclusive employment of CVC. *Md. Cas. Co. v. Crescent Valley Creamery*, 103 S.W.2d 880.

C. Leased Employees and Professional Employer Organizations

1. Commercial Crime Policies

1st Cir. 1998 (Mass.). The court denied coverage under a crime insurance policy, finding that there was no ambiguity in an exclusion for acts committed by authorized representatives. The court found that the insured's authorized representative could only act through the insured's officers and employees, and as such, where the policy at issue excludes illegal acts by employees, directors or authorized representatives, it is clear that the exclusion was designed to bar coverage of wrongs committed by persons who have been granted access to the corporate funds. *Stop & Shop Cos. v. Fed. Ins. Co.*, 136 F.3d 71.

9th Cir. 1989 (Cal.). Coverage was denied under a crime insurance policy where the court found that there was no ambiguity in the policy's exclusion for acts committed by authorized representatives. The court noted that the plain meaning of the authorized representative language in crime insurance policies is designed to bar coverage for wrongs committed by persons who have been granted access to the insured's funds. *Stanford Univ. Hosp. v. Fed. Ins. Co.*, 174 F.3d 1077.

S.D.N.Y. 1994. The court denied coverage under a 3-D policy based upon an exclusion for acts performed by authorized representatives. The court found that the wrongdoer did not meet the definition of an "employee" under the policy because the wrongdoer was an agent of the insured with only limited authority to select which investments would be made with monies held in an investment account. *Colson Servs. Corp. v. Ins. Co. of N. Am.*, 874 F. Supp. 65.

E.D. Pa. 1998. Workers, who were engaged to perform services for a customer of an outsourcing company, were not considered employees of the outsourcing company for purposes of "employee dishonesty" coverage under a commercial crime policy. Although the insured outsourcing company took the legal responsibility to pay taxes, unemployment insurance, and workers' compensation insurance for the workers, the customers of the insured outsourcing company maintained responsibility for the oversight of the workers. Accordingly, the court held that the workers did not meet the definition of "employees" under the policy because the insured did not have the right to direct and control the workers. *Omne Servs. Grp., Inc. v. Hartford Ins. Co.*, 2 F. Supp. 2d 714.

Ark. 1981. Coverage was provided under an insurance policy with a 3-D definition of "employee" where a temporary bookkeeper hired through an employment agency embezzled money. The court found that the temporary bookkeeper met the definition of "employee" under the policy because: (1) the duties performed by the temporary employee were identical to that of the employee she replaced; (2) the policy did not exclude temporary employees or make any distinctions between permanent and temporary employees; (3) the bookkeeper, although temporary, was in the regular service of the insured; and (4) the insured had control of the temporary bookkeeper and was responsible for paying her wages. *Radiology Assocs., P.A. v. Aetna Cas. & Sur. Co.*, 613 S.W.2d 106.

Mo. App. 2001. An office manager who was hired by an "employment contractor" for the insured met the definition of an "employee" under an employee dishonesty endorsement to an insurance policy because the policy defined "employees" as either (a) any direct employee of the insured, or (b) any person employed by an "employment contractor" while the person was performing services for the insured under the insured's direction and control. Noting that the term "employment contractor" was ambiguous, the court found in favor of the insured because the insured paid a third party to hire someone to staff its office. *Mansion Hills Condo. Ass'n v. Am. Fam. Mut. Ins. Co.*, 62 S.W.3d 633.

N.Y. App. 1980. The court determined that a manufacturer's blanket crime policy's definition of an "employee" created a "three pronged test" in which ". . .the individual must (1) be compensated by the insured by salary, wages or commission; (2) be subject to the insured's right to govern and direct at all times in the performance of his duties; and (3) not be a broker, agent, factor, commission merchant, consignee or contractor, or any other agent or representative of the same general character." The court remanded the case for a determination as to whether the insured paid the alleged employee's salary, and whether the insured controlled and directed the performance of the alleged employee. *Gross Veneer Co., Inc. v. Am. Mut. Ins. Cos.,* 424 N.Y.S.2d 743.

2.   Other Policies or Bond Forms

N.Y. App. 1983. A security guard, who was robbed while transporting money from the insured's place of business, met the definition of an "employee" under an insurance policy, even though he was paid by a separate security agency for his normal working hours. The court noted that the insured paid the security guard directly for overtime work, and had the sole right to direct and control the security guard's working activities. *Fortunoff Silver Sales, Inc. v. Hartford Acc. & Indem. Co.,* 459 N.Y.S.2d 866.

N.Y. App. 1919. Coverage was denied under a fidelity bond where the wrongdoer worked as a messenger for a telegraph company that had a contract with the insured. Although the insured utilized the services of the wrongdoer on a daily basis, every morning the wrongdoer reported to the telegraph company and was subject to being recalled at their discretion. The court therefore declined to find that the wrongdoer was the insured's employee under the bond. *Auchincloss v. U.S. Fid. & Guar. Co.,* 179 N.Y.S. 454.

D. Merger & Former Employees

1. Other Policies or Bond Forms

8th Cir. 1988 (Neb.). The court denied coverage under a bankers blanket bond because the insured discovered the dishonesty of a former employee before the effective date of the bond. The court noted, however, that if the discovery had been made during the policy period of the bond, coverage would have been upheld. *First Sec. Sav. v. Kansas Bankers Sur. Co.,* 849 F.2d 345.

8th Cir. 1971 (Mo.). The court upheld coverage under a bankers blanket bond where the insured discovered the dishonesty of a former executive vice president during the policy period of the bond. The court rejected the fidelity carrier's defense to coverage that the insured had failed to disclose suspicions about the former employee in its application for bond coverage because the bond application only concerned present employees, while the actual bond covered the acts of any employee sustained during the policy period. *USF&G v. Empire State Bank,* 448 F.2d 360.

8th Cir. 1942 (Mo.). A subsidiary of a finance company insured by a bankers blanket bond continued to be covered under the bond after its capital stock was assigned to a third corporation pursuant to a plan of reorganization. The court reasoned that coverage was clear because the subsidiary was specifically named on the bond. *Okla. Morris Plan Co. v. Sec. Mut. Cas. Co.,* 455 F.2d 1209.

9th Cir. 1945 (Ca.). A savings and loan that merged with the insured was denied coverage under a bankers blanket bond for attorneys' fees and costs in defending suits for allegedly fraudulent acts committed by the insured's employees prior to the merger. The court reasoned that the savings and loan did not sustain a new loss upon the acquisition of the insured through merger. *Fid. Sav. & Loan Ass'n v. Republic Ins. Co.,* 513 F.2d 954.

N.D. Cal. 2011. As the result of a merger, a pre-existing company became a subsidiary of the primary named insured under a Crime Protection Policy. Through an endorsement, the subsidiary and its own subsidiaries became joint insureds under the policy. A sub-subsidiary subsequently discovered a theft by one of its employees, which had occurred prior to the merger. The fidelity carrier denied the claim, emphasizing that the policy's definition of "employee" applied only to the acts of persons "while in your service," and arguing to the court that the employee was not in the service of a company that was a named insured at the time of the theft. The court, however, concluded that the policy provided coverage for loss discovered by the company after becoming a named insured, regardless of when the loss occurred. *Bei Sensors & Sys. Co., Inc. v. Great Am. Ins. Co.*, No. C 09-5819, 2011 WL 835769.

D. Mass. 2010. An employee of an insured signed up for direct deposits of his paychecks, but through an administrative error the insured's human resources department misdirected its president and C.E.O.'s much larger paychecks to the same employee's bank account. The employee did not notify the insured of the mistake, but left the company for a new employer, after which the erroneous payments continued to be made into his bank account for in excess of one year. The employer's financial institution bond defined employee as a person receiving direct compensation from the insured and who is subject to its right of direction and control. The definition, as quoted by the court, did not reference former employees. Nevertheless, the court found that because the employee's dishonesty in failing to disclose the payroll error began while he was still employed by the insured, the court concluded that the loss was caused by employee dishonesty and was covered by the bond. *FundQuest Inc. v. Travelers Cas. & Sur. Co.*, 715 F. Supp. 2d 202.

M.D.N.C. 1959. Coverage was denied under a bankers indemnity bond because the discovery of the loss occurred following the merger of the insured and the bond terminated upon merger. *Wachovia Bank & Trust Co. v. Mfrs. Cas. Ins. Co.*, 171 F. Supp. 369.

E. Managers, Directors, or Trustees

1. Commercial Crime Policies

N.D. Ga. 1962. The court refused to provide coverage under a comprehensive blanket policy for wrongful acts of directors because the directors did not meet the definition of "employees" under the policy. The subject directors of the insured assumed positions as officers of the insured and usurped the power of those offices. The court noted that the wrongdoers: (1) were purely intruders who acted with fraudulent purposes, (2) did not undertake normal operations of the insured, and (3) were not authorized to act on behalf of the insured through any valid act of the insured's board of directors. *Ga. Cas. & Sur. Co. v. Seaboard Sur. Co.*, 210 F. Supp. 644.

2. Other Policies or Bond Forms

5th Cir. 1970 (Tex.). A director of an insured bank met the definition of an "employee" under a bankers blanket bond because the director was authorized by the board of directors to act in an officer-like capacity for the corporation. As such, the director's actions met the definition of "acts coming within the scope of the usual duties of an employee," which were covered by the bond. *FDIC v. Aetna Cas. & Sur. Co.,* 426 F.2d 729.

9th Cir. 1991 (Or.). A director of an insured, who was also the president and sole shareholder of a company that fraudulently obtained a loan from the insured, met the definition of an "employee" under a fidelity bond. The court determined that the director was performing the functions of an employee when he made fraudulent representations to the board of directors so that the insured would issue the loan at issue. *Interstate Prod. Credit Ass'n v. Fireman's Fund Ins. Co.,* 944 F.2d 536.

10th Cir. 1969 (Okla.). A director exclusion in a blanket honesty bond (similar to commercial crime policies, 3-D policies, and financial institution bonds) was found to exclude from the definition of "employee" under the bond only those directors who functioned as outside directors, and not those directors who functioned both as a director and officer, and who received a salary for services rendered in such capacity. *Ins. Co. of N. Am. v. Greenberg,* 405 F.2d 330.

E.D. Mo. 1974. The fraudulent acts of the chairman of the board of directors of the insured were covered under a bankers blanket bond despite an exclusion in the bond for loss resulting for "any act or acts of any director of the insured." The court noted that the chairman of the board was an employee of the insured at all pertinent times. *First Nat'l Bank of Sikeston v. Transamerica Ins. Co.,* 377 F. Supp. 1041.

Kan. 1989. The court rejected an insurer's argument that a director was not an employee and excluded from coverage under a financial institution bond because the insured bank did not possess a right to control his activities as a director. The court noted that the bond obviously contemplated coverage beyond just persons who are employees in the classic, common law sense, or there would be no need for the language contained in the director's exclusion. *First Hays Banshares, Inc. v. Kan. Banker's Sur. Co.,* 769 P.2d 1184.

Wash. App. 1982. A director's actions in establishing a fraudulent program for insurance premium financing were covered by a financial institution bond because despite being a director, the director performed all of the acts coming within the scope of the usual duties of an employee. *Puget Sound Nat'l Bank v. St. Paul Fire & Marine Ins. Co.,* 645 P.2d 1122.

F. ERISA Trustees

1. Commercial Crime Policies

Or. Ct. App. 2010. Two ERISA trusts, each established by a separate union, sought to recover under identical "Welfare and Pension Plan ERISA Compliance" endorsements to commercial crime policies issued in favor of the unions as insureds. The endorsements defined "employee" as any "trustee, an officer, employee, administrator or a manager" of an ERISA plan "except an administrator or a manager who is an independent contractor." At issue was whether the principals of a third-party investment management company, contracted by the trusts to manage their investments, qualified as "employees" as defined in the endorsements. The trusts argued that the third-party investment managers met the policies' definition of "employee," that any other interpretation would render coverage illusory, and alternatively, that the policies should be read in conjunction with statutory and regulatory requirements that the trusts contended required fidelity coverage for persons managing the assets of ERISA plans. The court affirmed summary judgment in favor of the insurers, holding that the individuals in question were indisputably associated with an independent contractor, and because ERISA's bonding provision does not require a single insurance policy to cover every specific person for whom bonding is required. *Empr's-Shopmens Local 516 Pension Trust v. Travelers Cas. and Sur. Co. of America,* 235 P.3d 689.

2. Other Policies or Bond Forms

2d Cir. 2011 (N.Y.). A company ("Schupak") obtained an ERISA compliance bond, covering loss due to dishonest acts committed by any "employee," defined to include "[a] trustee, an officer, employee, administrator or manager, except an administrator or manager who is an independent contractor, of any Employee Welfare or Pension Benefit Plan . . . covered by this policy." Schupak alleged that its plan suffered a loss due to Bernie Madoff's Ponzi scheme, and further alleged that Madoff was its "Custodian and Investment Trustee" as "delegated by the Plan Trustee." Schupak, however, was unable to produce documentary evidence of either Madoff having been appointed a plan trustee or of his acceptance of that position. Affirming the dismissal of Schupak's complaint for failure to state a claim, the court noted that Schupak's complaint contained no factual allegations supporting the inference that Madoff was a "trustee" for the purposes of the bond. The court further noted that, as alleged in the complaint, plan funds were placed under Madoff's control only "after passing through a third party intermediary," which the court viewed as negating the plausibility of any assertion that Madoff was directly engaged by the ERISA plan as its trustee. *Schupak Group, Inc. v. Travelers Cas. and Sur. Co. of Am.*, 10-1873-cv, 425 Fed. Appx. 23, 2011 WL 2214756.

9th Cir. 1996 (Cal.). An alleged wrongdoer who provided investment advice to an ERISA plan did not meet the definition of an "employee" under an employee dishonesty bond. The insured argued that the bond provided coverage for "trustees." The court found that although the wrongdoer was a fiduciary, the definition of "trustee" cannot be read to embrace all fiduciaries. *Joseph Rosenbaum, M.D., Inc. v. Hartford Fire Ins. Co.,* 104 F.3d 258.

G. Unidentifiable Employees

1. Commercial Crime Policies

2d Cir. 1973 (N.Y.). Coverage was denied under a 3-D policy where the insured failed to prove that its losses were sustained by reason of fraudulent or dishonest acts of employees. The court rejected the insured's efforts to rely upon inventory computations, in light of an inventory exclusion within the policy. *Dunlop Tire & Rubber Corp. v. Fid. & Dep. Co. of Md.,* 479 F.2d 1243

5th Cir. 1964 (Ga.). The court upheld a jury instruction allowing the jury to consider an enumeration of missing merchandise from a current stock record to determine whether the insured incurred a loss under a 3-D policy resulting from unidentified employee dishonesty. Although the policy contained an inventory exclusion, the court reasoned that an enumeration of missing merchandise was permitted under the policy because it is not the same as a computed inventory loss based upon inventory computations. *Sun Ins. Co. of N.Y. v. Cullum's Men Shop, Inc.* 331 F.2d 988.

5th Cir. 1960 (Ga.). In evaluating a claim under a commercial crime policy without an inventory exclusion, the court allowed coverage after finding that the insured had provided proof of an apparent theft through a hatch in the insured's warehouse and had excluded every reasonable hypothesis other than employee dishonesty. *Savannah Wholesale Co. v. Cont'l Cas. Co.,* 279 F.2d 706.

7th Cir. 1966 (Ill.). The court denied coverage under a 3-D Policy containing an inventory exclusion because the insured's proof that certain of its employees had turned over a small quantity of merchandise was insufficient to establish that dishonest employees had stolen the large amount of merchandise for which a loss was being alleged. *Gillette Co. v. Travelers Indem. Co.,* 365 F.2d 7.

9th Cir. 1956 (Cal.). Coverage was upheld under an employee fraud and dishonesty policy where there was no dispute that currency was taken from a locked cash box in the insured's manager's office and circumstantial evidence suggested that the suspect employees had knowledge that a large sum of cash was left in the office over the weekend. The court rejected the fidelity carrier's argument that the insured failed to sustain its burden of proof since the employees should have been presumed innocent. *Gen. Accident, Fire & Life Assurance Corp. v. Indep. Military Air Transp. Ass'n,* 232 F.2d 439.

10th Cir. 1997 (Okla.). The court upheld coverage under a fidelity policy where the insured utilized an analysis of production levels on comparable oil drilling units to demonstrate employee dishonesty. The court rejected the fidelity carrier's claim that such evidence was barred under the policy's inventory exclusion because the policy did not exclude all speculative evidence—only the product of self-created inventory records. The court reasoned that the results of the analysis, when compared to the wrongdoer's records for the oil drilling unit at issue, utilized extrinsic evidence to demonstrate employee dishonesty and did not implicate the inventory calculation exclusion. *Producers Oil Co. v. Hartford Fire Ins. Co.,* 129 F.3d 131 (Table), No. 96-5071, 1997 WL 687709.

D.C. 1976. The court permitted the insured to plead alternative theories of coverage under a commercial crime policy where both employee dishonesty and burglary by outsiders were covered. The court found that the insured had demonstrated that the cause of the loss was either employee dishonesty or burglary by an outsider based upon the small size of the loss, the short time in which it occurred, and evidence of tampering with the insured's burglar alarm. *Alexandre of London v. Indem. Ins. Co. of N.A.,* 182 F. Supp. 748.

D. Idaho 1953. The court allowed coverage under an employee dishonesty policy where the insured demonstrated loss through a retail accounting method of inventory computation, and provided testimony that established, by process of elimination, that the loss must have been caused by employee theft. *Morrow Retail Stores, Inc. v. Hartford Acc. & Indem. Co.,* 111 F. Supp. 772.

N.D. Ill. 2011. A cable supply company suffered a series of thefts from its warehouse, and sought to recover from its fidelity carrier. The policy covered employee theft but specified that if the amount of the claimed loss was calculated based upon the insured's inventory records, coverage would exist only where the insured "wholly establishes" that it has sustained a loss "caused by an identified employee." The insured was able to produce strong evidence of thefts involving non-employees, but only limited circumstantial evidence as to the involvement of some of its employees in some of the thefts. However, the thefts involved the removal of tens of thousands of pounds of product using the insured's forklifts and padlock keys kept inside the insured's facilities, which the insured argued suggested the likelihood of the involvement of its employees in the theft. The court opined that the "identified employee" clause was ambiguous, and could be reasonably interpreted to mean "someone who can be identified as an employee," despite that his or her individual identity remained unknown, and denied the fidelity carrier's motion for summary judgment under that clause. The court's reasoning is difficult to reconcile with the plain meaning of the clause, inasmuch as it would allow coverage for loss caused by an unidentified employee. *Coleman Cable, Inc. v. Travelers Indem. Co.*, 790 F. Supp. 2d 742.

N.D. Ill. 1996. In interpreting an inventory exclusion under an employee dishonesty policy, the court determined that despite a factual dispute as to whether there was adequate evidence to support a finding of employee dishonesty, coverage for inventory losses was permitted where there was, at minimum, circumstantial evidence of employee dishonesty. *Blitz Corp. v. Hanover Ins. Co.*, No. 95-C2725, 1996 WL 308233.

S.D.N.Y. 1974. In interpreting an unidentifiable employee clause and an inventory exclusion clause under a 3-D policy, the court noted that where the insured claimed that a loss was caused by employee dishonesty, but the dishonest employee cannot be identified, the insured must submit evidence that "reasonably proves" that the loss was caused by the fraud or dishonesty of undesignated employees before inventory computations will be admitted as evidence in the insured's case in chief. The court found that this requires more than "some independent evidence," but less than a prima facie case. *U.S. Smelting Refining & Mining Co. v. Aetna Cas. & Sur. Co.*, 372 F. Supp. 489.

Ariz. Ct. App. 1977. The court held that under a fidelity insurance policy containing an inventory exclusion, the insured must first make a prima facie showing, other than through inventory computation or profit and loss computation, that some loss has occurred that is causally related to the insured misconduct of one or more employees. *J.R. Norton Co. v. Fireman's Fund Ins. Co.*, 116 Ariz. 427.

Cal. Ct. App. 1977. The court declined coverage under an employee fidelity policy where the only evidence submitted of employee dishonesty was that of an inventory computation. The use of inventory computations was not permitted under the policy's inventory exclusion, and without at least some other evidence of employee dishonesty, the court was constrained to deny coverage. *Prager & Bear, Inc. v. Fed. Ins. Co.*, 66 Cal.App.3d 970.

Ill. App. Ct. 1999. Coverage was denied under a commercial crime policy where the insured relied upon an inventory computation to demonstrate losses through the dishonesty of unidentified employees. Although the policy covered the "dishonest acts of 'employees' whether identified or not," the insured was not relieved of the burden of demonstrating that a loss occurred in excess of the policy deductible and that the loss was caused by employee dishonesty. *Reedy Indus., Inc. v. Hartford Ins. Co. of Ill.*, 715 N.E.2d 728.

Me. 1953. The court denied coverage under a 3-D policy because evidence of the theft of 29 chickens by several employees did not support the insured's loss ratio analysis that 5,449 chickens must have been stolen by other unidentifiable employees. *Lipman Bros., Inc. v. Hartford Acc. & Indem. Co.*, 100 A.2d 246.

Mass. 1976. The court found independent evidence of employee dishonesty despite the lack of direct evidence where an insured demonstrated that its property disappeared from a locked enclosure to that only employees had access. The court then accepted testimony of the insured's manager and accepted purchase records as reasonable proof of the amount of the loss under a blanket crime policy. *Popeo v. Liberty Mut. Ins. Co.*, 343 N.E.2d 417.

Mo. 1977. The court permitted coverage under a blanket crime policy for dishonest and fraudulent acts of unidentified employees where the insured demonstrated losses through an audit report of dry cleaning tickets. The court held that the audit report did not constitute an inventory computation because dry cleaning constitutes a bailment and did not meet the definition of "inventory." *Chenoweth-Chapman Corp. v. Am. Ins. Co.*, 553 S.W.2d 872.

Neb. 1968. Coverage was denied under a fidelity policy containing an inventory exclusion where the insured failed to introduce any evidence of employee dishonesty beyond an inventory computation. *Paramount Paper Prods. Co. v. Aetna Cas. & Sur. Co.*, 157 N.W.2d 763.

N.Y. 1983. In evaluating a 3-D policy with an inventory exclusion, the court held that the insured met the standard of reasonable proof necessary to establish employee dishonesty in order to defeat a motion for summary judgment. The court noted that the policy only required that the insured's "evidence reasonably proves that the loss was in fact due to the fraud or dishonesty of one or more" of its employees, and that this "requires more than 'some independent evidence' but less than a prima facie case as a condition to the use of inventory" records. *Ace Wire & Cable Co., Inc. v. Aetna Cas. & Sur. Co., 457 N.E.2d 761.*

N.Y. App. Div. 1983. The court upheld a denial of the fidelity carrier's motion for summary judgment finding that the deposition of one of the insured's officers presented enough evidence to create a triable issue of fact as to whether the insured could overcome an inventory exclusion clause to demonstrate employee dishonesty under a comprehensive and blanket crime policy. *Schenectady Hardware & Elec. Co., v. Hartford Acc. & Indem. Co.,* 464 N.Y.S.2d 50.

N.Y. Civ. Ct. 1975. The court denied coverage under a 3-D policy with an inventory exclusion where the insured failed to present any direct or independent proof of employee dishonesty beyond inventory computations. The court rejected the insured's argument that because the thefts occurred at a place of limited access, the thefts must have been committed by an employee. The court held that absent production of independent evidence of employee dishonesty, the claim must be dismissed pursuant to the inventory exclusion clause in the policy. *Kaplan Jewelers, Inc. v. Ins. Co. of N. Am.,* 383 N.Y.S.2d 127.

N.Y. Civ. Ct. 1981. The court denied coverage under an insurance policy for employee theft with an inventory exclusion because evidence of the arrest of an employee in unlawful possession of four garments was insufficient to establish proof of employee dishonesty independent of inventory computations. *Teviro Casuals, Inc. v. Am. Home Ass. Co.,* 439 N.Y.S.2d 145.

N.Y. Civ. Ct. 1970. The court dismissed an insured's claim for theft of inventory under a 3-D policy where the insured offered no proof of employee dishonesty, and merely offered evidence that there was limited access to the insured's premises. *Kernwood Mfg. Corp. v. Home Indem. Co.*, 317 N.Y.S.2d 113.

R.I. 1970. The court dismissed a claim against a 3-D policy based upon the insured's failure to prove by a preponderance of the evidence that it sustained a loss through the dishonesty of unidentified employees. The insured attempted to support its claim that 1000 metal alloy bars had been stolen by unidentified employees based upon a guilty plea of one employee for taking thirty bars. *Danal Jewelry Co. v. Fireman's Fund Ins. Co.*, 264 A.2d 320.

Tenn. Ct. App. 1996. The court allowed coverage under an employee dishonesty policy with an inventory exclusion where the insured reasonably proved employee dishonesty through evidence that: (1) missing inventory had been received, (2) the inventory had not been sold in the usual course of business, and (3) the inventory was kept in a locked area accessible only by two employees. The court found that evidence showing the purchase of the missing merchandise and the absence of the merchandise from the inventory, without evidence of a sale, was not an inventory computation contemplated by the policy. *Strings & Things in Memphis, Inc. v. State Auto Ins. Co.*, 920 S.W.2d 652.

2. Other Policies or Bond Forms

5th Cir. 1954 (Tex.). Holding that proof of loss by employee dishonesty under a fidelity bond must be established by conclusive evidence, the court upheld a finding of coverage because two of the three employees of the insured were proven to have engaged in theft of merchandise, and there was no evidence showing any probability that the loss was occasioned in any other manner. *New Amsterdam Cas. Co. v. W.D. Felder*, 214 F.2d 825.

5th Cir. 1941 (Tex.). The court denied coverage under a blanket position bond where the insured's only proof of theft by unidentified employees was in the form of inventory computations. *Cobb v. Am. Bonding Co. of Baltimore*, 118 F.2d 643.

7th Cir. 1945 (Ill.). An insured attempted to prove a claim of inventory loss through unidentified employee dishonesty under a fidelity bond by presenting: (1) evidence of the shortage in its inventory; (2) evidence of normal shrinkage due to shoplifting; and (3) evidence of measures taken to protect against burglary and shoplifting. The court denied coverage, noting that there was not direct or affirmative proof of employee dishonesty, and although unidentified employee dishonesty may be demonstrated by circumstantial evidence, it must be of such nature to fairly or reasonably exclude any other explanation. *Gaytime Frock Co. v. Liberty Mut. Ins. Co.,* 148 F.2d 694.

8th Cir. 1965 (Mo.). The court affirmed a jury decision that the insured's losses were covered under a fidelity bond as having been caused by unidentifiable employees. The court noted that loss concerned grain from a large grain elevator that was under almost constant supervision by employees. The court also noted that employee supervision would be required for any outside wrongdoer to accomplish a theft of the grain, and that the insured negated any inference that the grain shortage reasonably could have attributed to any other cause. The court held that "conclusive evidence" as required by the bond, requires only evidence that is "clear, satisfactory, and convincing to the trier of facts." *Lumbermens Mut. Cas. Co. v. Norris Grain Co.,* 343 F.2d 670.

W.D. La. 1946. An insured sought to recover fidelity losses under three separate blanket bonds where there were no identifiable employees whose acts resulted in the loss. Two bonds were commercial blanket bonds that did not refer to unidentifiable employees, but contained traditional coverage for losses resulting from dishonest acts of any employee. The court allowed coverage, holding that the insured was not required to prove which particular employee committed the dishonest acts. The third bond, however, covered $2,500 for dishonest acts of each identifiable employee, and $2,500 for losses resulting from the dishonesty of employees not identified. The court allowed $2,500 of coverage for the acts of unidentified employees. *United States v. Nat'l Cas. Co.,* 5 F.R.D. 275.

D. Nev. 1968. The court found that the insured provided adequate proof of employee dishonesty to establish coverage under two fidelity bonds with inventory exclusions. The insured's employees were stealing chips at the casino and cashing them at other casinos. The court, however, denied the use of win percentages as the basis for calculating losses, but allowed the insured to demonstrate losses calculated based on the testimony of those individuals who cashed the chips. *Mapes Casino, Inc. v. Md. Cas. Co.*, 290 F. Supp. 186.

N.D.N.Y. 2000. The court denied an insurer's motion for summary judgment to dismiss the insured's claim against a property insurance policy with an inventory exclusion, where the insured relied upon an inventory count to establish a loss of inventory by unidentifiable employee theft. The court reasoned that because the insured first visually observed that a portion of its inventory was missing and then performed an inventory count to confirm and quantify the loss, a question of fact existed as to whether the loss was disclosed by the process of taking inventory. *Better Env't, Inc. v. ITT Hartford Ins. Group*, 96 F. Supp. 2d 162.

E.D. Pa. 1971. The court rejected coverage under a fidelity bond with an inventory exclusion where the insured relied upon inventory computations to demonstrate loss through the dishonesty of unidentified employees. The court found that absent any independent evidence of employee dishonesty, the insured could not utilize inventory computations to support its claims because of an inventory exclusion in the bond. *York Lumber Co. v. Fid. & Dep. Co. of Md*, 331 F. Supp. 1131.

Fl. App. 1958. Summary judgment was affirmed denying coverage under an employee's fidelity bond where the insured attempted to establish theft by unidentified employees solely relying upon discrepancies in an audit report. *Gen. Truck Sales, Inc. v. Am. Fire & Cas. Co.*, 100 So. 2d 202.

N.J. App. Div. 1967. The court held that the insured could recover under an employee fidelity bond with an inventory exclusion without proof of employee-connected loss. The court noted, however, that inventory records constitute inherently indispensable proof of the full amount of a loss if there is some appreciable proof from other facts or circumstances that the loss was caused by employee dishonesty. *Hoboken Camera, Inc. v. Hartford Accident & Indem. Co.*, 93 N.J. Super. 484.

H. Endorsements or Other Policies Expanding the Definition of Employee

1. Attorneys

5th Cir. 1972 (Ga.). An approved attorney acting on behalf of an insured title company met the definition of "employee" under a fidelity bond. The bond's definition of "employee" included "all attorneys who perform legal services for the Insured . . . or any individual engaged by the Insured . . . including, but not limited to, all of the Insured's approved attorneys." *Pioneer Nat'l Title Ins. Co. v. Am. Cas. Co. of Reading, Pa.,* 459 F.2d 963.

M.D. Ga. 1959. An attorney retained by a borrower, who provided an opinion relied upon by the insured bank, did not meet the definition of an "employee" under a financial institution bond because the borrower's attorney was never seen, never contacted, and never retained by the insured bank. *Moultrie Nat'l Bank v. Travelers Indem. Co.,* 181 F. Supp. 444, *aff'd* 275 F.2d 903 (5th 1960).

N.D. Ga. 2010. A bank insured under a Financial Institution Bond sought to recover for loss caused by an attorney who performed certain services for each of the buyers, the sellers, and the bank at closings in connection a real estate development. The bond defined "employee" to include an attorney "retained by" the insured while performing legal services for the insured. Although the borrower initially selected this attorney to handle the closings, the bank approved of him and accepted his services. On those facts, the court concluded as a matter of law that the attorney was "retained by" the bank for purposes of qualifying as an employee under the bond. *Federal Ins. Co. v. United Community Banks, Inc.,* No. 2:08-cv-0128, 2010 WL 3842359.

S.D. Miss. 2014. A bank made loans purportedly secured by property for which it had received fraudulent certificates of title from an attorney. The bank's fidelity bond defined employee to include an attorney retained by the insured while performing legal services for the insured. The attorney in question was not retained or paid by the bank, and provided no legal services at the bank's request. The court therefore granted summary judgment against the bank and dismissed its claim under the bond.

Copiah Bank, N.A. v. Fed. Ins. Co., Inc., No. 3:12-cv-27, 2014 WL 172122.

D.N.J. 1977. An attorney, who was a director of the insured bank and a partner in a New York law firm, met the definition of an "employee" under a bankers blanket bond because the bond's definition of "employees" included "attorney, retained by the insured to perform legal services for the insured." The insurer argued that the attorney was not an employee because there was no retainer paid to the attorney. The court disagreed with this argument, reasoning that the word "retained" in the bond's definition of "employee," in addition to connoting the payment of a fee, referred to the engagement of the services of an attorney or counselor to manage a cause. The court reasoned that the payment of a fee was not necessary to give rise to an attorney-client relationship. *Midland Bank & Trust Co. v. Fid. & Dep. Co. of Md.*, 442 F. Supp. 960.

S.D. Tex. 2014. An attorney was retained solely to act as a title insurance agent for an insured under a financial institution bond, which defined "Employee" to include an attorney retained by the insured while performing "legal services" for it. The agreement between the insured and the attorney expressly provided that the relationship between the two parties was that of attorney and client. The attorney was also exempt from Florida's licensing requirements for title insurance agents solely by virtue of being a licensed attorney. On those facts, a Magistrate Judge recommended that partial summary judgment be entered in favor of the insured, finding that the attorney in question qualified as an employee under the bond. *Stewart Info. Servs. Corp. v. Great Am. Ins. Co.*, 997 F. Supp. 2d 650.

Minn. Ct. App. 2012. Several banks participated in loans purportedly secured by the fictitious assets of an airline company. The banks had fidelity coverage under financial institution bonds, which defined "employee" to include an attorney who was "retained by" and was "performing legal services for" the insureds. The borrower retained an investment broker to place the loans, which broker in turn retained an attorney to assist with closing the loans. Because the attorney was not retained by the insured banks and had not agreed to represent them as clients, the appellate tribunal sustained the motion court's award of partial summary judgment dismissing the banks' fidelity claims based upon the attorney's alleged misconduct in closing the loans. *Alerus Fin.*

Nat'l Ass'n v. St. Paul Mercury Ins. Co., No. A11-680, 2012 WL 254484.

2. Data Processors

N.D. Cal. 2004. An insured bank under a financial institution bond alleged that it suffered a loss due to thefts of cash by a vendor providing ATM and armored car services. The bond's definition of an "employee" included a person or organization contracted by the insured as an electronic data processor of checks or other accounting records. The insured argued that because the ATM vendor was contractually required to fill out inventory summary forms recording the balances for various ATMs and to transmit those forms to the bank by facsimile, the vendor qualified as an electronic data processor of accounting records. The court rejected that argument and entered summary judgment in favor of the insurer. The court observed that the vendor's primary responsibility was to transport currency, and that transmitting the forms to the bank was "at best a subsidiary function," which did not render the vendor an employee in the context of the definition of the bond. *Humboldt Bank v. Gulf Ins. Co.*, 323 F. Supp. 2d 1027, *aff'd* 189 Fed. Appx. 645.

D. Colo. 2008. A bank obtained a financial institution bond that defined an "employee" to include "each natural person, partnership or corporation authorized by the Insured to perform services as data processor of checks or other accounting records of the Insured . . . herein called Processor." The bond stated that coverage terminated as to any Employee as "soon as any Insured, or any director or officer not in collusion with such person, learns of any dishonest or fraudulent act committed by such person[.]" The bank engaged a third-party vendor, Century, to process credit card applications. Century later learned of, and participated in, a fraudulent scheme involving alleged employees of the bank. At issue before the court was whether coverage terminated as to one or more of the fraudsters when Century first learned of the fraud, which the court perceived as turning upon whether Century was a Processor under the policy. The court expressed skepticism as to whether Century qualified as a Processor because it did not appear to handle checks or other accounting records, and declined to grant summary judgment in favor of the insurer on the basis of when Century learned of the fraud. *F.D.I.C. v. St. Paul Cos.*, 634 F. Supp. 2d 1213.

S.D. Fl. 2012. An insurance premium financing agency obtained fidelity coverage under a financial institution bond, which defined "Employee" to include third parties "authorized by the insured to perform services as data processor of checks[.]" The bond excluded coverage for loss due to dishonest conduct "by any non-Employee" who is an insurance broker, agent, or other representative of the same character. A loss was allegedly caused by the principal of an insurance agency that did business with the insured pursuant to a written producer agreement. Although the broker otherwise fell within the "non-Employee" exclusion, the court found a question of fact as to whether the broker was nevertheless an employee, because there was some evidence that the broker also performed services for the insured by which he could be deemed a data processor of checks and, hence, an "Employee" under the bond. *Abco Premium Finance, LLC v. Am, Int'l Grp., Inc.*, No. 11-23020-CIV, 2012 WL 32786268, *aff'd on other grounds*, 518 Fed. Appx. 601 (11th Cir. 2013).

E.D. Pa 2001. An insured bank entered into an agreement with a premium financing company whereby the finance company was to establish and maintain a computer system and enter certain account information into the computer system for the insured bank. The premium financing company failed to report accurate information and instead transmitted incomplete and inaccurate data. The fidelity bond at issue included, in its definition of "employee," "each natural person, partnership or corporation authorized to perform services as data processors of checks or other accounting records of Insureds (not including preparation or modification of computer software programs)." The insurer filed a motion to dismiss the bank's complaint based upon the argument that the premium finance company modified computer programs. The court, however, denied the motion because the premium finance company met the definition of a "data processor" by entering accounting data, in addition to modifying computer programs. *Hudson United Bank v. Progressive Cas. Ins. Co.*, 152 F. Supp. 2d 751.

3. Investment Advisors

Del. Ch. 2010. An investment fund obtained a fidelity bond, with "Employee" defined broadly to include "an agent" of the insured and "an investment advisor." The insured invested funds with Bernard Madoff, was allegedly damaged as a result of the collapse of his Ponzi scheme, and brought suit against the fidelity carrier. The carrier moved to dismiss, arguing that Madoff was not an "Employee" under the bond. The court, however, held that the complaint proffered a sufficiently "reasonable" reading of bond to survive a motion to dismiss, suggesting that Madoff could be found to be an "Employee" either as an "investment advisor" or within the scope of the bond's "free-wheeling use of agency terms." *Mass. Mut. Life Ins. Co. v. Certain Underwriters at Lloyd's of London*, No. 4791-VCL, 2010 WL 2929552.

4. Other Endorsements

8th Cir. 1971 (S.D.). The insured requested an endorsement to its fidelity bond that deleted the insured's president and vice president from the definition of "employee" under the bond. As a result of the request, the insurer issued an endorsement exempting those two individuals. In a subsequent policy period, the insured then decided to cover the president and vice president. To effectuate the change, the fidelity carrier cancelled the special endorsement. The insured then made a claim as a result of its president having raided the company's assets. The fidelity carrier denied coverage arguing that the president was not an employee, and that the cancelled endorsement would have only applied if president met the definition of "employee" under the bond. The court found that the prior cancellation of the endorsement clearly indicated that absent a limiting endorsement, the bond covered the president as an employee of the insured. *Gen. Fin. Corp. v. Fid. & Cas. Co. of N.Y.*, 439 F.2d 981.

C.D. Cal. 1998. An employee of an independent contractor that provided certain services to an insured was accused of conduct that led to the insured being sued in connection with an alleged Ponzi scheme. The insured sought fidelity coverage under a series of crime policies, which defined "employee" similarly to the Commercial Crime Policy, but several of which also extended the definition to include "Independent Contractors." The court noted in *dicta* that the independent contractor clause "would possibly allow for coverage" as to the individual in question. However, that clause was not included during the policy periods when the subject company had served as an independent contractor for the insured. Thus, the court held that the individual in question was neither an employee nor a temporary employee of the insured. *Vons Cos., Inc. v. Fed. Ins. Co.*, 57 F. Supp. 2d 933, *aff'd on other grounds* 212 F.3d 489 (9th Cir. 2000).

Bankr. E.D. Pa. 1987. A fidelity carrier issued a rider to a fidelity bond excluding the insured's president from the definition of "employee" under the bond. The insured then brought claims against the fidelity bond with such rider as well as a second fidelity bond for dishonest acts of its president. The court held that there was coverage under the second fidelity bond without the rider because the existence of the rider on the first fidelity bond established that the president was considered to be an "employee" for the purpose of the fidelity clause. *In re Leedy Mort. Co.,* 76 B.R. 440.

I.   Other Circumstances

1.   Commercial Crime Policies

N.D. Cal. 2014. Two companies obtained commercial crime policies with endorsements extending coverage to loss involving the funds of clients while the insured was acting as a qualified intermediary in a tax-deferred exchange of property intended to qualify under I.R.S. Code 1031. The court read the endorsement to provide for coverage even where the loss was caused by the insured itself or its partners, who would otherwise not qualify as an employee under the policies. The two owners of the insureds, with the knowledge of all of the insureds' officers, stole client funds through a Ponzi scheme, and a receiver for the insured sought to recover under the policies for the purpose of reimbursing the victims. The court granted summary judgment in favor of the fidelity carrier, holding that under California Insurance Code Section 533, an insurer is not liable for loss caused by a willful act of an insured. Although the receiver sought recovery for the benefit of third parties, the court expressed its concern that to permit any recovery would allow criminals to insure against liability for their own misconduct. *Dillon v. Cont'l Cas. Co.,* No. 5:10-CV-05238, 2014 WL 1266124.

Kan. App. 2003. The court reversed summary judgment in favor of the insurer construing an exclusion within a commercial crime policy as ambiguous. The insured (the "City") sought coverage for the dishonest acts of a city manager who was required by statute to be bonded. The insurer argued that coverage was precluded under an exclusion for employees required by law to be individually bonded. The City argued that the policy referred to employees who must be separately bonded, and the statute at issue did not specify a requirement for an individual bond as opposed to coverage under a blanket bond. Accordingly, the court held that the exclusion in the policy, as applied to the facts of the case, was ambiguous and should be construed against the insurer. *City of Concordia v. Am. States Ins.,* No. 89,200, 2003 WL 21948009.

2. Other Policies or Bond Forms

2d Cir. 1970 (N.Y.). In light of certain rules of the New York Stock Exchange, an individual who managed a subsidiary corporation of the insured was treated as an employee of the insured for purposes of coverage under a fidelity bond. *Oscar Gruss & Son v. Lumbermens Mut. Cas. Co.,* 422 F.2d 1278.

9th Cir. 1979 (Cal.). A fidelity bond listed two companies as named insureds. The first company had employees and the second company did not. The first company was employed under a management contract to act as an investment advisor to the second company. The court determined that under these circumstances, it was intended that the second company be covered for the actions of an employee of the first company. Coverage was ultimately denied, however, under an exclusion for losses resulting for from the trading of securities. *Research Equity Fund, Inc. v. Ins. Co. of N. Am.,* 602 F.2d 200.

Mass. 1914. A wrongdoer and an insured entered into an agreement for the assignment and collection of accounts receivable assigned to the insured at a discount, and delivered back to the wrongdoer for collection on the insured's account. The insured obtained a fidelity bond covering the wrongdoer of an employee. The court reversed a lower court's finding of coverage because the risks involved were materially different from the normal risk of defalcation by an employee assigned to collect accounts receivable. The court noted that the fidelity bond was not intended to cover such a situation. *Coyle v. USG&G,* 104 N.E. 559.

J.   The Alter Ego Defense

1.   Commercial Crime Policies

9th Cir. 1991 (Cal.). Two of the insured's principal officers and directors were found to not meet the definition of "employees" under a 3-D policy that included "govern and direct" language as part of the definition. The court reasoned that the insured could not govern and direct the two individuals because they were the sole shareholders of the insured's parent company, and therefore they controlled the insured, rather than the insured controlling them. *Cal. Union Ins. Co. v. Am. Diversified Sav. Bank,* 948 F.2d 556.

Bankr. N.D. Ga. 1995. Although noting that the mere fact that the president and director owned a majority of shares of an insured corporation does not prove actual dominance, the court found that the insured's president and director was not restrained or controlled by anyone in the insured corporation, and dominated the insured corporation such that he did not meet the definition of an "employee" under the insured's commercial crime policy. *In re Prime Commercial Corp.,* 187 B.R. 785.

E.D. La. 2001. An insured's sole owner and president was found not to meet the definition of "employee" under a crime policy because he directed the insured and the insured did not have the right to govern and direct his performance. *Orleans Parish Sch. Bd. v. Chubb Custom Ins. Co.,* 162 F. Supp. 2d 506.

S.D.N.Y. 1997. The court declined coverage under employee dishonesty and crime policies where an insured was unable to govern and direct a defalcating shareholder. The court held that the shareholder did not meet the definition of "employee" under the policy because it was undisputed that the shareholder dominated and controlled the insured and that no one at the insured governed and directed the shareholder. *In re Payroll Express Corp.,* 216 B.R. 344.

S.D. Ohio 2005. The president and sole shareholder of an insured corporation did not meet the definition of an "employee" under a commercial crime policy because he was not subject to the direction and control of the insured. The insured attempted to argue that the president was an "employee" because he was subject to the control of the insured's "compliance officer." The court disagreed, finding that the insured must exercise control, and not just have a theoretical right to exert control. *Lutz v. St. Paul Fire & Marine Ins. Co.*, No. 1:03-CV-750, 2005 WL 2372871.

Mo. Ct. App. 2003. An insured corporation allegedly suffered a loss caused by its sole shareholder, who also served as its president and managing officer, but who was one of several directors. The insurer denied the claim, because the wrongdoer was not an employee as defined in the subject crime policy, which defined "employee" as a person subject to insured's right to direct and control. The lower court granted the fidelity carrier's summary judgment motion on that basis, but the appeals court reversed. The court stated its agreement with the courts of other jurisdictions that the "alter ego defense" has its basis in the language of the policy, and held that the defense could apply under Missouri law. Nevertheless, the court borrowed and applied concepts from corporate veil-piercing cases, which require absolute domination of a corporation by an individual before he is deemed an alter ego of the corporation, and found that the fidelity carrier had not established such dominance under summary judgment standards. In so holding, the court failed to recognize that the burden of proving a covered claim is ordinarily placed upon the insured, and that in order to avoid summary judgment the insured should have been required to introduce at least some evidence that the wrongdoer met the policy's definition of an "employee" and was subject to the insured's right to direct and control. *E. Attucks Cmty. Hous., Inc. v. Old Republic Sur. Co.*, 114 S.W.3d 311.

N.D. 1996. The court, in examining a fidelity coverage endorsement to an errors and omissions policy, determined that fidelity coverage cannot exist where the defalcating employee's control over, and ownership of, the insured corporation is "overwhelming." The court determined, however, that the individual's control was not so overwhelming as to eliminate his status as an "employee" under the policy. *Emp'rs Reins. Corp. v. Landmark*, 547 N.W.2d 527.

Ohio 1990. The president of the insured embezzled funds being held in trust. The court declined to allow coverage under a 3-D policy. The court did not analyze whether the president qualified as an "employee" under the policy. Rather, based upon admissions by the insured's counsel that the president was the insured's alter ego, the court declined to allow coverage under an exclusion for loss due to any fraudulent, dishonest, or criminal act by any insured. *Thrift Fed. Sav. & Loan v. Overton,* 563 N.E.2d 289.

2. Other Policies or Bond Forms

1st Cir. 1993 (Mass.). A commercial fidelity bond was issued to two corporations over which one president maintained complete control. The president was the sole shareholder of one corporation, and owned 50% of the stock of the other corporation (his wife owning the other 50%). The court determined that the president was the alter ego of the two corporations, rather than an employee, and therefore denied coverage under the bond for the president's fraudulent acts. The court focused on the "right to govern and direct" language in the bond's definition of "employee" and distinguished between a theoretical right to control and an actual right to control. Finding that the corporations never exercised their theoretical rights to control the president, and that the president controlled the corporations, the court denied coverage. *Bird. v. Centennial Ins. Co.,* 11 F.3d 228.

4th Cir. 1967 (Md.). The court of appeals reversed the dismissal of a claim brought under a savings and loan blanket bond, concluding that material issues of fact existed as to whether the dishonest executives that caused the loss exercised such dominance and control over the affairs of the insured corporation that their fraudulent acts and the knowledge thereof could be imputed to the corporation. *Phoenix Sav. & Loan, Inc. v. Aetna Cas. & Sur. Co.,* 381 F.2d 245.

4th Cir. 1965 (S.C.). A corporation's principal officers who were its only directors and owned 75% of its stock were not "employees" within the meaning of a commercial fidelity bond. The court noted that the bond was intended to protect the corporation from the fraud or dishonesty of its employees, not to protect its creditors from the fraud or dishonesty of its stockholders and directors. *Kerr. v. Aetna Cas. & Sur. Co.,* 350 F.2d 146.

5th Cir. 1993 (Tex.). An individual who, together with his former wife, owned 95% of the insured corporation's common stock and dominated control of the corporation, was found to not be an "employee" within the meaning of a commercial fidelity bond. The court reasoned that when one person owns a controlling interest in a corporation and dominates the corporation's actions, his acts are the corporation's acts. Allowing the corporation to recover for its owner's dishonest conduct would essentially allow the corporation to recover for its own dishonest acts. *In re World Hospitality Ltd.*, 983 F.2d 650.

5th Cir. 1985 (Tex.). The majority shares of an insured bank were owned by a holding company whose sole shareholders were the president and vice president of the insured bank. As a result of dishonest acts of the president, the insured bank sought coverage under a bankers blanket bond. The court denied coverage on equitable considerations, finding that the vice president's knowledge of the president's dishonest acts was imputed to the bank. *City State Bank in Wellington v. U. S. Fid. & Guar. Co.*, 778 F.2d 1103.

5th Cir. 1976 (Ala.). Two principals of an insured corporation acquired control of the holding company that owned the insured. Thereafter, the principals elected themselves officers and directors of both the holding company and the insured and thereafter raided the insured's coffers. The court denied coverage under the fidelity bond noting that the principals did not meet the bond's definition of "employee" because the insured never had the right to govern or direct the principals. Rather, the court concluded that the momentary status of the principals as officers never placed them "in the service" of the insured, "for they only served themselves." *First Nat'l Life Ins. Co. v. Fid. & Dep. Co. of Md.*, 525 F.2d 966.

5th Cir. 1972 (Tex.). A majority shareholder of the insured bank committed fraudulent acts that the bank contended were covered under a bankers blanket bond. The court rejected the insurer's argument that the majority shareholder was the bank's alter ego, and found that because the majority shareholder was to be specifically excluded from participating in any recovery, the bank was not being allowed profit from its own fraud. *FDIC v. Lott,* 460 F.2d 82.

5th Cir. 1963 (Fla.). In examining a commercial blanket bond, the court found that where a principal officer and shareholder who wholly owned the insured corporation took the corporation's money, the knowledge of the principal officer and shareholder was imputed to the insured corporation since there was no adverse interest. *McKee v. Am. Cas. Co.,* 316 F.2d 428.

6th Cir. 1991 (Tenn.). The court denied coverage under a bankers blanket bond where a director, president, and majority shareholder of an insured's parent company had caused the insured to make loans to associates of the director. The court ruled in favor of the insurer because the director did not possess the manifest intent to cause a significant injury to an entity in which he had a major financial stake. *FDIC v. St. Paul Fire & Marine Ins. Co.,* 942 F.2d 1032.

7th Cir. 1971 (Ill.). In deciding a summary judgment motion, the court found that there was an issue of fact as to whether two officers, who were two of the three owners of the insured corporation, were subject to the control of a six-member board of directors, and thus met the definition of "employees" under the fidelity bond at issue. *Charm Proms., Ltd. v. Travelers Indem. Co.,* 447 F.2d 607.

8th Cir. 1989 (Minn.). Coverage was denied under a bankers special bond where the fraudulent act was committed by the president of the bank. The court reasoned that the president, for all practical purposes, was the bank because he owned 92% of the shares of the bank, and, in addition to being president, was the chief operating officer, and director of the bank. *Red Lake County State Bank v. Emp'rs Ins. of Wausau,* 874 F.2d 546.

8th Cir. 1971 (S.D.). The court found that that the president and majority shareholder of a corporation who had committed fraudulent acts was an "employee" under a commercial fidelity bond because the president's majority stock ownership is not a basis for the surety to avoid liability. The court noted that the corporation was still subject to the control of the directors who at all times had the right to govern and direct the exercise of all corporate powers, business and property. *Gen. Fin. Corp. v. Fid. & Cas. Co. of N.Y.,* 439 F.2d 981.

10th Cir. 1994 (Utah). The F.D.I.C. brought suit in its corporate capacity against a surety seeking to recover under a savings and loan blanket bond for fraud committed by former officers of a savings and loan. Ignoring whether the former officer's knowledge was imputed to the savings and loan, the court that held the alter ego doctrine was inapplicable, reasoning that any payments under the fidelity bond would accrue to F.D.I.C. in its corporate capacity, and not to the persons responsible for the wrongdoing. *FDIC v. Oldenburg,* 34 F.3d 1529.

10th Cir. 1969 (Okla.). The court rejected the insurer's argument that two directors of the insured, who were also officers of the corporation, did not meet the fidelity bond's definition of "employee." The court declined to apply the alter ego doctrine because the two directors were neither the sole directors, nor the sole or majority shareholders. *Ins. Co. of N. Am. v. Greenberg,* 405 F.2d 330.

10th Cir. 1967 (Okla.). The surety on a bank employee dishonesty bond contended that the president of the insured bank was the bank's alter ego. The court rejected the argument because the insured bank's board of directors played a significant part in managing the bank. *USF&G. v. Oklahoma,* 383 F.2d 417.

D. Colo. 2008. The court granted partial summary judgment against the receiver of an insured bank under a financial institution bond, as to its claim under the bond's insuring agreement for Computer Systems Fraud. The court's stated basis for its holding was that coverage under that agreement was excluded for loss caused by an "employee," and the loss was caused by three individuals that the court clearly viewed as employees. The facts recited elsewhere in the opinion reveal that these three individuals included the Chief Executive Officer of the bank who owned one hundred percent of its stock, a member of the bank's Board of Directors who also served as the president of the bank, as well as the bank's Chief Financial Officer. The court did not expressly discuss whether the bond required that to qualify as an "employee" an individual must be subject to the insured's right to direct and control. However, the court observed that there was no evidence presented that the CEO exercised the level of dominance over the bank or the Board of Directors necessary for the CEO to be viewed as the bank's alter ego, such that the CEO's knowledge of his own wrongdoing could be imputed to the bank. *F.D.I.C. v. St. Paul Cos.,* 634 F. Supp. 2d 1213.

D. Del. 2011. The Chief Executive Officer of the insured under a financial institution bond was accused of causing the insured a loss. The bond defined "employee" to include an "officer" of the insured, and did not expressly require that the employee be subject to the direction and control of the insured. The court granted summary judgment against the fidelity carrier as to its "alter ego" defense, reasoning that the bond as drafted provided coverage for fraudulent acts committed by officers of the insured, regardless of the degree of control exercised by such officers over the insured. *Arrowood Indem. Co. v. Hartford Fire Ins. Co.* 774 F. Supp. 2d 636.

M.D. Fla. 1970. The court declined to apply an alter ego defense despite the parties' stipulation that a wrongdoer was the alter ego of the insured. The court reasoned that because the fidelity carrier knew everything about the insured's business at the time the fidelity bond was issued, the carrier knew that the wrongdoer controlled the insured, and that the carrier could not rely on other employees to receive notice of the wrongdoer's misconduct. The court thereby concluded that the carrier had waived the notice and discovery provisions in the bond. *Fid. & Dep. Co. of Md. v. USAFORM Hail Pool, Inc.,* 318 F. Supp. 1301.

M.D. Ga. 1967. In denying coverage under a bankers blanket bond, the court found that where a bank partner had sole and complete control of an insured bank, the bank partner's knowledge of misappropriation of bank funds would be imputed to the insured bank. *Hartford Acc. & Indem. Co. v. Hartley,* 275 F. Supp. 610.

N.D. Ohio 2013. A company ("PBA") was a third-party administrator of the ERISA health benefit plans of its clients. PBA obtained crime coverage for employee theft, covering not only PBA's own funds, but those of its clients as well. PBA agreed to segregate its clients' funds, but did not do so. Instead, PBA regularly deposited its clients' funds in PBA's general accounts, from which PBA paid its own operating expenses, including very generous payments and benefits for its executives. A creditor of PBA, invoking a direct action statute allowing it to stand in PBA's shoes, brought an action against the insurer. The insurer moved for summary judgment, arguing that the president and majority-owner of PBA, who was fully aware of and participated in the scheme, was not an "employee" as defined in the policy, because he was not subject to PBA's right of direction and control. The court, however, found it unnecessary to reach that argument, because a number of lower-level "employees" of PBA were actively involved in the diversions of client funds. *Guyan Int'l, Inc. v. Prof'l Benefits Adm'rs, Inc.*, No. 5:10-cv-823, 2013 WL 1338194.

E.D. Pa. 1993. In examining coverage under a commercial fidelity bond, the court found that knowledge of a corporation's sole directors, officers, and principals who engaged in a scheme of embezzlement and fraud was deemed the knowledge of the corporation. *In re Lloyd Sec., Inc.*, 153 B.R. 677.

Bankr. W.D. Pa. 1994. The court denied a surety's motion for summary judgment to deny coverage based upon the alter ego doctrine under a commercial fidelity bond. The court reasoned that although the alleged wrongdoer was president, director, and majority shareholder of the insured corporation, he was not the sole officer, and there was a board of directors consisting of three persons. The court therefore found that an issue of fact remained as to whether the control exercised by the non-fraudulent parties would be sufficient to establish that the alleged wrongdoer could be an "employee" within the meaning of the bond. *In re Mechem Fin, Inc.*, 167 B.R. 799.

Ariz. 1985. Two sole shareholders who acted as the officers and directors of the insured corporation were discovered to have embezzled funds from the insured. The court rejected a claim against a fidelity bond because the sole shareholders did not meet the bond's definition of "employee" whom the insured must have the right to control. The court rejected the suggestion that the theoretical right to control would satisfy this requirement, and held that there must be "actual control." *Emp'rs Admin. Servs., Inc. v. Hartford Acc. & Indem. Co.*, 709 P.2d 559.

Cal. Ct. App. 1936. The court denied coverage under a fidelity bond where the wrongdoers at issue owned all of the stock of the insured's ultimate owner and controlled the management, policies, and affairs of the insured. As such, the court imputed the knowledge possessed by the wrongdoers to the insured. *W. Am. Fin. Co. v. Pac. Indem. Co.*, 61 P.2d 963.

Ill. App. Ct. 1989. The court declined coverage under a bankers blanket bond for losses due to high-level decisions made by the insured's officers and directors to participate in certain acts alleged to be fraudulent. The court held that the fidelity carrier is not required to indemnify the insured for attorneys' fees and costs in defending litigation that results from those acts. *State St. Bank & Trust Co. v. USF&G*, 539 N.E.2d 779.

Ill. App. Ct. 1962. The court permitted coverage under a bankers blanket bond where the fidelity carrier failed to provide evidence that would create even a reasonable inference that the supervisory officials and partners of the insured were aware of and approved illegal sales by employees for which the insured was seeking the recovery of losses. *Home Indem. Co. v. Reynolds & Co.*, 187 N.E.2d 274.

Iowa 1979. The court rejected the insurer's attempt to deny coverage under a fidelity bond under the "sole actor" doctrine where the insured bank's losses were the result of the dishonest and fraudulent acts of the insured's president. Although the president was a substantial stockholder and "without question the most influential person in the management of the bank's business," the court found that there was no basis to hold that the insured's board of directors abdicated its responsibilities or was entirely subject to the president's control. *FDIC v. Nat'l Sur. Corp.*, 281 N.W.2d 816.

Md. 1989. The sole shareholder and director of a management company did not meet the definition of "employee" under a commercial blanket bond. The court noted that where the dishonesty that causes the loss is that of a person who is the only officer, director and shareholder of the insured corporation, the cases are nearly uniform in holding that the standard commercial blanket bond does not provide coverage. *Three Garden Village v. USF&G*, 567 A.2d 85.

Minn. 1992. The court rejected the surety's alter ego defense and held that the insured bank's president and majority shareholder was an "employee" under a financial institution bond. The bond defined "employee" simply as "an officer or other employee of the Insured, while employed in, at, or by any of the Insured's offices or premises located in the United States," without reference to the concept of control. The court opined that a successful "alter ego defense" would require evidence that the bank's board of directors abdicated its control of the corporation to such a degree that that the bank president ceased to be its employee. The evidence, however, was in the court's view insufficient to prevent summary judgment dismissing that defense. *Transamerica Ins. Co. v. F.D.I.C.,* 489 N.W.2d 224.

Minn. 1976. The board of directors of a bank jointly decided to participate in a fraudulent scheme. The court denied coverage under a bankers fidelity bond because the bond did not cover losses caused by reasons of fraud, dishonesty, or breach of fiduciary duty where the bank, through its board of directors, had knowledge of the acts complained of, appreciated their fraudulent nature, and condoned, acquiesced, or participated in them. The court stated that to allow otherwise would allow the bank to insure against its own dishonesty. *Farmers & Merchants St. Bank of Pierez v. St. Paul Fire & Marine Ins. Co.,* 242 N.W.2d 840.

N.J. App. Div. 2000. An insured title agency was run by a sole shareholder who acted as director and president. The sole shareholder supervised title closing and collected checks from homebuyers to be held in trust to pay off existing mortgages on purchased properties. The sole shareholder, however, stole the checks. The court rejected the argument that the fidelity bond provided coverage for the acts of a sole shareholder/director because the corporation had no control over the sole shareholder/director. The court found that the theoretical right to control the sole shareholder/director had no significance and that insurance coverage is not intended to insure a corporation against its own fraudulent and/or dishonest acts. *Conestoga Title Ins. Co. v. Premier Title Agency, Inc.,* 746 A.2d 462, *aff'd,* 763 A.2d 746 (N.J. 2000).

N.J. App. Div. 2000. A fidelity insurer filed an action to rescind a fidelity bond issued on behalf of a title company. All corporate affairs of the title company were controlled by its president. The president's wife was the sole director and stockholder, but had absolutely nothing to do with the title company. The court acknowledged that although the wife of the president theoretically had the ability to control the company and the president, it could not permit a recovery under the bond where a thief has utterly dominated a corporation and become its alter ego through placing formal ownership of the company in a spouse or confederate. *Hartford Fire Ins. Co. v. Conestoga Title Ins. Co.,* 746 A.2d 460.

N.Y. Civ. Ct. 1993. An insured was estopped from seeking coverage under bankers blanket bonds where the insured had plead guilty to federal indictments involving the same transactions that formed the basis of the bond claims. The court reasoned that the knowing participation in and benefiting for criminal conduct engaged in by its employees meant that the insured was seeking to recover for its own criminal conduct. *Drexel Burnham Lambert Group, Inc. v. Vigilant Ins. Co.*, 595 N.Y.S.2d 999.

S.D. 1911. An employee, by acquiring a majority share of the insured bank's stock, was found to have lost his employee status under the terms of a bankers blanket bond. The court noted that the individual "practically became the master of the corporation and ceased to be one of its servants." The court reasoned that the object of the bond was to insure an employer against the fraudulent acts of its employees, not to insure an employer against his own fraudulent acts. *Farmers' & Merchants' St. Bank of Verdon v. USF&G*, 133 N.W. 247.

Wash. 1932. Coverage was upheld under a fidelity bond despite the wrongdoer being the president, secretary, and treasurer of the insured. The court reasoned that the wrongdoer was an employee and was not the alter ego of the insured because at the time the wrongful acts occurred, the wrongdoer had not yet acquired a majority of the insured's stock even though it was being held in escrow for him. *Bryan v. Fid. & Cas. Co. of N.Y.*, 9 P.2d 86.

Wash. App. 1979. The court denied coverage under a fidelity bond where a president and sole shareholder of an insured bank stole money from the bank. The court found that the president and sole shareholder's act of theft was an act of the bank. *Seattle Int'l Corp. v. Commerce & Indus. Ins. Co.*, 600 P.2d 612.

SECONDARY RESOURCES

CharCretia V. DiBartolo, *Who's the Boss? The Impact of Professional Employer Organizations On Fidelity Coverage*, VIII FID. L. ASS'N. J. 75 (2002)

Cole S. Kain, *Alter Ego Defense*, VII FID. L. ASS'N. J. 217 (2001).

T. Scott Leo & Brandon G. Hummel, *Conditions and Limitations*, *in* ANNOTATED FINANCIAL INSTITUTION BOND 209 (Michael Keeley ed., 3d. ed. 2013)

Jeffrey M. Paskert, P. Keith Lichman & Dolores Parr, *Who Is An "Employee"?*, *in* COMMERCIAL CRIME INSURANCE COVERAGE 135 (Randall I. Marmor & Susan Koehler Sullivan eds. 2015)

Armen Shahinian & Andrew Kent, *Who is a Covered "Employee" Under The Financial Institution Bond*, *in* FINANCIAL INSTITUTION BONDS 113 (Duncan L. Clore ed., 3d ed. 2008)

Chapter 9

Definitions*

The newer versions of standard form commercial crime policies, such as the Crime Protection Policy[1] ("CPP") and the 2012 Commercial Crime Policy[2] (in both loss sustained and discovery versions) ("CCP") contain more defined terms than were contained in earlier forms. This section addresses the terms defined in the CPP and CCP, noting differences where appropriate.[3]

A. Banking Premises

"Banking premises" means the interior of that portion of any building occupied by a financial institution with which you have an account or which you have an account or which has custody of your money or security.

COMMENT

"Banking premises" is not a defined terms in the CCP. Often it is construed along with the more general defined term "premises," and, therefore, cases considering that definition also should be consulted. Courts construe both terms strictly such that activity occurring in locations other than the interior of a building, even if on a porch or deck attached to the building, will not be considered to be inside the premises.

---

*   By CharCretia V. Di Bartolo and Jamie L. Kessler, Hinshaw & Culbertson LLP, Boston, Massachusetts.
1   Crime Protection Policy, SP 00 01 04 12 (Sur. Ass'n of Am. 2012), *reprinted in* COMMERCIAL CRIME POLICY 769 (Randall I. Marmor & Susan Koehler Sullivan eds., 3d ed. 2014).
2   *E.g.*, Commercial Crime Policy, CR 00 23 08 13 (ISO Props, Inc. 2012) (Loss Sustained), *reprinted in* COMMERCIAL CRIME POLICY, *supra* note 1, at 799.
3   The defined terms "employee" and "discovery" are discussed at length in Chapters 8 and 12 herein, and therefore are not included in this Chapter.

The 2012 version of this definition uses only the term "financial institution" so that other depositary institutions, such as credit unions, are also covered by this definition.

ANNOTATIONS

7th Cir. 2005. A customer of the insured bank sued the bank for losses resulting from fraud committed by its employee. The Customer's employee embezzled from her employer by instructing the insured bank to prepare more than 570 cashier's checks drawn on customer's account and payable to employee's creditors. The bank sought defense and indemnity from insurer. The court affirmed summary judgment in favor of the insurer holding that the employee did not enter the premises of the bank to order the checks. Rather, she gave all instructions by phone. Accordingly, the on-premises insuring agreement of the financial institution bond did not apply. *Bankmanagers Corp. v. Fed. Ins. Co.*, 712 F.3d 1163.

7th Cir. 2005. The court affirmed summary judgment in favor of the insurer. An imposter opened an account in the name of the corporation and deposited stolen checks payable to the corporation. The bank did not require the imposter to endorse the checks. Instead, a bank employee placed a stamped endorsement on the checks. After the hold period expired, the imposter telephoned the bank and directed that most of the proceeds be transferred to the account of a legitimate commercial customer to pay for gold coins. A few days later, the imposter came to the bank to attempt to withdraw the remaining money and was arrested. The bank claimed coverage under the On Premises Insuring Agreement, arguing that the false pretenses were the misrepresentations in opening the account and depositing the checks and that the imposter was on bank premises at the time. The court disagreed, holding that for On Premises coverage, the perpetrator must be on the premises at the time the loss is sustained. Depositing money into the bank was not a loss. The loss occurred when the bank made the transfer in response to the perpetrator's telephone instructions and he was not on premises at the time. *The Private Bank v. Progressive Cas. Ins. Co.*, 409 F.3d 814.

S.D. Ind. 2006. In this unreported decision, the court held that phone cards stolen by an employee of a third party were not stolen on the insured's premises. The court rejected insured's argument that "premises" should include a location where an insured's employee continues to advance the interests of the insured. Here, an insured employee exchanged the phone cards off premises with a third party with whom the insured was doing business. The court held that the phone cards were never inside the building that the insured occupied or where it conducted its business. *Brightpoint, Inc. v. Zurich Am. Ins. Co.*, 2006 WL 693377.

Ohio App. 1998. The court reversed the trial court's summary judgment ruling in favor of the insurer, finding that questions of material fact existed regarding whether the loss to the bank resulting from the treasurer's diversion of funds through investments with son resulted directly from "theft." The court upheld the trial court's finding that the loss occurred inside the bank premises, that is, the treasurer's office, where the funds were improperly transferred or surrendered. *Columbiana County Bd. of Comm'rs v. Nationwide Ins. Co.*, 719 N.E.2d 561.

SECONDARY SOURCES

11 COUCH ON INS. §167:47 (Nov. 2014).

B. Cash

"Cash" means United States or Canadian bills and coins in current use and having a face value that are accepted by the United States or by the government of Canada as legal tender for the payment of debts.

COMMENT

The CPP incorporates this defined term into the broader term "money." In contrast, the CCP does not include a separate defined term but instead inserts the term "cash" directly into the defined term "money." The annotation for the definition of "money" should be consulted.

ANNOTATIONS

NONE

SECONDARY SOURCES

NONE

C. Computer Program

"Computer program" means a set of related electronic instructions, which direct the operation and function of a computer or devices connected to it, which enable the computer or devices to receive, process, store or send "electronic data."

COMMENT

"Computer program" is not a defined term in the CPP. This defined term is contained in Insuring Agreement 6 (Computer and Funds Transfer Fraud) in the CCP.

ANNOTATIONS

N.Y. Sup. 2013. The court granted the insurer's motion for summary judgment finding that the computer systems fraud rider was designed to cover wrongful acts in manipulating the computer system by hackers. Thus, there was no coverage for fraudulent content of a claim by bona fide doctors who were otherwise authorized to access the system. *Universal American Corp. v. Nat'l Union Fire Ins. Co. of Pittsburgh, PA*, 959 N.Y.S.2d 849, 2013 N.Y. Slip. Op. 23003, *modified by*, 110 A.D.3d 434.

SECONDARY SOURCES

Scott L. Schmookler, *Computer and Funds Transfer Fraud*, COMMERCIAL CRIME POLICY 297 (Randall I. Marmor & Susan Koehler Sullivan eds., 3d ed. 2014).

D. "Computer System"

"Computer system" means:
a. **Computers, including Personal Digital Assistants (PDAs) and other transportable or handheld devices, electronic storage devices and related peripheral components;**
b. **systems and applications software; and**
c. **related communications networks by which "electronic data" is collected, transmitted, processed, stored or retrieved.**

COMMENT

"Computer system" is not a defined term in the CPP. This defined term is contained in Insuring Agreement 6 (Computer And Funds Transfer Fraud) in the CCP.

ANNOTATIONS

N.Y. Sup. 2013. The court granted the insurer's motion for summary judgment finding that computer systems fraud rider was designed to cover wrongful acts in manipulating a computer system by hackers. Thus, there was no coverage for fraudulent content of a claim by bona fide doctors who were otherwise authorized to access the system. *Universal American Corp. v. Nat'l Union Fire Ins. Co. of Pittsburgh, PA*, 959 N.Y.S.2d 849, 2013 N.Y. Slip. Op. 23003, *modified by,* 110 A.D.3d 434.

SECONDARY SOURCES

Scott L. Schmookler, *Computer and Funds Transfer Fraud*, COMMERCIAL CRIME POLICY 297 (Randall I. Marmor & Susan Koehler Sullivan eds., 3d ed. 2014).

E. Counterfeit

"Counterfeit" means an imitation of an actual valid original which is intended to deceive and to be taken as the original.

COMMENT

This is a defined term contained in Insuring Agreement 6 (Money Orders and Counterfeit Paper Currency) in the CPP and Insuring Agreement A.7 (Money Orders and Counterfeit Money) in the CCP. The CPP contains a narrower definition ("counterfeit money") and provides that, in order to be within the defined term, the imitation of "money" must be intended to deceive "and to be taken as genuine." For purposes of determining whether something is counterfeit under this definition, the counterfeit must imitate an original document. Many of the cases dealing with whether there is a counterfeit document consider the definition used in the financial institution bond, which is substantially similar. These cases tend to look to whether the purported counterfeit was an attempt to imitate an actual document or was a fabrication in its entirety. The distinction between an imitation and an invention out of whole cloth is not always easily discernable. The Uniform Commercial Code does not define this term, but describes the term "genuine" to mean free of forgery or counterfeiting. U.C.C. §1-201(19) (2003).

ANNOTATIONS

5th Cir. 1990 (Tex.). Bogus stock certificates that were not imitations of genuine stock certificates were not "counterfeit" within the meaning of the definition in the financial institution bond. *Reliance Ins. Co. v. Capital Bancshares, Inc.*, 912 F.2d 756.

7th Cir. 1991 (Ill.). A bank customer deposited his employer's checks into his personal account at the insured bank by using a rubber stamp endorsement that stated the checks were for "deposit only" to the personal account. The stamp endorsement did not constitute a forgery under the definition in the financial institution bond. Forgery is the signing of the name of another with intent to deceive. *Alpine State Bank v. Ohio Cas. Ins. Co.*, 941 F.2d 554.

S.D. Ala. 2014. Certificate was not an imitation of an original and therefore was not "counterfeit" within coverage of a financial institution bond. Bank insured understood certificate to be a replacement for original and, in fact, significant terms, including certificate number, differed from the original. In order to be "counterfeit," the document must be "a fake version of an existing, genuine document and possess sufficient similarities to the original to render it plausible that it is the genuine original of that which it imitates." *Bank of Brewton v. The Travelers Cos.*, C.A. No. 13-0176-WS-B, 2014 WL 2113092.

N.D. Ill. 1999. Duplicate statements of origin used to induce a bank to extend a line of credit to a customer to purchase a boat were counterfeit because they were intended imitations of the originals. *State Bank of the Lakes v. Kan. Bankers Sur. Co.*, 1999 WL 674739.

M.D. La. 1993. A fake city ordinance is not a "counterfeit" within the meaning of the definitions of the bond because it is not an imitation of a specific original. Although there was an actual ordinance issued bearing the same public ordinance number as the fake ordinance, that ordinance differed from the fake ordinance substantially. The court found that there was no attempt to imitate an original as required by the definition. *FDIC v. Fid. & Dep. Co. of Md.*, 827 F. Supp. 385.

D.N.J. 1983. In a case involving claims of forgery, counterfeiting, and employee dishonesty under the 1969 Bankers Blanket Bond form, the court held that losses from loans secured by worthless certificates of deposit issued by an entity that had been chartered as a bank in the British West Indies, but which had no assets, were not losses under either Insuring Agreement D or E. The loss occurred because the CDs implicitly misrepresented fact of amounts available to issuing bank for its own account and therefore, were not counterfeited nor forged within the meaning of the bond. The court concluded that insured would be expected to protect itself against the risk posed by CDs that possibly had no value through its normal credit evaluation procedures. *Liberty Nat'l Bank v. Aetna Life & Cas. Co.*, 568 F. Supp. 860.

D.N.D. 2005. Faxed and unsigned "buyer's bill" that appeared to be from livestock seller and purported to memorialize sale of steer was not a "counterfeit" because it was not an imitation of a preexisting genuine "buyer's bill." Loan officer's subjective belief that the document was genuine is not determinative of whether "buyer's bill" was counterfeit. Summary judgment was upheld for the insurer on the credit union bond. *Dakota West Credit Union v. CUMIS Ins. Soc. Inc.*, 532 F. Supp. 2d 1110.

E.D. Wis. 2011. A fraudulent certificate of origin for vehicles did not imitate an "actual, valid original" certificate of origin. The loss resulted from bank's incomplete investigation of the document presented by fraudster. Coverage under Insuring Agreement E of financial institution bond precluded recovery. *Northshore Bank FSB v. Progressive Cas. Ins. Co.*, No. 10-C-71, 2011 WL 1457130.

La. App. 1995. Fake stock certificates that were imitations of real stock certificates were deemed to be counterfeit. *One Am. Corp. v. Fid. & Dep. of Md.*, 658 So. 2d 23.

Minn. 1989. Fake stock certificates that were not imitations of genuine certificates were not "counterfeits" as defined in the financial institution bond. *Nat'l City Bank of Minneapolis v. St. Paul Fire & Marine Ins. Co.*, 447 N.W.2d 171.

SELECTED SECONDARY SOURCES

Melissa L. Gardner & Jason Glasgow, *Check Exposures In Today's Electronic Banking Age: Is The Financial Institution Bond Keeping Stride With A Looming Paperless Society?*, 13 FID. L.J. 1 (2007).

T. Scott Leo & Brandon G. Hummel, *Conditions and Limitations: Definitions*, in ANNOTATED FINANCIAL INSTITUTION BOND 209, 218 (Michael Keeley ed., 3d ed. 2013).

F. Custodian

"Custodian" means you, or any of your partners or "members," or any "employee" while having care and custody of property inside the "premises," excluding any person while acting as a "watchperson" or janitor.

COMMENT

The defined term is the same in the CPP and the CCP, except that the CPP does not include the defined term "members."

The inclusion of the defined term "watchperson" is important because "watchperson" is defined as a party who is charged with the care and custody of property inside the "premises" and has no other duties. Thus, a loss of other property inside the "premises," involving a "watchperson" such as security guard, is not covered under Insuring Agreement 3(b)(1) (Inside the Premises) or Insuring Agreement A.4(a)(1) (Inside the Premises—Robbery or Safe Burglary of Other Property), whereas it would be covered if the employee had duties in addition to the care and custody of the property. Neither the CCP nor the CPP make this distinction for the loss of "money or "securities" from inside the premises resulting from "theft," disappearance or destruction, but only for the loss of "other property" resulting directly from an actual or attempted "robbery" of a "custodian."

ANNOTATIONS

Ill. App. 1930. In an appeal from a jury verdict in favor of the insured, the court refused to overturn a jury verdict on the issue of whether the employee was acting as a custodian, or as a watchman or porter, which was excluded from the policy, at the time of the robbery. *Ike Kaplan & Herman Kaplan v. USF&G*, 255 Ill. App. 437.

La. App. 1981. Grocery store cashier, who was responsible for office and its contents in absence of manager, was a "custodian" of insured property within the meaning of policy providing robbery coverage for taking of insured property, where "custodian" was defined as any employee in regular service of and duly authorized to have "care and custody" of insured property. *70th Street Food Store, Inc. v. Ne. Fire Ins. Co. of Pa.*, 408 So. 2d 958.

Mich. 1968. Money was taken at night from a locked safe on insured's bowling alley premises at a time when the insured had one employee on duty who had no duties with respect to the locked safe or the money contained therein except to keep others away from the area and who had no access to the money. The employee was forced, by threats of violence, to lie on the floor and be tied up while the intruders made their way to the insured's office and opened the locked safe. The court held there was no coverage under a robbery policy defining robbery as a taking of insured's property by putting a custodian in fear of violence, and defining a custodian as an employee who is duly authorized by the insured to have the care and custody of the insured property within the premises, excluding any person while acting as a watchman, porter or janitor because the employee was active as a watchperson and not a custodian. *Huron Bowl Inc. v. Sec. Ins. Co. of New Haven*, 14 Mich. App. 62, 165 N.W.2d 265.

SECONDARY SOURCES

COUCH, 10A COUCH ON INSURANCE. §151:28, 151:83.

G. Employee Benefit Plan(s)

"Employee benefit plan(s)" means any welfare or pension benefit plan shown in the Declarations that is subject to the Employee Retirement Income Security Act of 1974 (ERISA).

COMMENT

This defined term is included in both the CPP and the CCP, although the CCP includes the added requirement that the plan must also be sponsored by the insured. Condition 1(h) in the CCP provides that an "employee benefit plan" shown in the Declarations is included as an insured under Insuring Agreement A.1 (Employee Theft). It should be noted that "employee benefit plans" are provided with broader coverage than other insureds due to the requirements of ERISA, 29 U.S.C. §1001 *et seq.* Thus, with respect to losses sustained by an "employee benefit plan," Condition 1(h)(2) changes Insuring Agreement A.1 such that it pays for the loss of "funds" and "other property" resulting directly from fraudulent or dishonest acts by an "employee," rather than resulting simply from "theft." The regulations implementing ERISA state that the term "fraudulent or dishonest acts" encompasses such matters as "larceny, theft, embezzlement, forgery, misappropriation, wrongful abstraction, wrongful conversion, willful misapplication or any other fraudulent or dishonest acts." 29 C.F.R. §2580.412-9.

ANNOTATIONS

N.D. Cal. 1991. The court held that the sole remaining participant in an ERISA plan was an appropriate plaintiff as against the bonding company and could bring claims for an adjudication of fraud and dishonesty and for payment of policy proceeds directly into plan against plan trustee and bonding company. *Isola v. Hutchinson,* 780 F. Supp. 1299.

SECONDARY SOURCES

29 C.F.R. §2550.412-1 & §2580.412-1 - 412.20.

Employment Retirement Income Security Act (ERISA), 29 U.S.C. §1001 *et seq.*

EDWARD G. GALLAGHER ET AL., A COMPLETE GUIDE TO THE ERISA BONDING REQUIREMENT (1994).

H. Financial Institution

"Financial Institution" means:
a. **With regard to Insuring Agreement A.3.:**
   (1) **a bank, savings bank, savings and loan association, trust company, credit union or similar depository institution; or**
   (2) **an insurance company.**

b.   With regard to Insuring Agreement A.6.:

(1)   a bank savings bank, savings and loan association, trust company, credit union or similar depository institution;

(2)   an insurance company; or

(3)   a stock brokerage firm or investment company.

COMMENT

This defined term is contained in Insuring Agreement 6 (Computer And Funds Transfer Fraud) in the CCP. It is not a defined term in the CPP.

ANNOTATIONS

NONE

SECONDARY SOURCES

NONE

I.   Financial Institution Premises

"Financial institution premises" means the interior of that portion of any building occupied by a "financial institution.

COMMENT

This is a defined term in the CPP only. The annotations for "banking premises" and "premises" should be consulted as this term is substantially similar and limits its scope to the interior only of premises.

ANNOTATIONS

NONE

SECONDARY SOURCES

NONE

J. Forgery

"Forgery" means the signing of the name of another person or organization with intent to deceive; it does not mean a signature which consists in whole or in part of one's own name signed with or without authority, in any capacity, for any purpose.

COMMENT

The CPP and the CCP forms contain the same definition. The CPP provides, as respects Insuring Agreement 2 (Forgery or Alteration), that mechanically reproduced facsimile signatures are treated the same as handwritten signatures. The CCP extends this treatment in Condition E(3)(b) to electronically reproduced signatures, as well as to facsimile signatures.

State law generally determines what constitutes a forgery. However, while a forgery might exist under the law of the particular state, the CCP contains a narrower definition of "forgery," which will determine the question of coverage. Many of the cases considering the forgery definition involve the financial institution bond. Because the definition is substantially similar, these cases are of interest to cases involving the CCP. These cases often address whether another party's signature was signed with intent to deceive. A scheme perpetrated with one's own signature does not involve a forgery.

ANNOTATIONS

3d Cir. 2005. In this unpublished opinion, the court affirmed summary judgment for the insurer. The perpetrator obtained a legitimate check payable to a legitimate company in New York, formed a company of the same name in New Jersey, and used the New Jersey documents to open an account in the name of the New Jersey company at the insured bank.

She then deposited the check with an endorsement made up of an approximation of the company name, her own name and the account number. The court held that the perpetrator endorsed the check with the true name of her own business, her own true signature and her own true account numbers. Under the definition of "forgery" in the bond, the endorsement was not a forgery and the insured was entitled to coverage. *Lusitania Sav. Bank, FSB v. Progressive Cas. Ins. Co.*, 2005 WL 1586618.

7th Cir. 1991. A bank customer deposited his employer's checks into his personal account at the insured bank by using a rubber stamp endorsement that stated the checks were for "deposit only" to the personal account. The stamp endorsement did not constitute a forgery under the definition in the financial institution bond. Forgery is the signing of the name of another with intent to deceive. *Alpine State Bank v. Ohio Cas. Ins. Co.*, 941 F.2d 554.

9th Cir. 2005. In this unpublished opinion, the court affirmed summary judgment for the insurer on a commercial crime policy. The Casino's claim was under the forgery and theft coverages, but the withdrawal orders used by the perpetrator were neither altered nor forged, and theft coverage was foreclosed by an exclusion for property that the insured was induced to part with voluntarily. The court also held that the insured's promissory fraud count based on its broker's use of renewal summary failed because the summary clearly stated that the policy controlled, and any reliance on the summary to vary the policy was unreasonable as a matter of law. *Bell Gardens Bicycle Casino v. Great Am. Ins. Co.*, 24 Fed. Appx. 551.

9th Cir. 2001. Under the definition of "forgery" in a fiduciary bond, the court held that a signature was not a forgery because it did not purport to be the signature of a customer. *Universal Bank v. Northland & Ins. Co.*, 8 Fed. Appx. 784, 2001 WL 435072.

N.D. Ga. 2013. Construing Georgia law, the court held that falsely signing a name, even with a one-letter misspelling, is a "forgery" within the meaning of a bank insurance bond. Court also held that definition of "forgery" was ambiguous and included the signing of the name of a fictitious person. *F.D.I.C. v. Cincinnati Ins. Co.*, 981 F. Supp. 2d 1324.

M.D. Ga. 1996. A "forgery" within the meaning of the financial institution bond definition did not include the endorsement by an attorney of a draft payable to the attorney and his client. The attorney endorsed his own name and forged the client's endorsement to deposit the proceeds of a draft into his trust account, from which the attorney apparently converted the funds. The bank sought recovery for the loss it incurred after the attorney's client obtained a judgment against the bank for conversion, the bank having accepted the check with the forged endorsement of the client. Although the client's endorsement was apparently forged, the definition of "forgery" excludes a signature consisting, in whole or in part, of one's own name. *Reliance Ins. Co. v. First Liberty Bank*, 927 F. Supp. 448.

E.D. La. 1982. A bank sued its borrower's mother for outstanding loans and borrower offered to be responsible for his mother's indebtedness by giving new collateral and restructuring his own indebtedness to the bank. The new collateral consisted of a mortgage on property owned by a third party. The borrower signed the collateral mortgage and note as agent for the third party, even though he was not. The bank contended this was a forgery and the court, in denying the claim of forgery, pointed out that under Louisiana law, in direct contrast to New York law, signing one's own name and representing that one has authority to give writing is not forgery. The court noted that an authorized signature under the U.C.C. includes forgeries but they are not functional equivalents. *March Inv. Corp. v. Langford*, 554 F. Supp. 800.

D. Minn. 2005. The court granted summary judgment to BancInsure on an Insuring Agreement E claim because at the time the bank disbursed the loan proceeds it had possession of only a facsimile transmission of the forged personal guarantees. The insured argued that the phrase "a mechanically reproduced facsimile signature is treated the same as a handwritten signature" meant that the signatures on the documents sent by facsimile transmission were the same as handwritten signatures and thus the documents were originals and, in any case, the facsimile copies would have been enforceable against the guarantors but for the forgery. The court noted that the purpose of the requirement of possession of originals is to allow the bank to examine the signatures and detect forgeries, and that enforceability of a copy was not the question. The facsimile copies were copies, not originals, and there was thus no coverage under Insuring Agreement E. The court rejected the bank's argument that under modern banking practice literal enforcement of the original requirement rendered the coverage promised illusory. The court noted that the original documents could have been sent by overnight delivery. *BancInsure, Inc. v. Marshall Bank, N.A.*, 400 F. Supp. 2d 1140.

D. Neb. 1992. Absent evidence that someone signed a check with another party's name with intent to deceive, there is no "forgery" as that term is defined in the financial institution bond. There was no evidence that an individual signing a corporate check was either signing as a representative of the corporation or that someone other than the individual signed the check with intent to deceive. *Ralston Bank v. Kan. Bankers Sur. Co.*, 794 F. Supp. 896.

D.N.J. 2004. The perpetrator fraudulently opened an account in the name of TCS America and deposited a legitimate check made payable to TCS America, which is an actual company in New York. The criminal endorsed the check by signing "Deposit only TCS" with her own name under it and two numbers under her name. The check was for $198,124, and the insured eventually paid the drawee bank that amount under its warranty of the endorsement. The criminal received $59,801 while on the insured's premises, and the insurer paid that amount less the deductible under Insuring Agreement B. The insured claimed the balance under Insuring Agreement D. The definition of "forgery" in the bond included signing the name of an organization with intent to deceive, but not "a signature which consists in whole or in part of one's own name signed with or without authority, in any capacity, for any purpose." Because the endorsement included the criminal's own name, it was not a forgery as defined in the bond, and the court granted summary judgment to the insurer. *Lusitania Sav. Bank, FSB v. Progressive Cas. Ins. Co.*, 328 F. Supp. 2d 514.

D.N.J. 1983. In a case involving claims of forgery, counterfeiting, and employee dishonesty under the 1969 form of the Bankers Blanket Bond, the court held that losses from loans secured by worthless certificate of deposit issued by an entity that had been chartered as a bank in the British West Indies, but which had no assets, were not losses under either Insuring Agreement D or E. The loss occurred because the CDs implicitly misrepresented fact of amounts available to the issuing bank for its own account; therefore, they were not counterfeited nor forged within the meaning of the bond. The court concluded that the bank would be expected to protect itself against the risk posed by the possible worthlessness of CDs through its normal credit evaluation procedures. *Liberty Nat'l Bank v. Aetna Life & Cas. Co.*, 568 F. Supp. 860.

S.D.N.Y. 1990. Fictitious bills of lading that bore no signature were not "forgeries" within the meaning of the bond. To prove forgery, one must show the use of the name to falsely represent that another person signed the document in question. Fictitious bills of lading were not "counterfeit" as they did not imitate genuine, specific original documents. *French Am. Banking Corp. v. Flota Mercante Grancolombiana, S.A.*, 752 F. Supp. 83.

N.D. Tex. 2008. Definition of "forgery" in commercial crime policy not ambiguous and operates to bar coverage where an endorser signs his own true name in whole or in part. Forger had signed named of agency, which also contained his own name, with intent to deceive. *Great American Ins. Co. v. AFS/IBEX Financial Services, Inc.*, 2008 WL 2795205.

E.D. Wis. 2005. A crooked car dealer defrauded the insured bank by giving it carbon copies of phony leases on which the dealer had traced the signature of the supposed lessees. The leased cars either did not exist or were worth far less than the documents represented them to be. The bank loaned the dealer money to buy the cars that were then leased to the dealer's customers. The primary issues were whether the loss was caused by the forgery or by the fact that there were no cars, whether the insured had physical possession of the written instruments, and whether the loss was caused by the insured's own employees' negligence and sloppy practices. The court agreed that the forgeries did not cause the loss, but read Insuring Agreement E to cover losses from extending credit upon instruments containing a forgery even if the forgery did not cause the loss. The court also held that the insured had possession of the carbon copies before advancing the money and that there was no requirement for possession of an "original." Even if an original were required, the carbon copies were the originals because they were the only signed versions of the leases. *First Nat'l Bank in Manitowoc v. Cincinnati Ins. Co*, 2005 WL 2460719.

Ind. App. 2003. A title company that wrongfully deposited a mortgage check did not commit an act of "forgery" as defined in the financial institution bond. The act of improperly negotiating an instrument is not an alteration of the instrument. *Utica Mut. Ins. Co. v. Precedent Cos., LLC*, 782 N.E.2d 470.

SELECTED SECONDARY SOURCES

John V. Burch & Timothy J. Burson, *Other Insuring Agreements in Commercial Crime and Other Fidelity Policies—An Update, in* COMMERCIAL CRIME POLICY (Gilbert J. Schroeder, ed. 1997).

Michael R. Davisson, *The Other Insuring Agreements of Commercial Crime Policies, in* COMMERCIAL CRIME POLICY (Randall I. Marmor & John J. Tomaine, eds., 2d ed. 2005).

David T. DiBiase, Carleton R. Burch & David J. Billings, *The ABC's Of Insuring Agreement (D) Under The Financial Institution Bond*, 17 FID. L.J. 1 (2011).

T. Scott Leo, *Conditions and Limitations: Definitions, in* ANNOTATED FINANCIAL INSTITUTION BOND 315 (Michael Keeley ed., 2d ed. 2004).

Roger Nettie, Scott S. Spearing & Alexandra L. Geiger, *Fidelity Insurance Issues Related To The Paperless Office: The Effect of Electronic Signatures On Financial Institutions And Other Hot Coverage Issues*, 20 FID. L.J. 1 (2014).

K. Fraudulent Instruction

"Fraudulent instruction" means:
a.   With regard to Insuring Agreement A.6.a.(2):
(1)   A computer, telegraphic, cable, teletype, telefacsimile, telephone or other electronic instruction directing a "financial institution" to debit your "transfer account" and to transfer, pay or deliver "money" or "securities" from that

transfer account which instruction purports to have been issued by you, but which in fact was fraudulently issued by someone else without your knowledge or consent;

(2) A written instruction (other than those described in Insuring Agreement A.2.) issued to a "financial institution" directing the "financial institution" to debit your "transfer account" and to transfer, pay or deliver "money" or "securities" from that "transfer account" through an electronic funds transfer system at specified times or under specified conditions which instruction purports to have been issued by you, but which in fact was issued, forged or altered by someone else fraudulently without your knowledge or consent; or

(3) A computer, telegraphic, cable, teletype, telefacsimile, telephone or other electronic or written instruction initially received by you, which instruction purports to have been issued by an "employee" but which was in fact fraudulently issued by someone else without your or the "employee's" knowledge or consent.

COMMENT

This definition is relevant to Insuring Agreement A.6 (Computer and Funds Transfer Fraud) in the CCP. The CPP does not contain this insuring agreement or the definition. The key to both this definition and the insuring agreement is that the instruction must be fraudulent. Instructions sent by an authorized party that are subsequently misused or misdirected will not fall within the definition as they were not "fraudulent" at the time sent.

ANNOTATIONS

C.D. Cal. 2014. No coverage under Funds Transfer Fraud Insuring Agreement where no evidence of unauthorized access into insured's electronic funds transfer system. Instead, it was undisputed that the third party was authorized to access the insured's system in order to process its payroll and only diverted the funds after such authorized entry. *Pestmaster Services, Inc. v. Travelers Casualty & Surety Co. of America,* 2014 WL 3844627.

N.J. App. 2005. Insured submitted claim for indemnification for losses incurred under an Electronic Computer Crime Policy. Court held that facsimile instructions sent by authorized persons were not covered under an insuring agreement covering "fraudulent facsimile transfer instructions." The court dubbed this insuring agreement "imposter coverage" because the agreement limited coverage to situations were an unauthorized person posed as a customer or other authorized person to issue the fraudulent transfer instructions. *Morgan Stanley Dean Witter & Co. v. Chubb Group of Ins. Cos.,* 2005 WL 3242234.

N.Y. Sup. 2013. The court granted insurer's motion for summary judgment finding that computer systems fraud rider was designed to cover wrongful acts in manipulating computer system by hackers. Thus, no coverage for fraudulent content of claim by bona fide doctors who were otherwise authorized to access the system. *Universal American Corp. v. Nat'l Union Fire Ins. Co. of Pittsburgh, PA,* 959 N.Y.S.2d 849, 2013 N.Y. Slip. Op. 23003, *modified by,* 110 A.D.3d 434.

N.Y. Sup. 2010. No coverage under Funds Transfer Fraud Insuring Agreement for an insured's losses that occurred after it voluntarily wire transferred funds to Bernie Madoff for investment purposes. *Cumberland Packing Corp. v. Chubb Ins. Corp.,* 958 N.Y.S.2d 306.

Pa. Dist. 2001. Plaintiff bank sued the insurance carrier under a "community financial institution bond," which provided coverage for losses from fraudulent electronic fund transfers and computer crime. Court held that policy's definition of "fraudulent electronic instruction" was unambiguous and that the purpose of the coverage was to protect the bank from someone breaking into the electronic fund transfer system and pretending to be an authorized representative or altering the electronic instructions to divert monies from the rightful recipient. Because the bank's customer sent the instructions, which were neither altered nor modified by an unauthorized party, the coverage did not apply. *Northside Bank v. Am. Cas. Co. of Reading*, 60 Pa. D. & C. 4th 95, 2001 WL 34090139.

SECONDARY SOURCES

John J. McDonald, Jr., Joel T. Wiegert & Jason Glasgow, *Computer Fraud and Funds Transfer Funds Coverages*, 14 FID. L.J. 109 (2008).

Scott L. Schmookler, *Computer and Funds Transfer Fraud*, COMMERCIAL CRIME POLICY 297 (Randall I. Marmor & Susan Koehler Sullivan eds., 3d ed. 2014).

L. Manager

"Manager" means a natural person serving in a directorial capacity for a limited liability company.

COMMENT

"Manager" is not a defined term in the CPP, although it is used in the CPP's definition of "employee," as an undefined term as concerns "employee benefit plans" only.

In the CCP, the term "manager" appears in two exclusionary sections: in Exclusion D(1)(b), excluding loss from "theft" or other dishonest acts committed by any "employee," "managers," directors, trustees or representatives, except when covered under Insuring Agreement A.1; and in Definition 7(a)(4)(b) ("employee"), wherein a "manager" is excluded from the definition, unless performing acts within the scope of the usual duties of an "employee." The inclusion of "manager" in these sections logically follows the intent of Insuring Agreement A.1 to provide coverage only for acts of employees and not individuals serving in a directorial or ownership capacity. The term as defined by the CCP is more limited than the typical dictionary definition in that it is limited to a person acting in a "directorial capacity for a limited liability company."

ANNOTATIONS

NONE

SECONDARY SOURCES

NONE

M. Member

"Member" means an owner of a limited liability company represented by its membership interest who, if a natural person, also may serve as a "manager".

COMMENT

"Member" is not a defined term in the CPP. In the CCP, it is included within the definition of "custodian" and therefore the discussion of that term also should be consulted. The CCP adds this defined term to Exclusion D(1)(a), excluding acts by "You, your partners or 'members'" as well as to provisions relating to knowledge of the corporate insured, including the Joint Insured Condition E(1)(l)(2). Like the defined term "manager," "member" expands the universe of individuals considered by the CCP to operate at a management or ownership level and, thus, outside the scope of Insuring Agreement A.1 (Employee Theft).

ANNOTATIONS

NONE

SECONDARY SOURCES

NONE

N. Messenger

"Messenger" means you, or your relative, or any of your partners or "members", or any "employee" while having care and custody of property outside the "premises".

COMMENT

The CCP and CPP definitions are similar. The CPP does not include "relative" or "member" and instead includes your partners or "employees."

This definition is relevant to Insuring Agreement 4 (Outside the Premises) and Insuring Agreement A.5 (Outside the Premises). Cases construing the definition focus not so much on the definition itself but on whether the funds are being conveyed by the party at the time of theft or simply being stored. So, an employee who takes money home for the weekend for safekeeping would not be considered a "messenger," whereas an employee who stores the money in his car in the course of conveying the money to his employer may fall within the definition's scope. Similarly, property may be considered to be in the "care and custody" of the messenger if left unattended but only where the messenger takes care to secure the property; property left unattended in an unlocked vehicle, for example, would not satisfy this condition.

ANNOTATIONS

Fla. 1971. Construing mercantile robbery policies, the court held that money kept by the insured's president in his home from close of business on Saturday with the intention of depositing the money in bank on Monday was not in the process of "being conveyed by a messenger" and thus not covered by policy. *State Liquor Stores #1 v. U. S. Fire Ins. Co.*, 243 So. 2d 228.

Ga. App. 1969. The court reversed summary judgment in favor of insurer, finding that policy covered loss of money "conveyed" by an employee who was in regular service of insured employer, and who was duly authorized by employer to have "custody" of funds outside of premises and where employee on way back from bank to employer's

ANNOTATED COMMERCIAL CRIME INSURANCE POLICY

office with proceeds of check he had been sent to cash for employer left employer's automobile in parking area with money in glove compartment for ten minutes while he got a sandwich and during that time locked automobile broken into and money stolen. The decision includes lengthy dissent, which concluded that money was not being "conveyed" at time of theft, but rather was simply being stored, and thus not covered. *Atlanta Tallow Co., Inc. v. Fireman's Fund Ins. Co.*, 167 S.E.2d 361.

Ga. App. 1967. The insured's messenger left a zipped bag of money on the front seat of his car unlocked and went into his home to have lunch. The money was gone when he returned. The court held that the nature of the property must be taken into consideration when determining whether property was within the "care and custody" of the messenger when stolen. By leaving the car unlocked, the messenger did not take reasonable precautions to prevent the loss, thus forfeiting coverage under the "Outside The Premises" insuring agreement. *Cleveland Avenue Liquor Store v. Home Ins. Co.*, 156 S.E.2d 202.

La. 1960. The court held that insured/plaintiff was not acting as "messenger" when he conveyed two bags of money to his home and left the money in a cedar chest with the intention of taking the money to the bank later in the day. The court was construing a broad form theft policy wherein the definition itself did not include the "care and custody" provision included in the CCP definition. *Monteleone v. Am. Employers' Ins. Co.*, 120 So. 2d 70.

N.J. Super. 1977. A messenger left payroll monies under the seat of a locked van for thirty to thirty-five minutes while attending to other duties. When he returned to his van, the payroll had been stolen. The court considered that "care" is commonly defined as "charge or supervision" and that the payroll remained under the messenger's supervision and control, even though left unattended, because he had locked the vehicle, taken the keys with him and remained near where the vehicle was parked. *Deleson Steel Co., Inc. v. Hartford ins. Group*, 372 A.2d 663.

N.Y. App. 1960. The court reversed a decision in favor of the insured to find that "money" was not in custody of a "messenger" when the loss occurred. The insured's secretary and general manger took $600 of company funds with him for safekeeping because there was an excessive amount of cash on the premises at the close of business on a Friday night. The employee placed money in his wallet, which he then put in his trousers, discovering that the money was missing on Sunday morning. Under the circumstances, the court held that employee was acting merely as a custodian and not as a "messenger" within the meaning of the policy. The money was not being conveyed to a bank or other depository or to a person at another place. Rather, it was being carried solely for the purpose of safekeeping. *O.K. Express Corp. v. Md. Cas. Co.*, 198 N.Y.S.2d 105.

SECONDARY SOURCES

Mark Gamin, Armen Shahinian & Andrew Kent, *The Subtleties of Insuring Agreement (C) of the Financial Institution Bond*, 9 FID. L.J. 115 (2003).

Christopher C. Novak, Todd D. McCormick & Thomas R. Orofino, *The Other Insuring Agreement of Commercial Crime Policies*, COMMERCIAL CRIME POLICY 267 (Randall I. Marmor & Susan Koehler Sullivan eds., 3d ed. 2014).

O. Money

"Money" means:
a. **Currency, coins and bank notes in current use and having a face value;**
b. **Travelers checks and money orders held for sale to the public; and**
c. **In addition, includes:**
   (1) **Under Insuring Agreements A.1 and A.2, deposits in your account at any financial institution; and**
   (2) **Under Insuring Agreement A.6, deposits in your account at a "financial institution" as defined in Paragraph F.9.b.**

COMMENT

Both the CPP and the CCP include this definition but with slightly different wording. Both forms now include deposits held in accounts of a financial institution. The CPP includes the defined terms "cash." Given the requirement that currency, coins and bank notes must be in current use and have a face value, the definition is clearly limited to items used as a circulating medium of exchange and does not embrace notes, bonds or evidences of debt. At least one court has held that collectible coins were "money" rather than "other property," even though these items likely had value beyond the face value of the instruments, because the definition of "money" specifically includes "coins."

ANNOTATIONS

6th Cir. 2004. In this unpublished decision, the court held that $1.5 million in gambling credit from a casino constituted either "money" or "securities" under a blanket crime policy and that the policy exclusion for the "giving or surrendering of Money or Securities in any exchange or purchase" applied to exclude coverage for a gambler's use of fraudulent cashier's check to obtain gambling credit, which the gambler promptly lost at the casino. The court also determined that the cashier's checks could not be considered "express money orders" because that term does not naturally encompass a cashier's check issued by a bank. *Harrah's Entm't, Inc. v. ACE Am. Ins. Co.*, 100 Fed. Appx. 387.

9th Cir. 1990. An insured credit union brought an action against its insurer, seeking to recover under its fidelity bond losses suffered because of its loan officer's disbursement of proceeds from an improper loan on the construction of a new building. The court held that the loan loss did not qualify as a loss of money because it did not involve loss of "currency, coin, bank notes, Federal Reserve Notes, revenue stamps or postage stamps" as defined by the bond. *Portland Fed. Employees Credit Union v. Cumis Ins. Soc'y*, 894 F. 2d 1101.

D.C. Cir. 1970. In action on employee dishonesty policy, the court rejected the insured's argument that he policy covered only physical loss of "money," "securities" and "other property" due to the conduct of insured's employees, holding that a consequential pecuniary loss measured by payments to third parties was a covered loss under the policy. The court went on to reverse the lower court due to an erroneous jury instruction on an unrelated point. *Imperial Ins., Inc. v. Employers' Liab. Assur. Corp.*, 442 F.2d 1197.

Cal. Ct. App. 1983. The insured brought action against a homeowner's insurer for loss resulting from burglary of his silver coin collection. The insurance policy contained an exclusion limiting the insurer's liability to $100 for a loss by theft of "money, bullion, numismatic property and bank notes." The insured argued that his silver coins were not money because they were taken out of circulation and were an investment. The court disagreed, holding that "silver coins are most reasonably regarded as "money," and whether kept out of circulation by plaintiff or not, maintain their monetary character." *McKee v. State Farm Fire & Cas. Co.*, 145 Cal. App. 3d 772.

Conn. Super. Ct. 2010. An insured law firm sought coverage under a commercial crime policy's computer fraud coverage for a loss suffered by an e-mail scam. The law firm deposited fraudulent check later rejected by bank and sought coverage for loss. Insurer denied coverage, claiming that the alleged loss fell within Exclusion (F) as a loss resulting directly or indirectly from the insured's acceptance of money orders or counterfeit money. The court held that a bank check does not fall within the recognized definition of "money" as defined in the policy or its usual and ordinary meaning and, therefore, exclusion did not apply. *Owens, Schine & Nicola, P.C. v. Travelers*, No. CV095024601, 2010 WL 4226958, *vacated*, 2012 WL 12246940 (Conn. Super Ct. Apr. 18, 2012).

Fla. 2000. Rare collectible coins were "coins" within the meaning of a homeowner's insurance policy. Unlike CCP, policy did not limit coverage only to coins used as currency. *Walker v. State Farm Fire Ins. Co.*, 758 So. 2d 1161.

Minn. 1975. In a case arising from the infamous D.B. Cooper airline hijacking, the court rejected the insurer's position that the insured had not incurred a loss of money because the insured borrowed the money needed to pay the hijacker. The insurer argued that the policy only covered specific money that the insured might have on its premises at any particular time from ticket sales and did not include borrowed money. *Nw. Airlines, Inc. v. Globe Indem. Co.*, 225 N.W.2d 831.

Mo. App. 1965. The court held that, under a Money and Securities Broad Form Policy, which insured against loss of money, securities and other property by reason of safe burglary or robbery, rare coins kept by the insured as collector's items, having no relation to the insured's business as a department store, could be used in the conduct of the insured's business as a medium of exchange and therefore was insured as money at face value and not as other property at market value. "Coins' were expressly included in the definition of "money" and thus could not be considered to be "other property." *Cornblath v. Fireman's Fund Ins. Co.*, 392 S.W.2d 648.

N.C. 1992. An insured brought suit against its insurer seeking coverage for lost interest on sums stolen by its former president. The policy defined "money" as "currency, coins, bank notes and bullion, and travelers' checks, register checks and money orders held for sale to the public." The court held that "[i]nterest on stolen currency, coins, etc. is not included in the definition of 'money.'" Accordingly, the court reasoned that the fidelity policy only provided coverage for the principal amount stolen by the plaintiff's former president. *Empire of Carolina, Inc. v. Continental Cas. Co.*, 414 S.E.2d 389.

Vt. 2014. The court held that prejudgment interest on money embezzled by a town employee was covered by a commercial blanket bond. Rejecting the reasoning of *Empire of Carolina*, the court found that use of the term "money" referred to its liquidity not the form of the asset. Thus, the fact that interest did not one of the forms in the definition did not preclude recovery by insured. The court also noted that the bond did not contain a potential income exclusion, reinforcing its view that the definition was ambiguous and should be construed against the insurer. *Town of Ira v. Vermont League of Cities and Towns Property and Casualty Intermunicipal Fund, Inc.*, 109 A.3d 893.

SELECTED SECONDARY SOURCES

Bradford R. Carver & CharCretia V. DiBartolo, *Conditions and Limitations: Definitions*, *in* ANNOTATED FINANCIAL INSTITUTION BOND 209, 245 (Michael Keeley ed., 3d ed. 2013).

Scott S. Spearing et al., *What is Money in Today's Financial System?*, XVIII FID. L.J. 83 (2012).

U.C.C. §1-201(24), comment 24 (2001).

P. Occurrence

"Occurrence" means (CPP Version):
a.   As respects Insuring Agreement 1., all loss or losses caused by, or involving, any one employee, acting alone or in collusion with others.
b.   As respects Insuring Agreement 2., all loss or losses caused by any person or in which that person is involved, whether the loss involves one or more instruments.
c.   As respects all other Insuring Agreements, all loss or losses caused by:
  (1)   Any number of acts, involving one person whether acting alone or in collusion with others;
  (2)   Any number of acts involving a group of persons acting together; or
  (3)   An act or event, or any number of related acts or events, not involving any identifiable person.

"Occurrence" means (CCP Version)(Disc. Form):
a.   Under Insuring Agreement A.1.:
  (1)   An individual act;
  (2)   The combined total of all separate acts whether or not related; or
  (3)   A series of acts whether or not related;
    committed by an "employee" acting alone or in collusion with other persons, during the Policy Period shown in the Declarations, before such policy period or both.

b.   Under Insuring Agreement A.2.:
   (1)   An individual act;
   (2)   The combined total of all separate acts whether or not related; or
   (3)   A series of acts whether or not related; committed by a person acting alone or in collusion wither other persons, involving one or more instruments, during the Policy Period shown in the Declarations, before such policy period or both.
c.   Under all other Insuring Agreements:
   (1)   An individual act or event;
   (2)   The combined total of all separate acts or events whether or not related; or
   (3)   A series of acts ore vents whether or not related; committed by a person acting alone or in collusion wither other persons, or not committed by any person, during the Policy Period shown in the Declarations, before such policy period or both.

COMMENT

The majority of courts construing "occurrence" find the term to be unambiguous and limit coverage to all loss resulting from all acts of one employee, whether happening over a period of years or consisting of different means or methods as long as the loss results from the same scheme to defraud the employer. A minority of courts construe the definition more broadly, allowing insureds to recover under multiple policies for loss resulting from multiple acts of the same employee. Construction varies from jurisdiction to jurisdiction and therefore the law of the applicable jurisdiction must be consulted when considering this definition.

ANNOTATIONS

4th Cir. 2001. Construing South Carolina law, the court held that definition of "occurrence" was ambiguous as to whether a loss continuing over successive policies was intended to be covered under every policy in effect during the time span in which the employee dishonesty occurred or only the first of those policies. As a result, South Carolina law required that the ambiguity be resolved in favor of the insured. The insured allowed to recover up to the limit of liability in each year in which employee theft occurred. *Spartan Iron & Metal Corp. v. Liberty Insurance Corp.*, 5 Fed. Appx 176.

5th Cir. 2008 (Miss.). Applying Mississippi law, an employee's prolonged embezzlement from insured employer, comprising repeated, related acts throughout ten-year period that spanned multiple insurance contracts, constituted a single "occurrence" within employee dishonesty coverage of those contracts, not repeated occurrences. The policies defined occurrence as an "act or series of related acts involving one or more employees." The employee's acts that caused injury to the insured had a single cause, namely employee's dishonesty. *Madison Materials Co., Inc. v. St. Paul Fire & Marine Ins. Co.*, 523 F.3d 541.

9th Cir. 2009. Applying Arizona law, the fact that one employee was guilty of multiple embezzlements did not mean that there were multiple occurrences under policies defining an "occurrence" as "all loss caused by, or involving, one or more employees, whether the result of a single act or series of acts," and a new policy year did not trigger the beginning of a new "occurrence." *Superstition Crushing, Inc. v. Travelers Cas. & Surety Co.*, 360 Fed. Appx. 844.

9th Cir. 2000. Applying California law, the court held that the definition of "occurrence" was ambiguous such that the insured was not limited under only the last of three consecutive, one-year policies in effect during the three-year period that employee theft transpired. Rather, the insured could recover policy limits under each of three policies in effect during the period. *Karen Kane, Inc. v. Reliance Ins. Co.*, 202 F.3d 1180.

D. Colo. 2004. Applying Colorado law, various acts of embezzlement, accomplished by insured's employee by manipulating insured's refund and fax/copy accounts, booking paid rooms as "comps," allowing two customers to live in insured's motel for period of months for fee, which she kept, and stealing daily cash deposits and ski lift ticket sales, constituted single occurrence, for purposes of limitation of liability provision of commercial crime insurance policies defining "occurrence" as "all loss caused by, or involving, one or more 'employees', whether the result of a single act or series of acts"; cause of insured's loss was dishonesty of one employee. *Wausau Business Ins. Co. v. U.S. Motels Mgmt. Inc.*, 341 F. Supp. 2d 1180.

D. Md. 2005. Applying Maryland law, various acts of embezzlement by insured physician's employee were not rendered separate occurrences under employee dishonesty coverage provision of business insurance policy by virtue of fact that employee used different means to accomplish embezzlement, e.g., forged checks and unauthorized uses of credit card. The employee's acts had single cause, namely dishonesty of that employee, under the policy's definition of "occurrence" as "all loss caused by, or involving, one or more employees, whether the result of a single act or a series of acts." However, the court went on to find that the definition was ambiguous as to whether the "series of related acts" included acts occurring outside the policy period. Accordingly, the court found that the employee's acts of embezzlement constituted one occurrence in each policy year in which they occurred. *Glaser v. Hartford Cas. Ins. Co.*, 364 F. Supp. 2d 529.

W.D. Mich. 2011. Employees of company used income received from vehicle sales to pay current expenses rather than the lender on a floor plan financing agreement. The employees also provided inaccurate financial information thereby misstating the financial condition of the company. Construing Michigan law, the court held that payment of a legitimate debt of the business is neither a loss to the company nor a theft. As such, the insureds also failed to show an "occurrence" that would trigger coverage. *Coopersville Motors, Inc. v. Federated Mutual Co.*, 771 F. Supp. 2d 796.

D.N.J. 2008. An Employee embezzled money over a period of several years from his employer by fraudulently converting money orders. The court rejected *Auto Lenders v. Gentilini* to hold that "occurrence" was not ambiguous and that conversion of money orders was one "occurrence" because it was a part of a continuous scheme by the employee, despite "batching" by employee of money orders for deposit. *Pine Belt Automotive, Inc. v. Royal Indemnity Co.*, C.A. No. 06-5995, 2013 WL 4682582.

D. Nev. 2011. The court rejected the insured's interpretation of "occurrence" definition, such that "series of acts" limited occurrence to total amount of loss caused by the same employee in the same way. Instead, the court found that the term was unambiguous and included all acts of the same employee, no matter the manner in which theft occurred. The court found significant that the policy definition did not include relatedness within the concept of "series of acts." *APMC Hotel Mgmt. Inc. v. Fid. & Dep. Co. of Maryland*, 2:09-cv-2100, 2011 WL 5525966.

D.R.I. 2011. An insured landfill brought a declaratory judgment action seeking coverage for multiple alleged fraudulent acts by multiple employees over a multi-year period. The court held that the policy's definition of "single loss" was ambiguous, to the extent that the combined total of all separate acts. committed by more than one employee acting . . . in collusion with other persons" language could be construed to aggregate into a single loss acts of separate groups of employees that were connected by a common non-employee third actor. The court noted that this construction was intended to reach only situations where thefts would not be aggregated into a single loss but for the participation of "other persons" (i.e., non-employees or non-fiduciaries, as the case may be) in the thefts. *Rhode Island Resource Recovery Corp. v. Travelers Cas. & Sur. Co. of America*, C.A. No. 10-294-S, 2011 WL 2118808.

N.D. Tex. 2008. A commercial crime policy defined "occurrence" as "all loss or losses caused by any person or in which that person is involved, where the loss involves one or more instruments" for purpose of forgery coverage. The court held that, while the definition may prevent cumulation of policy limits, it did not unequivocally demonstrate that the parties intended that a prior policy would become entirely irrelevant, and allowed the insured to access the limits of a prior policy. *Great American Ins. Co. v. AFS/IBEX Financial Services, Inc.*, 2008 WL 2795205.

Ariz. 2008. In a case of first impression, the Arizona Supreme Court held that embezzlement by a single employee accomplished by the forging of multiple checks over multiple years constituted a "series of acts" and thus one "occurrence." The court also held that only acts from which the loss results are considered as part of the "occurrence." *Employers Mutual Cas. Co. v. DGG & Car, Inc.*, 183 P.3d 513, 218 Ariz. 262.

Conn. 2000. Construing add-on coverage to a commercial liability policy that did not include a definition of "occurrence," court found that the policy was ambiguous as to whether each check written from the insured's payroll account by its employee constituted a separate occurrence. Court held on summary judgment motions that each of the plaintiff's losses was caused by a separate act of embezzlement because it was always within the employee's control to stop stealing from her employer and because it was the employee's individual acts of theft that caused the plaintiff's losses, not her underlying dishonesty. *Shemitz Lighting Inc. v. Hartford Fire Ins. Co.*, 2000 WL 1781840.

Fla. 2005. Embezzlement by an employee over a four-year period constitutes a single "occurrence." *Reliance Ins. Co. v. Treasure Coast Travel Agency, Inc.*, 660 So. 2d 1136.

Ky. 2013. Employee used two methods to steal from her employer including writing unauthorized checks to herself and assisting her husband in purchasing vehicles without proper payment. The court held that all acts by the employee constituted one "occurrence" under a commercial crime policy and that the definition was not ambiguous. *Piles Chevrolet Pontiac Buick, Inc. v. Auto Owners Insurance Co*, C.A. No. 002317MR, 2013 WL 212039.

Ill. App. 2009. Even though the insured waived the issue on appeal, the Illinois appellate court held in *dicta* that the definition of "occurrence" was not ambiguous. The policy defined "occurrence" as a "single act or a series of acts." The court upheld the lower court ruling in favor of the insurer that the insured failed to provide evidence of the number of occurrences such that the determination could not be made as to whether the amount of occurrences fell within $10,000 deductible of a commercial crime policy. *Reedy Industries, Inc. v. Hartford Ins. Co. of Ill.*, 306 Ill. App. 3d 989.

Minn. 1996. The court held that the phrase "series of related acts" in business insurance policy was not ambiguous. Each of employee's acts of issuing unauthorized checks to herself formed part of one "series of related acts" and thus one occurrence, for purposes of coverage under business protection policy of employer, while each of the employee's unauthorized acts of taking funds received from customers formed part of another series of acts and constituted second occurrence for coverage purposes. *American Commerce Ins. Brokers, Inc. v. Minnesota Mutual Fire and Cas. Co.,* 551 N.W.2d 224.

Mo. 2007. An employee's embezzlement scheme was one "occurrence" under employee dishonesty coverage provided by commercial crime insurance policies maintained by two affiliated insured companies for which the employee worked, which policies defined an "occurrence" as "all loss caused by or involving, one or more employees, whether the result of a single act or series of acts." Insured companies were not entitled to coverage for each and every fraudulent check cashed as part of the embezzlement scheme because the losses occurred through one common cause, the employee's dishonesty. *Thornburgh Insulation, Inc. v. J.W. Terrill, Inc.,* 236 S.W.3d 651.

N.J. 2004. Submission of 27 fraudulent credit applications by dealership's finance manager to lender to induce it to finance car sales to high-risk customers were separate occurrences under employee dishonesty provision of commercial package insurance policy for which automobile dealership was entitled to recover up to $5000 for each fraudulently induced sale, even though each sale was similar and policy literally limited coverage to $5000 per employee. The court construed policy language to mean that for each loss of property there was only one recovery, regardless of number of employees involved, and each sale caused the insured a distinct loss. *Auto Lenders Acceptance Corp. v. Gentilini Ford, Inc.,* 181 N.J. 245.

N.C. 1996. A church treasurer's embezzlement of $32,760, which was accomplished by writing 24 checks over the course of several weeks, was one "occurrence" within meaning of the church's insurance policy, which provided up to $5,000 for any one occurrence of embezzlement under its employee dishonesty provision and which defined occurrence to be all loss involving a single act or series of related acts. The checks were all written in furtherance of one employee's dishonest acts, and each did not constitute a new and individual act of dishonesty, but were a continuum of wrongful actions. *Christ Lutheran Church v. State Farm Fire & Cas. Co.,* 122 N.C.App. 614.

Ohio 2014. Two insureds purchased and received commercial general liability policies over a period of several years with, endorsements extending coverage for employee dishonesty. Insureds claimed they were entitled to limits of insurance under each policy in effect during the years of embezzlement by joint employee. The appeals court reversed summary judgment in favor of the insurers, finding that each renewal created a separate contract of insurance and that the insureds were entitled to recover under each policy in effect during the years of embezzlement. The policies' discovery of loss provisions, however, limited the insureds' recovery and eliminated coverage under any policy that ended more than one year before discovery of loss. *E.J. Zeller Inc. v. Auto Owners Insurance Co.*, C.A. No. 4-14-04, 2014 WL 5803028.

Wash. App. 2009. An insured from which employee continued to steal cash after his thefts were discovered and after he began repaying stolen amounts through deductions from his pay sustained only one loss from one "occurrence" under commercial crime insurance policy that defined "occurrence" to include all separate acts committed by an employee during policy period. Therefore, the amount recovered from the employee was applied to the total amount stolen in determining whether the insured had been fully compensated for its loss, as necessary before the insurer could benefit from the insured's third-party recovery from the employee. *S&K Motors, Inc. v. Harco National Insurance Co.*, 15 Wash. App. 633, 213 P.3d 630.

SECONDARY SOURCES

Samuel J. Arena & A. Nicole Stover, *Limit of Liability*, COMMERCIAL CRIME POLICY 477 (Randall I. Marmor & Susan Koehler Sullivan eds., 3d ed. 2014).

Q. Other Property

"Other property" means any tangible property other than "money" and "securities" that has intrinsic value. Other property does not include "computer programs," "electronic data" or any property specifically excluded under this Policy.

COMMENT

This definition appears in both the CPP and the CCP. The CCP specifically excludes "computer programs" and "electronic data." This defined term limits the policy's coverage to losses of tangible property. Thus, choses in action would not fall within this definition or the policy's coverage. In addition, the item must have some intrinsic value. Customer lists have been excluded from coverage because such lists constitute proprietary information rather than tangible property. Similarly, the specific exclusion of "computer programs" and "electronic data" confirm the limitation of coverage to tangible property only.

ANNOTATIONS

3d Cir. 2002. Losses due to falsified pharmaceutical studies did not constitute a direct loss of money, but the court determined that the studies could be deemed "other property." The court did not consider whether the studies constituted tangible or intangible property. *Scirex Corp. v. Fed. Ins. Co.*, 313 F.3d 841.

4th Cir. 1984. Labor dishonestly diverted from one construction site to another was not property under either a Risk Policy or a Dishonesty Policy, even in the absence of a specific definition of the term "other property." *G&C Constr. Corp. v. St. Paul Fire & Marine Ins. Co.*, 731 F.2d 183.

4th Cir. 1964 (Va.). Construing an employee dishonesty policy, the court upheld a district court decision finding coverage for a scheme whereby a salesman gave his employer false data as to financial condition of the business operation by salesman personally, and thereby obtained large shipments of fertilizer on credit. The court held that the fertilizer, rather than the amounts due, evidenced by notes and open accounts, constituted other property within the coverage of policy. "Other property" was not a defined term in the policy at issue. The court rejected the insurer's argument that the loss constituted a chose in action and was not tangible or corporeal in nature, finding that the loss was the fertilizer itself, not the choses in action represented by the notes. *Virginia-Carolina Chem. Corp. v. Hartford Acc. & Indem. Co.*, 339 F.2d 413.

D.C. Cir. 1970. In an action on an employee dishonesty policy, the court rejected the insured's argument that the policy covered only physical loss of "money," "securities," and "other property" due to the conduct of the insured's employees, holding that a consequential pecuniary loss measured by payments to third parties was a covered loss under the policy. The court went on to reverse the lower court due to an erroneous jury instruction on an unrelated point. *Imperial Ins., Inc. v. Employers' Liab. Assur. Corp.*, 442 F.2d 1197.

C.D. Cal. 2000. The insured filed a declaratory judgment action against its insurer seeking coverage under its commercial crime policy for losses suffered from its employees' disclosure of insured's trade secrets to a third party in exchange for a cash payment. The court held that the loss of trade secrets was not covered under the policy. The court reasoned that tangible generally means corporeality and held that "[t]angible property does not encompass trade secrets." *Avery Dennison Corp. v. Allendale Mutual Ins. Co.*, No. CV 99-09217CM (cwx), 2000 WL 33964136.

S.D. Fla. 1995. This case involved the theft by an employee of lists of combinations of electronic serial numbers and mobile phone identification numbers used to program mobile phone "clones" that could be used with corresponding charges going to the insured's account with its cellular phone providers. The insured sought coverage for the cellular charges and deactivation and reactivation charges incurred in order to disconnect the stolen numbers and install new numbers on its cellular phone inventory. The court found that the number combinations were not tangible property but more closely resembled proprietary information that could be used or disclosed to cause economic damage. The court also opined that there was no real intrinsic value to the lists because they had no meaning or use without the reference to the cellular phones. *People's Telephone Co., Inc. v. Hartford Fire Ins. Co.*, 36 F. Supp. 2d 1335.

S.D. Ind. 2006. In this unreported decision, the court held that phone cards stolen by an employee of a third party constituted property within the meaning of a crime policy with computer and funds transfer fraud coverage. The court found that "intrinsic value" means "the inherent value of a thing, without any special features that might alter its market value." Although a cellular phone was necessary to extract the specific value from a prepaid telephone card, this "technological feature" did not detract from the value of the card itself. *Brightpoint, Inc. v. Zurich Am. Ins. Co.*, 2006 WL 693377.

Cal. App. 1986. Argentinian pesos were currency, not other property, despite foreign currency provisions in policy. *Levi Strauss & Co. v. Aetna Cas. & Sur.*, 229 Cal. Rptr. 434.

Mo. App. 1965. Under a Money and Securities Broad Form Policy, which insured against loss of money, securities and other property by reason of safe burglary or robbery, rare coins kept by an insured as collector's items, having no relation to the insured's business as a department store, could be used in the conduct of the insured's business as a medium of exchange and therefore was insured as money at face value and not as other property at market value. "Coins' were expressly included in the definition of "money" and thus could not be considered to be other property. *Cornblath v. Fireman's Fund Ins. Co.*, 392 S.W.2d 648.

N.Y. App. 2005. The court granted summary judgment to an insurer on a crime policy. The claim involved alleged losses from the theft of customer lists and trade secrets. The insurer argued that this intangible property was not covered and that the employees that the insured named as dishonest no longer worked for the insured during the coverage period of the policy. Although the opinion provides no details regarding the basis for the court's decision, it does say that the policies either exclude or do not cover consequential damages. *Duratech Indus., Inc. v. Cont'l Co.*, 800 N.Y.S.2d 182.

SECONDARY SOURCES

Joel P. Williams & Timothy E. Markey, *Loss and Valuation*, COMMERCIAL CRIME POLICY 323 (Randall I. Marmor & Susan Koehler Sullivan eds., 3d ed. 2014).

R. Premises

"Premises" means the interior of that portion of any building you occupy in conducting your business.

COMMENT

This definition is the same in the CPP and the CCP. It often is construed along with the more specific defined term "banking premises," and, therefore, cases considering that definition also should be consulted. Courts construe both terms strictly such that activity occurring in locations other than the interior, even if on a porch or deck attached to the building, will not be considered to be inside the premises.

ANNOTATIONS

S.D. Ind. 2006. In this unreported decision, the court held that phone cards stolen by an employee of a third party were not stolen on the insured's premises. The court rejected the insured's argument that "premises" should include a location where an insured's employee continues to advance the interests of the insured. Here, an insured employee exchanged the phone cards off premises with a third party with whom the insured was doing business. The court held that the phone cards were never inside the building that the insured occupied or where it conducted its business. *Brightpoint, Inc. v. Zurich Am. Ins. Co.*, 2006 WL 693377.

La. App. 1967. A pharmacist's loss by theft from an employee who was returning to the pharmacy from the bank and who had stepped up on to the porch and was about to enter the building when the money was taken was not covered because it did not occur "inside" the premises. The court found that the employee had not passed the threshold into the building when the theft occurred and therefore it did not occur inside the premises. *Singerman v. Nat'l Surety Corp.*, 196 So. 2d 291.

Mich. 1944. An insured operator of a café was insured under a mercantile robbery and safe burglary policy. The insured, his wife and two employees were in their cars in the parking lot of the business after hours when three masked men approached them and forced them out of their cars and back into the café. The cash receipts from the day's business were in the wife's purse, which she left in the car. Inside the café, the men threatened and physically beat the insured with a revolver until they divulged the location of the money, which the robbers then brought back into the café. The insurer denied coverage on the grounds that the robbery did not take place inside the premises as required by the policy. The court disagreed, finding that there are two distinct elements to robbery: (1) putting the victim in fear of violence to his person or property and (2) the taking of money, property, or thing of value from the person or in his presence. The court held that the offense of robbery was perpetrated against the insured inside the building when the robbers removed the money from the insured's wife's purse. The crime was not consummated until the whereabouts of the money was disclosed, it had been taken into the building, appropriated by the robbers and then taken away. *Saks v. St. Paul Mercury Indem. Co.*, 14 N.W.2d 547.

SECONDARY SOURCES

Christopher C. Novak, Todd D. McCormick & Thomas R. Orofino, *The Other Insuring Agreement of Commercial Crime Policies*, COMMERCIAL CRIME POLICY 267 (Randall I. Marmor & Susan Koehler Sullivan eds., 3d ed. 2014).

S. Robbery

"Robbery" means the unlawful taking of property from the care and custody of a person by one who has:
a.   Caused or threatened to cause that person bodily harm; or
b.   Committed an obviously unlawful act witnessed by that person.

COMMENT

This definition is the same in the CCP and the CPP, except that the CCP adds the word "unlawful" to the "taking of property." Robbery is clearly distinguishable from burglary or safe burglary in that is requires the use of threats or force along with the taking of the property. In other words, the taking must be witnessed by a person who is in fear of bodily harm. Courts have looked to state law to construe the term "robbery," along with the policy definition.

ANNOTATIONS

2d Cir. 2012. An insured operator of a check cashing store made a claim under the crime insurance policy after a group of criminals successfully tricked the check cashing employee to turn over $120,000 in cash to them. The insured asserted that the crime was covered under the policy's definition of "robbery." The insurer denied coverage on the basis that the provision provided that the unlawful taking must be done by an "overt felonious act." In this case, the insurer argued the felonious act was not overt, but covert, because the employee was unaware at the time that she was handing over the money to a criminal. The court disagreed and found that the event was covered because the most relevant act was the obvious, observable action of the criminal taking the box of cash. That act was clearly "felonious," was "overt" in the sense of being observable and was within the employee's physical "presence" and her "cognizance," since she was aware of his request for money. *VAM Check Cashing Corp. v. Federal Ins. Co.*, 699 F.3d 727.

Mich. 1944. An insured operator of a café was insured under a mercantile robbery and safe burglary policy. The insured, his wife and two employees were in their cars in the parking lot of the business after hours when three masked men approached them and forced them out of their cars and back into the café. The cash receipts from the day's business were in the wife's purse, which she left in the car. Inside the café, the men threatened and physically beat the insured with a revolver until they divulged the location of the money, which the robbers then brought back into the café. The insurer denied coverage on the grounds that the robbery did not take place inside the premises as required by the policy. The court disagreed, finding that there are two distinct elements to robbery: (1) putting the victim in fear of violence to his person or property, and (2) the taking of money, property, or thing of value from the person or in his presence. The court held that the offense of robbery was perpetrated against the insured inside the building when the robbers removed the money from the insured's wife's purse. The crime was not consummated until the whereabouts of the money was disclosed, it had been taken into the building, appropriated by the robbers and then taken away. *Saks v. St. Paul Mercury Indem. Co.*, 14 N.W.2d 547.

Pa. Dist. 1951. An insured made a claim on a policy providing robbery and safe burglary coverage after premises were burglarized and various items stolen. The court rejected the insured's argument that burglary and robbery are synonymous, finding instead that robbery is the stealing of goods from the person of another or from his immediate presence by force or by putting him in fear, while burglary results from the felonious entry of premises and the carrying away of good therein with the intent to steal. The court also noted that safe burglary was defined by the policy as the felonious abstraction of property from within a safe or vault by any person making felonious entry into such safe or vault when all doors thereto are closed and locked. The court agreed with the insurer that the cost of fixing the lock on the safe, $10, was covered. *Hunt Motor Co., Inc. v. Fid. & Cas. Co. of N.Y.*, 78 Pa. D & C. 49.

SECONDARY SOURCES

NONE

T. Safe Burglary

"Safe burglary" means the unlawful taking of:
a.   Property from within a locked safe or vault by a person unlawfully entering the safe or vault as evidenced by marks of forcible entry upon its exterior; or
b.   A safe or vault from inside the "premises".

COMMENT

This defined term is the same in both the CPP and the CCP. It is found in Insuring Agreement 3 (Inside the Premises) of the CPP and Insuring Agreement A.4 (Inside the Premises—Robbery or Safe Burglary of Other Property) in the CCP.

The definition includes both the unlawful taking of a safe or vault itself, as well as the unlawful taking of property within a locked safe or vault. As respects the unlawful taking of property from within a safe or vault, the definition requires evidence of forcible entry upon the exterior of the safe or vault, thus ensuring that the theft is by an intruder rather than an employee with authorized or unauthorized access to enter the safe or vault. Courts have upheld denials of coverage where no signs of forced entry were visible on the safe or vault in question. Another issue that arises in cases considering this definition is whether the compartment holding the money or property constitutes a safe or vault within the meaning of the policy. Because neither the CPP nor the CCP contain a definition of "safe or vault," courts have turned to both dictionary and common definitions of both to determine the issue, as illustrated in the cases below.

ANNOTATIONS

E.D. Pa. 1986. In this unreported decision, the court allowed recovery under a federal crime insurance policy where the insured's premises were forcibly entered and a substantial amount of cash and property removed from an unlocked safe. The criminal gained access to the building by forcibly tearing down a wall of the insured's premises. The court allowed recovery even though the safe was either left unlocked or opened without any signs of forcible entry because the policy defined "burglary" as the "felonious abstraction of insured property from within the premises by . . . felonious entry therein by actual force and violence," evidenced by visible marks or damage to the exterior of the premises. The building itself was clearly entered by force, thus justifying coverage as "burglary." *X-Press Check Cashing, Inc. v. Fed. Crime Program*, 1986 WL 10653.

Fla. 1975. The court rejected insured's argument that the "visible marks" requirement in the definition of "safe burglary" pertaining to a mercantile robbery and safe burglary endorsement was intended only as nonessential evidentiary assurance that the theft was by an intruder and not by an employee. The court concluded that there was no coverage under the endorsement for the claimed loss where money was taken from a locked safe during business hours after an employee had rotated the dial of the combination lock through the first two sequences, and the dial had only to be rotated to a stop in the proper direction for the intruder to gain entry, and where otherwise there were no signs of forcible entry into the safe itself. *Rosie O'Grady's Warehouse, Inc. v. Charter Oak Fire Ins. Co.*, 319 So. 2d 632.

Fla. 1956. The court upheld an insurer's denial of a claim where thieves forcibly opened doors leading to the office where the safe was situated and took the safe from the premises. The safe was never recovered. The court refused to infer that the opening of the safe left marks upon it and found that there could be no recovery where there was no evidence of visible marks of forcible entry on the safe itself. *A.L. Moore v. General Cas. Co. of Am.*, 91 So. 2d 341.

Neb. 1968. The court held that a loss of money from a safe, on which only the inner door had been pried open, was not covered by the policy. The exterior of the safe contained no marks indicating a forcible entry, and the combination lock was neither marked nor damaged. *Hazuka v. Md. Cas. Co.*, 160 N.W.2d 174.

N.Y. App. 1992. The court upheld the insurer's denial of coverage where a large safe showed signs of being tampered with but nothing was stolen therefrom, but a substantial amount of money was removed from a small safe, which showed no signs of forced entry, either on its exterior or interior. The court held that an insurer may require signs of visible force in a policy of insurance for burglary and that the policy provisions were unambiguous in this regard. *Prince Check Cashing Corp. v. Fed. Ins. Co.*, 582 N.Y.S. 2d 751.

Ohio App. 1996. The court considered the issue of whether a second-floor room in a bar/restaurant used both for balancing cash register receipts and for counting money, but also for the safekeeping of money, money in cash drawers, valuable liquors, and other valuables constituted a "vault" within the meaning of a commercial crime policy's robbery and safe burglary coverage form. The court disregarded the insurer's proffered expert testimony, in which its expert stated that a vault has certain physical requirements, including size and type of lock. Instead, the court referred to the definition of "vault" defined in the dictionary as "a room or compartment for the safekeeping of valuables." The court found that the insured used the room for that purpose and awarded coverage under the policy. *Slam Jams II, Etc. v. Capitol Indem. Corp.*, 1996 WL 403353.

Pa. Dist. 1951. The insured made claim on a policy providing robbery and safe burglary coverage after premises were burglarized and various items stolen. The court rejected the insured's argument that burglary and robbery are synonymous, finding instead that robbery is the stealing of goods from the person of another or from his immediate presence by force or by putting him in fear, while burglary results from the felonious entry of premises and the carrying away of good therein with the intent to steal. The court also noted that safe burglary was defined by the policy as the felonious abstraction of property from within a safe or vault by any person making felonious entry into such safe or vault when all doors thereto are closed and locked. The court agreed with the insurer that the cost of fixing the lock on the safe, $10, was covered. *Hunt Motor Co., Inc. v. Fid. & Cas. Co. of N.Y.*, 78 Pa. D & C. 49.

S.C. 2002. The court granted summary judgment to the insurer on a bad faith claim on the grounds that the issue of whether an ATM machine constituted a safe or a vault was a novel issue of first impression and therefore, the insurer had a reasonable basis to deny claim. The trial court held on summary judgment motions that the ATM constituted a safe under the common definition of the word, and because the policy contained no definition of "safe," or criteria for differentiating an ATM from a safe. *Mixson, Inc. v. Am. Loyalty Ins. Co.*, 562 S.E.2d 659.

SECONDARY SOURCES

NONE

U. Securities

"Securities" means negotiable and nonnegotiable instruments or contracts representing either "money or property" and includes:
a.   Tokens, tickets, revenue and other stamps (whether represented by actual stamps or unused value in a meter) in current use; and

b. **Evidences of debt issued in connection with credit or charge cards, which cards are not issued by you; but does not include "money."**

COMMENT

This definition is the same in the CPP and the CCP. In determining whether an item falls within the definition, it may be necessary to consult state law, including the commercial code, for the state law requirements for negotiable and nonnegotiable instruments. It is also important to note that this definition specifically excludes the defined term "money," which should also be consulted when reviewing whether an item falls within the definition.

ANNOTATIONS

5th Cir. 2004. A crooked lawyer operating a Ponzi scheme deposited fraudulently obtained funds in an account of the insured bank. He then used some of the money to purchase certificates of deposit from the bank and pledged the CDs as collateral for two personal lines of credit and personal credit cards from the bank. After he was arrested, the United States sought to forfeit the CDs and the defrauded "investors" sued the bank claiming the CDs. The bank asserted innocent ownership of the CDs to the extent of the loans they secured. The bank eventually settled with the "investors" and sought to recover its losses. The court affirmed summary judgment for the bank on the theory that Insuring Agreement E of the bond covered the loss. There was no dispute that the CDs were securities covered by that insuring agreement or that the bank extended credit in good faith reliance on them. The issues were whether they were "stolen" and whether the money paid to settle the "investors'" suit was a direct loss. The court resolved both issues in favor of the insured. *Brady Nat'l Bank v. Gulf Ins. Co.*, 2004 WL 734884.

D.C. Cir. 1970. In action on employee dishonesty policy, the court rejected the insured's argument that the policy covered only physical loss of "money," "securities," and "other property" due to the conduct of the insured's employees, holding that a consequential pecuniary loss measured by payments to third parties was a covered loss under the policy. The court went on to reverse the lower court due to an erroneous jury instruction on an unrelated point. *Imperial Ins., Inc. v. Employers' Liab. Assur. Corp.*, 442 F.2d 1197.

Or. App. 2003. A check is a negotiable instrument pursuant to Oregon statute and, as such, falls within the definition of "securities." *Robben & Sons Heating, Inc. v. Mid-Century Ins. Co.,* 74 P.3d 1141.

SELECTED SECONDARY SOURCES

Bradford R. Carver & CharCretia V. DiBartolo, *Conditions and Limitations: Definitions, in* ANNOTATED FINANCIAL INSTITUTION BOND 209 (Michael Keeley ed., 3d ed. 2013).

Gary J. Valeriano & Carleton Burch, *Insuring Agreement (E)— Securities, in* ANNOTATED FINANCIAL INSTITUTION BOND 118 (Michael Keeley ed., 3d ed. 2013).

V. Security Procedure

"Security procedure" means a procedure established by agreement of the Insured and its customer or financial institution for the purpose of (i) verifying that a payment order is that of the Insured, or (ii) detecting error in the transmission or the content of the payment order or communication. A security procedure may require the use of algorithms or other codes, identifying words or numbers, encryption, callback procedures or similar security devices.

COMMENT

This definition is not included in the CCP. In the CPP, the definition is relevant to Insuring Agreement 5 (Computer Fraud) and is contained within the exclusion specific to this insuring agreement, Exclusion 6 (a)(Failure to Follow Security Procedures).

The CPP definition follows closely the definition of "security procedure" provided by the U.C.C. Article 4A, which governs the rights, duties and liabilities of banks and their commercial customers with respect to electronic funds transfers. Non-insurance cases, as below, construing this Article's definition, including its requirements for commercial reasonableness of such procedures, may be instructive when considering this definition.

ANNOTATIONS

1st Cir. 2012 (Me.). A bank customer sued its bank to recover money lost through fraudulent entry into its account. The court found that the bank's security procedures were not commercially reasonable and thus the bank could not shift the risk of fraud to its customer. *PATCO Const. Co., Inc. v. People's United Bank*, 684 F.3d 197.

8th Cir. 2014 (Mo.). A bank's security procedures were commercially reasonable as required to shift the risk of fraud to its customer. *Choice Escrow and Land Title, LLC v. Bancorp South Bank*, 754 F.2d 611.

SECONDARY SOURCES

Melissa Waite, *In Search of the Right Balance: Patco Lays The Foundation For Analyzing The Commercial Reasonableness of Security Procedures under U.C.C. Article 4A*, 54 B.C. L. REV. E-SUPPLEMENT 217.

W. Theft

"Theft" means the unlawful taking of property to the deprivation of the Insured.

COMMENT

The CPP contains a completely different definition of "theft," defining it simply as "any act of stealing." In theory, this appears to be a narrower definition than that contained in the CCP, which defines "theft" as an "unlawful taking" of covered property "to the deprivation of the

Insured." Several of the cases construing the definition contained in the CCP look to state criminal law proscribing larceny and theft to determine the scope of the term. Thus, it is likely that those courts would reach similar results irrespective of whether the CPP or CCP definition was at issue.

Some courts have looked to the perpetrator's intent in taking the property, finding that intent to permanently deprive the insured of its property is a necessary element of "theft." Loss resulting directly from pure embezzlement of money or property clearly falls within the scope of this defined term. It remains unclear whether less traditional schemes involving, for example, loss resulting from fraudulent orders, unauthorized trading, unsupported lending or similar schemes are likewise covered. A few courts in some jurisdictions have adopted a more expansive view of this definition, resulting in coverage for less typical schemes, including schemes resulting in losses to third parties over whose property the insured has exercised care, custody or control.

ANNOTATIONS

11th Cir. 2011 (Ala). As head of a division of the insured's single-family home developments, an employee analyzed various properties and then provided a report and recommendation to the insured's board of directors, which would then be followed by a tour of the properties. Employee was involved in a series of self-dealing transactions either (1) recommending that the insured purchase properties that he owned individually or with another party; or (2) the employee received a portion of the sale proceeds after recommending purchase of property owned by the third party. Construing a CrimeShield policy that included employee theft coverage, the court held that this scheme did not constitute "theft." Although the employee had violated his fiduciary duty to the company, the insured was not deprived of "money" because the insured received "exactly what it had bargained for." The insured reviewed the property and ultimately authorized the purchase. According to the court, the insured had bargained for and received property that it could use for future development. *Hartford Fire Ins. Co. v. Mitchell Co., Inc.*, 440 Fed. Appx 759, 2011 WL 3925363.

Bankr. N.D. Ga. 1995. The court considered an employee dishonesty claim in which the president and chief executive officer of the insured caused the insured to engage in four separate questionable loan transactions with four separate customers. In addition to finding that the perpetrator was not an "employee" of the insured based on the alter ego doctrine, the court analyzed the definition of "theft" to find that the insured did not establish that two of the four transactions constituted "thefts" within the meaning of the policy. The court's analysis focused on what the defalcating party knew and when he knew it, finding that a theft took place if he was aware that a particular loan was based on fraudulent collateral. Because the trustee in bankruptcy could not prove that the perpetrator knew that two of the four transactions were based on false collateral, no "theft" was proven under the policy for those transactions. *In re Prime Commercial Corp.*, 187 B.R. 785.

N.D. Ill. 2009. The court broadly interpreted the term "theft" to find that an employee's scheme of selling false documents to customers to use to obtain loans and defraud third-party lenders with the false documents was covered as "theft." *Taylor Chrysler Dodge, Inc. v. Universal Underwriters Ins. Co.*, Case No. 08 C 4522, 2009 U.S. Dist LEXIS 91187.

N.D. Ill. 2000. In this unreported decision, the court considered a case that involved an allegation that a salesman for a third party bribed the purchasing agent for the insured to purchase the third party's component parts at inflated prices. In interpreting the commercial crime policy at issue, the court adopted a narrow interpretation of "theft," concluding that this type of loss was not covered by the plain language of the policy. "Theft" was defined as "the unlawful taking, including by violence or threat of violence, of assets to the deprivation of the Insured." The court found that this language was more restrictive than the traditional coverage for "any fraudulent or dishonest acts." Thus, these acts did not constitute "theft" under the policy definition because the purchase by the insured of the salesman's company's products at higher prices did not constitute a "taking" of the insured's assets. *Williams Electronics Games, Inc. v. Barry*, No. 97 C 3743, 2000 U.S. Dist. LEXIS 425.

E.D. La. 2004. An employee manipulated company accounts receivable to make them look current and collectible and to make herself and her department's performance look better. The insured alleged that the employee's actions resulted in additional merit pay and bonuses and a substantial uncollectible accounts receivable. The court held that the scheme was an "unlawful taking" but found that uncollectible accounts receivable did not constitute "other property," and therefore were not covered. The court did conclude, however, that the merit pay increases and bonuses were covered losses as out of pocket losses directly resulting from the scheme. *Morris Kirschman & Co. v. Hartford Fire Ins. Co.*, C.A. No. 03-1743, 2004 U.S. Dist. LEXIS 17427.

W.D. Mich. 2011. Employees of a company used income received from vehicle sales to pay current expenses rather than the lender on a floor plan financing agreement. The employees also provided inaccurate financial information thereby misstating the financial condition of the company. Construing Michigan law, the court held that payment of a legitimate debt of the business is neither a loss to the company nor a theft. As such, the insureds failed to show an "occurrence" that would trigger coverage. *Coopersville Motors, Inc. v. Federated Mutual Co.*, 771 F. Supp. 2d 796.

W.D. Mich. 2011. The insurer brought a subrogation action after paying a claim under the "employee theft" insuring agreement of its policy. The underlying claim involved a scheme whereby the insured's employee artificially inflated shipment invoices and then received kickbacks from the shipping company. The employee overcharged the insured employer for services never actually given or that were unreasonably priced. The carrier sought to recover from the shipping company and the two employees involved in the scheme. *Hartford Fire Ins. Co. v. Clark,* 771 F. Supp. 2d 796.

D.N.J. 2008. An employee of car dealership convinced his employer to make the first loan payment on car loans to help customers with bad credit be able to purchase cars. The employee would request checks for the initial loan payment from the accounting department made payable to the bank and then would take the requests to the bank and exchange them for blank money orders. The employee retained some of the blank money orders rather than remit to the lender. The insured also submitted false credit applications in order to induce the lender bank to issue loans to customers who did not meet credit standard. The insurer conceded that embezzlement of money orders was "theft" and the issue regarding that aspect of the loss involved the number of occurrences. The court held that the loss sustained as a result of the submission of false credit reports was not "theft" because it was not a taking of the insured's property. *Pine Belt Auto. v. Royal Indemnity Co.*, No. 06-5995 (JAP), 2013 WL 4682582.

S.D.N.Y. 1998. In this unreported decision, a federal district court found that fact issues existed with respect to whether losses caused by certain employees' false representations, false entries in company records and unauthorized advances would be covered under a crime policy. The court looked to state criminal law to analyze the meaning of the term "theft" and equated the term with the broader criminal term "larceny." The court found that a specific showing of intent would be required for coverage to exist given that the state law regarding larceny included "wrongful taking, obtaining or withholding of another's property . . . committed by . . . trespassory taking, common law larceny by trick, embezzlement, or obtaining property by false pretense." *Titan Indus. Corp. v. Fed. Ins. Co.*, No. 94 Civ. 0726.

N.D. Ohio 2014. Employee used her access to a customer's accounts to steal money from the customer. The court held that the amount paid by the insured to reimburse the customer was a covered loss, despite the third-party nature of the loss, finding that the definition of "theft" did not limit coverage to property that the insured company owns or holds; it merely requires that there be "deprivation" to the insured due to the unlawful taking of property. *Transtar Electric, Inc. v. Charter Oak Fire Ins. Co.*, No. 3:13CV1837, 2014 U.S. Dist. LEXIS 8000.

N.D. Ohio 2013. The insured administered accounts for its client's self-funded employee benefit plan. The client sued the insured when it learned that the insured had not paid all plan claims due. Referencing an exclusion to further define the term "theft," the court held that "theft" included both an "unlawful taking" and a "fraudulent, dishonest or criminal act." The insured's conduct in exercising control of its client's funds without consent, depriving the client of its funds, was dishonest and therefore covered. *Guyan International, Inc. v. Professional Benefits Administrators, Inc.*, No. 5:1-CV 823, 2013 U.S. Dist. LEXIS 46297.

W.D. Tenn. 2009. Employee stole money from the insured's president's personal account. The court held that the insured did not have physical possession, a bailment, or care, custody or control of money in the president's personal account and therefore did not "hold" the money for purposes of coverage under the "theft" insuring agreement. *Loeb Properties v. Federal Ins. Co.*, 663 F. Supp. 2d 640.

Ill. App. 1993. An insured paper distributor claimed a loss as a result of "unidentifiable employee theft." The court of appeals reversed summary judgment in favor of the insured on the grounds that there were fact issues regarding the claimed theft. The case focused not on the definition of "theft," but on whether a theft even occurred, given that the insured relied largely on a year-end physical inventory count to prove the purported theft. *Brander Central Co. v. Fed. Ins. Co.*, 628 N.E.2d 1129.

Mass. Super. 1992. In this unreported trial court decision, the court analyzed an employee dishonesty claim that was based upon losses that the insured incurred from unauthorized currency hedging transactions by an employee. The court, in interpreting the CCP "theft" language, considered Massachusetts law on theft or larceny and reviewed prior case law. The court concluded that the employee did not intend to permanently deprive his employer of its money or property but rather hoped to recoup the losses that he negligently caused by his error in keeping certain transactions open overnight. Thus, the court held that his conduct did not constitute theft under either Massachusetts law or the policy and held that there was no coverage. *Apollo Computer Inc. v. Fed. Ins. Co.,* No. 900-0288-C.

Ohio App. 1998. In determining that a question of fact existed as to whether a "theft" occurred when a county treasurer illegally invested and/or diverted county funds through his son, the court looked to the state law of "theft." The employee dishonesty policy defined "theft" as "any act of stealing." The court held that "theft" under Ohio law required an individual to knowingly exert or obtain control over the property of another with the purpose to deprive the owner of the property. Significantly, the court found that Ohio law no longer required a permanent deprivation of that property. Thus, the court held that a question of material fact existed as to whether a theft occurred. The trial court had based its summary judgment in favor of the carrier on the fact that the treasurer had not plead guilty to theft, but rather to having an unlawful interest in a government contract. The appellate court found not only that the policy does not require a conviction for theft, but also that personal gain is not a factor in determining the occurrence of a theft. The court went on to hold that a question existed as to whether the treasurer intended to use the funds, without giving proper consideration to the county in return for the money. *Columbiana County Bd. of Comm'rs v. Nationwide Ins. Co.*, 719 N.E.2d 561.

SECONDARY SOURCES

Toni Scott Reed, *Commercial Crime Coverage For The Twenty-First Century: Does A "Theft" Standard in Traditional Insuring Agreement (A) Broaden Or Narrow Coverage For Employee Dishonesty*, 14 FID. L.J. 137 (2008).

Toni Scott Reed, *Employee Theft Versus Manifest Intent: The Changing Landscape of Commercial Crime Coverage*, 36 TORT & INS. L.J. 43 (Fall 2000).

Toni Scott Reed, *What Is Employee Dishonesty And Employee Theft?*, COMMERCIAL CRIME POLICY 39 (Randall I. Marmor & Susan Koehler Sullivan eds., 3d ed. 2014).

X. Transfer Account

"Transfer account" means an account maintained by you at a "financial institution" from which you can initiate the transfer, payment or delivery of "money" or "securities":
a. By means of computer, telegraphic, cable, teletype, telefacsimile, telephone or other electronic instructions; or
b. By means of written instructions (other than those described in Insuring Agreement A.2) establishing the conditions under which such transfers are to be initiated by such "financial institution" through an electronic funds transfer system.

COMMENT

This definition is relevant to Insuring Agreement A.6 (Funds Transfer Fraud) in the CCP. Neither the insuring agreement nor the definition is included in the CPP. The defined terms "money," "securities," and "financial institution" also should be consulted. This definition also references Insuring Agreement A.2 (Forgery or Alteration), which provides that the company will pay for loss resulting directly from "forgery" or alteration of checks, draft, promissory notes, or "similar written promises, orders or directions to pay a sum certain in 'money.'" The written promises, orders or directions to pay referenced in Insuring Agreement A.2 are specifically excluded from this defined term.

ANNOTATIONS

NONE

SECONDARY SOURCES

NONE

Y. Watchperson

"Watchperson" means any person you retain specifically to have care and custody of property inside the "premises" and who has no other duties.

COMMENT

This definition is critical to a determination of coverage under Insuring Agreement 3(b) (Inside the Premises) and Insuring Agreement A.4 (Inside the Premises—Robbery or Safe Burglary of Other Property) because coverage is not available for loss or damage to "other property" resulting from "robbery" involving a "watchperson." Both insuring agreements provide coverage only if the actual or attempted "robbery" involves a "custodian," a defined term that specifically excludes "watchperson." The defined term "custodian" should be consulted.

ANNOTATIONS

La. App. 1981. A grocery store cashier, who was responsible for the office and its contents in absence of the manager, was a "custodian" of insured property within meaning of a policy providing robbery coverage for the taking of insured property, where a "custodian" was defined as any employee in regular service of and duly authorized to have "care and custody" of insured property. *70th Street Food Store, Inc. v. Ne. Fire Ins. Co. of Pa.*, 408 So. 2d 958.

Mich. 1968. Money was taken at night from a locked safe on the insured's bowling alley premises at a time when the insured had one employee on duty who had no duties with respect to the locked safe or the money contained therein except to keep others away from the area and who had no access to the money. The employee was forced by threats of violence to lie on the floor and be tied up while the intruders made their way to the insured's office and opened the locked safe. The court held there was no coverage under a robbery policy defining robbery as a taking of insured's property by putting a custodian in fear of violence, and defining a custodian as an employee who is duly authorized by the insured to have the care and custody of the insured property within the premises, excluding any person while acting as a watchman, porter or janitor because the employee was acting as a watchperson and not a custodian. *Huron Bow, Inc. v. Sec. Ins. Co. of New Haven*, 165 N.W.2d 265.

Ill. App. 1930. In an appeal from a jury verdict in favor of insured, the court refused to overturn a jury verdict on the issue of whether an employee was acting as a custodian or as a watchman or porter at the time of the robbery. The acts of the employee while acting as a "watchperson" were excluded from the policy. *Ike Kaplan & Herman Kaplan v. USF&G*, 255 Ill. App. 437.

SECONDARY SOURCES

NONE

Chapter 10

Inventory Loss Exclusion*

Insureds frequently attempt to rely upon a profit and loss statement or a computation of inventory before and after the alleged malfeasance to otherwise prove that a covered event has occurred and/or to quantify their resulting damages. The inherent flaw associated with this means of trying to prove up a claim lies in the irrefutable fact that inventory shortages or differences may be caused by any number of reasons for which no coverage shall reasonably be expected to exist. This might include breakage, waste, customer or third-party theft, or either negligent or intentional bookkeeping errors. One of the industry's logical reactions to these realities was the Inventory Loss Exclusion, which is a frequently litigated policy exclusion.

The primary purpose of the Inventory Loss Exclusion is to preclude an Insured from proving that a covered loss has occurred by relying in some meaningful way on a computation or comparison of inventory or a profit and loss statement, independent of some proof of actual employee dishonesty or theft. In theory, it may appear as though the Inventory Loss Exclusion is straightforward enough in its terms and application. But like many commercial crime or fidelity coverage provisions and exclusions, whether the Inventory Loss Exclusion ultimately is held to apply can turn sharply on the specific facts of the case, including but not limited to, the nature of the property at issue, security or other precautions against theft that the Insured has taken, relative access to the Insured's facility by employees as opposed to non-employees, and the accounting procedures and controls maintained by the Insured.

As is frequently the case when the jurisprudence on a policy term or exclusion begins to erode or chip away at the logical intention of such a term or exclusion, underwriters have reacted swiftly and frequently in revising and sharpening the language of the Inventory Loss Exclusion. Of course, due regard must be given to the policy terms at issue, including any applicable endorsements and riders. Depending upon the language utilized, the Insured may not be able to rely on an inventory or profit and loss computation either to prove that a theft occurred or to

---

* By D.M. Studler, SDC CPAS, LLC, Aurora, Illinois, and Brian M. Falcon, Frost Brown Todd, LLC, Indianapolis, Indiana.

demonstrate damages. In other situations though, documents related to inventory records or inventory counts may be used to at least quantify the loss, if the Insured has independently established a covered loss due to employee dishonesty.

Not only do the policy forms differ in their scope and limitations on the exclusion, but also different courts have treated the Inventory Loss Exclusion distinctly. Three standards have emerged: (1) the "Absolute" exclusion, where proof of the loss is dependent as to its existence or amount on an inventory computation or profit and loss computation; (2) the exclusion "with Exception," where inventory and profit and loss computations are excluded unless the Insured can prove employee dishonesty with evidence wholly apart from the computation; and (3) the "Conclusive Proof" standard, where conclusive proof of employee dishonesty is required if the loss involves an inventory shortage. While minimal decisions have applied the "Conclusive Proof" standard, case law abounds on the other two standards.

This chapter will discuss and examine in detail the history and evolution of the Inventory Loss Exclusion, as well as the case law from throughout the country analyzing and interpreting it.

This chapter addresses the history and evolution of the Inventory Loss Exclusion. Three typical exclusions can be found on the 1990 edition of the Employee Dishonesty Coverage Form,[1] the Insurance Services Offices (ISO) August 2013 Commercial Crime Policy[2] (in both the loss sustained and discovery forms) and the Surety & Fidelity Association of America (SFAA) 2012 Crime Protection Policy.[3]

---

1   Employee Dishonesty Coverage Form (Form A, Blanket), CR 00 01 10 90 (Sur. Ass'n of Am. 1997), *reprinted in* COMMERCIAL CRIME POLICY 725 (Randall I. Marmor & John J. Tomaine eds., 2d ed. 2005).
2   Commercial Crime Policy, CR 00 23 08 13 (ISO Props., Inc. 2012) (Discovery) & Commercial Crime Policy, CR 00 21 08 13 (ISO Props., Inc. 2012) (Loss Sustained).
3   Crime Protection Policy, SP 00 01 04 12 (Sur. Ass'n of Am. 2012).

Standard Forms and Coverage

A. 1990 ISO and SFAA Joint Policy CR 00 01 10 90 (D)(1)(b) (Employee Dishonesty Form)

D.   ADDITIONAL EXCLUSIONS, CONDITION AND DEFINITIONS: In addition to the provisions in the Crime General Provisions Form, this Coverage Form is subject to the following:
   1.   Additional Exclusions: We will not pay for loss as specified below:
      b.   Inventory Shortages: loss, or that part of any loss, the proof of which as to its existence or amount is dependent upon:
         (1)   An inventory computation; or
         (2)   A profit and loss computation.

B. 2013 ISO Loss Sustained Policy CR 00 23 08 13 (D)(2)(a)

ISO has had various editions over the last fifteen years as follows: March 2000, July 2002, May 2006, and August 2013. A comparison of the ISO forms indicates the forms are unchanged from 2000 to August 2013. Thus, this chapter discusses the August 2013 CR 00 23 form stand-alone Commercial Crime Policy. The CR 00 23 08 13 edition indicates:

D.   Exclusions
   2.   Insuring Agreement A.1. does not apply to:
      a.   Inventory Shortages
         Loss, or that part of any loss, the proof of which as to its existence or amount is dependent upon:
         (1)   An inventory computation; or
         (2)   A profit and loss computation.
         However, where you establish wholly apart from such computations that you have sustained a loss, then you may offer your inventory records and actual physical count of inventory in support of the amount of loss claimed.

  b. **Trading**
   Loss resulting from trading, whether in your name or in a genuine or fictitious account.

  c. **Warehouse Receipts**
   Loss resulting from the fraudulent or dishonest signing, issuing, cancelling of failing to cancel, a warehouse receipt or any papers connected with it.

C. 2013 ISO Loss Sustained Policy CR 00 23 08 13 (D)(3)(a) (Accounting or Arithmetical Errors)

The ISO Commercial Crime Policy also has additional exclusions applicable to other insuring agreements (Inside The Premises and Outside The Premises) but not Employee Theft.

  D. **Exclusions**
   3. **Insuring Agreements A.3, A.4 and A.5 do not apply to:**
    a. **Accounting Or Arithmetical Errors Or Omissions**
     Loss resulting from accounting or arithmetical errors or omissions.
    b. **Exchanges Or Purchases**
     Loss resulting from the giving or surrendering of property in any exchange or purchase.
    h. **Voluntary Parting Of Title To Or Possession Of Property**
     Loss resulting from your, or anyone else acting on your express or implied authority, being induced by any dishonest act to voluntarily part with title to or possession of any property.

D. 2012 SFAA Crime Protection Policy (E)(2) & (3)(as applicable to specific insuring agreements)

D.   EXCLUSIONS
Applicable to All Insuring Agreements, Except as Indicated
We will not pay for loss as specified below:
Applicable to Specific Insuring Agreements
We will not pay for loss as specified below:
1.   **Under Insuring Agreement 1**
Employee Canceled Under Prior Insurance
Loss caused by any employee of yours, or predecessor in interest of yours, for whom similar prior insurance has been canceled and not reinstated since the last such cancellation.
2.   **Under Insuring Agreements 1 and 5**
Inventory Shortages
Loss, or that part of any loss, the proof of which as to its existence or amount is dependent upon:
a.   **An inventory computation; or**
b.   **A profit and loss computation.**
3.   **Under Insuring Agreements 3 and 4**
a.   **Accounting or Arithmetical Errors or Omissions**
Loss resulting from accounting or arithmetical errors or omissions.
b.   **Money Operated Devices**
Loss of property contained in any money operated device unless the amount of money deposited in it is recorded by a continuous recording instrument in the device.
c.   **Transfer or Surrender of Property**
(1)   **Loss of property after it has been transferred or surrendered to a person or place outside the premises or banking premises:**
(i)   **On the basis of authorized instructions; or**
(ii)   **As a result of threat to do:**

                        (a)   **Bodily harm to any person; or**

                        (b)   **Damage to any property.**

        (2)   **But, this exclusion does not apply under Insuring Agreement 4. to loss of money, securities or other property while outside the premises or banking premises in the care and custody of a messenger if you:**

                (i)   **Had no knowledge of any threat at the time the conveyance began; or**

                (ii)   **Had knowledge of a threat at the time the conveyance began, but the loss was not related to the threat.**

    5.   **Under Insuring Agreements 3 and 4**

        a.   **Exchanges or Purchases**

        Loss resulting from the giving or surrendering of property in any exchange or purchase.

        b.   **Voluntary Parting of Title to or Possession of Property**

        Loss resulting from your, or anyone acting on your express or implied authority, being induced by any dishonest act to part voluntarily with title to or possession of any property.

Insuring Agreement 1 is Employee Theft. Insuring Agreement 3 is Inside the Premises. Insuring Agreement 4 is Outside the Premises. Thus, the exclusions specific to Insuring Agreements 3 and 4 are not applicable to Insuring Agreement 1.

COMMENT

A. Historical Review of the Inventory Shortage Exclusion

Fidelity losses are frequently discovered when:

1. An employer becomes aware of a minor act of employee theft or employee dishonesty. The employer then undertakes an

inventory count or profit and loss analysis. The employer presents the employee theft or employee dishonesty claim based upon maximum possible loss calculated by inventory count or profit and loss computation.

2. An employer, conducting a periodic inventory or preparing a profit and loss statement, notes a significant difference between the inventory amount calculated and the amount counted or a significant decrease in profits. Contending and determining the variances are not explained by market factors, operational issues or other reasons, the employer looks at employees as the only remaining plausible cause. Again, the employer submits the maximum amount as the claimed loss.

3. A company experiences losses (loss of profit) during an employee's oversight of a branch or manufacturing plant. After the employee is terminated or the employee resigns, the branch or manufacturing plant returns to being profitable.

The inventory exclusion language necessitates additional consideration. For example, an Insured has video footage for sixty days illustrating an employee loading raw material (copper) at a manufacturing plant The employee is seen taking approximately ten eight-foot copper pipes every Wednesday and Friday for eight weeks. Thus, we can verify: 160 (8 weeks x 2 days x 10 pieces) eight-foot copper pipes stolen.

The Insured uses an inventory computation to calculate 2,000 copper pipes are missing. The Insured is using an inventory computation to substantiate the claimed loss of 2,000 pipes. An inventory computation is a comparison of "recorded" inventory quantity to actual inventory quantity at a given time.

An everyday way to consider this concept is for the reader to compare his or her check register balance to what the bank indicates he or she actually has on deposit. A comparison of such quantum (amounts) is considered an inventory computation. Please note, the authors consider the inventory exclusion to be broader in concept than inventory records and actual physical count of inventory.

In addition, the quantum of claimed loss is different than a quantity of claimed loss. In our check register comparison to the bank records, there is a quantum difference of $100. What we do not know is whether

356 ANNOTATED COMMERCIAL CRIME INSURANCE POLICY

the $100 difference between the check register and bank records consists of two $50 denomination bills or five $20 denomination bills.

Thus, the inventory exclusion excludes an inventory computation of either quantity (number of pipes or number of $5 denomination bills) or quantum (value multiplied by units). If the condition or proof of the existence of employee dishonesty or employee theft is met, then the Insured may present inventory records and an actual physical count of inventory. Such language indicates the Insured must be able to substantiate quantity of inventory, not quantum or value. Value of inventory is addressed in the valuation portion of the policy and in a different section of the annotation.

So, when an Insured contends he or she is missing $20,000 quantum in copper, can the Insured provide inventory records and actual physical count of inventory? The exclusion by its wording requires the Insured to know the quantity (number) of pipes missing. Quantum is quantity multiplied by value per unit. If the Insured cannot provide the quantity of pipes missing, it is not likely the Insured has the requisite documentation to support a computation. From an accountant's perspective, the language in the inventory exclusion is to verify and avoid inclusion of lost value; meaning the value of copper pipes today will be different tomorrow. Thus, the Insured is required to support the quantity of missing pipe with records. The Insured is not allowed to convolute the computation with changing values per unit.

The exclusion does not allow profit and loss records to be included, as profit and loss amounts are normally quantum amounts (units x unit value). The profit and loss amounts are convoluted with not only costs but also with profit. Lost profit is excluded from coverage as an indirect loss. Any analysis or inclusion of profit records would allow for the possible inclusion of profit in any valuations.

Until 1957, the following language was used in an effort by carriers to describe the type of losses that they intended to cover. Fidelity losses were covered ". . . including that part of any inventory shortage which the Assured shall conclusively prove to have been caused by the fraud or dishonesty of any Employees . . . ."

Courts, however, began to construe the term "conclusively" broadly to mean by a preponderance of the evidence, thus resulting in unexpected adverse verdicts to surety companies. Because this provision was found to be inadequate, in 1957, the Surety Association revised the exclusion clause. Set forth in its entirety, the inventory exclusion provided:

Section 2: This Policy does not apply:

(B) . . . to loss, or that part of any loss, as the case may be, the proof of which either as to its factual existence or as to its amount, is dependent upon an inventory computation or a profit and loss computation; provided, however, that this paragraph shall not apply to loss of Money, Securities or other property which the insured can prove, through evidence wholly apart from such computations, if sustained by the insured through any fraudulent or dishonest act or acts committed by any one or more of the Employees. SAA CDDD P-Form A, March 1980.

As litigation became more frequent over the exclusion introduced in 1957, two lines of authority developed. One held that the exclusion operated to eliminate *any* use of such computations unless other evidence wholly apart from those computations verified the nature and extent of loss. The second line argued that the "proviso" operated to allow the use of such computations so long as there was *some* independent evidence relating to nature and extent of loss.

Despite the fact that this provision has been subject to considerable debate concerning alleged ambiguities, it remained an industry standard until 1977, when, subject to a split of judicial authority over the meaning of the latter half of the clause (beginning "provided however . . ."), the industry moved to clarify further its intent, by deleting the "provided" clause in its entirety.

The 1977 revision provided, as follows:

Section 2: This Bond does not apply.

(B) To loss, or that part of any loss as the case may be, the proof of which either as to its factual existence or to its amount, is dependent upon an inventory computation or a profit and loss computation.

In 1986, the Commercial Crime Policy was introduced. Although the language of the inventory exclusion was revised, the exclusion is similar to the 1977 language:

COMMERCIAL CRIME POLICY:
1.   **Additional Exclusions: We will not pay for loss as specified below:**
     b.   **Inventory Shortages: loss, or that part of any loss, the proof of which as to its existence or amount is dependent upon:**
          (1)   An inventory computation; or
          (2)   A profit and loss computation.

B. Current Status of the Inventory Exclusion

The CR 00 01 10 90—Form A Employee Dishonesty was one of a number of crime coverage forms available to be combined with Crime General Provision Form CR 10 00 to create a monoline commercial crime policy. Other crime forms available would include Form B—Forgery or Alteration or Form F—Computer Fraud.

The prior forms issued jointly supported ISO and SAA coverage forms. By using individual forms for coverages, the exclusions applicable to a coverage, such as an inventory shortage, were within the individual form for Employee Dishonesty. The inventory shortage exclusion is not listed on the Form B, as an inventory shortage would not result from Forgery or Alteration.

The 2002 ISO Commercial Crime Policy was one of ten forms and policies in the ISO New Crime program introduced in 2000. The ISO Crime policies and forms originally contained seven insuring agreements. The number of insuring agreements expanded to eight; after combining the Computer Fraud and Electronic Transfer Fraud insuring agreements in the August 2013 edition, the number of insuring agreements returned to seven. The ISO Crime Program requires fewer forms and endorsements than the jointly supported ISO and SAA coverage forms.

The exclusions in the ISO forms are in two categories: 1) exclusions that apply to all insuring agreements and 2) exclusions applicable to specific insuring agreements. The inventory shortage exclusion that applies to Employee Theft coverage under the ISO Program allows the Insured to offer inventory information to support the amount of loss if the Insured establishes that a loss has occurred without reliance on the inventory information.

C. Difference in the Exclusion Language between the ISO and SFAA Employee Dishonesty Form (CR 00 01 10 90), ISO CR 0023 0813 and 2012 SFAA Crime Protection Policy

There are differences in the description of the exclusion, as shown by the following:

b. **Inventory Shortages: loss, or that part of any loss, the proof of which as to its existence or amount is dependent upon:**
   (1) An inventory computation; or
   (2) A profit and loss computation.

and the ISO Policy (CR 00 23 08 13):

a. **Inventory Shortages**
   Loss, or that part of any loss, the proof of which as to its existence or amount is dependent upon:
   (1) An inventory computation; or
   (2) A profit and loss computation.
   However, where you establish wholly apart from such computations that you have sustained a loss, then you may offer your inventory records and actual physical count of inventory in support of the amount of loss claimed.

The ISO inventory shortage exclusion that applies to Employee Theft coverage allows the Insured to offer inventory information to support the amount of a loss if the Insured establishes, without reliance on the inventory computation information, a loss has occurred. The ISO language appears to deny the use of sales and cost of goods sold records to support use of a profit and loss computation, even though the Insured may have established, wholly apart from a profit and loss computation, an employee theft loss.

From an accounting perspective, an Insured who has discovered a loss through investigating a decrease in sales or decrease in profits, will need to use some other method, wholly apart from its profit calculation, to document and support the evidence of Employee Theft and the amount of Employee Theft. For example, the profit margin of the produce department of a grocery store has been decreasing. Even if the Insured can provide evidence, including but not limited to, witness affidavits or video, the Insured cannot utilize the loss of profit margin to determine the amount of loss that it sustained due to Employee Theft. Under the ISO form, the Insured must present inventory records and actual physical count of the inventory in support of its claim. No longer can the Insured contend there is an overall inventory shortage in the produce department; rather the Insured must provide the actual physical count sheets of apples, oranges, pears, et al. The Insured must also provide the inventory records of the products.

Employers often will provide other evidence such as that an employee has misappropriated monies by writing checks or submitting overstated expense reports. However, the fact monies were stolen has no relevance to missing inventory and the use of an inventory computation to calculate a loss amount. The misappropriation of checks is not evidence wholly apart to support missing inventory.

The exclusion in the SFAA form is broader than the exclusion contained in the current ISO form. In theory, at least, any claim in which an Insured relies on an inventory or profit and loss computation to support its claim is excluded under the SFAA form.

D. Claims for Employee's Taking of Client's Property

Many of the current policies provide "Client's Property" coverage either by endorsement or within the insuring agreements themselves. The client's property coverage is useful in the following situation:

ACME Transportation (ACME) provides inventory logistics services to Big Water Heater Company (BWH). BWH manufactures, distributes, and sells water heaters internationally. ACME employees work on the BWH facilities moving water heaters from various warehouses, stocks, and stores. At the end of last year, BWH took a complete physical inventory count and found they were missing 200 high-end water heaters. After investigations were concluded, it was determined an ACME employee misappropriated 200 water heaters.

ACME and BWH have a contract whereby ACME will provide licensed forklift drivers, licensed truck drivers, and other heavy equipment operators, as BWH needs the services. ACME also provides the necessary equipment, as needed, such as forklifts and truck tractors.

In most cases, without the client's property coverage, ACME's crime policy will not address the claimed misappropriation as discussed in detail in the ownership of property chapter of the annotation. However, if the policy provides the client's property coverage, there are usually similar conditions among the ISO, SFAA and proprietary forms as follows:

1) The theft must be committed by an identified employee of the Insured,
2) There must be a written agreement between the Insured and the client,
3) The inventory computation exclusion still applies with a condition of evidence of theft wholly apart, including an identified employee, and
4) Only the Insured may make the claim under the Insured's policy.

The language for ISO CR 04 01 08 13 is as follows:

A.   The following Insuring Agreement is added to Section A. Insuring Agreements:
We will pay for loss of or damage to "money", "securities" and "other property" sustained by your "client" resulting directly from "theft" committed by an identified "employee", acting alone or in collusion with other persons.

C.   Under Section E. Conditions
2.   The Ownership Of Property; Interests Covered Condition is replaced by the following:
Ownership Of Property; Interests Covered
The property covered under this Insuring Agreement is limited to property:
a.   That your "client" owns or leases; or
b.   That your "client" holds for others in any capacity; or
c.   For which your "client" is legally liable, provided your "client" was liable for the property prior to the time the loss was sustained.

D.   Under Section F. Definitions
1.   The following definitions are added:

> > **a.** **"Client" means any entity for whom you perform services under a written contract.**
> **2.** **The definition of "theft" is replaced by the following:**
> **"Theft" means the unlawful taking of property to the deprivation of your "client".**

The language for Crime Protection Policy SE 00 48 04 12 is as follows:

A. COVERAGE	**We will pay for loss of, and loss from damage to, money, securities and other property sustained by a client of yours, resulting directly from dishonest acts committed by an identified employee, acting alone or in collusion with other persons, with the manifest intent to:**
B. DEFINITION	**As used in this Insuring Agreement, client means an entity for which you perform services as specified in a written agreement.**
D. CONDITION	**For purposes of this Loss of Client's Property Insuring Agreement only, the Ownership of Property, Interests Covered condition is deleted and replaced with the following:**
	The property covered under this Loss of Client's Property Insuring Agreement is limited to property:
	a. That your client owns or holds; or
	b. For which your client is legally liable.
	However, this insurance is for your benefit only. It provides no direct rights or benefits to any other person or organization, including your client. Any claim for loss to your client that is covered under this insurance must be presented by you.

OUTLINE OF ANNOTATIONS

Over time, different solutions have evolved with regard to the use of inventory or profit and loss computation to establish or support a claim for loss resulting from employee dishonesty, described as follows:

A. Absolute Exclusion/Decisions Upholding Exclusion: Exclusion of loss dependent as to its existence or amount on an inventory computation or a profit and loss computation.
B. Exclusion With Exception: Exclusion of inventory and profit and loss computations with an exception for loss that the Insured can prove by evidence wholly apart from such computation was sustained through fraudulent or dishonest acts by an employee.
C. Conclusive Proof Standard: A requirement in the insuring agreement that there must be conclusive proof that the loss was due to employee dishonesty if the loss involved a shortage of inventory.[4]
D. Client's Property: Coverage for the loss of a client's property caused by the Insured's employee's dishonesty if there is a written agreement between the Insured and the client. Case law regarding this coverage, or at least the specific issues related to it, has been relatively slow to emerge.

Each of these is discussed in the Annotations.

ANNOTATIONS

A. Absolute Exclusion/Decisions Upholding Exclusion

1. Commercial Crime Policies

M.D. Ala. 2015. After the Insured's truck driver was terminated for causes unrelated to theft, the Insured audited its delivery and sales records and took a physical inventory of the driver's remaining inventory. Those findings were compared against the Insured's computer-generated inventory records and a prior physical inventory conducted six months earlier. Both comparisons yielded an inventory

---

4   Ronald G. Mund & DM Studler, *The Inventory Computation & Profit & Loss Exclusion: Separating the Wheat from the Chaff*, VII FID. L.J. 7 (2001).

shortage of 82,510 bottles of product. While the Insured admitted that its loss was "dependent upon" inventory calculations, it also claimed that the exclusion should apply only when proof of the loss was "wholly" dependent upon such calculations. The Insured asserted that it had other evidence of theft, including an affidavit from its CFO that the product was to remain locked in a storage unit or in the driver's truck. The court held that this evidence suggested only that the driver was responsible for the loss, rather than of independent proof of theft. The shortage could have resulted from negligence or waste. The inventory calculations constituted the sole evidence that the bottles were stolen by an employee. The court granted summary judgment in favor of the Insurer. In doing so, the court rejected an argument that the exclusion rendered the coverage illusory and that the Insurer had waived the defense by paying on a similar claim earlier. *W.L. Petrey Wholesale Co., Inc. v. Great American Insurance Co.*, 2015 WL 404523.

Ill. App. 1999. Insured determined that 439 canisters of Freon, valued at $83,584.80, were missing and that the loss resulted from employee dishonesty. The two-foot high, thirty-pound Freon canisters are stored in a locked "cage"—a twenty-foot by ten-foot section of the building, fenced off by a ten-foot to twelve-foot high chain link fence, open at the top. The court held that there was no evidence of employee dishonesty and that even if the computations do not fall within the inventory shortages exclusion and that the missing Freon was due to employee dishonesty, Insured failed to present any evidence as to the number of occurrences and which occurrences, if any, were in excess of the deductible. *Reedy Indus., Inc. v. Hartford Ins.*, 715 N.E.2d 728.

2. Other Policy or Bond Forms

2d Cir. 1973 (N.Y.). Insured submitted inventory computation to support its claims for loss due to employee dishonesty. The Insured had no evidence of employee dishonesty except by negative inference. The court held that an inventory shortage alone is not sufficient to show employee dishonesty. *Dunlop Tire & Rubber Corp. v. Fid. & Dep. Co. of Md.*, 479 F.2d 1243.

7th Cir. 1966 (Ill.). Action by assignee to recover upon an employee fidelity bond. In response to the Insured's argument that the inventory profit and loss exclusion was ambiguous and would tend to make the whole contract illusory, the court held that despite its sympathy with the argument, it must be rejected in view of the plain and unambiguous language of the policy. *Gillette Co. v. Travelers Indem. Co.*, 365 F.2d 7.

10th Cir. 1986 (Wyo.). Insurer was awarded declaratory judgment that: coverage did not apply; no breach of duty of good faith resulted from Insurer's failure to reveal clear and unambiguous limit; and Insurer had no duty to investigate when it was clearly not liable. The appellate court affirmed, stating that both the fact and the amount of the loss must be shown by independent evidence as the policy required. Independent evidence of the fact that employee stole inventory and cash was not enough when there was no independent evidence of the amount of the theft. *Sec. Ins. Co. of Hartford v. Wilson*, 800 F.2d 232.

11th Cir. 2010 (Ga). The policy excluded loss for missing property where the only evidence of loss was a shortage disclosed on taking inventory, or other instances where no physical evidence existed that showed what happened to the property. The Insured sought coverage for $200,000 worth of warehouse materials without knowing exactly what happened to the inventory. There were no signs of breaking and entering, no damaged locks and no broken doors or glass. The Insured relied on the testimony of one of its employees that he knew the materials had been stolen but he did not name the culprit. The court granted summary judgment in the Insurer's favor, relying on the lack of evidence explaining what exactly happened to the missing materials and noting that the employee's testimony did not constitute "physical evidence" in any event. *Seagull Enterprises, LLC v. Travelers Property Casualty Company of America*, 366 Fed. Appx. 979.

N.D. Ill. 1986. Insurer sought summary judgment based on inventory computation exclusion action brought by Insured alleging Insurer's bad faith refusal to pay claim of losses resulting from employee dishonesty. The Insured presented inventory computation as proof of loss; however, the Insurer refused to pay the claim, since such proof was expressly excluded under the policy. The court held that while the exclusion clause might be subject to eventual judicial interpretation, nevertheless the validity of the clause was supported by case law. Thus, the court concluded that the Insurer was entitled to reject inventory computation as proof of loss, at least pending judicial decision on the clause. *Barr Co. v. Safeco Ins. Co. of Am.*, No. 83-C-2711.

E.D. Mich. 2009. The policy excluded coverage for missing property where the only proof of loss was an unexplained or mysterious disappearance, an inventory shortage, or another instance where no physical evidence existed to show what happened to it. The Insured's President claimed to have witnessed individuals taking the Insured's lumber. The thieves' identity was never established and the Insured's security guard disavowed knowledge or awareness of a theft. Following this incident, the Insured took an inventory of the lumber and determined that a "substantial quantity" was missing. The court allowed that theft may have been a "plausible explanation" for the missing lumber, but it held that theft was not "deducible from the evidence as a reasonable inference." Without any physical evidence of employee theft, the Insurer's motion for summary judgment was granted. *Banner Lumber Co., Inc. v. Indiana Lumbermen's Mutual Insurance Co.*, 2009 WL 3462510.

D. Nev. 1968. Action to recover on two fidelity bonds brought by gambling casino. The court held that a preponderance of the evidence showed that while computation of percentage of win from a game and calculation of an unusually low percentage of win are reliable indicia for the guidance of management and a probable indication that something may be wrong, they were not reliable proof of loss due to employee dishonesty for the reason that too many variables existed. *Mapes Casino, Inc. v. Md. Cas. Co.*, 290 F. Supp. 186.

S.D.N.Y. 1974. Insured claimed a loss of over six tons of gold and silver valued at $395,000. Proof of loss included inventory computations, verified proof that one of several accused employees had been arrested with one bar of silver in his possession and circumstantial evidence relating to several other employees. The court denied recovery based upon the policy exclusion, holding that although the Insured presented some evidence other than inventory computations to prove employee dishonesty, the court was not persuaded that the Insured had made a prima facie case as to the existence of any loss other than through the inventory computations. *U. S. Smelting Refining & Mining Co. v. Aetna Cas. & Sur. Co.*, 372 F. Supp. 489.

E.D. Pa. 1971. The court denied recovery based upon Insured's failure to establish damages through something other than the use of negative inference. The Insured presented a claim for loss of roofing shingles from its locked warehouse. As evidence of loss through employee dishonesty, the Insured offered evidence tending to show that only its employees had access and opportunity to abscond with the missing property. The court held, however, that such evidence of employee dishonesty presupposes the factual existence of the loss and adds nothing by which its existence can be proved. The computations alone, even if accurate, were insufficient to prove the existence of the loss and support a claim under the policy exclusion. *York Lumber Co., Inc. v. Fid. & Dep. Co. of Md.*, 331 F. Supp. 1131.

Cal. App. 1977. Textile distributor procured policy of employee fidelity insurance after becoming aware of extensive inventory losses over a two-year period. The losses continued despite a tightening of security measures and Insured sought recovery under the policy. Insurer refused to pay, claiming that inventory exclusion barred recovery. The court agreed, noting that although there was verified proof of employee dishonesty for the period prior to the contract execution date, only inventory computation was available for the period upon which recovery was sought. *Prager & Bear, Inc. v. Fed. Ins. Co.*, 136 Cal. Rptr. 340.

Miss. 1966. Action by warehouse for shortage shown through inventory to amount to $13,671.15 following time of hiring of the only two employees having access to the warehouse other than the Insured's president. Insured also provided evidence that one of the employees sold one of the missing items and accepted a purchaser's check for $1,010 and appropriated the money to his own use. The court held, however, that comprehensive dishonesty, disappearance and destruction policy excluded recovery for any loss dependent for proof, either as to factual existence or amount, upon inventory or profit and loss computation. *Gotcher Engineering & Mfr. Co., Inc. v. U. S. Fid. & Guar. Co.*, 193 So. 2d 115.

Mo. 1966. The court held that, where bond specifically provided that it would not cover any loss, or part of loss, proof of which either as to its factual existence or amount was dependent on inventory computation, neither audit nor testimony of results of audit, insofar as related to beer shortage at plaintiff's warehouse, was competent evidence to establish liability under bond for shortage. *Locke Distr. Co. v. Hartford Acc. & Indem. Co.*, 407 S. W.2d 658.

Neb. 1988. Unexplained shortages of gasoline at various stations were only provable by the taking of inventory and, therefore, properly excluded under "all-risk" policy. The difference between the perpetual records kept by the company and the physical inventory taken was the only proof of the loss. The court noted that there was no independent corroborating evidence, so the inventory exclusion clause must be enforced. *Jones v. Employers Mut. Cas. Co.*, 432 N.W.2d 535.

Neb. 1968. Action in a blanket crime policy to recover for property loss allegedly due to employee dishonesty. Insured had knowledge of two thefts by employees and the merchandise lost as a result of those thefts was all recovered. Insured sought, however, to recover for greater loss based upon inventory computations. The court held that Insured, under fidelity policy containing exclusionary clause in effect restricting recovery to losses in regard to which proof was not dependent upon an inventory computation or profit and loss computation in absence of other evidence, was precluded from recovery for all losses revealed by the inventory computation despite the showing of certain specific losses due to employee dishonesty. *Paramount Paper Prods. Co., Inc. v. Aetna Cas. & Sur. Co.*, 157 N.W. 2d 763.

N.Y. App. 1981. Dress manufacturer sought recovery for lost inventory. The Insured offered as evidence the apprehension of a company employee in the possession of a small quantity of dresses alleged to be part of the larger total loss. In addition, the Insured sought to use inventory computations and a financial book audit to establish the extent of loss. The court denied recovery; although acknowledging that the majority view provides for the use of such computations as corroborative evidence, the court held under the insufficiency theory that proof of a $20 loss would not sustain a claim for an over $15,000 total loss. Under the old clause (1957), $15,209 jury verdict for plaintiffs was reversed on appeal because the only independent evidence offered by the employer was discovering $20 worth of stolen merchandise in employee's possession. *Teviro Casuals, Inc. v. Am. Home Assur. Co.*, 439 N.Y. S.2d 145.

N.Y. App. 1977. Under an old clause, the court affirmed judgment of trial court, which awarded employer $125 of $123,000 claim. Although employee admitted to stealing $1,600 worth of goods, those goods were returned to employer. The policy exclusion for losses only ascertainable by profit and loss or inventory computation was valid. The court determined that positive proof of minor loss would not in itself be sufficient; rather, independent evidence of a much larger sum was necessary to avoid the exclusion. *Am. Thermostat Corp. v. Aetna Cas. & Sur. Co.*, 399 N.Y.S. 2d 292.

N.C. App. 1987. Under an all risk policy, the Insured could not recover for losses disclosed in taking of regular monthly inventory of available store stock, given policy exclusion for losses due to unexplained or mysterious disappearance of property or shortage of property disclosed on taking inventory. *Blue Stripe, Inc. v. U. S. Fid. & Guar. Co.*, 360 S.E.2d 140.

R.I. 1970. Insured brought action to recover under comprehensive dishonesty, disappearance and destruction policy after it caught one of its 80 employees in possession of thirty bars of white metal. This was alleged to be sufficient proof of a larger loss, corroborated by an independent inventory computation. The court disallowed the claim, basing its decision upon the policy exclusion. *Danal Jewelry Co. v. Fireman's Fund Ins. Co.*, 264 A.2d 320.

Wash. App. 2007. The Insured was an additional Insured lessor that made a claim related to missing computer equipment. The policy excluded the loss of missing property where the only evidence of loss was a shortage disclosed on taking inventory, or where there was no physical evidence showing what happened to the property. The Insured argued that, as an additional Insured, it did not have to establish what happened to the property. The court disagreed, holding that such a construction only applied where the policy terms were ambiguous. Because there was no policy ambiguity, the additional Insured was still required to demonstrate what happened to the property with physical evidence. The Insured attempted to demonstrate theft by relying on the facts that a large number of employees had recently been laid off and that there had been three other reported thefts in the two years preceding the loss. The court held that such circumstantial evidence was not sufficient, as the loss was not discovered until the inventory count was taken. The court affirmed summary judgment in the Insurer's favor. *NCF Financial, Inc. v. St. Paul Fire & Marine Insurance Co.,* 137 Wash. App. 1016.

B. Exclusion with Exception

1. Commercial Crime Policies

N.D. Ill. 2011. The Insured submitted a claim after discovering the theft of copper wire. It was uncontested, through both surveillance videos and a discrepancy between the Insured's actual inventory and what was shown on its books, that the Insured was the victim of at least one theft. The Insured valued its loss with an inventory comparison. The court denied the Insurer's motion for summary judgment, finding that the Insured's surveillance evidence gave rise to a strong inference of employee involvement. The surveillance evidence showed an individual with significant knowledge unique to that of an employee of the Insured, including the direction and route the thief walked inside the premises and the fact the thief moved lower-value materials out of the way to take higher-value materials. This level of knowledge gave rise to a reasonable inference that an employee was involved. The policy required that the employee involved in the theft be "identified." The Insurer insisted that this meant that the specific identity of the thief be known; the Insured argued that it required only a showing that someone who could be identified as an employee contributed to the theft. Although the court determined that the Insured ultimately offered evidence of a specifically named employee, it agreed with the Insured's position, holding that the Insured had demonstrated evidence that the thief merely could be "identified" as one of its employees by virtue of his knowledge of the facility and movement of the materials within the facility. *Coleman Cable, Inc. v. Travelers Indemnity Co.,* 790 F. Supp. 2d 742.

N.D. Ill. 1996. In denying cross motions for summary judgment, the court read the inventory exclusion to exclude only losses the proof of which, as to factual existence or amount, turns upon probabilities deduced or estimations made from comparison of post-theft-discovery dollar, as distinct from unit, inventory amounts with a pre-discovery dollar amount, or of a post-theft unit number with a pre-theft number calculated from a pre-theft dollar inventory amount. The exclusion could not be construed to exclude a loss which can be established by showing that a particular item or unit of goods observed and identified as present at one physical inventory count is not present at the next. *Blitz Corp. v. Hanover Ins. Co.*, 1996 WL 308233 (1996).

N.Y. 1995. Insured discovered a substantial shortage of merchandise in the clothing department of one of the university bookstores. Insured determined that its general merchandise buyer had falsified order forms, invoices and shipping and receiving documents for items purchased from a vendor and concluded that its employee and vendor had acted together in a scheme to bill Insured for merchandise never received. Insured determined that its loss was more than $1.6 million. In denying the claim, the Insurer did not rely on the inventory exclusion. The court held that the inventory exclusion could apply if Insured did not establish as a matter of law that it could prove the *amount* of its loss by other than dollar estimates. *New York Univ. v. Cont'l Ins. Co.*, 639 N.Y.S.2d 283.

Pa. Super 1991. Insured had evidence that employees were stealing video tapes and based the amount of its claim for loss due to employee dishonesty on both an inventory and profit and loss computation. The court held that an inventory computation and profit and loss computation may be considered to substantiate an Insured's claim when independent evidence of the theft has been presented. *Movie Distr. Liquidating Trust v. Reliance Ins. Co.*, 595 A.2d 1302.

Tenn. App. 1995. Evidence showing that individual items were received for sale, that they were missing, and that they were not sold was not proof of loss via "inventory computation" such as would result in application of policy exclusion. *Strings & Things in Memphis, Inc. v. State Auto Ins. Cos.*, 920 S.W.2d.

    2.   *Other Policy or Bond Forms*

11th Cir. 1984 (Ga.). Insured alleged former vice president had converted construction materials. Trial court's directed verdict was reversed on appeal. The appellate court found that sufficient evidence existed in addition to inventory computation to avoid application of the pre-1977 exclusion clause. This other evidence included purchase orders, invoices (goods never delivered or to wrong site), monthly statements, canceled checks, building plans, job specifications, bid estimates, and independent witnesses. *Fid. & Dep. Co. of Md. v. Southern Utilities, Inc.*, 726 F.2d 692, *aff'g* 555 F. Supp. 206 (M.D.Ga. 1983).

Ariz. 1977. In this action on a fidelity insurance policy, the court held that under exclusionary clause prohibiting recovery for losses if proof was dependent upon inventory computation or profit and loss computation, once Insured made prima facie showing, other than through inventory computation or profit and loss computation, that some loss occurred which was causally related to misconduct by one or more of Insured's employees, Insured would be entitled to introduce inventory computations and profit and loss computations to corroborate the loss and prove the total amount. *J. R. Norton Co. v. Fireman's Fund Ins. Co.*, 569 P.2d 857.

Ga. 1973. The court allowed inventory-type computations to support other evidence which would, on its own, be insufficient. The court's decision was based in part upon the proviso language deleted from the 1977 standard exclusion. The case is important as it highlights the court's attempt to construe the exclusion to reach a desired result. In what has been called the "redefining theory," the court simply changed the name of what would normally be considered an inventory-type computation, thereby avoiding the effects of the exclusion. In this case, the court considered that a computation by means of daily sales tickets was distinguishable from standard inventory or profit or loss computations. *Atlanta Coca-Cola Bottling Co. v. Transamerica Ins. Co.*, 61 F.R.D. 120.

Mass. 1976. The court adopted the "redefining theory" to avoid the policy exclusion. The Insured's evidence consisted of testimony by a materials control manager to the effect that he put goods in a locked warehouse and later found them to be missing. The court upheld coverage and supported its decision with the following analogy: "If the owner of an automobile locks it in a garage and later finds the garage empty, it would be an unwarranted strain on the language to say that he had made an 'inventory computation.' The dollar amount of loss was computed, not from inventory records, but from purchase records." *Popeo v. Liberty Mut. Ins. Co.*, 343 N.E.2d 417.

Mich. 1975. The Insured restaurant owner sought recovery under its fidelity insurance policy. The court held that evidence showing that customers paid restaurant bills which were not marked as paid and that restaurant manager took money from cash register without leaving a receipt constituted evidence of restaurant manager's dishonesty, independent of evidence of inventory and/or profit and loss computations, so that evidence of such computations was admissible despite exclusion in policy. *NIB Foods, Inc. v. Ins. Co. of N. Am.*, 234 N.W.2d 725.

Mo. 1977. The court employed the "redefining theory" to provide employee dishonesty coverage under a blanket crime policy. The action was initiated by a laundry and dry cleaning business, which claimed a loss of $7,659.47 in cash which was allegedly brought about by the dishonest and fraudulent acts of its employees in failing to remit to the Insured money collected from customers. The court held that an audit report which determined the amount of the Insured's loss by totaling individual cleaning charges shown on computer cards for which a check of the clothing on the racks revealed there was no item of clothing with the corresponding number, did not constitute proof of loss by inventory computation within the meaning of that term as used in the exclusion. *Chenoweth-Chapman Corp. v. Am. Ins. Co.*, 553 S.W.2d 872.

Mo. 1968. The court held that the inventory exclusion, which provided that it should not apply to loss which Insured could prove through evidence wholly apart from such computation was ambiguous and thus could not be construed to exclude Insurer's liability to Insured who could prove amount of loss only by resort to inventory computation or profit and loss computation. *Meyer Ins. Co. v. General Ins. Co. of Am.*, 422 S.W.2d 617.

N.J. 1967. The court relied upon public policy rationale to support coverage despite the use of inventory computations. The court held that denial of right to adduce proof of inventory records as either the only available proof of the full amount of loss or as corroboration sufficient to make a case where independent proof existed, would defeat justice by precluding recovery on a meritorious claim by use of the only proof reasonably available to the Insured. "So to do would contravene public policy, not only in defeating the reasonable expectations of coverage of the purchaser of the insurance but also in allowing a private agreement to nullify the inherently probative effect of relevant evidence." *Hoboken Camera Center, Inc. v. Hartford Acc. & Indem. Co.*, 226 A.2d 439.

N.Y. App. 1983. The court affirmed judgment for the Insured, allowing use of inventory computations as corroborative evidence in case addressing the 1977 form policy exclusion. The theft of cable products by warehouse manager was sufficiently illustrated by testimony of company secretary and inventory records to avoid summary judgment under the inventory exclusion. "'[I]nventory computation' is to be construed to proscribe proof of the fact or amount of loss through a generalized estimate, calculated, for example, from sales records and average markup, of what the dollar value of inventory on hand should be. It does not, however, preclude proof of the fact or amount of loss through inventory records (whether perpetual or periodically made) detailing the actual physical count of individually identifiable units such as are described in the . . . affidavits." *Ace Wire & Cable Co., Inc. v. Aetna Cas. & Sur. Co.*, 454 N.Y.S.2d 897 (N.Y. 1982), *aff'd*, 457 N.E.2d 761.

Tenn. App. 2005. The court held that an inventory exclusion clause in an all-risk insurance policy was limited to cases in which the Insured sought to establish a loss only by comparing inventory calculations. Genuine issues of material fact existed as to whether Insured had evidence besides inventory calculations to establish the inventory loss, which precluded summary judgment on issue of whether coverage for the loss was barred by inventory exclusion clauses in the all-risk policies. This decision contains a lengthy discussion of inventory loss exclusion cases. *HCA, Inc. v. Am. Protection Ins. Co.*, 174 S.W.3d 184.

Wash. App. 1990. Meat tallow producer paid for supplies based on a yield formula for the final product. When the quality of the raw materials deteriorated, an employee was blackmailed into falsifying records. The appellate court held that, although one method of proof (the inventory records) involved an inventory computation, three other proof methods allowed the Insured to get around the inventory exclusion clause, namely: (1) yields of subsequent deliveries, (2) yield test on last load of supplies, and (3) amount paid versus amount received from all suppliers in 1981. The appellate court affirmed the jury verdict of damages, saying that the terms "fraud and dishonesty," "intent" and "result directly" were properly defined; damages were not too uncertain; and attorney fees were properly denied. It appears that the trial court let the inventory records go into evidence. The court held, though, that the quantum of other evidence was such that this would not work a reversal. *Hanson PLC v. Nat'l Union Fire Ins. Co. of Pittsburgh, Pa.* 894 P.2d 66.

Wis. 1963. Action in which a franchised automobile dealer sought to recover for stolen parts and accessories under a blanket crime policy. Insured's evidence included signed confessions by one employee and admissions by several other persons allegedly purchasing the stolen goods from that employee. A trial court awarded the Insured only $246 out of a total claimed loss of over $14,000. On appeal, the court acknowledged that inventory computations which had been excluded by the trial court should have been admitted to aid in the establishment of the total loss. The court affirmed the $246 verdict, however, holding that even if the computations were admitted, the loss remained so speculative as to eliminate the larger claim from jury consideration. *Tri-Motors Sales, Inc. v. Travelers Indem. Co.*, 119 N.W.2d 327.

C. Conclusive Proof Standard

1. Commercial Crime Policies

None.

2. Other Policy or Bond Forms

Ariz. App. 1977. The appellate court granted a new trial based on the fact that mismanagement by a feedlot manager could constitute dishonesty within the meaning of the fidelity policy in effect. In so doing, the court also determined that after a prima facie showing through means other than inventory computations or profit and loss computations has been made, either of those otherwise prohibited methods may be used to show the extent of the loss. This was under the old clause. *J. R. Norton Co. v. Fireman's Fund Ins. Co.*, 569 P.2d 857.

Mo. App. 1977. The trial court judgment, which awarded the Insured $7,659.47, was affirmed. The Insured supplied sufficient evidence to evade application of the inventory loss exclusion clause by showing that an audit had been performed which was admissible as a business record.

The audit compared IBM cards against clothing on the dry cleaner's racks to determine that cash was being received by employees and the cash was not being turned over to the business. This was under the old clause. *Chenoweth-Chapman Corp. v. Am. Ins. Co.*, 553 S.W.2d 872.

N.Y. App. 1983. The Insurer appealed from denial of summary judgment at trial court. The Insureds were entitled to present evidence at trial that may avoid the inventory exclusion clause. It is not clear whether this case is under the new clause or the old clause. *Schenectady Hardware & Elec. Co. v. Hartford Acc. & Indem. Co.*, 464 N.Y.S. 2d 50.

D. Client's Property

1. Commercial Crime Policies

D.N.J. 2009. The trial court granted the Insurer's motion to dismiss a claim brought by the Insured's client. Because the policy covered the loss of property belonging to a client of the Insured, the client argued it had standing to sue the Insurer directly. The trial court disagreed, relying on the policy language stating that the insurance was only for the Insured's benefit and conferred no rights or benefits on others. The trial court similarly rejected, again relying on the same policy language, the client's contention that a settlement agreement with the Insured conferred standing upon the client. *Carteret Ventures, LLC v. Liberty Mutual Insurance Co.,* 2009 WL 3230844.

D. Wash. 2013. The policy, which related to a Section 1031 exchange, provided for coverage for direct losses to the Insured's property and excluded losses suffered by the Insured's clients; however the policy was procured in accordance with a Washington statute requiring $1 million of protection for the benefit of the Insured's clients as part of Section 1031 exchanges. The client made a claim after the Insured's employee stole the client's money. The Insurer moved for summary judgment on the client's breach of contract, estoppel, and bad faith allegations and the trial court granted the motion. In so ruling, the court relied upon the exclusion for coverage related to the client's property and held that neither a state statute, nor an estoppel theory, could expand the reach of coverage beyond the policy terms. *Muse Apartments, LLC v. Travelers Cas. and Surety Co. of America,* 2013 WL 6062340.

2. Cases from Other Policies

6th Cir. 2012 (Ohio). Loss of Insured's clients' money through theft, where the Insured contracted with the clients to manage the clients' investment accounts, was covered. Summary judgment in favor of the Insured was affirmed. The policy requirement that the property be owned and held in such a manner that the Insured be responsible for the loss was satisfied based on the written agreement between the Insured and the client. *First Defiance Financial Corp. v. Progressive Casualty Ins. Co.,* 688 F.3d 265.

SECONDARY SOURCES

Annotation, *Construction and effect of clause in fidelity bond or insurance policy excluding from coverage losses proved by 'inventory computation' or 'profit and loss computation,'* 45 A.L.R.4th 1049 (1986).

Carleton Burch, Dee M. Studler & Amy L. White, *The Inventory and Profit and Loss Computation Exclusion,* Vol. XV The Fidelity Law Journal (2009).

Chelberg, *The Inventory Computation Exclusion—The Latest View,* 15 THE FORUM 930 (Summer 1980).

Commercial Crime Policy, CR 00 23 08 13 (ISO Props., Inc. 2012) (Discovery) & Commercial Crime Policy, CR 00 21 08 13 (ISO Props., Inc. 2012) (Loss Sustained).

Crime Protection Policy, SP 00 01 04 12 (Sur. Ass'n of Am. 2012).

Cushman, *An Up-To-Date Look at the Inventory Computation Exclusion in Fid. Ins. Policies,* 39 INS. COUNSEL J. 64 (1972).

Employee Dishonesty Coverage Form (Form A, Blanket), CR 00 01 10 90 (Sur. Ass'n of Am. 1997), *reprinted in* COMMERCIAL CRIME POLICY 725 (Randall I. Marmor & John J. Tomaine eds., 2d ed. 2005).

Ronald G. Mund & D.M. Studler, *The Inventory Computation & Profit & Loss Exclusion: Separating the Wheat from the Chaff*, VII FID. L.J. 7 (2001).

Chapter 11

Exclusions Other Than Inventory Loss*

Exclusions further define and reinforce which risks and losses commercial crime insurance does not cover. Where judicial decisions or insured interpretations of an insuring agreement differ from that of the underwriter, exclusions often serve to clarify the underwriter's intent. For this reason, exclusions not only play a critical role in defining the coverage afforded by commercial crime insurance, but they also often reflect more recent trends in coverage litigation. This chapter provides annotations to the exclusions other than the inventory loss exclusions found in the Insurance Services Office's Commercial Crime Policy, Form Nos. 00 22 08 13 (Discovery Form) and 00 23 08 13 (Loss Sustained Form) (collectively, "Commercial Crime Policy") and the Surety & Fidelity Association of America's Crime Protection Policy, Form No. SP 00 01 04 12 ("Crime Protection Policy").

A. Acts Committed By You, Your Partners Or Your Members

1. This Policy does not cover:
   a. **Acts Committed By You, Your Partners Or Your Members**
      Loss resulting from "theft" or any other dishonest act committed by:
      (1) You; or
      (2) Any of your partners or "members";
      whether acting alone or in collusion with other persons.

(Commercial Crime Policy)

---

* By Samuel J. Arena, Jr., Stradley Ronon Stevens & Young, LLP, Philadelphia, Pennsylvania, and A. Nicole Stover, Stradley Ronon Stevens & Young, LLP, Cherry Hill, New Jersey.

We will not pay for loss as specified below:
1. **Acts Committed by You or Your Partners**
   Loss resulting from any dishonest act committed by you or any of your partners whether acting alone or in collusion with other persons.

(Crime Protection Policy)

COMMENT

Commercial crime insurance provides coverage for loss from employee dishonesty and fraudulent acts of third parties. Acts committed by the insured or one of the insured's partners or members are not acts of an employee or a third party and, therefore, do not fall within the scope of the intended coverage. This exclusion expresses that intent by excluding acts committed by the insured or any of the insured's partners or members regardless of whether they are acting alone or in collusion with others. This exclusion works in conjunction with the policy definition of "you" and "your," referring to the Named Insured shown in the policy declarations.

OUTLINE OF ANNOTATIONS

A. Cases Decided Under Commercial Crime Policies
B. Cases Decided Under Other Policies or Bonds

ANNOTATIONS

A. Cases Decided Under Commercial Crime Policies

M.D. Pa. 2011. In coverage action arising from insurer's denial of coverage because theft was committed by a former member of the insured, insured sought discovery from former member. Former member disputed insurer's right to discovery, citing his Fifth Amendment right against self-incrimination. The court recognized that the privilege could limit discovery, but ordered former member to submit to the court a particularized explanation of the basis for claiming the privilege and the facts giving rise to a reasonable apprehension of self-incrimination. Former member was also directed to submit responsive documents for *in camera* review. *G & V Farms, LLC v. Hartford Fire Ins. Co.*, No. 1:09-CV-13242011, 2011 WL 4565632, at *1.

B. Cases Decided Under Other Policies or Bonds

1st Cir. 1993 (Mass.). Plaintiff was the general partner of fifteen limited partnerships owning housing projects subsidized by HUD. The partnerships entered into management agreements with two site management companies to assist in operating the housing projects. After Plaintiff learned that the president of the management companies was making improper payments from project funds and terminated the management agreements, Plaintiff filed suit against the management companies' fidelity insurer seeking to collect as a third-party beneficiary of the policies. Plaintiff then obtained an assignment of all the right, title and interest of the management companies' in the policies and amended the complaint to assert a direct breach of contract claim. The insurer moved for summary judgment on the ground that the dishonest acts giving rise to the claim were not committed by an employee of the insureds, but instead were committed by their "alter ego," and the trial court agreed. On appeal, the court found that the president of the management companies was not an "employee" because he was not subject to governance and direction by the companies. He was the dominant shareholder, who effectively ran the companies, and no formal directors' meetings were ever held. *Bird v. Centennial Ins. Co.*, 11 F.3d 228.

W.D. Mo. 2010. President and partial owner of insured used insured's operating account to transfer trust funds into his personal account. The crime policy excluded loss resulting from dishonest acts of any Officer-Shareholder "whether acting alone or in collusion with others." The insured admitted that the president was an "Officer-Shareholder" but argued that another employee assisted in concealing the transactions and therefore the exclusion did not apply. The court held that the exclusion did apply because the Officer-Shareholder participated in the entire theft and that collusion with other employees was expressly contemplated as resulting in application of the exclusion. *Tactical Stop-Loss LLC v. Travelers Cas. & Surety Co. of Am.*, No. 08-0962, 2010 WL 2802203.

S.D. Ohio 2005. A financial brokerage company sought coverage under its fidelity bond following embezzlement by individual who served as president, sole shareholder, and primary director of insured. The court held that the individual so controlled the company that he could not be considered a covered "employee" under the policy and highlighted that the bond contained an exclusion specifically disclaiming coverage for the dishonest acts of the named insured. The court also rejected the insured's contention that, by charging an additional premium to insure the individual as an at-risk employee, the insurer was estopped from denying coverage. The court found that the additional premium did not evidence the insurer's intent to cover the individual because the insurer also charged an additional premium for seven other employees of the company who posed a greater risk of loss because of the positions they held. *Lutz v. St. Paul Fire & Marine Ins. Co.*, No. 1:03-cv-750, 2005 WL 2372871, at *6.

W.D. Wash. 2012. A money-lending business wired $200,000 to an escrow service company in connection with a real estate transaction that would render the money-lending business the senior lienholder on a residential property. When it was discovered that the representative of the escrow service company failed to transfer the escrow funds as directed, the representative forged cancelled checks purporting to show payment of the escrow funds. The escrow company's fidelity insurer denied coverage on several grounds, including based on the exclusion for acts committed by "you" or "your partners." The court rejected this contention because, as a limited liability company, the escrow company only had "members" and not "partners," concluding that if the insurer wished to exclude acts of members of a limited liability company from coverage, "it was obligated to either do so expressly or to define 'partner' in a way that includes limited liability company members." *Ritchie v. Capitol Indemnity Corp.*, No. C11-1903RAJ, 2012 WL 3126809, at *7.

SECONDARY SOURCES

Samuel J. Arena, Jr., Daniel T. Fitch, Jeffrey S. Price & Justin D. Wear, *Key Exclusions*, in 10 NEW APPLEMAN ON INSURANCE 133.06(5) (2014).

Matt J. Farley, Richard E. Baudouin, and Rebecca B. Farina, *Ch. XI, Exclusions in the Commercial Crime Policy, in* COMMERCIAL CRIME INSURANCE COVERAGE 427, 459-462 (Randall I. Marmor and Susan Koehler Sullivan, eds., Am. Bar Ass'n 2015) [hereinafter COMMERCIAL CRIME INSURANCE COVERAGE].

Howard Marks, *The "Other" Exclusions of Commercial Blanket Bonds and Dishonesty Policies* (unpublished paper presented at Nat'l Inst. Fid. Bonds, Fid. & Sur. Law Comm., ABA, New York, N.Y., Nov. 1991).

Jeffrey M. Paskert, P. Keith Lichtman & Dolores A. Parr, *Ch. III, Who Is An "Employee"?, in* COMMERCIAL CRIME INSURANCE COVERAGE 135, 169-176.

B. Acts Committed By Your Employees Learned Of By You Prior To The Policy Period

    1.   **This Policy does not cover:**
        b.   **Acts Committed By Your Employees Learned Of By You Prior To The Policy Period**
            Loss caused by an "employee" if the "employee" had also committed "theft" or any other dishonest act prior to the effective date of this Policy and you or any of your partners, "members", "managers", officers, directors or trustees, not in collusion with the "employee", learned of such "theft" or dishonest act prior to the Policy Period shown in the Declarations.

(Commercial Crime Policy)

We will not pay for loss as specified below:

1.   **Under Insuring Agreement 1**
     Employee Canceled Under Prior Insurance
     Loss caused by any employee of yours, or predecessor
     in interest of yours, for whom similar prior insurance
     has been cancelled and not reinstated since the last such
     cancellation.

(Crime Protection Policy)

COMMENT

Where an insured chooses to continue to employ a dishonest employee, the insured has assumed the risk of loss arising from future actions by the employee and should not be permitted to pass that risk to the insurer. Where the theft or dishonest act was learned of prior to the Policy Period, the policy has never incepted as to that employee. Depending on the specific facts and circumstances, Commercial Crime Policy Condition 1.d (Concealment, Misrepresentation Or Fraud), Condition 1.g (Duties In The Event of Loss), and Condition 2.a. (Termination As To Any Employee) and Crime Protection Policy Condition E.3 (Concealment, Misrepresentation Or Fraud), Condition E.7 (Duties in the Event of Loss), and Condition 1 (Cancellation as to Any Employee), discussed in other chapters of this book, may also be implicated in the coverage analysis.

OUTLINE OF ANNOTATIONS

A.   Cases Decided Under Commercial Crime Policies
B.   Cases Decided Under Other Policies or Bonds

ANNOTATIONS

A.   Cases Decided Under Commercial Crime Policies

E.D. Ky. 2014. Employee of insured wholesale company admitted to owner of company in 2010 that he had collected payments from customers and failed to remit them to the company. Due to his friendship with the company's owner, the employee was not terminated from employment and was allowed to repay the funds. No report was made to the company's then-current insurer. Thereafter, plaintiff Westfield Insurance Company issued a commercial crime policy to the company effective April 1, 2012. The employee's actions from 2010 were not disclosed during underwriting. When the employee was discovered perpetrating the same exact scheme in November 2012, the company reported the claimed loss arising from the 2012 actions to Westfield and initially did not disclose that the employee had engaged in the same scheme two years prior. The court held that the claim for the 2012 scheme was excluded from coverage as a result of the company's prior knowledge of the 2010 scheme. The court rejected the company's attempt to argue that the 2010 scheme did not constitute a "theft," and held that, regardless, the 2010 scheme constituted a "dishonest act" subject to the same exclusion. *Westfield Ins. Co. v. Jackson Wholesale Co.*, No. 5:13-135, 2014 WL 104081, at *1-3.

W.D. Mich. 2011. Company officer's admission that he knew that employees used funds from the sale of vehicles to pay past due bills and of other improprieties before the policy period began required exclusion of claim from coverage, even if insured could otherwise bring the claim within the scope of coverage by demonstrating an "occurrence" of "employee theft" during the policy period. *Coopersville Motors, Inc. v. Federated Mutual Ins. Co.*, 771 F. Supp. 2d 796, 801.

N.D. Miss. 2006. Insured knew of employee's prior dishonest acts occurring twenty years prior to acts giving rise to claimed loss. When insurer denied coverage based on the knowledge of prior dishonesty, the insured contended that she was unaware of the exclusion because her agent never provided her the policy. In denying the insurer's motion for summary judgment, the court found that disputed issues of material fact precluded summary judgment. *Hodges v. Employers Mutual Cas. Co.*, No. 1:05CV161-D-A, 2006 WL 2033887.

B. Cases Decided Under Other Policies or Bonds

D.N.J. 1993. A manufacturing company had substantial information regarding an employee's dishonesty prior to inception of the policy. While the application for insurance was pending, the manufacturer had two undercover operatives watch the employee in the warehouse to determine the extent of his dishonesty. The court held that such information was sufficient to trigger the policy's exclusion providing that "[t]he coverage of Insuring Agreement I shall not apply to any Employee from and after the time that the Insured or any partner or officer thereof not in collusion with such Employee shall have knowledge or information that such Employee has committed any fraudulent or dishonest act in the service of the Insured or otherwise, whether such act be committed before or after the date of employment by the Insured." The court further held that "[t]he policy provision in question should be enforced for the additional reason that it simply embodies the equitable concept that it is unfair to impose upon an insurer the risk of loss from an employee whom the employer knows or has ample reason to suspect is dishonest, but continues to employ." *Cooper Sportswear Manufacturing Co. v. Hartford Cas. Ins. Co.*, 818 F. Supp. 721.

N.Y. App. Div. 2012. Senior Vice President forged insured bank President's name resulting in the approval of loans that were never repaid. Prior to the inception of the Financial Institution Bond, the President had discovered that the Senior Vice President had forged his signature on prior loan extensions that did not result in a loss to the bank. The bank contended that, because the prior dishonest acts did not result in a loss, they were not excluded by the policy. In rejecting this contention, the court held that loss is not an element of a dishonest or fraudulent act and that the Senior Vice President's forgeries established a pattern of dishonest behavior. *Capital Bank & Trust Co. v. Gulf Ins. Co.*, 937 N.Y.S.2d 463.

SECONDARY SOURCES

Farley et al., *Ch. XI, Exclusions in the Commercial Crime Policy, in* COMMERCIAL CRIME INSURANCE COVERAGE 427, 474-75.

C. Acts Committed By Your Employees, Managers, Directors, Trustees Or Representatives

    1.   This Policy does not cover:
        c.   Acts Committed By Your Employees, Managers, Directors, Trustees Or Representatives
            Loss resulting from "theft" or any other dishonest act committed by any of your "employees", "managers", directors, trustees or authorized representatives:
            (1)   Whether acting alone or in collusion with other persons; or
            (2)   While performing services for you or otherwise;
            except when covered under Insuring Agreement A.1.

(Commercial Crime Policy)

We will not pay for loss as specified below:
2.   Acts of Employees, Directors, Trustees or Representatives
We will not pay for loss resulting from any dishonest act committed by any of your employees, directors, trustees or authorized representatives:
a.   Acting alone or in collusion with other persons; or
b.   While performing services for you or otherwise;
except when covered under Insuring Agreement 1.

(Crime Protection Policy)

COMMENT

With the exception of the employee theft insuring agreement (Insuring Agreement A.1 of the Commercial Crime Policy or Insuring Agreement 1 of the Crime Protection Policy), none of the crime insuring agreements are intended to cover theft or other dishonest acts committed by the named insured's employees, managers, directors, trustees, or authorized representatives. This exclusion serves the public policy of placing the risk of choosing dishonest managers, directors, trustees or authorized representatives upon the insured. Insurers cannot underwrite risks which they cannot evaluate, and the insured is in the best position to determine the fidelity of its employees, managers, directors, trustees, or authorized representatives. This exclusion eliminates the unknown risk posed by such individuals within the insured's control and applies (1) whenever such individuals were acting alone or in collusion with other persons, and (2) while such persons are performing services for the named insured or otherwise.

OUTLINE OF ANNOTATIONS

A. Cases Decided Under Commercial Crime Policies
B. Cases Decided Under Other Policies or Bonds

ANNOTATIONS

A. Cases Decided Under Commercial Crime Policies

1st Cir. 1998 (Mass.). Insured sought coverage under commercial crime policy for losses resulting from tax service wrongfully diverting money, intended to pay insured's payroll taxes, for personal use. The insurer denied the claim on the ground that the policy's authorized representative exclusion barred recovery for theft perpetrated by the tax service's executives. The insured argued that the exclusion did not apply because the tax service executives diverted funds for their personal gain and not for the benefit of the company. The court found that the authorized representative exclusion in the policy was not ambiguous and barred recovery by the insured. The court interpreted "authorized representative" to mean "a person or company empowered to act on an entity's behalf," and found that the tax service satisfied this definition. The court also rejected the insured's argument that the exclusion did not apply because the wrong was perpetrated for the personal benefit of the wrongdoers, finding that the tax service could only act through its officers and employees, and that the grant of authority to the executives of the tax service enabled their diversion of funds. *Stop & Shop Co. v. Fed. Ins. Co.,* 136 F.3d 71.

9th Cir. 1999 (Cal.). Insured hospital incurred a loss caused by the dishonesty of several employees, including the president and sole shareholder of hospital's tax service provider. Hospital sought coverage under a commercial crime policy to recover for the loss. The Ninth Circuit reversed the trial court's grant of summary judgment in favor of the hospital, finding that the tax service was the hospital's "authorized representative," and that the policy excluded coverage for loss due to "theft or any other fraudulent, dishonest, or criminal act ... by any employee, director, trustee or authorized representative of the insured whether acting alone or in collusion with others." The court found that the hospital had authorized the tax service to act as its representative before tax authorities. The hospital also designated the tax service as its representative on forms submitted with the Internal Revenue Service. The court also found that employees of the tax service also were "authorized representatives" within the meaning of the exclusion because the tax service was merely an instrumentality through which its director served his own personal interests. *Stanford Univ. Hosp. v. Fed. Ins. Co.*, 174 F.3d 1077.

C.D. Cal. 2014. Payroll processer diverted funds from the insured's bank account that the processor was supposed to use to pay the insured's payroll taxes. The insured sought coverage for computer fraud. The court held that the claim was excluded because the payroll processor was the insured's authorized representative because the processor was authorized by the insured to have access to the insured's account. The court rejected the insured's argument that, because the processor never intended to apply the funds as directed, the agreement authorizing the processor to act on the insured's behalf was void *ab initio*, and, instead, held that the fraud in the inducement rendered the agreement voidable, not void. The insured intended to authorize the processor to act on its behalf and to hold otherwise "would render the authorized representative exclusion a nullity." *Southern California Counseling Ctr. v. Great Am. Ins. Co.*, No. 13-5468.

D. Kan. 1995. Insured subsidiary and parent corporations brought suit against insurer to recover under commercial crime policy for dishonest acts of parent corporation's president in appropriating money for his personal use. The insurer argued that the president was not an "employee" of the subsidiary as defined in the policy. The court noted that in order to show that the president was a covered employee, it must prove he was in the services of the subsidiary, the subsidiary compensated him directly by salary, wages or commissions, and subsidiary had right to direct and control president. The court found that the president was not an "employee" of the subsidiary because he was not compensated directly by the subsidiary but rather by the parent company, and that the phrase "compensated directly" was not ambiguous. *T.S.I. Holdings, Inc. v. Buckingham,* 885 F. Supp. 1457.

D. Mass. 1995. The Kendall Company ("Kendall") hired Hamilton Taft to provide payroll tax services. Hamilton Taft was responsible for depositing federal, state and local withholding tax payments for Kendall. Hamilton Taft paid any tax obligations out of funds deposited in its bank account pursuant to electronic automated clearinghouse transfers. Hamilton Taft's chief executive officer ("CEO") fraudulently induced Kendall to contract with Hamilton Taft as part of a fraudulent scheme, orchestrated by the CEO and other Hamilton Taft employees, to divert Kendall's tax payments. For two years, Hamilton Taft failed to pay Kendall's tax obligations, and instead diverted Kendall's funds to pay tax payments for other companies controlled by Hamilton Taft's CEO or for her own personal benefit. Hamilton Taft eventually declared bankruptcy, leaving approximately $85 million in unpaid taxes for its clients. Hamilton Taft's CEO and president were indicted by a federal grand jury for devising a scheme to defraud corporations by means of false and fraudulent pretenses. Kendall claimed coverage for its losses under a blanket crime insurance policy and argued that the term "authorized representative" was ambiguous. Kendall contended that the term related only "to someone with actual representational responsibilities ... and would not apply under the terms of the blanket crime policy to a tax paying service[.]" The insurer argued that Kendall's losses were caused by the criminal act of an "authorized representative" and were not covered by the policy. The court determined that, as a matter of law, the term "authorized representative" was not ambiguous because it was not susceptible to more than one construction. The court found that Kendall's losses were not covered by operation of the "authorized representative" exclusion. *The Kendall Co. v. Nat'l Union Ins. Co. of Pittsburgh, Pa.,* Civ. A. No. 93-10501-PBS (Unreported Memorandum and Order on Motion for Judgment on the Pleadings).

D.N.J. 2008. Car dealership employee embezzled funds by issuing checks from the dealer to cover customers' payments on installment sales, exchanging the checks for blank money orders, and then converting the money orders. The car dealership had to repurchase the loans from the lender after it was discovered the employee falsified credit information of borrowers. The insurer prevailed on summary judgment for several reasons. First, the conversion of the blank money orders was a single occurrence and subject to the policy's limit of insurance, as the single cause of the loss was the employee's embezzlement. Second, the falsifying of credit information was not an employee theft, and the policy excluded loss caused by employee dishonesty unless covered under the employee theft insuring agreement. Third, the policy had a Truth in Lending insuring agreement, but such coverage was excluded for the insured's dishonest or fraudulent acts. *Pine Belt Auto., Inc. v. Royal Indemnity Co.*, No. 06-5995, 2008 WL 4682582, *aff'd*, 400 F. App'x. 621 (3d Cir. 2008).

D.N.J. 1977. Bank sought recovery under Bankers Blanket Bond and employee dishonesty bond to recover losses incurred when two employees, one a director and the other a member of the board of directors, made fraudulent loans in excess of bank's lending limits. The member of board of directors was also a partner in a law firm providing counsel for the bank in connection with the loans. The surety argued that the acts of the board member were not covered because, *inter alia*, acts committed by a director were excluded by operation of the bond provision excluding losses "resulting wholly or partly from the wrongful act or default of any of the directors of the Insured who are not employed by the insured at a salary." The court held that the board member had been engaged to perform legal services for the bank and was an "employee" within the meaning of the bond. The court also found that the exception in the directors exclusion applied, which provided coverage for each director who "handles or has charge or custody of money, securities or other valuable property of the Insured or of its customers." *Midland Bank & Trust Co. v. Fid. & Dep. Co. of Md.*, 442 F. Supp. 960.

S.D. Ohio 2007. Payroll tax service filed false tax returns on behalf of insured and retained the excess payroll paid to it by the insured. Upon discovery by the Internal Revenue Service, the insured was required to

ANNOTATED COMMERCIAL CRIME INSURANCE POLICY

pay the underpayment, plus interest. The court denied coverage for employee dishonesty because the payroll service was not an employee. The court denied coverage under the Money and Securities coverage because it excluded dishonest acts of the insured or its "authorized representative," and the court held that the payroll tax service was an authorized representative. The court did find partial coverage under an employee benefits liability section of the policy. *Florists' Mut. Ins. Co. v. Ludy Greenhouse Mfg. Corp.*, 521 F. Supp. 2d 661.

W.D. Pa. 2014. Employee of insured became an independent contractor of insured pursuant to an addendum to an employment agreement. The insured sought coverage under its employee dishonesty insuring agreement for the former employee's failure to make payments owed to the insured pursuant to the addendum. The court granted the insurer's motion for summary judgment, holding that the individual was not an "employee" based on the addendum's designation of the individual as an independent contractor and regulations of the Internal Revenue Service regarding independent contractor status. *Management Recruiters of Pittsburgh-North, Inc. v. Travelers Indemnity Co. of America,* No. 13-201, 2014 WL 201070.

E.D. Pa. 1998. Insured temporary agency filed suit against insurer under commercial crime policy, alleging that an employee caused insured to enter into contracts with companies owned by Timothy Kraft to outsource employees to insured. As a result, insured was required to place the outsourced employees upon its payroll, pay taxes and insurance premiums, and assume workers compensation liability for the outsourced employees. Nevertheless, the employees continued to provide services to their companies after they were outsourced to insured. The insurer moved for partial summary judgment, arguing that Kraft was not an "employee" of insured within terms of policy. The court found that in order for Kraft to be an employee of insured, he had to be in the insured's services and insured must have the right to direct and control him. The court determined that at no time was Kraft in insured's services or subject to its control, and thus was not an employee as defined by the policy. *Omne Serv. Group, Inc. v. Hartford Ins. Co.,* 2 F. Supp. 2d 714.

S.D.N.Y. 1994. Colson, which acted as a collection and payment agent for various entities, sued its insurer seeking coverage under a commercial crime policy for losses caused by the actions of the National Bank of

Washington ("NBW"). NBW maintained the funds collected by Colson in an account, and was authorized to make conservative overnight investments with the collected funds. NBW made unauthorized purchases of commercial paper issued by its corporate parent, which subsequently defaulted on its commercial paper obligations. The insurer argued that Colson's losses were not covered by operation of the "authorized representative" exclusion in the policy. Colson claimed that NBW was not its authorized representative. The court determined that the exclusion applied as a bar to coverage because the losses resulted from the acts of an "authorized representative." *Colson Servs. Corp. v. Ins. Co. of N. Am.*, 874 F. Supp. 65.

W.D. Wash. 2005. Insured filed suit against its insurer to recover under commercial crime policy for losses sustained when an employee and his friend stole money from one of its stores. The insurer denied the claim on the ground that, among other things, it was barred by the "Employee Theft Exclusion" excluding any loss resulting from a theft or dishonest act committed by an employee, except when covered under Insuring Agreement A.1. The court agreed that this exclusion clearly barred coverage under Insuring Agreement A.3 because the thief was an employee of the insured. The court also considered whether there was coverage under Insuring Agreement A.1. Insuring Agreement A.1 required an interpretation of Condition E(1)(a), which bars coverage for any employee "discovered" to have committed theft or any other dishonest act before or after becoming employed by the insured. The court found that the word "discovery" was ambiguous, and therefore determined that Condition E(1)(a) did not apply because it was not clear the insured "discovered" the employee's prior conviction for grand theft auto. *Akins Foods, Inc. v. Am. & Foreign Ins. Co.*, No. C04-2195JLR, 2005 WL 2090678.

Kan. Ct. App. 2003. The City of Concordia brought an action to recover under a commercial crime policy when the city manager misused the proceeds of a loan from the city. The policy included an exclusion for any "loss caused by any 'employee' required by law to be individually bonded." The main issue before the court was whether the exclusion applied to the position of city manager, who, according to statute and city code, must give a bond for the faithful performance of his or her duties. The city claimed the exclusion was ambiguous because the policy did not define the phrase "individually bonded" and that the phrase was subject to multiple meanings. The court agreed that the provision was ambiguous and construed the ambiguity against the insurer, finding that the exclusion did not apply. *City of Concordia v. Am. States Ins.*, No. 89, 200, 2003 WL 21948009.

Wis. Ct. App. 2008. An independent adjuster hired by the insured submitted false ledgers showing workers compensation payments purportedly made from a disbursement account on behalf of the insured but issued checks to payees to whom the insured was not indebted. The checks were signed in the adjuster's own name. The insured claimed under the forgery and alteration coverage, but the ledgers were not "Covered Instruments," and the checks were not altered. The insured also claimed under the computer fraud coverage, based on the use of a computer to generate the false ledgers. The court declined to address whether the claim fell within the computer fraud coverage and instead determined that the claim was excluded because the adjuster was an authorized representative of the insured. In rejecting the insured's argument that the adjuster was not authorized to steal, the court determined that to so hold would render the exclusion meaningless, as no representative would ever be authorized to steal. The court also affirmed summary judgment for the second insurer under a second policy, because the checks signed by the adjuster to actual payees were genuine instruments, not forgeries. *Milwaukee Area Technical College v. Frontier Adjusters of Milwaukee*, 752 N.W. 2d 396, 402.

B. Cases Decided Under Other Policies Or Bonds

4th Cir. 1970 (Md.). The insured's losses arose from the defalcations of two individuals who served as directors of the insured from time to time. The insurer argued that the two individuals acted in the complained-of transactions as directors of the insured. The court reasoned that the acts of directors who were salaried employees of the insured, like the two individuals at issue, rendered them more like corporate officers than directors. Thus, the "directors" exclusion did not apply to preclude coverage. *Phoenix Sav. & Loan, Inc. v. Aetna Cas. & Sur. Co.*, 427 F.2d 862.

4th Cir. 1965 (S.C.). The insured misrepresented financial statements to deceive the insurance commissioner of the bank, which was considering the grant of a loan to the insured. The stockholders, who owned 75% of the insured's stock, were effectively the sole stockholders and the only directors of the closely held insured. The bond was intended to protect the corporation from the fraud or dishonesty of employees, not to protect its creditors from the fraud or dishonesty of the stockholders and directors. Here, the individuals were not "Employees" of the corporation, and, therefore, the exclusion was inapplicable. *Kerr v. Aetna Cas. & Sur. Co.*, 350 F.2d 146.

5th Cir. 1976 (Tex.). The insured suffered losses when purchasers of controlling stock in the insured's parent company manipulated the stocks and assets of the insured. The court found that the "director" exclusion covers the unfaithful activity that breaches the confidence of an insured in regular officials who serve as its directors, but it does not include the acts of outside directors not in the service of the insured. *First Nat'l Life Ins. Co. v. Fid. & Dep. Co. of Md.*, 525 F.2d 966.

5th Cir. 1970 (Tex.). Insured bank sought recovery under Bankers Blanket Bonds and an excess bank employee dishonesty bond, alleging it sustained losses when the bank purchased certain real estate notes in violation of the National Banking Act. The insured bank was controlled by two men who installed their agent as both the bank's president and chairman of the board. At the instruction of the two men, the president and chairman of the board purchased the notes in violation of law. The insurer argued that the acts of the president were within the bond's exclusion for acts of a director. The court construed the exclusion as not covering losses resulting from an act of a director of the insured unless the director is "employed as a salaried, pensioned or elected official of an Employee of the Insured." The exclusion contained an exception, however, if the director was performing acts within the scope of the usual duties of an employee, as distinguished from general, "directorial acts" on behalf of the insured. The court found that the president and chairman of the board was acting in an "officer-like" capacity in purchasing the notes, and found that an officer is an "employee" covered by the bond. The court therefore concluded that the exclusion did not apply. *FDIC v. Aetna Cas. & Sur. Co.*, 426 F.2d 729.

6th Cir. 1992 (Ky.). The insured sustained losses when a member of the insured's board of directors caused the insured to become insolvent by purposefully making poor recommendations for out-of-territory loans. The court noted that the insured's control over the director was insufficient to establish that the director was an employee. No evidence showed that any officer or supervisory agent of the insured gave instructions, directions, or supervision to the director regarding the performance of his duties, thereby leaving the reasonable conclusion that he was an independent contractor. Thus, the "director" exclusion was inapplicable. *Bank of Cumberland v. Aetna Cas. & Sur. Co.*, 956 F.2d 595.

7th Cir. 2009 (Ill.). Bank employees unknowingly cashed customer's bad checks. The insurer argued that the bank's losses were caused by its employees' failure to follow bank policy in accepting customer checks and, therefore, the Financial Institution Bond's Loss Caused by Employee exclusion should apply. The court disagreed, holding that such an "expansive interpretation of Exclusion (h) would swallow all—or nearly all—of the bond's coverage because a bank must necessarily operate through its employee." *First State Bank of Monticello v. Ohio Cas. Inc. Co.*, 555 F.3d 564.

7th Cir. 2007 (Wisc.). An insured bank sought coverage under a Bankers' Blanket Bond for losses it sustained when it relied upon forged automobile leases submitted by a car dealer, a bank customer. The car dealer's president submitted leases to the bank to obtain funds to purchase cars. The car dealership then leased the cars to customers. The car dealer's president began submitting forged leases to the bank for transactions that did not actually exist and for which the bank nonetheless provided funds to the car dealership. The insurer denied coverage for a number of reasons, including the existence of an exclusion for "loss caused by an Employee . . . ." The insurer argued that the bank's own employees caused the loss by failing to investigate the car dealership and to verify the legitimacy of the leases. The court rejected the insurer's argument, finding that, under the insurer's interpretation, there would never be coverage for forged documents because "bank employees are intermediaries in every forgery-related bank loss." *First Nat'l Bank in Manitowoc v. Cincinnati Ins. Co.*, 485 F.3d 971.

8th Cir. 1994 (Mo.). The insured bank sustained losses from cashing customer's checks and checks drawn by the customer's employees to third parties. The customer's employees signed the checks with the names of other persons and presented the checks with forged endorsements. The insured's employees never enforced the bank's policy of requiring endorsement by the presenter of third-party checks. The customer declared bankruptcy and sued the bank for the wrongful check-cashing transactions. The Eighth Circuit concluded that the "Employee" exclusion applied because the insured's losses resulted directly from the acts of the employees of the insured. Thus, the "Employee" exclusion precluded coverage under the bond. *Empire Bank v. Fid. Dep. Co. of Md.*, 27 F.3d 333.

C.D. Cal. 2012. Insured advanced funds for customers that either had not opened accounts or had not purchased the services attributed to them reflected in false financing documents submitted by insured's dealer. The policy excluded loss due to forgery "committed by any authorized representative of the Insured," unless an employee acted in collusion with the authorized representative. The court held that the loss was excluded because the terms of the agreements between the insured and the dealer indicated the dealer was an authorized representative. The court rejected the insured's contentions that the exclusion could only apply where the authorized representative has authority over the insured's funds or is the authorized representative of each insured sustaining the loss, or where the loss occurred within the scope of the representative's authority or was caused by the grant of that authority. The court held that the exclusion was not so limited. *Kubota Credit Corp., USA v. Fed. Ins. Co.*, No. 10-2521, 2012 WL 12033876.

N.D. Cal. 2004. Bank filed suit against its insurer to recover under Financial Institution Bond for losses resulting from theft of currency by owner of automated teller machines and armored car service that delivered cash from bank to automated teller machines. The court analyzed whether to apply an exclusion for losses "resulting directly or indirectly from the complete or partial nonpayment of or default upon any loan, or any transaction in the nature of a loan . . . or extensions of credit." The analysis turned on whether the thief was an "employee" of the insured bank. The bank argued that the thief was an "electronic data processor . . . of accounting records" for the bank because it was required to send to the bank an inventory summary every time it replenished the automated teller machines with cash. The court rejected this argument because the thief did not "process" data, but rather merely recorded balances of particular machines on a form provided to the bank. *Humboldt Bank v. Gulf Ins. Co.*, 323 F. Supp. 2d 1027.

N.D. Ga. 2013. Real estate developer forged a sales contract that resulted in insured bank issuing a loan to developer where part of the purported collateral was actually the bank's own loan proceeds. The bank's settlement attorney, who was an employee of the bank, falsified settlement statements and disbursed funds in violation of the insured bank's policies and closing instructions. The court held that the settlement attorney "caused" the loss and therefore fell within the exclusion applicable to "loss caused by an Employee." The court held the causation language to be ambiguous and that it only excludes coverage "if an employee acts with knowledge of or intent to further a forgery or intentionally disregards relevant bank policies." Nevertheless, the settlement attorney's actions met this heightened standard because the attorney intentionally disregarded the bank's policies by falsifying the settlement statements and improperly disbursing funds. *FDIC v. Cincinnati Ins. Co.*, 981 F. Supp. 2d 1324.

E.D. La. 2007. Employees of insured bank participated in a fraudulent mortgage scheme. The Financial Institution Bond excluded loss caused by an Employee except when covered under Insuring Agreement (A). Because the bank alleged that the two employees caused the loss, the exclusion applied and barred the Insuring Agreement (D)(2) and fraudulent mortgages coverage claims. Issues of fact precluded summary judgment on the Insuring Agreement (A) claim. *First Guaranty Bank v. BancInsure, Inc.*, No. 06-3497, 2007 WL 1232212.

D. Minn. 2014. Insured bank's employees accessed e-mail and Facebook on the bank's computers and would leave security tokens in USB ports to allow one employee to enter information on behalf of another employee. The employees introduced the Zeus virus by clicking on a link in an e-mail and their actions had allowed criminals to access the bank information needed to initiate wire transfers. The insurer denied coverage under the Financial Institution Bond on several bases, including the exclusion for "loss resulting directly or indirectly from theft of confidential information" because the employee's passwords and pass phrases were confidential and were used to make the wire transfers and "loss caused by a director or Employee of the Insured or by a person in collusion with any director or Employee of the Insured . . . except when loss is caused by an Employee and covered under Insuring Agreement (L) or (M)." The court applied Minnesota's concurrent causation doctrine: "When there are multiple causes of an insured's loss, one of which is a 'covered peril' and the other of which is an 'excluded peril,' Minnesota's concurrent causation doctrine provides that the availability of coverage or the applicability of the exclusion depends on which peril was the 'overriding cause' of the loss." The court found that, but for the hacker's fraudulent conduct, the funds would not have been transferred and that "neither the employees' violations of policies and practices (no matter how numerous), the taking of confidential passwords, nor the failure to update the computer's antivirus software was the efficient and proximate cause of Plaintiff's loss." The court rejected the insurer's arguments that the employee exclusion does not require that the employee's conduct be the only cause of the loss in order for the exclusion to apply; that the concurrent causation doctrine cannot apply in the context of the theft of confidential information or mechanical failure or gradual deterioration exclusions because those exclusions include losses "indirectly" caused by those perils; and that no Minnesota court had applied the concurrent causation doctrine to a Financial Institution Bond, and that other courts have declined to do so. *State Bank of Bellingham v. BancInsure, Inc.*, No. 13-0900, 2014 WL 4829184.

S.D. Miss. 2012. Bank's vice president forged signatures, made unauthorized withdrawals, and released collateral. The court determined that fidelity bond exclusion unambiguously excluded coverage for loss caused by an employee unless the loss is caused by the "misplacement, mysterious unexplainable disappearance or destruction of or damage to Property." *BancInsure v. Peoples Bank of the South*, 866 F. Supp. 2d 577.

W.D. Mo. 1993. The employee exclusion was applicable because the insured's losses were caused by the insured's employee's failure to comply with the insured's own internal policies and procedures. *Empire Bank v. Fid. & Dep. Co. of Md.*, 828 F. Supp. 675.

S.D.N.Y. 1984. A federally chartered credit union filed suit against insurer to recover under a Credit Union Discovery Bond following failure of bank which had issued insured certificates of deposit. The insured invested in the certificates of deposit based upon information received from an investment consulting firm. The insured alleged that the bank and consulting firm were "employees" of insured, that the loss was due to the fraud and misrepresentation of those "employees" and that the bond therefore provided coverage. The insurer moved for summary judgment and argued, among other things, that neither the bank nor the consulting firm was an "employee." The court agreed, finding that neither the bank nor the consulting firm received any wage, salary or commission from the insured, and that credit union did not submit any proof establishing an "employee" relationship. *IBM Poughkeepsie v. Cumis Ins. Soc'y,* 590 F. Supp. 769.

W.D. Pa. 2010. Insured added exclusion to policy for loss caused by "anyone authorized to sign checks for UBICS" after a loss in 2008. Insured's controller embezzled funds from the insured. Controller also was the employee who applied for the policy in 2008 and was authorized to sign checks. The insurer argued that the authorized signatory exclusion barred the claim and that the controller's knowledge should be imputed to the insured under the fraud, concealment, and misrepresentation condition. The insured counterclaimed for breach of contract, breach of the implied covenant of good faith and fair dealing, and punitive damages under Pennsylvania's insurance bad faith statute. In denying the insurer's motion to dismiss, the court held that the insured could plead alternative claims, although acknowledging that the contractual bad faith claim and breach of contract claim would merge. *One Beacon America Ins. Co. v. UBICS, Inc.,* No. 10-737, 2010 WL 5441677.

S.D. W. Va. 1969. Plaintiff, a wholesaler, discovered a shortage of certain products in one of its wholesale outlets. Following an audit, which revealed a loss of inventory, and an investigation by the state police department, plaintiff learned that seven men, three of whom were plaintiff's employees, had stolen the missing merchandise. Plaintiff sought coverage for its losses under a Comprehensive Business Policy, which insured plaintiff against loss of property except for losses caused by the dishonest or criminal act of any employee. Plaintiff argued that the exclusion only barred coverage for losses sustained by an insured when the loss was caused by an employee during working hours, and, because the missing merchandise was taken from plaintiff's property after business hours, the exclusion was inapplicable to plaintiff's losses. The court determined that the exclusion language precluding coverage for losses caused by "any employee while working or otherwise" encompassed the acts of plaintiff's employees. Thus, the court found that the exclusion barred any coverage for plaintiff's losses. *Sehon, Stevenson & Co., Inc. v. Buckeye Union Ins. Co.*, 298 F. Supp. 1168.

Kan. 1989. A director caused the insured bank to sustain losses when he fraudulently obtained several loans and deposited insufficient funds checks in substantial amounts with the insured. The court held that the "director" was an "employee" only for acts committed while he acted as a member of a committee of the insured, not merely because he was a member of a committee. *First Hays Banshares, Inc. v. Kansas Bankers Sur. Co.*, 769 P.2d 1184.

Minn. 1976. The court held that the insured's losses arising from allegedly fraudulent acts of the bank were not covered under the bond. The directors of the bank knew of the transactions at issue. The acts of the directors constituted the acts of the bank. The court concluded that because the bond was not intended to insure the bank against the acts taken by its directors, there was no coverage for the claimed losses under the bond. *Farmers Merch. State Bank of Pierz v. St. Paul Fire & Marine Ins. Co.*, 242 N.W.2d 840.

N.J. Super. Ct. App. Div. 2015. Former technician's assistant of insured pharmacy facilitated after-hours robbery of store by providing a security code and duplicate keys to robbers. The insurer paid the limit under the employee dishonesty coverage, but it denied liability under other coverages based on the exclusion for dishonest acts of employees. The court held the exclusion unambiguous and rejected the pharmacy's argument that the technician's assistant did not meet the definition of "employee" under the exclusion because she worked as a part-time, hourly employee and because she was not on duty at the time of the robbery. The court held that the exclusion does not apply only to an employee who commits dishonest acts during working hours and found that the employee used her knowledge as an employee to facilitate the crime. *Union Hill Supremo Pharmacy v. Franklin Mut. Ins. Co.*, No. 705-13, 2015 WL 893260.

N.Y. App. Div. 2015. Insured claimed loss resulting from Bernard Madoff Ponzi scheme and sought coverage under a rider to Financial Institution Bond for "Loss resulting directly from the dishonest acts of any Outside Investment Advisor, named in the Schedule below, solely for their duties as an Outside Investment Advisor," which scheduled Madoff as an Outside Investment Advisor. The court held that the rider did not cover the claimed loss because Madoff did not act "solely" as an Outside Investment Advisor, but also as a securities broker. The court also held that the exclusion for "dishonest acts of any securities . . . broker, agent or other representative of the same general character" excluded coverage, as the exclusion required only the individual to be a securities broker and did not require the individual to be acting as a broker in causing the loss. *Jacobson Family Inv., Inc. v. Nat'l Union Fire Ins. Co. of Pittsburgh, PA*, No. 601325, 2015 WL 3767850.

Wash. Ct. App. 1982. Bank's director was also a director of an insurance brokerage firm. The director implemented a program for insurance premium financing, which the director operated, under which the bank would loan money to the director's clients for their insurance premiums. An auditor hired by the bank discovered that many of the premium financing loans were fraudulent. The bank filed a proof of loss under two fidelity policies for losses resulting from the fraudulent scheme. The insurer contended that the director was not an "employee" of the bank, thereby barring coverage, and that the director did not perform acts within the scope of the usual duties of an "employee." The court found that coverage under the bond was not simply limited to acts by "employees" because such an interpretation would ignore the "director's exclusionary clause" in the policy. The court also found that the director was performing acts within the scope of the usual duties of an employee, which include holding loan collateral and interacting with bank borrowers in matters relating to their loans. *Puget Sound Nat'l Bank v. St. Paul Fire & Marine Ins. Co.*, 645 P.2d 1122.

SECONDARY SOURCES

Samuel J. Arena, Jr., Daniel T. Fitch, Jeffrey S. Price & Justin D. Wear, *Key Exclusions*, *in* 10 NEW APPLEMAN ON INSURANCE 133.06(2) (Michael Keeley et al. eds., 2014).

Bradford R. Carver, *The Authorized Representative Exclusion: Placing the Risk Where it Ought to Be* (unpublished paper presented at Annual Meeting of the Nat'l Bond Claim Ass'n, Oct. 3-4, 1996).

Farley et al., *Ch. XI, Exclusions In the Commercial Crime Policy*, *in* COMMERCIAL CRIME INSURANCE COVERAGE 427, 462-67.

Cole S. Kain, *Alter Ego Defense*, VII FID. L.J. 217 (2001).

David K. Kerr, *The Potential Income and Principal Other Exclusions*, *in* FINANCIAL INSTITUTION BONDS 221 (Duncan L. Clore ed., 1995).

Howard Marks, *The "Other" Exclusions of Commercial Blanket Bonds and Dishonesty Policies* (unpublished paper presented at Nat'l Inst. Fid. Bonds, Fid. & Sur. Law Comm., ABA, New York, N.Y., Nov. 1991).

Toni Scott Reed, *Ch. II, What Is Employee Dishonesty and Employee Theft?*, *in* COMMERCIAL CRIME INSURANCE COVERAGE 39, 107-109.

Scott L. Schmookler, *Ch. VII, Computer and Funds Transfer Fraud*, *in* COMMERCIAL CRIME INSURANCE COVERAGE 297, 317-320.

D. Confidential Or Personal Information

1.   **This Policy does not cover:**
   d.   **Confidential Or Personal Information**
   Loss resulting from:
   (1)   **The disclosure of your or another person's or organization's confidential or personal information   including, but not limited to, patents, trade secrets, processing methods, customer lists, financial information, credit**

**card information, health information or any
other type of nonpublic information; or**

**(2)   The use of another person's or
organization's confidential or personal
information including, but not limited to,
patents, trade secrets, processing methods,
customer lists, financial information, credit
card information, health information or any
other type of nonpublic information.**

(Commercial Crime Policy)

We will not pay for loss as specified below:
9.   Confidential Information
**Loss resulting from the theft, disappearance,
destruction or disclosure of confidential information
including, but not limited to, trade secrets, personal
information, customer lists and intellectual property.
For purposes of Insuring Agreement 5, confidential
information cannot itself be the other property
transferred, but a loss otherwise covered under
Insuring Agreement 5 shall not be excluded by the fact
that confidential information was used to gain access to
your computer system or to the computer system of
your financial institution, in order to cause the
fraudulent transfer.**

(Crime Protection Policy)

COMMENT

Loss resulting from the use or disclosure of confidential or personal
information is excluded from commercial crime insurance. As hacking
activities and data breaches have become more prevalent, this exclusion
may increasingly be implicated.

OUTLINE OF ANNOTATIONS

A. Cases Decided Under Commercial Crime Policies
B. Cases Decided Under Other Policies or Bonds

ANNOTATIONS

A. Cases Decided Under Commercial Crime Policies

6th Cir. 2012 (Ohio). Hackers infiltrated a retailer's network and downloaded customer credit card and checking account information. The store incurred liability for credit card charge backs, investigations by state and federal agencies, card reissuance, fines by credit card associations, and other customer-related public relations expenses. The insured filed a claim under the computer fraud endorsement to its crime policy. The endorsement excluded coverage for "any loss of proprietary information, Trade Secrets, Confidential Processing Methods, or other confidential information of any kind." The court refused to apply the exclusion. Applying the interpretive doctrine of *ejusdem generis* (the general term takes the meaning of the specific terms), the court found that the terms "Trade Secrets" and "Confidential Processing Methods" were limited to information about the insured's business and, thus, "other confidential information" refers to information belonging to the insured and not to customers' credit card information. *Retail Ventures, Inc. v. Nat'l Union Fire Ins. Co.*, 691 F.3d 821.

B. Cases Decided Under Other Policies Or Bonds

D. Minn. 2014. Insured bank's employees accessed e-mail and Facebook on the bank's computers and would leave security tokens in USB ports to allow one employee to enter information on behalf of another employee. The employees introduced the Zeus virus by clicking on a link in an e-mail and their actions had allowed criminals to access the bank information needed to initiate wire transfers. The insurer denied coverage under the Financial Institution Bond on several bases, including the exclusion for "loss resulting directly or indirectly from theft of confidential information" because the employee's passwords and pass phrases were confidential and were used to make the wire transfers and "loss caused by a director or Employee of the Insured or by a person in collusion with any director or Employee of the Insured . . . except when loss is caused by an Employee and covered under Insuring Agreement (L) or (M)." The court applied Minnesota's concurrent causation doctrine: "When there are multiple causes of an insured's loss, one of which is a 'covered peril' and the other of which is an 'excluded peril,' Minnesota's concurrent causation doctrine provides that the availability of coverage or the applicability of the exclusion depends on which peril was the 'overriding cause' of the loss." The court found that, but for the hacker's fraudulent conduct, the funds would not have been transferred and that "neither the employees' violations of policies and practices (no matter how numerous), the taking of confidential passwords, nor the failure to update the computer's antivirus software was the efficient and proximate cause of Plaintiff's loss." The court rejected the insurer's arguments that the employee exclusion does not require that the employee's conduct be the only cause of the loss in order for the exclusion to apply; that the concurrent causation doctrine cannot apply in the context of the theft of confidential information or mechanical failure or gradual deterioration exclusions because those exclusions include losses "indirectly" caused by those perils; and that no Minnesota court had applied the concurrent causation doctrine to a Financial Institution Bond, and that other courts have declined to do so. *State Bank of Bellingham v. BancInsure, Inc.*, No. 13-0900, 2014 WL 4829184.

Minn. Ct. App. 2004. The insured filed suit seeking coverage under excess crime loss policies for amounts paid to defend and settle previous litigation that arose when the employees of the insured wrongfully stole and used the proprietary agricultural products of competing companies. The policies followed the form of the underlying policy, which included an exclusion for "loss resulting directly or indirectly from the accessing of any confidential information, including, but not limited to, trade secret information, computer programs, confidential processing methods or other confidential information of any kind." The court determined that it was "undisputed that proprietary germplasm and seed lines are intellectual property and are protected trade secrets." The court rejected the insured's contention that the term "accessing" was ambiguous as used in the policy. The insured argued that the term referred only to computer files and not to the use of germplasm, in part because the insured's counsel and other employees regularly used the verb "access" to refer to the process of extracting the genetic information contained in germplasm for the purpose of incorporating the information into its breeding programs. *Cargill, Inc. v. Nat'l Union Fire Ins. Co. of Pittsburgh,* No. A03-187, 2004 WL 51671.

SECONDARY SOURCES

Farley et al., *Ch. XI, Exclusions in the Commercial Crime Policy, in* COMMERCIAL CRIME INSURANCE COVERAGE 427, 472-74.

Arthur N. Lambert et al., *Analysis of the "Computer Fraud" Insuring Agreement in the Commercial Crime Policy, in* 10 NEW APPLEMAN ON INSURANCE 125.01 (Michael Keeley et al. eds., 2014).

Toni Scott Reed, *Cybercrime: Losses, Claims, and Potential Insurance Coverage for the Technology Hazards of the Twenty-First Century,* 20 FIDELITY L.J. 55, 103-104 (2014).

E. Data Security Breach

1.   **This Policy does not cover:**
   e.   **Data Security Breach**
         Fees, costs, fines, penalties and other expenses incurred by you which are related to the access to or disclosure of another person's or organization's confidential or personal information including, but not limited to, patents, trade secrets, processing methods, customer lists, financial information, credit card information, health information or any other type of nonpublic information.

(Commercial Crime Policy)

We will not pay for loss as specified below:
9.   **Data Breach Costs**
      Expenses related to your obligations to comply with federal and state privacy laws and Payment Card Industry Data Security Standards (if applicable) arising

from a data security breach, including, but not limited to, expenses related to notifying affected individuals when the affected individuals' personally identifiable financial or medical information was stolen, accessed, downloaded, or misappropriated while in your care, custody or control, forensic audit expenses and fines and penalties.

(Crime Protection Policy)

COMMENT

This exclusion affirms that the insurer has no obligation to indemnify the insured for "expenses" such as fees, costs, fines or penalties related to the access to or disclosure of another person's or organization's confidential or personal information, including those resulting from a data security breach.

OUTLINE OF ANNOTATIONS

A. Cases Decided Under Commercial Crime Policies
B. Cases Decided Under Other Policies or Bonds

ANNOTATIONS

A. Cases Decided Under Commercial Crime Policies

NONE

B. Cases Decided Under Other Policies Or Bonds

NONE

SECONDARY SOURCES

Toni Scott Reed, *Cybercrime: Losses, Claims, and Potential Insurance Coverage for the Technology Hazards of the Twenty-First Century*, 20 FIDELITY L.J. 55, 103-104 (2014).

F. Governmental Action

1. **This Policy does not cover:**
   f. **Governmental Action**
   Loss resulting from seizure or destruction of property by order of governmental authority.

(Commercial Crime Policy)

We will not pay for loss as specified below:
4. **Governmental Action**
   Loss resulting from seizure or destruction of property by order of governmental authority.

(Crime Protection Policy)

COMMENT

As other commentators have noted, because commercial crime insurance's purpose is to protect against losses arising from the dishonest acts of employees and certain specified fraudulent acts of others, it is not readily apparent how an exclusion which provides that the policy does not apply to loss resulting from seizure or destruction of property by order of government authority might come into play in the context of an actual crime policy claim. This exclusion, like the nuclear power and war exclusions, exists to expressly exclude from coverage catastrophic events that are beyond coverage by the insurance industry. Most likely, this exclusion is a carryover from casualty insurance policies and included in the policy out of an abundance of caution.

OUTLINE OF ANNOTATIONS

A. Cases Decided Under Commercial Crime Policies
B. Cases Decided Under Other Policies or Bonds

ANNOTATIONS

A. Cases Decided Under Commercial Crime Policies

NONE

B. Cases Decided Under Other Policies Or Bonds

D. Colo. 2010. Sherriff's seizure of property pursuant to a writ of attachment on behalf of a private creditor fell within commercial property policy exclusion for losses due to seizure or destruction or property by government authority, despite insured's contention that seizure was in interest of a private creditor, not government. *Bigsky LLC v. Hartford Cas. Co.*, No 09-00893, 2010 WL 3075575.

E.D. Pa. 2010. In order for governmental acts exclusion in commercial property policy to apply, the government order must have been lawful, and authorities must have acted within the bounds of the governmental order. Thus, the exclusion did not apply to loss resulting from unlawfully executed police search. It was not bad faith for insurer to deny coverage in reliance on insured's representation that warrant was facially valid without first obtaining copy of warrant. *Kao v. Markel Ins. Co.*, 708 F. Supp. 2d 472.

Ill. App. Ct. 2011. Exclusion in fire insurance policy for loss resulting from seizure or destruction of property by order of governmental authority was clear and unambiguous, despite insured's contention that "governmental authority" was an ambiguous term. Loss resulting from search warrant ordered by judge was excluded from policy. *Pierce Food Serv. Equip. Co. v. Am. Econ. Ins. Co.*, No. 2-11-0333, 2011 WL 10457851.

Mich. Ct. App. 2013. The State Department of Agriculture ordered a recall of cheese product after it tested positive for listeria. The insured cheese manufacturer claimed loss relating to the seizure of non-contaminated cheese under its commercial property coverage. The loss resulted from the seizure or destruction of property by order of a governmental authority and therefore was excluded from coverage. *Torres Hillsdale Country Cheese v. Auto Owners Ass'n*, No. 308824, 2013 WL 5450284.

SECONDARY SOURCES

Farley et al., *Ch. XI, Exclusions in the Commercial Crime Policy, in* COMMERCIAL CRIME INSURANCE COVERAGE 427, 457-59.

G. Indirect Loss

1.   **This Policy does not cover:**
   g.   **Indirect Loss**
        Loss that is an indirect result of an "occurrence" covered by this Policy including, but not limited to, loss resulting from:
        (1)   Your inability to realize income that you would have realized had there been no loss of or damage to "money", "securities" or "other property";
        (2)   Payment of damages of any type for which you are legally liable. But, we will pay compensatory damages arising directly from a loss covered under this Policy; or
        (3)   Payment of costs, fees or other expenses you incur in establishing either the existence or the amount of loss under this Policy.

(Commercial Crime Policy)

We will not pay for loss as specified below:
5.   Indirect Loss

Loss that is an indirect result of an act or occurrence covered by this Policy including, but not limited to, loss resulting from:

a. **Your inability to realize income that you would have realized had there been no loss;**

b. **Payment of damages of any type for which you are legally liable unless you establish that the act or acts that gave rise to the damages involved conduct which caused a covered loss of money, securities or other property which was in your custody and control and for which you were responsible prior to the loss; or**

c. **Payment of costs, fees or other expenses you incur in establishing either the existence of the amount of loss under this insurance.**

(Crime Protection Policy)

COMMENT

This exclusion reinforces the language of the various insuring agreements that coverage is provided only for certain loss to the insured resulting "directly" from the specified causes. As one court has stated, this exclusion "reinforces the conclusion that the policy meant to insure . . . only against immediate harm from employee dishonesty but not for any obligations [the insured] might have to others as a result of that dishonesty." *Fireman's Fund Ins. Co. v. Special Olympics Int'l, Inc.*, 249 F. Supp. 2d 19 (D. Mass. 2003), *aff'd*, 346 F.3d 259 (5th Cir. 2003). This exclusion affirms that the policy only provides coverage for direct, out-of-pocket losses.

The indirect loss exclusion brings within its scope not only the three types of excluded indirect loss set forth in its subparagraphs (potential income, damages of any type for which the insured is legally liable and costs in establishing loss), but also "[l]oss that is an indirect result of any act or 'occurrence' covered by the policy."

OUTLINE OF ANNOTATIONS

ANNOTATIONS

A. Potential Income

1. Cases Decided Under Commercial Crime Policies

7th Cir. 1987 (Ill.). The insured brought an action under a comprehensive crime insurance policy for alleged loss of income as a result of an employee's leak of trade secrets to a competitor. The insured argued that the trade secret should be treated like property and that the lost income from the theft of the trade secret was the "actual liquidated value" of the stolen trade secret. The court held that loss of income suffered by the insured was loss of potential income rather than loss analogous to theft of property and, as such, was expressly excluded from coverage by the potential income exclusion. *U. S. Gypsum Co. v. Ins. Co. of N. Am.*, 813 F.2d 856.

C.D. Cal. 2014. Pest control company outsourced payroll function, only to later discover that payroll taxes were not paid to government, but instead were diverted to payroll company's own creditors. The pest control company sought coverage under the funds transfer fraud and computer fraud insuring agreements for claimed losses, including loss of business profits, loss of future earnings, loss of investment opportunities, out of pocket damages, and interest on loans, all of which the company contended resulted from the insurer's failure to pay the initial claimed loss for the unpaid paid payroll taxes. The court held that, even if there were coverage under the policy, all such claimed losses were indirect losses excluded as potential income. *Pestmaster Servs., Inc. v. Travelers Cas. & Sur. Co. of Am.*, No. 13-5039, 2014 WL 3844627.

2. Cases Decided Under Other Policies or Bonds

4th Cir. 1987 (N.C.). A bank brought an action for declaratory judgment regarding its right to recover under a Bankers Blanket Bond amounts lost through an employee's fraudulent loan scheme. The bank employee made loans to fictitious persons and deposited the loan proceeds into checking accounts the employee established under the corresponding fictitious names. When those loans became due, the employee either renewed the loan or created another fictitious loan and applied the proceeds to pay the loans. The surety claimed that interest repaid on the earlier loans should be subtracted from loss as potential income because that money represented a return on the bank's own money. The surety relied upon the exclusion in the bond for "potential income, including but not limited to interest and dividends, not realized by the Insured." The court held that the exclusion did not apply and that the insurer was liable for all of the outstanding principal balance of the notes, including interest. The court reasoned that, because the funds were "realized" when they reentered the bank as payment of the initial loans, the potential income exclusion did not apply. The exclusion did apply, however, to interest which had accrued but which had not yet been paid. *St. Paul Fire & Marine Ins. Co. v. Branch Bank & Trust,* 834 F.2d 416.

5th Cir. 1987 (La.). The insured under a Comprehensive Dishonesty, Disappearance and Destruction Policy sought recovery of lost profits sustained when two employees surreptitiously submitted a bid on behalf of their individual companies deliberately underbidding their employer. The employees were awarded a five-year contract as a result. The court held that the potential income exclusion excluded coverage for loss of future profits or future income flow resulting from fraudulent or dishonest acts of employees. The court reversed and remanded on the issue of whether other losses allegedly sustained by the employees, including travel expenses, salaries, telephone services and secretarial assistance, were also excluded under the policy. *Diversified Group, Inc. v. Van Tassel*, 806 F.2d 1275.

8th Cir. 1990 (Iowa). A bank brought an action against an insurer under the bank's fidelity bond where insurer denied coverage under the bond for bank losses resulting from fraudulent loan and commodity/cattle schemes involving two bank clients. False financial statements, falsified loan documents and elaborate withdrawal methods were used to conceal the nature of the transactions. Although the court held that the bank sustained losses under the bond when loan proceeds were transferred to third parties, the court also held that the future interest claimed by the insured was excluded by the potential income exclusion. The court held that, although the bank restructured the loan debt, sustaining a loss of future interest, the payments were not yet due and, therefore, not realized, falling squarely within the potential income exclusion. The court further held that the potential income exclusion is not ambiguous with regard to the treatment of future interest and, therefore, the court construed the provision according to its plain meaning. The bank also reached settlements with the two customers to avoid potentially large compensatory and punitive damage awards, and incurred attorneys' fees and costs incurred in negotiating the settlements. The court held that the bond provided coverage for the bank's settlement costs and stated that "a settlement precipitated by claims of fraud or dishonesty and paid to a third party by the insured is a covered loss." The court also found that the bond permitted the recovery of attorneys' fees and costs due to the bond provision allowing such recovery if expended in defending "any suit or legal proceeding." The court found that the attorneys' fees provision was not limited to formally commenced lawsuits, but also applied to settlement negotiations prior to any formal complaint. *First Am. State Bank v. Cont'l Ins. Co.*, 897 F.2d 319.

D. Kan. 1990. Insured sought coverage under fidelity policy for the value of oil taken by the dishonest acts of an employee. The court denied the insured's motion for summary judgment on the ground that the claim was barred by the potential income exclusion in the policy. In analyzing the exclusion, the court stated that every commercial asset represents "potential income" in the sense that "if it has value, it can be sold." The court rejected such an expansive interpretation, however, finding that the exclusion draws a line between the asset lost and the income that might be made using the asset, as in interest and dividends. The court concluded that the lost oil was not in the nature of interest and dividends, and thus the potential income exclusion did not apply. *Koch Indus., Inc. v. Nat'l Union Fire Ins. Co. of Pittsburgh, Pa.*, No. 89-1158-K, 1990 WL 20021.

E.D. La. 1994. After a finding of coverage under a Bankers Blanket Bond, a question arose concerning how recoveries by the insured of both principal and interest losses were to be applied. The parties questioned whether the recoveries obtained by the insured must be applied first to principal on the underlying loans to offset the surety's liability under the bond or whether they should be applied to accrued interest not covered under the bond. The court held that the potential income exclusion was not determinative of the manner in which recovery should be applied. The sureties were not bound to pay the insured for loss of income that was earned but not received. The court concluded that the funds actually collected and received by the insured on the underlying loans could not be used to offset an uncovered loss of accrued interest. The court further held that, even if the potential income exclusion had some bearing on the question of how to apply recoveries, the exclusion would not apply to the funds recovered by the insured because such income is both accrued and received, or "realized." *First Nat'l Bank of Louisville v. Lustig*, 847 F. Supp. 1322.

D. Minn. 1990. Bank brought action against surety under Bankers Blanket Bond to recover losses arising out of the dishonest and fraudulent conduct of three former employees in diverting bank funds for the benefit of third parties and implementing devices to conceal their actions. In its motion for summary judgment, the surety argued, *inter alia*, that the bond did not cover the bank's claims for the loss of accrued and capitalized interest, citing to the bond's exclusion of "potential income, including but not limited to interest and dividends, not realized by the insured." The insurer argued that the term "realized" meant "to convert into money." The bank argued that many banks rely upon the accrual basis of accounting, and that, under this practice, the term "realized" may mean the recognition of revenue by a seller of goods or services. The court denied the insurer's motion, finding the exclusion to be ambiguous and better left to the jury for interpretation. *Mid-Am. Bank v. Am. Cas. Co. of Reading, Pa.*, 745 F. Supp. 1480.

D.N.J. 1990. A savings and loan association brought an action seeking a declaratory judgment that the surety was obligated to indemnify it under savings and loan blanket bond and for bad faith damages. The insured argued that it was entitled to recover costs, prejudgment interest and attorneys' fees after the court held in its favor. The surety argued that prejudgment interest was excluded by an exclusion for "potential income, including but not limited to interest and dividends, not realized by the insured." The court found a distinction between interest that accrues, or could have been earned, between the time that a loss is suffered and a claim is paid, and the interest that accrues between the time that a claim is wrongfully denied and recovery is had under the contract. The court held that the purpose of the exclusionary section was to limit the bounds of insurance coverage as opposed to limiting the insurer's liability in the event of a lawsuit. The court, therefore, held that the insured was entitled to an award of prejudgment interest, not under the bond, but under the general principles regarding the award of prejudgment interest. *Oritani Sav. & Loan Ass'n v. Dep. Co. of Md.,* 744 F. Supp. 1311.

M.D. Tenn. 1982. The employee of a bank established 161 fictitious installment loans in a scheme to embezzle funds from the bank. Each loan included unearned interest and a $25 loan origination fee. The majority of the claim was settled, but the parties submitted the issue of the loan origination fee to the court for determination. Judgment was entered for the insured because the bond did not include a potential income exclusion. In reaching this decision, the court stated: "In the case of a blanket fidelity bond with a clause excluding potential income, the underwriter stands in the shoes of the unfaithful employee and a recovery is limited to the amount that went into his hands. However, without the exclusion of potential income, the underwriter stands in the shoes of each fictitious borrower at date of discovery. Therefore, recovery is for unpaid principal, accrued interest, and the loan original fee." *U.S. Bank of Sumner Cnty. v. Glens Falls Ins. Co.,* 548 F. Supp. 355.

S.D. W. Va. 1994. A bank brought an action against the surety on a Financial Institution Bond as a result of a former bank officer's embezzlement scheme. The former employee repaid the embezzled amount of money, but not any interest that would have accrued. The bank sought the interest on the amount stolen under the bond for the period between the notice of loss and the receipt of payment from the former employee. The court found that the bank effectively discharged its claim against the surety for interest on the amount repaid by the former employee by accepting settlement on the principal amount of the loss. The court cited state court precedent, *Bennett v. Federal Coal & Coke Co.*, 70 W. Va. 456 (1912), for the proposition that, "where the contract does not so specifically provide for payment of interest, but the right thereto is by an implication, interest is considered as damages, and not as forming the basis of the action, and is recoverable only along with the principal sum and as an incident thereto, and if the principal sum is accepted in settlement the right to damages is lost and no separate subsequent action can be maintained therefore." The court also noted that the policy specifically excluded "interest . . . not realized by the Insured." *Bank One, W. Va. v. USF&G*, 869 F. Supp. 426.

Iowa 1988. A bank brought an action on a Bankers Blanket Bond arising from an employee's embezzlement scheme. The court held that the "loss" under the bond refers to the actual depletion of the bank funds by the employee's dishonesty rather than the face amount of the notes. Thus, the court held that the "loss" does not include that portion of the outstanding notes that represents interest payments made to cover prior embezzlements. *Am. Trust & Sav. Bank v. USF&G*, 418 N.W.2d 853.

Md. 1964. Federal credit union filed suit against its insurer under Credit Union Blanket Bond for interest on the principal sums embezzled by an employee by making loans to fictitious persons and pocketing the proceeds. The court determined that the interest was recoverable because "the deprivation of the amount of the interest due the employer resulted directly, as a natural and continuing sequence, without efficient intervening cause, from the wrongful acts of the employee and so was a 'direct loss of, or damage to' money of the employer," as defined by the bond. *Soc. Sec. Admin., Baltimore Fed. Credit Union v. Emp'r's Mut. Liab. Ins. Co. of Wis.*, 199 A.2d 918.

Mass. App. Ct. 1992. The bank brought an action against its insurer on a Financial Institution Bond arising from losses sustained as a result of manipulation by an employee of a check proofing system. The court upheld the trial court's award of statutory prejudgment interest, finding that the exclusion applies to interest that might have been earned on the stolen money between the time of the theft and presentation to the insurer of a proof of loss. The exclusion does not include the period between the wrongful refusal of an insurer to pay a proper claim and ultimate recovery after litigation. *Cambridge Trust v. Commercial Union Ins. Co.,* 591 N.E.2d 1117.

Ohio Ct. App. 1993. Insured bank brought action against insurer under Financial Institution Bond to recover losses incurred when bank vice president created fictitious loans with his computer and diverted funds from those loans to actual delinquent loan accounts so it would appear that the bank received payments on the delinquent loan accounts. When a customer actually made payments on an account, the vice president diverted the funds to his own account. The bank's proof of loss included accrued interest on fictitious loans, which the insurer denied on the ground that it was "potential income" subject to exclusion. The court agreed with the bank, stating that "[w]hen fictitious loans are created and used to pay old interest on pre-existing loans, the face value of the fictitious loans, plus interest accrued on them, is the amount of loss to the bank. The fact that interest payments on pre-existing loans were made with the funds does not render those interest payments potential income." *First Nat'l Bank of Dillonvale v. Progressive Cas. Ins. Co.,* 640 N.E.2d 1147.

Tenn. Ct. App. 1981. A bank sued a former employee and its fidelity bond insurer to recover for loss of embezzled funds. The bank employee had embezzled funds from the bank over a period of years by forging signatures to interest bearing promissory notes and pocketing the proceeds. When the notes became due, the employee created new notes that he used to pay interest due on old notes, to pay off some notes in full and to obtain additional funds. The insurer conceded coverage for portion of the loss relating to funds retained by the employee, but denied coverage for interest, citing the exclusion. The court agreed that the exclusion applied to interest outstanding on unrepaid funds. The court held that the insured's loss included amounts borrowed by the employee in the form of new notes, the proceeds of which were used to pay off old loans, even though that amount essentially resulted in the payment of interest on the old notes to the bank. In addition, the court upheld the trial court's award of prejudgment interest on common law grounds. *Bank of Huntington v. Smothers,* 626 S.W.2d 267.

SECONDARY SOURCES

Martin J. Andrew, *Potential Income Exclusion* (unpublished paper presented at conference titled "Employee Dishonesty: Claims, Bond Coverages and Caveats," Fid. & Sur. Law. Comm., ABA, Nov. 4-5, 1983).

Samuel J. Arena, Jr., Daniel T. Fitch, Jeffrey S. Price, & Justin D. Wear, *Key Exclusions*, *in* 10 NEW APPLEMAN ON INSURANCE 133.03 (Michael Keeley et al. eds., 2014).

William T. Bogaert & Andrew F. Caplan, *Computing the Amount of Compensable Loss Under the Financial Institution Bond*, 33 TORT & INS. L.J. 807 (1998).

Farley et al., *Ch. XI, Exclusions In the Commercial Crime Policy*, *in* COMMERCIAL CRIME INSURANCE COVERAGE 427, 448-453.

David K. Kerr, *The Potential Income and Principal Other Exclusions*, *in* FINANCIAL INSTITUTION BONDS 224 (Duncan L. Clore ed., 1995).

Jacobsen, *Is Interest Covered by Fidelity and Financial Institution Bonds*, 3 FORUM 278 (1968).

Lentz, *Profit and the Potential Income Exclusion*, 19 FORUM 694 (1984).

Edgar L. Neel, *Financial Institution and Fidelity Coverage for Loan Losses*, 21 TORT & INS. L.J. 590 (1986).

Edgar L. Neel, *The Potential Income Exclusion* (unpublished paper presented at Nat'l Inst. Fid. Bonds, Fid. & Sur. Law Comm., ABA, New York, N.Y., Nov. 1991).

Edgar L. Neel, *The Potential Income Exclusion: Does a Phantom Still Live?*, *in* COMMERCIAL CRIME POLICY 8-1 (Gilbert J. Schroeder ed., 1997).

Patrick M. Pike, *Update on the Loan Loss and Potential Income Exclusions of the Financial Institution Bond* (unpublished paper presented at Annual Meeting of the Sur. Claims Inst., June 21-23, 1989).

Toni Scott Reed, *Ch. II, What Is Employee Dishonesty and Employee Theft?, in* COMMERCIAL CRIME INSURANCE COVERAGE 39, 117-121.

Gilbert J. Schroeder, *The Definition of Dishonesty, the Definition of Discovery, the Potential Income Exclusion and Other Sundry Topics* (unpublished paper presented at Annual Meeting of the Sur. Claims Inst., June 21, 1991).

Weldy, *A Survey of Recent Changes in the Financial Institution Bonds*, 12 FORUM 895 (1976).

Joel T. Wiegart, *Ch. V, Compensability of Third-Party Losses, in* COMMERCIAL CRIME INSURANCE COVERAGE 215, 253-255.

ANNOTATIONS

B. Damages For Which The Insured Is Legally Liable

1. Cases Decided Under Commercial Crime Policies

N.D. Ohio 2014. Employee of insured electrical contractor employee stole funds from a residential housing developer. The insured provided administrative services to the developer, which shared common ownership and facilities with the insured. After the insured contractor reimbursed the developer, the contractor filed a claim under the employee theft insuring agreement of the contractor's commercial crime policy. The court applied a proximate cause standard to determine that the insured had sustained a loss resulting directly from theft. The court then refused to apply the policy's indirect loss exclusion, determining that the exclusion "simply confirms the insurer's obligation to provide coverage for direct losses." *Transtar Elec. v. Charter Oak Fire Ins. Co.*, No. 3:13-1837, 2014 WL 252023.

2. Cases Decided Under Other Policies or Bonds

N.D. Miss. 1984. Plaintiff brought an action against a police officer, the police chief, the city, and its insurer seeking monetary damages for the deprivation of his constitutional rights when he was beaten by the police officer. The insurer issued a faithful performance blanket bond insuring the police department and naming the city as obligee. The insurer filed a motion to dismiss, or in the alternative, for summary judgment, arguing that the bond excluded losses to the insured as a result of damages for which the insured is legally liable as a result of deprivation of constitutional rights or tortious conduct of employees. The court found that the exclusion was not void as against public policy and enforced it as written. The court therefore granted the insurer's motion for summary judgment. *Simons v. City of Columbus,* 593 F. Supp. 876.

Mass. App. Ct. 2005. A secretary for the insured company was asked to keep the books for the insured company as well as a related company. The secretary began writing checks to herself using funds from both the insured company and the related company. The insured filed suit seeking coverage under its employee dishonesty policy, arguing that it was "legally liable" for the related company's funds and, therefore, sought indemnification, not only for the amounts taken from its account, but also for amounts taken from the related company's account. The insurer moved for summary judgment on the ground that the insured did not suffer a direct loss covered by the policy, citing the exclusion for indirect losses, including "payment of damages of any type for which you are legally liable." The insured argued that the phrase "the property covered under this insurance is limited to property: (a) That you own or hold; or (b) For which you are legally liable" in the "covered property" section provided coverage for the property for which the insured was legally liable. The court agreed with the insurer, finding that reimbursement by the insured to a harmed third party is an indirect loss and not a covered direct loss within the meaning of the policy. The court rejected the insured's interpretation because it overlooked the exclusion and would effectively "transform this employee dishonesty fidelity policy into a general liability policy, spreading risk exposure to a class of independent third-party business entities and persons far beyond the single named insured signatory to the policy." *Atlas Metals Prod. Co., Inc. v. Lumberman's Mut. Cas. Co.,* 829 N.E.2d 257.

N.Y. App. Div. 1998. Insurers filed declaratory judgment action to determine coverage owed under stockbroker blanket bonds for losses arising from insider trading schemes. The insurers argued, *inter alia*, that the bonds provided no coverage for insured's settlement of third-party claims. The trial court and the appellate division agreed, finding that such amounts were excluded as indirect or consequential damages under the bonds' exclusion for "damage of any type for which the insured is legally liable, except direct consequential damages." The court determined that the exclusion applied because the loss arose from the settlement with third parties who were the targets of the dishonest employee's acts. The court stated that the fidelity bonds did not cover an employee's dishonest acts toward third parties, absent an intent to cause a loss to the insured. *Aetna Cas. & Sur. Co. v. Kidder, Peabody & Co.,* 676 N.Y.S.2d 559.

N.Y. 1993. Drexel Burnham Lambert Group, the holding company for Drexel Burnham Lambert Inc., commenced a lawsuit seeking coverage for losses sustained through the fraud and dishonesty of Michael Milkin and Dennis Levine against insurers that had issued multiple bankers and brokers blanket bonds. Drexel alleged that by reason of the dishonest activities of these former employees, criminal and civil claims were made against Drexel as a result of which Drexel sustained and continued to sustain losses which were covered under the employee dishonesty coverage provisions of the bonds. The court granted the insurer's motions to dismiss on various grounds, including exclusions for losses resulting from the purchase and sale of securities, exemplary, punitive or consequential damages or consequential loss. The court held, in part, that the blanket bond's exclusion for "consequential damages" was applicable in that the fraud was committed not against Drexel, but against members of the investing public, against companies they manipulated and against federal regulatory agencies. The court held that the bond covered loss to the insured, not losses sustained by the outside world and claims against the insured. *Drexel Burnham Lambert Grp., Inc. v. Vigilant Ins. Co.,* 157 Misc. 2d 198.

D. Utah 2008. Fidelity bond's exclusion for "damages of any type for which the Insured is legally liable, except compensatory damages" does not transform the bond into a liability policy. Insurer had no liability for compensatory damages paid out by the insured based on liability to third parties arising out of a loss covered by the bond. *Direct Mortgage Corp. v. Nat'l Union Fire Ins. Co. of Pittsburgh, PA*, 625 F. Supp. 2d 1171.

SECONDARY SOURCES

David K. Kerr, *The Potential Income and Principal Other Exclusions*, in FINANCIAL INSTITUTION BONDS 224 (Duncan L. Clore ed., 1995).

Farley, et al., *Ch. XI, Exclusions In the Commercial Crime Policy*, in COMMERCIAL CRIME INSURANCE COVERAGE 427, 448-453.

Toni Scott Reed, *Ch. II, What Is Employee Dishonesty and Employee Theft?*, in COMMERCIAL CRIME INSURANCE COVERAGE 39, 117-121.

Joel T. Wiegart, *Ch. V, Compensability of Third-Party Losses*, in COMMERCIAL CRIME INSURANCE COVERAGE 215, 253-255.

ANNOTATIONS

C. Costs Establishing Loss

  1. Cases Decided Under Commercial Crime Policies

  NONE

  2. Cases Decided Under Other Policies or Bonds

S.D. Fla. 1970. Bank filed suit against sureties to recover under Bankers Blanket Bond following bank vice president's dishonest conduct in connection with the issuance of loans. The bank also sought expenses incurred in repossessing, servicing and disposing of vehicles involved in fraudulent loan transactions. The court found that the bond provided coverage for the loss, and also that the insured could recover the costs incurred in repossessing, servicing and disposing of the vehicles. *Miami Nat'l Bank v. Penn. Ins. Co.*, 314 F. Supp. 858.

N.D. Ill. 1992. A bank and a holding company were insureds under a Financial Institution Bond. On an insurer's motion to strike and dismiss portions of the complaint, the court granted the motion in its entirety on the grounds that a claim seeking attorneys' fees and consequential damages for breach of the terms of the bond was excluded from coverage under the bond. The court held that the bond exclusions clearly excluded coverage for attorneys' fees and consequential damages. *Beverly Bancorp., Inc. v. Cont'l Ins. Co.*, No. 92C4823, 1992 WL 345420.

La. Ct. App. 1969. Insured brought suit against insurer to recover under a fidelity bond following a series of thefts of money by an employee. The insured also sought recovery of the amounts it expended in conducting audits to ascertain the loss. The court held that the audit costs were not recoverable because the insured was able to ascertain the total amount of loss through its own records without resort to a special audit, and the insurer should not be required to shoulder the expense of the audit under such circumstances. *Am. Drug Stores, Inc. v. Home Indem. Co.*, 222 So. 2d 512.

N.J. 1963. Borough brought an action against surety to recover for losses sustained when the borough's tax collector, treasurer, and water registrar embezzled money. Borough's claim included losses incurred in reviewing the borough's books and the reconstruction of its records. The surety claimed such losses also served to assist the borough in prosecuting its claim under the bond and, thus, were not recoverable. The court disagreed with the surety and found that because the official mishandled his office such that his successor could not perform unless "the records are cleaned of the resulting taint," the investigation was necessary and not simply part of an expense of litigation to recover under the bond. *Borough of Totowa v. Am. Sur. Co. of N.Y.*, 188 A.2d 586.

N.Y. 1944. An employee falsified the records of a savings and loan association, which the association claimed resulted in the loss of the integrity of its records. The association claimed that the loss could only be repaired by the employment of competent accountants. The association filed suit under a fidelity bond to recover the reasonable value of the accounting services and expenses necessitated by the loss. The surety claimed that insured retained the accountants merely to ascertain the amount of its loss, and that professional services rendered in the enforcement and collection of any claim upon the bond was not a loss covered under the bond. The court found in favor of the association, finding that, because the bond covered "all losses arising from dishonesty, including loss of property," losses other than "property losses" must have been contemplated. The destruction of bank records by destroying their integrity was such a loss. The court concluded that the restoration of the records was not an expense incidental to the enforcement and collection of the association's claim, and that the bond was broad enough to embrace such a loss. *Ninth Fed. Savs. & Loan Ass'n of N.Y.C. v. USF&G*, 50 N.Y.S.2d 372.

Pa. 1956. Insured savings and loan association sought recovery on a fidelity bond for losses incurred when an employee embezzled funds from the association. The insured's claim included amounts incurred in examining and auditing its books following the embezzlement. The court determined that the insured was entitled to recover amounts paid to examiners in auditing its books. The court stated that these costs were necessary to restore the integrity of the insured's business records that were destroyed by the dishonest employee. *Edmunds-Bouvier Savs. & Loan v. New Amsterdam Cas. Co.,* 132 A.2d 181.

SECONDARY SOURCES

APPLEMAN, INSURANCE LAW AND PRACTICE §§ 5273, 5661.

Farley et al., *Ch. XI, Exclusions In the Commercial Crime Policy, in* COMMERCIAL CRIME INSURANCE COVERAGE 427, 448-453.

David K. Kerr, *The Potential Income and Principal Other Exclusions, in* FINANCIAL INSTITUTION BONDS 224 (Duncan L. Clore ed., 1995).

Toni Scott Reed, *Ch. II, What Is Employee Dishonesty and Employee Theft?, in* COMMERCIAL CRIME INSURANCE COVERAGE 39, 117-121.

Joel T. Wiegart, *Ch. V, Compensability of Third-Party Losses, in* COMMERCIAL CRIME INSURANCE COVERAGE 215, 253-255.

ANNOTATIONS

D. Other Cases

1. Cases Decided Under Commercial Crime Policies

5th Cir. 2003 (Tex.). Two vehicle dealerships filed suit against their commercial crime insurer seeking coverage for a loss incurred when the dealership's controller transferred title to a new car to her mother, purportedly in exchange for a $2,000 down payment and a trade-in, neither of which was received. The insurer refused to pay the claim for the value of the trade-in vehicle, arguing that the loss was not an "employee dishonesty" loss but rather a bad business deal, that there was no loss of "covered property" because the insured did not set forth evidence of the value of the trade-in, and that the claim was barred by the "indirect loss" exclusion. The court did not reach the indirect loss exclusion or whether there was "employee dishonesty" because it found that the insured did not make out a prima facie case of a covered loss by failing to show the value of the covered property. *Performance Autoplex II, Ltd. v. Mid-Continent Cas. Co.,* 322 F.3d 847.

6th Cir. 2012. "Indirect loss" exclusion implicated only where there is first a direct loss covered by the policy, from which the insured sustains indirect losses that are not covered by the policy. The claimed loss involved only one type of loss—diverted commissions—which were not a direct loss under the policy's insuring agreement. *Tooling, Mfg. & Techs. Ass'n v. Hartford Fire Ins. Co.,* 693 F.3d 665.

7th Cir. 2011 (Wis.). A mortgage lender warranted to investors that its mortgages met certain regulatory requirements. After one of the insured's office managers conspired with a mortgage broker to issue loans that did not meet down payment requirements, the insured was required to repurchase the mortgages. The fidelity bond insured against direct financial loss directly caused by employee dishonesty, but excluded loss from repurchasing a real estate loan from an investor. The court discussed the split of authority on what constitutes "direct loss," and applied Wisconsin's contract interpretation of direct means direct in order to determine that the mortgage repurchase was not a direct loss. The court rejected the insured's argument that it suffered a loss when it originally funded the substandard mortgages, finding instead that any such loss was recovered when the mortgages were sold. The court also held that the exclusion barred the claim. *Universal Mortg. Corp. v. Wurttembergische Versigherung, AG,* 651 F.3d 759.

D. Mass. 2003. The insurer filed a declaratory judgment action to determine whether it was responsible to indemnify insured for diversion of contributions by insured's employee for his personal use. The court held that this was not a direct loss because no funds were taken from any of the insured's authorized accounts and its assets were not diminished. The court therefore did not specifically reach whether the exclusion applied. The court did note, however, that the exclusion "reinforces the conclusion that the policy meant to insure . . . only against immediate harm from employee dishonesty but not for any obligations 'insured' might have to others as a result of that dishonest." *Fireman's Fund Ins. Co. v. Special Olympics Int'l, Inc.,* 249 F. Supp. 2d 19, *aff'd,* 346 F.3d 259 (5th Cir. 2003).

N.D. Tex. 1996. The insured filed suit against its commercial crime insurer after the insurer denied coverage for insured's replacement of funds, which its employee had embezzled from personal accounts maintained for a third party. The insurer moved for summary judgment on several grounds, including that the loss was not the "direct" result of employee dishonesty. The court agreed, finding that the direct result of the employee's embezzlement was a loss to the third party's personal funds. The court found that the loss to the insured to replace those funds was indirect. *Lynch Prop., Inc. v. Potomac Ins. Co. of Ill.,* 962 F. Supp. 956.

Minn. Ct. App. 2004. The insured filed suit seeking coverage under excess crime loss policies for amounts paid to defend and settle previous litigation that arose when the employees of the insured wrongfully stole and used the proprietary agricultural products of competing companies. The policies followed the form of the underlying policy, which included an exclusion for "indirect or consequential loss of any nature." The court found that the lawsuits with the competitors arose due to losses to the competitors incurred as a result of thefts by the insured's employees. The court determined that the insured's litigation costs were only indirect losses incurred due to direct losses to third parties. The court relied in part upon the indirect loss exclusion in reaching its conclusion. *Cargill,*

Inc. v. Nat'l Union Fire Ins. Co. of Pittsburgh, No. A03-187, 2004 WL 51671.

2. Cases Decided Under Other Policies Or Bonds

2d Cir. 2000 (N.Y.). FDIC, as receiver of a bank, brought a claim on a fidelity bond, claiming that fraudulent and dishonest acts of a trustee caused loss to the bank. The trustee of the bank failed to inform the bank of a construction manager's fraud in soliciting bribes and demanding kickbacks from subcontractors on a real estate venture funded by the bank. On appeal, the court upheld summary judgment in favor of FDIC. The court determined that the fraudulent non-disclosure resulted directly in loss to the bank because the bank would not have continued funding but for the non-disclosure. Thus, the court held that the amounts claimed constituted a "direct loss" to the insured. *FDIC v. Nat'l Union Fire Ins. Co. of Pittsburgh, Pa.*, 205 F.3d 66.

5th Cir. 1985 (Tex.). A savings association filed suit to recover under a fidelity bond the attorneys' fees and costs it incurred in successfully defending a fraud action arising out of a default under a loan commitment. The loan commitment fee allegedly had been embezzled by the association's president. The bond expressly included indemnification for attorneys' fees and court costs "incurred and paid by the Insured in defending any suit or legal proceeding brought against the insured to enforce the insured's liability. . . ." The insurer argued that it should be absolved from indemnity liability for indirect losses to the insured that were sustained in litigation brought by third parties defrauded by the insured's employee. The court disagreed, citing the coverage provision for attorneys' fees and costs, which the court determined clearly applied. *Cont'l Sav. Ass'n v. USF&G*, 762 F.2d 1239.

D. Minn. 2005. A securities broker sued its insurer to recover losses under a fidelity bond. A government computer sales company was a client of one of the broker's registered representatives, and the computer company borrowed up to $20 million from Finova Capital Corporation ("Finova"). As collateral for the borrowed funds, the computer company pledged the assets contained in certain accounts maintained by the securities broker. Pursuant to the pledge agreements, the computer company was permitted to make trades in the investment accounts but required Finova's approval to make any withdrawals. The computer company's financial condition deteriorated and one of the majority stockholders in the company devised a plan to remove funds from the pledged accounts through a fictitious offshore bank that had no assets. The stockholder ordered the securities broker's employee to sell all the securities in the pledged accounts by purchasing certificates of deposits purportedly issued by the fraudulent bank. The broker received copies of the certificates, and its employee directed another employee to fax wire instructions to the broker's headquarters. Two days later, the securities broker wire transferred more than $6 million to the fictitious bank. The computer company defaulted on its loan obligations, and Finova attempted to liquidate the investment account. The fictitious bank failed to redeem the certificates of deposit, and the fraudulent scheme was uncovered. The securities broker claimed that its losses were covered under the insurer's fidelity bond. The insurer argued that the bond did not cover losses "resulting from indirect or consequential loss of any nature," and that the broker's losses did not arise until it settled the underlying lawsuit, which thereby made the loss indirect or consequential. The court, however, rejected the insurer's argument, finding that the "loss" occurs "at the time of the activity giving rise to the claim against the insured and not at the time of trial proceedings or entry of a judgment." Accordingly, the court determined that the broker suffered a loss the instant that the money was wire transferred out of its account to the fictitious bank and that the indirect loss exclusion was not a bar to recovery. *RBC Dain Rauscher, Inc. v. Fed. Ins. Co.*, 370 F. Supp. 2d 886.

E.D. Ark. 2004. Insured bank filed suit against its insurer seeking coverage under a Financial Institution Bond for losses incurred as a result of the fraud perpetrated by one of its borrowers. The insurer moved for summary judgment, arguing, *inter alia*, that the bank would have suffered the same losses even if the signatures on the falsified leases at issue had been authentic. The insurer argued that the persons whose names were forged on the leases did not have authority to bind those entities to the leases under state law. In evaluating this argument, the court construed the phrase "loss resulting directly" from a forgery. The court construed the phrase as the equivalent to proximate causation, "[a] cause that directly produces an event and without which the event would not have occurred." The court found that the forgeries did cause a "direct loss" to the bank because the loss resulted directly from the bank "having extended credit on the faith of a Security Agreement which bears a signature of a lessee or another person which is a forgery." *Pine Bluff Nat'l Bank v. St. Paul Mercury Ins. Co.*, 346 F. Supp. 2d 1020.

D. Conn. 2002. A trustee for a bankrupt payroll administration company sought coverage under an Employee Dishonesty Protection Rider to a fidelity insurance policy for losses sustained when a director misappropriated customer funds that the company held in trust for the Internal Revenue Service. The insurer argued that the policy limited coverage to direct losses of property and did not insure against indirect losses such as legal liabilities due to the employee's dishonesty. The court granted insurer's motion for summary judgment on grounds that bankrupt company did not sustain a direct loss of money or property. The court relied upon the insuring agreement of the policy, which provided coverage for "loss or damage to, money, securities and other property that results directly from employee dishonesty." The policy also included an exclusion for "loss that is an indirect result of any act or event covered by this agreement, including . . . Payment of damages of any type for this you are legally liable." *Finkel v. St. Paul Fire & Marine Ins. Co.*, No. 3:00CV 1194, 2002 WL 1359672.

N.D. Ill. 1992. A bank and its holding company were insureds under a Financial Institution Bond. The bond included exclusions for "(u) all fees, costs and expenses incurred by the insured (1) in establishing the existence of or amount of loss covered under this bond, or (2) as a party to any legal proceeding, whether or not such legal proceeding exposes the insured to loss covered by this bond" and "(v) indirect of consequential loss of any nature." On an insurer's motion to strike and dismiss portions of the complaint, the court granted the motion in its entirety on the grounds that a count seeking attorneys' fees and consequential damages for breach of the terms of the bond was excluded by indirect loss exclusions (u) and (v). The court held that these exclusions clearly exclude coverage for attorneys' fees and consequential damages and that "parties to a contract can exclude or restrict the remedies that a party may have for breach of that contract when the only losses that are suffered on account of that breach are economic losses." *Beverly Bancorp., Inc. v. Cont'l Ins. Co.*, No. 92C4823, 1992 WL 345420.

D.N.J. 1990. A savings and loan association brought an action against its insurer on a Savings and Loan Blanket Bond. Among other things, the insured sought recovery of attorneys' fees incurred in connection with collection actions against the responsible parties. The insurer argued that the fees were consequential damages excluded by a provision stating that the bond does not cover "indirect or consequential loss of any nature." The court held that the insured was entitled to recover attorneys' fees incurred in connection with collection actions brought against responsible parties, but not attorneys' fees incurred in connection with its action against its insurer on the bond. The court held that the fees relating to the collection actions should not be characterized as "consequential damages," but as general damages flowing directly from the insurer's breach of contract. The court also found that these fees were costs incurred in mitigating losses and that, if the insurer had paid the loss, would not have accrued to insured. *Oritani Sav. & Loan Ass'n v. Fid. & Dep. Co. of Md.,* 744 F. Supp. 1311.

Kan. 1970. After a judgment creditor obtained a judgment against the insured corporation due to the fraudulent acts of an employee, the creditor brought a garnishment action against the corporation's insurer seeking recovery under a Blanket Honesty Bond issued to the corporation. The Bond protected against "any loss of money or other property, belonging to the Insured, or in which the Insured has a pecuniary interest, or for which the Insured is legally liable . . . through any fraudulent or dishonest act or acts committed by any of the Employees." The insurer argued that it owed no duty to indemnify the judgment creditor because the obligation of the bond ran only to the insured corporation, and not to third parties to whom the corporation may be liable. The court agreed with the insurer and determined that the bond issued to the corporation did not insure it against liabilities to third parties, but rather indemnified the corporation against direct losses of money or property through employee dishonesty. *Ronnau v. Caravan Int'l Ins. Corp.,* 468 P.2d 118.

Neb. 1976. After a judgment creditor obtained a judgment against the bank due to the fraudulent acts of a bank employee, the creditor brought a garnishment action against the bank's insurer seeking recovery under Blanket Dishonesty Bonds issued to the bank. The issue before the court was whether the judgment against the bank, resulting from the fraudulent acts of one its employees, was a loss within the contemplation of the bonds. Following *Ronnau v. Caravan International Ins. Corp.*, 468 P.2d 118 (Kan. 1970), the court found that nowhere in the bond did the insured assume an obligation to respond to the liability of the bank to third persons. The court concluded that the creditor's judgment was not a loss sustained by the bank within the contemplation of the bonds. *Foxley Cattle Co. v. Bank of Mead*, 244 N.W.2d 205.

Neb. 1973. Insured broadcasting company filed an action to recover losses allegedly suffered as a result of the fraudulent and dishonest acts of its general manager in forging the president's signature on a promissory note to a bank. The bank intimated that it would no longer advertise with the insured unless it paid the note. The insured paid the note, with interest, by executing to the bank a new promissory note. The insurer argued that there was no coverage under the bond because the insured was not legally liable for the forged note, yet paid it anyway. The court found that the insured suffered no direct loss as a result of the fraudulent acts of its manager. The court stated that "[t]he original loss suffered by the bank in this case is not, under the facts alleged, converted into a direct loss by the insured because it determined to pay the bank on an obligation for which it was not liable." *KAMI Kountry Broad. Co. v. USF&G*, 208 N.W.2d 254.

N.H. 1981. A bank's customer filed suit against it for negligence and breach of fiduciary duty, alleging that the bank knowingly and improperly permitted payment of certain checks for purposes that the customer did not intend. The insured bank then filed a petition for declaratory judgment to determine the extent of coverage the insurer owed to the bank under a blanket bond. Among other things, the insured argued that the bond did not cover losses which the insured bank might suffer as a result of its alleged liability to third parties for negligence and breach of fiduciary duty. The court determined that the bond did provide coverage for indirect losses which resulted from the bank's potential liability to its customer, noting that the bond neither excluded nor limited the insurer's liability for indirect losses. The court nevertheless found in favor of the insurer because the checks at issue were not stolen, and thus did not fall within the scope of the coverage afforded by the bond. The court also did not permit the recovery of attorney fees and costs incurred in litigating the declaratory judgment action and the prior action by the bank's customer, because the bond's attorney fees and costs provision did not apply where the claims were not covered by the bond. *Exeter Banking Co. v. New Hampshire Ins. Co.*, 438 A.2d 310.

N.Y. App. Div. 2005. The insured brought an action against its several insurers and the insurance agency that procured the policies to recover for losses incurred by the insured. The insurers filed motions for summary judgment as to various counts of the insured's complaint, including seeking dismissal of the insured's claim for consequential damages under the policies. The trial court entered an order dismissing the insured's claim for consequential damages, and the insured appealed. On appeal, the court affirmed the dismissal of the insured's claim for consequential damages, finding that the "insurance policies at issue either specifically exclude claims seeking to recover consequential damages or do not specifically provide coverage for them." *Duratech Indus., Inc. v. Cont'l Ins. Co.*, 800 N.Y.S.2d 182.

SECONDARY SOURCES

Samuel J. Arena, Jr., Daniel T. Fitch, Jeffrey S. Price & Justin D. Wear, *Key Exclusions*, *in* 10 NEW APPLEMAN ON INSURANCE 133.05 (Michael Keeley et al. eds., 2014).

David T. DiBiase et al., *"Direct Loss" Under Common Fidelity Coverages—"Direct Means Direct!"* (unpublished paper presented at Mid-Winter Meeting of Fid. & Sur. Law. Comm., ABA, New York, N.Y., Jan. 22, 1999).

Howard Marks, *The "Other" Exclusions of Commercial Blanket Bonds and Dishonesty Policies* (unpublished paper presented at Nat'l Inst. Fid. Bonds, Fid. & Sur. Law Comm., ABA, New York, N.Y., Nov. 1991).

Bradford A. Thomas, *Analysis of Direct Losses and Indirect Losses Under the Modern Financial Institution Bond's Fidelity Coverage and Exclusions* (unpublished paper presented at the 1st Annual S. Sur. & Fid. Claims Conf., Apr. 26-27, 1990).

H. Legal Fees, Costs And Expenses

1.   **This Policy does not cover:**
   h.   **Legal Fees, Costs and Expenses**
      Fees, costs and expenses incurred by you which are related to any legal action, except when covered under Insuring Agreement A.2.

(Commercial Crime Policy)

We will not pay for loss as specified below:
6.   **Legal Expenses**
   Expenses related to any legal action, except when covered under Insuring Agreement 2.

(Crime Protection Policy)

COMMENT

As cases denying coverage for attorneys' fees point out, commercial crime insurance does not provide liability coverage and, therefore, does not impose any duty on the insurer to provide a defense to its insured. Except when covered under Insuring Agreement A.2 (Forgery Or Alteration), this exclusion affirms that the insurer has no obligation to indemnify the insured for expenses "related to any legal action." Thus, this provision excludes from coverage legal expenses incurred in prosecuting claims under the policy, legal expenses incurred in pursuing third parties, and legal expenses incurred in defending claims against the insured. Given the broad language of the exclusion, this exclusion is not limited to "attorneys' fees" and should reasonably be interpreted to include other expenses such as filing fees, court costs, deposition costs and any other expenses relating to the legal action. This exclusion has no application with respect to legal expenses covered under Insuring Agreement A.2 (Forgery or Alteration) (reasonable legal expenses incurred and paid by the insured to defend against a suit against the insured for refusing to pay on a covered instrument on the basis that it has been forged or altered) of the Commercial Crime Policy or Insuring Agreement 2 (Forgery or Alteration) of the Crime Protection Policy.

OUTLINE OF ANNOTATIONS

A. Cases Decided Under Commercial Crime Policies
B. Cases Decided Under Other Policies or Bonds

ANNOTATIONS

A. Cases Decided Under Commercial Crime Policies

Miss. Ct. App. 2005. Employee dishonesty and forgery or alteration provisions provided no coverage for alleged liability for employee's alteration of power of attorney allowing agents to leave vehicle in principal's name. The relevant general employee dishonesty provisions of the policy provided for first party, not third-party coverage, as the policy expressly stated that the insurer would not pay either for indirect loss resulting from payment of damages of any type for which the insured is legally liable, or for any expenses related to any legal action. *Watson Quality Ford, Inc. v. Great River Ins. Co.*, 909 So. 2d 1196.

N.Y. App. Div. 1985. Comprehensive dishonesty, disappearance, and destruction policy did not obligate the insurer to defend the insured, pay the costs of defense of court actions, or to pay any judgments against them, as the policy was clearly an indemnity policy providing coverage against employee dishonesty, not a liability policy. *Kriegler v. Aetna Cas. & Sur. Co.*, 108 A.D.2d 708.

B. Cases Decided Under Other Policies or Bonds

N.D. Ill. 1992. A bank and a holding company were insureds under a Financial Institution Bond. The insurer moved to strike and dismiss portions of the complaint on the grounds that a claim seeking attorneys' fees and consequential damages for breach of the terms of the bond was excluded by the terms of the bond. The court held that the bond clearly excluded coverage for any claims for attorneys' fees and consequential damages. *Beverly Bancorp., Inc. v. Cont'l Ins. Co.*, No. 92C4823, 1992 WL 345420.

Ill. App. Ct. 1984. Four business partners sought coverage under two fidelity bonds issued for their losses and defense costs incurred in connection with an action initiated against them by the Commodities Futures Trading Commission ("CFTC"). Plaintiffs argued that the bonding companies' obligations arose whether or not the business partners' defense was successful. The bonding company countered that, notwithstanding plaintiffs' success in the CFTC action, the CFTC complaint alleged that the culpable acts were committed by the partners' "managing body," and that the actions of such "managing body" were not covered under the bonds. The court agreed with the bonding company and held that the fees expended in the defense of the CFTC action were not covered under the bonds. *Mortell v. Ins. Co. of N. Am.*, 458 N.E.2d 922.

N.C. Ct. App. 1984. Plaintiff, a dealer in cattle, sought reimbursement of his court costs incurred in connection with an earlier successful action brought against a cattle company to recover the purchase price of livestock that the dealer had sold. The surety had issued a bond to cover the purchases of livestock made by a cattle company. The cattle dealer claimed that after his unsuccessful attempts to obtain the purchase price of the cattle from the cattle company itself, he was obliged to retain legal counsel and obtain the money due through the courts. Because he was successful, he claimed that the bond's principal, the cattle dealer, and the bonding company itself were responsible for his legal fees. The court disagreed, holding that the terms of the bond did not provide coverage for his legal fees. *Martin v. Hartford Acc. & Indem. Co.*, 316 S.E.2d 126.

SECONDARY SOURCES

Farley et al., *Ch. XI, Exclusions in the Commercial Crime Policy, in* COMMERCIAL CRIME INSURANCE COVERAGE 427, 467-69.

Hull, *Surety's Liability for Attorney's Fees and Court Costs Under Fidelity Bonds*, 14 FORUM 634 (Winter 1979).

Gilbert J. Schroeder, *Court Costs and Attorneys' Fees, in* BANKERS AND OTHER FINANCIAL INSTITUTION BLANKET BONDS 243 (1979).

Gilbert J. Schroeder, *Court Costs and Attorneys' Fees, in* FINANCIAL INSTITUTION BONDS 370 (Duncan L. Clore ed., 1995).

I. Nuclear Hazard

    1. This Policy does not cover:
       i.   Nuclear Hazard
          Loss or damage resulting from nuclear reaction or radiation, or radioactive contamination, however caused.

(Commercial Crime Policy)

We will not pay for loss as specified below:
7.   Nuclear Chemical or Biological
      Loss resulting from nuclear reaction, nuclear radiation or radioactive, chemical or biological contamination, or any related act or incident.

(Crime Protection Policy)

COMMENT

This exclusion brings within its scope not only "loss resulting from nuclear reaction, nuclear radiation or radioactive contamination," but also "any related act or incident." Given that the purpose of commercial crime insurance is to protect against losses arising from dishonest acts of employees and certain specified fraudulent acts of others, it is not readily apparent how this exclusion would come into play other than in connection with a theft of nuclear or radioactive materials. While the theft of nuclear or radioactive materials by an employee may be covered, any loss resulting from nuclear reaction, nuclear radiation or radioactive contamination would be excluded by operation of the nuclear exclusion and also by operation of the exclusion for indirect loss. This exclusion, like the governmental actions and war exclusions exists to expressly exclude from coverage catastrophic events that are beyond coverage by the insurance industry. Most likely, these exclusions are carryovers from casualty insurance policies and are included in the policy out of an abundance of caution.

OUTLINE OF ANNOTATIONS

A. Cases Decided Under Commercial Crime Policies
B. Cases Decided Under Other Policies or Bonds

ANNOTATIONS

A. Cases Decided Under Commercial Crime Policies

NONE

B. Cases Decided Under Other Policies or Bonds

NONE

SECONDARY SOURCES

Farley et al., *Ch. XI, Exclusions in the Commercial Crime Policy, in* COMMERCIAL CRIME INSURANCE COVERAGE 427, 457-59.

J. Pollution

1. **This Policy does not cover:**
   j. **Pollution**
       Loss or damage caused by or resulting from pollution. Pollution means the discharge, dispersal, seepage, migration, release or escape of any solid, liquid, gaseous or thermal irritant or contaminant, including smoke, vapor, soot, fumes, acids, alkalis, chemicals and waste. Waste

includes materials to be recycled, reconditioned or reclaimed.

(Commercial Crime Policy)

COMMENT

Given that the purpose of commercial crime insurance is to protect against losses arising from dishonest acts of employees and certain specified fraudulent acts of others, it is not readily apparent how this exclusion would come into play other than in connection with a theft resulting in the discharge, dispersal, seepage, migration, release or escape of a pollutant. Any loss or damage caused by or resulting in pollution would be excluded by operation of the pollution exclusion and also by operation of the exclusion for indirect loss. This exclusion, like the governmental actions and war exclusions exists to expressly exclude from coverage catastrophic events that are beyond coverage by the insurance industry. Most likely, these exclusions are carryovers from casualty insurance policies and are included in the policy out of an abundance of caution.

OUTLINE OF ANNOTATIONS

A. Cases Decided Under Commercial Crime Policies
B. Cases Decided Under Other Policies or Bonds

ANNOTATIONS

A. Cases Decided Under Commercial Crime Policies

NONE

B. Cases Decided Under Other Policies or Bonds

N.D. Ala. 1998. Hotel owner claimed loss arising from Environmental Protection Agency's order to close and decontaminate hotel because an exterminator had used methyl parathion. Pollution exclusion barred

EXCLUSIONS OTHER THAN INVENTORY LOSS

coverage because the methyl parathion was a "pollutant," "irritant," or "contaminant" for purposes of the exclusion. *Haman, Inc. v. St. Paul Fire & Marine Ins. Co.*, 18 F. Supp. 2d 1306.

SECONDARY SOURCES

NONE

K. War And Military Action

1.   **This Policy does not cover:**
     k.   **War And Military Action**
          Loss or damage resulting from:
          (1)   War, including undeclared or civil war;
          (2)   Warlike action by a military force, including action in hindering or defending against an actual or expected attack, by any government, sovereign or other authority using military personnel or other agents; or
          (3)   Insurrection, rebellion, revolution, usurped power, or action taken by governmental authority in hindering or defending against any of these.

(Commercial Crime Policy)

We will not pay for loss as specified below:
8.   **War and Similar Actions**
     Loss resulting from war, whether or not declared, warlike action, insurrection, rebellion or revolution, or any related act or incident.

(Crime Protection Policy)

COMMENT

This exclusion brings within its scope not only loss resulting from "war, whether or not declared," but also loss resulting from "warlike action, insurrection, rebellion or revolution, or any related act or incident." Given that the purpose of commercial crime insurance is to protect against losses arising from dishonest acts by employees and certain specified fraudulent acts of others, it is not readily apparent how this exclusion would ever be involved in a commercial crime insurance claim. For example, in order for this exclusion to apply in the employee theft context there would have to be loss of or damage to covered property resulting from employee theft that also resulted from a war or one of the related acts or incidents described in this exclusion. Although there are no cases applying this exclusion, included in the annotations are two Circuit Court cases that address the application of a "war" exclusion in the property insurance context.

OUTLINE OF ANNOTATIONS

A. Cases Decided Under Commercial Crime Policies
B. Cases Decided Under Other Policies or Bonds

ANNOTATIONS

A. Cases Decided Under Commercial Crime Policies

NONE

B. Cases Decided Under Other Policies or Bonds

2d Cir. 1974 (N.Y.). The insured airline brought an action to recover against its property insurers after one of its planes was hijacked by two men acting for the Popular Front for the Liberation of Palestine. The terrorists forced the crew to fly the plane to Beirut, where a demolitions expert and explosives were put onboard. The terrorists then forced the crew to Cairo, where the passengers were evacuated and then the plane was totally destroyed. The insurer argued that the insured's claim was

EXCLUSIONS OTHER THAN INVENTORY LOSS

precluded by the war exclusion in the policy. The court found that the
exclusion was not applicable because the meaning of "war" in the
insurance provisions referred to hostilities by government entities.
Because the terrorist group was not acting on behalf of a government, the
court found that it did not apply. *Pan Am. World Airways v. Aetna
Cas. & Sur. Co.*, 505 F.2d 989.

3d Cir. 1996 (Pa.). Insureds owned businesses and properties in Liberia,
which were damaged by looting and fire at a time when Charles Taylor
and Prince Johnson led separate armies against the Liberian government.
The insureds filed a declaratory judgment action claiming benefits under
their property insurance policy. The policy contained exclusions for
losses caused by war, civil war, insurrection, rebellion or revolution. The
insurer claimed that the exclusion precluded coverage. The court found
that a state of insurrection existed in Liberia during the relevant time
period, and that the insurrection caused the insured's losses. The court
found that "insurrection" is "the most basic form of civil unrest" and
defined "insurrection or rebellion" within the meaning of property
insurance policy exclusions for insurrection and war as "a movement
accompanied by action specifically intended to overthrow the constituted
government and to take possession of the inherent powers thereof." The
court determined that insureds' losses resulted from looting caused by a
"total breakdown of civil authority," and that the soldiers under Taylor
and Johnson participated in the looting and destruction. As a result, the
court concluded that the exclusion applied to the insureds' claim. *Younis
Bros. v. CIGNA Worldwide Ins. Co.*, 91 F.3d 13.

SECONDARY SOURCES

Farley et al., *Ch. XI, Exclusions in the Commercial Crime Policy, in*
COMMERCIAL CRIME INSURANCE COVERAGE 427, 457-59.

Toni Scott Reed, *Cybercrime: Losses, Claims, and Potential Insurance
Coverage for the Technology Hazards of the Twenty-First Century*,
20 FIDELITY L.J. 55, 103-104 (2014).

Bert Wells, Rukesh Korde, Pamela Carter & Franciska Coleman, *Cyber-
Risk Insurance, in* 4 NEW APPLEMAN ON INSURANCE 29-54 - 29-58
(Aviva Abramovsky ed., 2014).

L. Trading

2.   Insuring Agreement A.1. does not cover:
b.   Trading
Loss resulting from trading, whether in your name or in a genuine or fictitious account.

(Commercial Crime Policy)

COMMENT

Commercial crime insurance excludes from coverage loss resulting directly or indirectly from trading, whether such trading is in the name of the insured or in a genuine or fictitious account. The objective of this exclusion is to remove from coverage any losses relating directly or indirectly to the purchasing or selling of securities. As stated by the Second Circuit, the purpose is to "exempt from coverage losses caused by market forces, misjudgments of those forces by buyers and sellers of securities, or various errors or omissions . . . in the course of trading." *Glusband v. Fittin Cunningham & Lauzon, Inc.*, 892 F.2d 208 (2d Cir. 1989). Although the trading loss exclusion has not been applied uniformly by the courts, most decisions focus on the actual cause of the loss. This exclusion has application only with respect to Insuring Agreement A.1 (Employee Dishonesty).

OUTLINE OF ANNOTATIONS

A. Cases Decided Under Commercial Crime Policies
B. Cases Decided Under Other Policies or Bonds

ANNOTATIONS

A. Cases Decided Under Commercial Crime Policies

E.D. La. 2011. The insured invested in a mutual fund that invested in hedge funds, one of which invested a portion of its holdings in a fund managed by Bernard Madoff. The insured claimed a loss resulting directly from computer fraud based on its allegation that Madoff used a computer to generate false documents. The court held that the insured did not sustain a direct loss as a result of Madoff's actions because the insured's loss "was too far removed from the Madoff scheme." The court also determined that investing in the mutual fund was "trading" within the meaning of the trading loss exclusion because "the purchase of shares in a mutual fund is equivalent to the buying and selling of securities." Relying on the policy's exclusion for losses "resulting directly or indirectly from trading," the court rejected the insured's contention that the exclusion should not apply because the insured's losses were not caused by its investment in the mutual fund, but rather Madoff's fraudulent misrepresentations, as the loss indirectly resulted from trading. The exclusion for parting with title to property also barred the claim, as the "dishonest act" under that exclusion may be committed by a third party who is not the party to whom the insured entrusted the property. The insured entrusted its investment to the mutual fund and any fund in which the mutual fund subsequently invested. The court declined to reach the issue of whether computer fraud caused the loss. *Methodist Health Sys. Found., Inc. v. Hartford Fire Ins. Co.*, 834 F. Supp. 2d 493.

B. Cases Decided Under Other Policies or Bonds

2d Cir. 1989 (N.Y.). The insured's employee induced investors to invest money based on employee's misrepresentations that he would follow a conservative investment strategy. The strategy was reckless, and the insured sustained losses. The insured sued the insurer for coverage under the bond. In reversing the trial court, the Second Circuit held that the losses resulted from bad trades. The exclusion's purpose is to "exempt from coverage losses caused by market forces, misjudgments of those forces by buyers and sellers of securities, or various errors or omissions . . . in the course of trading." Thus, the losses were not covered by operation of the "trading" exclusion. *Glusband v. Fittin Cunningham & Lauzon, Inc.*, 892 F.2d 208.

2d Cir. 1978 (N.Y.). A mutual fund, registered under the Investment Company Act of 1940, sought recovery for losses resulting from the acts of its president who was bribed to knowingly acquire securities at manipulated prices. Reversing the trial court, the Second Circuit noted that where the insured is a regulated investment company and not a broker, the fraudulent purchase of securities by an employee "may well be considered" outside the contemplated meaning of trading. Moreover, the bond at issue was a "statutory bond," which must be read to afford coverage for the "larceny and embezzlement" of a company officer. Thus, the court concluded that the trading loss exclusion was inapplicable, and the insurer was liable to the insured on the bond. In a lengthy dissenting opinion, mention was made of the insured's option to have acquired more expensive coverage, and an objection was raised to using the statute as a "bail out" device contradicting the obvious intent and understanding of the parties to the contract. *Index Fund, Inc. v. Ins. Co. of N. Am.*, 580 F.2d 1158.

3d Cir. 1954 (Pa.). A securities broker sought to recover for losses incurred when an employee made unauthorized use of a customer "mark-up account" to buy and sell securities. The Third Circuit determined that the trading loss exclusion was applicable to such transactions; the term "trading" is not to be equated solely with authorized trading; and, although protection against such losses may be of predominant importance to a securities broker, the clause cannot be ignored within the bond without doing violence to the plain meaning of the insurance contract. The court made passing mention of the insurer's assertion that such coverage is available at a "substantially higher premium." *Roth v. Md. Cas. Co.*, 209 F.2d 371.

4th Cir. 1938 (N.C.). A brokerage subsidiary sought recovery for a variety of losses, among which were funds that an employee wrongfully misappropriated to finance a series of securities trades which she carried out through another broker. The trading losses exclusion was held inapplicable because none of the transactions involved use of the insured's name or credit and the insured had no liability thereon. The loss resulted solely from the dishonest use of the insured's funds, and the claim was determined to be covered. *In re Schluter, Green & Co.*, 93 F.2d 810.

6th Cir. 1990 (Ohio). The insured made a claim for losses arising out of governmental securities underlying certain repurchase agreements the insured had purchased from a broker. The transactions involving the repurchase agreements were handled in a sloppy fashion. Upon reconciling the statements for the repurchase agreements, it was discovered that some of the securities underlying the repurchase agreements were missing. The Sixth Circuit determined that the insured's losses were not market losses, and, thus, the "trading" exclusion was not a bar to coverage. *First Fed. Sav. & Loan Ass'n of Toledo v. Fid. & Dep. Co. of Md.*, 895 F.2d 254.

7th Cir. 1939 (Ill.). A general securities and grain brokerage sought recovery under a bond for losses caused by a dishonest employee who set up a number of fictitious accounts to consummate various commodity trades on the insured's credit. Using checks that had been signed in blank, settlement of these checks was effectuated with the insured's funds. The court determined that the trading loss exclusion was inapplicable. The court construed the exclusion as a limitation only upon trading losses which are not dishonest and are caused either through the insured's own trading or trading by customers who fail to meet their commitments. Considering the nature of the insured's business, any other construction, the court reasoned, would "nullify" the basic insuring clause and reduce the protection to a "mere shadow." *Paddleford v. Fid. & Cas. Co. of N.Y.*, 100 F.2d 606.

8th Cir. 1985 (Neb.). An insured grain trading business sustained losses due to poor trades. An employee of the grain trading business forged the company's books to make the company look more profitable. In the meantime, the employee tried to improve the company's profitability in hopes that eventually the company would recoup the losses. The employee made bad trades, and the insured's loss worsened. The Eighth Circuit determined that the trading exclusion applied to the losses despite the fact that the insured was not a commodity brokerage house. The court relied on the trial court's consideration of the caption to the rider for the trading exclusion, the exclusion's endorsement, and extrinsic evidence to support its decision. *Lincoln Grain, Inc. v. Aetna Cas. & Sur. Co.*, 756 F.2d 75.

9th Cir. 1988 (Cal.). Insurer filed suit for declaratory judgment that trading loss exclusion barred insured broker's claim under Broker's Blanket Bond for losses incurred when an employee stole bearer bonds and wrongfully retained sales proceeds of the bonds. The court determined that the trading loss exclusion did not apply because the insured's losses did not occur at the time the employee traded the bonds, but rather at a later date when the thief retained the sales proceeds of the bonds or when the rightful owners claimed their bonds, and when the thief stole certain other bonds. The court noted that the insured would have suffered losses even if the bonds were not traded. The court found that the trading loss exclusion does not apply simply when a trade occurs anywhere in the chain of events that resulted in a loss to the insured. *Ins. Co. of N. Am. v. Gibralco,* 847 F.2d 530.

9th Cir. 1979 (Cal.). A mutual find, registered under the Investment Company Act of 1940, sought to recover for losses resulting from the acquisition of securities at manipulated prices upon the recommendation of a bribed employee of the insured's independent investment advisor. The Ninth Circuit affirmed the judgment for the insurer and determined that: (1) the term "trading" is not ambiguous; is not commonly understood to apply only to the activities of stockbrokers; and the exclusionary language could have been waived for an additional premium which the insured declined; and (2) statutory mandates of a fidelity bond, with which the trading loss exclusion is arguably in conflict, extend solely to the officers and employees of the mutual fund, not to the employees of an independent investment advisor. *Research Equity Fund, Inc. v. Ins. Co. of N. Am.,* 602 F.2d 200.

9th Cir. 1974 (Cal.). The trustee of a bankrupt municipal bond broker sought recovery for a variety of losses including the repurchase of depressed or delinquent issues for the personal benefit of controlling shareholders or in consequence of customer sales induced by fraudulent misrepresentations. The Ninth Circuit affirmed summary judgment for insurer and determined that the repurchase losses came within the trading loss exclusion and, to the extent customer monies were wrongfully diverted to payment of the insured's operating expenses, these are not direct losses, but third-party liabilities for which no coverage is afforded. *Bass v. Am. Ins. Co.,* 493 F.2d 590.

D.D.C. 1962. A stock brokerage sought recovery for losses resulting from customer's short check given to procure a stock purchase for its account. After first concluding that the employee's carelessness in accepting the check did not rise to the level of dishonest or fraudulent within the meaning of the bond, the trading loss exclusion was held applicable and precluded recovery for the customer's admitted fraud. While there may be, a technical distinction in the securities business between trading for one's own account and a purchase transacted for a customer's account, the term employed in the bond should not be given such restricted meaning, "but the same meaning it has in any mercantile business, namely, the buying and selling of commodities-in the instant case, the buying and selling of securities on a customer's account." *Sade v. Nat'l Sur. Corp.,* 203 F. Supp. 680.

W.D. Mo. 1984. A customer fraudulently used the securities account of his employer for his own securities transactions. The court determined that the "trading" exclusion applied to deny recovery. The court reasoned that the historical context of the exclusion, adoption of the clause from stockbroker's bonds, and discussions by the American Bankers Association publication indicate that a reasonable banker would understand the "trading" exclusion to bar recovery for losses resulting from the legal and illegal buying and selling of securities. *Shearson/Am. Express, Inc. v. First Cont'l Bank & Trust Co.,* 579 F. Supp. 1305.

S.D.N.Y. 1967. The insured stockbroker sought to recover for more than $1.2 million worth of short checks given by a corporate customer to procure delivery of various stocks. The trading loss exclusion was held applicable and judgment entered for the insurer on all of a variety of issues. Trading "means the operation of the usual occupation of buying and selling stocks," and even though the purchase by the insured had been completed, collection from the customer was still "an inherent part of the completion of the transaction." This case includes a lengthy analysis of several other points including (1) the customer's lack of fraudulent intent; (2) the inadmissibility of a guilty plea to related criminal charges; (3) the insured's extension of credit; and (4) the purview of the "in transit" provisions of Insuring Agreement (C). *Sutro Bros. & Co. v. Indem. Ins. Co. of N. Am.,* 264 F. Supp. 273.

E.D. Wis. 1997. Assignee of claim under directors and officers policy filed suit against insurer for coverage for losses a hospital suffered from insured advisor's investment in volatile derivative securities. The policy contained an exclusion for losses resulting from trading. The insurer contended that the exclusion applied and barred coverage for the claim. The court agreed, finding that the policy clearly excluded losses resulting from securities trades, whether the cause of action is for breach of fiduciary duty or negligence. It was ultimately trading that caused the loss. *Straz v. Kansas Bankers Sur. Co.,* 986 F. Supp. 563.

Cal. Ct. App. 1934. The insured sought to recover losses suffered for the declined market value of stock that a dishonest employee had purchased through unauthorized use of a customer's account. "Trading" has a well-understood meaning in connection with the purchase and sale of securities, and given that there was no question as to the term having any peculiar or limited meaning in the text of the bond, it was error to admit "expert" testimony on whether the insured's loss resulted from trading. *Rath v. Indem. Ins. Co. of N. Am.,* 38 P.2d 435.

Cal. Ct. App. 1934. The insured brokerage firm sought recovery for market decline in stock acquired for a customer who failed to settle his account. The trading loss exclusion held applicable. With no evidence that the term "trading" was used in other than its common meaning, these were clearly trading transactions and it was error to admit "expert" testimony to the contrary. *Earl v. Fid. & Dep. Co. of Md.,* 32 P.2d 409.

Del. Ch. 2010. Insured investment funds and their affiliates invested over $3 billion with Bernard Madoff, who allegedly stole the funds. As stated by the court, the trading loss exclusion was inapplicable because "Madoff did not lose money through reckless, improvident, or even dishonest trading. Madoff was a thief. He engaged in embezzlement and embezzlement-like acts. The trading exclusion does not apply to outright theft." *Massachusetts Mut. Life Ins. Co. v. Certain Underwriters of Lloyd's of London,* No. 4791-VCL, 2010 WL 2929552.

Ill. App. Ct. 1932. A bank obtained recovery for losses incurred on fictitious notes and conditional sale agreements discounted and purchased by a dishonest commission broker, found to have been an employee, acting in collusion with an outside motor vehicle dealer. Trading ordinarily implies a purchase and sale, and the trading loss exclusion, if extended to securities purchased for investment and not for the purpose of being sold, would "practically annul" all of the provisions for the insured's protection. *Am. Inv. Co. v. USF&G,* 267 Ill. App. Ct. 370.

La. Ct. App. 1970. A customer claiming to have been misled into unsuitable investments sought recovery against municipal bond broker.

The municipal bond broker later impleaded its insurer seeking indemnification for its defense costs and potential accountability to the plaintiff. The broker prevailed on the primary claim when no customer relationship was found to have existed, and the trading loss exclusion was held applicable to preclude any recovery against the insurer. In reaching its decision, the court found that, irrespective of employee fraud or dishonesty being at the root of the alleged loss, the claimed loss was at least the indirect result of trading and rejected "the premise that there can be no trading unless it is authorized, legally executed and honestly accomplished." *Hepler v. Fireman's Fund Ins. Co.*, 239 So. 2d 669.

Mass. 1927. A brokerage partnership sought recovery against its fidelity insurer for market losses on stock transactions that a dishonest employee carried out through the unauthorized use and manipulation of a customer account. The trading loss exclusion was held applicable and precluded the insured's recovery. The bond language is free of ambiguity, and "trading" should be given the same general meaning it has in any mercantile business; namely, the buying and selling of commodities. The term should not be given a restricted meaning as applicable only to buying and selling for the broker's own account as distinguished from transactions on behalf of customers. *Harris v. Nat'l Sur. Co.*, 155 N.E. 10.

N.J. Super. Ct. App. Div. 1993. The insured made a claim for recovery of losses arising out of mortgages and a mortgage pool. The insured argued in a prior action that the mortgage pools were "securities," and in this action, it contended that the mortgage pools were not securities and, therefore, not subject to the "trading loss" exclusion. The court determined that the doctrine of judicial estoppel precluded the insured's inconsistent positions, and the court declined to address the applicability of the exclusion. *N. J. Sav. & Loan Ass'n v. Fid. & Dep. Co. of Md.*, 660 A.2d 1287.

N.Y. App. Div. 1985. Insured filed suit for coverage under a blanket employee fidelity bond, which included an exclusion for trading losses. Part of the insured's complaint sought to recover for losses arising out of a "short-sale" of United States Treasury notes. The court dismissed the claims for "short-sale" losses because they were barred by the trading loss exclusion. *Flushing Nat'l Bank v. Transamerica Ins. Co.*, 491 N.Y.S.2d 793.

N.Y. App. Div. 1964. A brokerage firm sought recovery for losses resulting from the acknowledged fraud of one of its customers on whose behalf various purchase and separate short sale commitments were entered. The court reversed the judgment for the insured, following a line of cases in which trading was given its generally accepted meaning and not a restricted application to transactions for the broker's own account. *Condon v. Nat'l Sur. Corp.*, 254 N.Y.S.2d 620.

N.Y. App. Div. 1939. A securities broker sought recovery for market losses resulting from customer purchase and sale commitments entered wherein the insured relied upon the misinformation of a dishonest employee. In the face of conflicting expert testimony on construction of the term "trading," the court set aside a jury verdict for the insurer. The court gave the exclusionary language an interpretation most favorable to the insured and construed "trading" in the limited technical sense of the over-the-counter market. The court concluded that it did not embrace sales or purchases as brokers for the account of another. *Cohon v. USF&G*, 13 N.Y.S.2d 976.

N.Y. App. Div. 1927. A brokerage firm sought recovery for losses resulting from short checks given in payment of treasury certificates acquired for the account of a customer. The trading loss exclusion was held applicable to preclude recovery, and the term "trading" is not limited to include only those transactions in which the insured was acting as a seller as distinguished from a broker. *Kean v. Md. Cas. Co.*, 223 N.Y.S. 373.

SECONDARY SOURCES

Samuel J. Arena, Jr., Daniel T. Fitch, Jeffrey S. Price & Justin D. Wear, *Key Exclusions*, *in* 10 NEW APPLEMAN ON INSURANCE 133.02 (Michael Keeley et al. eds., 2014).

Stephen J. Beatty, *From Wall Street to Main Street: Employee Dishonesty Claims, the Trading Loss Exclusion, and Other Matters* (unpublished paper presented at Annual Meeting of the Sur. Claims Inst., June 22, 1989).

Farley et al., *Ch. XI, Exclusions in the Commercial Crime Policy, in* COMMERCIAL CRIME INSURANCE COVERAGE 427, 470-72.

Mark S. Gamell, *The Impact of the Securities Laws on the Financial Institution Bond* (unpublished paper presented at Annual Meeting of the Sur. Claims Inst., June 22-24, 1994).

John T. Harris & David R. Glissman, *Fidelity Exposure for Repo Losses: A Billion Dollar Time Bomb?* (unpublished paper presented at Annual Meeting of the Sur. Claims Inst., June 1986).

David K. Kerr, *The Potential Income and Principal Other Exclusions, in* FINANCIAL INSTITUTION BONDS 221 (Duncan L. Clore ed., 1995).

William P. Sullivan, Jr., *The Trading Exclusion in the Brokers Blanket Bond* (unpublished paper presented at Annual Meeting of ABA, Fid. & Sur. Law Comm., Aug. 12, 1979).

Robert K. Tucker, *Insuring Agreement (A) and Coverage Exclusions Under the Stockbroker's Blanket Bond* (unpublished paper presented at Annual Meeting of ABA, Fid. & Sur. Law Comm., Aug. 7, 1988).

M. Warehouse Receipts

2. Insuring Agreement A.1. does not cover:
c. Warehouse Receipts
Loss resulting from the fraudulent or dishonest signing, issuing, cancelling or failing to cancel, a warehouse receipt or any papers connected with it.

(Commercial Crime Policy)

COMMENT

Warehouse receipts are highly negotiable and, therefore, the likely subject of fraudulent or dishonest conduct. This exclusion makes clear that the policy excludes loss resulting from fraudulent or dishonest signing, issuing, canceling or failing to cancel, a warehouse receipt "or any papers connected with it." Such a loss could occur where an employee, in collusion with a customer of the employer, provides merchandise to the customer without canceling the warehouse receipt or when the employee, in collusion with a vendor, issues a receipt without having received the merchandise. The customer or vendor could then make a claim based on the fraudulent receipt. For coverage to apply the employee's acts must be "fraudulent or dishonest." Loss caused by unintentional error is not covered. This exclusion has application only with respect to Insuring Agreement A.1 (Employee Dishonesty).

OUTLINE OF ANNOTATIONS

A. Cases Decided Under Commercial Crime Policies
B. Cases Decided Under Other Policies or Bonds

ANNOTATIONS

A. Cases Decided Under Commercial Crime Policies

NONE

B. Cases Decided Under Other Policies or Bonds

NONE

SECONDARY SOURCES

NONE

N. Exchanges Or Purchases

3. Insuring Agreements A.3., A.4. and A.5 do not cover:
b. Exchanges Or Purchases
Loss resulting from the giving or surrendering of property in any exchange or purchase.
4. Insuring Agreement A.6 does not cover:
c. Exchanges Or Purchases
Loss resulting from the giving or surrendering of property in any exchange or purchase.

(Commercial Crime Policy)

We will not pay for loss as specified below:
5. Under Insuring Agreements 3 and 4
a. Exchanges or Purchases
Loss resulting from the giving or surrendering of property in any exchange or purchase.

(Crime Protection Policy)

COMMENT

This exclusion eliminates loss that sometimes occurs because of overcharges or undercharges in purchase transactions or when a person receives less than equivalent value for an exchange item. Crime insurance is just that, crime insurance. Its purpose is not to enable the insured to recoup losses caused by the insured's poor business practices when exchanging property or making purchases. This exclusion has application only with respect to Insuring Agreements A.3 (Inside The Premises—Theft of Money And Securities), A.4 (Inside The Premises—Robbery Or Safe Burglary Of Other Property), A.5 (Outside The Premises) and A.6 (Computer and Funds Transfer Fraud) of the Commercial Crime Policy and with respect to Insuring Agreements 3 (Inside the Premises) and 4 (Outside the Premises) of the Crime Protection Policy.

OUTLINE OF ANNOTATIONS

A. Cases Decided Under Commercial Crime Policies
B. Cases Decided Under Other Policies or Bonds

ANNOTATIONS

A. Cases Decided Under Commercial Crime Policies

6th Cir. 2004. A casino sought recovery under its manuscripted blanket crime policy, which the casino had drafted. The casino claimed losses resulting from two fraudulent cashier's checks presented to the casino by a customer and used to obtain $1.5 million from the casino. The customer lost virtually all of the money before the casino could discover that the checks were frauds. The casino filed a claim for its losses with the insurance company. The insurer, however, denied the claim, stating that the policy's provision excluding losses "due to the giving or surrendering of Money or Securities in any exchange or purchase" barred coverage. The court determined that the casino "gave or surrendered gambling credit," which constituted "Money or Securities" under the policy, in exchange for the forged checks. The court held that any coverage under the policy was barred by operation of the exclusion, which it construed against the casino as the drafter. *Harrah's Entm't, Inc. v. ACE Am. Ins. Co.*, 100 F. App'x 387.

Conn. Super. Ct. 2010. Law firm was retained to collect a debt by an alleged Chinese company and wired funds to an overseas account based on a purported check by the "debtor," which was discovered to be fraudulent. The law firm claimed a loss under the computer crime coverage of its policy, and the court applied a proximate cause standard to the direct loss insuring agreement requirement and rejected the insurer's argument that there was no coverage because there had been no computer hacking or manipulation of computer data. The policy excluded loss "resulting directly or indirectly from the giving or surrendering of Money, Securities or Other Property in exchange or purchase, whether or not fraudulent, with any party not in collusion with an Employee, except when covered under Insuring Agreement E." The court held the exclusion ambiguous and construed it against the insurer to find it inapplicable to the circumstances. The law firm had argued that the exclusion was inapplicable because it did not wire the funds in exchange for a fee for its services, but instead had received a retainer to cover future fees, and that therefore the law firm had not exchanged the wired funds for a fee. *Owens, Schine & Nicola, P.C. v. Travelers Cas. & Sur. Co. of Am.*, No. 095024601, 2010 WL 4226958, *vacated*, 2012 WL 12246940 (Conn. Super. Ct. Apr. 18, 2012).

B. Cases Decided Under Other Policies or Bonds

Cal. Ct. App. 2007. Insured designed an ad campaign and sent a media buyer funds to place and pay for advertisements with media companies. The insured's funds were placed in a commingled account, from which the owner of the media buyer embezzled funds. The policy excluded from coverage "loss or damage resulting from dissolution arising out of the giving or surrendering of assets in any exchange or purchase." Although the court agreed that the term "arising out of" was not ambiguous and required application of a broader standard than causation ("origination, growth, flow or connection to the event"), the court held the exclusion inapplicable based on the facts of the case. The transaction at issue involved the insured's transfer of funds to its agent as part of the purchase of ad time from media outlets; however, the theft of those funds once they came into possession of the media buyer was an independent and intervening act separate and apart from the purchase transaction and, therefore, the loss did not arise out of the giving or surrendering of assets in an exchange or purchase. *Sears Roebuck & Co. v. Nat'l Union Fire Ins. Co. of Pittsburgh, Pa.*, No. B187280, 2007 WL 2876149 (petition for rehearing granted).

SECONDARY SOURCES

Scott L. Schmookler, *Ch. VII, Computer and Funds Transfer Fraud, in* COMMERCIAL CRIME INSURANCE COVERAGE 297, 320-322.

O. Fire

> **3.   Insuring Agreements A.3., A.4. and A.5 do not cover:**
>
> **c.   Fire**
>
> **Loss or damage resulting from fire, however caused, except:**
>
> **(1)   Loss of or damage to "money" and "securities"; and**
>
> **(2)   Loss from damage to a safe or vault.**

(Commercial Crime Policy)

COMMENT

Although this exclusion carves out from its scope fire loss of or damage to "money" or "securities" or fire loss from damage to a safe or vault, the fire exclusion expressly excludes all other loss resulting from fire "however caused." Fire loss is covered under a variety of commercial property coverage forms available to the insured. This exclusion has application only with respect to Insuring Agreements A.3 (Inside The Premises—Theft of Money and Securities), A.4 (Inside The Premises—Robbery Or Safe Burglary Of Other Property) and A.5 (Outside The Premises).

OUTLINE OF ANNOTATIONS

A. Cases Decided Under Commercial Crime Policies
B. Cases Decided Under Other Policies or Bonds

ANNOTATIONS

A. Cases Decided Under Commercial Crime Policies

NONE

B. Cases Decided Under Other Policies or Bonds

NONE

SECONDARY SOURCES

NONE

P. Money Operated Devices

3. **Insuring Agreements A.3., A.4. and A.5 do not cover:**
   d. **Money Operated Devices**
      Loss of property contained in any money operated device unless the amount of "money" deposited in it is recorded by a continuous recording instrument in the device.

(Commercial Crime Policy)

We will not pay for loss as specified below:
5. **Under Insuring Agreements 3 and 4**
   b. **Money Operated Devices**
      Loss of property contained in any money operated device unless the amount of money deposited in it is recorded by a continuous recording instrument in the device.

(Crime Protection Policy)

COMMENT

Insureds often have vending machines or other "money operated devices" on their premises. Although the money operated device exclusion does not entirely eliminate coverage for loss from such machines, it provides that any loss of property contained in any money-operated device will be covered only if the amount of "money" deposited in the machine is recorded by a continuous recording instrument in the device. Without a continuous recording instrument, it would be difficult, if not impossible, to determine the amount of the loss. This exclusion applies with respect to Insuring Agreements A.3 (Inside The Premises— Theft Of Money And Securities), A.4 (Inside The Premises—Robbery Or Safe Burglary Of Other Property) and A.5 (Outside The Premises) of the Commercial Crime Policy and with respect to Insuring Agreements 3 (Inside the Premises) and 4 (Outside the Premises) of the Crime Protection Policy.

OUTLINE OF ANNOTATIONS

A. Cases Decided Under Commercial Crime Policies
B. Cases Decided Under Other Policies or Bonds

ANNOTATIONS

A. Cases Decided Under Commercial Crime Policies

NONE

B. Cases Decided Under Other Policies or Bonds

NONE

SECONDARY SOURCES

NONE

Q. Motor Vehicles or Equipment and Accessories

3.   Insuring Agreements A.3., A.4. and A.5 do not cover:
e.   Motor Vehicle Or Equipment And Accessories
Loss of or damage to motor vehicles, trailers or semitrailers or equipment and accessories attached to them.

(Commercial Crime Policy)

We will not pay for loss as specified below:
4.   Under Insuring Agreement 4
Motor Vehicles Or Equipment and Accessories
Loss of motor vehicles, trailers or semi-trailers or equipment and accessories attached to them.

(Crime Protection Policy)

COMMENT

Loss or damage to motor vehicles or equipment and accessories attached to them is not a matter for crime coverage. Such coverage can be obtained under a variety of automobile coverage forms and is expressly excluded from coverage under commercial crime insurance by operation of this exclusion. This exclusion has application only with respect to Insuring Agreements A.3 (Inside The Premises—Theft Of Money And Securities), A.4 (Inside The Premises—Robbery Or Safe Burglary Of Other Property) and A.5 (Outside The Premises) of the Commercial Crime Policy and with respect to Insuring Agreement 4 (Outside the Premises) of the Crime Protection Policy.

OUTLINE OF ANNOTATIONS

A. Cases Decided Under Commercial Crime Policies
B. Cases Decided Under Other Policies or Bonds

ANNOTATIONS

A. Cases Decided Under Commercial Crime Policies

NONE

B. Cases Decided Under Other Policies or Bonds

NONE

SECONDARY SOURCES

NONE

R. Transfer Or Surrender Of Property

    3.   Insuring Agreements A.3., A.4. and A.5 do not cover:

        f.   Transfer Or Surrender Of Property

            (1)   Loss of or damage to property after it has been transferred or surrendered to a person or place outside the "premises" or "financial institution premises":

                (a)   On the basis of unauthorized instructions; or

                (b)   As a result of a threat including, but not limited to:

                    (i)   A threat to do bodily harm to any person;

                    (ii)   A threat to do damage to any property;

                    (iii)   A threat to introduce a denial of service attack into any "computer system";

                    (iv)   A threat to introduce a virus or other malicious instruction into any "computer system" which is designed to damage, destroy or corrupt

"electronic data" or "computer programs" stored within the "computer system";

(v) A threat to contaminate, pollute or render substandard your products or goods; or

(vi) A threat to disseminate, divulge or utilize:

    i.   Your confidential information;

    ii. Confidential or personal information of another person or organization; or

    iii. Weaknesses in the source code within any "computer system."

(2) But, this exclusion does not apply under Insuring Agreement A.5. to loss of "money," "securities" or "other property" while outside the "premises" in the care and custody of a "messenger" if you:

(a) Had no knowledge of any threat at the time the conveyance began; or

(b) Had knowledge of a threat at the time the conveyance began, but the loss was not related to the threat.

(Commercial Crime Policy)

We will not pay for loss as specified below:
3. Under Insuring Agreements 3 and 4
    c.   Transfer or Surrender of Property

(1) Loss of property after it has been transferred or surrendered to a person or place outside the premises or banking premises:

(i) On the basis of unauthorized instructions; or

(ii) As a result of a threat to do:

(a) Bodily harm to any person; or

(b) Damage to any property.

    (2)   But this exclusion does not apply under Insuring Agreement 4 to loss of money, securities, and other property while outside the premises or banking premises in the care and custody of a messenger if you:

        (i)   Had no knowledge of any threat at the time the conveyance began; or

        (ii)   Had knowledge of a threat at the time the conveyance began, but the loss was not related to the threat.

(Crime Protection Policy)

COMMENT

It is possible for an insured to sustain a loss by voluntarily parting with property under the mistaken assumption that delivery was proper when in fact the instructions were unauthorized by the insured. Loss or damage to property after it has been transferred or surrendered to a person or place outside the "premises" or "banking premises" on the basis of unauthorized instructions is excluded. If the unauthorized instructions were by an employee to defraud an employer then there may be coverage under the employee theft insuring agreement. Coverage for property surrendered or transferred as a result of threat to do bodily harm to any person or as a result of a threat to do damage to any property also is expressly excluded. But this exclusion does not apply under Outside The Premises coverage (Insuring Agreement A.5) to loss while outside the "premises" in the care, custody and control of a "messenger" if (1) the insured had no knowledge of any threat at the time the conveyance began or (2) the insured had knowledge of a threat when the conveyance began, but the loss was not related to the threat. For example, if a messenger was robbed of the insured's bank deposit on the street at gunpoint, Insuring Agreement A.5 would cover the loss providing that there was no prior threat to the insured. However, if the messenger conveyed the insured's bank deposit under the threat of an extortionist who had kidnapped and threatened to injure the insured's family if the money was not given to him, Insuring Agreement A.5 would not cover the loss. This exclusion has application only with respect to Insuring Agreements A.3 (Inside the Premises—Theft Of Money And Securities),

A.4 (Inside The Premises—Robbery Or Safe Burglary Of Other Property) and A.5 (Outside The Premises) of the Commercial Crime Policy and with respect to Insuring Agreements 3 (Inside the Premises) and 4 (Outside the Premises) of the Crime Protection Policy.

OUTLINE OF ANNOTATIONS

A. Cases Decided Under Commercial Crime Policies
B. Cases Decided Under Other Policies or Bonds

ANNOTATIONS

A. Cases Decided Under Commercial Crime Policies

NONE

B. Cases Decided Under Other Policies Or Bonds

Ohio Ct. App. 1998. County Treasurer illegally invested and diverted county funds to his son. The County contended that the exclusion applies only to situations where the covered property is lost outside of the covered premises and that the loss occurred at the moment of the illegal funds transfer, which was consummated within the covered premises. The insurer countered that the Treasurer knowingly and intentionally transferred or surrendered covered property to a person outside the premises, thereby excluding coverage. The court determined that whether the exclusion applied hinged upon the disputed fact as to whether a theft actually occurred and therefore summary judgment applying the exclusion was inappropriate. "For instance, if it is determined that a theft did occur, it would necessarily follow that the county experienced a loss of funds the moment the funds were improperly transferred or surrendered. The moment the county was deprived of lawful possession of the funds marks the moment in which the loss of covered property occurred. Under this scenario, the exclusionary provision outlined in section (D)(1)(f)(1) would not be applicable as the loss would have occurred on premises rather than after the funds were transferred. In the event that it is determined a theft did not occur, the aforementioned 'outside the premises' exclusionary provision could be applicable as the loss would not have occurred until the investment soured." *Columbiana Cnty. Bd. Of Comm'rs. v. Nationwide Ins. Co.*, 719 N.E.2d 561.

SECONDARY SOURCES

NONE

S. Vandalism

3.   **Insuring Agreements A.3., A.4. and A.5 do not cover:**
g.   **Vandalism**
Loss from damage to the "premises" or its exterior, or to any safe, vault, cash register, cash

box, cash drawer or "other property" by vandalism or malicious mischief.

(Commercial Crime Policy)

We will not pay for loss as specified below:
3.   **Under Insuring Agreements 3 and 4**
(d)   **Vandalism**
Loss from damage to any safe, vault, or other property, or to the premises or its exterior, by vandalism or malicious mischief.

(Crime Protection Policy)

COMMENT

Vandalism is not a matter for crime coverage. Damage to property from vandalism and malicious mischief, including building damage caused by the breaking in or exiting or burglars, is covered under a variety of commercial property coverage forms available to the insured and expressly excluded from coverage under commercial crime insurance by operation of that exclusion. This exclusion applies only with respect to Insuring Agreements A.3 (Inside the Premises—Theft Of Money And Securities), A.4 (Inside The Premises—Robbery Or Safe Burglary Of Other Property) and A.5 (Outside The Premises) of the Commercial Crime Policy and with respect to Insuring Agreements 3 (Inside the Premises) and 4 (Outside the Premises) of the Crime Protection Policy.

OUTLINE OF ANNOTATIONS

A. Cases Decided Under Commercial Crime Policies
B. Cases Decided Under Other Policies or Bonds

ANNOTATIONS

A. Cases Decided Under Commercial Crime Policies

NONE

B. Cases Decided Under Other Policies or Bonds

3d Cir. 1986 (Pa.). Brinker's residence was insured under a Residential Crime Insurance Policy issued by the Federal Emergency Management Agency ("FEMA"), when the home was extensively damaged by fire. The fire marshal determined that the cause of the fire was arson, and the insured claimed that cash was stolen and the fire was a cover up for the burglary of the money. Notwithstanding federal regulations that required all residential policies issued by FEMA to cover damage to property by vandalism or malicious mischief, FEMA had issued a commercial policy to Brinker that provided coverage for property damage caused by vandalism or malicious mischief which occurs only during a burglary. The insured filed a timely claim under the policy, but because it appeared uncertain that a burglary had indeed occurred, FEMA denied the claim based upon the policy language limiting coverage for property damage arising only during a burglary. Finding FEMA's denial of coverage unjustified due to the factual errors as to the applicable policy and the mandated policy language, the trial court disagreed with FEMA and determined that the insured's losses were covered. *Brinker v. Guiffrida,* 798 F.2d 661.

SECONDARY SOURCES

NONE

T. Voluntary Parting Of Title To Or Possession of Property

3.   Insuring Agreements A.3., A.4. and A.5 do not cover:
h.   Voluntary Parting Of Title To Or Possession of Property
Loss resulting from your, or anyone else acting on your express or implied authority, being induced by any dishonest act to voluntarily part with title to or possession of any property.

(Commercial Crime Policy)

We will not pay for loss as specified below:
5.   Under Insuring Agreements 3 and 4
(b)   Voluntary Parting of Title to or Possession of Property
Loss resulting from your, or anyone acting on your express or implied authority, being induced by any dishonest act to part voluntarily with title to or possession of any property.

(Crime Protection Policy)

COMMENT

Loss resulting from the insured, or anyone acting with the insured's express or implied authority, being induced by a dishonest act to voluntarily part with title to or possession of any property is expressly excluded from coverage. The purpose of the voluntary parting exclusion is to eliminate coverage if the insured, or anyone acting with the insured's express or implied authority, is tricked into voluntarily turning over property to a thief. If there is any violence or threat of violence, so that the parting with the property is not completely voluntary, the exclusion does not apply. Likewise, if the property is taken without the involvement of the insured or someone acting on the insured's express or implied authority, there has not been a voluntary transfer and the exclusion does not apply. This exclusion has application only with respect to Insuring Agreements A.3 (Inside The Premises—Theft Of Money And Securities), A.4 (Inside The Premises—Robbery Or Safe Burglary Of Other Property) and A.5 (Outside The Premises) and A.6 (Computer and Funds Transfer Fraud) of the Commercial Crime Policy and with respect to Insuring Agreements 3 (Inside the Premises) and 4 (Outside the Premises) of the Crime Protection Policy.

OUTLINE OF ANNOTATIONS

A. Cases Decided Under Commercial Crime Policies
B. Cases Decided Under Other Policies or Bonds

ANNOTATIONS

A. Cases Decided Under Commercial Crime Policies

9th Cir. 2005 (Cal.). The casino made a claim for coverage under its crime insurance policy for losses sustained from a customer's deposit of signed withdrawal receipts. The casino honored the receipts in reliance upon the statement from the customer's bank that the customer's check had cleared. The insurer denied the casino's claim for coverage under the forgery and theft provisions of the policy because the policy excluded coverage for losses resulting from "you, or anyone acting on your express or implied authority, being induced by any dishonest act to voluntarily part with" property. The court determined that the receipts were not forged and the casino parted with its property voluntarily and as a result of the customer's dishonest act, thereby excluding the casino's claim from coverage under the policy. The court upheld the trial court's grant of summary judgment in favor of the insurer. *Bell Gardens Bicycle Casino v. Great Am. Ins. Co.*, 124 F. App'x 551.

E.D. La. 2011. The insured invested in a mutual fund that invested in hedge funds, one of which invested a portion of its holdings in a fund managed by Bernard Madoff. The insured claimed a loss resulting directly from computer fraud based on its allegation that Madoff used a computer to generate false documents. The court held that the insured did not sustain a direct loss as a result of Madoff's actions because the insured's loss "was too far removed from the Madoff scheme." The court also determined that investing in the mutual fund was "trading" within the meaning of the trading loss exclusion because "the purchase of shares in a mutual fund is equivalent to the buying and selling of securities." Relying on the policy's exclusion for losses "resulting directly or indirectly from trading," the court rejected the insured's contention that the exclusion should not apply because the insured's losses were not caused by its investment in the mutual fund, but rather Madoff's fraudulent misrepresentations, as the loss indirectly resulted from trading. The exclusion for parting with title to property also barred the claim, as the "dishonest act" under that exclusion may be committed by a third party who is not the party to whom the insured entrusted the property. The insured entrusted its investment to the mutual fund and any fund in which the mutual fund subsequently invested. The court declined to reach the issue of whether computer fraud caused the loss. *Methodist Health Sys. Found., Inc. v. Hartford Fire Ins. Co.*, 834 F. Supp. 2d 493.

B. Cases Decided Under Other Policies Or Bonds

N.D.N.Y. 2014. Businessowners Property Coverage Form excluded loss resulting from law firm's acceptance of cashier's check believed to represent payment of funds owed to lawyer's client and subsequent wire of funds to purported client, which was discovered to be a scam. The court held the voluntary parting exclusion unambiguous and rejected the law firm's contention that the exclusion did not apply to the claimed loss because it did not explicitly reference losses induced by scheme, fraud, or trick and because the law firm's reasonably expected larceny to be covered. *Martin, Shudt, Wallace, DiLorenzo & Johnson v. Travelers Indem. Co. of Conn.*, No. 13-0498, 2014 WL 460045.

S.D. Ohio 2015. Lawyer agreed to represent client in connection with recovery of unpaid settlement funds, and upon receipt of cashier's check purporting to be funds owed, wired the funds to the client less the lawyer's contingency fee. It was discovered that the cashier's check was fraudulent and the transaction a scam, and lawyer filed a claim under business owners insurance policy. The lawyer argued that the presence of fraud vitiated the ability to voluntarily part with the funds, citing to Ohio common law that a payment induced by fraud is not a voluntary payment. The court disagreed, finding that the claimed loss was "clearly excluded" by the voluntary parting exclusion. *Schmidt v. Travelers Indem. Co. of Am.*, No. 13-932, 2015 WL 1475100.

SECONDARY SOURCES

Farley et al., *Ch. XI, Exclusions in the Commercial Crime Policy, in* COMMERCIAL CRIME INSURANCE COVERAGE 427, 428-434.

U. Authorized Access

> 4. **Insuring Agreement A.6 does not cover:**
> a. **Authorized Access**
> **Loss resulting from a fraudulent:**
> **(1) Entry of "electronic data" or "computer program" into; or**
> **(2) Change of "electronic data" or "computer program" within**
> **any "computer system" owned, leased or operated by you by a person or organization with authorized access to that "computer system," except when covered under Insuring Agreement A.6.b.**

(Commercial Crime Policy)

COMMENT

Loss resulting from a person or organization with authorized access fraudulently entering electronic data or a computer program into or changing electronic data or a computer program within any computer system owned, leased or operated by the insured is expressly excluded from coverage, unless covered by Insuring Agreement A.6.b. This exclusion has application only with respect to Insuring Agreement A.6 (Computer and Funds Transfer Fraud).

OUTLINE OF ANNOTATIONS

A. Cases Decided Under Commercial Crime Policies
B. Cases Decided Under Other Policies or Bonds

ANNOTATIONS

A. Cases Decided Under Commercial Crime Policies

NONE

B. Cases Decided Under Other Policies Or Bonds

N.J. Super. Ct. App. Div. 2005. Electronic and Computer Crime Policy excluded coverage for "loss by reason of the input of Electronic Data at an authorized electronic terminal . . . or a Customer Communication System by a customer or other person who had authorized access to the customer's authentication mechanism." The court determined that the exclusion clearly and unambiguously barred coverage where a customer or authorized representative inputted data, but not where the data entry was accomplished by another individual such as an imposter or hacker. *Morgan Stanley Dean Witter v. Chubb Ins. Co.*, No. A-4124-03T2, 2005 WL 3242234.

N.Y. Super. Ct. 2013. Computer Systems Fraud Rider to Financial Institution Bond provided coverage for "loss resulting directly from a fraudulent (1) entry of Electronic Data or Computer Program into, or (2) change of Electronic Data or Computer Program within the Insured's proprietary Computer System . . . ." The court determined that coverage was only available for an unauthorized entry into the system by an unauthorized user, such as a hacker, or for unauthorized data, such as a computer virus. Coverage was not available for loss resulting from an authorized user's use of the system as intended to input medical claims, but where the claims themselves were fraudulent. *Univ. Am. Corp. v. Nat. Union Fire Ins. Co. of Pittsburgh, PA*, 959 N.Y.S.2d 849, *aff'd* 972 N.Y.S.2d 241 (2013).

SECONDARY SOURCES

NONE

V. Credit Card Transactions

4.   **Insuring Agreement A.6 does not cover:**
     b.   **Credit Card Transactions**
          Loss resulting from the use or purported use of credit, debit, charge, access, convenience, identification, stored-value or other cards or the information contained on such cards.

(Commercial Crime Policy)

We will not pay for loss as specified below:
6.   **Under Insuring Agreement 5**
     (b)   **Debit and Credit Cards**
           Loss resulting from the use or purported use of credit, debit, charge, access, convenience or other cards.

(Crime Protection Policy)

COMMENT

Loss resulting from not only the use or purported use of credit, debit, charge, access, convenience, identification, stored-value or other cards, but also the information contained on such cards, is excluded from coverage. This exclusion has application only with respect to Insuring Agreement A.6 (Computer and Funds Transfer Fraud) of the Commercial Crime Policy and with respect to Insuring Agreement 5 (Computer Fraud) of the Crime Protection Policy.

OUTLINE OF ANNOTATIONS

A. Cases Decided Under Commercial Crime Policies
B. Cases Decided Under Other Policies or Bonds

ANNOTATIONS

A. Cases Decided Under Commercial Crime Policies

NONE

B. Cases Decided Under Other Policies Or Bonds

D. Colo. 2015. Former officers of financial advisor allegedly fraudulently diverted funds, and insured sought coverage under its fidelity bond. In ruling on pre-trial motions *in limine*, the court cited the bond's credit card exclusion to exclude evidence with respect to credit card payments. The court granted the motion to exclude the evidence, despite the contention that the insurer sought dispositive relief on potential coverage issues through its motion. *In re Centrix Fin., LLC*, No. 09-01542, 2015 WL 3475730.

S.D.N.Y. 1991. Merchant posed as an art gallery, but was really a male escort service that created fraudulent credit card sales slips, which resulted in chargebacks to insured bank. The bank sought coverage under its Financial Institution Bond, and the court first addressed the bond's credit card exclusion, which excluded "loss resulting directly or indirectly from the use or purported use of credit, debit, charge, access, convenience, identification, or other cards (1) in obtaining credit or funds . . . whether such cards were issued, or purport to have been issued, by the Insured or by anyone other than the Insured." The court stated that the exclusion was potentially ambiguous as to whether the exclusion would apply to schemes where, rather than actual credit cards, authorization codes and card numbers serve as the basis for fraud. On the other hand, the court also noted that it may be the case that the exclusion of losses resulting "indirectly" from the "purported use" of credit would include the use of credit card numbers and codes to commit fraud, which was supported by the annotated bond's statement that the exclusion "address[es] the situation in which funds are obtained through the fraudulent use of the card number." The court declined to reach a determination on the credit card exclusion, however, as the court determined that the uncollected funds exclusion unambiguously excluded the claimed loss from coverage. *Broadway Nat'l Bank v. Progressive Cas. Ins. Co.*, 775 F. Supp. 123, *aff'd* 963 F.2d 1522 (2d Cir. 1992).

Del. Super. Ct. 2013. Insured bank contracted with Visa and MasterCard in connection with debit cards and with third party to service debit card transactions. Hackers accessed customer debit card and personal identification numbers in the service provider's system, resulting in unauthorized withdrawals from the customer accounts. Visa and MasterCard issued assessments against the bank pursuant to their contract. The bank sought coverage for assessments by Visa and MasterCard for expenses for blocking, monitoring, or reissuing compromised cards; compensation of issuers for a portion of the fraud loss; and cost reimbursements to issuers. The bank agreed that an additional assessment for failure to comply with stored account data security requirements was excluded from coverage, and it was not a part of the claim. The court determined that the claimed loss fell within the policy's "Electronic Risk Liability" section, which afforded coverage in relevant part for "all loss resulting from any electronic risk claim . . . that arises out of a loss event." The Policy defined "electronic risk claim" as "a written demand for monetary damages or nonmonetary relief," and a "loss event" as "any unauthorized use of, or unauthorized access to electronic data or software with a computer system." The court then reviewed whether the claimed loss fell within an exclusion in the policy for any claim against the insured "based upon or attributable to or arising from the actual or purported fraudulent use by any person or entity of any data or in any credit, debit, charge, access, convenience, customer identification, or other card, including, but not limited to the card number." The court determined that the exclusion was unambiguous and agreed with the insurer that the fraudulent use of data and subsequent assessments were meaningfully linked and qualified as "arising from" the fraudulent use, even though the court also agreed with the bank that a parallel basis for the assessments was the service provider's failure to ensure data security compliance. Despite finding that the claimed loss met the exclusion, the court determined that application of the claimed loss to the "Electronic Risk Liability" coverage section would render coverage illusory, and therefore declined to apply the exclusion to the claimed loss at issue. *First Bank of Del., Inc. v. Fid. & Deposit Co. of Md.*, No. CVN11CO8221MMJCCLD, 2013 WL 5858794.

SECONDARY SOURCES

Farley et al., *Ch. XI, Exclusions in the Commercial Crime Policy, in* COMMERCIAL CRIME INSURANCE COVERAGE 427, 434-437.

Gilbert J. Schroeder, *Claims Under Financial Institution Bonds for Losses Due to Credit Card Chargebacks*, Brief, Summer 2004, at 24, WL 33 SUM Brief 24.

W. Fraudulent Instructions

    4.   Insuring Agreement A.6 does not cover:
        d.   Fraudulent Instructions
            Loss resulting from an "employee" or "financial institution" acting upon any instruction to:
            (1)   Transfer, pay or deliver "money", "securities" or "other property", or
            (2)   Debit or delete your account;
            which instruction proves to be fraudulent, except when covered under Insuring Agreement A.6.a.(2) or A.6.b.

(Commercial Crime Policy)

COMMENT

Loss resulting from fraudulent instructions is excluded from coverage. This exclusion has application only with respect to Insuring Agreement A.6 (Computer and Funds Transfer Fraud).

OUTLINE OF ANNOTATIONS

A. Cases Decided Under Commercial Crime Policies
B. Cases Decided Under Other Policies or Bonds

ANNOTATIONS

A. Cases Decided Under Commercial Crime Policies

NONE

B. Cases Decided Under Other Policies Or Bonds

E.D. Pa. 2014. Credit union sought recovery under credit union bond after credit union employee authorized three separate wire transfers from member's account on basis of fraudulent e-mail instruction without a callback verification. The court held that the bond's exclusion for any "loss resulting directly or indirectly from a fraudulent instruction through E-mail, Telefacsimile, or Telephonic means, or ACH debit from the Accountholder's account that was originated through another financial institution, except as may be covered under the Employee or Director Dishonesty Insuring Agreement or the Funds Transfer Insuring Agreement" unambiguously barred coverage under any other bond provisions. The court rejected the credit union's contention that the phrase "originated through another financial institution" applied not only to ACH debits, but also instructions initiated by "E-mail, Telefacsimile, or Telephonic" means, and in so doing applied the rule of interpretation that a limiting clause in a policy is to be confined to the last antecedent unless the context or evident meaning requires a different construction. The court also found that the exclusion did not render coverage afforded for employee acts in conscious disregard of credit union policies illusory, as that coverage would still apply in situations in which employees act in conscious disregard of credit union policies not involving funds transfers. *Sb1 Fed. Credit Union v. FinSecure, LLC,* 14 F. Supp. 3d 651.

Cal. Ct. App. 2012. Credit union bond excluded coverage for "any loss directly or indirectly from . . . fraudulent instruction through 'e-mail,' 'telefacsimile' or 'telephonic' means . . . except as may be covered under . . . Funds Transfer Coverage." When credit union was not entitled to recover its loss under the funds transfer coverage because it did not use a "callback verification" procedure or a "procedure set forth in a written funds transfer agreement, signed by the member or the member's authorized representative, that governs the transaction and instruction," the credit union contended that the exclusion should not be enforced to prevent its recovery under other coverages. The court determined that the funds transfer exclusion was "conspicuous, plain, and clear" and understandable to a layperson and that therefore the exclusion would bar coverage under any other insuring agreement. *Universal City Studios Credit Union v. Cumis Ins. Soc'y, Inc.*, 145 Cal. Rptr. 3d 650.

SECONDARY SOURCES

NONE

X. **Failure To Follow Security Procedures**

We will not pay for loss as specified below:
6. **Under Insuring Agreement 5**
    (a) **Failure to Follow Security Procedures**
         (1) **Loss resulting from your failure to follow security procedures agreed to in writing with your customer or your financial institution;**
         (2) **Loss that would have been avoided if you had accepted and followed commercially reasonable security procedures that your financial institution made available for your account or accounts involved in the loss; or**
         (3) **Loss resulting from your failure to comply with security procedures that you represented to us you would follow.**

(Crime Protection Policy)

COMMENT

Loss resulting from failure to follow security procedures is expressly excluded by the Crime Protection Policy. This exclusion has application only with respect to Insuring Agreement 5 (Computer Fraud).

OUTLINE OF ANNOTATIONS

A. Cases Decided Under Commercial Crime Policies
B. Cases Decided Under Other Policies or Bonds

ANNOTATIONS

A. Cases Decided Under Commercial Crime Policies

NONE

B. Cases Decided Under Other Policies Or Bonds

NONE

SECONDARY SOURCES

NONE

Chapter 12

Discovery of Loss*

Coverage under the Commercial Crime Policy, as written today, is triggered by the insured's discovery of loss during the policy period. This means only one policy is triggered for a given loss. Discovery also starts the clock on the insured's claim prosecution duties, and has other functions too. Commonly used forms thus contain definitions of this term. This chapter reviews those definitions and case law arising under them.

The definitions used by the standard forms of the Insurance Service Office ("ISO") and the Surety & Fidelity Association of America ("SFAA") are as follows:

ISO Form

"Discover" or "discovered" means the time when you first become aware of facts which would cause a reasonable person to assume that a loss of a type covered by this Policy has been or will be incurred, regardless of when the act or acts causing or contributing to such loss occurred, even though the exact amount or details of loss may not then be known.

"Discover" or "discovered" also means the time when you first receive notice of an actual or potential claim in which it is alleged that you are liable to a third party under circumstances which, if true, would constitute a covered loss under this Policy.[1]

SFAA Form

Discovery of Loss

Discovery of loss occurs when you first become aware of facts which would cause a reasonable person to assume that a loss covered by this Policy has been or will be incurred

---

*   James A. Knox, Jr., Christensen Ehret, LLP, Chicago, Illinois.

1   Commercial Crime Policy, CR 00 22 08 13 at § F 5 (ISO Props., 2012) (Discovery Form), reprinted in COMMERCIAL CRIME INSURANCE COVERAGE 785, 791 (Randall I. Marmor & Susan Koehler Sullivan eds. 2014).

even though the exact amount or details of loss may not then be known.

Discovery also occurs when you receive notice of an actual or potential claim against you alleging facts that if true would constitute a covered loss under this insurance.[2]

COMMENT

These definitions of discovery of loss appear in the ISO's Commercial Crime Policy (Discovery Form) and the SFAA's Crime Protection Policy. Discovery is defined for the usual reason—to avoid dispute if possible about the meaning of a term, particularly when the term is used by the policy for many purposes. For one thing, discovery of loss during the policy period is a condition to coverage. Discovery also starts the clock on deadlines for prosecution of the claim.

The two forms take slightly different approaches. The ISO form undertakes the task in its definitions section. The term is defined as a verb—"discover" or "discovered." That verb is used as an element of what the insured must prove under each insuring agreement. In contrast, the SFAA form adheres to tradition by using the noun "discovery." The meaning of this noun is expressed in the same paragraph that makes it a condition of coverage. The definitions otherwise are nearly identical.

Both forms include provisions stating discovery also occurs on notice of an actual or potential claim against the insured, if facts are alleged that, if true, would give rise to coverage. Thus, discovery is deemed to occur on notice of a third-party claim making such allegations, even if the insured disputes the allegations or has yet to investigate them. This is an express exception to the rule discussed below that the insured itself must have knowledge sufficient to assume that a covered loss has actually occurred, as judged by a reasonable person standard.

One of the main functions of discovery of loss is to serve as a coverage trigger that will allow for coverage of a previously undetected embezzlement or the like that occurs or begins to occur before the policy period. Given the stealthy nature of employee dishonesty and some of the

---

2   Crime Protection Policy, reprinted in COMMERCIAL CRIME INSURANCE COVERAGE 785, 791 (Randall I. Marmor & Susan Koehler Sullivan eds. 2014).

other covered crimes, this is a frequent phenomenon, for which coverage is expected. The insured has the burden of proving it discovered the loss during the policy period,[3] and not sooner, but if it does so, then the insurer is willing to accept the risk of prior loss rather than limit its coverage to that part of the loss, if any, that occurred only during the policy period. However, the insurer does insist on limiting the amount of such coverage. The policy specifies that the insurer will provide no more than a single-policy limit for the total loss resulting from the occurrence.[4]

Requiring that the loss be discovered during the policy period achieves this. Assuming a string of discovery policies, only the policy in force at the time of discovery provides coverage, subject to the limits of that policy alone. Under the ISO form, for example, the employee dishonesty insuring agreement covers "loss that you sustain resulting directly from an 'occurrence' taking place at any time which is 'discovered' by you during the Policy Period."[5] The policy elsewhere states its limit of coverage amount for the occurrence, and also makes it clear that an ongoing loss involving the same employee, including a loss spanning policy periods, is only one occurrence.[6]

A crime policy may include a discovery period that extends beyond the end of the policy period, but this applies only in certain circumstances, beyond the scope of this commentary. In general, any such extension of the discovery period terminates as soon as a successor policy is issued, so there still is no overlap or stacking.[7] Moreover, the loss itself must still take place before the end of the policy period; a loss occurring only during the extended discovery period would not be covered.

---

3   FDIC v. N.H. Ins. Co., 953 F. 2d 478, 482-3 (9th Cir. 1991).

4   Commercial Crime Policy, CR 00 22 08 13, *supra* note 2, at § B.

5   *Id.* at § A (Insuring Agreement A).

6   Under an older alternative form known as "loss sustained," insureds sometimes maintained they were entitled to coverage under policies in force before the loss was discovered, so long as the loss had begun by then. Actually a loss sustained policy, if standard, was more restrictive. Other than under a limited prior loss exception, it required not only discovery during the policy period but also that the acts giving rise to the loss occur during that period. Nevertheless, the phasing out of the loss sustained form is a welcome development.

7   Commercial Crime Policy, *supra* note 2, at § E j (1).

A second major function of discovery of loss is to commence three countdowns for an insured making a claim. Meeting these deadlines is a condition to coverage. First, the insured must give notice of loss—notice of what it has discovered—to the insurer as soon as practicable after the discovery. Second, the insured must submit its proof of loss within a certain time after discovery as specified by the policy. Typically, the proof is due four to six months after discovery. Third, if suit is necessary, the insured must file the suit within the specified time after discovery. Usually this is two years. All these periods run from the actual discovery date, which may or may not correspond to the insured's alleged discovery date, as investigation may reveal.[8]

Discovery also automatically terminates any further coverage of the accused employee. Once the employee's dishonesty has been discovered, there is no coverage for loss thereafter caused by that employee. Not only that, but there is no coverage even for loss already suffered, if it occurs after discovery at any time of any dishonest act by the employee at any time. By "any" the policy does mean any—any act before or after the policy was issued and whether that act caused loss or not. Sometimes these terms are expressly softened. The automatic termination of coverage as to an employee and other duties on discovery are discussed at length in other chapters in this book.

Discovery also triggers the insured's duty not to prejudice the insurer's recovery rights against the employee or others who may be liable to the insured for the loss.[9] Discovery also is the operative date for valuation of a securities loss or of a foreign loss. A foreign loss may be paid either in the foreign currency or in dollars at the exchange rate in force on the date of discovery, at the insurer's option.[10]

So when, then, does discovery occur? The traditional judicial formulation, which the policy's discovery definition restates, is that a loss is discovered as soon as the insured obtains facts sufficient to cause a reasonable person to recognize dishonesty or fraud.[11] There must be

---

8   Commercial Crime Policy, *supra* note 2, at § E g (1) (notice of loss); § E g (2) (proof of loss); § E m(3) (suit). See Chapter 13, Duties of the Insured in the Event of a Loss. The duties to cooperate, produce records and submit to any requested examination under oath are also triggered by discovery. *Id.* at §§ E g(3), g(4) and g(5).

9   Commercial Crime Policy, *supra* note 2, at § E g (6).

10 Commercial Crime Policy, *supra* note 2, at § E x.

11 Drexel Burnham Lambert Group, Inc. v. Vigilant Ins. Co., 595 N.Y.S.2d 999, 1007 (Sup. Ct. 1993).

something more than suspicion. There also must be something more than loss. There must be knowledge of a covered cause of the loss.[12] Discovery means "that time when the insured gains sufficient factual knowledge, not mere suspicions, which would justify a careful and prudent [person] in charging another with dishonesty."[13]

The "discovery" definition (or if, the term is undefined in a particular policy, the judicial definition) imposes an objective standard, rather than determining the moment of discovery based on the insured's subjective belief alone.[14] Discovery occurs only once and the inquiry again is this: When would a reasonable person with the same growing awareness of facts as the actual insured, first be able to assume that a covered loss had occurred, or was going to occur? This could be rather early in the investigation. The definition expressly contemplates that discovery can occur before the insured knows the details or exact amount of the loss.

The discovery date thus does not shift forward as more and more details become known.[15] The date also does not move ahead when additional dishonest acts, employees or other facts revealing the full extent of the loss are discovered.[16] Nor does it wait on the insured's ability to ascertain and compute the resulting loss.[17] Indeed, in some cases, the actual loss may not have yet occurred, or it can be avoided. One of the reasons discovery triggers a notice obligation is to give the insurer a chance to participate in any opportunity to minimize the loss. The policy contemplates discovery typically will occur before the insured has enough information to provide a proof of loss—that is why the insured is given several months after discovery to file its proof.

---

12 Guyan Int'l, Inc. v. Travelers Cas. & Sur. Co., No. 3:10-1244, 2011 U.S. Dist. LEXIS 142828 (S.D. W. Va. Dec. 12, 2011).

13 Alfalfa Elec. Coop., Inc. v. Travelers Indem. Co., 376 F. Supp. 901, 906 (W.D. Okla. 1973).

14 FDIC v. Aetna Cas. & Sur. Co., 785 F. Supp. 867, 868 (D. Mont. 1990).

15 Magnolia Mgt. Corp. v. Fed. Ins. Co., No. 06-4447, 2007 U.S. Dist. LEXIS 85372 (W.D. La. Nov. 19, 2007).

16 Omega Advisors, Inc. v. Fed. Ins. Co., No. 10-912, 2010 U.S. Dist. LEXIS 125934, *20-22 (D.N.J. Nov. 30, 2010); United Ass'n Union Local No. 290 v. Fed. Ins. Co., No. 07-1521- HA, 2008 U.S. Dist. LEXIS 62746 (D. Or. Aug. 11, 2008).

17 Commodore Int'l, Ltd. v. Nat'l Union Fire Ins. Co. of Pittsburgh, Pa., 591 N.Y.S.2d 168 (App. Div. 1992).

This idea of objectively assessed awareness can be traced back to *Guarantee Co. v. Mechanics' Savings Bank & Trust Co.*[18] The insured in that case had a duty to investigate a suspicious situation rather than believe the employee's assertion that he was innocent. Unreasonable trust, naiveté, disbelief or denial does not push the date of discovery forward. Moreover, manifestations of subjective belief may be conclusive. The insured may be deemed to have discovered the loss, for example, by the date it filed a fraud suit against the employee or by the discovery date it gives in its sworn proof of loss.[19]

There is a flip side to consider as well. Sometimes the insured (or a successor) asserts a date of discovery that is found to be too early. Typically, this is an effort to reach back after actual discovery to obtain coverage under a terminated policy. It is improper to project discovery back to the date the conduct occurred or to any time before the dishonest or fraudulent nature of the conduct is appreciated by the insured, under the objective standard.[20] Reasonable inferences must be drawn from the known facts, as learned, but inferences of dishonesty may be unreasonable before a certain point. If a policy period, including any extended discovery period, terminates before actual discovery, it is too late for coverage under that policy.[21]

The remaining issue is who in the insured's organization must know the facts importing discovery of the loss? The question is one of agency law, subject to the terms of the policy[22] (which terms may even override ordinary agency law).[23] The insured is an organization, usually a corporation or a partnership. For an organization to discover a loss, one of its agents must discover the loss. The agent must be sufficiently aware of facts to meet the standard. Ordinarily, therefore, discovery of loss by

---

18   183 U.S. 402 (1902).

19   Livonia Volkswagen, Inc. v. Universal Underwriters Group, No. 06-13619, 2008 U.S. Dist. LEXIS 25519 (E.D. Mich. Mar. 31, 2008); Omega Advisors, Inc. v. Fed. Ins. Co., No. 10-912, 2010 U.S. Dist. LEXIS 125934, *20-22 (D.N.J. Nov. 30, 2010); United Ass'n Union Local No. 290 v. Fed. Ins. Co., No. 07-1521- HA, 2008 U.S. Dist. LEXIS 62746 (D. Or. Aug. 11, 2008); Bickerstaff Imports, Inc. v. Sentry Select Ins. Co., 682 S.E.2d 365 (Ga. Ct. App. 2009).

20   FDIC v. Aetna Cas. & Sur. Co., 903 F.2d 1073, 1079 (6th Cir. 1990).

21   *Id.*

22   Cal. Union Ins. Co. v. Am. Diversified Bank, 948 F.2d 556 (9th Cir. 1991).

23   Scottsdale Indem. Co. v. Martinez, Inc., CV-12-BE-2146-S, 2014 U.S. Dist. LEXIS 135129 (N. D. Ala. Sept. 25, 2014).

the insured occurs when a non-colluding director, officer, partner, manager or supervisor discovers the loss.

However, not every agent or employee's knowledge is always imputed to the insured. The dishonest or a colluding employee's knowledge ordinarily is not imputed to the insured.[24] Generally, if the discovering person is in a position of management, control or supervision above or at the same level as the dishonest officer or employee, the discovering person's knowledge is imputed.[25] Imputation could also occur upon discovery by a person at a lower level of authority, if that person has a duty to report wrongdoing.[26] Moreover, it must be the insured that discovers the loss, not a third party or even the insurer as informed by the third party only.[27]

The trend of current policies is to specify exactly which person or department must discover the loss. Some policies state that discovery occurs when an officer, director, insurance manager or risk manager first becomes aware of facts which would cause a reasonable person to assume that a covered loss has been or will be incurred. Other policies specify that discovery does not occur until the insured's risk manager or risk management department has such awareness. This kind of provision has been enforced as written[28] but courts may impute knowledge to the specified person if that person was kept in the dark by persons under a duty to communicate to that person.[29]

---

24   S.E. Bakery Feeds, Inc. v. Ranger Ins. Co., 974 S.W.2d 635, 639 (Mo. Ct. App. 1996).

25   E. Udolf, Inc. v. Aetna Cas. & Sur. Co., 573 A.2d 1211, 1213-15 (D. Conn. 1990).

26   People's State Bank v. Am. Cas. Co. of Reading, Pa., 818 F. Supp. 1073, 1076 (E.D. Mich. 1993).

27   Gray & Assoc., LLC v. Travelers Cas. & Sur. Co. of Am., No. CCB-07-2216, 2008 U.S. Dist. LEXIS 23903 (D. Md. Mar. 25, 2008).

28   EaglePitcher Mgt. Co. v. Zurich Am. Ins. Co., No. CV 04-870, 2009 U.S. Dist. LEXIS 68360, *23-24 (D. Ariz. July 30, 2009).

29   Magnolia Mgt. Corp. v. Fed. Ins. Co., No. 06-4447, 2007 U.S. Dist. LEXIS 85372 (W.D. La. Nov. 19, 2007); Hudson Ins. Co. v. Oppenheim, 916 N.Y.S.2d 68 (App. Div. 2011).

One further note, about the annotations below. Cases involving bonds issued to financial institutions and securities dealers are not included.[30]

ANNOTATIONS

1st Cir. 1990 (Mass.). Time within which to discover loss could not be equitably tolled on the basis that the employee exerted adverse domination and control over insured; that the employee did not exercise such control was undisputed. Discovery and notice provision made policy a "claims made and reported" type, so late notice could not be excused. *J.I. Corp. v. Fed. Ins. Co.,* 920 F.2d 118, 119-20.

2d Cir. 1984 (N.Y.). Discovery of a loss is governed by an objective standard based on conclusions that a reasonable person would reach from facts known to the insured. The insured discovered a loss when a committee met to discuss certain bond trades by its investment manager and prepared a memo referring to excessive broker commissions. Notice not given to the insurer until five months later was untimely. Insured was not justified in believing the conduct to be honest until informed by counsel that the trading was illegal. *Utica Mut. Ins. Co. v. Fireman's Fund Ins. Cos.,* 748 F.2d 118, 121-23.

2d Cir. 1935 (N.Y.). Discovery triggering notice and proof of loss conditions occurred when insured warehouse's representative discovered misappropriations while examining dishonest employee's accounts, not later when insured assembled sufficient details to submit proof of loss. *Pub. Warehouses of Matanzas, Inc. v. Fid. & Dep. Co. of Md.,* 77 F.2d 831, 832-33.

2d Cir. 1927 (N.Y.) Discovery requires that the insured actually learn of the thefts; the mere possibility of the insured informing itself from materials at its disposal is insufficient. *Mass. Bonding & Ins. Co. v. Norwich Pharmacal Co.,* 18 F.2d 934, 937.

---

30 *See* Toni Scott Reed, Discovery of Loss, ANNOTATED FINANCIAL INSTITUTION BOND 341 (Michael Keeley ed., 3d ed. 2013) for a comprehensive set of annotations on cases involving such bonds.

3d Cir. 2011 (N.J.). Discovery occurred under a commercial crime policy when the insured armored car company learned that money in its custody disappeared, as this was a type of loss covered by the policy. *Diebold Inc. v. Continental Cas. Co.*, 430 F. App'x 201, 206-7.

3d Cir. 1937 (Pa.). Discovery under a fidelity schedule bond meant "positive discovery which requires affirmative action, not mere or even real suspicion." Jury question existed as to whether vice president's understanding of president's conduct amounted to knowledge of embezzlement. *Hunt v. Fid. & Dep. Co. of Md.*, 92 F.2d 75, 77.

5th Cir. 1974 (Ala.). Loss was discovered only when it became clear that the employee had misappropriated the cash he received from sales. *Brad's Machine Prod., Inc. v. Phoenix Assur. Co. of N.Y.*, 489 F.2d 622, 624-25.

6th Cir. 1996 (Ohio). Insured's farm manager allegedly stole cattle and equipment from insured. The court held insured's suit on a crime policy was barred because it was filed more than a year after discovery of loss. The discovery date was established by the insured's admissions in its complaint, answers to interrogatories and sworn proof of loss. *Friendly Farms v. Reliance Ins. Co.*, 79 F.3d 541, 544-45.

6th Cir. 1975 (Ohio). Discovery of loss does not occur until the insured has had a reasonable time to discover the extent and amount of the loss. *Russell Gasket Co. v. Phoenix of Hartford Ins. Co.*, 512 F.2d 205, 208.

7th Cir. 1956 (Ill.) Insured meat packer investigating inventory losses had mere suspicions, not knowledge sufficient to constitute discovery of loss, until it learned that losses were result of theft by specific employees, so its notice the next day was prompt enough. *B. Constantino & Sons Co. v. New Amsterdam Cas. Co.*, 234 F.2d 902, 903-4.

8th Cir. 1992 (Mo.). Insured made loan to third party to enable it to buy insured's factory. Insured learned its president deposited third party's repayment of loan into president's personal account, rather than insured's account. President claimed he did this in repayment of a personal loan to the insured. Outside auditors did not reach a conclusion as to whether the president's conduct was improper. In determining whether insured discovered the loss during the policy period, court acknowledged mere suspicion of wrongdoing is insufficient; there must be some verification. If an outside auditor could not tell whether wrongdoing had occurred, then discovery had not occurred. Bankruptcy trustee's proof of loss giving discovery date after policy period did not necessarily preclude insured from establishing earlier discovery but lack of evidence that management had knowledge and not just suspicion was conclusive against insured. *Block v. Granite State Ins. Co.,* 963 F.2d 1127, 1129-30.

8th Cir. 1907 (Mo.). Notice is required on knowledge of facts that would justify a careful and prudent man to believe a crime had been committed. *Aetna Indemnity Co. v. J.R. Crowe Coal & Mining Co.,* 154 F. 545, 549.

9th Cir. 2001 (Idaho). Insured claimed theft by former management group through payment of excessively high fees to companies controlled by group. When group proposed merger of insured's subsidiary with another company, merger was opposed and shareholder derivative suit was filed, claiming transactions were fraudulent. The suit was dismissed and a new management group took over, investigated fraud and concluded old group had looted insured. Not until after renewing its crime policy did the new group report it had discovered the excessive fees. Insurer contended discovery occurred before the bond period. The court held that a fact issue existed as to whether insured had knowledge before the bond period, greater than mere suspicion, and with appreciation of the significance of the facts, sufficient to cause a reasonable person to assume that a fraudulent or dishonest act had occurred. *Gulf USA Corp v. Fed. Ins. Co.,* 259 F.3d 1049, 1058-60.

9th Cir. 2000 (Cal.). Insured's employee committed fraud over three policy years. The court held discovery provision in first of several consecutive policies precluded recovery under that policy because the insured discovered the loss more than six months after the policy's one-year period for notice to the insurer. The inception of the loss doctrine used in construing occurrence policies did not apply. There was no equitable tolling because the employee did not adversely dominate the insured. *Karen Kane, Inc. v. Reliance Ins. Co.,* 202 F.3d 1180, 1188-90.

9th Cir. 1992 (Cal.). A fact issue for jury existed as to whether ordinary, reasonable and sensible employer would have concluded that dishonesty had occurred but knowledge of insured's branch manager could be imputed to insured in determining when discovery of loss occurred. *Mercedes-Benz of N. Am. v. Hartford Acc. & Indem. Co.*, Nos. 89-56011, 89-56012, 1992 U.S. Dist. LEXIS 19825, *4-7.

9th Cir. 1912 (Cal.). Discovery occurs not on mere suspicion but on receipt of definite knowledge or information sufficient to justify insured in preferring charges against employee. *National Surety Co. v. Western Pac. Ry. Co.*, 200 F. 675, 682-4.

10th Cir. 1966 (N.M.). Discovery occurs when the insured is in possession of knowledge which would justify a careful and prudent person in charging another with fraud or dishonesty. "Suspicion" became "knowledge" when employee failed to attend a meeting where he had promised to explain mysterious disappearance. *Hidden Splendor Mining Co. v. Gen. Ins. Co. of Am.*, 370 F.2d 515, 517.

10th Cir. 1941 (N.M.). Employer is not bound to report merely suspicious conduct, but only knowledge which would justify a careful and prudent person in charging another with fraud or dishonesty. *Am. Employers' Ins. Co. v. Raton Wholesale Liquor Co.*, 123 F.2d 283, 285.

N.D. Ala. 2014. CEO signed insured's application for policy, made material misrepresentations therein and knew she had already embezzled from the insured. In addition to upholding a misrepresentation defense, the court deemed the insured to have discovered the loss before the bond period as a result of the CEO's knowledge of her own theft. The policy provided that discovery of loss occurred when an officer, director, insurance manager, or risk manager first becomes aware of facts which would cause a reasonable person to assume that a covered loss has been or will be incurred. A reasonable CEO would know her theft resulted in loss, and her knowledge had to be imputed to the insured even if the insured's other officer was not then aware of it. The policy specified that an officer's knowledge is imputed, so discovery occurred even if the CEO's knowledge would not have been imputed under general agency principles. Moreover, the sole representative doctrine applied as an exception to the rule that the knowledge of an agent acting adversely to the principal is not imputed. The CEO was the sole agent applying for the insurance. *Scottsdale Indem. Co. v. Martinez, Inc.,* CV-12-BE-2146-S, 2014 U.S. Dist. LEXIS 135129, *32-37.

D. Ariz. 2009. Policies specified risk manager had to know about loss for discovery to occur so knowledge of others including even the CEO was not imputed. Neither policy required notice until after the insured's risk manager learned of the loss. As a result, if any other individual working for the insured learned of the loss, it was insufficient to trigger notice. The court concluded that the risk manager did not discover the loss until after the employee's arrest, which fell after the first policy's sixty-day discovery tail, and, therefore, the second policy provided coverage. Only the risk manager's knowledge mattered. *EaglePitcher Mgt. Co. v. Zurich Am. Ins. Co.,* 640 F. Supp. 2d 1109, 1118-20.

N.D. Cal. 2014. Dishonest officers' collusive control of insured conducting Ponzi scheme precluded coverage and did not require tolling of discovery period. *Dillon v. Continental Cas. Co.,* No. 5:10-CV-05238, 2014 U.S. Dist. LEXIS 4170, *35.

D.D.C. 1980. Loss based on third-party claim is not discovered until such loss exists and such loss does not exist until third party demands indemnity from insured. *Fid. & Dep. Co. of Md. v. President & Directors of Georgetown College,* 483 F. Supp. 1142, 1147.

N.D. Ill. 2005. From 1998 to 2000, union's secretary-treasurer invested funds with consulting firm and misled union officials as to the investment's security. Union sued fidelity insurer more than two years after it filed proof of loss and insurer asserted suit was time-barred. The court agreed, rejecting union's argument that it did not discover loss until twenty months after it filed proof of loss, when it received a distribution of the consulting firm's assets from a receivership. *Bridge, Structural & Reinforcing Iron Workers v. Fid. & Dep. Co. of Md.,* No. 03 C 4207, 2005 U.S. Dist. LEXIS 8242, *7-12.

N.D. Ill. 1995. Real estate developer discovered officer's embezzlement after discovery period but argued officer's adverse domination tolled the period. The court disagreed. No inference could be drawn that the officer controlled the insured and the adverse domination argument had been applied only in the context of regulated mutual funds anyway. Difficulties in discovering a loss, including intentional concealment by the employee, do not excuse even a diligent insured from the need to discover the loss during the policy's discovery period. *Willow Mgmt. Co. v. Am. States Ins.*, No. 94 C 6994, 1995 U.S. Dist. LEXIS 467, *6-9.

N.D. Ill. 1990. The insured gave notice and proof of loss to its crime insurer after the subsidiary discovered employee theft. Insurer contended insured had earlier knowledge of an occurrence that could become a loss when it discovered third parties were selling inventory stolen from the insured. Insured argued it had yet to learn of any employee theft. The court held that a fact issue existed as to whether insured had such knowledge of employee involvement in the scheme as would require notice to its fidelity insurer. *Maytag Corp. v. Fed. Ins. Co.*, No. 89 C 9254, 1990 U.S. Dist. LEXIS 12358, *4-7.

D. Kan. 1989. Discovery of fraud or dishonesty is deemed to occur when the insured actually becomes aware of sufficient facts which would lead a reasonable person to believe that an insured loss has occurred. The earliest discovery could have occurred was when a security department employee informed his superiors in writing that he was investigating a rumor that a particular employee was using a dummy corporation to defraud the insured. Issue of fact still existed as to when insured acquired knowledge of the wrongdoing and not mere suspicion, but whenever that was, insured's notice of loss was timely. *Koch Indus., Inc. v. Nat'l Union Fire Ins. Co. of Pittsburgh, Pa.*, No. 89-1158-K, 1989 U.S. Dist. LEXIS 15703, *31-38.

W.D. La. 2007. Insured discovered loss when employee confessed theft and insured gave notice, even though insured had not completed its investigation or established the extent of its loss. Discovery of facts giving rise to a potential fidelity claim constitutes discovery, not later determination of the extent of loss. The policy defined discovery as knowledge or discovery by its designated insurance representative, but the court rejected a literal reading of that in the circumstances. In any event, discovery occurred when the representative contacted insurance agent about the claim more than two years before the insured filed suit. *Magnolia Mgt. Corp. v. Fed. Ins. Co.*, No. 06-4447, 2007 U.S. Dist. LEXIS 85372, *14-22.

E.D. La. 1997. HMO's officer negotiated HMO's dental plan contract with PPO. After officer resigned, HMO learned of discrepancy between contract price and amount paid PPO, and that officer was a co-owner of PPO. HMO terminated contract with PPO and PPO sued HMO. HMO countersued PPO and sued officer for self-dealing and breach of fiduciary duty. The court held HMO's crime policy did not cover the loss because these events established HMO discovered loss before inception of policy. A fidelity loss cannot be discovered twice. HMO's discovery was not postponed by officer's denials of wrongdoing until date when HMO first saw checks PPO used to pay HMO's officer. *USF&G v. Maxicare Health Plans,* No. CIV. A. 96-2457, 1997 U.S. Dist. LEXIS 12045, *11-18.

D. Md. 2008. A title company suffered losses as a result of fraud by an employee of a real estate settlement agency. The title company notified the settlement agency's crime insurer. The insured's receiver eventually made a claim but the crime insurer correctly denied coverage. Only the title company, not the insured, discovered the loss during the policy's discovery period. The title company's notice did not count because the policy required the insured to discover the loss, not the insurer or a third party. *Gray & Assoc., LLC v. Travelers Cas. & Sur. Co. of Am.,* No. CCB-07-2216, 2008 U.S. Dist. LEXIS 23903, *9-18.

D. Mass. 1994. Executive director of insured developer made illegal loan from reserve account to board of directors by forging signature of a board member. Discovery occurred when fraudulent loan was uncovered by auditors and reported to insured. Discovery did not occur later after insured had referred matter to crime investigation agency. Insured's delay in providing notice and proof of loss was patently unreasonable and precluded coverage. *United States v. Nat'l Grange Mut. Ins. Co.,* Civ. A. NO. 92-12813-MAP, 1994 U.S. Dist. LEXIS 13321, *10-11.

D. Mass. 1985. Bond required notice on discovery "of any act or circumstance indicating a probable claim." Insured's executives had a meeting to discuss whether a third-party administrator (who had previously been found to "misuse" premium funds) was cashing premium checks instead of depositing them, knew this was not allowed and had given false explanations for his conduct. This qualified as discovery. Coverage was denied due to the insured's failure to give written notice to the insurer after the meeting. *Boston Mut. Life Ins. Co. v. Fireman's Fund Ins. Co.*, 613 F. Supp. 1090, 1092-93.

E.D. Mich. 2008. A car dealer discovered thefts by its general manager. The insured fired the manager and then sued him. The court presumed that the insured discovered the loss not later than when it sued the manager, almost three years before it sued its crime insurer, which was too late. *Livonia Volkswagen, Inc. v. Universal Underwriters Group*, No. 06-13619, 2008 U.S. Dist. LEXIS 25519, *19-20.

D.N.J. 2010. The insured discovered its loss no later than when it sued the employee for taking bribes from foreign officials. There was no later discovery of a separate loss when the insured learned more facts because the bond defined all loss involving a single employee as a single loss. *Omega Advisors, Inc. v. Fed. Ins. Co.*, No. 10-912, 2010 U.S. Dist. LEXIS 125934, *20-22.

S.D.N.Y. 1974. Discovery of loss occurred upon actual knowledge, not mere suspicion, of gold and silver inventory loss and thus insured timely filed proof of loss and suit. *U. S. Smelting Refining & Mining Co. v. Aetna Cas. & Sur. Co.*, 372 F. Supp. 489, 491.

W.D. Okla. 1973. Discovery means that time when insured gains sufficient factual knowledge, not mere suspicion, which would justify a careful and prudent person in charging another with dishonesty. It means knowledge of the first dishonest act, not just acts for which claim is made. *Alfalfa Elec. Co-op, Inc. v. Travelers Indem. Co.*, 376 F. Supp. 901, 906-8.

D. Or. 2008. Insured was sued by SEC and ERISA plans and itself accused CEO and another officer of concealing fraudulent loan losses. Insured thus discovered loss before third fidelity policy was issued. The loss was an uninsurable known loss under that policy. Discovery date could not be pushed forward into third policy period on basis of insured's not learning until then that other employees had been involved in the fraud. They were all acting under the direction of the CEO. *United Ass'n Union Local No. 290 v. Fed. Ins. Co.*, No. 07-1521- HA, 2008 U.S. Dist. LEXIS 62746, *18-23.

D. Or. 1992. Insured suffered losses from loans made to company controlled by insured's director. Director induced the loans by understating the amount of collateral. Insurer contended insured failed to file timely notice or suit after discovering the loss on the basis of deficiencies in loan file. Insured contended at worst it should have discovered loss earlier but did not actually do so until the director disappeared, so notice and suit were timely. The court agreed with insured. Discovery occurs not on suspicion of dishonest conduct, but when the insured acquires knowledge of a specific fraudulent or dishonest act that might be covered. While an insured cannot disregard known facts, the insured's knowledge of the poor quality of its credit administration, and its feeling of concern, did not rise to the level of discovery of loss. There was no reckless or unreasonable disregard of known facts by a non-wrongdoing employee. *Interstate Prod. Credit Ass'n v. Fireman's Fund Ins. Co.*, 788 F. Supp. 1530, 1535-37.

E.D. Pa. 2015. Insured ESOP's CEO allegedly stole ESOP plan assets. Insured filed complaint alleging it discovered loss on a certain date several months after the date it "began to discover" the theft in July and August of 2012, according to the proof of loss form it filled out. Insurer asserted a contractual limitations defense on the basis that the insured did not file suit within two years of the discovery date given in the proof of loss. The court denied insurer's motion to dismiss on basis that issues of fact existed as to when insured actually discovered loss as raised by insured's affidavit stating it only suspected the theft by the date given in the proof of loss. Although the discovery threshold is low, it was unclear what facts the insured knew and when. The proof of loss form did not conclusively establish that the insured had in fact discovered the loss by the stated date. Nor did discovery necessarily occur in July 2012 when a court found the insured and its CEO liable to ESOP participants for breach of fiduciary duty. *Spear v. Westfield Ins. Co.*, 2015 U.S. Dist. LEXIS 75540, *10-16.

E.D. Pa. 1995. Sole director and president of nursing home was accused of embezzlement. President of insured, nursing home's parent company, confronted nursing home president over several years and told him he was "stealing" from the nursing home. Two of six proof of loss forms submitted by insured to its fidelity insurer claimed the losses were discovered in 1990; the rest claimed discovery in 1993. The proofs giving the 1990 date showed the insured had at least discovered a situation that may have resulted in loss, so insured's suit filed more than two years after that date was untimely. *Northwood Nursing & Convalescent Home, Inc. v. Continental Ins. Co.,* 902 F. Supp. 79, 82-84.

S.D. W. Va. 2011. The insured contracted with a corporate administrator for management of its employee benefit plan. On discovering a loss of funds, the insured terminated its contract with the administrator and procured a crime policy covering plan managers. An issue of fact existed as to whether the insured discovered the loss before it obtained the policy. Arguably, the insured knew funds had been lost but did not yet know that a theft had occurred. *Guyan Int'l, Inc. v. Travelers Cas. & Sur. Co.,* No. 3:10-1244, 2011 U.S. Dist. LEXIS 142828, *9-11.

Bankr. N.D. Ga. 1993. If an insured under a fidelity policy suspects fraud by an employee, a duty of inquiry arises that cannot be satisfied by the undocumented assertion of the employee that no problem exists or, if there is a problem, he will solve it. The failure of the insured to inquire promptly or to respond promptly in a manner that would cause a reasonable and prudent person to put aside his suspicion of fraud triggers duty to notify the insurer under a policy requiring notice of discovery of an "occurrence which may become a loss." The insured need not have actual knowledge of theft or fraud under this wording. *In re Prime Commercial Corp. v. Those Certain Underwriters at Lloyd's,* 187 B.R. 785, 800-06.

Ariz. Ct. App. 1971. Where employee had borrowed money from the insured in the past and repaid same, insured could not be held to know that the employee's continuation of the practice was dishonest. A presumption of honesty applies. If acts known are as consistent with the integrity of employees as their dishonesty, there is no discovery of loss, even if dishonest acts are found later. *Md. Cas. Co. v. Clements,* 487 P.2d 437, 442-46.

Ark. 1930. Unbusinesslike methods in and of themselves do not warrant notice to surety. *Fid. & Dep. Co. of Md. v. Cunningham,* 28 S.W.2d 715, 719.

Cal. Ct. App. 1931. Discovery triggering notice duty requires actual knowledge, not mere opportunity to investigate or means of knowledge. *Pac. Coast Adjustment Bureau v. Indem. Ins. Co. of N. Am.,* 2 P.2d 218, 219-20.

Cal. Ct. App. 1919. Discovery triggering notice duty requires knowledge of default or every opportunity of knowing of default, not mere suspicion. *L.A. Athl. Club v. USF&G,* 183 P. 174, 177.

Conn. 1990. Discovery occurs if employee in position of authority and with duty to report fraud knows of employee's dishonest conduct. *E. Udolf, Inc. v. Aetna Cas. & Sur. Co.,* 573 A.2d 1211, 1213-15.

Fla. Ct. App. 2003. Undisputed fact that loss was not discovered until after discovery period expired barred coverage. Discovery clause is enforceable and not an impermissible attempt to shorten the applicable statute of limitations, contrary to a Florida statute. *Fireman's Fund Ins. Co. v. Levine & Partners,* 848 So. 2d 1186, 1187.

Ga. Ct. App. 2009. The insured asserted it did not discover the loss until it learned its employee had been convicted. However, the insured's original proof of loss and correspondence asserted it had discovered the employee's dishonesty three years earlier. The date given with the proof of loss was controlling and the insured's suit filed more than two years after that date was time barred. *Bickerstaff Imports, Inc. v. Sentry Select Ins. Co.,* 682 S.E.2d 365, 367-68.

Ga. Ct. App. 1996. The insured asked the manager of its dealership to investigate his used car operation. The manager reported everything was okay. Accounting records revealed problems but the manager explained there had been a high volume of business. After the manager was fired, his successor continued the investigation. After the discovery period expired, an employee confessed embezzlement. An issue of fact existed whether the insured had discovered its loss before the discovery period expired. The insured did not have to identify the employee by then; it need only have known it was the victim of employee dishonesty. *Boomershine Pontiac v. Globe Indem. Co.,* 466 S.E.2d 915, 917-19.

Ga. Ct. App. 1989. Criminal trial of insured's former executive director for misappropriation of funds did not provide insured with sufficient knowledge to constitute discovery of loss. Although the trial led insured to believe it had sustained a loss, the director was acquitted and the prosecution did not share the results of its investigation with the insured. Only on receipt of an auditor's report a year later did the insured have the degree of knowledge sufficient to constitute discovery of loss. *USF&G v. Macon-Bibb County Econ. Opportunity Council, Inc.*, 381 S.E.2d 539, 540.

Ind. Ct. App. 1995. Fidelity bond automatically terminated on takeover of insured by liquidator and required discovery of loss before termination. The liquidator was allowed to continue investigating whether loss had been discovered before termination. Mere fact that wrongdoing officer, through subsidiaries, owned controlling interest in insured, did not factually establish adverse domination sufficient to equitably toll discovery period so court did not address whether doctrine legally applies to discovery of a fidelity loss. *Mut. Sec. Life Ins. Co. v. Fid. & Dep. Co. of Md.*, 659 N.E.2d 1096, 1102-03.

La. Ct. App. 1997. Loss claimed under consecutive policies could only be discovered once and was discovered during first policy when insured was sued for misrepresentations by salesman, not when final judgment was entered during second policy. The notice of loss given to insurer then was too late. *Newpark Res., Inc. v. Marsh & McLennan*, 691 So. 2d 208, 212-13.

La. Ct. App. 1938. Insured has no duty to inform its insurer of suspicions but only of knowledge of fraudulent or dishonest conduct on the part of its employee which might involve the liability of the insurer. *Inter-City Express Lines, Inc. v. Hartford Acc. & Indem. Co.*, 178 So. 280, 282.

Me. 2002. Proof of loss was not timely filed after insured was deemed to have discovered president's personal use of company credit cards. Ordinary standards of objective reasonableness applied to the determination of when discovery occurred. *Acadia Ins. Co. v. Keiser Indus., Inc.*, 793 A.2d 495, 498-99.

Mass. 1935. Discovery does not wait on actual ability to prove loss but occurs when inferences can be reasonably drawn from known facts that would inform an ordinary person that there had been a loss. *Gilmour v. Standard Sur. & Cas. Co. of N.Y.*, 197 N.E. 673, 675-6.

Minn. 1910. Insured is not bound to assume employee dishonesty until it has knowledge of acts that could be covered under fidelity bond; suspicions of irregularities or fraud do not suffice. *Gamble-Robinson Co. v. Mass. Bonding & Ins. Co.*, 129 N.W. 131, 132.

Miss. 1951. Awareness of loss sustained by reason of acts constituting larceny or embezzlement means knowledge of facts which would constitute the crime. The crime is so serious that a charge cannot safely be based upon mere inferences or suspicions arising from unexplained irregularities in the employee's accounts. A period of investigation after a well-founded suspicion has arisen may be needed before the charge can be made with sufficient certainty. *Hartford Acc. & Indem. Co. v. Hattiesburg Hardware Stores*, 49 So. 2d 813, 816-19.

Miss. 1921. Awareness of acts constituting larceny or embezzlement means knowledge of facts of the crime. Time to investigate may be needed. Mere suspicions arising from irregularities in the employee's accounts are insufficient. *Md. Cas. Co. v. Hall*, 88 So. 407, 409.

Mo. Ct. App. 1998. Insurer need not show prejudice from the insured's failure to discover an employee's check forgeries before the policies' discovery period expired. A commercial crime policy is not an occurrence policy, so prejudice is immaterial. The dishonest employee's knowledge could not be imputed to the insured. *S.E. Bakery Feeds, Inc. v. Ranger Ins. Co.*, 974 S.W.2d 635, 639.

Mont. 1924. Insured grain dealer was held not to know its manager had been gambling in grain despite having records to that effect in its custody, because only the employee knew about records. *Outlook Farmer's Elevator Co. v. Am. Sur. Co. of N.Y.*, 223 P. 905, 911.

N.Y. App. Div. 2011. A bond stated notice of loss had to be given as soon as practicable after discovery of loss by the "corporate risk manager." The insured argued its chief actuary held that title de facto and did not get notice until after the insurer got notice. However, general counsel knew about the loss a year earlier, and the bond required reasonable diligence to acquire knowledge of covered losses. The insured breached that duty, either because it did not inform its actuary sooner or the risk management function had been delegated to counsel so that counsel's knowledge was imputed to the chief actuary. *Hudson Ins. Co. v. Oppenheim*, 916 N.Y.S.2d 68, 69-70.

N.Y. App. Div. 1992. Insured learned employees were stealing its computer equipment and notified insurer. Insured and insurer could not agree over insured's request for extension of time to file its proof of loss. Insured filed proof of loss and filed suit over two years later. Insured argued this was timely on basis that discovery did not occur until it had information from which it could reasonably estimate the extent of the loss. The court disagreed. The insured's first knowledge of the thefts was its moment of discovery even if the amount of the loss had yet to be determined. *Commodore Int'l, Ltd. v. Nat'l Union Fire Ins. Co. of Pittsburgh, Pa.*, 591 N.Y.S.2d 168, 169-70.

N.Y. App. Div. 1934. Where dishonest act reasonably appeared to be one of casual irregularity or careless usurpation of authority without wrongful intent, insured had not yet become conclusively aware that acts were actually dishonest and fraudulent and therefore had not yet discovered loss. *Charles W. Schreiber Travel Bureau, Inc. v. Standard Sur. & Cas. Co. of N. Y.*, 269 N.Y.S. 804, 806-7.

Or. Ct. App. 2000. Policy required notice on discovery of loss or of an occurrence which may become a loss, but the time to sue was based only on discovery of loss. Discovery of loss does not occur until the insured has knowledge of specific facts that reasonably would cause a person to conclude that the employee had acted unlawfully. Factors to consider include whether the loss is covered, whether the insured is aware of sufficient facts that reasonably suggest that the loss would lead to coverage, and whether there are objective facts showing what a reasonable person should conclude from the available information. Insured's filing of complaint against its employee for breach of fiduciary duty did not demonstrate that it had knowledge of the employee's fraudulent intent so as to constitute discovery as a matter of law. Insurer was not entitled to summary judgment that suit was untimely. *Nike, Inc. v. N.W. Pac. Indem. Co.*, 999 P.2d 1197, 1203-4.

Tenn. Ct. App. 1984. Discovery of loss triggering time period to give proof of loss ran from knowledge of loss, not later knowledge of amount of loss. *Griffith Motors, Inc. v. Compass Ins. Co.*, 676 So. 2d 555, 558.

Tenn. Ct. App. 1965. Discovery means knowledge of facts and circumstances sufficient to satisfy persons of ordinary prudence that a loss had occurred. *World Secret Serv. Ass'n v. Travelers Indem. Co.*, 396 S.W.2d 848, 849.

Vt. 1940. Discovery occurs on knowledge or reasonable inferences from known fact that loss has occurred, not later when extent of loss is determined. *Brown v. Md. Cas. Co.*, 11 A.2d 222, 223-4.

Wash. 1966. Insured's knowledge that its manager had been late in making deposits did not by itself mean insured had actual knowledge of dishonesty sufficient to constitute discovery of loss. *Tradewell Stores, Inc. v. Fid. & Cas. Co. of N.Y.*, 410 P.2d 782, 784-85.

SECONDARY SOURCES

Paul Briganti, *Inside the Mind of the Reasonable Person: Determining When Discovery of Loss Has Occurred Under a Fidelity Bond in the Third Circuit*, 46 VILL. L. REV. 801 (2001).

Duncan L. Clore, *Discovery of Loss: The Contractual Predicate to the Claim*, in FINANCIAL INSTITUTION BONDS 193 (Duncan L. Clore ed., 3d ed. 2008).

Duncan L. Clore & Meredith Constant, *Discovery*, in ANNOTATED FINANCIAL INSTITUTION BOND 421 (Michael Keeley, ed. 2004).

Duncan L. Clore & Michael Keeley, *Discovery of Loss: The Contractual Predicate to the Claim*, in FINANCIAL INSTITUTION BONDS 137 (Duncan L. Clore ed., 2d ed. 1998).

Duncan L. Clore & John J. Tomaine, *Discovery of Loss*, in HANDLING FIDELITY BOND CLAIMS 431 (Michael Keeley & Sean Duffy, eds., 2d ed. 2005).

Paul R. Devin & Allen N. David, *Discovery Under Fidelity Bonds: The Emerging Concept of the Insured's Duty of Inquiry*, 21 TORT & INS. L.J. 543 (1986).

Edward Etcheverry, *Discovery, Notice, Proof of Loss and Suit Limitations*, in COMMERCIAL CRIME POLICY 12 (Gilbert J. Schroeder ed., 1997).

James A. Knox, Jr. & Sandra M. Stone, *Discovery of Loss*, in THE COMMERCIAL CRIME POLICY ANNOTATED, 2d Ed. (Cole S. Kain and Lana M. Glovach, eds. 2005).

G. Wayne Murphy, *Allegations, Assertions and Charges as Discovery of Loss*, 12 THE FORUM 986 (1977).

Toni Scott Reed, *Discovery*, in ANNOTATED FINANCIAL INSTITUTION BOND 341 (Michael Keeley ed., 3d ed. 2013).

Scott L. Schmookler & Bruce Robbibaro, *Discovery by the Risk Manager: The Effect of Noise Reducing Headphones on Fidelity Coverage*, XVII FID. L.J. 171 (2011).

Paul D. Schoonover, *Discovery, Notice and Automatic Cancellation Under Revised Form 24*, 16 THE FORUM 962 (1981).

Justin D. Wear, *Conditions of Coverage*, in COMMERCIAL CRIME INSURANCE COVERAGE 393 (Randall I. Marmor and Susan Koehler Sullivan eds. 2015).

Michael J. Weber & Ronald G. Mund, *Discovery—What Does It Do, What Is It and Who Must Discover?*, in COMMERCIAL CRIME POLICY 333 (Randall J. Marmor & John J. Tomaine eds., 2d ed. 2005).

Karen Wildau & Marlo Orlin Leach, *What Did They Know and When Did They Know It, Who Are "They" Anyway and What Difference Does It Make—Imputation Under the Financial Institution Bond And Its Implication for Coverage*, III FID. L.J. 1 (1997).

Chapter 13

Duties of Insured in the Event of a Loss*

This chapter discusses all the duties specified in the various standard forms of the insured once a loss is discovered. The topic of discovery has been extensively discussed by the courts in cases involving fidelity coverage for many years. Chapter 12, Discovery, deals with this topic in greater detail.

Discovery of "a loss or a situation that may result in loss," in the case of the Crime Protection Policy, or of "a loss or a situation that may result in loss of or damage to 'money,' 'securities' or 'other property'" in the case of the Commercial Crime Policy (Discovery Form and Loss Sustained Forms) triggers the accrual of the time period in which the insured must notify the carrier, submit a sworn proof of loss and later, if necessary, commence suit. These policies specifically require that the insured give notice to the carrier as soon as possible, provide a detailed, sworn proof of loss within 120 days of discovery, and file suit neither later than two years after the discovery of loss, nor earlier than 90 days after submitting the proof of loss.

Throughout the existence of fidelity coverage, the courts have employed a variety of definitions of knowledge or discovery of loss. While these formulations are not identical, they generally distinguish those circumstances when an insured merely suspects that a loss from a covered activity has occurred from actual knowledge or awareness of facts that would justify a reasonable person in charging that such activity has occurred.

---

*   By Keith Witten and Carol Z. Smith, Gilliland & Hayes, LLC, Overland Park, Kansas.

A. Notice of Loss

CRIME PROTECTION POLICY[1]
Section E. Conditions

7.   **After you discover a loss or a situation that may result in a loss you must:**
     a.   **Notify us as soon as possible.**

COMMERCIAL CRIME POLICY (DISCOVERY FORM and LOSS SUSTAINED FORM)[2] Section E. Conditions

1. g. Duties in the Event of Loss
     After you discover a loss or a situation that may result in loss of or damage to "money," "securities" or "other property" you must:
     (1)   Notify us as soon as possible. If you have reason to believe that any loss (except for loss covered under Insuring Agreements A.1. or A.2.) involves a violation of law, you must also notify the local law enforcement authorities; . . .

COMMENT

This section requires that notice of loss be given as soon as possible to the carrier. Courts generally construe "as soon as possible" to mean within a reasonable time under the circumstances. Frequently, compliance with this requirement is a question of fact for a jury or other fact finder, although in some instances the court itself may be able to determine as a matter of law that notice was either timely or untimely.

---

1   Crime Protection Policy, SP 00 01 04 12 (The Surety & Fidelity Association of America 2012), *reprinted in* COMMERCIAL CRIME INSURANCE COVERAGE 769 (Randall I. Marmor & Susan Koehler Sullivan, eds., 2015) [*see* App'x A].

2   Commercial Crime Policy, CR 00 22 08 13 and CR 00 23 08 13 (Insurance Services Office, Inc. 2012), *reprinted in* COMMERCIAL CRIME INSURANCE COVERAGE 785, 799 (Randall I. Marmor & Susan Koehler Sullivan, eds., 2015) [*see* App'x B and C].

Two schools of thought have emerged in regard to enforcement of the notice provision. Most jurisdictions have strictly construed this requirement as a condition precedent to recovery under the policy. In recent years, however, some courts have held that the carrier must prove it was prejudiced by the insured's failure to give notice in a timely fashion in order for non-compliance with the notice requirement to constitute a defense to a claim under the policy.

The carrier can waive or otherwise be estopped from asserting late notice as a defense in a number of ways. Waiver or estoppel may arise from assurances by the carrier that the late notice would not preclude recovery, the carrier failing to raise as a defense lack of compliance with the notice provision, or the carrier's commencement of investigation notwithstanding lack of notice without reserving its rights. Whether such a waiver took place is ultimately a question of law, but its determination may involve factual elements to be determined by the trier of fact.

It should be borne in mind that some older policy forms omitted the language *"a situation that may result in loss, . . ."* [emphasis added]. Consequently, under such forms, the time for providing notice, submitting proof of loss and filing suit did not begin to run until actual knowledge or discovery of loss by the insured. The newer language appears to create a stricter standard, obligating the insured to give notice and proof of loss to the carrier under circumstances that might not have required it to do so under the older forms that did not contain the italicized language. Some older forms also triggered the requirements of giving notice and proof of loss and commencement of suit on "knowledge or discovery." Few, if any, cases seem to make any distinction between these different formulations, however, and for the most part, courts have considered the notice, proof of loss, and commencement of action requirements within the context of the "knowledge or discovery" language alone.

OUTLINE OF ANNOTATIONS

2. Whether notice is timely
   (a) Cases Decided Under Commercial Coverages
   (b) Cases Decided Under Other Financial Institution Coverages
3. Effect of untimely notice
   (a) Cases Decided Under Commercial Coverages
   (b) Cases Decided Under Other Financial Institution Coverages
4. Whether the carrier must show prejudice from untimely notice
   (a) Cases Decided Under Commercial Coverages
   (b) Cases Decided Under Other Financial Institution Coverages
5. Waiver and estoppel
   (a) Cases Decided Under Commercial Coverages
   (b) Cases Decided Under Other Financial Institution Coverages

ANNOTATIONS

A. Notice of loss

1. What constitutes discovery

(a) Cases Decided Under Commercial Coverages

5th Cir. 1974 (Ala.). [Commercial Coverages]. A loss was discovered only when it became clear that the employee had misappropriated substantially all of the cash he had received from cash sales, which was against company policy. *Brad's Machine Products, Inc. v. Phoenix Assur. Co. of N. Y.*, 489 F.2d 622.

7th Cir. 1980 (Ill.). [Commercial Coverages]. When the vice president of an insurance company set premium rates too low, discovery of a loss occurred only when the insured learned that its employee was receiving kickbacks, and that the low rates were not just an error of judgment. The law presumes every man to be honest until the contrary is established. *Central Nat'l Life Ins. Co. v. Fidelity & Deposit Co. of Md.*, 626 F.2d 537.

9th Cir. 2001 (Idaho). [Crime Policy]. Under Idaho law, when the policy required the insured to provide notice of loss at the earliest practicable moment but in no event later than sixty days after discovery of loss, the district court erred in granting summary judgment to the carrier in that fact issues existed as to when the insured discovered the loss because discovery of the loss occurs only when the insured becomes aware of facts that would cause a reasonable person to assume a loss had been or would be incurred. *Gulf USA Corp. v. Fed. Ins. Co.*, 259 F.3d 1049.

10th Cir. 1966 (N.M.). [Commercial Coverages]. Discovery occurs when the insured is in possession of knowledge which would justify a careful and prudent man in charging another with fraud or dishonesty. "Suspicion" became "knowledge" when the principal failed to attend a meeting at which he had promised to explain a mysterious disappearance. *Hidden Splendor Mining Co. v. General Ins. Co. of Am.*, 370 F.2d 515.

N.D. Ohio 1964. [Primary Commercial Coverages]. A finance company's knowledge that its branch manager had lied as to challenged accounts, had knowingly permitted false documents and values to be the basis of disbursement of company funds, had permitted a check float, and had falsely certified the existence of nonexistent security, was knowledge of specific acts of dishonesty. Discovery does not depend on knowledge of total misconduct viewed in retrospect with the obvious advantage of hindsight, but rather upon knowledge of facts which, in light of the circumstances surrounding those facts and the reasonable inferences to be drawn from those facts, would inform an ordinary, reasonable and sensible employer that dishonesty has occurred which might involve the carrier in liability. *City Loan & Sav. Co. v. Employers' Liab. Assur. Corp.*, 249 F. Supp. 633.

(b) Cases Decided Under Other Financial Institution Coverages

S.D. Miss. 2012. [Financial Institution Bond]. In an action by the FDIC as receiver of a failed bank, a genuine issue of material fact precluded summary judgment as to whether the bank discovered a loss so as to trigger the duty to provide notice of loss at the earliest practicable moment, not to exceed within thirty days, because the teller operations officer believed the dishonest employee's explanation for a $30,000 shortage in the vault cash that a cash out ticket had not been run. *Federal Deposit Ins. Corp. v. Denson*, 908 F. Supp. 2d 792.

2d Cir. 1984 (N.Y.). [Fidelity Bond]. Under New York law, "discovery" of a loss is determined under an objective standard based on conclusions that a reasonable person would reach from facts known to the insured. The insured discovered a loss on February 22, when a committee met to discuss certain bond transactions initiated by its investment manager and a memo was circulated regarding these, including a reference to excessive broker commissions. Because no notice was given until July 23, the notice was untimely. Despite the insured's contentions that it justifiably believed in the investor's honesty until its counsel informed it that such trading was illegal, the court concluded that the notice of loss came too late. *Utica Mut. Ins. Co. v. Fireman's Fund Ins. Cos.*, 748 F.2d 118.

3d Cir. 1981 (N.J.). [Bankers Blanket Bond]. A bank is not under a duty to notify its insurance carrier of a loss until it has knowledge of some specific fraudulent act, and mere suspicion of dishonesty or wrongdoing is not enough. When the circumstances surrounding the losses presented serious symptoms which were not yet susceptible of final diagnosis, there was no discovery. *Fidelity & Deposit Co. of Md. v. Hudson United Bank*, 653 F.2d 766.

3d Cir. 1937 (Pa.). [Fidelity Schedule Bond]. Discovery means "positive discovery which required affirmative action, not mere or even real suspicion" and it was a jury question as to whether a vice president's understanding of the president's conduct amounted to knowledge of embezzlement. *Hunt v. Fidelity & Deposit Co. of Md.*, 92 F.2d 75.

5th Cir. 1972 (Tex.). [Bankers Blanket Bond]. Knowledge that the bank president had exceeded loan limits and had excessive cash items did not trigger an obligation to notify the carrier when the president had reasonable explanations for those issues. *Federal Deposit Ins. Corp. v. Lott*, 460 F.2d 82.

5th Cir. 1970 (Tex.). [Bankers Blanket Bond]. Discovery of loss occurred not when the insured discovered real estate notes that proved to be fraudulent that were not of a type the bank could legally purchase, but when it learned of its director's related conduct, even if it had earlier suspected fraud. *Federal Deposit Ins. Corp. v. Aetna Cas. & Sur. Co.*, 426 F. 2d 729.

6th Cir. 1934 (Mich.). [Bank Fidelity Schedule Bond]. Nothing short of knowledge that a loss had been or would be sustained constitutes discovery. The bank had no way to know that an overdraft of its president would result in a loss. *United States Fid. & Guar. Co. v. Barber*, 70 F.2d 220.

8th Cir. 1979 (Ark.). [Bankers Blanket Bond]. Discovery is deemed to occur when the insured actually becomes aware of sufficient facts which would lead a reasonable person to believe that an insured loss has occurred. Mere suspicion of an insured loss is not sufficient to trigger the notice requirement. Absent a specific provision requiring it, the insured had no duty to exercise diligence to search out facts which might lead to discovery of the loss. The test is whether a reasonable person was aware of facts which would convert his appreciation of those facts into actual knowledge of the alleged dishonesty. *Perkins v. Clifton State Bank*, 593 F.2d 327.

10th Cir. 1991 (Okla.). [Bankers Blanket Bond and Excess Bank Employee Dishonesty Blanket Bond]. Under Oklahoma law, when several relatives of the dishonest chairman of the board became aware of a check kiting scheme he perpetrated but failed to report his dishonest actions to the board of directors, they participated in his scheme so that their knowledge would not be imputed to the bank and, accordingly, the bank's failure to notify the carrier of the chairman's dishonesty within thirty days after their discovery of the loss did not preclude recovery. *Adair State Bank v. Am. Cas. Co.*, 949 F.2d 1067, *overruled on other grounds, Stauth v. National Union Fire Ins. Co. of Pittsburgh*, 236 F.3d 1260.

10th Cir. 1970 (Okla.). [Bankers Blanket Bond]. No discovery resulted from the directors' examination of a bank examiners' report disapproving a bookkeeper's "turn backs" when an officer-director recycled the overdrafts and covered them by granting fictitious loans because the report indicated only poor banking practices and not specific evidence of wrongdoing. *First Nat'l Bank of Cushing v. Security Mut. Cas. Co.*, 431 F.2d 1025.

Bankr. N.D. Ga. 1995. [Employee Fidelity Policy]. Under Georgia law, when a policy required that the insured provide notice within sixty days of discovery of an occurrence which might become a loss, the triggering of the notice requirement should be calculated to weed out as many false claims as possible while permitting the carrier to participate in the investigation of conduct that a prudent person would consider illicit or corrupt. If the insured discovered an employee's dishonesty that gave rise to a suspicion of fraud, a duty of inquiry arose that could not be satisfied by the undocumented assertion by the employee that no problem existed or that if there was one, he would solve it. The failure of the insured to inquire promptly or of the employee to respond promptly in a manner that would cause a reasonable person to put aside the suspicion of fraud triggered a duty to notify the carrier. *Ellenberg v. Underwriters at Lloyd's*, 187 B.R. 785.

D. Kan. 1984. [Bankers Blanket Bond]. Coverage was denied because a check kiting scheme could have been discovered by the bank officers exercising ordinary care and diligence. The bank had "knowledge of loss" when it "had knowledge which would justify a careful and prudent person in charging [the customer] with a check kiting scheme." *Security Nat'l Bank of Kansas City, Kansas v. Continental Ins. Co.*, 586 F. Supp. 139.

E.D. Ky. 1989. [Bankers Blanket Bond]. A material issue of fact precluded judgment in favor of the carrier on the issue of whether the insured gave timely notice because of a question as to when the insured's board of directors came to a realization that loan irregularities were the result of employee fraud of such magnitude that the insured would have to be closed. *Federal Deposit Ins. Corp. v. Reliance Ins. Co.*, 716 F. Supp. 1001.

D. Mass. 1998. [Bankers Blanket Bond]. Under Massachusetts law, the insured bank discovered a loss when it became aware of the results of a $45,000 confidential investigation, made a Report of Apparent Crime, met with an FBI agent, received two grand jury subpoenas, and became aware of its employee's extraordinary assets incommensurate with his salary and of a suspicious pattern of missing ownership interests in real estate partnerships involving the employee's friends and customers. Consequently, notice came too late and the carrier was not required to demonstrate actual prejudice from the delay in providing notice. *Federal Deposit Ins. Corp. v. Underwriters of Lloyd's of London*, 3 F. Supp. 2d 120.

D. Mass. 1995. [Fidelity Name Schedule Bond]. Under a bond requiring "that as soon as reasonably possible and in any event within fifteen days after discovery by the insured of any act or circumstance indicating a probable claim hereunder, written notice thereof to be given to the underwriter," the court interpreted "indicating a probable claim" to mean a "realization that the act or circumstance is such that at the moment it appears more probable than not that when more is known [the insured] will have a basis for making a claim . . ." *Boston Mut. Life Ins. Co. v. Fireman's Fund Ins. Co.*, 613 F. Supp. 1090.

D. Mass. 1985. [Fidelity Bond]. Because the bond required notice upon discovery "of any act or circumstance indicating a probable claim," the court held there was no coverage in that the insured had "discovered" a situation involving a probable claim at a meeting of executives when a discussion centered on the possibility that a third-party administrator (who previously had been found to have "misused" premium funds) was cashing premium checks instead of depositing them, that the administrator knew this to be a forbidden practice and that he had given false explanations for such delay. The insured failed to give written notice after meeting took place. *Boston Mut. Life Ins. Co. v. Fireman's Fund Ins. Co.*, 613 F. Supp. 1090.

W.D. Mo. 1980. [Bankers Blanket Bond]. Discovery occurred when the bank learned of a potential covered loss when it was informed of stops to be placed on checks made payable to the bankrupt company which were deposited to account of another company. *Columbia Union Nat'l Bank v. Hartford Acc. & Indem. Co.*, 496 F. Supp. 1263 (W.D. Mo. 1980), *aff'd*, 669 F.2d 1210.

D. Mont. 1990. [Fidelity Bond]. When more than one year before the FSLIC gave notice to the fidelity carrier, the FHLBB had requested the directors' resignation and reported the directors to FBI, the president received a letter from a director that mentioned essentially the same facts as those detailed in the proof of loss and letters between the FHLBB and board of directors showed the board was aware of potential problems ten months before it gave notice of loss to the carrier, the insured failed to comply with the bond requirement that the insured give notice of loss within thirty days after discovery of the loss and furnish a proof of loss within six months. The wrongdoers on the board of directors and those who colluded with them did not dominate the board so as to prevent discovery when two directors resigned long before the carrier was notified and the directors who were not accused of any wrongdoing learned of some losses almost a year before the carrier was notified. Under Montana law, the carrier did not have to show substantial prejudice to assert the failure to provide timely notice as a defense under the bond. *Federal Sav. & Loan Ins. Corp. v. Aetna Cas. & Sur. Corp.*, 785 F. Supp. 867.

D.N.J. 1971. [Bankers Blanket Bond]. The time to give notice of loss began when the bank knew all the facts on which its claim was based. *Essex County State Bank v. Fireman's Fund Ins. Co.*, 331 F. Supp. 931.

S.D.N.Y. 2007. [Unspecified coverage form]. When the insured's employee destroyed a database in an effort to sabotage the insured's business, but concealed his sabotage, the insured did not discover the loss until the sabotage was discovered. *Hewlett-Packard Co. v. Factory Mut. Ins. Co.*, No. 04 Civ. 2791 (TPG)(DCF), 2007 U.S. Dist. LEXIS 24146.

W.D. Okla. 1973. [Comprehensive Dishonesty, Disappearance and Destruction Policy]. When the insured delayed in providing notice of loss for at least seven and one-half months after the discovery of the loss, the notice was not provided within a reasonable time after discovery of a covered loss as required. *Alfalfa Elec. Corp., Inc. v. Travelers Indem. Co.*, 376 F. Supp. 901.

E.D. Pa. 1995. [Multi-Peril Package Policy]. When the insured discovered a loss at least three years before notifying the carrier and the policy required notice of loss as soon as possible and suit within two years, the claim was barred because the carrier suffered prejudice in that the losses incurred after the insured discovered them could have been avoided if the carrier had received timely notice. The insured was not so adversely dominated as to warrant tolling the contractual two-year suit limitation period when the insured had the right to and did receive financial records and the insured's controller was able to create ledger statements that revealed the misappropriated funds. *Northwood Nursing & Convalescent Home, Inc. v. Continental Ins. Co.*, 902 F. Supp. 79.

E.D. Pa. 1993. [Fidelity Bond]. When a fidelity bond required the insured to provide written notice of any loss at the earliest practicable moment after discovery of the loss, the underwriters failed to aver sufficient prejudice to warrant a finding that the notice was untimely. The doctrine of equitable tolling applied to postpone the date of discovery when the sole directors, officers and principals of the insured engaged in an extensive scheme of embezzlement and fraud so that adverse domination prevented imputing their knowledge to the insured. *In re Lloyd Sec., Inc.*, 153 B.R. 677.

N.D. Tex. 1997. [Bankers Blanket Bond]. When the bond provided that the insured must provide notice at the earliest practicable moment, not to exceed thirty days, after discovery of loss, and proof of loss within 100 days after discovery of the loss, because the facts were disputed, the question of when discovery of the loss occurred was a fact issue for determination by the jury and summary judgment was improper. *Federal Deposit Ins. Corp. v. Fidelity & Deposit Co. of Md.*, 1997 WL 560616.

E.D. Va. 1963. [Bankers Blanket Bond]. A loss occurred when the bank discovered a fraud, not when the bank was called upon to make the loss good. Loss referred to a condition in which the insured might be subjected to claim or demand out of which legal liability might arise. *Mount Vernon Bank & Trust Co. v. Aetna Cas. & Sur. Co.*, 224 F. Supp. 666.

Ariz. App. 1971. [Employee Fidelity Bond]. When the principal had in the past borrowed money from the obligee and repaid loans, the insured could not be held to know that the principal's continuation of the practice was dishonest. *Maryland Cas. Co. v. Clements*, 487 P.2d 437.

Ark. 1930. [Employee Fidelity Bond]. Knowledge of unbusinesslike methods in and of themselves did not warrant giving notice to the carrier. *Fidelity & Deposit Co. of Md. v. Cunningham*, 28 S.W.2d 715.

Cal. App. 1987. [Savings and Loan Blanket Bond]. When the bond provided indemnity against loss as opposed to liability, and the court deemed the phrase "discovery of loss" to require notice upon discovery of a real loss as opposed to an anticipated loss, the time for giving notice began running when the insured settled a lawsuit by paying $55,000 that arose out of the activities of the manager of the bank. *Downey Sav. & Loan Ass'n v. Ohio Cas. Ins. Co.*, 234 Cal. Rptr. 835.

Cal. App. 1981. [Savings and Loan Blanket Bond]. The insured discovers a loss when it should have recognized the dishonest and fraudulent character of conduct based on the then known facts. *USLIFE Sav. & Loan Ass'n v. National Sur. Corp.*, 171 Cal. Rptr. 393.

Conn. 1964. [Savings and Loan Blanket Bond]. A provision in the bond that the insured should give the underwriter notice of any loss at the earliest practicable moment after discovery was a condition precedent to the insured's recovery. There was no requirement to show prejudice. The insured did not make the claim regarding lost or stolen bonds for over two years despite suggestions to make the claim by the U.S. Treasury Department. A person of ordinary and reasonable prudence would have recognized that a loss had occurred. *Hartford Fed. Sav. & Loan Ass'n v. Aetna Cas. & Sur. Co.*, 206 A.2d 650.

Ind. App. 1931. [Bankers Blanket Bond]. When the bond required the insured to give notice of loss as soon as possible after learning of a loss and the insured learned of a loss committed over ten months after the expiration of a prior bond, it had no duty to give notice at that time and notice of loss given immediately after it discovered a subsequent covered loss was timely. Loss meant pecuniary damage for which the insured might be liable even though the extent of a loss might not be immediately ascertainable. *Fletcher Sav. & Trust Co. v. American Sur. Co. of N.Y.*, 175 N.E. 247.

Iowa 1979. [Bankers Blanket Bond]. When the bank directors knew of excessive loans but justifiably believed the bank president's representations that they were being paid back, they were not bound to notify the carrier. *Federal Deposit Ins. Corp. v. National Sur. Corp.*, 281 N.W.2d 816.

Ky. App. 1906. [Employee Fidelity Bond]. An employer was not bound to report his suspicions to the company even though they were strong enough in his opinion to discharge the employee, but after suspicion was aroused, reasonable diligence must be used in pursuing inquiries as to the facts. *Fidelity & Guar. Co. of N. Y. v. Western Bank*, 94 S.W. 3.

La. App. 1938. [Fidelity Bond]. The obligee had no obligation to inform its carrier of its suspicions but only of knowledge of fraudulent or dishonest conduct by its employee which might result in liability of the carrier. *Inter-City Express Lines, Inc. v. Hartford Acc. & Indem. Co.*, 178 So. 280.

Mass. 1935. [Employee Fidelity Bond]. To trigger the requirement of notice, something less than discovery of demonstrative loss is needed. The case distinguishes discovery of loss from a loss having occurred. Discovery occurs when the facts known and the inferences which should be reasonably drawn from those facts would inform an ordinary man that there had been a loss. *Gilmour v. Standard Sur. & Cas. Co. of N. Y.*, 197 N.E. 673.

Miss. 1951. [Blanket Position Bond]. To be aware of a loss sustained by reason of acts constituting larceny or embezzlement, the insured must have knowledge of facts which would constitute a crime. Such crimes are so serious that a charge cannot safely be based upon mere inferences or suspicions arising from unexplained irregularities or discrepancies in the books or accounts of the employee. Awareness of a loss with sufficient certainty to justify charging of larceny or embezzlement generally requires considerable time for investigation after a well-founded suspicion of wrongdoing has been aroused. *Hartford Acc. & Indem. Co. v. Hattiesburg Hardware Stores*, 49 So. 2d 813.

Mo. 1966. [Bankers Blanket Bond]. When judgment was rendered against the insured for improperly crediting a drawee's check to the account of the drawee, discovery occurred because the bank must have recognized that the drawee had suffered a loss and that it intended to attempt to hold the bank liable for the loss. *Jefferson Bank & Trust Co. v. Central Sur. & Ins. Corp.*, 408 S.W.2d 825.

Mont. 1924. [Employee Fidelity Bond]. An insured in the business of buying, selling, and storing grain was held not to know that its manager was "gambling in grain" despite having records to that effect in its custody because the employee was the only one who knew of the existence or significance of records. *Outlook Farmer's Elevator Co. v. American Sur. Co. of N.Y.*, 223 P. 905.

N.J. 1978. [Bankers Blanket Bond]. Discovery occurs when the insured learns facts which would justify a careful and prudent person in charging another with dishonesty or fraud; mere suspicions of irregularities or improper conduct do not require the insured to report such acts to the carrier. *National Newark & Essex Bank v. Am. Ins. Co.*, 385 A.2d 1216.

N.Y. Sup. 1993. [Bankers and Brokers Blanket Bonds]. A loss is discovered once the insured obtains facts sufficient to cause a reasonable person to recognize that there has been dishonesty or fraud resulting in a loss. The insured is required to give notice of discovery of a loss or of an occurrence which may give rise to a claim for a loss even though no loss has then been sustained. Particulars of a loss can come later with the proof of loss. *Drexel Burnham Lambert Group, Inc. v. Vigilant Ins. Co.*, 595 N.Y.S.2d 999.

N. Y. App. 1934. [Employee Fidelity Bond]. Because the insured could reasonably believe a dishonest act to be one of casual irregularity or of careless usurpation of authority without wrongful intent, the insured did not conclusively become aware that the act was actually dishonest and fraudulent. *Charles W. Schrieber Travel Bureau, Inc. v. Standard Sur. & Cas. Co. of N.Y.*, 269 N.Y.S. 804.

Pa. 1934. [Bank Employee Fidelity Bond]. A failure to give notice within ten days of discovery when a third party's claim was presented to the bank released the carrier from liability. *Gentile v. American Bank & Trust Co.*, 172 A. 303.

Tenn. App. 1965. [Employee Fidelity Bond]. Discovery means knowledge of facts and circumstances sufficient to satisfy a person of ordinary prudence that a loss had occurred. *World Secret Serv. Ass'n v. Travelers Indem. Co.*, 396 S.W.2d 848.

2.   *Whether notice is timely*

(a) Cases Decided Under Commercial Coverages

E.D. Ark. 1982. [Commercial Coverages]. A delay of one year and twenty-one days was not in compliance with a provision requiring notice as soon as is practicable. Another claim in the same case was not rejected for a ninety-one-day notice delay, but was rejected for the late filing of suit. *Chandler Trailer Co. v. Lawyer's Sur. Corp.*, 535 F. Supp. 204.

E.D.N.Y. 1997. [Commercial Crime Insurance Policy and Excess Policy]. Notice to the wholesale insurance broker was not notice to the carrier when the policy required the insured to immediately report any occurrence likely to result in a claim and the insurance broker was considered to be agent of the insured and not the carrier under New York law. The immediate notice requirement required notice within a reasonable time and a delay of as little as ten days might be deemed unreasonable. *M.Z. Discount Clothing v. Meyninger*, 983 F. Supp. 182.

(b) Cases Decided Under Other Financial Institution Coverages

U.S. 1902. [Bank Employee Fidelity Bond]. Notice of loss should be given as soon as reasonably practicable under the circumstances of a case. The bond required a full statement of all items of claimed misappropriation on which the right to recover on the bond was based. *Fidelity & Deposit Co. of Md. v. Courtney*, 186 U.S. 342.

U.S. 1898. [Employee Fidelity Bond]. Notice of loss was not required unless the bank had knowledge—not simply suspicion—of the existence of such facts as would justify a careful and prudent man in charging another with fraud or dishonesty. *American Sur. Co. of N.Y. v. Pauly*, *(Pauly I)*, 170 U.S. 133.

U.S. 1898. [Employee Fidelity Bond]. The insured became contractually bound to notify the carrier of loss when it was satisfied that the principal has committed some specific act or fraud or dishonesty likely to involve loss. *American Sur. Co. of N.Y. v. Pauly*, *(Pauly II)*, 170 U.S. 160.

1st Cir. 1966 (Mass.). [Bankers Blanket Bond]. A bank which first learned of unlawful conduct of a corporation's agent on November 28 on receipt of a phone call from the corporation was not required to give notice until November 29 when it first received a demand for payment on certain checks. *Aetna Cas. & Sur. Co. v. Guar. Bank & Trust Co.*, 370 F.2d 276.

3d Cir. 1981 (N.J.). [Bankers Blanket Bond]. A bank is not under a duty to notify its carrier of a loss until it has knowledge of some specific fraudulent act, and a mere suspicion of dishonesty or wrongdoing is not enough. When the circumstances surrounding the losses presented serious symptoms which were not yet susceptible of final diagnosis, there was no discovery. *Fidelity & Deposit Co. of Md. v. Hudson United Bank*, 653 F.2d 766.

5th Cir. 1987 (Miss.). [Public Official Liability Insurance]. The policy required the insured making a claim to notify the carrier of any loss "as soon as practicable." That phrase meant within a reasonable time under all the circumstances to effectuate the objects and purposes of the notice clause. Notice given so late that it is "unreasonable" or that prejudices the carrier bars recovery by the insured. *Mississippi ex rel. Hinds County v. Richardson*, 817 F.2d 1203.

5th Cir. 1985 (Tex.). [Fidelity Bond]. The insured sought recovery under the bond for attorney fees and costs expended in defending a suit which grew out of the activities of the insured's president. Notice on July 17, 1974, of a suit filed on May 13, 1974, was reasonable within the provisions of the bond. *Continental Sav. Ass'n v. United States Fid. & Guar. Co.*, 762 F.2d 1239.

5th Cir. 1972 (Tex.). [Bankers Blanket Bond]. Knowledge that the bank president had exceeded loan limits and had excessive cash items did not trigger an obligation to notify the carrier when the president had reasonable explanations for those issues. *Federal Deposit Ins. Corp. v. Lott*, 460 F.2d 82.

5th Cir. 1970 (Tex.). [Bankers Blanket Bond]. Discovery of a loss occurred not when the insured discovered that relevant notes were not of a type the bank could legally purchase, but when it learned of its director's related conduct, even if it had earlier suspected fraud. *Federal Deposit Ins. Corp. v. Aetna Cas. & Sur. Co.*, 426 F. 2d 729.

6th Cir. 1975 (Ohio). [Employee Fidelity Bond]. Discovery of a loss does not occur until the insured has had a reasonable time to discover the extent and amount of the loss. *Russell Gasket Co. v. Phoenix of Hartford Ins. Co.*, 512 F.2d 205.

6th Cir. 1932 (Tenn.). [Bank Employee Fidelity Bond]. A bank which gave notice two years after its discovery of a loss did not do so as soon as was practicable. *National City Bank v. National Sec. Co.*, 58 F.2d 7.

7th Cir. 1956 (Ill.). [Blanket Position Bond]. The insured's suspicions were merely gestating during the period when it was investigating a shrinking of gross or net profits as an inventory check. Prompt notice followed the insured's viable knowledge of specific culprits. *B. Constantino & Sons Co. v. New Amsterdam Cas. Co.*, 234 F.2d 902.

7th Cir. 1952 (Ind.). [Bankers Blanket Bond]. When the bond required that the insured give written notice to the underwriter of any loss within a reasonable time after the insured learned of such loss, a delay of nine months and twelve days in giving notice was not reasonable. *Muncie Banking Co. v. American Sur. Co. of N.Y.*, 200 F.2d 115.

8th Cir. 1979 (Ark.). [Bankers Blanket Bond]. Discovery is deemed to occur when the insured actually becomes aware of sufficient facts which would lead a reasonable person to believe that an insured loss has occurred. Mere suspicion of an insured loss is not sufficient to trigger the notice requirement. Absent specific provision, the insured had no duty to exercise diligence to search out facts which might lead to discovery of the loss. The test is whether a reasonable person was aware of facts which would convert his appreciation of those facts into actual knowledge of the alleged dishonesty. *Perkins v. Clifton State Bank*, 593 F.2d 327.

8th Cir. 1935 (Iowa). [Bank Cashier's Fidelity Bond]. A jury could reasonably conclude that notice was not late because the evidence supported the insured's contention that it was not aware of the principal's dishonesty until just three days before it gave notice. *Fidelity & Deposit Co. of Md. v. Bates*, 76 F.2d 160.

8th Cir. 1932 (Neb.). [Employee Fidelity Bond]. Ordinary fairness requires that when an obligee has reasonable grounds for believing that the terms of the bond have been violated, and that a loss has been sustained, it should give prompt notice to the carrier so that the carrier may take steps to protect its rights. A delay of four months and twenty-one days in giving notice did not comply with the notice condition requiring that notice be given as soon as practicable. *American Sur. Co. of N.Y. v. Bankers' Sav. & Loan Ass'n of Omaha, Neb.*, 59 F.2d 577, *aff'd*, 67 F.2d 803 (8th Cir. 1932), *cert. denied*, 291 U.S. 678 (1933).

9th Cir. 1912 (Cal.). [Employee Fidelity Bond]. Immediate notice means with no more than that degree of promptitude which is reasonable under the circumstances and whether the notice is given with due diligence under all the circumstances of a particular case is ordinarily a question for the jury. *National Sur. Co. v. Western Pac. Railway Co.*, 200 F. 675.

10th Cir. 1985 (N.M.). [Bankers Special Bond]. Under the law of New Mexico, substantial compliance with the notice and proof of loss requirements of an insurance policy is all that is required of the insured to collect under policy. The insured complied with the proof of loss requirement of the bond by providing full particulars as soon as they were known to the insured, even though the insured did not know the "full particulars" of the alleged loss within six months of discovery of the alleged loss. *Wells Fargo Bus. Credit v. American Bank of Commerce*, 780 F.2d 871.

10th Cir. 1941 (N.M.). [Employee Fidelity Bond]. An employer not bound to report merely suspicious conduct, but only knowledge which would justify a careful and prudent man in charging another with fraud or dishonesty. *Am. Employers' Ins. Co. v. Raton Wholesale Liquor Co.*, 123 F.2d 283.

E.D. Ark. 1903. [Employee Fidelity Bond]. When a bond required "immediate" notice, notice given after eleven days was insufficient. *National Sur. Co. v. Long*, 125 F. 887.

N.D. Cal. 1962. [Bankers Blanket Bond]. A five-month delay in giving notice of loss did not comply with the notice requirements of a bond requiring that the insured notify the underwriter within a reasonable time after learning of any occurrence or event which, in the judgment of the insured, might give rise to a claim. *St. Paul Fire & Marine Ins. Co. v. Bank of Stockton*, 213 F. Supp. 716.

S.D. Fla. 1970. [Financial Institution Bond]. When the bond required the insured to give notice to the underwriter at the earliest practicable moment, not to exceed thirty days, after discovery of loss and material issues of fact existed as to when the insured could have discovered the loss, summary judgment could not be entered in favor of the insured even though it argued that its actual discovery occurred within thirty days of providing notice to the carrier. *ABCO Premium Fin. LLC v. American Int'l Group, Inc.*, No. 11-23020-CISCOLA/Bandstra, 2012 U.S. Dist. LEXIS 111833.

S.D. Fla. 1970. [Bankers Blanket Bond]. Actual discovery of dishonesty took place only after a meeting among bank officials and the principal even though the bank had earlier had a general awareness of problems. *Miami Nat'l Bank v. Pennsylvania Ins. Co.*, 314 F. Supp. 858.

Bankr. N.D. Ga. 1995. [Employee Fidelity Policy]. When the policy required that the insured provide notice within sixty days of discovery of an occurrence which might become a loss, the triggering of the notice requirement should be calculated to weed out as many false claims as possible while permitting the carrier to participate in the investigation of conduct that a prudent person would consider illicit or corrupt. If the insured discovered the employee's dishonesty that gave rise to a suspicion of fraud, a duty of inquiry arose that could not be satisfied by the undocumented assertion by the employee that no problem existed or that if there was one, he would solve it. The failure of the insured to inquire promptly or of the employee to respond promptly in a manner that would cause a reasonable person to put aside suspicion of fraud triggered a duty to notify the carrier. *Ellenberg v. Underwriters at Lloyd's*, 187 B.R. 785.

D. Ga. 1972. [Bankers Blanket Bond]. Under the bond which required the insured to provide notice of loss "as soon as practicable" after discovery, notice within a reasonable time was sufficient. *Bank of Acworth v. Firemen's Ins. Co. of Newark, N.J.*, 339 F. Supp. 1229.

D. Kan. 1982. [Bankers Blanket Bond]. Because a bond required written notice at the "earliest practicable moment after discovery of any loss," a 17-day delay in giving notice after actual discovery did not comply with the notice provision in that the delay in providing notice resulted in prejudice to the carrier. *Security Nat'l Bank of Kansas City v. Continental Ins. Co.*, 586 F. Supp. 139.

D.N.J. 1977. [Bankers Blanket Bond]. The insured was not bound to give notice until it has acquired knowledge that some specific fraudulent or dishonest act has occurred which might make the carrier liable for misconduct; notice is not required when the obligee merely suspects or has reason to suspect wrongdoing. Knowledge of excessive loans alone did not amount to discovery. *Midland Bank & Trust Co. v. Fidelity & Deposit Co. of Md.*, 442 F. Supp. 960.

D. Minn. 2014. [Financial Institution Bond]. When a bank employee induced others to participate in an advance fee scheme in which he was involved and the carrier defended the resulting lawsuit under a D&O policy, but later declined coverage under the FIB, notice of the loss was timely because the insured notified the carrier of its suspicions within an hour. *Avon State Bank v. BancInsure, Inc.*, Civ. No. 12-2557 (RHK/LIB), 2014 U.S. Dist. LEXIS 3099.

S.D. Ohio 1974. [Indemnity Bond]. As soon as practicable means within a reasonable time—notice given six months after knowledge of an unauthorized expenditure was not as soon as practicable. *Sheet Metal & Roofing Contractors' Ass'n of Miami Valley, Ohio v. Liskany*, 369 F. Supp. 662.

W.D. Okla. 1973. [Comprehensive Dishonesty, Disappearance and Destruction Policy]. When a bank delayed in providing notice of loss for at least seven and one-half months after the discovery of the loss, the notice was not provided within a reasonable time after discovery of a covered loss as required in the bond. *Alfalfa Elec. Corp., Inc. v. Travelers Indem. Co.*, 376 F. Supp. 901.

E.D. Pa. 1995. [Multi-Peril Package Policy]. When the insured discovered a loss at least three years before notifying the carrier and the policy required notice of loss as soon as possible and suit within two years, the claim was barred because the carrier suffered prejudice in that the losses incurred after the insured discovered them could have been avoided if the carrier had received timely notice. The insured was not so adversely dominated as to warrant tolling the contractual two-year suit limitation period when the insured had the right to and did receive financial records and the insured's controller was able to create ledger statements that revealed the misappropriated funds. *Northwood*

Nursing & Convalescent Home, Inc. v. Continental Ins. Co., 902 F. Supp. 79.

E.D. Va. 1963. [Bankers Blanket Bond]. A nine-month delay in giving notice of loss was not at the earliest practicable moment after discovery of the loss as required by the bond. *Mount Vernon Bank & Trust Co. v. Aetna Cas. & Sur. Co.*, 224 F. Supp. 666.

E.D. Wis. 1945. [Fidelity Bond]. When the bond contained a requirement that the insured notify the carrier of a fraudulent or dishonest act by any employee within fifteen days after discovery and the company's officers were in collusion with the employee, such notification was timely because the notice was given within fifteen days from the date the insurance commissioner took charge of the insured company. *Duel v. National Sur. Corp.*, 64 F. Supp. 961, *aff'd,* 157 F.2d 516 (E.D. Wis. 1945).

Conn. 1979. [Bankers Blanket Bond]. A delay of more than twenty-two weeks between discovery and notification of a loss failed as a matter of law to constitute notice at the earliest practicable moment, as required by the bond. *Lafayette Bank & Trust Co. v. Aetna Cas. & Sur. Co.*, 411 A.2d 937.

Conn. 1964. [Savings and Loan Blanket Bond]. A provision in the bond that the insured should give the underwriter notice of any loss at the earliest practicable moment after discovery was a condition precedent to the insured's recovery. There was no requirement to show prejudice. The insured did not make the claim regarding lost or stolen bonds for over two years despite suggestions to make the claim by the U.S. Treasury Department. A person of ordinary and reasonable prudence would have recognized that a loss had occurred. *Hartford Fed. Sav. & Loan Ass'n v. Aetna Cas. & Sur. Co.*, 206 A.2d 650.

Conn. 1934. [Employee Fidelity Bond]. Giving notice of loss, as distinguished from proof of loss, within ten days after the ascertainment by an investigation of the actual amount of a loss sustained is not sufficient compliance with the terms of policy if such notice is not given within ten days after the discovery of dishonest acts of the employee which occasioned a loss. *Mutual Indus. Fin. Corp. v. American Sur. Co. of N.Y.*, 175 A. 777.

Ill. App. 1932. [Employee Fidelity Bond]. When an employee, unknown to his employer, falsely pretended to conduct an investigation as to the makers of fraudulent promissory notes, there was no discovery until the employer discovered the employee's lies. *American Investment Co. of Ill. v. United States Fid. & Guar. Co.*, 267 Ill. App. 370.

Ind. App. 1937. [Employee Fiduciary Bond]. Whether a notice sent ten days after discovery of a loss was timely was a question for the jury, the court being unable to hold that such notice was untimely as matter of law. *Fidelity & Deposit Co. of Md. v. Mesker*, 11 N.E.2d 528.

Ind. App. 1931. [Bankers Blanket Bond]. When the bond required the insured to give notice of loss as soon as possible after learning of a loss and the insured learned of a loss committed over ten months after the expiration of the bond, it had no duty to give notice at that time and notice given immediately after it discovered a covered loss was timely. Loss meant pecuniary damage for which the insured might be liable even though the extent of loss might not be immediately ascertainable. *Fletcher Sav. & Trust Co. v. American Sur. Co. of N.Y.*, 175 N.E. 247.

Iowa 1902. [Building and Loan Employee Fidelity Bond]. A six- or eight-day delay, when no prejudice resulted, was not as a matter of law a violation of the condition requiring immediate notice. *Perpetual Bldg. & Loan Ass'n v. United States Fid. & Guar. Co.*, 92 N.W. 686.

Kan. App. 1986. [Bankers Blanket Bond]. Whether notice was given as soon as practicable when there was an eighteen-month delay was a question of fact because the circumstances potentially explaining the delay were open to dispute. *Home Life Ins. Co. v. Clay*, 719 P.2d 756.

Kan. 1980. [Union Fidelity Bond]. A telephone call regarding a default substantially complied with a 30-day notice provision, even though a formal written notice not submitted until 6 months later. *Local No. 1179, Carpet, Linoleum & Resilient Floor Decorators Union v. Merchants Mut. Bonding*, 613 P.2d 944.

Kan. 1932. [Employee Indemnity Bond]. A delay of eighty-four days in giving notice was not in compliance with a clause requiring notice as soon as practicable but not later than 10 days after discovery of loss. *La Harpe Farmers' Union v. United States Fid. & Guar. Co.*, 8 P.2d 354.

Ky. App. 1938. [Employee Fidelity Policy]. When a policy required notice at the earliest practicable moment, but in any event not later than five days after discovery of loss, a two-year delay was too late. A notice requirement should be construed according to the parties' intentions and should be given a reasonable interpretation consistent with this language. *Jellico Grocery Co. v. Sun Indem. Co. of N.Y.*, 114 S.W.2d 83.

La. App. 1937. [Employee Fidelity Bond]. A letter sent to a former agent of the carrier indicating there might be a covered loss was insufficient notice of loss. *George J. Ricau & Co., Inc. v. Indemnity Ins. Co. of N. Am.*, 173 So. 217.

La. 1933. [Fiduciary Deposit Bond]. That savings and loan officers might have acquired knowledge of a defalcation by examining the treasurer's books was not a defense to the carrier, the employer only being required to notify the carrier of the facts actually coming to its knowledge. *Slidell Sav. & Homestead Ass'n v. Fidelity & Deposit Co. of Md.*, 152 So. 121.

La. 1932. [Blanket Fidelity Bond]. Before denouncing an employee to the bondsman as dishonest, an employer has the right to satisfy himself that the employee is in fact dishonest and need not do so on mere suspicion. *Bank of Commerce & Trust Co. v. Union Indem. Co.*, 142 So. 156.

Mich. App. 1970. [Employee Fidelity Bond]. A delay of seven months and eight days was prima facie evidence of a failure to give notice as soon as practicable. *Grand Rapids Auction, Inc. v. Hartford Acc. & Indem. Co.*, 178 N.W.2d 812.

Mich. 1957. [Fidelity Bond]. Notice of loss furnished to a local agent of the carrier was sufficient notice of loss. *Masters v. Massachusetts Bonding & Ins. Co.*, 84 N.W.2d 462.

Mich. 1954. [Employee Fidelity Bond]. The court strictly construed a fifteen-day notice provision as a condition precedent and held the carrier not liable when the insured provided notice thirty-four days after its discovery of a loss. *Continental Studios v. American Auto. Ins. Co.*, 64 N.W.2d 615.

Minn. 1957. [Bankers Blanket Bond]. The insured cannot wait for a determination of a loss before giving notice of loss. It does not have to give notice until it is justified in believing a loss occurred through dishonesty rather than through errors consistent with integrity. Mere suspicion of an irregularity does not require the insured to assume its employee is guilty of dishonest acts and to give notice based on such assumptions. *Prior Lake State Bank v. National Sur. Corp.*, 80 N.W.2d 612.

Minn. 1933. [Bank Employee Bond]. The running of the time for giving notice of loss did not occur until the bank was required to pay a judgment against it for the amount which the cashier had wrongfully withdrawn from his account in his name as guardian. *Cary v. National Sur. Co.*, 251 N. W. 123.

Minn. 1929. [Employee Fidelity Bond]. A delay of six and one-half months barred recovery of a portion of a claim when the bond required notice within ten days after discovery of loss, but not the remainder of the claim as to which the insured promptly notified the carrier. *Citizens' State Bank of St. Paul v. New Amsterdam Cas. Co.*, 224 N.W. 451.

Minn. 1910. [Employee Bond]. The court denied recovery when a fifty-six-day lapse in the giving of notice of loss occurred because the policy required that on the discovery of any fraud or dishonesty on the part of any employee, the employer should immediately give notice of loss to the carrier. *Gamble-Robinson Co. v. Massachusetts Bonding & Ins. Co.*, 129 N.W. 131.

Mo. 1941. [Bankers Blanket Bond]. When the bond required that a claim be submitted by the employer in writing, showing the items and the dates of the losses, and be delivered to the carrier within three months after such discovery and immediately upon the discovery of an irregularity, the bank notified the carrier of a shortage and the carrier sent representatives to check out the matter, there was sufficient notice of loss. *LeMay Ferry Bank v. New Amsterdam Cas. Co.*, 149 S.W.2d 328.

Mont. 1924. [Employee Fidelity Bond]. An insured in the business of buying, selling, and storing grain was held not to know its manager was "gambling in grain" despite having records to that effect in its custody because the employee was the only one who knew of the existence or significance of records. *Outlook Farmer's Elevator Co. v. American Sur. Co. of N.Y.*, 223 P. 905.

N.C. 1926. [Employee Fidelity Bond]. Reasonable notice complies with a requirement of immediate notice, and thus the insured did not have to give notice as soon as it discovered that an employee was short in his accounts. *Forest City Bldg. & Loan Ass'n. v. Davis*, 133 S.E. 530 (N.C. 1926), *modified on another ground*, 138 S.E. 338.

N.H. 1932. [Bank Treasurer's Fidelity Bond]. Whether a delay of over five months between the discovery of a loss and the giving of notice of loss constituted immediate notice was for a jury to decide. *Exeter Banking Co. v. Taylor*, 160 A. 733.

N.J. 1978. [Bankers Blanket Bond]. A letter advising the carrier that the insured had no tangible evidence of a covered loss, but that suspicious circumstances were under investigation was sufficient to constitute notice of loss. *National Newark & Essex Bank v. Am. Ins. Co.*, 385 A.2d 1216.

N.Y. Sup. Ct. 2011. [Unspecified policy form]. Under a policy that required the insured to provide notice of loss "[a]t the earliest practicable moment after discovery of [the] loss by the Corporate Risk Manager," and provided that "[d]iscovery occurs when the Corporate Risk Manager first becomes aware of facts which would cause a reasonable person to assume that a loss . . . has been or will be incurred," because there was no designated "Corporate Risk Manager" and the de facto corporate risk manager merely reminded subsidiaries to report claims to insurers and merely requested subsidiaries to copy him on claims, the insureds breached their duty to "exercise reasonable diligence . . . to acquire knowledge" of covered losses with reasonable celerity. Because the de facto risk manager delegated the risk management role to the legal department (by directing subsidiaries to report losses directly to the insurer), the general counsel's and assistant general counsel's knowledge of the claimed loss, and the corresponding duty to notify the underwriters, would be imputed to the risk manager. *Hudson Ins. Co. v Oppenheim*, 916 N.Y.S.2d 68.

Ohio 1912. [Bank Employee Fidelity]. A requirement that the insured provide notice of loss at the earliest practicable moment does not mean instantly, but it does mean very soon. Whether notice was timely when the possibility of employee dishonesty first arose on November 30, 1904, an investigation followed, and notice was given to the carrier on January 15, 1905, was an issue for the jury. *Rankin v. United States Fid. & Guar. Co.*, 99 N.E. 314.

Okla. 1932. [Bank Employee Fidelity Bond]. The time for giving notice of loss to a carrier on a terminated bond did not start until the officers of the insured discovered an embezzlement had occurred during the term of bond. *American Sur. Co. of N.Y. v. State ex rel. Shull*, 12 P.2d 212.

Pa. 1936. [Fidelity Bond]. When notice is required within ten days of discovery, notice given four days after an audit by state banking department disclosed irregularities in the principal's books was sufficient even though officers of the insured had had strong suspicions of embezzlement by the principal several months earlier. *Thomas Holme Bldg. & Loan Ass'n v. New Amsterdam Cas. Co.*, 188 A. 374.

Pa. 1928. [Employee Fidelity Bond]. When the bond required notice to be given as soon as possible, a five-month delay defeated the claim. *Morrellville Deposit Bank v. Royal Indem. Co.*, 294 Pa. 446.

Pa. 1915. [Employee Fidelity Bond]. Notice of loss given by telephone was sufficient. *Wachs & Co. v. Fidelity & Deposit Co. of Md.*, 93 A. 1007.

S.C. 1936. [Employee Fidelity Bond]. The carrier was not released by the bank's failure to give notice within ten days because the acting president of the bank had concealed the existence of the bond and there was nothing to show that anyone else knew that the bond existed. *Farley v. American Sur. Co. of N.Y.*, 188 S.E. 776.

S.C. 1935. [Bankers Blanket Bond]. When a shortage in a bank's accounts occurred, and had the bank immediately investigated, it would have discovered a loss due to dishonesty. However, the bank let one month pass before reporting it; it could not recover for that loss because the bond required notice at the earliest practicable moment, and not later than ten days. *Planter's Sav. Bank of Greer v. American Sur. Co. of N.Y.*, 181 S.E. 222.

Tenn. App. 1937. [Fidelity Bond]. A delay of over four months in providing notice of loss released the carrier from liability. *Nashville & Am. Trust Co. v. Aetna Cas. & Sur. Co.*, 110 S.W.2d 1041.

Tex. App. 1925. [Employee Fidelity Bond]. A provision in the bond requiring "immediate" notice was invalid under a statute barring clauses allowing less than ninety days after accrual of a cause of action for providing notice of loss to the carrier. "Immediately" ordinarily means less than such time. *Western Indem. Co. v. Free & Accepted Masons of Texas*, 268 S.W. 728.

Tex. 1922. [Employee Fidelity Bond]. A seventeen-month delay in giving notice of loss was unreasonable as a matter of law because the bond required immediate notice. *Texas Glass & Paint Co. v. Fidelity & Deposit Co. of Md.*, 244 S.W. 113.

Vt. 1940. [Bankers Blanket Bond]. An employer should have known of a defalcation after a second short inventory, and notice of loss provided after the fourth short inventory two months later was too late. *Brown v. Maryland Cas. Co.*, 11 A.2d 222.

Wash. 1966. [Comprehensive Fidelity Insurance Policy]. The insured's manager's tardiness in making deposits did not alone result in actual knowledge of dishonesty. *Tradewell Stores, Inc. v. Fidelity & Cas. Co. of N.Y.*, 410 P.2d 782.

Wash. 1935. [Bankers Blanket Bond]. A loss could not be discovered until the bank learned its president had caused the loss rather than a third party not associated with the bank. *Hansen v. American Bonding Co. of Baltimore*, 48 P.2d 653.

Wash. 1902. [Employee Fidelity Bond]. "Immediate" notice means within a reasonable time. Whether the insured acted with due diligence under circumstances of a particular case and without unnecessary or unreasonable delay when there was a forty-three-day delay in giving notice of loss created a question for a jury. *Remington v. Fidelity & Deposit Co. of Md.*, 67 P. 989.

W. Va. 1935. [Fidelity Bond]. Notice of loss furnished twelve weeks after discovery of loss by the insured precludes recovery when the bond requires notice within five days. *Greenbrier Laundry Co. v. Fidelity & Cas. Co. of N.Y.*, 178 S.E. 631 (W.Va. 1935).

Wis. 1974. [Bankers Blanket Bond]. Notice of loss served fifteen months after discovery was too late, because the bond required that the insured provide notice at the earliest practicable moment. *State Bank of Viroqua v. Capitol Indem. Corp.*, 214 N.W.2d 42.

Wis. 1912. [Employee Fidelity Bond]. An insured is only required to notify the carrier of dishonest acts actually coming to its knowledge. *First Nat'l Bank of Crandon v. United States Fid. & Guar. Co.*, 137 N.W. 742.

3. Effect of untimely notice

(a) Cases Decided Under Commercial Coverages

E.D. Ark. 1982. [Commercial Coverages]. A delay of one year and twenty-one days was not in compliance with a provision requiring notice as soon as practicable. Another claim in the same case was not rejected for a 91-day notice delay, but was rejected for the late filing of suit. *Chandler Trailer Co. v. Lawyer's Sur. Corp.*, 535 F. Supp. 204.

E.D.N.Y. 1997. [Commercial Crime Insurance Policy and Excess Policy]. Notice to the wholesale insurance broker did not constitute notice to the carrier because the policy required the insured to immediately report any occurrence likely to result in a claim. In addition, the insurance broker was considered to be the agent of the insured and not the carrier under New York law. The immediate notice requirement required notice within a reasonable time, and a delay of as little as ten days might be deemed unreasonable. *M.Z. Discount Clothing v. Meyninger*, 983 F. Supp. 182.

(b) Cases Decided Under Other Financial Institution Coverages

U.S. 1902. [Cashiers Bond and Tellers Bond]. When bank officers were told that its teller was speculating, the bank's failure to immediately convey the information to the carrier precluded recovery on the bond. *Guarantee Co. of N. Am. v. Mechanics' Sav. Bank & Trust Co.*, 183 U.S. 402.

1st Cir. 1997. [Financial Institution Bond]. The FDIC could not recover under a bond when it failed to comply with the requirement to provide notice of loss within 30 days of discovery. A Massachusetts statute adopting the notice-prejudice rule for certain types of liability insurance did not extend to financial institution bonds. *Federal Deposit Ins. Corp. v. Insurance Co. of N. Am.,* 105 F.3d 778.

2d Cir. 1935 (N.Y.). [Employee Fidelity Bond]. When the bond required notice to be provided within ten days but no notice was provided until the proof of loss was furnished eighty-five days after discovery of a loss (which was also out of compliance with the proof requirement), the suit was properly dismissed. *Public Warehouses of Matanzas v. Fidelity & Deposit Co. of Md.*, 77 F.2d 831.

4th Cir. 1927 (Md.). [Fidelity Bond]. A failure to give notice of loss did not defeat the insured's claim when notice of loss was not made a condition of recovery under the bond. *New Amsterdam Cas. Co. v. United States Shipping Bd. Emergency Fleet Corp.*, 16 F.2d 847.

5th Cir. 1934 (Fla.). [Blanket Employee Fidelity Bond]. A requirement for notice to the carrier within ten days after discovery of a loss was upheld when the insured delayed giving notice for sixty days. The carrier did not waive nor was it estopped to assert late notice as a defense. *Murray v. American Sur. Co. of N.Y.*, 69 F.2d 147.

8th Cir. 1932 (Neb.). [Fidelity Bond]. The insured presented its claim four months and twenty-one days after discovery. The court found in favor of the carrier on the basis that the requirements for giving notice must be strictly complied with. *American Sur. Co. of N.Y. v. Bankers' Sav. & Loan Ass'n of Omaha*, 59 F.2d 577, *later approved* 67 F.2d 803 (8th Cir. 1932), *cert. denied*, 291 U.S. 678 (1934).

10th Cir. 1966 (N.M). [Fidelity Bond]. Timely notice is a prerequisite to the carrier's liability in New Mexico and a notice requirement will be strictly enforced. *Hidden Splendor Mining Co. v. General Ins. Co. of Am.*, 370 F.2d 515.

S.D. Ala. 1934. [Employee Fidelity Bond]. Late notice did not defeat a claim when the bond contained no provision for forfeiture. *American Nat'l Bank & Trust Co. v. United States Fid. & Guar. Co.*, 7 F. Supp. 578.

S.D. Cal. 1898. [Employee Fidelity Bond]. A claim was barred when notice of loss was given seven months after discovery because the condition that any claim must be made as soon as practicable after discovery is strictly enforced. *California Sav. Bank of San Diego v. American Sur. Co. of N.Y.*, 87 F. 118.

D. Conn. 1997. [Financial Institution Bond Form A]. A savings bank that waited over two years after its discovery of a loss before it provided notice of loss to the carrier was barred from recovery when the bond required notice within 30 days of discovery of loss and the carrier was not required to show any prejudice arising out of the late notice. *Community Sav. Bank v. Federal. Ins. Co.*, 960 F. Supp. 16.

S.D. Idaho 1933. [Fidelity Bond]. Prompt notice of loss is a condition precedent to recovery under a fidelity bond. It was implicit that a 47-day delay was not in compliance with a provision requiring the insured to provide immediate notice of loss. *Thompson v. United States Fid. & Guar. Co.*, 3 F. Supp. 756.

D. Mass. 1985. [Fidelity Bond]. When a bond required notice upon discovery "of any act or circumstance indicating a probable claim," the court held there was no coverage in that the insured had "discovered" a situation involving a probable claim at a meeting of executives when the discussion centered on the possibility that a third-party administrator (who had previously been found to have "misused" premium funds) was cashing premium checks instead of depositing them, that the administrator knew this to be a forbidden practice, and that he had given false explanations for such delay. The insured failed to give written notice after meeting took place. *Boston Mut. Life Ins. Co. v. Fireman's Fund Ins. Co.*, 613 F. Supp. 1090.

S.D.N.Y. 2007. [Unspecified coverage form]. When the insured's employee destroyed a database in an effort to sabotage the insured's business, but concealed his sabotage, the insured did not discover the loss until the sabotage was discovered; consequently, the insured had no duty to provide notice upon the discovery of the destruction of the database and notice provided on discovery of the sabotage complied with the policy's requirement that the insured give immediate written notice. *Hewlett-Packard Co. v. Factory Mut. Ins. Co.*, No. 04 Civ. 2791 (TPG)(DCF), 2007 U.S. Dist. LEXIS 24146.

S.D. Ohio 1974. [Indemnity Bond]. In an action by a contractors' association and trustees of welfare and pension funds to recover under an indemnity bond, the trustees who, after discovering losses, elected not to give notice of loss to the carrier, could not recover because the requirement of timely notice of loss and proof of loss were conditions precedent. Acts or conduct of the fidelity carrier giving rise to a waiver or estoppel must have occurred within the time limitation for notice of loss, proof of loss, and filing of suit rather than after such limitations have run. *Sheet Metal & Roofing Contractor's Ass'n of Miami Valley, Ohio v. Liskany*, 369 F. Supp. 662.

W.D. Okla. 1973. [Comprehensive Dishonesty, Disappearance and Destruction Policy]. When a bank delayed in providing notice of loss for at least seven and one-half months after the discovery of the loss, the notice was not provided within a reasonable time after discovery of a covered loss as required in the bond. *Alfalfa Elec. Corp., Inc. v. Travelers Indem. Co.*, 376 F. Supp. 901.

Ala. 1933. [Employee Fidelity Bond]. Prompt notice of loss was an affirmative defense, not a condition precedent which must be pleaded in an insured's complaint. *National Sur. Co. v. Julian*, 150 So. 474.

Cal. App. 1919. [Employee Fidelity Bond]. A condition requiring prompt notice was to be strictly construed as a material part of a policy. *Los Angeles Athletic Club v. United States Fid. & Guar. Co.*, 183 P. 174.

Conn. 2007. [Unspecified coverage form]. Under Connecticut law, if the jury found that the insured delayed in notifying the carrier of a loss it discovered, and that the delay was unexcused and unreasonable, such a delay would constitute a failure to comply with the policy's notice condition and would excuse the carrier from liability, unless the jury found that the insured had proven by a fair preponderance of the evidence that the carrier had suffered no material prejudice due to the late notice. *National Publishing Co. v. Hartford Fire Ins. Co.*, 949 A.2d 1203.

Fla. App. 1977. [Fidelity Bond]. Actual damages resulting from a failure to give notice must be pleaded and proved as a defense—the failure to give a compensated surety notice of a principal's default does not relieve the surety when failure to do so results in no loss to it. *Carnival Cruise Lines, Inc. v. Financial Indem. Co.*, 347 So. 2d 825.

Ga. App. 1919. [Employee Fidelity Bond]. Compliance with the express terms of the bond regarding notice is a condition precedent which must be affirmatively pleaded. *Bank of Ball Ground v. National Sur. Co.*, 97 S.E. 892.

Ky. App. 1956. [Employee Fidelity Bond]. Notice and proof of loss must be given within the time limits fixed by a policy of fidelity insurance. *Shatz v. American Sur. Co. of N.Y.*, 295 S.W.2d 809.

Ky. App. 1943. [Employee Fidelity Bond]. A provision requiring an insured to give notice of loss within three months of the termination of a bond was consonant with public policy. *Wilhoit v. Furnish*, 174 S.W.2d 515.

Mass. 1935. [Employee Fidelity Bond]. Prompt notice of loss is a condition precedent to recovery under a fidelity bond. *Gilmour v. Standard Sur. & Cas. Co. of N.Y.*, 197 N.E. 673.

N.C. 1913. [Employee Fidelity Bond]. Because the bond provided for immediate notice of loss, but did not provide for forfeiture for a failure of compliance with the notice provision and notice was given five days after discovery, there was no breach of a condition precedent. *Dixie Fire Ins. Co. v. American Bonding Co.*, 78 S.E. 430.

N.Y. App. 1975. [Multi-Peril Bank Policy]. A two-year delay in providing notice of loss is unreasonable as a matter of law when the policy requires notice as soon as practicable. *Columbus Trust Co. v. Hanover Ins. Co.*, 375 N.Y.S.2d 628.

N.Y. App. 1906. [Fidelity Bond]. When the bond required immediate notice of any act that indicated an employee was dishonest and the employee failed to give the employer collections due on September 2nd, and broke a subsequent promise to pay such collections, notice given on October 7th was too late. *Supreme Ruling of Fraternal Mystic Circle v. Nation Sur. Co.*, 99 N.Y.S. 1033.

N.Y. App. 1905. [Employee Fidelity Bond]. The court denied recovery when the bond required immediate notice, but notice was not given until 19 days after the discovery of a shortage in petty cash, because of the violation of a condition precedent. The insured is not required to prove prejudice from late notice. *National Discount Co. v. United States Fid. & Guar. Co.*, 94 N.Y.S. 457.

N.Y. Sup. 2005. [Unspecified coverage form]. The carriers met their initial burden of establishing their entitlement to a judgment as a matter of law by demonstrating, with legally sufficient evidence, that the insured failed to provide prompt notice of covered losses under the subject insurance policies, which they required. *Duratech Industries, Inc., Respondent-Appellant v. Continental Insurance Company*, 800 N.Y.S.2d 182.

N.Y. Sup. 1997. [Fidelity Bond]. An apartment building owner's failure to provide prompt notice of a claim to the fidelity carrier of its management company did not bar a suit against the carrier when the policy did not name the owners as the insured and the notice was promptly given as soon as the owners learned the carrier's identity. *Woodburn Court Assocs. I v. Trans Urban Housing Sys., Inc.*, 663 N.Y.S.2d 445.

N.Y. Sup. 1993. [Bankers and Brokers Blanket Bonds]. A loss is discovered once the insured obtains facts sufficient to cause a reasonable person to recognize that there has been dishonesty or fraud resulting in a loss. The insured is required to give notice of discovery of a loss, or of an occurrence which might give rise to a claim for a loss, even though no loss has then been sustained. The particulars of a loss can come later with the proof of loss. *Drexel Burnham Lambert Group, Inc. v. Vigilant Ins. Co.*, 595 N.Y.S.2d 999.

Ohio App. 1978. [Deputy Registrar's Blanket Position Bond]. A failure to notify the carrier of a loss within six months as provided by the bond discharged the carrier. *Ohio v. Safeco Ins. Cos.*, 396 N.E.2d 794.

Ohio 1926. [Employee Fidelity Bond]. When the insuring contract provides that the employer shall, within a given time after becoming aware of any evidence of dishonesty of any employee, give notice to the carrier, such provision constitutes a condition precedent. When the employer fails to comply with that provision, it cannot recover, even though a defalcation has taken place and a loss ensued. *Kornhauser v. National Sur. Co.*, 150 N.E. 921.

Pa. 1934. [Bank Employee Fidelity Bond]. A failure to give notice of loss within ten days of discovery of loss, as required by the bond, released the carrier from liability when a third party's claim was presented to the bank. *Gentile v. American Bank & Trust Co.*, 172 A. 303.

S.C. 1935. [Bankers Blanket Bond]. A requirement that notice of shortage must be given to the carrier not later than ten days after discovery of such shortage was reasonable and was a condition precedent to recovery on the bond. *Planter's Sav. Bank of Greer v. American Sur. Co. of N.Y.*, 181 S.E. 222.

Tenn. App. 1979. [Bankers Blanket Bond]. A provision requiring that the insured furnish written notice to the carrier at the earliest practicable moment after discovery of any loss was not a condition precedent when it did not expressly provide that it was such. The burden of proof was on the carrier to show that the notice was faulty. *Union Planters Corp. v. Harwell*, 578 S.W.2d 87.

Tenn. App. 1965. [Employee Fidelity Bond]. The words "provided however" regarding a notice of loss term created a condition precedent such that the insured's failure to give notice within the specified time released the carrier from liability. *World Secret Serv. Ass'n v. Travelers Indem. Co.*, 396 S.W.2d 848.

Vt. 1940. [Bankers Blanket Bond]. When the bond provided that notice of loss must be given within ten days after discovery of loss, the failure to give such notice released the carrier from any obligations imposed by the bond. *Brown v. Maryland Cas. Co.*, 11 A.2d 222.

W. Va. 1935. [Fidelity Bond]. A notice of loss given twelve weeks after discovery precluded recovery because the bond required notice within five days after discovery. *Greenbrier Laundry Co. v. Fidelity & Cas. Co. of N.Y.*, 178 S.E. 631.

Wis. 1940. [Bank Employee Fidelity Bond]. A provision requiring notice "at the earliest practicable moment and in all events not later than 10 days" was valid and enforceable. *Bank of Kaukauna v. Maryland Cas. Co.*, 291 N.W. 319.

4. Whether the carrier must show prejudice from untimely notice

(a) Cases Decided Under Commercial Coverages

N.D. Cal. 2011. [Crime Protection Policy]. In order to demonstrate the requisite prejudice from late notice of loss, a carrier must show that, due to delay in reporting the loss, the carrier lost something that would have changed the handling of the underlying claim. A carrier must show that, but for the delay, there is a substantial likelihood that the carrier would have been able to garner a better result. *BEI Sensors & Sys. Co. v. Great American Ins. Co.*, No. C 09-5819 SBA, 2011 U.S. Dist. LEXIS 27996.

Mo. App. 2003. [Crime Policy]. While the conditions of a crime policy that require the insured to give notice of loss to the carrier within a certain time are valid, the insured will not be barred from recovery unless the carrier can demonstrate that it suffered prejudice as a result of the carrier's failure to comply with such provisions. *East Attucks Community Housing, Inc. v. Old Republic Sur. Co.*, 114 S.W.3d 311.

(b) Cases Decided Under Other Financial Institution Coverages

1st Cir. 1997 (Mass.). [Financial Institution Bond]. The FDIC could not recover under a bond when it failed to comply with the bond requirement of notice of loss within 30 days of discovery. A Massachusetts statute adopting a notice-prejudice rule for certain types of liability insurance did not extend to financial institution bonds. *Federal Deposit Ins. Corp. v. Insurance Co. of N. Am.*, 105 F.3d 778.

2d Cir. 1984 (N.Y.). [Fidelity Bond]. Once a loss has occurred, the carrier is entitled to the required notice of loss at the earliest practical time. Under New York law, the carrier may assert the defense of noncompliance without showing it was prejudiced by the untimely notice. *Utica Mut. Ins. Co. v. Fireman's Fund Ins. Cos*, 748 F.2d 118.

5th Cir. 1987 (Miss.). [Public Official Liability Insurance]. When the policy required the insured to notify the carrier of any loss "as soon as practicable," that phrase meant within a reasonable time, under all the circumstances, to effectuate the objects and purposes of the notice clause. Notice given so late that it was "unreasonable" or that prejudiced the carrier barred recovery by the insured. *Mississippi ex rel. Hinds County v. Richardson*, 817 F.2d 1203.

6th Cir. 1975 (Ohio). [Employee Fidelity Bond]. In Ohio, late notice of loss to the carrier is not a defense unless the carrier is prejudiced. *Russell Gasket Co. v. Phoenix of Hartford Ins. Co.*, 512 F.2d 205.

8th Cir. 1999 (Minn.). [Fidelity Bond]. Under Minnesota law, the carrier was prejudiced by the insured's untimely notice of loss when it was too late for the carrier to recover from the banks which paid the insured's checks altered by a dishonest employee and the insured had already assigned its claims against the employee to another carrier. *Winthrop & Weinstine, P.A. v. Travelers Cas. & Sur. Co.*, 187 F.3d 871.

9th Cir. 1981 (Cal.). [Savings and Loan Blanket Bond]. A delay between the closure of the bank and the providing of notice of loss to the carrier did not prejudice the carrier because the carrier had conducted its own investigation for over two years. *Fidelity Sav. & Loan Ass'n v. Aetna Life & Cas. Co.*, 647 F.2d 933.

10th Cir. 1994 (Utah). [Savings and Loan Blanket Bond]. A loss was discovered at the latest at the time when the FDIC issued cease and desist orders, which was prior to the termination of the bond. The carrier was required to show prejudice by reason of the late notice when the bond did not expressly make the giving of notice within a specified time a condition precedent. *Federal Deposit Ins. Corp. v. Oldenburg*, 34 F.3d 1529.

N.D. Cal. 1962. [Bankers Blanket Bond]. A five-month delay in giving notice of loss did not comply with the notice requirements of a bond requiring that the insured notify the underwriter within a reasonable time after learning of any occurrence or event which, in the judgment of the insured, might give rise to a claim. *St. Paul Fire & Marine Ins. Co. v. Bank of Stockton*, 213 F. Supp. 716.

D. Colo. 2008. [Financial Institution Bond]. The notice/prejudice rule does not extend to fidelity bonds under Colorado law. Even had the notice/prejudice rule applied, the carrier demonstrated prejudice by showing that it tripled the coverage amount following discovery of loss by the insured but before the insured gave notice to the carrier of a loss. *Federal Deposit Ins. Corp. v. St. Paul Cos.*, 634 F. Supp. 2d 1213.

D. Colo. 2015. [Financial Institution Bond]. The notice/prejudice rule does not extend to fidelity bonds under Colorado law because a Financial Institution Bond covers events discovered during the policy term, regardless of when the acts occurred; like a claims-made policy, the bond terminates once the bond period expires; the public policy concerns that prompted Colorado's adoption of the notice-prejudice rule in other contexts (the adhesive nature of the contract, the public's interest in compensating tort victims, and the inequity of an insurer's receiving a windfall from a technicality), are not present in a claim under a Financial Institution Bond; and the presence of seventeen riders to the bond suggested that the parties were capable of negotiating the bond's terms. *Centrix Fin., LLC v. Nat'l Union Ins. Co.*, No. 09-cv-01542-PAB-CBS, 2015 U.S. Dist. LEXIS 71122.

D. Conn. 1997. [Financial Institution Bond Form A]. A savings bank that waited over two years after discovery of loss before it provided notice of loss to the carrier was barred from recovery when the bond required notice within 30 days of discovery of loss and the carrier was not required to show any prejudice. *Community Sav. Bank v. Federal Ins. Co.*, 960 F. Supp. 16.

D. Kan. 1982. [Bankers Blanket Bond]. When the bank's knowledge of a check kiting scheme exceeded mere suspicion, the scheme was readily apparent from the bank's records, and the prejudice suffered by the carrier was great, coverage was denied under the bond as a result of delay in notice. *Security Nat'l Bank of Kansas City, Kansas v. Continental Ins. Co.*, 586 F. Supp. 139.

E.D. La. 1995. [Financial Institution Bond]. Because the bond did not make timely notice and proof of loss conditions precedent to coverage, the carrier had to demonstrate prejudice as result of late notice and proof of loss to avoid liability on the bond. *Resolution Trust Corp. v. Gaudet*, 907 F. Supp. 212.

D. Mass. 1998. [Bankers Blanket Bond]. Under Massachusetts law, the insured bank discovered a loss when it became aware of the results of a $45,000 confidential investigation, made a Report of Apparent Crime, met with an FBI agent, received two grand jury subpoenas, and became aware of its employee's extraordinary assets incommensurate with his salary and of a suspicious pattern of missing ownership interests in real estate partnerships involving the employee's friends and customers. Consequently, notice came too late and the carrier was not required to demonstrate actual prejudice from the delay in providing notice. *Federal Deposit Ins. Corp. v. Underwriters of Lloyd's of London*, 3 F. Supp. 2d 120.

D. Mass. 1994. [Position Fidelity Schedule Bond]. Under Massachusetts law, the notice-prejudice rule does not apply to fidelity insurance policies. Because the insured elected to pursue criminal proceedings against the wrongdoer rather than comply with a contractual provision requiring that notice of loss be given within a reasonable time after discovery and that a proof of loss be furnished within 180 days of discovery, the claim was barred. *United States v. National Grange Mut. Ins. Co.*, 1994 WL 511563.

W.D. Mo. 1980. [Fidelity Bond]. Under Missouri law, the unexcused failure to comply with a condition requiring notice to the carrier relieves the carrier from liability, if the carrier has been prejudiced by lack of notice. The issue of prejudice is ordinarily a question of fact on which the carrier has the burden of proof. Failure to give the required notice of loss prejudiced the carrier. *Columbia Union Nat'l Bank v. Hartford*

Acc. & Indem. Co., 496 F. Supp. 1263, *aff'd,* 669 F.2d 1210 (8th Cir. 1981).

D. Mont. 1990. [Fidelity Bond]. When more than one year before the FSLIC gave notice to the fidelity carrier, the FHLBB had requested the directors' resignation and reported the directors to FBI, the president received a letter from a director that mentioned essentially the same facts as those detailed in the proof of loss and letters between the FHLBB and board of directors showed the board was aware of potential problems ten months before the carrier was given notice of loss the insured failed to comply with the bond requirement that the insured give notice of loss within thirty days after discovery of the loss and file a proof of loss within six months. Wrongdoers on the board of directors and those who colluded with them did not dominate the board so as to prevent discovery; two directors resigned long before the carrier was notified, and the directors who were not accused of wrongdoing learned of some losses almost a year before the carrier was notified. Under Montana law, the carrier did not have to show substantial prejudice to assert the failure to provide timely notice as a defense under the bond. *Federal Sav. & Loan Ins. Corp. v. Aetna Cas. & Sur. Corp.*, 785 F. Supp. 867.

D.N.J. 1994. [Bankers Blanket Bond]. A New Jersey rule that the carrier must prove appreciable prejudice before denying a claim based on late notice applied to a "discovery" bond. The carrier's mere silence could not create a waiver of the proof of loss provision. *Resolution Trust Corp. v. Moskowitz*, 868 F. Supp. 634.

D.N.J. 1971. [Bankers Blanket Bond]. The time to give notice of loss began to run when the bank had all the facts on which its claim was based. The insured's delay in giving notice of the loss to the carrier prejudiced it because the maker of the allegedly dishonest loan had gone into bankruptcy before the bank gave notice of the loss. *Essex County State Bank v. Fireman's Fund Ins. Co.*, 331 F. Supp. 931.

E.D. Pa. 1995. [Multi-Peril Package Policy]. When the insured discovered a loss at least three years before notifying the carrier and the policy required notice of loss as soon as possible and suit within two years, the claim was barred because the carrier suffered prejudice in that further losses incurred after the insured first discovered the loss could have been avoided if the carrier had received timely notice. The insured was not so adversely dominated as to warrant tolling the contractual two-year suit limitation period when the insured had the right to and did receive financial records and the insured's controller was able to create ledger statements that revealed the misappropriated funds. *Northwood Nursing & Convalescent Home, Inc. v. Continental Ins. Co.*, 902 F. Supp. 79.

E.D. Pa. 1993. [Fidelity Bond]. When the fidelity bond required the insured to provide written notice of any loss at the earliest practicable moment after discovery of a loss, the underwriters failed to aver sufficient prejudice to warrant a finding that the notice of loss was untimely. The doctrine of equitable tolling applied to postpone the date of discovery when the sole directors, officers and principals of the insured engaged in an extensive scheme of embezzlement and fraud so that adverse domination prevented imputing their knowledge to the insured. *In re Lloyd Secs., Inc.*, 153 B.R. 677.

Bankr. W.D. Pa. 1994. [Fidelity Bond]. Under Pennsylvania law, carriers must show actual prejudice from late notice of a potential claim, as well as the insured's failure to submit a proper proof of loss, in order to be released from their responsibility under a fidelity bond. *In Re Mechem Fin., Inc.*, 167 B.R. 799.

D. Utah. 2013. [Credit Union Bond]. A jury could have found that the carrier was prejudiced by the insured's late notice. Prejudice is the loss of a valuable right or benefit, and occurs when a carrier suffers a material change in its ability to investigate, settle, or defend the claims at issue. The question of prejudice should be evaluated in light of the purposes of the notice requirements, namely to enable the carrier to investigate and take the necessary steps to protect its interests, including the loss of money or property value. *Transwest Credit Union v. CUMIS Ins. Soc'y*, No. 2:09-CV-297 TS 2013 U.S. Dist. LEXIS 61701.

Cal. App. 1987. [Savings and Loan Blanket Bond]. Although notice may not have been given at the "earliest practicable moment," in the absence of prejudice, the carrier may not rely on the breach of a notice clause. When the bond provided indemnity against loss, not liability, and no loss was suffered until the insured settled a third-party suit, the period for giving notice did not start to run until the date of that settlement (i.e., upon "discovery" of the loss). *Downey Sav. & Loan Ass'n v. Ohio Cas. Ins. Co.*, 234 Cal. Rptr. 835, *cert. denied*, 486 U.S. 1036 (1987).

Conn. App. 2006. [Employee Dishonesty Coverage]. The insured met its burden of proving that the carrier suffered no prejudice from late notice of loss when the carrier's sales agent testified that any delay did not prejudice the carrier because it was a property damage claim rather than a liability claim, the claims adjuster testified that he did not believe there was any prejudice to the carrier, the insured and its expert adjuster cooperated fully with the carrier in providing information regarding the claim, a computer expert did not testify as to any prejudice resulting from the delay in notice and even after receiving notice from its agent the carrier did not begin its investigation for several months. *National Publishing Co., Inc. v. Hartford Fire Ins. Co.*, 94 Conn. App. 234.

Conn. 1964. [Savings and Loan Blanket Bond]. A provision in the bond that the insured should give the underwriter notice of any loss at the earliest practicable moment after discovery was a condition precedent to the insured's recovery. There was no requirement to show prejudice. The insured did not make a claim regarding the lost or stolen bonds for over two years despite suggestions to make the claim by the U.S. Treasury Department. A person of ordinary and reasonable prudence would have recognized that a loss had occurred. *Hartford Fed. Sav. & Loan Ass'n v. Aetna Cas. & Sur. Co.*, 206 A.2d 650.

Fla. App. 1977. [Fidelity Bond]. Actual damages resulting from a failure to give notice must be pleaded and proved as a defense—the failure to give compensated surety notice of a principal's default does not relieve the surety when a failure to do so results in no loss to it. *Carnival Cruise Lines, Inc. v. Fin. Indem. Co.*, 347 So. 2d 825.

Iowa 1902. [Building & Loan Employee Fidelity Bond]. A six- or eight-day delay, when no prejudice resulted, was not, as a matter of law, a violation of a condition precedent requiring immediate notice. *Perpetual Bldg. & Loan Ass'n v. United States Fid. & Guar. Co.*, 92 N.W. 686.

Kan. App. 1986. [Bankers Blanket Bond]. A bank's failure to provide timely notice of loss does not preclude coverage unless the carrier can show it was prejudiced as result of the untimeliness in providing notice of loss. *Home Life Ins. Co. v. Clay*, 719 P.2d 756.

Mich. App. 1970. [Employee Fidelity Bond]. Prejudice to the rights of the carrier is a necessary element in determining if there has been an unreasonable delay in providing notice of loss. *Grand Rapids Auctions, Inc. v. Hartford Acc. & Indem. Co.*, 178 N.W.2d 812.

Miss. 1933. [Bankers Blanket Bond]. The failure of the bank to notify the carrier of a loss within 10 days after its discovery of defalcations by employees as required by a bankers blanket bond which neither provided that such failure relieved the carrier of liability nor made notice of the essence of the bond, did not preclude recovery by the bank on the bond, absent a showing of prejudice to the carrier. *Fidelity & Deposit Co. of Md. v. Merchants' & Marine Bank of Pascagoula*, 151 So. 373.

N.H. 1914. [Employee Fidelity Bond]. A mere delay by an employer in notifying the carrier of loss did not relieve the carrier of liability when it did not lose any means of securing itself as a result of the delay. *Peerless Cas. Co. v. Howard*, 92 A. 165.

N.Y. App. 1905. [Employee Fidelity Bond]. The court denied recovery when the bond required immediate notice, but notice was not given until 19 days after the discovery of a shortage in petty cash, because of the violation of a condition precedent. The insured is not required to prove prejudice from late notice. *National Discount Co. v. United States Fid. & Guar. Co.*, 94 N.Y.S. 457.

N.C. App. 1984. [Fidelity Bond]. An unexcused delay in notifying the carrier of a loss or claim does not relieve the carrier of its policy obligations if the delay does not materially prejudice the carrier and the insured acted in good faith. *B&H Supply Co., Inc. v. Insurance Co. of N. Am.*, 311 S.E.2d 643.

    5.   *Waiver and estoppel*

        (a) Cases Decided Under Commercial Coverages

        None

(b) Cases Decided Under Other Financial Institution Coverages

2d Cir. 1981 (N.Y.). [Fidelity Bond]. A repudiation of liability by the carrier on ground that a loss is not covered by the policy operates as a waiver of a notice requirement contained in policy. *H.S. Equities, Inc. v. Hartford Acc. & Indem. Co.*, 661 F.2d 264.

2d Cir. 1935 (N.Y.). [Employee Fidelity Bond]. No waiver of the notice or proof of loss provisions occurred when a local agent responded to a request for an extension of time by responding that the carrier wanted information regarding salvage before "passing on the claim." *Public Warehouses of Matanzas v. Fidelity & Deposit Co.*, 77 F.2d 831, *cert. denied*, 296 U.S. 633.

5th Cir. 1934 (Fla.). [Blanket Employee Fidelity Bond]. A requirement for notice to the carrier within ten days after discovery of loss was upheld when the insured delayed in giving notice for 60 days. The carrier did not waive nor was it estopped to assert late notice as a defense. *Murray v. American Sur. Co. of N.Y.*, 69 F.2d 147.

5th Cir. 1929 (Ala.). [Fidelity Bond]. When, after late notice, a bonding company failed to object but induced the insured to further document the claim, it waived the requirement of timely notice. *American Sur. Co. of N.Y. v. Blount County Bank*, 30 F.2d 882, *cert. denied*, 280 U.S. 561 (1930).

8th Cir. 1999 (Minn.). [Fidelity Bond]. Under Minnesota law, the carrier's payment of a claim under a first proof of loss and approval of a claim under a second proof of loss, neither of which were covered because they occurred when the insured was covered by a prior carrier, did not estop the carrier from denying coverage for losses under a third proof of loss absent evidence that the insured actually relied, to its detriment on the carrier's conduct such as by not notifying the prior carrier. *Winthrop & Weinstine, P.A. v. Travelers Cas. & Sur. Co.*, 187 F.3d 871.

8th Cir. 1935 (Iowa). [Fidelity Bond]. A bank advised the bonding company of the "possibility of liability under the bond in connection with acts of its cashier." The bonding company conducted an investigation. Later, the bank failed and its receiver filed proofs of loss.

The bonding company's adjuster continued its investigation without objection to the sufficiency or timeliness of the notice of loss or proof of loss and told the examiner in charge that a loss shown to be the result of dishonest act of the cashier would be paid. The court held that there was evidence to justify a jury in concluding that notice and proof of loss were timely submitted and further, there was "substantial evidence" that the bonding company had waived the requirement for timely notice of loss and proof of loss. *Fidelity & Deposit Co. of Md. v. Bates*, 76 F.2d 160.

9th Cir. 1934 (Wash.). [Blanket Position Bond]. The carrier waived defenses as to which corporation it covered when it accepted a notice of the loss. *Hansen & Rowland v. Fidelity & Deposit Co. of Md.*, 72 F.2d 151.

D.C. Cir. 1938. [Fidelity Bond]. When the insured discovered a loss in 1922 but did not give notice until 1928 and the bonding company investigated the claim and denied liability based in part on the lack of notice, there was no waiver of the notice requirement by the bonding company. Acceptance of notice of default is not a waiver. *United States Shipping Bd. Merch. Fleet Corp. v. Aetna Cas. & Sur. Co.*, 98 F.2d 238.

D. Nev. 1968. [Fidelity Bond]. A carrier's denial of liability on other grounds waived any defects in the notice of loss or the untimeliness of the proof of loss. *Mapes Casino, Inc. v. Maryland Cas. Co.*, 290 F. Supp. 186.

D.N.J. 1994. [Bankers Blanket Bond]. A New Jersey rule that the carrier must prove appreciable prejudice before denying a claim based on late notice applied to a "discovery" bond. The carrier's mere silence could not create a waiver of the proof of loss provision. *Resolution Trust Corp. v. Moskowitz*, 868 F. Supp. 634.

S.D. Ohio 1974. [Fidelity Bond]. In an action by a contractors' association and trustees of welfare and pension funds to recover under indemnity bond, the trustees who, after discovering losses, elected not to give notice of loss to the carrier, could not recover because notice of loss and the proof of loss were conditions precedent. Acts or conduct of the fidelity carrier giving rise to a waiver or estoppel must have occurred within the time limitation for notice of loss, proof of loss, and filing of suit rather than after such limitations have run. *Sheet Metal & Roofing Contractor's Ass'n of Miami Valley, Ohio v. Liskany*, 369 F. Supp. 662.

Bankr. N.D. Ohio 1988. [Fidelity Bond]. The carrier's failure to give timely notice of coverage excused a lack of prompt notice of loss and prompt submission of proof of loss by an insured. *Rafoth v. National Union Fire Ins. Co. of Pittsburgh, Pa.*, 93 B.R. 559.

Ark. 1915. [Fidelity Bond]. A carrier's unconditional denial of liability waived timely notice of loss under a bond. *Equitable Sur. Co. v. Bank of Hazen*, 181 S.W. 279.

Cal. App. 1981. [Blanket Fidelity Bond]. A carrier was entitled to summary judgment on the issues of waiver and estoppel. No facts were presented which indicated that the carrier intended to waive a limitation upon the period for discovery of a loss within coverage of the bond. *USLIFE Sav. & Loan Ass'n v. National Sur. Corp.*, 171 Cal. Rptr. 393.

Ga. App. 1936. [Fidelity Bond]. A failure by the bonding company to complain about the sufficiency of notice waived timely compliance with the notice provision; also a statement by the bonding company that other insurance would have to be exhausted before it could be called upon to pay a loss presented a fact issue as to whether the bonding company waived the limitation on filing suit. *American Sur. Co. of N.Y. v. Peoples Bank*, 189 S.E. 414.

Ga. App. 1919. [Employee Fidelity Bond]. An insured must affirmatively plead either that it complied with a notice of loss provision or that the carrier waived notice of loss. *Bank of Ball Ground v. National Sur. Co.*, 97 S.E. 892.

Ill. App. 1961. [Fidelity Bond]. When after the expiration of the time for giving notice and furnishing proof of loss, the local agent of the bonding company met with the insured, requested that the insured sign the proof of loss and said that a loss would be taken care of, the bonding company waived both the requirements for giving notice and furnishing proof of loss. *Royal Loan Corp. v. American Sur. Co. of N.Y.*, 173 N.E.2d 17.

La. App. 1963. [Fidelity Bond]. An investigation and denial of a claim constituted waiver of the notice of loss and proof of loss requirements despite the fact that the material furnished to the bonding company conclusively showed that the claim was not timely. *Standard Brass & Mfg. Co. v. Maryland Cas. Co.*, 153 So. 2d 475.

La. App. 1938. [Fidelity Bond]. A carrier must reserve its rights regarding untimely notice of loss. It cannot give the insured an impression that the matter will be settled and then bring up notice problems twelve months after having received notice of loss. The action of the agent in leading the insured to believe that notice to the agent was sufficient to waive the bond provision requiring notice to the bonding company "at its home office." *Inter-City Express Lines, Inc. v. Hartford Acc. & Indem. Co.*, 178 So. 280.

La. App. 1932. [Employee Indemnity Bond]. The carrier waived the requirement for notice by regular mail when it learned all necessary information from an actual inspection of the insured's records. *Shreveport Laundries, Inc. v. Massachusetts Bonding & Ins. Co.*, 142 So. 868.

Mass. 1931. [Bankers Blanket Bond]. The carrier's acceptance of a notice of loss by letter waived the bond requirement that notice be furnished by registered letter or telegram. A denial of liability did not waive the proof of loss requirement. *Fitchburg Sav. Bank v. Massachusetts Bonding & Ins. Co.*, 174 N.E. 324.

Mich. 1957. [Dishonesty Bond]. When the insured provided actual notice of a claim and furnished proof of loss within the time required by the bond and the carrier denied liability on other grounds, the carrier waived the bond requirements as to both notice of loss and proof of loss. *Masters v. Massachusetts Bonding & Ins. Co.,* 84 N.W.2d 462.

Mich. 1927. [Employee Fidelity Bond]. When a fidelity contract required notice of loss to be sent to the home office of the carrier within three months of the discovery of loss, and the insured sent a notice of loss to the defendant's local agent within that period, but did not send the notice to the carrier's home office, the notice either constituted proper notice or the notice provision was waived. The carrier's investigation without reference to the late notice and its general denial of liability waived the notice and proof of loss requirements as a matter of law. *Farmers' Produce Co. v. Aetna Cas. & Sur. Co.*, 213 N.W. 689.

Minn. 1933. [Fidelity Bond]. The bonding company could not assert a failure to comply with the notice and proof of loss requirements of a bond in view of its denial of liability, even though the bonding company also denied liability on the basis that the bond had been terminated and the time for discovering a loss had passed and further reserved its rights and defenses. The court did not use the words "waiver" or "estoppel." *Cary v. National Sur. Co.*, 251 N.W. 123.

Minn. 1925. [Fidelity Bond]. The conduct of the bonding company was sufficient to support a jury finding of waiver of the notice and proof of loss requirements of the bond. *Ceylon Farmers' Elevator Co. v. Fidelity & Deposit Co. of Md.*, 203 N.W. 985.

Mo. App. 1908. [Fidelity Bond]. The carrier's acceptance of late notice of loss without objection and causing the insured to go to additional trouble and expense to prove its loss waived the requirement of timely notice under the bond. *Roark v. City Trust, Safe Deposit & Sur. Co.*, 110 S.W. 1.

N.H. 1932. [Bank Treasurer's Fidelity Bond]. Whether the carrier's failure to object to a notice given five months after the discovery of loss constituted a waiver, when the bond required immediate notice, was a question for jury. *Exeter Banking Co. v. Taylor*, 160 A. 733.

N.D. 1927. [Employee Fidelity Bond]. When a bond provided coverage for losses discovered within six months of expiration of the bond, the carrier did not waive its rights when the notice did not state when a loss was discovered. *Baird v. Northwestern Trust Co.*, 217 N.W. 538.

N.Y. Sup. 1997. [Fidelity Bond]. The carrier did not waive and was not estopped to assert the "single loss" discovery and notice provisions of the bond by its investigation of a second claim or settlement of the initial claim. *Bank Saderat Iran N.Y. Agency v. National Union Fire Ins. Co. of Pittsburgh, Pa.*, 665 N.Y.S.2d 79.

Pa. 1934. [Tax Collector's Bond]. When a borough notified the carrier of a possible employee defalcation and the carrier responded that it would investigate, the carrier was estopped from asserting the defense of lack of notice when the borough discovered actual loss thereafter. *Borough of Nanty-Glo v. American Sur. Co. of N.Y.*, 175 A. 536.

Tenn. App. 1930. [Employee Fidelity Bond]. It is not necessary to give notice of each item of default after each discovery, one notice being sufficient. The carrier, having paid part of the loss on receipt of the first notice without raising a question as to delay in giving that notice, was estopped to raise that defense. *Fourth & First Bank & Trust Co. ex rel. Nashville Trustee Co. v. Standard Acc. Ins. Co.*, 12 Tenn. App. 311.

Wash. 1920. [Fidelity Bond]. When, after late notice, the bonding company sent proof of loss forms to the insured "for your convenience in stating any claim which you may have to make . . .," there was no implied waiver of the notice requirement. *Bankers' Trust Co. v. American Sur. Co.*, 191 P. 845.

W. Va. 1920. [Fidelity Bond]. A denial of liability on other grounds waived the requirement of timely notice under the bond. *Piedmont Grocery Co. v. Hawkins*, 104 S.E. 736.

Wis. 1974. [Bankers Blanket Bond]. When the carrier did not deny coverage within the time notice of loss was required to be given, and did not induce the bank to postpone giving notice by promises or action upon which the bank relied, the carrier was not estopped to raise untimeliness of notice as a defense. *State Bank of Viroqua v. Capitol Indem. Corp.*, 214 N.W.2d 42.

SECONDARY SOURCES

Annotation, *Effect of Failure to Give Notice, or Delay in Giving Notice or Filing of Proofs of Loss, upon Fidelity Bond or Insurance*, 23 A.L.R.2d 1065 (1952).

Annotation, *Subsequent denial of liability following promise or negotiations as affecting contractual limitation for action upon Insurance Policy*, 3 A.L.R 218 (1919).

Annotation, *Suspicion, or Reasons for Suspicion of Wrongdoing by Officer or Employee, Covered by Fidelity Bond or Policy, as Requiring Obligee to Comply with Conditions of Bond with Respect to Notice of Discovery of Knowledge of Loss*, 129 A.L.R. 1411 (1940).

Annotation, *Validity, Construction, & Effect of "Regulatory Exclusion" in Directors' and Officers' Liability Insurance Policy*, 21 A.L.R. 5th 292 (1994).

Annotation, *Validity, Construction & Application of Provision of Fidelity Bond as to Giving Notice of Loss or Claim within Specified Time after Close of Bond Year*, 149 A.L.R. 945 (1944).

William T. Atkins, *What Constitutes Discovery of Loss within the Meaning of the Word 'Loss' Under Financial Institution & Fidelity Bonds*, ABA SECTION OF INSURANCE, NEGLIGENCE AND COMPENSATION LAW PROCEEDINGS 1967, 73-79.

James E. Clark, *The Law of Fidelity Bonds*, 28 INS. COUNSEL J. 210 (1961).

Duncan L. Clore & John Tomaine, *Discovery of Loss*, *in* HANDLING FIDELITY BOND CLAIMS 431 (Michael Keeley & Sean Duffy eds., 2d ed. 2005).

Paul R. Devin & Allen N. David, *Discovery Under Fidelity Bonds: The Emerging Concept of the Insured's Duty of Inquiry*, 21 FORUM 543 (1985-86).

John C. Eichman, *Submission of the Insured's Claim*, *in* HANDLING FIDELITY BOND CLAIMS 37 (Michael Keeley & Sean Duffy eds., 2d ed. 2005).

Peter C. Haley, *"Loss" Containment Under the Financial Institution Bond*, II FID. L.J. 111 (1996).

Francis L. Kenney, Jr., *The Effect of Discovery of Loss Upon the Contract Rights, Duties & Obligations of the Parties*, ABA SECTION

OF INSURANCE, NEGLIGENCE AND COMPENSATION LAW PROCEEDINGS 1967, pp. 80-94.

Francis L. Kenney, Jr., *Notice—Its Place in Fidelity Insurance*, ABA SECTION OF INSURANCE, NEGLIGENCE AND COMPENSATION LAW PROCEEDINGS 1955, pp. 132-178.

Jack McNeil, *When Is the Failure to Comply with the Requirements for Timely Notice, Proof of Loss & Suit a Defense to a Surety?*, 16 FORUM 1139 (1981).

Ronald C. Mund, *The Claim Handler's Initial Analysis & Response to the Claim*, in HANDLING FIDELITY BOND CLAIMS 69 (Michael Keeley & Sean Duffy eds., 2d ed. 2005).

G. Wayne Murphy, *Allegations, Assertion, & Charges as Discovery of Loss*, 12 THE FORUM 986 (1976).

James Postula, *What Constitutes Timely Notice & Proof of Loss Under Fidelity & Financial Institution Bonds*, ABA SECTION OF INSURANCE, NEGLIGENCE AND COMPENSATION LAW PROCEEDINGS 1967, 108-115.

Scott L. Schmookler & Bruce Robbibaro, *Discovery by the Risk Manager: The Effect of Noise Reducing Earphones on Fidelity Coverage*, XVII FID. L.J. 171 (2011).

Paul D. Schoonover, *Discovery, Notice & Automatic Cancellation Under Revised Form 24*, 16 FORUM 962 (1981).

Lynn M. Schubert, Edward G. Gallagher & Marilyn Klinger, *Annual Survey of Fidelity & Surety Law*, 28 TORT & INS. L.J. 251 (1993).

Armen Shahinian & Scott D. Baron, *Notice/Proof—Legal Proceedings Against Underwriter*, in ANNOTATED FINANCIAL INSTITUTION BOND 470 (Michael Keeley ed., 2d ed. 2004).

Armen Shahinian & Scott D. Baron, *The Notice Defense to Financial Institution Bond Claims Dissected: No Showing of Prejudice From Late Notice Should Be Required*, II FID. L.J. 1 (1996).

Edward Allen Shure, *Contract Provisions for Notice & Proof after Discovery of Loss & Conditions Precedent to Insured's Right of Recovery*, ABA SECTION OF INSURANCE, NEGLIGENCE AND COMPENSATION LAW PROCEEDINGS 1967, 95-107.

Frank L. Skillern, Jr., *How to Prevent Loss of Fidelity Carriers' Rights by Waiver & Estoppel*, 10 FORUM 301 (1974).

Patricia H. Thompson & Lynn M. Schubert, *Annual Survey of Surety & Fidelity Law*, 29 TORT & INS. L.J. 412 (1994).

Karen Wildau, *Evolving Law of Third-Party Claims Under Fidelity Bond: When is Third-Party Recovery Allowed?*, 25 FORUM 92 (1989).

Mark E. Wilson, *How to Prepare & Present a Fidelity Claim: Advice for the Insured*, 28 THE BRIEF NO. 3, 54 (1999).

William H. Woods, *Condition & Limitations; Section 4—Notice/Proof—Legal Proceedings*, *in* ANNOTATED BANKERS BLANKET BOND 46 (Frank L. Skillern, Jr. ed., Supp. 1983).

William H. Woods, *Defense Based on Contractual Requirements for Timely Filing of Suit in Fidelity Cases*, 17 FORUM 1291 (1982).

Julie Fry Yanda & Mark Struthers, *The Insured's Duties Following Discovery of Loss*, XIX FID. L.J. 147 (2013).

Frederick Zauderer & Richard S. Mills, *At the Apex of the Arc of the Pendulum—Notice Prejudice Rule in Fidelity Cases*, IV FID. L.J. 127 (1998).

B. Proof of Loss

CRIME PROTECTION POLICY[3]
Section E. Conditions

7.   **After you discover a loss or a situation that may result in a loss you must:**
    c.   **Give us a detailed, sworn proof of loss within 120 days.**

COMMERCIAL CRIME POLICY (DISCOVERY FORM)[4]
Section E. Conditions

1. g. Duties in the Event of Loss
After you discover a loss or a situation that may result in loss of or damage to "money," "securities" or "other property" you must: . . .
(3)   Give us a detailed, sworn proof of loss within 120 days.

COMMENT

The purpose of the requirement that the insured provide a sworn proof of loss is to (1) furnish the carrier with the particulars of the loss and all data necessary to determine the fact and amount of its liability, (2) afford the carrier an adequate opportunity for investigation, 3) enable the carrier to form an intelligent estimate of its rights and liabilities before it is obligated to pay, and (4) prevent fraud and imposition upon the carrier.

Unless the policy specifically provides otherwise, the insured is not required to use any particular form of proof of loss, but whatever form is employed should enable the carrier to fairly and correctly assess its rights

3   Crime Protection Policy, SP 00 01 04 12 (The Surety & Fidelity Association of America 2012), *reprinted in* COMMERCIAL CRIME INSURANCE COVERAGE 769 (Randall I. Marmor & Susan Koehler Sullivan, eds., 2015) [*see* App'x A].
4   Commercial Crime Policy, CR 00 22 07 02 (ISO Props., Inc. 2001), *reprinted in* COMMERCIAL CRIME POLICY 785, 799 (Randall I. Marmor & Susan Koehler Sullivan, eds., 2015) [*see* App'x B and C].

and liabilities. Generally, provisions for the giving of proof of loss to a carrier are liberally construed in favor of the insured. Strict compliance is typically not required and substantial compliance with the policy's provisions frequently will suffice.

In some jurisdictions, the period fixed for submitting proof of loss is regarded as a condition precedent to the right of recovery, while in others it is deemed not to work a forfeiture in the absence of prejudice to the carrier. In many states, statutes determine whether contractual provisions in fidelity policies will be enforced or disregarded.

A carrier may be held to have waived the requirement for the insured to furnish proof of loss by its own acts or conduct, or that of its authorized agent. Such waiver may arise from conduct by the carrier which tends to create a belief in the mind of the insured that submission of proof of loss is unnecessary, conduct inconsistent with an intention to insist upon strict compliance with contractual requirements, or conduct that induces the insured to abstain from submitting proof of loss. However, some states have statutes that provide that certain acts of insurance companies will not be deemed to constitute a waiver of any policy provision or defense. For example, South Dakota Codified laws (2004), Vol. 32, Chapter 58-12, Section 58-12-2, which provides:

Acts of carrier not constituting waiver of defense. Without limitations of any right or defense of a carrier, none of the following acts by a carrier shall be deemed to constitute a waiver of any provision of a policy or of any defense of the insured thereunder:

1) Acknowledgement of the receipt of notice of loss or claim under the policy.

2) Furnishing forms for reporting a loss or claim, for giving information relative thereto, or for making proof of loss or receiving or acknowledging receipt of any such forms or proof completed or uncompleted.

3) Investigating any loss or claim under any policy.

OUTLINE OF ANNOTATIONS

A. Proof of Loss
    1. What proof of loss is adequate
        (a) Cases Decided Under Commercial Coverages
        (b) Cases Decided Under Other Financial Institution Coverages
    2. Whether proof of loss is timely
        (a) Cases Decided Under Commercial Coverages
        (b) Cases Decided Under Other Financial Institution Coverages
    3. Effect of untimely proof of loss
        (a) Cases Decided Under Commercial Coverages
        (b) Cases Decided Under Other Financial Institution Coverages
    4. Whether the carrier must show prejudice from untimely proof of loss
        (a) Cases Decided Under Commercial Coverages
        (b) Cases Decided Under Other Financial Institution Coverages
    5. Waiver and estoppel
        (a) Cases Decided Under Commercial Coverages
        (b) Cases Decided Under Other Financial Institution Coverages

ANNOTATIONS

A. Proof of Loss

1. What proof of loss is adequate

(a) Cases Decided Under Commercial Coverages

D. Nev. 1968. [Blanket Crime Policy and Comprehensive Dishonesty, Disappearance and Destruction Policy]. The proof of loss should identify the employee or employees charged with a loss and should put the carrier on notice of the claim within the coverage of the bond. The fear of a suit for defamation does not justify a failure to comply with the proof of loss requirement. *Mapes Casino, Inc. v. Maryland Cas. Co.*, 290 F. Supp. 186.

S.D.N.Y. 1974. [Blanket Crime Policy and Comprehensive Dishonesty, Disappearance and Destruction Policy]. A proof of loss with supporting papers which adequately notified the carrier of the factual basis of the insured's claim, a loss of more than six tons of gold and silver, was adequate. *United States Smelting Refining & Mining Co. v. Aetna Cas. & Sur. Co.*, 372 F. Supp. 489.

Ore. 1973. [Crime Policy]. Substantial, as distinguished from strict, compliance with the proof of loss provision is all that is required. A failure to sign the proof of loss under oath was not a failure to substantially comply with the proof of loss requirement of the policy. *Sutton v. Fire Ins. Exchange*, 509 P.2d 418.

(b) Cases Decided Under Other Financial Institution Coverages

2d Cir. 1935 (N.Y.). [Employee Fidelity Bond]. The insured is not required to follow instructions on the back of a proof of loss form. Such instructions cannot enlarge the terms of the bond, and the insured is required only to give the information which it has. *Public Warehouses of Matanzas v. Fidelity & Deposit Co.*, 77 F.2d 831, *cert. denied*, 296 U.S. 633.

2d Cir. 1927 (N.Y.). [Employee Fidelity Bond]. The proof of loss provision will not be construed to require the impossible and when it was not possible to provide the items and dates of the losses, as required in the policy, such would not be required. *Massachusetts Bonding & Ins. Co. v. Norwich Pharmacal Co.*, 18 F.2d 934.

5th Cir. 1917 (Ala.). [Bank Employee Fidelity Bond]. A proof of loss is adequate if it shows the information that must be alleged and proved in an action upon the bond. *Maryland Cas. Co. v. First Nat'l Bank*, 246 F. 892, *cert. denied*, 246 U.S. 670 (1918).

7th Cir. 1953 (Ill.). [Brokers Blanket Bond]. If a proof of loss is itemized to the extent that is reasonably possible under the circumstances and is sufficient for the bonding company to ascertain the nature of the different items upon which the claim is based, it is sufficient. *Irvin Jacobs & Co. v. Fid. & Deposit Co. of Md.*, 202 F.2d 794.

10th Cir. 1969 (Okla.). [School Official Bond]. The proof of loss must show not only misconduct but also actual damage. *Independent Sch. Dist. 93 Pottawatomie County, Oklahoma v. Western Sur.*, 419 F.2d 78.

W.D. Pa. 2006. [Theft Policy]. When the insured filed a proof of loss claiming that he suffered a loss of $428,534.12 and the carrier paid the loss in the full amount of the coverage of $150,000 and took an assignment of the insured's rights to the extent of its payment, and the insured subsequently obtained a recovery of $325,000 from the wrongdoer, the insured was not estopped from claiming that his loss was actually in excess of his total recovery of $475,000, even though the proof of loss showed a loss of lower amount, because the carrier failed to demonstrate that it actually relied on the proof of loss or suffered a detriment due to reliance on the amount of the loss stated in the proof of loss. Substantial compliance as opposed to strict and literal compliance with the proof of loss provision is all that is required for an effective proof of loss. *Hartford Fire Ins. Co. v. Spall*, 2006 WL 538938.

E.D. Wis. 1945. [Employee Fidelity Bond]. A proof of loss which states the nature and amount of the claim is sufficient. The bonding company was able to pay or adjust the claim without further expense if it chose to do so. *Duel v. National Sur. Corp.*, 64 F. Supp. 961, *aff'd*, 157 F.2d 516 (E.D. Wis. 1945).

Ala. 1970. [Employee Fidelity Bond]. Compliance with the proof of loss provision is a condition precedent to the right to bring suit, but a failure to comply with that provision does not void the policy or work a forfeiture of the claim in the absence of an express provision that the failure to file a proof of loss works a forfeiture. *American Fire & Cas. Co. v. Burchfield*, 232 So. 2d 606.

Ariz. App. 1971. [Employee Fidelity Bond]. Because the policy did not specifically require that any specific proof of loss forms be utilized, the insured's submission of an audit report prepared by certified public accountants setting forth each claimed defalcation and explaining in detail how and when it occurred, substantially complied with the policy's requirement that the insured file a detailed proof of loss, duly sworn to. *Maryland Cas. Co. v. Clements*, 487 P.2d 437.

Cal. App. 1919. [Employee Fidelity Bond]. A proof of loss is sufficient if it includes all information as to nature and amount of misappropriations which is available under the circumstances. *Los Angeles Athletic Club v. United States Fid. & Guar. Co.*, 183 P. 174.

Ind. App. 1931. [Fidelity Bond]. The insured was required to file a proof of loss with the bonding company itemized to the extent that was then reasonably possible under the circumstances. *Fletcher Sav. & Trust Co. v. American Sur. Co.*, 175 N.E. 247.

Mo. 1941. [Fidelity Bond]. The insured provided information regarding the total loss claimed and the method of the embezzlement. The insured offered to provide additional information and permitted inspection of its books and records. The insured substantially complied with the proof of loss provision even though it could not provide the dates of each loss. *Lemay Ferry Bank v. New Amsterdam Cas. Co.*, 149 S.W.2d 328.

N.C. 1926. [Employee Fidelity Bond]. The insured was not required to include every specific item in the proof of loss. The insured was required to furnish a verified statement sufficient to enable the bonding company to ascertain the nature of the different items upon which the claim was based. *Forest City Bldg. & Loan Ass'n. v. Davis*, 133 S.E. 530 (N.C. 1926), *modified on another ground*, 138 S.E. 338.

N.Y. Sup. 1975. [Comprehensive Dishonesty, Disappearance and Destruction Policy]. When the proof of loss stated that a specific employee had stolen property, but at trial, the insured contended that the property was stolen by unidentified employees, the entire proof of loss was fallacious and did not comply with the terms of the policy. *Kaplan Jewelers, Inc. v. Insurance Co. of N. Am.*, 383 N.Y.S.2d 127.

Tex. App. 1967. [Burglary Policy]. Substantial compliance with the proof of loss provision is all that is required. The insured is not bound by statements made in the proof of loss when the bonding company could have requested additional information and was not prejudiced by the statements in the proof of loss. *Great Central Ins. Co. v. Cook*, 422 S.W.2d 801.

2. *Whether proof of loss is timely*

(a) Cases Decided Under Commercial Coverages

S.D.N.Y. 1974. [Blanket Crime Policy and Comprehensive Dishonesty, Disappearance and Destruction Policy]. Discovery of loss required knowledge rather than mere suspicion and did not occur until an inventory was completed, even though the insured had earlier suspicions. When the carrier gave the insured several extensions of time to file its proof of loss and the insured submitted its proof of loss before the last extension of time expired, the proof of loss was timely. *United States Smelting Refining & Mining Co. v. Aetna Cas. & Sur. Co.*, 372 F. Supp. 489.

D.C. 1980. [Blanket Crime Policy]. An employee allegedly misappropriated government grants given to the insured. The employer informed the carrier of possible losses, but filed the proof of loss two years later after the government filed a formal claim against the employer for misappropriations. The policy required the filing of a proof of loss within four months of discovery of loss. A third-party loss does not arise until the third-party demands compensation from the insured so that the filing the proof of loss within four months of the demand complied with the timely filing requirement. *Fidelity & Deposit Co. of Md. v. President & Directors of Georgetown College*, 483 F. Supp. 1142.

(b) Cases Decided Under Other Financial Institution Coverages

5th Cir. 1980 (Tex.). [Blanket Fidelity Bond]. A delay of one year and three months in filing the proof of loss was held to be reasonable under the circumstances and in compliance with a condition of the bond which provided the insured "shall make every effort to file . . . affirmative proof of loss . . . as soon as practicable" when the evidence established that no administrative action could be taken until criminal matters were resolved by the Department of Justice. *United States v. Indiana Bonding & Sur. Co.*, 625 F.2d 26.

5th Cir. 1972 (Tex.). [Savings and Loan Blanket Bond]. Compliance with the proof of loss provision is a condition precedent to recovery. The bond required that the proof of loss be filed within 100 days after the discovery of loss. The failure of the insured to file the proof of loss for nearly two years after discovery of the loss barred the claim. *Abilene Sav. Ass'n. v. Westchester Fire Ins. Co.*, 461 F.2d 557.

5th Cir. 1938 (Ga.). [Employee Fidelity Bond]. A proof of loss which was mailed within the time stated in the bond, but not received by the bonding company until one day after the time for filing of the proof of loss substantially complied with the proof of loss condition. *Franklin Sav. & Loan Co. of Macon v. American Employers Ins. Co.*, 99 F.2d 494.

6th Cir. 1975 (Ohio). [Fidelity Bond]. The general manager of the insured defrauded it by stealing confidential records such as lists of sources of raw materials and customers and tools and dies. Within four months of the completion of an extensive, complicated investigation, during which the carrier offered no assistance, the insured filed the proof of loss. The insured should be allowed a reasonable time within which to discover the extent and amount of the loss before being required to file the proof of loss, so that filing within four months after a year-and-a-half discovery process was timely when the loss was extensive, complicated, and difficult of proof and the carrier suffered no prejudice. Discovery of the loss did not occur until the insured had a reasonable time to discover the extent and amount of the loss. *Russell Gasket Co. v. Phoenix of Hartford Ins. Co.*, 512 F.2d 205.

10th Cir. 1985 (N.M.). [Bankers Special Bond]. Under the law of New Mexico, substantial compliance with the notice and proof of loss requirements of insurance policy is all that is required of the insured to collect under policy. The insured complied with the proof of loss requirement of the bond by providing full particulars as soon as they were known to the insured, even though the insured did not know the "full particulars" of the alleged loss within six months of its discovery of the alleged loss. *Wells Fargo Bus. Credit v. American Bank of Commerce*, 780 F.2d 871.

S.D. Fla. 2012. [Financial Institution Bond]. When the bond required the insured to furnish a proof of loss to the underwriter within six months after discovery of loss, and material issues of fact existed as to when the insured could have discovered the loss, summary judgment could not be entered in favor of the insured even though it argued that its actual discovery occurred within six months of furnishing the proof of loss to the carrier. *ABCO Premium Fin. LLC v. American Int'l Group, Inc.*, No. 11-23020-CISCOLA/Bandstra, 2012 U.S. Dist. LEXIS 111833.

D. Minn. 2014. [Financial Institution Bond]. When a bank employee induced others to participate in an advance fee scheme in which he was involved and the carrier defended the resulting lawsuit under a D&O

policy, but later declined coverage under the FIB, notice of the loss was timely because the insured notified the carrier of its suspicions within an hour. *Avon State Bank v. BancInsure, Inc.*, Civ. No. 12-2557 (RHK/LIB), 2014 U.S. Dist. LEXIS 3099.

D. Mont. 1990. [Fidelity Bond]. When more than one year before the FSLIC gave notice to the fidelity carrier, the FHLBB had requested the directors' resignation and reported the directors to FBI, the president received a letter from a director that mentioned essentially the same facts as those detailed in the proof of loss and letters between the FHLBB and board of directors showed the board was aware of potential problems ten months before the carrier received notice, the insured failed to comply with the bond requirement that the insured give notice of loss within thirty days after discovery of the loss and file a proof of loss within six months. The wrongdoers on the board of directors and those who colluded with them did not dominate the board so as to prevent discovery when two directors resigned long before the carrier was notified and the directors who were not accused of any wrongdoing learned of some losses almost a year before the carrier was notified. Under Montana law, the carrier did not have to show substantial prejudice to assert a failure to provide timely notice as a defense under the bond. *Federal Sav. & Loan Ins. Corp. v. Aetna Cas. & Sur. Corp.*, 785 F. Supp. 867.

D.C. Cir. 1964. [Employee Fidelity Bond]. The failure to file a proof of loss within a period of ninety days after discovery of a loss as provided by the bond precluded recovery. The proof of loss was filed three weeks after the deadline for it. *Ace Van & Storage Co. v. Liberty Mut. Ins. Co.*, 336 F.2d 925.

Me. 2002. [Employee Dishonesty Coverage]. When the policy required the insured to provide a proof of loss within 120 days after discovery of loss and the proof of loss was filed more than 120 days after its employee failed to comply with a promise to the chairman of board that he would repay improper personal expenses charged on the corporate credit card, the proof of loss was untimely. *Acadia Ins. Co. v. Keiser Indus., Inc.*, 793 A.2d 495.

Neb. 1989. [Bankers Blanket Bond]. An untimely proof of loss which added a series of transactions not mentioned in the original proof of loss and increased the claim by more than $2 million did not relate back to the original proof of loss and justified the granting of summary judgment against the insured. *First Sec. Sav. v. Aetna Cas. & Sur. Co.*, 445 N.W.2d 596.

3. Effect of untimely proof of loss

(a) Cases Decided Under Commercial Coverages

E.D. Ark. 1982. [Commercial Coverages]. A requirement that a proof of loss be filed within four months of discovery of loss was not binding when the proof of loss was filed within a reasonable period and the carrier exercised an unreasonable amount of control over the filing procedure. *Chandler Trailer Co. v. Lawyer's Sur. Corp.*, 535 F. Supp. 204.

(b) Cases Decided Under Other Financial Institution Coverages

2d Cir. 1935 (N.Y.). [Employee Fidelity Bond]. The timely filing of a proof of loss is a condition precedent to liability. The bond required filing the proof of loss within thirty days after discovery of default. The proof of loss was not filed until eighty-five days after discovery. *Public Warehouses of Matanzas v. Fidelity & Deposit Co.*, 77 F.2d 831, *cert. denied*, 296 U.S. 633 (1935).

5th Cir. 1981 (Tex.). [Bankers Blanket Bond]. A rider to the bond required the insured to furnish "affirmative proof of loss with full particulars in writing," including the dates and items of a loss, duly sworn to within 100 days after discovery of the loss. The bank forwarded each of the seven complaints filed against it and a letter containing the details of an investigation conducted by the bank to the carrier. The bank did not make a claim on the bond. The bank successfully defended all seven suits and sought indemnity for attorneys' fees and expenses. Texas law only required "substantial compliance" with the proof of loss requirements and the bank substantially complied with requirements of the rider. *First Nat'l Bank of Bowie v. Fidelity & Cas. Co. of N.Y.*, 634 F.2d 1000.

5th Cir. 1954 (Tex.). [Comprehensive Dishonesty, Disappearance and Destruction Policy]. A failure to file the proof of loss required by the policy precludes recovery. *Lawson v. American Motorists Ins. Corp.*, 217 F.2d 724.

9th Cir. 1954 (Ariz.). [Blanket Position Bond]. The court affirmed a judgment in favor of the carrier because the insured did not comply with the proof of loss provision. *Alianza Hispano-America v. Hartford Acc. & Indem. Co.*, 209 F.2d 578.

S.D. Ala. 1934. [Employee Fidelity Bond]. In a pre-*Erie Railroad Co. v. Tompkins*, 304 U.S. 64 (1938), decision, the federal district court held that it would follow Alabama case law holding that a provision in a bond requiring that as soon as possible after the insured learned of a loss it must give to the underwriter a written notice of such loss and within ninety days file an itemized proof of claim duly sworn to, did not forfeit the insured's right to sue on the bond in the absence of a clause providing that failure to comply with those provisions resulted in a forfeiture. *American Nat'l Bank & Trust Co. v. United States Fid. & Guar. Co.*, 7 F. Supp. 578.

D.D.C. 2007. [Unspecified coverage form]. Because the policies required the insured to send the carrier a signed, sworn statement of loss containing the information the carrier requested to investigate the claim within sixty days after the carrier's request, and the policies further provided that no one could bring a legal action under the policies unless there had been full compliance with the terms of the policies and the insured failed to provide such information within that time period, the court granted summary judgment in favor of the carrier. *MDB Communs. v. Hartford Cas. Ins. Co.*, 479 F. Supp. 2d 136.

D.D.C. 2008. [Unspecified coverage form]. Because the policies required the insured to send the carrier a signed, sworn statement of loss containing the information the carrier requested to investigate the claim within sixty days after the carrier's request, and the policies further provided that no one could bring a legal action under the policies unless there had been full compliance with the terms of the policies and the insured failed to provide such information within that time period, the court granted summary judgment in favor of the carrier. *MDB Communs., Inc. v. Hartford Cas. Ins. Co.*, 531 F. Supp. 2d 75.

W.D. Okla. 1973. [Comprehensive Dishonesty, Disappearance and Destruction Policy]. A delay in giving proof of loss of at least seven and one-half months did not comply with the policy's requirement that the insured provide the proof of loss within a reasonable time after discovery. *Alfalfa Elec. Coop., Inc. v. Travelers Indem. Co.*, 376 F. Supp. 901.

Conn. 1929. [Employee Fidelity Bond]. Compliance with the proof of loss provision is not a condition precedent to liability in the absence of an express provision making compliance a condition precedent. In the absence of such a provision, a delay in filing the proof of loss postpones the time for payment and for bringing suit. The insured must bring suit within the time provided. *Elberton Cotton Mills, Inc. v. Indemnity Insurance Co. of N. Am.*, 145 A. 33.

Ga. App. 1929. [Employee Fidelity Bond]. In the absence of an explicit provision making compliance with the proof of loss provision a condition precedent to liability, a failure to comply with the proof of loss provision does not work a forfeiture. The insured must bring suit within time provided. *People's Loan & Sav. Co. v. Fidelity & Cas. Co.*, 147 S.E. 171.

Hawaii (1990). [Fidelity Bond]. Despite the insured's failure to give timely notice of loss or submit a proof of claim, the carrier was not relieved of liability entirely. *Employee's Retirement System of the State of Hawaii v. Real Estate Fin. Corp.*, 793 P.2d 170.

Ky. App. 1956. [Employee Fidelity Bond]. Notice and proof of loss must be given within the time limits fixed by the policy. *Shatz v. American Sur. Co. of N.Y.*, 295 S.W.2d 809.

N.Y. App. 1909. [Burglary or Larceny Policy]. Proofs of loss were retained by the carrier and certain claims were then passed for payment without any objection to the sufficiency of the proofs of loss. Such action on part of the carrier constituted waiver. *Monahan et al. v. Metro. Sur. Co.*, 114 N.Y. 862.

Ohio. App. 2009. [Fidelity Bond]. When non-colluding directors of the insured learned that the insured credit union had likely suffered losses through a corporate executive's pattern of misbehavior, including improper use of corporate assets, they had a duty to provide a proof of loss within sixty days. *American Mut. Share Ins. Corp. v. CUMIS Ins. Soc'y, Inc.*, No. 08AP-576, 2009 Ohio App. LEXIS 304.

4. *Whether the carrier must show prejudice from untimely proof of loss*

(a) Cases Decided Under Commercial Coverages

None

(b) Cases Decided Under Other Financial Institution Coverages

9th Cir. 1981 (Cal.). [Savings and Loan Blanket Bond]. California law does not require strict compliance with a condition governing the proof of loss unless the carrier can show actual prejudice. *Fidelity Sav. & Loan Ass'n v. Aetna Life Ins. Co.*, 647 F.2d 933.

E.D. La. 1995. [Financial Institution Bond]. Because a financial institution bond did not make timely notice and proof of loss condition precedents to coverage, the carrier had to demonstrate prejudice as result of late notice and proof of loss to avoid liability on the bond. *Resolution Trust Corp. v. Gaudet*, 907 F. Supp. 212.

E.D. La. 1990. [Savings and Loan Blanket Bond]. Although under Louisiana law time limits on providing notice and proof of loss are generally valid, the FDIC's failure to comply with the bond provisions requiring the giving of the proof of loss within 6 months of discovery of loss did not preclude recovery absent a showing of prejudice to the carrier from the late proof of loss. *Federal Deposit Ins. Corp. v. Aetna Cas. & Sur. Co.*, 744 F. Supp. 729.

D. Mass. 1994. [Position Fidelity Schedule Bond]. Under Massachusetts law, the notice-prejudice rule does not apply to fidelity insurance policies. Because the insured elected to pursue criminal proceedings against the wrongdoer rather than comply with a contractual provision requiring that notice of loss be given within a reasonable time after discovery and that a proof of loss be furnished within 180 days of discovery, the claim was barred. *United States v. National Grange Mut. Ins. Co.*, 1994 WL 511563.

Bankr. W.D. Pa. 1994. [Fidelity Bond]. Under Pennsylvania law, a carrier must show actual prejudice from a late notice of a potential claim and the insured's failure to provide the proof of loss in order to be released from its responsibility under a fidelity bond. *In re Mechem Fin., Inc.*, 167 B.R. 799.

W.D. Pa. 2006. [Theft Policy]. When the insured filed a proof of loss claiming that he suffered a loss of $428,534.12 and the carrier paid the loss in the full amount of coverage of $150,000 and took an assignment of the insured's rights to the extent of its payment, and the insured subsequently obtained a recovery of $325,000 from the wrongdoer, the insured was not estopped from claiming that his loss was actually in excess of his total recovery of $475,000, even though the proof of loss showed a loss of a lower amount, because the carrier failed to demonstrate that it actually relied on the proof of loss or suffered a detriment due to its reliance on the amount of the loss stated in the proof of loss. Substantial compliance as opposed to strict and literal compliance with the proof of loss provision is all that is required for an effective proof of loss. *Hartford Fire Ins. Co. v. Spall*, 2006 WL 538938.

S.D. Tex. 1985. [Bankers Blanket Bond and Excess Fidelity Bond]. Under Texas law, when a rider provided that a sworn written proof of loss must be provided within 100 days after a discovery of a loss and eliminated the provision that legal proceedings could not be brought prior to sixty days after the filing of the proof of loss, the court could not decide whether the filing of the proof of loss was a condition precedent to recovery without further consideration. *South Texas Nat'l Bank of Laredo v. United States Fire Ins. Co.*, 640 F. Supp. 278.

Kan. 1998. [Financial Institution Bond]. On a certified question, the Kansas Supreme Court held that the failure of the insured to provide a proof of loss within the time limit provided in a financial institution bond does not justify denial of coverage absent a showing by the carrier of substantial prejudice. *National Union Fire Ins. Co. of Pittsburgh, Pa. v. Federal Deposit Ins. Corp.*, 957 P.2d 357.

Kan. 1980. [Union Fidelity Bond]. The insured who notified the carrier by telephone in March or April that a claim might be submitted and actually submitted a written claim in September substantially complied with a thirty-day notice provision because the carrier could show no evidence of prejudice from the late notice. *Local No. 1179, Carpet, Linoleum & Resilient Floor Decorators Union v. Merchants Mut. Bonding Co.*, 613 P.2d 944.

Me. 2002. [Employee Dishonesty Coverage]. The carrier suffered prejudice from the untimely filing of a proof of loss due to the employee's dissipation of assets and the carrier's consequent inability to recoup part of the loss. *Acadia Ins. Co. v. Keiser Indus., Inc.*, 793 A.2d 495.

Pa.Ct.Comm.Pls. 2007. [Commercial Crime Coverage]. The insured's failure to submit a signed, sworn proof of loss as required by the Commercial Crime Coverage form that required the insured to submit a detailed, sworn proof of loss within 120 days of discovery of loss warranted denial of the claim. *Fair, Inc. v. Assurance Co. of America*, 2007 Phila. Ct. Com. Pl. LEXIS 276.

    5. *Waiver and estoppel*

        (a) Cases Decided Under Commercial Coverages

        None

        (b) Cases Decided Under Other Financial Institution Coverages

2d Cir. 1960 (N.Y). [Employee Indemnity Bond]. An independent adjuster had no authority to waive the requirement that the insured furnish a proof of loss. *Hotel Atlantis, Inc. v. Peerless Cas. Co.*, 285 F.2d 257.

3d Cir. 1947 (Pa.). [Bankers Blanket Bond]. A statement by the bonding company representative that the bank could not file a proof of loss until it knew what the loss was waived the requirement of furnishing the proof of loss. *Dubois Nat'l Bank v. Hartford Acc. & Indem. Co.*, 161 F.2d 132.

3d Cir. 1932 (N.J.). [Fidelity Bond]. When the bonding company had actual notice of the items in the claim and cooperated with the insured to reduce the loss, the filing of formal proof of loss was waived. *New Amsterdam Cas. Co. v. Basic Bldg. & Loan Ass'n*, 60 F.2d 950.

5th Cir. 1954 (Texas). [Blanket Fidelity Bond]. Denial of liability on the merits waived the proof of loss requirement. *New Amsterdam Cas. Co. v. W.D. Felder & Co.*, 214 F.2d 825.

5th Cir. 1934 (Fla.). [Fidelity Bond]. An employee fidelity bond was canceled on May 25, 1930, and by its terms covered only losses sustained prior to that date or discovered before the expiration of one year thereafter. The bank failed on February 2, 1931, the receiver discovered losses sued for on April 10, 1931, and notified the bonding company on June 10, 1931. The bonding company denied liability because of the cancellation of the bond and the expiration of the time limit for the discovery of the claim. The court held there was no waiver in connection with notice requirement because the bonding company did not know date of discovery until after suit was filed and no estoppel because the time for giving notice had expired on June 10th and the receiver was not misled. *Murray v. American Sur. Co. of N.Y.*, 69 F.2d 147.

6th Cir. 1969 (Mich.). [Fidelity Bond]. The conduct of the bonding company in continuously advising the insured that "the claim was under investigation and the defendant would advise" constituted a waiver of the proof of loss requirement and suit limitation period. *William H. Sill Mortgages, Inc. v. Ohio Cas. Co.*, 412 F.2d 341.

7th Cir. 1953 (Ill.). [Fidelity Bond]. Denial of liability on the ground that the employee's acts were not dishonest within the meaning of the bond waived the proof of loss requirement. *Irvin Jacobs & Co. v. Fid. & Deposit Co. of Md.*, 202 F.2d 794.

8th Cir. 1935 (Iowa). [Fidelity Bond]. The bank advised the bonding company of the "possibility of liability under the bond in connection with acts of its cashier." The bonding company conducted an investigation. Later, the bank failed and its receiver filed proofs of loss. The bonding company's adjuster continued its investigation without objection to the sufficiency or timeliness of the notice or proof of loss and told the examiner in charge that a loss shown to be result of dishonest act of cashier would be paid. The court held that there was evidence to justify a jury in concluding that the notice and proof of loss were timely submitted and further, there was "substantial evidence" that the bonding company had waived the requirement of a timely proof of loss. *Fidelity & Deposit Co. of Md. v. Bates*, 76 F.2d 160.

9th Cir. 1954 (Ariz.). [Blanket Position Bond]. The court affirmed a judgment in favor of the carrier because the plaintiff did not comply with the proof of loss provision. *Alianza Hispano-America v. Hartford Acc. & Indem. Co.*, 209 F.2d 578.

10th Cir. 1979 (Utah). [Fidelity Bond]. Employees of the insured, including its president, issued unauthorized shares of stock of one of its customers, which thereafter brought suit against the insured. The insured went into receivership and brought an action against the carrier to recover on the bond, but failed to provide a timely proof of loss. Though generally the requirement to file a timely proof of loss is not satisfied by the insured delivering to the carrier a copy of the complaint against the insured for damages caused by its employees' dishonesty, the carrier may be estopped from asserting the requirement on the basis of excuse or waiver when the persons expected to file the proof of loss perpetrated the fraud and the carrier had knowledge of the action against the insured. *Mascaro v. Fireman's Fund Ins. Co.*, 611 F.2d 338.

S.D. Ill. 1959. [Fidelity Bond]. The acts of the bonding company in receiving late proof of loss and denying liability on other grounds were not a waiver as a matter of law, because those acts occurred after the time for filing the proof of loss had expired. *Oakley Grain & Supply Co. v. Indemnity Insurance Co. of N. Am.*, 173 F. Supp. 419.

E.D. Mich. 1934. [Blanket Fidelity Bond]. When, after notice, the insured and the bonding company agreed that "without further preliminaries a suit at law should be instituted to determine the question of liability," the bonding company waived the necessity of a formal proof of loss. *Thomas v. Standard Acc. Ins. Co.*, 7 F. Supp. 205.

E.D. Mich. 2013. [Unspecified coverage form]. The insured's failure to provide a sworn proof of loss within sixty days of a request by the carrier constituted a defense to a claim for a loss through theft. The carrier's payment of other losses after the sixty-day period for providing sworn proof of loss had elapsed did not constitute a waiver or estop the carrier from relying on the insured's failure to provide a sworn proof of loss as a defense to the claim. Conduct constituting a waiver or estoppel must occur during the relevant time period. *Olivia Marie, Inc. v. Travelers Cas. Ins. Co. of America*, No. 2:11-cv-12394, 2013 U.S. Dist. LEXIS 19050.

D. Minn. 2014. [Financial Institution Bond]. When a bank employee induced others to participate in an advance fee scheme in which he was involved and the carrier defended the resulting lawsuit under a D&O policy, but later declined coverage under the bond, the filing of the proof of loss was waived because the carrier lead the insured to believe it was not necessary to file a proof of loss under the FIB. *Avon State Bank v. BancInsure, Inc.*, No. 12-2557 (RHK/LIB), 2014 U.S. Dist. LEXIS 3099.

D. Nev. 1968. [Comprehensive Dishonesty, Disappearance and Destruction Policy and Blanket Crime Policy]. A denial of liability on other grounds waived defects in the notice of loss or the timeliness of the proof of loss. *Mapes Casino, Inc. v. Maryland Cas. Co.*, 290 F. Supp. 186.

S.D. Ohio 2000. [Fidelity Bond]. The carrier did not waive the defense that the insured failed to provide a proof of loss because it reserved that defense by expressly stating in a letter to the insured that it "reserved all rights and defenses available to it under the bond and applicable law." *First Bank of Marietta v. Hartford Underwriters Ins. Co.*, 115 F. Supp. 898, *aff'd*, 307 F.3d 501 (6th Cir. 2002).

Bankr. N.D. Ohio 1988. [Fidelity Bond]. The carrier's failure to give a timely notice of coverage excused the lack of a prompt notice of loss and the prompt submission of the proof of loss by the insured. *Rafoth v. National Union Fire Ins. Co. of Pittsburgh, Pa.*, 93 B.R. 559.

W.D. Okla. 1973. [Fidelity Bond]. When the insured gave notice that it had tentatively discovered a discrepancy in its securities and other funds and had fired an employee; promised a complete audit; six months later and after the time for filing the proof of loss had expired the insured requested the bonding company to extend the period for filing proofs of loss; the extension was granted with a reservation of rights; and the proof of loss was subsequently filed and rejected; the carrier did not waive nor was it estopped to assert the requirement of a timely proof of loss. A delay of at least seven and one-half months in filing the proof of loss was not within a reasonable time after discovery as provided in the bond. *Alfalfa Elec. Coop., Inc. v. Travelers Indem. Co.*, 376 F. Supp. 901.

D.C. Cir. 1970. [Employees Fidelity Policy]. The time for filing the proof of loss could be waived orally or by conduct despite a provision in the policy stating that the terms of policy could not be waived except by an endorsement signed by an authorized representative of the company. *Imperial Ins., Inc. v. Employers' Liab. Assur. Corp.*, 442 F.2d 1197.

D.C. Cir. 1964. [Fidelity Bond]. Conduct by the bonding company after its receipt of a late proof of loss did not constitute a waiver or estoppel. *Ace Van & Storage Co. v. Liberty Mut. Ins. Co.*, 336 F.2d 925.

Del. 1964. [Fidelity Bond]. The court recognized the rule that the denial of liability during the period in which the proof of loss may be filed will constitute a waiver of that requirement; the court further stated that a mere request for more information would not be construed as a waiver, and a statement by the bonding company's agent that the company "was not going to do anything about the claim" could be construed as a denial of liability. *Standard Acc. Ins. Co. v. Pensell's Drug Store, Inc.*, 202 A.2d 271.

Ga. App. 1933. [Fidelity Bond]. When prior to the expiration of the time for filing a proof of loss, the insured asked that the matter be held in abeyance, and the bonding company did not insist on a proof of loss being filed and negotiated settlement both before and after this deadline, the filing of a proof of loss was waived. *Knights of the Ku Klux Klan v. Fidelity & Deposit Co. of Md.*, 169 S.E. 514.

Ga. App. 1929. [Fidelity Bond]. Accepting the proof of loss after the deadline in the bond had run and denying liability on another ground waived the timely filing of the proof of loss. *Peoples' Loan & Sav. Co. v. Fidelity & Cas. Co.*, 147 S.E. 171.

Ill. App. 1961. [Fidelity Bond]. When after the expiration of the time for giving notice and filing a proof of loss, the local agent of the bonding company met with the insured, requested that the insured sign the proof of loss and said that a loss would be taken care of, the bonding company waived both requirements. *Royal Loan Corp. v. American Sur. Co. of N.Y.*, 173 N.E.2d 17.

Iowa 1906. [Fidelity Bond]. The insured attempted to file two proofs of loss, one under the bond before its limits were increased and one under the increased bond. The bonding company retained the first proof of loss until the time limit expired and then returned to the insured demanding a new one. After the second proof of loss, the bonding company denied liability because of a want of authority on the part of the agent who granted the increase. The carrier's conduct after its receipt of the first proof of loss was a waiver of "any further proofs" and the denial of liability was a further waiver. *T.M. Sinclair & Co. v. National Sur. Co.*, 107 N.W. 184.

Kan. 1927. [Employee Fidelity Bond]. Discovery of loss occurs when a demand is made for repayment of a misapplication of funds, and that demand is not complied with. When the carrier made no objection that the proof of loss was not furnished in time, and when sued raised no such question in its answer, but denied that an embezzlement had occurred, and at trial raised for the first time the question that the proof of loss had not been made in time, the issue of untimely proof of loss was raised too late and had been waived. *Docking v. National Sur. Co.*, 252 P. 201.

La. App. 1963. [Fidelity Bond]. The investigation and denial of a claim constituted a waiver of the notice and proof of loss requirements despite the fact that material furnished to the bonding company conclusively showed that the claim was not timely. *Standard Brass & Mfg. Co. v. Maryland Cas. Co.*, 153 So. 2d 475.

Mass. 1951. [Fidelity Bond]. The insured gave notice of a loss, which the bonding company acknowledged, and stated that the claim was being turned over to the claim department. The bonding company later advised the insured that it would write to the insured when its investigation was complete. The insured never filed the proof of loss and after the time for filing had expired, the bonding company denied liability. Because of the first letter, the court held the bonding company was estopped to assert the insured's failure to comply with the notice requirement, but not estopped to assert the failure to timely file a proof of loss, as the denial of liability occurred after the time for filing a proof of loss had expired. *Star Fastener, Inc. v. Employers' Ins. Co.*, 96 N.W.2d 713.

Mass. 1945. [Fidelity Bond]. The carrier's receipt of an unsworn statement of loss without objection and its denial of liability on the ground that a loss was not covered by the bond waived the proof of loss requirement. *Fuller v. Home Indem. Co.*, 60 N.E.2d 1.

Mass. 1931. [Bankers Blanket Bond]. The carrier's acceptance of a notice of loss by letter waived the bond requirement that notice be furnished by registered letter or telegram. A denial of liability did not waive the proof of loss requirement. *Fitchburg Sav. Bank v. Massachusetts Bonding & Ins. Co.*, 174 N.E. 324.

Mich. 1957. [Dishonesty Bond]. The carrier waived the insured's lack of timeliness in filing a sworn proof of loss, where it furnished to the insured forms for the proof of loss and accepted them after the expiration of the time for such action provided in the bond, the carrier suffered no prejudice from the insured's failure of literal, as distinguished from substantial, compliance, and the carrier failed to plead that defense in its answer. *Masters v. Massachusetts Bonding & Ins. Co.,* 84 N.W.2d 462.

Mich. 1927. [Fidelity Bond]. The carrier's investigation without reference to late notice and its general denial of liability waived the notice and proof of loss requirements of the bond as a matter of law. *Farmers' Produce Co. v. Aetna Cas. & Sur. Co.*, 213 N.W. 685.

Mich. 1909. [Fidelity Bond]. The insured's furnishing proofs of loss and the carrier's acceptance of them without objection waived the timely furnishing of proofs of loss under the bond. *Crystal Ice Co. v. United Sur. Co.*, 123 N.W. 619.

Minn. 1933. [Fidelity Bond]. The bonding company could not assert a failure to comply with the notice and proof of loss requirements in view of its denial of liability, even though the bonding company also denied liability on the basis that the bond had been terminated and the time for discovering a loss had passed and further reserved its rights and defenses. The court did not use the words "waiver" or "estoppel." *Cary v. National Sur. Co.*, 251 N.W. 123.

Minn. 1925. [Fidelity Bond]. The conduct of the bonding company in failing to follow up on its request for a proof of loss and the insured's assumption that the carrier's local agent would provide the proof of loss was sufficient to support a jury finding of waiver of the proof of loss requirements. *Ceylon Farmers' Elevator Co. v. Fidelity & Deposit Co. of Md.*, 203 N.W. 985.

Mo. 1929. [Fidelity Bond]. Admission of liability for certain items in the claim after the deadline for filing the proof of loss and ultimate denial of liability on other grounds extended the time for filing the proof of loss by implication and made the defense of late proof of loss unavailable. *Exchange Bank of Novinger v. Turner*, 14 S.W.2d 425.

N.Y. App. 1965. [Comprehensive Dishonesty, Disappearance, and Destruction Policy]. When the issue was whether the carrier's denial of liability after the insured submitted its initial proof of loss statement waived this provision of policy so that the insured was not obligated to submit any further proof of loss statements, it was for the jury to determine whether the insured had so repudiated its liability as to release the insured from filing the proof of loss statement. *Silberblatt, Inc. v. Travelers Indem. Co.*, 259 N.Y.S.2d 673.

Okla. 1966. [Fidelity Bond]. The conduct of the bonding company in not denying liability but insisting that it could not pay the claim until the accused employee admitted the defalcation waived the proof of loss requirement and the suit limitation provision. *Hartford Acc. & Indem. Co. v. Luper*, 421 P.2d 811.

Okla. 1939. [Fidelity Bond]. After notice, an agent for the bonding company had the insured's books audited. At a meeting, the agent for the bonding company said: "We can just let this matter ride and when we can determine the exact amount of the shortage, we will get together on it." Thereafter, the proof of loss forms were sent to the insured but never completed and returned. The court upheld a jury finding of waiver of the proof of loss requirement. *Maryland Cas. Co. v. Tucker*, 96 P.2d 80.

Tex. App. 1969. [Fidelity Bond]. The fact that the proof of loss form was filed seven days late; within the time limit, the auditor of the insured submitted an unsworn report and the bonding company's auditor said he would let the auditor know if anything further was needed raised a fact issue of waiver (resolved by jury in favor of the insured). *Commercial Standard Ins. Co. v. J.D. Hufstedler Truck Co.*, 443 S.W.2d 54.

Wis. 1974. [Bankers Blanket Bond]. The bonding company's denial of liability following the time for filing a proof of loss did not constitute a waiver of the requirement that the insured provide a timely notice of loss or the filing of the proof of loss. *State Bank of Viroqua v. Capitol Indem. Corp.*, 214 N.W.2d 42.

SECONDARY SOURCES

Annotation, *Carrier's Admission of Liability, Offers of Settlement, Negotiations, and the Like, as a Waiver of, or Estoppel to Assert, Contractual Limitation Provision*, 29 A.L.R.2d 636 (1953).

Annotation, *Carrier's Demand for Additional or Corrected Proof of Loss as Waiver or Estoppel as to right to Assert Contractual Limitation Provision, or as Suspending Running Thereof*, 15 A.L.R.2d 955 (1951).

Annotation, *Carrier's Denial of Liability as Suspending Running of Statute of Limitation or Limitation Provision of Policy*, 171 A.L.R. 577 (1947).

Annotation, *Constitutionality, Construction, & Application of Statutes Related to Contractual Time Limitation Provisions of Insurance Policies*, 112 A.L.R. 1288 (1938).

Annotation, *Construction & Effect of Provision in Employee's Fidelity Bond Requiring Employer-Insured to File "Itemized" Proof of Claim or Proof of Loss with Particulars*, 37 A.L.R. 2d 900 (1954).

Annotation, *Effect of Failure to Give Notice, or Delay in Giving Notice or Filing of Proofs of Loss, upon Fidelity Bond or Insurance*, 23 A.L.R. 2d 1065 (1952).

Annotation, *Subsequent Denial of Liability Following Promise or Negotiations as Affecting Contractual Limitation for Action Upon Insurance Policy*, 3 A.L.R. 218 (1919).

Annotation, *Suspicion, or Reasons for Suspicion, of Wrong-Doing by Officer or Employee Covered by Fidelity Bond or Policy, as Requiring Obligee to Comply with Conditions of Bond with Respect to Notice of Discovery or Knowledge of Loss*, 129 A.L.R. 1411 (1940).

Annotation, *Validity of Contractual Time Period Shorter Than Statute of Limitations for Bringing Action*, 6 A.L.R.3d 1226 § 5(b), (1966).

Annotation, *Validity, Construction, and Application of Provision of Fidelity Bond as to Giving Notice of Loss or Claim within Specified Time after Close of Bond Year*, 149 A.L.R. 945 (1944).

Atkins, *What Constitutes Discovery of Loss Within the Meaning of the Word "Loss" Under Financial Institution and Fidelity Bonds*, ABA SECTION OF INSURANCE, NEGLIGENCE AND COMPENSATION LAW PROCEEDINGS, pp. 73-79, (1967).

James E. Clark, *The Law of Fidelity Bonds*, 28 INS. COUNSEL J. 210 (1961).

Duncan L. Clore & John Tomaine, *Discovery of Loss*, *in* HANDLING FIDELITY BOND CLAIMS 431 (Michael Keeley & Sean Duffy eds., 2d ed. 2005).

A. H. Denecke, *Surety and Fidelity Bonds*, 37 ORE. L. REV. 95 (1958).

Ronald Lee Gilman, *Dishonesty Alone Does Not Deck a Fidelity Carrier*, 51 INS. COUNSEL J. 529 (1984).

Robert C. Haase, Jr., *Proof of Loss in Fidelity Cases—Sufficiency & Requirements of Good Faith*, 12 FORUM 980 (1977).

Peter C. Haley, *"Loss" Containment Under the Financial Institution Bond*, II FID. L.J. 111 (1996).

Francis C. Kenney, Jr., *Notice—Its Place in Fidelity Insurance*, ABA SECTION OF INSURANCE, NEGLIGENCE AND COMPENSATION LAW PROCEEDINGS, pp. 132-178, (1955).

Francis L. Kenney, Jr., *The Effect of Discovery of Loss upon the Contract Rights, Duties & Obligations of the Parties*, ABA SECTION OF INSURANCE, NEGLIGENCE AND COMPENSATION LAW PROCEEDINGS, pp. 80-94 (1967).

Jack McNeil, *When is the Failure to Comply with Requirements for Timely Notice, Proof of Loss & Suit a Defense to a Surety?*, 16 FORUM 1139 (1981).

G. Wayne Murphy, *Allegations, Assertions & Charges as Discovery of Loss*, 12 THE FORUM 986 (1977).

Dolores Parr, *The Insured's Proof of Loss*, in HANDLING FIDELITY BOND CLAIMS 93 (Michael Keeley & Sean Duffy eds., 2d ed. 2005).

James Postula, *What Constitutes Timely Notice & Proof of Loss Under Fidelity & Financial Institution Bonds*, ABA SECTION OF INSURANCE, NEGLIGENCE AND COMPENSATION LAW PROCEEDINGS, pp. 108-115, (1967).

Paul D. Schoonover, *Discovery, Notice and Automatic Cancellation Under Revised Form 24*, 16 FORUM 962 (1981).

Edward Alan Shure, *Contract Provisions for Notice & Proof after Discovery of Loss are Conditions Precedent to Insured's Right of Recovery*, ABA SECTION OF INSURANCE, NEGLIGENCE AND COMPENSATION LAW PROCEEDINGS, pp. 95-107, (1967).

Frank L. Skillern, Jr., *How to Prevent Loss of Fidelity Carriers' Rights by Waiver & Estoppel*, 10 FORUM 301 (1974).

TORTS AND INSURANCE PRACTICE SECTION, COMMITTEE ON FIDELITY AND SURETY LAW, A NATIONAL INSTITUTE, EMPLOYEE DISHONESTY: CLAIMS, BOND COVERAGES AND CAVEATS, Tab 9 (1983).

Mark E. Wilson, *How to Prepare and Present a Fidelity Claim: Advice for the Insured*, 28 THE BRIEF NO. 3, 54 (1999).

William H. Woods & Robert D. Carnaghan, *Loss, Notice, Proof and Legal Proceedings, in* ANNOTATED BANKERS BLANKET BOND 132 (Frank N. Skillern, Jr., ed., 1980).

William H. Woods, *Defenses Based on Contractual Requirements for Timely Filing of Suit in Fidelity Cases*, 17 FORUM 1291 (1982).

William H. Woods, *Loss, Notice, Proof and Legal Proceedings, in* ANNOTATED BANKERS BLANKET BOND 26 (Frank N. Skillern, Jr., ed., 1st ed. 1980 & Supp. 1983).

Julie Fry Yanda & Mark Struthers, *The Insured's Duties Following Discovery of Loss*, XIX FID. L.J. 147 (2013).

C. Duty to Cooperate

CRIME PROTECTION POLICY[5]
Section E. Conditions

7. **After you discover a loss or a situation that may result in a loss you must:**
    b. **Submit to examination under oath at our request and give us a signed statement of your answers; . . .**
    d. **Cooperate with us in the investigation and settlement of any claim.**

---

5   Crime Protection Policy, SP 00 01 04 12 (The Surety & Fidelity Association of America 2012), *reprinted in* COMMERCIAL CRIME INSURANCE COVERAGE 769 (Randall I. Marmor & Susan Koehler Sullivan, eds., 2015) [*see* App'x A].

COMMERCIAL CRIME POLICY (DISCOVERY FORM)[6]
Section E. Conditions

1. g. Duties in the Event of Loss
    **After you discover a loss or a situation that may result
    in loss of or damage to "money," "securities" or "other
    property" you must: . . .**
    **(3)   Cooperate with us in the investigation and
           settlement of any claim. . . .**
    **(5)   Submit to examination under oath at our request
           and give us a signed statement of your
           answers. . . .**

COMMENT

Although there is very little case law on the subject of examination of the insured under oath and the insured's duty to cooperate under fidelity insurance, that does not mean that these duties lack importance. On the contrary, both are vital to the carrier. Without the right to insist on an examination under oath, cooperation in the investigation, and settlement of claims, a carrier would frequently find it all but impossible to conduct a reasonable investigation of a claim. Perhaps the self-evident necessity of these duties explains the fact that there is so little case law concerning them.

OUTLINE OF ANNOTATIONS

A. Insured's duty to cooperate
    1. Submission by the insured to examination under oath
        (a) Cases Decided Under Commercial Coverages
        (b) Cases Decided Under Other Financial Institution Coverages
    2. Other Instances of Lack of Cooperation

---

6   Commercial Crime Policy, CR 00 22 07 02 (ISO Props., Inc. 2001), *reprinted in* COMMERCIAL CRIME POLICY 786, 799 (Randall I. Marmor & Susan Koehler Sullivan, eds., 2015) [*see* App'x B and C].

ANNOTATIONS

A. Insured's duty to cooperate

1. Submission by the insured to examination under oath

(a) Cases Decided Under Commercial Coverages

Ind. Ct. App. 2006. [Unspecified coverage form]. The refusal of the insured's principal officer and owner to submit to an examination under oath despite the carrier's repeated requests constituted a breach of contract not excused by the insured's offer to stipulate that its principal officer and owner's previous interview was under oath and the insurer was not required to show prejudice in order to rely on it as a defense to a claim under the policy. *Knowledge A-Z, Inc. v. Sentry Ins.*, 857 N.E.2d 411.

Mo. App. 2003. [Crime Policy]. A genuine issue of material fact as to whether the failure of the insured's president to appear for examination under oath as required by policy was excused by the carrier's hiring of the law firm that had previously represented the insured's president, allegedly resulting in a conflict of interest, precluded summary judgment in favor of the carrier. *East Attucks Community Housing, Inc. v. Old Republic Sur. Co.*, 114 S.W.3d 311.

(b) Cases Decided Under Other Financial Institution Coverages

None

2. Other Instances of Lack of Cooperation

N.Y. Sup. 2009. [Crime Policy]. Before a carrier may disclaim coverage for an insured's lack of cooperation, it must show that the carrier acted diligently in seeking to bring about that cooperation, that its efforts were reasonably calculated to obtain the insured's cooperation, and that the insured's attitude after his cooperation was sought was one of willful and avowed obstruction. The insured's concealment of its settlement with the alleged wrongdoer, its obstruction of the carrier's efforts to contact him and its belated promise to allow him to be examined at some indefinite time in the future "under appropriate circumstances," justified the

584   ANNOTATED COMMERCIAL CRIME INSURANCE POLICY

carrier's denial of coverage. *Conference Assoc., Inc., v. Travelers Cas. and Sur. Co. of America*, No. 35341-08, 2009 N.Y. Misc. LEXIS 6813.

SECONDARY SOURCES

Scott D. Baron, *The Fidelity Loss Investigation in a Regulated Industry*, 28 THE BRIEF NO. 3, 12 (1999).

John V. Church, Gail D. Spielberger & Gerald N. Carroza, *The Insured's Duty to Cooperate, in* COMMERCIAL CRIME POLICY 611 (Randall I. Marmor & John J. Tomaine & eds., 2d ed. 2005).

Cole S. Kain & Cynthia Mellon, *Potential Conflicts Between Fidelity Carriers & Insureds: Parallel Proceedings, Interviewing Witnesses & Actions Against Third Parties*, IV FID. L.J. 1 (1999).

Michael Keeley & Sean Duffy, *Investigating the Employee Dishonesty Claim: Interviewing Witnesses, Obtaining Documents & Other Important Issues, in* HANDLING FIDELITY BOND CLAIMS 153 (Michael Keeley & Sean Duffy eds., 2d ed. 2005).

Michael Keeley, *Overcoming Attorney-Client, Work Product, Bank Privacy & Other Evidentiary Objections In Investigating Fidelity Bond Claims*, II FID. L.J. 51 (1996).

Michael Keeley, *The Attorney-Client Privilege & Work Product Doctrine—The Boundaries of Protected Communications by Insureds & Carriers*, 33 TORT & INS. L.J. 1169 (1998).

Patricia H. Thompson, *An Insured's Guide to Effective Claim Investigation, Presentation & Resolution, in* FINANCIAL INSTITUTION BOND 533 (Duncan L. Clore ed., 2d ed. 1998).

Mark E. Wilson, *How to Prepare & Present a Fidelity Claim: Advice for the Insured*, 28 THE BRIEF NO. 3, 54 (1999).

Julie Fry Yanda & Mark Struthers, *The Insured's Duties Following Discovery of Loss*, XIX FID. L.J. 147 (2013).

D. Timeliness of Suit

CRIME PROTECTION POLICY[7]
Section E. Conditions

Legal Action Against Us
    You may not bring any legal action against us involving loss:
    a.   **Unless you have complied with all the terms of this Policy;**
    b.   **Until 90 days after you have filed proof of loss with us; and**
    c.   **Unless brought within 2 years from the date you discover the loss.**

COMMERCIAL CRIME POLICY (DISCOVERY FORM)[8]
Section E. Conditions

m. Legal Action Against Us
    You may not bring any legal action against us involving loss:
    (1)   **Unless you have complied with all the terms of this Policy;**
    (2)   **Until 90 days after you have filed proof of loss with us; and**
    (3)   **Unless brought within 2 years from the date you discover the loss.**
    If any limitation in this condition is prohibited by law, such limitation is amended so as to equal the minimum period of limitation provided by such law.

---

7   Crime Protection Policy, SP 00 01 04 12 (The Surety & Fidelity Association of America 2012), *reprinted in* COMMERCIAL CRIME INSURANCE COVERAGE 769 (Randall I. Marmor & Susan Koehler Sullivan, eds., 2015) [*see* App'x A].

8   Commercial Crime Policy, CR 00 22 08 13 and CR 00 23 08 13 (Insurance Services Office, Inc. 2012), *reprinted in* COMMERCIAL CRIME INSURANCE COVERAGE 785, 799 (Randall I. Marmor & Susan Koehler Sullivan, eds., 2015) [*see* App'x B and C].

COMMENT

In addition to giving the carrier notice of loss as soon as possible and providing it with a detailed, sworn proof of loss within the time limits prescribed, the insured must file legal action within the time limits contained in the contract or those prescribed by statute, if a statute prohibits a contractual limitation of the time for filing suit. Virtually all commercial crime policies contain contractual limitation provisions which limit the time within which suit may be instituted on a claim under the policy. The period of limitation provided in the policy is almost always shorter than the period prescribed by state statutes of limitation.

Absent a statute to the contrary, a carrier may validly prescribe a reasonable contractual period for bringing an action on a fidelity policy which is less than the period prescribed by a state statute of limitation. However, numerous states have enacted statutes that specifically prohibit the parties from contracting for a shorter period of limitation than that prescribed by the statute of limitation. Consequently, some fidelity policies provide that if the minimum period in the policy is prohibited by statute, then the minimum period permitted by law becomes the contractual period. This provision is important because some states have both a statutory period of limitation and a minimum period of limitation for which the parties can contract, the latter being substantially shorter. Contractual limitation provisions in fidelity policies as short as one year have been held to be reasonable and valid. The limitation period in fidelity policies has also been held to be binding upon successors in interest of the insured such as receivers and trustees in bankruptcy.

Because fidelity policies are written by insurance companies and contain short contractual limitation periods like those found in other types of insurance policies, it is not surprising that courts treat them similarly. Many courts have held that a carrier may, by its conduct or representations, waive or be estopped from asserting a policy provision stipulating that the action be brought within a certain period of time. Application of the doctrine of equitable estoppel generally boils down to the balancing of a number of equities arising out of extremely varied fact situations. Consequently, this is not an apt field for the application of cut-and-dried principles of law.

The annotations demonstrate that if the insured was lulled into a false sense of security, was misled, or the conduct of the carrier was inconsistent with an intention to demand compliance with the provision (sometimes hopes of settlement held out by the carrier may be sufficient), then the carrier will not be permitted to enforce the provision.

When the carrier's conduct prevents the insured from complying with the contractual limitation provision, the limitation provision may be deemed to have been waived, or the carrier may be held to be estopped from asserting it, or the conduct may only suspend the running of the limitation period. Generally, conduct that operates as a waiver or estoppel must have continued through or began very near the end of the limitation period. If there is a reasonable time remaining after the conduct at issue in which to bring suit, then the insured may find it difficult to argue that the carrier has waived or is estopped to assert the contractual limitation period as a defense. While the cases involving waiver of limitation provisions in other types of insurance policies are legion, there have been relatively fewer such cases interpreting this provision in fidelity insurance.

OUTLINE OF ANNOTATIONS

ANNOTATIONS

A. Timeliness of Suit

1. *What constitutes discovery*

(a) Cases Decided Under Commercial Coverages

7th Cir. 1980 (Ill.). [Commercial Coverages]. When the vice president of the insured, an insurance company, set premium rates too low, the discovery of a loss occurred only when the insured learned that its employee was receiving kickbacks, and that the low rates were not just an error of judgment. The law presumes every man to be honest until the contrary is established. Whether the insured brought the action on the policy within 24 months after discovery of the loss was a question for the jury to decide. *Central Nat'l Life Ins. Co. v. Fidelity & Deposit Co. of Md.*, 626 F.2d 537.

N.D.N.Y. 2006. [Commercial Crime Policy]. Under New York law, when the bankruptcy trustee for the insured sent a letter to the carrier stating his intention to make a claim and requesting a claim form and a month and half later submitted a proof of loss "completed to the extent of information currently available," and the proof of loss specifically detailed the wrongdoer's diversion of funds, the trustee could not claim that he did not discover a loss until the wrongdoer was later indicted and, consequently, an action on the policy was untimely under the contractual limitation on the time for bringing suit. *Lawrence Group, Inc. v. Hartford Cas. Ins. Co.,* Case No. 1:02-CV-725 (unpublished slip opinion).

(b) Cases Decided Under Other Financial Institution Coverages

8th Cir. 1993 (S.D.). [Bankers Blanket Bond]. Under South Dakota law, when the bond required that suit be brought within 24 months of discovery of loss, the facts known to the board of directors when it reviewed a state examination report, even though the report criticized certain transactions, were not sufficient as a matter of law to cause a reasonable person to assume that an insured loss had been incurred so as to trigger the contractual time limitation for filing suit. Nor was the bank aware of sufficient facts after a meeting with the FDIC to have discovered that a covered loss had been incurred despite having been informed of the bank's weakened condition and of numerous apparent violations of federal banking laws and regulations. *First Dakota Nat'l Bank v. St. Paul Fire & Marine Ins. Co.*, 2 F.3d 801.

W.D. La. 2007. [Unspecified coverage form]. Because a nursing home bookkeeper confessed to taking some cash and checks on Jan. 26, 2004, and the insured's Insurance Administrator notified the carrier's agent on Feb. 3, 2004, of the confession, the insured's suit filed on Feb. 15, 2006, was not filed within 2 years of discovery, as required by the policy's crime coverage, and was untimely, despite the insured's argument that it was not certain it had sustained a loss until much later because the dishonest employee had offered to pay back the stolen funds. The insured's investigation into the extent of the loss did not delay the time when discovery occurred. *Magnolia Mgmt. Corp. v. Federal Ins. Co.*, NO. 06-0447, 2007 U.S. Dist. LEXIS 85372.

D. Minn. 1990. [Bankers Blanket Bond]. When the insured bank was aware of various acts that were not in line with accepted banking practice more than two years before it brought suit, but claimed that it attributed these acts to negligence or bad business judgment and only had suspicions of fraud or dishonesty, a material fact issue existed as to whether the bank brought suit within two years of discovery of loss as required by the bond. *Mid-Am. Bank of Chaska v. Am. Cas. Co. of Reading, Pa.*, 745 F. Supp. 1480.

D.N.J. 1971. [Bankers Blanket Bond]. The contractual time to file suit began to run when the bank had all the facts on which its claim was based. *Essex County State Bank v. Fireman's Fund Ins. Co.*, 331 F. Supp. 931.

D.N.J. 2010. [Financial Institution Bond]. An insured under a Financial Institution Bond discovered a loss committed by its employee no later than February 2, 2006, the date it sued the employee alleging fraud; its suit against the carrier filed more than two years later was not timely in view of a policy provision that required that legal proceedings for the recovery of any loss must not be brought after the expiration of twenty-four months from the discovery of such loss. *Omega Advisors, Inc. v.*

Federal Ins. Co., No. 10-912 (JAP), 2010 U.S. Dist. LEXIS 125934.

Bankr. W.D. Pa. 1994. [Fidelity Bond]. Under Pennsylvania law, a material issue of fact precluded summary judgment on the issue whether the carrier could deny coverage based on the insured's failure to comply with a contractual limitation period for filing suit when the carrier provided the bankruptcy trustee of the insured with a certified copy of policy that omitted the limitation provisions and failed to respond to the trustee's numerous requests for information regarding the policy. *In Re Mechem Fin., Inc.*, 167 B.R. 799.

D. Wis. 2009. [Unspecified coverage form]. The insured's suit for a loss arising out of employee theft was barred when brought more than four years after the insured provided notice to the carrier of the alleged thefts because a Wisconsin statute of limitations of one year for suits on fire insurance policies after the date of the occurrence applied to the claim and even under the policy's more generous two-year contractual limitation for bringing suits after the date on which the direct physical loss or damage occurred, the suit was untimely. *Ward Mgmt. Co. v. Westport Ins. Corp.*, 598 F. Supp. 2d 923.

Ga. App. 1989. [Public Employee Fidelity Bond]. The dispositive issue in this case was when the insured discovered its loss. The allegedly dishonest employee was the subject of a criminal investigation in May 1985. That investigation led to an indictment and the trial of the employee in February 1986. Following the trial, the insured hired the same accounting firm that had completed an audit for the district attorney's office to complete another audit. The results of that audit were received in February 1987. The proof of loss was filed in May 1987 and an action was filed in October 1987. The bond contained a contractual limitation period of one year for filing suit. Although the court recognized the insured "felt it had sustained a loss" as early as February 1986, the insured did not obtain the degree of knowledge necessary to constitute "discovery" until after its receipt of the auditor's report in February 1987. Thus, its action filed in October 1987 was within the one-year period of limitations. *United States Fid. & Guar. Co. v. Macon-Bibb County Econ. Opportunity Council, Inc.*, 381 S.E.2d 539.

N.Y. Sup. Ct. 2011. [Unspecified policy form]. Under a policy that required the insured to provide notice of loss "[a]t the earliest practicable moment after discovery of [the] loss by the Corporate Risk Manager," and provided that "[d]iscovery occurs when the Corporate Risk Manager first becomes aware of facts which would cause a reasonable person to assume that a loss . . . has been or will be incurred," because there was no designated "Corporate Risk Manager" and the de facto corporate risk manager merely reminded subsidiaries to report claims to insurers and merely requested subsidiaries to copy him on claims, the insureds breached their duty to "exercise reasonable diligence . . . to acquire knowledge" of covered losses with reasonable celerity. Because the de facto risk manager delegated the risk management role to the legal department (by directing subsidiaries to report losses directly to the insurer), the general counsel's and assistant general counsel's knowledge of the claimed loss, and the corresponding duty to notify the underwriters, would be imputed to the risk manager. In addition, because the insureds "discovered" the loss on July 23, 2002, given the twenty-four month limitations period contained in the policy, the action was untimely commenced on July 28, 2004, the date of a Standstill Agreement entered into by the parties. *Hudson Ins. Co. v. Oppenheim*, 916 N.Y.S.2d 68.

Ohio. App. 2009. [Fidelity Bond]. Non-colluding directors' knowledge that the insured credit union had likely suffered losses through a corporate executive's pattern of misbehavior including improper use of corporate assets constituted discovery of loss, which began the running of time for filing suit. *American Mut. Share Ins. Corp. v. CUMIS Ins. Soc'y, Inc.*, No. 08AP-576, 2009 Ohio App. LEXIS 304.

Or. App. 2000. [Fidelity Bond]. Under Oregon law, knowledge that an employee violated company policy did not necessarily imply discovery of employee theft and the circuit court erred in granting summary judgment in favor of the carrier on the grounds of the failure to comply with the contractual limitation for filing suit. *Nike v. Northwestern Pac. Indem. Co.*, 999 P.2d 1197; *petition for review granted & original opinion adhered to*, 1 P.3d 1060 (Or. 2001).

Tex. App. 1994. [Comprehensive Dishonesty, Disappearance and Destruction Policy]. A provision in a policy limiting the time for bringing suit to twenty-eight months after discovery of loss began to run when the carrier sent a letter denying coverage for losses, not when a judgment was entered against the insured in a suit brought by victim of employee theft, because the determination of the insured's liability for the losses was irrelevant to the question when the insured's claim accrued against the carrier. The carrier's failure to inform the insured that the claim could not be assigned to the victim of the theft did not estop the carrier from asserting that the claim was barred by the contractual twenty-eight month limitations period because the policy contained a non-assignment clause. *Amarco Petroleum, Inc. v. Texas Pac. Indem. Co.*, 889 S.W.2d 695.

2. Validity of contractual limitations on time for filing suit

(a) Cases Decided Under Commercial Coverages

E.D. Ark. 1982. [Commercial Coverages]. A delay of one year and twenty-one days in giving notice of an insured's first claim was not in compliance with a provision requiring notice as soon as practicable, and that claim was accordingly barred. The second claim in the same case was not rejected for a notice delay of ninety-one days, but was rejected for the late filing of suit against the carrier. *Chandler Trailer Co. v. Lawyer's Sur. Corp.*, 535 F. Supp. 204.

Ky. 1971. [Commercial Coverages]. A contractual provision requiring suit to be brought within one year after discovery of loss was reasonable, even though the general period of statutory limitations was fifteen years. The court rejected the contention that the period of limitation should commence with the expiration of a "no suit" period, the period of time after giving notice or filing the proof of loss during which bringing suit is prohibited by contract. Even if fairness were the test, which it was not, it was not unfair to include the non-suit period in the overall period allowed in which to bring suit. *Ashland Fin. Co. v. Hartford Acc. & Indem. Co.*, 474 S.W.2d 364.

Md. 2010. [Commercial Coverages]. Contrary to the holdings of courts in many other states, a Commercial Crime Policy that provided that the insured must bring suit within three years of discovery of loss violated a Maryland statute that made a provision in an insurance contract setting a shorter time to bring an action on the insurance contract than required by the law of the State illegal and void by fixing the time when the contractual period began to run as the discovery of loss because the statute of limitation did not begin to run on the Commercial Crime Policy until the carrier breached the contract by erroneously denying the claim in whole or in part, or by withholding any decision on the claim for an unreasonable length of time. *St. Paul Travelers v. Millstone*, 987 A.2d 116.

(b) Cases Decided Under Other Financial Institution Coverages

2d Cir. 1915 (N.Y.). [Employee Fidelity Bond]. The insured's failure to bring suit within the 12-month period from the filing of a claim as required by the bond was a condition precedent to recovery. *United States v. Fidelity & Deposit Co. of Md.*, 224 F. 866.

6th Cir. 1956 (Mich.). [Blanket Position Bond]. Noncompliance with a provision requiring that suit be brought within 15 months of discovery of fraudulent or dishonest acts of employees resulted in the proper dismissal of an action on the bond. *Goosen v. Indemnity Ins. Co.*, 234 F.2d. 463.

6th Cir. 1927 (Ohio). [Employee Fidelity Bond]. The trial court correctly directed verdict for the defendant on the basis of the insured's failure to comply with a one-year limitation period in which to bring suit after discovery of its employees' larceny or embezzlement. *Reynolds v. Detroit Fid. & Sur. Co.*, 19 F.2d 110.

8th Cir. 1994 (S.D.). [Savings and Loan Blanket Bond]. A savings and loan blanket bond was a surety contract within the meaning of a South Dakota statute that voided any contractual provision restricting the time within which suit could be brought except for those in surety contracts. Therefore, the bond's two-year limitation on bringing suit was valid and barred the suit by the RTC. *Resolution Trust Corp. v. Hartford Acc. & Indem. Co.*, 25 F.3d 657.

8th Cir. 1965 (Mo.). [Employee Fidelity Bond]. A Missouri statute that prohibited any contractual limitation of time in which any suit could be instituted rendered a contractual period of limitation in a bond invalid. *Lumbermens Mut. Cas. Co. v. Norris Grain Co.*, 343 F.2d 670.

S.D. Ind. 2014. [Financial Institution Bond]. A two-year contractual limitation on the time for filing suit after discovery of loss was valid under Indiana law. *Federal Deposit Ins. Corp. v. Fidelity & Deposit Co. of Md.*, 2014 U.S. Dist. LEXIS 166808 3:11-cv-00019-RLY-WGH.

D.N.J. 1952. [Insurance Policy]. In the absence of a controlling statute to the contrary, a provision in a contract may limit the time for bringing action on such contract to a period less than that prescribed in general statute of limitation, provided that it is reasonable. However, because contractual periods limitation are in derogation of the general statutes of limitation, not very stringent evidence of a waiver of the limitation period is required by the courts in order to defeat the application of a contracted for limitation period. *Sherwood Jewelers-Newark, Inc. v. Philadelphia Nat'l Ins. Co.*, 102 F. Supp. 103.

S.D.N.Y. 1978. [Stockholders' Blanket Bond]. Under New York law, the parties to a contract may designate a shortened period of limitation so long as the period designated is reasonable. The carrier was entitled to summary judgment upon the issues of waiver and estoppel. Waiver is a matter of intent. Consistent reservations of rights by the carrier negated any intention to waive the conditions of the bond. Estoppel requires an affirmative misrepresentation that compliance with the conditions of the bond will not be required. *Redington v. Hartford Acc. & Indem. Co.*, 463 F. Supp. 83.

E.D. Tenn. 1936. [Employee Fidelity Bond]. A contractual limitation on the time for filing suit is valid in the absence of a statute to the contrary or a finding that the period is so unfair and unreasonable that the court must strike it down. *Holland v. Fuller*, 14 F. Supp. 688.

Ariz. 1982. [Insurance Policy]. Although the court recognized that the carrier would not be estopped from enforcing a contractually shortened period of limitations under the ordinary application of estoppel principles, the legislature's intent in permitting the carriers to contractually shorten the period in which suit must be brought (to allow the carriers to protect themselves from fraudulent claims) made the limitation inapplicable when the claim was "patently just." *Zuckerman v. Transamerica Ins. Co.*, 640 P.2d 441.

Ariz. 1932. [Contract Performance Bond]. Bonds are within the ambit of the insurance code, and a statute limiting the minimum period of limitations to two years on insurance policies included bonds. *Massachusetts Bonding & Ins. Co. v. Lenitz*, 9 P.2d 408.

Ga. App. 1958. [Insurance Policy]. A policy provision requiring that no action could be maintained unless commenced within twelve months after a loss was valid. The claimant's contention that the twelve-month period did not commence until the carrier denied the claim was without merit, because the policy clearly stated that the limitation period began to run from the date of a loss. *General Ins. Co. of Am. v. Lee Chocolate Co.*, 103 S.E.2d 632.

Ind. App. 1984. [Honesty Blanket Bond]. Although the parties to a private bond may limit by contract the time in which suit must be brought, public officials cannot, on behalf of the public, set the terms of contracts to supersede those between private parties. A provision of a public bond which limited the time to bring suit to three years was void. *Indiana v. Lidster*, 467 N.E.2d 47.

Ky. 1977. [Employee Dishonesty Bond]. The court upheld a contractual limitations provision in a fidelity bond which specified that the time for filing suit on the claim was fifteen months after the proof of loss or some nineteen months from discovery of loss despite the fact that in the absence of a contractual limitation, the statute of limitations permits an action to be brought within fifteen years after occurrence. *United States Fire Ins. Co. v. American Turners of Louisville, Inc.*, 557 S.W.2d 905.

Minn. 1938. [Employee Fidelity Bond]. An action was barred by the insured's failure to bring suit within one year of its discovery of loss as required by the bond. *Hayfield Farmers Elevator & Mercantile Co. v. New Amsterdam Cas. Co.*, 282 N.W. 265.

Miss. 1972. [Employee Fidelity Bond]. When a statute made insurance contracts subject to the general six-year statute of limitations, provisions in a fidelity bond providing that all actions against the carrier had to be commenced within one year from date the insured discovered a loss were null and void and of no binding force. *Latham v. United States Fid. & Guar. Co.*, 267 So. 2d 895.

N.M. 1991. [Public Employees Faithful Performance Blanket Bond]. Contractual limitations on the time for suit provisions in bonds covering state employees for faithful performance of their duties were not void as against public policy, absent evidence that the parties' agreement was unconscionable or one of adhesion, or that state was in an unequal bargaining position with the carriers. The court found none of those conditions present and upheld the time-to-sue provision. *State ex rel. Udall v. Colonial Penn Ins. Co.*, 812 P.2d 777.

N.D. 1927. [Employee Fidelity Bond]. A statute limiting the minimum period for bringing suit on insurance contracts was inapplicable to suits on fidelity bonds. *Storing v. National Sur. Co.*, 215 N.W. 875.

Pa. Commw. 1974. [Public Employee Faithful Performance Blanket Position Bond]. The court held valid a contractual provision that required suit to be brought within three years after the cancellation of a bond. The underwriter did not waive the contractual limitations period. *Pennsylvania v. Transamerica Ins. Co.*, 316 A.2d 85.

S.D. 2014. In answer to a certified question from the United States District Court for the District of South Dakota, the Supreme Court of South Dakota concluded that a South Dakota statute allowing contractual limitations on the time in which to bring suit on "a surety contract" if not less than two years did not apply to a suit on a financial institution bond. *First Dakota Nat'l Bank v. BancInsure, Inc.*, 851 N.W.2d 924.

3. *Waiver and estoppel*

    (a) Cases Decided Under Commercial Coverages

6th Cir. 1927 (Ohio). [Fidelity Bond]. After discussing the ways that the bonding company could have waived the bond's requirement that suit be brought within 12 months of the discovery of loss, the court held there was no evidence in the record showing any such conduct by the bonding company. In the absence of conduct creating an estoppel, waiver must be supported by an agreement founded on a valuable consideration. *Reynolds v. Detroit Fid. & Sur. Co.*, 19 F.2d 110.

W.D. Mich. 2010. [Commercial Crime Coverage]. Although the policy provided that the insured could not bring a legal action against the carrier unless it was brought within two years from the date the insured discovered the loss, the insured's claim that the carrier's representatives advised the insured that the loss was not discovered until the carrier completed its investigation precluded summary judgment, because the insured could be estopped to raise the contractual limitation if the insured's claim was true. *Coopersville Motors, Inc. v. Federated Mut. Ins. Co.*, No. 1:09-CV-1110, 2010 U.S. Dist. LEXIS 116094.

6th Cir. 1996 (Ohio). [Crime Insurance Policy]. Under Ohio law, when the insured admitted it discovered a loss more than one year before it instituted suit and the policy required that suit be brought within one year of discovery, the suit was barred. The carrier did not waive the suit limitations provision in the policy by investigating the claim and offering to settle the suit after the suit limitation had expired. *Friendly Farms v. Reliance Ins. Co.*, 79 F.3d 541.

(b) Cases Decided Under Other Financial Institution Coverages

6th Cir. 1969 (Mich.). [Employee Fidelity Bond]. Under a fidelity bond with a 12-month period of limitation, the insured made frequent inquiries to the carrier about its claim, was told that the matter was under investigation, and that the carrier would advise the insured. Because the carrier did not deny liability until after the limitations period had run, the carrier waived the limitations period. *William H. Sill Mortgages, Inc. v. Ohio Cas. Ins. Co.*, 412 F.2d 341.

6th Cir. 1956 (Mich.). [Blanket Employee Fidelity Bond]. In an action by the insured's trustee in bankruptcy, the claimant had the burden of establishing that the conditions and time limitations specified in the bond were fulfilled or waived. *Goosen v. Indemnity Insurance Co. of N. Am.*, 234 F.2d 463.

6th Cir. 1927 (Ohio). [Employee Fidelity Bond]. When the carrier received the proof of loss, agreed to review it and in response to a later inquiry, informed the insured that it had turned the claim over to its attorneys for investigation and the insured filed suit one month and fifteen days after the limitations period expired, the court noted that waiver in the absence of conduct creating estoppel must be supported by consideration, and there can be no waiver unless so intended by one party and understood by the other, but when one party has so acted as to mislead another, an estoppel is created. The court concluded that conduct on the part of the carrier was no more than a delay in announcing its action, which did not create a waiver or estoppel upon which the insured could rely. The burden of proof as to waiver was upon the party asserting it. *Reynolds v. Detroit Fid. & Sur. Co.*, 19 F.2d 100.

8th Cir. 1996 (S.D.). [Savings and Loan Blanket Bond]. A two-year contractual limitation period was not tolled during the carrier's fifteen-- month investigation of the claim. The carrier did not waive nor was it estopped from denying the claim because of a breach of that provision, when the denial of coverage occurred seven months prior to the expiration of the limitations period. *Federal Deposit Ins. Corp. v. Hartford Acc. & Indem. Co.*, 97 F.3d 1148.

10th Cir. 1960 (Colo.). [Employee Indemnity Bond]. After the insured made its written claim, the carrier extended three offers of settlement, which were rejected by the insured. One of the offers was made almost one month after the contractual limitations period had expired. These acts estopped the carrier from denying liability on the basis of a fifteen- month contractual limitations period contained in the bond. *Home Indem. Co. v. Midwest Auto Auction, Inc.*, 285 F.2d 708.

N.D. Ga. 1979. [Insurance Policy]. The carrier's failure to formally deny the claim within the applicable period of limitations created a question of fact regarding the carrier's implied waiver of a twelve-month limitation period; summary judgment in favor of the carrier was inappropriate. *Forrester v. Aetna Cas. & Sur. Co.*, 478 F. Supp. 42.

W.D. La. 2008. Because a Louisiana statute expressly provided that investigating a loss or claim or engaging in negotiations looking toward a possible settlement of any such loss or claim did not constitute a waiver of any provision of a policy or of any defense of the insurer, the carrier's letter to its insured offering to continue to investigate the claim or engage in negotiations did not waive the two-year contractual limitation on bringing suit. *Korean War Veterans Ass'n v. Federal Ins. Co.*, Civil Action No. 07-0690, 2008 U.S. Dist. LEXIS 4682.

E.D. Mich. 2008. [Unspecified form]. Because the insured discovered that its General Manager/General Sales Manager had engaged in dishonest conduct no later than the date it sued him, the policy required that suit be brought within one year of the discovery of a loss, contractual provisions limiting the time within which the claimants may bring suit are enforceable under Michigan law, the carrier continually reserved its rights in all communications with its insured, and the carrier neither made any false representation nor concealed any fact that caused the insured to delay in filing its action within the one-year contractual limitations period, the carrier did not waive nor was it estopped to assert the contractual limitation on time for filing suit as a defense to suit filed after the limitation period had passed. *Livonia Volkswagen, Inc. v. Universal Underwriters Group*, No. 06-13619, 2008 U.S. Dist. LEXIS 25519.

D. Minn. 2014. [Financial Institution Bond]. When a bank employee induced others to participate in an advance fee scheme in which he was involved and the carrier defended the resulting lawsuit under a D&O policy, but later declined coverage under an FIB, the carrier was estopped from asserting the 2-year suit limitation because it would be unjust, inequitable, or unconscionable to claim a defense under the FIB when the insured defended the lawsuit against Bank under the D&O policy. *Avon State Bank v. BancInsure, Inc.*, Civ. No. 12-2557 (RHK/LIB), 2014 U.S. Dist. LEXIS 3099.

S.D.N.Y. 1978. [Stockholders' Blanket Bond]. Even if the claimant were to establish that the underwriter was estopped from asserting a shortened period of limitations, the claimant's delay in filing a lawsuit after the underwriter's denial of the claim barred the claimant from claiming estoppel due to his own laches. *Redington v. Hartford Acc. & Indem. Co.*, 463 F. Supp. 83.

S.D. Ohio 1974. [Indemnity Bond]. When the acts of the carrier upon which a waiver was claimed occurred after the limitations period had expired, the carrier was not estopped to assert the limitations period as a defense. Summary judgment was appropriate when the insured failed to provide evidence that the underwriter's alleged conduct giving rise to the defenses of waiver or estoppel occurred prior to the expiration of the time limitation contained in the bond. *Sheet Metal & Roofing Contractors Ass'n of Miami Valley, Ohio v. Liskany*, 369 F. Supp. 662.

N.D.N.Y. 2000. [Credit Union Bonds]. Under New York law, when the carrier disclaimed coverage on certain grounds—, not because suit was untimely under a contractual limitation of time for filing suit, although it possessed sufficient actual or constructive knowledge of the circumstances regarding the unasserted defense of untimely suit—, the carrier was conclusively deemed to have waived the untimely filing of suit. *Nestegg Fed. Credit Union v. Cumis Ins. Soc'y, Inc.*, 87 F. Supp. 2d 144.

Ariz. 1982. [Insurance Policy]. Although the court recognized that the carrier would not be estopped from enforcing contractually shortened period of limitations under ordinary application of estoppel principles, the legislature's intent in permitting the carriers to contractually shorten the period in which suit must be brought (to allow the carriers to protect themselves from fraudulent claims) made the limitation inapplicable when the claim was "patently just." *Zuckerman v. Transamerica Ins. Co.*, 640 P.2d 441.

Ga. App. 2009. [Commercial Crime Policy]. The carrier did not waive a 2-year suit limitation because it consistently denied liability and never entered into negotiations. Mere negotiation for a settlement is not the type of conduct designed to lull the claimant into a false sense of security so as to constitute a waiver of the limitation defense, nor was there any evidence of an affirmative promise, statement or other act or any evidence of actual or constructive fraud to lead the insured into believing that the insurer intended to enlarge the limitation period. *Bickerstaff Imports, Inc. v. Sentry Select Ins. Co.*, 682 S.E.2d 365.

Ga. App. 1936. [Bank Cashier's Indemnity Bond]. A petition alleging that the carrier had misled the bank to believe that the claim would be paid without suit if the bank first sued another carrier which had bonded the employee in his capacity as administrator of estate from which funds had been embezzled was sufficient, if proved, to support a jury verdict when the bank lost the suit and the carrier refused to pay, claiming that the period of limitations had expired. *American Sur. Co. of N.Y. v. Peoples Bank*, 189 S.E. 414.

Ga. App. 1933. [Employee Fidelity Bond]. The court stated the rule that, when the carrier, by its acts in negotiating settlement, has led the insured to believe that he will be paid without suit, the carrier cannot invoke a policy provision which requires that an action on the bond be brought within a specified time. *Knights of Ku Klux Klan v. Fidelity & Deposit Co. of Md.*, 169 S.E. 514.

Ill. 1925. [Accident Insurance Policy]. Questions of waiver of the contractual limitations period for bringing suit on a bond are ordinarily for the jury. *Dickenson v. Pacific Mut. Life Ins. Co.*, 150 N.E. 256.

N.Y. App. 2003. [Fidelity Bond]. When the insured failed to show its detrimental reliance on the carrier's conduct, the carrier was not estopped to rely on the insured's failure to comply with contractual provisions limiting the time for filing suit. *Empire Blue Cross & Blue Shield v. Various Underwriters at Lloyd's*, 767 N.Y.S.2d 432.

Ohio App. 1940. [Name Schedule Bond]. The carrier could not rely on a limitation clause in a fidelity bond requiring an action to be brought within twelve months after the filing of the proof of loss, when the carrier over a period of time had attempted to collect from the employee the amount of the embezzlement, and had recovered part, but finally denied liability on the bond entirely. The facts as plead, if proved, were an admission of liability by conduct, and the limitation period could not commence until the insured knew the company had changed its mind or had closed negotiations. *Walton Baking Co. v. Hartford Acc. & Indem. Co.*, 34 N.E.2d 78.

Tex. App. 1994. [Comprehensive Dishonesty, Disappearance and Destruction Policy]. A provision in a policy limiting the time for bringing suit to twenty-eight months after the discovery of a loss began to run when the carrier sent a letter denying coverage for the losses, not when a judgment was entered against the insured in a suit brought by a victim of employee theft, because the determination of the insured's liability for the losses was irrelevant to the question when the insured's claim accrued against the carrier. The carrier's failure to inform the insured that the claim could not be assigned to the victim of the theft did not estop the carrier from asserting that the claim was barred by contractual 28-month limitations period because the policy contained a non-assignment clause. *Amarco Petroleum, Inc. v. Texas Pac. Indem. Co.*, 889 S.W.2d 695.

4. *Tolling of time for filing suit*

   (a) Cases Decided Under Commercial Coverages

   None

   (b) Cases Decided Under Other Financial Institution Coverages

8th Cir. 1996 (S.D.). [Savings and Loan Blanket Bond]. A two-year contractual limitation period was not tolled during the carrier's 15-month investigation of the claim. The carrier did not waive nor was it estopped from denying the claim because of a breach of that provision, when the denial of coverage occurred seven months prior to the expiration of the limitations period. *Federal Deposit Ins. Corp. v. Hartford Acc. & Indem. Co.*, 97 F.3d 1148.

N.D. Ill. 2012. [Unspecified coverage form]. Because the policy required that the insured give the carrier a detailed sworn proof of a loss, but the proof of loss supplied by the insured was not sworn, an Illinois statute tolling the time for filing suit from the date the proof of loss is filed, in whatever form is required by the policy, until the date the claim is denied in whole or in part, did not apply to toll the time for filing suit. *Wallis v. Card Servs. Int'l, Inc.*, No. 10 C 7250 2012 U.S. Dist. LEXIS 70932.

E.D. Tenn. 1988. [Savings and Loan Blanket Bond]. The court employed, at least in part, a "tolling approach" to the consideration of limitations on the time for bringing suit, under which the time for bringing a claim against the bond was tolled between the time the notice of loss was sent to the carrier until the carrier denied liability. *Federal Sav. & Loan Ins. Corp. v. Aetna Cas. & Sur. Co.*, 701 F. Supp. 1357.

N.J. 1978. [Bankers Blanket Bond]. A bank's letter to the bonding company was sufficient to provide notice of loss and the limitation period to file suit was tolled until the bonding company formally denied liability. *National Newark & Essex Bank v. Am. Ins. Co.*, 385 A.2d 1216.

SECONDARY SOURCES

Annotation, *Carrier's Admission of Liability, Offers of Settlement, Negotiations, and the Like, as a Waiver of, or Estoppel to Assert, Contractual Limitation Provision*, 29 A.L.R.2D 636 (1953).

Annotation, *Carrier's Demand for Additional or Corrected Proof of Loss as Waiver or Estoppel as to the Right to Assert Contractual Limitation Provision, or as Suspending Running Thereof*, 15 A.L.R.2d 955 (1951).

Annotation, *Carrier's Denial of Liability as Suspending Running of Statute of Limitation or Limitation Provision of Policy*, 171 A.L.R. 577 (1947).

Annotation, *Constitutionality, Construction, & Application of Statute Related to Contractual Time Limitation Provisions of Insurance Policies*, 112 A.L.R. 1288 (1938).

Annotation, *Notice of Loss or Claim within Specified Time after Close of Bond Year*, 149 A.L.R. 945 (1944).

Annotation, *Validity of Contractual Time Period Shorter Than Statute of Limitations for Bringing Action*, 6 A.L.R.3d 1197 (1966).

A. H. Denecke, *Surety and Fidelity Bonds*, 37 ORE. L. REV. 95 (1958).

Jack McNeil, *When Is the Failure to Comply with the Requirements for Timely Notice, Proof of A Loss & Suit a Defense to a Surety?*, 16 FORUM 1130 (1981).

Frank L. Skillern, Jr., *How to Prevent Loss of Fidelity Carrier's Rights by Waiver & Estoppel*, 10 FORUM 302 (1984).

George W. Terrell, *How to Prevent Loss of a Contract Surety's Rights by Waiver & Estoppel*, 10 FORUM 878 (1975).

Chapter 14

Cancellation and Termination*

This chapter analyzes the conditions required in order to end the contractual obligations owed under a crime policy.[1] These conditions are typically contained in two different provisions of the crime policy, a cancellation provision and a termination provision. The cancellation provision, which is discussed first, sets forth the specific requirements for the insured or the insurer to effectively cancel the policy. In addition to the technical requirements set forth in the cancellation provision, each jurisdiction typically also has statutory provisions that govern termination, and the contractual and statutory provisions should both be complied with to ensure a proper cancellation. This chapter then moves to the termination provision, which generally provides that the policy will not provide coverage for theft or other dishonest conduct of an employee once the insured has knowledge of the employee's dishonest acts. The termination provision requires an analysis of who knew what, and when. This type of fact-intensive analysis occurs frequently under fidelity bonds in determining when a loss was first "discovered" by the insured, and those cases provide considerable guidance.

---

*   Susan Koehler Sullivan, Sedgwick, LLP, Los Angeles, California, and Thomas R. Orofino, Sedgwick, LLP, New York, New York.

[1]   The authors acknowledge the scholarship of Martha L. Perkins and Lana M. Glovach, the authors of the chapter on this topic that appears in the Second Edition of this work. This revision builds upon, in no small part, the work of these distinguished authors.

A. Cancellation of the Policy[2]

(1) The first Named Insured shown in the Declarations may cancel this policy by mailing or delivering to us advance written notice of cancellation.

(2) We may cancel this policy by mailing or delivering to the first Named Insured written notice of cancellation at least:

   (a) 10 days before the effective date of cancellation if we cancel for non-payment of premium; or

   (b) 30 days before the effective date of cancellation if we cancel for any other reason.

(3) We will mail or deliver our notice to the first Named Insured's last mailing address known to us.

(4) Notice of cancellation will state the effective date of cancellation. The policy period will end on that date.

(5) If this Policy is cancelled, we will send the first Named Insured any premium refund due. If we cancel, the refund will be pro rata. If the first Named Insured cancels, the refund may be less than pro rata. The cancellation will be effective even if we have not made or offered a refund.

(6) If notice is mailed, proof of mailing will be sufficient proof of notice.

COMMENT

Commercial crime policies allow either the first named insured or the insurer to cancel the policy prior to the end of the policy period. The first named insured may cancel the policy by: (1) mailing or delivering to the insurer; (2) written notice of cancellation; and (3) specifying the desired effective date of cancellation. If the insured's cancellation notice is mailed, then proof of such mailing will be deemed proof that the cancellation notice was provided to the insurer. Per the standard

---

2   This identical language appears in the following forms: Crime Protection Policy, SP 00 01 04 12, § E.1. (Sur. & Fid. Ass'n of Am. 2012); and Commercial Crime Policy, CR 00 22 08 13, § E.1.b (Ins. Servs. Offices, Inc. 2012) (Discovery).

cancellation language such as noted above, if the first named insured decides to cancel the crime policy, the premium refund may be less than pro rata (i.e., the short-term rate).

Should the insurer decide to cancel the crime policy, the company must: (1) mail or deliver; (2) to the first named insured; (3) a written notice of cancellation; (4) at least 10 days before the effective date of cancellation if cancelling for non-payment of premium or at least 30 days before the effective date of cancellation if cancelling for any other reason; (5) to the first named insured's last known mailing address; and (6) such notice must specify the effective date of cancellation. As with cancellation by the insured, if the notice is mailed, proof of mailing is sufficient proof of notice. If the insurer cancels the policy, the premium refund will be pro-rata. Pursuant to the standard cancellation language, an insurer's otherwise valid cancellation notice will be deemed effective even if the insurer has not made or offered a premium refund.[3]

While the standard cancellation provision is relatively straightforward, in almost all cases, the standard cancellation language will be modified by endorsement to comply with particular state requirements with respect to cancellation of an insurance policy prior to the original expiration date. Further, some states, by law or regulation, restrict the ability of an insurer to cancel the policy or may only permit cancellation on specified grounds. Such cancellation and notice requirements are beyond the scope of this chapter, but it is essential that in addition to any applicable endorsements, that the practitioner also consult the insurance statutes or regulations in the pertinent jurisdiction.

As the case summaries below reflect, generally speaking, an insurer seeking to cancel a commercial crime policy must comply with both the policy language and state regulations. Given the potentially serious implications of an improper cancellation notice, insurers are advised to

---

3   Most commercial crime policies also provide another method for their cancellation: by the same insurer issuing a new policy. The Declarations Page of such policies generally contains an item entitled "Cancellation of Prior Insurance," which item provides: "by acceptance of this policy, you [the insured] give us notice canceling a prior policy Nos. _____." *See, e.g.,* Crime Protection Policy, SP 00 01 04 12, at CPP-1. If the same insurer issues a new policy at the expiration date of the prior policy, the prior policy is cancelled automatically and the new policy becomes effective. The purpose of this provision is to prevent two policies from being issued to the same insured by the same company at the same time.

carefully draft cancellation notices, including confirming the effective date of cancellation in compliance with both the policy dictates and state law. Best practices such as ensuring notice of cancellation is mailed to all required parties (which can vary by jurisdiction), at the proper addresses, and by certified mail return receipt requested, are important in order to avoid a determination that cancellation was not properly effected.

OUTLINE OF ANNOTATIONS

A. Commercial Crime Policies
B. Other Policy or Bond Forms

ANNOTATIONS

A. Commercial Crime Policies

2d Cir. 1999 (N.Y.). A Crime Insurance Policy provided that it would be terminated effective thirty days after the insured's receipt of the insurer's written notice of termination. Endorsements prohibited either party from canceling, without first giving written notice to certain customers of the insured (loss payees). The insured Payroll Express sought to non-renew and signed a cancellation notice prepared by the insurer. After the effective date of that cancellation notice, Payroll did not pay further premium and obtained substitute coverage for the loss payees from the date of cancellation of the prior policy. The court rejected the trustee's assertion that the cancellation was ineffective because of the failure to comply with the notice requirements as to the loss payees, for the following reasons: (1) no premium had been paid to the first insurer since the cancellation notice; (2) the policy had no language that it was self-renewing upon ineffective notice of cancellation to the loss payees; and (3) the purpose of the cancellation notice is to protect the insured from being left without coverage, which was not offended when Payroll cancelled and then obtained substitute coverage for the loss payees who were to be notified of such cancellation. *In re Payroll Express Corp.*, 186 F.3d 196.

B. Other Policy or Bond Forms

5th Cir. 1932 (Tex.). A fidelity bond covered losses the insured bank sustained during the bond period and discovered before the expiration of one year from the date of the bond's cancellation. The bond provided that it could be cancelled "upon the effective date specified in a written notice served by either party hereto on the other or sent by registered mail." The insurer contended that the bond was cancelled on July 6, 1929, and discovery of loss occurred on September 4, 1930, such that there was no coverage. The trial and appellate courts found otherwise, concluding there was no proof of any formal written cancellation notice at any time or of discovery of loss until September 4, 1930. This conclusion was belied by the record which reflected: the bank's vice president told the insurance agent that the bank did not wish the bond's $25,000 coverage spread over several years and, in order to have the full coverage for each year, the insured wished to change its bond to another company; the agent wrote a bond with another surety on July 6, 1929; the insured neither was charged nor paid further premium for the bond at issue; the agent asked the insured to surrender the bond and, while it was not surrendered, on January 6, 1930, the insured signed a release of the surety "from liability for any and all acts committed by various employees . . . on and after the sixth day of July 1929," and there was evidence of a misunderstanding about the parties' intent. The court noted that, prior to the signing of the release, the bond had not been terminated in the manner set forth in it, nor was there clear proof that the parties by consent had substituted another method. *Aetna Cas. & Sur. Co. v. First Trust & Sav. Bank*, 62 F.2d 316.

M.D. Ga. A Bankers Blanket Bond provided three methods for termination or cancellation in its entirety: (1) by the underwriter; (2) by the insured; and (3) by the appointment of a receiver for the insured. The court also recognized cancellation by mutual assent. In this case, it did not matter which cancellation method was chosen because discovery of loss did not occur prior to the effective termination of the bond. The bank's receiver failed to avail himself of a bond provision providing for an additional discovery period. The court also rejected the receiver's argument that the underwriter knew that the insured bank was insolvent and cancelled the bond for that reason because, even if true, the underwriter's reservation of rights did not affect the validity of the cancellation: "when the right to cancel has been reserved by the parties they may do so regardless of their reason or motive." *Hartley v. Hartford Acc. & Indem. Co.*, 275 F. Supp. 610.

W.D. Mo. 1991. A one-year Property Owners Policy contained Comprehensive Crime Coverage. Due to non-payment of premium, the policy was canceled before the expiration date stated in the policy. The policy covered a loss from employee dishonesty if the insured discovered the loss by April 18, 1985, and reported it to the insurer "as soon as practicable" after discovery. The insured's bankruptcy trustee submitted the insured's claim stating that the insured discovered the loss in July 1985. The insurer denied the claim because discovery of loss was outside the policy period. The trustee challenged delivery of the notice of cancellation to the insured and the effective date of cancellation. As to delivery, uncontroverted evidence established that the insurer mailed the cancellation notice to the insured by certified mail. Pointing to the policy provision that proof of mailing is sufficient proof of notice, the court found that proof of mailing was sufficient to cancel the policy whether or not the insured actually received the notice. As to the effective date of cancellation, the notice stated that cancellation could not become effective until at least ten days after the notice was mailed. There were fewer than ten days between the mailing of the notice and its effective date. The court concluded that, while the notice was ineffective, cancellation occurred on the earliest date that it would comply with the policy. Because discovery of loss was still after that date, there was no coverage. *Block v. Granite State Ins. Co.*, 963 F.2d 1127.

D.R.I. 1992. A Small Loan Companies Blanket Bond provided for termination in its entirety thirty days after the insured's receipt of the underwriter's written cancellation notice. Although the underwriter followed the bond's cancellation provision, neither the underwriter nor the insured notified the Rhode Island Department of Business Regulation ("DBR") that the underwriter had cancelled the bond, as required by a state statute. The court concluded that the cancellation notice did not effectively terminate coverage because the DBR was never notified; rather, the bond remained in effect until a receiver took over (the later receivership terminated the bond in its entirety under another bond provision), and the receiver's claim was timely. *Paradis v. Aetna Cas. & Sur. Co.*, 796 F. Supp. 59.

E.D. Wis. 2004. The insured, a national bank, cancelled its Community Financial Institution Bond, received unearned premium, and obtained a replacement bond—with no gap in coverage—from another insurer. The original bond contained a rider requiring that the insurer give identified state agencies written notice of the cancellation in order for the cancellation to be effective. The cancelled carrier denied the insured's claim on the basis that discovery of loss occurred after the bond was canceled; the insured argued that the cancellation was not effective because the insurer failed to notify the state agencies per the rider. The court concluded that the state agencies did not regulate national banks for insurance purposes and, thus, had no authority to act on any such notice. Notwithstanding the rider, the insurer's failure to perform what all conceded would have been a useless act had no impact on its cancellation of the bond. *First Nat'l Bank v. Cincinnati Ins. Co.,* 321 F. Supp. 2d 988.

Fla. 1961. The fidelity bond provided that the effective cancellation date would not be less than thirty days after the insured received notice by registered mail. The defalcating employee received the notice only twenty-six days before the specified termination date. The trial court held that the cancellation was effective thirty days after the insured's receipt, despite the date given in the notice. The Florida Supreme Court disagreed, holding that the notice was ineffectual to cancel the risk because it violated the bond's thirty-day period. *Graves v. Iowa Mut. Ins. Co.,* 132 So. 2d 393.

Ind. App. 1929. A fidelity bond permitted the insurer to terminate its obligations by giving the insured written notice stating the effective termination date. The bond did not specify the method of delivery of that notice, but the insurer sent it by registered mail, return receipt requested. The defalcating employee signed for the letter, but the insured claimed never to have seen it. The court concluded that, under these circumstances, the cancellation notice fell short of being personal notice that the court determined the law required. *Andrews v. Minter Coal & Coke Co.,* 168 N.E. 869.

N.Y. 1936. Shortly after a fidelity bond was issued, the insured instructed the surety that communications should be referred to the insured's secretary/treasurer. For several years the surety had communications with the insured's officers other than the defalcating treasurer, but subsequently all such communications were with the defalcating treasurer. The treasurer, in the insured's name, wrote the surety canceling the bond. There was evidence that this letter was written without the authority, knowledge, approval, or ratification of the insured's board of directors, executive committee, or any other officer other than the defalcating treasurer. The trial court held, and the appellate court affirmed, that the bond had been canceled as a result of the communication between the surety and the treasurer (whose defalcations were at issue) who for many years represented the insured in dealings concerning the bond. Accordingly, the insured was estopped from asserting that the surety should have communicated with another representative of the insured. *Dry Good Alliance, Inc. v. Stewart*, 3 N.E.2d 206.

SECONDARY SOURCES

David E. Bordon et al., *Conditions to Recovery: Termination and Cancellation, in* FINANCIAL INSTITUTION BONDS 315 (Duncan L. Clore ed., 1995).

Michael R. Davisson, *Conditions to Recovery: Termination and Cancellation, in* FINANCIAL INSTITUTION BONDS 471 (Duncan L. Clore ed., 2d ed. 1998).

Michael R. Davisson, *Section 12—Termination or Cancellation, in* ANNOTATED FINANCIAL INSTITUTION BOND 544 (Michael Keeley ed., 2d ed. 2004).

John B. Hayes, *Cancellation as to any Employee and Cancellation of Bond, in* THE COMMERCIAL BLANKET BOND ANNOTATED (William F. Haug ed., 1985).

Robert J. Heyne et al., *The Simplified Commercial Crime Forms, or "A Jabberwock Meets the Flesch Test,"* (unpublished paper presented at Annual Meeting of the ABA, Fid. & Sur. Law Comm., New York, N.Y, Aug. 1986).

Victor B. Levitt, *The Pitfalls and Windfalls of Policy Cancellations*, *(unpublished paper presented at Annual Meeting of ABA, Fid. & Sur. Law Comm., Aug. 1983).*

Michael B. McGeehon & Martin J. O'Leary, *Termination of Coverage*, *in* HANDLING FIDELITY BOND CLAIMS 445 (Michael Keeley & Timothy Sukel eds., 1999).

Martha L. Perkins & Lana M. Glovach, *Cancellation and Termination of Coverage*, *in* COMMERCIAL CRIME POLICY 471 (Randall I. Marmor & John J. Tomaine eds., 2d ed. 2005).

Edward T. Stork, *Termination of Coverage*, *in* HANDLING FIDELITY BOND CLAIMS 499 (Michael Keeley & Sean Duffy eds., 2d ed. 2005).

Cheryl J. Wickham et al., *Cancellation*, *in* COMMERCIAL CRIME POLICY 11-5 (Gilbert J. Schroeder ed., 1997).

B. Termination as to Any Employee[4]

This Insuring Agreement[5] terminates as to any "employee":

---

4   The "Termination" provision in the most recent Commercial Crime Policy, CR 00 22 08 13, appears at § E.2.a, (Ins. Servs. Offices, Inc. 2012) (Discovery). Note that earlier editions of the commercial crime policy have provided a substantially similar condition to coverage; however, the condition was titled "Cancellation as to Any Employee" instead of "Termination as to Any Employee."
Although titled "Cancellation as to Any Employee," substantially similar language appears in the most recent Crime Protection Policy, SP 00 01 04 12, *Conditions Applicable to Specific Insuring Agreements*, §E.1 (Sur. & Fid. Ass'n of Am. 2012). Note that the SFAA policy includes an additional clause that the policy is canceled as to any employee upon discovery by: "As to **Employee benefit plan(s)**, any trustee, fiduciary or plan administrator not in collusion with the **employee** . . . ."

5   The Termination provision now appears in the Commercial Crime Policy in the section titled "Conditions Applicable to Insuring Agreement A.1.[Employee Theft]." Some earlier editions of the commercial crime

(1)   As soon as:

    (a)   You; or

    (b)   Any of your partners, "members", "managers", officers, directors or trustees not in collusion with the "employee";

learn of "theft" or any other dishonest act committed by the "employee" whether before or after becoming employed by you; or

(2)   On the date specified in a notice mailed to the first Named Insured. That date will be at least 30 days after the date of mailing.

We will mail or deliver our notice to the first Named Insured's last mailing address known to us. If notice is mailed, proof of mailing will be sufficient proof of notice.

COMMENT

The "termination" provision in the commercial crime policy provides that coverage terminates, immediately and automatically, as to any "employee" as soon as the named insured, or the specific delineated individuals not in collusion with the employee, learn of "theft" or any other dishonest act committed by that employee. The intent of this provision is plain: to place the risk of employees known to have been dishonest with the insured, not the insurer. Should the named insured, or one of the persons identified in the provision and not in collusion with the insured, learn that one of its employees has committed "theft" or any other dishonest act, coverage is no longer provided for future losses caused by that employee. The immediate termination of coverage as to any employee upon the employer's discovery of prior dishonesty not only incentivizes the insured employer to be diligent both in its hiring practices and in supervising its employees, but properly places the risk of hiring a dishonest employee on the insured employer, which is in the best position to guard against the hiring and retention of dishonest employees.

---

policy included this provision in the conditions section applicable to all insuring agreements.

Additionally, pursuant to subpart (2) of the Termination provision, the insurance company may cancel coverage as to any employee if: (i) the insurer mails a notice to the first named insured; (ii) specifying the date coverage will terminate as to the employee; (iii) which date must be at least thirty days after the date the notice is mailed. The insurer must mail or deliver the termination notice to the insured's last known mailing address. If mailed, proof of mailing is sufficient to show proof of notice to the insured.

These "automatic" termination provisions typically provide that coverage will automatically terminate as to a specific employee (1) upon discovery of a dishonest act; (2) regardless of when the act took place, whether prior to, or after, the inception of the policy; and (3) regardless of whether the employee committed the act while employed by the insured. As always, there are various iterations of the termination provision, and the specific language of the relevant policy should be carefully reviewed when invoking the termination provision.

Cases interpreting the termination provision often focus on: (1) what acts constitute "dishonesty," an undefined term, to trigger the termination clause; (2) who knew of the employee's dishonest acts and whether that person's knowledge will be imputed to the insured; and (3) the extent of information that must be known, or when the insured or management "discovers" the employee's prior dishonesty.

In recent years, a few courts have questioned the breadth of certain automatic termination provisions, and held that the coverage automatically terminates or cancels only if the insured learns of the employee's prior dishonesty *after* the inception of the policy. These cases generally note that the termination or cancellation of coverage as to an employee presupposes the inception of coverage as to that employee, thus discovery of prior dishonesty can only occur after the policy incepts. These cases, however, deviate from the majority of courts, which have agreed that the risk of employing known bad actors properly lies with the insured, not the insurer.[6]

---

6   The minority view cases may also be nullified by recent versions of the ISO and SFAA crime policies. *See*, ISO Commercial Crime Policy, CR 00 22 08 13, Exclusion, 1.b., *Acts Committed By Your Employees Learned of by You Prior to the Policy Period*; and SFAA Crime Protection Policy, SP 00 01 04 12, *Conditions Applicable to Specific Insuring Agreements*, §E.1 ("coverage under this policy is canceled as to any employee immediately upon discovery by You . . . of any dishonest act committed by that employee

616 ANNOTATED COMMERCIAL CRIME INSURANCE POLICY

In order for the automatic cancellation provision to be triggered, the particular "dishonest" act does not have to be an act that would qualify for coverage under the policy. Moreover, it does not matter when the dishonest act occurred or whether it occurred when the employee was in the employment of the insured or otherwise. The disqualifying act could have occurred at any time, in the recent past or the distant past, because the cancellation clause generally contains no temporal limitation. Nor, unless the policy language provides otherwise, must the dishonest act involve a large sum of money, if any money at all.

In spite of the breadth indicated by the term "dishonesty" for purposes of automatic cancellation, some courts have strained to avoid the effect of the clause. Thus, some courts have found that prior acts of dishonesty are matters of "mistake," "negligence," "inefficiency," or "poor business practices" rather than dishonest conduct that triggers cancellation as to an employee.

The language of the various standard and manuscripted policies expressly states the categories of persons by whom discovery will terminate coverage. Depending on the specific policy language, coverage is canceled when the "Insured" or any "officer," "member," "director," "trustee," or "partner," not in collusion with the employee discovers the dishonest act. Inclusion of specific categories is not intended as a limitation on the word "insured." Discovery by the insured can occur even if the discovery is made by an individual who would not qualify under the specified categories of persons. Because an insured can only learn information through its officers, agents, and employees, of necessity, the issue becomes whose knowledge will be imputed to the insured (other than those categories of individuals denominated in the policy) to constitute "discovery" by the insured. The courts generally rely on traditional agency principles to resolve the issue of whether the individual is deemed "the insured." Often, discovery will be imputed to the insured when it is made by an employee acting within the scope of his or her employment under circumstances where the employee would be expected to communicate the information to his or her employer. Typically, the more senior the person who has discovered the prior

---

whether before or after becoming employed by you ... *whether such discovery occurs prior to or after the commencement of this Policy*, there is no coverage under Insuring Agreement 1. for loss or losses resulting from acts committed by that employee after the date of such discovery ...") (emphasis added).

dishonest act, the more likely it is that a court will conclude that the insured was aware of the prior act.

It is important to note that, as evidenced in the case law, crime policies and bond forms often use slightly different language to express the automatic termination clause (i.e., "cancellation" versus "termination" and "discover" versus "learns of"). As always, care should be taken to compare the applicable termination language against the language identified in case law to determine whether the case law is apposite. Similarly, case law regarding what is "dishonest" and when the insured will be charged with knowledge of such conduct is highly fact specific and will typically require a detailed comparison with the facts at hand.

OUTLINE OF ANNOTATIONS

A. Validity in General
   1. Commercial Crime Policies
   2. Other Policy or Bond Forms
B. What Act(s) Constitute "Dishonesty" Under the Termination Provision?
   1. Commercial Crime Policies
   2. Other Policy or Bond Forms
C. Who Must Learn of the Dishonesty to Trigger the Termination Provision?
   1. Commercial Crime Policies
   2. Other Policy or Bond Forms
D. What Constitutes Discovery or Knowledge of Dishonesty?
   1. Commercial Crime Policies
   2. Other Policy or Bond Forms
E. When Must the Dishonesty be Discovered?
   1. Before or After the Bond/Policy Incepts
   2. Only After Inception of the Bond/Policy

ANNOTATIONS

A. Validity in General

1. Commercial Crime Policies

5th Cir. 1967 (Fla.). A provision that terminates coverage after the insured gains knowledge that an employee has committed any fraudulent or dishonest act is reasonable, valid, and enforceable. *St. Joe Paper Co. v. Hartford Acc. & Indem. Co.*, 359 F.2d 579.

8th Cir. 1970 (Ark.). A bond provision that automatically cancels coverage as to a particular employee upon the insured's discovering the employee's dishonesty is reasonable and valid. *Ritchie Grocer Co. v. Aetna Cas. & Sur. Co.*, 426 F.2d 499.

2. Other Policy or Bond Forms

5th Cir. 1981 (La.). The court held that a provision in a Bankers Blanket Bond expressly excluding coverage for losses resulting from dishonest acts of any employee that occurred after the insured employer had knowledge of the employee's dishonesty is valid. *Central Progressive Bank v. Fireman's Fund Ins. Co.*, 658 F.2d 377.

5th Cir. 1957 (La.). A provision that a fidelity bond is canceled as to any employee upon discovery of that employee's dishonesty is valid. The operation of such a clause, in the absence of ambiguity, should be construed in the plain, ordinary, and popular sense of the language used, and if any of the terms are ambiguous, the construction most favorable to the insured will be adopted. *J.S. Fraering, Inc. v. Employers Mut. Liab. Ins. Co.*, 242 F.2d 609.

8th Cir. 1991 (Mo.). The automatic termination provision (in a Brokers Blanket Bond) serves a valid public policy. "[I]t rests upon the policy that the employer should responsibly supervise its employees, particularly since the insured is in a better position than the insurer to monitor the activities of its employees. By terminating indemnification for the further fraudulent conduct of an employee after the employer has learned that the employee defrauded clients, the termination clause encourages employers to supervise their employees. This incentive minimizes fraud, thus, [sic] benefiting both the investment industry and its customers." *Newhard, Cook & Co. v. Ins. Co. of N. Am.*, 929 F.2d 1355.

D. Idaho 2010. Termination provisions, such as the one appearing in the credit union bond at issue, are "common[ly] . . . found in fidelity bonds and such provisions are legally enforceable." Fidelity coverage "can be cancelled as to certain employees upon the insured's discovery of dishonest or fraudulent acts by that employee." *Pioneer Federal Credit Union v. CUMIS Ins. Soc'y, Inc.*, No. 08-CV-496, 2010 U.S. Dist. LEXIS 145761, at *13.

Ill. App. 1995. Automatic cancellation provisions, such as the one in a Public Employees' Bond, are "well recognized as being reasonable; to conclude otherwise would be contrary to fundamental fairness and public policy—the City [insured] should not be compensated for losses caused by the misconduct of its employees of which it was aware and did nothing to prevent." *Kinzer v. Fid. & Dep. Co. of Md.*, 652 N.E.2d 20.

Utah 1991. The court discussed the public policy behind the automatic termination provision. "The hiring or retention of an employee who is known to be dishonest is effectively a conscious decision to increase the risk of loss due to employee dishonesty. [Automatic termination] provisions properly shift such increased fidelity loss risk to the employer." *Home Sav. & Loan v. Aetna Cas. & Sur. Co.*, 817 P.2d 341.

B. What Act(s) Constitute "Dishonesty" Under the Termination Provision?

1. Commercial Crime Policies

8th Cir. 1970 (Ark.). The insured, while investigating the background of a job applicant, discovered that the applicant, a teenager, had stolen some tires and money. The judge and sheriff believed the theft a youthful indiscretion and dismissed the charges. The insured's branch manager, with this knowledge, hired the teenager as a truck driver for the insured. When the teenager embezzled from the insured, the court found that the coverage had terminated as to that employee. The court opined that the fact that the judge and authorities had refrained from imposing the penalty of the law on the teenager was immaterial to whether the act was a dishonest act or whether the insured had prior knowledge of the dishonest deed. *Ritchie Grocer Co. v. Aetna Cas. & Sur. Co.*, 426 F.2d 499.

Cal. App. 1959. A bookkeeper's act, prior to the bond being issued, of taking $20 from petty cash, which he later repaid, was sufficient knowledge on the part of the insured to prevent the bookkeeper from ever being covered under a newly issued bond. *Ciancetti v. Indem. Ins. Co. of N. Am.*, 335 P.2d 1048.

2. Other Policy or Bond Forms

4th Cir. 1979 (S.C.). An insured mortgage broker, prior to the effective date of fidelity policies, discovered during the course of a routine audit that the vice president was falsely certifying pre-advances for certain HUD/FHA loans. The court held that the bonding companies were not liable for losses sustained by the insured because of the vice president's false certification of letters of credit after the effective date of the policies. *C. Douglas Wilson & Co. v. Ins. Co. of N. Am.*, 590 F.2d 1275.

Bankr. N.D. Ga. 1995. The court reviewed a coverage exclusion in a fidelity policy for a loss caused by an employee if the insured had knowledge of dishonest acts committed by the employee (1) while employed by the insured, or (2) prior to employment by the insured, if such conduct involved money, securities, or other property valued at $10,000 or more. The court observed that, if the policy provides that the prior dishonest act must have involved loss of a specified amount, then that qualification will be enforced. Thus, for the automatic termination clause to be triggered, the requisite dollar amount of the loss sustained by the prior employer must be established. *In re Prime Commercial Corp.*, 187 B.R. 785.

Bankr. S.D.N.Y. 1992. In a Securities Dealer Blanket Bond case, the court granted summary judgment in favor of the insurer, concluding that the stockbroker/employee's trading for his own account, although a violation of company policy, did not qualify as dishonest or fraudulent acts within the meaning of the bond. Furthermore, the court held that, even if such acts did qualify as dishonest or fraudulent under the bond, coverage terminated pursuant to the automatic termination provision because of the insured's knowledge of such trading by the employee on one prior occasion. The insured permitted the employee to continue his brokerage activities after the first violation because the employee covered the loss. *In re J.T. Moran Fin. Corp.*, 147 B.R. 335.

Kan. App. 2005. The insured bank discovered that an employee had surreptitiously raised the limit on her credit card issued by the bank. The bank disciplined the employee, required her to pay off the credit card account, and gave the insurer, BancInsure, notice of the incident. BancInsure drafted a response stating that coverage for the employee was terminated but never sent the response to the bank. Two years later, the employee stole $53,000 from customer accounts and the bank submitted a claim. BancInsure denied the claim based on the automatic termination provision. The appellate court reversed the initial judgment for the bank, finding the automatic termination provision clear and unambiguous: "Under the law, [the employee's] surreptitious and unauthorized act of raising her personal credit limit constituted dishonest conduct within the meaning of Section 12 of the bond. The fact that the plaintiff suffered no economic loss and that [the employee] intended no financial loss to her employer does not make the conduct honest." The court rejected the bank's argument that failure to respond to the notice letter was a breach of BancInsure's obligation to the bank. *Troy State Bank v. BancInsure, Inc.*, 109 P.3d 203.

La. 1969. The court held that the State's pardon for the employee's prior dishonesty, for which he has been incarcerated in the penitentiary, did not change the fact that the employee had committed a dishonest act. Thus, the automatic termination clause precluded coverage for that employee's succeeding dishonest acts. *Verneco, Inc. v. Fid. & Cas. Co. of N.Y.*, 219 So. 2d 508.

La. App. 1961. A fidelity bond was canceled under a termination provision providing for termination upon discovery by the employer of any act that "may be made basis of any claim" upon the employer's discovery of the bookkeeper's dishonesty several years prior to the time the claims was made, even though the bookkeeper made restitution of funds embezzled on the prior occasion. *Employers' Liab. Assur. Co. v. S. Produce Co.*, 129 So. 2d 247.

Mich. App. 1997. The court enforced the "clear and specific" automatic termination clause in the employee dishonesty policy because the insured knew when it hired the embezzling employee, that the employee had just completed serving a sentence for breaking and entering and larceny. The court was unpersuaded by the insured's suggested interpretation of the automatic termination clause that all "dishonest acts" must be committed in the course of employment with the insured. *F.L. Jursik v. Travelers Indem. Ins. Co.*, No. 199913, 1997 WL 33332724.

Miss. 1963. The court held that a salesman, who was known by his employer to have embezzled money, was excluded from coverage under the blanket employees' fidelity bond, despite the fact that the dishonest employee made restitution for the prior embezzlement. *Frank Gardner Hardware & Supply Co. v. St. Paul Fire & Marine Ins. Co.*, 148 So. 2d 190.

Miss. 1963. A fidelity bond provided that coverage would terminate immediately upon discovery by the employer of any dishonest or criminal act committed by the employee. The court held that conflicting testimony sustained a finding that earlier acts of an employee were "mere matters of mistake or inefficiency." Such acts, observed the court, did not constitute dishonest or criminal conduct and did not terminate coverage. *USF&G v. Constantin*, 157 So. 2d 642.

N.Y. App. 2012. The court held that "the act of forging another's name without consent in order to approve transactions in which [the employee] d[id] not have authority to approve, with the admitted purpose of avoiding detection," constitutes a "dishonest act" as a matter of law. According to the court, "dishonest or fraudulent acts" were not defined in the termination provision, thus they must be given their ordinary meaning and "broadly include acts that demonstrate a want of integrity, breach of trust or moral turpitude affecting the official fidelity or character or the employee . . . the conduct need not amount to a crime to constitute dishonesty." Additionally, the court found that the fidelity bond does not require that a loss occur in order for conduct to be considered "dishonest or fraudulent" under the termination provision: "The express terms of the bond provide that dishonest or fraudulent acts *plus* loss presents the basis for a claim; hence, loss is not an element of a dishonest or fraudulent act" *Capital Bank & Trust Co. v. Gulf Ins. Co.*, 91 A.D.3d 1251 (emphasis added).

N.Y. App. 1993. The Banker's and Broker's Blanket Bonds provided that coverage terminated as to any partner or employee of the insured when any supervisory employee not in collusion learned of any dishonest act on the part of such partner or employee. The court found that the insured was not entitled to coverage for claims arising from transactions as to which the insured had pleaded guilty to criminal charges, claims for third-party indemnification based on the insured's willful acts, and all transactions involving employees whose names became known to the insured's management during the criminal investigation. *Drexel Burnham Lambert Group, Inc. v. Vigilant Ins. Co.*, 595 N.Y.S.2d 999.

Tex. App. 1962. Where an employer knew that this employee had misappropriated $500 of the employer's funds before the fidelity bond was issued covering such employee, the subsequent misappropriation by that employee was excluded from coverage under the bond's automatic termination provision. *Larson v. Peerless Ins. Co.*, 362 S.W.2d 863.

Utah App. 1991. The court held that the automatic termination provision of a Savings and Loan Blanket Bond can apply to bar coverage even if the conduct that reveals the dishonesty is unrelated to the subsequent conduct that causes the loss. *Home Sav. & Loan v. Aetna Cas. & Sur. Co.*, 817 P.2d 341.

Va. 1946. The court determined that the insured's practice of permitting its salesmen to overdraw commission accounts or pay themselves out of cash collections, with later repayments, did not automatically terminate coverage under a Blanket Position Bond for the subsequent loss caused by a salesman. The court observed that, because the practice was permitted by the employer, there was "no moral turpitude or breach of honesty or want of integrity." The court determined that violation of good business practices did not rise to the requisite level of "dishonesty." *Hartford Acc. & Indem. Co. v. Singer*, 39 S.E.2d 505.

Wis. 1917. An insured bank's directors falsely certified its cashier's reports to the bank commissioner and examiner. The court held that the insured bank was precluded from recovery under the bond for losses resulting from the cashier's larceny or embezzlement. *Eland State Bank v. Mass. Bonding & Ins. Co.*, 162 N.W. 662.

C. Who Must Learn of the Dishonesty to Trigger the Termination Provision?

1. Commercial Crime Policies

6th Cir. 2005 (Ohio). The president of the insured, a subsidiary of a larger corporation, "borrowed" funds from client accounts and executed promissory notes for the "loans." The general manager learned about the loans. An officer of the parent corporation learned about the loans and terminated the president, who was subsequently convicted of wire fraud. The policies provided for termination as to any employee upon discovery of dishonesty by "you" or by "any of your partners, officers or directors" not in collusion with the employee. The first issue on appeal was whether the general manager's discovery terminated coverage. The Sixth Circuit declined to consider whether the general manager was an "officer" because that argument was not made below in the district court. The court then held that "you" as applied to a corporation was ambiguous, without discussing the definition of "you" in the policy. *Century Bus. Servs., Inc. v. Utica Mut. Ins. Co.*, 122 F. App'x 196.

8th Cir. 1970 (Ark.). The knowledge possessed by a branch manager of one of the insured's grocery stores that an employee had previously committed burglary and larceny was imputed to the insured to preclude coverage under the employee dishonesty policy. *Ritchie Grocer Co. v. Aetna Cas. & Sur. Co.*, 426 F.2d 499.

9th Cir. 1992 (Cal.). The branch manager's knowledge of an employee's dishonesty was imputed to the insured such that coverage was canceled as to that employee. The insured argued that the employee's dishonesty, if any, had not been discovered by the insured because the branch manager was neither the "insured" nor a "partner or officer." The court rejected this argument. Branch managers, the court noted, are agents of the corporation; and corporations cannot act apart from their agents. Accordingly, the branch manager was the "insured" for purposes of the cancellation clause. *Mercedes-Benz of N. Am. v. Hartford Acc. & Indem. Co.*, 974 F.2d 1342.

D. Mass. 1985. The court imputed the controller's knowledge and that of "other executives" to the insured to trigger the automatic termination provision. *Boston Mut. Life Ins. Co. v. Fireman's Fund Ins. Co.*, 613 F. Supp. 1090.

W.D. Wash. 2005. After an employee robbed the insured, a food grocer, the loss was presented under a commercial crime policy. Although the employee had previously submitted an employment application disclosing a prior conviction for grand theft auto, the court denied the carrier's motion for summary judgment based on the automatic termination provision because the factual record did not establish knowledge by the partners, members, managers, etc., of this prior dishonesty. The employment application was given to a "cashier/bookkeeper" who appeared to have performed a "ministerial role in accepting applications." Thus the court would not impute the cashier's actual knowledge of prior dishonesty to the Named Insured. *Akins Foods, Inc. v. Am. & Foreign Ins. Co.*, No. C04-2195JLR, 2005 WL 2090678.

Conn. 1990. The knowledge of an employee may be imputed to an employer if the employee holds a position of management or control, with either an explicit or an inferred duty to report known dishonesty of a fellow employee. A store manager and bookkeeper discovered that an employee had embezzled $6,000. They arranged for the employee to repay the amount, which she did. The store owner was not notified of the employee's theft. The store brought an action on its fidelity bond two years later when the employee was again caught embezzling funds. Denying coverage under the employee dishonesty insurance policy, the court held that the store manager's and the bookkeeper's knowledge of the employee's prior embezzlements terminated coverage. *E. Udolf, Inc. v. Aetna Cas. & Sur. Co.*, 573 A.2d 1211.

Me. 2002. The chairman of the board became aware that the company's president made unauthorized personal use of the corporate credit card. The chairman did not notify the insurer of the president's acts. The company accepted the president's agreement to discontinue use and repay the charges. The president instead continued his unauthorized use of the credit card and was subsequently terminated. The court held that the chairman's knowledge of the president's unauthorized use and non-payment of the debt triggered both an obligation to notify the insurer and the automatic termination provision. *Acadia Ins. Co. v. Keiser Indus., Inc.*, 793 A.2d 495.

Mo. App. 2003. The court addressed whether commercial crime policies had been automatically terminated at the time of employee thefts, due to one party's discovery of another's dishonest acts. The court determined that the control necessary to invoke the "alter ego rule" is not just majority or complete stock control but complete domination of finances, policy, and business practices. The court thus held summary judgment on the automatic termination issue was improper. *East Attucks Cmty. Hous., Inc. v. Old Republic Sur. Co.*, 114 S.W.3d 311.

N.C. 1984. The court held that knowledge by the insured of an employee's first series of embezzlements precluded recovery, under the terms of the theft and embezzlement provisions of an insurance policy, for a subsequent series of embezzlements. *B&H Supply Co. v. Ins. Co. of N. Am.* 311 S.E.2d 643.

2.   Other Policy or Bond Forms

4th Cir. 1967 (Md.). Analyzing a Savings and Loan Blanket Bond (Form No. 22), the court held that summary judgment should not have been granted in favor of Aetna by the lower court where a question of fact remained as to whether an employee's defalcations were known to any of the officers and directors of the bank. Although some of the losses claimed by the bank allegedly resulted from a conspiracy among the employee and the officers and directors, the bank also contended that certain losses resulted through the acts of the employee without the knowledge or participation by those same officers and directors. *Phoenix Sav. & Loan, Inc. v. Aetna Cas. & Sur. Co.*, 381 F.2d 245.

5th Cir. 1985 (Tex.). The court held that a Bankers Blanket Bond (1969 Form 24) was terminated before it was renewed due to the bank vice president's knowledge of the bank president's dishonest and fraudulent acts relating to use of bank funds. The court reasoned that, because the bank was wholly owned by the vice president, his knowledge of the president's activity of using funds to finance a side business barred the claim made under the bankers blanket bond for losses resulting from the dishonest activity of the president. *City State Bank in Wellington v. USF&G*, 778 F.2d 1103.

5th Cir. 1981 (La.). A bank president made fictitious loans to allow use of bank funds for political contributions, in order to gain business for the bank. The evidence showed that the board of directors of the insured bank had knowledge or information of prior fraudulent or dishonest activities of the bank president. Finding for the insurer, the court held that a bond provision excluding coverage after knowledge of an employee's dishonesty is valid. *Century Progressive Bank v. Fireman's Fund Ins. Co.*, 658 F.2d 377.

5th Cir. 1972 (Tex.). That the president of the insured bank was the controlling shareholder and actually ran the bank did not justify imputing his knowledge of his own fraudulent acts to the insured bank so as to terminate the insurer's liability under the Bankers Blanket Bond, where there was no showing that other directors neglected their duties and responsibilities or that the directors knew of the fraudulent acts of the president. *FDIC v. Lott*, 460 F.2d 82.

5th Cir. 1968 (Ga.). The knowledge of a partner who had sole and complete management of operations of the insured unincorporated bank as to his own misappropriation was imputable to the insured bank at the time the partner made the application for a Bankers Blanket Bond, even though the application provided that such knowledge as to any officer signing for the bank may have with respect to his own personal acts and conduct is not imputable to the bank. *Harley v. Hartford Acc. & Indem. Co.*, 389 F.2d 91 (Fifth Circuit essentially adopted the district court's opinion in *Hartford Acc. & Indem. Co. v. Hartley*, 275 F. Supp. 610 (M.D. Ga. 1967)).

8th Cir. 1993 (S.D.). First Dakota National Bank, after buying failed American State Bank, sued its fidelity insurer for losses allegedly caused by dishonest former employees of American, seeking recovery under two fidelity bonds. The insurer contended that American was aware of dishonest acts by the employees as of a given date, which terminated coverage for such employees thereafter. The court held that the knowledge of the two dishonest employees themselves could not be imputed to the bank because their interests were adverse to those of the bank, and there was insufficient evidence that a non-colluding officer learned of a loss covered under the bond as of the given date. *First Dakota Nat'l Bank v. St. Paul Fire & Marine Ins. Co.*, 2 F.3d 801.

8th Cir. 1971 (S.D.). Fidelity insurer failed to establish as a matter of law that board of directors or employees of the insured corporation were aware of the insured president's conduct in improperly transferring funds to related companies and to himself. *Gen. Fin. Corp. v. Fid. & Cas. Co. of N.Y.*, 439 F.2d 981.

10th Cir. 1994 (Utah). The FDIC, in its corporate capacity, sued fidelity insurers to recover on two Savings and Loan Blanket Bonds for losses caused by alleged fraud and negligence of former officers and directors of a failed savings and loan. Both bonds provided for termination of coverage as to any employee upon the insured's learning of any dishonest act committed by such person. The court held that the automatic termination provision would apply only if a non-colluding person learned of the dishonest acts prior to the latest date of the relevant transactions in the case. *FDIC v. Oldenburg*, 34 F.3d 1529.

10th Cir. 1991 (Okla.). Where bank officer was aware of a check kiting scheme by the bank's chairman and withheld such information from her monthly reports, the court held such actions constituted collusion and did not trigger the automatic termination provision of the policy. Alternatively, the court held that applying the automatic termination provision would be contrary to the legislative intent of the Oklahoma insurance statutes. *Adair State Bank v. Am. Cas. Co. of Reading, Pa.*, 949 F.2d 1067.

10th Cir. 1936 (Okla.). The insured's board of directors made a decision to procure blanket position bonds. The insured's secretary-treasurer certified in the applications that the insured had no knowledge of employees' infidelity. The secretary-treasurer's knowledge that he and two others had embezzled money from the company was not imputable to the company so as to preclude recovery on the bonds for subsequent embezzlement of the secretary-treasurer and others. *Maryland Cas. Co. v. Tulsa Indus. Loan & Inv. Co.*, 83 F.2d 14.

D. Ariz. 1994. The RTC brought an action to recover on a fidelity bond issued to a savings and loan association when losses were sustained from an illegal loan approved by the insured's president. Testimony by the insured's CFO and vice president revealed that both knew the president had authorized the illegal loan and suspected that the president had lied about how the loan would be handled. The court found that this evidence was sufficient to terminate coverage. *RTC v. Aetna Cas. & Sur. Co.*, 873 F. Supp. 1386.

D. Conn. 1997. An insured savings institution sought coverage for loan losses allegedly caused by its president's presentation to the insured's board of directors of nine loans in which the president maintained an undisclosed interest. The court entered summary judgment in favor of the insurer because prior to the initiation of the bond period, non-colluding members of the insured's board learned of the president's dishonesty with respect to the first of the nine loans, but did not take action because the loan was performing. *Community Sav. Bank v. Fed. Ins. Co.*, 960 F. Supp. 16.

E.D. La. 1993. Discovery by the insured can occur even if the discovery is made by an individual not in the specified categories. The court imputed the knowledge of the insured's outside counsel to the insured for purposes of applying the automatic termination clause in Section 12 of the Bankers Blanket Bond. The court observed that the "inclusion of the words 'or any director or officer' does not restrict the insured to directors and officers." *First Nat'l Bank of Louisville v. Lustig*, 150 F.R.D. 548.

Bankr. W.D. Pa. 1994. The insured's president/majority shareholder/director completed a fidelity policy application but failed to disclose that he had engaged in embezzlement. The insurer argued that, because the president knew he was guilty of embezzlement at the time the application was prepared, his knowledge was imputed to the insured and coverage was terminated. The policy application, however, provided that the knowledge of any officer signing for the insured applicant, unknown to the applicant, was not imputable to the applicant. The court held that this language reflected an intent that the knowledge of the individual who provided the information for the applicant would not be imputed to the insured. *Mecum Fin., Inc. v. Md. Ins. Group*, 167 B.R. 799.

Bankr. E.D. Pa. 1993. The court applied the adverse domination theory to the automatic termination provision in a fidelity bond. The two sole corporate officers of the insured egregiously misappropriated customers' funds. The court declined to impute the defalcators' knowledge of their wrongdoing to the insured so as to terminate coverage at the commencement of their wrongdoing. *Lloyd Sec., Inc. v. Nat'l Union Fire Ins. Co. of Pittsburgh, Pa.*, 153 B.R. 677.

E.D. Wis. 1945. The court held that the cancellation provision of a fidelity bond had no application where the evidence showed that every officer and employee of the insured, with respect to the employee's acts, was in collusion with the defalcating employee. *Duel v. Nat'l Sur. Corp.*, 64 F. Supp. 961.

Ga. App. 1995. An insurer sought a declaratory judgment that its fidelity bond was terminated as to allegedly dishonest acts of employees of the insured bank. The court held that the termination provision did not apply to the employees collectively but applied instead to individuals. Therefore, the insurer was required to show prior knowledge of dishonest acts with regard to each of the ten allegedly dishonest employees, each individually. *Banca Nazionale del Lavoro v. Lloyds*, 458 S.E.2d 142.

Iowa 1968. The knowledge of the managing agent of the insured bank, who was also active in management of an insurance agency partially owned by the insured bank, that he had been embezzling funds was not imputable to the insured bank and did not preclude recovery under the Bankers Blanket Bond obtained by him. *Mechanicsville Trust & Sav. Bank v. Hawkeye-Security Ins. Co.*, 158 N.W.2d 89.

Minn. 1976. Members of the insured bank's board of directors were aware of the bank's relationship to customers at the same time the board decided that the bank should buy property for which the same customers were seeking a loan from the bank. The court held there was no coverage under the Bankers Blanket Bond issued to the insured bank for the bank's liability, if any, to the customers. Thus, the insurer had no duty to defend the action brought by the customers charging the bank with fraud, dishonesty, and breach of fiduciary relationship. *Farmers & Merch. State Bank of Pierz v. St. Paul Fire & Marine Ins. Co.*, 242 N.W.2d 840.

Miss. 1969. An employer had no obligation to volunteer information about his knowledge of a re-employed employee's previous defalcation and the employer's knowledge thereof did not preclude coverage for subsequent defalcations by the same employee, where the issuance of a one-man fidelity bond for such employee had been a condition precedent to the employee's re-employment and was a transaction entirely between the employee and the insurer. *St. Paul Fire & Marine Ins. Co. v. Comer*, 227 So. 2d 859.

Miss. 1934. A Bankers Blanket Bond was terminated as to the president of the insured bank when he loaned money to himself without approval of the board of directors, if the misappropriation was then known to the cashier and vice president. Alternatively, the bond was terminated when the board subsequently approved the loan. *Fid. & Dep. Co. v. Merchs. & Marine Bank*, 151 So. 373.

Va. 1946. A Blanket Position Bond issued to a partnership in the installment jewelry business provided that the bond is canceled as to any employee, if the insured is a co-partnership, immediately upon discovery by any partner thereof of any fraudulent or dishonest act by the employee. The court held that the cancellation clause did not become operative when the manager discovered the employee's overdraft, as such knowledge was not imputable to the partnership. *Hartford Acc. & Indem. Co. v. Singer*, 39 S.E.2d 505.

Wash. 1939. The president of a corporation fraudulently concealed his previous acts of dishonesty in order to induce the carrier to issue a fidelity bond. The court held that there was no coverage under the bond because the previous defalcations were not disclosed in the application for the bond. The court found that the bond was void from its inception. *Post v. Md. Cas. Co.*, 97 P.2d 173.

D. What Constitutes Discovery or Knowledge of Dishonesty?

1. Commercial Crime Policies

D. Ariz. 2009. Analyzing "what discovery meant under the Federal policy," the court held that "discovery" occurs when the insured [has] knowledge—not merely suspicion—of the existence of such facts as would justify a careful and prudent man in charging another with fraud or dishonesty." *EaglePitcher Mgmt. Co. v. Zurich Am. Ins. Co.*, 640 F. Supp. 2d 1109.

D. Kan. 1989. The termination language in a Comprehensive Dishonesty, Disappearance and Destruction Policy precludes recovery for losses from dishonest acts only if it is established that the insured had "'actual knowledge and not mere suspicion or a reason to know of the wrongdoing.'" *Koch Indus., Inc. v. Nat'l Union Fire Ins. Co. of Pittsburgh, Pa.*, No. 89-1158-K, 1989 WL 158039.

D.N.J. 1993. The insurer denied a claim under a Comprehensive Dishonesty, Disappearance, and Destruction Policy for losses from an employee's dishonest acts because the insured had prior information about the employee's dishonesty. The court observed that the insured had "sufficient 'information,' if not 'knowledge'" of the employee's dishonesty to trigger the termination provision. Applying the policy term "information," the court adopted a state-of-mind standard and entered summary judgment for the insurer. *Cooper Sportswear Mfg. Co. v. Hartford Cas. Ins. Co.*, 818 F. Supp. 721.

W.D. Okla. 1973. A Comprehensive Dishonesty, Disappearance and Destruction Policy (Form B) provided that coverage was terminated as to any employee immediately upon discovery by the insured of any fraudulent or dishonest act on the part of that employee. The court observed that, in order for the automatic termination provision to be triggered, the particular dishonest act does not have to qualify for coverage under a fidelity insuring agreement. The court held that the insured had discovered its manager's dishonesty so as to terminate coverage no later than April, when the board of directors of the insured had authorized loan transitions in February, March, and April nearly identical to that for which the claim was asserted. *Alfalfa Elec. Coop., Inc. v. Travelers Indem. Co.*, 376 F. Supp. 901.

W.D. Wash. 2005. After the employee had worked at a grocery store for several months, the store manager had him fill out an employment application. On it the employee revealed a prior conviction for grand theft auto. The store manager denied seeing the application, which was given to the store's cashier/bookkeeper. The employee later participated in a robbery. The prior dishonesty condition provided that the insurance was canceled as to any employee immediately upon discovery of theft or any other dishonest act by "You" or by "[a]ny of your partners, members, managers, officers, directors or trustees not in collusion with the employee." The court held that "discovery" required actual knowledge, not constructive knowledge. The cashier/bookkeeper had actual knowledge, but the court stated that "given the undeveloped factual record, the court refrains from imputing [the bookkeeper's] actual knowledge to [the Insured]." *Akins Foods, Inc. v. Am. & Foreign Ins. Co.*, No. C04-2195JLR, 2005 WL 2090678.

La. App. 1974. The court found that the insured under a Commercial Blanket Bond did not have knowledge or information that an employee was engaged in continuous acts of theft and, therefore, the automatic termination provision did not bar coverage. The court observed that Hall, apparently president or CEO of the insured, had been wrong to trust his defalcating manager but that Hall's mistaken trust did not constitute knowledge of the employee's thefts. *Harris W. Hall Co. v. Security Ins. Co.*, 289 So. 2d 832.

La. App. 1969. A Blanket Crime Policy provided for termination of coverage as to any employee from the time that the insured or any partner or officer thereof not in collusion has knowledge of any fraudulent or dishonest act by such employee. The court held that an employee who, eight years prior to the embezzlement, was "short" in his accounts and paid appropriate adjustments, did not commit dishonest acts within the meaning of the termination clause because "every man is presumed to be honest until the contrary is established." *Salley Grocer Co. v. Hartford Acc. & Indem. Co.*, 223 So. 2d 5.

Me. 2002. The insured's chairman of the board discovered that the insured's president made unauthorized personal use of the corporate credit card. The chairman did not notify the insurer of the president's acts. The insured accepted the president's agreement to discontinue use of the corporate credit card and to repay the charges. The president instead continued his unauthorized use of the credit card and subsequently was terminated. The court held that the chairman's knowledge of the president's unauthorized use and non-payment of the debt triggered both an obligation to notify the insurer and the application of the automatic termination clause. *Acadia Ins. Co. v. Keiser Indus., Inc.*, 793 A.2d 495.

N.Y. App. 2005. The appellate court affirmed summary judgment for the insurer on a commercial crime policy because the insured knew, before it submitted the application that its employee had been found civilly liable for fraud and had made money transfers that other officers questioned. In this "prior knowledge" case, the court applied an objective standard of discovery of the defalcator's dishonesty prior to inception of the policy: "Under these circumstances, plaintiff cannot claim, as represented in its application for the insurance, that it then had no reason to suspect this person's honesty . . . ." *Am. Rice, Inc. v. Nat'l Union Fire Ins. Co. of Pittsburgh, Pa.*, 795 N.Y.S.2d 191.

2. Other Policy or Bond Forms

U.S. 1898. The insurer denied coverage on the basis that the notice of loss was furnished too late under the bond language, which required notice "as soon as practicable." The court found that the notice provision was not triggered by the facts known to the insured. The court observed that "mere suspicion" of dishonesty is insufficient for notice purposes and that the insured has no obligation to provide notice until it has acquired "knowledge" of some specific fraudulent or dishonest act. *Am. Sur. Co. v. Pauly*, 170 U.S. 133.

4th Cir. 1970 (Md.). The corporate successor of a savings and loan association on a Savings and Loan Blanket Bond (Form No. 22) failed to establish as a matter of law that discovery of any defalcation by the insured occurred before the conservatorship began. Thus, the automatic termination provision was inapplicable to bar coverage. *Phoenix Sav. & Loan, Inc. v. Aetna Cas. & Sur. Co.*, 427 F.2d 862.

5th Cir. 1981 (La.). A bank's president made fictitious loans to allow use of bank funds for political contributions, the purpose of which was to gain business for the bank. The board of directors of the insured bank had knowledge of prior fraudulent or dishonest activities of the bank president. The court held that coverage terminated under the Bankers Blanket Bond. *Century Progressive Bank v. Fireman's Fund Ins. Co.*, 658 F.2d 377.

5th Cir. 1970 (Tex.). The insured under a Bankers Blanket Bond is not required to give notice when the insured merely suspects or has reason to suspect wrongdoing, but only when it has acquired knowledge of some specific fraudulent or dishonest act. The insured bank was not required to give notice to the insurer when it discovered that real estate notes purchased by the insured bank did not conform to the type authorized for purchase by a national bank, even if it did have reason to suspect wrongdoing but had not yet discovered the fraudulent conduct of the director. *FDIC v. Aetna Cas. & Sur. Co.*, 426 F.2d 729.

5th Cir. 1939 (Tex.). The Fifth Circuit affirmed the judgment against the insurer on a bank's fidelity bond because the evidence established that the insured had no knowledge or belief that the defalcating employee was dishonest. The court declined to adopt the carrier's argument that, if the insured had undertaken inquiries more diligently, it could have discovered that the employee was untrustworthy. The court observed that the case authorities "make it clear that neither negligence nor inattention, nor any failure to discover what by diligence might have been discovered, nothing, in fact, short of actual discovery by the bank of dishonesty or a positive breach of an imperative condition, will defeat claims for loss caused by that dishonesty, unless it is otherwise provided in the contract." *Am. Employers' Ins. Co. v. Cable*, 108 F.2d 225.

6th Cir. 1982 (Mich.). The insurer denied coverage under a Brokers Blanket Bond based on the insured's knowledge of an employee's unauthorized purchase of stock for a customer's account from a prior employer. The court held that the termination provision was ambiguous because the language implied there would be prior effective coverage for an employee who was hired with insured's knowledge of the dishonest conduct. The court, however, refused to construe the ambiguity against the insurer due to the prior course of conduct between the insurer and the insured, whereby the insurer had twice contacted the insurer prior to employment of individuals with tarnished pasts, for purposes of determining whether coverage could be obtained. *William C. Roney & Co. v. Fed. Ins. Co.*, 674 F.2d 587.

8th Cir. 1991 (Mo.). The court held that the automatic termination clause of the Brokers Blanket Bond (Form 14) was triggered to bar coverage. The Eighth Circuit affirmed the denial of coverage because the broker had knowledge of at least four complaints by clients alleging dishonesty and fraud by the same employee. In finding that the insured had learned of the employee's prior dishonesty, the court emphasized, in particular, that the insured broker's vice president characterized the employee's unauthorized limited partnership offering as "at best, deceitful." *Newhard, Cook & Co. v. Ins. Co. of N. Am.*, 929 F.2d 1355.

8th Cir. 1975 (Mo). The insured bank knew that its president was part owner of a livestock company, that the president had previously used his position as a bank officer to give the livestock company immediate credit on checks deposited but not yet collected, and that this practice had been criticized by the comptroller of the currency. Additionally, the bank knew that the president had made arrangements with another bank to cover checks drawn on the livestock company's account on the day they arrived at that bank. The court held that the bank had knowledge of dishonest and fraudulent acts of the bank president, thus terminating the bankers blanket bond as to the president. *First Nat'l Bank of Sikestown v. Transamerica Ins. Co.*, 514 F.2d 981.

8th Cir. 1971 (Mo.). The court held that discovery of the bank vice president's dishonesty occurred either when the insured bank verified that the vice president had received payoff for a loan, or when the vice president's statements to a bank investigator were found to be in conflict with documentary evidence already in the insured bank's possession. The court noted that, in determining when discovery of an employee's fraud has occurred, the trier of fact must find the pertinent underlying facts known to the insured and determine the subjective conclusions reasonably drawn therefrom by the insured. In addition, the court observed that suspicion alone does not rise to the level of discovery. *USF&G v. Empire State Bank*, 448 F.2d 360.

10th Cir. 1970 (Okla.). The court held that the evidence supported the finding that the bank board of directors' review of a national bank examiner's report disapproving certain practices did not constitute notice of the bank president's fraudulent acts involving fictitious loans. Thus, the court affirmed the district court's judgment that the Bankers Blanket Bond and excess fidelity policy covered the loss resulting from the president's fraudulent acts. *First Nat'l Bank of Cushing v. Sec. Mut. Cas. Co.*, 431 F.2d 1025.

10th Cir. 1941 (N.M.). The court determined that the insured on a fidelity bond was not required to report "merely suspicious conduct" but only "knowledge that would justify a careful and prudent man in charging another with fraud or dishonesty." Thus, the court found that the insured's acceptance of the defalcating employee's explanation of dishonored checks was reasonable under all the circumstances. *Am. Employers' Ins. Co. v. Raton Wholesale Liquor Co.*, 123 F.2d 283.

N.D. Ill. 1990. The court found the terms of the automatic termination provision in an Executive Risk Policy ambiguous and held that knowledge of an employee's prior acts of dishonesty had to be actual and not imputed for the automatic termination provision to bar coverage. *Foote, Cone & Belding Commc'ns, Inc. v. Fed. Ins. Co.*, 749 F. Supp. 892.

E.D. Ky. 1989. The court held that the termination clause of the Bankers Blanket Bond had not been triggered even though the board of directors should have known not only that the scope of certain loans had reached alarming levels but also that the loans were well in excess of the employees' personal lending limits. The court opined as follows: "While a Board may not hide from liability behind poor management practices, case law requires actual knowledge of some specific fraudulent or dishonest act which might involve the insurer." *FDIC v. Reliance Ins. Corp.*, 716 F. Supp. 1001.

E.D. La. 1993. A bank brought an action against its insurer under a Bankers Blanket Bond, claiming damages for losses allegedly caused by a former loan officer who issued fraudulent reports in connection with proposed loans. The court held that the termination clause of the bond, ending coverage for employee dishonesty when the insured "learned" of the employee's dishonest or fraudulent act, applied when the bank had actual knowledge of facts that would cause a reasonable person in the bank's position to infer that the employee had committed dishonest acts. *First Nat'l Bank of Louisville v. Lustig*, 150 F.R.D. 548.

D. Mass. 1985. An insured brought an action against an insurer under a fidelity bond, seeking to recover on a Fidelity Name Schedule Bond for losses resulting from dishonest acts of an administrator. The court held that the insurer could not recover because of its failure to give notice as required under the bond. Applying a pure subjective standard, the court found that the insured had subjective awareness of the employee's prior dishonesty. *Boston Mut. Life Ins. Co. v. Fireman's Fund Ins. Co.*, 613 F. Supp. 1090.

M.D.N.C. 1959. Knowledge available to the insured must rise above a mere suspicion of loss to invoke the automatic termination clause. Knowledge of inefficient business procedures or irregularities and discrepancies in accounts, if it is as consistent with the integrity of bank employees as with their dishonesty, does not constitute "discovery" within a Bankers Blanket Bond provision. *Wachovia Bank & Trust Co. v. Mfrs. Cas. Ins. Co.*, 171 F. Supp. 369.

D.N.J. 2006. An insured stockbroker's knowledge of its former employee's dishonesty prior to the commencement date of coverage under a fidelity bond constituted discovery and barred the insured's claim. The bond specified that it terminated as to an employee upon the insured's learning of any dishonest activities on the part of that employee. *Inv. Center v. Great Am. Ins.*, No. 04-CV-6204, 2006 WL 1074676.

D.N.J. 1977. The court held that the fact that the board of directors of the insured bank may have had knowledge, by virtue of state banking department reports of examination, that the amount of ship loans was excessive and their documentation poor was not by itself sufficient to warrant a conclusion by the board that the bank president and an attorney/director had committed dishonest acts. *Midland Bank & Trust Co. v. Fid. & Dep. Co. of Md.*, 442 F. Supp. 960.

N.D. Ohio 1964. The court found that officers of a savings and loan company had actual knowledge of specific acts constituting dishonesty that terminated coverage as to the defalcating employee: the dishonest branch manager had lied as to challenged accounts, had knowingly permitted false documents and values to be the basis of disbursements of company funds, had permitted a check float, and had falsely certified that he had inspected a nonexistent security. "Knowledge or discovery of dishonesty does not depend upon knowledge of the total misconduct when viewed in retrospect and with the obvious advantages of hindsight, but rather upon knowledge of facts which, in the light of proven circumstances surrounding those facts and in the light of reasonable inferences which can be drawn from those facts, would inform the ordinary, reasonable and sensible employer that dishonesty has occurred . . . ." *City Loan & Sav. Co. v. Employers' Liab. Assur. Corp.*, 249 F. Supp. 633.

D.P.R. 1991. The FDIC brought an action against an insurer on a Savings and Loan Blanket Bond seeking indemnification for alleged fraudulent acts of an employee of the failed bank. The court denied the insurer's motion for summary judgment, noting that, unless the bond provides otherwise, even the strongest suspicion does not amount to knowledge or discovery of an employee's dishonesty. Nothing short of actual discovery of dishonesty or positive breach of a condition by the employee would terminate the bond as to the defalcating employee. *FDIC v. CNA Cas.*, 786 F. Supp. 1082.

D.P.R. 1972. Although there were suspicions material to the risk that should in good conscience have been reported to the insurer as a condition to obtaining increased bond coverage, there was no actual knowledge of losses or unlawful, fraudulent acts, the concealment of which would breach the conditions of the bond. *Banco de San German Inc. v. Maryland Cas. Co.*, 344 F. Supp. 496.

M.D. Tenn. 1990. The FDIC, as receiver for a closed bank, filed an action against the bank's insurer on a Bankers Blanket Bond for damages due to defalcations by the bank president. The court held that knowledge by junior officers of the executive committee did not constitute the insured's knowledge of dishonest acts. The court noted that an officer's suspicion that payments are dishonest is insufficient to constitute discovery of dishonesty; discovery of dishonesty occurs only where the officer has "knowledge which would justify a careful and prudent man in charging another with fraud or dishonesty." *FDIC v. St. Paul Fire & Marine Ins. Co.*, 738 F. Supp. 1146.

Ariz. App. 1971. The court analyzed whether acts prior to coverage under a fidelity bond were dishonest so as to preclude coverage. The court observed that, in determining the insured's knowledge of prior acts of the employee, the question is not whether the employee's acts were in fact dishonest, but rather whether, based on the facts known to the employer, the employer should reasonably have perceived the dishonesty. *Md. Cas. Co. v. C.A. Clements*, 487 P.2d 437.

Ill. App. 1995. The insured brought a coverage action under a Public Employees' Bond containing an automatic cancellation provision canceling coverage as to any employee immediately upon discovery of any act that would constitute liability under the bond. The court held that the cancellation provision is governed by a subjective standard and was triggered when the insured had actual knowledge that its employees were involved in the unauthorized expenditure of funds. *Kinzer v. Fid. & Dep. Co. of Md.*, 652 N.E.2d 20.

Iowa 1979. The court found that, under a banker's fidelity bond, the insured did not have prior knowledge of the defalcating employee's misconduct that would trigger the automatic termination clause. While an earlier bank examination disclosed to the board of directors three loans made in excess of the bank's authority, the court found this knowledge immaterial because these loans, standing alone, did not amount to dishonest or fraudulent acts. In addition, the board of directors had reason to believe the practice had been discontinued. *FDIC v. Nat'l Sur. Corp.*, 281 N.W.2d 816.

Kan. 1989. The termination language in a Bankers Blanket Bond required the insured to have actual knowledge and not mere suspicion or reason to know of wrongdoing in order for coverage to terminate as to an employee. *First Hays Banshares, Inc. v. Kansas Bankers Sur. Co.*, 769 P.2d 1184.

Me. 1941. Discovery by the insured employer, after the inception of the fidelity policy, that an employee had embezzled funds prior to the commencement thereof, did not terminate the bond as to that employee. The relevant termination language provided that coverage would terminate as to any employee "upon discovery of loss through that employee." The court observed that the language did not unambiguously provide that discovery of losses incurred before the execution of the bond would terminate coverage as that employee. *Reliable Furniture Co. v. Union Safe Dep. & Trust Co. of Del.*, 21 A.2d 834.

N.J. App. 1993. Mere suspicions by a savings and loan about irregularities or improper conduct in its contractor's servicing of mortgages did not require the savings and loan to report those acts to its fidelity bond carrier under the bond's automatic termination clause. *N.J. Sav. & Loan Ass'n v. Fid. & Dep. Co. of Md.*, 660 A.2d 1287.

N.Y. 1930. The court stated an objective standard for automatic termination in a fidelity bond, a quotation that is frequently cited: "The appeal is to the mores rather than to the statutes. Dishonesty, unlike embezzlement or larceny, is not a term of art. Even so, the measure of its meaning is not a standard of perfection, but an infirmity of purpose so opprobrious or furtive as to be fairly characterized as dishonest in the common speech of men. 'Our guide is the reasonable expectation and purpose of the ordinary business man when making an ordinary business contract.'" *World Exch. Bank v. Commercial Cas. Ins. Co.*, 173 N.E. 902.

Okla. 1916. Even where there is no bond provision concerning automatic cancellation upon the insured's learning of the employee's prior dishonesty, the insured must nonetheless deal with the underwriter consistent with "good faith and fair dealing." The insurer should not, therefore, be liable for losses that occur after the insured learns the employee is embezzling. *Phoenix Ins. Co. of Hartford v. Newell*, 159 P. 1127.

Pa. 1935. A Bankers Blanket Bond was procured upon the false statement of the chief executive officer that no similar losses had been sustained. The insured bank had no information that indicated any officers were dishonest. The court, nonetheless, held that the chief executive officer's knowledge that he himself had embezzled a large amount of the bank's funds was imputable to the insured bank so as to defeat recovery on the bond for his subsequent embezzlements. *Gordon v. Cont'l Cas. Co.*, 181 A. 574.

Pa. App. 1956. The court held that the cancellation clause of the policy referred only to dishonesty of an employee while in the employ of the insured and declined to deem the policy cancelled as to the defalcating employee whom the insured's service manager knew was discharged from his prior employment for equipment theft. The relevant language of the policy stated that the policy shall be "cancelled as to any employee: (a) Immediately upon discovery by the assured . . . of any fraudulent or dishonest act on the part of such employee." The court observed that the cancellation clause contained no express provision for discovery of the employee's dishonesty during prior employment. *Ne. Lincoln-Mercury v. Century Indem. Co. of Hartford*, 124 A.2d 420.

Tex. App. 1984. A bank brought suit to recover under a Bankers Blanket Bond (Form 24) for loan losses resulting from dishonest acts of a former bank president. That bank president, as a member of the Executive Loan Committee, approved loans to a borrower with whom he was a partner in trading securities without disclosing this relationship to the directors. The court held that coverage terminated as to the bank president when the board of directors became aware of facts from which they could infer dishonesty and, therefore, the insurer was liable only for losses on loans made before coverage terminated. In addition, renewal of the bond did not reinstate coverage for the bank president because coverage had already been terminated as to the president. *Fid. & Cas. Co. v. Central Bank of Houston*, 672 S.W.2d 641.

Utah App. 1991. In 1982 Home Savings and Loan replaced its F&D Savings and Loan Blanket Bond with a similar Aetna bond. Home Savings truthfully stated in the Aetna application that it had incurred no insurable losses over the $5,000 deductible within the past five years. At the time the Aetna bond was completed, an action by second mortgage loan recipients was pending that involved a Home Savings employee whom it had learned was engaged in fraudulent and dishonest acts and had fired in December 1981. The court held that neither Aetna nor F&D was liable for losses caused by dishonest acts by the employee that occurred after the December 1981 discovery, but both were liable for such acts prior to that time that were discovered within their successive bond periods. *Home Sav. & Loan Co. v. Aetna Cas. & Sur. Co.*, 817 P.2d 341.

E. When Must the Dishonesty be Discovered to Terminate Coverage?

1. Before or After the Bond/Policy Incepts

4th Cir. 1979 (S.C.). An insured mortgage broker, prior to the effective date of fidelity policies, discovered during the course of a routine audit that the vice president was falsely certifying pre-advances for certain HUD/FHA loans. The court held that the bonding companies were not liable for losses sustained by the insured because of the vice president's false certification of letters of credit after the effective date of the policies. *C. Douglas Wilson & Co. v. Ins. Co. of N. Am.*, 590 F.2d 1275.

D. Ariz. 1994. RTC brought an action to recover on a fidelity bond issued to a savings and loan association when losses were sustained from an illegal loan approved by the insured's president. The fidelity bond contained a termination provision providing that the bond would be deemed terminated or cancelled as to any employee "as soon as any insured or any director or officer not in collusion with such person, shall learn of any dishonest or fraudulent act committed by such person at any time against the insured or any person or entity." Testimony by the insured's CFO and vice president revealed that both knew that the president had authorized the illegal loan and suspected that the president had lied about how the loan would be handled. The court found that this evidence was sufficient to terminate coverage: "Under the termination provision, the policy never goes into effect with respect to an employee if, before the effective date of the policy, directors or officers of the policyholder were aware of the employee's dishonest or fraudulent act and failed to report it." *RTC v. Aetna Cas. & Sur. Co.*, 873 F. Supp. 1386.

D. Del. 2011. While the court found that fact issues remained as to whether the relevant persons possessed knowledge of dishonest or fraudulent acts by the employee, thus terminating coverage going forward, the court seemed to acknowledge that knowledge obtained prior to the fidelity bond's inception would trigger the automatic termination provision. The carrier argued that the insured had knowledge of dishonesty "prior to the bond's inception," however, the court found that because of remaining fact issues, the carrier "is not entitled to summary judgment on the ground that the bond's coverage for [the employee] terminated at inception." *Arrowood Indem. Co. v. Hartford Fire Ins. Co.*, 774 F. Supp. 2d 636.

Bankr. N.D. Ga. 1995. The fidelity policy provided that: (i) "coverage of an employee terminates when a noncolluding officer discovers 'any act of theft or other fraudulent or dishonest act by the Employee"; and (ii) excluded coverage for loss caused by an Employee if an officer of the insured knows of acts of theft or other fraudulent conduct committed during employment or prior to employment. The court found that "the purpose of the exclusion and termination provisions is to limit the surety's exposure to liability due to a known risk." *In re Prime Commercial Corp.*, 187 B.R. 785.

D.N.J. 2006. The court noted that under a fidelity bond issued to a securities broker-dealer, "the bond terminates upon [the firm] learning of any 'dishonest' activities on the part of the employee." After submitting a loss, the carrier declined coverage citing prior knowledge of the employee's fraudulent activity prior to the inception of the bond. The court granted Great American's summary judgment motion, citing both the termination provision and the fact that the firm had knowledge of the particular loss prior to the inception of the discovery based fidelity bond. *The Inv. Ctr. v. Great Am. Ins.*, 2006 WL 1074676 (D.N.J. April 20, 2006).

D.N.J. 1993. The insurer denied a claim under a Comprehensive Dishonesty, Disappearance, and Destruction Policy for losses from an employee's dishonest acts because the insured had prior information about the employee's dishonesty. Analyzing both a policy exclusion precluding coverage for loss if the insured knew of prior employee dishonesty "whether committed before or after the date of employment by the insured" and a cancellation provision providing that the policy shall be cancelled "immediately upon discovery" of dishonest or fraudulent act by the employee, the court held that there was no coverage. Additionally, the court stated that "the policy provision in question should be enforced for the additional reason that it simply embodies the equitable concept that it is unfair to impose upon an insurer the risk of loss from an employee whom the employer knows or has ample reason to suspect is dishonest, but continues to employ." *Cooper Sportswear Mfg. Co. v. Hartford Cas. Ins. Co.*, 818 F. Supp. 721.

D. Or. 2008. Federal issued a Pension and Welfare Fund Fiduciary Dishonesty Policy containing a "Termination as to Any Employee" provision, which provided: "this policy shall terminate as to any Employee (1) immediately upon discovery by any officer of the Insured (not in collusion with such Employee) of any fraudulent or dishonest act on the part of such Employee . . ." Allegations regarding employee fraud emerged in September 2000 and the policy did not incept until November 2000. Thus, the insured had knowledge of fraudulent acts by the employee at the policy's inception. According to the court, since the insured was "already aware of dishonest acts when the [policy] began, [the employee] was never a covered 'employee' under that policy." *United Ass'n Union Local No. 290 ex rel. U.A.U. Local No. 290 Plumber, Steamfitter & Shipfitter Indus. 401(k) Plan & Trust v. Fed. Ins. Co.*, No. CIV.07-1521-HA, 2008 WL 3523271.

La. 1969. The employee cancellation provision in question read: "The coverage of this policy shall not apply to any employee from and after the time that the insured or any partner of officer thereof not in collusion with such employee shall have knowledge or information that such employee has committed any fraudulent or dishonest act in the service of the insured or otherwise, whether such act be committed before or after the date of employment by the insured." Before hiring Mr. Walden, the employer knew of his previous theft conviction and incarceration, and despite the fact that Walden had been pardoned, the knowledge of his previous dishonesty was known prior to the policy inception. The court held that the automatic cancellation clause precluded coverage under the policy for subsequent dishonesty by Walden: "[I]f the insured, then has knowledge of a dishonest person in his employ . . . he is not insured for the dishonest acts of that employee." *Verneco, Inc. v. Fid. & Cas. Co. of N.Y.*, 219 So. 2d 508.

Mich. App. 1997. An auto supply business hired an ex-con through a public "transition of prisoners" program to work at its supply counter. The individual had just completed serving a sentence for breaking and entering and larceny and the employer knew this fact before employing the individual. After the ex-con stole truck parts and equipment from his new employer a loss was submitted to Travelers. Travelers denied coverage under the automatic termination provision, and in subsequent litigation asserted that the policy was automatically canceled as to the employee the moment he was hired because his employer knew he had a criminal record. The court agreed, holding that there was "nothing ambiguous in the policy's cancellation clause." *F.L. Jursik Co. v. Travelers Indem. Ins. Co.*, No. 199913, 1997 WL 33332724.

N.Y. App. 2012. Under the Termination provision in a fidelity bond issued to a bank, coverage terminated as to any employee as soon as an officer or director of the bank learned of any dishonest or fraudulent act committed by such employee. Following a coverage dispute, the bank's president was deposed and he admitted to knowledge of the employee's previous forgeries, which were a violation of the bank's policies. The president stated that the employee was a top performer, thus he was not terminated at the time and remained employed at the bank when the policy was issued. The court held that because the previous forgeries committed by the employee constituted dishonest acts and the president "was aware of this conduct in 2001, prior to the issuance of the bond, coverage as to [the employee] terminated immediately upon inception of the bond." *Capital Bank & Trust Co. v. Gulf Ins. Co.*, 91 A.D.3d 1251.

2. Only After Inception of the Bond/Policy

E.D. Wis. 2011. Waupaca, a supplier of lawn and garden products, purchased a commercial crime policy from Travelers that included a provision that the coverage "terminates as to any employee as soon as your . . . Management Staff Members . . . becomes aware of any dishonest or fraudulent employment related act . . . ." One of Waupaca's managers knew of prior dishonesty by a current Waupaca employee that resulted in that employee being terminated from his previous employer. The employee engaged in additional dishonesty at Waupaca by stealing inventory and supplies. Analyzing Travelers' denial of coverage under the termination provision, the court held that the language was ambiguous because of the "present tense" used in the provision: "[T]he policy suggests that coverage will exist for some given period of time before it could terminate. It could not, in other words, 'terminate' upon its very inception." Given the triggering event for the termination is stated "as soon as" the manager "becomes aware," the court held that a reasonable person would likely expect that the provision is aimed only at knowledge that is gained after the effective date of the policy, not before." As noted above, this decision is a deviation from prior case law and raises a number of public policy concerns. *Waupaca Northwoods, LLC v. Travelers Cas. & Sur. Co. of Am.*, No. 10-C-459, 2011 WL 1563278.

Conn. Super. Ct. 2009. In another departure from prior case law, the court found that the cancellation provision was ambiguous and that a "common sense" reading of the provision meant that coverage only terminated as to the employee if knowledge of prior dishonesty was discovered *after* the policy became effective. The policy provided that the insurance would be cancelled "immediately upon discovery by You . . . of any dishonest acts committed by that 'employee' whether before or after becoming employed by you." After reporting a loss sustained after its bookkeeper committed dishonest acts, the insured company admitted that the same employee had previously stole money from the company nearly a decade earlier. Despite this dishonesty, the bookkeeper was retained as an employee. Travelers moved for summary judgment based upon the policy's cancellation provision. The court denied the motion, noting that: (i) "the word 'cancellation' . . . assumes there is an operative policy providing coverage prior to any cancellation"; and (ii) "[the policy language] 'immediately upon discovery'" . . . clearly seems to indicate the discovery contemplated is contemplated as taking place during the term of the current contract of insurance and operation of the fidelity bond." *C.A. White, Inc. v. Travelers Cas. & Sur. Co. of Am.*, 47 Conn. L. Rptr. 687, *aff'd on reh'g* 52 Conn. L. Rptr. 20.

N.C. App. 2004. Analyzing a slightly modified version of the SFAA's Standard Form 24 Financial Institutions Bond, the court held that the automatic termination provision was ambiguous and that coverage terminates under the provision only if the insured bank discovers the employee's dishonesty *after* coverage incepts. The bank knew that its employee, Ms. Gibson, had been convicted in 1981 of embezzling fund from a previous employer, yet decided to keep the employee. Colonial issued the FI Bond in January 2001 and in May 2001 it was discovered that Gibson had embezzled over one million dollars from the bank. Colonial denied coverage solely based on the termination provision based on the bank's undisputed knowledge of Gibson's earlier conviction for embezzlement. On appeal, the court found that use of the present tense in "terminates . . . as soon as" the insured "learns" of any dishonest conduct "suggests an intent by the parties that coverage under the bond must first commence before discovery of an employee's dishonesty will operate to terminate it." *Home Sav. Bank, SSB v. Colonial Am. Cas. & Sur. Co.*, 598 S.E.2d 265.

SECONDARY SOURCES

Annotation, *Agent's Knowledge of His Own Embezzlement or Other Misconduct as Imputable to Principal in Latter's Suit on Fidelity Bond or Insurance*, 105 A.L.R. 535 (1936).

Annotation, *Bankers Blanket Bond's Termination of Coverage Upon FDIC Takeover Did Not Violate Public Policy*, 12 INS. LITIG. RPTR. 349 (1990).

Annotation, *Construction and Application of Provisions of Bond or Policy Insuring Fidelity of Employees, Regarding Termination as to Employees Guilty of Default or Other Acts of Dishonesty*, 104 A.L.R. 1174 (1936).

Annotation, *Duty of Employer Applying for Fidelity Insurance to Notify Insurer That Employee Had Overdrawn His Account*, 4 A.L.R. 558 (1919).

Annotation, *Duty of Employer to Notify Surety that Employee was Dilatory, Slow, or Negligent in Settling Account*, 60 A.L.R. 160 (1929).

Annotation, *Federal Deposit Insurance Corporation May Not Recover Under Insolvent Thrift's Fidelity Bond*, 14 INS. LITIG. RPTR. 170 (1992).

Annotation, *Fiduciary Insurance and Financial Institution in the Post—FIRREA Era*, 14 INS. LITIG. RPTR. 40 (1992).

Annotation, *Obligee's Concealment of Facts or Evasive Answers as Fraud against Surety*, 8 A.L.R. 1485 (1920).

Annotation, *Obligee's Concealment or Misrepresentation Concerning Previous Defalcation as Affecting Liability on Fidelity Bond or Contract*, 4 A.L.R. 3d 1197 (1965).

Annotation, *Suspicion, or Reasons for Suspicion, of Wrongdoing by Officer or Employee Covered by Fidelity Bond or Policy, as Requiring Obligee to Comply with Conditions of Bond with Respect to Notice of Discovery or Knowledge of Loss*, 129 A.L.R. 1411 (1940).

Atkins, *What Constitutes Loss within the Meaning of the Word "Loss" Under Financial Institution and Fidelity Bonds*, 1967 ABA Section on Insurance, Negligence, and Compensation Law 73 (1967).

D. Baudler et al., *Fraud and Dishonesty Under the Blanket Bond*, 9 FORUM 229 (Winter 1973).

David E. Bordon et al., *Conditions to Recovery: Termination and Cancellation, in* FINANCIAL INSTITUTION BONDS 315 (Duncan L. Clore ed., 1995).

David E. Bordon, *Current Issues and Positions Taken by the RTC and FDIC in Litigation Arising Under the Standard Forms 22 and 24, in* FINANCIAL INSTITUTION BONDS (Duncan L. Clore ed., 1992).

David E. Bordon, *Termination of Coverage Under the Banker's Blanket Bond* (unpublished paper presented to the Annual Meeting of the ABA, Fid. & Sur. Law Comm., New York, N.Y, Aug. 1986).

Lee McGraw Brewer, *Prior Dishonesty and Automatic Termination— Has Tom the Piper's Son Ruined His Life Forever?* (unpublished paper presented at Annual Meeting of Nat'l Bond Claims Ass'n, Oct. 1993)

Duncan L. Clore & John Tomaine, *Discovery of Loss, in* HANDLING FIDELITY BOND CLAIMS 431 (Michael Keeley & Sean Duffy eds., 2d ed. 2005).

Michael R. Davisson, *Conditions to Recovery: Termination and Cancellation, in* FINANCIAL INSTITUTION BONDS 471 (Duncan L. Clore ed., 2d ed. 1998).

Michael R. Davisson, *Section 12—Termination or Cancellation, in* ANNOTATED FINANCIAL INSTITUTION BOND 544 (Michael Keeley ed., 2d ed. 2004).

Paul R. Devin & Allen N. David, *Discovery Under Fidelity Bonds: The Emerging Concept of the Insured's Duty of Inquiry*, 21 TORT & INS. L.J. 543 (1986).

Edward Etcheverry & Guy W. Harrison, *Employee Dishonesty—When Does Your Bond "Automatically Terminate"? in* VI FID. L.J. 71 (2000).

Mark S. Gamell & Whitney J. Drasin, *Cancellation and Termination of Coverage, Commercial Crime Insurance Coverage*, (Marmor & Sullivan, 3rd ed. 2015).

John B. Hayes, *Cancellation as to any Employee* and *Cancellation of Bond*, *in* THE COMMERCIAL BLANKET BOND ANNOTATED (William F. Haug ed., 1985).

Robert J. Heyne et al., *The Simplified Commercial Crime Forms, or "A Jabberwock Meets the Flesch Test,"* (unpublished paper presented at Annual Meeting of the ABA, Fid. & Sur. Law Comm., New York, N.Y, Aug. 1986).

Charles H. Hoens, Jr., *When Can the Bankers Blanket Bond Be Rescinded for Fraud or Misrepresentation?* 16 FORUM 1102 (1981).

Michael Keeley & Toni Scott Reed, *"Superpowers" of Federal Regulators: How the Banking Crisis Created an Entire Genre of Bond Litigation*, 31 TORT & INS. L.J. 817 (1996).

David A. Lewis, *Continuing to Make Questionable Loans to Same Customer As Constituting Dishonesty*, 10 FORUM 115 (1974).

John Michael McCormick, *Frauds of the Insured, Imputation of Knowledge and Impleading the Employee in Fidelity Cases*, 4 FORUM 204 (Spring 1969).

Michael B. McGeehon & Martin J. O'Leary, *Termination of Coverage*, *in* HANDLING FIDELITY BOND CLAIMS 445 (Michael Keeley & Timothy Sukel eds., 1999).

George C. Montgomery, *The Alter Ego Type Defenses Reconsidered*, 14 FORUM 615 (1973).

G. Wayne Murphy, *Allegations, Assertions, and Charges as Discovery of Loss*, 12 FORUM 986 (Summer 1977).

Murry, *Conditions to Recovery Under the Bankers Blanket* Bond, 50 INS. COUNSEL J. 125 (1983).

John D. O'Malley, *Dishonesty within the Meaning of Bankers Blanket Bonds*, 81 BANKING L.J. 941 (1964).

Martha L. Perkins & Lana M. Glovach, *Cancellation and Termination of Coverage*, in COMMERCIAL CRIME POLICY 471 (Randall I. Marmor & John J. Tomaine eds., 2d ed. 2005).

Carol A. Pisano, *Pulling the Trigger on Fidelity Coverage: Termination of Coverage Based on Discovery or Warping Time*, unpublished paper delivered at 2003 Surety Claims Institute Meeting.

Andrew M. Reidy & Barbara M. Tapscott, *The Pitfalls of Fidelity Insurance; Banks Seeking Coverage for Employee Fraud Face Four Hurdles: Timely Notice, Discovery, Termination and Manifest Intent*, 18 NAT'L L.J. 137 (Mar. 1, 1996).

Douglas M. Reimer & William F. Haug, *Fraudulent or Dishonest Acts*, 8 FORUM 615 (Summer 1973).

Bernard A. Reinert, *Court's Failure to Terminate Coverage Where Owner Knows of Dishonesty*, 11 FORUM 1014 (Spring 1976).

Hugh E. Reynolds, Jr., & James Dimos, *Symposium: The Restatement of Suretyship: Fidelity Bonds and the Restatement*, 34 WM. & MARY L. REV. 1249 (1993).

Paul D. Schoonover, *Discovery, Notice and Automatic Termination under Revised Form 24*, 16 FORUM 962 (1981).

Frank L. Skillern, *When Dishonesty by Officers of Insured Becomes Dishonesty of Insured to Preclude Recovery Under Fidelity Bond*, 5 FORUM 235 (Spring 1970).

Sandra M. Stone & Barry F. MacEntee, *Defining Employee Dishonesty Within the Framework of the Automatic Termination Provision and the Fidelity Insuring Agreement*, 17 FID. L.J. 143 (2011).

Edward T. Stork, *Termination of Coverage*, in HANDLING FIDELITY BOND CLAIMS 499 (Michael Keeley & Sean Duffy eds., 2d ed. 2005).

Bryan W. Tabor, *Timely Review of Bankers Blanket Bond*, 23 INS. COUNSEL J. 121 (1956)

Cheryl J. Wickham et al., *Cancellation, in* COMMERCIAL CRIME POLICY 11-5 (Gilbert J. Schroeder ed., 1997).

Karen Wildau & Marlo Orlin Leach, *What Did They Know and When Did They Know It, Who are "They" Anyway, and What Difference Does It Make—Imputation Under the Financial Institution Bond and Its Implication for Coverage, in* III FID. L. ASS'N J. 1 (1997).

Charles H. Witherwax, *Bad Banking and Poor Judgment Constituting Dishonesty Under the Banker's Blanket Bond*, 10 FORUM 101 (Fall 1974).

Chapter 15

Limit of Insurance*

This chapter is an update to Section 13—Limit of Liability—of the American Bar Association's 2006 Annotated Commercial Crime Policy, Second Edition.[1] This chapter includes annotations of decisions involving Commercial Crime Loss Sustained and Discovery Policies, and in some instances, under Employee Dishonesty coverage, claims in which the court's discussion turns on Limit of Liability issues.[2]

So often a sophisticated crime scheme, whether it be employee embezzlement or other forms of fraud, is carried out over a number of years before the scheme is discovered. Often, this complicates efforts by the insured attempting to put the pieces of the scheme together in a discernible manner when presenting its verified proof of loss. It also presents issues for the carrier when evaluating applicable coverage issues, including the maximum liability potentially facing the carrier affording coverage under a specific insuring agreement.

There are numerous decisions across jurisdictions addressing the definition of "occurrence." Should a series of dishonest acts constitute multiple, independent events availing the insured to the potential for multiple recoveries up to the policy limit for each act? Is the series of dishonest acts one occurrence subject to a maximum recovery of one policy limit? What factors come into play when an employee is in collusion with multiple individuals or groups, not all of whom are involved in all aspects of the scheme or involved to the same extent?

---

* By Michael J. Weber, Grace Winkler Cranley, Leo & Weber, Chicago, Illinois, and Ginger Johnson, The Hanover Insurance Group, Itasca, Illinois.

1 *See* Edward G. Gallagher, *Limits of Liability, in* ANNOTATED COMMERCIAL CRIME POLICY 495 (Cole S. Kain & Lana M. Glovach eds., 2d ed. 2006).

2 Note that in some instances this chapter cites to Crime General Provisions (Loss Sustained Form), Standard Form CR 1000 (Revised to 04-97); Crime General Provisions (Discovery Form), Standard Form CR 1100 (Revised to 04-97); Employee Dishonesty Coverage Form A—Blanket, B, Standard Form CR 0001 (Revised to 10-90); and Forgery or Alteration Coverage Form, Standard Form CR 0003 (Revised to 01-86). These forms are predecessor forms that are no longer supported by the SFAA or ISO.

Each of these are significant and repeating issues addressed by the courts to determine a carrier's limit of liability.

This chapter also includes annotations addressing the impact of losses occurring over multiple policy periods, including multiple policies issued by the same carrier or different carriers. The type of policy (discovery or loss sustained), timing of discovery, as well as the express terms of the policy, including prior insurance provisions and non-cumulation clauses, are each a significant factor in determining maximum exposure and the limit of liability for a carrier in response to a valid claim.

When confronting complex crime claims, an analysis of a carrier's liability can be an onerous task—always subject to the specific facts of the underlying loss, as well as to the policy or possibly multiple policies in issue, and their terms, conditions, and definitions, each of which have an impact on the analysis of the limit of liability.

A. Limit of Insurance

The Commercial Crime Protection Policy (Standard Form)[3], the Employee Dishonesty Coverage Form A—Blanket[4] and the Forgery or Alteration Coverage Form[5] contain the same language, stating:

Limit of Insurance
The most we will pay for loss in any one "occurrence" is the applicable Limit of Insurance shown in the Declarations.

The Commercial Crime Policy[6] contains the following language, stating:

---

3   Crime Protection Policy, Standard Form No. SP 0001 (Revised to 04 12), Condition 13.

4   Employee Dishonesty Coverage Form A—Blanket, B, Standard Form CR 0001 (Revised to 10-90).

5   Forgery or Alteration Coverage Form, Standard Form CR 0003 (Revised to 01-86).

6   The Commercial Crime Policy (Loss Sustained Form), Standard Form No. CR 00 23 08 13 (Revised to 08-13) and the Commercial Crime Policy (Discovery Form), Standard Form No. CR 00 22 (Revised to 08-13) contain the same language at B. Limit of Insurance.

B. Limit of Insurance

The most we will pay for all loss resulting directly from an "occurrence" is the applicable Limit of Insurance shown in the Declarations.

If any loss is covered under more than one Insuring Agreement or coverage, the most we will pay for such loss shall not exceed the largest Limit of Insurance available under any one of those Insuring Agreements or coverages.

ANNOTATIONS

N.D. Ill. 1993. Employer Diamond Transportation claimed the $250,000 limit under each of three annual policies. Travelers paid a single $250,000 limit. The court granted Travelers' motion to dismiss. The court found that the limit of insurance provision clearly stated a single $250,000 limit. *Diamond Transp. Sys., Inc. v. Travelers Indem. Co.*, 817 F. Supp. 710.

Ga. 2004. The parties stipulated that there were two three-year policies and that the employee stole during all three years of the first policy and the first year of the second policy. The limit of liability was $50,000. The trial court awarded the employer its losses up to $50,000 for each year it had coverage. The court of appeals reversed as to the three years of the first policy but still permitted cumulation between the first policy and the first year of the second policy. The Georgia supreme court affirmed. The court stated, "The policy unambiguously stated that for that three year period, the most Cincinnati would pay for losses due to employee dishonesty was $50,000 per occurrence." *Sherman & Hemstreet, Inc. v. Cincinnati Ins. Co.*, 594 S.E.2d 648.

SECONDARY SOURCES

David T. DiBiase, *Fidelity Claims in Excess of Policy Limits—Problems and Solutions,* 52 INS. COUNSEL J. 660 (1985).

Edward G. Gallagher, *Limit of Liability, in* COMMERCIAL CRIME POLICY 451 (Randall I. Marmor & John J. Tomaine eds., 2d ed. 2005).

Edward G. Gallagher, *Limits of Liability, in* ANNOTATED COMMERCIAL CRIME POLICY 495 (Cole S. Kain & Lana M. Glovach eds., 2d ed. 2006).

William J. Hacker, *Limit of Liability, in* COMMERCIAL CRIME POLICY 14-1 (Gilbert J. Schroeder ed., 1997).

Tracey Haley, Cumulation of Crime Policy Limits—The Impact of A.B.S. Clothing *(unpublished paper presented at Annual Meeting of ABA, Fid. & Sur. Law Comm. 1998))* (on file at the Stradley Library, No. 2873).

Patrick O'Connor & D. M. Studler, *Limits of Liability: A Multi-Faceted Perspective*, (unpublished paper presented at Annual Meeting of Sur. Claims Inst. 1999).

Robert Olausen, *Commercial Crime Insurance: The Changing Landscape* (unpublished paper presented at Annual Meeting of Sur. Claims Inst. 1997).

Tracey Santor et al., *Limits of Liability, in* HANDLING FIDELITY BOND CLAIMS 319 (Michael Keeley & Sean Duffy eds., 2d ed. 2005).

John J. Tomaine, *Through the Looking Glass: Determining the Applicable Limit of Liability and Deductible in Multiple Check Claims* (unpublished paper presented at Annual Meeting of ABA, Fid. & Sur. Law Comm. 2001) (on file at the Stradley Library, No. 3170).

Christopher R. Ward et al., *Recent Developments in Fidelity and Surety Law*, 46 TORT TRIAL & INS. PRAC. L.J. 371, 382-84 (Winter 2011).

Christopher R. Ward et al., *Recent Developments in Fidelity and Surety Law*, 45 TORT TRIAL & INS. PRAC. L.J. 367, 375-76 (Winter 2010).

B. Definition of Occurrence

The Commercial Crime Protection Policy (Standard Form)[7] defines "Occurrence" as follows:

Occurrence means
a. **As respects Insuring Agreement I, all loss or losses caused by, or involving, any one employee, acting alone or in collusion with others.**
b. **As respects Insuring Agreement 2, all loss or losses caused by any person or in which that person is involved, whether the loss involves one or more instruments.**
c. **As respects all other Insuring Agreements, all loss or losses caused by:**
    (1) Any number of acts, involving one person whether acting alone or in collusion with others;
    (2) Any number of acts involving a group of persons acting together; or
    (3) An act or event, or any number of related acts or events, not involving any identifiable person.

The Employee Dishonesty Coverage Form A—Blanket[8] defines "Occurrence" as follows:

"Occurrence" means all loss caused by, or involving, one or more "employees", whether the result of a single act or series of acts.

The Forgery or Alteration Coverage Form B[9] defines "Occurrence" as follows:

---

7 Crime Protection Policy, Standard Form No. SP 0001 (Revised to 04 12), Definition 10.
8 Employee Dishonesty Coverage Form A—Blanket, B, Standard Form CR 0001 (Revised to 10-90), Additional Exclusions, Condition and Definitions 3.b.
9 Forgery or Alteration Coverage Form, Standard Form CR 0003 (Revised to 01-86), Additional Exclusion, Conditions and Definition 3.

"Occurrence" means all loss caused by any person or in which that person is involved, whether the loss involves one or more instruments.

The Commercial Crime Policy (Discovery Form)[10] defines "Occurrence" to mean:

"Occurrence" means:
a. **Under Insuring Agreement A.1.:**
   (1) **An individual act;**
   (2) **The combined total of all separate acts whether or not related; or**
   (3) **A series of acts whether or not related**
   committed by an "employee" acting alone or in collusion with other persons, during the Policy Period shown in the Declarations, before such policy period or both.
b. **Under Insuring Agreement A.2.:**
   (1) **An individual act;**
   (2) **The combined total of all separate acts whether or not related; or**
   (3) **A series of acts whether or not related,**
   committed by an person acting alone or in collusion with other persons, involving one or more instruments, during the Policy Period shown in the Declarations, before such policy period or both.
c. **Under all other Insuring Agreements**
   (1) **An individual or event;**
   (2) **The combined total of all separate acts whether or not related; or**
   (3) **A series of acts or events whether or not related**
   committed by a person acting alone or in collusion with other persons, or not committed by any person, during the Policy Period shown in the Declarations, before such policy period or both.

---

10   Commercial Crime Policy (Discovery Form), Standard Form No. CR 00 22 (Revised to 08-13) Definition 17.

The Commercial Crime Policy (Loss Sustained Form)[11] defines "Occurrence" to mean:

> **"Occurrence" means:**
> a. **Under Insuring Agreement A.1.:**
>   **(1)** **An individual act;**
>   **(2)** **The combined total of all separate acts whether or not related; or**
>   **(3)** **A series of acts whether or not related**
>   **committed by an "employee" acting alone or in collusion with other persons, during the Policy Period shown in the Declarations, except as provided under Condition E.1.o. or E.1.p.**
> b. **Under Insuring Agreement A.2.:**
>   **(1)** **An individual act;**
>   **(2)** **The combined total of all separate acts whether or not related; or**
>   **(3)** **A series of acts whether or not related,**
>   **committed by an person acting alone or in collusion with other persons, involving one or more instruments, during the Policy Period shown in the Declarations, except as provided under Condition E.1.o. or E.1.p.**
> c. **Under all other Insuring Agreements**
>   **(1)** **An individual or event;**
>   **(2)** **The combined total of all separate acts whether or not related; or**
>   **(3)** **A series of acts or events whether or not related**
>   **committed by a person acting alone or in collusion with other persons, or not committed by any person, during the Policy Period shown in the Declarations, except as provided under Condition E.1.o. or E.1.p.**

COMMENT

Whether a series of acts constitute multiple acts subject to multiple limits (and deductibles) or one occurrence is often debated and is the

---

11 Commercial Crime Policy (Loss Sustained Form), Standard Form No. CR 00 23 08 13 (Revised to 08-13), Definitions 17.

subject of many court decisions. In conjunction with an analysis of the underlying scheme's chain of events, including parties involved, courts will look to whether the definition of "occurrence" in the policy is ambiguous or whether a series of events constitute a single loss under the policy. The court's analysis also comes into play when analyzing a series of events occurring over multiple or continuous policy periods.

ANNOTATIONS

3d Cir. 2002 (Pa.). Scirex conducted drug trials for pharmaceutical companies. Nurses employed by Scirex let patients leave early and falsified data reports to indicate the patients had been observed for the required period. Scirex had to re-perform several trials at substantial expense. There were four studies, and Scirex claimed the value of each up to the limit of insurance. Federal Insurance argued that there was only one occurrence or event and one limit. The court agreed with Federal. [Note, the policy was not a standard commercial crime policy and the language of the applicable provisions differed somewhat from the SFAA/ISO form]. *Scirex Corp. v. Fed. Ins. Co.*, 313 F.3d 841.

4th Cir. 2001 (S.C.). There were two successive one-year policies with different policy numbers. An employee stole in excess of the $100,000 per occurrence limit during each of the two policy years. The employer claimed $200,000. Liberty tendered $100,000. The Fourth Circuit affirmed summary judgment for the employer. The court thought that the definition of "occurrence" was ambiguous because it did not affirmatively say whether the series of acts included acts occurring outside of the policy period. [Note, this is an unpublished decision and pursuant to Fourth Circuit Rule 36c is not supposed to be cited as precedent]. *Spartan Iron & Metal Corp. v. Liberty Ins. Corp.*, 6 F. App'x 176.

5th Cir. 2008 (S.D. Miss.). Fifth Circuit affirmed district court holding on summary judgment. Employee's related acts of embezzlement over a decade and spanning multiple policy periods constituted only one occurrence and employer Madison was entitled to recover no more than the limits of the policy in effect when the theft was discovered. Mississippi courts recognize that an "occurrence" is determined by the cause or causes of the resulting injury. Although employee committed multiple related acts throughout the decade, court found there was only one cause of the injury sustained by Madison and that was the employee's dishonesty. The court looked to the unambiguous terms of policy stating that multiple related acts may constitute a single occurrence. The court further held under Prior Insurance clause that only way Madison could recover for losses in a prior policy period would be if the losses incurred in the current policy period totaled less than the current limits, and then only to bring Madison's recovery up to the current policy's limits. *Madison Materials Co., Inc. v. St. Paul Fire & Marine Ins. Co.*, 523 F.3d 541.

5th Cir. 2001 (Tex.). Two employees working independently each stole in excess of the limit of insurance. General Accident argued that this was only one occurrence because it was all loss involving one or more employees. The court held that there were two occurrences and stated, "The more natural reading of the policy, however, is that the 'involving' clause signifies a group of employees working together." *Ran-Nan, Inc. v. General Acc. Ins. Co. of Am.*, 252 F.3d 738.

9th Cir. 2009 (D. Ariz.). Ninth Circuit affirms district court holding on summary judgment that Superstition is limited to one limit of insurance per occurrence, which the court equated to entire embezzlement regardless of fact that the employee was guilty of multiple embezzlements. Losses discovered within the one-year tail from the end of the policy period were limited to single-policy limits, regardless of whether loss took place over more than one policy period. The court held that a new policy period does not trigger the beginning of a new occurrence, rather the term, "occurrence" can span more than one policy period. Further, certain losses occurring before the beginning of the policy period are part of, and not in addition to, the current policy limits. *Superstition Crushing, LLC v. Travelers Cas. and Surety Co. of America*, 360 Fed. Appx. 844.

9th Cir. 2000 (Cal.). Karen Kane, Inc. claimed losses during three policy periods. Reliance Insurance Company paid a single limit, and the district court granted summary judgment to Reliance. On appeal, the Ninth Circuit held that *A.B.S. Clothing* was the law of California and that the definition of "occurrence" was ambiguous. The court thought that a temporal condition could be read into the definition and each series of

ANNOTATED COMMERCIAL CRIME INSURANCE POLICY

acts during a policy period could be a separate occurrence. *Karen Kane, Inc. v. Reliance Ins. Co.*, 202 F.3d 1180.

10th Cir. 1984 (Ok.). An employee embezzled $53,036.86 by forging 31 checks and altering nine other checks. The limit of liability was $10,000. Aetna Casualty & Surety claimed that each check was a separate occurrence. The court affirmed summary judgment for Aetna and held that the cause of the loss was the continued dishonesty of the one employee and only one limit could be recovered. Although this case predates the 1986 Commercial Crime Policy and involved somewhat different policy terms, it is often relied upon to reject the multiple occurrences theory asserted by the insured. *Bus. Interiors, Inc. v. Aetna Cas. & Sur. Co.*, 751 F.2d 361.

C.D. Cal. 1998. Karen Kane, Inc. suffered losses during three consecutive policy periods. The court granted summary judgment to Reliance Insurance Company and rejected Karen Kane's argument that the definition of "occurrence" was ambiguous. The court distinguished the *A.B.S. Clothing* decision on the ground that the California Court of Appeals considered the definition only in deciding whether there was one continuous policy or a series of separate policies, and that issue was not in the case because Reliance conceded that there were three separate policies. The court held, "Dantzler's conduct falls squarely within the definition of "occurrence" provided by the policy: his fraud constituted a 'series of acts' that caused the insured a loss." The insured also argued that each fraudulent transaction was a separate series of acts, but conceded that it claimed only the $250,000 policy limit per year, not per fraudulent transaction. The court held that the reasonable expectation of the parties was that the series of thefts was one occurrence. [Note, this decision was reversed by the Ninth Circuit]. *Karen Kane, Inc. v. Reliance Ins. Co.*, No. CV 97-3295-WMB, 1998 WL 476454, *aff'd in part, rev'd in part* by 202 F.3d 1180 (9th Cir. 2000).

D. Colo. 2004. A dishonest employee used several different schemes to steal money over a four-year period. During the last two years, the employer had coverage under policies written by the Wausau. The issue was the applicable limit of insurance. The employer argued that the dishonest employee's various embezzlement methods were each a separate occurrence. The court held that there was a single occurrence and stated, "The cause of defendant's loss was the dishonesty of one employee. Although the employee appears to have been particularly creative in finding ways to bilk defendant, her intent throughout undoubtedly was the same: to steal defendant's money." *Wausau Bus. Ins. Co. v. U.S. Motels Mgmt., Inc.*, 341 F. Supp. 2d 1180.

N.D. Ill. 2008. Over an eight-year period employee diverted monies from company Aldridge Electric profit-sharing plan using two distinct methods. Aldridge sought recovery alleging that the employee either committed three separate schemes representing separate occurrences, or that employee's embezzlement from each of the eighty-three plan participants constituted a separate occurrence. The district court followed the Illinois Supreme Court's holding that the cause theory (number of occurrences is determined by referring to the cause or causes of the damages rather than by the effect theory, which looks at how many individual claims resulted from the occurrences) is Illinois law with respect to defining occurrences. The court held that as a matter of law on summary judgment, employee's acts constituted one occurrence. *Aldridge Electric, Inc. v. Fidelity & Deposit Co. of Maryland*, No. 04 C 4021, 2008 WL 4287639.

N.D. Ill. 1993. Employer Diamond Transportation claimed the $250,000 limit under each of three annual policies. Travelers paid a single $250,000 limit. The court granted Travelers' motion to dismiss. The court found the entire loss was a single occurrence. *Diamond Transp. Sys., Inc. v. Travelers Indem. Co.*, 817 F. Supp. 710.

D. Md. 2013. Two former executives of Emcor defrauded the company over a six-year period. Emcor sought recovery against GAIC under all three of GAIC's successive policies, as well as for losses for the period covered by the prior insurer. GAIC argued under terms of the Loss Sustained During Prior Insurance section that each policy offered coverage only for conduct occurring during the specified policy period, as well as for the period of coverage under the policy that immediately preceded. Emcor sought recovery for losses spanning each policy period. The district court refused to afford coverage for losses that occurred during prior policy periods and that were not known to Emcor until after the discovery window, including the one-year tail, had expired. The court held that GAIC policies clearly provided for loss sustained coverage for a finite period of time. GAIC's motion for partial summary judgment was granted. *Emcor Group, Inc. v. Great American Ins. Co.*, No. ELH-12-0142, 2013 WL 1315029.

D. Md. 2005. Glaser argued two theories in an attempt to recover more that its $25,000 limit of liability for thefts by a single employee. The employee used forged checks, fraudulent credit card charges and a fraudulent payroll instruction to steal $168,493.12 spread over the periods of three consecutive annual policies. Glaser argued there were seven occurrences and it should receive its losses up to seven limits. The court held that there was only one cause of loss, the employee's dishonesty, and thus only one occurrence not separate occurrences for each method of theft. On the other hand, the court held that there was no temporal limit in the definition of "occurrence" and found separate occurrences for each policy during which the thefts occurred. The result was a recovery of the $25,000 limit for each of the first two annual policies and the amount stolen, which was less than the limit, in the third policy year. *Glaser v. Hartford Cas. Ins. Co.*, 364 F. Supp. 2d 529.

D. Mass. 2010. An employee requested that his employer send his payroll direct deposits to a different bank. In addition to the employee's salary, the employer inadvertently began depositing the CEO's salary by direct deposit into the employee's account. The employee quit, but continued to receive the CEO's salary by direct deposit. It took 16 months for the CEO to discover he was not receiving his paychecks. The employer reimbursed the CEO and submitted an employee dishonesty claim under Traveler's policy. Travelers paid the claim for the period while the employee was employed and denied the claim for the period after he quit. The District Court of Massachusetts agreed with the employer that the employee committed acts that caused the entire loss while he was employed. Therefore, the court concluded that there was one occurrence for the entire loss, both during and after the time period in which employee was employed. *FundQuest Inc. v. Travelers Cas. and Surety Co.*, 715 F. Supp. 2d 202.

E.D. Mich. 2009. An employer alleged that Federal breached its obligations under a commercial crime policy by failing to indemnify it for losses resulting from an embezzlement scheme by an employee. The employer contended that there were at least three losses based on the acts of three individuals. The court found that the employee was integral to the scheme and there was only a single loss under the policy. The court also rejected the employer's argument that the Prior Loss provision provides recovery for losses sustained prior to the inception of the current policy. The court found the language was clear and the employer was not entitled to recover beyond the policy limit even though a portion of the loss was sustained in a prior, insured year. *Hartman & Tyner, Inc. v. Federal Ins. Co.*, No. 08-12461, 2009 WL 3152957.

E.D. Mo. 2005. Acid Piping had employee dishonesty coverage as part of a package policy. There was a $5,000 single loss limit for the coverage. An employee stole several hundred thousand dollars by submitting dozens of fraudulent invoices. The issue before the court was whether the $5,000 limit applied to all loss caused by the employee or applied separately to each fraudulent invoice. The policy did not define occurrence or loss, but did say that the carrier's maximum liability was $5,000 "for any loss caused by any employee whether acting alone or in collusion with others, either resulting from a single act or any number of acts, regardless of when those acts occurred, during the policy period of this insurance or prior insurance." The court held that the policy was ambiguous and that the $5,000 limit was per invoice not per employee. *Acid Piping Tech., Inc. v. Great N. Ins. Co.*, No. 4:04-CV 1667 CDP, 2005 WL 3008512.

D. Nev. 2011. Embezzlement over a three-year period involving theft of cash, theft of accounts payable, and theft of daily deposits was determined to be one occurrence under an unambiguous definition of "occurrence." The court also held that occurrence did not contain a limitation, which raised ambiguity about whether occurrence pertained to all loss, or was limited to loss arising in the policy period. The court held that a series of acts are related when committed by an employee, and did not consider the particular manner in which the loss was caused. *APMC Hotel Management, LLC v. Fidelity and Deposit Co. of Maryland*, No. 2:09-cv-2100-LDG-VCF, 2011 WL 5525966.

D.N.J. 2009. Credit manager for an auto dealership was involved in an embezzlement with others over two policy periods with separate insurers. The auto dealership sought recovery of multiple limits after receiving the single loss limit amount from the second carrier. The dealership argued that the definition of "occurrence" was ambiguous and could mean multiple acts of theft. The court held that the scheme involving the conversion of multiple money orders constituted a single occurrence. The prior carrier, Royal Indemnity, denied coverage on the basis that the loss was not discovered by Pine Belt within the extended period to discover the loss after termination of the policy. Royal Indemnity argued that the extended period to discover loss terminated immediately upon the effective date of the policy from the successor carrier, Granite State, which became effective immediately upon termination of Royal Indemnity's coverage. Pine Belt argued that Royal Indemnity's policy was ambiguous because it was unclear whether the commercial crime coverage was written on a loss sustained or discovery form. The court found no ambiguity existed in determining that the policy was written on a loss sustained form and granted Royal Indemnity's motion for summary judgment. *Pine Belt Automotive, Inc. v. Royal Indemnity Co.*, No. 06-5995 (JAP), 2009 WL 1025564.

D. Or. 2003. Harrington had annual polices with American Economy Insurance Company from 1989 through 2002. The limit of liability for employee dishonesty was $15,000. Harrington claimed the limit for each year in which the embezzlements by a former employee occurred over a thirteen-year period. American Economy paid the one limit under the last policy. The court held that under Oregon law thefts during each separate annual policy were separate occurrences. *Harrington v. Am. Econ. Ins. Co.* No. 03-712-MO, 2003 WL 23190177.

E.D. Pa. 1998. An employee acted in collusion with two different customers to place phantom employees on the insured's payroll. The employer argued that there were two separate schemes and so two occurrences. The court held that there was one cause of loss, the dishonest employee, either acting alone or in collusion with others, and so one occurrence. *Omne Servs. Group, Inc. v. Hartford Ins. Co.*, 2 F. Supp. 2d 714.

D.R.I. 2011. Employer incurred losses as a result of many years of theft caused by various employees and third parties. A claim was submitted under Travelers' commercial crime coverage. The District of Rhode Island denied Travelers' summary judgment motion seeking to limit coverage to a single loss. The court found the definition of "single loss" to be ambiguous and was in contradiction to the clause providing that there was no aggregate limit. The facts of the claim left open whether employees acted independently or in groups that may have constituted multiple losses. *Rhode Island Resource Recovery Corp. v. Travelers Indemnity Co.,* No. 10-294, 2011 U.S. Dist. LEXIS 58007.

S.D. Tex. 1996. An employee stole funds during the terms of three successive policies. Atlantic Mutual, the carrier on the first two policies, paid for the losses sustained during the terms of its policies (which were less than the limit of insurance). Preferred Risk, the carrier on the third policy, however, argued that there was a single occurrence and it owed only the single loss limit minus what the other insurer paid. The court held that the definition of "occurrence" was unambiguous and all thefts by a single employee were one occurrence. *Bethany Christian Church v. Preferred Risk Mut. Ins. Co.,* 942 F. Supp. 330.

N.D. Tex. 1994. An employee stole during the terms of two policies. The court held that the definition of "occurrence" was clear and unambiguous and limited the employer to recovery of a single limit under the second policy. *Potomac Ins. Co. of Ill. v. Lone Star Web, Inc.,* Civ. No. 3:93-CV-2122-H, 1994 WL 494784.

E.D. Va. 2008. The court found that term, "occurrence" in the employee dishonesty policy was ambiguous as dishonesty occurred over a span of years and multiple policy periods. While acts were considered one occurrence, question was whether the occurrences were limited to the temporal policy limits or whether they were covered under the policy in effect when the dishonesty was discovered. The court held that occurrence took place over several policy periods and awarded plaintiff recovery up to the limit of insurance under each policy in effect during the time the dishonesty took place. *Adolf Jewelers, Inc. v. Jewelers Mutual Ins.,* 614 F. Supp. 2d 648.

S.D. West V.A. 2009. On summary judgment plaintiff contended that multiple acts of embezzlement involving 293 checks bookkeeper wrote to herself over several years constituted separate occurrences. The court found that the definition of, "occurrence" for purposes of the employee dishonesty provision to be unambiguous regardless that bookkeeper was charged with six separate counts of embezzlement and six counts of falsifying accounts. In granting defendant's motion for summary judgment, the court held that a series of acts is considered one occurrence. Affirmed on appeal. *Beckley Mechanical, Inc. v. Erie Ins.*

Co., No. 5:07-cv-00652, 2009 WL 973358, *aff'd* 374 Fed. Appx. 381 (4th Cir. 2010).

Ariz. 2008. Employee embezzled from employer by forging company checks over a five-year period. The Supreme Court of Arizona vacated the appellate court decision and reversed the judgment of the superior court in finding under insured's employee dishonesty policy that a series of acts was one occurrence. Although there may be more than one occurrence per year under the policy, it does not follow that losses resulting from an employee's embezzlement scheme are each separate occurrences. *Employers Mutual Cas. Co. v. DGG & CAR, Inc.*, 183 P.2d 513.

Cal. Ct. App. 1995. Two employees embezzled from July 1988 to May 1991. Home Insurance Company issued a $100,000 policy commencing April 4, 1989, and twice renewed it for annual period starting April 4, 1990, and April 4, 1991. There were different policy numbers, but the coverage and limits were not changed. Home Insurance paid the single loss limit of $100,000. A.B.S. claimed $100,000 per year, including the year preceding the first policy, and sued. The trial court granted summary judgment to Home Insurance. The court of appeals thought the issue was whether there was a single, continuous policy or multiple annual policies. In a 2-1 decision, the court of Appeals reversed summary judgment and remanded the case. The court thought that the definition of "occurrence" was ambiguous because, although "all loss" suggested there could be only one occurrence, the limit of liability for "any one occurrence" suggested there could be more than one occurrence. The court ignored the fact that there could be a separate occurrence if there was another dishonest employee operating separately. *A.B.S. Clothing Collection, Inc. v. Home Ins. Co.*, 41 Cal. Rptr. 2d 166.

Conn. Super. Ct. 2000. Over an eighteen-month period Shemitz Lighting's bookkeeper embezzled money by forging checks on Shemitz's accounts and diverting checks payable to Shemitz. Shemitz claimed a loss of $209,000. The limit of liability was $10,000 per occurrence. The court thought that "occurrence" was not defined and could "mean that their recovery is limited to: $10,000 for each act of dishonesty; $10,000 for each employee; $10,000 for each policy period; or $10,000 for each coverage period." The court then construed the ambiguous term against Hartford and granted summary judgment to

Shemitz holding that each act of embezzlement was a separate occurrence. *Shemitz Lighting, Inc. v. Hartford Fire Ins. Co.*, No. CV960052970, 2000 WL 1781840.

Fla. Dist. Ct. App. 1995. The insured had annual policies issued from February 1988 to February 1991. A dishonest employee embezzled throughout this period. The trial court granted summary judgment, finding coverage under all four policies. The court of appeals reversed. Even though the embezzlements took place over a four-year period, they were one occurrence. *Reliance Ins. Co. v. Treasure Coast Travel Agency, Inc.*, 660 So. 2d 1136.

Ga. 2004. The parties stipulated that there were two three-year policies and that the employee stole during all three years of the first policy and during the first year of the second policy. The limit of liability was $50,000. The trial court awarded the employer its losses up to $50,000 for each year it had coverage. The court of appeals reversed as to the three years of the first policy but still permitted cumulation between the first policy and the first year of the second policy. The state supreme court affirmed. The court held that a series of embezzlements by a single employee over the course of the three years of the first policy was a single occurrence. *Sherman & Hemstreet, Inc. v. Cincinnati Ins. Co.*, 594 S.E.2d 648.

Ga. Ct. App. 2003. An employee stole from its employer during each of the three years of the first policy and the first year of the second, renewal policy. The limit of insurance was $50,000, which Cincinnati Insurance paid. The trial court agreed with the employer that the limit was $50,000 per year. Cincinnati appealed, and the court held that the applicable limit for the three years of the first policy was $50,000 but that the amount stolen during the first year of the second policy was subject to another $50,000 limit. The court of appeals held that the stipulation that the first three years was a single policy foreclosed recovery of more than one limit for those years, but that the definition of "occurrence" was ambiguous because it did not have a temporal limit. Thus, all thefts by one employee during the policy period were one occurrence subject to one limit, but thefts during the period of the second policy could be a separate occurrence subject to a separate limit. *Cincinnati Ins. Co. v. Sherman & Hemstreet, Inc.*, 581 S.E.2d 613.

Ill. App. Ct. 1991. Two employees used similar schemes to steal money from their employer. The issue was whether they acted in collusion with each other. If so, the employer was entitled to one limit. The court affirmed summary judgment for Transportation Insurance Company finding that, under the admitted facts, the employees acted in collusion with each other. The controlling provisions of the policy differed substantially from the standard form. *Purdy Co. of Ill. v. Transp. Ins. Co.*, 568 N.E.2d 318.

Kan. Ct. App. 1990. The court affirmed summary judgment for the employer allowing recovery of two policy limits. There were two successive one-year policies. The non-standard conditions included that a series of similar or related acts during the policy period would be one occurrence. The employer argued that meant that acts outside of the policy period would be a separate occurrence subject to a separate limit. The court thought that a reasonable person would expect that a second policy meant a second limit and would understand the occurrence provision to mean only that all loss in one policy period was one occurrence. *Penalosa Coop. Exch. v. Farmland Mut. Ins. Co.*, 789 P.2d 1196.

Ky. Ct. App. 2013. In unpublished opinion Kentucky Appellate Court affirmed circuit court's granting of summary judgment in favor of Auto Owners holding that employer was entitled to recovery for one occurrence of employee embezzlement under three provisions of a Commercial Umbrella Policy. Employee had engaged in twenty-eight fraudulent vehicle transactions and forty-five unauthorized check transactions. The court upheld the circuit court ruling that Piles was entitled to the policy limits for one occurrence under each applicable provision of the policy—commercial crime caused by employee dishonesty; loss of property caused by employee dishonesty; and loss of property caused by forgery or alterations to negotiable instruments. *Piles Chevrolet Pontiac Buick, Inc. v. Auto Owners Ins. Co.*, Nos. 2011-CA-002317-MR, 2011-CA-002340-MR, 2013 WL 2120319.

La. Ct. App. 1996. The clerk's office generated insufficient funds to cover all of its expenses. The clerk diverted monies from the health insurance trust fund for other uses. The court held that this was one scheme and one occurrence under the commercial crime policy. The court affirmed judgment for a single limit of liability. *Jefferson Parish*

Clerk of Court Health Ins. Trust v. Fid. & Dep. Co. of Md, 673 So. 2d 1238.

Minn. 1996. The insured was an insurance agency specializing in insurance for taxicabs. Many of the taxi owners paid with cash or cashier's checks. The dishonest employee took cash payments and checks without the payee filled in, and also issued fraudulent checks to herself. She stole over $190,000. The limit of liability was $10,000. Minnesota Mutual first paid the $10,000 but later conceded that the employee had used two "methods" of embezzlement. The trial court thought there were two occurrences. The court of appeals thought that the meaning of occurrence was ambiguous. The Supreme Court disagreed, thought the meaning was unambiguous and that there were two occurrences. Minnesota Mutual argued that there were two occurrences because the employee used two methods of embezzlement. The insurance agency argued there were 155 occurrences based on 155 separate thefts or seven occurrences based on seven distinct methods used by the employee. The court rejected the 155 occurrences argument both because it would mean multiple deductibles and because potentially unlimited numbers of $10,000 recoveries "is simply incommensurate with the $563 per-year premium under the policy." The court held that courts should consider the extent to which acts in a "series of related acts" are "connected by time, place, opportunity, pattern, and, most importantly, method or modus operandi." In this case, that meant two occurrences. *Am. Commerce Ins. Brokers, Inc. v. Minn. Mut. Fire & Cas. Co.*, 551 N.W.2d 224.

Minn. Ct. App. 1997. An employee embezzled during the periods of two consecutive annual policies. American Family Mutual argued that its obligation was one limit. The court found that the definition of "occurrence" contained no temporal restriction. The definition was unambiguous and not restricted to acts within the policy period. The court concluded, "The policy unambiguously limits recovery on claims arising from one employee's misconduct to the stated limit." *Landico, Inc. v. Am. Family Mut. Ins. Co.*, 559 N.W.2d 438.

Miss. 1999. An employee misappropriated money on 175 separate occasions from 1984 to 1988. Universal Underwriters provided a series of one-year package policies with employee dishonesty coverage, but no definition of "occurrence." The court held that coverage for loss resulting from any fraudulent of dishonest act provided separate coverage for each theft. The court distinguished cases involving policies that defined occurrence and limited recovery to a single limit for each occurrence. *Universal Underwriters Ins. Co. v. Buddy Jones Ford, Lincoln-Mercury, Inc.*, 734 So. 2d 173.

Mo. Ct. App. 2007. Office manager/bookkeeper embezzled monies by issuing a series of fraudulent checks on two company accounts with common ownership. Each company purchased separate commercial crime policies from Travelers. Travelers paid the policy limits to each company based on the series of acts being one occurrence for each company. On appeal, the companies sought recovery of additional losses they incurred, arguing that each fraudulent check was a separate occurrence of employee dishonesty and that they were entitled to recover the amount of their loss up to the policy limits for each check. The Missouri Court of Appeals reversed the trial court's entry of summary judgment in favor of the companies, holding that the definition of "occurrence" is unambiguous, and the cause of the losses to the companies was an embezzlement scheme consisting of a series of acts by one employee. Therefore, each company suffered only one occurrence of employee dishonesty subject to the limit of liability previously paid by Travelers. *Thornburgh Insulation, Inc. v. J.W. Terrill, Inc.*, 236 S.W. 3d 651.

N.J. 2004. An employee falsified financial information in 27 separate automobile installment sale transactions. The employer auto dealership was obligated to repurchase loans made in reliance on the fraudulent information. The policy's limit of liability was $5,000. The employer claimed a separate limit for each transaction. The supreme court held that each transaction was a separate occurrence. The court recognized that "read literally" the definition of "occurrence" would make all employee dishonesty losses a single occurrence, but thought that would "nullify the protections afforded by the policy" and therefore could be ignored. Disregarding what the policy actually said, the court then stated that the definition simply means that there can be only one recovery regardless of the number of employees involved. The court contrasted the 27 separate car sales with an embezzlement in which an employee steals cash or checks as part of an ongoing scheme to defraud, and held that the car sales were not a single act or series of related acts, and the $5,000 limit and $250 deductible applied separately to each one. *Auto Lenders Acceptance Corp. v. Gentilini Ford, Inc.*, 854 A.2d 378.

N.J. Super. Ct. App. Div. 2013. An employee of the surgical center stole upwards of $1 million over several years. The surgical center recovered approximately $830,000 under a separate employee dishonesty policy and sought to recover the balance from Franklin Mutual (FMI) under a business owners policy. FMI determined that the loss constituted one occurrence under the policy and paid the policy limit of $10,000. The center contended that each theft was a separate occurrence and argued for a separate limit of recovery for each theft. The appellate court affirmed summary judgment for FMI and found the provision "series of similar or related acts is one occurrence" to be unambiguous. *North Fullerton Surgery Center v. Franklin Mutual Ins. Co.*, No. L-45-11, 2013 WL 5762560.

N.C. Ct. App. 1996. The treasurer of Christ Lutheran Church wrote 24 fraudulent checks, totaling $32,760. The limit of liability was $5,000. The court rejected the church's argument that each check was a separate occurrence, and held that there was one occurrence and one limit: "These checks were all written in furtherance of one employee's dishonest acts. They do not constitute a new and individual act of dishonesty." *Christ Lutheran Church v. State Farm Fire & Cas. Co.*, 471 S.E.2d 124.

Or. Ct. App. 2003. An employee stole during two consecutive policy periods. Mid-Century Insurance Company argued that this was one occurrence and therefore subject to one limit. The employer argued that when the policy was renewed and it paid a new premium, it received a new limit. The court thought that the policy as a whole indicated an intent that a renewal was a new, separate insurance contract and coverage under each policy was limited to each period. The court held that thefts during the period of the renewal policy were another occurrence. The court did not mention a "prior insurance written by us" provision. *Robben & Sons Heating, Inc. v. Mid-Century Ins. Co.*, 74 P.3d 1141.

Pa. Super. Ct. 2006. A Superior Court of Pennsylvania held that successive fidelity bonds issued over several years represented continuous insurance, subject to a single limit, rather than multiple contracts. Bond included a non-accumulation clause in which no limit of insurance accumulates from year to year. *Reliance Insurance Company v. IRPC, Inc.*, 904 A.2d 912.

Wash. Ct. App. 2009. This case addresses whether excluded losses occurring after discovery of employee dishonesty should be considered when determining whether the auto dealership was fully compensated for a series of thefts. The auto dealership fell victim to one of its salesmen's thefts both prior to and after discovery of his actions. For a period of time, the dealership agreed to keep him on, but unbeknownst to them the employee continued to steal. Through garnishment of the employee's wages, the dealership recovered its losses from the thefts that occurred prior to the discovery of the employee's actions. Harco denied the claim based on the recovery, arguing that those were the only amounts covered under the insured's policy. The Washington Appellate Court, in reversing the lower court's decision, found that the series of thefts constituted one occurrence. In so holding, the Appellate Court held that the term "occurrence" would include all of the dealership's lost funds. In distinguishing between coverage obligations and reimbursement obligations, the court looked to whether the dealership had been fully compensated for its losses. Reimbursement was not determinative on whether the loss was fully insured. Even though an entire occurrence was not covered (the thefts occurring after discovery of the employee's actions), Harco could not set off the garnished wages recovered by the dealership against its liability under the insured's crime policy. The court reasoned that after Harco reimbursed the dealership for the amount of pre-discovery losses, it was no worse off had the employee been fired immediately upon discovery of the occurrence. *S&K Motors, Inc. v. Harco National Ins. Co.*, 213 P.3d 630.

Wash. Ct. App. 2001. An employer's payroll manager issued extra checks to herself and two other employees, in addition to stealing merchandise. All of the thefts were accomplished by not reporting accurate information to the outside company that prepared the employer's payroll checks. The employer claimed three limits because three employees were involved. The court held that there was one series of related acts and so one occurrence. *Valley Furniture & Interiors, Inc. v. Transp. Ins. Co.*, 26 P.3d 952.

SECONDARY SOURCES

Dennis J. Bartlett, *Stacking of Limits—A Cosmetic Approach to the Uninsured Fidelity Loss*, 15 FIDELITY L.J. 111 (Oct. 2009)

David T. DiBiase & Gary J. Valeriano, *Stacking Takes a Turn*, 77 DEF. COUNS. J. 503 (Oct. 2010)

David T. DiBiase, *Fidelity Claims in Excess of Policy Limits—Problems and Solutions* 52 INS. COUNSEL J. 660 (1985).

Keith Flanagan, *The Death of A.B.S. and Karen Kane: An Update on The Insurer's Liability for Multiple Limits*, (unpublished paper presented at Annual Meeting of Sur. Claims Inst. 2010).

Adam P. Friedman, *Fidelity Claims—The Year in Review 2011-2012* (unpublished paper submitted at the 23rd Annual Northeast Surety and Fidelity Claims Conference, Sept. 20-21, 2012)

Edward G. Gallagher, *Limits of Liability, in* ANNOTATED COMMERCIAL CRIME POLICY 495 (Cole S. Kain & Lana M. Glovach eds., 2d ed. 2006).

Edward G. Gallagher, *Limit of Liability, in* COMMERCIAL CRIME POLICY 451 (Randall I. Marmor & John J. Tomaine eds., 2d ed. 2005).

William J. Hacker, *Limit of Liability, in* COMMERCIAL CRIME POLICY 14-1 (Gilbert J. Schroeder ed., 1997).

Tracey Haley, *Cumulation of Crime Policy Limits—The Impact of A.B.S. Clothing* (unpublished paper presented at Annual Meeting of ABA, Fid. & Sur. Law Comm. 1998)) (on file at the Stradley Library, No. 2873).

Patrick O'Connor & D. M. Studler, *Limits of Liability: A Multi-Faceted Perspective*, (unpublished paper presented at Annual Meeting of Sur. Claims Inst. 1999).

Robert Olausen, *Commercial Crime Insurance: The Changing Landscape* (unpublished paper presented at Annual Meeting of Sur. Claims Inst. 1997).

Tracey Santor et al., *Limits of Liability, in* HANDLING FIDELITY BOND CLAIMS 319 (Michael Keeley & Sean Duffy eds., 2d ed. 2005).

Carol Z. Smith et al., *Recent Developments in Fidelity and Surety Law*, 50 TORT TRIAL & INS. PRAC. L.J. 367, 373 (Winter 2015).

John J. Tomaine, *Through the Looking Glass: Determining the Applicable Limit of Liability and Deductible in Multiple Check Claims* (unpublished paper presented at Annual Meeting of ABA, Fid. & Sur. Law Comm. 2001) (on file at the Stradley Library, No. 3170).

Christopher R. Ward et al., *Recent Developments in Fidelity and Surety Law*, 47 TORT TRIAL & INS. PRAC. L.J. 216, 229 (Fall 2012).

Christopher R. Ward et al., *Recent Developments in Fidelity and Surety Law*, 46 TORT TRIAL & INS. PRAC. L.J. 371, 382-84 (Winter 2011).

Christopher R. Ward et al., *Recent Developments in Fidelity and Surety Law*, 45 TORT TRIAL & INS. PRAC. L.J. 367, 375-76 (Winter 2010).

Christopher R. Ward et al., *Recent Developments in Fidelity and Surety Law*, 44 TORT TRIAL & INS. PRAC. L.J. 459, 471-74 (Winter 2009).

Christopher R. Ward et al., *Recent Developments in Fidelity and Surety Law*, 43 TORT TRIAL & INS. PRAC. L.J. 437, 447 (Spring 2008).

C. Discovery Period for Loss

The Commercial Crime Protection Policy (Standard Form)[12] provides as follows:

---

12   Crime Protection Policy, Standard Form No. SP 0001 (Revised to 04 12), Condition 9.

Extended Period to Discover Loss

a. **We will pay for loss that you sustained prior to the effective date of termination or cancellation of this insurance, which is discovered by you**

(1) **Within 60 days following the date of termination or cancellation; and**

(2) **As respects any employee benefit plan(s), within one year following the date of termination or cancellation.**

b. **However, this extended period to discover loss terminates immediately upon the effective date of any other insurance obtained by you replacing in whole or in part the insurance afforded by this Policy whether or not such insurance provides coverage for loss sustained prior to its effective date.**

The Commercial Crime Policy (Discovery Form)[13] provides as follows:

Extended Period to Discovery Loss
We will pay for loss that you sustained prior to the effective date of cancellation of this Policy, which is "discovered" by you:

(1) **No later than 60 days from the date of that cancellation. However, this extended period to "discover" loss terminates immediately upon the effective date of any other insurance obtained by you, whether from us or another insurer, replacing in whole or in par the coverage afforded under this Policy, whether or not such other insurance provides coverage for loss sustained prior to its effective date.**

(2) **No later than one year from the date of that cancellation with regard to any "employee benefit plan."**

The Commercial Crime Policy (Loss Sustained Form)[14] provides:

---

13 Commercial Crime Policy (Discovery Form), Standard Form No. CR 00 22 (Revised to 08-13) Condition 1.j.

14 Commercial Crime Policy (Loss Sustained Form), Standard Form No. CR 00 23 08 13 (Revised to 08-13), Condition 1.j.

Extended Period to Discovery Loss
We will pay for loss that you sustained prior to the effective date of cancellation of this Policy, which is "discovered" by you:

> **(1)   No later than one year from the date of that cancellation. However, this extended period to "discover" loss terminates immediately upon the effective date of any other insurance obtained by you, whether from us or another insurer, replacing in whole or in par the coverage afforded under this Policy, whether or not such other insurance provides coverage for loss sustained prior to its effective date.**
>
> **(2)   No later than one year from the date of that cancellation with regard to any "employee benefit plan."**

The Crime General Provisions (Loss Sustained Form)[15] provides:

> **Extended Period to Discovery Loss: We will pay only for covered loss discovered no later than one year from the end of the Policy Period.**

The Crime General Provisions (Discovery Form)[16] provides:

> **Extended Period to Discovery Loss: We will pay for loss that you sustained prior to the effective date of termination or cancellation of this insurance, which is discovered by you no later than 60 days from the date of that termination or cancellation.**
>
> **However, this extended period to discover loss terminates immediately upon the effective date of any other similar insurance obtained by you that covers the loss in whole or in part.**

---

15   Crime General Provisions (Loss Sustained Form), Standard Form CR 1000 (Revised to 04-97), General Condition 10.

16   Crime General Provisions (Discovery Form), Standard Form CR 1100 (Revised to 04-97), General Condition 6.

COMMENT

The courts enforce the extended discovery provision period when analyzing whether a loss was discovered during the policy period or during the extended tail period. Depending on the timing of the discovery, this can act to limit claims for loss to two policies.

ANNOTATIONS

5th Cir. 2008 (W.D. La.). St. Paul issued five one-year policies to Whitaker for the years 1998-2002. After filing for bankruptcy in 2003, Whitaker discovered that its employee embezzled in excess of $500,000 over several years through a forged check scheme. Whitaker filed a claim under each of the St. Paul polices. St. Paul paid Whitaker $110,000 under the 2002 policy and declined coverage under the prior policies. St. Paul relied upon the terms of the policy extending the discovery period for an additional one year after expiration for losses under the current policy. Since Whitaker failed to discover the losses within one year of the prior policies the bankruptcy court granted Whitaker's motion for summary judgment. The district court subsequently reversed and granted St. Paul's motion for summary judgment, which was affirmed by the Fifth Circuit. *In re Whitaker Constr. Co., Inc.,* 288 Fed. Appx. 153.

6th Cir. 2008 (W.D. Tenn.). Employer did not discover employee theft occurring over a seven-year period until after one year from the expiration of two insurer commercial crime policies. The Sixth Circuit Court of Appeals affirmed the district court's granting of summary judgment for FCCI because discovery of the theft occurred after the one-year tail provided after expiration of the policy. Although Tennessee courts had not yet addressed whether a finding of prejudice is required upon late notice under a commercial crime policy, the court reasoned that the prejudice rule applicable to untimely notice in occurrence policies does not extend to the discovery clause in indemnity agreements. *Stewart's Wholesale Electric Supply, Inc. v. FCCI Ins. Group,* No. 07-5895, 2008 WL 7768692.

9th Cir. 2000 (Cal.). Karen Kane, Inc., claimed losses during three policy periods. Reliance Insurance Company paid a single limit, and the district court granted summary judgment to Reliance. The Ninth Circuit reversed as to the definition of "occurrence," but held that the discovery condition was enforceable and excluded any claim under the first of the three policies. The court stated, "The language of the one-year discovery rule is quite plain and would appear to apply in straightforward fashion." *Karen Kane, Inc. v. Reliance Ins. Co.*, 202 F.3d 1180.

C.D. Cal. 1998. Karen Kane, Inc., suffered losses during three consecutive policy periods. The court granted summary judgment to Reliance Insurance Company and rejected Karen Kane's argument that the definition of "occurrence" or loss under "prior insurance issued by us" provisions were ambiguous. It also noted that the one-year discovery period barred any claim under the first of the three policies. *Karen Kane, Inc. v. Reliance Ins. Co.*, No. CV 97-3295-WMB, 1998 WL 476454, *aff'd in part, rev'd in part* by 202 F.3d 1180 (9th Cir. 2000).

N.D. Ill. 2013. Federated issued Midway Truck Parts a commercial lines insurance policy that contained a Crime and Fidelity Coverage Part with language similar to the Commercial Crime Loss Sustained Form on Extended Period to Discovery Loss. Prior to the expiration of the Federated policy on October 6, 2009, Midway purchased a policy from Travelers. On September 30, 2010, Midway discovered that a former employee had stolen $1 million from Midway. Midway notified both Federated and Travelers and Travelers paid the policy limit of $500,000. Federated declined coverage on the basis that its coverage terminated on October 6, 2009 and the one-year tail period terminated upon the effective date of the Travelers policy replacing the Federated policy. The court agreed finding that the term "replace" was unambiguous. *Midway Truck Parts, Inc. v. Federated Ins. Co.*, No. 11 CV 9060, 2013 WL 593860.

N.D. Ill. 1995. The policy expired in March 1992 and the complaint alleged that the loss was discovered in April 2003. The court granted American States' motion to dismiss. The employer argued that the embezzled money was under the domination and control of the dishonest employee and the discovery period should be tolled. The court noted that in the cases cited by the employer, the adverse domination and control was of the insured itself. *Willow Mgmt., Co. v. Am. States Ins. Co.*, No. 94 C 6994, 1995 WL 22862.

D.N.J. 2009. Credit manager for an auto dealership was involved in an embezzlement with others over two policy periods with separate insurers. The auto dealership sought recovery of multiple limits after receiving the single loss limit amount from the second carrier. The dealership argued that the definition of, "occurrence" was ambiguous and could mean multiple acts of theft. The court held that the scheme involving the conversion of multiple money orders constituted a single occurrence. The prior carrier, Royal Indemnity, denied coverage on the basis that the loss was not discovered by Pine Belt within the extended period to discover the loss after termination of the policy. Royal Indemnity argued that the extended period to discover loss terminated immediately upon the effective date of the successor carrier, Granite State's, policy, which became effective immediately upon termination of Royal Indemnity's coverage. Pine Belt argued that Royal Indemnity's policy was ambiguous since it was unclear whether the commercial crime coverage was written on a loss sustained or discovery form. The court found no ambiguity existed in determining that the policy was written on a loss sustained form and granted Royal Indemnity's motion for summary judgment. *Pine Belt Automotive, Inc. v. Royal Indemnity Co.,* No. 06-5995 (JAP), 2009 WL 1025564.

N.D. Tex. 1994. An employee stole during the terms of three policies, and the loss was discovered more than one year after the expiration of the first policy. The court noted that, "the First Policy plays no part in this case" because the one-year discovery period had expired. *Potomac Ins. Co. of Illinois v. Lone Star Web, Inc.,* Civ. No. 3:93-CV-2122-H, 1994 WL 494784.

Cal. Ct. App. 1995. Two employees embezzled from July 1988 to May 1991. Home Insurance Company issued a $100,000 policy commencing April 4, 1989, and twice renewed it for annual periods starting April 4, 1990, and April 4, 1991. There were different policy numbers, but the coverage and limits were not changed. Home Insurance paid the single loss limit of $100,000. A.B.S. claimed $100,000 per year, including the year preceding the first policy, and sued. The trial court granted summary judgment to Home Insurance. The court of appeals thought the issue was whether there was a single, continuous policy or multiple annual policies. In a 2-1 decision, the court of appeals reversed summary judgment and remanded the case. The court thought that the one-year discovery provision was evidence that the parties intended separate, independent annual contracts because under a continuous contract the discovery period would run from the end of the last policy period. *A.B.S. Clothing Collection, Inc. v. Home Ins. Co.*, 41 Cal. Rptr. 2d 166.

Fla. Dist. Ct. App. 1995. The employer had annual policies issued from February 1988 to February 1991. The dishonest employee embezzled throughout this period. The trial court granted summary judgment finding coverage under all four policies. The court of appeals reversed. The discovery of loss provision barred coverage under either of the first two policies. *Reliance Ins. Co. v. Treasure Coast Travel Agency, Inc.*, 660 So. 2d 1136.

Ga. Ct. App. 2003. An employee stole from its employer during each of the three years of the first policy and the first year of the second, renewal policy. The limit of insurance was $50,000, which Cincinnati Insurance paid. The trial court agreed with the employer that the limit was $50,000 per year. Cincinnati appealed, and the court held that the applicable limit for the three years of the first policy was $50,000 but that the amount stolen during the first year of the second policy was subject to another $50,000 limit. The court of appeals held that the stipulation that the first three years was a single policy foreclosed recovery of more than one limit for those years, but since the loss was discovered during the first year of the second policy, it was within the one-year discovery period of the first policy and thefts during the first policy could be claimed under the first policy. *Cincinnati Ins. Co. v. Sherman & Hemstreet, Inc.*, 581 S.E.2d 613.

Iowa 1994. Hopkins Sporting Goods had two package policies with employee dishonesty endorsements. The first policy ran from 1986 through 1989, and the second from 1989 to 1992. The loss was sustained during 1987 through 1991 and discovered in 1992. Hopkins claimed the $15,000 limit for each year. Cincinnati Insurance paid a single $15,000, arguing that the one-year discovery provision barred recovery for any year before 1989. The court agreed that the discovery clause clearly supported that position, but thought that the provision was "clouded" by the prior insurance provision. The court ignored the part of the prior insurance provision that made the coverage part of the current policy. *Cincinnati Ins. Co. v. Hopkins Sporting Goods, Inc.*, 522 N.W.2d 837.

Minn. Ct. App. 1992. An employee stole over the course of three years. The employer argued that there were three separate policies in force. Millers Mutual Insurance argued that there was one continuous policy and one limit of liability. The employer eventually conceded that "its failure to report the theft loss within one year, as required by the policy, precluded coverage for losses" during the term of the first policy. *Prairie Land & Cooperative v. Millers Mut. Ins. Ass'n of Illinois*, No. C2-91-1503, 1992 WL 20705.

Miss. 1999. An employee misappropriated money on 175 separate occasions from 1984 to 1988. Universal Underwriters provided a series of one-year package policies with employee dishonesty coverage, but no definition of "occurrence." The policies each required that loss be discovered within one year of the end of the Coverage Part period. The trial court held that recovery was limited by the discovery provision, but the state supreme court reversed because it thought that a prior insurance clause could be read to extend the discovery clause through each successive policy period. *Universal Underwriters Ins. Co. v. Buddy Jones Ford, Lincoln-Mercury, Inc.*, 734 So. 2d 173.

SECONDARY SOURCES

Edward G. Gallagher, *Limits of Liability, in* ANNOTATED COMMERCIAL CRIME POLICY 495 (Cole S. Kain & Lana M. Glovach eds., 2d ed. 2006).

D. Non-Cumulation

The Commercial Crime Protection Policy (Standard Form)[17] provides as follows:

Non-Cumulation of Limit of Insurance
Regardless of the number of years this Policy remains in force or the number of premiums paid, no Limit of

---

17   Crime Protection Policy, Standard Form No. SP 0001 (Revised to 04 12), Condition 15.

Insurance cumulates from year to year or Policy Period to Policy Period.

The Crime General Provisions (Discovery Form)[18] provides:

Non-Cumulation of Limit of Insurance
Regardless of the number of years this insurance remains in force or the number of premiums paid, no Limit of Insurance cumulates from year to year or period to period.

COMMENT

Courts often are faced with the issue of whether the non-cumulation clause impacts limits by policy period to policy period, or over each year of a multi-year policy. While some courts find the clause to be ambiguous, the practitioner should remain cognizant of the necessity for a thorough analysis as to how limits, including unused limits, are applied in determining liability.

ANNOTATIONS

2d Cir. 1971 (N.Y.). In 1965, Scranton obtained coverage in the amount of $4,000 and paid a yearly premium through 1969, when it discovered that its treasurer had embezzled funds each year, totaling in excess of $14,500. USF&G contended that its liability was limited to $4,000 since the position schedule bond provided that the Underwriter "shall not be liable under this bond on account of any employee for a larger amount in the aggregate than the amount stated opposite the position occupied by such employee." Scranton claimed that the language was both ambiguous and unconscionable. The court held that no ambiguity existed and the language clearly limited the Underwriter's liability to the specified amount throughout the life of the agreement. *Scranton Vol. Fire Co. v. USF&G,* 450 F.2d 775.

---

18 Crime General Provisions (Discovery Form), Standard Form CR 1100 (Revised to 04-97), General Condition 11.

4th Cir. 2001 (S.C.). There were two successive one-year policies with different policy numbers. An employee stole in excess of the $100,000 per occurrence limit during each of the two policy years. The employer claimed $200,000. Liberty tendered $100,000. The court thought that the non-cumulation provision was ambiguous because other courts had disagreed on its meaning. The Fourth Circuit did not suggest a reading of the provision that would support awarding two limits. [Note, this is an unpublished decision and pursuant to Fourth Circuit Rule 36c is not supposed to be cited as precedent]. *Spartan Iron & Metal Corp. v. Liberty Ins. Corp.*, 6 F. App'x 176.

5th Cir. 2008 (S.D. Miss.). Fifth Circuit affirmed district court holding on summary judgment. Employee's related acts of embezzlement over a decade and spanning multiple policy periods constituted only one occurrence and employer Madison was entitled to recover no more than the limits of the policy in effect when the theft was discovered. Mississippi courts recognize that an "occurrence" is determined by the cause or causes of the resulting injury. Although employee committed multiple related acts throughout the decade, court found there was only one cause of the injury sustained by Madison and that was the employee's dishonesty. The court looked to the unambiguous terms of the policy stating that multiple related acts may constitute a single occurrence. The court further held under Prior Insurance clause that only way Madison could recover for losses in a prior policy period would be if the losses incurred in the current policy period totaled less than the current limits, and then only to bring Madison's recovery up to the current policy's limits. *Madison Materials Co., Inc. v. St. Paul Fire & Marine Ins. Co.*, 523 F.3d 541.

8th Cir. 1983 (N.D.). Surety issued bonds for a trustee appointed in Chapter X reorganization proceedings. The bonds did not contain language proscribing cumulative liability. However, certificates of continuance that included annual premium statements provided that the liability of the company "shall not be cumulative." Although copies of these certificates were filed with the bankruptcy court, each renewal was found to be a separate contract with a separate limit of liability in that the bankruptcy judge did not formally approve the certificates, nor was there any indication that he had actual knowledge of the limiting language contained therein. *In re Endeco, Inc. U.S. f/u/o McMerty v. Fid. & Cas. Co. of N.Y.,* 718 F.2d 879.

8th Cir. 1960 (Mo.). A position schedule bond, periodically renewed during a fourteen-year period, provided that the underwriter's aggregate liability on account of any one employee would not exceed the sum scheduled for said employee and that coverage would not be cumulative. Upon discovery that its bookkeeper had embezzled funds over a number of years, the employer submitted a proof of loss for $11,600, notwithstanding the fact that the bookkeeper's scheduled coverage never exceeded $2,000. The court stated that there was no ambiguity in the limiting language and, when coupled with the indefinite term of the carrier's obligation, evidenced an intent to limit liability for losses on account of the particular employee to $2,000. *Mass. Bonding & Ins. Co. v. Julius Seidel Lumber Co.,* 279 F.2d 861.

11th Cir. 2009 (S.D. Fla.). An employee stole $42 million from his employer over a thirteen-year period. PBSJ sought recovery of the $2 million limit for each policy in effect during the entire period. The Eleventh Circuit affirmed summary judgment in favor of Federal, which paid a single limit of $2 million. The court looked to the language of the crime coverage, which stated that prior policies were terminated and would not afford coverage if not discovered and reported before the effective date of the current policy. Each policy also included a non-cumulation clause and limits on recovery up to $2 million. *PBSJ Corp. v. Federal Ins. Co.,* 347 Fed. Appx. 532.

C.D. Ca. 2010. This case involved fraudulent mortgages in excess of $30,000,000 and involved two policies. Both the primary policy and excess policies had limits of $15 million each. Fremont's claims against the excess carrier survived upon the court's ruling that Fremont's claim against the excess carrier alleged a loss that exceeded the primary carrier's limits. The excess carrier was subject to a valid claim if the loss exceeds the primary limits regardless whether the primary policy had yet to be exhausted. *Fremont Reorganizing Group v. Federal Ins. Co.,* No. SACV 09-01208 JVS (ANx), 2010 WL 444718.

D.C. Cir. 1951. A hospital bookkeeper embezzled in excess of $5,000 per year during a three-year period and approximately $3,900 during a fourth year. The hospital submitted a claim for $18,975 although the blanket position bond contained only $5,000 in scheduled coverage and a non-cumulation clause. In finding the carrier liable for a total of $5,000 the court rejected the hospital's argument that cumulative meant "carry-over" of unused coverage from year to year and stated that courts have consistently held liability to be limited, in the aggregate, to the amount stated where unambiguous language to that effect is included in coverage documentation. *Columbia Hosp. for Women & Lying-in Asylum v. USF&G,* 188 F. 2d 654.

D. Colo. 2004. A dishonest employee used several different schemes to steal money over a four-year period. During the last two years, the employer had coverage under policies written by Wausau. The issue was the applicable limit of insurance. The employer argued that the non-cumulation provision was ambiguous, citing cases from other jurisdictions. The court distinguished the cases by pointing to the loss under a "prior insurance written by us" provision. It did not address the non-cumulation provision in isolation. *Wausau Bus. Ins. Co. v. U.S. Motels Mgmt., Inc.,* 341 F. Supp. 2d 1180.

N.D. Ill. 1968. Savings & Loan sought recovery, up to the stated penalty for each of a multitude of covered activities committed by one of its directors. Held: The language employed by the Underwriter indicated an intention to limit liability as to any one individual to the specified amount. *Fed. Sav. & Loan Corp. v. Aetna Ins. Co.,* 279 F. Supp. 161.

M.D. Ala. 1963. St. Paul issued three successive fidelity policies covering losses up to $2,500, $10,000, and $10,000 respectively. During the same three-year period an employee embezzled in excess of $43,000. The policies were similar, covering losses discovered within three years of cancellation, and each provided that where the period allowed for discovery of loss under prior insurance had not elapsed, "the Company's liability under this bond and under such prior insurance shall not be cumulative." The dairy contended that St. Paul's liability under the three policies in question was $22,500. St. Paul sought to limit its liability to a maximum of $10,000 by virtue of the quoted provision. Held: The provision could only be interpreted as preventing any loss in excess of the stated limit from being carried forward and claimed under the terms of any succeeding policies so as to achieve a similar result had the dairy obtained coverage with separate and independent insurers for each of the three years. Based upon the evidence presented in connection with losses sustained during each period, the court found that the dairy was entitled to recover $2,500 for the first year of coverage, $2,500 for the second, and $10,000 for the third. *White Dairy Co., Inc. v. St. Paul Fire & Marine Ins. Co.*, 222 F. Supp. 1014.

M.D. La. 1974. A tax collector embezzled approximately $180,000 during a three-year period. Language contained in certificates renewing a position bond provided that liability "shall not be cumulative." held: Plaintiffs recovery limited to the stated penalty, and limiting language in the contract was clear and unambiguous. *Parish of East Baton Rouge v. Fid. & Cas. of N.Y.*, 373 F. Supp. 440.

D. Md. 2013. Two former executives of Emcor defraud company over a six-year period. Emcor sought recovery against GAIC under all three of GAIC's successive policies, as well as for losses for the period covered by prior insurer. GAIC argued under terms of the Loss Sustained During Prior Insurance section that each policy offered coverage only for conduct occurring during specified policy period, as well as for the period of coverage under immediately preceding policy. Emcor sought recovery for losses spanning over each policy period. The district court refused to afford coverage for losses that occurred during prior policy periods, and which were not known to Emcor until after the discovery window, including the one-year tail, had expired. The court held that GAIC policies clearly provided for loss sustained coverage for a finite period of time. GAIC's motion for partial summary judgment was granted. *Emcor Group, Inc. v. Great American Ins. Co.*, No. ELH-12-0142, 2013 WL 1315029.

D. Md. 2005. Various acts of embezzlement by physician's employee over three policy periods constituted one occurrence under employee dishonesty coverage of business insurance policy regardless of fact that employee used different means to embezzle funds. Plaintiff contended that Hartford sold a series of independent insurance policies over multiple policy years and that it was entitled to coverage for seven separate occurrences up to the limit of $25,000 for each occurrence under each of the three policy years. Hartford contended that acts embezzlement constituted one occurrence under the policy terms and that the maximum coverage of $25,000 is cumulative across all three policy years. However the court concluded that since the physician's five successive policies required different premiums to account for varied levels of coverage over different property each of the five policies was independent of each other. In looking at the occurrence definition, non-cumulation provision and the effect of prior insurance section, the court concluded that the employee's acts of embezzlement constitute one occurrence in each policy period and that the policies afforded coverage up to the $25,000 limit per policy year for each successive policy year during which the embezzlement occurred. *Glaser v. Hartford Cas. Ins. Co.*, 364 F. Supp. 2d 529.

D. Or. 2008. This case involved a $77 million claim under Federal Insurance's Pension and Welfare Fund Fiduciary Dishonesty Policy effective from 1993-2003. During the ten-year period the policy was renewed three times. The current policy included Non-Accumulation and Limits of Liability sections. As a result of a sophisticated Ponzi-like scheme, plaintiffs amassed losses in excess of $180 million, approximately $100 million of which were recovered through a receivership and third parties. Federal asserted that it paid the $1 million policy limit, which it contended was the total amount of its exposure under the bond for one loss. In granting summary judgment, the district court agreed with Federal in concluding that to allow plaintiff to recover $1 million for each fraudulent act would render the Total Liability clause in the bond meaningless. The court stated that the clause specifies that the policy limit applies to either a loss or losses caused by dishonesty. The court interpreted the clause to establish that a single-policy limit applies to every loss involving the dishonest fiduciary for a total of $1 million. Plaintiff also argued that it was entitled to recover the policy limits three times, once for each renewal period—equating to $3 million. In addressing the legal theories applicable to the earliest bond period, the court did not find the bond periods to be discrete as the forms had the same bond numbers, replacement forms were not issued and the renewal statement issued by Federal at the end of the period referenced a three-year premium bill for a "continuous" policy period. In referencing the Non-Accumulation of Liability clause, the court found that the losses were not cumulative from year to year. *United Association Union Local No. 290 ex rel. U.A.U. Local No. 290 Plumber, Steamfitter & Shipfitter Industry 401(k) Plan and Trust v. Federal Ins. Co.*, No. 07-1521-HA, 2008 WL 3523271.

Cal. Ct. App. 1995. Two employees embezzled from July 1988 to May 1991. Home Insurance issued a $100,000 policy commencing April 4, 1989, and twice renewed it for an annual period starting April 4, 1990, and April 4, 1991. There were different policy numbers, but the coverage and limits were not changed. Home Insurance paid the single loss limit of $100,000. A.B.S. claimed $100,000 per year, including the year preceding the first policy, and sued. The trial court granted summary judgment to Home Insurance. The court of appeals thought the issue was whether there was a single, continuous policy or multiple annual policies. In a 2-1 decision, the court of appeals reversed summary judgment and remanded the case. The court thought that the non-cumulation clause was ambiguous because it could mean that an unused portion of the limit of one policy or one year could not be carried forward and applied to loss under another policy or another year. *A.B.S. Clothing Collection, Inc. v. Home Ins. Co.*, 41 Cal. Rptr. 2d 166.

Conn. Super. Ct. 2000. Over an eighteen-month period, Shemitz Lighting's bookkeeper embezzled money by forging checks on Shemitz's accounts and diverting checks payable to Shemitz. Shemitz claimed a loss of $209,000. The limit of liability was $10,000 per occurrence. The court thought that the non-cumulation provision could mean only that unused limits from one period cannot be carried forward to the next period. The court held that the combination of the non-cumulation clause and the provision limiting recovery in a single occurrence were ambiguous, and granted summary judgment to Shemitz holding that each act of embezzlement was a separate occurrence. *Shemitz Lighting, Inc. v. Hartford Fire Ins. Co.*, No. CV960052970, 2000 WL 1781840.

Fla. Ct. App. 1995. The employer had annual policies issued from February 1988 to February 1991. The dishonest employee embezzled throughout this period. The trial court granted summary judgment finding coverage under all four policies. The court of appeals reversed. The non-cumulation provision alone probably would not have been sufficient to limit the recovery to one policy, but in combination with the "prior insurance issued by us" clause, "we think that this insurer has accomplished what insurers with non-cumulation provisions alone apparently intended, but failed to state with sufficient clarity . . . ." *Reliance Ins. Co. v. Treasure Coast Travel Agency, Inc.*, 660 So. 2d 1136.

Fla. Dist. Ct. App. 1978. City sought to recover for an employee's misappropriations over a two-year period covered by successive "package" policies. Distinguishing fidelity policies that provide multi-year coverage from separate, successive obligations, the court held that language to the effect that liability under consecutive bonds would not be cumulative could not be interpreted so as to allow the insurer to avoid liability for losses incurred during each policy period. *City of Miami Springs v. Travelers Indem. Co.*, 365 So. 2d 1030.

Ga. 2004. The parties stipulated that there were two three-year policies and that the employee stole during all three years of the first policy and the first year of the second policy. The limit of liability was $50,000. The trial court awarded the employer its losses up to $50,000 for each year it had coverage. The court of appeals reversed as to the three years of the first policy but still permitted cumulation between the first policy and the first year of the second policy. The supreme court affirmed. The court held that the non-cumulation clause was ambiguous as between one policy and the next because it could mean that an unused limit was not carried forward to future years. The court, therefore, permitted the insured to recover up to a new limit for the thefts in the first year of the renewal policy. The court did not mention the "prior insurance written by us" provision that would have prevented this result. For each of the three years of the first policy, however, the court applied the non-cumulation clause to bar any argument that the limit of insurance increased because of payment of annual premiums or the three-year term of the policy. The court pointed out that there was no annual limit to carry forward. *Sherman & Hemstreet, Inc. v. Cincinnati Ins. Co.*, 594 S.E.2d 648.

Ga. Ct. App. 2003. An employee stole from its employer during each of the three years of the first policy and the first year of the second, renewal policy. The limit of insurance was $50,000, which Cincinnati Insurance paid. The trial court agreed with the employer that the limit was $50,000 per year. Cincinnati appealed, and the court held that the applicable limit for the three years of the first policy was $50,000 but that the amount stolen during the first year of the second policy was subject to another $50,000 limit. The court of appeals held that the stipulation that the first three years was a single policy foreclosed recovery of more than one limit for those years, but that the non-cumulation provision was ambiguous because it could mean that the insured could not carry unused

ANNOTATED COMMERCIAL CRIME INSURANCE POLICY

parts of a limit forward to the next policy period. *Cincinnati Ins. Co. v. Sherman & Hemstreet, Inc.*, 581 S.E.2d 613.

Iowa 1994. Hopkins Sporting Goods had two package policies with employee dishonesty endorsements. The first policy ran from 1986 through 1989 and the second from 1989 to 1992. The loss was sustained during 1987 through 1991 and discovered in 1992. Hopkins claimed the $15,000 limit for each year. Cincinnati Insurance paid a single $15,000. The court thought that the non-cumulation language was ambiguous and thus did not bar allowance of $15,000 per year. *Cincinnati Ins. Co. v. Hopkins Sporting Goods, Inc.*, 522 N.W.2d 837.

Kan. Ct. App. 1990. The court affirmed summary judgment for an employer allowing recovery of two policy limits. There were two successive one-year policies. The employer argued that the non-cumulation provision could mean that there was no liability under the current policy for losses under prior policies. The court admitted that the Farmland Mutual Insurance meant to limit its liability to a single limit and that the employer's construction was "strained," but cited several pre-1986 cases supporting it. *Penalosa Coop. Exch. v. Farmland Mut. Ins. Co.*, 789 P.2d 1196.

Ky. Ct. App. 2014. The Providence City Clerk was found guilty of embezzling close to $1 million from the City's utility fund over multiple years. The City submitted a claim under Ohio Casualty's bond and argued that the bond, written over seven years, was a series of separate, independent contracts that renewed annually and allowed the City to recover $300,000 in losses every year the bond was in effect.[19] The Kentucky Court of Appeals granted Ohio Casualty's motion for summary judgment and held that Ohio Casualty was liable for one limit of $300,000, concluding that the bond was written for an indefinite period, regardless of the fact that renewal notices for renewal premiums were issued each year, and the policy was not renewed each year during the relevant period. The court noted that the City Clerk's position was by appointment, not election, which supported the position that the bond was written for an indefinite period rather than a specific term. The court looked further at the facts of the claim in determining that the bond was

---

19   The issues in this case dealt with non-cumulation in a surety public official bond.

continuous for an indefinite period of time, inclusive of the length of time the City Clerk remained in her position. *Ohio Casualty Ins. Co. v. City of Providence,* No. 2012-CA-002204-MR, 2014 WL 92268.

La. Ct. App. 1982. The state sought to recover in excess of $75,000 under a public employees blanket bond that had been renewed annually for six years. Held: Non-cumulation clause explicit and unambiguous and not against public policy. *State of Louisiana ex rel. Guste v. Aetna Cas. & Sur. Co.,* 417 So. 2d 404, *aff'd,* 429 So. 2d 106.

Md. Ct. App. 1970. Non-cumulation provision applied to limit recovery to the stated penalty. *Comm'r of Leonardtown v. Fid. Cas. Co. of N.Y.,* 270 A.2d 788.

Mich. 1984. Statute required licensed mobile home dealers to obtain a "properly executed bond or renewal certificate." Where renewal certificates were used, the statute provided that such be "in the same amount and with the same effect as an original bond." The court found the surety liable up to the extent of the policy limit for each year, despite a policy provision limiting aggregate liability to the stated penalty. Since existing law must be read in conjunction with statutory bonds, the court concluded that the scope of the surety's obligation must be determined according to statutory requirements. *General Elect. Credit Corp. v. Wolverine Ins. Co.,* 362 N.W.2d 595.

Minn. 1979. In light of the ambiguity that existed concerning the accumulation of liability, the court interpreted policy so as to allow recovery in excess of the policy's aggregate limits. *Columbia Heights Motors v. Allstate Ins. Co.,* 275 N.W.2d 32.

Minn. Ct. App. 1997. An employee embezzled during the periods of two consecutive annual policies. The court held that American Family Mutual's obligation was to pay only one limit. The employer argued that the non-cumulation provision was ambiguous. The court noted that the provision was not to be read in isolation and that with the occurrence definition recovery was unambiguously limited. The court stated, "Thus, the occurrence definition and the non-cumulation clause work in conjunction with each other to restrict Landico's recovery. The non-cumulation clause limits recovery vertically, within each year of coverage, while the occurrence definition limits recovery horizontally, across multiple years of coverage." *Landico, Inc. v. Am. Family Mut. Ins. Co.*, 559 N.W.2d 438.

Minn. Ct. App. 1992. An employee stole over the course of three years. The employer argued that there were three separate policies in force. Millers' Mutual Insurance argued that there was one continuous policy and one limit of liability. The court thought that there were three policies and that the non-cumulation provision was inconsistent with the declarations pages, which had new policy periods, and ambiguous in that it could mean the insured could not carry unused parts of the limit forward to another policy period. The court affirmed summary judgment for the employer allowing recovery of two limits. *Prairie Land & Cooperative v. Millers Mut. Ins. Ass'n of Illinois*, No. C2-91-1503, 1992 WL 20705.

Mo. 1968. State sought to recover on two, successive, one-year blanket position policies for losses occurring during both periods. Held: Language limiting the underwriter's liability to the amount of the later policy, in the aggregate, was unambiguous. *State ex rel. State Dep't of Public Health & Welfare v. Hanover Ins. Co.*, 431 S.W.2d 141.

N.Y. App. Div. 2001. Plaintiff had renewal commercial crime policy for the period 1993-1996 with Firemen's Insurance, a subsidiary of Continental Insurance. Plaintiff subsequently had renewal polices from 1996-1999 following Continental's merger with CNA. The CNA policy included both prior insurance section and non-cumulation sections. Shared-Interest sought recovery for thefts committed by employee between 1994-1997 in the amount of $460,316.15. CNA paid the policy limit of $100,000 in exchange for a release under the Fireman's policy in effect during the CNA policy period. Plaintiff filed a claim for an additional $100,000 under the policy in effect during the Continental period. CNA denied the claim relying upon the terms of the policy, which permitted recovery of no more than the policy limit during the effective period of the policy including renewals. Upon cross motions for summary judgment, the Supreme Court granted plaintiff's motion. The appellate court reversed. The court agreed with CNA that what plaintiff attempted to characterize as three separate policy periods were in actuality three-year premium terms. The court also rejected plaintiff's argument that following Continental's merger with CNA, Fireman's became a different insurance company from the one who issued the initial policy. Last, while the court did not need to review a stacking of coverages issue, the court did note that even if the policy in effect during the Continental period and the CNA period were treated as two separate policies, that anti-stacking provisions of the Crime General Provisions Form were unambiguous and prevented double recovery. *Shared-Interest Mgmt. Inc. v. CNA Fin. Ins. Group*, 725 N.Y.S.2d 469.

Ohio Ct. App. 2014. A bookkeeper for E.J. Zeller began working for another company, City Rentals, in the same capacity in 2005. On August 8, 2008, it was discovered that the bookkeeper had embezzled from both companies. Zeller purchased an Auto Owner's policy that covered acts of employee dishonesty with an endorsement that extended coverage to losses up to a $10,000 limit. A crime endorsement included additional coverage up to $50,000. The initial policy period was August 12, 2003 to August 12, 2004 and similar policies covered all periods through August 12, 2009. The declarations provided that acceptance of the next year's coverage was notice that the prior year's coverage had been canceled. City Rentals purchased similar policies from Auto Owners with a policy period of June 10, 2005 to June 10, 2006 and renewed it on June 10, 2006. At renewal on June 10, 2007, City Rentals discontinued the crime endorsement. On June 10, 2008, City Rentals renewed the policy increasing the limit of insurance in the property endorsement for employee dishonesty from $10,000 to $15,000. Auto Owners paid $60,000 to Zeller and $10,000 to City Rentals as the maximum coverage. The court held that the non-cumulation provision in the policies did not operate to exclude coverage for employee dishonesty under prior policies, the provision was specifically limited to "this insurance" and did not apply to prior policies. *E.J. Zeller, Inc. v. Auto Owners Ins. Co.*, No. 4-14-04, 2014 WL 5803028.

Pa. Super. Ct. 2006. Reliance wrote a single policy for a one-year period. It was extended three times by endorsements. An employee embezzled substantial sums during the period the policy was in force. The employer claimed a policy limit for each year. The court affirmed summary judgment for Reliance on the ground that there was a continuous bonding scheme, which, under Pennsylvania law, permits recovery of a single limit. The court also noted that the non-cumulation and prior insurance provisions were unambiguous and did not support the employer's argument. *Reliance Ins. Co. v. IRPC, Inc.*, 904 A.2d 912.

Pa. Super. Ct. 1981. Three successive policies were issued by different entities within the Continental Companies. In all other respects, the policies were identical and provided that the aggregate liability of the "Company" was limited to the stated penalty. *Held*: Since each instrument was identical, each included reference to "Continental Insurance Companies," and each was signed by the same person as secretary of the three entities, the parties intended to continue the coverage afforded by the preceding policy for a new period, and therefore carrier's liability was limited in the aggregate to $5,000. *Eddystone Fire Co. No. 1 v. Cont'l Ins. Co.*, 425 A.2d 803.

Pa. 1962. Carrier issued successive policies with stated limits of $5,000 and $2,000 respectively. Both policies provided that the carrier's aggregate liability would be limited to the larger of the penalties, provided that the period for discovery under the earlier coverage had not expired. *Held*: Liability limited to the later, $2,000 penalty, since the loss was not discovered before the expiration of the one-year period for discovery under prior coverage. *Exch. Bldg. Ass'n v. Indem. Ins. Co. of N. Am.*, 12 A.2d 924.

Va. 1990. An employee stole more than the $10,000 limit in each of the four years coverage was in place. The court reversed the trial court and held that the non-cumulation provision limited Graphic Arts Mutual Insurance Company's liability to one $10,000 limit. The court stated, "The insurance contract explicitly limits Graphic Arts' liability to a maximum of $10,000 for the entire coverage period, regardless of the number of years the coverage was in effect." *Graphic Arts Mut. Ins. Co. v. C.W. Warthen Co.*, 397 S.E.2d 876.

SECONDARY SOURCES

David T. DiBiase, *Fidelity Claims in Excess of Policy Limits—Problems and Solutions,* 52 INS. COUNSEL J. 660 (1985).

Edward G. Gallagher, *Limits of Liability, in* ANNOTATED COMMERCIAL CRIME POLICY 495 (Cole S. Kain & Lana M. Glovach eds., 2d ed. 2006).

Edward G. Gallagher, *Limit of Liability, in* COMMERCIAL CRIME POLICY 451 (Randall I. Marmor & John J. Tomaine eds., 2d ed. 2005).

William J. Hacker, *Limit of Liability, in* COMMERCIAL CRIME POLICY 14-1 (Gilbert J. Schroeder ed., 1997).

Tracey Haley, *Cumulation of Crime Policy Limits—The Impact of A.B.S. Clothing* (unpublished paper presented at Annual Meeting of ABA, Fid. & Sur. Law Comm. 1998)) (on file at the Stradley Library, No. 2873).

Patrick O'Connor & D. M. Studler, *Limits of Liability: A Multi-Faceted Perspective,* (unpublished paper presented at Annual Meeting of Sur. Claims Inst. 1999).

Robert Olausen, *Commercial Crime Insurance: The Changing Landscape* (unpublished paper presented at Annual Meeting of Sur. Claims Inst. 1997).

Tracey Santor et al., *Limits of Liability, in* HANDLING FIDELITY BOND CLAIMS 319 (Michael Keeley & Sean Duffy eds., 2d ed. 2005).

Tracey Santor, *Fidelity Casenotes*, NEWSLETTER (Sur. & Fid. Claims Inst., Overland Park, Kan.) May 10, 2010, at 17-22.

John J. Tomaine, *Through the Looking Glass: Determining the Applicable Limit of Liability and Deductible in Multiple Check Claims* (unpublished paper presented at Annual Meeting of ABA, Fid. & Sur. Law Comm. 2001) (on file at the Stradley Library, No. 3170).

Christopher R. Ward et al., *Recent Developments in Fidelity and Surety Law*, 46 TORT TRIAL & INS. PRAC. L.J. 371, 382-84 (Winter 2011).

Christopher R. Ward et al., *Recent Developments in Fidelity and Surety Law*, 45 TORT TRIAL & INS. PRAC. L.J. 367, 375-76 (Winter 2010).

E. Prior Insurance

The Commercial Crime Policy (Loss Sustained Form)[20] provides:

Loss Sustained Entirely During Prior Insurance Not Issued By Us or Any Affiliate

(1) If you "discover" loss during the Policy Period shown in the Declarations, resulting directly from an "occurrence" taking place during the policy period of any prior cancelled insurance that was issued to you or a predecessor in interest by another company, and the period of time to discover loss under that insurance had expired, we will pay for the loss under this Policy; provided:

   (a) This Policy became effective at the time of cancellation of the prior insurance; and

   (b) The loss would have been covered under this Policy had it been in effect at the time of the "occurrence."

The Crime General Provisions (Loss Sustained Form)[21] provides:

Loss Sustained During Prior Insurance

a. If you, or any predecessor in interest, sustained loss during the period of any prior insurance that you or the predecessor in interest could have recovered under that insurance except that the time within which to discover loss had expired, we will pay for it under this insurance, provided:

   (1) This insurance became effective at the time of cancellation or termination of the prior insurance; and

---

20 Commercial Crime Policy (Loss Sustained Form), Standard Form No. CR 00 23 08 13 (Revised to 08-13), Condition 1.p. Note this provision contains additional language relating to the application of deductibles and limits of amounts to be paid.

21 Crime General Provisions (Loss Sustained Form), Standard Form CR 1000 (Revised to 04-97), Condition 10.

(2) **The loss would have been covered by this insurance had it been in effect when the acts or events causing the loss were committed or occurred.**

b. **The insurance under this condition is part of, not in addition to, the Limits of Insurance applying to this insurance and is limited to the lesser of the amount recoverable under:**

(1) **This insurance as of its effective date; or**

(2) **The prior insurance had it remained in effect.**

COMMENT

The prior insurance provision serves the crucial function of giving the insured coverage for loss sustained during the term of a prior policy if the loss was discovered too late to claim under the prior policy. This is a departure from a true loss sustained policy and significantly increases the protection afforded the insured.

There are conditions on this coverage extension. The insured cannot receive more under the prior insurance provision than it would have received under the prior policy had it remained in effect. Therefore, the limit of liability of the prior policy cuts off what can be carried forward to the current policy.

Most importantly, any recovery under the prior insurance provision is a recovery under the current policy, not under the prior policy, and is subject to the limit of insurance of the current policy.

ANNOTATIONS

5th Cir. 2008 (W.D. La.). St. Paul issued five one-year policies to Whitaker for the years 1998-2002. After filing for bankruptcy in 2003, Whitaker discovered that its employee embezzled in excess of $500,000 over several years through a forged check scheme. Whitaker filed a claim under each of the St. Paul polices. St. Paul paid Whitaker $110,000 under the 2002 policy and declined coverage under the prior policies. St. Paul relied upon the terms of the policy extending the discovery period for an additional one year after expiration for losses under the current policy. Since Whitaker failed to discovery the losses within one year of the prior policies, the bankruptcy court granted Whitaker's motion for summary judgment. The district court subsequently reversed and granted St. Paul's motion for summary judgment, which was affirmed by the Fifth Circuit. *In re Whitaker Constr. Co., Inc.,* 288 Fed. Appx. 153.

8th Cir. 1999 (Minn.). An employee stole during the terms of successive policies written by USF&G and Travelers. The loss was discovered within the one-year discovery period of the USF&G, but the insured law firm initially notified only Travelers, the insurer on the second policy. Travelers paid for losses incurred during the term of its policy, but denied liability for earlier losses. The court agreed that the loss under prior insurance clause of the second policy did not apply because the loss was discovered in time to claim under the first (USF&G's) policy. Late notice barred the claim on the first policy not late discovery. If the first, three-year policy were regarded as separate annual policies, then the loss would have been discovered too late to claim under the first two such policies, but Travelers's policy would not have become effective at the time of their cancellation or termination. *Winthrop & Weinstine, P.A. v. Travelers Cas. & Sur. Co.,* 187 F.3d 871.

9th Cir. 2009 (D. Ariz.). Ninth Circuit affirms district court holding on summary judgment that Superstition is limited to one limit of insurance per occurrence, which the court equated to entire embezzlement regardless of fact that the employee was guilty of multiple embezzlements. Losses discovered within the one-year tail from the end of the policy period were limited to single-policy limits regardless of whether the loss took place over more than one policy period. The court held that a new policy period does not trigger the beginning of a new occurrence, rather the term, "occurrence" can span more than one policy period. Further, certain losses occurring before the beginning of the policy period are part of, and not in addition to, the current policy limits. *Superstition Crushing, LLC v. Travelers Cas. and Surety Co. of America,* 360 Fed. Appx. 844.

10th Cir. 1992 (Utah). The university suffered a loss of works of art over the course of ten to twelve years. Lumbermens Mutual was the insurer on the policy in force when the loss was discovered. Lumbermens acknowledged liability under the prior insurance provision, but argued that the amounts carried forward from earlier years were limited by the limits of insurance under the prior year policies. The court agreed. *Brigham Young Univ. v. Lumbermens Mut. Cas. Co.*, 965 F.2d 830.

10th Cir. 1971 (Kan.). Bank discovered losses from a check kiting scheme during term of bond written by National Surety on a "loss discovered" basis. After National Surety cancelled this bond, the bank obtained a second bond from Continental written on a "loss sustained" basis. The second bond also covered losses sustained during the prior bond, if the losses "would have been recoverable" under the prior bond. After National Surety paid the bank the face amount of the bond, the bank discovered that the perpetrator of the check kiting scheme had also caused losses on forged notes during the term of the first bond. *Held*: Bank could not recover face amount of bond from Continental. This loss would not have been "recoverable" under the prior bond, because National Surety had already paid the face amount of other losses caused by the same person. *Traders State Bank, Glen Elder, Kansas v. Cont'l Ins. Co.*, 448 F.2d 280.

11th Cir. 2009 (S.D. Fla.). An employee stole $42 million from his employer over a thirteen-year period. PBSJ sought recovery of the $2 million limit for each policy in effect during the entire period. The Eleventh Circuit affirmed summary judgment in favor of Federal, which paid a single limit of $2 million. The court looked to the language of the crime coverage, which stated that prior policies were terminated and would not afford coverage if not discovered and reported before the effective date of the current policy. Each policy also included a non-cumulation clause and limits on recovery up to $2 million. *PBSJ Corp. v. Federal Ins. Co.,* 347 Fed. Appx. 532.

W.D. Ark. 1962. Fort Smith Tobacco & Candy discovered losses from employee dishonesty several months after one bond had terminated and been replaced by a second. Fort Smith notified only the second carrier, not the first. More than one year after the first bond had terminated, the second carrier denied coverage. *Held*: Fort Smith did not meet its burden of proving that losses in question occurred during term of second bond, and second carrier was not estopped from asserting this defense. *Fort Smith Tobacco & Candy Co. v. Am. Guar. & Liab. Ins. Co.*, 208 F. Supp. 244.

D. Ariz. 2009. EaglePitcher's (EPI) employee embezzled millions of dollars from corporate assets and pension fund assets. Employee Brock was terminated from EPI in March 2002. EPI claimed his termination was due to the company's transfer from Cincinnati to Phoenix. Brock continued to work for EPI through an entity called Interconnect to assist in the transition to Phoenix until July 31, 2002. EPI's investigation into Brock's activities was kept within a small inner circle, which did not include EPI's Risk Manager. The policy in effect during much of Brock's investigation was issued by Federal Insurance. Federal's policy expired on August 1, 2002. At that time, a new policy was issued by Zurich. Both policies included reporting requirements upon discovery of loss. By endorsement, both reporting requirements were triggered only by discovery of the loss by the company's Risk Manager. Notice was ultimately submitted to Zurich in November 2002 and to Federal in March 2003. Federal declined coverage based upon the policy terms requiring discovery and notice within sixty days of the expiration of the policy. Zurich denied liability based on the "Cancellation As to Any Employee" condition and also asserted that EPI discovered the loss in time to report it under Federal's policy. Upon careful analysis of the timing and circumstances of the discovery of the loss by the Risk Manager, and in conjunction with the Loss Sustained During Prior Insurance section of Zurich's policy, the court granted EPI's motion for summary judgment finding that EPI did not discover its loss from Brock's actions until after the reporting time required under the Crime Coverage section of Federal's policy had expired. Thus, the court held that by the terms of its policy, Zurich agreed to cover losses that Federal would have covered but for the termination of Federal's policy. *EaglePitcher Management Co. v. Zurich American Ins Co.*, 640 F. Supp. 2d 1109.

D. Colo. 2004. A dishonest employee used several different schemes to steal money over a four-year period. During the last two years, the employer had coverage under policies written by Wausau. The issue was the applicable limit of insurance. The court rejected the employer's argument that the prior insurance clause entitled it to additional sums for losses during the terms of prior policies written by other insurers. Wausau had already paid the limit of the current policy, and that was all the employer was entitled to receive. *Wausau Bus. Ins. Co. v. U.S. Motels Mgmt., Inc.*, 341 F. Supp. 2d 1180.

N.D. Ill. 2008. From 2000-2005, American was insured under six policies issued by both General Casualty and Acuity that covered employee dishonesty. In 2005, American discovered that an employee had embezzled funds and notified Acuity of the claim. The fraudulent checks had been issued during policies issued by both carriers. The court held that Acuity's annual renewals created three-year-long one-year policies rather than three-year-long continuous policy and that the termination of each policy period started new one-year discovery period for claims under that policy. *American Auto Guardian, Inc. v. Acuity Mutual Ins. Co.*, 548 F .Supp. 2d 624.

E.D. La. 1997. Reliance moved for summary judgment on the grounds that the dishonest acts took place prior to the commencement of its policy but were discovered within the discovery period of the prior policy and so there was no prior insurance coverage. The court found genuine issues of fact as to when the dishonest acts occurred and denied the motion. *Maxicare Health Plans v. Reliance Ins. Co.*, No. CIV. A. 96-2477, CIV.A. 96-2457, 1997 WL 472667.

E.D. La. 1997. The court granted summary judgment to USF&G because the loss was discovered prior to commencement of the policy. The prior insurance provision extends coverage to losses sustained during the period of certain prior policies, but only if the loss is discovered during the period of the current policy. *USF&G v. Maxicare Health Plans*, No. CIV.A.96-245, 1997 WL 466802.

D. Md. 2013. Two former executives of Emcor defraud company over a six-year period. Emcor sought recovery against GAIC under all three of GAIC's successive policies, as well as for losses for the period covered by prior insurer. GAIC argued under terms of the Loss Sustained During Prior Insurance section that each policy offered coverage only for conduct occurring during specified policy period, as well as the period of coverage under immediately preceding policy. Emcor sought recovery for losses spanning over each policy period. District court refused to afford coverage for losses that occurred during prior policy periods and were not known to Emcor until after the discovery window, including the one-year tail, had expired. The court held that GAIC policies clearly provided for loss sustained coverage for a finite period of time. GAIC's motion for partial summary judgment granted. *Emcor Group, Inc. v. Great American Ins. Co.*, No. ELH-12-0142, 2013 WL 1315029.

E.D. Mich. 2009. Hartman & Tyner owned and managed over thirty apartment complexes. An employee in cahoots with outside vendors embezzled $4.6 million over many years. Federal offered to pay one single loss of $1 million, which was the limit on the current policy. Hartman & Tyner sought to recover three separate limits, one for each person involved in the fraud. The Eastern District of Michigan concluded that the employee was an integral part of each element of the fraud. Since the policy provided that a series of acts by an employee constituted one occurrence, the court agreed with Federal that there was a single loss. The court also noted that the policy provided that recovery under more than one policy was precluded. *Hartman & Tyner, Inc. v. Federal Ins. Co.*, No. 08-12461, 2009 WL 3152957.

D. Minn. 1998. An employee stole over the course of four years. For the first three, the insured law firm had coverage from USF&G. During the fourth year, when the loss was discovered, it had coverage with Travelers. Travelers, the second insurer paid for losses sustained during the term of its policy. The law firm argued that the prior insurance provision made Travelers liable for losses sustained during the terms of the USF&G's policy. The court disagreed and granted summary judgment to Travelers. The prior insurance provision did not obligate Travelers to pay for losses sustained during the terms of the prior policy because the loss was discovered in time to claim under the prior policy. Even if the prior policy were treated as three separate policies and the loss discovered too late to claim under the first two, Travelers' policy did not become effective at the termination or cancellation of the first two policies. *Winthrop & Weinstine, P.A. v. Travelers Cas. & Sur. Co.*, 993 F. Supp. 1248.

D.N.J. 2009. Credit manager for an auto dealership was involved in an embezzlement with others over two policy periods with separate insurers. The auto dealership sought recovery of multiple limits after receiving the single loss limit amount from the second carrier. The dealership argued that the definition of, "occurrence" was ambiguous and could mean multiple acts of theft. The court held that the scheme involving the conversion of multiple money orders constituted a single occurrence. The prior carrier, Royal Indemnity, denied coverage on the basis that the loss was not discovered by Pine Belt within the extended period to discover loss after termination of the policy. Royal Indemnity argued that the extended period to discover the loss terminated immediately upon the effective date of the successor carrier, Granite State's, policy, which became effective immediately upon termination of Royal Indemnity's coverage. Pine Belt argued that Royal Indemnity's policy was ambiguous since it was unclear whether the commercial crime coverage was written on a loss sustained or discovery form. The court found no ambiguity existed in determining that he policy was written on a loss sustained form and granted Royal Indemnity's motion for summary judgment. *Pine Belt Automotive, Inc. v. Royal Indemnity Co.*, No. 06-5995 (JAP), 2009 WL 1025564.

D.R.I. 2006. An employee stole during the terms of three policies. The amount taken during the term of the third policy was less than the deductible. The court rejected the employer's argument that there was coverage under the prior insurance provision. The third policy overlapped with, and therefore did not become effective upon the termination or cancellation of, the second policy. It was also a matter of disputed facts whether the time to discover the loss under the second policy had expired. *Armbrust Int'l, Ltd. v. Travelers Cas. & Sur. Co. of Am.*, No. C.A. 04-212 ML, 2006 WL 1207659.

Cal. Ct. App. 1995. Two employees embezzled from July 1988 to May 1991. Home Insurance Company issued a $100,000 policy commencing April 4, 1989, and twice renewed it for annual periods starting April 4, 1990, and April 4, 1991. There were different policy numbers, but the coverage and limits were not changed. Home Insurance paid the single loss limit of $100,000. A.B.S. claimed $100,000 per year, including the year preceding the first policy. The trial court granted summary judgment to Home Insurance. The court of appeals thought the issue was whether there was a single, continuous policy or multiple annual policies. In a 2-1 decision, the court of appeals reversed summary judgment and remanded the case. The court thought that the prior insurance provision could mean that the insured had coverage for losses sustained under prior policies but discovered too late to claim under the prior policies. The court concluded, "Thus, the parties' intent to enter into one continuous contract cannot be clearly and unambiguously established by the 'prior loss' provision of the contract." *A.B.S. Clothing Collection, Inc. v. Home Ins. Co.*, 41 Cal. Rptr. 2d 166.

Ga. Ct. App. 2003. An employee stole from its employer during each of the three years of the first policy and the first year of the second, renewal policy. The limit of insurance was $50,000, which Cincinnati Insurance paid. The trial court agreed with the employer that the limit was $50,000 per year. Cincinnati appealed, and the court held that the applicable limit for the three years of the first policy was $50,000 but that the amount stolen during the first year of the second policy was subject to another $50,000 limit. The court of appeals held that the stipulation that the first three years was a single policy foreclosed recovery of more than one limit for those years. The court correctly noted that the prior insurance provision did not apply because the loss was discovered during the one-year discovery period of the first policy. *Cincinnati Ins. Co. v. Sherman & Hemstreet, Inc.*, 581 S.E.2d 613.

Iowa 1994. Hopkins Sporting Goods had two package policies with employee dishonesty endorsements. The first policy ran from 1986 through 1989 and the second from 1989 to 1992. The loss was sustained during 1987 through 1991 and discovered in 1992. Hopkins claimed the $15,000 limit for each year. Cincinnati Insurance paid a single $15,000 arguing that the one-year discovery provision barred recovery for any year before 1989. The court agreed the discovery clause clearly supported that position, but thought that the provision was "clouded" by the prior insurance provision. The court ignored the part of the prior insurance provision that made the coverage part of the current policy. *Cincinnati Ins. Co. v. Hopkins Sporting Goods, Inc.*, 522 N.W.2d 837.

Ky. Ct. App. 1939. Fidelity & Deposit Company wrote banker's blanket bonds covering a bank and then the bank's successor. More than one year after the first bond terminated, defalcations of an employee of the original bank were discovered. The pertinent bond provision was held to be ambiguous and, therefore, to provide coverage of losses under the prior bond, which were discovered more than one year after its term had ended. *Fid. & Dep. Co. of Md. v. Lyon*, 124 S.W.2d 74.

La. 1983. The State's blanket fidelity bond contained no specific termination or cancellation date and was continued in force for six years by an annual premium. The bond further provided that the stated amount of coverage did not cumulate from year to year. Acknowledging contrary opinions, the court held the bond to be one continuous contract instead of a series of successive contracts. Consequently, the State, who sustained losses over each of the six years covered by the bond, could recover the amount of liability coverage only once. The non-cumulation clause precluded collection of the bond's coverage for each year the State sustained a loss. *State ex rel. Guste v. Aetna Cas. & Sur. Co.*, 429 So. 2d 106.

Miss. 1999. An employee misappropriated money on 175 separate occasions from 1984 to 1988. The insurer provided a series of one-year package policies with employee dishonesty coverage, but no definition of "occurrence." The policies each required that loss be discovered within one year of the end of the Coverage Part period. The trial court held that recovery was limited by the discovery provision, but the Supreme Court reversed because it thought that a prior insurance clause could be read to extend the discovery clause through each successive policy period. *Universal Underwriters Ins. Co. v. Buddy Jones Ford, Lincoln-Mercury, Inc.*, 734 So. 2d 173.

Mo. 1968. Employee misappropriated funds during the terms of two consecutive bonds issued by the same insurer. The loss was discovered within the time permitted for suit on the first bond. A bond provision limiting aggregate recovery to the larger of either bond amount was unambiguous, and liability was limited to judgment for amount of later bond. *State ex. rel. State Dep't of Health & Welfare, Division of Welfare, v. Hanover Ins. Co.*, 431 S.W. 2d 141.

N.D. 1993. An employee embezzled during the terms of three consecutive policies. The court held that the employer could recover no more than a single limit because the prior insurance provision showed an intent to have one continuous policy. Although not the standard policy, the prior insurance clause clearly limited the recovery to the smaller of the limit of the current policy or the limit of the prior policy. The court seemed wedded to the idea of a single versus continuous policy and reached the right result by forcing a finding of a continuous policy. *Kavaney Realtor & Developer, Inc. v. Travelers Ins. Co.*, 501 N.W.2d 335.

Pa. Super. Ct. 2006. Reliance wrote a single policy for a one-year period. It was extended three times by endorsements. An employee embezzled substantial sums during the period the policy was in force. The employer claimed a policy limit for each year. The court affirmed summary judgment for Reliance on the ground that there was a continuous bonding scheme, which, under Pennsylvania law, permits recovery of a single limit. The court also noted that the non-cumulation and prior insurance provisions were unambiguous and did not support the employer's argument. *Reliance Ins. Co. v. IRPC, Inc.*, 904 A.2d 912.

Pa. 1940. Corporation reduced its fidelity coverage but discovered dishonest acts of a former secretary exceeding even the larger of the bonds over two years later. The first bond covered only losses discovered within one year after cancellation. The second bond contained a superseded surety rider, which covered any loss under the prior bond "which would have been recoverable under said prior bond had it continued in force," but limited in amount to "no more than amount recoverable under the attached bond." *Held*: The corporation can recover only the smaller of the two bonds. *Exch. Bldg. Ass'n of Fairhill v. Indem. Ins. Co.*, 12 A.2d 924.

Va. 1988. An employee stole in excess of the $20,000 limit during the terms of successive policies written by different carriers. The loss was discovered during the term of the second policy, and that carrier paid its limit. The employer also sought the limit from the first carrier. The court rejected the carrier's argument that the prior insurance provision limited the employer to the payment already received from the other carrier because the other carrier's policy was not for a prior period. *White Tire Distribs., Inc. v. Pa. Nat'l Mut. Cas. Ins. Co.*, 367 S.E.2d 518.

SECONDARY SOURCES

David T. DiBiase, *Fidelity Claims in Excess of Policy Limits—Problems and Solutions*, 52 INS. COUNSEL J. 660 (1985).

Keith Flanagan, *The Death of A.B.S. and Karen Kane: An Update on The Insurer's Liability for Multiple Limits*, (unpublished paper presented at Annual Meeting of Sur. Claims Inst. 2010).

Edward G. Gallagher, *Limits of Liability, in* ANNOTATED COMMERCIAL CRIME POLICY 495 (Cole S. Kain & Lana M. Glovach eds., 2d ed. 2006).

Edward G. Gallagher, *Limit of Liability, in* COMMERCIAL CRIME POLICY 451 (Randall I. Marmor & John J. Tomaine eds., 2d ed. 2005).

William J. Hacker, *Limit of Liability, in* COMMERCIAL CRIME POLICY 14-1 (Gilbert J. Schroeder ed., 1997).

Tracey Haley, *Cumulation of Crime Policy Limits—The Impact of A.B.S. Clothing* (unpublished paper presented at Annual Meeting of ABA, Fid. & Sur. Law Comm. 1998)) (on file at the Stradley Library, No. 2873).

Robert M. Konop, *The Loss Sustained Policy and Multiple Year Losses: Keeping it Simple*, 18 Fidelity L.J. 193 (November, 2012).

Patrick O'Connor & D. M. Studler, *Limits of Liability: A Multi-Faceted Perspective*, (unpublished paper presented at Annual Meeting of Sur. Claims Inst. 1999).

Robert Olausen, *Commercial Crime Insurance: The Changing Landscape* (unpublished paper presented at Annual Meeting of Sur. Claims Inst. 1997).

Tracey Santor et al., *Limits of Liability, in* HANDLING FIDELITY BOND CLAIMS 319 (Michael Keeley & Sean Duffy eds., 2d ed. 2005).

Carol Z. Smith et al., *Recent Developments in Fidelity and Surety Law*, 49 TORT TRIAL & INS. PRAC. L.J. 207, 215 (Winter 2013).

John J. Tomaine, *Through the Looking Glass: Determining the Applicable Limit of Liability and Deductible in Multiple Check Claims* (unpublished paper presented at Annual Meeting of ABA, Fid. & Sur. Law Comm. 2001) (on file at the Stradley Library, No. 3170).

F. Prior Insurance Issued by Us

The Commercial Crime Policy (Loss Sustained Form)[22] provides:

Loss Sustained Entirely During Prior Insurance
If you "discover" loss during the Policy Period shown in the
Declarations, resulting directly from an "occurrence" taking
place entirely during the policy period(s) of any prior
cancelled insurance that we or any affiliate issued to you or
any predecessor in interest, we will pay for the loss,
provided:
(a)   This Policy became effective at the time of cancellation
of the prior insurance; and
(b)   The loss would have been covered under this Policy had
it been in effect at the time of the "occurrence."
We will first settle the amount of loss that you sustained
during the most recent prior insurance. We will then settle
any remaining amount of loss that you sustained during the
policy period(s) of any other prior insurance.

The Crime General Provisions (Loss Sustained Form)[23] provides:

Loss Covered Under This Insurance and Prior Insurance
Issued by Us or Any Affiliate:
If any loss is covered:
a.   Partly by this insurance; and
b.   Partly by any prior cancelled or terminated insurance
that we or any affiliate had issued to you or any
predecessor in interest;
the most we will pay is the larger of the amount recoverable
under this insurance or the prior insurance.

---

22 Commercial Crime Policy (Loss Sustained Form), Standard Form No. CR
00 23 08 13 (Revised to 08-13), Condition 1.o.(2). This Policy also contains
specific provisions in the same section relating to Loss Sustained Partly
During This Policy and Partly During Prior Insurance.
23 Crime General Provisions (Loss Sustained Form), Standard Form CR 1000
(Revised to 04-97), 11.

Regardless of the number of years this insurance remains in force or the number of premiums paid, no Limit of Insurance cumulates from year to year or period to period.

COMMENT

The one-year discovery period afforded under the policy means that a loss can be covered under two consecutive policies. The part of the loss sustained during the term of the first policy can be claimed under the first policy if its discovery period has not expired. The part of the loss sustained during the term of the second policy can be claimed under the second policy.

If the first and second policies were written by different insurers, the insured gets whatever it is entitled to under the separate contracts. If the two policies were written by the same insurer or affiliated insurers, the insured is limited to the larger of the amount recoverable under the first policy or the amount recoverable under the second policy.

ANNOTATIONS

2d Cir. 1971 (N.Y.). In 1965 Scranton obtained coverage in the amount of $4,000 and paid a yearly premium through 1969, when it discovered that its treasurer had embezzled funds each year totaling in excess of $14,500. USF&G contended that its liability was limited to $4,000 since the position schedule bond provided that the Underwriter "shall not be liable under this bond on account of any employee for a larger amount in the aggregate than the amount stated opposite the position occupied by such employee." Scranton claimed that the language was both ambiguous and unconscionable. The court held that no ambiguity existed and the language clearly limited the Underwriter's liability to the specified amount throughout the life of the agreement. *Scranton Vol. Fire Co. v. USF&G,* 450 F.2d 775.

4th Cir. 2001 (S.C.). There were two successive one-year policies with different policy numbers. An employee stole in excess of the $100,000 per occurrence limit during each of the two policy years. The employer claimed $200,000. Liberty tendered $100,000. The Fourth Circuit affirmed summary judgment for the employer. The court thought that the prior insurance provision was ambiguous because other courts had disagreed on its meaning. The Fourth Circuit did not suggest a reading of the provision that would support awarding two limits. [Note, this is an unpublished decision and pursuant to Fourth Circuit Rule 36c is not supposed to be cited as precedent]. *Spartan Iron & Metal Corp. v. Liberty Ins. Corp.*, 6 F. App'x 176.

5th Cir. 2008 (S.D. Miss.). Fifth Circuit affirmed district court holding on summary judgment. Employee's related acts of embezzlement over a decade and spanning multiple policy periods constituted only one occurrence and employer Madison was entitled to recover no more than the limits of the policy in effect when the theft was discovered. Mississippi courts recognize that an "occurrence" is determined by the cause or causes of the resulting injury. Although employee committed multiple related acts throughout the decade, court found there was only one cause of the injury sustained by Madison and that was the employee's dishonesty. The court looked to the unambiguous terms of policy stating that multiple related acts may constitute a single occurrence. The court further held under Prior Insurance clause that only way Madison could recover for losses in a prior policy period would be if the losses incurred in the current policy period totaled less than the current limits, and then only to bring Madison's recovery up to the current policy's limits. *Madison Materials Co., Inc. v. St. Paul Fire & Marine Ins. Co.*, 523 F.3d 541.

8th Cir. 1983 (N.D.). Insurer issued bonds for a trustee appointed in Chapter X reorganization proceedings. The bonds did not contain language proscribing cumulative liability. However, certificates of continuance that included annual premium statements provided that the liability of the company "shall not be cumulative." Although copies of these certificates were filed with the bankruptcy court, each renewal was found to be a separate contract with a separate limit of liability in that the bankruptcy judge did not formally approve the certificates, nor was there any indication that he had actual knowledge of the limiting language contained therein. *In re Endeco, Inc. U.S. f/u/o McMerty v. Fid. & Cas. Co. of N.Y.*, 718 F.2d 879.

8th Cir. 1960 (Mo.). A position schedule bond, periodically renewed during a fourteen-year period, provided that the underwriter's aggregate liability on account of any one employee would not exceed the sum scheduled for said employee and that coverage would not be cumulative. Upon discovery that its bookkeeper had embezzled funds over a number of years, the employer submitted a proof of loss for $11,600 notwithstanding the fact that the bookkeeper's scheduled coverage never exceeded $2,000. The court stated that there was no ambiguity in the limiting language and, when coupled with the indefinite term of the carrier's obligation, evidenced an intent to limit liability for losses on account of the particular employee to $2,000. *Mass. Bonding & Ins. Co. v. Julius Seidel Lumber Co.*, 279 F.2d 861.

10th Cir. 1992 (Utah). The university suffered a loss of works of art over the course of ten to twelve years. The court rejected the university's argument that the loss under a "prior insurance written by us" provision applied. The prior insurance was written by other carriers and the loss was not discovered within the discovery periods of the prior policies. *Brigham Young Univ. v. Lumbermens Mut. Cas. Co.*, 965 F.2d 830.

M.D. Ala. 1963. St. Paul issued three successive fidelity policies covering losses up to $2,500, $10,000 and $10,000 respectively. During the same three-year period an employee embezzled in excess of $43,000. The policies were similar, covering losses discovered within three years of cancellation, and each provided that where the period allowed for discovery of loss under prior insurance had not elapsed, "the Company's liability under this bond and under such prior insurance shall not be cumulative." The dairy contented that St. Paul's liability under the three policies in question was $22,500. St. Paul sought to limit its liability to a maximum of $10,000 by virtue of the quoted provision. The court held that the provision could only be interpreted as preventing any loss in excess of the stated limit from being carried forward and claimed under the terms of any succeeding policies so as to achieve a similar result had the dairy obtained coverage with separate and independent insurers for each of the three years. Based upon the evidence presented in connection with losses sustained during each period, the court found that the dairy was entitled to recover $2,500 for the first year of coverage, $2,500 for the second, and $10,000 for the third. *White Dairy Co., Inc. v. St Paul Fire & Marine Ins. Co.*, 222 F. Supp. 1014.

C.D. Cal. 1998. Karen Kane, Inc. insured suffered losses during three consecutive policy periods. The court granted summary judgment to Reliance and rejected Karen Kane's argument that the loss under a "prior insurance issued by us" provision was ambiguous or that it did not apply because the prior policies were not cancelled or terminated. [Note, this case was reversed by the 9th Circuit]. *Karen Kane, Inc. v. Reliance Ins. Co.*, No. CV 97-3295-WMB, 1998 WL 476454, *aff'd in part, rev'd in part* by 202 F.3d 1180 (9th Cir. 2000).

D.C. Cir. 1951. A hospital bookkeeper embezzled in excess of $5,000 per year during a three-year period, and approximately $3,900 during a fourth year. The hospital submitted a claim for $18,975 although the blanket position bond contained only $5,000 in scheduled coverage and a non-cumulation clause. In finding the carrier liable for a total of $5,000 the court rejected the hospital's argument that cumulative meant "carry-over" of unused coverage from year to year and stated that courts have consistently held liability to be limited, in the aggregate, to the amount stated where unambiguous language to that effect is included in coverage documentation. *Columbia Hosp. for Women & Lying-in Asylum v. USF&G,* 188 F. 2d 654.

D. Colo. 2004. A dishonest employee used several different schemes to steal money over a four-year period. During the last two years, the employer had coverage under policies written by Wausau. The issue was the applicable limit of insurance. The court held that the "prior insurance written by us" provision unambiguously limited the employer to the larger of the amount recoverable under either of the two policies—in this case the single limit of $100,000. *Wausau Bus. Ins. Co. v. U.S. Motels Mgmt., Inc.*, 341 F. Supp. 2d 1180.

N.D. Ill. 1993. Employer Diamond Transportation claimed the $250,000 limit under each of three annual policies. Travelers paid a single $250,000 limit. The court granted Travelers' motion to dismiss. The court found that the "prior insurance written by us" provision limited Diamond to a single $250,000 limit. *Diamond Transp. Sys., Inc. v. Travelers Indem. Co.*, 817 F. Supp. 710.

N.D. Ill. 1968. Savings & Loan sought recovery, up to the stated penalty, for each of a multitude of covered activities committed by one of its directors. The court concluded that the language employed by the

Underwriter indicated an intention to limit liability as to any one individual to the specified amount. *Fed. Sav. & Loan Corp. v. Aetna Ins. Co.*, 279 F. Supp. 161.

M.D. La. 1974. A tax collector embezzled approximately $180,000 during a three-year period. Language contained in certificates renewing a position bond provided that liability "shall not be cumulative." Plaintiffs recovery was limited to the stated penalty, and the court found that the limiting language in the contract was clear and unambiguous. *Parish of East Baton Rouge v. Fid. & Cas. of N.Y.*, 373 F. Supp. 440.

D. Md. 2013. Two former executives of Emcor defraud company over a six-year period. Emcor sought recovery against GAIC under all three of GAIC's successive policies, as well as for losses for the period covered by prior insurer. GAIC argued under terms of the Loss Sustained During Prior Insurance section that each policy offered coverage only for conduct occurring during specified policy period, as well as the period of coverage under immediately preceding policy. Emcor sought recovery for losses spanning over each policy period. District court refused to afford coverage for losses that occurred during prior policy periods and were not known to Emcor until after the discovery window, including the one-year tail, had expired. The court held that GAIC policies clearly provided for loss sustained coverage for a finite period of time. GAIC's motion for partial summary judgment was granted. *Emcor Group, Inc. v. Great American Ins. Co.*, No. ELH-12-0142, 2013 WL 1315029.

Cal. Ct. App. 1995. Two employees embezzled from July 1988 to May 1991. Home Insurance Company issued a $100,000 policy commencing April 4, 1989, and twice renewed it for annual periods starting April 4, 1990, and April 4, 1991. There were different policy numbers, but the coverage and limits were not changed. Home Insurance paid the single loss limit of $100,000. A.B.S. claimed $100,000 per year, including the year preceding the first policy, and sued. The trial court granted summary judgment to Home Insurance. The court of appeals thought the issue was whether there was a single, continuous policy or multiple annual policies. In a 2-1 decision, the court of appeals reversed summary judgment and remanded the case. The court thought that the "true purpose" of the "prior insurance written by us" provision was to prevent recovery of the same loss under both policies. The court concluded that this provision did not show an intent to enter into a single, continuous contract. *A.B.S. Clothing Collection, Inc. v. Home Ins. Co.*, 41 Cal. Rptr. 2d 166.

Fla. Dist. Ct. App. 1995. The employer had annual policies issued from February 1988 to February 1991. The dishonest employee embezzled throughout this period. The trial court granted summary judgment finding coverage under all four policies. The court of appeals reversed. The non-cumulation provision alone probably would not have been sufficient to limit the recovery to one policy, but in combination with the "prior insurance issued by us" clause, "we think that this insurer has accomplished what insurers with non-cumulation provisions alone apparently intended, but failed to state with sufficient clarity . . . ." *Reliance Ins. Co. v. Treasure Coast Travel Agency, Inc.*, 660 So. 2d 1136.

Fla. Dist. Ct. App. 1978. City sought to recover for an employee's misappropriations over a two-year period covered by successive "package" policies. Distinguishing fidelity policies that provide multi-year coverage from separate, successive obligations, the court held that language to the effect that liability under consecutive bonds would not be cumulative could not be interpreted so as to allow the Travelers to avoid liability for losses incurred during each policy period. *City of Miami Springs v. Travelers Indem. Co.*, 365 So. 2d 1030.

Ga. Ct. App. 2003. An employee stole from its employer during each of the three years of the first policy and the first year of the second, renewal policy. The limit of insurance was $50,000, which Cincinnati Insurance paid. The trial court agreed with the employer that the limit was $50,000 per year. Cincinnati appealed, and the court held that the applicable limit for the three years of the first policy was $50,000 but that the amount stolen during the first year of the second policy was subject to another $50,000 limit. The court of appeals held that the stipulation that the first three years was a single policy foreclosed recovery of more than one limit for those years, but thought that the "prior insurance written by us" provision was not applicable because "there was no showing that any loss was covered partly by it and partly by the renewal policy." The court itself awarded recoveries under both policies for thefts by a single employee, so it is hard to understand why it thought there was no such loss. *Cincinnati Ins. Co. v. Sherman & Hemstreet, Inc.*, 581 S.E.2d 613.

La. Ct. App. 1982. The state sought to recover in excess of $75,000 under a public employees' blanket bond that had been renewed annually for six years. The court held that the non-cumulation clause was explicit and unambiguous and not against public policy. *State of Louisiana ex rel. Guste v. Aetna Cas. & Sur. Co.*, 417 So. 2d 404, *aff'd*, 429 So. 2d 106.

Md. 1970. Non-cumulation provision applied to limit recovery to the stated penalty. *Com'r of Leonardtown v. Fid. Cas. Co. of N.Y.*, 270 A.2d 788.

Mich. 1984. Statute required licensed mobile home dealers to obtain a "properly executed bond or renewal certificate." Where renewal certificates were used, the statute provided that such be "in the same amount and with the same effect as an original bond." The court found the surety liable up to the extent of the policy limit for each year despite a policy provision limiting aggregate liability to the stated penalty. Since existing law must be read in conjunction with statutory bonds, the court concluded that the scope of the surety's obligation must be determined according to statutory requirements. *General Elec. Credit Corp. v. Wolverine Ins. Co.*, 362 N.W.2d 595.

Minn. 1979. In light of the ambiguity that existed concerning the accumulation of liability, the court interpreted policy so as to allow recovery in excess of the policy's aggregate limits. *Columbia Heights Motors v. Allstate Ins. Co.*, 275 N.W.2d 32.

Mo. 1968. State sought to recover on two successive, one-year blanket position policies for losses occurring during both periods. Held: Language limiting the Underwriter's liability to the amount of the later policy, in the aggregate, was unambiguous. *State ex rel. State Dep't of Public Health & Welfare v. Hanover Ins. Co.*, 431 S.W.2d 141.

N.Y. App. Div. 2001. The insurance policy issued in 1990 was good until cancelled. It had a series of three year premium terms. A dishonest employee stole during two of the premium terms, and because of a merger, CNA changed the policy number. The court held that there was a single policy and a single limit but that even of the policies were separate, the anti-stacking provisions, and particularly the "prior insurance issued by us" clause, would bar the claim for more than one limit. The trial court erred in limiting the word "terminated" to the insured's election to end coverage. *Shared-Interest Mgmt. Inc. v. CNA Fin. Ins. Group*, 725 N.Y.S.2d 469.

Ohio Ct. App. 2014. A bookkeeper for E.J. Zeller began working for another company, City Rentals, in the same capacity in 2005. On August 8, 2008, it was discovered that the bookkeeper had embezzled from both companies. Zeller purchased an Auto Owner's policy that covered acts of employee dishonesty with an endorsement that extended coverage to losses up to a $10,000 limit. A crime endorsement included additional coverage up to $50,000. The initial policy period was August 12, 2003 to August 12, 2004, and similar policies covered all periods through August 12, 2009. The declarations provided that acceptance of the next year's coverage was notice that the prior year's coverage had been canceled. City Rentals purchased similar policies from Auto Owners with a policy period of June 10, 2005, to June 10, 2006, and renewed it on June 10, 2006. At renewal on June 10, 2007, City Rentals discontinued the crime endorsement. On June 10, 2008, City Rentals renewed the policy increasing the limit of insurance in the property endorsement for employee dishonesty from $10,000 to $15,000. Auto Owners paid $60,000 to Zeller and $10,000 to City Rentals as the maximum coverage. Each endorsement contained a prior insurance provision similar to the Crime General Provisions (Loss Sustained Form) wording. The court found that provision limits recovery for an individual loss that spans multiple policy periods abut does not otherwise exclude coverage under prior policies that are attributable to acts that occurred solely during the policy period. *E.J. Zeller, Inc. v. Auto Owners Ins. Co.*, No. 4-14-04, 2014 WL 5803028.

Pa. Super. Ct. 1981. Three successive policies were issued by different entities within the Continental Companies. In all other respects, the policies were identical and provided that the aggregate liability of the "Company" was limited to the stated penalty. The court held that because each instrument was identical, each included reference to "Continental Insurance Companies," and each was signed by the same person as secretary of the three entities, the parties intended to continue the coverage afforded by the preceding policy for a new period, and therefore carrier's liability was limited in the aggregate to $5,000. *Eddystone Fire Co. No. 1 v. Cont'l Ins. Co.*, 425 A.2d 803.

Pa. 1962. Carrier issued successive policies with stated limits of $5,000 and $2,000, respectively. Both policies provided that the carrier's aggregate liability would be limited to the larger of the penalties, provided that the period for discovery under the earlier coverage had not expired. The court found that liability was limited to the later, $2,000 penalty, since the loss was not discovered before the expiration of the one-year period for discovery under prior coverage. *Exch. Bldg. Ass'n v. Indem. Ins. Co. of N. Am.*, 12 A.2d 924.

Va. 1988. An employee stole in excess of the $20,000 limit during the terms of successive policies written by different carriers. The loss was discovered during the term of the second policy, and that carrier paid its limit. The employer also sought the limit from the first carrier. The court rejected arguments based on another insurance "written by us" provision because the other policy was written by an unrelated company. *White Tire Distribs., Inc. v. Pa. Nat'l Mut. Cas. Ins. Co.*, 367 S.E.2d 518.

SECONDARY SOURCES

David T. DiBiase, *Fidelity Claims in Excess of Policy Limits—Problems and Solutions,* 52 INS. COUNSEL J. 660 (1985).

Edward G. Gallagher, *Limits of Liability, in* ANNOTATED COMMERCIAL CRIME POLICY 495 (Cole S. Kain & Lana M. Glovach eds., 2d ed. 2006).

Edward G. Gallagher, *Limit of Liability, in* COMMERCIAL CRIME POLICY 451 (Randall I. Marmor & John J. Tomaine eds., 2d ed. 2005).

William J. Hacker, *Limit of Liability, in* COMMERCIAL CRIME POLICY 14-1 (Gilbert J. Schroeder ed., 1997).

Tracey Haley, *Cumulation of Crime Policy Limits—The Impact of A.B.S. Clothing* (unpublished paper presented at Annual Meeting of ABA, Fid. & Sur. Law Comm. 1998)) (on file at the Stradley Library, No. 2873).

Patrick O'Connor & D. M. Studler, *Limits of Liability: A Multi-Faceted Perspective*, (unpublished paper presented at Annual Meeting of Sur. Claims Inst. 1999).

Robert Olausen, *Commercial Crime Insurance: The Changing Landscape* (unpublished paper presented at Annual Meeting of Sur. Claims Inst. 1997).

Tracey Santor et al., *Limits of Liability, in* HANDLING FIDELITY BOND CLAIMS 319 (Michael Keeley & Sean Duffy eds., 2d ed. 2005).

John J. Tomaine, *Through the Looking Glass: Determining the Applicable Limit of Liability and Deductible in Multiple Check Claims* (unpublished paper presented at Annual Meeting of ABA, Fid. & Sur. Law Comm. 2001) (on file at the Stradley Library, No. 3170).

G. Cancellation of Prior Insurance

The Commercial Crime Protection Policy (Standard Form)[24] Declarations Page provides,

> **Item 5. CANCELLATION OF PRIOR INSURANCE**
> **By acceptance of this Policy you give us notice cancelling prior policy Nos. _____.**

COMMENT

If a single policy is renewed or extended for another policy period and the policy keeps the same number, there is nothing to put in the blank on the Declarations page. The parties cannot simultaneously extend and cancel the one policy. If a new policy is written, or a new number assigned, the expired policy number can be entered in the blank. Sometimes, whoever prepares the policy form neglects to fill in the blank.

---

24 Crime Protection Policy, Standard Form No. SP 0001 (Revised to 04 12), Condition 13.

Although omission of the policy number of the expiring policy does not change the fact that it has terminated, insureds sometimes argue either that the empty blank shows an intent to "keep the policy open" for cumulative claims or that the policy is not cancelled or terminated within the meaning of the "prior insurance written by us" condition.

ANNOTATIONS

4th Cir. 2001 (S.C.). There were two successive one-year policies with different policy numbers. An employee stole in excess of the $100,000 per occurrence limit during each of the two policy years. The employer claimed $200,000. Liberty tendered $100,000. The Fourth Circuit affirmed summary judgment for the employer. In the context of examining whether there was one continuous policy or two successive policies, the court noted that the blank in the Cancellation of Prior Insurance item was not filled in and stated, "it is reasonable to conclude that the parties intended to leave the prior policies open as independent avenues for recovery . . . ." [Note, this is an unpublished decision and pursuant to Fourth Circuit Rule 36c is not supposed to be cited as precedent]. *Spartan Iron & Metal Corp. v. Liberty Ins. Corp.*, 6 Fed. Appx, 176.

11th Cir. 2009 (S.D. Fla.). An employee stole $42 million from his employer over a thirteen-year period. PBSJ sought recovery of the $2 million limit for each policy in effect during the entire period. The Eleventh Circuit affirmed summary judgment in favor of Federal, which paid a single limit of $2 million. The court looked to the language of the crime coverage, which stated that prior policies were terminated and would not afford coverage if not discovered and reported before the effective date of the current policy. Each policy also included a non-cumulation clause and limits on recovery up to $2 million. *PBSJ Corp. v. Federal Ins. Co.*, 347 Fed. Appx. 532.

C.D. Cal. (1998). Karen Kane, Inc. insured suffered losses during three consecutive policy periods. The court interpreted the cancellation of prior insurance provision on the declaration page to mean that there was no distinction between a cancelled policy and one that expired according to its terms. *Karen Kane, Inc. v. Reliance Ins. Co.*, No. CV 97-3295-WMB,

1998 WL 476454, *aff'd in part, rev'd in part* by 202 F.3d 1180 (9th Cir. 2000).

N.D. Ill. 1993. Employer Diamond Transportation claimed the $250,000 limit under each of three annual policies. Travelers paid a single $250,000 limit. The court granted Travelers' motion to dismiss. The court found that the cancellation of a prior insurance provision meant that there was only one bond in effect at any one time. *Diamond Transp. Sys., Inc. v. Travelers Indem. Co.*, 817 F. Supp. 710.

N.D. Tex. 2008. District court addressed multiple issues in conjunction with Great American's declaratory judgment motion that crime policies issued to AFS/IBEX Financial do not provide coverage for losses stemming from checks issued by AFS/IBEX to Charles McMahon Insurance Agency. AFS/IBEX provides premium financing in the insurance industry. AFS/IBES entered into an agreement with McMahon. He was to create and sign premium finance applications on behalf of insureds. AFS/IBEX would then send a check to the insurance company for the premium amounts and the insureds would send regular payments to AFS/IBEX. Unbeknownst to McMahon Sr., McMahon Sr.'s son, the office manager for the agency, issued 122 false applications, causing AFS/IBEX to issue checks for premium financing. The checks were deposited by McMahon, Jr., in his personal bank account. AFS/IBEX submitted a claim for forgery coverage under Great American's policies. In addressing the Cancellation of Prior Insurance section within two policies, the court found the terms, "cancel" and "cancellation" to be ambiguous, leaving open the possibility that the terms have both a retroactive and prospective effect. Further, the court held that the cancellation of prior insurance section operates to terminate the policy period under the current policy, but does not rescind the policy, which remedy is retroactive as if the policy had never been issued, with respect to a loss sustained during the prior policy. *Great American Insurance Co. v. AFS/IBEX Financial Services, Inc.*, Civil Action No. 3:07-CV-924-O, 2008 WL 2795205.

Ohio Ct. App. 2014. A bookkeeper for E.J. Zeller began working for another company, City Rentals, in the same capacity in 2005. On August 8, 2008, it was discovered that the bookkeeper had embezzled from both companies. Zeller purchased an Auto Owner's policy that covered acts of employee dishonesty with an endorsement that extended coverage to losses up to a $10,000 limit. A crime endorsement included additional coverage up to $50,000. The initial policy period was August 12, 2003, to August 12, 2004, and similar policies covered all periods through August 12, 2009. The declarations provided that acceptance of the next year's coverage was notice that the prior year's coverage had been canceled. City Rentals purchased similar policies from Auto Owners with a policy period of June 10, 2005, to June 10, 2006, and renewed it on June 10, 2006. At renewal on June 10, 2007, City Rentals discontinued the crime endorsement. On June 10, 2008, City Rentals renewed the policy increasing the limit of insurance in the property endorsement for employee dishonesty from $10,000 to $15,000. Auto Owners paid $60,000 to Zeller and $10,000 to City Rentals as the maximum coverage. The court found that each policy was a new, separate policy of insurance. *E.J. Zeller, Inc. v. Auto Owners Ins. Co.*, No. 4-14-04, 2014 WL 5803028.

SECONDARY SOURCES

David T. DiBiase, *Fidelity Claims in Excess of Policy Limits—Problems and Solutions,* 52 INS. COUNSEL J. 660 (1985).

Edward G. Gallagher, *Limits of Liability, in* ANNOTATED COMMERCIAL CRIME POLICY 495 (Cole S. Kain & Lana M. Glovach eds., 2d ed. 2006).

Edward G. Gallagher, *Limit of Liability, in* COMMERCIAL CRIME POLICY 451 (Randall I. Marmor & John J. Tomaine eds., 2d ed. 2005).

William J. Hacker, *Limit of Liability, in* COMMERCIAL CRIME POLICY 14-1 (Gilbert J. Schroeder ed., 1997).

Tracey Haley, *Cumulation of Crime Policy Limits—The Impact of A.B.S. Clothing* (unpublished paper presented at Annual Meeting of ABA, Fid. & Sur. Law Comm. 1998)) (on file at the Stradley Library, No. 2873).

Patrick O'Connor & D. M. Studler, *Limits of Liability: A Multi-Faceted Perspective,* (unpublished paper presented at Annual Meeting of Sur. Claims Inst. 1999).

Robert Olausen, *Commercial Crime Insurance: The Changing Landscape* (unpublished paper presented at Annual Meeting of Sur. Claims Inst. 1997).

Tracey Santor et al., *Limits of Liability, in* HANDLING FIDELITY BOND CLAIMS 319 (Michael Keeley & Sean Duffy eds., 2d ed. 2005).

John J. Tomaine, *Through the Looking Glass: Determining the Applicable Limit of Liability and Deductible in Multiple Check Claims* (unpublished paper presented at Annual Meeting of ABA, Fid. & Sur. Law Comm. 2001) (on file at the Stradley Library, No. 3170).

Chapter 16

Third-Party Losses*

An employer's potential risk of loss from employee dishonesty is not limited to embezzlement of its money or property. When an employee misappropriates property belonging to a third party or otherwise perpetrates a fraud on a third party, he exposes the employer to a risk of liability. An employer may be vicariously liable for the employee's fraud, even if the employer was entirely innocent and received no benefit.

Faced with this exposure, employers commonly seek indemnity under their Commercial Crime Policy. Courts construing pre-1980 commercial crime policies were split over the compensability of such third-party losses. Because the policies covered "loss through any dishonest or fraudulent act of any of the Employees...,"[1] courts disagreed as to whether it provided coverage for indirect losses resulting from an employee's fraudulent misconduct. A majority of courts refused to inject a direct loss requirement into fidelity bonds and found the "through" standard was sufficiently broad to cover both direct and indirect losses, meaning that claims based upon an insured's vicarious liability to a third party were, subject to other defenses, covered under fidelity bonds. However, a minority of courts rejected the notion that fidelity bonds must cover indirect losses simply because they did not exclude such losses, holding that the inherent nature of coverage afforded by fidelity bonds prohibited coverage for indirect losses.

The addition of the ownership provision in 1980 resolved this split of authority. Pulling together concepts found in several places in the pre-1980 bonds, this provision distinguishes between claims based upon the insured's liability for damages caused by an employee's perpetration of fraud on a third party and claims based upon the employee's misappropriation of a third party's property while in the possession of

---

*   Scott Schmookler, Gordon & Reese, LLP, Chicago, Illinois.
1   *See* Financial Institution Bond, Standard Form No. 24 (revised to April 1969), *reprinted in* STANDARD FORMS OF THE SURETY ASSOCIATION OF AMERICA; Comprehensive Dishonesty Disappearance and Destruction Policy (revised to March 1940), *reprinted in* STANDARD FORMS OF THE SURETY ASSOCIATION OF AMERICA (Surety Ass'n of America).

the insured. Claims falling within the latter category are generally covered, but the former are not.

Although the employee's conduct might be characterized as fraudulent or dishonest and the employer's liability to its customer might result in an out-of-pocket loss to the employer, an insured's vicarious liability for an employee's fraud on a third party is outside the scope of coverage afforded by a Commercial Crime Policy for one of three reasons: first, commercial crime policies are not liability policies; second, an insured's liability is an indirect loss outside the scope of coverage afforded under the bond; and third, an employee's misconduct does not constitute "employee dishonesty" or "theft" as defined in the policy.

Conversely, the bond does cover (subject to other potential defenses) the misappropriation of a third party's property while in the possession or control of the insured. Such claims are covered not because the insured may be liable to the owner for the misappropriation of its property, but because the ownership provision extends coverage to loss of a third party's property while in the possession or control of the insured.

Courts analyzing the compensability of a third-party loss have not always addressed the ownership provision. This chapter, therefore, will summarize cases interpreting the ownership provision, and cases analyzing the compensability of third-party losses under other provisions. Because the nature of the claim and terms of the policy impact the compensability of a third-party loss, the cases analyzing the compensability of third-party losses under other provisions are subdivided by the nature of the claim, and finally, by the type of policy at issue in the case (i.e., Pre-1980 Policy, Post-1980 Policy, Non-Standard Policy).

> **The property covered under this policy is limited to property:**
> **(1)   That you own or lease;**
> **(2)   That you hold for others; or**
> **(3)   For which you are legally liable, except for property inside the premises of a "client" of yours.**
> **However, this policy is for your benefit only; it provides no rights or benefits to any other person or organization. Any claim for loss that is covered under this policy must be presented by you.**

OUTLINE OF ANNOTATIONS

A. Ownership Provision
B. Cases Addressing Coverage for an Insured's Vicarious Liability
   Compensability of Losses Under Pre-1980 Policies
C. Compensability of Losses Under "Manifest Intent Policies"
D. Compensability of Loss Under Non-Standard Policies

ANNOTATIONS

A. Ownership Provision

3d Cir. 2013 (Pa.). There was a genuine dispute of fact of whether an investment firm owned, held, or was legally liable for embezzled funds. *Marion v. Hartford Fire Ins. Co.*, 2013 U.S. App. LEXIS 9825.

8th Cir. 2015 (Minn.). The bond provided coverage because the bank held the funds and thus, the loss to the bank from the employee's fraudulent conduct was a direct loss. *Avon State Bank v. BancInsure, Inc.*, 787 F.3d 952.

5th Cir. 1969 (Tex.). The court granted summary judgment against intervenor claiming third-party beneficiary status for loss of premium account monies due to fraudulent acts not covered as there was no intent to create legal liability to third party. *Am. Empire Ins. Co. v. Fidelity & Dep. Co.*, 408 F.2d 72.

9th Cir. 2000 (Cal.). A grocer sought indemnity under a commercial crime policy after its alleged employees engaged in a Ponzi scheme. The insured argued that the ownership provision implied coverage for third-party loss, but the court rejected that argument and held that the claim was not covered unless the insured could prove that it sustained a direct loss as a result of its employees' misconduct. While the insured was ultimately required to reimburse the victims of the fraud, the court held that the settlement of these claims did not constitute a direct loss under the bond. *Vons Cos. v. Fed. Ins. Co.*, 212 F.3d 489.

10th Cir. 1994 (Okla.). A title company sought indemnity under a financial institution bond after its employee embezzled money from escrow accounts. Although the insured did not own money held in the escrow accounts, the court nonetheless held that its loss was covered because the ownership provision extended coverage to the loss of property held by the insured or for which it is legally liable. *Spears v. St. Paul Fire Ins. Co.*, 40 F.3d 318.

D. Ca. 2014 (Cal.). Insured satisfied the direct loss element because it was legally liable for the funds held in escrow. *Fid. Nat'l Fin., Inc. v. Nat'l Union Fire Ins. Co.*, 2014 U.S. Dist. LEXIS 140030, *reconsideration denied by*, 2015 U.S. Dist. LEXIS 46822.

D. Colo. 1967. An accounting firm sought indemnity under a dishonesty, disappearance, and destruction policy after its employee embezzled checks issued by the firm's customers. Although the checks were issued by the firm's customer, the court held that the claim was nonetheless covered because the policy covered loss of property held by the firm and the firm "held" the funds on behalf of its customers. *Elmer Fox & Co. v. Commercial Union Ins. Co. of N.Y.*, 274 F. Supp. 235.

W.D. Tenn. 2009. Insured could not recover under a commercial crime policy because it could not prove that it owned, held, or was legally liable for stolen property. *Loeb Props. v. Fed. Ins. Co.*, 663 F. Supp. 2d 640, 649.

W.D. Pa. 2001. A commercial crime policy did not cover an estate's loss caused by insured's employee, who stole the estate's money, in absence of evidence of the employee's purpose to cause loss. *Shoemaker v. Lumbermens Mut. Cas. Co.*, 176 F. Supp. 2d 449.

Cal. App. 1948. The owners of a hotel sought indemnity under a commercial blanket bond after its employee embezzled money from a number of guests. Because the policy provided coverage for loss of property for which the insured was "legally liable," the court held that the bond covered the insured's vicarious liability for its employee's misconduct. *Alberts v. Am. Cas. Co. of Reading, Pa.*, 88 Cal. App. 2d 891.

Miss. 1968. An insurance company sought to garnish a commercial crime policy issued to a loan collection agent after the agent misappropriated loan proceeds. The court held that the insurance company could garnish the policy because the policy covered the misappropriation of the loan proceeds. Although the insured did not own the loan proceeds, the court found coverage because the bond also covered property held by the insured. *Am. Nat'l Ins. Co. v. USF&G*, 215 So. 2d 245.

B. Cases Addressing Coverage for an Insured's Vicarious Liability Compensability of Losses Under Pre-1980 Policies

1st Cir. 1966 (Mass.). Although the court recognized that a bankers blanket bond did not cover judicially imposed liability, it held that the bond covered settlement of claims brought against the bank for loss sustained by the third party as a result of wrongful cashing of checks because settlements were a determination of total loss, not a judicially imposed liability. *Aetna Cas. & Sur. Co. v. Guar. Bank & Trust Co.*, 370 F.2d 276, 280.

5th Cir. 1985 (Tex.). The insured, after it successfully defended a lawsuit that alleged that its employee had engaged in fraudulent conduct, brought an action against its fidelity insurer seeking reimbursement for attorneys' fees incurred in defending the claim. The court held that although the insured's liability was an indirect loss, it was nonetheless covered under the bond because the bond did not specifically exclude coverage for indirect losses. *Cont. Sav. Ass'n v. USF&G*, 762 F.2d 1239.

5th Cir. 1980 (Fla.). A lender could not recover under a bankers blanket bond issued to a borrower because the bond did not cover a loss sustained by a third party and the lender sought to recover a loss it sustained after the borrower defaulted on a loan. *Everhart v. Drake Mgmt., Inc.*, 627 F.2d 686, 691-92.

5th Cir. 1967 (Tex.). A security broker sought coverage under a brokers blanket bond after its employee fraudulently induced customers to purchase securities. Because the policy covered all losses "through" the dishonest acts of an employee, the court held that the insured's liability resulting from its employee's dishonest conduct was covered under the bond. *Nat'l Sur. Corp. v. Rauscher, Pierce & Co.*, 369 F.2d 572.

6th Cir. 1962 (Tenn.). Insured sought coverage under a bankers blanket bond after a bankruptcy trustee sought to void payments on a loan. The court held that the claim was not covered because the bond only covered losses sustained by the insured, not an insured's liability to third parties. *First Nat'l Bank of Memphis v. Aetna Cas. & Sur. Co.*, 309 F.2d 702.

D.D.C. 1980. A college sought recovery under a blanket crime policy for losses sustained when an employee exploited grants from the National Institutes of Health. Although not addressing the compensability of third-party losses in detail, the court noted that the bond did cover an insured's liability to a third party for losses caused by employee dishonesty. *Fid. & Dep. Co. of Md. v. President & Dir. of Georgetown College*, 483 F. Supp. 1142.

W.D. Ky. 1940. An insured sought indemnity under a bankers blanket bond for losses resulting from its settlement of a third-party claim. The court held that the insured's payment of a legal liability caused by the dishonest act of the employee was the equivalent of an embezzlement and therefore, was covered under the bond. *Hooker v. New Amsterdam Cas. Co.*, 33 F. Supp. 672.

S.D. W. Va. 1973. A bank sought indemnity under a bankers blanket bond for losses sustained when an employee fraudulent induced a third party to purchase defective promissory notes. The court held that the insured's liability to the third party was covered because the bond covered all losses "through any dishonest, fraudulent or criminal act" and the insured's liability resulted from the employee's fraudulent conduct. *First Nat'l Bank of West Hamlin v. Md. Cas. Co.*, 354 F. Supp. 189.

Kan. 1970. After the insured was held vicariously liable for the fraudulent acts of its employee, the judgment creditor sought to garnish the insured's fidelity bond. Affirming judgment in favor of the insurer, the court held that the creditor was not entitled to garnish the bond because the bond only covered losses sustained by the insured and did not cover an insured's liability for losses sustained by a third party as a result of employee dishonesty. *Ronnau v. Caravan Int'l Ins. Corp.*, 468 P.2d 118.

Minn. 1976. A bank sought indemnity under a bankers blanket bond after it was held liable for losses sustained by a third party as a result of its employee's fraudulent loan scheme. The court held that the claim was covered because the bond was broad enough to cover an insured's liability to a third party as a result of the dishonest or fraudulent acts of an employee. *Farmers & Merch. State Bank of Pierz v. St. Paul Fire & Marine Ins. Co.*, 242 N.W.2d 840.

Neb. 1981. A bank sought indemnity for losses resulting from its vicarious liability to a third party for the fraudulent acts of an employee. Affirming summary judgment for the insurer, the court held that the claim was not covered because a financial institution bond did not insure the bank against the consequences of its own torts, even if committed by an employee otherwise covered under the bond. *Omaha Bank for Coop. v. Aetna Cas. & Sur. Co.*, 301 N.W.2d 564.

Neb. 1979. A bank sought indemnity under a financial institution bond after its employee defrauded a customer. The court held that insured's liability was not covered under the bond because financial institution bonds only cover losses sustained by the insured, not an insured's liability to a third party. *Bank of Mead v. St. Paul Fire & Marine Ins. Co.*, 244 N.W.2d 205.

Neb. 1973. A broadcasting company sought indemnity under a commercial crime policy after it was required to honor a promissory note forged by its general manager. Although the insured was liable under the note, the court held that its liability was not covered because the insured's liability did not constitute a direct loss. The original loss was sustained by the holder of the note. The fact that the insured reimbursed the holder of the note for its loss did not transfer the holder's loss into a direct loss. *Kami Kountry Broadcasting Co. v. USF&G*, 208 N.W.2d 254.

N.M. 1980. A state livestock board sought indemnity under a faithful performance bond after its employees stole a third parties' livestock. Although the policy covered losses "through" an employee's dishonest or fraudulent acts, the New Mexico Supreme Court held that the insured's liability to a third party for losses caused by its employee misconduct was not covered because the bond only covered losses sustained by the insured, not losses sustained by third parties. In so holding, the court rejected the argument that the bond, as a statutory bond, should be interpreted to provide such coverage on the grounds that the statute did not expressly require coverage for third-party losses. *N.M. Livestock Board v. Dose*, 607 P.2d 606.

N.Y. 1980. A commercial crime policy covering loss "through" fraudulent and dishonest acts is not governed by the New York direct action statute because it does not cover insured's liability to a third party. *175 E. 74th Corp. v. Hartford Acc. & Indem. Co.*, 416 N.E.2d 584, 587-88.

Tex. App. 1932. An accounting firm sought indemnity under a commercial fidelity bond after its employee embezzled money from its clients. The court held that the claim was covered because the bond expressly provided coverage for loss of property "for which the employer is responsible." Because the insured was liable for its employee's misconduct, the court held that its liability was covered under the bond. *Am. Employers Ins. Co. v. Johnson*, 47 S.W. 463.

C. Compensability of Losses Under "Manifest Intent Policies"

1st Cir. 2003 (Mass.). A not-for-profit organization sought indemnity under a commercial crime policy for losses sustained when an employee fraudulently induced third parties to make contributions. The court held that the claim was not covered because insured did not sustain an actual loss as a result of the employee's scheme. While a third party sustained a loss, that loss was not covered because the employee did not act with the manifest intent to cause the insured a loss. *Fireman's Fund Ins. Co. v. Special Olympics Int'l, Inc.*, 346 F.3d 259.

2d Cir. 1989 (N.Y.). After the owner of an investment management firm fraudulently induced third parties to invest money in risky investments, the insured sought indemnity under a financial institution bond. The court held that the claim was not covered because the owner did not have the manifest intent to cause the firm to suffer a loss, but instead were performed with the intent to benefit the insured. *Glusband v. Fittin Cunningham & Lauzon*, 892 F.2d 208.

5th Cir. 1998 (Tex.). A property management company sought indemnity under a commercial crime policy after its employee misappropriated money from a customer's account. The insured argued that the policy's ownership provision implied coverage for losses sustained by third parties, but the court held that the provision only provided coverage for losses of property owned by or held by the insured. Since the insured did not hold the customer's account (but instead simply had access to her checkbook), the court held that the insured's liability was outside the scope of coverage. *Lynch Props. Inc. v. Potomac Ins. Co. of Ill., Inc.*, 140 F.3d 622.

6th Cir. 2012 (Ohio). A bank's liability to repay customers for loss customers suffered after its employee embezzled money held in brokerage account constituted a loss "resulting directly from" employee dishonesty. *First Defiance Fin. Corp. v. Progressive Cas. Ins. Co.*, 688 F.3d 265, 270.

6th Cir. 1997 (Ohio). The insured sought indemnity under a financial institution bond after its officers fraudulently induced third parties to purchase a restaurant. The court held that the claim was not covered because the officers did not act with the manifest intent to cause the insured a loss, but instead acted with the manifest intent to cause the third parties to suffer a loss. *Peoples Bank & Trust Co. v. Aetna Cas. & Sur. Co.*, 113 F.3d 629.

7th Cir. 2011 (Wis.). A mortgage banker's liability to repurchase loan induced by employee dishonesty did not constitute a "direct financial loss" within the meaning of a financial institution bond because the banker did not suffer a loss until it received and honored a repurchase demand. *Universal Mortg. Corp. v. Württembergische Versicherung AG*, 651 F.3d 759, 763-64.

8th Cir. 1990 (Iowa). Third parties threatened to sue a bank as a result of an employee's fraudulent loan scheme. After the bank settled the suits, it sought coverage under its financial institution bond. Relying upon cases interpreting a predecessor version of the financial institution bond, the court held that the insured's liability was covered because, in its opinion, fidelity bonds were intended to cover losses derived from vicarious liability. *First Am. State Bank v. Cont'l Ins. Co.*, 897 F.2d 319.

8th Cir. 1987 (Iowa). A bankers blanket bond is not a form of liability insurance and therefore did not cover judgment entered against insured and was not subject to garnishment, even though judgment was based upon employee's embezzlement of grain from the judgment creditors. *Anderson v. Emp'rs Ins. of Wausau*, 826 F.2d 777, 780.

9th Cir. 2002 (Cal.). A fidelity bond issued to title company did not cover the amount the title company was required to contribute to make up deficiencies in title company's escrow account. *United Gen. Title Ins. Co. v. Am. Int'l Grp., Inc.*, 51 Fed. Appx. 224, 226.

9th Cir. 2000 (Cal.). Amounts paid to settle two lawsuits that alleged that insured was vicariously liable for employee's fraud on a third party did not constitute a "direct loss" under a commercial crime policy. *Vons Cos. Inc., v. Fed. Ins. Co.*, 212 F.3d 489, 492.

9th Cir. 2000 (Cal.). A bank's liability to a customer for an unauthorized withdrawal from the customer's account did not constitute a loss resulting directly from a fraud on the premises of the insured. *Cal. Korea Bank v. Va. Sur. Co.*, No. 98-56778, No. 98-56806, 2000 U.S. App. LEXIS 12306, *4-5.

9th Cir. 1991 (Cal.). A title insurer sought coverage under an Insurance Company Blanket Bond after its employee embezzled money from an escrow account. The court held that the insured's liability was covered under the bond because the bond contained a provision providing for reimbursement of defense costs incurred in defending third-party suits. *First Am. Title Ins. Co. v. St. Paul Fire & Marine Ins. Co.*, 951 F.2d 1134.

D. Conn. 2002. A commercial crime policy did not cover insured's liability to reimburse customers from money embezzled from trust accounts because the payment of a liability is not a loss resulting directly from employee dishonesty. *Finkel v. St. Paul Fire & Marine Ins. Co.*, No. 3:00CV1194 (AHN), 2002 WL 1359672, *8.

N.D. Ill. 2000. The insured sought coverage under a commercial crime policy for liability resulting from its employee's payment of kickbacks to a customer's salesman. The court held that the claim was not covered because the employee's payment of kickbacks were intended to benefit the insured, and were not performed with the manifest intent to cause it a loss. *Williams Elec. Games, Inc. v. Barry*, No. 97 C 3743, 2000 WL 106672.

D. Kan. 1993. Although an Arkansas statute required a securities broker and its agents to post bond that authorized direct suits thereon by third parties, that statute did not provide implied direct action on a fidelity bond because a fidelity bond is a form of first-party coverage and it does not cover insured's liability to a third party. *Sch. Emps. Credit Union v. Nat'l Union Fire Ins. Co. of Pittsburgh, Pa.*, 839 F. Supp. 1477, 1482, *aff'd sub nom. Sch. Employees Credit Union v. Nat'l Union Fire Ins. Co.*, 52 F.3d 338 (10th Cir. 1995).

E.D. Ky. 1990. A fidelity bond issued to a city does not cover loss suffered by the public as a result of police officer's performance of his duties because the bond was only intended to cover loss to the city. *Thornsberry v. W. Sur. Co.*, 738 F. Supp. 209, 211-12.

E.D. Mich. 2008. Insured's liability for money stolen from escrow account represented a loss resulting directly from employee dishonesty because insured held the money at the time of its theft. *Phillip R. Seaver Title Co. v. Great Am. Ins. Co.*, No.08-CV-11004, 2008 U.S. Dist. LEXIS 78568, *9-12, *amended in part, reconsideration granted in part, reconsideration denied in part by Phillip R. Seaver Title Co. v. Great Am. Ins. Co.*, 2008 U.S. Dist. LEXIS 95267 (E.D. Mich., Nov. 17, 2008).

E.D. Mich. 1992. A stock brokerage partnership sought coverage under a blanket bond after its employee fraudulently induced a third party to invest in certain securities. The court held that the insured's liability was covered under the bond because the bond did not specifically limit coverage to losses sustained by the insured. *Manley, Bennett, McDonald & Co. v. St. Paul Fire & Marine Ins. Co.*, 792 F. Supp. 1070.

D. Minn. 2005. A stock broker suffered loss when its registered representative initiated an unauthorized wire transfer of funds from client's account (rather than when broker settled secured lender's lawsuit) and thus, the loss did not fall within indirect loss exclusion. *RBC Dain Rauscher, Inc. v. Fed. Ins. Co.*, 370 F. Supp. 2d 886, 890.

D. Minn. 2001. The insured bank was sued by a customer and his creditor after a loan officer embezzled funds using the customer's line of credit. The court held that there was a genuine issue of fact as to whether the employee's misconduct occurred in connection with the embezzlement or whether it was an unrelated act intended to benefit the bank as his employer. *First Nat'l Bank of Fulda v. BancInsure, Inc.*, No. 00-2002 DDA/FLN, 2001 WL 1663872, *3.

W.D. Mo. 1993. A bank's claimed loss did not result directly from a forgery, but resulted directly from the bank's failure to follow proper procedures because. The bank's procedures required it to reject the transaction and loss occurred solely because the bank violated procedure and accepted the check for deposit. *Empire Bank v. Fid. & Dep. Co. of Md.*, 828 F. Supp. 675, 679-80, *aff'd*, 27 F.3d 333 (8th Cir. 1994).

Bank. N.D. Ohio. 1988. Liability arising after an employee falsely represented that he had authority to sell large blocks of insured's stock at a discount (in order to defraud investors) was a loss "resulting directly from" employee dishonesty because the employee's conduct contemporaneously caused the insured to sustain a loss. *In re Baker & Getty Fin. Servs., Inc.*, 93 B.R. 559, 566.

D. Utah. 2008. A bank's liability to repurchase a loan induced by employee dishonesty did not constitute a loss resulting directly from employee dishonesty because the bank did not suffer a loss until it received and honored a repurchase demand. *Direct Mortg. Corp. v. Nat'l Union Fire Ins. Co. of Pittsburgh, Pa.*, 625 F. Supp. 2d 1171, 1176-78.

W. Va. 1985. A direct action statute did not authorize suit against a financial institution bond carrier because the bond limited coverage to loss "resulting directly" from employee dishonesty and did not cover liability incurred by the insured. *Commercial Bank of Bluefield v. St. Paul Fire. & Marine Ins. Co.*, 336 S.E.2d 552, 556.

W.D. Wash. 2011. Insured that sustained chargeback losses as a result of fraudulent credit card transactions processed through its computer system by several retail merchants did not suffer a direct loss because the loss did not occur until it was unable to recover the chargeback funds from the merchant banks, the bank deducted funds from insured's reserve account, and the insured fulfilled its contractual obligation to replace those deducted funds. *Pinnacle Processing Grp., Inc. v. Hartford Cas. Ins. Co.*, No.C10-1126-RSM, 2011 U.S. Dist. LEXIS 128203, *16-17, *motion denied by Pinnacle Processing Group, Inc. v. Hartford Cas. Ins. Co.*, 2011 U.S. Dist. LEXIS 138862 (W.D. Wash., Dec. 2, 2011).

D. Vt. 2001. A customer who obtained a judgment against the insured for loss sustained by the customer as a result of an employee's embezzlement scheme could not (even with an assignment) recover on a commercial crime policy because the embezzlement scheme did not cause the insured a direct loss and insured's liability represented an indirect loss. *Patrick v. St. Paul Fire & Marine Ins. Co.*, No.1:99CV314, 2001 U.S. Dist. LEXIS 26434, *8.

Cal. App. 2007. Insured's liability for a stolen game piece did not constitute a direct loss within the meaning of a commercial crime policy because the insured did not own the game piece, hold the game piece, and, aside from tort liability, was not legally liable for the game piece. *Simon Mktg., Inc. v. Gulf Ins. Co.*, 149 Cal. App. 4th 616, 625-26.

Conn. Super. 1997. An insurance agent sought indemnity under a commercial crime policy after it fraudulently induced third parties to purchase annuity contracts. The court held that the insured's liability for its employee's conduct was not covered, even though the employee acted dishonestly, because a fidelity bond is an indemnity policy (not a liability policy) and therefore, does not cover an insured's liability to a third party. While the insured might be obligated to reimburse the third party for its losses, the court held that the settlement of a claim did not transform an indirect loss into a direct loss. *IIT Hartford Life Ins. Co. v. Pawson Assocs., Inc.*, No. CV 940361910S, 1997 WL 345345.

Del. Ch. 2010. Interpreting Massachusetts law, the court held that the insured could recover only defense costs expended defending suits for loss of property owned or held by insured. *Mass. Mut. Life Ins. Co. v. Certain Underwriters at Lloyd's of London*, No. 4791-VCL, 2010 Del. Ch. LEXIS 156, *77-78.

Ill. App. 2004. A mortgage broker sought indemnity under a financial institution bond after its employees engaged in a loan fraud scheme. The court held that insured's liability was not covered because a financial institution bond is an indemnity policy (not a liability policy) and the insured's liability did not "result directly" from employee dishonesty.

RBC Mortgage Co. v. Nat'l Union Fire Ins. Co. of Pittsburgh, Pa., 812 N.E.2d 728.

Iowa 1999. A fire department sought indemnity under a commercial crime policy after it was held liable for losses sustained by a third party as a result of its employee's fraudulent conduct. Because the bond covered only losses caused to the insured through dishonest or fraudulent acts, the court held that the claim was not covered. The insured argued that it sustained a loss because it was required to reimburse the third party for its loss, but the court held that the insured's liability was not covered because a fidelity bond is not an indemnity policy and does not cover indirect losses sustained as a result of employee dishonesty. *City of Burlington, Iowa v. Western Sur. Co.*, 599 N.W.2d 469.

Iowa 1994. An insurance company sought coverage under a financial institution bond after its employee defrauded a third party. The court held that the insured's liability was not covered because a financial institution bond is an indemnity policy that covers actual losses sustained by insured, not insured's liability to a third party. *Central Nat'l Ins. Co. of Omaha v. Ins. Co. of N. Am.*, 522 N.W.2d 39.

Ka. 2007. A bank's liability to a third party arising from a deposit of fiduciary funds into personal and business bank accounts did not constitute a loss of property resulting directly from theft on the premises of the insured. *Citizens Bank, N.A. v. Kan. Bankers Sur. Co.*, No. 95,136, 2007 Kan. App. Unpub. LEXIS 524, at *11-15.

La. App. 1994. A commercial crime policy issued to the police department did not cover liability to the state for amounts state paid on fraudulent invoices because the policy limited coverage to direct losses. The state, therefore, could not pursue a direct claim on the policy pursuant to Louisiana's direct action statute. *State ex rel. Dept. of Transp. & Dev. v. Acadia Parish Police Jury*, 631 So. 2d 611, 613-14.

Md. 1989. Fidelity bonds are a form of first-party coverage indemnifying the insured for its loss and not a form of third-party coverage indemnifying the insured for its liability to third persons. *Three Garden Vill. v. U.S. Fid. & Guar. Co.*, 567 A.2d 85, 93.

Mass App. 2005. Theft from a bank account maintained by a noninsured third party did not result in a direct loss to the insured, even if the insured is liable to the third party. *Atlas Metals Prods. Co. v. Lumbermans Mut. Cas. Co.*, 63 Mass. App. Ct. 738, 742.

Mich. App. 1992. A third party brought a garnishment action against a brokers blanket fidelity bond. The court held that the third party was not entitled to garnish the bond because the bond only covered losses sustained by the insured, and did not cover the insured's liability to a third party, even if that liability was predicated upon an employee's dishonest conduct. *Bralko Holdings, Ltd. v. Ins. Co. of N. Am.*, 483 N.W.2d 929.

Mont. 2006. Addressing a certified question from the United States District Court for the District of Montana, the court held that "direct loss" within the context of a business owner's policy means all losses proximately caused by an employee's dishonesty. Distinguishing cases involving liability to a third party, the court held that the insured was entitled to recover costs incurred to investigate the extent of an employee dishonesty and remedy the discovered damages. *Frontline Processing Corp. v. Am. Econ. Ins. Co.*, 149 P.3d 906, 911.

N.J. 2004. A car dealer sought coverage under a fidelity policy after its employee fraudulently induced a third party to approve loans. Although the insured was seeking coverage for losses sustained as a result of its vicarious liability for its employee's conduct, the court held that the claim was covered because the "resulting directly" standard requires only proof of proximate causation. *Auto Lenders Acceptance Corp. v. Gentilini Ford, Inc.*, 854 A.2d 378.

N.Y. App. 2003. Addressing a policy that covered the theft of client funds while in the possession of the insured, the court held that the insured could recover only the amount embezzled and could not recover fees, interest, and costs caused by the theft. *Ernst & Young LLP v. Nat'l Union Fire Ins. Co. Pittsburgh, Pa.*, 758 N.Y.S.2d 304, 305.

N.Y. App. 1998. An investment broker sought indemnity under a financial institution bond after its employees engaged in insider trading. The court held that the claim was not covered because the insured did not sustain a loss as a result of the employee's misconduct. While third parties sustained a loss and the insured was liable for those losses, the court held that the insured's liability was not covered because: (1) a financial institution bond is an indemnity policy, not a liability policy; (2) the insured's liability does not result directly from employee dishonesty; and (3) the employees did not act with the manifest intent to cause the insured a loss. *Aetna Cas. & Sur. Co. v. Kidder, Peabody & Co, Inc.*, 676 N.Y.S.2d 559.

N.Y. App. 1985. A union sought indemnity under a comprehensive dishonesty, disappearance, and destruction policy for expenses it sustained in defending third-party lawsuits brought to recover damages sustained as a result of an employee's fraud. The court held that the insurer was not required to reimburse the union for defense costs because the bond is not a liability policy and as such, does not cover an insured's liability to a third party. *Kriegler v. Aetna Cas. & Sur. Co.*, 485 N.Y.S.2d 1017.

N.Y. Sup. Ct. 2010. A commodities futures merchant's payment of a loss suffered on personal trades conducted by a broker constituted a "direct financial loss" within the meaning of a financial institution bond. *N.H. Ins. Co. v. MF Global, Inc.*, 958 N.Y.S.2d 309, *aff'd as modified by* 970 N.Y.S.2d 16, 19 (2013).

N.Y. Sup. Ct. 1995. A brokerage firm sought indemnity under a financial institution bond for losses sustained when an employee conducted unauthorized trades on a customer's account. The court held that the insured's liability to the customer was not covered because the employee did not act with the manifest intent to cause the insured a loss and the insured did not suffer a direct loss as a result of the employee's conduct. *Cont. Bank, N.A. v. Aetna Cas. & Sur. Co.*, 626 N.Y.S.2d 385.

N.Y. Sup. Ct. 1993. Investment broker sought recovery under a financial institution bond after its employees fraudulently induced third parties to invest in securities. The court held that the insured's liability was not covered because an insured's liability to a third party is a consequential loss outside the scope of coverage. *Drexel Burnham Lambert Group, Inc. v. Vigilant Ins. Co.*, 595 N.Y.S.2d 999.

W. Va. 1985. A third party brought an action against an insurer who issued a commercial crime policy to a payroll service. Although the payroll service's employee had defrauded the third party and the third party had obtained a judgment against the payroll service, the court held that the third party could not garnish the payroll service's fidelity bond because the bond covered only losses sustained by the insured, and did not cover the insured's liability to a third party, even if predicated upon an employee's dishonest conduct. *Commercial Bank of Bluefield v. St. Paul Fire & Marine Ins. Co.*, 336 S.E.2d 552.

Wis. App. 2003. Insured sought indemnity under a financial institution bond after its employees conspired with third parties to obtain loans. The court held that the claim was not covered because the insured did not sustain a direct loss as a result of the employees' misconduct. While the employees' misconduct caused a third party to sustain a loss and the insured was ultimately liable to the third party for its loss, the court held that the insured's liability was not covered because it was an indirect loss and financial institution bonds are not intended to cover third-party losses. *Tri City Nat'l Bank v. Fed. Ins. Co.*, 674 N.W.2d 617.

D. Compensability of Losses Under Non-Standard Policies

8th Cir. 1990 (Ark.). After the insured's owner defrauded investors, the investors sought indemnity under a statutory bond required by the Arkansas Security Act. Although the bond excluded coverage for third-party losses, the court nonetheless held that the claim was covered. The court reasoned that the exclusion of coverage for third-party losses was unenforceable because the bond was issued pursuant to a statute and the statute contemplated that the bond would cover losses sustained by third parties. *Foster v. Nat'l Union Fire Ins. Co. of Pittsburgh, Pa.*, 902 F.2d 1316.

D. Kan. 1993. A third party sought recovery under a statutory fidelity bond after it was defrauded by an investment advisor. The court held that the insured did not have standing to seek coverage under the bond because it did not cover losses sustained by third parties. The third party argued that the bond, as a statutory bond, should be interpreted to provide such coverage, but the court rejected that argument because the statute did not expressly require the bond to cover losses sustained by third parties. *Sch. Employees Credit Union v. Nat'l Union Fire Ins. Co. of Pittsburgh, Pa.*, 839 F. Supp. 1477.

Ill. App. 1991. A computer company sought indemnity under a general liability insurance policy after its employee fraudulently ordered computers on its corporate account. Although the policy covered losses through employee dishonesty, the court held that the insured's liability for the computers was not a covered loss because the insured's liability was not a loss of "money, property or securities." *Travelers Ins. Co. v. P.C. Quote, Inc.*, 570 N.E.2d 614.

Ill. App. 1990. A printing company sought indemnity under an insurance policy for losses sustained when employee destroyed a third party's property. The court held that the insured's liability was covered because the policy specifically afforded coverage for sums that the insured "shall become legally obligated to pay as damages because of bodily injury or property damage . . . ." *Northbrook Nat'l Ins. Co. v. Nehoc Adver. Servs.*, 554 N.E.2d 251.

Wash. 1993. A third party sought recovery under a statutory fidelity bond after its real estate agent embezzled escrow funds. The court held that the insured's liability was covered because the bond was statutorily required to cover any fraudulent or dishonest act committed by the insured's employees. *Estate of K.O. Jordan v. Hartford Acc. & Indem. Co.*, 844 P.2d 403.

SECONDARY SOURCES

John W. Bassett, *Direct Loss Under the Fidelity Insuring Agreement of the Financial Institution Bond*, 54 DEF. COUNS. J. 487 (1987).

Lisa Block & Dirk E. Ehlers, *Aetna v. Kidder Peabody: Trend or Anomaly?*, in AMERICAN BAR ASSOCIATION'S 1999 SURVEY: TOP TEN LIST OF MOST VEXING FIDELITY CLAIMS ISSUES (1999).

Joseph J. Brenstrom, *Third Party Losses: Causational Approach to Resolving Claims on Fidelity Bonds and Other Common Crime Coverages Based Upon Losses To An Insured Arising out of Claims*

Against the Insured By Third Parties (unpublished paper presented at the annual meeting of the Surety Claims Institute, Miami, Florida in June, 1997).

Bradford Carver, *Loss and Causation, in* HANDLING FIDELITY BOND CLAIMS (Michael Keeley & Timothy M. Sukel eds., 2005).

Duncan L. Clore, *Suits Against Financial Institutions: Coverage and Considerations,* 20 FORUM 83 (1984).

Paul R. Devin & R. Allan Fryer, *Third-Party Claims Against the Insured, in* HANDLING FIDELITY BOND CLAIMS (Michael Keeley and Timothy M. Sukel eds., 1999).

Lawrence R. Fish, *Ownership of Property—Interest Covered, in* COMMERCIAL CRIME POLICY, (Gilbert J. Schroeder, ed., 1996).

Christopher Franklin, *Legal Liability for Third Party Losses under Commercial Crime Policies* (unpublished paper presented at the Fidelity and Surety Annual Mid-Winter Meeting of the Fidelity and Surety Law Committee of TIPS in New York, New York, January 27, 1995).

Mark S. Gamell, *Third Party Claims and Losses under the Financial Institution Bond,* I FID. L.J. 75 (1995).

Peter C. Haley & Sarah Mubashir, *How to Combine Fact-Finding and Legal Research in the Investigation of a Clause (E) Claim, in* HANDLING FIDELITY BOND CLAIMS (Michael Keeley & Timothy M. Sukel eds., 2005).

Peter C. Haley, *Clause (E): The Continued Importance of Defined Terms and Causation Theories, in* FINANCIAL INSTITUTION BONDS (Duncan L. Clore ed., 1998).

Peter C. Haley, *Paradigms of Proximate Cause,* 36 TORT & INS. L.J. 147 (2000).

Stephen M. Kranz, Patricia H. Thompson & Ashley M. Daugherty, *Can Direct mean Direct? Untangling the Web of Causation in Fidelity Coverage*, XVI FID. L.J. 153 (2010).

John F. Kruger & Linda Sorensen, *Causation in Fidelity Cases*, 12 FORUM 420 (1976).

John A. Nocera, *Third Party Claims Under Fidelity Bonds* (unpublished paper presented at Surety Claims Institute Annual Meeting in Williamsburg, Virginia, June, 1995).

Maura Z. Pelleteri, *Causation in Loan Loss Cases*, *in* LOAN LOSS COVERAGE UNDER FINANCIAL INSTITUTION BONDS (Gilbert Schroeder and John J. Tomaine eds., 2007).

Scott L. Schmookler, *The Compensability of Third-Party Losses Under Fidelity Bonds*, VII FID. L.J. 115 (2001).

Scott L. Schmookler, *The Compensability of Warehouse Lending Losses*, *in* LOAN LOSS COVERAGE UNDER FINANCIAL INSTITUTION BONDS (Gilbert Schroeder and John J. Tomaine eds., 2007).

Scott L. Schmookler, *Third Party Claims and Losses under the Financial Institution Bond*, I FID. L.J. 75 (1995).

Susan Sullivan & Teresa Jones, *The Question of Causation in Loan Loss Cases*, XI FID. L.J. 97 (2005).

Bradford A. Thomas, *Analysis of Direct Losses and Indirect Losses Under the Modern Financial Institution Bonds Fidelity Coverage and Exclusions* (unpublished paper presented at the Southern Surety and Fidelity Claims Conference, April 1990).

Karen Wildau, *Evolving Law of Third-Party Claims Under Fidelity Bonds: When Is Third-Party Recovery Allowed?*, 25 TORT & INS. L.J. 92 (1989).

Chapter 17

Concealment, Misrepresentation or Fraud (Including Rescission)*

The Concealment, Misrepresentation or Fraud provision has its origin in the statutory New York State Fire Policy. The condition was introduced into the Commercial Crime form in 1994 as the ISO sought uniformity in the General Conditions of its mercantile property policies. The provision was subsequently incorporated into the Surety Association of America's Commercial Crime Forms beginning in 1996.

The provision serves to void the policy and release the insurer from any policy liability due to the named insured's fraud relating to the policy or for the intentional concealment or misrepresentation of any material fact by any insured concerning either the policy, the property covered under the policy, the interest of the named insured in that property, or a claim made under the policy.

E. **CONDITIONS**
   1. **Concealment, Misrepresentation or Fraud**
      This Policy is void in any case of fraud by you as it relates to this Policy at any time. It is also void if any insured, at any time, intentionally conceals or misrepresents a material fact concerning:
      a. **This insurance;**
      b. **The covered property;**
      c. **Your interest in the covered property; or**
      d. **A claim under this insurance.**[1]

---

* By William T. Bogaert and Sa'adiyah K. Masoud, Wilson Elser Moskowitz Edelman & Dicker LLP, Boston, Massachusetts.

1 Crime Protection Policy, SP 00 01 04 12 (Sur. Ass'n of Am. 2012). This recent version of this condition substantially follows the language of the condition when it was introduced in the Commercial Crime form in 1994, other than changing "insurance" to "Policy," and replacing "you or any other insured" with a more surgical "any insured." Crime General Provisions, CR 10 00 06 95, § B.1. (Ins. Servs. Office, Inc., 1994), A-25

COMMENT

The Concealment, Misrepresentation or Fraud condition applies to misstatements or nondisclosures in the application process, as well as in other circumstances. The provision also is applicable if an insured intentionally conceals or misrepresents material information in connection with a claim presented under the policy.

The condition also voids the policy where the insured has failed to disclose a material fact to the insurer. While most states have enacted statutes governing an insurer's right to rescind insurance policies for misrepresentations, the insurer's right to rescind the policy due to an insured's non-disclosure or concealment of information is commonly not governed by statute, but is frequently guided by common law principles of contract.

The provision is limited to the concealment or misrepresentation of "material facts." Determination of whether a fact is material is a matter of state law. Generally, material facts are those facts that would have influenced the judgment of the insurer in assessing the risk or in evaluating a claim. In some jurisdictions, the insurer's proof of the materiality of concealed or misrepresented facts may include proof that the insurer relied on those facts to its detriment.

Under the common law of most states, in order for an insurer to establish fraud, it must prove that the insured made a false statement either with knowledge of its falsity or with reckless disregard to its truth. The insurer must further demonstrate that it relied upon the fraudulent statement to its detriment.

The provision only voids the policy for fraud or an intentional misrepresentation or concealment. Whether an innocent misrepresentation or non-disclosure of a fact that increases the risk of loss to the insurer voids the policy is statutory and varies from state to state.

(Gilbert J. Schroeder ed., 1997). This condition appears as General Condition E.1.d of the Crime General Provisions, in both the Loss Sustained and Discovery Forms is identical with slightly varied language from the SFAA. Form *See* Commercial Crime Policy CR 00 22 08 13 (ISO Props., Inc. 2012) (Discovery) & Commercial Crime Policy, CR 00 23 08 13 (ISO Props., Inc. 2012) (Loss Sustained). Despite the minor language variations in the different forms, the scope and substance of this condition are similar.

OUTLINE OF ANNOTATIONS

A. Cases Interpreting the Concealment, Misrepresentation and Fraud General Condition
   1. Cases Involving Commercial Crime Policies
   2. Cases Involving Other Policies
B. Cases Decided On Material Misrepresentation or Concealment in Policy or Bond Application
   1. Cases Involving Commercial Crime Policies
   2. Cases Involving Other Policy or Bond Forms

ANNOTATIONS

A. Cases Interpreting the Concealment, Misrepresentation and Fraud General Condition

1. Cases Involving Commercial Crime Policies

N.D. Ga. 2013. The insurance contract provision voided the entire policy if the insured ever intentionally concealed or misrepresented a material fact, regarding any claim under the policy. The Policy condition provided:

> CONCEALMENT, MISREPRESENTATION OR FRAUD: This Coverage Part is void in any case of fraud by you as it relates to this Coverage Part at any time. It is also voice if you or any other insured, at any time, intentionally conceal or misrepresent a material fact concerning: 1. This Coverage Part; 2. The Covered Property; 3. Your interest in the Covered Property; or 4. A claim under this Coverage Part.

The court found that the accountant's different valuation of less than four thousand dollars (or 2% of the plaintiff's claim) was insufficient to conclude that the business intentionally lied about the value of its loss. *OSA Healthcare, Inc. v. Mount Vernon Fire Insurance Co.*, 975 F. Supp. 2d 1316 (2013).

N.D. Ga. 2006. The court, in construing an identical Concealment, Misrepresentation or Fraud provision as noted in *OSA Healthcare, Inc. v.*

Mount Vernon Fire Insurance Co., 975 F. Supp. 2d 1316, 1324 (N.D. Ga. 2013), *supra*, voided the policy as a matter of law and concluded that no reasonable trier of fact could believe that business had not lied on his sworn proof of loss. The business's proof of loss claim of a burglary loss of $190,123.33 could not be duplicated by the business' own forensic accountant and that accountant was unable to account for one-fourth of the business' claim. *Perspolis, Inc. v. Federated Mutual Insurance Co.*, No. 1:03-CV-2456, 2006 WL 826469.

W.D. Mich. 2011. The court rescinded the commercial crime policy, finding there was a material misrepresentation by the owner of the car dealership concerning his knowledge of claims. The owner admitted knowing of the dishonest acts of two employees, did not disclose these facts and specifically obtained additional coverage for employee theft committed by these two employees. The policy contained the following condition to coverage:

> b.   Concealment, Misrepresentation or Fraud
> This insurance is void in any case of fraud by you as it relates to this insurance at any time. It is also void if you or any other Insured, at any time, intentionally conceal or misrepresent a material fact concerning:
>> (1)   This insurance;
>> (2)   The property covered under the insurance;
>> (3)   Your interest in the property covered under this insurance; or
>> (f)   A claim under this insurance.

The court deemed the concealed facts material as a matter of law and voided the policy. *Coopersville Motor, Inc. v. Federated Mutual Insurance Co.*, 771 F. Supp. 2d 796.

E.D. Va. 2014. The court voided the policy issued to the volunteer fire department where the treasurer and later insurance agent of the fire department answered "yes" on the Renewal Survey to the question "whether there were any changes in the operations or exposures of the organization" and requested an increase in coverage where treasurer was embezzling monies from the fire department. The court held that the treasurer answered truthfully not making an affirmative misrepresentation by omitting facts that were not specifically asked of him. The court, however, read the 1994 ISO version of this condition in conjunction with the "Joint Insured" section of the policy to rescind the policy holding the treasurer's actions was an intentional concealment of a clearly material fact within the meaning of the Concealment, Misrepresentation or Fraud provision and the "you" in the provision extended to the fire department via the "Joint Insured," i.e., imputation clause, thereby imputing to the fire department knowledge of the treasurer's embezzling activities notwithstanding the treasurer's status as an agent for both parties. *Middleburg Volunteer Fire Department v. McNeil & Co.*, 60 F. Supp. 3d 640, *appeal filed*, No. 14-2330.

Wash. App. 1996. The policyholder failed to cooperate with the insurance company in its investigation of his claim for stolen business property, leading to suspicions that the claim was fraudulent. The appellate court reversed grant of summary judgment to the insurance company based on a language of concealment clause, on the basis that there was a genuine issue of material fact as to whether the claim by policyholder was fraudulent. *Tran v. State Farm Fire & Cas. Co.*, 1996 Wash. App. LEXIS 460.

2. Cases Involving Other Policies

8th Cir. 1996 (Neb.). Arson by the insured on his video store and his report to the insurer that fire was accidental constituted fraud and material misrepresentation and so voided the policy, thereby precluding coverage under policy for burglary of the video store, committed subsequent to the arson and by unrelated parties. *McCullough v. State Farm Fire & Cas. Co.*, 80 F.3d 269.

E.D. Mo. 2006. Where an insurance policy listed the corporation owning a supermarket as insured, the court held that the director and holder of fifty percent of the corporation's stock was included within the meaning of "any insured" under Missouri law, even though he was not listed as such on the policy. As a result, the policy was declared void on several grounds, including on the basis that the director had concealed his role in arson that destroyed the supermarket. *State Auto Prop. & Cas. Ins. Co. v. St. Louis Supermarket #3, Inc.*, 2006 U.S. Dist. LEXIS 240.

E.D. Mo. 1998. Policy language was clear and unambiguous and prevented recovery by insured married couple, where one spouse committed arson that destroyed property, and then concealed this material fact from insurance company and other spouse was barred from recovery under the policy by the language "It is also void if you or any other insured, at any time, intentionally conceal or misrepresent a material fact . . . ." *Employers Mut. Cas. Co. v. Tavernaro*, 4 F. Supp. 2d 868.

S.D.N.Y. 2013. The concealment of nonpayment of $600,000 in rent at one insured location and misrepresentations regarding damages by one of the owners of a family business conglomerate could void the policy under the Concealment, Misrepresentation or Fraud provision. The policy's "Concealment, Misrepresentation or Fraud" provision provided:

> This policy is void in any case of fraud by the Insured as it relates to this policy at any time. It is also void if the Insured or any other person or entity insured under this policy, at any time, intentionally conceals or misrepresents a material fact concerning:
> 1.   This policy;
> 2.   The Covered Property;
> 3.   The Insured's interest in the Covered Property; or
> 4.   A claim under this policy.

The court found the provision clear and unambiguous holding that the excess and surplus lines insurer could void the policy in its entirety in the event of a concealment, misrepresentation or fraud by any insured under the policy. The court rejected an argument that policy fraud provisions were severable and voidable as to each insured and property and read the second sentence of the above provision to plainly contemplate voiding the entire policy on the basis of concealment or misrepresentation, which included "fraud" by any covered person or entity under the policy and the first sentence as addressing the same in regards to fraud by the primary insured under the policy. *Mon Chong Loong Trading Corp. v. Travelers Excess and Surplus Lines Co.*, No. 12-civ-6509, 2013 WL 3326662.

E.D. Pa. 1996. Insurance company moved for summary judgment on policyholder's claims for breach of contract, bad faith, and deceit on the grounds that the policyholder made material misrepresentations regarding a loss claim under the policy, which misrepresentations voided the policy. Misrepresentations alleged by the insurance company included misrepresentation regarding the amount of cash lost in a fire at insured business, as well as misrepresentation of the income earned by the business. The court found that whether these were material misrepresentations presented issues of fact to be decided by a jury and could not form a basis for summary judgment. *Garvey v. Nat'l Grange Mut. Ins. Co.,* 1996 U.S. Dist. LEXIS 5782.

S.D. Texas 2013. A homeowner who intentionally made material misrepresentations and concealed material facts regarding fire damage claimed that first letter from State Farm adjuster seeking to void policy relative to certain claims for debris removal, personal property and storage should limit the second letter from State Farm that generally sought to void entire policy to only those claims specified in first letter. The court upheld voiding entire policy as there were no qualifying terms in the second letter and State Farm had the right to void entire policy under the Concealment or Fraud provision "if you or any other insured under the policy has intentionally concealed or misrepresented any material fact or circumstances relating to this insurance, whether before or after a loss." *Alexander v. State Farm Lloyds,* No. 4:12-cv-490, 2013 WL 49719.

La. App. 1997. Louisiana's law provided that "misrepresentations in a proof of loss will void coverage only if the insured knowingly and intentionally makes such misrepresentations with the intent to deceive and defraud the insurer. Fraud will never be presumed from acts which may be accounted for on the basis of honesty and good faith." Though issue was not briefed, the court found no manifest error in jury's verdict that plaintiff manufacturing company made no willful concealment or material misrepresentation of material fact in violation of the policy condition. *B. Bennett Mfg. Co. v. S. Carolina Ins. Co.,* 692 So. 2d 1258.

B. Cases Decided Using Material Misrepresentation in Policy or Bond Application

1.   Cases Involving Commercial Crime Policies

8th Cir. 2011 (Minnesota). The chief financial officer of a paper recycling company, whose duties included completing insurance applications, made material misrepresentations on six different insurance applications for commercial crime insurance. The representations included claims that all company locations were independently audited on an annual basis, had certain internal controls, and that the bank accounts were reconciled by someone not authorized to deposit to or withdraw from accounts. These statements were not true as to all locations or accounts and allowed the CFO to embezzle over $500,000 by controlling accounts that were never audited or reconciled. The court allowed the insurance to be rescinded in accordance with Minnesota law finding that Minn. Stat. § 60A. 08(9) which provided that "[n]o oral or written misrepresentation made by the assured . . . in the negotiation of insurance, shall be deemed material, or defeat or avoid the policy . . . unless the matter misrepresented increased the risk of loss") contemplated and governed misrepresentations made in applications for insurance, that the CFO made the misrepresentations within the scope of his employment and was specifically authorized to purchase the company's insurance and therefore any misrepresentations were attributable to the company. The court also considered and rejected the company's argument that Minnesota law imposed a "but for" requirement and so the insurance company did not have to prove it would not have issued the policy all but for the misrepresentations but only that the "matter misrepresented increase[d] the risk of loss." *Pioneer Industries, Inc. v. Hartford Fire Insurance Co.*, 639 F.3d 461.

9th Cir. 2001 (Idaho). The court refused to rescind fidelity insurer's commercial crime policy because policyholder failed to disclose pertinent loss history information in its renewal application form. There was an issue of fact about whether the policyholder suffered a material loss. The court reasoned that if the insured company did not suffer a material loss, its failure to include the circumstance on the application would not have constituted a material misrepresentation justifying rescission. *Gulf USA Corp. v. Fed. Ins. Co.*, 259 F.3d 1049.

Bankr. D.N.J. 2005. The insurance company sought declaration in a bankruptcy proceeding that comprehensive commercial crime policy issued to the policyholder did not provide coverage for conversion of customer funds by employees where policyholder made material misrepresentations in the policy renewal application. The misrepresentations included failure to reveal known past losses, caused by employee dishonesty, and claims against policyholder. The court found that these misrepresentations were objectively untruthful and that the question on the application seeking this information was not ambiguous. Therefore, the policies were void *ab initio*. In addition, an untruthful answer constituted equitable fraud, making rescission possible even where misrepresentation may have been innocent. *In the matter of Tri-State Armored Services, Inc. (Great Am. Ins. Co. v. Subranni)* 332 B.R. 690.

S.D.N.Y. 1983. The policyholder's failure to make a good faith effort to provide a reasonable estimate of gross receipts on an application for federal crime insurance constituted a material misrepresentation, which warranted denial of coverage under the policy. *Nyasco Sports, Inc. v. Fed. Emergency Mgmt. Agency,* 561 F. Supp. 864.

2. Cases Involving Other Policy or Bond Forms

U.S. 1902. A recovery was denied to a bank on a cashier's bond due to the bank president's misrepresentation in the application where the bank's president had received reports of cashier's unlawful speculation. In finding for the bond issuer, the Supreme Court relied on bond provisions "that any written answers (in the application) . . . shall be held to be a warranty." *Guar. Co. of N. Am. v. Mechanics' Sav. Bank & Trust Co.,* 183 U.S. 402.

2d Cir. 2010 (Conn.). The court held that bank's fidelity bond was an "asset" that the FDIC acquired as a receiver but refused to apply Section 1823(a) holding there was nothing secret about the misrepresentation defense where the grounds for rescission were plainly stated on the face of the bond. The insurance company could rescind for material misrepresentations in the fidelity bond. *F.D.I.C. v. Great American Ins. Co.,* 607 F. 3d 288.

2d Cir. 1999 (N.Y.). A Chapter 11 trustee appealed a judgment in favor of a surety company that policyholder's CEO material misrepresentations on the application regarding diverting of funds for personal use can be imputed to the policy-holding corporation to void policies *ab initio*. The court found that adverse domination and adverse interest doctrines were inapplicable and that the policies were void *ab initio* because of materially false answers given by the CEO in response to question, "whether there was any other information material to the proposed insurance." *In re Payroll Express Corp.,* 186 F.3d 196.

2d Cir. 1935 (N.Y.). Statements about an employee's indebtedness to his employer that were not embodied in the policy were not warranties, but were representations "on the faith of which the bond was delivered, and, if material to the risk, must have been true, or the bond could not survive." *Becker, Moore & Co., Inc., v. USF&G,* 74 F.2d 687.

5th Cir. 1919 (Ala.). Action by receiver of bank against fidelity insurer on bank's bond subject to a provision "all . . . statements the obligee hereby warrants to be true." Despite evidence that the cashier was in default, bank certified that the books and accounts were examined and correct and that the cashier was not in default upon subsequent renewals. The court held that the bank had notice of the terms of the original bond, including the warranty provision, and that therefore, "there is no room for holding the surety company bound by a continuation certificate issued on the faith of a statement which was warranted to be true, but was false . . . ." *Green v. Interstate Cas. Co.,* 256 F. 81.

6th Cir. 1994 (N.J.). The insurance company brought declaratory judgment action against the receiver of an insolvent financial institution seeking to rescind financial institution bond. The court held that FIRREA did not create a jurisdictional bar to the affirmative defense of rescission. *Nat'l Union Fire Ins. Co. of Pittsburgh, Pa. v. City Sav., F.S.B.,* 28 F.3d 376.

6th Cir. 1991 (Tenn.). The insurance company refused payment under a bankers blanket bond due to alleged misrepresentations on its bond application about whether the insured bank was under investigation in regard to its banking practices. Sixth Circuit held that the *D'Oench* doctrine or 12 U.S.C. §1823(e) was inapplicable to the bankers blanket bond and that the FDIC acquires such a bond with knowledge of the recognized defenses available under insurance law. *FDIC v. Aetna Cas. & Sur. Co.*, 947 F.2d 196.

8th Cir. 1935 (Ark.). A policyholder brought action against its insurance company to recover upon a fidelity bond after the bank's collecting agent embezzled funds. The bank stated on its bond application that it checked the account of the bank's collecting agent on a monthly basis. In fact, the account was never checked and the bank's noncompliance with this warranty prevented recovery. The court relied on the bond provision and application, which expressly made the bank's statements warranties and not representations. *Employers Liab. Assur. Corp. v. Wasson*, 75 F.2d 749.

9th Cir. 1925 (Wash.). The court affirmed lower court decision that surety issued fidelity bond in reliance of continuation certificate, which constituted a contract between the bank and the surety and "if it made false material representations or warranties relied upon by defendant, the contract . . . is subject to avoidance." Bond provision stated application answers as to the bank's cashier were "warranties and form part of and be conditions precedent to the issuance . . ." *Duke v. Fid. & Dep. Co. of Md.*, 5 F.2d 305.

9th Cir. 1919 (Cal.). Company charged with knowledge of one of its employee's embezzlement when account books clearly demonstrated that embezzlement. Consequently, statements in an application for bond, which warranted that employee was trustworthy, prevented recovery under the bond. *Nat'l Sur. Co. v. Globe Grain & Milling Co.*, 256 F. 601.

9th Cir. 1904 (Wash.). An insured savings and loan association brought action to recover upon a fidelity bond after the saving and loan association's secretary embezzled funds. The bond issuer defended on grounds that answers in application relating to being short on accounts that were warranted to be true were, in fact, false. The court held that provision in fidelity bond "[t]hat all the representations made by the employer . . . to the surety . . . are warranted by the employer to be true . . ." was not a warranty. The court reasoned that other language requiring knowledge of the employer qualified this statement. *Am. Bonding Co. of Baltimore v. Spokane Bldg. & Loan Soc'y*, 130 F. 737.

10th Cir. 1994 (Utah). The court held that the D'Oench doctrine or 12 U.S.C. §1823(e) applied to fidelity bonds. Therefore, the insurer's misrepresentation defense based on untruthful assertions made in the bond application failed. *FDIC v. Oldenburg,* 34 F.3d 1529.

10th Cir. 1930 (Okla.). In action to recover on a fidelity bond executed by cashier of the bank, bond provision stated that representations on application were warranties by bank. The court held that application answers to questions concerning whether applicant was in debt to the bank were not false. However, court found that bond should have terminated after discovery of defalcation. *USF&G v. State of Oklahoma ex rel. Shull,* 43 F.2d 532.

E.D. Ark. 1923. The court held that fidelity bond condition stating that "all written statement made in connection with this bond or any renewal thereof are warranted to be true" must clearly be limited to the time the questions in the application were answered. The court further held that insurance company by issuing the bond without an answer to an application question constituted a waiver. *Bank of England, Ark., v. Md. Cas. Co.,* 293 F. 783.

D. Del. 2011. The sole shareholder of the student loan servicing company, Student Financing Corporation, committed fraudulent acts in placing or acquiring thousands of student loans that failed to meet the company's underwriting guidelines. The credit risk policy insurer for the company made a claim against the fidelity policy insurer who asserted a counterclaim for rescission on the grounds that the company failed to disclose the fraudulent nature of its business, or that it was near collapse, and moreover that the company's shareholder provided fraudulent and misleading information on the application that voided the policy *ab initio* all of which was imputed to the credit risk policy insurer. The court held that the policy was not void *ab initio* discussing the difference between fraud in the inducement and fraud in the factum determining that this was a case of fraud in the inducement. There remained questions of fact precluding summary judgment as to whether the fidelity insurer had knowledge of facts supporting rescission for nine years, and unreasonably delayed its decision and whether it failure to return the bond's premium prevented it from seeking rescission. The court also found that there were questions of fact as to whether the company's officers knew of the alleged fraud. *Arrowood Indemnity Co. v. Hartford Fire Insurance Co.*, 774 F. Supp. 2d 636.

M.D. Fla. 2014. The court determined that the parties contracted out of the Florida statutory standard permitting rescission of a policy for a "misrepresentation, omission, concealment of fact, or incorrect statement" in a professional liability policy that required an intentional misrepresentation to void the policy. Therefore, it was held an issue of fact whether the principal of a law firm when answering inaccurately on several questions on an application were made with the intent to deceive. *Travelers Cas. and Sur. Co. of America v. Mader Law Group, LLC*, No. 8:13-cv-2577, 2014 WL 5325745.

M.D. Ga. 1967. The bond was void *ab initio* where applicant bank, through managing partner, warranted it had no knowledge of any employee dishonesty. At time of application, managing partner was in fact misappropriating bank funds. The court held that managing partner's knowledge could be imputed to bank because he was the only active partner and was in fact the bank's alter ego. *Hartford Acc. & Indem. Co. v. Hartley*, 275 F. Supp. 610.

N.D. Ill. 2014. Illinois court found that it was an issue of fact whether executive had lied on renewal application and declined to settle whether adverse interest exception was recognized by Illinois where state law requires an insurer to show an "actual intent to deceive" if the insured has made representations in a policy application on "knowledge and belief." *FDIC v. OneBeacon Midwest Ins. Co.*, No. 11-C-3972, 2014 WL 1292833.

N.D. Ill. 2012. The insurance company could bring an affirmative defense that the FDIC's claims for coverage, as a receiver of a failed bank, were barred "because the insurance contract was unenforceable and/or void *ab initio* due to concealment, material misrepresentation and/or material breach of warranty by the Bank." The court held that neither the financial institution bond nor application was an asset governed by the requirements of 18 U.S.C. § 1823 and the *D'Oench, Duhme* doctrine the continued viability of which it questioned and nevertheless found to be inapplicable. *F.D.I.C. v. OneBeacon Midwest Insurance Co.*, 883 F. Supp. 2d 754.

N.D. Ill. 1989. Illinois law does not impose a duty on the policyholder to volunteer to the insurance company information material to the risk involved, where the insurer has not specifically requested such information. Thus, savings and loan association's failure to inform insurance company that it was operating pursuant to cease and desist order did not provide grounds for rescission of bond. *FSLIC v. Transamerica Ins. Co.*, 705 F. Supp. 1328.

E.D. Ky. 2011. The president and CEO of a corporation made false and intentional misrepresentations on policy applications for coverage under financial institution bond and professional liability policy given she was embezzling funds. The court held that her actions could not be imputed to corporation and insurance could not be rescinded for representations. The court declined to rescind policies because the officer's representations were adverse to corporation's interests, she was not the "sole actor" for corporation where corporation had a Board of Directors that regularly met and discussed these matters, and there was no benefit to the corporation for her actions. The adverse interest exception applied and the officer's knowledge could not be imputed because in concealing her fraudulent activity she acted adversely to corporation. *BancInsure v. U.K. Bancorporation Inc./United Kentucky*, 830 F. Supp. 2d 294.

D. Mass. 1998. The court granted Lloyd's summary judgment motion and held that misrepresentations in application rendered bond void *ab initio*. FDIC, as receiver for the insured bank, brought action against the bond underwriters to recover on a banker's blanket bond. Lloyd's argued that it was entitled to rescind the bond under Mass. Gen. Laws c. 175 § 186 due to material misrepresentations by the bank on its application. The court found misrepresentations by the insured bank in withholding critical information about the misconduct of two discharged loan officers in answering "no," to an application question asking the bank to state any irregularities in banking or financial operations known to the bank. *FDIC v. Underwriters of Lloyd's of London Fid. Bond No. 834/FB9010020*, 3 F. Supp. 2d 120.

D. Md. 2011. A fund that invests in other companies, in particular a laboratory that was involved in the sale and distribution of a tainted drug sought insurance coverage for itself and its purported subsidiaries for two classes of lawsuits. The general commercial liability and umbrella insurers sought to rescind and reform the relevant insurance contracts because of certain material and intentional false representations in a series of insurance applications. The court rejected the fund's argument that the parol evidence rule, given a merger/integration clause in the policy, foreclosed any consideration of the pre-contractual representations as evidence of fraud, and held that such evidence was admissible because "if a contract carries no legal effect from the start, a court should treat the integration clause included within the contract as equally worthless." *Charter Oak Fire Insurance Co. v. American Capital, Ltd.*, CA No. DKC 09-0100, 2011 WL 856374.

S.D. Miss. 2012. In Mississippi, to establish that a material misrepresentation has been made on an insurance application "(1) it must contain answers that are false, incomplete, or misleading, and (2) the false, incomplete, or misleading answers must be material to the risk insured against or contemplated by the policy. The party seeking to void the insurance contract . . . must establish the existence of a factual misrepresentation and its materiality by *clear and convincing evidence*. Whether the misrepresentation was intentional, negligent, or the result of mistake or oversight is of no consequence." The court held that bank's application responses in regards to internal control over cash, especially as to whether it maintained dual control over main and reserve cash vaults in each location, and the bank's representation as to whether reasonable efforts had been made to obtain sufficient information from each and every individual or entity proposed for insurance were questions of fact given that bank's dual control policy was disregarded in one location. *FDIC v. Denson*, 908 F. Supp. 2d 792.

D.N.J. 1996. The court granted insurance company's summary judgment motion brought against FDIC as successor to receiver of the insured insolvent bank. Insurance company sought summary judgment seeking rescission of Financial Institution Bond issued in 1989 on grounds that the insolvent bank misrepresented material information on the application with respect to whether the bank had received criticism from regulators. Interpreting New Jersey law, the court held that the bank knowingly and falsely misrepresented that regulators had not criticized operations, which materially affected the insurance company's decision to issue the 1989 bond. *FDIC v. Moskowitz*, 946 F. Supp. 322.

S.D.N.Y. 2001. A receiver of investment firm brought a third-party action against the firm's London insurers who issued blended fidelity and professional liability policies. Both parties sought summary judgment based on the insurers' allegations that they were induced to sell policies by misrepresentations on an unsigned bankers blanket bond application and in the underwriting process. The court held that where the insurers had knowledge of the basis to rescind after the policy was issued (but prior to the claim), but chose not to, they were deemed to have ratified the coverage. *SEC v. Credit Bancorp, Ltd.,* 147 F. Supp. 2d 238.

E.D. Pa. 1993. The court erred in determining that fidelity bond was subject to rescission for failure of insured savings & loan association to list all losses sustained by officers in past three years. Under Pennsylvania law, the insurer must establish that (1) that the declaration by the insured was false; (2) that the false declaration was material to the risk; and (3) that the insured knew it to be false. The court concluded that there was no evidence to support the materiality element. *Fid. Fed. Sav. & Loan Ass'n v. Felicetti,* 813 F. Supp. 332.

Bankr. E.D. Pa. 1992. Trustee in a securities fraud case brought an action against the insurance company to collect upon a securities dealers bond. In its summary judgment motion the insurance company argued that the policyholder's principals failed to disclose in the bond application their participation in fraudulent activity justifying rescission of the bond. The bankruptcy court denied the insurance company's motion holding that the policyholder's principals' knowledge of their own fraudulent acts may not be imputed to the insured corporation. However, the court also denied the trustee's summary judgment motion because "[i]t appears grossly unfair to allow the principal of a corporation, knowing not only of his own fraud, but also that his actions cannot be imputed to his corporation, to load upon on purchases of fidelity bonds in order to replenish the corporation at the expense of an innocent and ignorant insurance company." *In re Lloyd Sec., Inc.* 1992 Bankr. LEXIS 764.

W.D. Tenn. 1986. An insured bank moved for summary judgment on the insurance company's affirmative defense that fidelity bond was void because of the bank's misrepresentations in the application. The court, applying Tenn. Code Ann. Section 56-7-103, held that the insurance company's misrepresentation defense was not valid to the extent the company conducts an in-depth inquiry and the policyholder's nondisclosure pertains to a subject about which the insurance company did not inquire. However, the court stated that the insurance company's misrepresentation defense would not be stricken to the extent that it was based on alleged affirmative representations by the policyholder in connection with its fidelity bond application. The insurance company's failure to inquire about certain subjects on the application does not permit a policyholder to affirmatively misrepresent information. *United Am. Bank in Memphis v. Aetna Cas. & Sur. Co.*, 1986 U.S. Dist. LEXIS 27619.

Ark. 1909. The court held that statements by the insured bank that are made part of the basis of the cashier's bond issued by the bond issuer are treated as representations if not labeled as warranties and will not avoid the bond except for fraud or misrepresentation. The court found that statements representing condition of the bank and the accounts of the bank and the character of the bank's employees were mere representations, which were made honestly, and thus did not vitiate the bond because bond provision failed to state it was a warranty but only said such representations constituted part of the basis and consideration of the contract. *Title Guar. & Sur. Co. v. Bank of Fulton*, 117 S.W. 537.

Ark. 1908. The court held that the bank's representations in application concerning frequency of checking its employee's account constituted a warranty that was breached. Bond included provisions that statements by the employer were warranted to be true, were considered conditions precedent and would void the policy if untrue. *USF&G v. Bank of Batesville*, 112 S.W. 957.

Ark. 1906. A fidelity bond contained a provision stating "[t]hat all the representations made by the employer . . . are warranted by the employer to be true" and the application for the bond contained similar language. However, the court found that bank did not breach any conditions or warranties of the bond as the alleged misstatements were not material. *Am. Bonding Co. of Baltimore v. Morrow*, 96 S.W. 613.

Cal. App. 1914. Stipulation in policy made statements or answers in letter containing the bank's responses to casualty company's questions for purposes of procuring the bond warranties and part of the contract.

The court held that policy was void *ab initio* due to warranties being false and policy issued in reliance upon them. The court reasoned that when a warranty is broken at its inception the policy never attaches to the risk, which it purports to cover. *Wolverine Brass Works v. Pac. Coast Cas. Co. of San Francisco,* 146 P. 184.

Colo. 1906. Provision that bond was issued and accepted upon the condition that all the representations made by the investment company to the surety company were warranted by the investment company to be true permitted voiding of bond. The court explained that a material misrepresentation made in response to a specific inquiry upon which the surety company relies avoids the policy, whether or not the questions were warranties or representations. The court held that answers in connection with questions relating to examination of accounts/books and shortages were untrue, material to the risk and within the knowledge of the officer who completed the application. *Am. Bonding & Trust Co. v. Burke,* 85 P. 692.

Colo. 1906. The court reversed ruling for an insured union on action to recover on bond. The secretary of the union answered questions in the application, which bond deemed, ". . . are to be considered warranties, and they shall form the basis of the guarantee hereby applied for." The court held that the union's misrepresentation regarding checking accounts and financial books was an absolute breach of contract made to induce bond issuer into the issuing of the bond. The court reasoned that the bond made the answers material to the risk and that bond issuer would not have issued the bond had the union not made answers that it did. *USF&G v. Downey,* 88 P. 451.

Ind. App. 2010. The homeowner's answer on application that she had never had an insurance policy cancelled was a material misrepresentation as a matter of law given that she had a prior history of cancellation(s) with other insurance carriers. The court found that the application question "coverage ever declined, cancelled, or non-renewed" was unambiguous and declined to consider the homeowner's argument that she interpreted the question to specifically address only the insurance policy in effect and whether it had ever been declined, cancelled or non-renewed. Moreover, the court credited an affidavit from an underwriter stating he would not issue the subject policy had he known of the cancellation history. The court reviewed several decisions from various jurisdictions and determined that representations in regards to cancellation were material as a matter of law, and the insurance company had met its burden by submitting the affidavit, which was not disputed by the homeowner. The dissent disagreed with the construction of the policy, finding the homeowner's interpretation of the policy reasonable given particularly the section heading stated "Insurance Coverage" and not "Prior Insurance Coverage" "Coverage History or the Like." Moreover, the dissent doubted the underwriter's affidavit given that in another part of the application insured had answered "yes" to having a loss history without any further detail and the insurance company had not investigated "[I]t cannot be heard to complain now that it was misled on one issue when it conduct reveals that, on a related issue with materiality to the underwriting risk, it had notice but made no inquiry." *Allied Property and Casualty Insurance Co. v. Good*, 938 N.E.2d 227.

Ky. App. 1918. Employer's fraudulent misrepresentation in application for renewal of cashier's bond made knowingly, which was material to the risk that the insurer relies upon and induces execution of the bond prevents, recovery upon the bond. Bond provision provided that the representations made by the bank were warranted to be true and that bond was executed upon that condition. The court reasoned that where the bank fails to use due diligence to learn the truth of his application answers recovery upon bond is not permitted if the bond issuer relies upon the answer. *Fid. & Dep. Co. v. Kane*, 206 S.W. 888.

Ky. App. 1915. Notwithstanding bond provision that all statements made by the employer are warranted to be true, the court held that a bond executed to insure a bank against the dishonesty of its employee was not void on account of misrepresentations made by the employer in the application relating to indebtedness and honesty if the bank does not know or should not know that the representation was false. The court further stated that if the bank knowingly made a false answer, it would be fatal to recovery under the bond. *Am. Bonding Co. of Baltimore v. Ballard County Bank's Assignee*, 176 S.W. 368.

Ky. App. 1903. The court deemed employer's statements in application, which were false, to be warranties and fatal to an action upon the bond despite Kentucky Statute Section 639 (1899) declaring insurance application statements representations. Bond recited that the bank's statements constitute an essential part of the bond and form the basis of the contract. The court held that the application of the statute was immaterial because the misrepresentations were material to the risk. *Warren Dep. Bank v. Fid. & Dep. Co. of Md*, 74 S.W. 1111.

La. App. 1937. Bank answered in statement that bank would systematize its books, check employee's books on a bi-annual basis and that the last check of the accounts showed all accounts to be correct in every respect. Bond provision stated, "statements . . . are warranted by the employer to be true, and shall constitute part of the basis and consideration of the contract . . . ." The court held that the bank's false answers made it impossible for the bond to be effective because the answers were warranties and the questions asked were highly material to the interest of the bond issuer and the truth of the answers were indispensable prerequisites to the issuance of the bond. *City Bank & Trust Co. v. Commercial Cas. Co.*, 176 So. 27.

Mass. 2009. The State Treasurer's office's inaccurate representations on its application for an employee dishonesty bond did not provide a basis for the insurance company to rescind the bond because the representations were substantially true and correct and were not made with the intent to defraud. The Department's answer "yes" to question "Are bank accounts reconciled monthly by someone not authorized to deposit or withdraw" was substantially true although certain checks issued by the UCF, the fund that was the source of the thefts were not because those checks approximated 2,500 of the eight to nine million checks annually that were reconciled independently. Similarly, the court held that the state voucher system did not address UCF checks was not a misrepresentation given that eight to nine million checks were subject to the voucher system. Finally, the Department's inaccurate representation that "yes" there was "an internal audit by an Internal Audit Department under the control of an employee who is a public accountant, or the equivalent?" was not a material misrepresentation given the testimony of the senior underwriter for the insurance company that the presence of an internal auditor was not an important factor in determining whether to issue a bond. *Hanover Ins. Co. v. Treasurer and Receiver General*, 74 Mass. App. Ct. 725.

Minn. 1919. Insured company stated, on its bond application, that to the best of its knowledge, no employee had committed a dishonest act. The bond provided that all employer-furnished statements concerning the employee and his accounts were warranted to be true. After employee embezzled funds, the surety company refused to pay on the bond prompting an action by the employer. Evidence established that insured company knew of dishonest acts by the employee and made misrepresentations in the application regarding such. The insured company claimed that they were not made with the intent to deceive. The court stated that the misrepresentations avoided the contract regardless of intent under statute because the matter misrepresented increased the risk of loss. *W.A. Thomas Co. v. Nat'l Sur. Co.,* 172 N.W. 697.

Mo. App. 1916. Bond provision stated "bond was . . . renewed upon the following condition . . . (2) representations made by employer were warranted to be true; that the employee has not to the knowledge of the employer . . . been in arrears or a defaulter in the position covered by this bond or in any other position . . ." The court held that the statements made in the renewal certificate, that the employee had faithfully, honestly and punctually accounted for all moneys and property and always had proper securities, property and funds on hand to balance his accounts, and was not then in default, were nothing more than misrepresentations. *Commercial Bank v. Am. Bonding Co.,* 187 S.W. 99.

Mo. App. 1915. Bond recited that it was issued upon the faith of the statements made by the packing company, which were warranted to be true. The court affirmed lower court's ruling for the bond issuer denying recovery on bond due to the packing company's false statement in the application for the bond. In so deciding, the court stated that whether statements were warranties was immaterial because statements were highly material to the risk. *Krey Packing Co. v. USF&G,* 175 S.W. 322.

Neb. 1909. Bond recites that "it is issued . . . upon the faith of said statements, which plaintiff warrants to be true, and as a condition precedent to the employer's right to recover upon the bond; that if said written statement is in any respect untrue, the bond shall be void." The court affirmed district court's judgment for bond issuer due to fact that the policyholder made no effort, successful or not, to examine accounts and due to fact that policyholder permitted cashier to perform tasks that it warranted in the application the cashier would not perform. The court explained that common honesty dictates that the policyholder should neither be untruthful nor negligent in answering questions propounded to it for the purpose of securing material information concerning the risk that a bonding company is asked to assume. *Sunderland Roofing & Supply Co. v. USF&G,* 122 N.W. 25.

N.Y. Sup. Ct. 2011. The court interpreted a financial institution bond rider as limiting the right to rescind the policy only for intentionally made misrepresentations, omissions, concealment, or incorrect statements even though New York law and General Agreement Provision D in the financial institution bond permitted rescission based upon an innocent or unintentional material omission. The rider in the insurance policy titled "Intentional Misrepresentation of Insured Rider," which deleted General Agreement Provision D, the court held clearly required an intentional element although language itself was subject to two interpretations, "Any intentional misrepresentation, omission, concealment or any incorrect statement of a material fact, in the application or otherwise, shall be grounds for rescission of the bond." Whether statements by limited liability investment companies were material and were intentional misrepresentations was an issue of fact that could not disposed of at summary judgment. The court disregarded the insurance underwriter's affidavit stating that he would have denied coverage had he known of the facts, finding the affidavit was conclusory and unsupported by documentary evidence. *US Fire Insurance Co. v. Nine Thirty FEF Investments, LLC and Nine Thirty VC Investments, LLC,* No. 603284/09, 2011 WL 2552335.

N.Y. Sup. Ct. 2006. The response on an application for business property insurance indicating that there were no deep fat fryers in use in the building, when there was such a fryer in use in the building, rendered the policy void as material misrepresentation. *Bleecker Street Health & Beauty Aids v. Granite State Ins. Co.,* 11 Misc. 3d 1091A.

Okla. 1914. The court held that insurance company was estopped from denying liability on a cashier's bond based on alleged misrepresentations on application question regarding frequency of examinations of cashier's account. The court cited bond provision that stipulated that representations of the bank were expressly warranted to be true. Although it considered these representations warranties for the sake of argument, court found representations relating to frequency of examination and examiner to be true. *USF&G v. Boley Bank & Trust Co.*, 144 P. 615.

Okla. 1911. The court held that the answers in questions submitted by the policyholder in connection with the bond constituted warranties. Bond provision stated that "representations are hereby expressly warranted to be true" and "Employer's Statement" showed that it was the express intention of the parties that the answers relating to examination of accounts were warranties and conditions precedent. However, court failed to find evidence to establish that there were any false representations establishing a breach of the bond. *S. Sur. Co. v. Tyler & Simpson Co.*, 120 P. 936.

Okla. 1906. The court found that "where statement and representations have been made by the insured as the basis for insurance, and by the terms of the policy . . . said statements are made part of the policy itself, any material, false, and fraudulent statement made by the insured will avoid the policy." The court ultimately held that representations of assistant cashier that president was not indebted to bank were "outrageously untrue" and were known to be untrue, thereby avoiding liability of the insurance company. *J.A. Willoughby v. Fid. & Dep. Co. of Md.*, 85 P. 713.

Or. 1917. Finding for insurer, the court held that the policyholder's written answers to the bond issuer's questions regarding custody of securities and examination of books were warranties based on express declaration contained in the application and in the bond. The application stated that the answers were warranted to be true and the bond stated that it was executed in reliance upon the faith of the policyholder's written statements that were warranties and conditions precedent to recovery on the policy. *Bissinger & Co. v. Mass. Bonding Ins. Co.* 163 P. 592.

Pa. 1933. Casualty company issued a bankers blanket bond to title company based on a written application completed by the company's secretary/treasurer, who was embezzling money from the company at the time he signed the application. At trial, the lower court applying state law excluded the application from evidence because it was not attached to the bond at issuance. However, the Supreme Court held that the rule excluding the application did not exclude proof otherwise. Bond provision stated that "no statement . . . made in the application for this bond or otherwise submitted by or on behalf of the insured shall be deemed a warranty of anything except the fact that the statement is true to the best of the knowledge . . . of the person making it." The court stated warranty was broken as soon as it was made. The court also stated that the misstatement that was "otherwise submitted" may be a complete defense to the suit on the bond if the statement as to the honesty of the employees whose fidelity was to be insured was applied. *Gordon v. Cont'l Cas. Co.*, 166 A. 557.

S.D. 1939. In an action against the issuer of a cashier's bond for the cashier's allegedly misappropriated bank funds during the bond's term, the original bond had been continued "in reliance upon the statements contained in the Clearance Certificate [which] are to be deemed warranties and a part of this contract." The court held that statements in certificate were intended warranted representations and that such warranty was breached pursuant to statute and case law when an examination of the books was not made and shortages were known in the cashier's account. *FDIC v. Western Sur. Co.*, 285 N.W. 909.

Tenn. 1914. Bank's Continuation Certificate to insured to renew cashier's bond certifying that books of the cashier were examined and found correct was held not to be a warranty of the correctness of such accounts but only that such examinations were made and no errors were discovered. Bond provision stating "[w]hereas the employer has heretofore delivered to the company certain representations and promises relative to the duties and accounts of the employee and other matters, it is hereby understood and agreed that those representations and such promises . . . shall constitute part of the basis and consideration of the contract" did not defeat payment under the bond. *Hunter v. USF&G*, 167 S.W. 692.

Utah App. 1991. The casualty company appealed the trial court ruling that employee dishonesty loss was covered by a Savings and Loan blanket bond arguing that coverage for loss should be barred because the policyholder failed to reveal an employee's dishonesty and pending lawsuits when it applied for the bond. The majority held that because the omitted material information was not asked for in the bond application and because the policyholder did not intentionally withhold information from the casualty company, bond could not be voided under Utah Code

Ann. § 31-19-8. The bond provision read: "[m]isrepresentations . . . shall not prevent recovery . . . unless (a) fraudulent; or (b) material either to acceptance of risk, or to hazard assumed by the insurer; or (c) the insurer in good faith either would not have either issued contract. . . , or would not have provided coverage with respect to hazard resulting in the loss, if the true facts had been made known to the insurer as required . . . ." *Home Sav. & Loan v. Aetna Cas. & Sur. Co.,* 817 P.2d 341.

Wash. App. 1980. Where bond application did not request any information regarding non-work-related defalcations of employees, insured school district was not required to give any, and bond was upheld, despite evidence that employee who embezzled funds had previously committed a non-work-related forgery. *State of Washington v. United Pac. Ins. Co.,* 612 P.2d 809.

Wash. 1910. The court overruled the lower court's ruling for a policyholder allowing recovery on a fidelity bond. The president of the company answered, in application for the bond, that accounts were examined and in every respect correct, with funds on hand to balance the accounts. The bond was issued and recited, "[i]f the employee's written statement herein before referred to shall be found in any respect untrue this bond shall be void." The court held that the representation that the books were examined and found to balance was a warranty of a material fact; that it was known, or should have been known, by the respondent that the representation was false, and without it appellant would not have assumed the risk. *Poultry Producers' Union v. F.C. Williams,* 107 P. 1040.

Wis. 1942. In an action against a casualty company on its fidelity bond, the court held that the application question relating to the examination and checking of accounts, which was breached by the policyholder, prevented recovery. The court relied, in part, on the bond provision that "[a]ll written statements made . . . by the employer in connection with this bond . . . are warranted . . . to be true" and the application stipulation that "[i]t is agreed that the above answers . . . constitute the basis of and form a part of the consideration of the bond." *Bloedow v. Nitschke,* 1 N.W.2d 762.

Wis. 1911. A bond provision stated that all "the representations made by the employer . . . are warranted to be true." However, the court stated that whether representations on the application concerning the frequency of inspection of the agent's books were warranties was not material. The court then held that provisions in the bond regarding supervision of the agent and inspection of accounts superseded the application and were held to be conditions subsequent and not conditions precedent, which must be plead by the insurance company to defeat the employer's recovery. *United Am. Fire Ins. Co. v. Am. Bonding Co. of Baltimore*, 131 N.W. 994.

SECONDARY SOURCES

Romualdo P. Eclavea, J.D., *Concealment, Representations, and Warranties*, 35A Am. Jur. 2d Fidelity Bonds and Insurance (2015).

Robert M. Horkovich et al., *Insurance Coverage for Employee Theft Losses: A Policyholder Primer on Commonly Litigated Issues*, 29 U. MEM. L. REV. 363 (1999).

Paul R. Koepff, *Fraud, Misrepresentation and Incontestability Provisions*, 3 Law and Prac. of Ins. Coverage Litig. § 37:4 (2014).

David J. Krebs & Diane L. Matthews, *Judicial Rescission of Fidelity Coverage*, VII FID. L.J. 89 (2001).

DAVID KREBS AND MAURA Z. PELLETERI, 10-131 NEW APPLEMAN ON INSURANCE LAW LIBRARY EDITION § 131.04, *General Agreement (D)—Representation of Insured* (2015).

Joseph Powers, *Pulling the Plug on Fidelity, Crime, and All Risk Coverage: The Availability of Rescission as a Remedy or Defense*, 32 TORT & INS. L.J. 905 (1997).

LEE RUSS AND THOMAS F. SEGALLA, 7 COUCH ON INSURANCE 3d § 100.1 (3d. ed. 1997).

J.F. Rydstrom, Annotation, *Obligee's Concealment or Misrepresentation Concerning Previous Defalcation as Affecting Liability on Fidelity Bond or Contract*, 4 A.L.R.3d 1197 (1998).

Christopher R. Ward et al., *Recent Developments in Fidelity and Surety Law*, 45 Tort Trial & Ins. Prac. L.J. 365 (Winter, 2010).

Cynthia H. Young, *Misrepresentations in the Financial Institution Bond Application*, II. FID. L.J. 21 (1996).

Chapter 18

Salvage and Recovery*

The various forms of commercial crime policies contain fairly standard policy language relating to recovery. These provisions are generally referred to in this chapter as the "Recovery Provisions." The Recovery Provisions describe how monetary recoveries from third-party sources that were responsible for, or somehow otherwise benefited from, dishonest activity that triggered coverage should be distributed.

The "Recoveries" provision cited below is one of the Recovery Provisions available to the Insurer for recovering losses incurred under a commercial crime policy. According to this typical provision, if assets are recovered through the recovery process, then the costs for pursuing the recovered assets are first deducted and paid before any recovered funds are distributed. After deducting costs of recovery, the recovered assets are distributed to the Insured until the Insured is reimbursed for any loss that exceeded the limit of insurance. If any recovered amounts remain, then the remaining amount goes to the Insurer until it is reimbursed for the amount paid to the Insured. Finally, if recovered amounts still remain after paying the above, then those amounts are paid to the Insured until it is reimbursed for the part of the loss that equals the deductible amount. It is very rare that there are sufficient recoveries to make both the Insured and the Insurer whole.

The various "Transfer of Rights" provisions cited below address how the Insurer obtains ownership of the recovery claim after paying the Insured's claim. These contractual rights are significant because some states impose defenses to common law subrogation claims (an Insurer that pays the Insured's claim likely obtained a common law right of subrogation to the Insured's recovery claim against the third party that caused the loss). To potentially avoid those defenses, it is important for the Insurer to obtain an assignment of the Insured's claim. Therefore, it is common for crime policies, bonds, and other insurance agreements to contain language that requires the Insured to assign its claim to the Insurer upon the Insurer's payment of the claim.

---

*   Brandon J. Held and Brett D. Drivers, Mills Paskert Divers, Tampa, Florida.

The Transfer of Rights provisions typically also require that the Insured do everything in its power both to secure the potential recovery rights, and to not impair those rights. This can be a bit of a gray area. To avoid potential issues, it is often appropriate for the Insurer and the Insured to discuss potential recovery even while the claim is pending. For example, the statute of limitations might run on a potential recovery claim before the claim is paid. While the language in the particular policy requires that the Insured take action to "secure" the recovery rights, it does not provide that the Insured must take action to obtain potential sources of recovery while the claim is pending.

Many cases involving the Recovery Provisions relate either to the Insurer's subrogation rights, or to defenses against the Insurer's subrogation rights. The Recovery Provisions also are addressed, although not always cited, in decisions involving claims against the various recovery targets (third parties, banks, etc.). Those cases are included below. The authors have not attempted to include every reported case that relates to recovery, but have limited the annotation to cases that address an issue pertinent to the Recovery Provisions of the policy in those instances.

There are not many cases specifically decided under the "Recoveries" provisions of commercial crime policies. Since this provision is so similar to recovery provisions in the Financial Institution Bond ("FIB"), a sampling of cases relevant to FIBs are included in this annotation. Also, many cases cited in the Recoveries Chapter of the *First Supplement* to the *Commercial Blanket Bond Annotated* are included, with credit to the authors of that work, James A. Knox and Stephen L. Baskind. Likewise, many cases from the *Financial Institution Bond Annotated, Third Edition* are included, with credit to the editor of that work, Michael Keeley.

The relevant bond provisions (with few minor differences among various forms) are as follows:

19. Recoveries[1]
a. **Recoveries, whether effected by you or us, shall be applied, net of the expenses of such recovery, in the following manner and order:**
(1) **To the satisfaction of your loss which would otherwise have been paid under this Policy but for**

---

[1] Crime Protection Policy, SP 00 01 04 12, (The Surety & Fidelity Ass'n of Am., 2012).

the fact that it is in excess of the Limit of Insurance and the Deductible Amount, if any;

    (2)   Then to us, until we are reimbursed for the settlement made;

    (3)   Then to you, until you are reimbursed for that part of the loss equal to the Deductible Amount, if any;

    (4)   Then to you for any loss not covered by this Policy.

b.   Recoveries do not include any recovery from insurance, suretyship, reinsurance, security or indemnity taken for our benefit.

c.   If original securities are recovered after duplicates of such securities have been issued, the original securities shall be surrendered to us.

21. Transfer of Your Rights and Duties Under This Policy[2]

Your rights and duties under this Policy may not be transferred without our written consent except in the case of death of an individual named insured. If you die, your rights and duties will be transferred to your legal representative but only while acting within the scope of duties as your legal representative. Until your legal representative is appointed, anyone having proper temporary custody of your property will have your rights and duties but only with respect to the property.

22. Transfer of Your Rights of Recovery Against Others to Us[3]

You must transfer to us all your rights of recovery against any person or organization for any loss you sustained and for which we have paid or settled. You must also do everything necessary to secure those rights and do nothing after loss to impair our actual or potential rights of recovery.

---

2   *Id.*
3   *Id.*

OUTLINE OF ANNOTATIONS

A. Cases Decided Under Commercial Crime Policy
B. Cases Decided Under Similar Clauses of Other Policies
   1. Subrogation and Assignment
   2. Compensated Surety and Superior Equities Defenses and Issues
   3. Insured's Impairment of Subrogation Rights
   4. Issues Concerning the Allocation of Recoveries
   5. Issues Concerning Third-Party Defenses
   6. Recovery Targets
      (a) Recovery Claims Against Dishonest Employees
      (b) Recovery Claims Against Accountants
      (c) Recovery Claims Against Officers and Directors
      (d) Recovery Claims Against Banks

ANNOTATIONS

A. Cases Decided Under Commercial Crime Policy

9th Cir. 2001 (Id.). Federal Insurance Co. sought summary judgment in a declaratory judgment action regarding claims made against the "Employee Theft Coverage" clause of a "crime policy." Federal alleged, among other things, that the insured breached the policy's subrogation clause and impaired Federal's subrogation rights by granting the wrongdoers a general release of liability. The Ninth Circuit Court of Appeals reversed the lower court's grant of summary judgment and held that material facts precluded entry of summary judgment because the insured may not have been aware of the fraud the wrongdoers allegedly committed when it agreed to their release. The case also turned on application of English law. *Gulf USA Corp. v. Fed. Ins. Co.*, 259 F.3d 1049.

S.D. Ala. 2006. Continental Casualty Co. sued a bank after paying the claims of its insured under a commercial crime policy. The court denied Continental's motion for partial summary judgment on the issue of whether the bank failed to exercise ordinary care and acted in good faith pursuant to Alabama's commercial code. *Cont'l Cas. Co. v. Compass Bank*, 2006 WL 644472, Case No. 04-0766-KD-C.

E.D. La. 1997. After F&D paid its insured's loss under a commercial crime policy, it then sued Rebecca and Reynolds Gaspard to recover the loss Rebecca Gaspard caused. The Gaspards moved to dismiss and asserted that the insured was a real party in interest and had to be a party to the lawsuit. The court rejected that assertion and ruled that the insured's assignment to F&D was valid and, therefore, the insured was not a party required to be named in the lawsuit. *Fid. & Dep. Co. of Md. v. Gaspard*, 1997 WL 335598, Case No. 96-3468.

S.D. Miss. 1997. Aetna paid its insured's claim under a commercial crime policy and received an assignment of all of its insured's rights against Pendleton. Pendleton claimed that Aetna could not proceed against him without including the insured in the litigation as a real party in interest. The court rejected this conclusion and found that the insured's assignment gave Aetna the exclusive right to litigate the claim against Pendleton. The court found that this assignment was valid under Mississippi law. *Aetna Cas. & Sur. Co. v. Pendleton Detectives of Miss., Inc.*, 969 F. Supp. 415.

N.D. Ohio 2006. The insurer paid a claim under a commercial crime policy in a case where an insurance agent deposited $500,000 of premium payments into his personal account instead of his company's account. The insurer asserted its subrogation rights and sued the depository bank. The court held that none of the bank's defenses against the insurer's subrogation claims had merit, including the bank's defense under the voluntary payment doctrine, (i.e., alleging that the insurer was not required to pay under its policy and was a volunteer), estoppel, and waiver. The court also found the voluntary payment doctrine inapplicable to conventional subrogation. *Cont'l Cas. Co. v. Fifth/Third Bank*, 418 F. Supp. 2d 964, 971.

N.Y. 2011. Travelers sought summary judgment against the insured because the insured allegedly failed to preserve Travelers' subrogation rights. The court denied Travelers' motion because Travelers had not paid its insured's claim. The court found that the commercial crime policy's provisions required Travelers to pay the claim before it was entitled to any subrogation rights. The court noted that any ambiguity in the policy regarding Travelers' rights would be construed against

Travelers. *Gould Investors, L.P. v. Travelers Cas. & Sur. Co. of Am.*, 83 A.D.3d 660, 661.

Pa. Super Ct. 2001. A bank sued the insurer and claimed it was an insured under the Depositors Forgery Coverage Provision of a commercial crime policy issued to an aluminum and chemical company. The insured company claimed losses resulting from the forgery of two checks, which the bank should not have paid. The insurer paid the company's claim under the policy and received assignment and subrogation rights. Even though the bank paid on the improper endorsement, it claimed it was an insured under the policy issued to the insured company. The court held that subrogation is equitable in nature, regardless of any applicable contract language, and applied the doctrine of superior equities to cases involving subrogation. The court remanded the case to determine whether the bank or the insurer had superior equities. *Mellon Bank N.A. v. Nat'l Union Ins. Co. of Pittsburgh, Pa.*, 768 A.2d 865.

B. Cases Decided Under Similar Clauses of Other Policies

1. Subrogation and Assignment

2d Cir. 1992 (Conn.). The general rule of subrogation—that only a full payment of the debt owed to the subrogor permits subrogation—protects the subrogor, who can waive the protection by agreeing to a partial subrogation. *Grant Thornton v. Syracuse Sav. Bank*, 961 F.2d 1042.

5th Cir. 1965 (Ga.). An insurer paid a loss under a bankers blanket bond and, by assignment, sued a bank that held funds from forged checks. The bank argued that the assignment was not enforceable under an election of remedies theory. The court ruled that it was not inconsistent, but alternative, for the insurer to sue as the bank's assignee and depositor. *Citizens & S. Nat'l Bank v. Am. Sur. Co. of N. Y.*, 347 F.2d 18.

5th Cir. 1949 (Tex.). USF&G paid a claim for losses based upon forged endorsements of the insured's checks by the insured's employee. The court ruled that neither a written assignment nor equitable subrogation favored USF&G over the bank paying the forged endorsements. Because the bank and USF&G were equally blameless, subrogation did not shift the loss. The assignment failed because USF&G, by paying the loss of its insured, elected a remedy inconsistent with recovery from the bank. *USF&G v. First Nat'l Bank in Dallas*, 172 F.2d 258.

8th Cir. 2001 (N.D.). The court discussed general principles of subrogation and distinguished between conventional subrogation and legal subrogation. It explained that conventional subrogation generally is contractual, which occurs when a party having no interest pays the debt of the other, and by agreement, is entitled to the other's rights. Legal subrogation, in contrast, is equitable. It ensures justice by requiring payment from the party who in equity and good conscience should pay it. *BancInsure, Inc. v. BNC Nat'l Bank*, 263 F.3d 766.

8th Cir. 1974 (Ark.). After payment of a fidelity claim, Globe Indemnity Co. became subrogated to its insured's rights and was subject to the same three-year statute of limitations applicable to the insured in the claim against the wrongdoer. Globe's claim against the wrongdoer was time-barred because Globe failed to sue within the three-year limitations period. The court rejected the argument that Globe's claim did not accrue under the statute of limitations until its payment to the insured. *Williams v. Globe Indem. Co.*, 507 F.2d 837.

9th Cir. 1977 (Cal.). The insurer settled a loss under a bankers blanket bond and then sued a party to the scheme that had defrauded the insured bank. The Ninth Circuit reversed summary judgment against the insurer. It held that another California State court decision changed the law and allowed independent tort liability to a third party by an insurer. *Community Nat'l Bank v. Fid. & Dep. Co. of Md.*, 563 F.2d 1319.

N.D. Ala. 1961. Applying Alabama law, the court ruled that a subrogation claim must be brought in the name of the subrogating insurance carrier under the real party in interest doctrine. *USF&G v. Slifkin*, 200 F. Supp. 563.

S.D. Fla. 1980. A fidelity bond insurer was not entitled to a declaratory judgment holding that any judgment it might obtain in a separate action against a debtor for indemnification would be deemed non-dischargeable in the debtor's bankruptcy action. *In re Harris*, 7 B.R. 284.

D. Kan. 1995. During insurance coverage litigation, the court allowed a fidelity insurance carrier to file third-party claims for subrogation. It held that the insurer could implead the third-party defendants even before the subrogation claims accrued. The court also held that the statute of limitations could be tolled so long as the third-party complaints were filed within the limitations period. *Nat'l Union Fire Ins. Co. v. FDIC*, 887 F. Supp. 262.

M.D. La. 1984. The insurer sued for contribution and indemnity under a directors and officer liability insurance policy after it paid loss that resulted from fraud. The district court held that no right to indemnity or contribution existed. However, the insurer did have conventional subrogation rights. But, the insurer failed to join the directors and officers in the lawsuit, and also failed to assert conventional subrogation. Consequently, the court found no valid subrogation claim existed. *Fid. Nat'l Bank of Baton Rouge v. Aetna Cas. & Sur. Co.*, 584 F. Supp. 1039.

E.D. Mo. 1983. A bank sued the insurer under a Bankers Blanket Bond for coverage. The insurer wanted to pursue potential subrogation claims and filed third-party claims against two bank officers. The court denied the bank officers' motion to dismiss, reasoning that the bank had a cause of action against its officers, and the insurer would "step into the shoes" of the bank if it paid a loss. *Mfr. Bank & Trust Co. of St. Louis v. Transamerica Ins. Co.*, 568 F. Supp. 790.

E.D. Mo. 1963. Federal Insurance Co. paid its insured bank's claim for loans made on forged notes. Although FHA insured the notes, FHA denied coverage because the notes were signed with fictitious names. After paying the bank's claim, Federal sued FHA. The court denied recovery. It ruled that Federal was not entitled to rights as assignee because the bank's assignment did not comply with federal statutes. It also ruled that Federal was not entitled to subrogation rights because it was neither a party to the contract of insurance nor held insurance under the National Housing Act. *Fed. Ins. Co. v. Hardy*, 222 F. Supp. 68.

D.N.J. 1977. F&D denied its insured bank's claim under an employee blanket bond and an excess bank employee dishonesty bond. The bank sued F&D, and F&D asserted that the insured bank prejudiced its subrogation rights by settling with a third party for less than the claimed loss. The court first cited the subrogation provision of the policy and held that F&D's right to subrogation would not arise unless the bank had been reimbursed for the total amount of its loss. In this case, however, the bank's loss exceeded the amount of coverage that the bond provided. In addition, because subrogation is an equitable principle, equity would not be served if F&D were permitted to escape its liability under the bonds because the bank tried to mitigate its losses after F&D denied its liability. *Midland Bank & Trust Co v. Fid. & Dep. Co. of Md.*, 442 F. Supp. 960.

D.N.J. 1975. The court ruled that an insurer on a stockbrokers blanket bond is entitled to subrogation. However, the insurer could not recover until it first sustained a loss. *Fid. & Cas. Co. of New York v. First Nat'l Bank in Fort Lee*, 397 F. Supp. 587.

E.D.N.Y. 1978. The court ruled that a bank's insurers had no subrogation claim against the United States simply by reason of the United States' regulation of the bank. However, the court noted that a claim might exist on an allegation that the United States' involvement was so pervasive as to result in the United States and its agencies essentially running the bank. *In Re: Franklin Nat'l Bank Sec. Litig.*, 445 F. Supp. 723.

W.D. Okla. 1976. A bankers blanket bond surety did not have a valid subrogation claim against the brokerage firm. The surety contended that an officer of the insured invested embezzled funds in a margin account, and sued a brokerage firm for failing to follow the New York Stock Exchange's rules for handling the subject account. The brokerage firm filed a motion to dismiss, which the court granted. *Hartford Acc. & Indem. Co. v. Merrill Lynch, Pierce, Fenner & Smith, Inc.*, 74 F.R.D. 357.

E.D. Pa. 1984. The insurer brought third-party claims before paying an insurance claim under a blanket bond. The third-party defendants moved to dismiss the claims. The court denied the motions to dismiss and held that the insurer, if found to be liable to its insured, is legally subrogated to any rights its insured would have against the third-party defendants. *Gen. Acc. Ins. Co. of Am. v. Fid. & Dep. Co. of Md.*, 598 F. Supp. 1223.

Ark. App. 1997. The court found that Shelter Insurance Co. was subject to the same statute of limitations as its insured would be if insured were pursuing the claim, even if Shelter pursues the claim as a subrogation action. *Shelter Ins. Co. v. Arnold*, 940 S.W.2d 505.

Cal. App. 1990. The insurers settled a claim that the court later determined was not covered by the relevant policies. After recoveries were made, one insurer filed a declaratory judgment action challenging the arbitrator's apportionment of recoveries. The court ruled that equitable doctrines of subrogation did not apply because there was no coverage under the policies. *United Pac. Ins. Co. v. Hanover Ins. Co.*, 266 Cal. Rptr. 231.

Cal. App. 1978. An employee who purchased property with stolen funds is a constructive trustee of the property. An insurer is subrogated to its insured's rights against that employee. These subrogation rights include the right to enforce constructive trust and receive profit from the sale of trust property. An assignment from the insured to the insurer results in the same conclusion. *Haskel Eng'g & Supply Co. v. Hartford Acc. & Indem. Co.*, 144 Cal. Rptr. 189.

Cal. App. 1977. The court found that the insurer that paid part of a claim is partially subrogated to the insured's claim. *Bank of the Orient v. Superior Ct. San Francisco County*, 136 Cal. Rptr. 741.

Fla. App. 1999. The court ruled that a bank's fidelity insurer could assert its insured's rights and sue an auditor for accounting malpractice based on conventional and equitable subrogation. *Nat'l Union Fire Ins. Co. v. KPMG Peat Marwick*, 742 So. 2d 328, 332.

Fla. App. 1972. Aetna paid its insured's loss under a dishonesty bond and sued the bank that cashed checks that the insured's employee forged. The court held that Aetna was a conventional subrogee of its insured by contract and was entitled to pursue depositor's (its insured's) contract action against the bank without showing equities superior to those of the bank. *Dispatch Serv., Inc. v. Airport Bank of Miami*, 266 So. 2d 127.

Ga. App. 1983. The insurer paid bank's loss under a fidelity bond and received an assignment of the bank's rights to pursue all claims. The person accused of dishonesty in the proof of loss sued the bank for libel and slander because of allegations the bank made in the proof of loss. The bank eventually settled with the allegedly dishonest employee. The settlement agreement prevented the bank from pursuing claims against this person for fraudulent issuance of promissory notes. The court ruled that this settlement agreement barred the insurer's subrogation claims. *Bank of Danielsville v. Seagraves*, 305 S.E.2d 790.

Minn. 1953. Fidelity insurer was subrogated to its insured's claims against a party wrongfully receiving the proceeds of forged instruments. *New York Cas. Co. v. Sazenski*, 60 N.W.2d 368.

Mo. App. 1966. The insurer on a stockbrokers bond paid for loss and sued the stockbroker's customer for conversion. The court ruled that the loss was caused by conversion, which was covered under the policy. Thus, the insurer was not a volunteer in making payment and could recover under a subrogation claim. *Fireman's Fund Ins. Co. v. Trippe*, 402 S.W. 2d 577.

Ore. 1977. The court allowed an insurer to pursue subrogation claims and have a constructive trust imposed on embezzled funds and traceable proceeds. *Lane County Escrow Serv., Inc. v. Smith*, 560 P.2d 608.

Wis. 1978. A fidelity bond insurer became a secured creditor when insured assigned its rights to the insurer after payment of claim. Thus, the insurer could sue to enforce the rights to purchase stock because it received its insured's rights to participate in a note secured by the stock. The court rejected the defendant's argument that the insurer was estopped from pursuing the claim because of the assignment. *Kornitz v. Commonwealth Land Title Ins. Co.*, 260 N.W.2d 680.

2. Compensated Surety and Superior Equities Defenses and Issues

7th Cir. 2001 (Ill.). The court did not allow a bank to assert a compensated surety defense against the insurer's contract-based subrogation claim. The court noted that compensated surety defense was a variant of the superior equities doctrine. After noting the split in jurisdictions regarding application of the compensated surety defense, the court found that even if the Illinois Supreme Court recognized the defense in cases of equitable subrogation, it would not permit the defense in cases of contractual subrogation. *Mut. Servs. Cas. Ins. Co. v. Elizabeth State Bank*, 265 F.3d 601.

11th Cir. 1985 (Fla.). The insurer settled a claim and received a written assignment of the bank's rights. The insurer sued the bank directors, as third-party defendants, for negligence. The district court entered summary judgment in favor of the directors. The court concluded that the insurer did not have a cause of action in subrogation, but the Eleventh Circuit certified two questions on appeal to the Supreme Court of Florida. The first asked whether an assignment and subrogation action required an insurer to establish superior equities against the directors in order to recover. The second question asked whether an insurer's status as a paid surety established the superior equities in the directors' favor when the directors were accused only of negligence. The court's answer to the first question: the insurer's right of subrogation required a showing of superior equities, and the written assignment by the bank did nothing to change that requirement. The court's answer to the second question: equitable principles required an insurer to first establish the directors' bad faith, actual knowledge, or fraud to maintain a negligence subrogation action. *Dixie Nat'l Bank of Dade County v. Employer's Commercial Union Ins. Co. of Am.*, 759 F.2d 826.

N.D. Ill. 1989. The surety sued an accounting firm after paying its insured's claims. The court ruled that the doctrine of superior equities applied and needed to be balanced in this case. The court noted that when balancing equities, the court must not only consider the accountant's negligence, but also whether the surety's risk was modified by its subrogation rights. *Fed. Ins. Co. v. Basabe*, 1989 WL 134799, Case No. 88 C 10504.

E.D.N.Y. 1977. The court allowed officers and directors to assert the superior equities defense to an insurer's subrogation claim. *FDIC v. Nat'l Sur. Corp.*, 434 F. Supp. 61.

E.D. Tenn. 1988. A fidelity bond insurer brought a third-party claim against directors and officers of the insured bank. The court ruled that the insurer could only sue the bank officers and directors when their alleged wrongdoing, whether it was negligence or fraud, was equal to or greater than the alleged wrongdoing covered by the bond in question. *FSLIC v. Aetna Cas. & Sur. Co.*, 696 F. Supp. 1190.

W.D. Tenn. 1998. The court applied the compensated surety defense to insurer's subrogation claims. It did not make an exception for subrogation based on contract or an assignment. *Lawyers Title Ins. Corp. v. United Am. Bank of Memphis*, 21 F. Supp. 2d 785.

Ala. 2002. Alabama Supreme Court rejected the superior equities defense in a subrogation claim an insurer brought against a bank. The court noted that Alabama has never specifically adopted the "superior-equities doctrine." The court further noted that Alabama state and federal courts have accepted the right of subrogation without challenge or mention of "superior equities." *Am. Liberty Ins. Co. v. AmSouth Bank*, 825 So. 2d 786, 791.

Ariz. 1976. The court ruled that a bank could not assert compensated surety defense to prevent a fidelity bond surety from pursuing its assigned claims against bank after the surety paid claim. The court found that claim for conventional subrogation was contract based, and therefore, equity defenses such as the compensated surety defense do not apply. *Liberty Mut. Ins. Co. v. Thunderbird Bank*, 555 P.2d 333.

Cal. App. 1978. The court found that the equities favored a brokerage firm in action by bank's insurer to recover from broker that dealt in securities stolen from bank. *Cont'l Ins. Co. v. Morgan, Olmstead, Kennedy & Gardner, Inc.*, 148 Cal. Rptr. 57.

Cal. App. 1978. When the fidelity bond insurer's equities are superior to those of a third-party wrongdoer, the insurer can be subrogated to its insured's rights after the insurer pays the claim. *Fireman's Fund Ins. v. Sec. Pac. Nat'l Bank*, 149 Cal. Rptr. 883.

Cal. App. 1970. An employee stole tires and sold them to an innocent third party. The court found that the fidelity insurance carrier that paid its insured's claim did not stand in the shoes of its insured. The court then ruled that the equities of the insurer were inferior to the third party who purchased stolen tires. *Fed. Ins. Co. v. Allen*, 92 Cal. Rptr. 125.

Cal. App. 1963. The surety on a forgery bond reimbursed its insured title insurance company for loss and received an assignment of the title insurance company's rights. A property manager for foreign property owners forged property owners' names to a mortgage note and used the borrowed funds to pay liens on the property. The appellate court affirmed the trial court's dismissal of the surety's complaint against the property owners. The court found that the owners were innocent with respect to their employee's fraud, and implicitly held that the surety did not have superior equities to the property owners. The court also held that if the surety is not entitled to subrogation, an assignment by the creditor will be ineffectual to give the surety a right of subrogation it would not otherwise have. *Fid. & Dep. Co. of Md. v. De Strajman*, 29 Cal. Rptr. 855.

Cal. App. 1963. A fidelity bond insurer paid loss and sued in subrogation. The court noted that subrogation is applicable to fidelity bonds if the insurer's equities are superior to those of the third party. The court found that the equities weighed in favor of subrogated insurer in its action against drawee bank. *Hartford Acc. & Indem. Co. v. All Am. Nut Co.*, 34 Cal. Rptr. 23.

Cal 1938. The doctrine of superior equities prevents an insurer from being subrogated to its insured's right against a bank unless the equities weigh in favor of the insurer. An insurer could not avoid this superior equities defense when it sued under an assignment as opposed to common law subrogation. *Meyers v. Bank of Am. Nat'l Trust & Sav. Ass'n*, 77 P.2d 1084.

D.C. 1994. The court held that the doctrine of superior equities did not apply in an insurer's lawsuit to recover as a conventional (contractual) subrogee, as opposed to as an equitable subrogee. *Nat'l Union Fire Ins. Co. v. Riggs Nat'l Bank*, 646 A.2d 966.

Fla. App. 1981. The insurer paid loss under fidelity bond. Both the insurer and the insured filed suit against collecting bank for negligence and conversion. The appellate court disagreed with the bank's assertion that the trial court should have instructed the jury that the insurer, as a compensate surety, had a heavier burden of proof than its insured against the bank regarding the negligence claim. The appellate court held that the trial court properly refused to make the instruction regarding the burden of proof to the jury. *Travelers Ins. Co. v. Jefferson Nat'l Bank*, 404 So. 2d 1131.

Fla. App. 1972. Aetna paid its insured's loss under a dishonesty bond and sued the bank that cashed checks that the insured's employee forged. The court held that Aetna was a conventional subrogee of its insured by contract and was entitled to pursue depositor's (its insured's) contract action against bank without showing equities superior to those of bank. *Dispatch Serv., Inc. v. Airport Bank of Miami*, 266 So. 2d 127.

Kan. App. 1979. A surety on a fidelity bond for a county treasurer who was required to pay the county as a result of the treasurer's dishonest actions was subrogated to the county's right of action against a third party who was responsible for the loss. In this case, the third party was an accounting firm. The appellate court noted that it was necessary for the surety to prove its equites superior to those of the accounting firm. The court concluded that the trial judge erred by concluding that subrogation did not apply. *Western Sur. Co. v. Loy*, 594 P.2d 257.

Mo. App. 1961. A fidelity bond insurer sued collecting bank after paying claim for a check the bank cashed on unauthorized endorsements. The court ruled that the insurer did not have burden of establishing superior equities to bank to recover. But, even if it did, trial court erred in failing to find that the insurer's equities were superior because the bank cashed the checks. *Aetna Cas. & Sur. Co. v. Lindell Trust Co.*, 348 S.W.2d 558, 570-71.

Nev. 1966. A fidelity bond surety sued a bank that cashed checks with unauthorized endorsements. The court disapproved of the "weighing of the equities" doctrine and found no significance in the fact that the subrogated surety was compensated. The court, therefore, held that a subrogated surety succeeds to all rights of its insured and is subject only to those defenses the bank may have raised against the insured. The insurer that paid the loss under a fidelity bond could pursue subrogation claims on all of its insured's rights against bank without regard to any weighing of equities or consideration of fact that the insurer was compensated. *Fed. Ins. Co. v. Toiyabe Supply Co.*, 409 P.2d 623.

N.J. 1984. The court discussed whether a surety asserting its subrogation rights must show superior equities before it could pursue a subrogation claim. The court ultimately selected the standard of giving the surety the benefit of the insured's contractual rights against the third person. The court reasoned its holding gave force to the contractual relationship between the parties and because it was in harmony with the rule adopted in the state in all other forms of insurance. *Standard Acc. Ins. Co. v. Pellecchia*, 104 A.2d 288.

N.Y. 1990. The court refused to apply the doctrine of superior equities to prevent an insurance company's subrogation claim when the third party was an alleged negligent wrongdoer. The court reasoned that the superior equities doctrine is designed to ensure equity and justice among the parties. It ruled that the doctrine should not be applied if its intended result would not be achieved. *Fed. Ins. Co. v. Arthur Andersen & Co.*, 552 N.E.2d 870.

N.Y. Super Ct. 1985. The insured sustained a loss when its officer received unauthorized salary payments over a five-year period. As subrogee and assignee of the insured's rights, Hartford sought recovery from the insured's auditors for negligence and breach of contract for their failure to detect the apparent embezzlement. Auditors moved to dismiss the suit based on the doctrine of superior equities. The court agreed that the doctrine of superior equities barred Hartford's suit for subrogation. However, the superior equities doctrine did not apply to Hartford's assignment claim. Thus, Hartford's claims were allowed to proceed. *Hartford Acc. & Indem. Co. v. Peat, Marwick, Mitchell & Co.*, 494 N.Y.S. 821.

Okla. 1963. The insurer lost a subrogation claim against the bank because the court found that the insurer's equities were not superior to those of the bank. *Fid. & Cas. Co. of N.Y. v. Nat'l Bank of Tulsa*, 388 P.2d 497.

S.C. 1964. The insurer paid losses covered by an employee fidelity bond. The insurer then filed a subrogation action against the bank that had paid forged and altered checks by the defalcating employee. The court considered the equities between the positions of the insurer and the bank. As to some checks, bank's position was superior to compensated insurer; as to others, the insurer's position held superior. *U. S. Fid. & Guar. Co. v. First Nat'l Bank*, 137 S.E.2d 582.

S.C. 1963. A fidelity bond insurer avoided application of the superior equities doctrine by entering into a "loan receipt" arrangement with its insured when it pursued a claim against a bank that cashed forged checks for the insured's employee. *W. Wesley Singletary & Son, Inc. v. Lake City State Bank*, 133 S.E.2d 118.

Wis. 1978. The insurer lost its subrogation claim against directors and officers of the insured bank. The court ruled that the fidelity insurance carrier did not have an equitable position superior to that of the officers and directors. *First Nat'l Bank of Columbus v. Hansen*, 267 N.W.2d 367.

3. Insured's Impairment of Subrogation Rights

2d. Cir. 1981 (N.Y.). The court held that Hartford, which issued a broker's blanket bond, could not pursue subrogation against the insured's employee. The insured impaired Hartford's subrogation rights because the insured took responsibility for employee's defense and did not inform employee that pursuant to settlement between Hartford and the insured, the employee may be liable to Hartford. *H.S. Equities, Inc. v. Hartford Acc. & Indem. Co.*, 661 F.2d 264.

6th Cir. 1975 (Ohio). Phoenix of Hartford Insurance Co. denied its insured's claim. The insured then pursued wrongdoers, and Phoenix did not assist. The court found that Phoenix waived its rights, and was estopped from asserting any rights, against the insured for impairment of subrogation by denying claim and failing to assist its insured in seeking recovery for its losses. *Russell Gasket Co. v. Phoenix of Hartford Ins. Co.*, 512 F.2d 205.

8th Cir. 1999 (Minn.). The court held that the insured's failure to give notice of loss to the first insurer of employee dishonesty policies, even though it gave notice to second insurer, prejudiced the first insurer and, therefore, precluded coverage. The insured's untimely notice prevented first insurer from pursuing recovery from banks that paid fraudulent checks because statute of limitations expired. *Winthrop & Weinstein, P.A. v. Travelers Cas. & Sur. Co.*, 187 F.3d 871.

D. Kan. 1982. The court found that the insured who released an alleged check kiter from liability without the consent of its insurance carrier, Continental Insurance Co., released Continental under a banker's blanket bond because the insured impaired Continental's subrogation rights. *Sec. Nat. Bank of Kansas City, Kan. v. Cont'l Ins. Co.*, 586 F. Supp. 139.

E.D. Mo. 1987. The court held that the insured's bank's claim against its blanket bond insurer, F&D, was barred. The bank released the defalcating employee without F&D's knowledge or consent, which impaired F&D's subrogation rights. *St. Louis Fed. Sav. & Loan Ass'n v. Fid. & Deposit Co. of Md.*, 654 F. Supp. 314, 315.

D.N.J. 1977. F&D denied its insured bank's claim under an employee blanket bond and an excess bank employee dishonesty bond. Bank sued F&D, and F&D asserted that the insured bank prejudiced its subrogation rights by settling with a third party for less than the claimed loss. The court first cited the subrogation provision of the policy and held that F&D's right to subrogation would not arise unless bank had been reimbursed for the total amount of its loss. In this case, however, the bank's loss exceeded the amount of coverage the bond provided. In addition, because subrogation is an equitable principle, equity would not be served if F&D were permitted to escape its liability under the bonds because the bank tried to mitigate its losses after F&D denied its liability. *Midland Bank & Trust Co v. Fid. & Dep. Co. of Md.*, 442 F. Supp. 960.

Ga. App. 1983. The insurer paid bank's loss under a fidelity bond and was assigned the bank's rights to pursue all claims. The person accused of dishonesty in the proof of loss sued the bank for libel and slander because of allegations bank made in the proof of loss. The bank eventually settled with the allegedly dishonest employee. The settlement agreement prevented the bank from pursuing claims against this person for fraudulent issuance of promissory notes. The court ruled that this settlement agreement barred the insurance carrier's subrogation claims. *Bank of Danielsville v. Seagraves*, 305 S.E.2d 790.

Kan. 1989. A fidelity insurer denied the insured bank's claim. The bank then pursued the dishonest employee and reached a settlement with the dishonest employee. The insurer argued that the settlement agreement voided coverage because it destroyed its subrogation rights. The court rejected this argument. It ruled that the insurer's denial of claim forfeited its rights to prior approval of any settlement agreements the bank entered. *First Hays Banshare, Inc. v. Kansas Bankers Sur. Co.*, 769 P.2d 1184, 1187.

Kan. App. 1988. The insured refused to allow F&D to use the insured's name in a suit against the insured's directors and officers for negligent supervision of the dishonest employee. The court held that the policy did not require the insured to allow its name to be used in a subrogation action. The court also ruled that this refusal did not prejudice F&D's

subrogation action. *Fid. & Dep. Co. of Md. v. Shawnee State Bank*, 766 P.2d 191.

N.J. 1953. The insured bank and third party were aware of a surety's subrogation interest in a bank's claim against a third party. Consequently, the bank and the third party that deliberately entered into a settlement, which released the third party, without consulting the surety, did not impair the surety's subrogation rights against the third party. *Standard Acc. Ins. Co. v. Pellechia*, 104 A.2d 288.

Tex. App. 1979. The insured's failure to timely sue responsible party, which resulted in permanent bar to claim, impaired USF&G's subrogation rights. Consequently, USF&G's was not obligated to pay the insured's claim under a dishonesty bond. *Republic Nat'l Life Ins. Co. v. U. S. Fire Ins. Co.*, 589 S.W.2d 737 (Tex. Civ. App.–Dallas (1979), *rev'd on other grounds*, 602 S.W.2d 527.

4. Allocation of Recoveries

5th Cir. 1996 (La.). The court allowed the insured to allocate the sales of loan collateral against unpaid interest instead of distributing the recoveries to the surety. The court ruled that the proceeds from the collateral sale were not related to the loss claimed against the surety. *First Nat'l Bank of Louisville v. Lustig*, 96 F.3d 1554, 1569.

7th Cir. 1940 (Ill.). Where the insured partially recovered stolen funds before Lloyd's payment of loss, the insured was required to turn those proceeds over to Lloyd's pursuant to a manuscript version of the "Recoveries" provision. The insured was not entitled to apply the funds to an uncovered portion of its loss. *City Trust & Sav. Bank of Kankakee, Illinois v. Underwriting Members of Lloyds*, 109 F.2d 110.

10th Cir. 1994 (Utah). In a dispute over the application of recoveries to loan losses that resulted from employee dishonesty, the court held that the FDIC was entitled to recover its administrative expenses incurred in settling claims with third parties. The court found that settlements were "recoveries." As a result, the court ruled the cost of obtaining such recoveries should be deducted from the recovered amount. The court also held that the collateral source rule did not exclude evidence of a settlement with a separate party relating to loss on the same loan. The collateral source rule should not prevent an insurer under a fidelity bond from receiving credit for a settlement with a separate party. *FDIC v. United Pac. Ins. Co.*, 20 F.3d 1070.

M.D. La. 1993. With regard to a loan loss covered under a financial institution bond, any recovery must first be applied to satisfy the insured's covered loss in excess of the amount paid under the bond. When the loss involves fraudulently made loans, any payments received on the loans after discovery must be applied to the principal amount of the loan, not to interest. *FDIC v. Fid. & Dep. Co. of Md.*, 827 F. Supp. 385.

D. Me. 1970. A fidelity insured under an unidentified fidelity policy owed commissions to dishonest employee. The dishonest employee owed the insured because the dishonest employee had received certain advances. The commissions and advances were not related to the acts of dishonesty. The fidelity insurer argued that it was entitled to subrogate to the insured's claim to commissions without regard to the advances. The insured argued that its right to offset the commissions against the advances was superior to the fidelity insurer's argument. The court sided with the insured and ruled that the insured's right to offset was superior to the insurer's salvage rights. *Mutual Trust Life Ins. Co. v. Wemyss*, 309 F. Supp. 1221.

Cal. App. 1971. This case involved both uncovered and covered loss in excess of the policy limits, with the issue being how to allocate the salvage recoveries. The court prorated this recovery between that part of the loss that would be covered if there was no policy limit, and that part of the loss that was not within the terms of the policy. It held that the insured should receive towards the uncovered loss that prorated proportion of the recovered amounts that the uncovered loss bore compared to the entire loss. Until the excess covered loss was reimbursed, the insured should receive the balance of the salvage as well. After that point, the court ruled the insurer would receive the covered loss percentage while the insured received the uncovered loss percentage until the entire loss was fully reimbursed. *Graydon-Murphy Oldsmobile v. Ohio Cas. Ins. Co.*, 93 Cal. Rptr. 684.

D.C. 2001. This case involved a dispute over the interpretation of a settlement agreement in which Travelers and its insured were to share recovery. The insured claimed that it was entitled to recover losses that Travelers did not reimburse before any recovery was paid to Travelers. The court disagreed. The court noted that the non-covered losses were taken into consideration when the parties entered into the settlement agreement. Thus, the court ordered that recoveries were to be shared as set forth in the agreement. The make-whole doctrine, which provides that the insurer cannot exercise a right of reimbursement or subrogation until the insured's entire loss has been compensated, can be altered by contract. *District No.1-Pac. Coast Dist., Marine Eng'rs' Beneficial Ass'n v. Travelers Cas. & Sur. Co.*, 782 A.2d 269.

Iowa 1997. A fidelity insurer of the state tax department sought a declaration that the department had to treat assets later seized from the embezzlers as "recoveries" under the policy. The court refused to issue such a declaration and ruled that the assets seized from the dishonest employee were not recoveries for purposes of the subrogation clause. *Lumbermen Cas. Co. v. State of Iowa*, 564 N.W.2d 431.

D.N.J. 1977. F&D denied its insured bank's claim under an employee blanket bond and an excess bank employee dishonesty bond. Bank sued F&D, and F&D asserted that the insured bank prejudiced its subrogation rights by settling with a third party for less than the claimed loss. The court first cited the subrogation provision of the policy and held that F&D's right to subrogation would not arise unless bank had been reimbursed for the total amount of its loss. In this case, however, the bank's loss exceeded the amount of coverage the bond provided. In addition, because subrogation is an equitable principle, equity would not be served if F&D were permitted to escape its liability under the bonds because the bank tried to mitigate its losses after F&D denied its liability. *Midland Bank & Trust Co v. Fid. & Dep. Co. of Md.*, 442 F. Supp. 960.

5. Claims Are Subject to Third-Party Defenses

5th Cir. 1955 (Ala.). A fidelity bond insurer sued a bank to recover amounts it paid to the insured for a claim that involved checks deposited with unauthorized endorsements. The court held that the insurer was subject to all claims and credits that could have been asserted against the subrogee bank. *First Farmers & Merchants Nat'l Bank of Troy v. Columbia Gas. Co.*, 226 F.2d 474.

6th Cir. 1988 (Ohio). The insurer brought a subrogation action against the insured's directors and officers to recover amounts paid in settlement of claims under a fidelity bond. The court held that a fidelity insurer, in the absence of fraud, bad faith, or evidence that the individual directors derived a benefit from the defaulting employer's dishonesty, cannot recover from the insured's officer and directors. *Home Indem. Co. v. Shaffer*, 860 F.2d 186.

7th Cir. 1982 (Ill.). The insurer paid a bankers blanket bond claim and filed a third-party claim against an allegedly dishonest bank president. The court found that the insurer's subrogation claim seeking tort liability was barred by the five-year limitations period, and that the insurer waived its claim that the claim should be viewed as an indemnity claim. The court also found that that the insurer did not have an independent cause of action based on indemnity, which may have permitted suit despite the expiration of the limitations period on the tort claim. *Rock Island Bank v. Aetna Cas. & Sur. Co.*, 692 F.2d 1100.

8th Cir. 1974 (Ark.). After payment of a fidelity claim, Globe Indemnity Co. became subrogated to its insured's rights and was subject to the same three-year statute of limitations applicable to the insured in the claim against the wrongdoer. Globe's claim against the wrongdoer was time-barred because it failed to sue within the three-year limitations period. The court rejected the argument that Globe's claim did not accrue under the statute of limitations until its payment to the insured. *Williams v. Globe Indem. Co.*, 507 F.2d 837.

11th Cir. 1985 (Fla.). The insurer settled a claim and received a written assignment of the bank's rights. The insurer sued the bank directors, as third-party defendants, for negligence. The district court entered summary judgment in favor of the directors. The court concluded that the insurer did not have a cause of action in subrogation, but the Eleventh Circuit certified two questions on appeal to the Supreme Court of Florida. The first asked whether an assignment and subrogation action required an insurer to establish superior equities against the directors in order to recover. The second question asked whether an insurer's status as a paid surety established the superior equities in the directors' favor when the directors were only accused of negligence. The court's answer to the first question: the insurer's right of subrogation required a showing of superior equities, and the written assignment by the bank did nothing to change that requirement. The court's answer to the second question: equitable principles required an insurer to first establish the directors' bad faith, actual knowledge, or fraud to maintain a negligence subrogation action. *Dixie Nat'l Bank of Dade County v. Employer's Commercial Union Ins. Co. of Am.*, 759 F.2d 826.

E.D. Mo. 1963. The insurer paid its insured bank's claim for loans made on forged notes. Although FHA insured the notes, FHA denied coverage because the notes were signed with fictitious names. After paying the bank's claim, the insurer sued FHA. The court denied recovery. It ruled that the insurer was not entitled to rights as assignee because the bank's assignment did not comply with federal statutes. It also ruled that the insurer was not entitled to subrogation rights because it was neither a party to the contract of insurance nor held insurance under the National Housing Act. *Fed. Ins. Co. v. Hardy*, 222 F. Supp. 68.

E.D.N.Y. 1978. The court ruled that a bank's insurers had no subrogation claim against the United States simply by reason of the United States' regulation of the bank. However, the court noted a claim might exist on an allegation that the United States' involvement was so pervasive as to result in the United States and its agencies essentially running the bank. *In Re: Franklin Nat'l Bank Sec. Litig.*, 445 F. Supp. 723.

W.D. Okla. 1976. A bankers blanket bond surety did not have a valid subrogation claim against a brokerage firm. The surety contended that an officer of the insured invested embezzled funds in a margin account, and sued a brokerage firm for failing to follow the New York Stock Exchange's rules for handling the subject account. Brokerage firm filed motion to dismiss, which the court granted. *Hartford Acc. & Indem. Co. v. Merrill Lynch, Pierce, Fenner & Smith, Inc.*, 74 F.R.D. 357.

E.D. Pa. 1983. The insurer's subrogation action against the probate estate of a person who had delivered stolen bearer bonds to a broker was barred by the statute of limitations. The limitations applicable to the insured's rights against the estate applied to subrogated insurer's rights. *Ins. Co. of N. Am. v. United States*, 561 F. Supp. 106.

Ark. App. 1997. The insurer is subject to the same statute of limitations as the insured would be if the insured were pursuing the claim, even if the insurer pursues the claim as a subrogation action. *Shelter Ins. Co. v. Arnold*, 940 S.W.2d 505.

D.C. App. 1976. When an insurer pursues its subrogation rights, it does so subject to all defenses that could have been asserted against the insured, including statute of limitations. *Aetna Cas. & Sur. Co. v. Windsor*, 353 A.2d 684.

W.D. Okla. 1976. The court dismissed subrogated insurer's negligence claim against a broker for lack of proximate cause. *Hartford Acc. & Indem. Co. v. Merrill, Lynch, Pierce, Fenner & Smith, Inc.* 74 F.R.D. 357.

6. *Recovery Targets*

(a) Recovery Claims Against Dishonest Employees

4th Cir. 2003 (Va.). The court ruled that the spouse of the deceased dishonest employee was liable to subrogating the insurance carrier under theories of conversion, money had and received, and unjust enrichment. Spouse had been enriched by the use of the stolen funds to pay off her debts. *Fed. Ins. Co. v. Smith*, 63 Fed. Appx. 630.

7th Cir. 1982 (Ill.). The insurer paid a bankers blanket bond claim and filed a third-party claim against allegedly dishonest bank president. The court found that the insurer's subrogation claim seeking tort liability was barred by the five-year limitations period, and that the insurer waived its claim that the claim should be viewed as an indemnity claim. The court also found that that the insurer did not have an independent cause of action based on indemnity, which may have permitted suit despite the expiration of the limitations period on the tort claim. *Rock Island Bank v. Aetna Cas. & Sur. Co.*, 692 F.2d 1100.

D.C. 1997. The surety was subrogated to the claims of trust beneficiaries and the successor trustee against a Chapter 7 bankruptcy debtor, and to the nondischargeable nature of the claims in the bankruptcy. Debtor had been trustee of a trust and used trust monies for his personal expenses. Debtor's actions were a defalcation in a fiduciary capacity, which was within the exceptions to discharge under the bankruptcy code. *Old*

Republic Sur. Co v. Richardson, 193 B.R. 378, *aff'd*, 107 F.3d 923 (D.C. Cir.), *cert. denied*, 522 U.S. 851.

S.D. Fla 1970. The insurer lost coverage lawsuit and had to pay its insured bank's losses covered by the policy related to unauthorized loans. The insurer then sued and was awarded a judgment against the loan officer who approved unauthorized loans. *Miami Nat'l Bank v. Pa. Ins. Co.*, 314 F. Supp. 858.

W.D. Okla. 1976. The court dismissed subrogated insurer's negligence claim against the broker for lack of proximate cause. *Hartford Acc. & Indem. Co. v. Merrill, Lynch, Pierce, Fenner & Smith, Inc.* 74 F.R.D. 357.

Iowa 1965. Subrogated insurer pursued claim against a dishonest principal's ex-wife. The court granted insurer a lien on property the dishonest principal gave to his ex-wife in a divorce settlement agreement because the court found that a fraudulent conveyance was involved. *Travelers Indem. Co. v. Cormaney*, 138 N.W.2d 50.

N.Y. App. Div. 1986. Subrogated insurer pursued claim against a dishonest employee and his attorney because the insurer argued that the transfer of real estate from the employee to the attorney was a fraudulent conveyance. *USF&G v. Byrnes*, 497 N.Y.S.2d 719.

Pa. Comm. Ct. 1988. The court ruled that a prior criminal conviction was conclusive as to a bank director's liability to Aetna in a civil suit where the conduct for which the director was convicted was precisely the same conduct that made Aetna liable to the insured under a bankers blanket bond. *Luzerne Nat'l Bank v. Hanover Ins. Co.*, 1988 WL 163999, Case No. 3600-C of 1984.

(b) Recovery Claims Against Accountants

N.D. Ill. 1989. The surety sued an accounting firm after paying its insured's claims. The court ruled that the doctrine of superior equities applied and needed to be balanced in this case. The court noted that when balancing equities, the court must not only consider the accountant's negligence, but also whether the surety's risk was modified by its subrogation rights. *Fed. Ins. Co. v. Basabe*, 1989 WL 134799, Case No. 88 C 10504.

E.D. Mich. 1940. Sureties on a city's treasurer bonds were, after making payment on the claims, subrogated to the city's right of action against the public accountant for negligence in auditing the city's books. *Md. Cas. Co. v. Cook*, 35 F. Supp. 160.

Cal. App. 1980. The insured sued Liberty Mutual Insurance Co. and General Insurance Company of America after denial of claim. In the coverage litigation, Liberty and General filed cross complaints against the insured's accountants. The court ruled that Liberty and General were entitled to declaratory judgment as to whether the accountants were negligent and therefore liable to Liberty and General, even though Liberty and General had not yet paid the claim. *Liberty Mut. Ins. Co. v. Harris, Kerr, Forster, & Co.*, 89 Cal. Rptr. 437.

Fla. 2000. The court ruled that a bank's fidelity insurance carrier could assert a claim of professional malpractice against an independent accounting firm responsible for preparing an audit. *KPMG Peat Marwick v. Nat'l Union Fire Ins. Co.* 765 So. 2d 36 *receded from in part by Cowan Liebowitz & Latman, P.C. v. Kaplan*, 902 So. 2d 755, 756 (Fla. 2005).

Fla. 1934. The surety on a fidelity bond was subrogated to its insured's right against public accountant for alleged negligent failure to discover employee embezzlements in audit. *Dantzler Lbr. & Export Co. v. Columbia*, 156 So. 116.

Kan. App. 1979. The surety that paid claim under a county treasurer's fidelity bond asserted a claim against accountants for negligently auditing the county's books. The court held that a surety, in asserting its subrogation rights, steps into the shoes of its insured and privity of contract is not necessary in suit against third parties responsible for the loss. *Western Sur. Co. v. Loy*, 594 P.2d 257.

N.Y. 1990. The court refused to apply the doctrine of superior equities to prevent an insurance company's subrogation claim against an accountant, which was an alleged negligent wrongdoer. The court reasoned that the superior equities doctrine is designed to ensure equity and justice among the parties. It ruled that the doctrine should not be applied if its intended result would not be achieved. *Fed. Ins. Co. v. Arthur Andersen & Co.*, 552 N.E.2d 870.

N.Y. App. Div. 1939. Subrogating fidelity insurance carrier was entitled to pursue claims against accountants for negligence. The court held that the claim should have gone to the jury and it was error for the trial court to dismiss the claim. *Nat'l Sur. Corp. v. Lybrand*, 9 N.Y.S.2d 554.

N.Y. Super Ct. 1985. The insured sustained a loss when its officer received unauthorized salary payments over a five-year period. As subrogee and assignee of the insured's rights, the insurer sought recovery from the insured's auditors for negligence and breach of contract for their failure to detect the apparent embezzlement. Auditors moved to dismiss the suit based on the doctrine of superior equities. The court agreed that the doctrine of superior equities barred the insurer's suit for subrogation. However, the assignment from the insured to the insurer did not bar the suit. Thus, the claims were allowed to proceed. *Hartford Acc. & Indem. Co. v. Peat, Marwick, Mitchell & Co.*, 494 N.Y.S. 821.

(c) Recovery Claims Against Officers and Directors

6th Cir. 1988 (Ohio). The insurer brought a subrogation action against the insured's directors and officers to recover amounts paid in settlement of claims under a fidelity bond. The court held that a fidelity insurer, in the absence of fraud, bad faith, or evidence that the individual directors derived a benefit from the defaulting employer's dishonesty, cannot recover from the insured's officer and directors. *Home Indem. Co. v. Shaffer*, 860 F.2d 186.

11th Cir. 1985 (Fla.). The insurer settled a claim and received a written assignment of the bank's rights. The insurer sued the bank directors, as third-party defendants, for negligence. The district court entered summary judgment in favor of the directors. The court concluded that the insurer did not have a cause of action in subrogation, but the Eleventh Circuit certified two questions on appeal to the Supreme Court of Florida. The first asked whether an assignment and subrogation action required an insurer to establish superior equities against the directors in order to recover. The second question asked whether an insurer's status as a paid surety established the superior equities in the directors' favor when the directors were only accused of negligence. The court's answer to the first question: the insurer's right of subrogation required a showing of superior equities, and the written assignment by the bank did nothing to change that requirement. The court's answer to the second question: equitable principles required an insurer to first establish the directors' bad faith, actual knowledge, or fraud to maintain a negligence subrogation action. *Dixie Nat'l Bank of Dade County v. Employer's Commercial Union Ins. Co. of Am.,* 759 F.2d 826.

C.D. Ill. 1989. For insurer to recover in subrogation claim against bank officers, it must first establish fraud, bad faith or some other evidence that the bank officers derived a personal benefit from the defaulting employee's dishonesty, or that the officers actually discovered the conduct causing the loss. *Employers Ins. of Wausau v. Doonan,* 712 F. Supp. 1368.

M.D. La. 1984. The insurer paid claim under a fidelity bond and sought to recover from Directors and Officers Liability Policy issued to the insured. The insurer asserted that the bank's officers and directors negligently failed to discover a fraudulent credit card scheme. The court held that the directors' and officers' insurer was not primarily or actually responsible for the debt. *Fid. Nat'l Bank of Baton Rouge v. Aetna Cas. & Sur. Co.,* 584 F. Supp. 1039.

E.D. Mo. 1983. The court did not dismiss the third-party action of a savings and loan blanket bond insurer against an officer. The court found that the complaint stated a cause of action despite an officer's assertion that the insurer failed to assert superior equities compared to third-party defendants accused of mere negligence. *Community Fed. Sav. & Loan v. Transamerica Ins. Co.,* 559 F. Supp. 536.

E.D. Mo. 1983. A bank sued the insurer under a Bankers Blanket Bond. The insurer wanted to pursue potential subrogation claims and filed third-party claims against two bank officers. The court denied the bank officers' motion to dismiss. The court reasoned that the bank had a cause of action against its officers, and the insurer would "step into the shoes" of the bank if it paid a loss. *Mfr. Bank &Trust Co. of St. Louis v. Transamerica Ins. Co.,* 568 F. Supp. 790.

E.D.N.Y. 1977. The surety companies filed third-party claims against directors of corporations involved in dishonest activity. The court held that if the surety companies pay the claims on the bond to the plaintiff, then the surety companies will be subrogated to the claims of the plaintiffs. The court ruled that the surety companies had standing to assert their claims against the directors. *FDIC v. Nat'l Sur. Corp.*, 434 F. Supp. 61.

E.D. Tenn. 1988. Fidelity bond insurer brought third-party claim against directors and officers of the insured bank. The court ruled that the insurer could only sue the bank officers and directors when their alleged wrongdoing, whether it was negligence or fraud, was equal to or greater than the alleged wrongdoing covered by the bond in question. *FSLIC v. Aetna Cas. & Sur. Co.*, 696 F. Supp. 1190.

Tex. App. 1943. The court allowed a fidelity bond insurer to maintain third-party actions for equitable subrogation against the insured's president, who misappropriated funds even though insurer had not yet paid the claim. *Am. Employer's Ins. Co. v. Dallas Joint Stock Land Bank*, 170 S.W.2d 546.

Wis. 1978. The insurer lost its subrogation claim against directors and officers of the insured bank. The court ruled that the fidelity insurer did not have an equitable position superior to that of the officers and directors. *First Nat'l Bank of Columbus v. Hansen*, 267 N.W.2d 367.

(d) Recovery Claims Against Banks

4th Cir. 1965 (N.C.). The insurer paid an employee dishonesty claim under a fidelity bond and sued the depository bank. The Fourth Circuit affirmed the holding that the insurer was subrogated to its insured's rights against the bank. *Md. Cas. Co. v. Bank of Charlotte*, 340 F.2d 550.

5th Cir. 1965 (Ga.). An insurer paid a loss under a bankers blanket bond and, by assignment, sued a bank that held funds from forged checks. The bank argued that the assignment was not enforceable under an election of remedies theory. The court ruled that it was not inconsistent, but alternative, to sue as the bank's assignee and depositor. *Citizens & S. Nat'l Bank v. Am. Sur. Co. of N. Y.*, 347 F.2d 18.

5th Cir. 1955 (Ala.). A fidelity bond insurer sued a bank to recover amounts it paid to the insured for a claim that involved checks deposited with unauthorized endorsements. The court held that the insurer was subject to all claims and credits that could have been asserted against the subrogee bank. *First Farmers & Merchants Nat'l Bank of Troy v. Columbia Gas. Co.*, 226 F.2d 474.

7th Cir. 2004 (Ill.). The court rejected affidavits that subrogated insurer offered at trial against bank as hearsay. The insurer could not get the insured's witnesses to appear live at trial and tried to offer their testimony via affidavit, which the court rejected. *Travelers Cas. & Sur. Co. v. Wells Fargo Bank, N.A.*, 374 F.3d 521.

Cal. App. 1967. A fidelity bond insurer paid a claim and then sued the bank that paid the checks that were the subject of the claim. The bank paid the checks in violation of the bank's own rules. The court found the bank liable to the insurer. *Pac. Indem. Co. v. Sec. First Nat'l Bank*, 56 Cal. Rptr. 142.

Fla. App. 1972. Aetna paid its insured's loss under a dishonesty bond and sued the bank that cashed checks that the insured's employee forged. The court held that Aetna was a conventional subrogee of its insured by contract and was entitled to pursue depositor's (its insured's) contract action against bank without showing equities superior to those of bank. *Dispatch Serv., Inc. v. Airport Bank of Miami*, 266 So. 2d 127.

Mich. App. 1978. The insurer on an unidentified bond sued bank for value of checks as assignee and subrogee of its insured, which was the payee-owner of checks paid on forged endorsements. The court allowed recovery under an implied contract theory. *Cont'l Cas. Co. v. Huron Valley Nat'l Bank*, 85 Mich. App. 319.

Mo. 1961. A fidelity bond insurer sued the collecting bank after paying a claim for a check the bank cashed on unauthorized endorsements. The court ruled that the insurer did not have the burden of establishing superior equities to the bank to recover. But, even if it did, trial court erred in failing to find that the insurer's equities were superior because the bank cashed the checks. *Aetna Cas. & Sur. Co. v. Lindell Trust Co*, 348 S.W.2d 558.

N.Y. App. 1970. The insurer on a brokers bond paid loss and sued the bank for paying on forged endorsements. The court held that the insured/broker's negligence substantially contributed to the forgeries. Therefore, recovery against the bank was denied. *Fid. & Dep. Co. of Md. v. Chemical Bank N.Y. Trust Co.*, 318 N.Y.S.2d 957.

Tex. 1901. The court allowed an insurer under a county treasurers bond to maintain a third-party equitable subrogation claim against the bank receiving misappropriated money even though the insurer had not yet paid claim. *Skipwith v. Hurt*, 60 S.W. 423.

SECONDARY SOURCES

Brett D. Divers & Brandon J. Held, *The Parties Rights to which the Contract Bond Surety is Subrogated, in* THE CONTRACT BOND SURETY'S SUBROGATION RIGHTS (George D. Bachrach, James D. Ferruci, and Dennis J. Bartlett, eds., 2013).

Karen K. Fitzgerald, *Salvage and Recovery, in* COMMERCIAL CRIME POLICY 535 (Randall Marmor & John Tomaine, eds., 2d ed. 2005).

Michael R. Davisson & Susan Koehler Sullivan, *Subrogation and Mitigation, in* HANDLING FIDELITY BOND CLAIMS 573 (Michael Keeley & Timothy Sukel eds., 1999).

Judy J. Hlafcsak, *The Nature and Extent of Subrogation Rights of Fidelity Insurers Against Officers and Directors of Financial Institutions*, 47 U. PITT. L. REV. 727-47 (Spr. 1986).

James A. Knox, *Recovery From Principal, Bank, Co-Conspirators, Other Carriers and Officers and Directors,* (ABA National Institute 1983).

Peter D. Sullivan, *Subrogation against Accountant, in* THE PURSUIT OF SUBROGATION AND INDEMNITY CLAIMS (Lawrence W. Moelmann, ed. 1991)

Richard S. Wisner & Scott O. Reed, *Salvage and Subrogation Rights, in* FINANCIAL INSTITUTION BONDS (Harvey C. Koch ed., 1989).

Richard Wisner & Scott Leo, *Subrogation Rights of Surety on a Fidelity Bond Against Officers and Directors of Insured Corporation,* 18 FORUM 320 (1983).

Chapter 19

Other Common Conditions*

This chapter addresses common conditions typically found in commercial crime policies, comparing and contrasting provisions found in the 1996 edition of the Insurance Services Office ("ISO") Crime General Provisions,[1] the 2012 ISO Commercial Crime Policy[2] (in both the loss sustained and discovery forms), and the 2012 Crime Protection Policy.[3]

A. Records (Inspections)

1996 Crime General Provisions:

(B) General Conditions
(15) Records: You must keep records of all Covered Property so we can verify the amount of any loss.

2012 ISO Commercial Crime Policy (Records):

---

*   By Matt J. Farley and Richard E. Baudouin, Krebs Farley, PLLC, New Orleans, Louisiana.
1   Crime General Provisions, CR 10 00 04 97, § B.1. (Ins. Servs. Office, Inc., 1996) (Loss Sustained) Crime General Provisions, CR 11 00 04 97 (Ins. Servs. Office, Inc., 1996) (Discovery), *reprinted in* COMMERCIAL CRIME POLICY 815 & 819 (Randall I. Marmor & Susan Koehler Sullivan eds., 2d ed. 2014).
2   Commercial Crime Policy, CR 00 22 08 13 (ISO Props., Inc. 2012) (Discovery) & Commercial Crime Policy, CR 00 23 08 13 (ISO Props., Inc. 2012) (Loss Sustained), *reprinted in* COMMERCIAL CRIME POLICY, *supra* note 2, 785 & 799.
3   Crime Protection Policy, SP 00 01 04 12 (Sur. & Fid. Ass'n of Am. 2012), *reprinted in* COMMERCIAL CRIME POLICY, *supra* note 2, at 677.

(E)   Conditions
  (1)   Conditions Applicable to All Insuring Agreements
    i.   Examination Of Your Books And Records
          We may examine and audit your books and records as they relate to this Policy at any time during the Policy Period shown in the Declarations and up to three years afterward.

2012 ISO Commercial Crime Policy (Inspections and Surveys):

(E)   Conditions
  (1)   Conditions Applicable to All Insuring Agreements
    k.   Inspections And Surveys
      (1)   We have the right to:
        (a)   Make inspections and surveys at any time;
        (b)   Give you reports on the conditions we find; and
        (c)   Recommend changes.
      (2)   We are not obligated to make any inspections, surveys, reports or recommendations and any such actions we do undertake relate only to insurability and the premiums to be charged. We do not make safety inspections. We do not undertake to perform the duty of any person or organization to provide for the health or safety of workers or the public. And we do not warrant that conditions:
        (a)   Are safe or healthful; or
        (b)   Comply with laws, regulations, codes or standards
      (3)   Paragraphs k.(1) and k.(2) apply not only to us, but also to any rating, advisory, rate service or similar organization which makes insurance inspections, surveys, reports or recommendations.

COMMENT

All three of the standard forms contain similar language concerning the insured's retention of records. While the retention condition is tied to the insurer's ability to verify any loss, the 2012 ISO Commercial Crime Policy contains two provisions that permit the insurer to make inspections outside the context of a loss or claim. Condition (i) permits the insurer to "examine and audit" the insured's books and records at any time during the policy period and three years thereafter. Condition (k) permits the insurer to make inspections, while clarifying that the purpose of such inspections take on an underwriting function and not to warrant or otherwise approve of the safety of the insureds' premises. Failure to comply with Condition (i) may provide a defense to coverage. While not a fidelity case, the policy at issue in *Tran v. State Farm Fire & Cas. Co.*, 961 P.2d 358 (Wash. 1998) contained a provision identical to Condition (i) of the 2012 ISO Commercial Crime Policy. The insured submitted a claim for stolen property following an alleged burglary. State Farm became suspicious and requested that the insured submit personal financial information for review. The insured refused. In finding that the insured breached the policy, the court held that State Farm had the right to "examine and audit" the insured's "books and records," which included his personal financial information.

OUTLINE OF ANNOTATIONS

A. Examination of Records
B. Inspection of Premises

ANNOTATIONS

A. Examination of Records

NONE

B. Inspection of Premises

NONE

SECONDARY SOURCES

NONE

B. Valuation

1996 Crime General Provisions:[4]

(B)   General Conditions
    (19)   Valuation—Settlement:
        a.   Subject to the applicable Limit of Insurance provision we will pay for:
            (1)   Loss of "money" but only up to and including its face value. We may, at our option, pay for loss of "money" issued by any country other than the United States of America:
                (a)   At face value in the "money" issued by that country; or
                (b)   In the United States of America dollar equivalent determined by the rate of exchange on the day the loss was discovered.
            (2)   Loss of "securities" but only up to and including their value at the close of business on the day the loss was discovered. We may, at our option:
                (a)   Pay the value of such "securities" or replace them in kind, in which event you must assign to us all your rights, title and interest in and to those "securities"; or
                (b)   Pay the cost of any Lost Securities Bond required in connection with issuing duplicates of the "securities". However, we will be liable only for the

---

4   Crime General Provisions, CR 10 00 06 95, § B.20 (Ins. Servs. Office, Inc., 1994), *reprinted in* COMMERCIAL CRIME POLICY, *supra* note 1, at A-25.

payment of so much of the cost of the bond as would be charged for a bond having a penalty not exceeding the lesser of the:

i. Value of the "securities" at the close of business on the day the loss was discovered; or

ii. Limit of Insurance.

(3) Loss of, or loss from damage to, "property other than money and securities" or loss from damage to the "premises" for not more than the:

(a) Actual cash value of the property on the day the loss was discovered;

(b) Cost of repairing the property or "premises"; or

(c) Cost of replacing the property with property of like kind and quality.

We may, at our option, pay the actual cash value of the property or repair or replace it.

If we cannot agree with you upon the actual cash value or the cost of repair or replacement, the value or cost will be determined by arbitration.

b. We may, at our option, pay for loss of, or loss from damage to, property other than "money":

(1) in the "money" of the country in which the loss occurred; or

(2) in the United States of America dollar equivalent of the "money" of the country in which the loss occurred determined by the rate of exchange on the day the loss was discovered.

c. Any property that we pay for or replace becomes our property.

2012 ISO Commercial Crime Policy:

(E) Conditions
    (1)   Conditions Applicable to All Insuring Agreements
        x.   **Valuation—Settlement**
            The value of any loss for purposes of coverage under this Policy shall be determined as follows:
            (1) Money
                Loss of "money" but only up to and including its face value. We will, at your option, pay for loss of "money" issued by any country other than the United States of America:
                (a) At face value in the "money" issued by that country; or
                (b) In the United States of America dollar equivalent, determined by the rate of exchange published in The Wall Street Journal on the day the loss was "discovered".
        (2) Securities
        Loss of "securities" but only up to and including their value at the close of business on the day the loss was "discovered". We may, at our option:
        (a) Pay the market value of such "securities" or replace them in kind, in which event you must assign to us all your rights, title and interest in and to those "securities"; or
        (b) Pay the cost of any Lost Securities Bond required in connection with issuing duplicates of the "securities". However, we will be liable only for the payment of so much of the cost of the bond as would be charged for a bond having a penalty not exceeding the lesser of the:
            (i) Market value of the "securities" at the close of business on the day the loss was "discovered"; or

(ii) Limit of Insurance applicable to the "securities".

(3) **Property Other Than Money And Securities**

(a) Loss of or damage to "other property" or loss from damage to the "premises" or its exterior for the replacement cost of the property without deduction for depreciation. However, we will not pay more than the least of the following:

(i) The Limit of Insurance applicable to the lost or damaged property;

(ii) The cost to replace the lost or damaged property with property of comparable material and quality and used for the same purpose; or

(iii) The amount you actually spend that is necessary to repair or replace the lost or damaged property.

(b) We will not pay on a replacement cost basis for any loss or damage to property covered under Paragraph x.(3)(a):

(i) Until the lost or damaged property is actually repaired or replaced; and

(ii) Unless the repair or replacement is made as soon as reasonably possible after the loss or damage.

If the lost or damaged property is not repaired or replaced, we will pay on an actual cash value basis.

(c) We will, at your option, pay for loss or damage to such property:

(i) In the "money" of the country in which the loss or damage was sustained; or

(ii) In the United States of America dollar equivalent of the "money" of the country in which the loss or damage was sustained, determined by the rate of exchange published in The Wall

> **Street Journal on the day the loss was "discovered".**
>
> **(d) Any property that we pay for or replace becomes our property.**

COMMENT

All three forms contain similar language for settlement valuation, with a few notable distinctions. The 2012 ISO Commercial Crime Policy changed the election in (x)(1) and (x)(3)(c) from the previous form and now permits the insured to choose whether to value the loss of money or damage to property (other than securities) in the currency of the country where it was sustained, or in its United States Dollar equivalent. In the 2012 Crime Protection Policy and 1996 General Conditions Form, this election remains the insurer's decision to make. With respect to settlement for loss of or damage to property (other than money), all three forms generally provide for the payment of either replacement cost or actual cash value.

ANNOTATIONS

3d Cir. 2002 (Pa.). A pharmaceutical testing company suffered a loss when its nurses rendered worthless the clinical studies conducted for client drug companies. Federal Insurance Company argued that, upon discovery, the studies had no value. The court rejected the literal application of the provision and held that coverage would be illusory if only damaged or destroyed property could be valued for loss. Instead, the court considered the day-of-discovery provision to apply when property value is subject to market fluctuation, not for custom-made property. *Scirex Corp. v. Fed. Ins. Co.,* 313 F.3d 841.

9th Cir. 1986 (Ca.). The court measured the insured's equipment loss (caused by an employee's fraudulent sales) by stipulated fair market value or wholesale list price and not by insured's cost to remanufacture. It found that the provisions setting loss valuation at actual cash value or actual cost of replacement were ambiguous for failing to specify value or cost to whom—manufacturer, wholesaler, retailer, or purchaser in the market. The court refused to require insured in effect to make more equipment at cost to replace what was stolen. *James B. Lansing Sound, Inc. v Nat'l Union Fire Ins. Co. of Pittsburgh, Pa.*, 801 F.2d 1560.

Cal. App. 1986. The insured's dishonest employee stole money in Argentina years before discovery. Because the policy was silent on when the foreign currency would be valued, the court used the date of the insurer's "breach of contract" to determine the foreign currency conversion rate, i.e., the date when insured submitted proof of loss. *Levi Strauss & Co. v. Aetna Cas. & Sur. Co.,* 184 Cal. App. 3d 1479.

SECONDARY SOURCES

Joel P. Williams & Timothy E. Markey, *Loss and Valuation, in* COMMERCIAL CRIME POLICY 323 (Randall I. Marmor & Susan Koehler Sullivan, eds., 3d ed. 2015).

C. Liberalization

1996 Crime General Provisions:

(B) General Conditions
(8) Liberalization: If we adopt any revision that would broaden the coverage under this insurance without additional premium within 45 days prior to or during the Policy Period, the broadened coverage will immediately apply to this insurance.

COMMENT

This provision is virtually identical across all forms. In the event the insurer issues a revision that broadens coverage and does not charge any additional premium, the broader coverage applies immediately.

ANNOTATIONS

NONE

SECONDARY SOURCES

Justin P. Wear, *Conditions of Coverage, in* COMMERCIAL CRIME POLICY 393 (Randall I. Marmor & Susan Koehler Sullivan, eds., 3d ed. 2015).

D. Territory

1996 Crime General Provisions:

(B) General Conditions
   (17) Territory: This insurance covers only acts committed or events occurring within the United States of America, U.S. Virgin Islands, Puerto Rico, Canal Zone, or Canada.

2012 ISO Commercial Crime Policy:

(E) Conditions
   (1)   Conditions Applicable to All Insuring Agreements
      (u)   Territory: This policy covers loss that you sustain resulting directly from an "occurrence" taking place within the United States of America (including its territories and possessions), Puerto Rico and Canada.
   (2)   Conditions Applicable To Insuring Agreement A.1.
      (b)   Territory
         We will pay for loss caused by any "employee" while temporarily outside the territory specified in Territory Condition E.1.u. for a period of not more than 90 consecutive days.

(3) Conditions Applicable to Insuring Agreement A.2.
(d) Territory
We will cover loss that you sustain resulting directly from an "occurrence" taking place anywhere in the world. Territory Condition E.1.u. does not apply to Insuring Agreement A.2.

(5) Conditions Applicable to Insuring Agreement A.6.
(b) Territory
We will cover loss that you sustain resulting directly from an "occurrence" taking place anywhere in the world. Territory Condition E.1.u. does not apply to Insuring Agreement A.6.

COMMENT

This provision limits the territorial reach of covered acts or occurrences. The 2012 ISO Commercial Crime Policy's reference to "territories and possessions" expands its geographic scope to unlisted places such as Guam and America Samoa. Unlike the 1996 General Conditions, the 2012 ISO Commercial Crime Policy permits coverage for employee dishonesty (Insuring Agreement A.1) while the employee is temporarily out of the normal territorial boundary. The 2012 ISO Commercial Crime Policy also allows for worldwide coverage for forgery coverage (Insuring Agreement A.2) and computer and funds transfer fraud (Insuring Agreement A.6). While it does not include the broader reach of the 2012 ISO Commercial Crime Policy, the 2012 Commercial Crime Protection Policy contains a similar carve-out for employee dishonesty, but not for its forgery and computer fraud coverages.

ANNOTATIONS

A. Cases Under Previous Forms

5th Cir. 2006 (La.). Bulk-Pack's employee in Mexico embezzled money by inducing extra funds to be transferred from the company's bank in the

United States into its bank in Mexico, from which account the employee stole. Bulk-Pack pointed to the transfer from the U.S. account and tried to analogize to federal venue law in mail-fraud cases. The court held that the policy was clear and unambiguous in requiring the dishonest activity to be committed in the U.S. Because all of the employee's dishonesty occurred in Mexico, no covered acts fell within the territory covered by the policy. *Bulk Pack, Inc. v. Fid. & Dep. Co. of Md,* 163 Fed. Appx. 298.

SECONDARY SOURCES

John W. Hinchey, *General Agreements (Bond Period, Discovery, Multiple Coverages, Multiple Insureds, Territory, Consolidation/ Merger)*, *in* FIDELITY BONDS 39 (Michael Keeley & Timothy M. Sukel, eds., 1991).

Cynthia A. Mellon, *General Conditions: Who, Where and What, in* COMMERCIAL CRIME POLICY 6 (Gilbert J. Schroeder, ed., 1997).

E. Other Insurance

2012 ISO Commercial Crime Policy:

(E) Conditions
   (1)   Conditions Applicable to All Insuring Agreements
      (o)   Other Insurance
         If other valid and collectible insurance is available to you for loss covered under this Policy, our obligations are limited as follows:
         (1)   Primary Insurance
            When this Policy is written as primary insurance, and:
            (a)   You have other insurance subject to the same terms and conditions as this Policy, we will pay our share of the covered loss. Our share is the proportion that the applicable Limit Of Insurance shown in the

Declarations bears to the total limit of all insurance covering the same loss.

(b) You have other insurance covering the same loss other than that described in Paragraph o.(1)(a), we will only pay for the amount of loss that exceeds:

(i) The Limit of Insurance and Deductible Amount of that other insurance, whether you can collect on it or not; or

(ii) The Deductible Amount shown in the Declarations;

whichever is greater. Our payment for loss is subject to the terms and conditions of this Policy.

(2) **Excess Insurance**

(a) When this Policy is written excess over other insurance, we will only pay for the amount of loss that exceeds the Limit of Insurance and Deductible Amount of that other insurance, whether you can collect on it or not. Our payment for loss is subject to the terms and conditions of this Policy.

(b) However, if loss covered under this Policy is subject to a deductible, we will reduce the Deductible Amount shown in the Declarations by the sum total of all such other insurance plus any Deductible Amount applicable to that other Insurance.

2012 Crime Protection Policy:

(E) Conditions

(16) Other Insurance

a. This Policy does not apply to loss recoverable or recovered under other insurance or

ANNOTATED COMMERCIAL CRIME INSURANCE POLICY

indemnity. However, if the limit of the other insurance or indemnity is insufficient to cover the entire amount of the loss, this Policy will apply to that part of the loss, other than that falling within any Deductible Amount, not recoverable or recovered under the other insurance or indemnity. However, this Policy will not apply to the amount of loss that is more than the applicable Limit of Insurance shown in the Declarations.

b. Under Insuring Agreement 4., we will pay only for the amount of loss that you cannot recover:

(1) Under your contract with the armored motor vehicle company; and

(2) From any insurance or indemnity carried by, or for the benefit of customers of, the armored motor vehicle company.

COMMENT

The Other Insurance provision in the 1996 General Conditions Form is virtually identical to the provision in the 2012 Crime Protection Policy. Those forms make the policy an excess policy, only covering that portion of the loss that exceeds the limit of the other policy that provides coverage. Application of the provision becomes complicated when the other applicable insurance contains a similar provision. Reference should be made to how the particular jurisdiction handles the conflict. The 2012 ISO Commercial Crime Policy, to a certain extent, anticipates the issue. Where both policies are primary and the other insurance is subject to the same terms and conditions, the policy will indemnify its "share," which is defined as the proportion of its limit when combined with the limit of the other policy. But where the other insurance covers the same loss but is not subject to the same terms and conditions, then the policy becomes excess. Again, the practitioner will need to assess how the particular jurisdiction handles the situation where the other insurance policy contains the same provision.

OUTLINE OF ANNOTATIONS

A. Crime Policies
B. Other Similar Policies

ANNOTATIONS

A. Crime Policies

S.D. Tex. 1996. A church sustained employee dishonesty losses during three policy periods, the two earlier periods being with another insurer. Having settled with that insurer, the church sought to recover the limits of the third policy covering the latest time period. The court held that the entire loss was one occurrence under all three policies, and one occurrence could trigger only one limit of liability. The "other insurance" provision in Preferred Risk's policy required payment only of the loss, within limits, not recovered from the other insurer, so Preferred Risk received full credit against its limits for the prior insurer's payment. *Bethany Christian Church v. Preferred Risk Mut. Ins. Co.,* 942 F. Supp. 330.

D. Kan. 1995. Applying Illinois law to the "other insurance" clause in the 1995 Crime General Provisions, the court held that the identical clauses in both insurance policies cancel each other out and liability must be divided equally between the two carriers. *T.S.I. Holdings, Inc. v. Buckingham,* 885 F. Supp. 1457.

B. Other Similar Policies

Mo. App. 2006. Insured claimed for uncollectible chargebacks under two merchant chargeback indemnity policies (Utica and BancInsure). After settling with BancInsure, insured sought to recover from Utica, who defended under an "other insurance" provision in its policy that was essentially identical to the one in BancInsure's policy. The court held that the provisions may authorize pro rata contribution between the insurers, but they are "mutually repugnant" and to be disregarded under Missouri law as to the insured. Consequently, the insured was allowed to recover all of its covered loss from Utica without an instruction to the jury about the BancInsure policy. *Heartland Payment Sys, L.L.C. v. Utica Mut. Ins. Co.*, 185 S.W.3d 225.

Cal. App. 1978. Because two brokers blanket bonds covered the same risk and both contained "excess insurance" clauses, the court held that neither clause could be given effect. Both loss and defense costs were prorated between the two carriers in proportion to their respective amounts of coverage. *Cont'l Ins. Co. v. Morgan, Olmstead, Kennedy & Gardner, Inc.*, 83 Cal. App. 3d 593.

SECONDARY SOURCES

John W. Hinchey, *General Agreements (Bond Period, Discovery, Multiple Coverages, Multiple Insureds, Territory, Consolidation/ Merger), in* FIDELITY BONDS 39 (Michael Keeley & Timothy M. Sukel, eds., 1991).

Justin D. Wear, *Conditions of Coverage, in* COMMERCIAL CRIME POLICY 393 (Randall I. Marmor & Susan Koehler Sullivan, eds., 3d ed. 2015).

F. Consolidation/Merger

1996 Crime General Provisions:

(B) General Conditions
    (2) Consolidation—Merger: If through consolidation or merger with, or purchase or acquisition of assets or liabilities of, some other entity:
        a. Any additional persons become "employees"; or
        b. You acquire the use and control of any additional "premises";
        any insurance afforded for "employees" or "premises" also applies to those additional "employees" and "premises", for a period of 60 days after the effective date of such

consolidation, merger, or purchase or acquisition of assets or liabilities.

You must give us written notice within this 60 day period and obtain our written consent to extend this insurance to such additional "employees" or "premises". Upon obtaining our written consent, you must pay us an additional premium.

If you fail to notify us in writing within this 60 day period, then this insurance shall automatically terminate as to such additional "employees" or "premises".

2012 ISO Commercial Crime Policy:

(E) Conditions

    (1) Conditions Applicable to All Insuring Agreements

        (e) Consolidation—Merger or Acquisition

If you consolidate or merge with, or purchase or acquire the assets or liabilities of, another entity:

    (1) You must give us written notice as soon as possible and obtain our written consent to extend the coverage provided by this Policy to such consolidated or merged entity or such purchased or acquired assets or liabilities. We may condition our consent by requiring payment of an additional premium; but

    (2) For the first 90 days after the effective date of such consolidation, merger or purchase or acquisition of assets or liabilities, the coverage provided by this Policy shall apply to such consolidated or merged entity or such purchased or acquired assets or liabilities, provided that all "occurrences" causing or contributing to a loss involving such

> **consolidation, merger or purchase or acquisition of assets or liabilities, must take place after the effective date of such consolidation, merger or purchase or acquisition of assets or liabilities.**

2012 Crime Protection Policy:

(E)   Conditions

    (4)   Consolidation and Merger

      If through consolidation or merger with, or purchase or acquisition of assets or liabilities of, some other entity, any additional persons become employees or you acquire the use and control of any additional premises:

      a.   You must give us written notice and obtain our written consent to extend this Policy to such additional employees or premises. We may condition our consent upon payment of an additional premium; but

      b.   For the first 60 days after the effective date of such consolidation, merger or purchase or acquisition ι of assets or liabilities, any insurance afforded for employees or premises also applies to these additional employees or premises for acts committed or events occurring within said 60 day period.

COMMENT

The Consolidation/Merger condition anticipates that the insured may expand its business to acquire other assets during the policy period. The 1996 General Conditions Form covers the employees or premises of the acquired assets, but only if written notice is given to the insurer within 60 days and the insurer consents. The 2012 ISO Commercial Crime Policy and the 2012 Crime Protection Policy require written notice and consent of the insurer after the acquisition to cover the newly acquired premises and employees. But unlike the 1996 General Conditions, these forms provide for a short period of coverage following the acquisition for the new employees and premises regardless of whether the insured gives notice. The period is 90 days for the 2012 ISO Commercial Crime Policy and 60 days for the 2012 Crime Protection Policy.

OUTLINE OF ANNOTATIONS

A. Cases Under Prior Forms
B. Cases Under Similar Coverages

ANNOTATIONS

A. Cases Under Prior Forms

N.D. Ill. 1994. Interpreting a consolidation/merger clause identical to the 1995 Crime General Provisions, the court determined that the insurer did not intend, without notice, to extend coverage to employees or assets added other than through internal growth. *Newman v. Hartford Ins. Co. of Ill.*, 1994 WL 247071.

B. Cases Under Similar Coverages

N.C. App. 2003. The merger clause in Form 25 Financial Institution Bond excluded coverage for embezzlement by an insurance agent of the company acquired by insured's subsidiary. The insured had failed to satisfy the written notice and consent requirements for extension of coverage. The court rejected the argument that the merger clause did not apply to the rider under which the claim was made; all riders become incorporated into the bond. *Jefferson Pilot Fin. Ins. Co. v. Marsh USA Inc.*, 582 S.E.2d 701.

SECONDARY SOURCES

John W. Hinchey, *General Agreements (Bond Period, Discovery, Multiple Coverages, Multiple Insureds, Territory, Consolidation/ Merger), in* FIDELITY BONDS 39 (Michael Keeley & Timothy M. Sukel, eds., 1991).

Justin D. Wear, *Conditions of Coverage*, *in* COMMERCIAL CRIME POLICY 393 (Randall I. Marmor & Susan Koehler Sullivan, eds., 3d ed. 2015).

G. Joint Insured

1996 Crime General Provisions:

(B) General Conditions
   (6) Joint Insured:
   a.   **If more than one Insured is named in the Declarations, the first named Insured will act for itself and for every other Insured for all purposes of this insurance. If the first named Insured ceases to be covered, then the next named Insured will become the first named Insured.**
   b.   **If any Insured or partner or officer of that Insured has knowledge of any information relevant to this insurance, that knowledge is considered knowledge of every Insured.**
   c.   **An "employee" of any Insured is considered to be an "employee" of every Insured.**
   d.   **If this insurance or any of its coverages is cancelled or terminated as to any Insured, loss sustained by that Insured is covered only if discovered no later than 1 year from the date of that cancellation or termination.**
   e.   **We will not pay more for loss sustained by more than one Insured than the amount we would pay if all the loss had been sustained by one Insured.**

2012 Commercial Crime Policy:

(E) Conditions

(1) Conditions Applicable To All Insuring Agreements

(l) Joint Insured

(1) If more than one Insured is named in the Declarations, the first Named Insured will act for itself and for every other Insured for all purposes of this Policy. If the first Named Insured ceases to be covered, then the next Named Insured will become the first Named Insured.

(2) If any Insured, or partner, "member" or officer of that Insured has knowledge of any information relevant to this Policy, that knowledge is considered knowledge of every Insured.

(3) An "employee" of any Insured is considered to be an "employee" of every Insured.

(4) If this Policy or any of its coverages are cancelled as to any Insured, loss sustained by that Insured is covered only if it is "discovered" by you:

(a) No later than 60 days from the date of that cancellation. However, this extended period to "discover" loss terminates immediately upon the effective date of any other insurance obtained by that Insured, whether from us or another insurer, replacing in whole or in part the coverage afforded under this Policy, whether or not such other insurance provides coverage for loss sustained prior to its effective date.

> (b)   No later than one year from the date
> of that cancellation with regard to any
> "employee benefit plan".

2012 Crime Protection Policy:

(E) Conditions
    (10) Joint Insured

        a.   The first named Insured shown in the Declarations is responsible for the payment of all premiums and will be the payee for any return premiums we pay.

        b.   If more than one Insured is named in the Declarations, the first named Insured will act for itself and for every other Insured for all purposes related to this insurance. If the first named Insured ceases to be covered, then the next named Insured will become the first named Insured.

        c.   If any Insured or partner or officer of that Insured has knowledge of any information relevant to this insurance, that knowledge is considered knowledge of every Insured.

        d.   An employee of any Insured is considered to be an employee of every Insured.

        e.   If this Policy or any of its coverage is canceled or terminated as to any Insured, Condition E.9. Extended Period to Discover Loss applies separately to that Insured.

        f.   We will not pay more for loss sustained by more than one Insured than the amount we would pay if all the loss had been sustained by one Insured.

COMMENT

The Joint Insured Condition governs circumstance where an entity that is insured, but not named, incurs a loss. In such a case, the Named Insured has the right of action even where the other entity may ultimately receive the indemnity. The provisions also impute to all other insureds any discovery or knowledge of other insureds.

OUTLINE OF ANNOTATIONS

A. Fidelity Cases under Standard Forms
B. Cases Under Other Bonds

ANNOTATIONS

A. Fidelity Cases under Standard Forms

6th Cir. 2012 (Mich.). The Named Insured, a trade association, controlled an insurance agency that collected commissions on policies it sold to the trade association's members. An employee of the trade association diverted commissions intended for the insurance agency to himself. The court held that the trade association could not recover the insurance agency's loss under its commercial crime policy because the insurance agency was not a Named Insured and so it did not qualify as an insured. Even though the companies were closely related, they remained distinct corporate entities and there was no intent to cover the insurance agency.

S.D. Fla. 2011. The plaintiffs sued Travelers Casualty and Surety Company of America under a crime policy for losses caused by a joint employee of the plaintiffs and the Named Insured. Travelers argued that the plaintiffs had no standing because the complaint contained no allegations concerning the corporate relationship between the plaintiffs and the Named Insured. Accepting, for the sake of argument, that the plaintiffs were "insureds" under the policy by virtue of their status as subsidiaries of the Named Insured, Travelers argued that the Joint Insured Condition required the joinder of the Named Insured as a party plaintiff. Applying the provision that the Named Insured "will act for itself and for every other Insured for all purposes," the court held that where the Named Insured "consists of more than one entity," it must be joined as a plaintiff even where the constituent parts incurred the loss. *Fireman v. Travelers Cas. & Sur. Co. of Am.*, 2011 U.S. Dist. LEXIS 18426.

E.D. Va. 2014. Arch Insurance argued that an insurance policy was void due to concealment made by an officer of the insured Fire Department on the policy application. The officer also happened to be the insurance broker. The Fire Department argued that the officer's status as an Arch's agent meant that Arch could not use his misrepresentations to void the policy. The court disagreed and applied the language in the Joint Insured Condition that imputed the knowledge of an officer to the insured. *Middleburg Volunteer Fire Dep't, Inc. v. McNeil & Co.*, 2014 U.S. Dist. LEXIS 159701.

N.Y. App. 2012. Insurers issued layered fidelity bonds to an investment company that managed the investments of various family-held companies, which also qualified as insureds. The investment company submitted a single proof of loss, alleging coverage for investments made by the various other companies in Bernard Madoff's Ponzi scheme. The insurers argued that, in the aggregate, the various companies did not incur a net loss because they withdrew more money than they invested. Among other things, the insurers cited the Joint Insured Provision. The court held the Joint Insured Provision is merely a "housekeeping measure" that does not impact accounting for individual claims, and ultimately considered each individual company that incurred a loss, a "single loss." *Jacobson Family Inv., Inc. v. National Union Fire Ins. Co. of Pittsburgh, PA*, 102 A.D.3d 223.

Wisc. Ct. App. 2008. A medical services holding company sought indemnity under its commercial crime policy for losses caused by its employee's theft of money deposited in an account belonging to a constituent hospital's medical staff. The entity set up by the medical staff was not the Named Insured and did not qualify as an insured under the policy. The court held that the policy did not provide coverage because the holding company did not own or hold the account and was not legally liable for it. *Meriter Health Services, Inc. v. Travelers Casualty & Surety Co. of America*, 758 N.W.2d 112.

B. Cases Under Other Bonds

9th Cir. 1994 (Mont.). A schedule bond purchased by an escrow agent made the "Owners" of the escrow accounts the insureds, but the insurer never required a schedule listing the identities of the owners. The insurer argued that the escrow agent was the insured, but the court held that the owners, and thus insureds, could be identified by extrinsic evidence and that the insurer waived or was estopped to assert the absence of the schedule that had been intended to identify the insureds by name. *Transamerica Premier Ins. Co. v. Miller*, 41 F.3d 438.

SECONDARY SOURCES

Adam D. Cornett & Andrew S. Kent, *Who Can Recover Under a Fidelity Policy?*, 20 FID. L.J. 139 (2014).

John W. Hinchey, *General Agreements (Bond Period, Discovery, Multiple Coverages, Multiple Insureds, Territory, Consolidation/ Merger), in* FIDELITY BONDS 39 (Michael Keeley & Timothy M. Sukel eds., 1991).

Justin D. Wear, *Conditions of Coverage, in* COMMERCIAL CRIME POLICY 393 (Randall I. Marmor & Susan Koehler Sullivan, eds., 3d ed. 2015).

H. Transfer of Insured's Rights and Duties

2012 Commercial Crime Policy:

(E) Conditions
    (1) Conditions Applicable To All Insuring Agreements
      (v) Transfer Of Your Rights And Duties Under This Policy
        (1) Your rights and duties under this Policy may not be transferred without our written consent except in the case of death of an individual Named Insured.
        (2) If you die, your rights and duties will be transferred to your legal representative but only while acting within the scope of duties as your legal

representative. Until your legal representative is appointed, anyone having proper temporary custody of your property will have your rights and duties but only with respect to that property.

COMMENT

The 2012 ISO Crime Protection Policy and 2012 ISO Commercial Crime Policy contain virtually identical language. The provisions require the insurer's written consent before the insured may assign its rights under the policy. Application of this provision must include consideration of each state's treatment of "anti-assignment" clauses, particularly where the assignment occurs after the loss has already been incurred.

ANNOTATIONS

S.D. Fla. 2011. The plaintiff was the named insured but lost existence in a corporate reorganization that post-dated the allegedly covered loss. Travelers Casualty and Surety Company of America argued that statutory transfer of the interest from the named insured to the surviving entity violated the policy's Transfer Condition. The court disagreed, reasoning that the assignment did not increase Travelers' exposure because the loss occurred before the merger and that the assignment of interest in an insurance claim was "completely permissible." The court further distinguished the fact that the assignment was a result of law following a merger as opposed to a contract with the surviving entity. *Fireman v. Travelers Cas. & Sur. Co. of Am.*, 2011 U.S. Dist. LEXIS 107116.

N.D. Ill. 1994. A commercial crime policy with a transfer of rights clause did not cover the late-incorporated division of the named insured. The court held that the transfer of rights clause, among others, did not allow the new corporation to have the benefits of the crime policy without the insurer's consent. Neither successor-in-interest status nor assignment could have overcome the policy restrictions, although the court held that the evidence did not support such findings anyway. *Newman v. Hartford Ins. Co. of Ill.,* 1994 U.S. Dist. LEXIS 7366.

D.N.J. 2009. Plaintiff sued Liberty Mutual, who had issued a commercial crime policy to another entity. In response to Liberty Mutual's argument that Plaintiff had no standing under the policy, Plaintiff pointed to a prior settlement between it and the insured entity that effectively assigned its rights under the policy. The court held that the Transfer Condition prevented such an assignment without the insurer's consent. *Carteret Ventures, LLC v. Liberty Mut. Ins. Co.,* 2009 U.S. Dist. LEXIS 91919.

SECONDARY SOURCES

NONE

I. Cooperation

2012 ISO Commercial Crime Policy:

(E) **Conditions**
(1) **Conditions Applicable To All Insuring Agreements**
(f) **Cooperation**
You must cooperate with us in all matters pertaining to this Policy as stated in its terms and conditions.

COMMENT

The duty to cooperate is particularly important in the initial stages of reviewing a proof of loss, when insureds may seek to constrain the insurer's investigation. With respect to the 2012 ISO Commercial Crime Policy, this provision should be read in conjunction with the records examination and condition to permit a broad ability to review the insured's books and records and interview all relevant parties. As always, documentation of an insured's obstruction is essential to proving breach of the duty to cooperate.

ANNOTATIONS

9th Cir. 1992 (Cal.). The trial court presented the issue of whether the insured breached the policy's cooperation clause to the jury as an issue of breach of contract. The jury returned a verdict in favor of the insurer and awarded damages. The appellate court reversed, holding that the policy's language established that it was a condition precedent to coverage and not a promise subject to damages for breach. *Mercedes-Benz of North America, Inc. v. Hartford Acci. & Indem. Co.*, 1992 U.S. App. LEXIS 19825.

N.D. Tex. 2006. The cooperation clause in a commercial crime policy does not act as a waiver of the attorney-client privilege. *Kimberly-Clark v. Cont'l Cas. Co.*, 2006 U.S. Dist. LEXIS 63576.

Sup. Ct. N.Y. 2009. Insured asserted a claim against a crime policy after it discovered embezzlement by its chief financial officer. The court held that the insured breached the contract by delaying and obstructing the insurer's interview of the officer, which would have revealed a partial settlement of the loss. The court found that while the burden is on the insurer to prove that the insured's failure to cooperate was deliberate, that burden is not as heavy where there is a first-party claim against an indemnity policy. The court also noted that the right to examine under the cooperation clause is broader than rights under discovery in litigation. *Conference Associates, Inc. v. Travelers Cas. & Sur. Co. of Am.*, 2009 N.Y. Misc. LEXIS 6813.

SECONDARY SOURCES

Justin D. Wear, *Conditions of Coverage*, *in* COMMERCIAL CRIME POLICY 393 (Randall I. Marmor & Susan Koehler Sullivan, eds., 3d ed. 2015).

Julie Fry Yanda & Mark Struthers, *The Insured's Duties Following Discovery of Loss*, 19 FID. L.J. 147 (2013).

J. Loss Sustained During Prior Insurance Issued By Us Or Any Affiliate

2012 Commercial Crime Policy:

(E) Conditions
    (1) Conditions Applicable To All Insuring Agreements
        (o) Loss Sustained During Prior Insurance Issued By Us Or Any Affiliate
            (1) Loss Sustained Partly During This Policy And Partly During Prior Insurance

If you "discover" loss during the Policy Period shown in the Declarations, resulting directly from an "occurrence" taking place:

    (a) Partly during the Policy Period shown in the Declarations; and

    (b) Partly during the policy period(s) of any prior cancelled insurance that we or any affiliate issued to you or any predecessor in interest;

and this Policy became effective at the time of cancellation of the prior insurance, we will first settle the amount of loss that you sustained during this policy period. We will then settle the remaining amount of loss that you sustained during the policy period(s) of the prior insurance.

            (2) Loss Sustained Entirely During Prior Insurance

If you "discover" loss during the Policy Period shown in the Declarations, resulting directly from an "occurrence" taking place entirely during the policy period(s) of any prior cancelled insurance that we or any affiliate issued to you or any predecessor in interest, we will pay for the loss, provided:

(a) This Policy became effective at the time of cancellation of the prior insurance; and

(b) The loss would have been covered under this Policy had it been in effect at the time of the "occurrence".

We will first settle the amount of loss that you sustained during the most recent prior insurance. We will then settle any remaining amount of loss that you sustained during the policy period(s) of any other prior insurance.

(3) In settling loss under Paragraphs o.(1) and o.(2):

(a) The most we will pay for the entire loss is the highest single Limit of Insurance applicable during the period of loss, whether such limit was written under this Policy or was written under the prior insurance issued by us.

(b) We will apply the applicable Deductible Amount shown in the Declarations to the amount of loss sustained under this Policy. If no loss was sustained under this Policy, we will apply the Deductible Amount shown in the Declarations to the amount of loss sustained under the most recent prior insurance.

If the Deductible Amount is larger than the amount of loss sustained under this Policy, or the most recent prior insurance, we will apply the remaining Deductible Amount to the remaining amount of loss sustained during the prior insurance.

We will not apply any other Deductible Amount that may have been applicable to the loss.

(4) The following examples demonstrate how we will settle losses subject to this condition:

Example Number 1

The Insured sustained a covered loss of $10,000 resulting directly from an "occurrence" taking place during the terms of Policy A and Policy B.

Policy A

The current policy. Written at a Limit of Insurance of $50,000 and a Deductible Amount of $5,000.

Policy B

Issued prior to Policy A. Written at a Limit of Insurance of $50,000 and a Deductible Amount of $5,000.

The amount of loss sustained under Policy A is $2,500 and under Policy B, $7,500.

The highest single Limit of Insurance applicable to this entire loss is $50,000 written under Polity A. The Policy A Deductible Amount of $5,000 applies. The loss is settled as follows:

(a) The amount of loss sustained under Policy A ($2,500) is settled first. The amount we will pay is nil ($0.00) because the amount of loss is less than the Deductible Amount (i.e., $2,500 loss - $5,000 deductible = $0.00).

(b) The remaining amount of loss sustained under Policy B ($7,500) is settled next. The amount recoverable is $5,000 after the remaining Deductible Amount from Policy A of $2,500 is applied to the loss (i.e.,

$7,500 loss - $2,500 deductible = $5,000).

The most we will pay for this loss is $5,000.

Example Number 2

The Insured sustained a covered loss of $250,000 resulting directly from an "occurrence" taking place during the terms of Policy A and Policy B.

Policy A

The current policy. Written at a Limit of Insurance of $125,000 and a Deductible Amount of $10,000.

Policy B

Issued prior to Policy A. Written at a Limit of Insurance of $150,000 and a Deductible Amount of $25,000.

The amount of loss sustained under Policy A is $175,000 and under Policy B, $75,000.

The highest single Limit of Insurance applicable to this entire loss is $150,000 written under Policy B. The Policy A Deductive Amount of $10,000 applies.

The loss is settled as follows:

(a)   The amount of loss sustained under Policy A ($175,000) is settled first. The amount we will pay is the Policy A Limit of $125,000 because $175,000 loss - $10,000 deductible = $165,000, which is greater than the $125,000 policy limit.

(b)   The remaining amount of loss sustained under Policy B ($75,000) is settled next. The amount we will pay is $25,000 (i.e., $150,000 Policy B limit - $125,000 paid under Policy A = $25,000).

The most we will pay for this loss is $150,000.

Example Number 3

The Insured sustained a covered loss of $2,000,000 resulting directly from an "occurrence" taking place during the terms of Policies A, B, C, and D.

Policy A

The current policy. Written at a Limit of Insurance of $1,000,000 and a Deductible Amount of $100,000.

Policy B

Issued prior to Policy A. Written at a Limit of Insurance of $750,000 and a Deductible Amount of $75,000.

Policy C

Issued prior to Policy B. Written at a Limit of Insurance of $500,000 and a Deductible Amount of $50,000.

Policy D

Issued prior to Policy C. Written at a Limit of Insurance of $500,000 and a Deductible Amount of $50,000.

The amount of loss sustained under Policy A is $350,000; under Policy B, $250,000; under Policy C, $600,000; and under Policy D, $800,000.

The highest single Limit of Insurance applicable to this entire loss is $1,000,000 written under Policy A. The Policy A Deductible Amount of $100,000 applies. The loss is settled as follows:

(a)   The amount of loss sustained under Policy A ($350,000) is settled first. The amount we will pay is $250,000 (i.e., $350,000 loss - S100,000 deductible = $250,000).

(b)   The amount of loss sustained under Policy B ($250,000) is settled next.

> **The amount we will pay is $250,000 (no deductible is applied).**
>
> **(c)   The amount of loss sustained under Policy C ($600,000) is settled next. The amount we will pay is $500,000, the policy limit (no deductible is applied).**
>
> **(d)   We will not make any further payment under Policy D, as the maximum amount payable under the highest single Limit of Insurance applying to the loss of $1,000,000 under Policy A has been satisfied.**
>
> **The most we will pay for this loss is $1,000,000.**

COMMENT

The 2012 Commercial Crime Policy, Loss Sustained Form, contains provisions that address circumstances where losses are incurred over multiple policy periods. The language contemplates the situation where the occurrence takes place during a prior policy period or during both the prior and current policy period. In such situations, the condition provides a guide for determining the applicable limit of liability and deductibles in adjusting the total amount of coverage.

ANNOTATIONS

NONE

SECONDARY SOURCES

Robert M. Konop, *The Loss Sustained Policy and Multiple Year Losses: Keeping it Simple*, 18 FID. L.J. 195 (2012).

Appendix

Exhibit A

CRIME POLICY (LOSS SUSTAINED FORM)
STANDARD FORM NO. CR 00 23 05 06

CRIME AND FIDELITY
CR 00 23 05 06

COMMERCIAL CRIME POLICY
(LOSS SUSTAINED FORM)

Various provisions in this policy restrict coverage. Read the entire policy carefully to determine rights, duties and what is or is not covered.

Throughout this policy the words "you" and "your" refer to the Named Insured shown in the Declarations. The words "we", "us" and "our" refer to the Company providing this insurance.

Other words and phrases that appear in quotation marks have special meaning. Refer to Section **F.** Definitions.

A. Insuring Agreements

Coverage is provided under the following Insuring Agreements for which a Limit of Insurance is shown in the Declarations and applies to loss that you sustain resulting directly from an "occurrence" taking place during the Policy Period shown in the Declarations, except as provided in Condition **E.1.o.** or **E.1.p.**, which is "discovered" by you during the Policy Period shown in the Declarations or during the period of time provided in the Extended Period To Discover Loss Condition **E.1.j.**:

1. Employee Theft

We will pay for loss of or damage to "money", "securities" and "other property" resulting directly from "theft" committed by an "employee", whether identified or not, acting alone or in collusion with other persons.

For the purposes of this Insuring Agreement, "theft" shall also include forgery.

2. Forgery Or Alteration

a. We will pay for loss resulting directly from "forgery" or alteration of checks, drafts, promissory notes, or similar written promises, orders or directions to pay a sum certain in "money" that are:

   (1) Made or drawn by or drawn upon you; or

   (2) Made or drawn by one acting as your agent;

   or that are purported to have been so made or drawn.

   For the purposes of this Insuring Agreement, a substitute check as defined in the Check Clearing for the 21st Century Act shall be treated the same as the original it replaced.

b. If you are sued for refusing to pay any instrument covered in Paragraph **2.a.**, on the basis that it has been forged or altered, and you have our written consent to defend against the suit, we will pay for any reasonable legal expenses that you incur and pay in that defense. The amount that we will pay is in addition to the Limit of Insurance applicable to this Insuring Agreement.

3. Inside The Premises – Theft Of Money And Securities

a. We will pay for loss of "money" and "securities" inside the "premises" or "banking premises":

   (1) Resulting directly from "theft" committed by a person present inside such "premises" or "banking premises"; or

   (2) Resulting directly from disappearance or destruction.

b. We will pay for loss from damage to the "premises" or its exterior resulting directly from an actual or attempted "theft" of "money" and "securities", if you are the owner of the "premises" or are liable for damage to it.

c. We will pay for loss of or damage to a locked safe, vault, cash register, cash box or cash drawer located inside the "premises" resulting directly from an actual or attempted "theft" of or unlawful entry into those containers.

4. Inside The Premises – Robbery Or Safe Burglary Of Other Property

a. We will pay for loss of or damage to "other property":

   (1) Inside the "premises" resulting directly from an actual or attempted "robbery" of a "custodian"; or

   (2) Inside the "premises" in a safe or vault resulting directly from an actual or attempted "safe burglary".

b. We will pay for loss from damage to the "premises" or its exterior resulting directly from an actual or attempted "robbery" or "safe burglary" of "other property", if you are the owner of the "premises" or are liable for damage to it.

c. We will pay for loss of or damage to a locked safe or vault located inside the "premises" resulting directly from an actual or attempted "robbery" or "safe burglary".

5. Outside The Premises

a. We will pay for loss of "money" and "securities" outside the "premises" in the care and custody of a "messenger" or an armored motor vehicle company resulting directly from "theft", disappearance or destruction.

b. We will pay for loss of or damage to "other property" outside the "premises" in the care and custody of a "messenger" or an armored motor vehicle company resulting directly from an actual or attempted "robbery".

6. Computer Fraud

We will pay for loss of or damage to "money", "securities" and "other property" resulting directly from the use of any computer to fraudulently cause a transfer of that property from inside the "premises" or "banking premises":

a. To a person (other than a "messenger") outside those "premises"; or

b. To a place outside those "premises".

7. Funds Transfer Fraud

We will pay for loss of "funds" resulting directly from a "fraudulent instruction" directing a financial institution to transfer, pay or deliver "funds" from your "transfer account".

8. Money Orders And Counterfeit Money

We will pay for loss resulting directly from your having accepted in good faith, in exchange for merchandise, "money" or services:

a. Money orders issued by any post office, express company or bank that are not paid upon presentation; or

b. "Counterfeit money" that is acquired during the regular course of business.

B. Limit Of Insurance

The most we will pay for all loss resulting directly from an "occurrence" is the applicable Limit of Insurance shown in the Declarations.

If any loss is covered under more than one Insuring Agreement or Coverage, the most we will pay for such loss shall not exceed the largest Limit of Insurance available under any one of those Insuring Agreements or Coverages.

C. Deductible

We will not pay for loss resulting directly from an "occurrence" unless the amount of loss exceeds the Deductible Amount shown in the Declarations. We will then pay the amount of loss in excess of the Deductible Amount, up to the Limit of Insurance.

D. Exclusions

1. This policy does not cover:

a. Acts Committed By You, Your Partners Or Your Members

Loss resulting from "theft" or any other dishonest act committed by:

(1) You; or

(2) Any of your partners or "members";

whether acting alone or in collusion with other persons.

b. Acts Of Employees Learned Of By You Prior To The Policy Period

Loss caused by an "employee" if the "employee" had also committed "theft" or any other dishonest act prior to the effective date of this policy and you or any of your partners, "members", "managers", officers, directors or trustees, not in collusion with the "employee", learned of that "theft" or dishonest act prior to the Policy Period shown in the Declarations.

c. Acts Of Employees, Managers, Directors, Trustees Or Representatives

Loss resulting from "theft" or any other dishonest act committed by any of your "employees", "managers", directors, trustees or authorized representatives:

(1) Whether acting alone or in collusion with other persons; or

(2) While performing services for you or otherwise;

except when covered under Insuring Agreement **A.1.**

d. Confidential Information

Loss resulting from:

(1) The unauthorized disclosure of your confidential information including, but not limited to, patents, trade secrets, processing methods or customer lists; or

(2) The unauthorized use or disclosure of confidential information of another person or entity which is held by you including, but not limited to, financial information, personal information, credit card information or similar non-public information.

 CR 00 23 05 06

e. **Governmental Action**

Loss resulting from seizure or destruction of property by order of governmental authority.

f. **Indirect Loss**

Loss that is an indirect result of an "occurrence" covered by this policy including, but not limited to, loss resulting from:

(1) Your inability to realize income that you would have realized had there been no loss of or damage to "money", "securities" or "other property".

(2) Payment of damages of any type for which you are legally liable. But, we will pay compensatory damages arising directly from a loss covered under this policy.

(3) Payment of costs, fees or other expenses you incur in establishing either the existence or the amount of loss under this policy.

g. **Legal Fees, Costs And Expenses**

Fees, costs and expenses incurred by you which are related to any legal action, except when covered under Insuring Agreement A.2.

h. **Nuclear Hazard**

Loss or damage resulting from nuclear reaction or radiation, or radioactive contamination, however caused.

i. **Pollution**

Loss or damage caused by or resulting from pollution. Pollution means the discharge, dispersal, seepage, migration, release or escape of any solid, liquid, gaseous or thermal irritant or contaminant, including smoke, vapor, soot, fumes, acids, alkalis, chemicals and waste. Waste includes materials to be recycled, reconditioned or reclaimed.

j. **War And Military Action**

Loss or damage resulting from:

(1) War, including undeclared or civil war;

(2) Warlike action by a military force, including action in hindering or defending against an actual or expected attack, by any government, sovereign or other authority using military personnel or other agents; or

(3) Insurrection, rebellion, revolution, usurped power, or action taken by governmental authority in hindering or defending against any of these.

2. Insuring Agreement **A.1.** does not cover:

a. **Inventory Shortages**

Loss, or that part of any loss, the proof of which as to its existence or amount is dependent upon:

(1) An inventory computation; or

(2) A profit and loss computation.

However, where you establish wholly apart from such computations that you have sustained a loss, then you may offer your inventory records and actual physical count of inventory in support of the amount of loss claimed.

b. **Trading**

Loss resulting from trading, whether in your name or in a genuine or fictitious account.

c. **Warehouse Receipts**

Loss resulting from the fraudulent or dishonest signing, issuing, cancelling or failing to cancel, a warehouse receipt or any papers connected with it.

3. Insuring Agreements **A.3., A.4.** and **A.5.** do not cover:

a. **Accounting Or Arithmetical Errors Or Omissions**

Loss resulting from accounting or arithmetical errors or omissions.

b. **Exchanges Or Purchases**

Loss resulting from the giving or surrendering of property in any exchange or purchase.

c. **Fire**

Loss or damage resulting from fire, however caused, except:

(1) Loss of or damage to "money" and "securities"; and

(2) Loss from damage to a safe or vault.

d. **Money Operated Devices**

Loss of property contained in any money operated device unless the amount of "money" deposited in it is recorded by a continuous recording instrument in the device.

e. **Motor Vehicles Or Equipment And Accessories**

Loss of or damage to motor vehicles, trailers or semi-trailers or equipment and accessories attached to them.

f. Transfer Or Surrender Of Property

(1) Loss of or damage to property after it has been transferred or surrendered to a person or place outside the "premises" or "banking premises":

(a) On the basis of unauthorized instructions;

(b) As a result of a threat to do bodily harm to any person;

(c) As a result of a threat to do damage to any property;

(d) As a result of a threat to introduce a denial of service attack into your computer system;

(e) As a result of a threat to introduce a virus or other malicious instruction into your computer system which is designed to damage, destroy or corrupt data or computer programs stored within your computer system;

(f) As a result of a threat to contaminate, pollute or render substandard your products or goods; or

(g) As a result of a threat to disseminate, divulge or utilize:

(i) Your confidential information; or

(ii) Weaknesses in the source code within your computer system.

(2) But, this Exclusion does not apply under Insuring Agreement **A.5.** to loss of "money", "securities" or "other property" while outside the "premises" in the care and custody of a "messenger" if you:

(a) Had no knowledge of any threat at the time the conveyance began; or

(b) Had knowledge of a threat at the time the conveyance began, but the loss was not related to the threat.

g. Vandalism

Loss from damage to the "premises" or its exterior, or to any safe, vault, cash register, cash box, cash drawer or "other property" by vandalism or malicious mischief.

h. Voluntary Parting Of Title To Or Possession Of Property

Loss resulting from your, or anyone acting on your express or implied authority, being induced by any dishonest act to voluntarily part with title to or possession of any property.

4. Insuring Agreement **A.6.** does not cover:

a. Credit Card Transactions

Loss resulting from the use or purported use of credit, debit, charge, access, convenience, identification, stored-value or other cards or the information contained on such cards.

b. Funds Transfer Fraud

Loss resulting from a "fraudulent instruction" directing a financial institution to transfer, pay or deliver "funds" from your "transfer account".

c. Inventory Shortages

Loss, or that part of any loss, the proof of which as to its existence or amount is dependent upon:

(1) An inventory computation; or

(2) A profit and loss computation.

5. Insuring Agreement **A.7.** does not cover:

COMPUTER FRAUD

Loss resulting from the use of any computer to fraudulently cause a transfer of "money", "securities" or "other property".

E. Conditions

1. Conditions Applicable To All Insuring Agreements

a. Additional Premises Or Employees

If, while this policy is in force, you establish any additional "premises" or hire additional "employees", other than through consolidation or merger with, or purchase or acquisition of assets or liabilities of, another entity, such "premises" and "employees" shall automatically be covered under this policy. Notice to us of an increase in the number of "premises" or "employees" need not be given and no additional premium need be paid for the remainder of the Policy Period shown in the Declarations.

b. Cancellation Of Policy

(1) The first Named Insured shown in the Declarations may cancel this policy by mailing or delivering to us advance written notice of cancellation.

(2) We may cancel this policy by mailing or delivering to the first Named Insured written notice of cancellation at least:

(a) 10 days before the effective date of cancellation if we cancel for nonpayment of premium; or

(b) 30 days before the effective date of cancellation if we cancel for any other reason.

(3) We will mail or deliver our notice to the first Named Insured's last mailing address known to us.

(4) Notice of cancellation will state the effective date of cancellation. The policy period will end on that date.

(5) If this policy is cancelled, we will send the first Named Insured any premium refund due. If we cancel, the refund will be pro rata. If the first Named Insured cancels, the refund may be less than pro rata. The cancellation will be effective even if we have not made or offered a refund.

(6) If notice is mailed, proof of mailing will be sufficient proof of notice.

c. Changes

This policy contains all the agreements between you and us concerning the insurance afforded. The first Named Insured shown in the Declarations is authorized to make changes in the terms of this policy with our consent. This policy's terms can be amended or waived only by endorsement issued by us and made a part of this policy.

d. Concealment, Misrepresentation Or Fraud

This policy is void in any case of fraud by you as it relates to this policy at any time. It is also void if you or any other Insured, at any time, intentionally conceal or misrepresent a material fact concerning:

(1) This policy;

(2) The property covered under this policy;

(3) Your interest in the property covered under this policy; or

(4) A claim under this policy.

e. Consolidation – Merger Or Acquisition

If you consolidate or merge with, or purchase or acquire the assets or liabilities of, another entity:

(1) You must give us written notice as soon as possible and obtain our written consent to extend the coverage provided by this policy to such consolidated or merged entity or such purchased or acquired assets or liabilities. We may condition our consent by requiring payment of an additional premium; but

(2) For the first 90 days after the effective date of such consolidation, merger or purchase or acquisition of assets or liabilities, the coverage provided by this policy shall apply to such consolidated or merged entity or such purchased or acquired assets or liabilities, provided that all "occurrences" causing or contributing to a loss involving such consolidation, merger or purchase or acquisition of assets or liabilities, must take place after the effective date of such consolidation, merger or purchase or acquisition of assets or liabilities.

f. Cooperation

You must cooperate with us in all matters pertaining to this policy as stated in its terms and conditions.

g. Duties In The Event Of Loss

After you "discover" a loss or a situation that may result in loss of or damage to "money", "securities" or "other property" you must:

(1) Notify us as soon as possible. If you have reason to believe that any loss (except for loss covered under Insuring Agreement **A.1.** or **A.2.**) involves a violation of law, you must also notify the local law enforcement authorities.

(2) Submit to examination under oath at our request and give us a signed statement of your answers.

(3) Produce for our examination all pertinent records.

(4) Give us a detailed, sworn proof of loss within 120 days.

(5) Cooperate with us in the investigation and settlement of any claim.

h. Employee Benefit Plans

(1) The "employee benefit plans" shown in the Declarations (hereafter referred to as Plan) are included as Insureds under Insuring Agreement **A.1.**

(2) If any Plan is insured jointly with any other entity under this policy, you or the Plan Administrator must select a Limit of Insurance for Insuring Agreement **A.1.** that is sufficient to provide a Limit of Insurance for each Plan that is at least equal to that required if each Plan were separately insured.

(3) With respect to loss sustained or "discovered" by any such Plan, Insuring Agreement **A.1.** is replaced by the following:

We will pay for loss of or damage to "funds" and "other property" resulting directly from fraudulent or dishonest acts committed by an "employee", whether identified or not, acting alone or in collusion with other persons.

(4) If the first Named Insured is an entity other than a Plan, any payment we make for loss sustained by any Plan will be made to the Plan sustaining the loss.

(5) If two or more Plans are insured under this policy, any payment we make for loss:

(a) Sustained by two or more Plans; or

(b) Of commingled "funds" or "other property" of two or more Plans;

resulting directly from an "occurrence" will be made to each Plan sustaining loss in the proportion that the Limit of Insurance required for each Plan bears to the total Limit of Insurance of all Plans sustaining loss.

(6) The Deductible Amount applicable to Insuring Agreement **A.1.** does not apply to loss sustained by any Plan.

i. Examination Of Your Books And Records

We may examine and audit your books and records as they relate to this policy at any time during the Policy Period shown in the Declarations and up to 3 years afterward.

j. Extended Period To Discover Loss

We will pay for loss that you sustained prior to the effective date of cancellation of this policy, which is "discovered" by you:

(1) No later than 1 year from the date of that cancellation. However, this extended period to "discover" loss terminates immediately upon the effective date of any other insurance obtained by you, whether from us or another insurer, replacing in whole or in part the coverage afforded under this policy, whether or not such other insurance provides coverage for loss sustained prior to its effective date.

(2) No later than 1 year from the date of that cancellation with regard to any "employee benefit plans".

k. Inspections And Surveys

(1) We have the right to:

(a) Make inspections and surveys at any time;

(b) Give you reports on the conditions we find; and

(c) Recommend changes.

(2) We are not obligated to make any inspections, surveys, reports or recommendations and any such actions we do undertake relate only to insurability and the premiums to be charged. We do not make safety inspections. We do not undertake to perform the duty of any person or organization to provide for the health or safety of workers or the public. And we do not warrant that conditions:

(a) Are safe or healthful; or

(b) Comply with laws, regulations, codes or standards.

(3) Paragraphs **k.(1)** and **k.(2)** apply not only to us, but also to any rating, advisory, rate service or similar organization which makes insurance inspections, surveys, reports or recommendations.

l. Joint Insured

(1) If more than one Insured is named in the Declarations, the first Named Insured will act for itself and for every other Insured for all purposes of this policy. If the first Named Insured ceases to be covered, then the next Named Insured will become the first Named Insured.

(2) If any Insured, or partner, "member" or officer of that Insured has knowledge of any information relevant to this policy, that knowledge is considered knowledge of every Insured.

(3) An "employee" of any Insured is considered to be an "employee" of every Insured.

                   CR 00 23 05 06   ☐

(4) If this policy or any of its coverages is cancelled as to any Insured, loss sustained by that Insured is covered only if it is "discovered" by you:

(a) No later than 1 year from the date of that cancellation. However, this extended period to "discover" loss terminates immediately upon the effective date of any other insurance obtained by that Insured, whether from us or another insurer, replacing in whole or in part the coverage afforded under this policy, whether or not such other insurance provides coverage for loss sustained prior to its effective date.

(b) No later than 1 year from the date of that cancellation with regard to any "employee benefit plans".

(5) We will not pay more for loss sustained by more than one Insured than the amount we would pay if all such loss had been sustained by one Insured.

(6) Payment by us to the first Named Insured for loss sustained by any Insured, other than an "employee benefit plan", shall fully release us on account of such loss.

m. Legal Action Against Us

You may not bring any legal action against us involving loss:

(1) Unless you have complied with all the terms of this policy;

(2) Until 90 days after you have filed proof of loss with us; and

(3) Unless brought within 2 years from the date you "discovered" the loss.

If any limitation in this Condition is prohibited by law, such limitation is amended so as to equal the minimum period of limitation provided by such law.

n. Liberalization

If we adopt any revision that would broaden the coverage under this policy without additional premium within 45 days prior to or during the Policy Period shown in the Declarations, the broadened coverage will immediately apply to this policy.

o. Loss Sustained During Prior Insurance Issued By Us Or Any Affiliate

(1) Loss Sustained Partly During This Policy And Partly During Prior Insurance

If you "discover" loss during the Policy Period shown in the Declarations, resulting directly from an "occurrence" taking place:

(a) Partly during the Policy Period shown in the Declarations; and

(b) Partly during the Policy Period(s) of any prior cancelled insurance that we or any affiliate issued to you or any predecessor in interest;

and this policy became effective at the time of cancellation of the prior insurance, we will first settle the amount of loss that you sustained during this Policy Period. We will then settle the remaining amount of loss that you sustained during the Policy Period(s) of the prior insurance.

(2) Loss Sustained Entirely During Prior Insurance

If you "discover" loss during the Policy Period shown in the Declarations, resulting directly from an "occurrence" taking place entirely during the Policy Period(s) of any prior cancelled insurance that we or any affiliate issued to you or any predecessor in interest, we will pay for the loss, provided:

(a) This policy became effective at the time of cancellation of the prior insurance; and

(b) The loss would have been covered under this policy had it been in effect at the time of the "occurrence".

We will first settle the amount of loss that you sustained during the most recent prior insurance. We will then settle any remaining amount of loss that you sustained during the Policy Period(s) of any other prior insurance.

(3) In settling loss subject to this Condition:

(a) The most we will pay for the entire loss is the highest single Limit of Insurance applicable during the period of loss, whether such limit was written under this policy or was written under the prior insurance issued by us.

(b) We will apply the applicable Deductible Amount shown in the Declarations to the amount of loss sustained under this policy. If no loss was sustained under this policy, we will apply the Deductible Amount shown in the Declarations to the amount of loss sustained under the most recent prior insurance.

If the Deductible Amount is larger than the amount of loss sustained under this policy, or the most recent prior insurance, we will apply the remaining Deductible Amount to the remaining amount of loss sustained during the prior insurance.

We will not apply any other Deductible Amount that may have been applicable to the loss.

(4) The following examples demonstrate how we will settle losses subject to this Condition **E.1.o.**:

EXAMPLE NO. 1:

The insured sustained a covered loss of $10,000 resulting directly from an "occurrence" taking place during the terms of Policy **A** and Policy **B**.

POLICY A

The current policy. Written at a Limit of Insurance of $50,000 and a Deductible Amount of $5,000.

POLICY B

Issued prior to Policy **A**. Written at a Limit of Insurance of $50,000 and a Deductible Amount of $5,000.

The amount of loss sustained under Policy **A** is $2,500 and under Policy **B** is $7,500.

The highest single Limit of Insurance applicable to this entire loss is $50,000 written under Policy **A**. The Policy **A** Deductible Amount of $5,000 applies. The loss is settled as follows:

1. The amount of loss sustained under Policy **A** ($2,500) is settled first. The amount we will pay is nil ($0.00) because the amount of loss is less than the Deductible Amount (i.e., $2,500 loss - $5,000 deductible = $0.00).

2. The remaining amount of loss sustained under Policy **B** ($7,500) is settled next. The amount recoverable is $5,000 after the remaining Deductible Amount from Policy **A** of $2,500 is applied to the loss (i.e., $7,500 loss - $2,500 deductible = $5,000).

The most we will pay for this loss is $5,000.

EXAMPLE NO. 2:

The insured sustained a covered loss of $250,000 resulting directly from an "occurrence" taking place during the terms of Policy **A** and Policy **B**.

POLICY A

The current policy. Written at a Limit of Insurance of $125,000 and a Deductible Amount of $10,000.

POLICY B

Issued prior to Policy **A**. Written at a Limit of Insurance of $150,000 and a Deductible Amount of $25,000.

The amount of loss sustained under Policy **A** is $175,000 and under Policy **B** is $75,000.

The highest single Limit of Insurance applicable to this entire loss is $150,000 written under Policy **B**. The Policy **A** Deductible Amount of $10,000 applies. The loss is settled as follows:

1. The amount of loss sustained under Policy **A** ($175,000) is settled first. The amount we will pay is the Policy **A** Limit of $125,000 because $175,000 loss - $10,000 deductible = $165,000 which is greater than the $125,000 policy limit.

2. The remaining amount of loss sustained under Policy **B** ($75,000) is settled next. The amount we will pay is $25,000 (i.e., $150,000 Policy **B** limit - $125,000 paid under Policy **A** = $25,000).

The most we will pay for this loss is $150,000.

EXAMPLE NO. 3:

The insured sustained a covered loss of $2,000,000 resulting directly from an "occurrence" taking place during the terms of Policies **A, B, C** and **D**.

POLICY A

The current policy. Written at a Limit of Insurance of $1,000,000 and a Deductible Amount of $100,000.

POLICY B

Issued prior to Policy A. Written at a Limit of Insurance of $750,000 and a Deductible Amount of $75,000.

POLICY C

Issued prior to Policy B. Written at a Limit of Insurance of $500,000 and a Deductible Amount of $50,000.

POLICY D

Issued prior to Policy C. Written at a Limit of Insurance of $500,000 and a Deductible Amount of $50,000.

The amount of loss sustained under Policy A is $350,000, under Policy B is $250,000, under Policy C is $600,000 and under Policy D is $800,000.

The highest single Limit of Insurance applicable to this entire loss is $1,000,000 written under Policy A. The Policy A Deductible Amount of $100,000 applies. The loss is settled as follows:

1. The amount of loss sustained under Policy A ($350,000) is settled first. The amount we will pay is $250,000 (i.e., $350,000 loss - $100,000 deductible = $250,000).

2. The amount of loss sustained under Policy B ($250,000) is settled next. The amount we will pay is $250,000 (no deductible is applied).

3. The amount of loss sustained under Policy C ($600,000) is settled next. The amount we will pay is $500,000, the policy limit (no deductible is applied).

4. We will not make any further payment under Policy D as the maximum amount payable under the highest single Limit of Insurance applying to the loss of $1,000,000 under Policy A has been satisfied.

The most we will pay for this loss is $1,000,000.

p. **Loss Sustained During Prior Insurance Not Issued By Us Or Any Affiliate**

(1) If you "discover" loss during the Policy Period shown in the Declarations, resulting directly from an "occurrence" taking place during the Policy Period of any prior cancelled insurance that was issued to you or a predecessor in interest by another company, and the period of time to discover loss under that insurance had expired, we will pay for the loss under this policy, provided:

(a) This policy became effective at the time of cancellation of the prior insurance; and

(b) The loss would have been covered under this policy had it been in effect at the time of the "occurrence".

(2) In settling loss subject to this Condition:

(a) The most we will pay for the entire loss is the lesser of the Limits of Insurance applicable during the period of loss, whether such limit was written under this policy or was written under the prior cancelled insurance.

(b) We will apply the applicable Deductible Amount shown in the Declarations to the amount of loss sustained under the prior cancelled insurance.

(3) The insurance provided under this Condition is subject to the following:

(a) If loss covered under this Condition is also partially covered under Condition E.1.o., the amount recoverable under this Condition is part of, not in addition to, the amount recoverable under Condition E.1.o.

(b) For loss covered under this Condition that is not subject to Paragraph (3)(a), the amount recoverable under this Condition is part of, not in addition to, the Limit of Insurance applicable to the loss covered under this policy and is limited to the lesser of the amount recoverable under:

(i) This policy as of its effective date; or

(ii) The prior cancelled insurance had it remained in effect.

q. Other Insurance

If other valid and collectible insurance is available to you for loss covered under this policy, our obligations are limited as follows:

(1) Primary Insurance

When this policy is written as primary insurance, and:

(a) You have other insurance subject to the same terms and conditions as this policy, we will pay our share of the covered loss. Our share is the proportion that the applicable Limit of Insurance shown in the Declarations bears to the total limit of all insurance covering the same loss.

(b) You have other insurance covering the same loss other than that described in Paragraph **(1)(a)**, we will only pay for the amount of loss that exceeds:

(i) The Limit of Insurance and Deductible Amount of that other insurance, whether you can collect on it or not; or

(ii) The Deductible Amount shown in the Declarations;

whichever is greater. Our payment for loss is subject to the terms and conditions of this policy.

(2) Excess Insurance

(a) When this policy is written excess over other insurance, we will only pay for the amount of loss that exceeds the Limit of Insurance and Deductible Amount of that other insurance, whether you can collect on it or not. Our payment for loss is subject to the terms and conditions of this policy.

(b) However, if loss covered under this policy is subject to a Deductible, we will reduce the Deductible Amount shown in the Declarations by the sum total of all such other insurance plus any Deductible Amount applicable to that other insurance.

r. Ownership Of Property; Interests Covered

The property covered under this policy is limited to property:

(1) That you own or lease; or

(2) That you hold for others whether or not you are legally liable for the loss of such property.

However, this policy is for your benefit only. It provides no rights or benefits to any other person or organization. Any claim for loss that is covered under this policy must be presented by you.

s. Premiums

The first Named Insured shown in the Declarations:

(1) Is responsible for the payment of all premiums; and

(2) Will be the payee for any return premiums we pay.

t. Records

You must keep records of all property covered under this policy so we can verify the amount of any loss.

u. Recoveries

(1) Any recoveries, whether effected before or after any payment under this policy, whether made by us or you, shall be applied net of the expense of such recovery:

(a) First, to you in satisfaction of your covered loss in excess of the amount paid under this policy;

(b) Second, to us in satisfaction of amounts paid in settlement of your claim;

(c) Third, to you in satisfaction of any Deductible Amount; and

(d) Fourth, to you in satisfaction of any loss not covered under this policy.

(2) Recoveries do not include any recovery:

(a) From insurance, suretyship, reinsurance, security or indemnity taken for our benefit; or

(b) Of original "securities" after duplicates of them have been issued.

v. Territory

This policy covers loss that you sustain resulting directly from an "occurrence" taking place within the United States of America (including its territories and possessions), Puerto Rico and Canada.

w. Transfer Of Your Rights And Duties Under This Policy

(1) Your rights and duties under this policy may not be transferred without our written consent except in the case of death of an individual Named Insured.

© ISO Properties, Inc., 2005

(2) If you die, your rights and duties will be transferred to your legal representative but only while acting within the scope of duties as your legal representative. Until your legal representative is appointed, anyone having temporary custody of your property will have your rights and duties but only with respect to that property.

x. **Transfer Of Your Rights Of Recovery Against Others To Us**

You must transfer to us all your rights of recovery against any person or organization for any loss you sustained and for which we have paid or settled. You must also do everything necessary to secure those rights and do nothing after loss to impair them.

y. **Valuation – Settlement**

(1) The value of any loss for purposes of coverage under this policy shall be determined as follows:

(a) Loss of "money" but only up to and including its face value. We will, at your option, pay for loss of "money" issued by any country other than the United States of America:

(i) At face value in the "money" issued by that country; or

(ii) In the United States of America dollar equivalent determined by the rate of exchange published in *The Wall Street Journal* on the day the loss was "discovered".

(b) Loss of "securities" but only up to and including their value at the close of business on the day the loss was "discovered". We may, at our option:

(i) Pay the market value of such "securities" or replace them in kind, in which event you must assign to us all your rights, title and interest in and to those "securities"; or

(ii) Pay the cost of any Lost Securities Bond required in connection with issuing duplicates of the "securities". However, we will be liable only for the payment of so much of the cost of the bond as would be charged for a bond having a penalty not exceeding the lesser of the:

i. Market value of the "securities" at the close of business on the day the loss was "discovered"; or

ii. The Limit of Insurance applicable to the "securities".

(c) Loss of or damage to "other property" or loss from damage to the "premises" or its exterior for the replacement cost of the property without deduction for depreciation. However, we will not pay more than the least of the following:

(i) The cost to replace the lost or damaged property with property of comparable material and quality and used for the same purpose;

(ii) The amount you actually spend that is necessary to repair or replace the lost or damaged property; or

(iii) The Limit of Insurance applicable to the lost or damaged property.

With regard to Paragraphs **y.(1)(c)(i)** through **y.(1)(c)(iii)**, we will not pay on a replacement cost basis for any loss or damage:

i. Until the lost or damaged property is actually repaired or replaced; and

ii. Unless the repairs or replacement are made as soon as reasonably possible after the loss or damage.

If the lost or damaged property is not repaired or replaced, we will pay on an actual cash value basis.

(2) We will, at your option, settle loss or damage to property other than "money":

(a) In the "money" of the country in which the loss or damage occurred; or

(b) In the United States of America dollar equivalent of the "money" of the country in which the loss or damage occurred determined by the rate of exchange published in *The Wall Street Journal* on the day the loss was "discovered".

(3) Any property that we pay for or replace becomes our property.

2. Conditions Applicable To Insuring Agreement A.1.

a. Termination As To Any Employee

This Insuring Agreement terminates as to any "employee":

(1) As soon as:

(a) You; or

(b) Any of your partners, "members", "managers", officers, directors, or trustees not in collusion with the "employee";

learn of "theft" or any other dishonest act committed by the "employee" whether before or after becoming employed by you.

(2) On the date specified in a notice mailed to the first Named Insured. That date will be at least 30 days after the date of mailing.

We will mail or deliver our notice to the first Named Insured's last mailing address known to us. If notice is mailed, proof of mailing will be sufficient proof of notice.

b. Territory

We will pay for loss caused by any "employee" while temporarily outside the territory specified in the Territory Condition **E.1.v.** for a period of not more than 90 consecutive days.

3. Conditions Applicable To Insuring Agreement A.2.

a. Deductible Amount

The Deductible Amount does not apply to legal expenses paid under Insuring Agreement **A.2.**

b. Electronic And Mechanical Signatures

We will treat signatures that are produced or reproduced electronically, mechanically or by other means the same as handwritten signatures.

c. Proof Of Loss

You must include with your proof of loss any instrument involved in that loss, or, if that is not possible, an affidavit setting forth the amount and cause of loss.

d. Territory

We will cover loss that you sustain resulting directly from an "occurrence" taking place anywhere in the world. Territory Condition **E.1.v.** does not apply to Insuring Agreement **A.2.**

4. Conditions Applicable To Insuring Agreements A.4. And A.5.

a. Armored Motor Vehicle Companies

Under Insuring Agreement **A.5.**, we will only pay for the amount of loss you cannot recover:

(1) Under your contract with the armored motor vehicle company; and

(2) From any insurance or indemnity carried by, or for the benefit of customers of, the armored motor vehicle company.

b. Special Limit Of Insurance For Specified Property

We will only pay up to $5,000 for any one "occurrence" of loss of or damage to:

(1) Precious metals, precious or semi-precious stones, pearls, furs, or completed or partially completed articles made of or containing such materials that constitute the principal value of such articles; or

(2) Manuscripts, drawings, or records of any kind, or the cost of reconstructing them or reproducing any information contained in them.

5. Conditions Applicable To Insuring Agreement A.6.

a. Special Limit Of Insurance For Specified Property

We will only pay up to $5,000 for any one "occurrence" of loss of or damage to manuscripts, drawings, or records of any kind, or the cost of reconstructing them or reproducing any information contained in them.

b. Territory

We will cover loss that you sustain resulting directly from an "occurrence" taking place anywhere in the world. Territory Condition **E.1.v.** does not apply to Insuring Agreement **A.6.**

F. Definitions

1. "Banking premises" means the interior of that portion of any building occupied by a banking institution or similar safe depository.

2. "Counterfeit money" means an imitation of "money" that is intended to deceive and to be taken as genuine.

3. "Custodian" means you, or any of your partners or "members", or any "employee" while having care and custody of property inside the "premises", excluding any person while acting as a "watchperson" or janitor.

4. "Discover" or "discovered" means the time when you first become aware of facts which would cause a reasonable person to assume that a loss of a type covered by this policy has been or will be incurred, regardless of when the act or acts causing or contributing to such loss occurred, even though the exact amount or details of loss may not then be known.

"Discover" or "discovered" also means the time when you first receive notice of an actual or potential claim in which it is alleged that you are liable to a third party under circumstances which, if true, would constitute a loss under this policy.

5. "Employee":

a. "Employee" means:

(1) Any natural person:

(a) While in your service and for the first 30 days immediately after termination of service, unless such termination is due to "theft" or any other dishonest act committed by the "employee";

(b) Who you compensate directly by salary, wages or commissions; and

(c) Who you have the right to direct and control while performing services for you;

(2) Any natural person who is furnished temporarily to you:

(a) To substitute for a permanent "employee" as defined in Paragraph **a.(1)**, who is on leave; or

(b) To meet seasonal or short-term workload conditions;

while that person is subject to your direction and control and performing services for you, excluding, however, any such person while having care and custody of property outside the "premises";

(3) Any natural person who is leased to you under a written agreement between you and a labor leasing firm, to perform duties related to the conduct of your business, but does not mean a temporary employee as defined in Paragraph **a.(2)**;

(4) Any natural person who is:

(a) A trustee, officer, employee, administrator or manager, except an administrator or manager who is an independent contractor, of any "employee benefit plan"; and

(b) A director or trustee of yours while that person is engaged in handling "funds" or "other property" of any "employee benefit plan";

(5) Any natural person who is a former "employee", partner, "member", "manager", director or trustee retained as a consultant while performing services for you;

(6) Any natural person who is a guest student or intern pursuing studies or duties, excluding, however, any such person while having care and custody of property outside the "premises";

(7) Any "employee" of an entity merged or consolidated with you prior to the effective date of this policy; or

(8) Any of your "managers", directors or trustees while:

(a) Performing acts within the scope of the usual duties of an "employee"; or

(b) Acting as a member of any committee duly elected or appointed by resolution of your board of directors or board of trustees to perform specific, as distinguished from general, directorial acts on your behalf.

b. "Employee" does not mean any agent, broker, factor, commission merchant, consignee, independent contractor or representative of the same general character not specified in Paragraph **5.a.**

6. "Employee benefit plan" means any welfare or pension benefit plan shown in the Declarations that you sponsor and which is subject to the Employee Retirement Income Security Act of 1974 (ERISA) and any amendments thereto.

7. "Forgery" means the signing of the name of another person or organization with intent to deceive; it does not mean a signature which consists in whole or in part of one's own name signed with or without authority, in any capacity, for any purpose.

8. "Fraudulent instruction" means:

a. An electronic, telegraphic, cable, teletype, telefacsimile or telephone instruction which purports to have been transmitted by you, but which was in fact fraudulently transmitted by someone else without your knowledge or consent;

b. A written instruction (other than those described in Insuring Agreement **A.2.**) issued by you, which was forged or altered by someone other than you without your knowledge or consent, or which purports to have been issued by you, but was in fact fraudulently issued without your knowledge or consent; or

c. An electronic, telegraphic, cable, teletype, telefacsimile, telephone or written instruction initially received by you which purports to have been transmitted by an "employee" but which was in fact fraudulently transmitted by someone else without your or the "employee's" knowledge or consent.

9. "Funds" means "money" and "securities".

10. "Manager" means a person serving in a directorial capacity for a limited liability company.

11. "Member" means an owner of a limited liability company represented by its membership interest, who also may serve as a "manager".

12. "Messenger" means you, or a relative of yours, or any of your partners or "members", or any "employee" while having care and custody of property outside the "premises".

13. "Money" means:

a. Currency, coins and bank notes in current use and having a face value; and

b. Travelers checks, register checks and money orders held for sale to the public.

14. "Occurrence" means:

a. Under Insuring Agreement **A.1.**:

(1) An individual act;

(2) The combined total of all separate acts whether or not related; or

(3) A series of acts whether or not related;

committed by an "employee" acting alone or in collusion with other persons, during the Policy Period shown in the Declarations, except as provided under Condition **E.1.o.** or **E.1.p.**

b. Under Insuring Agreement **A.2.**:

(1) An individual act;

(2) The combined total of all separate acts whether or not related; or

(3) A series of acts whether or not related;

committed by a person acting alone or in collusion with other persons, involving one or more instruments, during the Policy Period shown in the Declarations, except as provided under Condition **E.1.o.** or **E.1.p.**

c. Under All Other Insuring Agreements:

(1) An individual act or event;

(2) The combined total of all separate acts or events whether or not related; or

(3) A series of acts or events whether or not related;

committed by a person acting alone or in collusion with other persons, or not committed by any person, during the Policy Period shown in the Declarations, except as provided under Condition **E.1.o.** or **E.1.p.**

15. "Other property" means any tangible property other than "money" and "securities" that has intrinsic value. "Other property" does not include computer programs, electronic data or any property specifically excluded under this policy.

16. "Premises" means the interior of that portion of any building you occupy in conducting your business.

17. "Robbery" means the unlawful taking of property from the care and custody of a person by one who has:

a. Caused or threatened to cause that person bodily harm; or

b. Committed an obviously unlawful act witnessed by that person.

18. "Safe burglary" means the unlawful taking of:

a. Property from within a locked safe or vault by a person unlawfully entering the safe or vault as evidenced by marks of forcible entry upon its exterior; or

b. A safe or vault from inside the "premises".

19. "Securities" means negotiable and nonnegotiable instruments or contracts representing either "money" or property and includes:

a. Tokens, tickets, revenue and other stamps (whether represented by actual stamps or unused value in a meter) in current use; and

b. Evidences of debt issued in connection with credit or charge cards, which cards are not issued by you;

but does not include "money".

20. "Theft" means the unlawful taking of property to the deprivation of the Insured.

21. "Transfer account" means an account maintained by you at a financial institution from which you can initiate the transfer, payment or delivery of "funds":

  a. By means of electronic, telegraphic, cable, teletype, telefacsimile or telephone instructions communicated directly through an electronic funds transfer system; or

  b. By means of written instructions (other than those described in Insuring Agreement **A.2.**) establishing the conditions under which such transfers are to be initiated by such financial institution through an electronic funds transfer system.

22. "Watchperson" means any person you retain specifically to have care and custody of property inside the "premises" and who has no other duties.

Exhibit B

COMMERCIAL CRIME POLICY (DISCOVERY FORM)
STANDARD FORM NO. CR 00 22 05 06

CRIME AND FIDELITY
CR 00 22 05 06

COMMERCIAL CRIME POLICY
(DISCOVERY FORM)

Various provisions in this policy restrict coverage. Read the entire policy carefully to determine rights, duties and what is or is not covered.

Throughout this policy the words "you" and "your" refer to the Named Insured shown in the Declarations. The words "we", "us" and "our" refer to the Company providing this insurance.

Other words and phrases that appear in quotation marks have special meaning. Refer to Section **F.** Definitions.

A. Insuring Agreements

Coverage is provided under the following Insuring Agreements for which a Limit of Insurance is shown in the Declarations and applies to loss that you sustain resulting directly from an "occurrence" taking place at any time which is "discovered" by you during the Policy Period shown in the Declarations or during the period of time provided in the Extended Period To Discover Loss Condition **E.1.j.:**

1. Employee Theft

We will pay for loss of or damage to "money", "securities" and "other property" resulting directly from "theft" committed by an "employee", whether identified or not, acting alone or in collusion with other persons.

For the purposes of this Insuring Agreement, "theft" shall also include forgery.

2. Forgery Or Alteration

a. We will pay for loss resulting directly from "forgery" or alteration of checks, drafts, promissory notes, or similar written promises, orders or directions to pay a sum certain in "money" that are:

(1) Made or drawn by or drawn upon you; or

(2) Made or drawn by one acting as your agent;

or that are purported to have been so made or drawn.

For the purposes of this Insuring Agreement, a substitute check as defined in the Check Clearing for the 21st Century Act shall be treated the same as the original it replaced.

b. If you are sued for refusing to pay any instrument covered in Paragraph **2.a.**, on the basis that it has been forged or altered, and you have our written consent to defend against the suit, we will pay for any reasonable legal expenses that you incur and pay in that defense. The amount that we will pay is in addition to the Limit of Insurance applicable to this Insuring Agreement.

3. Inside The Premises – Theft Of Money And Securities

a. We will pay for loss of "money" and "securities" inside the "premises" or "banking premises":

(1) Resulting directly from "theft" committed by a person present inside such "premises" or "banking premises"; or

(2) Resulting directly from disappearance or destruction.

b. We will pay for loss from damage to the "premises" or its exterior resulting directly from an actual or attempted "theft" of "money" and "securities", if you are the owner of the "premises" or are liable for damage to it.

c. We will pay for loss of or damage to a locked safe, vault, cash register, cash box or cash drawer located inside the "premises" resulting directly from an actual or attempted "theft" of or unlawful entry into those containers.

4. Inside The Premises – Robbery Or Safe Burglary Of Other Property

a. We will pay for loss of or damage to "other property":

(1) Inside the "premises" resulting directly from an actual or attempted "robbery" of a "custodian"; or

(2) Inside the "premises" in a safe or vault resulting directly from an actual or attempted "safe burglary".

b. We will pay for loss from damage to the "premises" or its exterior resulting directly from an actual or attempted "robbery" or "safe burglary" of "other property", if you are the owner of the "premises" or are liable for damage to it.

c. We will pay for loss of or damage to a locked safe or vault located inside the "premises" resulting directly from an actual or attempted "robbery" or "safe burglary".

5. Outside The Premises

a. We will pay for loss of "money" and "securities" outside the "premises" in the care and custody of a "messenger" or an armored motor vehicle company resulting directly from "theft", disappearance or destruction.

b. We will pay for loss of or damage to "other property" outside the "premises" in the care and custody of a "messenger" or an armored motor vehicle company resulting directly from an actual or attempted "robbery".

6. Computer Fraud

We will pay for loss of or damage to "money", "securities" and "other property" resulting directly from the use of any computer to fraudulently cause a transfer of that property from inside the "premises" or "banking premises":

a. To a person (other than a "messenger") outside those "premises"; or

b. To a place outside those "premises".

7. Funds Transfer Fraud

We will pay for loss of "funds" resulting directly from a "fraudulent instruction" directing a financial institution to transfer, pay or deliver "funds" from your "transfer account".

8. Money Orders And Counterfeit Money

We will pay for loss resulting directly from your having accepted in good faith, in exchange for merchandise, "money" or services:

a. Money orders issued by any post office, express company or bank that are not paid upon presentation; or

b. "Counterfeit money" that is acquired during the regular course of business.

B. Limit Of Insurance

The most we will pay for all loss resulting directly from an "occurrence" is the applicable Limit of Insurance shown in the Declarations.

If any loss is covered under more than one Insuring Agreement or Coverage, the most we will pay for such loss shall not exceed the largest Limit of Insurance available under any one of those Insuring Agreements or Coverages.

C. Deductible

We will not pay for loss resulting directly from an "occurrence" unless the amount of loss exceeds the Deductible Amount shown in the Declarations. We will then pay the amount of loss in excess of the Deductible Amount, up to the Limit of Insurance.

D. Exclusions

1. This policy does not cover:

a. **Acts Committed By You, Your Partners Or Your Members**

Loss resulting from "theft" or any other dishonest act committed by:

(1) You; or

(2) Any of your partners or "members";

whether acting alone or in collusion with other persons.

b. **Acts Of Employees Learned Of By You Prior To The Policy Period**

Loss caused by an "employee" if the "employee" had also committed "theft" or any other dishonest act prior to the effective date of this policy and you or any of your partners, "members", "managers", officers, directors or trustees, not in collusion with the "employee", learned of that "theft" or dishonest act prior to the Policy Period shown in the Declarations.

c. **Acts Of Employees, Managers, Directors, Trustees Or Representatives**

Loss resulting from "theft" or any other dishonest act committed by any of your "employees", "managers", directors, trustees or authorized representatives:

(1) Whether acting alone or in collusion with other persons; or

(2) While performing services for you or otherwise;

except when covered under Insuring Agreement **A.1.**

d. **Confidential Information**

Loss resulting from:

(1) The unauthorized disclosure of your confidential information including, but not limited to, patents, trade secrets, processing methods or customer lists; or

© ISO Properties, Inc., 2005   CR 00 22 05 06

(2) The unauthorized use or disclosure of confidential information of another person or entity which is held by you including, but not limited to, financial information, personal information, credit card information or similar non-public information.

e. Governmental Action

Loss resulting from seizure or destruction of property by order of governmental authority.

f. Indirect Loss

Loss that is an indirect result of an "occurrence" covered by this policy including, but not limited to, loss resulting from:

(1) Your inability to realize income that you would have realized had there been no loss of or damage to "money", "securities" or "other property".

(2) Payment of damages of any type for which you are legally liable. But, we will pay compensatory damages arising directly from a loss covered under this policy.

(3) Payment of costs, fees or other expenses you incur in establishing either the existence or the amount of loss under this policy.

g. Legal Fees, Costs And Expenses

Fees, costs and expenses incurred by you which are related to any legal action, except when covered under Insuring Agreement **A.2.**

h. Nuclear Hazard

Loss or damage resulting from nuclear reaction or radiation, or radioactive contamination, however caused.

i. Pollution

Loss or damage caused by or resulting from pollution. Pollution means the discharge, dispersal, seepage, migration, release or escape of any solid, liquid, gaseous or thermal irritant or contaminant, including smoke, vapor, soot, fumes, acids, alkalis, chemicals and waste. Waste includes materials to be recycled, reconditioned or reclaimed.

j. War And Military Action

Loss or damage resulting from:

(1) War, including undeclared or civil war;

(2) Warlike action by a military force, including action in hindering or defending against an actual or expected attack, by any government, sovereign or other authority using military personnel or other agents; or

(3) Insurrection, rebellion, revolution, usurped power, or action taken by governmental authority in hindering or defending against any of these.

2. Insuring Agreement **A.1.** does not cover:

a. Inventory Shortages

Loss, or that part of any loss, the proof of which as to its existence or amount is dependent upon:

(1) An inventory computation; or

(2) A profit and loss computation.

However, where you establish wholly apart from such computations that you have sustained a loss, then you may offer your inventory records and actual physical count of inventory in support of the amount of loss claimed.

b. Trading

Loss resulting from trading, whether in your name or in a genuine or fictitious account.

c. Warehouse Receipts

Loss resulting from the fraudulent or dishonest signing, issuing, cancelling or failing to cancel, a warehouse receipt or any papers connected with it.

3. Insuring Agreements **A.3., A.4.** and **A.5.** do not cover:

a. Accounting Or Arithmetical Errors Or Omissions

Loss resulting from accounting or arithmetical errors or omissions.

b. Exchanges Or Purchases

Loss resulting from the giving or surrendering of property in any exchange or purchase.

c. Fire

Loss or damage resulting from fire, however caused, except:

(1) Loss of or damage to "money" and "securities"; and

(2) Loss from damage to a safe or vault.

d. Money Operated Devices

Loss of property contained in any money operated device unless the amount of "money" deposited in it is recorded by a continuous recording instrument in the device.

e. Motor Vehicles Or Equipment And Accessories

Loss of or damage to motor vehicles, trailers or semi-trailers or equipment and accessories attached to them.

f. Transfer Or Surrender Of Property

(1) Loss of or damage to property after it has been transferred or surrendered to a person or place outside the "premises" or "banking premises":

(a) On the basis of unauthorized instructions;

(b) As a result of a threat to do bodily harm to any person;

(c) As a result of a threat to do damage to any property;

(d) As a result of a threat to introduce a denial of service attack into your computer system;

(e) As a result of a threat to introduce a virus or other malicious instruction into your computer system which is designed to damage, destroy or corrupt data or computer programs stored within your computer system;

(f) As a result of a threat to contaminate, pollute or render substandard your products or goods; or

(g) As a result of a threat to disseminate, divulge or utilize:

(i) Your confidential information; or

(ii) Weaknesses in the source code within your computer system.

(2) But, this Exclusion does not apply under Insuring Agreement **A.5.** to loss of "money", "securities" or "other property" while outside the "premises" in the care and custody of a "messenger" if you:

(a) Had no knowledge of any threat at the time the conveyance began; or

(b) Had knowledge of a threat at the time the conveyance began, but the loss was not related to the threat.

g. Vandalism

Loss from damage to the "premises" or its exterior, or to any safe, vault, cash register, cash box, cash drawer or "other property" by vandalism or malicious mischief.

h. Voluntary Parting Of Title To Or Possession Of Property

Loss resulting from your, or anyone acting on your express or implied authority, being induced by any dishonest act to voluntarily part with title to or possession of any property.

4. Insuring Agreement **A.6.** does not cover:

a. Credit Card Transactions

Loss resulting from the use or purported use of credit, debit, charge, access, convenience, identification, stored-value or other cards or the information contained on such cards.

b. Funds Transfer Fraud

Loss resulting from a "fraudulent instruction" directing a financial institution to transfer, pay or deliver "funds" from your "transfer account".

c. Inventory Shortages

Loss, or that part of any loss, the proof of which as to its existence or amount is dependent upon:

(1) An inventory computation; or

(2) A profit and loss computation.

5. Insuring Agreement **A.7.** does not cover:

COMPUTER FRAUD

Loss resulting from the use of any computer to fraudulently cause a transfer of "money", "securities" or "other property".

E. Conditions

1. **Conditions Applicable To All Insuring Agreements**

a. Additional Premises Or Employees

If, while this policy is in force, you establish any additional "premises" or hire additional "employees", other than through consolidation or merger with, or purchase or acquisition of assets or liabilities of, another entity, such "premises" and "employees" shall automatically be covered under this policy. Notice to us of an increase in the number of "premises" or "employees" need not be given and no additional premium need be paid for the remainder of the Policy Period shown in the Declarations.

b. Cancellation Of Policy

(1) The first Named Insured shown in the Declarations may cancel this policy by mailing or delivering to us advance written notice of cancellation.

(2) We may cancel this policy by mailing or delivering to the first Named Insured written notice of cancellation at least:

(a) 10 days before the effective date of cancellation if we cancel for non-payment of premium; or

(b) 30 days before the effective date of cancellation if we cancel for any other reason.

(3) We will mail or deliver our notice to the first Named Insured's last mailing address known to us.

(4) Notice of cancellation will state the effective date of cancellation. The policy period will end on that date.

(5) If this policy is cancelled, we will send the first Named Insured any premium refund due. If we cancel, the refund will be pro rata. If the first Named Insured cancels, the refund may be less than pro rata. The cancellation will be effective even if we have not made or offered a refund.

(6) If notice is mailed, proof of mailing will be sufficient proof of notice.

c. Changes

This policy contains all the agreements between you and us concerning the insurance afforded. The first Named Insured shown in the Declarations is authorized to make changes in the terms of this policy with our consent. This policy's terms can be amended or waived only by endorsement issued by us and made a part of this policy.

d. Concealment, Misrepresentation Or Fraud

This policy is void in any case of fraud by you as it relates to this policy at any time. It is also void if you or any other Insured, at any time, intentionally conceal or misrepresent a material fact concerning:

(1) This policy;

(2) The property covered under this policy;

(3) Your interest in the property covered under this policy; or

(4) A claim under this policy.

e. Consolidation – Merger Or Acquisition

If you consolidate or merge with, or purchase or acquire the assets or liabilities of, another entity:

(1) You must give us written notice as soon as possible and obtain our written consent to extend the coverage provided by this policy to such consolidated or merged entity or such purchased or acquired assets or liabilities. We may condition our consent by requiring payment of an additional premium; but

(2) For the first 90 days after the effective date of such consolidation, merger or purchase or acquisition of assets or liabilities, the coverage provided by this policy shall apply to such consolidated or merged entity or such purchased or acquired assets or liabilities, provided that all "occurrences" causing or contributing to a loss involving such consolidation, merger or purchase or acquisition of assets or liabilities, must take place after the effective date of such consolidation, merger or purchase or acquisition of assets or liabilities.

f. Cooperation

You must cooperate with us in all matters pertaining to this policy as stated in its terms and conditions.

g. Duties In The Event Of Loss

After you "discover" a loss or a situation that may result in loss of or damage to "money", "securities" or "other property" you must:

(1) Notify us as soon as possible. If you have reason to believe that any loss (except for loss covered under Insuring Agreement A.1. or A.2.) involves a violation of law, you must also notify the local law enforcement authorities.

(2) Submit to examination under oath at our request and give us a signed statement of your answers.

(3) Produce for our examination all pertinent records.

(4) Give us a detailed, sworn proof of loss within 120 days.

(5) Cooperate with us in the investigation and settlement of any claim.

h. Employee Benefit Plans

(1) The "employee benefit plans" shown in the Declarations (hereafter referred to as Plan) are included as Insureds under Insuring Agreement **A.1.**

(2) If any Plan is insured jointly with any other entity under this policy, you or the Plan Administrator must select a Limit of Insurance for Insuring Agreement **A.1.** that is sufficient to provide a Limit of Insurance for each Plan that is at least equal to that required if each Plan were separately insured.

(3) With respect to loss sustained or "discovered" by any such Plan, Insuring Agreement **A.1.** is replaced by the following:

We will pay for loss of or damage to "funds" and "other property" resulting directly from fraudulent or dishonest acts committed by an "employee", whether identified or not, acting alone or in collusion with other persons.

(4) If the first Named Insured is an entity other than a Plan, any payment we make for loss sustained by any Plan will be made to the Plan sustaining the loss.

(5) If two or more Plans are insured under this policy, any payment we make for loss:

(a) Sustained by two or more Plans; or

(b) Of commingled "funds" or "other property" of two or more Plans;

resulting directly from an "occurrence", will be made to each Plan sustaining loss in the proportion that the Limit of Insurance required for each Plan bears to the total Limit of Insurance of all Plans sustaining loss.

(6) The Deductible Amount applicable to Insuring Agreement **A.1.** does not apply to loss sustained by any Plan.

i. Examination Of Your Books And Records

We may examine and audit your books and records as they relate to this policy at any time during the Policy Period shown in the Declarations and up to 3 years afterward.

j. Extended Period To Discover Loss

We will pay for loss that you sustained prior to the effective date of cancellation of this policy, which is "discovered" by you:

(1) No later than 60 days from the date of that cancellation. However, this extended period to "discover" loss terminates immediately upon the effective date of any other insurance obtained by you, whether from us or another insurer, replacing in whole or in part the coverage afforded under this policy, whether or not such other insurance provides coverage for loss sustained prior to its effective date.

(2) No later than 1 year from the date of that cancellation with regard to any "employee benefit plans".

k. Inspections And Surveys

(1) We have the right to:

(a) Make inspections and surveys at any time;

(b) Give you reports on the conditions we find; and

(c) Recommend changes.

(2) We are not obligated to make any inspections, surveys, reports or recommendations and any such actions we do undertake relate only to insurability and the premiums to be charged. We do not make safety inspections. We do not undertake to perform the duty of any person or organization to provide for the health or safety of workers or the public. And we do not warrant that conditions:

(a) Are safe or healthful; or

(b) Comply with laws, regulations, codes or standards.

(3) Paragraphs **k.(1)** and **k.(2)** apply not only to us, but also to any rating, advisory, rate service or similar organization which makes insurance inspections, surveys, reports or recommendations.

l. Joint Insured

(1) If more than one Insured is named in the Declarations, the first Named Insured will act for itself and for every other Insured for all purposes of this policy. If the first Named Insured ceases to be covered, then the next Named Insured will become the first Named Insured.

       CR 00 22 05 06

(2) If any Insured, or partner, "member" or officer of that Insured has knowledge of any information relevant to this policy, that knowledge is considered knowledge of every Insured.

(3) An "employee" of any Insured is considered to be an "employee" of every Insured.

(4) If this policy or any of its coverages is cancelled as to any Insured, loss sustained by that Insured is covered only if it is "discovered" by you:

(a) No later than 60 days from the date of that cancellation. However, this extended period to "discover" loss terminates immediately upon the effective date of any other insurance obtained by that Insured, whether from us or another insurer, replacing in whole or in part the coverage afforded under this policy, whether or not such other insurance provides coverage for loss sustained prior to its effective date.

(b) No later than 1 year from the date of that cancellation with regard to any "employee benefit plans".

(5) We will not pay more for loss sustained by more than one Insured than the amount we would pay if all such loss had been sustained by one Insured.

(6) Payment by us to the first Named Insured for loss sustained by any Insured, other than an "employee benefit plan", shall fully release us on account of such loss.

m. Legal Action Against Us

You may not bring any legal action against us involving loss:

(1) Unless you have complied with all the terms of this policy;

(2) Until 90 days after you have filed proof of loss with us; and

(3) Unless brought within 2 years from the date you "discovered" the loss.

If any limitation in this Condition is prohibited by law, such limitation is amended so as to equal the minimum period of limitation provided by such law.

n. Liberalization

If we adopt any revision that would broaden the coverage under this policy without additional premium within 45 days prior to or during the Policy Period shown in the Declarations, the broadened coverage will immediately apply to this policy.

o. Other Insurance

If other valid and collectible insurance is available to you for loss covered under this policy, our obligations are limited as follows:

(1) Primary Insurance

When this policy is written as primary insurance, and:

(a) You have other insurance subject to the same terms and conditions as this policy, we will pay our share of the covered loss. Our share is the proportion that the applicable Limit of Insurance shown in the Declarations bears to the total limit of all insurance covering the same loss.

(b) You have other insurance covering the same loss other than that described in Paragraph **(1)(a)**, we will only pay for the amount of loss that exceeds:

(i) The Limit of Insurance and Deductible Amount of that other insurance, whether you can collect on it or not; or

(ii) The Deductible Amount shown in the Declarations;

whichever is greater. Our payment for loss is subject to the terms and conditions of this policy.

(2) Excess Insurance

(a) When this policy is written excess over other insurance, we will only pay for the amount of loss that exceeds the Limit of Insurance and Deductible Amount of that other insurance, whether you can collect on it or not. Our payment for loss is subject to the terms and conditions of this policy.

(b) However, if loss covered under this policy is subject to a Deductible, we will reduce the Deductible Amount shown in the Declarations by the sum total of all such other insurance plus any Deductible Amount applicable to that other insurance.

p. Ownership Of Property; Interests Covered

The property covered under this policy is limited to property:

(1) That you own or lease; or

(2) That you hold for others whether or not you are legally liable for the loss of such property.

However, this policy is for your benefit only. It provides no rights or benefits to any other person or organization. Any claim for loss that is covered under this policy must be presented by you.

q. Policy Bridge – Discovery Replacing Loss Sustained

(1) If this policy replaces insurance that provided you with an extended period of time after cancellation in which to discover loss and which did not terminate at the time this policy became effective:

(a) We will not pay for any loss that occurred during the Policy Period of that prior insurance which is "discovered" by you during the extended period to "discover" loss, unless the amount of loss exceeds the Limit of Insurance and Deductible Amount of that prior insurance. In that case, we will pay for the excess loss subject to the terms and conditions of this policy.

(b) However, any payment we make for the excess loss will not be greater than the difference between the Limit of Insurance and Deductible Amount of that prior insurance and the Limit of Insurance shown in the Declarations. We will not apply the Deductible Amount shown in the Declarations to this excess loss.

(2) The Other Insurance Condition **E.1.o.** does not apply to this Condition.

r. Premiums

The first Named Insured shown in the Declarations:

(1) Is responsible for the payment of all premiums; and

(2) Will be the payee for any return premiums we pay.

s. Records

You must keep records of all property covered under this policy so we can verify the amount of any loss.

t. Recoveries

(1) Any recoveries, whether effected before or after any payment under this policy, whether made by us or you, shall be applied net of the expense of such recovery:

(a) First, to you in satisfaction of your covered loss in excess of the amount paid under this policy;

(b) Second, to us in satisfaction of amounts paid in settlement of your claim;

(c) Third, to you in satisfaction of any Deductible Amount; and

(d) Fourth, to you in satisfaction of any loss not covered under this policy.

(2) Recoveries do not include any recovery:

(a) From insurance, suretyship, reinsurance, security or indemnity taken for our benefit; or

(b) Of original "securities" after duplicates of them have been issued.

u. Territory

This policy covers loss that you sustain resulting directly from an "occurrence" taking place within the United States of America (including its territories and possessions), Puerto Rico and Canada.

v. Transfer Of Your Rights And Duties Under This Policy

(1) Your rights and duties under this policy may not be transferred without our written consent except in the case of death of an individual Named Insured.

(2) If you die, your rights and duties will be transferred to your legal representative but only while acting within the scope of duties as your legal representative. Until your legal representative is appointed, anyone having proper temporary custody of your property will have your rights and duties but only with respect to that property.

w. Transfer Of Your Rights Of Recovery Against Others To Us

You must transfer to us all your rights of recovery against any person or organization for any loss you sustained and for which we have paid or settled. You must also do everything necessary to secure those rights and do nothing after loss to impair them.

                   CR 00 22 05 06

x. **Valuation – Settlement**

(1) The value of any loss for purposes of coverage under this policy shall be determined as follows:

(a) Loss of "money" but only up to and including its face value. We will, at your option, pay for loss of "money" issued by any country other than the United States of America:

(i) At face value in the "money" issued by that country; or

(ii) In the United States of America dollar equivalent determined by the rate of exchange published in *The Wall Street Journal* on the day the loss was "discovered".

(b) Loss of "securities" but only up to and including their value at the close of business on the day the loss was "discovered". We may, at our option:

(i) Pay the market value of such "securities" or replace them in kind, in which event you must assign to us all your rights, title and interest in and to those "securities"; or

(ii) Pay the cost of any Lost Securities Bond required in connection with issuing duplicates of the "securities". However, we will be liable only for the payment of so much of the cost of the bond as would be charged for a bond having a penalty not exceeding the lesser of:

i. Market value of the "securities" at the close of business on the day the loss was "discovered"; or

ii. The Limit of Insurance applicable to the "securities".

(c) Loss of or damage to "other property" or loss from damage to the "premises" or its exterior for the replacement cost of the property without deduction for depreciation. However, we will not pay more than the least of the following:

(i) The cost to replace the lost or damaged property with property of comparable material and quality and used for the same purpose;

(ii) The amount you actually spend that is necessary to repair or replace the lost or damaged property; or

(iii) The Limit of Insurance applicable to the lost or damaged property.

With regard to Paragraphs **x.(1)(c)(i)** through **x.(1)(c)(iii)**, we will not pay on a replacement cost basis for any loss or damage:

i. Until the lost or damaged property is actually repaired or replaced; and

ii. Unless the repairs or replacement are made as soon as reasonably possible after the loss or damage.

If the lost or damaged property is not repaired or replaced, we will pay on an actual cash value basis.

(2) We will, at your option, settle loss or damage to property other than "money":

(a) In the "money" of the country in which the loss or damage occurred; or

(b) In the United States of America dollar equivalent of the "money" of the country in which the loss or damage occurred determined by the rate of exchange published in *The Wall Street Journal* on the day the loss was "discovered".

(3) Any property that we pay for or replace becomes our property.

2. **Conditions Applicable To Insuring Agreement A.1.**

a. **Termination As To Any Employee**

This Insuring Agreement terminates as to any "employee":

(1) As soon as:

(a) You; or

(b) Any of your partners, "members", "managers", officers, directors or trustees not in collusion with the "employee";

learn of "theft" or any other dishonest act committed by the "employee" whether before or after becoming employed by you.

(2) On the date specified in a notice mailed to the first Named Insured. That date will be at least 30 days after the date of mailing.

We will mail or deliver our notice to the first Named Insured's last mailing address known to us. If notice is mailed, proof of mailing will be sufficient proof of notice.

b. Territory

We will pay for loss caused by any "employee" while temporarily outside the territory specified in the Territory Condition **E.1.u.** for a period of not more than 90 consecutive days.

3. Conditions Applicable To Insuring Agreement A.2.

a. Deductible Amount

The Deductible Amount does not apply to legal expenses paid under Insuring Agreement **A.2.**

b. Electronic And Mechanical Signatures

We will treat signatures that are produced or reproduced electronically, mechanically or by other means the same as handwritten signatures.

c. Proof Of Loss

You must include with your proof of loss any instrument involved in that loss, or, if that is not possible, an affidavit setting forth the amount and cause of loss.

d. Territory

We will cover loss that you sustain resulting directly from an "occurrence" taking place anywhere in the world. Territory Condition **E.1.u.** does not apply to Insuring Agreement **A.2.**

4. Conditions Applicable To Insuring Agreements A.4. And A.5.

a. Armored Motor Vehicle Companies

Under Insuring Agreement **A.5.**, we will only pay for the amount of loss you cannot recover:

(1) Under your contract with the armored motor vehicle company; and

(2) From any insurance or indemnity carried by, or for the benefit of customers of, the armored motor vehicle company.

b. Special Limit Of Insurance For Specified Property

We will only pay up to $5,000 for any one "occurrence" of loss of or damage to:

(1) Precious metals, precious or semi-precious stones, pearls, furs, or completed or partially completed articles made of or containing such materials that constitute the principal value of such articles; or

(2) Manuscripts, drawings, or records of any kind, or the cost of reconstructing them or reproducing any information contained in them.

5. Conditions Applicable To Insuring Agreement A.6.

a. Special Limit Of Insurance For Specified Property

We will only pay up to $5,000 for any one "occurrence" of loss of or damage to manuscripts, drawings, or records of any kind, or the cost of reconstructing them or reproducing any information contained in them.

b. Territory

We will cover loss that you sustain resulting directly from an "occurrence" taking place anywhere in the world. Territory Condition **E.1.u.** does not apply to Insuring Agreement **A.6.**

F. Definitions

1. "Banking premises" means the interior of that portion of any building occupied by a banking institution or similar safe depository.

2. "Counterfeit money" means an imitation of "money" that is intended to deceive and to be taken as genuine.

3. "Custodian" means you, or any of your partners or "members", or any "employee" while having care and custody of property inside the "premises", excluding any person while acting as a "watchperson" or janitor.

4. "Discover" or "discovered" means the time when you first become aware of facts which would cause a reasonable person to assume that a loss of a type covered by this policy has been or will be incurred, regardless of when the act or acts causing or contributing to such loss occurred, even though the exact amount or details of loss may not then be known.

APPENDIX 871

"Discover" or "discovered" also means the time when you first receive notice of an actual or potential claim in which it is alleged that you are liable to a third party under circumstances which, if true, would constitute a loss under this policy.

5. "Employee":

a. "Employee" means:

(1) Any natural person:

(a) While in your service and for the first 30 days immediately after termination of service, unless such termination is due to "theft" or any other dishonest act committed by the "employee";

(b) Who you compensate directly by salary, wages or commissions; and

(c) Who you have the right to direct and control while performing services for you;

(2) Any natural person who is furnished temporarily to you:

(a) To substitute for a permanent "employee" as defined in Paragraph a.(1), who is on leave; or

(b) To meet seasonal or short-term work load conditions;

while that person is subject to your direction and control and performing services for you, excluding, however, any such person while having care and custody of property outside the "premises";

(3) Any natural person who is leased to you under a written agreement between you and a labor leasing firm, to perform duties related to the conduct of your business, but does not mean a temporary employee as defined in Paragraph a.(2);

(4) Any natural person who is:

(a) A trustee, officer, employee, administrator or manager, except an administrator or manager who is an independent contractor, of any "employee benefit plan"; and

(b) A director or trustee of yours while that person is engaged in handling "funds" or "other property" of any "employee benefit plan";

(5) Any natural person who is a former "employee", partner, "member", "manager", director or trustee retained as a consultant while performing services for you;

(6) Any natural person who is a guest student or intern pursuing studies or duties, excluding, however, any such person while having care and custody of property outside the "premises";

(7) Any "employee" of an entity merged or consolidated with you prior to the effective date of this policy; or

(8) Any of your "managers", directors or trustees while:

(a) Performing acts within the scope of the usual duties of an "employee"; or

(b) Acting as a member of any committee duly elected or appointed by resolution of your board of directors or board of trustees to perform specific, as distinguished from general, directorial acts on your behalf.

b. "Employee" does not mean any agent, broker, factor, commission merchant, consignee, independent contractor or representative of the same general character not specified in Paragraph 5.a.

6. "Employee benefit plan" means any welfare or pension benefit plan shown in the Declarations that you sponsor and which is subject to the Employee Retirement Income Security Act of 1974 (ERISA) and any amendments thereto.

7. "Forgery" means the signing of the name of another person or organization with intent to deceive; it does not mean a signature which consists in whole or in part of one's own name signed with or without authority, in any capacity, for any purpose.

8. "Fraudulent instruction" means:

a. An electronic, telegraphic, cable, teletype, telefacsimile or telephone instruction which purports to have been transmitted by you, but which was in fact fraudulently transmitted by someone else without your knowledge or consent;

b. A written instruction (other than those described in Insuring Agreement A.2.) issued by you, which was forged or altered by someone other than you without your knowledge or consent, or which purports to have been issued by you, but was in fact fraudulently issued without your knowledge or consent; or

CR 00 22 05 06   © ISO Properties, Inc., 2005   **Page 11 of 13**

c. An electronic, telegraphic, cable, teletype, telefacsimile, telephone or written instruction initially received by you which purports to have been transmitted by an "employee" but which was in fact fraudulently transmitted by someone else without your or the "employee's" knowledge or consent.

9. "Funds" means "money" and "securities".

10. "Manager" means a person serving in a directorial capacity for a limited liability company.

11. "Member" means an owner of a limited liability company represented by its membership interest, who also may serve as a "manager".

12. "Messenger" means you, or a relative of yours, or any of your partners or "members", or any "employee" while having care and custody of property outside the "premises".

13. "Money" means:

   a. Currency, coins and bank notes in current use and having a face value; and

   b. Travelers checks, register checks and money orders held for sale to the public.

14. "Occurrence" means:

   a. Under Insuring Agreement A.1.:

      (1) An individual act;

      (2) The combined total of all separate acts whether or not related; or

      (3) A series of acts whether or not related;

      committed by an "employee" acting alone or in collusion with other persons, during the Policy Period shown in the Declarations, before such Policy Period or both.

   b. Under Insuring Agreement A.2.:

      (1) An individual act;

      (2) The combined total of all separate acts whether or not related; or

      (3) A series of acts whether or not related;

      committed by a person acting alone or in collusion with other persons, involving one or more instruments, during the Policy Period shown in the Declarations, before such Policy Period or both.

   c. Under All Other Insuring Agreements:

      (1) An individual act or event;

      (2) The combined total of all separate acts or events whether or not related; or

      (3) A series of acts or events whether or not related;

      committed by a person acting alone or in collusion with other persons, or not committed by any person, during the Policy Period shown in the Declarations, before such Policy Period or both.

15. "Other property" means any tangible property other than "money" and "securities" that has intrinsic value. "Other property" does not include computer programs, electronic data or any property specifically excluded under this policy.

16. "Premises" means the interior of that portion of any building you occupy in conducting your business.

17. "Robbery" means the unlawful taking of property from the care and custody of a person by one who has:

   a. Caused or threatened to cause that person bodily harm; or

   b. Committed an obviously unlawful act witnessed by that person.

18. "Safe burglary" means the unlawful taking of:

   a. Property from within a locked safe or vault by a person unlawfully entering the safe or vault as evidenced by marks of forcible entry upon its exterior; or

   b. A safe or vault from inside the "premises".

19. "Securities" means negotiable and nonnegotiable instruments or contracts representing either "money" or property and includes:

   a. Tokens, tickets, revenue and other stamps (whether represented by actual stamps or unused value in a meter) in current use; and

   b. Evidences of debt issued in connection with credit or charge cards, which cards are not issued by you;

   but does not include "money".

20. "Theft" means the unlawful taking of property to the deprivation of the Insured.

21. "Transfer account" means an account maintained by you at a financial institution from which you can initiate the transfer, payment or delivery of "funds":

    a. By means of electronic, telegraphic, cable, teletype, telefacsimile or telephone instructions communicated directly through an electronic funds transfer system; or

    b. By means of written instructions (other than those described in Insuring Agreement **A.2.**) establishing the conditions under which such transfers are to be initiated by such financial institution through an electronic funds transfer system.

22. "Watchperson" means any person you retain specifically to have care and custody of property inside the "premises" and who has no other duties.

Exhibit C

COMMERCIAL CRIME POLICY (DISCOVERY FORM) STANDARD FORM NO. CR 00 22 08 13

CRIME AND FIDELITY
CR 00 22 08 13

COMMERCIAL CRIME POLICY
(DISCOVERY FORM)

Various provisions in this Policy restrict coverage. Read the entire Policy carefully to determine rights, duties and what is or is not covered.

Throughout this Policy, the words "you" and "your" refer to the Named Insured shown in the Declarations. The words "we", "us" and "our" refer to the company providing this insurance.

Other words and phrases that appear in quotation marks have special meaning. Refer to Section **F.** Definitions.

A. Insuring Agreements

Coverage is provided under the following Insuring Agreements for which a Limit Of Insurance is shown in the Declarations and applies to loss that you sustain resulting directly from an "occurrence" taking place at any time which is "discovered" by you during the Policy Period shown in the Declarations or during the period of time provided in the Extended Period To Discover Loss Condition **E.1.j.:**

1. Employee Theft

We will pay for loss of or damage to "money", "securities" and "other property" resulting directly from "theft" committed by an "employee", whether identified or not, acting alone or in collusion with other persons.

For the purposes of this Insuring Agreement, "theft" shall also include forgery.

2. Forgery Or Alteration

a. We will pay for loss resulting directly from "forgery" or alteration of checks, drafts, promissory notes, or similar written promises, orders or directions to pay a sum certain in "money" that are:

(1) Made or drawn by or drawn upon you; or

(2) Made or drawn by one acting as your agent;

or that are purported to have been so made or drawn.

For the purposes of this Insuring Agreement, a substitute check as defined in the Check Clearing for the 21st Century Act shall be treated the same as the original it replaced.

b. If you are sued for refusing to pay any instrument covered in Paragraph **2.a.**, on the basis that it has been forged or altered, and you have our written consent to defend against the suit, we will pay for any reasonable legal expenses that you incur and pay in that defense. The amount that we will pay for such legal expenses is in addition to the Limit of Insurance applicable to this Insuring Agreement.

3. Inside The Premises – Theft Of Money And Securities

We will pay for:

a. Loss of "money" and "securities" inside the "premises" or "financial institution premises":

(1) Resulting directly from "theft" committed by a person present inside such "premises" or "financial institution premises"; or

(2) Resulting directly from disappearance or destruction.

b. Loss from damage to the "premises" or its exterior resulting directly from an actual or attempted "theft" of "money" and "securities", if you are the owner of the "premises" or are liable for damage to it.

c. Loss of or damage to a locked safe, vault, cash register, cash box or cash drawer located inside the "premises" resulting directly from an actual or attempted "theft" of, or unlawful entry into, those containers.

4. Inside The Premises – Robbery Or Safe Burglary Of Other Property

We will pay for:

a. Loss of or damage to "other property":

(1) Inside the "premises" resulting directly from an actual or attempted "robbery" of a "custodian"; or

(2) Inside the "premises" in a safe or vault resulting directly from an actual or attempted "safe burglary".

ANNOTATED COMMERCIAL CRIME INSURANCE POLICY

b. Loss from damage to the "premises" or its exterior resulting directly from an actual or attempted "robbery" or "safe burglary" of "other property", if you are the owner of the "premises" or are liable for damage to it.

c. Loss of or damage to a locked safe or vault located inside the "premises" resulting directly from an actual or attempted "robbery" or "safe burglary".

5. Outside The Premises

We will pay for:

a. Loss of "money" and "securities" outside the "premises" in the care and custody of a "messenger" or an armored motor vehicle company resulting directly from "theft", disappearance or destruction.

b. Loss of or damage to "other property" outside the "premises" in the care and custody of a "messenger" or an armored motor vehicle company resulting directly from an actual or attempted "robbery".

6. Computer And Funds Transfer Fraud

a. We will pay for:

  (1) Loss resulting directly from a fraudulent:

    (a) Entry of "electronic data" or "computer program" into; or

    (b) Change of "electronic data" or "computer program" within;

  any "computer system" owned, leased or operated by you, provided the fraudulent entry or fraudulent change causes, with regard to Paragraphs **6.a.(1)(a)** and **6.a.(1)(b)**:

    (i) "Money", "securities" or "other property" to be transferred, paid or delivered; or

    (ii) Your account at a "financial institution" to be debited or deleted.

  (2) Loss resulting directly from a "fraudulent instruction" directing a "financial institution" to debit your "transfer account" and transfer, pay or deliver "money" or "securities" from that account.

b. As used in Paragraph **6.a.(1)**, fraudulent entry or fraudulent change of "electronic data" or "computer program" shall include such entry or change made by an "employee" acting, in good faith, upon a "fraudulent instruction" received from a computer software contractor who has a written agreement with you to design, implement or service "computer programs" for a "computer system" covered under this Insuring Agreement.

7. Money Orders And Counterfeit Money

We will pay for loss resulting directly from your having, in good faith, accepted in exchange for merchandise, "money" or services:

a. Money orders issued by any post office, express company or "financial institution" that are not paid upon presentation; or

b. "Counterfeit money" that is acquired during the regular course of business.

B. Limit Of Insurance

The most we will pay for all loss resulting directly from an "occurrence" is the applicable Limit Of Insurance shown in the Declarations.

If any loss is covered under more than one Insuring Agreement or coverage, the most we will pay for such loss shall not exceed the largest Limit of Insurance available under any one of those Insuring Agreements or coverages.

C. Deductible

We will not pay for loss resulting directly from an "occurrence" unless the amount of loss exceeds the Deductible Amount shown in the Declarations. We will then pay the amount of loss in excess of the Deductible Amount, up to the Limit of Insurance.

D. Exclusions

1. This Policy does not cover:

  a. **Acts Committed By You, Your Partners Or Your Members**

    Loss resulting from "theft" or any other dishonest act committed by:

    (1) You; or

    (2) Any of your partners or "members";

    whether acting alone or in collusion with other persons.

© Insurance Services Office, Inc., 2012

b. Acts Committed By Your Employees Learned Of By You Prior To The Policy Period

Loss caused by an "employee" if the "employee" had also committed "theft" or any other dishonest act prior to the effective date of this Policy and you or any of your partners, "members", "managers", officers, directors or trustees, not in collusion with the "employee", learned of such "theft" or dishonest act prior to the Policy Period shown in the Declarations.

c. Acts Committed By Your Employees, Managers, Directors, Trustees Or Representatives

Loss resulting from "theft" or any other dishonest act committed by any of your "employees", "managers", directors, trustees or authorized representatives:

(1) Whether acting alone or in collusion with other persons; or

(2) While performing services for you or otherwise;

except when covered under Insuring Agreement **A.1.**

d. Confidential Or Personal Information

Loss resulting from:

(1) The disclosure of your or another person's or organization's confidential or personal information including, but not limited to, patents, trade secrets, processing methods, customer lists, financial information, credit card information, health information or any other type of nonpublic information; or

(2) The use of another person's or organization's confidential or personal information including, but not limited to, patents, trade secrets, processing methods, customer lists, financial information, credit card information, health information or any other type of nonpublic information.

e. Data Security Breach

Fees, costs, fines, penalties and other expenses incurred by you which are related to the access to or disclosure of another person's or organization's confidential or personal information including, but not limited to, patents, trade secrets, processing methods, customer lists, financial information, credit card information, health information or any other type of nonpublic information.

f. Governmental Action

Loss resulting from seizure or destruction of property by order of governmental authority.

g. Indirect Loss

Loss that is an indirect result of an "occurrence" covered by this Policy including, but not limited to, loss resulting from:

(1) Your inability to realize income that you would have realized had there been no loss of or damage to "money", "securities" or "other property";

(2) Payment of damages of any type for which you are legally liable. But, we will pay compensatory damages arising directly from a loss covered under this Policy; or

(3) Payment of costs, fees or other expenses you incur in establishing either the existence or the amount of loss under this Policy.

h. Legal Fees, Costs And Expenses

Fees, costs and expenses incurred by you which are related to any legal action, except when covered under Insuring Agreement **A.2.**

i. Nuclear Hazard

Loss or damage resulting from nuclear reaction or radiation, or radioactive contamination, however caused.

j. Pollution

Loss or damage caused by or resulting from pollution. Pollution means the discharge, dispersal, seepage, migration, release or escape of any solid, liquid, gaseous or thermal irritant or contaminant, including smoke, vapor, soot, fumes, acids, alkalis, chemicals and waste. Waste includes materials to be recycled, reconditioned or reclaimed.

k. War And Military Action

Loss or damage resulting from:

(1) War, including undeclared or civil war;

(2) Warlike action by a military force, including action in hindering or defending against an actual or expected attack, by any government, sovereign or other authority using military personnel or other agents; or

(3) Insurrection, rebellion, revolution, usurped power, or action taken by governmental authority in hindering or defending against any of these.

2. Insuring Agreement **A.1.** does not cover:

a. **Inventory Shortages**

Loss, or that part of any loss, the proof of which as to its existence or amount is dependent upon:

(1) An inventory computation; or

(2) A profit and loss computation.

However, where you establish wholly apart from such computations that you have sustained a loss, then you may offer your inventory records and actual physical count of inventory in support of the amount of loss claimed.

b. **Trading**

Loss resulting from trading, whether in your name or in a genuine or fictitious account.

c. **Warehouse Receipts**

Loss resulting from the fraudulent or dishonest signing, issuing, cancelling or failing to cancel, a warehouse receipt or any papers connected with it.

3. Insuring Agreements **A.3., A.4.** and **A.5.** do not cover:

a. **Accounting Or Arithmetical Errors Or Omissions**

Loss resulting from accounting or arithmetical errors or omissions.

b. **Exchanges Or Purchases**

Loss resulting from the giving or surrendering of property in any exchange or purchase.

c. **Fire**

Loss or damage resulting from fire, however caused, except:

(1) Loss of or damage to "money" and "securities"; and

(2) Loss from damage to a safe or vault.

d. **Money Operated Devices**

Loss of property contained in any money operated device unless the amount of "money" deposited in it is recorded by a continuous recording instrument in the device.

e. **Motor Vehicles Or Equipment And Accessories**

Loss of or damage to motor vehicles, trailers or semitrailers or equipment and accessories attached to them.

f. **Transfer Or Surrender Of Property**

(1) Loss of or damage to property after it has been transferred or surrendered to a person or place outside the "premises" or "financial institution premises":

(a) On the basis of unauthorized instructions; or

(b) As a result of a threat including, but not limited to:

(i) A threat to do bodily harm to any person;

(ii) A threat to do damage to any property;

(iii) A threat to introduce a denial of service attack into any "computer system";

(iv) A threat to introduce a virus or other malicious instruction into any "computer system" which is designed to damage, destroy or corrupt "electronic data" or "computer programs" stored within the "computer system";

(v) A threat to contaminate, pollute or render substandard your products or goods; or

(vi) A threat to disseminate, divulge or utilize:

i. Your confidential information;

ii. Confidential or personal information of another person or organization; or

iii. Weaknesses in the source code within any "computer system".

(2) But, this exclusion does not apply under Insuring Agreement **A.5.** to loss of "money", "securities" or "other property" while outside the "premises" in the care and custody of a "messenger" if you:

(a) Had no knowledge of any threat at the time the conveyance began; or

(b) Had knowledge of a threat at the time the conveyance began, but the loss was not related to the threat.

g. **Vandalism**

Loss from damage to the "premises" or its exterior, or to any safe, vault, cash register, cash box, cash drawer or "other property" by vandalism or malicious mischief.

h. Voluntary Parting Of Title To Or Possession Of Property

Loss resulting from your, or anyone else acting on your express or implied authority, being induced by any dishonest act to voluntarily part with title to or possession of any property.

4. Insuring Agreement **A.6.** does not cover:

a. Authorized Access

Loss resulting from a fraudulent:

(1) Entry of "electronic data" or "computer program" into; or

(2) Change of "electronic data" or "computer program" within;

any "computer system" owned, leased or operated by you by a person or organization with authorized access to that "computer system", except when covered under Insuring Agreement **A.6.b.**

b. Credit Card Transactions

Loss resulting from the use or purported use of credit, debit, charge, access, convenience, identification, stored-value or other cards or the information contained on such cards.

c. Exchanges Or Purchases

Loss resulting from the giving or surrendering of property in any exchange or purchase.

d. Fraudulent Instructions

Loss resulting from an "employee" or "financial institution" acting upon any instruction to:

(1) Transfer, pay or deliver "money", "securities" or "other property"; or

(2) Debit or delete your account;

which instruction proves to be fraudulent, except when covered under Insuring Agreement **A.6.a.(2)** or **A.6.b.**

e. Inventory Shortages

Loss, or that part of any loss, the proof of which as to its existence or amount is dependent upon:

(1) An inventory computation; or

(2) A profit and loss computation.

E. Conditions

1. **Conditions Applicable To All Insuring Agreements**

a. Additional Premises Or Employees

If, while this Policy is in force, you establish any additional "premises" or hire additional "employees", other than through consolidation or merger with, or purchase or acquisition of assets or liabilities of, another entity, such "premises" and "employees" shall automatically be covered under this Policy. Notice to us of an increase in the number of "premises" or "employees" is not required, and no additional premium will be charged for the remainder of the Policy Period shown in the Declarations.

b. Cancellation Of Policy

(1) The first Named Insured shown in the Declarations may cancel this Policy by mailing or delivering to us advance written notice of cancellation.

(2) We may cancel this Policy by mailing or delivering to the first Named Insured written notice of cancellation at least:

(a) 10 days before the effective date of cancellation if we cancel for nonpayment of premium; or

(b) 30 days before the effective date of cancellation if we cancel for any other reason.

(3) We will mail or deliver our notice to the first Named Insured's last mailing address known to us.

(4) Notice of cancellation will state the effective date of cancellation. The policy period will end on that date.

(5) If this Policy is cancelled, we will send the first Named Insured any premium refund due. If we cancel, the refund will be pro rata. If the first Named Insured cancels, the refund may be less than pro rata. The cancellation will be effective even if we have not made or offered a refund.

(6) If notice is mailed, proof of mailing will be sufficient proof of notice.

c. Changes

This Policy contains all the agreements between you and us concerning the insurance afforded. The first Named Insured shown in the Declarations is authorized to make changes in the terms of this Policy with our consent. This Policy's terms can be amended or waived only by endorsement issued by us and made a part of this Policy.

d. Concealment, Misrepresentation Or Fraud

This Policy is void in any case of fraud by you as it relates to this Policy at any time. It is also void if you or any other Insured, at any time, intentionally conceals or misrepresents a material fact concerning:

(1) This Policy;

(2) The property covered under this Policy;

(3) Your interest in the property covered under this Policy; or

(4) A claim under this Policy.

e. Consolidation – Merger Or Acquisition

If you consolidate or merge with, or purchase or acquire the assets or liabilities of, another entity:

(1) You must give us written notice as soon as possible and obtain our written consent to extend the coverage provided by this Policy to such consolidated or merged entity or such purchased or acquired assets or liabilities. We may condition our consent by requiring payment of an additional premium; but

(2) For the first 90 days after the effective date of such consolidation, merger or purchase or acquisition of assets or liabilities, the coverage provided by this Policy shall apply to such consolidated or merged entity or such purchased or acquired assets or liabilities, provided that all "occurrences" causing or contributing to a loss involving such consolidation, merger or purchase or acquisition of assets or liabilities, must take place after the effective date of such consolidation, merger or purchase or acquisition of assets or liabilities.

f. Cooperation

You must cooperate with us in all matters pertaining to this Policy as stated in its terms and conditions.

g. Duties In The Event Of Loss

After you "discover" a loss or a situation that may result in loss of or damage to "money", "securities" or "other property", you must:

(1) Notify us as soon as possible. If you have reason to believe that any loss (except for loss covered under Insuring Agreement A.1. or A.2.) involves a violation of law, you must also notify the local law enforcement authorities;

(2) Give us a detailed, sworn proof of loss within 120 days;

(3) Cooperate with us in the investigation and settlement of any claim;

(4) Produce for our examination all pertinent records;

(5) Submit to examination under oath at our request and give us a signed statement of your answers; and

(6) Secure all of your rights of recovery against any person or organization responsible for the loss and do nothing to impair those rights.

h. Employee Benefit Plans

The "employee benefit plans" shown in the Declarations (hereafter referred to as Plan) are included as Insureds under Insuring Agreement A.1., subject to the following:

(1) If any Plan is insured jointly with any other entity under this Policy, you or the Plan Administrator is responsible for selecting a Limit of Insurance for Insuring Agreement A.1. that is sufficient to provide a Limit of Insurance for each Plan that is at least equal to that required under ERISA as if each Plan were separately insured.

(2) With respect to loss sustained or "discovered" by any such Plan, Insuring Agreement A.1. is replaced by the following:

We will pay for loss of or damage to "money", "securities" and "other property" resulting directly from fraudulent or dishonest acts committed by an "employee", whether identified or not, acting alone or in collusion with other persons.

(3) If the first Named Insured is an entity other than a Plan, any payment we make for loss sustained by any Plan will be made to the Plan sustaining the loss.

                   CR 00 22 08 13

(4) If two or more Plans are insured under this Policy, any payment we make for loss:

(a) Sustained by two or more Plans; or

(b) Of commingled "money", "securities" or "other property" of two or more Plans;

resulting directly from an "occurrence", will be made to each Plan sustaining loss in the proportion that the Limit of Insurance required under ERISA for each Plan bears to the total of those limits.

(5) The 'Deductible Amount applicable to Insuring Agreement **A.1.** does not apply to loss sustained by any Plan.

i. Examination Of Your Books And Records

We may examine and audit your books and records as they relate to this Policy at any time during the Policy Period shown in the Declarations and up to three years afterward.

j. Extended Period To Discover Loss

We will pay for loss that you sustained prior to the effective date of cancellation of this Policy, which is "discovered" by you:

(1) No later than 60 days from the date of that cancellation. However, this extended period to "discover" loss terminates immediately upon the effective date of any other insurance obtained by you, whether from us or another insurer, replacing in whole or in part the coverage afforded under this Policy, whether or not such other insurance provides coverage for loss sustained prior to its effective date.

(2) No later than one year from the date of that cancellation with regard to any "employee benefit plan".

k. Inspections And Surveys

(1) We have the right to:

(a) Make inspections and surveys at any time;

(b) Give you reports on the conditions we find; and

(c) Recommend changes.

(2) We are not obligated to make any inspections, surveys, reports or recommendations and any such actions we do undertake relate only to insurability and the premiums to be charged. We do not make safety inspections. We do not undertake to perform the duty of any person or organization to provide for the health or safety of workers or the public. And we do not warrant that conditions:

(a) Are safe or healthful; or

(b) Comply with laws, regulations, codes or standards.

(3) Paragraphs **k.(1)** and **k.(2)** apply not only to us, but also to any rating, advisory, rate service or similar organization which makes insurance inspections, surveys, reports or recommendations.

l. Joint Insured

(1) If more than one Insured is named in the Declarations, the first Named Insured will act for itself and for every other Insured for all purposes of this Policy. If the first Named Insured ceases to be covered, then the next Named Insured will become the first Named Insured.

(2) If any Insured, or partner, "member" or officer of that Insured has knowledge of any information relevant to this Policy, that knowledge is considered knowledge of every Insured.

(3) An "employee" of any Insured is considered to be an "employee" of every Insured.

(4) If this Policy or any of its coverages are cancelled as to any Insured, loss sustained by that Insured is covered only if it is "discovered" by you:

(a) No later than 60 days from the date of that cancellation. However, this extended period to "discover" loss terminates immediately upon the effective date of any other insurance obtained by that Insured, whether from us or another insurer, replacing in whole or in part the coverage afforded under this Policy, whether or not such other insurance provides coverage for loss sustained prior to its effective date.

(b) No later than one year from the date of that cancellation with regard to any "employee benefit plan".

(5) We will not pay more for loss sustained by more than one Insured than the amount we would pay if all such loss had been sustained by one Insured.

(6) Payment by us to the first Named Insured for loss sustained by any Insured, or payment by us to any "employee benefit plan" for loss sustained by that Plan, shall fully release us on account of such loss.

m. Legal Action Against Us

You may not bring any legal action against us involving loss:

(1) Unless you have complied with all the terms of this Policy;

(2) Until 90 days after you have filed proof of loss with us; and

(3) Unless brought within two years from the date you "discovered" the loss.

If any limitation in this condition is prohibited by law, such limitation is amended so as to equal the minimum period of limitation provided by such law.

n. Liberalization

If we adopt any revision that would broaden the coverage under this Policy without additional premium within 45 days prior to or during the Policy Period shown in the Declarations, the broadened coverage will immediately apply to this Policy.

o. Other Insurance

If other valid and collectible insurance is available to you for loss covered under this Policy, our obligations are limited as follows:

(1) **Primary Insurance**

When this Policy is written as primary insurance, and:

(a) You have other insurance subject to the same terms and conditions as this Policy, we will pay our share of the covered loss. Our share is the proportion that the applicable Limit Of Insurance shown in the Declarations bears to the total limit of all insurance covering the same loss.

(b) You have other insurance covering the same loss other than that described in Paragraph o.(1)(a), we will only pay for the amount of loss that exceeds:

(i) The Limit of Insurance and Deductible Amount of that other insurance, whether you can collect on it or not; or

(ii) The Deductible Amount shown in the Declarations;

whichever is greater. Our payment for loss is subject to the terms and conditions of this Policy.

(2) **Excess Insurance**

(a) When this Policy is written excess over other insurance, we will only pay for the amount of loss that exceeds the Limit of Insurance and Deductible Amount of that other insurance, whether you can collect on it or not. Our payment for loss is subject to the terms and conditions of this Policy.

(b) However, if loss covered under this Policy is subject to a deductible, we will reduce the Deductible Amount shown in the Declarations by the sum total of all such other insurance plus any Deductible Amount applicable to that other insurance.

p. Ownership Of Property; Interests Covered

The property covered under this Policy is limited to property:

(1) That you own or lease;

(2) That is held by you in any capacity; or

(3) For which you are legally liable, provided you were liable for the property prior to the time the loss was sustained.

However, this Policy is for your benefit only. It provides no rights or benefits to any other person or organization. Any claim for loss that is covered under this Policy must be presented by you.

q. Policy Bridge – Discovery Replacing Loss Sustained

(1) If this Policy replaces insurance that provided you with an extended period of time after cancellation in which to discover loss and which did not terminate at the time this Policy became effective:

(a) We will not pay for any loss that occurred during the policy period of that prior insurance which is discovered by you during such extended period to discover loss, unless the amount of loss exceeds the Limit of Insurance and Deductible Amount of that prior insurance. In that case, we will pay for the excess loss subject to the terms and conditions of this Policy.

(b) However, any payment we make for the excess loss will not be greater than the difference between the Limit of Insurance and Deductible Amount of that prior insurance and the Limit Of Insurance shown in the Declarations. We will not apply the Deductible Amount shown in the Declarations to this excess loss.

(2) Other Insurance Condition **E.1.o.** does not apply to this condition.

r. Premiums

The first Named Insured shown in the Declarations:

(1) Is responsible for the payment of all premiums; and

(2) Will be the payee for any return premiums we pay.

s. Records

You must keep records of all property covered under this Policy so we can verify the amount of any loss.

t. Recoveries

(1) Any recoveries, whether effected before or after any payment under this Policy, whether made by us or by you, shall be applied net of the expense of such recovery:

(a) First, to you in satisfaction of your covered loss in excess of the amount paid under this Policy;

(b) Second, to us in satisfaction of amounts paid in settlement of your claim;

(c) Third, to you in satisfaction of any Deductible Amount; and

(d) Fourth, to you in satisfaction of any loss not covered under this Policy.

(2) Recoveries do not include any recovery:

(a) From insurance, suretyship, reinsurance, security or indemnity taken for our benefit; or

(b) Of original "securities" after duplicates of them have been issued.

u. Territory

This Policy covers loss that you sustain resulting directly from an "occurrence" taking place within the United States of America (including its territories and possessions), Puerto Rico and Canada.

v. Transfer Of Your Rights And Duties Under This Policy

(1) Your rights and duties under this Policy may not be transferred without our written consent except in the case of death of an individual Named Insured.

(2) If you die, your rights and duties will be transferred to your legal representative but only while acting within the scope of duties as your legal representative. Until your legal representative is appointed, anyone having proper temporary custody of your property will have your rights and duties but only with respect to that property.

w. Transfer Of Your Rights Of Recovery Against Others To Us

You must transfer to us all your rights of recovery against any person or organization for any loss you sustained and for which we have paid or settled. You must also do everything necessary to secure those rights and do nothing after loss to impair them.

x. Valuation – Settlement

The value of any loss for purposes of coverage under this Policy shall be determined as follows:

(1) **Money**

Loss of "money" but only up to and including its face value. We will, at your option, pay for loss of "money" issued by any country other than the United States of America:

(a) At face value in the "money" issued by that country; or

(b) In the United States of America dollar equivalent, determined by the rate of exchange published in The Wall Street Journal on the day the loss was "discovered".

(2) Securities

Loss of "securities" but only up to and including their value at the close of business on the day the loss was "discovered". We may, at our option:

(a) Pay the market value of such "securities" or replace them in kind, in which event you must assign to us all your rights, title and interest in and to those "securities"; or

(b) Pay the cost of any Lost Securities Bond required in connection with issuing duplicates of the "securities". However, we will be liable only for the payment of so much of the cost of the bond as would be charged for a bond having a penalty not exceeding the lesser of the:

(i) Market value of the "securities" at the close of business on the day the loss was "discovered"; or

(ii) Limit of Insurance applicable to the "securities".

(3) Property Other Than Money And Securities

(a) Loss of or damage to "other property" or loss from damage to the "premises" or its exterior for the replacement cost of the property without deduction for depreciation. However, we will not pay more than the least of the following:

(i) The Limit of Insurance applicable to the lost or damaged property;

(ii) The cost to replace the lost or damaged property with property of comparable material and quality and used for the same purpose; or

(iii) The amount you actually spend that is necessary to repair or replace the lost or damaged property.

(b) We will not pay on a replacement cost basis for any loss or damage to property covered under Paragraph x.(3)(a):

(i) Until the lost or damaged property is actually repaired or replaced; and

(ii) Unless the repair or replacement is made as soon as reasonably possible after the loss or damage.

If the lost or damaged property is not repaired or replaced, we will pay on an actual cash value basis.

(c) We will, at your option, pay for loss or damage to such property:

(i) In the "money" of the country in which the loss or damage was sustained; or

(ii) In the United States of America dollar equivalent of the "money" of the country in which the loss or damage was sustained, determined by the rate of exchange published in The Wall Street Journal on the day the loss was "discovered".

(d) Any property that we pay for or replace becomes our property.

2. Conditions Applicable To Insuring Agreement A.1.

a. Termination As To Any Employee

This Insuring Agreement terminates as to any "employee":

(1) As soon as:

(a) You; or

(b) Any of your partners, "members", "managers", officers, directors or trustees not in collusion with the "employee";

learn of "theft" or any other dishonest act committed by the "employee" whether before or after becoming employed by you; or

(2) On the date specified in a notice mailed to the first Named Insured. That date will be at least 30 days after the date of mailing.

We will mail or deliver our notice to the first Named Insured's last mailing address known to us. If notice is mailed, proof of mailing will be sufficient proof of notice.

b. Territory

We will pay for loss caused by any "employee" while temporarily outside the territory specified in Territory Condition **E.1.u.** for a period of not more than 90 consecutive days.

3. Conditions Applicable To Insuring Agreement A.2.

a. Deductible Amount

The Deductible Amount does not apply to legal expenses paid under Insuring Agreement **A.2.**

b. Electronic And Mechanical Signatures

We will treat signatures that are produced or reproduced electronically, mechanically or by other means the same as handwritten signatures.

c. Proof Of Loss

You must include with your proof of loss any instrument involved in that loss or, if that is not possible, an affidavit setting forth the amount and cause of loss.

d. Territory

We will cover loss that you sustain resulting directly from an "occurrence" taking place anywhere in the world. Territory Condition **E.1.u.** does not apply to Insuring Agreement **A.2.**

4. Conditions Applicable To Insuring Agreements A.4. And A.5.

a. Armored Motor Vehicle Companies

Under Insuring Agreement **A.5.**, we will only pay for the amount of loss you cannot recover:

(1) Under your contract with the armored motor vehicle company; and

(2) From any insurance or indemnity carried by, or for the benefit of customers of, the armored motor vehicle company.

b. Special Limit Of Insurance For Specified Property

We will only pay up to $5,000 for any one "occurrence" of loss of or damage to:

(1) Precious metals, precious or semiprecious stones, pearls, furs, or completed or partially completed articles made of or containing such materials that constitute the principal value of such articles; or

(2) Manuscripts, drawings, or records of any kind, or the cost of reconstructing them or reproducing any information contained in them.

5. Conditions Applicable To Insuring Agreement A.6.

a. Special Limit Of Insurance For Specified Property

We will only pay up to $5,000 for any one "occurrence" of loss of or damage to manuscripts, drawings, or records of any kind, or the cost of reconstructing them or reproducing any information contained in them.

b. Territory

We will cover loss that you sustain resulting directly from an "occurrence" taking place anywhere in the world. Territory Condition **E.1.u.** does not apply to Insuring Agreement **A.6.**

F. Definitions

1. "Computer program" means a set of related electronic instructions, which direct the operation and function of a computer or devices connected to it, which enable the computer or devices to receive, process, store or send "electronic data".

2. "Computer system" means:

a. Computers, including Personal Digital Assistants (PDAs) and other transportable or handheld devices, electronic storage devices and related peripheral components;

b. Systems and applications software; and

c. Related communications networks;

by which "electronic data" is collected, transmitted, processed, stored or retrieved.

3. "Counterfeit money" means an imitation of "money" which is intended to deceive and to be taken as genuine.

4. "Custodian" means you, or any of your partners or "members", or any "employee" while having care and custody of property inside the "premises", excluding any person while acting as a "watchperson" or janitor.

5. "Discover" or "discovered" means the time when you first become aware of facts which would cause a reasonable person to assume that a loss of a type covered by this Policy has been or will be incurred, regardless of when the act or acts causing or contributing to such loss occurred, even though the exact amount or details of loss may not then be known.

"Discover" or "discovered" also means the time when you first receive notice of an actual or potential claim in which it is alleged that you are liable to a third party under circumstances which, if true, would constitute a loss under this Policy.

6. "Electronic data" means information, facts, images or sounds stored as or on, created or used on, or transmitted to or from computer software (including systems and applications software) on data storage devices, including hard or floppy disks, CD-ROMs, tapes, drives, cells, data processing devices or any other media which are used with electronically controlled equipment.

7. "Employee":

   a. Means:

      (1) Any natural person:

         (a) While in your service and for the first 30 days immediately after termination of service, unless such termination is due to "theft" or any other dishonest act committed by the "employee";

         (b) Whom you compensate directly by salary, wages or commissions; and

         (c) Whom you have the right to direct and control while performing services for you;

      (2) Any natural person who is furnished temporarily to you:

         (a) To substitute for a permanent "employee", as defined in Paragraph 7.a.(1), who is on leave; or

         (b) To meet seasonal or short-term workload conditions;

         while that person is subject to your direction and control and performing services for you;

      (3) Any natural person who is leased to you under a written agreement between you and a labor leasing firm, to perform duties related to the conduct of your business, but does not mean a temporary "employee" as defined in Paragraph 7.a.(2);

      (4) Any natural person who is:

         (a) A trustee, officer, employee, administrator or manager, except an administrator or manager who is an independent contractor, of any "employee benefit plan"; or

      (b) Your director or trustee while that person is engaged in handling "money", "securities" or "other property" of any "employee benefit plan";

      (5) Any natural person who is a former "employee", partner, "member", "manager", director or trustee retained by you as a consultant while performing services for you;

      (6) Any natural person who is a guest student or intern pursuing studies or duties;

      (7) Any natural person employed by an entity merged or consolidated with you prior to the effective date of this Policy; and

      (8) Any natural person who is your "manager", director or trustee while:

         (a) Performing acts within the scope of the usual duties of an "employee"; or

         (b) Acting as a member of any committee duly elected or appointed by resolution of your board of directors or board of trustees to perform specific, as distinguished from general, directorial acts on your behalf.

   b. Does not mean:

      Any agent, broker, factor, commission merchant, consignee, independent contractor or representative of the same general character not specified in Paragraph 7.a.

8. "Employee benefit plan" means any welfare or pension benefit plan shown in the Declarations that you sponsor and that is subject to the Employee Retirement Income Security Act of 1974 (ERISA) and any amendments thereto.

9. "Financial institution" means:

   a. With regard to Insuring Agreement A.3.:

      (1) A bank, savings bank, savings and loan association, trust company, credit union or similar depository institution; or

      (2) An insurance company.

   b. With regard to Insuring Agreement A.6.:

      (1) A bank, savings bank, savings and loan association, trust company, credit union or similar depository institution;

      (2) An insurance company; or

      (3) A stock brokerage firm or investment company.

10. "Financial institution premises" means the interior of that portion of any building occupied by a "financial institution".

11. "Forgery" means the signing of the name of another person or organization with intent to deceive; it does not mean a signature which consists in whole or in part of one's own name signed with or without authority, in any capacity, for any purpose.

12. "Fraudulent instruction" means:

a. With regard to Insuring Agreement **A.6.a.(2)**:

(1) A computer, telegraphic, cable, teletype, telefacsimile, telephone or other electronic instruction directing a "financial institution" to debit your "transfer account" and to transfer, pay or deliver "money" or "securities" from that "transfer account", which instruction purports to have been issued by you, but which in fact was fraudulently issued by someone else without your knowledge or consent.

(2) A written instruction (other than those covered under Insuring Agreement **A.2.**) issued to a "financial institution" directing the "financial institution" to debit your "transfer account" and to transfer, pay or deliver "money" or "securities" from that "transfer account", through an electronic funds transfer system at specified times or under specified conditions, which instruction purports to have been issued by you, but which in fact was issued, forged or altered by someone else without your knowledge or consent.

(3) A computer, telegraphic, cable, teletype, telefacsimile, telephone or other electronic or written instruction initially received by you, which instruction purports to have been issued by an "employee", but which in fact was fraudulently issued by someone else without your or the "employee's" knowledge or consent.

b. With regard to Insuring Agreement **A.6.b.**:

A computer, telegraphic, cable, teletype, telefacsimile, telephone or other electronic, written or voice instruction directing an "employee" to enter or change "electronic data" or "computer programs" within a "computer system" covered under the Insuring Agreement, which instruction in fact was fraudulently issued by your computer software contractor.

13. "Manager" means a natural person serving in a directorial capacity for a limited liability company.

14. "Member" means an owner of a limited liability company represented by its membership interest who, if a natural person, may also serve as a "manager".

15. "Messenger" means you, or your relative, or any of your partners or "members", or any "employee" while having care and custody of property outside the "premises".

16. "Money" means:

a. Currency, coins and bank notes in current use and having a face value;

b. Traveler's checks and money orders held for sale to the public; and

c. In addition, includes:

(1) Under Insuring Agreements **A.1.** and **A.2.**, deposits in your account at any financial institution; and

(2) Under Insuring Agreement **A.6.**, deposits in your account at a "financial institution" as defined in Paragraph **F.9.b.**

17. "Occurrence" means:

a. Under Insuring Agreement **A.1.**:

(1) An individual act;

(2) The combined total of all separate acts whether or not related; or

(3) A series of acts whether or not related;

committed by an "employee" acting alone or in collusion with other persons, during the Policy Period shown in the Declarations, before such policy period or both.

b. Under Insuring Agreement **A.2.**:

(1) An individual act;

(2) The combined total of all separate acts whether or not related; or

(3) A series of acts whether or not related;

committed by a person acting alone or in collusion with other persons, involving one or more instruments, during the Policy Period shown in the Declarations, before such policy period or both.

c. Under all other Insuring Agreements:

(1) An individual act or event;

(2) The combined total of all separate acts or events whether or not related; or

(3) A series of acts or events whether or not related;

committed by a person acting alone or in collusion with other persons, or not committed by any person, during the Policy Period shown in the Declarations, before such policy period or both.

18. "Other property" means any tangible property other than "money" and "securities" that has intrinsic value. "Other property" does not include "computer programs", "electronic data" or any property specifically excluded under this Policy.

19. "Premises" means the interior of that portion of any building you occupy in conducting your business.

20. "Robbery" means the unlawful taking of property from the care and custody of a person by one who has:

a. Caused or threatened to cause that person bodily harm; or

b. Committed an obviously unlawful act witnessed by that person.

21. "Safe burglary" means the unlawful taking of:

a. Property from within a locked safe or vault by a person unlawfully entering the safe or vault as evidenced by marks of forcible entry upon its exterior; or

b. A safe or vault from inside the "premises".

22. "Securities" means negotiable and nonnegotiable instruments or contracts representing either "money" or property and includes:

a. Tokens, tickets, revenue and other stamps (whether represented by actual stamps or unused value in a meter) in current use; and

b. Evidences of debt issued in connection with credit or charge cards, which cards are not issued by you;

but does not include "money".

23. "Theft" means the unlawful taking of property to the deprivation of the Insured.

24. "Transfer account" means an account maintained by you at a "financial institution" from which you can initiate the transfer, payment or delivery of "money" or "securities":

a. By means of computer, telegraphic, cable, teletype, telefacsimile, telephone or other electronic instructions; or

b. By means of written instructions (other than those covered under Insuring Agreement A.2.) establishing the conditions under which such transfers are to be initiated by such "financial institution" through an electronic funds transfer system.

25. "Watchperson" means any person you retain specifically to have care and custody of property inside the "premises" and who has no other duties.

Exhibit D

COMMERCIAL CRIME POLICY
(LOSS SUSTAINED FORM)
STANDARD FORM NO. CR 00 23 08 13

CRIME AND FIDELITY
CR 00 23 08 13

COMMERCIAL CRIME POLICY
(LOSS SUSTAINED FORM)

Various provisions in this Policy restrict coverage. Read the entire Policy carefully to determine rights, duties and what is or is not covered.

Throughout this Policy, the words "you" and "your" refer to the Named Insured shown in the Declarations. The words "we", "us" and "our" refer to the company providing this insurance.

Other words and phrases that appear in quotation marks have special meaning. Refer to Section **F.** Definitions.

A. Insuring Agreements

Coverage is provided under the following Insuring Agreements for which a Limit Of Insurance is shown in the Declarations and applies to loss that you sustain resulting from an "occurrence" taking place during the Policy Period shown in the Declarations, except as provided in Condition **E.1.o.** or **E.1.p.**, which is "discovered" by you during the Policy Period shown in the Declarations or during the period of time provided in the Extended Period To Discover Loss Condition **E.1.j.**:

1. Employee Theft

We will pay for loss of or damage to "money", "securities" and "other property" resulting directly from "theft" committed by an "employee", whether identified or not, acting alone or in collusion with other persons.

For the purposes of this Insuring Agreement, "theft" shall also include forgery.

2. Forgery Or Alteration

a. We will pay for loss resulting directly from "forgery" or alteration of checks, drafts, promissory notes, or similar written promises, orders or directions to pay a sum certain in "money" that are:

 (1) Made or drawn by or drawn upon you; or

 (2) Made or drawn by one acting as your agent;

 or that are purported to have been so made or drawn.

 For the purposes of this Insuring Agreement, a substitute check as defined in the Check Clearing for the 21st Century Act shall be treated the same as the original it replaced.

b. If you are sued for refusing to pay any instrument covered in Paragraph **2.a.**, on the basis that it has been forged or altered, and you have our written consent to defend against the suit, we will pay for any reasonable legal expenses that you incur and pay in that defense. The amount that we will pay for such legal expenses is in addition to the Limit of Insurance applicable to this Insuring Agreement.

3. Inside The Premises – Theft Of Money And Securities

We will pay for:

a. Loss of "money" and "securities" inside the "premises" or "financial institution premises":

 (1) Resulting directly from "theft" committed by a person present inside such "premises" or "financial institution premises"; or

 (2) Resulting directly from disappearance or destruction.

b. Loss from damage to the "premises" or its exterior resulting directly from an actual or attempted "theft" of "money" and "securities", if you are the owner of the "premises" or are liable for damage to it.

c. Loss of or damage to a locked safe, vault, cash register, cash box or cash drawer located inside the "premises" resulting directly from an actual or attempted "theft" of, or unlawful entry into, those containers.

4. Inside The Premises – Robbery Or Safe Burglary Of Other Property

We will pay for:

a. Loss of or damage to "other property":

 (1) Inside the "premises" resulting directly from an actual or attempted "robbery" of a "custodian"; or

 (2) Inside the "premises" in a safe or vault resulting directly from an actual or attempted "safe burglary".

b. Loss from damage to the "premises" or its exterior resulting directly from an actual or attempted "robbery" or "safe burglary" of "other property", if you are the owner of the "premises" or are liable for damage to it.

c. Loss of or damage to a locked safe or vault located inside the "premises" resulting directly from an actual or attempted "robbery" or "safe burglary".

5. Outside The Premises

We will pay for:

a. Loss of "money" and "securities" outside the "premises" in the care and custody of a "messenger" or an armored motor vehicle company resulting directly from "theft", disappearance or destruction.

b. Loss of or damage to "other property" outside the "premises" in the care and custody of a "messenger" or an armored motor vehicle company resulting directly from an actual or attempted "robbery".

6. Computer And Funds Transfer Fraud

a. We will pay for:

(1) Loss resulting directly from a fraudulent:

(a) Entry of "electronic data" or "computer program" into; or

(b) Change of "electronic data" or "computer program" within;

any "computer system" owned, leased or operated by you, provided the fraudulent entry or fraudulent change causes, with regard to Paragraphs **6.a.(1)(a)** and **6.a.(1)(b):**

(i) "Money", "securities" or "other property" to be transferred, paid or delivered; or

(ii) Your account at a "financial institution" to be debited or deleted.

(2) Loss resulting directly from a "fraudulent instruction" directing a "financial institution" to debit your "transfer account" and transfer, pay or deliver "money" or "securities" from that account.

b. As used in Paragraph **6.a.(1)**, fraudulent entry or fraudulent change of "electronic data" or "computer program" shall include such entry or change made by an "employee" acting, in good faith, upon a "fraudulent instruction" received from a computer software contractor who has a written agreement with you to design, implement or service "computer programs" for a "computer system" covered under this Insuring Agreement.

7. Money Orders And Counterfeit Money

We will pay for loss resulting directly from your having, in good faith, accepted in exchange for merchandise, "money" or services:

a. Money orders issued by any post office, express company or "financial institution" that are not paid upon presentation; or

b. "Counterfeit money" that is acquired during the regular course of business.

B. Limit Of Insurance

The most we will pay for all loss resulting directly from an "occurrence" is the applicable Limit Of Insurance shown in the Declarations.

If any loss is covered under more than one Insuring Agreement or coverage, the most we will pay for such loss shall not exceed the largest Limit of Insurance available under any one of those Insuring Agreements or coverages.

C. Deductible

We will not pay for loss resulting directly from an "occurrence" unless the amount of loss exceeds the Deductible Amount shown in the Declarations. We will then pay the amount of loss in excess of the Deductible Amount, up to the Limit of Insurance.

D. Exclusions

1. This Policy does not cover:

a. **Acts Committed By You, Your Partners Or Your Members**

Loss resulting from "theft" or any other dishonest act committed by:

(1) You; or

(2) Any of your partners or "members";

whether acting alone or in collusion with other persons.

b. Acts Committed By Your Employees Learned Of By You Prior To The Policy Period

Loss caused by an "employee" if the "employee" had also committed "theft" or any other dishonest act prior to the effective date of this Policy and you or any of your partners, "members", "managers", officers, directors or trustees, not in collusion with the "employee", learned of such "theft" or dishonest act prior to the Policy Period shown in the Declarations.

c. Acts Committed By Your Employees, Managers, Directors, Trustees Or Representatives

Loss resulting from "theft" or any other dishonest act committed by any of your "employees", "managers", directors, trustees or authorized representatives:

(1) Whether acting alone or in collusion with other persons; or

(2) While performing services for you or otherwise;

except when covered under Insuring Agreement **A.1.**

d. Confidential Or Personal Information

Loss resulting from:

(1) The disclosure of your or another person's or organization's confidential or personal information including, but not limited to, patents, trade secrets, processing methods, customer lists, financial information, credit card information, health information or any other type of nonpublic information; or

(2) The use of another person's or organization's confidential or personal information including, but not limited to, patents, trade secrets, processing methods, customer lists, financial information, credit card information, health information or any other type of nonpublic information.

e. Data Security Breach

Fees, costs, fines, penalties and other expenses incurred by you which are related to the access to or disclosure of another person's or organization's confidential or personal information including, but not limited to, patents, trade secrets, processing methods, customer lists, financial information, credit card information, health information or any other type of nonpublic information.

f. Governmental Action

Loss resulting from seizure or destruction of property by order of governmental authority.

g. Indirect Loss

Loss that is an indirect result of an "occurrence" covered by this Policy including, but not limited to, loss resulting from:

(1) Your inability to realize income that you would have realized had there been no loss of or damage to "money", "securities" or "other property";

(2) Payment of damages of any type for which you are legally liable. But, we will pay compensatory damages arising directly from a loss covered under this Policy; or

(3) Payment of costs, fees or other expenses you incur in establishing either the existence or the amount of loss under this Policy.

h. Legal Fees, Costs And Expenses

Fees, costs and expenses incurred by you which are related to any legal action, except when covered under Insuring Agreement **A.2.**

i. Nuclear Hazard

Loss or damage resulting from nuclear reaction or radiation, or radioactive contamination, however caused.

j. Pollution

Loss or damage caused by or resulting from pollution. Pollution means the discharge, dispersal, seepage, migration, release or escape of any solid, liquid, gaseous or thermal irritant or contaminant, including smoke, vapor, soot, fumes, acids, alkalis, chemicals and waste. Waste includes materials to be recycled, reconditioned or reclaimed.

k. War And Military Action

Loss or damage resulting from:

(1) War, including undeclared or civil war;

(2) Warlike action by a military force, including action in hindering or defending against an actual or expected attack, by any government, sovereign or other authority using military personnel or other agents; or

(3) Insurrection, rebellion, revolution, usurped power, or action taken by governmental authority in hindering or defending against any of these.

2. Insuring Agreement **A.1.** does not cover:

   a. **Inventory Shortages**

      Loss, or that part of any loss, the proof of which as to its existence or amount is dependent upon:

      (1) An inventory computation; or

      (2) A profit and loss computation.

      However, where you establish wholly apart from such computations that you have sustained a loss, then you may offer your inventory records and actual physical count of inventory in support of the amount of loss claimed.

   b. **Trading**

      Loss resulting from trading, whether in your name or in a genuine or fictitious account.

   c. **Warehouse Receipts**

      Loss resulting from the fraudulent or dishonest signing, issuing, cancelling or failing to cancel, a warehouse receipt or any papers connected with it.

3. Insuring Agreements **A.3.**, **A.4.** and **A.5.** do not cover:

   a. **Accounting Or Arithmetical Errors Or Omissions**

      Loss resulting from accounting or arithmetical errors or omissions.

   b. **Exchanges Or Purchases**

      Loss resulting from the giving or surrendering of property in any exchange or purchase.

   c. **Fire**

      Loss or damage resulting from fire, however caused, except:

      (1) Loss of or damage to "money" and "securities"; and

      (2) Loss from damage to a safe or vault.

   d. **Money Operated Devices**

      Loss of property contained in any money operated device unless the amount of "money" deposited in it is recorded by a continuous recording instrument in the device.

   e. **Motor Vehicles Or Equipment And Accessories**

      Loss of or damage to motor vehicles, trailers or semitrailers or equipment and accessories attached to them.

f. **Transfer Or Surrender Of Property**

   (1) Loss of or damage to property after it has been transferred or surrendered to a person or place outside the "premises" or "financial institution premises":

      (a) On the basis of unauthorized instructions; or

      (b) As a result of a threat including, but not limited to:

         (i) A threat to do bodily harm to any person;

         (ii) A threat to do damage to any property;

         (iii) A threat to introduce a denial of service attack into any "computer system";

         (iv) A threat to introduce a virus or other malicious instruction into any "computer system" which is designed to damage, destroy or corrupt "electronic data" or "computer programs" stored within the "computer system";

         (v) A threat to contaminate, pollute or render substandard your products or goods; or

         (vi) A threat to disseminate, divulge or utilize:

            i. Your confidential information;

            ii. Confidential or personal information of another person or organization; or

            iii. Weaknesses in the source code within any "computer system".

   (2) But, this exclusion does not apply under Insuring Agreement **A.5.** to loss of "money", "securities" or "other property" while outside the "premises" in the care and custody of a "messenger" if you:

      (a) Had no knowledge of any threat at the time the conveyance began; or

      (b) Had knowledge of a threat at the time the conveyance began, but the loss was not related to the threat.

g. **Vandalism**

   Loss from damage to the "premises" or its exterior, or to any safe, vault, cash register, cash box, cash drawer or "other property" by vandalism or malicious mischief.

h. Voluntary Parting Of Title To Or Possession Of Property

Loss resulting from your, or anyone else acting on your express or implied authority, being induced by any dishonest act to voluntarily part with title to or possession of any property.

4. Insuring Agreement **A.6.** does not cover:

a. Authorized Access

Loss resulting from a fraudulent:

(1) Entry of "electronic data" or "computer program" into; or

(2) Change of "electronic data" or "computer program" within;

any "computer system" owned, leased or operated by you by a person or organization with authorized access to that "computer system", except when covered under Insuring Agreement **A.6.b.**

b. Credit Card Transactions

Loss resulting from the use or purported use of credit, debit, charge, access, convenience, identification, stored-value or other cards or the information contained on such cards.

c. Exchanges Or Purchases

Loss resulting from the giving or surrendering of property in any exchange or purchase.

d. Fraudulent Instructions

Loss resulting from an "employee" or "financial institution" acting upon any instruction to:

(1) Transfer, pay or deliver "money", "securities" or "other property"; or

(2) Debit or delete your account;

which instruction proves to be fraudulent, except when covered under Insuring Agreement **A.6.a.(2)** or **A.6.b.**

e. Inventory Shortages

Loss, or that part of any loss, the proof of which as to its existence or amount is dependent upon:

(1) An inventory computation; or

(2) A profit and loss computation.

E. Conditions

1. Conditions Applicable To All Insuring Agreements

a. Additional Premises Or Employees

If, while this Policy is in force, you establish any additional "premises" or hire additional "employees", other than through consolidation or merger with, or purchase or acquisition of assets or liabilities of, another entity, such "premises" and "employees" shall automatically be covered under this Policy. Notice to us of an increase in the number of "premises" or "employees" is not required, and no additional premium will be charged for the remainder of the Policy Period shown in the Declarations.

b. Cancellation Of Policy

(1) The first Named Insured shown in the Declarations may cancel this Policy by mailing or delivering to us advance written notice of cancellation.

(2) We may cancel this Policy by mailing or delivering to the first Named Insured written notice of cancellation at least:

(a) 10 days before the effective date of cancellation if we cancel for nonpayment of premium; or

(b) 30 days before the effective date of cancellation if we cancel for any other reason.

(3) We will mail or deliver our notice to the first Named Insured's last mailing address known to us.

(4) Notice of cancellation will state the effective date of cancellation. The policy period will end on that date.

(5) If this Policy is cancelled, we will send the first Named Insured any premium refund due. If we cancel, the refund will be pro rata. If the first Named Insured cancels, the refund may be less than pro rata. The cancellation will be effective even if we have not made or offered a refund.

(6) If notice is mailed, proof of mailing will be sufficient proof of notice.

c. Changes

This Policy contains all the agreements between you and us concerning the insurance afforded. The first Named Insured shown in the Declarations is authorized to make changes in the terms of this Policy with our consent. This Policy's terms can be amended or waived only by endorsement issued by us and made a part of this Policy.

d. Concealment, Misrepresentation Or Fraud

This Policy is void in any case of fraud by you as it relates to this Policy at any time. It is also void if you or any other Insured, at any time, intentionally conceals or misrepresents a material fact concerning:

(1) This Policy;

(2) The property covered under this Policy;

(3) Your interest in the property covered under this Policy; or

(4) A claim under this Policy.

e. Consolidation – Merger Or Acquisition

If you consolidate or merge with, or purchase or acquire the assets or liabilities of, another entity:

(1) You must give us written notice as soon as possible and obtain our written consent to extend the coverage provided by this Policy to such consolidated or merged entity or such purchased or acquired assets or liabilities. We may condition our consent by requiring payment of an additional premium; but

(2) For the first 90 days after the effective date of such consolidation, merger or purchase or acquisition of assets or liabilities, the coverage provided by this Policy shall apply to such consolidated or merged entity or such purchased or acquired assets or liabilities, provided that all "occurrences" causing or contributing to a loss involving such consolidation, merger or purchase or acquisition of assets or liabilities, must take place after the effective date of such consolidation, merger or purchase or acquisition of assets or liabilities.

f. Cooperation

You must cooperate with us in all matters pertaining to this Policy as stated in its terms and conditions.

g. Duties In The Event Of Loss

After you "discover" a loss or a situation that may result in loss of or damage to "money", "securities" or "other property", you must:

(1) Notify us as soon as possible. If you have reason to believe that any loss (except for loss covered under Insuring Agreement **A.1.** or **A.2.**) involves a violation of law, you must also notify the local law enforcement authorities;

(2) Give us a detailed, sworn proof of loss within 120 days;

(3) Cooperate with us in the investigation and settlement of any claim;

(4) Produce for our examination all pertinent records;

(5) Submit to examination under oath at our request and give us a signed statement of your answers; and

(6) Secure all of your rights of recovery against any person or organization responsible for the loss and do nothing to impair those rights.

h. Employee Benefit Plans

The "employee benefit plans" shown in the Declarations (hereafter referred to as Plan) are included as Insureds under Insuring Agreement **A.1.**, subject to the following:

(1) If any Plan is insured jointly with any other entity under this Policy, you or the Plan Administrator is responsible for selecting a Limit of Insurance for Insuring Agreement **A.1.** that is sufficient to provide a Limit of Insurance for each Plan that is at least equal to that required under ERISA as if each Plan were separately insured.

(2) With respect to loss sustained or "discovered" by any such Plan, Insuring Agreement **A.1.** is replaced by the following:

We will pay for loss of or damage to "money", "securities" and "other property" resulting directly from fraudulent or dishonest acts committed by an "employee", whether identified or not, acting alone or in collusion with other persons.

(3) If the first Named Insured is an entity other than a Plan, any payment we make for loss sustained by any Plan will be made to the Plan sustaining the loss.

(4) If two or more Plans are insured under this Policy, any payment we make for loss:

   (a) Sustained by two or more Plans; or

   (b) Of commingled "money", "securities" or "other property" of two or more Plans;

resulting directly from an "occurrence", will be made to each Plan sustaining loss in the proportion that the Limit of Insurance required under ERISA for each Plan bears to the total of those limits.

(5) The Deductible Amount applicable to Insuring Agreement **A.1.** does not apply to loss sustained by any Plan.

i. Examination Of Your Books And Records

We may examine and audit your books and records as they relate to this Policy at any time during the Policy Period shown in the Declarations and up to three years afterward.

j. Extended Period To Discover Loss

We will pay for loss that you sustained prior to the effective date of cancellation of this Policy, which is "discovered" by you:

(1) No later than one year from the date of that cancellation. However, this extended period to "discover" loss terminates immediately upon the effective date of any other insurance obtained by you, whether from us or another insurer, replacing in whole or in part the coverage afforded under this Policy, whether or not such other insurance provides coverage for loss sustained prior to its effective date.

(2) No later than one year from the date of that cancellation with regard to any "employee benefit plan".

k. Inspections And Surveys

(1) We have the right to:

   (a) Make inspections and surveys at any time;

   (b) Give you reports on the conditions we find; and

   (c) Recommend changes.

(2) We are not obligated to make any inspections, surveys, reports or recommendations and any such actions we do undertake relate only to insurability and the premiums to be charged. We do not make safety inspections. We do not undertake to perform the duty of any person or organization to provide for the health or safety of workers or the public. And we do not warrant that conditions:

   (a) Are safe or healthful; or

   (b) Comply with laws, regulations, codes or standards.

(3) Paragraphs **k.(1)** and **k.(2)** apply not only to us, but also to any rating, advisory, rate service or similar organization which makes insurance inspections, surveys, reports or recommendations.

l. Joint Insured

(1) If more than one Insured is named in the Declarations, the first Named Insured will act for itself and for every other Insured for all purposes of this Policy. If the first Named Insured ceases to be covered, then the next Named Insured will become the first Named Insured.

(2) If any Insured, or partner, "member" or officer of that Insured has knowledge of any information relevant to this Policy, that knowledge is considered knowledge of every Insured.

(3) An "employee" of any Insured is considered to be an "employee" of every Insured.

(4) If this Policy or any of its coverages are cancelled as to any Insured, loss sustained by that Insured is covered only if it is "discovered" by you:

   (a) No later than one year from the date of that cancellation. However, this extended period to "discover" loss terminates immediately upon the effective date of any other insurance obtained by that Insured, whether from us or another insurer, replacing in whole or in part the coverage afforded under this Policy, whether or not such other insurance provides coverage for loss sustained prior to its effective date.

   (b) No later than one year from the date of that cancellation with regard to any "employee benefit plan".

(5) We will not pay more for loss sustained by more than one Insured than the amount we would pay if all such loss had been sustained by one Insured.

(6) Payment by us to the first Named Insured for loss sustained by any Insured, or payment by us to any "employee benefit plan" for loss sustained by that Plan, shall fully release us on account of such loss.

m. Legal Action Against Us

You may not bring any legal action against us involving loss:

(1) Unless you have complied with all the terms of this Policy;

(2) Until 90 days after you have filed proof of loss with us; and

(3) Unless brought within two years from the date you "discovered" the loss.

If any limitation in this condition is prohibited by law, such limitation is amended so as to equal the minimum period of limitation provided by such law.

n. Liberalization

If we adopt any revision that would broaden the coverage under this Policy without additional premium within 45 days prior to or during the Policy Period shown in the Declarations, the broadened coverage will immediately apply to this Policy.

o. Loss Sustained During Prior Insurance Issued By Us Or Any Affiliate

(1) Loss Sustained Partly During This Policy And Partly During Prior Insurance

If you "discover" loss during the Policy Period shown in the Declarations, resulting directly from an "occurrence" taking place:

(a) Partly during the Policy Period shown in the Declarations; and

(b) Partly during the policy period(s) of any prior cancelled insurance that we or any affiliate issued to you or any predecessor in interest;

and this Policy became effective at the time of cancellation of the prior insurance, we will first settle the amount of loss that you sustained during this policy period. We will then settle the remaining amount of loss that you sustained during the policy period(s) of the prior insurance.

(2) Loss Sustained Entirely During Prior Insurance

If you "discover" loss during the Policy Period shown in the Declarations, resulting directly from an "occurrence" taking place entirely during the policy period(s) of any prior cancelled insurance that we or any affiliate issued to you or any predecessor in interest, we will pay for the loss, provided:

(a) This Policy became effective at the time of cancellation of the prior insurance; and

(b) The loss would have been covered under this Policy had it been in effect at the time of the "occurrence".

We will first settle the amount of loss that you sustained during the most recent prior insurance. We will then settle any remaining amount of loss that you sustained during the policy period(s) of any other prior insurance.

(3) In settling loss under Paragraphs o.(1) and o.(2):

(a) The most we will pay for the entire loss is the highest single Limit of Insurance applicable during the period of loss, whether such limit was written under this Policy or was written under the prior insurance issued by us.

(b) We will apply the applicable Deductible Amount shown in the Declarations to the amount of loss sustained under this Policy. If no loss was sustained under this Policy, we will apply the Deductible Amount shown in the Declarations to the amount of loss sustained under the most recent prior insurance.

If the Deductible Amount is larger than the amount of loss sustained under this Policy, or the most recent prior insurance, we will apply the remaining Deductible Amount to the remaining amount of loss sustained during the prior insurance.

We will not apply any other Deductible Amount that may have been applicable to the loss.

(4) The following examples demonstrate how we will settle losses subject to this condition:

Example Number 1

The Insured sustained a covered loss of $10,000 resulting directly from an "occurrence" taking place during the terms of Policy **A** and Policy **B.**

Policy A

The current policy. Written at a Limit of Insurance of $50,000 and a Deductible Amount of $5,000.

Policy B

Issued prior to Policy **A.** Written at a Limit of Insurance of $50,000 and a Deductible Amount of $5,000.

The amount of loss sustained under Policy **A** is $2,500 and under Policy **B,** $7,500.

The highest single Limit of Insurance applicable to this entire loss is $50,000 written under Policy **A.** The Policy **A** Deductible Amount of $5,000 applies. The loss is settled as follows:

(a) The amount of loss sustained under Policy **A** ($2,500) is settled first. The amount we will pay is nil ($0.00) because the amount of loss is less than the Deductible Amount (i.e., $2,500 loss - $5,000 deductible = $0.00).

(b) The remaining amount of loss sustained under Policy **B** ($7,500) is settled next. The amount recoverable is $5,000 after the remaining Deductible Amount from Policy **A** of $2,500 is applied to the loss (i.e., $7,500 loss - $2,500 deductible = $5,000).

The most we will pay for this loss is $5,000.

Example Number 2

The Insured sustained a covered loss of $250,000 resulting directly from an "occurrence" taking place during the terms of Policy **A** and Policy **B.**

Policy A

The current policy. Written at a Limit of Insurance of $125,000 and a Deductible Amount of $10,000.

Policy B

Issued prior to Policy **A.** Written at a Limit of Insurance of $150,000 and a Deductible Amount of $25,000.

The amount of loss sustained under Policy **A** is $175,000 and under Policy **B,** $75,000.

The highest single Limit of Insurance applicable to this entire loss is $150,000 written under Policy **B.** The Policy **A** Deductible Amount of $10,000 applies. The loss is settled as follows:

(a) The amount of loss sustained under Policy **A** ($175,000) is settled first. The amount we will pay is the Policy **A** Limit of $125,000 because $175,000 loss - $10,000 deductible = $165,000, which is greater than the $125,000 policy limit.

(b) The remaining amount of loss sustained under Policy **B** ($75,000) is settled next. The amount we will pay is $25,000 (i.e., $150,000 Policy **B** limit - $125,000 paid under Policy **A** = $25,000).

The most we will pay for this loss is $150,000.

Example Number 3

The Insured sustained a covered loss of $2,000,000 resulting directly from an "occurrence" taking place during the terms of Policies **A, B, C** and **D.**

Policy A

The current policy. Written at a Limit of Insurance of $1,000,000 and a Deductible Amount of $100,000.

Policy B

Issued prior to Policy **A.** Written at a Limit of Insurance of $750,000 and a Deductible Amount of $75,000.

Policy C

Issued prior to Policy **B.** Written at a Limit of Insurance of $500,000 and a Deductible Amount of $50,000.

Policy D

Issued prior to Policy **C.** Written at a Limit of Insurance of $500,000 and a Deductible Amount of $50,000.

The amount of loss sustained under Policy **A** is $350,000; under Policy **B,** $250,000; under Policy **C,** $600,000; and under Policy **D,** $800,000.

The highest single Limit of Insurance applicable to this entire loss is $1,000,000 written under Policy **A**. The Policy **A** Deductible Amount of $100,000 applies. The loss is settled as follows:

(a) The amount of loss sustained under Policy **A** ($350,000) is settled first. The amount we will pay is $250,000 (i.e., $350,000 loss - $100,000 deductible = $250,000).

(b) The amount of loss sustained under Policy **B** ($250,000) is settled next. The amount we will pay is $250,000 (no deductible is applied).

(c) The amount of loss sustained under Policy **C** ($600,000) is settled next. The amount we will pay is $500,000, the policy limit (no deductible is applied).

(d) We will not make any further payment under Policy **D**, as the maximum amount payable under the highest single Limit of Insurance applying to the loss of $1,000,000 under Policy **A** has been satisfied.

The most we will pay for this loss is $1,000,000.

p. Loss Sustained During Prior Insurance Not Issued By Us Or Any Affiliate

(1) If you "discover" loss during the Policy Period shown in the Declarations, resulting directly from an "occurrence" taking place during the policy period of any prior cancelled insurance that was issued to you or a predecessor in interest by another company, and the period of time to discover loss under that insurance had expired, we will pay for the loss under this Policy, provided:

(a) This Policy became effective at the time of cancellation of the prior insurance; and

(b) The loss would have been covered under this Policy had it been in effect at the time of the "occurrence".

(2) In settling loss subject to this condition:

(a) The most we will pay for the entire loss is the lesser of the Limits of Insurance applicable during the period of loss, whether such limit was written under this Policy or was written under the prior cancelled insurance.

(b) We will apply the applicable Deductible Amount shown in the Declarations to the amount of loss sustained under the prior cancelled insurance.

(3) The insurance provided under this condition is subject to the following:

(a) If loss covered under this condition is also partially covered under Condition **E.1.o.**, the amount recoverable under this condition is part of, not in addition to, the amount recoverable under Condition **E.1.o.**

(b) For loss covered under this condition that is not subject to Paragraph **p.(3)(a)**, the amount recoverable under this condition is part of, not in addition to, the Limit of Insurance applicable to the loss covered under this Policy and is limited to the lesser of the amount recoverable under:

(i) This Policy as of its effective date; or

(ii) The prior cancelled insurance had it remained in effect.

q. Other Insurance

If other valid and collectible insurance is available to you for loss covered under this Policy, our obligations are limited as follows:

(1) **Primary Insurance**

When this Policy is written as primary insurance, and:

(a) You have other insurance subject to the same terms and conditions as this Policy, we will pay our share of the covered loss. Our share is the proportion that the applicable Limit Of Insurance shown in the Declarations bears to the total limit of all insurance covering the same loss.

(b) You have other insurance covering the same loss other than that described in Paragraph **(1)(a)**, we will only pay for the amount of loss that exceeds:

(i) The Limit of Insurance and Deductible Amount of that other insurance, whether you can collect on it or not; or

(ii) The Deductible Amount shown in the Declarations;

whichever is greater. Our payment for loss is subject to the terms and conditions of this Policy.

(2) Excess Insurance

(a) When this Policy is written excess over other insurance, we will only pay for the amount of loss that exceeds the Limit of Insurance and Deductible Amount of that other insurance, whether you can collect on it or not. Our payment for loss is subject to the terms and conditions of this Policy.

(b) However, if loss covered under this Policy is subject to a deductible, we will reduce the Deductible Amount shown in the Declarations by the sum total of all such other insurance plus any Deductible Amount applicable to that other insurance.

r. Ownership Of Property; Interests Covered

The property covered under this Policy is limited to property:

(1) That you own or lease;

(2) That is held by you in any capacity; or

(3) For which you are legally liable, provided you were liable for the property prior to the time the loss was sustained.

However, this Policy is for your benefit only. It provides no rights or benefits to any other person or organization. Any claim for loss that is covered under this Policy must be presented by you.

s. Premiums

The first Named Insured shown in the Declarations:

(1) Is responsible for the payment of all premiums; and

(2) Will be the payee for any return premiums we pay.

t. Records

You must keep records of all property covered under this Policy so we can verify the amount of any loss.

u. Recoveries

(1) Any recoveries, whether effected before or after any payment under this Policy, whether made by us or by you, shall be applied net of the expense of such recovery:

(a) First, to you in satisfaction of your covered loss in excess of the amount paid under this Policy;

(b) Second, to us in satisfaction of amounts paid in settlement of your claim;

(c) Third, to you in satisfaction of any Deductible Amount; and

(d) Fourth, to you in satisfaction of any loss not covered under this Policy.

(2) Recoveries do not include any recovery:

(a) From insurance, suretyship, reinsurance, security or indemnity taken for our benefit; or

(b) Of original "securities" after duplicates of them have been issued.

v. Territory

This Policy covers loss that you sustain resulting directly from an "occurrence" taking place within the United States of America (including its territories and possessions), Puerto Rico and Canada.

w. Transfer Of Your Rights And Duties Under This Policy

(1) Your rights and duties under this Policy may not be transferred without our written consent except in the case of death of an individual Named Insured.

(2) If you die, your rights and duties will be transferred to your legal representative but only while acting within the scope of duties as your legal representative. Until your legal representative is appointed, anyone having temporary custody of your property will have your rights and duties but only with respect to that property.

x. Transfer Of Your Rights Of Recovery Against Others To Us

You must transfer to us all your rights of recovery against any person or organization for any loss you sustained and for which we have paid or settled. You must also do everything necessary to secure those rights and do nothing after loss to impair them.

y. Valuation — Settlement

The value of any loss for purposes of coverage under this Policy shall be determined as follows:

(1) Money

Loss of "money" but only up to and including its face value. We will, at your option, pay for loss of "money" issued by any country other than the United States of America:

(a) At face value in the "money" issued by that country; or

(b) In the United States of America dollar equivalent, determined by the rate of exchange published in The Wall Street Journal on the day the loss was "discovered".

(2) Securities

Loss of "securities" but only up to and including their value at the close of business on the day the loss was "discovered". We may, at our option:

(a) Pay the market value of such "securities" or replace them in kind, in which event you must assign to us all your rights, title and interest in and to those "securities"; or

(b) Pay the cost of any Lost Securities Bond required in connection with issuing duplicates of the "securities". However, we will be liable only for the payment of so much of the cost of the bond as would be charged for a bond having a penalty not exceeding the lesser of the:

(i) Market value of the "securities" at the close of business on the day the loss was "discovered"; or

(ii) Limit of Insurance applicable to the "securities".

(3) Property Other Than Money And Securities

(a) Loss of or damage to "other property" or loss from damage to the "premises" or its exterior for the replacement cost of the property without deduction for depreciation. However, we will not pay more than the least of the following:

(i) The Limit of Insurance applicable to the lost or damaged property;

(ii) The cost to replace the lost or damaged property with property of comparable material and quality and used for the same purpose; or

(iii) The amount you actually spend that is necessary to repair or replace the lost or damaged property.

(b) We will not pay on a replacement cost basis for any loss or damage to property covered under Paragraph **y.(3)(a):**

(i) Until the lost or damaged property is actually repaired or replaced; and

(ii) Unless the repair or replacement is made as soon as reasonably possible after the loss or damage.

If the lost or damaged property is not repaired or replaced, we will pay on an actual cash value basis.

(c) We will, at your option, pay for loss or damage to such property:

(i) In the "money" of the country in which the loss or damage was sustained; or

(ii) In the United States of America dollar equivalent of the "money" of the country in which the loss or damage was sustained, determined by the rate of exchange published in The Wall Street Journal on the day the loss was "discovered".

(d) Any property that we pay for or replace becomes our property.

2. Conditions Applicable To Insuring Agreement A.1.

a. Termination As To Any Employee

This Insuring Agreement terminates as to any "employee":

(1) As soon as:

(a) You; or

(b) Any of your partners, "members", "managers", officers, directors or trustees not in collusion with the "employee";

learn of "theft" or any other dishonest act committed by the "employee" whether before or after becoming employed by you; or

(2) On the date specified in a notice mailed to the first Named Insured. That date will be at least 30 days after the date of mailing.

We will mail or deliver our notice to the first Named Insured's last mailing address known to us. If notice is mailed, proof of mailing will be sufficient proof of notice.

b. **Territory**

We will pay for loss caused by any "employee" while temporarily outside the territory specified in Territory Condition **E.1.v.** for a period of not more than 90 consecutive days.

3. **Conditions Applicable To Insuring Agreement A.2.**

a. **Deductible Amount**

The Deductible Amount does not apply to legal expenses paid under Insuring Agreement **A.2.**

b. **Electronic And Mechanical Signatures**

We will treat signatures that are produced or reproduced electronically, mechanically or by other means the same as handwritten signatures.

c. **Proof Of Loss**

You must include with your proof of loss any instrument involved in that loss or, if that is not possible, an affidavit setting forth the amount and cause of loss.

d. **Territory**

We will cover loss that you sustain resulting directly from an "occurrence" taking place anywhere in the world. Territory Condition **E.1.v.** does not apply to Insuring Agreement **A.2.**

4. **Conditions Applicable To Insuring Agreements A.4. And A.5.**

a. **Armored Motor Vehicle Companies**

Under Insuring Agreement **A.5.**, we will only pay for the amount of loss you cannot recover:

(1) Under your contract with the armored motor vehicle company; and

(2) From any insurance or indemnity carried by, or for the benefit of customers of, the armored motor vehicle company.

b. **Special Limit Of Insurance For Specified Property**

We will only pay up to $5,000 for any one "occurrence" of loss of or damage to:

(1) Precious metals, precious or semiprecious stones, pearls, furs, or completed or partially completed articles made of or containing such materials that constitute the principal value of such articles; or

(2) Manuscripts, drawings, or records of any kind, or the cost of reconstructing them or reproducing any information contained in them.

5. **Conditions Applicable To Insuring Agreement A.6.**

a. **Special Limit Of Insurance For Specified Property**

We will only pay up to $5,000 for any one "occurrence" of loss of or damage to manuscripts, drawings, or records of any kind, or the cost of reconstructing them or reproducing any information contained in them.

b. **Territory**

We will cover loss that you sustain resulting directly from an "occurrence" taking place anywhere in the world. Territory Condition **E.1.v.** does not apply to Insuring Agreement **A.6.**

F. **Definitions**

1. "Computer program" means a set of related electronic instructions, which direct the operation and function of a computer or devices connected to it, which enable the computer or devices to receive, process, store or send "electronic data".

2. "Computer system" means:

a. Computers, including Personal Digital Assistants (PDAs) and other transportable or handheld devices, electronic storage devices and related peripheral components;

b. Systems and applications software; and

c. Related communications networks;

by which "electronic data" is collected, transmitted, processed, stored or retrieved.

3. "Counterfeit money" means an imitation of "money" which is intended to deceive and to be taken as genuine.

4. "Custodian" means you, or any of your partners or "members", or any "employee" while having care and custody of property inside the "premises", excluding any person while acting as a "watchperson" or janitor.

5. "Discover" or "discovered" means the time when you first become aware of facts which would cause a reasonable person to assume that a loss of a type covered by this Policy has been or will be incurred, regardless of when the act or acts causing or contributing to such loss occurred, even though the exact amount or details of loss may not then be known.

"Discover" or "discovered" also means the time when you first receive notice of an actual or potential claim in which it is alleged that you are liable to a third party under circumstances which, if true, would constitute a loss under this Policy.

6. "Electronic data" means information, facts, images or sounds stored as or on, created or used on, or transmitted to or from computer software (including systems and applications software) on data storage devices, including hard or floppy disks, CD-ROMs, tapes, drives, cells, data processing devices or any other media which are used with electronically controlled equipment.

7. "Employee":

   a. Means:

      (1) Any natural person:

         (a) While in your service and for the first 30 days immediately after termination of service, unless such termination is due to "theft" or any other dishonest act committed by the "employee";

         (b) Whom you compensate directly by salary, wages or commissions; and

         (c) Whom you have the right to direct and control while performing services for you;

      (2) Any natural person who is furnished temporarily to you:

         (a) To substitute for a permanent "employee", as defined in Paragraph 7.a.(1), who is on leave; or

         (b) To meet seasonal or short-term workload conditions;

         while that person is subject to your direction and control and performing services for you;

(3) Any natural person who is leased to you under a written agreement between you and a labor leasing firm, to perform duties related to the conduct of your business, but does not mean a temporary "employee" as defined in Paragraph 7.a.(2);

(4) Any natural person who is:

   (a) A trustee, officer, employee, administrator or manager, except an administrator or manager who is an independent contractor, of any "employee benefit plan"; or

   (b) Your director or trustee while that person is engaged in handling "money", "securities" or "other property" of any "employee benefit plan";

(5) Any natural person who is a former "employee", partner, "member", "manager", director or trustee retained by you as a consultant while performing services for you;

(6) Any natural person who is a guest student or intern pursuing studies or duties;

(7) Any natural person employed by an entity merged or consolidated with you prior to the effective date of this Policy; and

(8) Any natural person who is your "manager", director or trustee while:

   (a) Performing acts within the scope of the usual duties of an "employee"; or

   (b) Acting as a member of any committee duly elected or appointed by resolution of your board of directors or board of trustees to perform specific, as distinguished from general, directorial acts on your behalf.

   b. Does not mean:

   Any agent, broker, factor, commission merchant, consignee, independent contractor or representative of the same general character not specified in Paragraph 7.a.

8. "Employee benefit plan" means any welfare or pension benefit plan shown in the Declarations that you sponsor and that is subject to the Employee Retirement Income Security Act of 1974 (ERISA) and any amendments thereto.

9. "Financial institution" means:

   a. With regard to Insuring Agreement **A.3.**:

      (1) A bank, savings bank, savings and loan association, trust company, credit union or similar depository institution; or

      (2) An insurance company.

   b. With regard to Insuring Agreement **A.6.**:

      (1) A bank, savings bank, savings and loan association, trust company, credit union or similar depository institution;

      (2) An insurance company; or

      (3) A stock brokerage firm or investment company.

10. "Financial institution premises" means the interior of that portion of any building occupied by a "financial institution".

11. "Forgery" means the signing of the name of another person or organization with intent to deceive; it does not mean a signature which consists in whole or in part of one's own name signed with or without authority, in any capacity, for any purpose.

12. "Fraudulent instruction" means:

   a. With regard to Insuring Agreement **A.6.a.(2)**:

      (1) A computer, telegraphic, cable, teletype, telefacsimile, telephone or other electronic instruction directing a "financial institution" to debit your "transfer account" and to transfer, pay or deliver "money" or "securities" from that "transfer account", which instruction purports to have been issued by you, but which in fact was fraudulently issued by someone else without your knowledge or consent.

      (2) A written instruction (other than those covered under Insuring Agreement **A.2.**) issued to a "financial institution" directing the "financial institution" to debit your "transfer account" and to transfer, pay or deliver "money" or "securities" from that "transfer account", through an electronic funds transfer system at specified times or under specified conditions, which instruction purports to have been issued by you, but which in fact was issued, forged or altered by someone else without your knowledge or consent.

      (3) A computer, telegraphic, cable, teletype, telefacsimile, telephone or other electronic or written instruction initially received by you, which instruction purports to have been issued by an "employee", but which in fact was fraudulently issued by someone else without your or the "employee's" knowledge or consent.

   b. With regard to Insuring Agreement **A.6.b.**:

      A computer, telegraphic, cable, teletype, telefacsimile, telephone or other electronic, written or voice instruction directing an "employee" to enter or change "electronic data" or "computer programs" within a "computer system" covered under the Insuring Agreement, which instruction in fact was fraudulently issued by your computer software contractor.

13. "Manager" means a natural person serving in a directorial capacity for a limited liability company.

14. "Member" means an owner of a limited liability company represented by its membership interest who, if a natural person, may also serve as a "manager".

15. "Messenger" means you, or your relative, or any of your partners or "members", or any "employee" while having care and custody of property outside the "premises".

16. "Money" means:

   a. Currency, coins and bank notes in current use and having a face value;

   b. Traveler's checks and money orders held for sale to the public; and

   c. In addition, includes:

      (1) Under Insuring Agreements **A.1.** and **A.2.**, deposits in your account at any financial institution; and

      (2) Under Insuring Agreement **A.6.**, deposits in your account at a "financial institution" as defined in Paragraph **F.9.b.**

17. "Occurrence" means:

   a. Under Insuring Agreement **A.1.**:

      (1) An individual act;

      (2) The combined total of all separate acts whether or not related; or

      (3) A series of acts whether or not related;

committed by an "employee" acting alone or in collusion with other persons, during the Policy Period shown in the Declarations, except as provided under Condition **E.1.o.** or **E.1.p.**

b. Under Insuring Agreement **A.2.:**

(1) An individual act;

(2) The combined total of all separate acts whether or not related; or

(3) A series of acts whether or not related;

committed by a person acting alone or in collusion with other persons, involving one or more instruments, during the Policy Period shown in the Declarations, except as provided under Condition **E.1.o.** or **E.1.p.**

c. Under all other Insuring Agreements:

(1) An individual act or event;

(2) The combined total of all separate acts or events whether or not related; or

(3) A series of acts or events whether or not related;

committed by a person acting alone or in collusion with other persons, or not committed by any person, during the Policy Period shown in the Declarations, except as provided under Condition **E.1.o.** or **E.1.p.**

18. "Other property" means any tangible property other than "money" and "securities" that has intrinsic value. "Other property" does not include "computer programs", "electronic data" or any property specifically excluded under this Policy.

19. "Premises" means the interior of that portion of any building you occupy in conducting your business.

20. "Robbery" means the unlawful taking of property from the care and custody of a person by one who has:

a. Caused or threatened to cause that person bodily harm; or

b. Committed an obviously unlawful act witnessed by that person.

21. "Safe burglary" means the unlawful taking of:

a. Property from within a locked safe or vault by a person unlawfully entering the safe or vault as evidenced by marks of forcible entry upon its exterior; or

b. A safe or vault from inside the "premises".

22. "Securities" means negotiable and nonnegotiable instruments or contracts representing either "money" or property and includes:

a. Tokens, tickets, revenue and other stamps (whether represented by actual stamps or unused value in a meter) in current use; and

b. Evidences of debt issued in connection with credit or charge cards, which cards are not issued by you;

but does not include "money".

23. "Theft" means the unlawful taking of property to the deprivation of the Insured.

24. "Transfer account" means an account maintained by you at a "financial institution" from which you can initiate the transfer, payment or delivery of "money" or "securities":

a. By means of computer, telegraphic, cable, teletype, telefacsimile, telephone or other electronic instructions; or

b. By means of written instructions (other than those covered under Insuring Agreement **A.2.**) establishing the conditions under which such transfers are to be initiated by such "financial institution" through an electronic funds transfer system.

25. "Watchperson" means any person you retain specifically to have care and custody of property inside the "premises" and who has no other duties.

Exhibit E

Crime Protection Policy
Standard Form No. SP 00 01 04 12

CRIME PROTECTION POLICY

Edition of April 1, 2012

Policy No.

(Herein called Company)

DECLARATIONS

Item 1.   Name of Insured (herein called Insured):

Principal Address:

Item 2.   Policy Period: from 12:01 a.m. on _____ to 12:01 a.m. on _____

(MONTH, DAY, YEAR)   (MONTH, DAY, YEAR)

Item 3.   **INSURING AGREEMENTS, LIMITS OF INSURANCE AND DEDUCTIBLES**

Insuring Agreement	Limit of Insurance Per Occurrence	Deductible Amount Per Occurrence
1. Employee Dishonesty	$	$
2. Forgery or Alteration	$	$
3. Inside the Premises	$	$
4. Outside the Premises	$	$
5. Computer Fraud	$	$
6. Money Orders and Counterfeit Paper Currency	$	$
If added by Endorsement, Insuring Agreement(s):		
	$	$
	$	$
	$	$

If "Not Covered" is inserted above opposite any specified Insuring Agreement, or if no amount is inserted, such Insuring Agreement and any other reference thereto in this Policy shall be deemed to be deleted.

Item 4.   **ENDORSEMENTS FORMING PART OF THIS POLICY WHEN ISSUED**

Item 5.   **CANCELLATION OF PRIOR INSURANCE**

By acceptance of this Policy you give us notice cancelling prior policy Nos.

SP 00 01 04 12
Printed in U.S.A.

Copyright, The Surety & Fidelity Association of America, 2012

CPP-1

CRIME PROTECTION POLICY
TABLE OF CONTENTS

CRIME PROTECTION POLICY	Throughout this Policy the words "you" and "your" refer to the Insured(s) shown in the Declarations. The words "we", "us" and "our" refer to the Company providing this insurance. Read the entire Policy carefully to determine rights, duties and what is or is not covered. Words and phrases defined in the Policy are in **bold** type.
A. CONSIDERATION CLAUSE	In return for the payment of the premium, and subject to the Declarations, Insuring Agreements, Definitions, Exclusions, Conditions and other terms of this Policy, we will pay for loss covered by an Insuring Agreement of this Policy that you sustain resulting directly from acts committed or events occurring at any time and discovered by you during the Policy Period shown in the Declarations or during the period of time provided in the Extended Period to Discover Loss, Condition E. 9.

B. INSURING AGREEMENTS

1. Employee Dishonesty

We will pay for loss resulting directly from dishonest acts committed by an **employee**, whether identified or not, acting alone or in collusion with other persons, with the manifest intent to:

a. Cause you to sustain loss; and

b. Obtain an improper financial benefit for:

(1) The **employee**; or

(2) Any person or organization intended by the **employee** to receive that benefit.

As used in this Insuring Agreement, an improper financial benefit does not include any employee benefits received in the course of employment, including: salaries, commissions, fees, bonuses, promotions, awards, profit sharing or pensions.

2. Forgery or Alteration

a. We will pay for loss resulting directly from **forgery** or alteration of checks, drafts, promissory notes, or similar written promises, orders, or directions to pay a sum certain in **money** that are:

(1) Made or drawn by or drawn upon you;

(2) Made or drawn by one acting as your agent;

or that purport to have been so made or drawn.

b. If you are sued for refusing to pay any instrument covered in paragraph 2 a. on the basis that it has been forged or altered, and you have our written consent to defend against the suit, we will pay for any reasonable legal expenses that you incur and pay in that defense. The amount that we will pay for such legal expenses is in addition to the Limit of Insurance applicable to this Insuring Agreement.

3. Inside the Premises

a. We will pay for loss of **cash** and **securities** inside the **premises** or **banking premises** resulting directly from **theft**, disappearance or destruction. Provided, however, in the case of **theft**, the **theft** was committed by a person physically present in the **premises** or **banking premises** at the time of loss of such **cash** or **securities**.

b. We will pay for loss of, and loss from damage to, **other property**:

(1) Inside the **premises** resulting directly from an actual or attempted **robbery** of a **custodian**; or

(2) Inside the **premises** in a safe or vault, resulting directly from an actual or attempted **safe burglary**.

c. We will pay:

(1) For loss from damage to the **premises** or its exterior; or

(2) For loss of, and loss from damage to, a locked safe, vault, cash register, cash box or cash drawer located in the **premises**;

resulting directly from an actual or attempted **theft**, **robbery** or **safe burglary**, if you are the owner of the **premises** or are liable for damage to it.

4. Outside the Premises

We will pay for loss of, and loss from damage to, **cash,**, **securities** and **other property** outside the **premises** while in the care and custody of a **messenger** or armored motor vehicle company:

a. For **cash** and **securities** resulting from **theft**, disappearance or destruction; and

b. For **other property** resulting from actual or attempted **robbery**.

5. Computer Fraud

We will pay for loss resulting directly from the use of any computer to impersonate you, or your authorized officer or **employee**, to gain direct access to your computer system, or to the computer system of your financial institution, and thereby fraudulently cause the transfer of **money**, **securities** or **other property** from your **premises** or **banking premises** to a person, entity, place or account outside of your control.

6. Money Orders and Counterfeit Paper Currency

We will pay for loss resulting directly from your having accepted in good faith and in the regular course of business, in exchange for merchandise, **money** or services:

a. Money orders issued by any post office, express company or bank in the United States or Canada that are not paid upon presentation; or

b. **Counterfeit** United States or Canadian paper currency.

C. DEFINITIONS

1. **Banking premises** means the interior of that portion of any building occupied by a financial institution with which you have an account or which has custody of your **money** or **securities**.

2. **Cash** means United States or Canadian bills and coins in current use and having a face value that are accepted by the United States or by the government of Canada as legal tender for the payment of debts.

3. **Counterfeit** means an imitation of an actual valid original which is intended to deceive and to be taken as the original.

4. **Custodian** means you, any of your partners or any **employee** while having care and custody of property inside the **premises**, excluding any person while acting as a **watchperson** or janitor.

5. **Employee** means:

    a. Any natural person:

        (1) While in your service or for 30 days after termination of service; and

        (2) Whom you compensate directly by salary, wages or commissions; and

        (3) Whom you have the right to direct and control while performing services for you.

    b. Any natural person who is furnished temporarily to you to:

        (1) Substitute for a permanent **employee** as defined in (a) above who is on leave; or

        (2) Meet seasonal or short-term workload conditions;

        while that person is subject to your direction and control and performing services for you excluding, however, any such person while having care and custody of property outside the **premises**.

    c. Any natural person who is:

        (1) A trustee, officer, employee, administrator or manager, except an administrator or manager who is an independent contractor, of any **employee benefit plan(s)** insured under this insurance; and

        (2) Your director or trustee while that person is handling **funds** or **other property** of any **employee benefit plan(s)** insured under this insurance.

    d. **Employee** does not mean any:

(1) Agent, broker, person leased to you by a labor leasing firm (except when furnished on a temporary basis under the circumstances set forth in Definition 5.b.), factor, commission merchant, consignee, independent contractor or representative of the same general character; or

(2) Director or trustee except while performing acts within the scope of the usual duties of an employee.

6. **Employee benefit plan(s)** means any welfare or pension benefit plan listed in the Declarations that is subject to the Employee Retirement Income Security Act of 1974 (ERISA).

7. **Forgery** means the signing of the name of another person or organization with intent to deceive; it does not mean a signature which consists in whole or in part of one's own name signed with or without authority, in any capacity, for any purpose.

8. **Messenger** means you, any of your partners or **employees** while having care and custody of property outside the **premises**.

9. **Money** means:

   a. **Cash**;

   b. Demand and savings deposits at financial institutions; and

   c. Travelers checks, register checks and money orders held for sale to the public.

10. **Occurrence** means:

    a. As respects Insuring Agreement 1., all loss or losses caused by, or involving, any one **employee**, acting alone or in collusion with others;

    b. As respects Insuring Agreement 2., all loss or losses caused by any person or in which that person is involved, whether the loss involves one or more instruments.

    c. As respects all other Insuring Agreements, all loss or losses caused by:

       (1) Any number of acts involving one person whether acting alone or in collusion with others;

       (2) Any number of acts involving a group of persons acting together; or

       (3) An act or event, or any number of related acts or events, not involving any identifiable person.

11. **Other property** means any tangible property other than **money** and **securities** that has intrinsic value but does not include any property excluded under this insurance.

12. **Payment order** means an instruction of a sender to a receiving bank, transmitted orally, electronically, or in writing, to pay, or to cause another bank to pay, a fixed or determinable amount of money to a another person.

13. **Premises** means the interior of that portion of any building you occupy in conducting your business.

14. **Robbery** means the taking of property from the care and custody of a person by one who has:

    a. Caused or threatened to cause that person bodily harm; or

    b. In the presence of that person, caused or threaten to cause bodily harm to someone else.

15. **Safe burglary** means the taking of:

    a. Property from within a locked safe or vault by a person unlawfully entering the safe or vault as evidenced by marks of forcible entry upon its exterior; or

    b. A safe or vault on the **premises** by a person without your permission.

16. **Securities** mean negotiable and nonnegotiable instruments or contracts representing either **money** or property and includes:

a. Tokens, tickets, revenue and other stamps (whether represented by actual stamps or unused value in a meter) in current use; and

b. Evidences of debt issued in connection with credit or charge cards, which cards are not issued by you;

but does not include **money**.

17. **Security procedure** means a procedure established by agreement of the Insured and its customer or financial institution for the purpose of (i) verifying that a **payment order** is that of the Insured, or (ii) detecting error in the transmission or the content of the **payment order** or communication. A **security procedure** may require the use of algorithms or other codes, identifying words or numbers, encryption, callback procedures, or similar security devices.

18. **Theft** means any act of stealing.

19. **Watchperson** means any person you retain specifically to have care and custody of property on the **premises** and who has no other duties.

D. EXCLUSIONS Applicable to All Insuring Agreements, Except as Indicated

We will not pay for loss as specified below:

1. Acts Committed by You or Your Partners

Loss resulting from any dishonest act committed by you or any of your partners whether acting alone or in collusion with other persons.

2. Acts of Employees, Directors, Trustees or Representatives

We will not pay for loss resulting from any dishonest act committed by any of your **employees**, directors, trustees or authorized representatives:

a. Acting alone or in collusion with other persons; or

b. While performing services for you or otherwise;

except when covered under Insuring Agreement 1.

3. Fire

Loss from damage to the **premises** resulting from fire, however caused.

4. Governmental Action

Loss resulting from seizure or destruction of property by order of governmental authority.

5. Indirect Loss

Loss that is an indirect result of any act or **occurrence** covered by this Policy including, but not limited to, loss resulting from:

a. Your inability to realize income that you would have realized had there been no loss;

b. Payment of damages of any type for which you are legally liable unless you establish that the act or acts that gave rise to the damages involved conduct which caused a covered loss of **money**, **securities** or **other property** which was in your custody and control and for which you were responsible prior to the loss; or

c. Payment of costs, fees or other expenses you incur in establishing either the existence or the amount of loss under this insurance.

6. Legal Expenses

Expenses related to any legal action, except when covered under Insuring Agreement 2.

7. Nuclear Chemical or Biological

Loss resulting from nuclear reaction, nuclear radiation or radioactive, chemical or biological contamination, or any related act or incident.

8. War and Similar Actions

Loss resulting from war, whether or not declared, warlike action, insurrection, rebellion or revolution, or any related act or incident.

6

9. **Confidential Information**

Loss resulting from the theft, disappearance, destruction or disclosure of confidential information including, but not limited to, trade secrets, personal information, customer lists and intellectual property. For purposes of Insuring Agreement 5, confidential information cannot itself be the **other property** transferred, but a loss otherwise covered under Insuring Agreement 5 shall not be excluded by the fact that confidential information was used to gain access to your computer system or to the computer system of your financial institution, in order to cause the fraudulent transfer.

10. **Data Breach Costs**

Expenses related to your obligations to comply with federal and state privacy laws and Payment Card Industry Data Security Standards (if applicable) arising from a data security breach, including, but not limited to, expenses related to notifying affected individuals when the affected individuals' personally identifiable financial or medical information was stolen, accessed, downloaded or misappropriated while in your care, custody or control, forensic audit expenses and fines and penalties.

Applicable to Specific Insuring Agreements

We will not pay for loss as specified below:

1. **Under Insuring Agreement 1**

   Employee Canceled Under Prior Insurance

   Loss caused by any **employee** of yours, or predecessor in interest of yours, for whom similar prior insurance has been canceled and not reinstated since the last such cancellation.

2. **Under Insuring Agreements 1 and 5**

   Inventory Shortages

   Loss, or that part of any loss, the proof of which as to its existence or amount is dependent upon:

   a. An inventory computation; or

   b. A profit and loss computation.

3. **Under Insuring Agreements 3 and 4**

   a. **Accounting or Arithmetical Errors or Omissions**

   Loss resulting from accounting or arithmetical errors or omissions.

   b. **Money Operated Devices**

   Loss of property contained in any **money** operated device unless the amount of **money** deposited in it is recorded by a continuous recording instrument in the device.

   c. **Transfer or Surrender of Property**

   (1) Loss of property after it has been transferred or surrendered to a person or place outside **the premises** or **banking premises**:

      (i) On the basis of unauthorized instructions; or

      (ii) As a result of a threat to do:

         (a) Bodily harm to any person; or

         (b) Damage to any property.

   (2) But, this exclusion does not apply under Insuring Agreement 4, to loss of **money**, **securities** and **other property** while outside the **premises** or **banking premises** in the care and custody of a **messenger** if you:

      (i) Had no knowledge of any threat at the time the conveyance began; or

      (ii) Had knowledge of a threat at the time the conveyance began, but the loss was not related to the threat.

   d. **Vandalism**

   Loss from damage to any safe, vault or **other property**, or to the **premises** or its exterior, by vandalism or malicious mischief.

7

CPP-8

4. **Under Insuring Agreement 4**

   Motor Vehicles or Equipment and Accessories

   Loss of motor vehicles, trailers or semi-trailers or equipment and accessories attached to them.

5. **Under Insuring Agreements 3 and 4**

   a. **Exchanges or Purchases**

   Loss resulting from the giving or surrendering of property in any exchange or purchase.

   b. **Voluntary Parting of Title to or Possession of Property**

   Loss resulting from your, or anyone acting on your express or implied authority, being induced by any dishonest act to part voluntarily with title to or possession of any property.

6. **Under Insuring Agreement 5**

   a. **Failure to Follow Security Procedures**

   (1) Loss resulting from your failure to follow **security procedures** agreed to in writing with your customer or your financial institution;

   (2) Loss that would have been avoided if you had accepted and followed commercially reasonable **security procedures** that your financial institution made available for your account or accounts involved in the loss; or

   (3) Loss resulting from your failure to comply with **security procedures** that you represented to us you would follow.

   b. **Debit and Credit Cards**

   Loss resulting from the use or purported use of credit, debit, charge, access, convenience, or other cards.

E. CONDITIONS

Applicable to All Insuring Agreements

1. **Cancellation**

   a. The first named Insured shown in the Declarations may cancel this Policy by mailing or delivering to us advance written notice of cancellation.

   b. We may cancel this Policy by mailing or delivering to the first named Insured written notice of cancellation at least:

   (1) 10 days before the effective date of cancellation if we cancel for nonpayment of premium; or

   (2) 30 days before the effective date of cancellation if we cancel for any other reason.

   c. We will mail or deliver our notice to the first named Insured's last mailing address known to us.

   d. Notice of cancellation will state the effective date of cancellation. The Policy Period will end on that date.

   e. If this Policy is canceled, we will send the first named Insured any premium refund due. If we cancel, the refund will be pro rata. If the first named Insured cancels, the refund may be less than pro rata. The cancellation will be effective even if we have not made or offered a refund.

   f. If notice is mailed, proof of mailing will be sufficient proof of notice.

2. **Changes**

   This Policy contains all the agreements between you and us concerning the insurance afforded. The first named Insured shown in the Declarations is authorized on behalf of all insureds to agree with us on changes in the terms of this Policy. If the terms are changed, the changes will be shown in an endorsement issued by us and made a part of this Policy.

3. Concealment, Misrepresentation or Fraud

This Policy is void in any case of fraud by you as it relates to this Policy at any time. It is also void if any insured, at any time, intentionally conceals or misrepresents a material fact concerning:

a. This insurance;

b. The covered property;

c. Your interest in the covered property; or

d. A claim under this insurance.

4. Consolidation and Merger

If through consolidation or merger with, or purchase or acquisition of assets or liabilities of, some other entity any additional persons become **employees** or you acquire the use and control of any additional **premises**:

a. You must give us written notice and obtain our written consent to extend this Policy to such additional **employees** or **premises**. We may condition our consent upon payment of an additional premium; but

b. For the first 60 days after the effective date of such consolidation, merger or purchase or acquisition of assets or liabilities, any insurance afforded for **employees** or **premises** also applies to these additional **employees** or **premises** for acts committed or events occurring within said 60 day period.

5. Deductible

a. We will not pay for loss in any one **occurrence** unless the amount of loss exceeds the Deductible Amount shown in the Declarations. We then will pay the amount of loss in excess of the Deductible Amount, up to the Limit of Insurance. In the event more than one Deductible Amount could apply to the loss, only the highest Deductible Amount will be applied.

b. For losses covered under Insuring Agreement 1. you must:

    (1) Give us notice as soon as possible even though the loss falls entirely within the Deductible Amount; and

    (2) Upon our request, give us a statement describing the loss.

c. The deductible does not apply to loss sustained by any **employee benefit plan(s)**.

6. Discovery of Loss

Discovery of loss occurs when you first become aware of facts which would cause a reasonable person to assume that a loss covered by this Policy has been or will be incurred, even though the exact amount or details of the loss may not then be known.

Discovery also occurs when you receive notice of an actual or potential claim against you alleging facts that if true would constitute a covered loss under this insurance.

7. Duties in the Event of Loss

After you discover a loss or a situation that may result in a loss you must:

a. Notify us as soon as possible;

b. Submit to examination under oath at our request and give us a signed statement of your answers;

c. Give us a detailed, sworn proof of loss within 120 days, and

d. Cooperate with us in the investigation and settlement of any claim.

8. Employee Benefit Plan(s)

a. If any **employee benefit plan(s)** is insured jointly with any other entity under this insurance, you or the plan administrator must select a Limit of Insurance for Insuring Agreement 1. that is sufficient to provide a limit of insurance for each plan that is at least equal to that required if each plan were separately insured.

b. If the first named Insured is an entity other than a plan, any payment we make to that Insured for loss sustained by any plan will be held by that Insured for the use and benefit of the plan(s) sustaining the loss.

c. If two or more plans are insured under this insurance, any payment we make for loss:

    (1) Sustained by two or more plans; or

    (2) Of commingled **funds** or **other property** of two or more plans;

that arises out of one **occurrence**, is to be shared by each plan sustaining loss in the proportion that the limit of insurance required for each such plan bears to the total of those limits.

9. Extended Period to Discover Loss

a. We will pay for loss that you sustained prior to the effective date of termination or cancellation of this insurance, which is discovered by you:

    (1) Within 60 days following the date of termination or cancellation; and

    (2) As respects any **employee benefit plan(s)**, within one year following the date of termination or cancellation.

b. However, this extended period to discover loss terminates immediately upon the effective date of any other insurance obtained by you replacing in whole or in part the insurance afforded by this Policy whether or not such insurance provides coverage for loss sustained prior to its effective date.

10. Joint Insured

a. The first named Insured shown in the Declarations is responsible for the payment of all premiums and will be the payee for any return premiums we pay.

b. If more than one Insured is named in the Declarations, the first named Insured will act for itself and for every other Insured for all purposes related to this insurance. If the first named Insured ceases to be covered, then the next named Insured will become the first named Insured.

c. If any Insured or partner or officer of that Insured has knowledge of any information relevant to this insurance, that knowledge is considered knowledge of every Insured.

d. An **employee** of any Insured is considered to be an **employee** of every Insured.

e. If this Policy or any of its coverage is canceled or terminated as to any Insured, Condition E.9. Extended Period to Discover Loss applies separately to that Insured.

f. We will not pay more for loss sustained by more than one Insured than the amount we would pay if all the loss had been sustained by one Insured.

11. Legal Action Against Us

You may not bring any legal action against us involving loss:

a. Unless you have complied with all the terms of this Policy; and

b. Until 90 days after you have filed proof of loss with us; and

c. Unless brought within 2 years from the date you discover the loss.

12. Liberalization

If we adopt any revision that would broaden the coverage under this Policy without additional premium within 45 days prior to or during the Policy Period, the broadened coverage will immediately apply to this insurance.

13. Limit of Insurance

The most we will pay for loss in any one **occurrence** is the applicable Limit of Insurance shown in the Declarations.

14. Loss Covered Under More Than One Coverage

If two or more coverages of this Policy apply to the same loss, we will pay the lesser of:

a. The actual amount of loss; or

b. The highest single Limit of Insurance applicable to those coverages.

15. Non-Cumulation of Limit of Insurance

Regardless of the number of years this Policy remains in force or the number of premiums paid, no Limit of Insurance cumulates from year to year or Policy Period to Policy Period.

16. Other Insurance

a. This Policy does not apply to loss recoverable or recovered under other insurance or indemnity. However, if the limit of the other insurance or indemnity is insufficient to cover the entire amount of the loss, this Policy will apply to that part of the loss, other than that falling within any Deductible Amount, not recoverable or recovered under the other insurance or indemnity. However, this Policy will not apply to the amount of loss that is more than the applicable Limit of Insurance shown in the Declarations.

b. Under Insuring Agreement 4., we will pay only for the amount of loss that you cannot recover:

   (1) Under your contract with the armored motor vehicle company; and

   (2) From any insurance or indemnity carried by, or for the benefit of customers of, the armored motor vehicle company.

17. Ownership of Property, Interests Covered

The property covered under this Policy is limited to property:

a. That you own or hold; or

b. That is owned and held by someone else under circumstances that made you responsible for the property prior to, and independent of, the loss.

However, this Policy is for your benefit only. It provides no rights or benefits to any other person or organization.

18. Records

You must keep records of all covered property so we can verify the amount of any loss.

19. Recoveries

a. Recoveries, whether effected by you or us, shall be applied, net of the expense of such recovery, in the following manner and order:

   (1) To the satisfaction of your loss which would otherwise have been paid under this Policy but for the fact that it is in excess of the Limit of Insurance and the Deductible Amount, if any;

   (2) Then to us, until we are reimbursed for the settlement made;

   (3) Then to you, until you are reimbursed for that part of the loss equal to the Deductible Amount, if any;

   (4) Then to you for any loss not covered by this Policy.

b. Recoveries do not include any recovery from insurance, suretyship, reinsurance, security or indemnity taken for our benefit.

c. If original securities are recovered after duplicates of such securities have been issued, the original securities shall be surrendered to us.

20. Territory

This Policy covers only acts committed or events occurring within the United States of America, U.S. Virgin Islands, Puerto Rico or Canada. In addition, under Insuring Agreement 1., we will pay for loss caused by any **employee** while temporarily outside of said territories for a period of not more than 90 days.

21. Transfer of Your Rights and Duties Under This Policy

Your rights and duties under this Policy may not be transferred without our written consent except in the case of death of an individual named insured. If you die, your rights and duties will be transferred to your legal representative but only while acting within the scope of duties as your legal representative. Until your legal representative is appointed, anyone having proper temporary custody of your property will have your rights and duties but only with respect to that property.

22. Transfer of Your Rights of Recovery Against Others to Us

You must transfer to us all your rights of recovery against any person or organization for any loss you sustained and for which we have paid or settled. You also must do everything necessary to secure those rights and do nothing after loss to impair our actual or potential rights of recovery.

23. Valuation — Settlement

    a. Subject to the applicable Limit of Insurance provision we will pay for:

        (1) Loss of **money** but only up to and including its face value. We may, at our option, pay for loss of **money** issued by any country other than the United States of America:

            (i) At face value in the **money** issued by that country; or

            (ii) In the United States of America dollar equivalent determined by the rate of exchange on the day the loss was discovered.

        (2) Loss of **securities** but only up to and including their value at the close of business on the day the loss was discovered. We may, at our option:

            (i) Pay the value of such **securities**, or replace them in kind, in which event you must assign to us all your rights, title and interest in and to those **securities**; or

            (ii) Pay the cost of any Lost Securities Bond required in connection with issuing duplicates of the **securities**. However, we will be liable only for the payment of so much of the cost of the bond as would be charged for a bond having a penalty not exceeding the lesser of the:

                (a) Value of the **securities** at the close of business on the day the loss was discovered; or

                (b) Limit of Insurance.

        (3) Loss of, or loss from damage to, **other property** or loss from damage to the **premises** or its exterior for the replacement cost of the property without deduction for depreciation. However, we will not pay more than the least of the following:

            (i) The Limit of Insurance applicable to the lost or damaged property;

            (ii) The cost to replace the lost or damaged property with property:

                (a) Of comparable material and quality; and

                (b) Used for the same purpose; or

            (iii) The amount you actually spend that is necessary to repair or replace the lost or damaged property.

        (4) We will not pay on a replacement cost basis for any loss or damage:

            (i) Until the lost or damaged property actually is repaired or replaced; and

            (ii) Unless the repairs or replacement are made as soon as reasonably possible after the loss or damage.

        If the lost or damaged property is not repaired or replaced, we will pay on an actual cash value basis.

    b. We may, at our option, pay for loss of, or loss from damage to, property other than **money**:

        (1) In the **money** of the country in which the loss occurred; or

        (2) In the United States of America dollar equivalent of the **money** of the country in which the loss occurred determined by the rate of exchange on the day the loss was discovered.

    c. Any property that we pay for or replace becomes our property.

Applicable to Specific Insuring Agreements

1. **Insuring Agreement 1**

   Cancellation as to Any Employee

   Coverage under this Policy is canceled as to any **employee**:

   a. Immediately upon discovery by:

      (1) You; or

      (2) Any of your partners, officers or directors not in collusion with the employee; or

      (3) As to **Employee benefit plan(s)**, any trustee, fiduciary or plan administrator not in collusion with the **employee**;

      of any dishonest act committed by that **employee** whether before or after becoming employed by you. Whether such discovery occurs prior to or after commencement of this Policy, there is no coverage under Insuring Agreement 1, for loss or losses resulting from acts committed by that **employee** after the date of such discovery.

   b. On the date specified in a notice mailed to you. That date will be at least 30 days after the date of mailing. The mailing of notice to you at the last mailing address known to us will be sufficient proof of notice. Delivery of notice is the same as mailing.

2. **Insuring Agreement 2**

   a. **Deductible**

      The deductible does not apply to legal expenses paid under Insuring Agreement 2.

   b. **Facsimile Signatures**

      We will treat a reproduction of a handwritten signature the same as a handwritten signature. An electronic or digital signature is not treated as a reproduction of a handwritten signature.

   c. **Proof of Loss**

      You must include with your proof of loss any instrument involved in that loss, or, if that is not possible, an affidavit setting forth the amount and an explanation of the absence of the instrument.

   d. **Territory**

      We will cover loss you sustain anywhere in the world. The Territory Condition 20 does not apply to Insuring Agreement 2.

3. **Insuring Agreements 3 and 4**

   a. **Special Limit of Insurance for Specified Property**

      We only will pay up to $5,000 for any one **occurrence** of loss of, and loss from damage to:

      (1) Precious metals, precious or semi-precious stones, pearls, furs, or completed or partially completed articles made of or containing such materials that constitute the principal value of such articles; or

      (2) Manuscripts, drawings, or records of any kind or the cost of reconstructing them or reproducing any information contained in them.

   b. **Duties in the Event of Loss**

      If you have reason to believe that any loss of, or loss from damage to, **money, securities** or **other property** involves a violation of law, you must notify the police.

4. **Insuring Agreement 5**

   a. **Special Limit of Insurance for Specified Property**

      We only will pay up to $5,000 for any one **occurrence** of loss of, and loss from damage to, manuscripts, drawings, or records of any kind or the cost of reconstructing them or reproducing any information contained in them.

    b. **Duties in the Event of Loss**

       If you have reason to believe that any loss of, or loss from damage to, **money, securities** or **other property** involves a violation of law, you must notify the police.

    c. **Territory**

       We will cover loss you sustain anywhere in the world. The Territory Condition 20 does not apply to Insuring Agreement 5.

5. **Insuring Agreement 6**

    a. **Duties in the Event of Loss**

       You must notify the police if you have reason to believe you have accepted a **counterfeit** money order or **counterfeit** paper currency.

IN WITNESS WHEREOF, we have caused this Policy to be executed on the Declarations page.

Exhibit F

CRIME PROTECTION POLICY
FOR PUBLIC ENTITIES
STANDARD FORM NO. SP 00 02 04 12

CRIME PROTECTION POLICY FOR PUBLIC ENTITIES

Edition of April 1, 2012

Policy No.

(Herein called Company)

DECLARATIONS

Item 1. Name of Insured (herein called Insured):

Principal Address:

Item 2. Policy Period: from 12:01 a.m. on _____ to 12:01 a.m. on _____
(MONTH, DAY, YEAR)   (MONTH, DAY, YEAR)

Item 3. **INSURING AGREEMENTS, LIMITS OF INSURANCE AND DEDUCTIBLES**

Insuring Agreement	Limit of Insurance Per Occurrence	Deductible Amount Per Occurrence
1. Employee Dishonesty	$	$
2. Forgery or Alteration	$	$
3. Inside the Premises	$	$
4. Outside the Premises	$	$
5. Computer Fraud	$	$
6. Money Orders and Counterfeit Paper Currency	$	$
If added by Endorsement, Insuring Agreement(s):	$	$
	$	$
	$	$

If "Not Covered" is inserted above opposite any specified Insuring Agreement, or if no amount is inserted, such Insuring Agreement and any other reference thereto in this Policy shall be deemed to be deleted.

Item 4. **ENDORSEMENTS FORMING PART OF THIS POLICY WHEN ISSUED**

Item 5. **CANCELLATION OF PRIOR INSURANCE**

By acceptance of this Policy you give us notice cancelling prior policy Nos.

SP 00 02 04 12
Printed in U.S.A.   Copyright, The Surety & Fidelity Association of America, 2012
                                         CPP-16

CRIME PROTECTION POLICY FOR PUBLIC ENTITIES
TABLE OF CONTENTS

CRIME PROTECTION POLICY	Throughout this Policy the words "you" and "your" refer to the Insured(s) shown in the Declarations. The words "we", "us" and "our" refer to the Company providing this insurance. Read the entire Policy carefully to determine rights, duties and what is or is not covered. Words and phrases defined in the Policy are in **bold** type.
A. CONSIDERATION CLAUSE	In return for the payment of the premium, and subject to the Declarations, Insuring Agreements, Definitions, Exclusions, Conditions and other terms of this Policy, we will pay for loss covered by an Insuring Agreement of this Policy that you sustain resulting directly from acts committed or events occurring at any time and discovered by you during the Policy Period shown in the Declarations or during the period of time provided in the Extended Period to Discover Loss, Condition E. 8.
B. INSURING AGREEMENTS	**1. Employee Dishonesty**

We will pay for loss resulting directly from dishonest acts committed by an **employee**, whether identified or not, acting alone or in collusion with other persons, with the manifest intent to:

a. Cause you to sustain loss; and

b. Obtain an improper financial benefit for:

    (1) The **employee**; or

    (2) Any person or organization intended by the **employee** to receive that benefit.

As used in this Insuring Agreement, an improper financial benefit does not include any employee benefits received in the course of employment, including: salaries, commissions, fees, bonuses, promotions, awards, profit sharing or pensions.

2. Forgery or Alteration

a. We will pay for loss resulting directly from **forgery** or alteration of checks, drafts, promissory notes, or similar written promises, orders, or directions to pay a sum certain in **money** that are:

    (1) Made or drawn by or drawn upon you;

    (2) Made or drawn by one acting as your agent;

    or that purport to have been so made or drawn.

b. If you are sued for refusing to pay any instrument covered in paragraph 2 a. on the basis that it has been forged or altered, and you have our written consent to defend against the suit, we will pay for any reasonable legal expenses that you incur and pay in that defense. The amount that we will pay for such legal expenses is in addition to the Limit of Insurance applicable to this Insuring Agreement.

3. Inside the Premises

a. We will pay for loss of **cash** and **securities** inside the **premises** or **banking premises** resulting directly from **theft**, disappearance or destruction. Provided, however, in the case of **theft**, the **theft** was committed by a person physically present in the **premises** or **banking premises** at the time of loss of such **cash** or **securities**.

b. We will pay for loss of, and loss from damage to, **other property**:

    (1) Inside the **premises** resulting directly from an actual or attempted **robbery** of a **custodian**; or

    (2) Inside the **premises** in a safe or vault, resulting directly from an actual or attempted **safe burglary**.

c. We will pay:

    (1) For loss from damage to the **premises** or its exterior; or

    (2) For loss of, and loss from damage to, a locked safe, vault, cash register, cash box or cash drawer located in the **premises**;

    resulting directly from an actual or attempted **theft**, **robbery** or **safe burglary**, if you are the owner of the **premises** or are liable for damage to it.

4. Outside the Premises

We will pay for loss of, and loss from damage to, **cash**, **securities** and **other property** outside the **premises** while in the care and custody of a **messenger** or armored motor vehicle company:

a. For **cash** and **securities** resulting from **theft**, disappearance or destruction; and

b. For **other property** resulting from actual or attempted **robbery**.

5. Computer Fraud

We will pay for loss resulting directly from the use of any computer to impersonate you, or your authorized officer or **employee**, to gain direct access to your computer system, or to the computer system of your financial institution, and thereby fraudulently cause the transfer of **money**, **securities** or **other property** from your **premises** or **banking premises** to a person, entity, place or account outside of your control.

6. Money Orders and Counterfeit Paper Currency

We will pay for loss resulting directly from your having accepted in good faith and in the regular course of business, in exchange for merchandise, **money** or services:

a. Money orders issued by any post office, express company or bank in the United States or Canada that are not paid upon presentation; or

b. **Counterfeit** United States or Canadian paper currency.

C. DEFINITIONS

1. **Banking premises** means the interior of that portion of any building occupied by a financial institution with which you have an account or which has custody of your **money** or **securities**.

2. **Cash** means United States or Canadian bills and coins in current use and having a face value that are accepted by the United States or by the government of Canada as legal tender for the payment of debts.

3. **Counterfeit** means an imitation of an actual valid original which is intended to deceive and to be taken as the original.

4. **Custodian** means you, any of your officials or any **employee** while having care and custody of property inside the **premises**, excluding any person while acting as a **watchperson** or janitor.

5. **Employee** means:

   a. Any natural person:

      (1) While in your service or for 30 days after termination of service; and

      (2) Whom you compensate directly by salary, wages or commissions; and

      (3) Whom you have the right to direct and control while performing services for you.

   b. Any natural person who is furnished temporarily to you to:

      (1) Substitute for a permanent **employee** as defined in (a) above who is on leave; or

      (2) Meet seasonal or short-term workload conditions;

      while that person is subject to your direction and control and performing services for you excluding, however, any such person while having care and custody of property outside the **premises**.

   c. **Employee** does not mean any:

      (1) Agent, broker, person leased to you by a labor leasing firm(except when furnished on a temporary basis under the circumstances set forth in Definition 5.b.), factor, commission merchant, consignee, independent contractor or representative of the same general character; or

      (2) Member of any legislative board or council or any advisory commission, except while performing acts within the scope of the usual duties of an employee

6. **Forgery** means the signing of the name of another person or organization with intent to deceive; it does not mean a signature which consists in whole or in part of one's own name signed with or without authority, in any capacity, for any purpose.

7. **Messenger** means any of your officials or **employees** while having care and custody of property outside the **premises**.

8. **Money** means:

   a. **Cash**;

   b. Demand and savings deposits at financial institutions; and

   c. Travelers checks, register checks and money orders held for sale to the public.

9. **Occurrence** means:

   a. As respects Insuring Agreement 1., all loss or losses caused by, or involving, any one **employee**, acting alone or in collusion with others;

   b. As respects Insuring Agreement 2., all loss or losses caused by any person or in which that person is involved, whether the loss involves one or more instruments.

   c. As respects all other Insuring Agreements, all loss or losses caused by:

      (1) Any number of acts, involving one person whether acting alone or in collusion with others;

      (2) Any number of acts involving a group of persons acting together; or

      (3) An act or event, or any number of related acts or events, not involving any identifiable person.

10. **Other property** means any tangible property other than **money** and **securities** that has intrinsic value but does not include any property excluded under this insurance.

11. **Payment order** means an instruction of a sender to a receiving bank, transmitted orally, electronically, or in writing, to pay, or to cause another bank to pay, a fixed or determinable amount of money to a another person.

12. **Premises** means the interior of that portion of any building you occupy in conducting your business.

13. **Robbery** means the taking of property from the care and custody of a person by one who has:

    a. Caused or threatened to cause that person bodily harm; or

    b. In the presence of that person, caused or threaten to cause bodily harm to someone else.

14. **Safe burglary** means the taking of:

    a. Property from within a locked safe or vault by a person unlawfully entering the safe or vault as evidenced by marks of forcible entry upon its exterior; or

    b. A safe or vault on the **premises** by a person without your permission.

15. **Securities** mean negotiable and nonnegotiable instruments or contracts representing either **money** or property and includes:

    a. Tokens, tickets, revenue and other stamps (whether represented by actual stamps or unused value in a meter) in current use; and

    b. Evidences of debt issued in connection with credit or charge cards, which cards are not issued by you;

    but does not include **money**.

16. **Security procedure** means a procedure established by agreement of the Insured and its customer or financial institution for the purpose of (i) verifying that a **payment order** is that of the Insured, or (ii) detecting error in the transmission or the content of the **payment order** or communication. A **security procedure** may require the use of algorithms or

Copyright. The Surety & Fidelity Association of America. 2012
CPP-21

other codes, identifying words or numbers, encryption, callback procedures, or similar security devices.

17. **Theft** means any act of stealing.

18. **Watchperson** means any person you retain specifically to have care and custody of property on the **premises** and who has no other duties.

D. EXCLUSIONS

Applicable to All Insuring Agreements, Except as Indicated

We will not pay for loss as specified below:

1. **Acts Committed by You**

    Loss resulting from any dishonest act committed by you whether acting alone or in collusion with other persons.

2. **Acts of Employees, Directors, Trustees or Representatives**

    We will not pay for loss resulting from any dishonest act committed by any of your **employees**, directors, trustees or authorized representatives:

    a. Acting alone or in collusion with other persons; or

    b. While performing services for you or otherwise;

    except when covered under Insuring Agreement 1

3. **Fire**

    Loss from damage to the **premises** resulting from fire, however caused.

4. **Governmental Action**

    Loss resulting from seizure or destruction of property by order of governmental authority.

5. **Indirect Loss**

    Loss that is an indirect result of any act or **occurrence** covered by this Policy including, but not limited to, loss resulting from:

    a. Your inability to realize income that you would have realized had there been no loss;

    b. Payment of damages of any type for which you are legally liable unless you establish that the act or acts that gave rise to the damages involved conduct which caused a covered loss of **money**, **securities** or **other property** which was in your custody and control and for which you were responsible prior to the loss; or

    c. Payment of costs, fees or other expenses you incur in establishing either the existence or the amount of loss under this insurance.

6. **Legal Expenses**

    Expenses related to any legal action, except when covered under Insuring Agreement 2.

7. **Nuclear Chemical or Biological**

    Loss resulting from nuclear reaction, nuclear radiation or radioactive, chemical or biological contamination, or any related act or incident.

8. **War and Similar Actions**

    Loss resulting from war, whether or not declared, warlike action, insurrection, rebellion or revolution, or any related act or incident.

9. **Confidential Information**

    Loss resulting from the theft, disappearance, destruction or disclosure of confidential information including, but not limited to, trade secrets, personal information, customer lists and intellectual property. For purposes of Insuring Agreement 5, confidential information cannot itself be the **other property** transferred, but a loss otherwise covered under Insuring Agreement 5 shall not be excluded by the fact that confidential information was used to gain access to your computer system or to the computer system of your financial institution, in order to cause the fraudulent transfer.

6

10. Data Breach Costs

Expenses related to your obligations to comply with federal and state privacy laws and Payment Card Industry Data Security Standards (if applicable) arising from a data security breach, including, but not limited to, expenses related to notifying affected individuals when the affected individuals' personally identifiable financial or medical information was stolen, accessed, downloaded or misappropriated while in your care, custody or control, forensic audit expenses and fines and penalties.

Applicable to Specific Insuring Agreements

We will not pay for loss as specified below:

1. **Under Insuring Agreement 1**

   a. **Employee Canceled Under Prior Insurance**

      Loss caused by any **employee** of yours, or predecessor in interest of yours, for whom similar prior insurance has been canceled and not reinstated since the last such cancellation.

   b. **Bonded Employee**

      Loss caused by any **employee** required by law to be individually bonded.

   c. **Damages**

      Damages for which you are legally liable as a result of:

      (1) The deprivation or violation of the civil rights of any person by an **employee**; or

      (2) The tortious conduct of an **employee** except conversion of property of **other** parties held by you in any capacity.

   d. **Treasurer or Tax Collector**

      Loss caused by a treasurer or tax collector by whatever name known.

2. **Under Insuring Agreements 1 and 5**

   Inventory Shortages

   Loss, or that part of any loss, the proof of which as to its existence or amount is dependent upon:

   a. An inventory computation; or

   b. A profit and loss computation.

3. **Under Insuring Agreements 3 and 4**

   a. **Accounting or Arithmetical Errors or Omissions**

      Loss resulting from accounting or arithmetical errors or omissions.

   b. **Money Operated Devices**

      Loss of property contained in any **money** operated device unless the amount of **money** deposited in it is recorded by a continuous recording instrument in the device.

   c. **Transfer or Surrender of Property**

      (1) Loss of property after it has been transferred or surrendered to a person or place outside **the premises** or **banking premises**:

      (i) On the basis of unauthorized instructions; or

      (ii) As a result of a threat to do:

      (a) Bodily harm to any person; or

      (b) Damage to any property.

      (2) But, this exclusion does not apply under Insuring Agreement 4, to loss of **money**, **securities** and **other property** while outside the **premises** or **banking premises** in the care and custody of a **messenger** if you:

      (i) Had no knowledge of any threat at the time the conveyance began; or

      (ii) Had knowledge of a threat at the time the conveyance began, but the loss was not related to the threat.

d. **Vandalism**

Loss from damage to any safe, vault or **other property**, or to the **premises** or its exterior, by vandalism or malicious mischief.

4. **Under Insuring Agreement 4**

Motor Vehicles or Equipment and Accessories

Loss of motor vehicles, trailers or semi-trailers or equipment and accessories attached to them.

5. **Under Insuring Agreements 3 and 4**

a. **Exchanges or Purchases**

Loss resulting from the giving or surrendering of property in any exchange or purchase.

b. **Voluntary Parting of Title to or Possession of Property**

Loss resulting from your, or anyone acting on your express or implied authority, being induced by any dishonest act to part voluntarily with title to or possession of any property.

6. **Under Insuring Agreement 5**

a. **Failure to Follow Security Procedures**

(1) Loss resulting from your failure to follow **security procedures** agreed to in writing with your customer or your financial institution;

(2) Loss that would have been avoided if you had accepted and followed commercially reasonable **security procedures** that your financial institution made available for your account or accounts involved in the loss; or

(3) Loss resulting from your failure to comply with **security procedures** that you represented to us you would follow.

b. **Debit and Credit Cards**

Loss resulting from the use or purported use of credit, debit, charge, access, convenience, or other cards.

E. CONDITIONS

Applicable to All Insuring Agreements

1. **Cancellation**

a. The first named Insured shown in the Declarations may cancel this Policy by mailing or delivering to us advance written notice of cancellation.

b. We may cancel this Policy by mailing or delivering to the first named Insured written notice of cancellation at least:

(1) 10 days before the effective date of cancellation if we cancel for nonpayment of premium; or

(2) 30 days before the effective date of cancellation if we cancel for any other reason.

c. We will mail or deliver our notice to the first named Insured's last mailing address known to us.

d. Notice of cancellation will state the effective date of cancellation. The Policy Period will end on that date.

e. If this Policy is canceled, we will send the first named Insured any premium refund due. If we cancel, the refund will be pro rata. If the first named Insured cancels, the refund may be less than pro rata. The cancellation will be effective even if we have not made or offered a refund.

f. If notice is mailed, proof of mailing will be sufficient proof of notice.

2. **Changes**

This Policy contains all the agreements between you and us concerning the insurance afforded. The first named Insured shown in the Declarations is authorized on behalf of all insureds to agree with us on changes in the terms of this Policy. If the terms are changed, the changes will be shown in an endorsement issued by us and made a part of this Policy.

3. **Concealment, Misrepresentation or Fraud**

    This Policy is void in any case of fraud by you as it relates to this Policy at any time. It is also void if any insured, at any time, intentionally conceals or misrepresents a material fact concerning:

    a.   This insurance;

    b.   The covered property;

    c.   Your interest in the covered property; or

    d.   A claim under this insurance.

4. **Consolidation and Merger**

    If through consolidation or merger with, or purchase or acquisition of assets or liabilities of, some other entity any additional persons become **employees** or you acquire the use and control of any additional **premises**:

    a.   You must give us written notice and obtain our written consent to extend this Policy to such additional **employees** or **premises**. We may condition our consent upon payment of an additional premium; but

    b.   For the first 60 days after the effective date of such consolidation, merger or purchase or acquisition of assets or liabilities, any insurance afforded for **employees** or **premises** also applies to these additional **employees** or **premises** for acts committed or events occurring within said 60 day period.

5. **Deductible**

    a.   We will not pay for loss in any one **occurrence** unless the amount of loss exceeds the Deductible Amount shown in the Declarations. We then will pay the amount of loss in excess of the Deductible Amount, up to the Limit of Insurance. In the event more than one Deductible Amount could apply to the loss, only the highest Deductible Amount will be applied.

    b.   For losses covered under Insuring Agreement 1. you must:

    (1) Give us notice as soon as possible even though the loss falls entirely within the Deductible Amount; and

    (2) Upon our request, give us a statement describing the loss.

6. **Discovery of Loss**

    Discovery of loss occurs when you first become aware of facts which would cause a reasonable person to assume that a loss covered by this Policy has been or will be incurred, even though the exact amount or details of the loss may not then be known.

    Discovery also occurs when you receive notice of an actual or potential claim against you alleging facts that if true would constitute a covered loss under this insurance.

7. **Duties in the Event of Loss**

    a. After you discover a loss or a situation that may result in a loss you must:

    (1) Notify us as soon as possible;

    (2) Submit to examination under oath at our request and give us a signed statement of your answers;

    (3) Give us a detailed, sworn proof of loss within 120 days; and

    (4) Cooperate with us in the investigation and settlement of any claim.

    b. If you have reason to believe that any loss involves a violation of law, you must notify the police.

8. **Extended Period to Discover Loss**

   a. We will pay for loss that you sustained prior to the effective date of termination or cancellation of this insurance, which is discovered by you within 60 days following the date of termination or cancellation.

   b. However, this extended period to discover loss terminates immediately upon the effective date of any other insurance obtained by you replacing in whole or in part the insurance afforded by this Policy whether or not such insurance provides coverage for loss sustained prior to its effective date.

9. **Joint Insured**

   a. The first named Insured shown in the Declarations is responsible for the payment of all premiums and will be the payee for any return premiums we pay.

   b. If more than one Insured is named in the Declarations, the first named Insured will act for itself and for every other Insured for all purposes related to this insurance. If the first named Insured ceases to be covered, then the next named Insured will become the first named Insured.

   c. If any Insured or official of that Insured has knowledge of any information relevant to this insurance, that knowledge is considered knowledge of every Insured.

   d. An **employee** of any Insured is considered to be an **employee** of every Insured.

   e. If this Policy or any of its coverage is canceled or terminated as to any Insured, Condition E.8. Extended Period to Discover Loss applies separately to that Insured.

   f. We will not pay more for loss sustained by more than one Insured than the amount we would pay if all the loss had been sustained by one Insured.

10. **Legal Action Against Us**

    You may not bring any legal action against us involving loss:

    a. Unless you have complied with all the terms of this Policy; and

    b. Until 90 days after you have filed proof of loss with us; and

    c. Unless brought within 2 years from the date you discover the loss.

11. **Liberalization**

    If we adopt any revision that would broaden the coverage under this Policy without additional premium, within 45 days prior to or during the Policy Period, the broadened coverage will immediately apply to this insurance.

12. **Limit of Insurance**

    The most we will pay for loss in any one **occurrence** is the applicable Limit of Insurance shown in the Declarations.

13. **Loss Covered Under More Than One Coverage**

    If two or more coverages of this Policy apply to the same loss, we will pay the lesser of:

    a. The actual amount of loss; or

    b. The highest single Limit of Insurance applicable to those coverages.

14. **Non-Cumulation of Limit of Insurance**

    Regardless of the number of years this Policy remains in force or the number of premiums paid, no Limit of Insurance cumulates from year to year or Policy Period to Policy Period.

15. **Other Insurance**

    a. This Policy does not apply to loss recoverable or recovered under other insurance or indemnity. However, if the limit of the other insurance or indemnity is insufficient to cover the entire amount of the loss, this Policy will apply to that part of the loss, other than that falling within any Deductible Amount, not recoverable or recovered under the other insurance or indemnity. However, this Policy will not apply to the amount of loss that is more than the applicable Limit of Insurance shown in the Declarations.

b. Under Insuring Agreement 4., we will pay only for the amount of loss that you cannot recover:

   (1) Under your contract with the armored motor vehicle company; and

   (2) From any insurance or indemnity carried by, or for the benefit of customers of, the armored motor vehicle company.

16. Ownership of Property, Interests Covered

The property covered under this Policy is limited to property:

a. That you own or hold; or

b. That is owned and held by someone else under circumstances that made you responsible for the property prior to, and independent of, the loss.

However, this Policy is for your benefit only. It provides no rights or benefits to any other person or organization.

17. Records

You must keep records of all covered property so we can verify the amount of any loss.

18. Recoveries

a. Recoveries, whether effected by you or us, shall be applied, net of the expense of such recovery, in the following manner and order:

   (1) To the satisfaction of your loss which would otherwise have been paid under this Policy but for the fact that it is in excess of the Limit of Insurance and the Deductible Amount, if any;

   (2) Then to us, until we are reimbursed for the settlement made;

   (3) Then to you, until you are reimbursed for that part of the loss equal to the Deductible Amount, if any;

   (4) Then to you for any loss not covered by this Policy.

b. Recoveries do not include any recovery from insurance, suretyship, reinsurance, security or indemnity taken for our benefit.

c. If original securities are recovered after duplicates of such securities have been issued, the original securities shall be surrendered to us.

19. Territory

This Policy covers only acts committed or events occurring within the United States of America, U.S. Virgin Islands, Puerto Rico or Canada. In addition, under Insuring Agreement 1., we will pay for loss caused by any **employee** while temporarily outside of and territories for a period of not more than 90 days.

20. Transfer of Your Rights and Duties Under This Policy

Your rights and duties under this Policy may not be transferred without our written consent.

21. Transfer of Your Rights of Recovery Against Others to Us

You must transfer to us all your rights of recovery against any person or organization for any loss you sustained and for which we have paid or settled. You also must do everything necessary to secure those rights and do nothing after loss to impair our actual or potential rights of recovery.

22. Valuation — Settlement

a. Subject to the applicable Limit of Insurance provision we will pay for:

   (1) Loss of **money** but only up to and including its face value. We may, at our option, pay for loss of **money** issued by any country other than the United States of America:

     (i) At face value in the **money** issued by that country; or

     (ii) In the United States of America dollar equivalent determined by the rate of exchange on the day the loss was discovered.

    (2) Loss of **securities** but only up to and including their value at the close of business on the day the loss was discovered. We may, at our option:

        (i) Pay the value of such **securities**, or replace them in kind, in which event you must assign to us all your rights, title and interest in and to those **securities**; or

        (ii) Pay the cost of any Lost Securities Bond required in connection with issuing duplicates of the **securities**. However, we will be liable only for the payment of so much of the cost of the bond as would be charged for a bond having a penalty not exceeding the lesser of the:

           (a) Value of the **securities** at the close of business on the day the loss was discovered; or

           (b) Limit of Insurance.

    (3) Loss of, or loss from damage to, **other property** or loss from damage to the **premises** or its exterior for the replacement cost of the property without deduction for depreciation. However, we will not pay more than the least of the following:

        (i) The Limit of Insurance applicable to the lost or damaged property;

        (ii) The cost to replace the lost or damaged property with property:

           (a) Of comparable material and quality; and

           (b) Used for the same purpose; or

        (iii) The amount you actually spend that is necessary to repair or replace the lost or damaged property.

    (4) We will not pay on a replacement cost basis for any loss or damage:

        (i) Until the lost or damaged property actually is repaired or replaced; and

        (ii) Unless the repairs or replacement are made as soon as reasonably possible after the loss or damage.

    If the lost or damaged property is not repaired or replaced, we will pay on an actual cash value basis.

b. We may, at our option, pay for loss of, or loss from damage to, property other than **money**:

    (1) In the **money** of the country in which the loss occurred; or

    (2) In the United States of America dollar equivalent of the **money** of the country in which the loss occurred determined by the rate of exchange on the day the loss was discovered.

c. Any property that we pay for or replace becomes our property.

Applicable to Specific Insuring Agreements

1. **Insuring Agreement 1**

Cancellation as to Any Employee

Coverage under this Policy is canceled as to any **employee**:

a. Immediately upon discovery by:

    (1) You; or

    (2) Any person who is an official or department or division head authorized to manage, govern or control your **employees** in the performance of their duties and who is not in collusion with the employee;

of any dishonest act committed by that **employee** whether before or after becoming employed by you. Whether such discovery occurs prior to or after commencement of this Policy, there is no coverage under Insuring Agreement 1. for loss or losses resulting from acts committed by that **employee** after the date of such discovery.

     b.   On the date specified in a notice mailed to you. That date will be at least 30 days after the date of mailing. The mailing of notice to you at the last mailing address known to us will be sufficient proof of notice. Delivery of notice is the same as mailing.

2.   Insuring Agreement 2

     a.   **Deductible**

         The deductible does not apply to legal expenses paid under Insuring Agreement 2.

     b.   **Facsimile Signatures**

         We will treat a reproduction of a handwritten signature the same as a handwritten signature. An electronic or digital signature is not treated as a reproduction of a handwritten signature.

     c.   **Proof of Loss**

         You must include with your proof of loss any instrument involved in that loss, or, if that is not possible, an affidavit setting forth the amount and an explanation of the absence of the instrument.

     d.   **Territory**

         We will cover loss you sustain anywhere in the world. The Territory Condition 19 does not apply to Insuring Agreement 2.

3.   Insuring Agreements 3 and 4

Special Limit of Insurance for Specified Property

         We only will pay up to $5,000 for any one **occurrence** of loss of, and loss from damage to:

     a.   Precious metals, precious or semi-precious stones, pearls, furs, or completed or partially completed articles made of or containing such materials that constitute the principal value of such articles; or

     b.   Manuscripts, drawings, or records of any kind or the cost of reconstructing them or reproducing any information contained in them.

4.   Insuring Agreement 5

     a.   **Special Limit of Insurance for Specified Property**

         We only will pay up to $5,000 for any one **occurrence** of loss of, and loss from damage to, manuscripts, drawings, or records of any kind or the cost of reconstructing them or reproducing any information contained in them.

     b.   **Territory**

         We will cover loss you sustain anywhere in the world. The Territory Condition 19 does not apply to Insuring Agreement 5.

IN WITNESS WHEREOF, we have caused this Policy to be executed on the Declarations page.

Table of Cases

The following is an alphabetical listing of all cases annotated in this book. Although the cases that were annotated were shepardized, the subsequent history of the cases was not cited at the end of the individual annotations. As a result, the following list also does not include the subsequent history of the case. As is always prudent, a case should be shepardized before it is relied upon. Additionally, although this book generally follows *The Bluebook*,[1] editorial discretion was used when deemed appropriate. Thus, for instance, although *The Bluebook* requires citation to a specific date for an electronic database case citation, such a requirement did not seem necessary for purposes of this book. Thus, the reader, hopefully, will understand why the electronic database citations that follow do not include the complete dates.

---

1   THE BLUEBOOK: A UNIFORM SYSTEM OF CITATION (Columbia Law Review Association et al. eds., 19th ed. 2010).